The ALA Yearbook
of Library and
Information
Services

1989

The ALA Yearbook of Library and Information Services

A review of
library events 1988
Volume 14 (1989)

American Library Association
Chicago, Illinois

Composed by Precision Typographers, Inc.
Michigan City, Indiana, in Melior.
Printed on 50-pound Glatfelter,
a pH-neutral stock, and bound
by Braun-Brumfield, Inc.

Volume 1 (1976)
Volume 2 (1977)
Volume 3 (1978)
Volume 4 (1979)
Volume 5 (1980)
Volume 6 (1981)
Volume 7 (1982)
Volume 8 (1983)
Volume 9 (1984)
Volume 10 (1985)
Volume 11 (1986)
Volume 12 (1987)
Volume 13 (1988)
Volume 14 (1989)

ISBN 0-8389-0514-5
ISSN 0740-042X

Copyright © 1989 by the American Library Association

All rights reserved. No part of this publication may be reproduced in any form without permission in writing from the publisher, except by a reviewer who may quote brief passages in a review.

Printed in the United States of America.

EDITOR
Roger H. Parent

MANAGING EDITOR
Helen K. Wright

COPY EDITOR
Dorothy Parr Riesen

CONTRIBUTING EDITOR
Emily Melton, *Awards; Notables*

EDITORIAL ASSISTANT
Mary E. Wasser

INDEXERS
Bernard S. Schlessinger,
Texas Woman's University
June H. Schlessinger,
University of North Texas
Rashelle S. Karp,
Clarion University of Pennsylvania

PROOFREADERS
Karen Christopher
Bruce Frausto
Sara Guth
Debra M. Hall
Mary Rose McCudden
Paula M. Sedor
Pamala Spiegel

PRODUCTION MANAGER
Peter Broeksmit

LAYOUT
Joseph Szwarek

THE AMERICAN LIBRARY ASSOCIATION

PRESIDENT
F. William Summers

PRESIDENT-ELECT
Patricia W. Berger

TREASURER
Carla J. Stoffle

EXECUTIVE DIRECTOR
Thomas J. Galvin

DEPUTY EXECUTIVE DIRECTOR
Roger H. Parent

ASSOCIATE EXECUTIVE DIRECTOR FOR PUBLISHING
Edgar S. McLarin

ADVISERS

Toni C. Bearman, Dean,
School of Library and Information Science,
University of Pittsburgh

Miriam A. Drake, Director of Libraries,
Georgia Institute of Technology,
Atlanta

Norman Horrocks, Vice President,
Editorial, Scarecrow Press,
Metuchen, New Jersey

Barbara E. Markuson, Executive Director,
Indiana Cooperative Library Service Authority,
Indianapolis

Marilyn Gell Mason, Director,
Cleveland Public Library,
Cleveland

Frank W. Miller, Vice President/
Director, Marketing,
The H. W. Wilson Company,
Bronx

Marilyn Lea Miller, Chair,
Department of Library Science/Educational Technology,
University of North Carolina
at Greensboro

Samuel F. Morrison, Deputy Commissioner and
Chief Librarian,
Chicago Public Library

William H. Nault, Publisher and Chairman
of the Editorial Board,
World Book Inc., Chicago

Patrick M. O'Brien, Director of Libraries,
Dallas Public Library

Gail Ann Schlachter, President,
Reference Service Press,
San Carlos, California

Brooke E. Sheldon, Dean,
School of Library Science,
Texas Woman's University,
Denton

Gary E. Strong, California State Librarian,
Sacramento

Robert D. Stueart, Dean,
Graduate School of Library and
Information Science,
Simmons College,
Boston

Peggy Sullivan, Dean,
College of Professional Studies,
Northern Illinois University,
DeKalb

F. William Summers, Dean,
School of Library and Information Studies,
Florida State University,
Tallahassee

Alphonse Trezza, Professor,
School of Library and Information
Studies, Florida State University,
Tallahassee

Christina Carr Young,
National Commission on Libraries
and Information Science,
Washington, D.C.

EDITOR'S PREFACE

With this 1989 *ALA Yearbook* we continue our efforts to provide an authoritative and illustrated source of information about events that occurred during the past year and that reflect the many diverse interests and activities of librarianship and information science. These authoritative articles on subjects of enduring and current interest include annual topical articles on such issues as standards, information technology, and international relations; local correspondents reports from the states; a directory of library and library related organizations with information about officers, membership and activities; and biographies and obituaries of persons of note.

In this edition we include two feature articles. Over the past few years there has been a renewed interest among leaders on issues involving service to diverse populations. This interest has been sparked by a number of developments. ALA Past President, Regina Minudri, Director, Berkeley Public Library, focused on the diversity of populations requiring library service during her year as ALA President, 1986–87. Californians recognize the importance of these changing demographics of our population. They also see decrease in federal support for programs and services that address the needs and interests of a growing population of ethnic minorities.

In their feature article Yolanda J. Cuesta, Chief of Library Development Services, California State Library, and Roberto G. Trujillo, Community Information Services Consultant, California State Library, report on the recent conference, "A State of Change and Awareness Forum: California's Ethnic Future and Libraries," supported by a LSCA grant from the California State Library. The authors provide a brief historical perspective on outreach services in public libraries. They point out a retreat and some complacency in ethnic library service development since the high point of social consciousness in the 1960s. They attribute this in part to a paucity of innovative services that were once prompted by LSCA funding and other social legislation. They suggest weaknesses in our current approaches to library services to ethnic minorities and point out that there is a need for a renewed commitment to community information and referral services. Cuesta and Trujillo note that librarians must reallocate currently available library resources to develop new information systems that serve these constituencies.

On a different topic of significant current interest Lisa L. Fox, Preservation Program Director, Southeastern Library Network, Inc., discusses management strategies for disaster preparedness. Such catastrophic disasters as the fire at the Los Angeles Public Library on April 29, 1986 and the conflagration at the Leningrad Libraries on February 14, 1988 raised increased awareness of the importance of disaster preparedness. Fox also attributes this increased attention to the broader awareness and commitment to improved preservation techniques for library materials. She highlights trends and identifies such key management strategies as protection to minimize damage in the event of a disaster; written plans for recovering from such minor or cataclysmic disasters as fires and floods; and staff preparation. These strategies include broad-based participation in planning and full integration of plans into other library operations, and effective use of cooperative opportunities for disaster preparedness that may exist with other libraries, networks and agencies. Within the limits of this article, Fox provides a thorough discussion and many useful ideas.

My introduction to the *Yearbook* would be incomplete without recognizing and thanking Bernard Schlessinger for his outstanding efforts on the *Yearbook*'s index, and Helen K. Wright and Mary E. Wasser for their considerable effort in supporting the Editor and keeping the *Yearbook* on schedule. I also thank the Advisors who met with us twice this year to discuss the strengths and weaknesses of the *Yearbook* and who provided many useful suggestions for improvements.

ROGER H. PARENT
EDITOR

INFORMATION ACCESS IN THE 1990s

This is the 14th edition of *The ALA Yearbook of Library and Information Services*. As with the earlier volumes, it constitutes an important component of our profession's collective memory. It also chronicles the library events, trends, triumphs, and frustrations of 1988—a year marked by change and changing relationships in many areas of our national and professional lives. We, the people, elected a new President to lead us and chose our Representatives and Senators for the coming years as well. We, the members of the library profession, reacted decisively and with a passionate, resounding "no" to requests from the Federal Bureau of Investigation to subvert the privacy of some of our library patrons. Similarly, we registered our dismay and disgust regarding the National Commission on Libraries and Information Science's support of the FBI's so-called Library Awareness Program.

Within the American Library Association, our concerns regarding access to information were further manifested through the intensified efforts of members of ALA's Coalition on Government Information and by the establishment of a new information access coordinating committee. In addition, ALA's legislative and intellectual freedom programs continued to provide visible, tangible evidence of the Association's firm commitment to the right of all library patrons to unfettered information access and information use.

As we make ready for the 1990s, certain issues and challenges loom large on the horizon. We profess to be absolutely devoted to the principle of open access for all. But, what good is access if better than two-thirds of the information we possess is in such disrepair that it cannot be used, read, or even handled without crumbling? How helpful is open access to the functionally illiterate, and what are we as librarians prepared to do to assure that this nation does *not* enter the 21st century with two-thirds of our people unable to read or write? How will we avert the specter of becoming a bifurcated nation of information haves and information have-nots by the year 2000? Are we doing enough to reverse the rising tide of censorship? Given the politicization in recent years of the National Commission on Libraries and Information Science, what kind of a White House Conference on Libraries and Information Services can we expect in 1990 or 1991?

Obviously, you will not find all the answers to these difficult and disturbing questions in the pages of this *Yearbook*. What you *will* find however, is an authoritative and detailed account of 1988 accomplishments and trends in literacy, democratization, and access to information as well as a chronicle of the activities of present leaders and members of the profession. Further, you will gain a sense of the goals librarians and information specialists strive for and how they intend to achieve those goals. *The 1989 ALA Yearbook of Library and Information Services* is an incredibly rich, substantial, and diverse record of the progress, intentions, hopes, and disappointments of a noble profession!

PATRICIA W. BERGER

CONTENTS

Features

1 Management Strategies of Disaster Preparedness
LISA L. FOX, Preservation Program Director, Southeastern Library Network, Inc., Atlanta, Georgia

7 Service to Diverse Populations
YOLANDA J. CUESTA, Chief; ROBERTO G. TRUJILLO, Community Information Services Consultant, Library Development Services, California State Library, Sacramento

Special Reports

23 ALA/AASL and NCATE
MARILYN L. MILLER, Professor and Chair, Department of Library Science/Educational Technology, University of North Carolina at Greensboro

52 Twenty-fifth Anniversary of *Choice*
PATRICIA E. SABOSIK, Editor and Publisher, *Choice*, Middletown, Connecticut

81 Bibliotheca Alexandrina
MOHAMMED M. AMAN, Dean and Professor, School of Library and Information Science, University of Wisconsin at Milwaukee

90 Latchkey Children
STEVEN HERB, Coordinator of Children's Services, Dauphin County Library System, Harrisburg, Pennsylvania

125 The FBI Library Awareness Program
C. JAMES SCHMIDT, Vice-President, Research Libraries Group, Inc., Stanford, California

131 U.S./U.S.S.R. Seminar on Access to Library Resources Through Technology and Preservation
ROBERT P. DOYLE, Director, Library/Book Fellows Program, ALA

187 Retail Shops in Public Libraries: A Survey
MARCIA J. KUSZMAUL, Marketing Manager, Public Information Office, ALA

193 The Year of the Librarian: Ask a Professional. Ask a Librarian
LINDA WALLACE, Director, Public Information Office, ALA

199 Desktop Publishing and Its Applications for Libraries
MARVIN I. GARBER, Science/Technology Librarian, Sulzer Regional Library, Chicago

209 Library Statistics: A Current Review
MARY JO LYNCH, Director, Office for Research, ALA

250 Pay Equity in Minnesota
JANICE FEYE-STUKAS, Library Specialist, Office for Library Development and Services, Minnesota State Library, St. Paul

Review of Library Events 1988

13 Abstracting and Indexing
BETTY L. UNRUH, Executive Director, National Federation of Abstracting and Information Services, Philadelphia

14 Academic Libraries
MARILYN MITCHELL, Assistant Director, Auraria Library, Denver, Colorado

18 Accreditation
HERMAN L. TOTTEN, Professor, School of Library and Information Sciences, North Texas University, Denton

19 Adults, Library Services to
GARY O. ROLSTAD, Adult Services Consultant, Queens Borough Public Library, Jamaica, New York

21 American Association of Law Libraries
MARGARET A. LEARY, Director, Law Library, University of Michigan, Ann Arbor

22 American Association of School Librarians
KAREN A. WHITNEY, Aqua Fria High School, Avondale, Arizona

25 American Indians
VIRGINIA H. MATHEWS, Vice-President, Shoe String Press, Inc., Hamden, Connecticut

27 American Library Association
EMILY MELTON, Associate Librarian for Public Services, Indiana University/Purdue University at Indianapolis

32 American Library Association Awards
EMILY MELTON, Associate Librarian for Public Services, Indiana University/Purdue University at Indianapolis

41 American Library Trustee Association
SHARON L. JORDAN, Executive Director, American Library Trustee Association, ALA

42 American Society for Information Science
LINDA RESNIK, Executive Director, American Society for Information Science, Washington, D.C.

44 American Theological Library Association
SARA J. MYERS, Director, Ira J. Taylor Library, Iliff School of Theology, Denver

44 Archives
DONN C. NEAL, Executive Director, The Society of American Archivists, Chicago

46 Armed Forces Libraries
TONY DAKAN, Director, Air Forces Library and Information System, Randolph AFB, Texas

47 Art Libraries
JEFFREY L. HORRELL, Assistant University Librarian for Personnel, Budget, and Planning, Syracuse University

48 Asian Pacific American Librarians Association
CONCHITA J. PINEDA, President, APALA; Manager, Citicorp Information Services, New York

49 Association for Library and Information Science Education
LEIGH ESTABROOK, President of ALISE, Dean, Graduate School of Library and Information Science, University of Illinois, Urbana

50 Association for Library Service to Children
MARY R. SOMERVILLE, Children's Coordinator, Broward County Library, Ft. Lauderdale, Florida

51 Association of College and Research Libraries
JOANNE R. EUSTER, University Librarian, Rutgers University, New Brunswick, New Jersey

54 Association of Jewish Libraries
LINDA P. LERMAN, Judaica Bibliographer, Yale University Library, New Haven, Connecticut

55 Association of Research Libraries
NICOLA DAVAL, Program Officer, Association of Research Libraries, Washington, D.C.

61 Association of Specialized and Cooperative Library Agencies
BRUCE E. DANIELS, Director, Rhode Island Department of State Library Services, Providence

62 Beta Phi Mu
EWARD G. HOLLEY, Professor, School of Information and Library Science, University of North Carolina at Chapel Hill

63 Bibliographies, Indexes, and Other Reference Books
JAMES RETTIG, Assistant University Librarian for Reference and Information Services, College of William and Mary, Williamsburg, Virginia

64 Biographies
HELEN K. WRIGHT, Assistant Director for New Product Planning, ALA Publishing Services

76 Black Caucus of ALA
JESSIE CARNEY SMITH, University Librarian, Fisk University, Nashville

77 Blind and Physically Handicapped Library Services
STEVEN PRINE, JR., Network Consultant, National Library Service for the Blind and Physically Handicapped, Library of Congress, Washington, D.C.

78 Bookselling
BERNARD E. RATH, Executive Director, American Booksellers Association, New York

79 Buildings
ANDERS C. DAHLGREN, Consultant for Public Library Construction and Planning, Wisconsin Division for Library Services, Madison

83 Canadian Library Association
JANE COONEY, Executive Director, Canadian Library Association, Ottawa

84 Canadian Report
TERRI TOMCHYSHYN, Director, Professional Development, Canadian Library Association, Ottawa

86 Cataloging and Classification
JANET SWAN HILL, Assistant Director for Technical Services, University of Colorado Libraries, Boulder

87 **Catholic Library Association**
JOHN T. CORRIGAN, C.F.X., Executive Director, CLA, Haverford, Pennsylvania

88 **Children's Book Council**
JOHN DONOVAN, President, Children's Book Council, New York

90 **Children's Library Services**
JANE BOTHAM, Coordinator of Children's Services, Milwaukee Public Library

93 **Children's Literature**
JUNE H. SCHLESSINGER, Assistant Professor, School of Library and Information Sciences, University of North Texas, Denton

98 **Chinese American Librarians Association**
AMY SEETOO WILSON, Executive Director, CALA; Manager, Marketing Support Services and China Liaison, Dissertation Information Service, University of Michigan, Ann Arbor

98 **Collection Building and Management**
BONITA BRYANT, Head, Collection Development Department, State University of New York, Albany

100 **Continuing Library Education Network and Exchange Round Table**
SHERRIE E. SNYDER, President, CLENE Round Table; Director, Moline (Illinois) Public Library

101 **Copyright**
WILLIAM Z. NASRI, Professor, School of Library and Information Science, University of Pittsburgh

103 **Databases, Computer-Readable**
MARJORIE M. K. HLAVA, President, Access Innovations Inc., Albuquerque; GREG MACELWAIN, Access Innovations

105 **Education, Library**
PHYLLIS J. VAN ORDEN, Professor, School of Library and Information Studies, Florida State University, Tallahassee

108 **ERIC**
BARBARA B. MINOR, Publications Coordinator; JANE K. JANIS, Operations Manager, ERIC Clearinghouse of Information Resources, Syracuse University

108 **Ethnic Materials and Information Exchange Round Table**
MARIE F. ZIELINSKA, Chief, Multilingual Biblioservice, National Library of Canada, Ottawa

109 **Federal Librarians Round Table**
DORIA BEACHELL GRIMES, Database Product Specialist, National Technical Information Service, Springfield, Virginia

110 **Film and Video**
WILLIAM J. SLOAN, Librarian, Circulating Film Library, The Museum of Modern Art, New York

112 **Film and Video, Children's**
MARILYN BERG IARUSSO, Assistant Coordinator, Children's Services, The New York Public Library

115 **Foundations, Private**
JEANNE L. BOHLEN, Independent Sector, Washington, D.C.

116 **Freedom to Read Foundation**
JUDITH SESSIONS, Dean and University Librarian, Miami University, Oxford, Ohio

118 **Friends of Libraries**
FRANK W. MILLER, Vice-President, H. W. Wilson Company, Bronx, New York

119 **Government Documents Round Table**
CAROLYN C. JAMESON, Foreign Documents Librarian, Pennsylvania State University, University Park

119 **Government Publications and Depository System**
LEROY C. SCHWARZKOPF, Library Consultant, Greensbelt, Maryland

121 **Health and Rehabilitation Library Services**
SHARRON MC FARLAND, Systems Librarian Supervisor, NASA Scientific and Technical Facility, RMS Associates, Baltimore

122 **Information Technology**
RICHARD W. BOSS, Senior Consultant, Information Systems Consultants, Inc., Washington, D.C.

124 **Intellectual Freedom**
GORDON M. CONABLE, Director, Monroe County Library System, Monroe, Michigan

128 **Intellectual Freedom Round Table**
JUDITH SEREBNICK, Associate Professor, School of Library and Information Science, Indiana University, Bloomington

129 **IFLA**
HANS-PETER GEH, Director, International Federation of Library Associations and Institutions, The Hague

130 **International Relations**
MOHAMMED M. AMAN, Dean and Professor, School of Library and Information Science, University of Wisconsin-Milwaukee; MARY JO AMAN, Reference Librarian, University of Wisconsin-Milwaukee

134 **International Relations Round Table**
THEODORE F. WELCH, Director of Libraries, Northern Illinois University, DeKalb

135 **Junior Members Round Table**
DIANE J. CIMBALA, Northeast Regional Representative, F. W. Faxon Company, Leonia, New Jersey

136 **Law and Law Libraries**
JULIUS J. MARKE, Professor of Law and Law Librarian, St. John's University School of Law, Jamaica, New York

138 **Libraries and Literacy**
JANE C. HEISER, Administrator, Office of Lifelong Learning, Enoch Pratt Free Library, Baltimore

140 **Library Administration and Management Association**
ANN HEIDBREDER EASTMAN, Blacksburg, Virginia

144 **Library and Information Technology Association**
WILLIAM GRAY POTTER, Associate University Librarian for Technical Services, Automation, and Systems, Arizona State University, Tempe

145 **Library Association (of the United Kingdom of Great Britain and Northern Ireland)**
GEORGE CUNNINGHAM, Chief Executive, The Library Association, London

145 **Library History**
DONALD G. DAVIS, JR., Professor, Graduate School of Library and Information Science, University of Texas at Austin

147 **Library History Round Table**
WAYNE A. WIEGAND, Associate Professor, School of Library and Information Studies, University of Wisconsin-Madison

147 **Library Instruction Round Table**
THELMA H. TATE, Coordinator of Public Services, Douglas College, Rutgers University, New Brunswick, New Jersey

149 **Library of Congress**
GAIL M. FINEBERG, Writer-Editor, Federal Library and Information Center, Library of Congress, Washington, D.C.

151 **Library Press**
RICHARD D. JOHNSON, Director of Libraries, State University College, Oneonta, New York

153 **Library Programs, Department of Education**
ROBERT KLASSEN, Director, Public Library Support Staff, U.S. Department of Education, Washington, D.C.

154 **Library Research Round Table**
BARBARA FROLING IMMROTH, Graduate School of Library and Information Science, University of Texas, Austin

155 **Library Service to Older Adults**
JANE ANGELIS, Project Director, Academic Affairs & Research; DOUGLAS BEDIENT, Director, Learning Resources Service, Southern Illinois University, Carbondale

157 **Map and Geography Round Table**
MARY L. LARSGAARD, Assistant Head, Map and Imagery Laboratory, University of California, Santa Barbara

157 **Medical Libraries**
JAMES F. WILLIAMS, Director, University of Colorado at Boulder Libraries

159 **Medical Library Association**
RAYMOND A. PALMER, Executive Director, Medical Library Association, Chicago

161 **Mountain Plains Library Association**
DUANE F. JOHNSON, State Librarian, Kansas State Library, Topeka

162 **Music Library Association**
SUSAN T. SOMMER, President-Elect, Music Library Association, New York Public Library

163 **National Agricultural Library**
JOSEPH H. HOWARD, Director, National Agricultural Library, U.S. Department of Agriculture

165 **National Commission on Libraries and Information Science**
SANDRA N. MILEVSKI, Research Associate, National Commission on Libraries and Information Science

166 **National Endowment for the Humanities**
THOMAS C. PHELPS, Senior Program Officer, Division of General Programs, National Endowment for the Humanities

167 **National Library of Canada**
GWYNNETH EVANS, Director, External Relations, National Library of Canada, Ottawa

169 **National Library of Medicine**
ROBERT MEHNERT, Public Information Officer, Department of Health and Human Services, National Library of Medicine

169 **National Technical Information Service**
ALAN R. WENBERG, Program Analyst, National Technical Information Service, Springfield, Virginia

171 **Networks**
ALPHONSE F. TREZZA, Professor, School of Library and Information Studies, Florida State University, Tallahassee

172 **Notables**
EMILY MELTON, Associate Librarian for Public Services, Indiana University/Purdue University at Indianapolis

176 **Obituaries**
HELEN K. WRIGHT, Assistant Director for New Product Planning, ALA Publishing Services

178 **Oral History Association**
RONALD JOHN GRELE, Director, Oral History Office, Columbia University, New York

179 **Pacific Northwest Library Association**
GEORGE V. SMITH, President, Pacific Northwest Library Association, Deputy Director, Alaska State Library, Juneau

179 **Personnel and Employment: Compensation and Pay Equity**
PAUL M. GHERMAN, Director of Libraries; FRANCES O. PAINTER, Personnel Officer, Newman Library, Virginia Polytechnic Institute, Blacksburg

181 **Personnel and Employment: Continuing Education and Staff Development**
ELIZABETH W. STONE, Professor Emerita and Former Dean, Catholic University of America, Washington, D.C.

183 **Preservation of Library Materials**
ANN G. SWARTZELL, Associate Librarian (Conservation), New York State Library, Albany

185 **Public Libraries**
DONALD J. SAGER, City Librarian, Milwaukee Public Library

190 **Public Library Association**
KATHLEEN MEHAFFEY BALCOM, Library Director, Downers Grove (Illinois) Public Library

191 **Public Relations and Marketing**
JON ELDREDGE, Chief, Collection and Information Resources Development, Medical Center Library, University of New Mexico, Albuquerque

195 **Publishing, Book**
SANDY WHITELEY, Editor, Reference Books Bulletin, ALA

197 **Publishing, Electronic**
FRANK J. FARRELL, Group Vice-President, U.S. Reference; RICHARD TOWNLEY, Grolier, Inc., Danbury, Connecticut

201 **Publishing, Serials**
WILLIAM A. KATZ, Professor, School of Information Science and Policy, State University of New York at Albany

202 **Reference and Adult Services Division**
GAIL A. SCHLACHTER, President, Reference Service Press, San Carlos, California

204 **Reference Services**
MARGARET POWER, Reference Librarian, DePaul University, Chicago

206 **REFORMA**
INGRID BETANCOURT, Head, Ethnic Services and Collections, Newark Public Library

208 **Research**
PETER HERNON, Professor, Simmons College, Graduate School of Library and Information Science, Boston; C. D. Hurt, Director, Graduate Library School, University of Arizona, Tucson

216 **Resources and Technical Services Division**
MARION T. REID, Associate Director for Technical Services, Louisiana State University, Baton Rouge

218 **Risk Management for Libraries**
ROBERT A. SEAL, University Librarian, The University of Texas at El Paso

221 **School Library Media Programs**
DANIEL D. BARRON, College of Library and Information Science, University of South Carolina, Columbia

223 **Seminar on the Acquisition of the Latin American Library Materials**
SUZANNE HODGMEN, Executive Secretary, SALALM; Bibliographer for Ibero-American Studies, University of Wisconsin-Madison

224 **Serials**
ROBERT L. HOUBECK, JR., Head, Serials Division, University of Michigan Library, Ann Arbor

225 **Social Responsibilities**
ELLA GAINES YATES, State Librarian, Virginia State Library and Archives, Richmond

228 **Social Responsibilities Round Table**
JOHN HOSTAGE, Harvard Law School Library, Cambridge, Massachusetts

228 **Sound Recordings**
RICHARD SWEENEY HALSEY, Dean, School of Information Science and Policy, State University of New York at Albany

232 **Southeastern Library Association**
CLAUDIA H. MEDORI, Executive Secretary, Southeastern Library Association, Tucker, Georgia

232 **Special Libraries Association**
JOE ANN CLIFTON, Manager, Information Services, Litton Industries Guidance and Control Systems, Woodland Hills, California

234 **Standards**
SALLY H. MC CALLUM, Chief, Network Development and MARC Standards Office, Processing Services, Library of Congress, Washington, D.C.

237 **State Libraries**
LORRAINE SCHAEFFER SUMMERS, Assistant State Librarian, State Library of Florida, Tallahassee

239 **Theatre Library Association**
RICHARD M. BUCK, Assistant to the Chief, Performing Arts Research Center, The New York Public Library at Lincoln Center

241 **Trustees**
BARBARA COOPER, Chair, ALTA White House Conference Subcommittee, Fort Lauderdale

242 **United States Board on Books for Young People**
JEAN E. KARL, President, USBBYP, Wilmington, Delaware

243 **Universal Bibliographic Control**
WINSTON D. ROBERTS, Programme Officer, IFLA UBCIM Programme, British Library Bibliographic Services, London

244 **Universal Serials and Book Exchange**
CLAUDE L. HOOKER, Managing Director, Universal Serials and Book Exchange, Inc., Washington, D.C.

245 **Urban Libraries Council**
KEITH DOMS, Executive Director, Urban Libraries Council

245 **Video in Libraries**
RANDY PITMAN, Editor, *The Video Librarian*, Bremerton, Washington

247 **Washington Report**
EILEEN D. COOKE, Director, ALA Washington Office

249 **Women in Librarianship**
SANDRA K. PETERSON, Documents Librarian, Yale University, New Haven, Connecticut

254 **Women's National Book Association**
CATHY RENTSCHLER, President, WNBA; Editor, Library Lebererature, The H. W. Wilson Company

255 **Young Adult Library Services**
PATSY H. PERRITT, Associate Professor, School of Library and Information Science, Louisiana State University, Baton Rouge

257 **Young Adult Literature**
PAMELA SPENCER, Librarian, Thomas Jefferson High School for Science and Technology, Alexandria, Virginia

258 **Young Adult Services Division**
SUSAN B. MADDEN, Young Adult Coordinator, King County Library System, Seattle, Washington

State Reports
260

Alabama. FRED D. NEIGHBORS, Assistant Director, Alabama Public Library Service, Montgomery

Alaska. ANN K. SYMONS, Librarian, Juneau-Douglas High School, Juneau

Arizona. JUNE GARCIA, Library Extension Services Administrator, Phoenix Public Library

Arkansas. ROBERT RAZER, Head of Technical Services, Central Arkansas Library System, Little Rock

California. BETTY J. BLACKMAN, Dean, University Library, California State University, Carson City

Colorado. S. JANE ULRICH, System Director, Southwest Regional Library Service System, Durango; DANIEL W. LESTER, Director, John F. Reed Library, Fort Lewis College, Durango

Connecticut. SHARON BRETTSCHNEIDER, Assistant Executive Director, Capitol Region Library Council, Windsor

Delaware. GRACE S. HUSTED, Director of Libraries, New Castle

District of Columbia. MARY E. RAPHAEL, Executive Assistant to the Director, District of Columbia Public Library

Florida. ETHEL A. HUGHES, Library Consultant, State Library of Florida, Tallahassee

Georgia. HELEN CITRON WILTSE, Associate Director, Georgia Institute of Technology Library, Atlanta

Hawaii. SUSAN F. MAESATO, Public Services Librarian; KENNETH R. HERRICK, Director of Libraries, University of Hawaii at Hilo

Idaho. PAUL HOLLAND, Director, Idaho Falls Public Library

Illinois. PATRICIA M. HOGAN, Director, Poplar Creek Public Library, Streamwood

Indiana. MARTHA E. (CATT) FEDERSPIEL, Public Information Director, Indiana State Library, Indianapolis

Iowa. CARL F. ORGREN, Director, School of Library and Information Science, University of Iowa, Iowa City

Kansas. ROY BIRD, LSCH Coordinator/Public Library Consultant, Kansas State Library, Topeka

Kentucky. EDWARD KLEE, Assistant Director, Field Services, Kentucky Department for Libraries and Archives, Frankfort

Maine. NANN BLAINE HILYARD, Director, Auburn Public Library

Maryland. J. MAURICE TRAVILLIAN, Assistant State Superintendent for Libraries, Baltimore

Massachusetts. MARGARET L. CRIST, Assistant Director of Planning and Administrative Coordinator, Boston Public Library

Minnesota. EDWARD SWANSON, Principal Cataloger, Minnesota Historical Society, St. Paul

Mississippi. JAMES F. PARKS, JR., Librarian, Millsaps College, Jackson

Missouri. MADELINE MATSON, Associate, Publications, Missouri State Library, Jefferson City

Montana. ELLEN J. NEWBERG, Director, Parmly Billings Library, Billings

Nebraska. E. LA VERNE HASELWOOD, Professor, University of Nebraska, Omaha

Nevada. JOAN G. KERSCHNER, State Librarian, Reno

New Hampshire. LOUISE C. PRICE, Deputy Director, Manchester City Library

New Jersey. DANILO H. FIGUEREDO, Executive Director, New Jersey Library Association, Trenton

New Mexico. LOWELL DUHRSEN, Associate Dean, New Mexico State University Library, Las Cruces

New York. ROBERT E. BARRON, Chief, Bureau of School Library Media Programs, New York State Educational Department, Albany

North Carolina. HOWARD F. MCGINN, State Librarian, Raleigh

North Dakota. NEIL V. PRICE, Assistant Professor and Chairperson, Department of Library Science, University of North Dakota, Grand Forks

Ohio. HANNAH V. MC CAULEY, Director of the Library, Ohio University-Lancaster

Oklahoma. WILLIAM R. YOUNG, Information Representative, The Oklahoma Department of Libraries, Oklahoma City

Oregon. CAROL VENTGEN, Director, Coos Bay Public Library

Pennsylvania. PRISCILLA GRECO MCFERREN, Director, Hanover Public Library

Rhode Island. CAROL DI PRETE, Roger Williams College Library, Bristol

South Carolina. CARL STONE, Director, Anderson County Library

South Dakota. PHILIP BROWN, Documents Librarian, Hilton M. Briggs Library, South Dakota University, Brookings

Tennessee. CAROLYN C. DANIEL, School Library Media Specialist, McGavock High School, Nashville

Texas. MARGARET IRBY NICHOLS, Assistant Dean, School of Library and Information Sciences, University of North Texas, Denton

Utah. NATHAN M. SMITH, Director, School of Library and Information Sciences, Brigham Young University, Provo

Vermont. MILTON H. CROUCH, Assistant Director for Reader Services, University of Vermont, Burlington

Virginia. SANDRA WOOD HEINEMANN, Editor, *Virginia Library Association Newsletter*, Hampden-Sydney

Washington. MARGARET CHISHOLM, Director, Graduate School of Library and Information Science, University of Washington, Seattle

West Virginia. SHIRLEY A. SMITH, Field Consultant, West Virginia Library Commission, Charleston

Wisconsin. SARAH M. MCGOWAN, Library Director, Ripon College, Ripon

Wyoming. PAUL B. CORS, Catalog Librarian, University of Wyoming, Laramie

Management Strategies for Disaster Preparedness

by Lisa L. Fox

The ALA/RTSD (Resources and Technical Services Division) Preservation of Library Materials Section (PLMS) adopted a new section structure during 1988. That structure is significant in the development of the preservation field as a whole, for it transforms the Section's Executive Committee from its previous role of acting as a monitor of PLMS committee activities to a new one of building links and alliances between PLMS and the RTSD and ALA communities. The creation of a new committee for Program Management reflects the fact that preservation does not consist simply of such discrete activities as binding, repair, and education, but entails management of a complex library problem.

The reorganization of PLMS reflects a growing sophistication in the preservation field as a whole. Less visible is the fact that the profession's knowledge of specific areas of preservation such as disaster preparedness, book repair, and microfilming matured significantly in the past ten years and seems now to have reached a new plateau. That maturation can be seen especially as one examines emerging views toward disaster preparedness, views that increasingly focus on improved strategies for management.

Early Developments. The 1966 flood of the Arno River and consequent devastation of cultural institutions in Florence, Italy, is commonly credited with stimulating the library profession's awareness that disaster preparedness is an important activity. Conservators, librarians, and curators from all over the world converged on Florence to help pull priceless documents and art works from the mud and begin salvaging them. The participants in this massive effort realized that little was known about how to cope with such damage, but many important recovery techniques were developed or refined in that project. The second major result of the Florence flood was the vivid realization that all cultural institutions are vulnerable to such disasters, and that most are unprepared to deal with them. Soon thereafter, the enormity of the problem was brought closer to American librarians with the fires at Temple University's Klein Law Library (1972) and the Military Records Center (1973) and the 1972 floods in the Northeast following Hurricane Agnes.

Veterans of disasters quickly began using their experiences to teach and write on the subject. This publishing output created many works now considered classics in the field of disaster preparedness, including Peter Waters' *Procedures for Salvage of Water Damaged Library Materials* (1st ed., 1975) and John Martin's *The Corning Flood: Museum Under Water* in 1977. These works, like most of those written in the 1970s and early '80s, focused on articulating sound, practical procedures for salvaging wet materials from libraries, archives, and museums.

Elements of Disaster Preparedness. Over

the course of the past 20 years, consensus has emerged on most facets of this field. Disaster preparedness is the comprehensive term that describes strategies employed to protect library resources from unexpected or accidental loss from external causes, whether these be minor (as those resulting from broken plumbing) or cataclysmic (flooding, fire, and the like). Disaster preparedness includes three facets: protection, recovery, and planning.[1]

Protection involves activities taken to prevent or minimize damage to collections. It requires, first, that a library assess its vulnerability to such natural disasters as floods, earthquakes, and hurricanes, and to other incidents such as roof leaks, plumbing malfunctions, fire, and mold outbreaks. Second, it necessitates taking steps to prevent or to reduce the impact of disasters. Such protection takes a variety of forms: installing fire detectors and sprinkler systems, bracing shelves to resist earthquake damage, regularly maintaining plumbing and drainage systems, and storing collections in areas unlikely to sustain water damage from floods, roof leaks, or broken windows.

Recovery begins only after a disaster has occurred and involves three stages: response, salvage, and rehabilitation. In the response stage, the staff organizes the recovery project by notifying necessary personnel, procuring supplies and services for recovery, stabilizing the building's environment, and assessing the damage. The salvage stage involves packing and removing materials from the affected site, stabilizing them (most often through freezing), and drying them by any of a variety of processes (including air-drying, dehumidification, and vacuum thermal- or freeze-drying). The rehabilitation stage for books and documents may include such steps as cleaning, fumigation, repair, rebinding, affixing new labels and plates, reshelving, rehousing archival materials, and deodorization and removal of smoke or soot from fire-damaged materials. Rehabilitation of non-paper materials such as photographic and magnetic media often involves reprocessing and/or copying the salvaged item onto a new, stable medium.

The third element of disaster preparedness—and one that overarches protection and recovery—is the most critical: *planning*. In this activity, discrete lists of facts, resources, procedures, priorities, and options are brought together to form a coherent working document that will guide library policy and staff action on a day-to-day basis and in a disaster situation. The disaster plan should include such informational components as floor plans, lists of suppliers and other resources, personnel directories, insurance and accounting instructions, and various checklists. Perhaps more importantly, it should serve as a guide for the staff in recovering from disasters of various scopes, and it should include instructions and procedures that will be relevant in various scenarios. That is, it should reflect in some detail the library's plans for coping with incidents ranging from small water leaks to mold outbreaks to devastating fire or flood.

Current Situation. Certain activities that comprise disaster preparedness have been exceedingly well documented. Many excellent publications are available to help librarians implement a disaster preparedness project, and many organizations and institutions are willing to share their resource lists and information sheets with their colleagues.[2] For the most part, however, available resources focus on protection and recovery; they lack detailed guidance on planning.

Over the course of some 20 years, the library profession has generated a vast array of content-oriented information on disaster preparedness. Luckily, most disasters have increased librarians' knowledge of recovery procedures, and an increasing number of commercial firms that offer recovery services have emerged. Librarians' knowledge has also increased through the many articles, books, and workshops that offer sound, detailed advice on what to include in vulnerability assessments, the pros and cons of various sprinkler systems, and detailed procedures for drying wet books. Preservation specialists clearly have been guided by the belief that this information would make it simple for institutions to develop disaster plans.

Such content-oriented resources have almost succeeded in developing a "cookbook" approach to protection and recovery. However, most emphasize the *content* of disaster preparedness, but do not adequately address the *process* by which a coherent whole is formed. Thus, even after a librarian has filled in all the blanks in the useful workbooks that attempt to systematize the disaster preparedness process, the result is a compendium of solid information, but not actually a plan. Disaster planning can no more be reduced to a "recipe" than can automation planning. In each case, experts can offer guidance on technical matters; they can outline options and discuss their merits; they can suggest issues to be addressed; they can describe how others have addressed them, but they cannot develop a modus operandi. In the final analysis, each library must develop its own plan.

In the past two decades, the profession's

understanding of disaster preparedness has grown significantly, and a consensus has emerged about what constitutes disaster preparedness and the critical role of planning. Many excellent resources are available. And there is a growing awareness (spurred most recently by the fires at the Los Angeles Central Library and the Leningrad Library) that libraries must have disaster plans. Yet, many libraries still have not developed a disaster plan, and too few existing plans are workable documents that are well incorporated into the institution's operations. Few go beyond the stage of list-compilation.

Recognizing these problems, PLMS members, during the 1987 ALA Midwinter Meeting, proposed an intensive conference on disaster preparedness. The proposal was approved by RTSD; the PLMS planning committee was formed;[3] and on July 8, 1988, RTSD held a preconference on "Management Strategies for Disaster Preparedness."[3]

The program title, like its content, reflected the planners' awareness that what was lacking in disaster preparedness was attention to the *management* of the process.

Emerging Management Strategies. It is evident that further thought and work must be concentrated on disaster preparedness. Preservation librarians, especially those involved in teaching and writing, must develop or adapt better ways for managing the planning process and for incorporating disaster preparedness into the daily work of a library. The profession has begun to explore more effective management strategies for developing and implementing disaster preparedness. Some of the more promising strategies are: (1) more broad-based participation in the planning process, (2) greater integration of disaster preparedness into other library operations, (3) adoption of a phased implementation strategy, and (4) more effective use of cooperative opportunities. Discussion of these four prospects forms the core of this article.

Participation. As preservation specialists analyze the obstacles to disaster preparedness, it is becoming clear that the "Lone Ranger" approach to disaster planning seldom works. Early preservation programs frequently developed in libraries due to the impetus and energy (if not outright nagging) of one dedicated, motivated individual on the staff. Typically, this person became committed to the goal of preservation, became knowledgeable about the field, and began advocating and/or implementing changes in library operations.

Similarly, many disaster plans have evolved from one individual's growing awareness that libraries are vulnerable to (or are frequently experiencing) disasters of various types—the dramatic hurricane or the more common roof leak. While many such disaster plans exist on paper, few have an impact on the regular operation of libraries. Stipulated schedules for roof inspections are not followed; in-house recovery supply stockpiles are not maintained; insurance policies are not updated, and fire safety recommendations are not implemented.

The basic failure of disaster plans developed by "Lone Rangers" arises primarily from lack of participation. Because other staff members are not given an opportunity to develop a sense of "ownership" toward the disaster preparedness effort, they develop no sense of responsibility for its success.

As long as disaster preparedness seemed simply to require training a few people in how to air-dry damp books, it "may" have seemed simple for libraries to permit one individual to develop procedures. However, in the wake of recent disasters and the concomitant maturation of the field, it has become evident that an effective disaster plan must reflect hard choices. Many of the questions to consider cut to the heart of library priorities and staff allegiances: Which will we save first, the reference books or the special collections? Who will have final authority for directing the recovery project, the director or the local preservation librarian? Should our capital budget proposal include a new sprinkler system or an online catalog?

Such questions are difficult to answer, and they require broad-based input from the library staff. If the plan is to work, such questions must be faced directly, and voices on all sides must be heard. The dialogue must include administrative, professional, and support staff; and the perspectives of bibliographers and reference staff, catalogers, circulation and loan services personnel, media specialists, and other technical and public services departments must be sought. Each staff member has a unique perspective on the collection and its users; each will play a valuable role in disaster preparedness.

Others beyond the walls of the library must help shape the disaster preparedness program. Depending on the library's governance structure and other alliances or dependencies, input from the university, county, and community may be needed. Very often these institutions have disaster plans or resources that can be shared. The library's plan must be compatible with that of relevant organizations. For example, a university library's disaster plans must be coordinated with that of the parent institution, and a public library may need to incorporate existing provisions in a county-wide disaster plan. The staff must know whether the library already has been mandated with disaster preparedness responsibilities as is the case with some state library agencies. And the library must discover how it may draw upon existing networks such as the state emergency management agency or local civil defense. Contacts made during this process will ensure the compatibility of the library's plans with existing ones and will often strengthen ties to the larger community.

Only through seeking broad-based input and discussion (even heated debate) will the final product be a disaster plan that the staff and community will support. And only then will the plan be a workable document that does not gather dust in the files.

Integration. Just as the "Lone Ranger" approach must give way to a more participative process, disaster preparedness activities also must be integrated with ongoing library operations. In the early days of disaster preparedness (as of preservation in general), specialists set themselves apart, declaring the importance and uniqueness of their activities. While that philosophy was important during the establishment phase of this field, it has now become counterproductive. Effective disaster preparedness must be viewed as only one component of a library's overall planning and activities. Preservation librarians have a much better chance of building alliances with others and of accomplishing their mutual goals by becoming partners in the coalition for the good of the library.

One example of the integrative approach is the coordination of collection development or assessment activities and the establishment of salvage priorities. Disaster specialists have long urged librarians to set salvage priorities—that is, to identify those parts of the collection that must be given primary, secondary, and tertiary attention during recovery from a disaster. However, few librarians have actually set such priorities. Planning for salvage tends often to be avoided, even in libraries that have a fledgling disaster plan. Resistance to articulating salvage priorities can be reduced by integrating this activity into an overall collection management plan. It may be useful, while conducting a collection assessment or developing a collection development policy, to query: What parts of the collection are most important in the long term and which are most crucial to our daily operations? Discussion of these issues can bring collection development priorities into sharper focus and can establish the library's salvage priorities. Of course, the final decision about whether a particular library will give first priority to the collections with immediate value or to those with long-term research significance will depend on local circumstances and needs.

Space planning provides another opportunity to integrate disaster preparedness into more traditional activities. When a library plans new construction, renovation, or rearrangement of existing space, disaster preparedness merits consideration. For example, significant collections can be moved from basements and away from windows to reduce their vulnerability to flooding or hurricane. When acquiring new shelving, libraries can procure units with a canopy and with lowest shelves four inches off the floor—thus affording some protection from water. To reduce the risk of arson, book returns that open into the library can be enclosed or replaced with free-standing units away from the building.

There are other simple ways of integrating disaster preparedness into the library's day-to-day activities. Various ongoing prevention measures can prevent disasters or minimize their effects. For example, staff responsible for closing the building can check to see that all windows and doors are closed and securely locked. Workers in acquisitions and cataloging departments can routinely put such important records as on-order and in-process files in cabinets at the end of the day, rather than leaving them on desktops where they are more vulnerable to water, fire, and smoke damage. Step stools in stack areas can be marked with phosphorescent tape so that they will be visible in a darkened or smoke-filled building. Individually, none of these strategies are particularly difficult to implement, and together they can be important building blocks in the library's disaster preparedness program.

Phased Implementation. Integration, a building-block approach, suggests the third management strategy for disaster preparedness. For too long, many librarians have felt that no disaster preparedness activity could begin until the entire disaster plan had been completed. Others who have learned how far-reaching and complex the subject is have, despite their good intentions, simply left it undone. Both attitudes fail to recognize the benefits of "phased disaster preparedness." Librarians must begin to acknowledge that any single step taken to protect the collection from disaster is a valid achievement toward the goal of disaster preparedness. Planners need to segment the job into manageable tasks, phasing in each step over time as the staff gains more knowledge and commitment.

Employing a phased disaster preparedness strategy one library may begin by implementing such protective measures as regular roof inspections and preventive maintenance or by shifting collections so that lower shelves are not used. This may be especially prudent in a library that regularly experiences roof leaks, flooding, or similar incidents. Alternatively, the same institution might initiate its disaster preparedness effort simply by developing resource lists of suppliers, services, and sources that may be called upon when the collection sustains damage. Another library might begin by identifying salvage priorities. Eventually, such discrete steps will build toward a coherent disaster preparedness plan. In the meantime, these individual actions will have begun educating the staff, developing an organization-wide sensitivity to disaster preparedness issues, and cultivating a belief that progress can be achieved.

To ensure successful implementation, a few preservation librarians suggest that a disaster plan including strategies for protection and recovery must not only be created, but that a strategy for implementing the disaster schemes must be articulated. One of the chief problems in disaster preparedness is that too many written disaster plans are never incorporated into the institution's real goals, plans, and operations. In this context, budgeting, formal designation of staff responsibility, and ongoing staff training and support must be dealt with. In preparing a disaster plan, staff must frequently ask, How will this be achieved so that the plan will be a feasible one for the library? Whether written or existing primarily in the minds of the planners, a strategy must be articulated for ensuring that the disaster preparedness plan is actually implemented and receives ongoing attention.

Librarians are often dismayed to discover the challenges inherent in implementing a disaster preparedness plan, and the preservation field itself is partly responsible for the existing inertia. Practitioners have sought to promote disaster preparedness (and preservation in general) by talking about its importance and its benefits, but they have not acknowledged on the attendant difficulties or costs. Because obstacles have been unseen or dismissed in the planning stages, staff becomes disheartened when their disaster plan is not met with instant acceptance. By acknowledging and identifying difficulties in the early stages, planners can increase the staff's eventual acceptance of the disaster preparedness effort.

In developing a successful implementation plan, staff must recognize that disaster preparedness is difficult, because all organizational change is difficult. Some aspects of disaster preparedness will challenge such long-standing attitudes as "we'll never experience a flood," and such ingrained habits as leaving fire doors open or smoking in the building. Specific plans must be laid to motivate and educate the staff so that they will embrace changes that accompany authentic disaster preparedness.

Cooperation. Another management strategy for disaster preparedness is cooperative involvement. For several years, many writers and speakers have discussed the benefits of cooperation, but few real examples yet exist. Most purported cooperatives actually consist of a few individuals who are willing to make their services available to other institutions when they suffer disasters. While these important services meet a real need, they are more "benevolent parasitism" than cooperation.

More can be accomplished in truly cooperative disaster preparedness, and a few groups are beginning to realize benefits. A consortium of six small libraries, none of which had particular expertise in disaster preparedness, jointly retained a consultant to assess their individual vulnerabilities and to identify areas of common concern among the consortium members. Based on this consultation, staff members of the libraries drew up a "model" disaster plan that could be adapted by each, and the libraries are now exploring the potential of developing a common stockpile of recovery supplies. Other groups have concentrated efforts on training staff members locally so that each is prepared to develop and execute a disaster plan either in his/her own institution or in concert with others. Still other consortia have shared the work of identifying services and suppliers. Most successful projects have been marked by the willingness of each participating library to shoulder its share of the responsibility for becoming educated and of acting upon that knowledge. In these cases, the cooperative effort has increased the overall knowledge level of the staffs involved and has reduced the time that individual participants must devote to gathering basic information.

An additional, little acknowledged benefit of cooperative disaster planning is the maintenance of momentum. For a single library acting alone it is all too easy to let disaster preparedness activities slip to one side. However, if several institutions are working together, they often motivate or goad one another to continue the activity; for if deadlines for action are set, each participant will feel pressure to deliver on his/her commitment.

Cooperation in disaster preparedness, especially at local and state levels, is increasing. As librarians seek greater participation from their own staff, and then turn to the surrounding community or network, it is not surprising that common needs are identified and cooperative solutions begin to emerge. This bodes well for the field: the number and quality of successful disaster preparedness activities will increase.

Conclusion. The 1988 RTSD preconference, "Management Strategies for Disaster Preparedness," stands as a benchmark in the development of the field. It reflected the recognition that disaster preparedness—like the whole arena of preservation—must rest upon an overall management approach and must be well incorporated into a library's ongoing operations. It sought to communicate that recognition to a national audience.

However, while the conference was designed to accept more than 100 attendees, only about 40 registered, confirming the notion that most librarians still focus on the content- or information-oriented aspect of disaster preparedness, and not on the planning process. Thus, many librarians are not aware of the management issues whose significance is now emerging in preservation. Also highlighted is the fact that more library administrators must accept disaster preparedness as a serious professional responsibility. The willingness of administrators and other professionals to undertake this responsibility may grow as they recognize that libraries can improve disaster preparedness significantly without creating massive new programs. Even with limited personnel and financial resources, application of the management strategies outlined in this paper and at the preconference can accomplish much.

NOTES
1. At the outset, it should be acknowledged thet there is some blurring of the distinction between the terms "disaster planning" and "disaster preparedness." This is true because disaster planning should incorporate the whole gamut of disaster preparedness activities, and the sum of the disaster preparedness activities are reflected in the written disaster plan. While no strict distinction has emerged, disaster preparedness is the term used here to encompass all other disaster-related activities.
2. Some of the more useful longer publications dealing with these topics are John P. Barton and Johanna G. Wellheiser, eds., *An Ounce of Prevention*, Toronto, Toronto Area Archivists Group Education Foundation, 1985; John Morris, *Managing the Library Fire Risk*, 2d ed. Berkeley, University of California, 1979; New York University Libraries Preservation Committee, *Disaster Plan Workbook*, New York, NYU Libraries, 1984; Peter Waters, *Procedures for Salvage of Water Damaged Library Materials*, 3d ed. at press, Washington, D.C., Government Printing Office, 1989.
In addition, a wide variety of informational leaflets, resource lists, and other sources of guidance are available from such organizations as the Illinois State Library Preservation Office, Los Angeles Preservation Network, New York State Library Conservation/Preservation Program, Northeast Document Conservation Center, and SOLINET Preservation Program.
3. Planning committee members were: Merrily Smith (Library of Congress), Chair; Sally Buchanan (University of Pittsburgh), Christopher Coleman, (University of California at Los Angeles), Nancy Elkington, (University of Michigan), and Lisa Fox, (Southeastern Library Network/SOLINET). I am indebted to these individuals who served, along with Connie Brooks (now at Stanford University), as the faculty for the preconference. Our discussions prompted much of my thought on this subject.

Service to Diverse Populations

by Roberto G. Trujillo and Yolanda J. Cuesta

Twenty-five years have passed since the political and social turmoil of the 60s exerted its influence over the library profession and prompted the first major emphasis on serving ethnic minority groups. Prior to the 1960s public library efforts to serve ethnic minority communities were few and far between. The public library movement of the mid-nineteenth century with its goal of educating the masses and serving the "common man" largely excluded the ethnic minority segments of the population. Library services available to ethnic minorities were severely restricted for some groups and virtually nonexistent for others.

The focus here will be on the four generally recognized major minority and cultural groups: African Americans, American Indians, Asian Americans, and Hispanics.

For African Americans, public library service was generally unavailable prior to the Civil War. When public libraries finally began extending services to African Americans it was typically through restricted privileges or separate facilities. Services to African Americans gained a foothold under the public administration programs of the Great Depression and received more impetus during the early years of the Civil Rights movement of the late 1950s.

For American Indians early library services consisted mostly of bookmobile services in rural areas and reservations. For Asian Americans and Hispanics ongoing library service programs before the 1960s were isolated and rare.

The decade of the sixties raised the consciousness of the library profession to the disparity between its ideal of "service to all" and reality. Libraries began opening their doors to ethnic minority groups that had been excluded from the benefits of public library services. Evidence of this positive response abounds in the library literature of the 60s and 70s. Descriptions and examples of many of the early attempts to design and develop library services to meet the needs of ethnic groups comprise a large percentage of the early documentation on the evolution of ethnic library services.[1]

Undoubtedly the availability of federal funds through the passage of the Library Services and Construction Act (LSCA) in 1964 was the principal catalyst in the development of library services to ethnic groups. For the first time federal funds were made available to assist in the improvement of library services for several underserved groups including the physically handicapped, the institutionalized, and the disadvantaged. Other major pieces of social legislation enacted during the decade, including the Economic Opportunity Act, the Model Cities Act, and the Higher Education Act, also impacted on the development of library services to ethnic groups. Using federal funds, many exemplary and innovative programs were initiated and began successfully attracting ethnic minorities to libraries.

One of the most outstanding early programs serving African Americans was the

Langston Hughes Community Library and Cultural Center in New York. Its success was largely attributed to the involvement of community residents in the development and implementation of services. The services program that evolved was one designed by the community itself, and it inspired similar programs in other libraries. In California, the Los Angeles Public Library utilized a strong corps of community aides and dynamic cultural programs to extend services to the Watts community as well as to other ethnic neighborhoods.

The National Indian Education Association (NIEA) library program of the early 1970s built on early attempts at serving Indians in rural areas and reservations and demonstrated three successful and effective patterns of service to Indian communities. A library and cultural center, a tribal library system, and a community school library all drew heavy use by the communities. LSCA funds were also responsible for the first experiments in serving American Indians living in urban areas. The Milwaukee Public Library and the Chicago Public Library received attention in the literature for their successful programs.

Special services for Hispanics also parallel the availability of LSCA funds. One of the most successful early projects was the South Bronx project of the New York Public Library, which served a predominantly Puerto Rican community. Along with the Latin American Library in Oakland, these projects became models for other libraries developing programs for Hispanics. In California their influence can be seen in later LSCA-funded projects such as the outreach project at Union City Library in Alameda County and the Biblioteca Latinoamericana in San Jose.

Using LSCA funds, several major libraries opened branches in Asian communities and began developing Asian language collections. In California, San Francisco and Oakland initiated or expanded their services and even today continue to serve as examples of successful, ongoing, dynamic services to Asian communities. The influx of Southeast Asian refugees was the focus of several experimental library programs at the Hennepin County Library and Fairfax County Public Library.

These early attempts at service varied widely in their effectiveness. Many libraries seized the opportunity to use the available federal funds with little planning and assessment of needs prior to the development of services. Nevertheless, these programs identified quite clearly some of the major factors that contribute to successful development and delivery of services to ethnic groups. Successful programs had adequate funding levels to provide the needed services and to allow for experimentation. Federal funds enabled libraries to make a significant and visible impact by providing a major infusion of staff and materials into the community. Libraries' ability to experiment with the types and level of staff needed and to provide materials in a variety of formats was facilitated through LSCA funds.

One of the factors characteristic of successful programs was the recruitment of appropriate staff to move out into the community and identify information needs and promote library programs and services. The recognition that staff needed to interact daily with the community and the encouragement, and sometimes requirement, that they do so was crucial. Another critical factor to success was the involvement and participation by the community in the planning and development of services. Successful programs were able to develop mechanisms that enabled the community to identify its own needs and were successful in linking these needs to the expertise of librarians in retrieving and accessing that information. These programs dealt successfully with information sources they had not used before; they showed a willingness and an eagerness to seek out the nontraditional and nonconventional information sources in the community and made full use of formal and informal information networks.

Clearly a significant amount of work has been done by and on behalf of ethnic communities within the library profession. There has been a concerted effort, with moderate success, to recruit members of ethnic and racial groups into the profession—the numbers have at least doubled in the past 20 years. Collections of materials by and about African Americans, American Indians, Asian Americans, and Hispanics are part of American library resources, though perhaps not in proportion to the need. There are concerted efforts in different parts of the country to continue developing collections and to continue recruitment and training efforts, and there are attempts to incorporate bibliographic data about ethnic collections into national, local, state, and regional bibliographic utilities. There are successful community information and referral programs within libraries, and many of them attempt to deal with information needs of ethnic communities. Library literature is replete with reports of special services to targeted communities, and more often than not libraries report some success.

Why then the new initiatives and attempts to refocus library and information services to racial and ethnic communities? Why the recent California conference "A

State of Change: California's Ethnic Future and Libraries?"[2] Why a renewed interest in policy research to affect information services to these communities, e.g., the RAND Corporation report *Public Libraries Face California's Ethnic and Racial Diversity?*[3] And are not these reports related to others such as *One-Third of a Nation*[4], the report of the Commission on Minority Participation in Education and American Life? *One-Third of a Nation* acknowledges that "in the last ten years not only have we lost the momentum of earlier minority progress, we have suffered actual reversals" (p.11). The report also acknowledges that "with progress in key areas having come to a halt or even moving into reverse, the American people are at a critical point of decision: Will we rekindle our commitment to eliminating those disparities, a commitment that in the past has borne remarkable fruit? Or are we resigned to a long-term retreat, in which the gaps between minorities and the majority will widen, and continuing inequality will be tolerated?" (p.15)

In her paper "Library Services to Ethnic Groups Research and Implications" Cheryl Duran provides a timely review of the literature and a critique of research methodology—really the lack of rigorous research, and an agenda of research topics for the next five years. Significant work has been done by and on behalf of the ethnic community within the library profession, and for the most part it has been done within the past two decades. Nevertheless, evidence of actual reversal, or at the very least, an element of complacency can be seen in many areas of ethnic library service development. For example, in the key areas of recruitment and training of ethnic librarians clear indications of stagnation are evident. Since 1978, when the last of the special "institutes" to train ethnic librarians was phased out, the number of ethnic librarians entering the profession has been low. Compare this to the more than 100 Hispanic librarians who graduated between 1973 and 1978 from the graduate library institutes at the University of Arizona and from California State University, Fullerton. The stimulation that focused an interest for ethnic library service development through a major infusion of ethnic librarians has been missing from the profession for several years. The growing gap between the size of the ethnic librarian pool and that of California's diverse population prompted the California State Library Minority Recruitment Project to expand and revise its program to restimulate California's ability to develop more ethnic librarians.

There are also strong indications that the impact and use of LCSA monies for ethnic library services development has gradually dropped during the last ten years. As early as 1981, *An Evaluation of Title I Library Services and Construction Act* by Applied Management Science, Inc., found significant decreases in direct expenditures of Library Services and Construction Act Title I funds for priority groups identified in the Act. From Fiscal Year 1975 to Fiscal Year 1978, expenditures for the urban disadvantaged dropped 3.6 percent, and for limited English speaking persons expenditures dropped 1.3 percent. In contrast, expenditures for the general public increased from 41.2 percent of the total amount to 50.3 percent. The implications of the demographic statistics of the RAND report and *One-Third of a Nation* and the clear signs of retrenchment for serving ethnic communities cannot be ignored: a renewed and refocused effort to serve ethnic communities is needed.

Thus far we have provided a general historical context for understanding the renewed thrust on developing and improving library and information services to ethnic groups. The works cited provide important literature and research reviews, and all of them, including the RAND Report and the Report of The Commission on Minority Participation in Education and American Life, pose important, fundamental questions. The Duran paper suggests a research agenda, and the Tarin piece attempts to focus on problems and suggests that nothing less than the full commitment of library directors, "the group that can make the single biggest difference," will be necessary so that libraries can be truly responsive to community information needs and not just adapt services to reflect what the library perceives as the information needs of ethnic communities. The fundamental question that is implied but seldom asked directly is, what are the information needs of ethnic minority communities and how do libraries then work to meet them?

We have suggested that developing a staff that reflects society—that is, a staff that is diverse culturally and representative of the major racial and ethnic groups—is not enough. We also implied that developing ethnic and foreign language collections and developing sophisticated bibliographic control mechanisms is not enough. Staffing, appropriate collections, and bibliographic control and access to these collections are certainly important, but something is still missing. Are libraries that have been responsive and that have diverse staffing patterns, foreign language and ethnic collections, and access to these materials underutilized by minority communities? Does this then suggest that perhaps libraries are not identifying, collecting, and organizing for retrieval certain types of information that are important to minorities? Is the general restriction to bibliographic information (books, periodicals, films, videos, recordings, archives, manuscripts, etc.) a particular issue for minorities? Need libraries, particularly public libraries, revisit the notion of community information services?

Community information services have a history in libraries not unlike that of library service for minorities. The relationship between community information services and information and referral programs needs to be explored more fully. Many public libraries and public library systems have developed comprehensive information and referral services and programs. Most include information of particular importance to minority clients, and most attempt to respond to the status of individuals within diverse communities. Given the history of library services to minority communities, given the many successes and the many failures, and given the state of the art and the library profession's aspirations to really understand the information needs of new user or potential user communities, how must libraries focus their energy and resources?

At the State of Change conference in California, the need to explore how libraries allocate resources to meet particular library and information service needs was stressed. Implicity, the concern must also be on how libraries reallocate resources to meet information needs of realigned communities? Information needs may well be quite different from traditional bibliographic information services provided by libraries; needs may well encompass the necessity for developing new information systems, databases, retrieval systems, delivery systems, and access programs. Libraries and librarians are particularly qualified to identify information sources, acquire them, and process them for access. Why are libraries not doing what they do best by exploring sources of information that are organized differently from bibliographic information? Certainly the examples of information systems for information and referral programs are models; technology is such that library patrons should be able to access from their local public library, or their home or office, databases that provide information of a nonbibliographic nature. Access to such information sources does not preclude access to more traditional types of library information; it simply expands access to information that may force libraries to be all the more "networked." Technology is also such that language need not be a barrier. Libraries can and should play a pivotal role in enabling ethnic communities to become more self-sufficient in how they access information. Existing literature and programs provide ample evidence of how libraries have not become central in meeting the information needs of minority communities. The library community has not identified all the information sources utilized and needed by ethnics. Libraries are not linked and networked, and generally the public does not access information sources from libraries. Yet libraries exist to meet and serve the information needs of their respective communities. What will happen when someone other than an Anglo will make the decision on what information agencies to fund and not fund? Which information and cultural agencies will reflect and be responsive to the total community?

Libraries are inexperienced in these areas, though certainly there is a dearth of current successful programs. If libraries choose to continue to restrict themselves only to more traditional information sources, they may well find themselves all the more out of touch with the real information needs of emerging communities. Should not public libraries push the concepts and successes of the Detroit TIP (The Information Place) programs, the Los Angeles County Public Library's CALL (Community Access Library Line), and the Peninsula Library System's CIP (Community Information Place) program (San Mateo County, California)? Should not public libraries push the concept and principles of reference services to include reference tools (automated and otherwise) that provide community information? Should not public libraries also be at the forefront of developing community information databases just as they are leading in the development of national and regional bibliographic databases? Should not public libraries be able to provide access to information sources and not just refer clients to the source? How can libraries link technology and the traditional functions of identification, acquisition, processing, reference, and access to the specific information needs of minority communities?

Information services to minority communities should not be "special," and information sources important to diverse communities are not limited to bibliographic data. Demographic changes in communities require a rethinking, a new analysis, and a reallocation of resources to meet different information needs.

The work by Cheryl Duran and Edith Fisher suggests that even in more traditional roles, libraries have not fully documented the pre-civil rights era in African American librarianship; nor has there been full documentation of the African American experience from the civil rights era to the present. Duran points further to the lack of documentation and research on the information needs of American Indians. Likewise there are classification and bibliographic access issues that affect access to information by all minority groups. The information needs of Asian Americans are the least well documented. Over and over again librarians speak of and call for research that focuses on the information needs of minorities within the context of their total community information environment. The profession continues to call for ongoing personnel development programs, including recruitment into the profession. Libraries continue to request adequate funding to serve nontraditional information needs, and librarians continue to voice concern for a mechanism to deal with issues of reallocation of existing funds given new information need realities.

The minority population growth in the United States is phenomenal—the RAND Report provides clear evidence of this for California. As ethnic people become major players in government at city, county, state and national levels, libraries will find that the need to respond to demographically different communities has once again become imperative.

NOTES

1. Edith M. Fisher, "Minority Librarianship Research: A State-of-the-Art Review," *Library and Information Science Research* (Spring 1982): 5–65.
2. Nora Jacob, editor. *A State of Change: California's Ethnic Future and Libraries, Conference and Awareness Forum Proceedings 1988*. Stanford, California: Planning Group for "A State of Change," Stanford University Libraries and the California State Library, 1988.
3. Judith Payne, *Public Libraries Face California's Ethnic and Racial Diversity*, Santa Monica: RAND Corporation, May 1988.
4. *One-Third of a Nation*, A Report of The Commission on Minority Participation in Education and American Life, Washington, D.C., American Council on Education and Education Commission of the States, May 1988.
5. Cheryl Duran, "Library Services to Ethnic Groups: Research and Implications," paper presented at the California Library Association Annual Conference, Fresno, California, November 12, 1988.
6. Patricia A. Tarin, "RAND Misses the Point: A 'Minority' Report," *Library Journal*, November 1, 1988, 31–34.

Review of the Library Year

Abstracting and Indexing Services

The year 1988 brought analysis, expansion, and change—particularly with regard to electronic distribution—for the abstracting and indexing (A&I) community. The year also marked intrusion of the outside world prompting the information community to awake, unite, and react.

Technology is in the forefront of the industry. Despite uncertainty about the ultimate viability of CD-ROM, more databases were announced in that format than for online. Most CD-ROM products mirrored databases available for years, although some were developed directly from print versions such as Phonedisc. The majority of new databases are scientific or technological, even though business information is thought to receive the most usage and earn the most money. Beilstein is the standout among all the sci/tech databases introduced. A cooperative project of $15,000,000 to $20,000,000, funded by the Beilstein Institute, the German government, and Springer–Verlag, the publisher of the *Beilstein Handbook* and supplier of the database, Beilstein is the authoritative information source in organic chemistry, dating back to 1830. The database, the first third of which was available in December, was created by rekeying data from the more than 300 volumes of the handbook series, some 495,000 pages. The extraordinary effort and cost required to create this database as well as the heightened anticipation of its debut made it the "new product of the year."

Product and product-line improvements helped mark the maturing of an industry that observed the 16th anniversary of online availability in 1988. INSPEC introduced indexing to retrieve numerical data; Sociological Abstracts put its recently developed thesaurus online. A major technological breakthrough occurred when Dialog and Thomson & Thomson introduced images in the Trademarkscan database. Repackaging to meet a market need or to enhance the product line is exemplified by Congressional Information Service's index to statistical data and Congressional publications in the health and health-care areas as well as Petroleum Abstracts' (University of Tulsa) PA-Plus, which packaged *Bulletin*, database license, and search aids for one price to educational institutions. In the system sector, Dialog merged split databases into megafiles and introduced 2400 Baud DIALNET nodes.

Another critical movement was the reevaluation of and changes in pricing online information. The importance of the issue is illustrated by the fact that many conferences, including the NFAIS Annual Meeting, featured sessions on pricing; ASIDIC made pricing the subject of both its meetings in 1988. The trend to lower connect time charges has begun in earnest. Chemical Abstracts Service (CAS) began 1988 with the first phase-in stage of its pricing plan to charge for information searched and retrieved rather than time spent. Many online systems modified their pricing policies by introducing fixed price passwords or subscriptions offering unlimited usage. Some systems moved toward lower hourly charges. BRS reduced its per-hour search costs, but it was an ESA/IRS announcement that bordered on revolutionary. The Frascati-based online host proposed moving the bulk of the fee algorithm to data retrieved. ESA would have only minimum hourly fees for system housekeeping activities and database access fees. The access fees are initiated by entering the database but are independent of the length of time spent on the search. The success of the ESA-

IRS plan is yet to be determined, as is the level of cooperation from database producers. The ESA-IRS plan, the CAS pricing scheme, and the other pricing activities during 1988 intimate changes that are both inevitable and overdue.

Business may view 1988 as the year of aquisition and takeover. The A&I community was certainly not immune to the fever. Some acquisitions brought a needed or complementary technology or expanded a product line (Bowker–Library Database Division of EIC/Intelligence or Predicasts–BIS Infomat, Ltd.). The acquisition of the year was Knight Ridder's purchase of Dialog Information Services from Lockheed. The undisputed leader among online services, Dialog had flourished under a company whose product, business, and corporate philosophy were alien to its own. In spite of the mismatch and because of the leadership and personnel within Dialog, the company prospered. Knight Ridder paid $353,000,000, a premium price, for a virtually intangible product made possible only through the contracts/agreements with product owners. While the effect of the purchase on DIALOG (both philosophically and on product offering) or its users remains unknown, the identity of the buyer was welcomed by the A&I community: the premier U.S. system would remain U.S.-owned.

A&I companies continued to cooperate and expand vertically. Joint efforts added technology (CAS–Evans & Sutherland); permitted hybrid products (EMBASE–NLM—*Yearbook of Cancer* via SilverPlatter or NLM–EPA Toxic Chemical Release Inventory database); expanded product utility (IAC offering non-IAC CD-ROMs on its InfoTrac Reference Center); and increased market penetration (Bowker distribution of MicroSoft's Bookshelf CD-ROM Reference Library). A&I companies also added to their product lines. BIOSIS introduced its own online system, the BIOSIS Connection, designed to reach the life scientist. CAS announced on-demand searches in protein and nucleotide sequences; Dialog expanded its OnDisc product offering.

In its quest for the elusive enduser, the A&I community recognized that past efforts had been generally unsuccessful and that future economic stability requires market expansion beyond the nearly saturated library/information center area. While gateway development and growth may contribute to this goal, A&I services, online systems, and independent firms actively pursued new markets by developing software packages to simplify searching and/or increase data manipulation possibilities. CAS introduced STN EXPRESS; Derwent—PATSTAT PLUS; Dun's Marketing Services—Dun's Market Searcher Software; NLM—Grateful Med Version 3. Battelle introduced PATENTS–PC, with merge and edit capabilities. Tome Associates, Ltd., Verity, Inc., and Information Access System, Inc., marketed Tome, Searcher, TOPIC, and Intelligent Test Management System. Each software utilizes vocabularies or boolean operations/logic differently, enabling the occasional searcher to find information regardless of the protocol requirements of the database or the online system.

In the education arena, there were further attempts to reach unreached markets. In 1988, A&I services produced a record number of videotapes, videodiscs, and floppy discs that offered self-instruction options and learning flexibility. In addition, online systems produced education alternatives in print (Dialog), on videotape (BRS), on floppy (STN), and online (Westlaw). The emphasis the industry put on education was formally recognized by Dialog's introduction of an award for excellence in online education.

Although activity within the A&I community was substantial, 1988 will be remembered for outside events that affect all information companies. The disregard of states to copyright terms and conditions and any subsequent infringement litigation under the cloak of states' immunity was introduced into the corporate consciousness by a software duplication case in California. In an industry that sells, frequently at preferred rates, to such state entities as universities, the realization of what is currently legal was a harsh reality that provoked a cry for legislative cure. The FBI Library Awareness Program, and the levels of oversight and usage restriction it implied, was spotlighted. The revised Trade Bill put to rest for this year the issue of privatizing NTIS, and Congress finally took the steps necessary for the U.S. to become a signatory to the Berne Convention. The decision of the Copyright Office, Library of Congress, to re-evaluate its deposit requirements will affect each A&I organization. The Library also initiated a one-year pilot program for a Machine Readable Collections Reading Room.

The year began with a report from Carlos Cuadra that noted a slowdown in industry growth of both databases and online systems. At the same time, the number of gateways had increased during 1987 by 15, for a total of 59. Cuadra emphasized the attention that A&I services should pay to gateways by diagramming the 23 routes, 19 of which are gateways, a user can take to a database. As an increasing number of companies publicly endorsed the NFAIS Gateway Code of Practice, Judge Harold Greene, who had overseen the breakup of AT&T, issued his long-awaited decision on the extent of allowable activity by the Regional Bell Operating Companies (RBOCs). His approval of their offering access to information, without offering the information itself, effectively introduced seven companies, each of which has more money, market, and clout than most A&I services, into information dissemination via gateways. While the full effect of the Greene decision will not be known for years, 1988 is the year that we can record as the beginning.

ELIZABETH L. UNRUH

Academic Libraries

Creativity, Innovation and Research. Nineteen eighty-eight produced a collage of recurring concerns in academic librarianship. ALA president Margaret Chisholm challenged the profession to identify and develop its leadership. ACRL president Joanne Euster promoted the importance of creativity and innovation as functions of leadership. She stressed social innovation, i.e., new organizational structures, new service designs, new ways of seeing the world, as well as technological innovation. Her call for ideas resulted in the "Innovations" column in *College and Research Libraries News*. Topics in 1988 included humor, hypercard CAI, favorite books exhibits, automated access, special collections, and others.

Richard M. Dougherty was honored as the first recipient of the Hugh Craig Atkinson Memorial Award. Dougherty, Professor of Information and Library Studies, University of Michigan, was Director of Libraries until his resignation this fall. The Atkinson award recognized his achievements (including risk taking) that contributed significantly to improvements in the area of library automation, library management, and library development and research.

A second theme in the professional literature in 1988 questioned the intellectual content of the profession. Pauline Wilson asked: "Mission and Information: What Business Are We In?" in *The Journal of Academic Librarianship*, May. Richard Dougherty asked librarians to examine the influence of technology on the information environment. *(The Journal of Academic Librarianship*, September.) Charles Martell's editorials asked: What is research? And is there a research agenda for academic libraries? *(College and Research Libraries*, January and September.) Robert Grover and Martha L. Hale concluded in "The Role of the Librarian in Faculty Research." *(College and Research Libraries*, January) that librarians must assume a proactive role in the research process by understanding the function of research in information transfer and becoming key members of research networks.

Service. New services were offered, traditional services were expanded and the delivery of all services was analyzed. A third theme focused on the needs of new clientele as well as improved delivery to all clientele.

Links between academic libraries and the business community became increasingly important. Northwestern University Library's NQUERY provides Chicago area business and trade oganizations with books, journal articles, and access to data on optical disk on a cost–recovery basis. The Self Management Laboratory in the Undergraduate Library of the University of Illinois, Urbana–Champaign, links the library and counseling center through 300 non–circulating books, pamphlets, and audiocassettes and computer–based self-help programs. Peter G. Watson developed a program of library support for administrators at California State University, Chico *(College and Research Libraries News*, January). Improved service to the disabled, to ESL students, the print handicapped and to off–campus program is also promoted through the program.

The future of reference service was discussed at a program sponsored by the Reference and Information Services Committee of the University of Texas at Austin Library.

With the revision of the ACRL Model Statement, Bibliographic Instruction process and content were given considerable interest throughout the year. Sonia Bondi argued for BI as a teaching strategy that reinforced the development of critical thinking in the college curriculum ("Critical Thinking and Bibliographic Instruction," *The Journal of Academic Librarianship*, July). Chemistry professor John Lanning stressed information literacy as essential to the development of critical thinking ("Library Faculty Partnership in Curriculum Development," *College and Research Libraries News*, January).

Richard Feinberg and Christine King questioned whether current BI standards were practical in "Short–Term Library Skill competencies: Arguing for the Achievable," *College and Research Libraries*, January.

Collection Development. Conspectus–based collection development was promoted by Anthony W. Ferguson, Joan Grant and Joel Rutstein to foster cooperation between libraries and manage resources within individual libraries ("The RLG Conspectus: Its Use and Benefit," *College and Research Libraries*, May). Peggy Forcier and Larry R. Oberg, working on the Library and Information Resources for the Northwest (LIRN) Program demonstrated its value in smaller libraries. A more fundamental approach was presented by Catherine E. Pasterczyk in the form of a checklist for the new selector *(College and Research Libraries News*, July/August).

Reliance on approval plans by ARL libraries increased to 93.6 percent from 85 percent in 1982.

The ACRL Western European Specialists Section held its second international conference in

The new Macalester College (St. Paul, Minnesota) Library cost $10,000,000, is on five levels, and contains 69,000 square feet. The building has a 450,000 volume capacity and seats 600.

One of the largest and most ambitious new academic buildings in recent years, the Benjamin S. Rosenthal Library at Queens College, Flushing, New York, was dedicated on September 15. The 230,000-square-foot facility houses some 2,000,000 items, a conference center/lecture hall, and the Graduate School of Library and Information Services.
[© Katherine McGlynn, C.I.M.S. Queens College]

Florence, Italy, April 4–8. The philosophical differences between the European curatorial role and the American information delivery role was a recurring theme.

Collections continued to grow. The University of Virginia added its 3,000,000th volume, while Johns Hopkins and Southern Illinois University, Carbondale acquired their 2,000,000th volumes and the University of Louisville and Georgia State University reported their 1,000,000th volumes.

Many significant collections were added to the nation's academic libraries. The University of Texas at El Paso received $1,642,287 from the estate of Lucille B. Pillow for the purchase of books and new materials. Million-dollar grants were received by New York University, Johns Hopkins University, and the University of Illinois to improve their collections. The latter two were National Endowment for the Humanities challenge grants designed to strengthen their humanities collections. The University of Tulsa (Oklahoma) received a $1,500,000 matching grant from University Microfilms, Incorporated to acquire microfilm backruns of materials owned in incomplete sets.

Preservation. A major theft from the California Polytechnic State University at San Luis Obispo by author and 1988 Academy Award nominee Jerry Gustav Hasford, and the conviction of former University of Georgia rare book curator Robert "Skeet" Willingham emphasized the importance of this year's publication of the *Guidelines Regarding Thefts in Libraries*. Major grant support of preservation activity included $1,000,000 from the National Endowment for the Humanities to Yale University, an NEH grant to the Rochester Institute of Technology to fund a study on the preservation of deteriorating film, and Andrew F. Mellon grants to the University of Iowa and Columbia University to support training in conservation and preservation administration internships.

Funding. Another major concern throughout 1988 was the escalating price of serials. The 28th annual survey of U.S. periodical prices reported a 9.1 percent increase which was down from the 9.9 percent increase of 1987 but still more than two and a half times the U.S. rate of inflation (*Library Journal*, April 15). Librarians from nine research libraries, meeting in Lawrence, Kansas in January, reported increases of 12 to 20 percent in foreign and domestic titles.

Meanwhile, Stanford University announced it was canceling approximately $100,000 of its science subscriptions, and other libraries discussed boycotts or taking some other action to confront publishers. Results of a survey of ARL library directors, "Paying the Piper: ARL Libraries Respond to Skyrocketing Journal Subscription Costs," appeared in *The Journal of Academic Librarianship*, March. In the same issue, Dogherty's editorial, "Serial Prices: Outrageous or Just the Price of Doing Business?" identified elements in the serial publishing cycle contributing to the rise in domestic prices.

Application of the 6 percent standard (i.e., the library should receive a budget equal to 6 percent of the institutional budget) was promoted by librarians, although most library budgets experienced little growth. Federally funded increases for library programs were eliminated in the deficit reduction package, but start-up funding was provided for the new Title II–D technology and cooperation for academic libraries.

An additional $2,500,000 was authorized for Title II–D funding for library activities that supported initiatives funded under the Education and Training for American Competitiveness Act of 1987.

Technology. Automated catalogs became realities in increasing numbers with installations of NOTIS, CARLYLE, UNISYS, INOVAQUE, ALOHA, GEAC and a number of internally and externally developed systems nationwide. Several larger multitype networks were funded. The University of Michigan M–Link will electronically connect the university library system with the libraries of five Michigan communities; the Southeast Florida Library Network linked the databases of six Miami–area academic and public libraries and promised 24–hour document delivery. Electronic networks will join all seven University of Maine campuses electronically with public libraries and private college libraries statewide to be added. Fenway Libraries Online (FLO) links a group of eight specialized academic libraries in the Boston area that will share resources of over 900,000 volumes; the University of Missouri–Columbia and Case Western Reserve University, Cleveland, Ohio, will provide statewide dial-up access through their respective library computer networks. The ARL SPEC kit #142, "Remote Access to Online Catalogs," surveyed the technical issues, user instruction needs, management questions, and trends and needs of 57 ARL libraries.

Growth in state and regional networking was accompanied by expanded service provided by the bibliographical utilities. RLIN initiated the Research Access Project (RAP) in 11 RLG libraries that provided end-user searching to faculty at a cost of $99 per 10–hour blocks of search time. Indiana University Libraries, Bloomington, was the first OCLC/National Coordinated Cataloging Operations (NACO) institution to begin contributing authority records to the Library of Congress via the Linked Systems Project. The Linked Systems Project provides direct computer links between LC, RLIN, and OCLC and eventually will be used to transfer bibliographic records among them. The potential of CD-ROM to increase both bibliographic access and information delivery was demonstrated to about 11,000 participants at 335 receiving sites by a national CD-ROM teleconference broadcast from Oakton Community College in Des Plaines, Illinois, April 27. Telefacsimile transmission of documents has become an increasingly standard form of information delivery with an anticipated growth of about 600 new installations as reported in the upcoming fourth edition of *Telefacsimile Sites in the Libraries of the United States and Canada*. Idaho received an LSCA Title III grant for $41,800 to establish and operate a pilot telefacsimile network.

The U.S./USSR Seminar on Access to Library Resources Through Technology and Preservation, held at the Library of Congress July 5–8, gathered 12 Soviet and 30 American participants. For more on this subject see the Special Report in this volume.

Buildings. New buildings dedicated included Queens College, Flushing, New York; Arizona State University, West Campus, Phoenix; Colby–Sawyer College, New London, New Hampshire; Macalester College; and additions to the Oberlin College Conservatory of Music and the College of William and Mary. The University of Southern California, Los Angeles, received $11,500,000 of grants for a new teaching library to house 200,000 volumes and provide for hundreds of computers and individualized audiovisual work stations. Duke University, Durham, North Carolina obtained a Pew Charitable Trust Grant of $785,000 for the purchase of movable compact shelving to be installed in an off-campus warehouse accessible via daily courier.

Personnel. The *Library Journal* (October 15) reported that the number of library school graduates continued to rise, the average salary increase for new hires was the highest since 1981, and there were more jobs than qualified people to fill them. The latter confirmed the ALA placement report of a surplus of positions over applicants in all categories except administration. The average salary for entry level college and university librarians was $21,208, up 7 percent from the previous year. Roxanne Sellberg reported a disturbing lack of correlation between the amount of professional preparation and the salary received. (*The Journal of Academic Librarianship*, January). Another disquieting trend was the continued lack of equity in women's salaries. A study by David R. Dowell indicated that while level of position was the most powerful predictor of salary, accounting for 60 percent of all variance, men still earned almost $1,200 more per year than women ("Sex and Salary in a Female Dominated Profession," *The Journal of Academic Librarianship*, May).

Appointments. Included among the persons selected during 1988 to direct U.S. college, university and research libraries were: Dale E. Casper, Sam Houston State University, Huntsville, Texas; Kay Ann Cassell, New School for Social Research, New York, New York; Karen Cole, Fort Hays State University, Kansas; Joe Dahlstrom, University of Houston/Victoria, Texas; Peter V. Deekle, Susquehanna University, Selinsgrove, Pennsylvania; Adele S. Dendy, Prairie View A&M University, Texas; Douglas M. Ferrier, Texas Wesleyan College, Fort Worth, Texas; Robert A. Foley, Fitchburg State College, Massa-

Fletcher Library, Arizona State University (Tempe), West Campus.

chusetts; Eileen Agard Glickstein, Barnard College, New York, New York; Michael Gorman, California State University, Fresno; Joan Gotwals, Emory University, Atlanta, Georgia; B. Donald Grose, University of North Texas, Denton; Eleanor L. Heishman, State University of New York at Binghamton; Norma J. Hervey, Luther College, Decorah, Iowa; Ralph W. Holibaugh, Kenyon College, Gambier, Ohio; Margaret Johnson, University of Minnesota, Duluth; Ruth Katz, University of New Hampshire, Durham; Paula T. Kaufman, University of Tennessee, Knoxville; Jean Kindlen, University of Pittsburgh, Pennsylvania; Michael M. Lee, University of Houston/Clear Lake, Texas; James R. Martin, University of Southern Mississippi, Hattiesburg; Stanley Joe McCord, Lamar University, Beaumont, Texas; Aroland Meissner, Alfred University, New York; Thomas J. Moore, Central Michigan University, Mount Pleasant; Paul H. Mosher, University of Pennsylvania, Philadelphia; Cerise Oberman, State University of New York at Plattsburgh; Sarah Pedersen, Evergreen State College, Olympia, Washington; Richard C. Pollard, California State University, Fullerton; Ann E. Prentice, University of South Florida, Sarasota; Judith Sessions, Miami University, Oxford, Ohio; Elaine F. Sloan, Columbia University, New York, New York; Carol M. Spawn, Academy of Natural Sciences, Philadelphia, Pennsylvania; Thomas F. Staley, University of Texas at Austin, Harry Ransom Humanities Research Center; Susan A. Stussy, Saint Norbert College, De Pere, Wisconsin; Donald G. Sweet, University of Arkansas at Little Rock; Clarence Toomer, Greensboro College, North Carolina; J. Daniel Vann, III. Bloomsburg University of Pennsylvania; Bob Walter, Pittsburgh State University, Kansas; Peter Watson, Idaho State University, Pocatello; James F. Williams, II, University of Colorado, Boulder; and Ward M. Woodward, Northern State College, Aberdeen, South Dakota.

Duane Webster was appointed Association of Research Libraries (ARL)Executive Director and Elaine F. Sloan assumed the Presidency of ARL. Joseph Boisse assumed the ACRL Presidency; William Moffett was elected Vice President/President Elect of ACRL.

Awards. Academic or research librarian of the year: Edward G. Holley, former dean of the School of Information and Library Science, University of North Carolina, Chapel Hill; Miriam Dudley Bibliographic Instruction Librarian of the Year: Sharon A. Hogan, Director of Libraries, Louisiana State University, Baton Rouge; Samuel Lazerow Fellowship for Research in Acquisitions or Technical Services: Carol M. Kelley, Head of Acquisitions, Texas Technological College, Lubbock; K.G. Saur Award for Best Article Published in *College and University Libraries*: "Librarians and Faculty Members: Coping With Pressures to Publish," by Robert Boice, Jordan M. Scepanski, and Wayne Wilson; Doctoral Dissertation Fellowship: Sarla R. Murgar, "Managerial Motivation and Career Aspirations of Library/Information Science Students"; Bowker/Ulrich Serials Librarianship Award: Marjorie E. Bloss, Manager of Resource Sharing Department, OCLC, Dublin, Ohio. MARILYN MITCHELL

Accreditation

Standards Review. The accreditation by the American Library Association of programs that award the first professional degree for the practice of librarianship is guided by the *Standards for Accreditation*, adopted by the ALA Council in 1972. The ALA Committee on Accreditation (COA) has the responsibility for applying these standards and carrying out the accreditation process. For some time, COA has been exploring ways to involve a variety of interested associations more actively in the accreditation process. Late in 1987, the Committee concluded that an important step in moving this exploration forward would be a review and reassessment of the *Standards* to determine their need for revision. Early in 1988, the Committee decided that this investigation would be conducted by a subcommittee appointed to insure participation of a wide constituency from the library and information science professions served by the accreditation process. The American Association of Law Librarians, American Society for Information Science, Association for Library and Information Science Education, Canadian Association of Library Schools, Canadian Library Association, Medical Library Association, Society of American Archivists, Special Libraries Association, and the ALA Standing Committee on Library Education were asked for recommendations for the subcommittee.

At its spring meeting, COA developed a charge to the Standards Review Subcommittee that included (1) a review of the *Standards* for their relevancy, appropriateness, adequacy, and utility in light of changes in societal needs for and uses of information and changes in the library and information profession since their promulgation; and (2) provision of advice to COA on the nature of any changes or revisions needed in the *Standards* and specification of areas that should be studied further. The subcommittee's timetable included a final report to COA at the ALA Annual Conference in June 1989, with progress reports at the midwinter and spring meetings of the Committee. COA anticipated that, while funding for the review by the subcommittee could be found within ALA, outside funding would be sought for any extensive revision process that might be required.

The Standards Review Subcommittee, appointed by COA Chair Herman L. Totten in September 1988, held its first meeting in November, with COA member Suzanne O. Frankie as Chair. Members of the subcommittee are Francis X. Blouin, Jr.; Sandra S. Coleman; Marianne Cooper; Linda D. Crowe; Beth Miller; Emily Mobley; Jane Robbins; Fred W. Roper; Michele M. Thompson; Herbert White; and Herman L. Totten, ex officio. The meeting resulted in a preliminary report to COA, which was presented at the ALA Midwinter meeting in January 1989. The draft of the interim report paid special tribute to the wisdom and foresight of the drafters of the 1972 document for producing standards that have served well as a framework for assessing program quality and for encouraging the self-improvement of programs. The draft report also indicated that, while the Subcommittee concluded that the *Standards* need revision, this revision is not of a major substantive nature, but is rather a general broadening and updating of their tone and language to reflect changes that the profession, including graduate education programs, have undergone in the past two decades. Work toward a final Subcommittee report and COA action on it will take place during 1989.

Continuing Recognition by COPA. The Council on Postsecondary Accreditation (COPA) is a nongovernmental authorizing agency that grants the right to accredit to various bodies in their respective fields. In January 1988, COA submitted an application for continued recognition as the accrediting body for programs awarding the master's degree as the first professional degree in librarianship. In July, COA representatives attended a COPA review session on COA's application, and in October the COPA Board acted positively on the application and continued COA recognition for five years.

Site-visit Team Members. Site-visits to schools requesting accreditation of professional education programs are a very important part of the accreditation process. Members of site-visit teams include COA members and others chosen for their knowledge and experience in the diverse aspects of library and information services. During 1988, COA took several steps to maintain the high quality of site-visit team members. The pool of persons willing and able to serve as team members was reconstituted by asking those in the pool to reaffirm their willingness to serve, by examining the profile of the pool for gaps in coverage of the various aspects of library and information services, and by identifying additional persons to be added to the pool. Programs to train new members of the site-visitor pool and to retrain continuing members were redesigned, and a policy on evaluation of site-visit team members was approved and implemented.

Procedural Matters. During 1988, COA continued to consider its procedures and working documents for means of increasing the effectiveness of the Committee's activities. For some time, Committee members and staff have been concerned about the inequitable distribution of costs to support the Committee and the declining non-personnel budget under which the Committee operates. For example, the regular spring meeting of the Committee, considered imperative by COA members with an increasingly heavy workload, was eliminated in 1983. The committee revised its fee structure to add a system of fees required of schools applying for initial accreditation of programs, and an annual report review fee was assessed to schools applying for continued accreditation through the submission of an annual report. The additional revenue produced by the fees will be used by COA to meet its service responsibilities, including the reinstatement of the spring meeting of the Committee more effectively.

The *Manual of Procedures* and other working documents that guide the accreditation process were revised variously during the year. For example, the statement regarding conflicts of interest for persons associated with the accreditation process was revised; the policy on the official spokesperson for a school seeking accreditation was clarified; and several guidelines designed to aid interpretation and application of the *Standards* were revised.

Ongoing Activities. During 1988, COA received eleven self-study reports from schools requesting site visits for accreditation of education programs. Ten of the reports were accepted as useful working documents, and one was not acceptable. During the Midwinter and Annual ALA conferences, the Committee heard reports from eight teams of site visitors to schools. Based on these reports, COA continued the accreditation of five programs, removed the conditional status from the accreditation of another, and granted initial accreditation to two programs. Members of nine teams appointed to conduct site visits to schools during 1988 were briefed by COA members. Committee members met with representatives of several schools to discuss various matters regarding the accreditation of their programs. COA received reports that two accredited programs had been discontinued. Because of the nature of its work, most meetings of COA are held in executive session. Frequently, COA holds open meetings for the exchange of information with interested persons, as it did at the 1988 ALA Midwinter Conference.

Annually, each school with an accredited program submits a report to COA that is a partial application for continued accreditation. Only those programs scheduled to be visited in the current academic year are excused from reporting. Annual reports from 49 schools were considered by the Committee at its fall meeting. Based on the Committee's review of these reports, accredited status was continued for 43 programs, and action was delayed on 6 reports, pending receipt of additional information requested by the Committee.

COA Members. At the conclusion of the 1988 ALA Annual Conference, Elizabeth Boris, Edwin M. Cortez, Robert B. Croneberger, and Margo McBurney retired from the Committee. New appointees were Charles A. Bunge, Gwynneth Evans, Lauren Kelly, and Timothy W. Sineath. Continuing members were Trudi Bellardo, Keith M. Cottam, Linda D. Crowe, Suzanne O. Frankie, Michele M. Thompson, Herman L. Totten (Chair), Pat Woodrum, and E. Blanche Woolls.

HERMAN L. TOTTEN

Adults, Library Services to

The demand on frontline librarians is to understand, create, promote, implement, and evaluate the greatest diversity of programs and services ever. By the end of the 1980s, adult services librarians will have consolidated outstanding efforts in services to the illiterate, special programs for ethnic minorities, family education, health information services, online text and citation assistance, cultural and entertainment performances, and a growing diversity of offerings in literary development and readers' advisories.

In 1988, the Reference and Adult Services Division (RASD) continued to provide the organizational impetus through committees such as the Library Services to Adults Committee or the Adult Library Materials Committee. The two

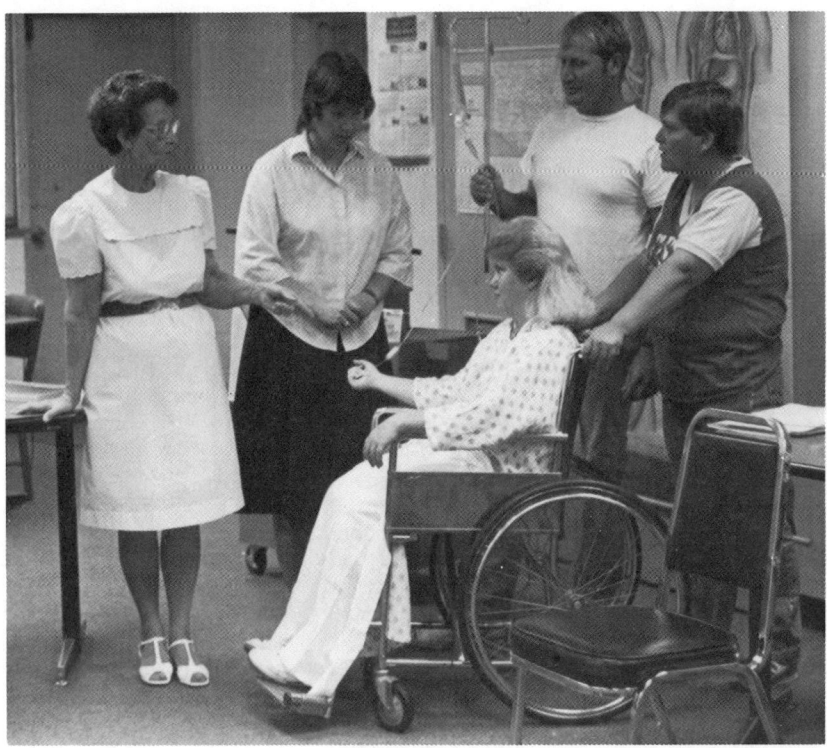

Oklahoma's Western Plains Library System and a local technical school conduct a class on Nurses Aids skills as part of the 1988 Employment Quick Start Program.

Writing to Win. The Champaign (Illinois) Public Library was the site of a three-day statewide poetry conference. The conference was sponsored by the READ Illinois Project, Stormline Press, and the Champaign library. This event also led to the publication of an anthology titled *Benchmark*. ALA's Communications Department has initiated a national project utilizing the PBS series "Voices and Visions." Funded with the help of a $358,000 grant from the National Endowment for the Humanities, this is a library-based reading, viewing, and discussion series on modern American poets.

Cultural and informational video programs have become bases for other library efforts. Brooklyn (New York) Public Library made a commitment to purchase "quality videos in such areas as science, ballet, opera, and language instruction." The MacArthur Foundation made available to libraries numerous PBS series at a greatly reduced price, which included public performance rights, so that the programs may be used in library meeting rooms and at media desks for individual viewing.

Librarians have shown a solid commitment to video programs of travel, educational topics, how-tos, PBS series, and other "classics." The Metropolitan Library System in Oklahoma County reported that 2,236 videotapes circulated 92,069 times in 11 months, and attributes heavy use to an offering of nonfiction materials.

A resurgence in the educational information center (EIC), for other continuing education information and for job assistance, may be emerging. In 1988, the Kellogg Foundation stepped up its long-standing support of adult education efforts, and sought the opinion of prominent librarians in the planning of its future activities. The Public Library Association Conference in April included a focus on programs in Pennsylvania where the state works cooperatively with libraries to provide EIC materials and personnel. The Earning and Learning Connection program at Queens Borough (New York) Public Library provides job assessment tests, résumé workshops, interviewing skills instruction, and other job-searching programs and support.

groups cooperated in a successful program at the New Orleans conference called "Discovering Literary Voices," a panel presentation addressing the selection and promotion of small presses, literary magazines, and local authors.

The strength of literary programming was evidenced in local, state, and national promotions. For example, the Patchogue-Medford (New York) Library sponsored a contest, with the aid of their Friends group, that honored writer Phyllis Whitney. Local authors submit creative works in the annual event. The library, cooperating with the Suffolk County (New York) Library System, produced a publication of the prizewinning selections.

The Adult Services in the Eighties (ASE) Project, funded by an ALA Goal Award and centered at Louisiana State University's School of Library and Information Science (Baton Rouge), was completed after working with the Adult Services Committee for five years. Library school instructors, public librarians, and other educators and researchers eagerly await its final form to be published by ALA in 1989. The preliminary reports provided to the Adult Services Committee, the "ASE Updates" in RQ (the official quarterly journal of RASD), and the hearings and programs over the last several years at conferences indicate that adult services are extraordinarily diverse, but also customized and carefully focused on individual issues in neighborhood and community libraries. All in all, the planning, implementation, and analysis of this research is groundwork for further understanding and even expansion of adult services.

RQ's "Adult Services" column has addressed personnel, technology, multicultural programs, and rural library services in this past year. The

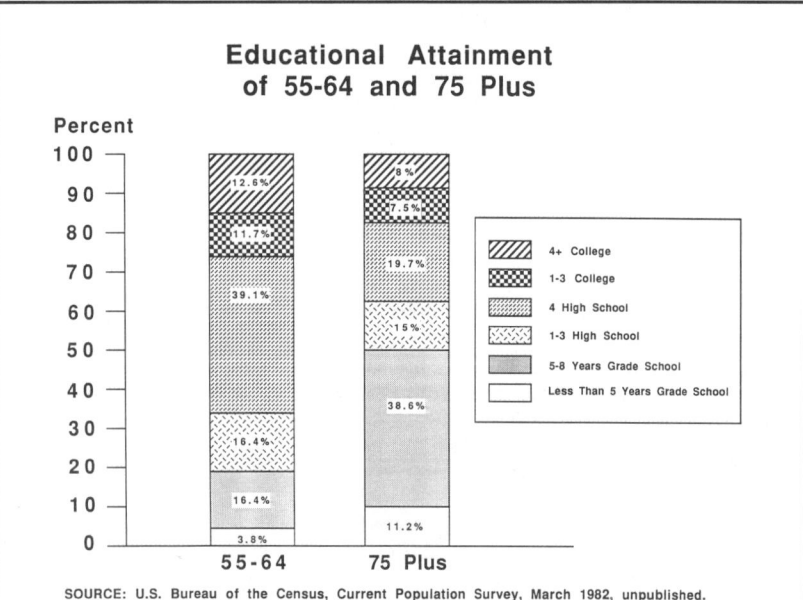

current editor of the column is Elizabeth Curry of the Southeastern Library Network.

The Margaret Monroe Library Adult Services Award honors a librarian who has made a significant contribution to and has had an impact on library adult services. Jane K. Hirsch of Montgomery County Department of Public Libraries (Maryland) was the 1988 recipient for her work in intellectual freedom programming, responsive collection development, and staff training.

Adult Services librarians have worked individually, organizationally, and theoretically toward access to and awareness of relevant programs and services for library users. Whether they promote the discovery of alternative voices in the world of publishing, provide multimedia resources and programs for information, education, and cultural enrichment, and/or seek cooperation with other program providers to develop programs of community interest, librarians through the 1980s responded to the upper limits of possibility with diverse programs and services.

Important partnerships of local and state libraries continue to facilitate many programs and services. The bridge between library educators and researchers also is well trafficked and undergirded by new offerings such as requests for proposals sought by the Council on Library Resources (CLR), which made funds available for Cooperative Research grants. Faculty in library schools and librarians in public libraries cooperate in researching topics of mutual interest.

The strengths of the book and of reading programs and discussions survive in a multimedia environment. The integration of books with other services is more easily accomplished when librarians respond to the multifaceted lives of library users.

GARY O. ROLSTAD

American Association of Law Libraries

The American Association of Law Libraries (AALL), founded in 1906, has continued as the professional organization for librarians employed in libraries of the legal profession: courts, government agencies, law firms and corporations, and law schools. Private sector libraries have continued to supply the largest part of the Association's growth in membership, although state, court, and county libraries have also grown fast:

Class of Membership	1988	1981	1976
Academic	1,390	1,256	1,018
Firm and corporate	1,678	1,136	794
State, court, and county	748	395	251
Foreign	480	116	140

The decade of the eighties has brought increased professionalization of headquarters' activities: the first Executive Director came in 1981; the Association occupied and renovated much larger office space in 1987; a Professional Development Officer was hired in early 1988. Later that year, a professional editor took over from member volunteers the editing and production of the *AALL Newsletter,* and a convention manager was used for the first time to plan the 1989 annual meeting to be held in Reno June 16–21. Throughout that period, the functions of keeping track of members and producing the annual *AALL Directory,* as well as daily document production, were computerized with the help of an outside consultant.

A major assignment for the new Professional Development Office was to coordinate AALL's educational activities with those of other professional organizations. The theme of looking outside the Association continued in other ways. The number of members who function as liaisons to other professional organizations—among librarians and among lawyers—continued to increase, and in 1988 there were 36 such representatives. Two Special Committees appointed for 1988–89 were especially concerned with events outside AALL's part of the profession: National Information Policy and Preservation Needs of Law Libraries. Each committee focused on meshing AALL's activities with those of other professional organizations.

The Standing Committee on National Legal Resources sponsored a by-invitation workshop at the Supreme Court in October 1988, "Setting the Legal Information Action Agenda for the Year 2000." Representatives from other types of libraries, the Library of Congress, the computing community, and scholars joined Committee members in outlining the major legal information needs for the rest of the century, and in determining how to meet those needs. Again, the theme was to get AALL more into the mainstream as a participant at the national level.

The Association's commitment to its educational function continued as some $53,000 were awarded as scholarships to attend law or library school and as grants to help attend the annual meeting. Of this, $3,500 is specifically for a minority scholarship.

The Association's concern with education was expressed by two other committees during the year. One, a Special Committee on Educational Policy, wrote a document describing the desirable characteristics of programs training law librarians that was sent to ALA's Committee on Accreditation. The other, a long-range planning subcommittee of the Standing Committee on Education worked to develop new organizational, policy, and procedural mechanisms to adjust AALL's operation to make optimum use of the Professional Development Officer.

The Association has 28 chapters, whose members need not be members of the national organization. Those groups' membership in 1988 totaled nearly 5,600—a better measure of the number of law librarians than AALL's count alone. The chapters range from very large groups in such cities as Washington, D.C., and New York, to much more scattered chapters in the Midwest, Southeast, and Northwest.

Twelve Special Interest Sections are tightly connected subgroups of the national organization. These represent types of law libraries (Academic; State, Court, County, and Private) and types of activities (technical services, reader services) as well as special topics (contemporary so-

American Association of Law Libraries

PRESIDENT (June 1988–July 1989):
Margaret A. Leary, University of Michigan Law Library

VICE-PRESIDENT/PRESIDENT-ELECT:
Richard Danner, Duke University Law Library

SECRETARY:
Gitelle Seer, Dewey, Ballantine, Bushby, Palmer and Wood (New York)

TREASURER:
Alan S. Holoch, Ohio State University Law Library

Membership (December 1988): 4,296
Headquarters: 53 W. Jackson Blvd., Chicago, Illinois 60604, Telephone 312-939-4764, telefax 312-431-1097
Interim Executive Director: William Murphy
Professional Development Officer: Martha S. Brown

---

cial problems). As AALL headquarters professionalizes, and the size and number of committees diminish as a result, the chapters and special interest sections have become increasingly important sources of energy in the Association.

To alleviate the impersonality of an increasingly larger and more complex Association, a special mentoring program is used at the national meeting, linking experienced members with new members. The special Conference of Newer Law Librarians continues to orient new members on the day before the annual meeting begins.

The Association continued to pay close attention to the needs of minority members and prospective members. A special brochure to attract minorities to law librarianship, and recruiting visits to minority student groups in law and library schools were carried out by the Standing Committee on Minorities. The President worked with major sponsors of events at the annual meeting to attain a better balance between education and entertainment.

Law librarianship remains a profession unique for its close connection to practitioners and academics, because the legal system in the U.S. relies on the doctrine of precedent and the existence of written law.

MARGARET A. LEARY

American Association of School Librarians

1988. The year 1988 lived up to expectation as a banner year for AASL. The major event was the publication of *Information Power: Guidelines for School Library Media Programs*. This document was developed jointly by AASL and the Association for Educational Communications and Technology (AECT). Published by the American Library Association in April, the first print run of 25,000 copies was sold out within two months.

Information Power was introduced to the educational community via an international teleconference that originated from the University of South Carolina/Columbia and featured representatives of AASL and AECT and a sampling of educators for around the nation along with a library media consultant from Vancouver, British Columbia. A toll-free number enabled viewers in every state in the U.S. and every province in Canada to phone in questions during the live question/answer segments. Based on attendance reports from the site coordinators and the number of calls received during the teleconference, approximately 10,000 people participated. Sponsors for a 1989 teleconference include AASL, AECT, and the National Association of Elementary School Principals (NAESP), with support from the National Association of Secondary School Principals (NASSP).

Implementation Activities. "Information Power: How to Get It, How to Keep It, How to Pass It On" was the title of AASL's preconference in New Orleans. Approximately 275 people attended the day-and-a-half program. Paul Jung, Superintendent of the Des Plaines, Illinois, School District #62, was the keynote speaker.

Companion documents by AASL and AECT members were published to further the implementation of *Information Power*. Implementation workshops were held in Park City (Utah), Chicago, Washington, D.C., and Dallas during August, September, and October.

Statement on Education for Library Media Specialists. AASL presented and ALA Council adopted a statement concerning the appropriate education for library media specialists, along with a statement developed by the ALA Standing Committee on Library Education (SCOLE) regarding the appropriate education for a librarian. SCOLE proposed, and ALA Council accepted, the following statement: "The master's degree from a program accredited by the American Library Association is the appropriate professional degree for librarians."

Planning for the Information Literacy Seminar. A major 1988 initiative was planning a symposium on information literacy to be held in April 1989. In 1986, the National Commission on Libraries and Information Services (NCLIS) commissioned a paper devoted to the role of the library media program in the development of students' critical thinking skills. This paper, coupled with the emphasis in *Information Power* on the need to develop an information studies curriculum, led AASL and NCLIS to plan a symposium entitled, "Information Literacy and Education for the 21st Century: Toward an Agenda for Action." The meeting will bring together members and staff from major educational associations and educational policy makers to address information literacy in our K–12 educational systems. The work of the ALA Presidential Commission on Information Literacy will provide background information and direction for the symposium.

AASL's Response to ALA Priorities and Goals. Access to Information, a major concept in *Information Power: Guidelines for School Library Media Programs* is the necessity for these programs to provide both intellectual and physical access to information and ideas. The document urges leaders in each school to identify and implement an information studies curriculum,

ALA/AASL and NCATE

In June 1987 the American Library Association (ALA) and its American Association for School Librarians (AASL) joined the National Association for Teacher Education (NCATE) in order to participate in the process of accreditation of higher education programs for school media specialists. The ALA Council in January 1988, had delegated management of ALA's participation in NCATE to AASL. ALA's decision to become involved in the approval of programs for school library media specialists in schools or departments of education not eligible for accreditation by ALA's Committee on Accreditation recognized two major problems that had been growing for more than a decade: (1) the failure of higher education to prepare enough school library media specialists to serve the nation's 100,000 plus public and private schools and (2) the documented variance of quality nationwide preparation standards for preparing school library media personnel.

For several years, school library leaders had been concerned about mounting evidence that a shortage of school librarians would materialize in the nineties. The 1977 and 1983 Miller-Downen[1] studies of AASL membership revealed startingly low numbers of beginning librarians in the work force. Studies done in the early eighties by Learmont[2] (1980), Heim[3] (1981), and King Research[4] (1983), revealed that the numbers of graduates of ALA-accredited library education programs being placed in educational settings were steadily declining. Turner's[5] study for AASL of the supply and demand of school library media specialists revealed that (1) a shallow pool of qualified library media specialists exists nationally, but particularly in the Middle Atlantic and Southeast; (2) school district personnel directors perceive that the quality, and quantity, of applicants for school library media professionals is declining; and (3) retirements in the nineties will intensify the problem of less-than-adequate pools of candidates for school library media positions.

Recruitment to the field suffered a setback in the seventies when the focus of federal funding was changed and many schools eliminated positions in their library media programs. The general disinclination of young people to enter the teaching profession also affected recruitment to the school library media field. The recruitment problem was further exacerbated by declining opportunities in ALA-accredited programs for pre-

service school library media specialists. The closing of some programs, the geographical dislocation for those that remain, and the failure of many ALA programs to provide the curriculum needed by school personnel resulted in a downward trend in students electing a school library media specialization.

During this same period of time, a variety of programs were developing or "hanging on" in schools of education. Generally speaking, most of these programs responded to state requirements for the certification of school personnel, resulting in certification programs at either the graduate or undergraduate level, and graduate degrees in education with a concentration in media. Usually these programs concentrated on school library media personnel, but many also prepared people for positions in small public libraries and community colleges—the latter due to the availability of courses in instructional design and technology. If accreditation was desired for any of these programs, only NCATE was available at the national level. For many years, the Association for Educational Communications and Technology (AECT) an NCATE member, had provided the only national standards for the preparation of school library media personnel.

In 1985, NCATE revised its organizational structure and developed a new approach to accreditation. This paved the way for ALA membership because, under the reorganization, any professional group that developed standards for training school personnel could join NCATE and could present for approval a set of guidelines for reviewing training programs.

All NCATE member professional organizations also have representatives on NCATE's governance boards, including the Board of Examiners that provides qualified teams of educators for evaluating universities and colleges that request accreditation.

At the end of 1988, ALA's participation in NCATE was fully underway. The Association has three persons on the Board of Examiners who will be trained in site evaluation and who will serve for three-year terms. The ALA Executive Board, makes all ALA appointments to NCATE governance boards and will appoint a fourth person to the Board of Examiners in 1989, and a fifth in 1990. One ALA representative serves on the NCATE Specialty Areas Studies Board, which reviews and accepts or rejects new or revised curriculum guidelines submitted by professional organization members and which manages and oversees implementation of program review.

The review process is the heart of NCATE's accreditation program. Representatives of appropriate professional organizations review specialty area professional school personnel programs at regular intervals to determine whether the educational program meets the guidelines for the particular profession.

The ALA/AASL guidelines, *Competencies for the Initial Preparation of School Library Media Specialists*, were adopted by the Specialty Areas Studies Board in September 1988. They include 56 professional competency statements that describe entry-level qualifications. Competencies are organized around professionalism, management, communication and group dynamics, collection management, organization, administration, instructional leadership, and access.

ALA's review process, designed, implemented, and managed by AASL will begin in May 1989, with the review of folios from several institutions, and will consist of evaluation of the program's documentation submitted to determine adequacy of syllabi, activities, assignments, and practices.

In order to appreciate fully the importance of ALA's decision to become involved in the NCATE accreditation process, it is necessary to review briefly the accreditation institutions that prepare teachers and school library media specialists in the U.S. Many states have three levels of accreditation: state approval, regional accreditation, and national accreditation.

The total impact of ALA's involvement in NCATE has yet to be revealed. Casual observers of the effect of accreditation on program development predict that the preparation programs in units of education

American Association of School Librarians

will change and perhaps improve. The influence of ALA, the largest national organization of librarians will lend support to faculties needing to improve and expand programs or move them to the graduate level as recommended by the latest national guidelines, *Information Power*, developed by AASL and AECT and published in 1988 by ALA.

One important secondary benefit for both ALA and AASL will come from opportunities for communication and liaison with other professional organizations that perceive librarianship as either unknown or arcane. Opportunities for the American Library Association to interpret the role of libraries in producing an information–literate society may be the primary benefit of the new ALA/NCATE relationship.

ENDNOTES

1. Miller, Marilyn L. and Thomas W. Downen, "A Look at AASL Membership" *School Media Quarterly* 7, no. 1 1978 40–47.
   Miller and Downen, "A Profile of Two National Organizations Serving School Library Media Specialists," *School Library Media Annual*, v.2, 1984.
2. Learmont, Carol L. "Placements and Salaries, 1979: Wider Horizons." *Library Journal* 105:2271–7, Nov. 1, 1980.
3. Helm, Kathleen McEntee, "Toward a Work–Force Analysis of the School Library Media Professional," *School Library Media Quarterly*, 9:235–249, Summer, 1981.
4. King Research, Inc., *Library Human Resources: A Study of Supply and Demand*, Chicago, ALA, 1983.
5. Turner, Phillip M. and J. Gordon Coleman, Jr., "School Library Media Specialists in the United States: Supply and Demand." Unpublished report for School Library Media Educators Section of the American Association of School Librarians, 1987.

MARILYN L. MILLER

Jacqueline G. Morris, Occidental College.

to be taught through the existing curricula, that will ensure all students become effective and efficient users on information. The document also recognizes that a major challenge facing school library media programs is to provide equal access to information to all students regardless of gender, economic level, geographic location, race, or religion. To meet that challenge, school library media collections must provide access to the information resources available beyond the confines of the school.

Special initiative legislative funding provided through the ALA Strategic Long-Range Planning Process provided support to AASL, the ALA Office for Research, and the ALA Washington Office to focus attention on the need for adequate funding of school library media programs. A colorful brochure entitled "Want a Hot Investment Tip?", a fact sheet on school library media programs, and a cover letter from the AASL President were prepared for distribution to approximately 40,000 district superintendents and school board presidents nationwide. Responses to date have been very positive. Additional brochures for distribution at the local level are available at cost from ALA/AASL.

The recent federal reauthorization of ECIA (HR5) includes school library resources as a category for funding. Members of AASL and the AASL Legislative Committee worked with Eileen Cooke of the ALA Washington Office in a concerted effort to have school library resources listed in the legislation as a category to receive funds. As a result of a resolution passed by the AASL Board of Directors at its Midwinter Meeting in San Antonio, several state affiliate associations sent a delegate to participate in the National Library Legislative Day. AASL's White House Conference Task Force developed a plan for AASL participation in the White House Conference on Libraries and Information Services. The detailed plan included involving AASL affiliate associations in the identification of issues and grassroots efforts to get those issues onto the national agenda.

AASL's Intellectual Freedom Committee is preparing a packet of materials on intellectual freedom issues that will help school library media specialists prepare for challenges to materials. AASL's Intellectual Freedom Committee joined with other division IFCs to jointly sponsor a program at the Annual Conference in New Orleans.

On public awareness AASL participated in the Association Collaborative on Teaching Thinking, and recently co-sponsored a meeting with the Association for Supervision and Curriculum Development (ASCD) on the use of instructional resources to teach students to think. A presentation was made in May at the International Reading Association (IRA) Conference held in Toronto. AASL prepared articles for publication in the National Association of Secondary School Principals (NASSP) *Bulletin*, *Reading Teacher*, and *PTA Today*. AASL also presented a program at the American Vocational Association Conference in St. Louis in December 1988 that highlighted the need for vocational students to develop their abilities to use information.

On personnel resources AASL eagerly addressed the responsibilities for participation in the National Council for the Accreditation of Teacher Education (NCATE) given to the division by ALA Council. Curriculum guidelines for school library media preparation programs were prepared by an AASL Task Force chaired by Marilyn Miller. The guidelines, reviewed by many educators and practitioners across the country, were approved by the AASL Board of Directors in New Orleans and by NCATE in September. Marilyn Miller represents ALA on the NCATE Specialty Area Studies Board. ALA appointees to the NCATE Board of Examiners are Roger Ashley, Pauletta Bracy, and Marilyn Greenberg. AASL is currently planning training sessions of those who will serve as folio reviewers with the first session to be held during 1989 Midwinter Conference.

AASL contacted the National Board for Professional Teaching Standards (NBPTS), a group proposed by the Carnegie Forum on Education and the Economy, to establish and maintain high standards for teaching. Prior to the contact, NBPTS had not considered school library media specialists as candidates for certification. It is now likely that library media specialists will be involved in the process.

Recognizing the Association's responsibility to help library media specialists develop the competencies needed to carry out the program described in *Information Power*, AASL made the commitment to develop a continuing education

AMERICAN ASSOCIATION OF SCHOOL LIBRARIANS

PRESIDENT (July 1988–July 1989):
Jacqueline G. Morris, Indiana Department of Education, Indianapolis

FIRST VICE-PRESIDENT/PRESIDENT-ELECT:
Retta B. Patrick, Library Media Consultant, Little Rock, Arkansas

EXECUTIVE DIRECTOR:
Ann Carlson Weeks

Membership (August 31, 1988): 6,243 (5,565 personal; 678 organizational)
Expenditures (August 31, 1988): $312,410

---

program by adding a Coordinator for Professional Development. Anne-Therese Costello joined the AASL staff in June 1988.

Planning continues for the fifth national division conference, "Access to Excellence," that will be held in Salt Lake City, Utah, in October 1989. More than 3,500 individuals are expected to attend the five-day conference.

On development and technology AASL continued its efforts this year to collect data on regional accrediting standards and to develop a plan for improving these standards in the area of library media programs. Carolyn Markuson, chair of the Task Force charged with this responsibility, reported to the AASL Board of Directors in New Orleans. Future action on the recommendations made by the Task Force will be considered at Midwinter, 1989.

AASL's monograph series, "Focus on Issues and Trends," was revitalized during 1988. Eleanor Kulleseid of Bank Street College, New York, will edit the series that will focus on major issues of the profession, blending theory and practice. Topics to be addressed include the teaching role of the library media specialist, the instructional consultant role of the library media specialist, facilities design, subject access, and the role of the library media program in the whole language movement.

Barbara Stripling and Judy Pitts of Fayetteville, Arkansas, were named co-editors of *School Library Media Quarterly* for a three-year term beginning with the Fall 1988 issue. See their biographies in this *Yearbook*.

Summary. Recent accomplishments will enable AASL to continue and increase its membership growth. The publication of revised national guidelines affirms our professional leadership. The teleconference, ongoing implementation activities, and our contacts with other educational associations will continue to increase the visibility and the importance of school library media programs to school administrators and teachers. ALA's membership in NCATE and ALA Council's adoption of the policy statement on the appropriate education for library media specialists demonstrate the Association's concern for the educational preparation of our members. In 1988, AASL undertook a long-range plan that will ensure that the Association is responsive to and anticipates the needs of the profession. The expanding publications program and the fifth AASL national conference indicate that 1989 will be equally eventful.

KAREN A. WHITNEY

American Indians

The addition of Title IV to the Library Services and Construction Act (LSCA) of 1984 was one of the most directly positive outcomes of the first White House Conference on Libraries and Information services in 1979. Since 1985, the first year of funding for the program, modest but stable funding earmarked for library services has been brought to American Indian tribes, and tribal effort and interest in libraries has been greatly stimulated. Most important, to Indian people on reservations were the benefits of community library services as an essential ingredient of effective programs for early childhood, literacy, employment, adult education, and the elderly. LSCA IV has engendered self-esteem and a sense of identity to young and older Indians alike. Having their own libraries has lent impetus to parents' efforts to participate in their children's learning and to continue their own.

Each fiscal year, two program cycles are completed: the Basic Grant program with separate appropriations for Indian tribes and Hawaiian Natives. All federally recognized Indian tribes are eligible to apply for basic grants, and the single organization approved to receive monies may apply for Hawaiian Natives. The appropriation is divided by the total number of eligible entries; in FY 1987—$3,572 for each tribe; in 1988—$3,550; for Hawaiian Natives—$602,500 in FY 1987; and $601,250 in FY 1988. The second funding, Special Project Grants, awards, can be sought after the Basic Grants are awarded. Grantees must share a minimum of 20 percent of total project costs, and a librarian must administer the funds. Money is awarded for a one-year phase of a three-to-five-year long-range plan for library development. Seventeen tribes received Special Project Grants in the last two fiscal years.

Authorized activities for the Basic Grants include library needs assessments, purchase of materials, dissemination of information about services, transportation to services, special programs, construction, and contracts to provide services. By far the greatest amount of money is spent for personnel and materials, more than $200,000 for personnel costs, and nearly $300,000 for materials in 1987.

The Poarch Band of Creek Indians at Atmore, Albama, only recently recognized as a tribe by the federal government, received its first project grant in 1988—a first for Alabama. The tribe will build a 2,800 square foot library learning resource center to improve library and information services to 1,831 tribal members between the multipurpose building and the Senior Tribal Housing. The federal portion was $93,744, with a nonfederal contribution of $28,900.

In its third year of special project funding, the Morongo Band of Mission Indians in Banning, California, will pay the salaries of a librarian and an assistant, increase the core collection to 3,500 volumes, and provide training for the library staff with a total of $31,452. Also in their third year of funding and developing services, the Miccosukee Tribe of Miami, Ohio, will pay the salary of a media specialist and will purchase computers to automate library management.

With its first successful application for a total

The Morongo Band of Mission Indians Library in Banning, California, has been funded for three successive years under the Special Projects Program of Title IV of LSCA, Library Services for Indian Tribes.

of $55,918 in special funding, the Fort Belknap Assiniboine/Gros Ventre Tribes of Harlem, Montana, plan to build a 2,875 square foot addition to the tribal recreation complex for library collections, children's services, tribal archives, and special collections.

A Nevada tribe, the Pyramid Lake Paiutes, received its first special grant for a total of $71,833 to support salaries of a librarian and aide to provide services to tribal members. The state library provides technical assistance.

In North Dakota, the Three Affiliated Tribes won its 4th year of development funding for a total (with its contribution) of $77,054 to pay salaries, increase the core collection to 3,500, and provide training for support staff. The Turtle Mountain Band of Chippewas, also in North Dakota, received $150,479 to expand its existing facility and children's services. Development was aided by a grant in the first year (1985) of $100,000.

In South Dakota, the Oglala Sioux Tribe of Pine Ridge, received its first grant of $117,197 to improve library services on the reservation through distribution of resources in nine district centers, using a van to coordinate program and transport materials.

In Washington, the Lummi Indian Tribe came back for a second grant having received its first in 1985, the latest to be used for renovating and furnishing an existing building as the tribal library facility and for partially supporting the salaries of two technicians. Their total expenditure is $61,056. The Nisqually Tribe, in its third year of funding, continued library staff training, purchased materials, developed a learning skills center, and implemented a community reading program and library services for special populations.

It is plain even with the relatively small amounts of money expended among the American Indian people on reservations that, as with other people, the appetite for library services grows as it is fed, and benefits are diverse and widespread. It is incumbent upon the Indian people and their many friends and well-wishers to fight to retain authorization for categorical funds and appropriations, when the next authorization for a Library Services and Construction Act comes before the Congress. They will have the opportunity to do this as the national White House Conference on Libraries process unfolds. Indian tribes are again to be accorded the status of a state or a territory as far as the planning process and the funding are concerned. They will have their own national preconference to develop objectives and recommendations to take to the larger body—as they did so successfully the first time around. Both the ALA Office for Library Outreach Service Subcommittee on Library Service for American Indian People and the American Indian Library Association are standing by, ready to go into action when the trumpet blows! Meanwhile American Indians are forging alliances with other groups within and outside ALA. American Indian people have glimpsed a future rich in the opportunities that libraries bring, and they have staked their claim to them.

VIRGINIA H. MATHEWS (OSAGE)

AMERICAN INDIAN LIBRARY ASSOCIATION

PRESIDENT (January 1988–December 1989):
Rhonda Harris Taylor, Route 2, Box 410, Bullard, Texas 75757

VICE-PRESIDENT:
Janice Beaudin, College Library, 600 N. Park Street, Madison, Wisconsin 53706

SECRETARY:
Naomi Caldwell-Woods, Providence Public Schools, Educational Technology Department, 480 Charles Street, Providence, Rhode Island 02904

TREASURER:
Sally Rogia, University of Wisconsin–Madison, 4252 Helen C. White Hall, 600 N. Park Street, Madison, Wisconsin 53706

EDITOR OF NEWSLETTER:
Kathy Kaya, The Libraries, Montana State University, Bozeman, Montana 59717-0022

Headquarters: ALA, 50 East Huron, Chicago, Illinois 60611

American Library Association

"It was the best of times, it was the worst of times" aptly describes the year 1988 for the American Library Association. A steady increase in membership, a highly successful Midwinter Meeting and Annual Conference, and an Association in sound fiscal health created a mood of optimism among members and staff. However, the FBI Library Awareness Program and the relationship between the American Library Association and the National Commission on Libraries and Information Science became matters of increasing concern for the Association.

Membership. Membership increased 4.7 percent during the year ending August 31, 1988. ALA's total membership figures stood at 47,249, with 44,308 personal members and 2,941 organizational members. According to data collected on the membership renewal forms, 31 percent of the Association's personal members currently work in public libraries, 26 percent in academic libraries, and 13 percent in school libraries.

The Public Library Association experienced an 8.3 percent increase in total membership, the largest increase among the divisions. The Association of College and Research Libraries remains the largest division, with more than 10,000 members.

In response to member requests, the Association will soon offer a preferred automobile and homeowners insurance package to members as part of an expanded member benefits program.

Conferences. The 1988 Midwinter Meeting, held in San Antonio, Texas, attracted record crowds. Snowstorms and bad weather in other parts of the country grounded many flights into the conference city, but despite these problems, 6,550 members, guests, and exhibitors attended the Midwinter Meeting. A new record of 450 exhibitors was set.

New Orleans, the site of the 1988 Annual Conference, proved to be a big hit with the 16,500 conference attendees. Even the heat and humidity of New Orleans in July could not keep conference attendees from enjoying the attractions of Bourbon Street, the Riverwalk, New Orleans–style jazz, the French Quarter, and Louisiana gumbo. Members gave rave reviews to New Orleans and will return there for the 1993 Annual Conference.

FBI Library Awareness Program. The Association viewed the FBI's Library Awareness Program with alarm as the Bureau's activity in that area continued. During the Midwinter Meeting in San Antonio, members of the National Commission on Libraries and Information Science and representatives of the FBI held a closed-door session from which all non-commissioners were excluded. Despite numerous requests from ALA that the transcript of the meeting be made public, NCLIS and the FBI refused to cooperate. Judith Krug, Director of the Office for Intellectual Freedom at ALA, and C. James Schmidt, chair of the Intellectual Freedom Committee, worked diligently to inform the FBI about ALA's stand on the protection of patron privacy and library records. At the Annual Conference in New Orleans, Council called for immediate cessation of the FBI's program, and Krug and Schmidt were asked to appear on ABC's "Nightline" to discuss ALA's opposition to the FBI program.

Executive Director Thomas Galvin reported at the Annual Conference that Toby McIntosh of the Bureau of National Affairs had been able to obtain a copy of the 50-page transcript of the closed meeting held between NCLIS and the FBI in January. Unfortunately, the document had been heavily censored, but the remaining portions portrayed NCLIS commissioners as highly critical of ALA's Office for Intellectual Freedom and the Intellectual Freedom Committee. Both Council and the Executive Board expressed their grave concern and dismay over NCLIS' criticism. Council directed the Legislation Committee to review the policies and activities of NCLIS on an annual basis and urged NCLIS to become informed about the privacy rights of all patrons. On September 9, ALA President-elect Patricia Berger, ALA legal counsel Mary Hutchings Reed, and representatives of the Intellectual Freedom Committee met with the FBI in Washington, D.C., to hear an explanation of the FBI's program and to discuss the matter in further detail.

Council, Executive Board, Other Association Activities. Although the FBI Library Awareness Program occupied much of the Association's attention during the year, there was also much activity in other areas. The National Library Card Campaign, which proved a resounding success in 1987, entered its second phase with a special focus on teenagers and older children. *Information Power: Guidelines for School Library Media Programs*, a joint effort by the American Association of School Librarians and the Association for Educational Communications and Technology, was presented to Council for approval at the Annual Conference. The document outlines new guidelines to replace those that had undergone revisions during the past 13 years.

In other action, Council passed resolutions opposing mandatory drug testing for library employees and directing ALA management to submit a proposal for a funded affirmative action program at ALA Headquarters. Council also adopted a statement on educational requirements for librarians submitted by the Standing Committee on Library Education and voted to approve a separate document on education for school library media specialists submitted by the American Association of School Librarians. As a result of the report of the Special Committee on Freedom and Equality of Access to Information, Council voted to form a new Standing Committee on Access and to refer the resolution to ALA's Committee on Organization for recommendations on the structure and composition of the new committee. Robert Stueart, chair of the Review Committee on the Staff Committee on Mediation, Arbitration, and Inquiry, presented the report of his committee's work, which Council adopted with all recommendations contained therein.

At the Annual Conference Membership Meeting, members expressed concern about a perceived lack of program activities, and membership voted to submit an advisory statement to Council requesting that COPES, the Executive Board, Council, and management "take all nec-

American Library Association

essary steps to ensure that 50 percent of ALA expenditures be directed to program activities" and that this goal be reached in five years. Council also voted to approve a recommendation that the eligibility period for student dues be extended from two years to three years.

Executive Director Galvin reported that the Association had experienced a "spectacular" financial year. Retiring Treasurer Patricia Schuman noted that ALA's net worth had increased 48 percent since she had been elected in 1984 and that the Association was currently in sound fiscal health. Schuman will spearhead a three-year fund drive, approved by the Executive Board, to increase the ALA Endowment Fund.

ALA Headquarters. In staff changes at ALA Headquarters, Thomas H. Gaughan was appointed Managing Editor of *American Libraries* in February. Joel Lee, who joined ALA in 1977 as Headquarters Librarian, left the Association in August to join Autographics. Lee was the first manager of ALANET, ALA's electronic information system, and had served as Senior Manager, Information Technology Publishing, since 1986. Paul Kobasa, Assistant Director for Marketing, ALA Publishing Services, resigned to join the staff of World Book. Leonard Kniffel, a former staff member at the Detroit Public Library, was appointed Associate Editor of *American Libraries* to replace Lois Pearson, who retired in September. Pearson, perhaps best known as the editor of "Action Exchange," had been with *American Libraries* since 1976. Anne E. Levinson, formerly an attorney in private law practice, was appointed Assistant Director of the Office for Intellectual Freedom. Emily Melton, Headquarters Librarian since 1984, left the Association in November to join the library faculty at Indiana University/Purdue University–Indianapolis.

EMILY MELTON

ALA Report

AMERICAN LIBRARY ASSOCIATION HIGHLIGHTS AND ORGANIZATION

The American Library Association is the oldest and largest library association in the world. ALA was founded in 1876. The first meeting, organized by Melvil Dewey, was held in Philadelphia, October 4–6, and drew 103 librarians. ALA membership was 43,397 in 1986, 45,145 in 1987, and 47,249 as of August 31, 1988.

The ALA Council is the governing body of the Association. It comprises 100 Councilors elected at large and Councilors representing each state, provincial, and territorial chapter. Council convenes at two meetings held each year: Midwinter (early each year) and Annual Conference (summer). The management arm of the Association is the Executive Board, which comprises the officers of the Association, the immediate Past President, and eight members elected by Council from its membership.

The goal of the Association is the promotion of libraries and librarianship to assure the delivery of user-oriented library information service to all. Much of its work is done through ALA Committees.

ACTIVITIES of the Association include:
  Research on library problems
  Development of standards and guidelines
  Accreditation of library education
    programs
  Clarification of legislative issues
  Vigorous support for intellectual freedom
  Publishing
  Awards
  Library cooperation
  Continuing education

ALA UNITS

Divisions of ALA are membership units that provide resources for special knowledge and for advancing knowledge and service through publications and professional programs. See in this volume:
  American Association of School
    Librarians
  American Library Trustee Association

AMERICAN LIBRARY ASSOCIATION COUNCIL

PRESIDENT (June 1988–July 1989):
F. William Summers, Dean, School of Library & Information Science, Florida State University, Tallahassee, Florida

VICE-PRESIDENT/PRESIDENT-ELECT:
Patricia Wilson Berger, Chief, Information Resources and Services Division, National Bureau of Standards, Gaithersburg, Maryland

SECRETARY:
Thomas J. Galvin, Executive Director, ALA

Council Membership: 100 councilors at large (25 elected by members each year); 1 councilor from each state, provincial, and territorial chapter (52); 1 councilor from each division of ALA (11); 12 members of the **Executive Board**

MEMBERSHIP:
44,308 personal members; 2,941 organization members; total (August 31, 1988) 47,249

ANNUAL EXPENDITURES: (August 31, 1988)
Payroll and Related Expenses	$ 8,303,605
Outside Services	1,352,132
Travel and Related Expenses	1,009,544
Meetings and Conferences	1,124,344
Publication-Related Expenses	5,079,039
Operating Expenses	3,916,624
	$20,785,288

ANNUAL REVENUES: (August 31, 1988)
Membership Dues	$ 4,309,612
Sale of Books and Materials	3,851,508
Subscriptions	3,442,269
Advertising, Net	2,393,550
Meetings and Conferences	4,012,315
Graphics Program	1,059,081
Grants	1,330,444
Other—	
Interest and Dividends	377,621
Rental—Huron Plaza	492,721
Miscellaneous	590,466
	$21,859,587

ANNUAL CONFERENCES:
Dallas, June 24–29, 1989; Chicago, June 23–28, 1990; Atlanta, June 29–July 4, 1991.

Association for Library Service
  to Children
Association of College and Research
  Libraries
Association of Specialized and Cooperative
  Library Agencies
Library Administration and Management
  Association
Library and Information Technology
  Association
Public Library Association
Reference and Adult Services Division
Resources and Technical Services
  Division
Young Adult Services Division

Round tables are membership units that deal with aspects of librarianship outside the scope of a Division. See in this volume:
  Continuing Library Education Network &
    Exchange Round Table and
  Ethnic Materials Information and Exchange
    Round Table
  Exhibits Round Table
  Federal Librarians Round Table
  Government Documents Round Table
  Independent Librarians Exchange
    Round Table
  Intellectual Freedom Round Table
  International Relations Round Table
  Junior Members Round Table
  Library History Round Table
  Library Instruction Round Table
  Library Research Round Table
  Map and Geography Round Table
  Social Responsibilities Round Table
  Staff Organization Round Table

ALA offices are headquarters staff units that address issues affecting the entire profession: Intellectual Freedom, Library Outreach Services, Research, Library Personnel Resources, and the Washington Office (Legislation). See articles in this volume on these subjects.

Other units comprising the program services of ALA are: American Libraries, the Committee on Accreditation, and the Headquarters Library.

ALA AFFILIATES are:
  American Association of Law Libraries
  American Indian Library Association
  American Society for Information Science
  Asian/Pacific American Librarians
    Association
  Association for Library and Information
    Science Education
  Association of Research Libraries
  Canadian Library Association
  Chinese-American Librarians Association
  Council on Library/Media Technical
    Assistants
  Friends of Libraries USA
  Laubach Literacy International (NALA)
  Literacy Volunteers of America
  Medical Library Association
  Music Library Association
  National Librarians Association
  Oral History Association
  REFORMA (National Association
    to Promote Library Services to the
    Spanish-speaking)
  Sociedad de Bibliotecarios de Puerto Rico
  Theatre Library Association
  Ukrainian Library Association of America
  Urban Libraries Council

ALA CHAPTERS are covered under State Reports, the final section of this volume.

HEADQUARTERS
  50 E. Huron St., Chicago, IL 60611
  Telephone: (312) 944-6780; for member hotline information, telephone 1-800-545-2433; 1-800-545-2444 (Illinois); 1-800-545-2455 (Canada).

Table 1. ALA Publishing Services, September 1, 1987–August 31, 1988

Publishing Services	Actual Expenditures	Income
Books	$2,381,693	$2,644,112
Booklist and *RBB*	2,248,406	2,576,322
Library Technology Reports	314,027	481,883
Information Technology Publishing	865,917	694,904
American Libraries	810,079	810,079

Source: ALA Treasurer's Report, August 31, 1988.

Table 2. ALA Membership (as of August 31, 1988)*

Personal members	44,308
Organizational members	2,941
Total	47,249
Membership in ALA units	
Divisions	
AASL	6,389
ACRL	10,170
ALTA	1,734
ASCLA	1,363
ALSC	3,578
LITA	4,829
LAMA	5,074
PLA	6,298
RASD	5,217
RTSD	6,037
YASD	2,488
Total Divisional membership	53,177
Members selecting no Division	36.21%
Members selecting one Division	36.38%
Members selecting two Divisions	18.11%
Members selecting three or more Divisions	9.3 %
Round Tables	
CLENE	378
EMIERT	545
ERT	268
FLRT	472
GODORT	1,381
IFRT	1,554
ILERT	279
IRRT	739
JMRT	918
LHRT	341
LIRT	1,118
LRRT	769
MAGERT	415
SRRT	990
SORT	246
Total Round Table membership	10,413

*Source: Membership statistics, monthly report August 31, 1988 (ALA Administrative Services).

American Library Association

Washington Office: 110 Maryland Ave., N.E., Washington, DC 20002
CHOICE (magazine): 100 Riverview Center, Middletown, CT 06457

FINDING OUT ABOUT ALA: SELECTED REFERENCES

These key sources provide a wealth of information about ALA, its organization and units, its publications and services, in addition to the many reports in this *ALA Yearbook.*

ALA Handbook of Organization and Membership Directory

The annual *Handbook* is a guide to the structure of ALA, with names of current officials, committee members, councilors, and representatives. It includes information about Divisions, Round Tables, and other units. Key documents include the Charter, ALA calendar, Constitution and Bylaws, and Policy Manual.

The *Membership Directory* includes the names and brief addresses of personal and organizational members, as well as historical listings of conferences, presidents, executive secretaries and executive directors.

The *Handbook* is available separately, free to personal members upon request to the Executive Office and for $10 to others. The combined handbook and directory is sent to organizational members and is $20 to others.

ALA Publications Checklist

This is an annual comprehensive bibliography of *all* materials currently available from *all* ALA units. It describes books, pamphlets, audiovisual materials, and periodicals available from ALA and its units. The *Checklist* contains detailed indexes by subject, issuing unit, and personal author, along with complete ordering instructions

Periodical	Editor(s)	Publication Frequency	Subscription*
ALA Washington Newsletter	Eileen D. Cooke and Carol C. Henderson, Editors ALA Washington Office	Irregular (minimum of 12 issues)	$20 per year.
ALSC Newsletter	Carla D. Hayden, Editor 50 E. Huron St. Chicago, Illinois	2 issues a year	Free to Division members.*
ALTA Newsletter	Nancy Stiegemeyer, Editor 215 Camellia Drive Cape Girardeau, Missouri	6 issues a year	Free to Division members.*
American Libraries	Arthur Plotnik, Editor ALA, Chicago	11 issues a year; July/August combined	Free to ALA members; available to institutions at $40 per year.
base line (MAGERT)	Carol A. Collier, Editor Library University of Wyoming, Laramie, Wyoming	Bimonthly	Free to Round Table members; subscription $15 per year.
Booklist	Bill Ott, Editor ALA, Chicago	22 issues a year	$56 per year; single issues, $4.50.
CHOICE (ACRL)	Patricia Sabosik, Editor 100 Riverview Center Middletown, Connecticut	11 issues a year; July/August combined	$125 per year.
College & Research Libraries (ACRL)	Charles Martell, Editor California State University, Sacramento, California	6 issues a year	Free to Division members; subscription $35 per year; single issues $7.50.
C&RL News (ACRL)	George Eberhart, Editor ACRL/ALA ALA, Chicago	11 issues; July/August combined	Free to Division members; subscription $15 per year; single issues $3.50.
Documents to the People (GODORT)	Diane L. Garner, Editor Pennsylvania State University, University Park, Pennsylvania	Bimonthly	Free to Round Table members; subscription $15 per year.
EMIE Bulletin (EMIERT)	David Cohen, Editor Queens College Flushing, New York	Quarterly	Free to Round Table members; subscription $10 per year; single issues $1.50.
The Federal Librarian (FLRT)	Grace T. Waibel, Editor 2500 Wisconsin Ave., N.W. #852, Washington, D.C.	3 issues a year	Free to Round Table members.*
Footnotes (JMRT)	Thomas Lawrence, Editor Southern New York Library Resources, Highland, New York	Quarterly	Free to Round Table members.*
IFRT Report	Scott Kass, Editor Florida International University North Miami, Florida	Irregular	Free to Round Table members.*

Table 3. Selected ALA Periodicals (1988), *Continued*			
Information Technology and Libraries (LITA)	William Potter, Editor Hayden Library Arizona State University Tempe, Arizona	Quarterly	Free to Division members; subscription $35 per year; single issues $12.50.
Interface (ASCLA)	Mary Redmond, Editor State Library Cultural Education Center, Albany, New York	Quarterly	Free to Division members; subscription $10 per year; single issues $3.
Journal of Youth Services in Libraries (formerly *Top of the News*) (ALSC/YASD)	Josette Lyders, Editor University of Houston Clear Lake, Texas	Quarterly	Free to Division members; subscription $30 per year.
LHRT Newsletter	Joanne Passet, Editor University of California at Los Angeles	Semiannually	Free to Round Table members.*
Library Administration & Management (LAMA)	Donald Riggs, Editor 2120 E. Knoll Circle Mesa, Arizona	Quarterly	Free to Division members; subscription $35 per year; single issues $8.50.
Library Instruction Round Table News (LIRT)	Co-editors: E. Dailey White Branch Library Syracuse, New York; E. Okada Indiana University Bloomington, Indiana	Quarterly	Free to Round Table members.
Library Resources & Technical Services (RTSD)	Sheila Intner, Editor P.O. Box 151 Monterey, Massachusetts	Quarterly	Free to Division members; subscription $30 per year; single issues $7.50.
Library Systems Newsletter (LTR)	Howard S. White, Editor ALA, Chicago	Monthly	$35 per year.
Library Technology Reports (LTR)	Howard S. White, Editor ALA, Chicago	Bimonthly	$175 per year; single copies $45.
Library Video Magazine (ALA Video)	Donna Kitta ALA, Chicago	Quarterly	VHS, Beta, 3/4 inch cassettes; subscription $249.95 per year.
LITA Newsletter	Walt Crawford, Editor Research Libraries Group Stanford, California	Quarterly	Free to Division members; subscription $15 per year; single issues $5.
Newsletter on Intellectual Freedom (IFC)	Judith F. Krug, Editor ALA, Chicago	6 issues a year	$25 per year; single issues $4.
Public Libraries (PLA)	Kenneth Shearer, Editor 1205 LeClair St. Chapel Hill, North Carolina	Quarterly	Free to Division members; subscription $18 per year.
RASD Update (RASD)	Constance Miller, Editor Indiana University Bloomington, Indiana	6 issues a year	Free to Division members; subscription $10 per year; single issues $3.
RQ (RASD)	Kathleen M. Heim, Editor Louisiana State University School of Library and Information Science Baton Rouge, Louisiana	Quarterly	Free to Division members; subscription $25 per year; single issues $8.
RTSD Newsletter	Thomas W. Leonhardt, Editor 3550 Knob Hill Lane Eugene, Oregon	8 issues a year	Free to Division members and *Library Resources & Technical Services* subscribers; subscription $15 per year.
School Library Media Quarterly (AASL)	Marilyn Greenberg, Editor California State University Los Angeles, California	Quarterly	Free to Division members; subscription $35 per year.
SORT Bulletin	Sharon K. Adley, Editor Lake County Public Library Merrillville, Indiana	Semiannually	Free to Round Table members.*
SRRT Newsletter	Jeanne Kocsis, Editor University of Massachusetts Library, Amherst, Massachusetts	3 issues a year	Free to Round Table members; $20 to institutions; single issues $2.

*Asterisk indicates not available by subscription (December 1988).

American Library Association Awards

and order forms. It is available for $2 from the Order Department.

Announcements of new ALA publications appear regularly in *American Libraries*, as well as in *electroCitations: ALA Publications News* in ALANET.

American Libraries

ALA's official journal reports regularly on ALA activities, policies, publications, and other highlights. It is sent to all ALA members and is also available by subscription to others for $40 from the Subscriptions Department.

Legislative Report of the Washington Office

Issued twice a year, this report summarizes ALA's many legislation-related activities.

Minutes

These are prepared by the Council and Executive Board Secretariat and are indexed annually. For information on current minutes, write to the Executive Office. The Headquarters Library holds complete, indexed minutes of the Executive Board (1906–) and Council (1963–); earlier Council minutes are found in *Library Journal* (1876–1902) and the *ALA Bulletin* (1902–63).

Treasurer's Report

Submitted at the Midwinter Meeting for the fiscal year (September 1–August 31); for information, contact Fiscal Services Department, ALA Headquarters.

For other sources and special files, contact the ALA Headquarters Library.

American Library Association Awards

This article covers selected awards, grants, and scholarships presented by the American Library Association as well as honors and awards presented by the divisions, offices, round tables and other units of the association during the 1988 calendar year. The awards vary widely in nature but generally seek to honor those who have contributed to libraries and librarianship. Scholarships are awarded to promising candidates who plan to enter the field of librarianship or to those persons already in the field who wish to pursue a course of advanced studies. Grants are given to encourage individuals and groups to undertake research or special projects which will contribute to libraries and librarianship.

The list of awards and recipients that follows covers January through December 1988. For previous recipients, see the editions of this *Yearbook* published since 1976. *See also* Biographies, State Reports, and the Index.

AASL/ABC–CLIO Leadership Development Award

An annual award of $1,750 to enable an AASL Affiliate Organization to plan and implement a leadership development program. Donated by ABC/CLIO. Administered by the American Association of School Librarians.

1988 RECIPIENT: New York Library Association, School Library Media Section.

AASL/Baker and Taylor President's Award

An annual award of $3,000 presented to an individual who has demonstrated excellence and provided an outstanding national or international contribution to school librarianship and school library media development. Donated by Baker and Taylor. Administered by the American Association of School Librarians.

1988 RECIPIENT: Margaret I. Rufsvold, Professor Emeritus, Indiana University Library School.

AASL/SIRS Intellectual Freedom Award

An annual award consisting of $2,000 and an engraved plaque presented to a school library media specialist at any level who has upheld the principles of intellectual freedom as set forth in "Policies and Procedures for Selection of Instructional Materials." The award also provides a grant of $1,000 and a framed certificate to a school library media center designated by the recipient. Donated by Social Issues Resources Series, Inc.

1988 RECIPIENT: Nancy Quesada Moreno, Austin (Texas) Independent School District.

ACRL Academic/Research Librarian of the Year

An annual award of $3,000 presented to an individual who has made an outstanding national or international contribution to academic and research librarianship and library development. Donated by Baker and Taylor. Administered by the Association of College Research Libraries.

1988 RECIPIENT: Edward G. Holley, ALA Past President, University of North Carolina at Chapel Hill.

ACRL K.G. Saur Award for "Best *College & Research Libraries* Article"

A cash award of $500 presented to an author to recognize the most outstanding article published in *College and Research Libraries* during the preceeding volume year. Donated by K.G. Saur. Administered by the Association of College and Research Libraries.

1988 RECIPIENT: Robert Boice, Jordan M. Scepanski, and Wayne Wilson for "Librarians and Faculty Members: Coping with Pressures to Publish" in *College & Research Libraries* November 1987.

ACRL/LAMA/LITA/RTSD Hugh C. Atkinson Memorial Award

An annual award for outstanding accomplishments of an academic librarian who has worked in the areas of library automation or library management and has made contributions toward the improvement of library services or to library development or research. Citation and cash award endowed by library vendors and members of ALA. Interdivisional award administered by the Association of College and Research Libraries.

1988 RECIPIENT: Richard M. Dougherty, University of Michigan.

Advancement of Literacy Award

An award presented to an American publisher or bookseller who has made a significant contribution to the advancement of literacy. Administered by the Alternative Education Programs Section of the Public Library Association.

1988 RECIPIENT: Gannett Foundation.

ALTA Literacy Award

An annual award given to an individual who has made an outstanding contribution toward the extirpation of illiteracy. Donated and administered by the American Library Trustee Association.

1988 RECIPIENTS: Richard C. Torbert, Friends of Libraries USA, and Tyrone Bryant, Broward County (Florida) Library System.

ALTA Major Benefactors Honor Award

An annual award consisting of a citation to recognize benefactors to public libraries. The recipient may be a person, institution, agency, or organization. The significance of the gift is measured from the point of view of the recipient library.

1988 RECIPIENT: Rhoda Krasner, Denver (Colorado) Public Library, and Fred K. Darrah, Little Rock, Arkansas.

Armed Forces Library Achievement Citation

An annual citation presented to a member of the Armed Forces Library Section of the Public Library Association who has made significant contributions to the development of armed forces library service and to organizations encouraging an interest in libraries and reading. Donated and administered by the Armed Forces Library Section of the Public Library Association.

NOT AWARDED in 1988.

ASCLA Exceptional Achievement Award

A citation presented to recognize leadership and achievement in the following areas of activity: consulting, multitype library cooperation, and state library development.

NOT AWARDED in 1988.

ASCLA Exceptional Service Award

A citation presented to recognize exceptional service to patients, the homebound, medical, nursing, and other professional staff in hospitals, and inmates, as well as to recognize professional leadership, effective interpretation of programs, pioneering activity, and significant research. Donated and administered by the Association of Specialized and Cooperative Library Agencies.

NOT AWARDED in 1988.

(Carroll Preston) Baber Research Award

An annual cash award of $10,000 and a citation presented to a person who encourages innovative research in the field of library science in the areas of improving library services to specific groups of people, new uses of technology, and cooperative projects. Donated by Eric R. Baber. Administered by the ALA Awards Committee.

1988 RECIPIENT: Dr. Melvin M. Bowie, University of Georgia Instructional Technology Department, with David V. Loertscher, Libraries Unlimited, and May Lien Ho, University of Arkansas College of Education, for a project entitled, "Computerized Collection Development Research in School Libraries."

(Mildred L.) Batchelder Award

A citation presented to an American publisher for a children's book considered to be the most outstanding of those books originally published in a foreign language in a foreign country and subsequently published in the United States during the year preceding presentation of the award. Donated and administered by the Association for Library Service to Children.

1988 RECIPIENT: Margaret McElderry Books for publication of *If You Didn't Have Me* by Ulf Nilsson, translated from Swedish by Lone Thygesen Blecher and George Blecher.

"Best of LRTS" Award

An annual citation given to the author(s) of the best paper published each year in the division's official journal. Criteria for selection of the winning paper include its value to technical services librarians, the inclusion of accurate supporting data and documentation, and a clear and readable writing style.

NOT AWARDED in 1988.

Beta Phi Mu Award

An annual award consisting of $500 and a citation of achievement presented to a library school faculty member or to an individual for distinguished service to education for librarianship. Donated by Beta Phi Mu International Library Science Honorary. Administered by the ALA Awards Committee.

1988 RECIPIENT: Samuel Rothstein, Professor Emeritus, University of British Columbia library school.

(Randolph) Caldecott Medal

A medal presented annually to the illustrator of the most distinguished American picture book for children published in the United States in the preceding year. The recipient must be a citizen or resident of the United States. Donated by Daniel Melcher. Administered by the Association for Library Service to Children.

1988 RECIPIENT: John Schoenherr, illustrator of *Owl Moon*, written by Jane Yolen, published by Philomel Books of the Putnam & Grosset Group, 1987.

(Francis Joseph) Campbell Citation

An annual award consisting of a citation and a medal and presented to a person who has made an outstanding contribution to the advancement of library service for the blind and physically handicapped. This contribution may take the form of an imaginative and constructive program

ALA awards program

in a particular library; a recognized contribution to the national library program for blind persons; creative participation in library associations or organizations that advance reading for the blind; a significant publication or writing in the field; imaginative contributions to library administration or services; or any activity of recognized importance. Donated and administered by the Libraries Serving Special Populations Section of the Association of Specialized and Cooperative Library Agencies.

1988 RECIPIENT: James G. Chandler, College Park, Maryland.

(James Bennett) Childs Award

An annual award, consisting of an engraved plaque, presented to a librarian or other individual for distinguished contributions to documents librarianship. Donated and administered by the Government Documents Round Table.

1988 RECIPIENT: Patricia Reeling, Rutgers University.

(John Cotton) Dana Public Relations Awards

An annual citation made to libraries or library organizations of all types submitting materials representing the year's public relations program or a special project terminated during the year 1987. Donated by the H.W. Wilson Company, the awards program is sponsored jointly with the Public Relations Section of the Library Administration and Management Association.

1988 RECIPIENTS:
Academic Library and Consortia Category: McGoogan Library of Medicine, Omaha, Nebraska; University of Texas/Arlington; Montana's Libraries, Bozeman.
Public Library Category: Alameda County Library, Haywood, California; Dauphin County Library System, Harrisburg, Pennsylvania; East Brunswick (New Jersey) Public Library; Farmers Branch (Texas) Manske Library; Greenville County (South Carolina) Library; John C. Hart Memorial Libary, Shrub Oak, New York; Louisville (Kentucky) Free Public Library; Middle Country Public Library, Centereach, New York; Orange County (California) Public Library; San Francisco Public Library; Sierra Madre (California) Public Library.
Service Library Category: RAF Upper Heyford Base Library, England.
School Library Category: Kenmore West High School, Buffalo, New York.
Special Library Category: Cargill Information Center, Minneapolis, Minnesota.

Dartmouth Medal

A medal honoring achievement in the creation of reference works of outstanding quality and significance. Creating reference works may include writing, compiling, editing, or publishing books or providing information in other forms for reference use.

1988 RECIPIENT: *Encyclopedia of Religion*, published by Macmillan, Mircea Eliade, editor-in-chief.

(Melvil) Dewey Medal

An engraved medal and a citation presented annually to an individual or a group for recent creative professional achievement of a high order, particularly in those fields in which Melvil Dewey was actively interested: library management, library training, cataloging and classification, and the tools and techniques of librarianship. Donated by Forest Press, Inc. Administered by the ALA Awards Committee.

1988 RECIPIENT: Herbert Goldhor, Professor Emeritus, University of Illinois.

(AASL/SIRS) Distinguished Library Service Award for School Administrators

An annual grant of $2,000 presented to a person directly responsible for the administration of a school or group of schools who has made an outstanding and sustained contribution toward furthering the role of the library and its development in elementary and/or secondary education. Sponsored by the American Association of School Librarians and Social Issues Resources Series, Inc.

1988 RECIPIENT: Ralph E. Ricardo, Ascension Parish School Board, Donaldsonville, Louisiana.

(GODORT) Documents to the People Award

An annual award consisting of a citation of achievement and a cash stipend of $2,000 to be used to promote professional advancement in the field of librarianship. The award is presented to the individual, library, organization, or other appropriate noncommercial group that has most effectively encouraged the use of federal documents in support of library services. Donated by the Congressional Information Service, Inc. Administered by the Government Documents Round Table.

1988 RECIPIENT: Agnes Ferruso, Library of Congress.

(Miriam) Dudley Award for Bibliographic Instruction

An annual award of $900 presented to a librarian who has made an especially significant contribution to the advancement of bibliographic instruction through development and implementation of courses or programs; through research and publication; or through participation in organizations promoting bibliographic instruction. Donated by Mountainside Publishing Company. Administered by the Association of College and Research Libraries.

1988 RECIPIENT: Sharon A. Hogan, Louisiana State University.

Equality Award

A certificate and a cash award of $500 given to an individual or group for an outstanding contribution toward promoting equality between women and men in the library profession in such areas as pay equity, affirmative action, legislative work, and nonsexist education. Donated by the Scarecrow Press. Administered by the ALA Awards Committee.

1988 RECIPIENT: Kathleen Weibel, Ohio Wesleyan University, Delaware, Ohio.

Facts on File Award

A cash grant of up to $1,000 awarded to a library for imaginative programming which makes current affairs more meaningful to an adult audience.

1988 RECIPIENT: Chicago Public Library Social Science and History Department.

Federal Librarians Achievement Award

An annual citation and gift for leadership or achievement in the promotion of library and information science in the federal community. Donated and administered by the Federal Librarians Round Table.

1988 RECIPIENT: Anne A. Heanue, ALA Washington Office.

Gale Research Company Financial Development Award

An annual award of $2,500 and a certificate presented to a library organization that exhibits meritorious achievement in carrying out a library financial development project to secure new funding resources for a public or academic library. Donated by the Gale Research Company. Administered by the ALA Awards Committee.

1988 RECIPIENT: Texas A&M University for its Library Excellence Dinners, created by Development and Promotion Coordinator Charlene Clark.

Gay and Lesbian Book Award

An annual award honoring a book or books of exceptional merit relating to the gay/lesbian experience. The form of the award is not fixed but is designated by the Gay Book Award committee each year as appropriate. Donated and administered by the Social Responsibilities Round Table Gay and Lesbian Task Force.

1988 RECIPIENT: Joan Nestle, author of *A Restricted Country*, published by Firebrand Books, and Randy Shilts, author of *And the Band Played On: Politics, People, and the AIDS Epidemic*, published by St. Martin's Press.

Grolier Foundation Award

An annual award consisting of $1,000 and a citation of achievement presented to a librarian who has made an unusual contribution to the stimulation and guidance of reading by children and young people. The award is given for outstanding work with children and young people through high school age, for continuing service, or in recognition of one particular contribution of lasting value. Donated by the Grolier Foundation. Administered by the ALA Awards Committee.

1988 RECIPIENT: Lucille C. Thomas, adjunct professor at Queens College library school, City University of New York.

(G.K.) Hall Award for Library Literature

A $500 cash award and a citation presented to an individual who makes an outstanding contribution to library literature; publications issued during the three years preceding the presentation are considered. Donated by G.K. Hall and Company, Inc. Administered by the ALA Awards Committee.

1988 RECIPIENT: Wayne A. Wiegand, Professor, University of Wisconsin, Madison, for *The Politics of an Emerging Profession 1876–1917*, published by Greenwood Press.

Hammond, Inc./MAGERT Award

An award honoring the year's best paper on map librarianship. Criteria for the award include originality and creativity, evidence of thorough research, up-to-date documentation, and critical evaluation. The paper must make a significant contribution to the field of map librarianship and provide new insights and methods of applications. The award consists of a certificate and $300. Donated by Hammond, Inc. Administered by the Map and Geography Round Table.

NOT AWARDED in 1988.

(Frances) Henne Award

An annual grant of $1,250 to enable a school library media specialist with five or fewer years of experience in the profession to attend an AASL Regional Conference or an ALA Annual Conference. Donated by the R.R Bowker Company. Administered by the American Association of School Librarians.

1988 RECIPIENT: Jane Louise Thomas, Lake Travis, Texas.

(John Ames) Humphry/Forest Press Award

This $1,000 award is made to a librarian or other person who has made significant contributions to international librarianship. The contribution may include publication of significant professional literature, participation in library organizations, the introduction of new technologies or theories, or outstanding teaching. Primary consideration is given to contributions in the field of classification and subject analysis and to work in Third World countries. Donated by the Forest Press. Administered by the International Relations Committee.

1988 RECIPIENT: Joel C. Downing, United Kingdom.

(John Phillip) Immroth Memorial Award for Intellectual Freedom

An annual award consisting of $500 and a citation presented to an individual who has made a notable contribution to intellectual freedom and demonstrated remarkable personal courage. Donated and administered by the Intellectual Freedom Round Table.

1988 RECIPIENT: Elliot and Eleanor Goldstein of SIRS, Inc.

Intellectual Freedom Round Table State Program Award

An annual award consisting of $1,000 and a citation presented to the state intellectual freedom committee that has implemented the most suc-

awards program

35

cessful and creative state IFC project during the calendar year. Donated by Social Issues Resources Series, Inc. Administered by the Intellectual Freedom Round Table.

1988 RECIPIENT: New York Library Association Intellectual Freedom Committee and Intellectual Freedom Round Table.

(SRRT Coretta Scott) King Awards

These annual awards are given to a black author and a black illustrator for an outstanding inspirational and educational contribution. The awards commemorate the life and works of the late Dr. Martin Luther King, Jr. and honor Mrs. Coretta Scott King for her courage and determination to continue the work for peace and world brotherhood. The award consists of plaques, World Book and Encyclopaedia Britannica sets, and cash awards of $250. Donated by Johnson Publications and Famous Amos Cookies. Administered by the Social Responsibilities Round Table.

1988 RECIPIENTS: Mildred D. Taylor for her book, *The Friendship*, published by Dial Books for Young Readers, and John Steptoe for his illustrations in *Mufaro's Beautiful Daughters: An African Tale*, published by Lothrop, Lee & Shepard.

(Exhibits Round Table) Kohlstedt Exhibit Awards

These annual awards consist of citations recognizing the best single, multiple, and island booth displays at the ALA Annual Conference. The award is named after Donald W. Kohlstedt in recognition of his hard work for better library conference exhibits. Administered by the Kohlstedt Committee of the Exhibits Round Table.

1988 RECIPIENTS: *Single Booth Category*: Mysterious Press; *Multiple Booth Category*: UMI; *Island Booth Category*: F.W. Faxon.

(Katherine Kyes) Leab and Daniel J. Leab American Book Prices Current Award

Three annual awards for the best catalog published by American or Canadian institutions in conjunction with exhibitions of books and/or manuscripts. The awards are presented in three categories: expensive, moderately expensive, and inexpensive, based upon production costs of the catalogs. Criteria for selecting winners include accuracy, consistency, clarity, quality of design, and usefulness to the intended audience. Endowed by Katherine Kyes Leab and Daniel J. Leab. Administered by the Rare Books and Manuscripts Section of the Association of College and Research Libraries.

1988 RECIPIENTS: *Expensive Category*: "The Larder Invaded: Reflections on Three Centuries of Philadelphia Food and Drink" and "35 Receipts from 'The Larder Invaded' " by The Library Company of Philadelphia; "Time: The Greatest Innovator" from the Folger Shakespeare Library. *Moderate Category*: "Marianne Moore: Vision Into Verse," Rosenbach Museum and Library. *Inexpensive Category*: "The Virgin & the Witch," Harvard Law School Library.

(AIA/ALA–LAMA) Library Buildings Award Program

An award cosponsored by the American Institute of Architects and the Library Administration and Management Association to encourage excellence in the architectural design and planning of libraries. Citations are presented to the winning architectural firms and to the winning libraries.

NOT AWARDED in 1988.

(Joseph W.) Lippincott Award

An award consisting of $1,000 and a citation of achievement, presented annually to a librarian for distinguished service to the profession of librarianship, including participation in the activities of professional library associations, notable published professional writing, or other significant activity. Donated by Joseph W. Lippincott Jr. Administered by the ALA Awards Committee.

1988 RECIPIENT: Henriette D. Avram, Assistant Librarian for Processing Services at the Library of Congress.

LITA/Gaylord Award for Achievement in Library and Information Technology

An annual award of $1,000 presented to recognize achievement in library and information technology. The award is intended to recognize distinguished leadership, notable development or application of technology, superior accomplishments in research or education, or original contributions to the literature of the field. Donated by Gaylord Brothers, Inc. Administered by the Library and Information Technology Association.

1988 RECIPIENT: Barbara E. Markuson, Indiana Cooperative Library Services Authority.

MAGERT Honors Award

An award established by the Map and Geography Round Table to recognize outstanding contributions by a MAGERT personal member to map librarianship, MAGERT, and/or a special MAGERT project. The award includes a citation and a cash award of $25. Donated and administered by the Map and Geography Round Table.

1988 RECIPIENT: Ralph E. Ehrenberg, Library of Congress.

(Margaret) Mann Citation

An annual citation made to a cataloger or classifier, not necessarily an American, for outstanding professional achievement in the areas of cataloging or classification, either through publication of significant professional literature, participation in professional cataloging associations, introduction of new techniques of recognized importance, or outstanding work in the area of teaching within the past five years. Donated and administered by the Cataloging and Classification Section, Resources and Technical Services Division.

1988 RECIPIENT: Ben R. Tucker, Library of Congress.

(Allie Beth) Martin Award

An award of $3,000 and a citation presented to a

librarian who, in a public library setting, has demonstrated an extraordinary range and depth of knowledge about books or other library materials and has exhibited a distinguished ability to share that knowledge. Donated by the Baker and Taylor Company. Administered by the Public Library Association.

1988 RECIPIENT: Daniel O. Robles, Santa Paula (California) Public Library District.

(AASL/Follett Software Company) Microcomputer in the Media Center Award

This award recognizes and honors library media specialists who have demonstrated innovative approaches to microcomputer applications in their respective libraries or media centers. The award may be presented for the use of the microcomputer as a library management tool and/or for its application as an educational tool in the learning center. Each recipient librarian receives a $1,000 cash award and funds to travel to the award ceremony. Each recipient library receives a $500 cash award.

1988 RECIPIENTS: *Category 1*: Nancy Everhart, Preparatory School Library, Freeland, Pennsylvania. *Category 2*: Linda Carol Hartman, Truman Elementary School, Kansas City, Missouri.

(Margaret E.) Monroe Library Adult Services Award

This award consists of a citation given to a librarian who has made significant contributions to and an impact on library adult services. The person may be a practicing librarian, a library and information science researcher or educator, or a retired librarian who has brought distinction to the profession's understanding and practice of services for adults. Donated and administered by the Reference and Adult Services Division.

1988 RECIPIENT: Jane K. Hirsch, retired from Montgomery (Maryland) Public Library.

(Isadore Gilbert) Mudge Citation

This annual award consists of a citation presented to a person who has made a distinguished contribution to reference librarianship. The contribution may take the form of an imaginative and constructive program in a particular library; the writing of a significant book or articles in the reference field; creative teaching of reference service; active participation in professional associations devoted to reference services; or other noteworthy activities which stimulate reference librarians to more distinguished performance. Donated and administered by the Reference and Adult Services Division.

1988 RECIPIENT: James R. Rettig, College of William and Mary.

(AASL/Encyclopaedia Britannica) National School Library Media Program of the Year Award

Three cash awards of $2,500 each presented annually to school districts which display outstanding achievement in exemplary library media programs. School districts representing elementary schools, secondary schools, or a combination of both may apply. Awards donated by Encyclopaedia Britannica. Administered by the American Association of School Librarians.

1988 RECIPIENTS: West Bloomfield Schools, West Bloomfield, Michigan; Round Rock Independent School District, Round Rock, Texas.

(John) Newbery Medal

A medal presented annually to the author of the most distinguished contribution to American literature for children published in the United States in the preceding year. The recipient must be a citizen or resident of the United States. Donated by Daniel Melcher. Administrated by the John Newbery Award Committee of the Association for Library Service to Children.

1988 RECIPIENT: Russell Freedman, author of *Lincoln: A Photobiography*, published by Clarion Books, a division of Houghton Mifflin Company, 1987.

Oberly Award for Bibliography in the Agricultural Sciences

A biennial award given in odd-numbered years, consisting of a citation and a cash award from the income of the Oberly Memorial Fund, presented to an American citizen who compiles the best bibliography in the field of agriculture or one of the related sciences in the two-year period preceding the year in which the award is made. Made possible by a fund established by colleagues in memory of Eunice Rockwood Oberly. Administered by the Science and Technology Section of the Association of College and Research Libraries.

NOT AWARDED in 1988.

(Eli M.) Oboler Memorial Award

A biennial award of $500 presented to the author or authors of an article, a series of thematically connected articles, a book, or a manual published on the local, state, or national level, in English or English translation. The works to be considered must have as their central concern one or more issues, events, questions, or controversies in the area of intellectual freedom, including matters of ethical, political, or social concerns related to intellectual freedom. Donated by HBW Associates. Administered by the Intellectual Freedom Round Table.

1988 RECIPIENT: Ann Bastian, editor, *Choosing Equality: The Case for Democratic Schooling*, published by Temple University Press, 1986.

(Esther J.) Piercy Award

An annual citation presented in recognition of a contribution to librarianship in the field of technical services by younger members of the profession. The recipient must be a librarian with not more than ten years of professional experience who has shown outstanding promise for contributions and leadership in any of the fields comprising technical services. Donated and administered by the Resources and Technical Services Division.

1988 RECIPIENT: Karen Markey, University of Michigan Library School.

ALA awards program

ALA awards program

Readex/GODORT/ALA Catherine J. Reynolds Award

An annual award to present grants to documents librarians for travel and/or study in the field of documents librarianship or in an area of study that will directly benefit their performance as a documents librarian. The award is supported by a $2,000 contribution from the Readex Corporation. Administered by the Government Documents Round Table.

1988 RECIPIENTS: Sheila H. Nollen, Macomb, Illinois, and Steven D. Zink, University of Nevada, Reno.

Reference Service Press Award

An annual award of $500 presented to recognize the author of the most outstanding article published in RQ during the preceding two volume years and to reward the author. The winning article is selected on the basis of originality, timeliness, relevance to RASD areas of interest and concern, and quality of writing. Donated by Reference Service Press, Inc. Administered by the Reference and Adult Services Division.

1988 RECIPIENT: Elfreda A. Chatman, author of "Opinions Leadership, Poverty, and Information Sharing," published in RQ, Spring 1987.

(Serials Section/Bowker/Ulrich's) Serials Librarianship Award

An annual award consisting of a citation and a $1,500 cash award for distinguished contributions to serials librarianship within the previous three years, demonstrated through participation in professional associations and/or library education programs, contributions to the body of serials literature, conduct of research in the area of serials, development of tools or methods to enhance access to or management of serials, or other advances leading to a better understanding of the field of serials.

1988 RECIPIENT: Marjorie E. Bloss, OCLC, Dublin, Ohio.

(John) Sessions Memorial Award

A plaque presented to a library or library system in recognition of significant work with the labor community. Such efforts may include outreach projects to local labor unions; the establishment of, or significant expansion of, special labor collections; initiation of programs of special interest to the labor community; or other library activities that serve the labor community. Donated by the AFL/CIO. Administered by the Reference and Adult Services Division.

1988 RECIPIENT: Southern Labor Archives, Georgia State University, Atlanta.

(Jesse H. Shera) Award for Research

An award established by the Library Research Round Table to encourage excellence in library research. The $500 award is presented to the person submitting the best completed research paper. Donated by the Library Research Round Table. Administered by the Shera Award Committee of LRRT.

1988 RECIPIENT: Danny P. Wallace and Bert R. Boyce for the paper, "Holdings as a Measure of Journal Value."

Trustee Citations

An ALA citation presented to each of two outstanding trustees who have served during part of the calendar year preceding the presentation. The citations are given for distinguished service to library development on the local, state, or national level. Administered by the American Library Trustee Association.

1988 RECIPIENTS: Jane Norcross, Atlanta, Georgia, and Francis H. Naftalin, Minneapolis, Minnesota.

(Leonard) Wertheimer Multilingual Award

An award presented to a person, group, or organization in recognition of work that enhances and promotes multilingual public library service. Supported by the National Textbook Company. Administered by the Public Library Association.

NOT AWARDED in 1988.

(Laura Ingalls) Wilder Medal

A medal presented every three years to an author or illustrator whose books have been published in the United States and who has, over a period of years, made a substantial and lasting contribution to children's literature. Donated and administered by the Association for Library Service to Children.

NOT AWARDED in 1988.

(H.W.) Wilson Library Periodical Award

An annual award consisting of $500 and a certificate, presented for a periodical which has made an outstanding contribution to librarianship and which is published by a local, state, or regional library, library group, or library association in the United States or Canada. The award is based on sustained excellence in content, format, and purpose. Donated by the H.W. Wilson Company. Administered by the ALA Awards Committee.

1988 RECIPIENT: *California State Library Foundation Bulletin*, edited by California State Librarian Gary Strong.

(Justin) Winsor Prize Essay

An award of $500 for an essay on some aspect of library history. The award was established to encourage excellence in research in library history. The winner is invited to submit his or her paper for publication in a future issue of *The Journal of Library History*. Donated and administered by the Library History Round Table.

1988 RECIPIENT: Brother Thomas O'Connor, St. Mary's College of California, for "Library Service to the American Committee to Negotiate Peace and to the Preparatory Inquiry, 1917–1919."

SCHOLARSHIPS
ACRL Doctoral Dissertation Fellowship

An annual award of $1,000 presented to a doctoral student in the field of academic librarianship whose research indicates originality, creativity, and interest in scholarship. The purpose of the fellowship is to foster research in academic librarianship by encouraging and assisting doctoral students in the field with their dissertation research. Funded by the Institute for Scientific Information. Administered by the Association of College and Research Libraries.

1988 RECIPIENT: Sarla Murgai, University of Tennessee/Knoxville.

Bound to Stay Bound Books Scholarships

Two annual $1,500 scholarships established to assist individuals who wish to work in the field of library service to children. The scholarships may be used for study toward the MLS or graduate study beyond the MLS degree at an ALA-accredited library school. Donated by Bound to Stay Bound Books, Inc. Administered by the Association for Library Service to Children.

1988 RECIPIENTS: Birgit Nicolaisen, Binghamton, New York, and Susan Valtfort, Santa Fe, New Mexico.

(David H.) Clift Scholarships

The ALA Scholarship Program, established in 1969, provides the David H. Clift Scholarship in the amount of $3,000 annually to help a worthy student begin a program of library education at the graduate level. The scholarship is funded by individual contributions and proceeds from the ALA President's Dance. As many scholarships as possible are awarded, depending upon the total amount of contributed funds. Administered by the ALA Awards Committee and the Office for Library Personnel Resources.

1988 RECIPIENTS: Linda Hilton, Pottstown, Pennsylvania; Donna Chen, Storm Lake, Iowa; Sheryl Davis, Redlands, California.

(Frederich Winthrop) Faxon Scholarship

Established in 1981 by the ALA Council, the Faxon Scholarship is a cash award of $3,000 and an optional expense-paid internship of up to ten weeks at the Faxon Company in Westwood, Massachusetts. The award is made to a worthy student to begin an ALA-accredited master's program in library or information science. Recipients should have a specific interest in the field of serials management and control. Funded by an annual contribution from the Faxon Company. Administered by the ALA Awards Committee and the Office for Library Personnel Resources.

1988 RECIPIENT: Michael Whetzel, Miami, Florida.

(Louise) Giles Minority Scholarships

Established in 1972 by the ALA Council, and named in memory of Louise Giles in 1977, the Minority Scholarship is a $3,000 cash award made to a worthy student who is a U.S. or Canadian citizen and a member of a principal minority group. The recipient must enter a formal ALA-accredited library program of graduate study leading to a master's degree. The scholarship is funded by individual contributions and proceeds from the ALA President's Dance. As many scholarships as possible are awarded depending upon the total amount of contributed funds. Administered by the ALA Awards Committee and the Office for Library Personnel Resources.

1988 RECIPIENTS: Victor Lui, Haslett, Michigan; Stephanie Sterling, Culver City, California; Rita Jimenez, Tucson, Arizona.

JMRT EBSCO Scholarship

The scholarship is a cash award of $1,000 made possible through the support of EBSCO Subscription Services. Applicants must enroll in an ALA-accredited library program and must be a U.S. or Canadian citizen and a member of ALA and JMRT prior to acceptance of the award.

1988 RECIPIENT: Janice Pardoe, University of California/Berkeley.

(Samuel) Lazerow Fellowship

An annual award of $1,000 established to foster advances in acquisitions or technical services by providing librarians in those fields with a fellowship for research, travel, or writing. Proposals are judged on their potential significance, originality, and clarity. Funded by the Institute for Scientific Information. Administered by the Association of College and Research Libraries.

1988 RECIPIENT: Carol M. Kelley, Texas Tech University.

LITA/CLSI Scholarship in Library and Information Technology

This scholarship is awarded to a beginning student in an ALA-accredited master's degree program in library and information science with emphasis on library automation. The purpose of the scholarship is to encourage the entry into the library automation field of qualified persons who plan to follow a career in that field and who evidence leadership and a strong commitment to the use of automated systems in libraries. The scholarship was established in 1984 by the Library and Information Technology Association and C.L. Systems, Inc. (CLSI) and consists of a cash award of $1,500.

1988 RECIPIENT: Walter Stine, Ashland, Oregon.

(Frederic G.) Melcher Scholarship

Two annual $4,000 scholarships established by the Association for Library Service to Children in honor of Frederic G. Melcher to encourage and assist persons who wish to enter the field of library service to children and who have been admitted to a graduate library school program accredited by ALA. Donated and administered by the Association for Library Service to Children.

1988 RECIPIENTS: Lisa Griest and Jeffrey Dufty.

RTSD Resources Section/Blackwell North America Scholarship Award

An annual award consisting of a citation, which

ALA awards program

awards program

is given to the winner, and a $1,000 scholarship, which is donated by Blackwell/North America to the library school of the winner's choice. The citation is presented to the author(s) of an outstanding monograph, published article, or original paper in the field of acquisition, collection development, or related areas of resources development in libraries.

1988 RECIPIENT: Joe A. Hewitt and John S. Shipman for "Cooperative Collection Development among Research Libraries in the Age of Networking: Report on a Survey of ARL Libraries," *Advances in Library Automation and Networking*, 1, 1987 and the University of North Carolina/Chapel Hill.

GRANTS
Bogle International Travel Fund Grants

An annual award consisting of a $300 cash grant to assist ALA members attending an international library conference for the first time. The award is named after Sarah Bogle, director of the Paris library school from 1924 to 1929 and an assistant secretary of the American Library Association at the time of her death in 1932.

1988 RECIPIENTS: Robert K. Bruce, ALA–USIA Library Fellow, Jakarta, Indonesia; Ann Kelsey, County College of Morris Learning Resource Center, Randolph Township, New Jersey; Maria Otero-Boisvert, University of Nevada/Reno Library; Carolyn A. W. Snyder, Indiana University/Bloomington Libraries; Betty L. Tsai, Bucks County Community College Library, Newtown, Pennsylvania.

Carnegie Reading List Awards

Carnegie Reading List Awards are granted to official units of the American Library Association and are based on a special fund created by Andrew Carnegie in 1902. The awards are for the creation of "reading lists, indexes, and other bibliographical and library aids as will be especially useful in the circulating libraries of this country." The awards are chosen annually by the ALA Publishing Committee.

1988 RECIPIENTS: Association for Library Service to Children for *Summertime Family Reading*, $1,600; Association for Library Service to Children for *Professional Literature for Children's Librarians*, $1,200; American Association of School Librarians for *Selection Tools: A Guide for Choosing Materials for K-12 Students*, $2,265; Office for Library Outreach Services for *Coretta Scott King Award Books*, $2,065; Young Adult Services Division, in conjunction with ALA's Public Information Office, for *A Series of Genre Booklists for Young Adults*, $5,675.

Grolier National Library Week Grant

An annual $1,000 cash award presented to the school media or state library association that submits the best plan for a public relations program to be conducted in the year in which the grant is presented. Donated by Grolier Educational Corporation. Administered by the National Library Week Committee of the American Library Association.

1988 RECIPIENT: Kentucky Library Association.

Martinus Nijhoff International West European Specialist Study Grant

An annual grant for an ALA member to visit the Netherlands and to spend ten consecutive working days visiting two other West European countries in order to study some aspect of West European librarianship or bibliography. The grant covers travel, room, and board. The primary consideration in selecting the recipient of the grant is the significance and utility of the proposed research as a contribution to the study of the acquisition, organization, or use of library materials from or relating to Western Europe. Funded by Martinus Nijhoff International. Administered by the Western European Specialists Section of the Association of College and Research Libraries.

NOT AWARDED in 1988.

(Shirley) Olofson Memorial Award

An annual cash award to help individuals attend their second ALA Annual Conference. The recipients must be members of ALA and potential or current members of the Junior Members Round Table. Donated and administered by the Junior Members Round Table.

1988 RECIPIENTS: James L. Huessmann; Judy Jeng.

(3M/JMRT) Professional Development Grants

The purpose of these grants is to encourage professional development and participation by new librarians in national ALA and JMRT activities. Cash awards are given to librarians to help defray the cost of attending an ALA Annual Conference. The recipients must be current members of ALA and the Junior Members Round Table. Administered by the Junior Members Round Table.

1988 RECIPIENTS: Joan Jobson, Dallas Public Library; Nancy Palma, Lock Haven (Pennsylvania) University Library; Linda Scott, Manhattan (Kansas) Public Library.

Putnam and Grosset Group Award

Four annual cash awards of $400 presented to four children's librarians to defray the costs of attending an ALA Annual Conference. The recipients must be members of the Association for Library Service to Children and have one to ten years of library experience. They must work directly with children and never have attended an ALA Annual Conference. Donated by Putnam and Grosset Group. Administered by the Association for Library Service to Children.

1988 RECIPIENTS: Katherine Louise Kan, Aiea Public Library, Pearl City, Hawaii; Lesly Ann Kaplan, Lynwood Branch Library, Marysville, Washington; Cynthia M. Olsen, San Bernardino (California) Library; Timothy R. Wadham, Dallas (Texas) Public Library.

(Herbert W.) Putnam Honor Award

An award of $500 presented as a grant-in-aid to an American librarian of outstanding ability to improve his or her service to the library profession or to society. The $500 grant is made possible by the income received from the Herbert W.

Putnam Honor Fund. Administered by the ALA Awards Committee.

1988 RECIPIENT: Charles A. Seavey, Assistant Professor, University of Arizona Library School.

Whitney–Carnegie Fund Grants

Whitney–Carnegie Awards are granted to individuals for the preparation of bibliographic aids for research. The aids must be aimed at a scholarly audience but must have general applicability. The awards cover costs appropriate to the preparation of a useful product, including the cost of research and compilation. The maximum award is $2,500, but the amounts and numbers of awards are made at the discretion of the ALA Publishing Committee and vary from year to year.

1988 RECIPIENTS: Bettina J. Manzo for *Guide to the Animal Rights Movement in the United States, 1972-1987*, $1,650; Blanche E. Woolls for *Reference Sources to Aid Public Librarians in Small Libraries to Meet the Needs of Small Business in Their Communities*, $2,498; Robert L. Wick for *Bibliography on Electronic and Computer Music*, $1,540; Rod Henshaw and Mary E. Jackson for *Creating Access: A Bibliographic Guide to the Purposes and Practices of Library Resource Sharing*, $2,000; Susan Steadman for *Feminist Dramatic Criticism, 1972-1988: An Annotated Bibliography*, $1,000; Joni Bodart-Talbot for *Researching Adolescence: Resources across Disciplines*, $2,000.

(H.W.) Wilson Library Staff Development Grant

A cash grant of $2,500 awarded to a library organization for a current or proposed program designed to further that organization's goals and objectives. The criteria for selection of a grant winner include clearly defined documentation of need in relation to staff development, a well-defined program to meet the organization's needs, and the commitment and demonstrated ability to implement the program. Donated by the H.W. Wilson Company. Administered by the ALA Awards Committee.

1988 RECIPIENT: Fairfax County (Virginia) Public Library for "Recognizing Cultural Differences: A Training Program for Staff," Nancy C. Woodall, Training Coordinator, and Edwin S. Clay III, Director.

World Book–ALA Goal Awards

World Book–ALA Goal Awards are two annual grants of $5,000 made to units of the American Library Association by World Book, Inc., to encourage and advance the development of public, academic, and/or school library service and librarianship through recognition and support of programs which implement the goals and objectives of ALA. Committees, joint committees, divisions, round tables, and chapters of the association are eligible.

1988 RECIPIENTS: Chapter Relations Committee, CLENE Round Table, and the Chapter Relations Office for "Improving Chapter Conferences"; Committee on the Status of Women in Librarianship for "Minority Women Librarians' Personal Perspectives on Librarianship."

YASD/Baker and Taylor Conference Grants

Two annual awards of $750 awarded to librarians who work directly with young adults in either a public library or a school library. The awards are used to help defray the costs of attending ALA's Annual Conference. Candidates must be members of YASD, have one to 10 years of library experience, and never have attended an ALA Annual Conference. Donated by Baker and Taylor. Administered by the Young Adult Services Division.

1988 RECIPIENTS: Barbara A. Carmody, Renton, Washington; Gloria L. Rhodes, Oceanside, California.

YASD/Frances Henne/Voice of Youth Advocates Research Grant

An annual grant of $500 to provide seed money for small scale projects which will encourage significant research that will have an influence on library service to young adults. Applicants must be members of the Young Adult Services Division, although the research project may be undertaken by an individual, an institution, or a group. Donated by *Voice of Youth Advocates (VOYA)*. Administered by the Young Adult Services Division.

NOT AWARDED in 1988.

EMILY MELTON

American Library Trustee Association

In 1988, the American Library Trustee Association (ALTA) emphasized connecting with trustees nationwide to raise their level of awareness of trustee issues and what should be trustee concerns. In pursuit of this goal, units in the ALTA structure employed varying, but unified tactics to achieve success.

Committees. The Publications Committee produced three new works in the ALTA series, increasing the number of publications to nine. The new publications are "A Questionnaire to Evaluate Your Library and Library Board," "Major Duties, Functions, and Responsibilities of Public Library Trustees—An Outline," and "Library Boards—Who Are They and How Do They Get There? A Survey." The Legislation Committee developed the ALTA Legislation Network whereby committee members will monitor the legislative activities of each member of the U.S. House and Senate Appropriations Committee, the House Education and Labor Committee, and the Senate Labor and Human Resources Committee. The White House Conference Subcommittee continued to monitor legislative activities in Congress for a White House Conference on Library and Information Services in 1990. This subcommittee continued to serve as the ALTA liaison to the White House Conference on Library and Information Services Task Force (WHCLIST), the National Commission on Libraries and Information Science (NCLIS), Friends of Libraries U.S.A. (FOLUSA), Chief Officers of State Library Agencies (COSLA), and Association of

American Society for Information Science

Specialized and Cooperative Library Agencies (ASCLA).

The Action Development Committee reviewed the ALTA long-range plan. While recognizing that the present goals are appropriate, the committee recommended that the language be updated to reflect the current and evolving needs of trustees. The ALTA/PLA Common Concerns Committee sponsored a program at the PLA National Conference in Pittsburgh. The program, "So You Think You Need a Consultant, Now What Do You Do?" was well attended and well received.

The Membership Committee conducted a regional membership promotion campaign in states contiguous to Louisiana, the state in which the 1988 ALA Annual Conference was held. In response to a request from ALA's Committee on Program Evaluation and Support that divisions develop a five-year financial plan, the Financial Planning Task Force was established. The group reviewed and assessed ALTA's financial situation and initiated the development of a divisional financial plan.

Conference Programs. An outstanding schedule of Annual Conference programs was coordinated by the Conference Program and Evaluation Committee co-chaired by Judith Baker and Patricia Turner. The program, "WHCLIS II: How to Get Glitz and Guts from the Process," was sponsored by the ALTA White House Conference Subcommittee. Among the seven speakers were Peggy Barber, Associate Executive Director, ALA Communications; William Asp, Director, Minnesota Library Development and Services; and Roslyn Kurland, Executive Board, Urban Libraries Council, all of whom presented descriptions of major trends that can be promoted through the White House Conference process at both state and national levels.

The Education of Trustees Committee sponsored "Great Expectations! Evaluating the Director/Evaluating the Board." Panelists and presenters were Nancy Stiegemeyer, Editor, *ALTA Newsletter*; Ron Dubberly, Director, Atlanta-Fulton Public Library; Eloise Fasold, Director, Arapahoe Library District; and Patricia Turner, Trustee, Baltimore County Public Library.

Walter Dean Myers, author of young adult books, was the keynote speaker at the luncheon sponsored by the Specialized Outreach Services Committee. Other programs included "Boardsmanship," of which Dorothy Gallagher, Chair, Nevada National Bank, was the featured speaker, and "Founding a Foundation and Funding It," with Norman Kelinson, Trustee, Bettendorf (Iowa) Public Library and Faye Clow, Director, Bettendorf (Iowa) Public Library.

Awards. Jane M. Norcross, Atlanta, Georgia, and Frances H. Naftalin, Minneapolis, Minnesota, were named Cited Trustees for 1988. Both outstanding trustees received their citations at the opening general session of the 1988 Annual Conference. Cited trustees are selected because of their library-related activities and accomplishments.

Richard Torbert, Swarthmore, Pennsylvania, and Tyrone Bryant, Ft. Lauderdale, Florida, were honored as recipients of the ALTA Literacy Award with a plaque presented at the Special-

Norma Buzan, Bloomfield Hills (Michigan) Township.

AMERICAN LIBRARY TRUSTEE ASSOCIATION

PRESIDENT (July 1988–June 1989):
Norma Buzan, Bloomfield Hills, Michigan

VICE-PRESIDENT/PRESIDENT-ELECT:
Norman Kelinson, Bettendorf, Iowa

EXECUTIVE DIRECTOR:
Sharon L. Jordan

Membership (August 31, 1988): 1,724

---

ized Outreach Services Committee Luncheon at the 1988 Annual Conference.

Rhoda Krasner of Wheatland, Colorado, and Fred K. Darragh, Jr. of Little Rock, Arkansas, were the two recipients selected for the 1988 Major Benefactors Honor Awards. Krasner's contribution of Lakeside Amusement Park admission passes and ride coupons to the Denver Public Library allowed the library to offer incentives to young readers to participate in the annual summer Reading Program. Darragh challenged the public libraries in the 75 Arkansas county seats to raise $500, and he matched this sum with a personal contribution of $36,000. The resulting funds were to be used to purchase Arkansas-related materials to improve state history and literature collections.

Affiliation Subscription Program. As increasing numbers of library trustees and directors recognized the value of the Affiliation Subscription Program, participation enrollment surged to more than 200 library boards. This trustee networking opportunity provided participants with four issues of the *Trustee Digest*, a four-page summary of articles and informative reports; various timely news releases; business information brochure; *ALA Washington Newsletter*; conference program information, and a copy of each new ALTA publications.

ALTA Newsletter. Aimed at making the division's primary source of communication to members even more readable, informative, and efficient, the *ALTA Newsletter* adopted a new format and appearance. The response from members indicated their approval and appreciation.

SHARON L. JORDAN

American Society for Information Science

After several years of planning and anticipation, and the major kickoff in late 1987 at its 50th Anniversary Conference, the American Society for Information Science celebrated its first half-century of service to the information profession throughout 1988. Calling upon members and supporters from all segments of the information community, ASIS sponsored events worldwide to emphasize the broad and ubiquitous role of information in today's society.

Virtually every ASIS Chapter and Special Interest Group participated in at least one 50th anniversary activity designed to draw attention to the important contributions made by information professionals in a variety of environments.

In Columbus, Ohio, a city in which numerous major information companies operate, the Central Ohio ASIS chapter celebrated the contributions and achievements of such organizations as Battelle, Chemical Abstracts Service, and ASIS at a day-long symposium which led to the publication of a booklet of the speeches presented. The Los Angeles Chapter of ASIS held a 50th anniversary gala party to honor the dozens of national information leaders who work or live in Southern California.

ASIS Special Interest Groups (SIGs) on Medical Information Systems and Biological and Chemical Information Systems, among others, received corporate sponsorship to further their goals toward broadening the reach of their respective organizations into new market areas. SIG/Personal Computers introduced an important new service for the information community with its directory of bulletin boards in use in libraries and similar organizations.

By October, when the anniversary celebration ended in Atlanta at the 51st ASIS Annual Meeting, the membership was infused with a new level of enthusiasm that underpinned the process of setting the profession's agenda for the next 50 years.

"Information and Technology: Planning for the Second 50 Years," the theme of the Annual Meeting, set the tone for both the technical elements of the annual gathering, as well as the governance activities in which members are involved. Throughout the week's activities, more than 1,000 members and colleagues discussed the areas of greatest personal and professional interest on which they hoped that ASIS would focus attention. By the end of the week, the beginnings of the new agenda were firmly in place.

Special Initiatives. At the beginning of her term, ASIS President Martha E. Williams, professor of information science at the University of Illinois, announced plans for an Information Science Indicators project to quantify information science and establish it as a recognized discipline of stature. Williams initiated the ASIS 2000 project in which the organization's leadership and membership would participate in an intensive effort to define the information science field as it would exist in the year 2000.

ASIS continued in-depth development of a major topic within the information industry at the 1988 Mid-Year Meeting. "Artificial Intelligence: Expert Systems and Other Applications" drew some 400 attendees for a detailed view of the directions in which new techniques are moving the information profession.

At the end of October 1988, incoming President W. David Penniman, AT&T Bell Laboratories, announced that he would continue to pursue the Information Science Indicators and ASIS 2000 projects, while embarking on a major recruitment effort in which every ASIS member is asked to become a mentor to a new member of the organization.

Awards. Winners of the 1988 ASIS annual awards were honored at the Society's 51st Annual Meeting in Atlanta. The 1988 Award of Merit, the society's highest honor, was presented to Professor F. Wilfrid Lancaster, University of Illinois, in recognition of his outstanding contributions as a researcher, teacher, and author. Other 1988 ASIS award winners include Harold Borko, professor at the University of California, Los Angeles, Outstanding Information Science Teacher; *Federal Information Policies in the 1980s: Conflicts and Issues*, by Peter Hernon and Charles R. McClure, published by Ablex Publishing Corporation, Best Information Science Book; Susanne M. Humphrey and Nancy E. Miller, "Knowledge-Based Indexing of the Medical Literature: The Indexing Aid Project," Best *JASIS* Paper; Stephanie W. Haas, ISI Information Science Doctoral Dissertation Scholarship; Elizabeth DuRoss Liddy and Clifford A. Lynch, Doctoral Forum Award; and Charlotte Weise and Stuart McLean, Student Paper Award. Bonnie C. Carroll, Oak Ridge, Tennessee, received the Watson Davis Award, given annually to an individual or individuals for outstanding continuous service to the Society.

Publications. In celebration of the ASIS anniversary, the Society published a special commemorative magazine highlighting many of the accomplishments in the field of information science during its first 50 years. Almost an immediate classic, the magazine is being used in library and information science schools throughout the United States as a resource in the teaching of the historical perspective of the field.

New volumes of two successful ASIS series were introduced in 1988: volume 23 of the prestigious *Annual Review of Information Science and Technology* (ARIST), edited by Martha E. Williams and published for ASIS by Elsevier Science Publishers, and volume 24 of the *Proceedings of the ASIS Annual Meeting*, edited by Christine Borgman and Edward Pai and published by Learned Information, Inc. ASIS continued publication of two of the leading periodicals in the field of information science: *The Journal of the American Society for Information Science*, published by John Wiley & Sons, is a fully refereed scholarly and technical publication and the *Bulletin of the American Society for Information Science*, published by ASIS.

History of ASIS. Since its founding in 1937 as the American Documentation Institute (ADI), ASIS has served the specialized information

---

AMERICAN SOCIETY FOR INFORMATION SCIENCE

PRESIDENT (October 1988–October 1989):
W. David Penniman, Director of Libraries and Information Systems, AT&T Bell Laboratories, Murray Hill, New Jersey

PRESIDENT-ELECT:
Toni Carbo Bearman, Dean, School of Library and Information Science, University of Pittsburgh, Pennsylvania

PAST PRESIDENT:
Martha E. Williams, Professor of Information Science, Coordinated Science Laboratory, College of Engineering, University of Illinois, Urbana

TREASURER:
N. Bernard (Buzzy) Basch, Vice-President, EBSCO Service, Chicago, Illinois

EXECUTIVE DIRECTOR:
Linda Resnik

Membership (September 30, 1988): 3,900
Headquarters: 1424 Sixteenth Street, NW, Suite 404, Washington, D.C. 20036

needs of a diverse group of professionals in scientific and professional organizations, companies, foundations, and government agencies.

The earliest focus of the Society was on a promising new medium—microfilm—that offered the first practical alternative to paper documentation and represented an exponential increase in the amount of information that could be stored and transmitted.

In later years, the emphasis switched from an emphasis on the specific media of information to the burgeoning requirements of the science of information. In the late 1960s, ADI changed its name to the American Society for Information Science and expanded its membership to serve a broader constituency.

ASIS has expanded its role within the information profession to become the most active information organization in the development and application of information technologies.

LINDA RESNIK

American Theological Library Association

AMERICAN THEOLOGICAL LIBRARY ASSOCIATION

PRESIDENT (June 1988–1989):
Channing R. Jescke, Pitts Theology Library, Emory University, Atlanta, Georgia 30322

VICE-PRESIDENT/PRESIDENT-ELECT:
H. Eugene McLeod, Southeastern Baptist Theological Seminary Library, Box 752, Wake Forest, North Carolina 27587

EXECUTIVE SECRETARY:
Simeon Daly, Archabbey Library, St. Meinrad School of Theology, Saint Meinrad, Indiana 47577

Membership (June 1988): 645 (469 personal; 176 institutional)

Annual Conference. Asbury Theological Seminary, Wilmore, Kentucky, hosted the 42nd annual conference of the American Theological Library Association at the Radisson Plaza Hotel, Lexington, Kentucky, June 20–24, 1988. Two continuing education workshops were held prior to the conference: "Getting Started in Desktop Publishing," by Dr. John Abercrombie, Assistant Dean for Computing (Humanities) and Director of the Center for Computer Analysis of Texts, University of Pennsylvania, Philadelphia, and "Advanced Searching Workshop," by the ATLA Religion Indexes Staff and Julie Hurd, Graduate Library School, University of Chicago. Rosalyn Lewis, United Methodist Publishing House, Nashville, Tennessee, delivered the presidential address, "Theological Librarianship: Service, Not Servitude." A plenary address by Herbert S. White, Dean, School of Library and Information Science, Indiana University, on "The Changing Role of Technical Services in the Theological Library" focused on the challenges of the cataloging profession. During another plenary session, Dr. Richard L. Harrison, Jr., Divinity School, Vanderbilt University, delivered a paper entitled, "Alexander Campbell, American Church Reformer," in commemoration of the bicentennial of the Disciples of Christ.

Additional papers included "Current Issues in Patristic Studies," by Dr. Frederick Norris, Emmanuel School of Religion; "Communitarian Movements: A Potpourri," by Dr. Philip N. Dare, Lexington Theological Seminary; "The Myth of the Automated Catalogue Environment," by Melinda Reagor, Rutgers University Libraries; and "The Interpretation of Matthew's Gospel in the Twentieth Century," by David Bauer, Asbury Theological Seminary.

Workshops, which concentrated on specialized needs of libraries, included "The Library's Role in Media and Instructional Design Services," led by Dr. Ken Boyd, Asbury Theological Seminary; and "Developing a Special Collections Program," organized by Sylvia Brown, Asbury Theological Seminary, and Dr. William J. Marshall, University of Kentucky. A panel discussion, "Censorship and Selection of Controversial Materials: Constitutional Issues in Theological Libraries," was moderated by Dr. Cecil R. White, West Oahu College.

Program Boards. The Religion Indexes Board plans to publish a revised edition of *Religion Index Two: Multi-Author Works, 1976–1980,* funded in part by a grant from the National Endowment for the Humanities. Other products produced include *Religion Index One: Periodicals Index to Book Reviews in Religion* (1987), and *Religion Index Two: Multi-Author Works* (1987). The Preservation Board has begun Phase Three of the Religion Monograph Preservation Program while progress continues on Phase Two. The Board received grants of $50,000 from the Henry Luce Foundation and $210,000 from the National Endowment for the Humanities. A Preservation Filming in Religion (PREFIR) Program, initiated in 1988, offers various subscription options for the monograph program, a limited number of on-demand monograph titles and serials at discounted prices, and interlibrary loans of titles in the program for non-members. Following the resignation of Robert P. Markham, Director of Programs for the Preservation Board, the Preservation and Religion Indexes boards, agreed to consider index and preservation matters as an Executive Committee. Albert E. Hurd serves as Executive Director of Programs.

Activities. The Board of Directors established a Task Force on Strategic Planning charged with investigating the structure and organization of ATLA and dissolved the Future Site Committee. The Board also voted to form an Ad Hoc Committee on Automation and Technology to coordinate automation concerns of other committees, facilitate automation activities and suggest conference programs relating to automation.

SARA J. MYERS

Archives

Archivist of the United States. In an impressive ceremony on December 4, 1987, the National Archives and Records Administration and hundreds of guests, including President Ronald Reagan, welcomed Don W. Wilson as the first permanent Archivist of the United States since the National Archives achieved independence in 1984. To many, Wilson's swearing-in marked completion of that independence as well as the beginning of a new era at NARA.

Throughout 1988, Wilson vigorously promoted his goal for NARA and began to reorient the agency in order to accomplish those goals. Wilson's top priority became planning for a major new NARA facility, "Archives II," to be built by 1994 near the University of Maryland campus.

Other elements in Wilson's goals for NARA include: continuing work on computerization and developing policies for machine-readable records; continuing to emphasize access; ensuring that NARA remains the repository for all federal records of enduring value; emphasizing and improving preservation efforts; expanding outreach; creatively utilizing NARA's field units; offering career-development opportunities for staff members; seeking a balance between research use and protection of records; and assuming a leadership role in formulating a national collection polcy.

Given the high visibility and key leadership role of the National Archives, its evolution under Wilson's direction is likely to have an important impact on the state of archives in the United States for years to come.

Certification. The Society of American Archivists in 1988 continued to develop a plan for voluntary certification of individual archivists. Progress was made on three fronts: devising a petition process to get certification started, preparing for a certification examination, and building awareness and support of the program among archivists throughout the profession.

SAA's Interim Board for Certification created a petition form to collect information about the education and experience of eligible archivists and established procedures for evaluating information submitted by those archivists requesting certification. The forms were distributed at the SAA annual meeting and will be available throughout the one-year period (ending September 30, 1989) when certification by petition is possible. The initial group of certified archivists will be announced early in 1989. Once 100 archivists are certified, an autonomous Academy of Certified Archivists can be created.

The Interim Board selected an experienced testing firm to assist in developing an objective, practice-based certification examination. This examination is to be administered initially at SAA's 1989 annual meeting and at least once a year thereafter. The process of preparing a reliable and comprehensive examination began with a role-delineation meeting at which a group of representative archivists defined the tasks that archivists perform and the knowledge needed to perform them in a competent manner.

The role-delineation document, once validated by about 200 other archivists, will guide a series of four item-development workshops. These workshops, which will involve still more archivists, will write at least 200 potential examination questions, from which an examination-development committee will select the 100 items for the first examination. In succeeding years, additional item development workshops will enlarge and refresh the pool of potential questions so that the examination keeps current with an evolving profession and maintains its integrity.

The two phases of certification (the immediate phase that employs petitions, and the examination process that will replace it in 1989) will entitle a certified archivist to eight years of certification, after which recertification will be necessary for those wishing to remain certified. The fee for either phase will be $275.

The Interim Board, along with other proponents of certification, also strove during 1988 to increase awareness of the new initiative and its benefits. Written communications, presentations at professional meetings, and individual discussions helped to circulate news of the evolving plans for certification and the reasons for an archivist to consider seeking certification. A large minority of archivists remained opposed to certification in principle, skeptical about the specific plan that had been announced, or dissatisfied with the certification fee.

With the SAA Council's final approval of a certification program, however, the issue shifted to whether enough archivists would actually become certified, first through petitions and then by examination. Only time will tell whether SAA's venture to provide the archival profession with a visible credential based upon an objective standard of archival competence will succeed.

Annual Meeting. Atlanta was the site of SAA's 52nd annual meeting, attended by 1,100 persons. In addition to providing the occasion for approximately 100 program sessions, numerous preconference workshops, dozens of meetings of all types, and a variety of other professional and cultural activities, the Society's annual meeting saw the installation of new officers and Council members.

SAA also presented its annual awards. Receiving the Society's highest individual honor, designation as Fellow, were Bruce Dearstyne, Anne Diffendal, Lawrence Dowler, and James Fogerty. The Bentley Historical Library/Michigan Historical Collections at the University of Michigan was the recipient of SAA's most prestigious award, the Distinguished Service Award.

The Waldo Gifford Leland Prize for superior writing in the archival field was presented to Nancy Gwinn (American Library Association) for *Preservation Microfilming*. Nancy Bartlett and Kathleen Koehler, both of the Bentley Historical Library, won the Philip M. Hamer-Elizabeth Hamer Kegan Award for their work on *A Book Of Days: 150 Years of Student Life at Michigan*.

Brother Denis Sennett, S.A., Friars of Atone-

SOCIETY OF AMERICAN ARCHIVISTS

PRESIDENT (October 1988–October 1989):
Frank B. Evans, National Archives and Records Administration, Washington, D.C.

VICE-PRESIDENT/PRESIDENT-ELECT:
John A. Fleckner, Smithsonian Institution, Washington, D.C.

EXECUTIVE DIRECTOR:
Donn C. Neal

Membership (December 1987): 4,400 (2,800 individual; 800 institutional; 800 subscribers)
Headquarters: 600 S. Federal, Suite 504, Chicago, Illinois 60605

Armed Forces Libraries

ment, received the Sister M. Claude Lane Award, given each year to an outstanding religious archivist. Avra Michelson, Smithsonian Institution, won the Fellows Posner Prize for the outstanding article in *The American Archivist* during 1987, while Gregory Kinney, a student at the University of Michigan, received the new Theodore Calvin Pease Award that recognizes superior writing by a student of archival administration.

A software system developed by Frederick Honhart at Michigan State University was awarded the C.F.W. Coker Prize as an outstanding finding aid. The Colonial Dames Scholarships went to Doris Martinson, Knox County Archives, and Margaret Nelson, Smithsonian Institution. Three foreign archivists, Jan Boomgaard (The Netherlands), Alan Ives (Australia), and Ann Pederson (Australia), shared the Oliver Wendell Holmes Award. A book edited by Pederson, *Keeping Archives*, received a special certificate of commendation.

DONN C. NEAL

Armed Forces Libraries

General Background. Each branch of the Armed Forces provides library service from general, special, scientific and technical research, medical research, legal and academic libraries. While each branch of service operates independently, crossfeed is transmitted by a Department of Defense subcommittee on libraries, the Military Librarians Division of SLA's annual Military Librarians Workshop, various user groups and through meetings of national, international, regional, state, and local library associations.

Air Force Libraries. The Air Force Library Program changed its name to Air Force Library and Information System, and adopted a new logo in 1988. The system includes all libraries in the Air Force except medical and legal libraries, and is under the direction of the Chief, Library and Information Branch, Directorate of Morale, Welfare and Recreation, and a Command Librarian assigned to each of 10 functional major commands and the Air University and Air Force Academy.

Library service is provided to Air Force personnel and their families worldwide. Each Air Force base has a general library or library system that equates to a public library; special, research, and academic libraries may coexist on the base.

A bare room in Kleine Brogel, Belgium, is the first in a series of "instant mini-libraries" planned for Air Forces personnel in Europe. The project is a cooperative effort by the Air Force and the Army.

Three overseas major commands operate library service centers which provide additional extension services.

Ratification of the INF treaty resulted in the immediate closure of missile site libraries in Belgium and The Netherlands. Two "instant mini-libraries," developed by the Army in Europe and made available to the Air Force, were installed in Germany and Belgium.

Air Force libraries worldwide are joining an electronic network for information and data transfer that utilizes the Faxon Company's MicroLinx/DataLinx system. This is in addition to access of OCLC and other national networks. At year's end, more than 40 libraries were online and had received on-site staff training by Faxon. Seventy-two Air Force librarians from bases around the world attended the annual ALA convention in New Orleans. Joe Burke, Base Librarian, RAF Upper Heyford, United Kingdom, was presented with the John Cotton Dana Library Public Relations Contest award for Military Libraries at the annual H. W. Wilson tea during the conference. Lee McLaughlin, Beulah Phillips, and Joe Burke were presented with Air Force outstanding librarian award plaques at the Armed Forces Library Section membership meeting.

Army Libraries. The Army Library System (ALS) is administered by the staff agencies or major commands served, while central guidance is provided by the Army Library Management Office (ALMO), under Dorothy Fisk McDysan, with advice from the Army Library Committee (ALC), made up of representatives from staff and command agencies. ALMO focuses on Army-wide library matters and encourages the integration and coordination of library activities. It collects, compiles, analyzes, and distributes statistical data on library resources expended and services provided and coodinates library automation efforts, in-service training, and the Army Librarian Career Program. It publishes the *ALMO Information Update* at irregular intervals, and published the *Army Library Directory* in 1988.

The ALS consists of 27 academic, 13 consolidated, 114 general, 258 law, 59 medical, and 83 technical libraries, and 12 headquarters/system offices. A major effort of ALS in 1988 was the production of a 12-module, self-paced library technician training package consisting of videotapes, workbooks, training exercises, and study guides. Reproduction rights were extended to other Department of Defense library systems.

Army general library service is directed by the Library Division of the U.S. Army Community and Family Support Center, which provides central funding, acquisition, and distribution of materials to libraries and personnel assigned to isolated locations, on maneuvers, etc. It also continued monitoring Army library participation in the Federal Library Network (FEDLINK) Interlibrary Loan Payment Program.

Automation was one of the bright spots for general libraries, with the installation of microcomputer systems at all libraries in the U.S., Panama, and Puerto Rico, and the continued development and expansion of the GEAC Patron-Oriented Automated Library System (PALS) in Europe. The PALS integrated system will link all Army libraries in Germany, Belgium, and Italy, as well as Air Force libraries in Germany.

A one-year moratorium on contracting out of libraries helped to make up for a dissappointing record of construction and upgrading of libraries.

Navy Libraries. The Coordinator of Naval Libraries, who is also the Director of the Navy Department Library in the Washington Navy Yard, D.C., is responsible for encouraging resource sharing, providing technical guidance, and maintaining close working relationships among some 150 special, research and academic libraries which are administered independently by the organizations they serve. Both Navy and Marine Corps general libraries constitute the Naval General Library Program, which is administered by the Naval Education and Training Program Management Support Activity, Pensacola, Florida. Regional librarians provide technical guidance and assistance, and coordinate ship and shore programs within their geographic areas.

During 1988, the program supported 154 Navy and 27 Marine Corps shore libraries, including main, branch, hospital patient, confinement library, and bookmobiles; and 158 libraries aboard major ships and Trident submarines. It also provided reference and paperback collections aboard 380 smaller ships and submarines and at 167 and 168 Marine Corps remote sites.

Armed Forces Libraries Section (AFLS). The section is part of the Public Library Association of the American Library Association. Membership is open to all armed forces librarians, institutions, and friends.

TONY DAKAN

Art Libraries

ARLIS/NA Conference Activities. The 1988 Annual Conference of ARLIS/NA marked the conclusion of the 16th anniversary year of the Society. The conference in Dallas, Texas, included a convocation with an address by Decherd Turner, Director of the Harry Ransom Humanities Research Center of the University of Texas at Austin, held at the Dallas Museum of Art; tours of the Fort Worth Art Museum, the Amon Carter Museum and the Kimbell Art Museum; and a variety of programs related to art librarians and visual resource professionals. The conference was cochaired by Milan Hughston of the Amon Carter Museum and Lois Swan Jones of the University of North Texas, Denton, Texas.

Sessions focused on such topics as Meeting the Challenges of Patrons' Needs, Prints in the Art Library, Cataloging Artists' Books, Indexing and Search Strategy Using the Art and Architecture Thesaurus (AAT), Visual Resources Collection Management, and Exhibition Catalogs. Preconference workshops included Self-study Process for Art Library and Visual Resources Collections: Use of Performance Measures, Preservation Options for Art Librarians, and Planning the Space Needs of the Art Library. The Art and Architecture Program Committee of RLG sponsored a program entitled "One Stop Shopping: Access to Visual and Archival Materials—Use of VIM and AMC-MARC Formats."

Several important issues affecting ARLIS/NA were discussed at the annual membership meeting. The Society's membership voted for affiliation with ARLIS/Australia-New Zealand and with ARLIS/Norge. ARLIS/NA also is affiliated with ARLIS/UK and Eire. An initial report was given on the results of a Members' Satisfaction Survey. Thirty-three percent of the members of the Society replied to the Survey and the results will be used in future planning for the organization. Vice President Ann Abid presented three models for restructuring the organization of ARLIS/NA. As a result of the ensuring discussions, a bylaws change is being written and will be voted upon by the membership at the next annual meeting. The membership of ARLIS/NA also unanimously passed a motion endorsing the use of permanent/durable paper in art publications, including those by ARLIS/NA, applauding those publishers now using this type of paper and encouraging others to do so.

Art and Architecture Thesaurus. The Art and Architecture Thesaurus (AAT) Project continued to progress in a number of areas during the past year. The AAT has registered all distributed hierarchies with the U.S. Copyright Office in advance of official publication sometime in 1988. The AAT was represented by Toni Petersen, its director, at the mid-year meeting of the American Society of Information Science in Ann Arbor in May. Her paper was titled "Constructing a Language of the Arts: Knowledge Representation in Thesauri." Plans are underway for a preconference program related to implementing the AAT at the 1989 ARLIS/NA Conference.

Museum Computer Network. A related organization to many art libraries, the Museum Computer Network, chose Deirdre C. Stam as its Executive Director during 1988. The MCN is housed in the School of the Information Studies, Syracuse University. Through its journal *Spectra*, its annual meeting and other publications and educational programs, the Museum Computer Network supports cooperative efforts that will enable museums and their libraries to play an effective role in the creation and dissemination of cultural and scientific knowledge as represented by their collections and related documentation. The MCN encourages the sharing of experience with automated collection information projects and with other computer applications.

Special Libraries Association. The Museum, Arts and Humanities Division of SLA presented two programs, "Contemporary Fine Printing and Small Press Publishing: The Book in Los Angeles" and "Collected Regional Planning Records," at the SLA annual conference. The conference, held in June 1988 in Los Angeles, also included tours of the Getty Conservation Institute and the Getty Center for the History of Art and the Humanities as well as the Huntington Library.

IFLA Art Section. The Art Section of the International Federation of Library Associations (IFLA) promotes international understanding, cooperation, research and development in the documentation of art, architecture, and design. During 1988, two publications were completed that record the proceedings of the First and Second European Conferences of the Art Section.

47

Work progressed on a third publication, *Bibliography of Bibliographies of Art Serials,* which is edited by Art Section Chairperson, Margaret Shaw, Librarian, Australian National Gallery. An Art Preconference session in Sydney, Australia, prior to the opening of the 54th IFLA General Conference provided a unique opportunity for Australian, Asian, European, and American colleagues to meet. In November the Third European Conference was held in Florence, Italy, with an international panel of speakers focusing on exhibition catalogs. Topics included the history of exhibition catalogs, their production and distribution, and bibliographic and physical access to exhibition catalogs. The Art Section also produces the *Section of Art Libraries, Special Libraries Division Newsletter,* which includes conference information and a professional literature update.

RLG Art and Architecture Program Committee. The Art and Architecture Program Committee (AAPC) of the Research Libraries Group (RLG) is charged with advising the Board of Governors about special requirements of art and architecture within the principal programs of RLG and with identifying projects which would address the specific information needs of art and architectural historians, architects, and curators. During 1988 the AAPC participated in a shared cataloging project for monographic series and in a joint acquisitions and cataloging project focusing on exhibition catalogs from American museums. Approximately 150 19th and 20th century art periodical titles have been identified for a microfilming preservation project. The AAPC is involved in the creation and maintenance of several special databases available on the Research Libraries Information Network (RLIN). By 1988 more than 25,000 records were contained in Online Avery Index to Architectural Periodicals and over 90,000 records available in the Sales Catalog Index Project Input On-line (SCIPIO). Working with the J. Paul Getty Trust the decision was made to mount the Art and Architecture Thesaurus as a special database to offer more than 40,000 art and architecture related terms for controlled vocabulary in cataloging and indexing projects for books, journals, visual resources, archives and art objects. With the support of staff at RLG, the AAPC continued to offer an effective method of cooperating on projects that widen the scope of art information available to the research community.

The sixth annual conference of the Visual Resources Association held in Houston, Texas, February 11–12, 1988, included three programs: "Trends in Automation IV," "Graphic Documentation in the Administration of Visual Resource Collections," and "Special Collections." Incoming President Eleanor Fink, from the Getty Art History Information Program, chaired the business meeting. The agenda included professional status, membership, and publications. A slide exchange, a walking tour of Houston and a reception following the College Art Association convocation were some of the highlights of the meeting.

Awards. The Ninth Annual George Wittenborn Memorial Award for outstanding art publications of 1987 was given to *The Art That is Life:*

ART LIBRARIES SOCIETY OF NORTH AMERICA

PRESIDENT (February 1988–February 1989):
Ann Abid, Cleveland Museum of Art, Ohio

VICE PRESIDENT/PRESIDENT-ELECT:
Clive Philpot, Museum of Modern Art, New York

SECRETARY:
Helene Roberts, Harvard University

TREASURER:
Jack Robertson, University of Virginia

PAST PRESIDENT:
Jeffrey Horrell, Syracuse University

EXECUTIVE DIRECTOR:
Pamela J. Parry

Membership (December 1988): 1,312 members/subscribers
Headquarters: 3900 E. Timrod St., Tucson, Arizona 85711

The Arts and Crafts Movement in America, 1875–1920 by Wendy Kaplan, published by the Museum of the Arts, Boston, in association with Little, Brown, and Company, and *The Eloquent Object: The Evolution of American Art in Craft Media Since 1945,* edited by Marcia and Tom Manhart and published by the Philbrook Museum of Art, Tulsa, Oklahoma, in association with the University of Washington Press.

JEFFREY L. HORRELL

Asian/Pacific American Librarians Association

In 1988 the Asian/Pacific American Librarians Association (APALA) continued to promote the Association's six major objectives: (1) providing a forum for discussion of problems and concerns of Asian/Pacific American librarians; (2) providing a forum for the exchange of ideas among Asian Pacific American librarians and other librarians; (3) supporting and encouraging library services to the Asian/Pacific American communities; (4) recruiting and supporting Asian/Pacific Americans in the library information science professions; (5) seeking funds for scholarships and fellowships in library information science schools for Asian/Pacific Americans; and (6) providing a vehicle whereby Asian/Pacific American librarians can cooperate with other associations and organizations having similar or allied interests.

APALA, established in 1980, is affiliated with the American Library Association and conducts its annual program and membership meeting in conjunction with the ALA Annual Conference.

Programs and Activities. As a result of increased demand for information and library services and the growing pool of highly qualified librarians, an increased number of Asian/Pacific American librarians worked in American libraries and information centers in 1988. APALA's meetings and round table discussions were designed to promote the awareness of all librarians about the problems and needs of minority library users. These activities provided an important forum for library professionals concerned with the problems and challenges fac-

O-Bon originated in 657 A.D. to worship Spirits of the Dead

Orange County (California) Public Library celebrates Asian-Pacific Americans.

ing ethnic minorities and their future information needs.

APALA members were active in exchange programs between the United States and Asian countries that include visits, teaching, lectures, and consultation on library matters and participation in international conferences and professional development that includes discussions of the appropriate treatment of Chinese, Japanese, and Korean materials by libraries, collection development for Asian/Pacific international business, Asian bibliographies, and research activities.

APALA continued to publish a quarterly newsletter that covers news, employment advertisements, book reviews, and other items of interest. It also published Proceedings of the 1988 Conference.

Conference in New Orleans. At the annual conference in New Orleans, the Asian/Pacific American Librarians Association focused on the extremely important and timely topic: "The Educational Excellence of Asian Americans: Myth or Reality?" Speakers were Linus Wright, Undersecretary, U.S. Department of Education; Tobin Barrozo, Provost and Vice President for Academic Affairs, Metropolitan State College in Denver, Colorado; and Chizuko Izawa, Professor of Psychology at Tulane University in New Orleans. In conjunction with the program, Professor Augurio Collantes of the Hostos Community College, (New York) City College, prepared an annotated bibliography of selected sources on the educational excellence of Asian Americans. At the conclusion, there was a reception and a well-attended and warmly received program of Filipino dances.

Profiles of Asian/Pacific American Librarians. Augurio Collantes prepared a profile of APALA membership. As of May 1986, membership, including institutions, was 177, with the greatest number (54) of Chinese ancestry, followed by Korean (27), Japanese (25), and native American (18). More than half (100) of the members were in academic libraries; special libraries (25) claimed the next largest group, followed by public libraries (10) and teachers of librarianship (12).

As of October 1988, 194 individual and 10 institutional members had renewed their membership.
CONCHITA J. PINEDA

Association for Library and Information Science Education

The Association for Library and Information Science Education [ALISE], in response to comments by library education facilities of its member schools, concentrated in 1988 on strategic planning. The first step in a process expected to take several years was revision of the Association's statement of mission and goals. The revised statement, approved by the Board at its July, 1988, meeting in New Orleans, will be brought to the membership for general discussion at the January 1989 conference.

In 1988 the Association continued its work to promote excellence in library and information science education through the following activities:

Awards. The two highest awards given by ALISE are the Award for Professional Contribution to Library and Information Science Education and the ALISE Service Award. Samuel Rothstein [University of British Columbia] received the professional contribution award; Mohammed M. Aman [University of Wisconsin–Milwaukee] received the service award. Annual awards encourage and support research by ALISE members and doctoral students in programs of library and information science. The research grant was awarded to John V. Richardson, Jr. and Donald O. Case [both from University of California at Los Angeles] for a study entitled "Gender and Ethnic Determinants of Success in Graduate School: A Mathematical Modeling of

---

ASIAN PACIFIC AMERICAN LIBRARIANS ASSOCIATION

PRESIDENT (July 1988–July 1989):
Conchita J. Pineda, Manager, Information Center, City Corp. City Bank, 153 E. 53rd Street, New York 10043

VICE-PRESIDENT/PRESIDENT-ELECT:
Ichiko Morita, Ohio State, University Libraries, 1858 Neil Avenue Mall, Columbus, Ohio 43210

SECRETARY:
Dallas R. Shawkey, Brooklyn Public Library, 109 Montgomery Street, Brooklyn, New York 11225

TREASURER:
Abdul J. Miah, Director, Learning Resources Center, J. Sargeant Reynolds Community College, 700 East Jackson Street, Richmond, Virginia 23240

JOURNAL EDITOR:
Sharad Karkhanis, Kingsborough Community College, Oriental Boulevard, Brooklyn, New York 11235

Membership (December 1987): 200

the Admissions Process in Library and Information Science."

Verna L. Pungitore [Indiana University] and Pamela Spence Richards [Rutgers University] were recognized in the Research Paper competition. In the Doctoral Dissertation Competition there also were two awards: to Prudence Dalrymple [University of Wisconsin–Madison] for "Retrieval by Reformulation in Two Library Catalogs: Toward a Cognitive Model of Searching Behavior"; and to Edward Anthony Olden [University of Illinois–Champaign–Urbana] for "The Beneficiaries of Library and Information Policy in British and Ex-British Africa: Steps from the White Women's League to the Electronic Library."

Activities. "Faculty Participation in Policy Formulation" was the theme of the well-received 1988 conference, planned by 1987 President Kathleen M. Heim. ALISE also co-sponsored a number of conferences. In May, members of the Association joined with AIESI's Francophone schools in a conference entitled "Bridging the Gap Between Theory and Practice." The Association for Research Libraries' Institute for Library Educators, another joint venture, received support from the Council on Library Resources. ALISE also worked with ALA to co-sponsor preconferences on recruitment and racism.

Members of the Association completed arrangements for a visit of Soviet librarians to the 1989 ALISE conference. The project, sponsored by the American Council of Learned Societies, is the initial exchange between library and information science educators in the United States and in the Soviet Union.

Publications. Under its new editor, Rosemary R. Du Mont, *The Journal of Education for Library and Information Science Education* published articles on far-ranging topics such as library education in Nicaragua and Brazil, and devoted one issue to summary papers presented at a conference of library assistants. The *Statistical Report*, edited by Timothy Sineath, cited positive indicators of the strength of library and information science education, including steady growth in the number of students and graduates per year and a rise in annual income for ALISE schools.

The Future. Growth in membership, both personal and institutional [including several new international schools], and the successful transition of the secretariat generated optimism and vitality in the Association. The ongoing strategic planning project provides a mechanism for members of ALISE to consider how library and information science education can be responsive to changes brought about by the rapidly shifting boundaries of this field.

LEIGH ESTABROOK

Association for Library Service to Children

If "Money and Power" constituted a major program theme for the 1988 New Orleans Conference, that phrase also characterized ALSC's 1988 financial viability and collaborative spirit. Thanks largely to the efforts of Executive Director Susan Roman, the Association for Library Service to Children (ALSC) reaped the benefits of interest income from grants, endowments, and added publishing ventures. Increased human resources in the form of new members helped solidify ALSC's standing as a division.

Grants. ALSC worked with the Home and School Institute to provide a "New Partnerships for Student Achievement" project at two locations: the Sulzer Regional Branch of the Chicago Public Library and Miami–Dade's North Dade facility. The three-year project, in which librarians work with parents to help children succeed in school, is funded by the John D. and Catherine T. MacArthur Foundation. In cooperation with AASL, the division accepted a Phase I, $43,000 grant from Houghton Mifflin for a single district, demonstration pilot project supporting the role of public and school librarians in promoting reading. The program is designed to foster a cooperative relationship among those most influential in a child's reading life, including public and school librarians, teachers, administrators, and parents, as part of introducing a reading textbook in the target community. The ALSC Board also accepted a new award from Econo-Clad for librarians attending ALA conferences.

A "Past Response Survey" Grant from the U.S. Department of Education promised baseline statistics in children's services, and a Computer Software Committee focused on new technology.

Publications and Videos. With a $1,350 grant from the Whitney–Carnegie Fund, an *AIDS Bibliography for Youth*, prepared by the Library Service to Children with Special Needs Committee was published with ALA graphics. "U.S.A. Through Children's Books" was prepared by the International Relations Committee and published by *Booklist*. ALSC and ALA Video produced "Caldecott at 50," based on the 1987 program about Charlemae Rollins Program. Yearly media evaluation pamphlets on the 1988 Newbery Award, Caldecott Award, Notable Chil-

---

ASSOCIATION FOR LIBRARY AND INFORMATION SCIENCE EDUCATION

PRESIDENT (January 1988–January 1989):
Leigh S. Estabrook, Graduate School of Library and Information Science, University of Illinois, Champaign–Urbana

PRESIDENT-ELECT:
Miles Jackson, School of Library and Information Studies, University of Hawaii at Manoa

SECRETARY/TREASURER:
Linda C. Smith, Graduate School of Library and Information Science, University of Illinois, Champaign–Urbana

EXECUTIVE SECRETARY:
Ilse Moon, Sarasota, Florida

EDITOR: *Journal of Education for Library and Information Science*
Rosemary R. Du Mont, School of Library Science, Kent State University, Ohio

Membership (June, 1988): 686 (602 personal; 84 institutional)
Headquarters: 5623 Palm Aire Drive, Sarasota, Florida 34243

dren's Books, Recordings, Films and Video, Filmstrips, and booklists were published. The 1989 Caldecott Calendar, available at the New Orleans Conference, enjoyed brisk sales. The 1988 edition of *The Newbery/Caldecott Awards and Honor Books: A Complete Listing* was published, along with a retrospective bibliography entitled *Notable Children's Films and Videos, Filmstrips, and Recordings, 1973-1986*.

Josette Lyders was appointed editor of a newly named JYSL (formerly TON). Elizabeth Huntoon served as guest editor for the special Caldecott 50th Anniversary issue.

Projects. Cooperation also marked two ventures with PLA: establishment of a Joint Task Force on Output Measures for Children's Services, and publication of a Position Paper on Latchkey Children, co-authored by PLA's Service to Children Committee and ALSC's Library Services to Children with Special Needs Committee. A joint dues project for recruiting new members was conducted with AASL and YASD. ALSC continued to work with OLPR to develop a recruitment program for children's librarians; a new brochure featured Steve Herb of Pennsylvania as one of four representative librarians. YASD and ALSC continued to consult with the Library of Congrees on "The Year of the Young Reader" through ALA Communication Service.

The Library Card Campaign, initiated by ALSC and carried out primarily by public children's librarians across the country in concert with their AASL colleagues, yielded dramatic results: 100,000 new cards in West Virginia and 50,000 in Louisville, Kentucky. ALA is committed to continue the campaign, which ultimately will be an annual canvas of early elementary grades.

The ALSC Education Committee produced a draft statement on Competencies for Librarians Serving Children. Through newsletter publication, the draft was shared with members, whose suggestions were encouraged.

Cooperative outreach to other organizations impacting children resulted in these actions: appointment of Margaret Mary Kimmel to the Advisory Committee of the California Reading Initiative, representation at the conference of the NAEYC (National Association for the Education of Young Children) and appointment of an advisory committee for the establishment of a book award from the Association for the Care of Children's Health (ACCH). Susan Roman explored the possibility of a health information network with ACCH.

Conferences and Programs. ALSC participated in a panel on "The Business of Video for Children" at Harvard University, and assisted WGBH Educational Television in formulating a new series, "Long Ago and Far Away," launched in early 1989. The division also initiated plans to send a delegation to Russia in 1989. The President and Executive Director spoke in the following states, promoting ALSC: Florida, Connecticut, Iowa, Oklahoma, Kentucky, North Carolina, Illinois, Pennsylvania, and Massachusetts.

A Russian delegation visited the ALSC Membership Meeting in New Orleans, bringing books, medals, and formal greetings. This dramatic presentation by a Ukrainian librarian served as a perfect accompaniment to the International Preconference, "Going Global." Participants in the "Going Global" event learned of the complexities of children's book production abroad, tips on book talks, facts on Batchelder Award titles, and data on international storytelling from a host of world-renowned guests.

ASSOCIATION FOR LIBRARY SERVICE TO CHILDREN

PRESIDENT (June 1988–July 1989):
Marilyn Berg Iarusso, New York Public Library, New York, New York

VICE-PRESIDENT/PRESIDENT-ELECT:
Barbara F. Immroth, University of Texas at Austin, Graduate School of Library and Information Science

EXECUTIVE DIRECTOR:
Susan Roman

Membership (August 31, 1988): 3,578 (3,055 personal; 523 organizational)
Expenditures (August 31, 1988): $248,953

The Membership Meeting honored Preconference speaker Margaret K. McElderry, recipient of the Batchelder Award, for her substantive contribution to publication of foreign children's books in the United States. The ALSC President's Program, part of a joint effort with YASD, focused on "Money and Power: How To Get It and Use It." Panelists plugged positive PR, grants, community coalition-building, and effective communication with boards and directors.

The highlight of the annual ALSC conference was the Newbery–Caldecott banquet. Twin themes of Mardi Gras and The Thirties added sparkle to the occasion. The evening commemorated the first ALSC banquet held in New Orleans in 1932. Russell Freedman received the Newbery Medal for *Abraham Lincoln*, and John Schoenherr was given the Caldecott for illustrating Jane Yolen's *Owl Moon*.

Continuing the "Caldecott at 50" celebration, Caldecott banner contest winners—all by school children—were displayed prominently in ALA's Great Hall, site of ALA Membership meetings.

The University of Oklahoma at Norman hosted the Arbuthnot Lecture, which featured folklorist John Bierhorst and attracted many native Americans who respect Bierhorst's role in preserving their culture. This event was a reminder of the far-reaching effect of ALSC awards.

MARY R. SOMERVILLE

Marilyn Berg Iarusso, The New York Public Library.

Association of College and Research Libraries

Nineteen eighty-eight brought new accomplishments and challenges to the Association of College and Research Libraries, the largest ALA division. Membership and expenditures grew to all-time highs as the Association saw many "firsts" and planned for the celebration of its 50th anniversary at the Fifth ACRL National Conference April 5–8, 1989 in Cincinnati.

Planning. While new initiatives and discussions of values dominated much of ACRL's

Association of College and Research Libraries

agenda, activities and planning continued to take place in the context of the 1986 Strategic Plan. The first annual Operating Plan was developed by Executive Director JoAn Segal and the Planning Committee, under Chair Carolyn Dusenbury. A planning cycle and calendar for succeeding years was developed and approved, and the Five-Year Financial Plan, through the work of the Budget and Finance Committee chaired by Patricia Wand, reached its penultimate draft for member hearings and Board approval during 1989. ACRL's plans for the year were also cast in terms of ALA's Mission, Priority Areas and Goals, both for the ALA Action Inventory and for the 1987–88 division annual report to ALA.

ACRL continued to maintain its Board-mandated financial reserve. Utilizing reserves above that level, the Board approved contracting for an output measures handbook, continued support for the publication of *Books for College Libraries*, third edition, and the Hugh Craig Atkinson Memorial Award, and created the Special Grants Fund. As a result, at the beginning of the 1989 fiscal year, reserve funds were at no more than the six-month level.

Performance Measures. Following ACRL Board approval in January, a contract was signed with Nancy Van House for the testing and writing of an *Output Measures Manual* for academic libraries, with completion scheduled for 1989.

Publishing Activities. The six-volume *Books for College Libraries*, third edition, 1988, was published jointly by ACRL and ALA. As a standard reference work in academic libraries, the second edition was badly out of date and the new edition was eagerly awaited by librarians. Publication of the third edition was subsidized by funds from ACRL's fiscal reserve. Patricia Sabosik, Editor and Publisher of *Choice*, was project officer for the publication.

ACRL continues to publish *Choice*, which offers more than 6,000 book reviews a year, the greatest number of any English-language reviewing medium; *College & Research Libraries*; *College & Research Libraries News*; *Rare Books and Manuscripts Librarianship (RBML)*; *Chapter Topics*, and regular newsletters for 12 ACRL sections. Alice Schreyer was appointed Editor of RBML for a three-year term.

Continuing Education. The Western European Studies Section sponsored ACRL's first overseas conference, "Shared Resources, Shared Responsibilities," in Florence, Italy, April 4–8, 1988. Participants comprised 90 Americans and 80 Europeans. A teleconference on CD-ROM technology was sponsored by the Community and Junior College Section in cooperation with the Community College Association for Instruction and Technology/Association for Educational Communications and Technology. The event drew an estimated audience of 10,000 to 11,000 at more than 320 sites in 47 states. At the Annual Conference in New Orleans, the Rare Books and Manuscripts Section held its 29th preconference, "Libraries and Museums: Leaves from Each Other's Books." The Bibliographic Instruction Section also held a preconference in New Orleans, "The Future of BI: Approaches in the Electronic Age."

Continuing the Historically Black Colleges

Twenty-fifth Anniversary of *Choice*

The first issue of *Choice* was published in March 1964 after more than five years of planning by the American Library Association (ALA). The Council on Library Resources (CLR) gave an initial grant to ALA to start a review journal for scholarly books appropriate for undergraduate libraries. The eve of the anniversary issue, and well into the 26th volume, is a time to reflect on the history of the publication and major events that helped shape the review service that has evolved today.

The idea of a review journal that would be used for selection and for improving undergraduate library collections originated with Verner Clapp, President of CLR, who proposed that ALA undertake the development and publication of this new journal. ALA's Executive Director, David Clift, and the ALA Executive Board accepted the proposal and appointed the Association of College and Research Libraries (ACRL) as the division responsible for the management and editorial policy of the new journal. In the 1970s, fiscal management was added to ACRL's responsibilities for *Choice*. Richard K. Gardner, the first editor, wrote a detailed history of the beginning of *Choice* that was published in the April 1984 issue.

The decision to locate the editorial office away from ALA's Chicago headquarters was made early in the planning process and it was strongly supported by Clapp. As a review journal of scholarly books, *Choice* would benefit greatly from proximity to, or operation in, an academic environment. Faculty reviewers would be close at hand and library resources would be readily available. Proximity to the New York publishing community was also a strong consideration.

Wesleyan University in Middletown, Connecticut, was willing to rent space for a nominal amount in Olin Library to ACRL for the new journal and the *Choice* Editor and Editorial Board accepted the offer. Within four years, the *Choice* operation grew too large to be supported by the library's facilities and *Choice* moved to commercial space in Middletown, just a few blocks from the Wesleyan Campus, and it has remained there to this day.

The new journal was aimed at undergraduate college libraries, and it also planned to use subject experts—college and university professors active in undergraduate teaching—to review new scholarly works. The initial pool of *Choice* reviewers, numbering just over 1,000, was recruited from the faculty of first-rate independent four-year colleges, representatives of the institutions *Choice* was designed to serve. The first group of reviewers was recruited by Richard K. Gardner, Virginia Clark, and Mary E. Poole, the founding editorial staff.

The number of reviewers grew to 1,359 by the end of 1964 and to approximately 3,000 a few years later; the pool continues at that level today. *Choice* reviewers are profiled in an editorial published in the January 1987 issue, and some of the statistics from that editorial appear below. The reviewers are the most important asset of the *Choice* review service.

Of the 3,000 reviewers on file, approximately 2,700 are faculty and 300 are librarians. The dominant gender is male, paralleling the gender distribution in academia. Men account for 77 percent of the reviewers. Of the male reviewers, 82 percent hold the Ph.D.; of the women, 64 percent do.

Choice reviewers are from 864 institutions, an increase of 509 over the 355 campuses represented in the first few issues. There are approximately 100 reviewers from community or junior colleges, 840

and Universities (HBCU) project begun in 1987, chaired by Beverly Lynch, an ACRL grant was received from the National Endowment for the Humanities. It will fund a humanities programming workshop specifically targeted at HBCUs, scheduled for 1989. A preconference on preparation for accreditation at HBCUs was approved for the 1989 Dallas Annual Conference. Plans for a statistical survey of HBCU libraries are under way.

Continuing Education. Continuing education courses developed by ACRL and offered throughout the nation, as well as in conjunction with Annual Conferences, continued to draw large audiences. During 1987–88, 24 local presentations reached 825 people, while another 163 participated in courses preceding the New Orleans conference. The development and offering of new courses is an ongoing process based on regular evaluations under the purview of the Course Advisory Committee.

The ACRL President's Program in New Orleans, "Creativity in the Workplace: From Conception to Application," featured Scott Isaksen, director of the Center for Studies in Creativity in Buffalo, New York, as keynote speaker. Susan Jurow, program officer for training of the Association of Research Libraries Office of Management Services, led attendees in creative problem–solving exercises.

Awards. Two new awards were presented in 1988. The Hugh C. Atkinson Award, jointly sponsored by ACRL, the Library Administration and Management Association, the Library Information and Technology Association and the Resources and Technical Services Division, was given to Richard M. Dougherty. The first K. G. Saur Award for the best article appearing in *College & Research Libraries* went to Robert Boice, Jordan Scepanski, and Wayne Wilson for "Librarians and Faculty Members: Coping with Pressures to Publish." Edward G. Holley was named Academic or Research Librarian of the Year at a ceremony during the ACRL President's Program in New Orleans. The Doctoral Dissertation Fellowship was awarded to Sarla Murgai; Carol M. Kelley received the Samuel Lazerow Fellowship for Research in Acquisitions or Technical Services. Sharon A. Hogan was named Miriam Dudley Bibliographic Instruction Librarian of the Year. The Katharine Kyes Leab and Daniel J. Leab American Book Prices Current Exhibition Catalogue Awards went to the Library Company of Philadelphia and the Historical Society of Pennsylvania, the Folger Shakespeare Library, the Rosenbach Museum and Library, and the Harvard Law School Library.

Standards. Three new guidelines were distributed: *Guidelines on the Selection of General Collection Materials for Transfer to Special Collections*, *Mission of a University Undergraduate Library: Model Statement*, and *Guidelines for Audiovisual Services in Academic Libraries*. The *Model Statement of Objectives for Academic Bibliographic Instruction* and *Guidelines Regarding Thefts in Libraries* were approved. *Standards for University Libraries: Evaluation of Performance* was published in draft form in the June 1988 *College & Research Libraries News*; open hearings were held in New Orleans. The third draft of *Guidelines for Conservators and Cura-*

---

reviewers from four-year institutions, and 1,980 reviewers from universities. The last figure indicates in part a migration of original reviewers to larger institutions as their careers matured. The average length of time a reviewer has written evaluations for Choice is 9.2 years; 42 percent have been reviewing for 11 or more years.

The subject editors at Choice select the books that are distributed for review. They follow guidelines set down in the Choice Selection Policy that was published in the September 1983 issue, paying special attention to the appropriateness of the title for undergraduate use. The title is then matched with a reviewer who has a research and/or teaching background on the topic of the book and who can write an authoritative critique of the work. The subject editors then edit reviews, checking for clarity, accuracy, and house style. Richard D. Johnson, while serving as Acting Editor, wrote a feature on the process of reviewing for Choice that was published in the September 1982 issue.

The first issue of Choice, containing approximately 300 reviews, was assembled by the three original editors. The number of reviews quickly increased to 600 an issue or more than 6,000 reviews a year by 1966 to keep up with increases in American book publishing. The editorial staff grew over the years to its present level of seven (three are part-time editors) plus one contributing editor for database reviews. Editorial responsibilities have increased over the past 25 years to include supervision of the support staff; management of relations with more than 2,000 publishers and 200 audiovisual producer/distributors on file; coordination of an online editorial system for the production of reviews; and the ongoing recruitment of reviewers.

Choice has responded to the changing information needs of academic libraries during the last quarter century by changing its reviewing coverage to meet these needs. Within a few years, purely liberal arts coverage had broadened to include other areas of undergraduate study. Choice began reviewing audiovisual and other nonprint material in 1980. The nonprint section was expanded in 1984 to include reviews of microcomputer software. In 1986, online databases and CD-ROM products were added to Choice's reviewing coverage. Expanded coverage of periodical reviews, particularly of new serial titles, began in 1987, and further plans to broaden Choice's reviewing coverage in this area are on the drawing boards. A significant change in reviewing policy occurred in 1984 when Choice adopted a new policy of signed reviews, reversing a 20-year practice of anonymous reviewing.

To complete Verner Clapp's vision of a current scholarly review service that would complement and update Charles B. Shaw's List of Books for College Libraries, Choice worked closely in the compilation of the three editions of Books for College Libraries that replaced the Shaw list.

Choice has matured over the past 25 years from a fledgling publication to a respected scholarly review journal. During this time, Choice has published more than 155,000 reviews (primarily book reviews) and approximately 250 bibliographic essays and related bibliographies listing more than 200,000 titles referenced in the essays. The subject editors and the reviewers, through their selections and evaluations of new academic titles, have helped shape undergraduate library collections. Thus Choice continues to provide quality selection and collection development information for the library community.

PATRICIA E. SABOSIK

Association of Jewish Libraries (AJL)

tors was published in the May 1988 *College & Research Libraries News* pending review by the Rare Books and Manuscripts Section Standards committee.

New Task Forces. President Joseph A. Boisse, who took office at the conclusion of the New Orleans conference, appointed new Task Forces: Paraprofessionals in Academic Libraries; Small College Assessment Program; Recruitment of Underrepresented Minorities, chaired by Edith Fisher; and Library School Curriculum, chaired by William Studer. A Task Force was formed to explore the possibility of starting a service corps of retired librarians, chaired by Evan Ira Farber, who proposed the concept. A Task Force was created to oversee the writing of a grant proposal to study sources of revenue in academic libraries, chaired by Anne Beaubien.

Chapters and Discussion Groups. Chapters continue to contribute vitality to the grass roots strength of ACRL. In addition to publication of *Chapter Topics*, ACRL officers and staff sponsored visits and speaking appearances at chapter meetings throughout the country, and provided advice and consultation on program planning and other chapter operations.

Two new discussion groups were approved: Journal Costs in Academic Libraries and Popular Culture and Libraries.

ACRL and ALA. ACRL worked closely with ALA in implementing ALA's strategic plan and articulating it with ACRL's plan. ACRL plans and activities were included in ALA's Action Inventory, and the annual report included a section enumerating ACRL's activities in terms of ALA's Mission, Priorities and Goals document.

ALA continued discussions with its divisions on revisions of the operating agreement. The ACRL staff and officers participated in discussions at Midwinter and Annual Conferences, as well as at the joint meeting of division executive committees in October, and a meeting of ALA's Committee on Program Evaluation and Support (COPES) with division representatives in November.

ACRL and Higher Education Groups. The Professional Association Liaison Committee awarded 10 librarians stipends to attend non-library conferences to present papers. The Committee also recommended 11 organizations where informal liaisons with ACRL should be established. Librarians were conspicuously in attendance at the October EDUCOM conference in Washington, D.C. The Library Directors Position Roundtable, chaired by ACRL President Joanne Euster, met at the American Association for Higher Education conference in March.

JOANNE R. EUSTER

Joseph A. Boisse, University of California at Santa Barbara.

ASSOCIATION OF COLLEGE AND RESEARCH LIBRARIES

PRESIDENT: (June 1988–July 1989)
Joseph A. Boisse, University of California, Santa Barbara, California

VICE-PRESIDENT/PRESIDENT-ELECT:
William A. Moffett, Oberlin College, Oberlin, Ohio

EXECUTIVE DIRECTOR:
JoAn S. Segal

Membership (August 31, 1988): 10,170 (9,044 personal; 1,126 organizational)
Expenditures, ACRL and *Choice* (August 31, 1988): $2,117,343

Association of Jewish Libraries (AJL)

The Association focuses on the specialized interests and needs of the Judaica library and its librarians. Our membership, which numbers more than 800, is primarily from the United States and Canada and also includes members from Latin America, Israel, Great Britain, France, and Germany.

The high point of 1989 was the 23rd Annual Convention of AJL held June 19-22 in Kansas City, Missouri coordinated by Beverly Newman and Fran Wolf. Sessions included a tour of the Harry Truman Library and a discussion by Frank Adler on "Researching Local Jewish History."

Other highlights in programing were separate sessions held for each of the two divisions: Synagogue, School and Center (SSC) and Research and Special Libraries (R&S). SSC programming included workshops on Synagogue libraries, Day Schools, Centers, Storytelling, and Cataloging. Other sessions included "Book Activities for Young Children," "Library Facility Planning," "Reference Materials for Your Library," "Library Games & Activities," "Periodicals for Your Library," "Jewish Books for Teenagers," "Bibliotherapy," and "Legal Aspects of Media." The R&S programing including a presentation on the Judaica Conservancy Foundation, a Cataloging Workshop and sessions on Hebraica implementation of RLIN and "Bibliography of Jewish Music." The president of the Council of Archives and Research Libraries in Jewish Studies (CARLJS), Pearl Berger, reported to the R&S membership on CARLJS activities.

Awards. The following book awards were announced for 1987: the Sydney Taylor Awards for Jewish Children's Literature were presented to David Adler for *The Number of My Grandfather's Arm* and Sonia Levitin for *The Return*. The Manuscript Competition award for unpublished writers of juvenile literature was presented to Frances Wissenberg for *The Streets are Paved with Gold*. The Harold Mason Judaica Reference Book Award was presented to Shimeon Brisman for his *History and Guide to Judaic Encyclopedias and Lexicons*.

Scholarship Funds. The Doris Orenstein fund supports needy AJL members for their first attendance at an annual convention. The May K. Simon Scholarship Fund was created for library or Jewish studies students who pledge to go into Judaica librarianship.

Chapters. Most of the 13 affiliated chapters of AJL are regional: Capital Area, Delaware Valley/Philadelphia, Greater Cleveland, Jewish Federation Libraries, Judaica Library Network of Metropolitan Chicago, Long Island, Metropolitan Detroit, Montreal, New England, New Jersey, New York Metropolitan Area, South Florida, Southern California, and the Southwest Region.

Activities. Aside from the planning of the 24th Annual AJL Convention, which will be held in Washington, D.C., June 18–21, 1989, AJL has initiated and begun planning for the First International Conference of Judaica and Israeli Libraries. Coinciding with the 25th anniversary of AJL, the July 3–5, 1990, Conference in Jerusalem will bring together Judaica librarians from around the world. Co-chairs Amnon Zipin and Edith Lubetski are coordinating programming, travel, funding and related tours in Israel. The 25th Annual Convention of AJL is planned to take place concurrently with the International Conference in Jerusalem.

Other activities during 1988 included a joint project with the Jewish Welfare Board on Library Certification for SSC libraries and a newly appointed Recruitment Task Force that arranges talks on Judacia librarianship as a profession. A day of continuing education with CEU credits for AJL members was scheduled in conjunction with the 23rd Annual Convention.

After actively seeking a change in the LCSH for materials denying the Holocaust and its related classification number, AJL formally recommended at its 1988 annual convention that all libraries comply with LC changes and use the newly assigned classification number (D804.35) and the specific subject heading: Holocaust, Jewish (1939–1945)—Errors, Inventions, etc.)

AJL has liaisons with several other organizations such as ALA Jewish Librarians Caucus, NISO, CNLIA, CARLJS, Jewish Book Council, Coalition of Alternatives in Jewish Education, and the Church and Synagogue Library Association.

Publications. Volume 4, no. 1 (fall 1987–winter 1988) of *Judaica Librarianship* appeared in late August. Highlights of the issue include articles on Hebrew word processing packages, theoretical and practical issues associated with retrospective conversion of Hebraica, archives, children's literature, acquisitions of Judaica, description of a graduate-level course on Hebraica and Judaica cataloging, a pathfinder on American Jewish literature, and several articles on synagogue libraries. The *AJL Newsletter* co-edited by Irene Levin and Hazel Karp appears four times a year and carries timely news of publications, book reviews, job announcements, and other information related to AJL and the profession.

LINDA P. LERMAN

ASSOCIATION OF JEWISH LIBRARIES

PRESIDENT (1988–1990):
Marcia Posner, Judaica Library Consultant, Federation of Jewish Philanthropies Library, New York 10022

VICE-PRESIDENT-ELECT:
Linda P. Lerman, Library of the Jewish Theological Seminary of America, New York 10027–9985

PRESIDENT OF RESEARCH AND SPECIAL LIBRARIES DIVISION:
Robert Singermore, Head Librarian, University of Florida Libraries, Gainesville 32611

PRESIDENT OF SYNAGOGUE, SCHOOL, AND CENTER DIVISION:
Sue Barancik, Temple Adath B'nai Israel, Evansville, Indiana 47715

General mailing address: c/o National Foundation for Jewish Culture, 122 E. 42nd Street, Room 1512, New York 10068

Association of Research Libraries

Nineteen eighty-eight marked the final year of the Association of Research Libraries' Five-Year Plan, that was adopted by the membership in 1983 and implemented in 1984. New planning efforts were launched in 1988 and will continue into 1989. Additional highlights of 1988 included developments in increasing serial prices, renewed emphasis on preservation of research library materials, legislative matters related to access to information, completion of a project to build a national inventory of research library collections, a joint conference with British research library directors, and a number of important staff changes.

Staff Changes. Duane E. Webster was appointed Executive Director of the Association in February 1988. Webster, who was previously Director of the Office of Management Studies, (OMS) and ARL Deputy Executive Director, succeeded Shirley Echelman, who had served as ARL Executive Director from May 1981 through October 1987. Jeffrey Gardner, formerly Associate Director of the Office of Management Services, was appointed Director of OMS in May 1988. In June, Jaia Barrett, ARL Program Officer for Federal Relations, was appointed ARL Assistant Executive Director, and Susan Jurow, OMS Program Officer for Training, was named OMS Associate Director.

Serials Prices. Rapidly rising serial prices continued to be a major focus of attention for ARL. In the spring, ARL contracted with Economic Consulting Services, (ECS) to conduct analyses of serials prices and the costs of serials publishing as part of a feasibility study on alternative methods of distributing scholarly information, including consideration of alternative publishing organizations as well as alternative modes and formats for scholarly communication. A major goal of the project was to determine the possibility of introducing new competition into the serials publishing industry in order to moderate pricing behavior. The analyses will look at price trends of a selected group of serials titles over a 15-year period, and will investigate factors contributing to price increases, e.g., currency fluctuations—such increased costs as postage, paper, and staff—associated with publication, distribution, and profit motivation. The study will also include a thorough assessment of the impact of serial price trends on research library collections and the libraries' ability to serve their users, evaluation of the impact on scholarly material in various fields, and review of the specific responses of libraries.

The serials pricing study, scheduled for completion in 1989, evolved from the Association's member libraries' concern with the impact of sharply rising serials costs on their ability to serve the research and scholarly communities. The results of the study will clarify the eco-

Association of Research Libraries

nomics of the journals industry and should lead to further consideration of strategies for influencing costs and the availability of scholarly communication in both the short- and long-term. Current efforts of ECS are directed toward developing cost indexes for publishing and distributing scientific and technical journals for publishers in the U.S. and three Western European countries. In addition, price–per–page data from 1973 to the present for a sample of 165 journal titles, representing four major publishers, will be analyzed. The long-term objective of the project is to moderate the rate of serials price increases, particularly those from the commercial sector. A strategic emphasis of the study will be to determine the potential for introducing elements of competition into the technical and scientific journal market in an attempt to moderate the rate of price increases.

An early product of the Serials Project was *ARL Briefing Package 1988-2: Rising Serials Prices and Research Libraries*, distributed to the membership in August. The package provides member libraries with descriptive, statistical, and analytical information that can be used to inform and educate libraries' various constituencies on the seriousness of problems related to rising serials prices.

Collections Inventory. The third phase of the North American Collections Inventory Project (NCIP) ended in June 1988; the project has become an ongoing, self-supporting ARL program. NCIP was designed to develop an online inventory of North American research library collections, building on work of the Research Libraries Group, begun in 1979, and collaborative efforts of RLG and ARL since 1983 to develop a standard approach to describing and assessing research library collections in specific subject areas covering a full range of scholarly interests. This approach has led to the Online Conspectus database, that provides information on the location of specific subject collections and relative collections' strengths and language coverage. The database, managed by RLG, is also available in printed form. The ARL Office of Management Services operates NCIP, and serves as distributor for Conspectus materials to non–RLG libraries.

NRMM Project. During 1987, in partnership with the Library of Congress, ARL negotiated an agreement with The Computer Company of Richmond, Virginia, for retrospective conversion of all monographic reports in the *National Register of Microform Masters*. During the project, the Computer Company will produce about 460,000 machine-readable records, between 30 and 40 percent of them not previously converted. Staff in LC's MARC Editorial and Cataloging Management and Publications Divisions review converted records to ensure that they conform to guidelines established by ARL and LC, based on ARL's *Guidelines for Retrospective Conversion of Bibliographic Records for Monographs*. Beginning in 1989, LC's Cataloging Distribution Services will compile tapes containing the records and sell them with no constraints on further reproduction or distribution to libraries, networks, and other organizations. As of November 30, 1988, 70,000 records had been converted. The project is supported by grants from the National Endowment for the Humanities and the Andrew W. Mellon Foundation and is expected to be completed at the end of 1989.

Preservation. The preservation of the intellectual content and, to the extent possible, the physical form of research library materials was identified as one of ARL's six major objectives in 1983. Since then, ARL has supported efforts to increase awareness of preservation problems in the higher education and Federal arenas and to work for legislative support for preservation activities. In March 1988, ARL was represented at Congressional hearings on the brittle books problem, and at appropriations hearings for the National Endowment for the Humanities, emphasizing the need for accelerated Endowment support for preservation efforts. Growing interest in encouraging the use of permanent paper by publishers led to ARL's third *Executive Briefing Package* in November 1988, this one focusing on *Preserving Knowledge: The Case for Alkaline Paper*. The package was produced in conjunction with the Commission on Preservation and Access and the National Humanities Alliance, with funding from the Commission. It has been distributed to the ARL membership, to publishers, to legislators, to scholars, and to others interested in the preservation of research materials.

In December, *Meeting the Preservation Challenge*, the papers from the October 1987 ARL Membership Meeting were published. The program, "Preservation: A Research Library Priority for the 1990s," covered a number of preservation issues from the perspectives of library directors, preservation administrators, and foundation representatives.

Assisting ARL libraries in improving preservation activities continued to be a major emphasis for the Office of Management Services. OMS received a three-year grant of $145,167 from the National Endowment for the Humanities to help support (a) the training of six experienced preservation librarians to serve as consultants to libraries in the OMS Preservation Planning Program, (b) the participation of ten member libraries in completing the Preservation Planning Program and (c) a formal evaluation of the program.

Legislative Affairs. A number of legislative issues captured the attention of ARL during 1988. As in the past, funding for library programs was a primary focus, in particular appropriations for Title II of the Higher Education Act and the FY 1989 budgets for the Library of Congress, the Government Printing Office, and the National Endowment for the Humanities. Increased funding for library preservation efforts also received a substantial amount of attention in 1988.

Limitations on access to information continues to be a major area of concern to ARL. A primary focus is the FBI Library Awareness Program. ARL issued The FBI in Libraries *Briefing Packing 1988-1*, in June, and participated in Congressional hearings. The ARL membership also adopted a "Statement on Library Users' Right to Confidentiality" at the May 1988 Membership Meeting. Other issues that continued to be monitored are the Federal Depository Library Program, copyright—including electronic formats, proposed privatization of the National Technical

Information Services, and other legislation and federal regulations that affect the public's access to information.

Government Information in Electronic Format. In May 1988, the ARL membership adopted a statement of six principles on access to government information in electronic format. The principles were prepared by the Task Force on Government Information in Electronic Format and issued in the task force's 1987 report, *Technology & U.S. Government Information Policies: Catalysts for New Partnerships*. In addition, ARL has been active in encouraging Congress and the Government Printing Office to proceed with a series of projects to test the use of electronic formats in the Depository Library Program.

Library Education. The ARL Office of Management Services conducted its third Institute on Research Libraries for Library and Information Science Faculty in Chicago during the summer of 1988. The Institute was co-sponsored by the Association of Library and Information Science Educations (ALISE) and the Association of College and Research Libraries (ACRL) and funded by the Council on Library Resources. Twelve faculty members from the U.S. and Canada participated; concentration was on collection development.

Meetings. The 112th ARL Membership Meeting, held in Oakland, California, in May, had two primary focuses: planning for ARL's future and a program exploring the background, technical aspects, application, and future implications of linked systems. The papers from the latter session, *Linked Systems*, were published during the summer. The 113th membership meeting was a joint meeting with the Standing Conference on National and University Libraries (SCONUL), held in York, England. The program, "Collec-

Association of Research Libraries

Table 1. ARL Library Data Totals

			Collections				
Volumes in Library	Volumes Added (Gross)	Volumes Added (Net)	Monographs Purchased	Current Serials Purchased	Current Serials Not Purchased	Current Serials Total	Total Microform Units in Library
1	2	3	4	5	6	7	8
University Median							
2,123,050	64,600	57,352	28,278	16,038	3,200	20,871	2,274,245
University High							
11,496,906	313,922	201,831	129,155	42,659	33,033	102,000	5,137,087
University Low							
1,140,108	27,701	21,013	5,194	6,792	0	7,317	172,234
Totals—University Libraries							
290,340,374	8,362,893	7,196,193	2,660,660	1,261,947	345,147	2,950,051	246,075,630
Totals—Nonuniversity Libraries							
48,652,153	966,256	842,534	493,165	142,230	202,860	520,125	25,902,022
Grand Totals—All ARL Libraries							
338,992,527	9,329,149	8,038,727	3,153,825	1,404,177	548,007	3,470,176	271,977,652

Table 2. ARL Library Data Totals

Interlibrary Loans		Personnel (FTE)				Expenditures			
Total Loaned	Total Borrowed	Professional Staff	Non-Professional Staff	Student Assistants	Total Staff	Monographs	Current Serials	Other Library Materials	Miscellaneous Materials Expenditures
9	10	11	12	13	14	15	16	17	18
University Median									
18,198	8.078	70	140	62	269	$1,142,923	$1,947,558	$127,121	$82,421
University High									
154,287	164,950	325	575	278	1,049	4,557,947	4,027,414	1,377,412	3,282,900
University Low									
2,260	1,211	30	47	7	112	291,947	965,471	3,159	0
Totals—University Libraries									
2,531,336	1,055,214	8,880	17,607	7,779	34,466	135,417,562	221,780,566	13,878,221	13,658,967
Totals—Nonuniversity Libraries									
996,365	40,324	3,914	3,876	241	8,031	12,509,078	16,015,013	4,193,725	639,063
Grand Totals—All ARL Libraries									
3,527,701	1,095,538	12,794	21,483	8,020	42,497	147,926,640	237,795,579	18,071,946	14,298,030

Table 3. ARL Library Data Totals

Total Library Materials	Contract Binding	Salaries & Wages Prof.	Salaries & Wages Non-Prof.	Salaries & Wages Student Assistants	Total Salaries & Wages	Other Operating Expend.	Total Library Expend.
19	20	21	22	23	24	25	26
Expenditures							

University Median

| $3,369,896 | $144,161 | $2,156,222 | $2,227,604 | $503,265 | $4,848,267 | $1,205,015 | $9,557,623 |

University High

| 9,968,054 | 779,542 | 10,119,557 | 9,384,046 | 4,383,357 | 20,464,069 | 5,991,495 | 37,196,490 |

University Low

| 1,621,181 | 46,781 | 1,093,203 | 522,641 | 108,183 | 1,873,275 | 318,313 | 4,473,279 |

Totals—University Libraries

| 394,539,591 | 20,123,465 | 259,019,831 | 274,848,018 | 62,587,253 | 623,342,533 | 155,556,758 | 1,193,562,457 |

Totals—Nonuniversity Libraries

| 39,979,365 | 2,338,865 | 22,398,562 | 24,622,355 | 1,257,014 | 229,369,665 | 143,452,769 | 415,140,664 |

Grand Totals—All ARL Libraries

| 434,518,956 | 22,462,330 | 281,418,393 | 299,470,373 | 63,844,267 | 852,712,198 | 299,009,527 | 1,608,703,121 |

Table 4. Number and Average Salaries of ARL University Librarians, fiscal year 1989

Position	Number of staff			Average salaries		
	Total	Men	Women	Combined	Men	Women
Director	98	70	28	$82,073	$81,636	$83,166
Associate director	159	71	88	57,033	57,188	56,908
Assistant director	240	105	135	50,513	51,455	49,781
Branch head	563	195	368	37,978	40,686	36,544
Subject specialist	760	377	383	34,515	36,138	32,919
Functional specialist	532	236	296	32,368	33,170	31,728
Department head: Reference	121	43	78	38,340	38,374	38,322
Cataloging	117	34	83	39,616	41,807	38,719
Acquisition	111	34	77	37,710	38,732	36,817
Serials	58	15	43	38,377	37,132	38,811
Documents/Maps	114	46	68	36,059	35,358	36,533
Circulation	98	42	56	33,737	34,693	33,021
Special Collections	102	67	35	41,306	43,989	36,169
Computer	59	36	23	44,556	45,210	43,533
Other	635	243	392	36,335	38,019	35,291
Reference: Over 15 years experience	460	142	318	34,527	35,114	34,265
10–15 years experience	261	82	179	30,776	31,472	30,457
5–10 years experience	250	80	170	27,441	27,939	27,207
Under 5 years experience	300	90	210	23,731	23,786	23,708
Catalog: Over 15 years experience	505	155	350	34,009	34,125	33,958
10–15 years experience	175	47	128	29,888	30,165	29,786
5–10 years experience	197	45	152	27,088	28,023	26,812
Under 5 years experience	238	69	169	23,472	23,942	23,281
Other: Over 15 years experience	272	79	193	36,074	38,254	35,182
10–15 years experience	123	37	86	31,121	32,204	30,655
5–10 years experience	147	35	112	28,262	29,982	27,725
Under 5 years experience	180	48	132	22,864	22,521	22,989
All Positions	6,875	2,523	4,352	$34,941	$37,395	$33,519

tions: Their Development, Management, Preservation, and Sharing," drew substantial numbers of ARL and SCONUL directors interested in this unique opportunity to meet and confer with colleagues facing similar challenges and obligations but in very different local environments. The meeting concluded with a call for closer ties between the two organizations. The papers from the York meeting will be published in 1989.

Publications. In addition to the Linked Systems and the three Briefing Packages, ARL published five issues of the ARL Newsletter and its regular statistical publications, the 1987 ARL Annual Salary Survey and the 1986–87 ARL Statistics.

Membership. The University of Illinois at Chicago (UIC) became ARL's 119th member late in 1988. UIC is the first institution invited to join ARL under membership criteria adopted by the ARL membership in May 1987.

Visiting Program Officers. During 1988, ARL initiated a new program designed to provide personal growth and professional development opportunities for mid- and senior-level staff in ARL libraries while at the same time allowing the Association to tap the pool of talented staff in its member libraries to work directly on its agenda of issues and projects. Two librarians were selected as the first participants. Diane H. Smith of the Pennsylvania State Libraries will work on access and information policy issues, and Rhonda MacInnes of the National Library of Canada will work with the OMS training program. The home institution provides financial support for program participants.

Management Services. The ARL Office of Management Studies was renamed in May 1988, and is now the ARL Office of Management Ser-

Association of Research Libraries

Table 5. Number and Average Salaries of U.S. ARL University Minority Librarians, fiscal year 1989

Position	Number of staff			Average salaries		
	Total	Men	Women	Combined	Men	Women
Director	3	2	1	$ *	$ *	$ *
Associate director	9	1	8	63,720	*	*
Assistant director	13	5	8	48,701	47,062	49,724
Branch head	44	14	30	38,084	43,066	35,759
Subject specialist	92	40	52	35,602	40,299	31,990
Functional specialist	42	14	28	32,987	33,395	32,783
Department head: Reference	6	1	5	33,427	*	*
Cataloging	11	3	8	39,922	*	*
Acquisition	5	0	5	34,431		34,431
Serials	3	1	2	*	*	*
Documents/Maps	6	2	4	41,169	*	*
Circulation	5	2	3	28,759	*	*
Special Collections	4	2	2	40,345	*	*
Computer	2	0	2	*		*
Other	52	23	29	37,098	38,835	35,721
Reference: Over 15 years experience	44	9	35	35,225	35,758	35,088
10–15 years experience	39	9	30	31,551	31,805	31,475
5–10 years experience	24	7	17	27,170	25,597	27,818
Under 5 years experience	31	11	20	23,999	25,363	23,249
Catalog: Over 15 years experience	97	26	71	33,088	33,402	32,974
10–15 years experience	18	5	13	28,484	27,107	29,014
5–10 years experience	19	2	17	26,015	28,435	25,730
Under 5 years experience	30	8	22	23,911	24,646	23,644
Other: Over 15 years experience	25	8	17	38,620	41,975	37,041
10–15 years experience	5	2	3	28,449	*	*
5–10 years experience	8	2	6	28,817	*	*
Under 5 years experience	14	1	13	22,151	*	*
All Positions	651	200	451	$33,904	$36,449	$32,776

*Salary information is not published when fewer than 4 individuals are involved.

Table 6. Number and Average Salaries of ARL University Librarians by Type of Institution, fiscal year 1989

Position	All combined (107)*		Public (63)		Private (30)	
	Number	Average salary	Number	Average salary	Number	Average salary
Director	98	$82,073	57	$79,247	28	$95,304
Associate director	159	57,033	92	56,418	48	60,448
Assistant director	240	50,513	143	50,341	83	51,365
Branch head	563	37,978	340	37,399	155	39,305
Subject specialist	760	34,515	428	34,832	255	33,851
Functional specialist	532	32,368	280	32,862	208	31,107
Department head: Reference	121	38,340	66	38,783	41	37,858
Cataloging	117	39,616	62	40,774	44	37,108
Acquisition	111	37,710	63	36,463	36	35,502
Serials	58	38,377	33	39,246	19	37,732
Documents/Maps	114	36,059	72	36,354	27	34,650
Circulation	98	33,737	56	34,143	32	31,742
Special Collections	102	41,306	57	42,770	35	40,081
Computer	59	44,556	32	45,231	20	43,701
Other	635	36,335	355	36,268	225	36,384
Reference: Over 15 years experience	460	34,527	295	34,766	93	33,093
10–15 years experience	261	30,776	158	30,557	67	30,997
5–10 years experience	250	27,441	164	27,415	57	27,375
Under 5 years experience	300	23,731	208	23,645	64	24,099
Catalog: Over 15 years experience	505	34,009	259	34,490	176	32,635
10–15 years experience	175	29,888	85	28,758	65	30,155
5–10 years experience	197	27,088	107	27,091	71	27,291
Under 5 years experience	238	23,472	134	22,933	91	24,080
Other: Over 15 years experience	272	36,074	186	36,678	52	32,584
10–15 years experience	123	31,121	72	31,563	39	30,409
5–10 years experience	147	28,262	85	28,635	52	27,660
Under 5 years experience	180	22,864	119	22,658	50	23,278
All Positions	6,875	$34,941	4,008	$34,905	2,133	$34,784

*Includes 13 Canadian libraries not included in public/private columns.
( ) Number of ARL libraries included.

Table 7. Number and Average Salaries of ARL University Librarians by Size of Professional Staff, fiscal year 1989

Position	Staff over 124(5)		Staff 75–124 (22)		Staff 50–74 (36)		Staff 1–49 (44)	
	Number	Salary	Number	Salary	Number	Salary	Number	Salary
Director	5	$95,501	18	$94,631	33	$82,898	42	$74,444
Associate director	11	66,178	43	60,089	57	57,286	48	51,900
Assistant director	15	56,538	77	53,084	73	50,402	75	46,777
Branch head	72	45,107	222	37,450	150	38,542	119	33,942
Subject specialist	113	39,192	298	33,713	232	35,459	117	30,171
Functional specialist	86	36,016	177	31,614	156	31,711	113	31,678
Department head: Reference	10	43,460	31	39,713	37	37,989	43	36,463
Cataloging	16	41,095	26	41,932	35	40,030	40	37,158
Acquisition	7	48,526	19	39,649	40	37,277	45	35,594
Serials	6	44,191	13	39,471	16	36,454	23	37,579
Documents/Maps	10	45,004	29	34,714	32	37,410	43	33,880
Circulation	16	33,633	17	34,311	30	34,210	35	33,102
Special Collections	9	41,592	24	42,886	34	42,699	35	38,795
Computer	5	60,629	14	48,762	19	41,677	21	40,530
Other	55	44,275	248	36,885	184	35,058	148	34,049
Reference: Over 15 years experience	39	41,866	121	32,416	159	35,793	141	32,882
10–15 years experience	23	36,231	79	30,471	68	30,764	91	29,670
5–10 years experience	16	32,909	78	26,968	82	27,740	74	26,427
Under 5 years experience	14	27,152	81	24,731	102	23,846	103	22,367
Catalog: Over 15 years experience	83	40,580	132	31,774	165	34,130	125	31,848
10–15 years experience	28	33,647	49	28,910	52	29,871	46	28,661
5–10 years experience	29	30,177	49	26,678	74	27,526	45	24,826
Under 5 years experience	29	25,863	74	24,118	86	22,872	49	22,136
Other: Over 15 years experience	70	42,678	74	32,768	83	35,468	45	32,354
10–15 years experience	23	37,079	28	29,726	48	30,800	24	27,680
5–10 years experience	9	33,528	32	27,986	54	27,789	42	26,700
Under 5 years experience	3	*	57	23,296	85	22,770	35	22,293
All Positions	812	$40,003	2,110	$34,591	2,186	$34,753	1,767	$33,264

( ) Number of ARL libraries included.
* Salary information is not published when fewer than 4 individuals are involved.

vices. The new name reflects more accurately the emphasis of the Office in helping research libraries meet the challenges of rapidly developing technology, new organizational demands, and changing economic conditions.

OMS offered six assisted self–studies through its Academic Library Program. Three studies—the Collection Analysis Project, the Public Services Studies, and the Preservation Planning Program—continued to be used frequently by academic libraries. As already noted, OMS has integrated the North American Collections Inventory Project into its regular ongoing operations.

More than 400 librarians attended public or institutionally–sponsored OMS programs in 1988. OMS Management Skills Institutes were held in eleven locations, along with two Analytical Skills Institutes and one Managing the Learning Process Institutes. Special Focus Workshops, short programs commissioned by individual libraries, focused on a variety of topics, including teambuilding, motivation, and planning for change. A new program, the Creativity to Innovation Workshop, was introduced in 1988. This workshop focuses on techniques to build personal and organizational capacity for creativity, and is designed to develop creative problem solving skills among librarians and library managers.

In the OMS publication program, staffing and user services provided the focus for new materials. The System and Procedures Exchange Center (SPEC) produced kits covering: performance appraisal, approval plans, remote access to online catalogs, search procedures for administrators, building use policies, library publications programs, fundraising, serials cancellation projects, use surveys, and electronic mail.

Other publications provided a more in–depth look at selected automation and staffing issues. *Toward Telecommunications Strategies in Academic and Research Libraries* (OP14, Thomas Kinney, October 1988) explores recent developments in the application of telecommunications technology and recommends ways library managers may better understand issues and make decisions. *Selection of the University Librarian* (OP13, Ruth J. Person and George C. Newman, February 1988) provides practical observations, conclusions, and common themes for a successful search, based on interviews at five large universities. *The Automation Inventory of Research Libraries, 1988* (PB13, annual, Maxine K. Sitts, with analysis by Emily Fayen and Arnold Hirshon, October 1988) features an expanded analysis that examines trends and vendor changes over the past two years.

OMS continued to offer a *Subject Index to SPEC Kits* (PBO6, compiled by Joann Treadwell, 1988), which provides a working index to SPEC

ASSOCIATION OF RESEARCH LIBRARIES

PRESIDENT (October 1988–October 1989):
Charles E. Miller, Director, Florida State University Library

VICE-PRESIDENT/PRESIDENT-ELECT:
Martin D. Runkle, Director, University of Chicago Library

EXECUTIVE DIRECTOR:
Duane E. Webster

Membership (December 1988): 119
Headquarters: 1527 New Hampshire Avenue, NW, Washington, D.C. 20036

kits and fliers. Also available are sets of binders and tabs (BT1, 1988) for the 1987 edition of the *Preservation Planning Program Resources Notebook* (SS02, Wesley Boomgaarden, 1987), which was previously available only as an unbound compilation.

NICOLA DAVAL

Association of Specialized and Cooperative Library Agencies

The Association of Specialized and Cooperative Library Agencies (ASCLA) is the division of the American Library Association that represents state library agencies, specialized library agencies and multitype library cooperatives. The year of 1988 for ASCLA was marked by growth in membership and a return to program planning and development.

Publications. *Interface,* ASCLA's quarterly publication, continued to offer information on issues of interest to membership groups within the division. David Karre of the North Central Library Cooperative was appointed Advertising Manager. Jan Smithee of the Central New York Library Resources Council was appointed Assistant Editor/Editor-Elect by the ASCLA Board of Directors.

The 7th edition of *The State Library Agencies: A Survey Project Report* was published in 1988. This biennial resource provides information and statistical data on the 50 state library agencies. Information is included on the state library agency's location in state government, powers and duties, major functional areas, notable activities, personnel, publications, and an organizational chart for each state library agency. Appendices include significant comparative data for each state on functions and services, materials collections, budget, staffing, and amount and use of federal and state aid to libraries. F. William Summers, Dean, School of Library and Information Studies, Florida State University, Tallahassee, Florida, provided an introduction and overview of the data.

Nancy L. Wareham compiled and edited the sixth edition of *The Report on Library Cooperation.* This biennial compilation is a valuable source of information about library cooperation and networking. It provides broad coverage of cooperative library activities of systems, consortia, cooperatives, and networks.

Standards. During 1988 ASCLA devoted considerable attention to the development of standards. The ASCLA Board of Directors authorized the preparation of the revision of the *Standards for Juvenile Correctional Institutions* and the *Library Standards for Jails and Detention Centers.* In addition, committees reviewed a draft revision of the *Standards for Adult Correctional Institutions* and a draft for new standards relating to multitype library cooperatives and networks.

Awards. On July 9, 1988 at the Latter Branch of the New Orleans Public Library, the Francis Joseph Campbell Award was presented to James Chandler. The Campbell award is given to a person who has made an outstanding contribution to the advancement of library service for the

blind and physically handicapped. Mr. Chandler was recognized for inventing the Voice Indexing Technique, which is used to index audiovisual tapes.

Conference Programs. During the 1988 Annual Conference in New Orleans, ASCLA sponsored a pre-conference and 10 conference programs. In addition, ASCLA sponsored the Multi-LINCS Network Assembly and State Library Agency Section/Chief Officers of State Library Agencies information and update session.

ASCLA's pre-conference—"Sharpen Your Consulting Skills"—was planned for state agency, regional and system consultants who had had little or no training in consultant skills. Sandra S. Stephan of the Maryland Division of Library Development and Services focused on various aspects of the consultant process—the roles of a consultant, basic consulting skills, and the balance between the client's needs and the resources and abilities available. Dr. Sara Fine, a psychologist and professor at the University of Pittsburgh's School of Library and Information Science, addressed the consultant interview, conflict resolution and problem solving, and group behavior. A total of 114 people from 34 states participated.

The Multitype Library Cooperatives and Networks Section (Multi-LINCS) sponsored three programs. "Planning for New Services in Multitype Libraries and Cooperatives—Factors and Consideration," cosponsored with the State Library Agency Section, examined factors involved in selecting new or additional services for multitype networks. An overview of automation activity in state networks and a discussion of specific strategies to be used in assessing changing technologies in a network environment were the themes of the "Impact of New Technologies on Library Networking, Cooperation, and Resource Sharing." The Network Assembly's program consisted of an open forum for discussing the Library of Congress Network Advisory Commit-

ASSOCIATION OF SPECIALIZED AND COOPERATIVE LIBRARY AGENCIES

PRESIDENT (July 1988–July 1989):
Joseph F. Shubert, State Librarian, New York State Library, Albany, New York 12230

VICE-PRESIDENT/PRESIDENT-ELECT:
William G. Asp, Director, Minnesota Library Development and Services, St. Paul, Minnesota

ALA STAFF LIAISON:
Andrew M. Hansen

Membership (August 31, 1988): 1,363 (1,012 personal; 351 organizational)
Expenditures (August 31, 1988): $53,717

Joseph F. Shubert, New York State Library.

tee's "Library Networking: Statement of a Common Vision."

The State Library Agency Section (SLAS) sponsored the "State of States in Youth Services." A panel identified the national trends in services to children and young adults. In addition, SLAS sponsored an Issues Forum, which dealt with cooperative collection development and the state library's role in library development.

The Library Services to Special Populations Section (LSSPS) sponsored six programs. The Library Service to the Impaired Elderly Forum's "What's Out on Aging: Frontline Developments," featured presentations from practitioners, governmental and organizational officials, and researchers discussing trends and developments in the field of aging. "AIDS Information: Focus on the Institutional Library," sponsored by the Library Service to Prisoners Forum, examined the best ways to disseminate AIDS information in an institutional environment. The Bibliotherapy Forum presented "Bibliotherapy 101: Getting Trained and Getting Started," which examined basic techniques, training options and the literature of the field.

"Weighing the Hard Choices: the Dilemmas of Health Care," planned by the Health Care Libraries Forum, provided an assessment of the moral issues and ethical questions raised by advanced techniques in research and an overview of bioethics as a discipline. The Library Service to the Blind and Physically Handicapped Forum sponsored "On the Air—In the News," which examined three approaches to radio information services: straight newspaper/periodicals, old-style radio and a mix of reading/call-in information shows. "Awareness Begins at Home," presented by the Library Service to the Deaf Forum, focused on the importance of staff attitudes to the deaf and on organizations useful to libraries in serving the deaf community.

ASCLA's Ad Hoc Committee on the Decade of the Disabled presented "Managing Effective Programs for Disabled Persons." The program examined management issues related to services for disabled persons.

In 1988 the Association of Specialized and Cooperative Library Agencies had a positive and productive year. Stability was restored and a framework was created for members to continue their programs and activities.

BRUCE E. DANIELS

Beta Phi Mu

At the ALA Conference in New Orleans, Past President Ed Holley presided at the initiation ceremony for new members, conducting the new ritual which was approved that same day by the Beta Phi Mu Executive Council. The meeting, held in the Counting Room at the Historic New Orleans Collection, museum and library, attracted the largest attendance in several years. The event also marked the 40th anniversary of this international library and information science honorary society.

During the ALA conference Samuel Rothstein, Professor Emeritus, School of Library, Archival and Information Studies, University of British Columbia, received the Beta Phi Mu Award for Distinguished Contributions to Education for Librarianship.

The Advisory Assembly chose Diane Carothers, Alpha Chapter, University of Illinois, Urbana, and Josephine McSweeney, Theta Chapter, Pratt Institute, Brooklyn, New York, for three-year terms as representatives on the Executive Council, 1988–91.

Publications. During 1988 the newsletter appeared under a new editor, Charles Seavey, Assistant Professor at the University of Arizona.

Preparations were completed for the first volume of the new Beta Phi Mu monographs to be distributed by Greenwood Press. The first title in this series, *An Active Instrument for Propaganda: American Public Libraries During World War I*, by Wayne Wiegand, will appear early in 1989.

Plans progressed for a Beta Phi Mu Distinguished Lecture series, whose lectures will subsequently replace the chapbook series given to new initiates. They will be similar to the earlier chapbooks in format, retaining typographic excellence of the previous series.

Scholarships. Beta Phi Mu's chief purpose is to recognize and encourage scholarship.

BETA PHI MU OFFICERS

PRESIDENT (July 198&–July 1989):
Elaine Sloan, Vice President for Information Studies and University Librarian, Columbia University, New York

VICE-PRESIDENT/PRESIDENT-ELECT:
Joseph J. Mika, Director, Library Science Program, Wayne State University, Detroit, Michigan

EXECUTIVE SECRETARY:
Blanche Woolls, Professor, School of Library Science, University of Pittsburgh

TREASURER:
Dennis K. Lambert, Eisenhower Library, Johns Hopkins University, Baltimore, Maryland

ADMINISTRATIVE SECRETARY:
Mary Y. Tomaino, School of Library and Information Science, University of Pittsburgh, Pennsylvania 15260

Membership (1988): 44 chapters, 21,500 members
Annual budget (1988): $40,500, Income (1987) $36,163

Winner of the Sarah Rebecca Reed Scholarship of $1,500, given annually to a beginning student, was Victor Liu who began his program at the University of Michigan.

Pamela Spence Richards, Rutgers University, received the $1,000 Harold Lancour Scholarship for Foreign Study to present a paper at a seminar at Wolfenbuttel, Germany.

The Frank B. Sessa Award for Continuing Education was not awarded in 1988.

Members and chapters continued their generous contributions to the scholarship funds.

EDWARD G. HOLLEY

Bibliographies, Indexes, and Other Reference Books

During 1988 the pattern of unabated publishing of printed reference works and the accelerating release of reference works on high density CD-ROM continued full force. Entries in the 1988 issue of *American Reference Books Annual* (Littleton, Colorado, Libraries Unlimited), the only reviewing source that attempts comprehensive coverage of the year's reference output in English, declined to about 1,600 entries in its 1988 issue. *CD-ROMs in Print*, published by Meckler, exploded in 1988 to 239 titles.

Outstanding Reference Works. Some of the reference works on CD-ROMs were updates of old standards. *Books in Print* (New York, Bowker) on its fortieth anniversary listed approximately 770,000 titles. In an apparent response to EBSCO's *Serials Directory*, Bowker combined separate works covering regular and irregular serials to create a three-volume *Ulrich's International Periodicals Directory*. The third edition of *Books for College Libraries* (Chicago: American Library Association) appeared and was also released on magnetic tape and online. In 1986 H. W. Wilson began producing *Readers' Guide Abstracts* in microfiche format only. In 1988 it became a print product as well and was issued in paperback 10 times a year and cumulated in hardback semiannually. The *Directory of Library and Information Professionals*, published by Research Publications, appeared early in 1988. It is significant that all of these reference works are also available in CD-ROM or some other machine-readable medium. Significant new printed reference works available only in print include *Reference Books for Young Readers* and *General Reference Books for Adults* from Bowker. Gale introduced two new titles, *Short Story Criticism* and *Classical and Medieval Literature Criticism* to its literary criticism series. Save for the index volume due in 1989, Scribner's completed its *Dictionary of the Middle Ages* and Grove's Dictionaries of Music issued the *New Grove Dictionary of Jazz*. In a departure from its long-standing "self-indexing" practice. *The New Standard Encyclopedia* introduced a separate index in its 1988 edition. The 1988 edition of the perennial best seller among encyclopedias, *World Book*, underwent a major redesign.

A program jointly sponsored by the Reference and Adult Services Division (RASD) and the *Reference Books Bulletin* Editorial Board at the annual conference of the American Library Association in New Orleans featured discussion by publishers of major subject encyclopedias and dictionaries. In RASD's program, "Twelve Years till 2000: Preparing for 21st Century Reference," Peter Watson of Idaho State University predicted that in the future much more information will become available in electronic formats, resulting in more personalized, or customized, reference works. Gale Research Company launched a program to acquire ideas for new reference works by offering a $500 "reward" to anyone submitting an idea that results in a new title published by Gale. RASD awarded the 1988 Dartmouth Medal to Macmillan for Mircea Eliade's monumental *The Encyclopedia of Religion* (1987).

CD-ROM. Among 1988's new CD-ROM products were standard printed reference works such as *Facts on File News Digest* and Gale's *Encyclopedia of Associations* and its extended family of directories, the latter released as *Associations CD*. Grolier announced an enhanced version of its *Electronic Encyclopedia* (based on the *Academic American Encyclopedia*) to run on the new Apple CD drive. The long-awaited machine-readable version of the *Oxford English Dictionary* became available on CD-ROM from Bowker. SilverPlatter, one of CD-ROM's pioneers, added SOFTWARE-CD, a database of information about software for business applications. Bowker's *Books In Print Plus* added reviews from *Sci-Tech Books News* and *Reference and Research Books News*. Ellis Enterprises of Oklahoma City introduced *The Bible Library*, a CD-ROM collection of seven English translations of the Bible, the original Greek and Hebrew texts in Romanized alphabet, and nine biblical reference works. At the fourth international AIDS conference in Stockholm in June, the Massachusetts Medical Society unveiled its *Compact Library: AIDS*, combining articles from medical journals and an electronic textbook maintained by physicians at San Francisco General Hospital. University Microfilms, already a player in the CD-ROM field with its *Dissertation Abstracts*, increased its presence with the release of *ABI/Inform*, *Newspaper Abstracts*, and *Periodical Abstracts*. The last seemed designed to compete head-to-head with CD-ROM indexes to popular periodicals available from H. W. Wilson and Information Access Co. IAC abandoned the large-format optical disk for its InfoTrac database, converting it to CD-ROM and reserving the InfoTrac name for the system. The database formerly known by that name became the *General Periodicals Index* available in two special editions designed for public and academic libraries respectively.

In 1988 various companies attacked the problem of providing a separate work station for each CD-ROM database and the inability to search large files stored on more than one disk without swapping disks. Information Access announced its Reference Center, which allows a library to link up to eight microcomputers and 16 CD drives running products from IAC, SilverPlatter, Disclosure, and DIALOG. Meridian Data of Capitola, California, unveiled CD Net, a means of networking as many as 21 CD-ROM drives. And

Biographies

Table 1. Bibliographies and Indexes in *American Book Publishing Record:* 1984–1988

Subject	Category	1984	1985	1986	1987	1988	Change 1987–1988
000	General	16	16	18	14	12	−2
100	Philosophy, Psychology	7	14	6	15	11	−4
200	Religion	12	10	14	14	12	−2
300	Social sciences, Education	182	162	84	107	97	−10
400	Language	4	8	0	0	8	+8
500	Pure science	12	13	17	20	7	−13
600	Applied science	52	81	34	93	59	−34
700	Fine arts	128	195	54	85	68	−17
800	Literature	74	64	54	88	67	−21
900	Travel, History, other	70	57	44	44	42	−2
	Total	557	530	325	480	383	−97

All data based on titles in 016 class in *American Book Publishing Record*. Because December data were unavailable for 1984 and 1985, extrapolation was based on the previous 11 months. For 1986, extrapolation was based on the year's first 10 months. Figures for 1987 and 1988 were extrapolated from the year's first nine months.

UMI offered a station able to access stacked CD drives and H. W. Wilson introduced networking capability among its CD products.

Laserdisk Professional, edited by Nancy Herther and published by Online, Inc., joined *CD-ROM Librarian*, edited by Nancy Melin and published by Meckler, to help librarians keep abreast of rapid developments in the field.

Even as small-scale networking of CD-ROM stations got under way, some libraries were working on what some predict will be the next step in information access and delivery. The library at Carnegie-Mellon University, was the first in the nation to provide access to Grolier's *Academic American Encyclopedia Online* through the campuswide network. The Colorado Alliance of Research Libraries (CARL) established its Article Access System, an enhancement of CARL's online catalog that enables users to search the contents pages of more than 10,000 serials. Cambridge Scientific Abstracts, a producer of CD-ROM products, offered academic libraries free sample tapes to test this mode of access to its 10 science databases. OCLC's announcements of plans to release its Online Reference Service in early 1989 whetted librarians' appetite for subject access to the rich OCLC database.

Major Projects. Work progressed on two major long-term projects. A team at the University of California, Riverside, continued to work on the *Eighteenth Century Short Title Catalog*. This comprehensive database of eighteenth-century English-language books in British and American libraries, funded in large part by the National Endowment for the Humanities, will be complete early in the next decade. In 1986 work began on the second series of the *Nineteenth Century Short Title Catalogue (NSTC)*, published by Avero and distributed by Chadwyck-Healey. An attempt to record as comprehensively as possible all English-language books published in Britain, the United States, and the British colonies between 1801 and 1918, the *NSTC*'s second series, includes cataloging information from six major British libraries as well as the Library of Congress and Harvard University. To be completed in 55 volumes, *NSTC* had progressed through 15 volumes at year's end.

Topical Bibliographies. The number of topical bibliographies published during 1988 declined about 20 percent from 1987's level (see table). Six publishers (ABBE, Garland, Greenwood, G. K. Hall, Oryx, and Scarecrow) accounted for more than half of the monographic bibliographies. Greenwood alone produced approximately one of every seven.

JAMES RETTIG

Biographies

Henriette D. Avram

AVRAM, HENRIETTE D.
Henriette D. Avram, Assistant Librarian for Processing Services, Library of Congress since 1983, was awarded the 1988 ALA Joseph W. Lippincott Award for distinguished service to the profession. She began at the Library of Congress in 1965 as Assistant Coordinator of Information Systems, became Chief of The MARC Development Office in 1970, was elevated to Director of the Network Development Office in 1976, and spent 1980 to 1983 as Director for Processing Systems, Networks and Automation Planning. Since 1966, Mrs. Avram has been regaled with honors, among them: Library of Congress (LC) Outstanding Performance Rating, 1966, 1967, 1981, 1982; L.C. Superior Service Award in 1968; The Margaret Mann Citation in Cataloging and Classification in 1971; The Federal Women's Award in 1974; The LITA Award for Achievement in Library and Information Technology in 1980; ALA's Melvil Dewey Award in 1981; and Appreciation Award for Extraordinary Contributions to Library and Information Science and The Development of Library Automation from the National Central Library in Taipei, Taiwan, September 3, 1986; and election as Honorary Fellow of the International Federation of Library Associations and Institutions (IFLA) August 21, 1987.

Mrs. Avram has lectured as consultant throughout the United States and the world, including Australia, Brazil, China, Denmark, France, Japan, Indonesia, Mexico, Poland, Sweden, the United Kingdom, and Venezuela. Since 1965 she has written some 100 books, papers, and articles on library automation, networking, standards, bibliographic control, and the implications of technology for libraries. For more on Henriette Avram, see her biography in *The ALA Yearbook* for 1982.

BERGER, PATRICIA WILSON
Patricia Wilson Berger, Chief Information Resources and Services Division, National Institute of Stan-

dards and Technology (formerly National Bureau of Standards), was elected Vice-President/President-Elect of the American Library Association for 1988-89. Berger came to the National Bureau of Standards in 1976, and left in 1978 to become Chief, Information Resources and Services Branch, Environmental Protection Agency (1978-79). She returned to NBS in 1979. Berger was Deputy Chief Librarian, Scientific Library, Patent and Trademark Office (1972-76); and Chief Librarian, Commission on Government Procurement (1971-72). Her earlier posts were with the Operations Research of the Johns Hopkins University, the Human Resources Research Office of the American University, the Institute for Defense Analyses, and the Lambda Corporation.

Born May 1, 1926 in Washington, D.C., Patricia Wilson Berger is currently a Trustee of the Freedom to Read Foundation; a member of the State Library Board of Virginia; a Nominating Committee member, Section T, American Association for the Advancement of Science; and a member of the Editorial Board, *Science and Technology Libraries*. She holds a 1965 B.A. from George Washington University and a 1974 M.L.S. from the Catholic University of America.

Among Berger's numerous awards and honors are listings in *Who's Who in America* since 1978; the Department of Commerce Bronze and Silver Medals for "outstanding administration of library services and outstanding contributions in managing, automating, and distributing scientific information at the National Bureau of Standards"; election as a Fellow in Special Libraries Association "in recognition of outstanding service to the special libraries profession and significant contributions to the Association"; 1988 recipient of the Federal Librarians Round Table Achievement Award, 1988 recipient of the Alumni Achievement Award in Library and Information Science from Catholic University; and 1988 recipient of a resolution from the Library Board of the Commonwealth of Virginia expressing their "pride and esteem" for "a national reputation enhanced by a 30-year career of outstanding service to the library and information science community in Virginia and the nation."

Over the years, Berger's writings have been published in a number of monographs, reference books, and professional journals including *Bowker Annual of Library and Book Trade, Information, The ALA Yearbook of Library and Information Services, Science and Technology Libraries, Journal of Chemical Information and Computer Science, Special Libraries, Library Administration and Management, Education For Professional Librarians* (White Plains, NY., Knowledge Industry Publications, 1986), and *Libraries in the 90s: What the Leaders Expect*, compiled by Donald E. Riggs and Gordon A. Sabine (Phoenix, Oryx, 1988).

BETANCOURT, INGRID

Ingrid Betancourt, Principal Librarian, Public Service/Head, Ethnic Services and Collections, Newark Public Library, was elected President of REFORMA, the National Association to Promote Library Services to the Spanish Speaking. She brings strong administrative experience and training to the post; she has participated in the Hispanic Leadership Opportunity Program, a 15-week seminar sponsored by La Casa de Don Pedro, Inc., The Ford Foundation, and the New Jersey Institute of Technology; the Projecto LEER Institute on Materials and Services to the Spanish-Speaking at Rutgers Graduate School of Library and Information Services; and seminars on Bilingual Education and Librarianship sponsored by the MERIT (Multilingual Education Resource Information Training) Center of Temple University. Betancourt is completing requirements to obtain the title of Certified Public Manager of New Jersey. She is conversant with American sign language and is certified to train people to use the Kurzweil Reading Machine for the blind. Betancourt is English/Spanish bilingual and has a working knowledge of Italian.

Born November 13, 1956 in San Juan, Puerto Rico, Betancourt earned a B.A. in English at Northwestern State University, Natchitoches, Louisiana, in 1978 and a M.L.S. in 1980 from Rutgers, the State University, Graduate School of Library and Information Services. She has been at Newark Public Library since 1980; successively promoted from Junior Librarian-Reference Humanities Division/Spanish Language Specialist in 1983 to Senior Librarian-Reference/Coordinator, Hispanic Services in 1984 to her present post which she has held since 1987.

Betancourt has developed a core collection of Spanish library materials for children and adults for Baker and Taylor's *Books in Spanish* catalog; she aids libraries throughout New Jersey in developing and evaluating Spanish language collections; and she develops and conducts workshops in cross-cultural differences and their impact on library service to an ethnically diverse public. She was a panelist for the July 12, 1988, ALA New Orleans program on "Is 'English-Only' Enough? Cultural Heritage, Language, and Libraries"; she was moderator/presenter at the May 25-26, 1988, Seton Hall University Second Annual Library Assistants Conference on "Bilingual and English as Second Language Programs in Libraries"; and she spoke at the New Jersey Library Association Conference May 13, 1988, on "Gente y Cuentos/People and Stories: An Intergenerational Approach to Literature."

Betancourt edited the *REFORMA Newsletter* in 1987; she wrote a library column for a Newark-based Spanish-language weekly, and her articles have appeared in both professional journals and English and Spanish newspapers in New Jersey.

BLOSS, MARJORIE E.

Marjorie E. Bloss, Manager, Resource Sharing, Marketing and User Services Division, OCLC, received the Bowker/Ulrichs' Serials Librarianship Award for contribution to serials librarianship in the areas of professional library education serials literature, and research and development of tools in union lists of serials and serials holdings statement. This is a well-deserved honor for one who has been involved in cataloging and classifying serials since July 1971 when she went to the Rochester (New York) Institute of Technology as Serials Cataloger, was promoted to Head, Serials Department in 1974, and was upgraded in 1976 to Head, Technical Services. Simultaneously, she taught Library of Congress classification, serials, and advanced cataloging at the State University College of Geneseo on a part-time basis. Between 1979 and 1983 Bloss served as Project Director at the Rochester Regional Library Council where she planned, organized, coordinated, and implemented a union list of serials project using OCLC for a five-county area comprised of 60 independent libraries. From Rochester she went to the Illinois Institute of Technology as Assistant Director for Technical Services and Automation, remaining there until December 1987 when she went to OCLC.

Born March 5, 1944, in Brooklyn, New York, Bloss holds a 1965 B.A. in English and Foreign and Comparative Literature from the University of Rochester and a 1966 M.L.S. from Case Western Reserve University. She was working on a Masters in Public Administration when she left the Illinois Institute of Technology. She is professionally active in the American Library Association's Resources and Technical Services Division serials sec-

Biographies

Ingrid Betancourt

Marjorie E. Bloss

Biographies

Joe Ann Clifton

Richard M. Doughterty

Ralph E. Ellsworth

tion, American National Standards Institute, ILLNET/OCLC Steering Committee, Illinois OCLC Users' Group, IFLA's Serials Publications Section and Working Group on Union Catalogues of Serials, the OCLC User's Council, and the Library of Congress Online Subcommittee. Bloss edited the Union List of Serials Section of *Serials Review* from 1984 to 1986 and is currently a member of its Advisory Board.

Marjorie E. Bloss is a recognized speaker on serials. She has written four books: *Serial Holdings Statements at the Summary Level: Recommendations* (London, IFLA International Programme for UBC, 1985); *A User Guide to the American National Standard for Serial Holdings Statements at the Summary Level*, with the OCLC Union List Task Force (Dublin, Ohio, OCLC, 1983); *Guidelines for Union Lists of Serials*, with the ALA, Ad Hoc Committee on Union Lists of Serials (Chicago, ALA Resources and Technical Services Division, 1982); and *Directory of Union Lists of Serials* (Chicago, ALA Resources and Technical Services Division, 1981). Her professional journal articles have been published in such magazines as *Serials Librarian*, *Serials Review*, *LRTS*, *Drexel Library Quarterly*, *Technical Services Quarterly*, and *Cataloging and Classification Quarterly*.

CLIFTON, JOE ANN

Joe Ann Clifton, Manager of Information Services for Litton Industries in Woodland Hills (California) a Los Angeles suburb, served as President of the Special Library Association (SLA) in 1988. She has been very active in the information profession, serving as President, Southern California Chapter, SLA, Chair of its Aerospace, Library Management, and Information Technology committees, and member of the National Board of Directors. In the American Society for Information Science, she has been Chair of the Los Angeles Chapter and a member of the National Board of Directors for eight years.

Clifton is a member of the California State Networking Task Force, the OCLC Advisory Committee for Special Libraries, and the AFIPS History of Computing Committee. She is an Associate Editor of *Journal of Cost Analysis*. Clifton is Editor of *Entrepreneurship and Intrapreneurship in Corporate Libraries* (SLA), *Directory of Speakers on the History of Computing* (AFIP Press, 1981); she is co-editor of *Computers in Information Data Centers* (AFIPS, 1973; and she has written a number of journal articles.

Clifton was born in Alton, Illinois. She was John Cotton Dana Lecturer for Immaculate Heart, the University of California at Los Angeles. She also lectured at the University of Southern California's School of Library and Information Science and has been the Shirley Alldredge Lecturer in Colorado, and the Alice Rankin Distinguished Lecturer in New Jersey. Clifton received the ASIS Watson Davis Award for Continuous Dedicated Service to the Membership and the Los Angeles Chapter of ASIS Award for Outstanding Membership in 1976.

DOUGHERTY, RICHARD M.

Richard M. Dougherty was born January 17, 1935, in East Chicago, Indiana. He is a graduate of Purdue University with a B.S. in Forestry. He received his M.L.S. (1961) and Ph.D. (1963) from Rutgers University. He is currently Professor of Information and Library Studies at the University of Michigan, Ann Arbor. Dougherty served as Director of the Library of Michigan from 1978 until May 31, 1988. During the 1984–85 academic year he also served as Acting Dean of the School of Library Science (now called the School of Information and Library Studies). Other positions he has held in the library profession include Head, Acquisitions Department, University of North Carolina, Chapel Hill; Associate Director of Libraries, University of Colorado, Boulder; and University Librarian, University of California, Berkeley from 1972 to 1978. He was Professor of Information Studies at the Graduate School of Library and Information Studies, Syracuse University, New York, and he served as a Visiting Lecturer at several other library schools.

Dougherty has been active in the profession for many years, having been elected to the Executive Board of both the American Library Association and the Association of Research Libraries. He was a member of the Board of Governors of the Research Libraries Group and served as its Chairman of its Board during 1986–1987.

Dougherty is the author of several books, most notably *Scientific Management of Library Operations* (2d. ed., Scarecrow, 1982) and *Improving Access to Library Resources* (Scarecrow, 1974). He has edited several journals, and for five years was editor of *College and Research Libraries*. In 1975 he launched the *Journal of Academic Librarianship*, which he continues to edit. In 1981 he began publishing *Library Issues: Briefings for Faculty and Administrators*; he also serves as its editor.

In 1959 Dougherty received the first Esther Piercy Award. In 1983 he was chosen Academic Librarian of the Year by the Association of College and Research Libraries. In 1988 he was the first recipient of ALA's Hugh C. Atkinson Memorial Award for outstanding accomplishments as an academic librarian who has worked in the areas of library automation or library management and has made contributions (including risk taking) toward the improvement of library services or to library development or research.

ELLSWORTH, RALPH E.

Ralph E. Ellsworth, Library Director Emeritus, University of Colorado at Boulder since 1972, was selected as an Honorary Life Member of the American Library Association in 1988. He was born September 22, 1907, in Forest City, Iowa and earned an A.B. from Oberlin College in 1924, a B.S. in L.S. from Western Reserve University in 1931, a Ph.D. from the University of Chicago in 1937, an honorary Doctor of Laws degree from Western Reserve University, and an honorary Doctor of Humane Letters conferred upon him in 1983 by Oberlin College. Ellsworth's career began in 1930 when he managed the Cleveland (Ohio) branch of Burrows Brothers Bookstore. Between 1931 and 1934, he was Librarian, Adams State College Alamosa (Colorado); after that he was Director of Libraries and Professor at the University of Colorado (1937–1943), at the University of Iowa (1944–1958), and at the University of Colorado (1958–1972).

Ellsworth's honors include University of Chicago Fellowships, a Midwest Interlibrary Center Special Citation of Appreciation, a Colorado Library Association Outstanding Achievement Award, the Denver Public Library Neil Scott Memorial Award, a Mountain-Plains Library Association Certificate of Recognition, and Western Reserve University's Alumni Association of the School of Library Science Certificate of Honor. He is listed in *Who's Who in America* and other biographical directories.

Ellsworth's publications include more than 50 journal articles, *Planning the College and University Library* (1960), *The American Right Wing* (1962), *The School Library* (1963), *The Economics of Book Storage* (1969), *Academic Library Buildings* (1973), *Planning Manual for Academic Library Buildings* (1973), and *Ellsworth on Ellsworth* (1983).

Ralph E. Ellsworth's monumental and lasting contributions to the profession include first and major promotor of the concept of modular planning, leadership in the drive for centralized cataloging, a developer for the Association of Research Libraries with University Microfilm of *Doctoral Dissertations Abstracts,* a member of the ALA committee that wrote the Library Bill of Rights, Chair of the organizing committee for the Colorado Associated University Press, and consultant for more than 200 library buildings projects (six of them outside the United States).

ESTABROOK, LEIGH STEWART
Leigh S. Estabrook, Dean and Professor, Graduate School of Library and Information Science, University of Illinois at Urbana–Champaign, served as President of the Association for Library and Information Science Education during 1988. Estabrook has a 1964 A.B. in history from Northwestern University, a 1969 M.S. in library science from Simons College, and a 1980 Ph.D. in sociology from Boston University.

Estabrook was born in Washington, D.C., May 1, 1942. She has been a bibliographer, community information specialist, a teacher of sociology and library and information science, and an associate editor of *Book Research Quarterly.* Since a biographical sketch of her appeared in *The 1987 ALA Yearbook of Library and Information Services,* Estabrook has served as Chair, Ad Hoc Commission to Accredit Public Libraries, as a consultant to Murphy–Jahn Architects for the Chicago Public Library Design–Build Competition, and Chair, Chancellor's Council to Combat Discrimination at the University of Illinois. With Margaret N. Kimmel she wrote "Accrediting Public Libraries: An Update," *Library Journal* May 15, 1988. Currently she is researching the effect of technological change on the nature of library work and the structure of the library labor force. This study of 14 research libraries is partially funded by the Research Board of the University of Illinois.

FISHER, EDITH MAUREEN
Edith M. Fisher, Ethnic Studies Subject Specialist/Bibliographer and Reference Librarian, Reference and Research Services Department, Central University Library, University of San Diego (UCSD) since 1972, was elected Chair of the Black Caucus of ALA for the period from 1988 to 1990. She is also Chair of the ACRL Task Force on Minority Recruitment for the same period, and has chaired ALA's Ethnic Materials Information Exchange Round Table for the past two years.

Fisher earned her B.A. in American Studies from the University of California at Los Angeles in 1969, her M.L.S. from the University of Illinois in 1972; since 1987 she has been a doctoral student in behavioral science at the University of Pittsburgh, School of Library Information Science. Among her research and publications are "Race, Class, and Ethnicity," *Choice* bibliographic essay (research in progress); "Behavioral Research Studies on Race Relationships in Librarianship, 1968–1988: State-of-the-Art Essay" (unpublished research in progress); "Academic Librarian's Awareness of Racialistic Incidents and Attitudes About Race: A California Study," dissertation research (in progress); "Race and Ethnic Studies," in *Selection on Library Materials in Applied and Interdisciplinary Fields,* ALA, 1987; "Women of Color: Observations About Library Access," *Ethnic Forum,* 1986; "Minority Librarianship Research: A State-of-the-Art Review," *Library & Information Science Research: An International Journal,* Spring, 1983; and "Academic Library Collection Development in Ethnic Studies: Issues for Concern," *Bookmark,* 1982.

FOSTER, ELOISE CANTZON
Eloise C. Foster, Director of the American Hospital Association (AHA) Resource Center, was President of the Medical Library Association for 1988/1989. She has been with AHA since 1975, having served as Manager of the Association's library until 1984 when she was promoted to her present post. Before coming to Chicago, she headed the Southeastern Regional Medical Library Program at Emory University, Atlanta (1972–75), and she was Technical Services Librarian and Regional Reference Librarian (1969–1972). Between 1965 and 1968, Foster taught for the Alfred I. DuPont Special School District, Wilmington (Delaware).

Born in Wilmington, Eloise C. Foster earned a B.S. in 1965 from Pennsylvania State University and a Master of Librarianship degree from Emory University in 1969. The Medical Library Association conferred the Ida and George Eliot Prize upon her in 1980 for her article titled "Library Development and the Joint Commission on Accreditation of Hospital Standards." Foster has written numerous journal articles, and she has been a committee member or officer of the Special Libraries Association, the Medical Library Association, and the American Library Association.

FREEDMAN, RUSSELL
Russell Freedman was awarded the 1988 Newbury Medal as author of the most distinguished contribution to American literature for children published in the U.S. The winning book, *Lincoln: A Photobiography,* published by Clarion Books, was the sixth nonfiction book to receive the Newbery medal since the inception of the award in 1922, and the first since 1956.

Born October 11, 1929, in San Francisco, Freedman graduated from the University of California at Berkeley with a B.A. in 1951. After serving with the U.S Army's Second Infantry Division during the Korean War, he joined the Associated Press bureau in San Francisco as a reporter and editor. In 1957 he moved to New York City where he worked as a publicity writer for such network television shows as "Kraft Television Theatre" and "Father Knows Best."

Since 1961 When Holiday House published his first book, *Teenagers Who Made History,* Russell Freedman has written more than 30 nonfiction books. Between 1969 and 1986, he was a member of the Writing Workshop faculty at the New School for Social Research. His many awards and honors include the 1988 Jefferson Cup Award for *Lincoln* and the 1984 Western Heritage Award for *Children of the Wild West* (Clarion). Five of Freedman's books have ben honored by ALA as Notable Children's Books.

FUTAS, ELIZABETH
Elizabeth Futas, librarian, library educator, and member of the ALA Executive Board, was selected as new editor until 1991 of *RQ,* the quarterly publication of the Reference and Adult Services Division. She is Director, Graduate School of Library and Information Studies University of Rhode Island, where since 1986 she has also held the rank of Professor. She taught at Emory University, Division of Library and Information Management from 1977 to 1985. Between 1974 and 1977,Futas was Co-Adjunct Lecturer at the Graduate School of Library and Information Studies, Rutgers University. She has also served as Reference Librarian at Georgia State University and Cataloger, Acquisitions, Reference Bibliographer, and Deputy Head, Reference–Social Science and Humanities Library, Queens College, and Cataloger, Ford Foundation.

Elizabeth Futas, who was born in Brooklyn, New York, May 8, 1944, holds a 1965 B.A. in Political Science from Brooklyn College, a 1966 M.A. in Librarianship from the University of Minnesota, and a 1980 Ph.D. in Information Studies

Biographies

Leigh Stewart Estabrook

Edith Maureen Fisher

Eloise Cantzon Foster

Russell Freedman

Biographies

Elizabeth Futas

Herbert Goldhor

Ronald Grele

Edward G. Holley

from Rutgers University. Between 1968 and 1972 she studied theater at New York University, and 1972 to 1974, she was engaged in cinema studies at New York University.

Futas has been a consultant and speaker at many state, local and national library gatherings and at universities. She is the author of *Library Acquisition Policies and Procedures* (Oryx, 1977 and 2d ed. 1984) and of *Library Forms: An Illustrated Handbook* (Neal-Schuman, 1984). Futas has also written numerous journal articles and chapters in books. Her research reports include "Sexism in Encyclopedias," "Communication and Information Patterns in the Emerging, Interdisciplinary Areas of Women's Studies," "Women in ALA" "Women in Library Education," and "Collection Development in Professional School Collections." Currently she and Kay Cassell are writing a *Collection Development Process Manual* to be published by ALA.

GOLDHOR, HERBERT
Herbert Goldhor, retired as of August 1987 Director, Library Research Center, Graduate School of Library and Information Science, University of Illinois, received the 1988 Melvil Dewey Medal for exemplary creative professional achievement in those fields in which Dewey was most actively interested. Goldhor's career began in 1938 as Assistant to the Librarian, Iowa State College, Ames. Between 1946 and 1951 he served as Assistant Professor and Associate Professor at the University of Illinois Library School. He moved to Evansville (Indiana) where he was Chief Librarian at the Evansville and Vanderburg County Public Library (1952-1961). Returning to the University of Illinois Graduate School of Library Science in 1962, he was promoted from Associate Director to Director of the School. From 1975 to his retirement, Goldhor directed the Library research Center.

Born February 8, 1917, Herbert Goldhor served in the U.S. Army between 1944 and 1946. He holds a 1935 B.A. from Dana College (now Newark College of Rutgers University), a 1938 B.S. in L.S. from Columbia University School of Library Service, and a 1942 Ph.D. from the Graduate Library School of the University of Chicago. He is well-known as a library consultant and surveyer and has assisted in the New York State Library evaluation of regional public library systems, upstate and in New York City, 1965-66; the Minneapolis-St. Paul (Minnesota) survey of public library service, 1965-67; the 1967 survey with Alphonse F. Trezza and Agnes Crawford of army library service in Europe; and the 1974 Library of the Art Institute of Chicago (with Elizabeth Usher). Goldhor was a 1977 consultant to the Department of Library Science, University of Azarabadegan, Tabriz, Iran, and a 1978 UNESCO consultant to the Department of Library Economy, University of Brasilia (Brazil).

Goldhor's publications number more than 200, including book reviews. More recent significant writings include *Practical Administration of Public Libraries* (with Joseph L. Wheeler), New York Harper, 1962; *An Introduction to Scientific Research in Librarianship*, monograph no. 12, University of Illinois Graduate School of Library Science, 1972; "Experimental Effects on the Choice of Books Borrowed by Public Library Adult Patrons," *Library Quarterly*, v/51, p.253-68, July 1981; and "Public Library Circulation and Expenditures, 1939-1983: United States, Canada, and Great Britain," *Bowker Annual of Library and Book Trade Information*, 1986.

GRELE, RONALD J.
Ronald J. Grele, Director, Oral History Research Office Columbia University, became President of the Oral History Association in 1988. Before coming to Columbia in 1981, he was Director, Oral History Program, University of California at Los Angeles. His previous experience includes directorship of the Oral History Office, New Jersey Historical Commission from 1977 to 1978 and Research Director of the Commission from 1978 to 1980. Between 1971 and 1975, he was Assistant Director of the Ford Foundation Oral Program. He served as Archivist and Interviewer, John F. Kennedy Library from 1965 to 1966, and he taught at Kingsborough Community College (1970-71), The California State University at Long Beach (1967-69), and at Lafayette College (1964-65).

Born June 8, 1934 in Naugatuck, Connecticut, Grele earned a B.A. from the University of Connecticut in 1958, a 1959 M.A from the same University, and a Ph.D. from Rutgers University in 1971. His dissertation was titled "The Structure of Urban Liberalism in the Fourth Congressional District of New Jersey, 1930-1960." Grele's fields of special interest are U.S. social history, urban history, oral history, and historiography. His writings include *Where Cities Meet: The Urbanization of New Jersey*, New York, Van Nostrand, 1965, *Envelopes of Sound: Six Practitioners Discuss the Theory and Practice of Oral History*, Precedent, 1975 (re-issued and expanded as *Envelopes of Sound: The Art of Oral History*, Precedent, 1985) and *1968: A Student Generation In Revolt*, New York, Pantheon, 1988.

HOLLEY, EDWARD GAILON
In 1988 ALA again honored Edward G. Holley, library science educator and historian, former university dean, Past President of ALA, Dean Emeritus and Professor, School of Information and Library Science, The University of North Carolina at Chapel Hill, and recipient of the prestigious Melvil Dewey medal in 1983, and the 1987 Joseph W. Lippincott award for notable achievement in librarianship. On July 11, 1988 Holley received the ACRL Academic or Research Librarian of the Year Award "not only for the significant and numerous contributions he has made to the published literature and library education programs but also for his leadership role and consulting activities. He has been an exemplary career, and throughout he has served as a role model and mentor for academic librarians. Dr. Holley has without question distinguished himself in virtually every major area of our library profession." Thus, Donna M. Goehner, Chair of the award jury described one of the giants of the profession.

Holley has written a number of *ALA Yearbook of Library and Information Sciences* articles during his distinguished career. For more on him, see his biographies in the 1988 and 1976 yearbooks.

JENSEN, MARY ANN
Mary Ann Jensen, Curator of the William Seymour Theatre Collection at Princeton University Library and Archivist since 1966 for McCarter Theatre at Princeton, was re-elected President of the Theatre Library Association—by acclamation. She has broadly-based background in theatre having attended Lawrence College in Appleton, Wisconsin and Milwaukee-Downer College between 1954 and 1958. She earned a B.A. from the latter institution with a major in Speech/Theatre. Between 1962 and 1964 she pursued graduate studies at the University of Wisconsin-Madison. Jensen was a 1958 summer stock apprentice at Ivoryton, Connecticut, a winter stock Assistant Stage Manager at the Fred Miller Theatre, Milwaukee during the 1958-59 season, and an Assistant to Dave Miller, Dave Miller Costume Shop, Milwaukee from 1959 to 1960. From

1962 to 1966 she worked in various posts at the University of Wisconsin Madison: Teaching Assistant, Fundamentals of Speech, and Voice Training; Assistant Director, Wisconsin Center for Theatre Research (WCTR) and Acting Director, WCTR. Jensen has held her current position at Princeton since 1966.

Born in Milwaukee, Mary Ann Jensen has delivered a number of papers and lectures on theater; one of them delivered on April 20, 1985 at a conference in Rutherford, New Jersey titled "From Strolling Players to Steven Spielberg: Two Hundred Years of a Theatrical Family" was published with her compilation of a seven-generation Barrymore family genealogy in *Performing Arts Resources* (Theatre Library Association, 1988). She edited the *American Society Research Newsletter* from 1968 to 1972; in 1972–73 she was theater critic for the Princeton Town Topics; from time to time she reviews drama for *The Daily Princetonian;* and in 1981, she compiled *Let Joy Be Unconfined: A Catalogue of the Ballet Exhibition Held at Princeton University Library in 1981*. Her various articles have been published in *Performing Arts Resources, The Princeton University Library Chronicle,* and elsewhere.

Jensen has curated a number of exhibitions held in the main gallery at Princeton University Library, and between 1967 and 1985, she acted in or directed more than a dozen productions both on and off the Princeton campus. She has served on the Theatre Library Association (TLA) Board since 1980; she was Vice–President of TLA, 1983–85; she was Chair of the George/Freedley/TLA Awards, 1984–85; and since 1981, she has been the TLA representative to the Council of National Library and Information Associations.

LEARY, MARGARET A.
Margaret A. Leary, Director of the Law Library, University of Michigan, began a one-year term as President of the American Association of Law Libraries in June 1988. Before that she had served as Vice–President/President–Elect and had been a member of the Association's Executive Board from 1983 to 1986, and she was Program Chair for the 1982 Annual Meeting of the Association.

Margaret A. Leary was born July 2, 1942 in Oberlin, Ohio, where she grew up with part-time jobs in school, public, and college libraries. In 1964, she received a B.A. in government from Cornell University, and in 1966 she earned an M.A. in library science at the University of Minnesota. She was a cataloger in the University's main library, and then in the law library, until she began law school at William Mitchell College of Law in St. Paul, where she worked for the next two years. During her last year at William Mitchell she was a student practitioner at the Legal Aid Society of Minnesota. In 1973, she was appointed Assistant Director of the University of Michigan Law Library. In 1982, she was promoted to Associate Director, and in 1984, to Director.

Leary has written on the use of microfilms in law libraries, on international executive agreements in legal research, and on the process of planning law libraries, topics on which she has frequently spoken at professional meetings. She helped develop a special program in law librarianship at the University of Michigan's School of Information and Library Studies, and taught courses in sources of legal information and law librarianship/administration. Leary also teaches advanced legal research in the University of Michigan Law School.

LEE, CHANG C.
Chang C. Lee, University Librarian and Archivist, The University of Central Florida since 1983, was elected president of the Chinese American Librarians Association for 1988–89. Born November 18, 1935, in Tainan Hsien, Taiwan, Republic of China, he earned an LL.B. in journalism in 1959 from National Chengchi University, a M.S. in Library Science in 1969 from Florida State University, and a Ph.D. in education from the same institution in 1976.

Lee has been on the faculty at The University of Central Florida since 1985. Between 1978 and 1983 he was Visiting Professor at National Chengchi University; from 1978 to 1981 he was Head Librarian, Pennsylvania State University, Behrend College; and from 1969 to 1978 Lee was Assistant and Associate Librarian at Florida A & M University.

Chang C. Lee's professional activities include President of the Mid–Atlantic Chapter, Chinese–American Librarians Association (1979–81), Chairperson of Subcommittee on Publications, Middle Management Discussion Group Committee, ALA Library Administration and Management Association (1970–80), Chairperson of Intellectual Freedom Committee, Florida Library Association (1986–87), and Chairperson, Lending Services Caucus at the same institution (1984–85). Lee served as Chairperson of Staff Development committee, as a member of the Collection Development Policy Committee of the International Education Council, as Advisor of the Chinese American Student Association at the University of Central Florida, and as advisor on library automation and member of the Curriculum Committee at National Chengchi University. Lee was Chair of the School Board Chinese Language School, Orlando (Florida) 1984–85. He was president of the Chinese Association of North Florida; the Chinese Association of Erie, Pennsylvania; and the Chinese American Association of Central Florida.

Since 1985, Lee has been Executive Editor of *Journal of Educational Media and Library Science;* from 1980 to 1982 he was Executive Editor of *Journal of Education Media Science;* and he was a member of the Editorial Board of *Education and Psychology* (1981–82). Chang C. Lee has written numerous journal and newspaper articles for *Journal of Educational Media Science, Educational Forum, Teachers' Friend, United Daily News, Central Daily News, Taiwan Education Review,* and *Flash.* His presentation for the 1988 Education Development Group, the National Development Seminar (Ministry of Education, Republic of China) was titled "The Importance of General Education."

LYDERS, JOSETTE ANNE
Josette Anne Lyders has been appointed Editor for ALA's *Journal of Youth Services in Libraries* for 1988 to 1991. She was highly qualified for the post having edited the *Texas Library Journal* since 1986, *A Review Sampler* (published by the University of Houston–Clear Lake) since 1984, the *ALA Chapter Handbook* in 1983, the *Houston Academy of Medicine–Texas Medical Center Library Annual Report* in 1983, and newsletters and conference kits since 1974.

Since 1984, Lyders has been an Assistant Professor and Chair of the Learning Resources Program at the University of Houston–Clear Lake; during the summers she is an Adjunct Assistant Professor at the University of Vermont. Between 1971 and 1980, Lyders was a high school librarian at Spaulding High School, Arre, Vermont. Between 1968 and 1971 she was Head of the Extension Division of the Oshkosh (Wisconsin) Public Library, and in 1967–68 she served as Children's Services Consultant for the State of Vermont's Free Public Library Service.

Lyders was born June 29, 1942, in Elmhust, Long Island, New York. She earned a B.A. in French from Stonehill College, North Easton, Massachusetts, in 1964; an M.S. in Library Science from Simmons College in 1967; an M.A. in

Biographies

Margaret A. Leary

Chang Chen Lee

Josette Anne Lyders

Biographies

Karen Markey

Susan K. Martin

Charles E. Miller

Liberal Studies from Dartmouth College in 1978; and a Doctor of Arts in Library Administration from Simmons in 1983, where she was elected to Beta Phi Mu.

Lyders has been active for 22 years in state and national library associations. Among other activities, she served for five years on the ALA Council, worked as a member of the 1975 Newbery-Caldecott Awards Committee, and chaired the ALA Chapter Relations Committee. She is currently a member of the ALA Standing Committee on Library Education. She has also written articles, editorials, and book reviews published in professional journals.

MARKEY, KAREN

Karen Markey, Assistant Professor and Teacher of organization of information resources, searching automated databases, and library automation at the School of Information and Library Studies, The University of Michigan, received the Esther J. Piercy Award in 1988. Between 1981 and 1987 she was Research Scientist at the OCLC Online Computer Library Center. In Spring 1986 she was Visiting Professor at the Graduate School of Library and Information Science, University of California, Los Angeles where she taught subject control of library materials; in 1978 she worked at ERIC Clearinghouse/Information Resources where she investigated online database coverage and overlap for developing a tertiary database and where she participated in online searching of BOOKS database (i.e., subject-enhanced MARC database). In 1977 Markey was a Library Intern at the National Trust for Historic Preservation where she designed and implemented an access and delivery system for newsletter and periodical collections, and from 1975 to 1976, she served as Reference Assistant at Milton S. Eisenhower Library, The Johns Hopkins University, in which posts she provided bibliographic instruction and prepared user aids to art and education references.

Born in Buffalo, New York, in 1953, Markey earned a 1975 B.A. in the History of Art at Johns Hopkins, a 1977 M.L.S. in Information Studies from Syracuse University, and a 1981 Ph.D. in Library and Information Science from Syracuse. Her dissertation was titled "Computer-assisted Construction of a Guide to Themes and Concepts in Medieval Art and their Essential Attributes."

Markey's sponsored research includes being Co-Principal Investigator for "Increasing Accessibility of the Library of Congress Subject Headings in Online Catalogs;" (a Council on Library Resources grant), Principal Investigator for "Dewey Decimal Classification Online Project" (financed by the Council on Library Resources, OCLC, and Forest Press), and Project Manager of the "Nationwide Online Catalog Project" (also financed by CLR).

Markey's monographs include *Subject Access to Visual Resources Collections* (Greenwood, 1986) and *Subject Searching in Library Catalogs: Before and After the Introduction of Online Catalogs* (OCLC, 1984). She has written chapters in Joseph R. Matthews *The Impact of Online Catalog* (Neil-Schuman, 1986), *Annual Review of Information Science and Technology*, edited by Martha E. Williams (Knowledge Industry Publications, 1984), and *Online Catalogs, Online Reference: Converging Trends*, edited by Brian Aveny and Brett Butler (ALA, 1984). Markey has written articles for such journals as *Library Trends, Library Resources and Technical Services, Cataloging and Classification Quarterly, Visual Resources, Preservation News*, and several reports in the *OCLC Research Report* series.

MARTIN, SUSAN KATHERINE (OROWAN)

On August 1, 1988 Susan K. Martin, library systems specialist, library educator, and library administrator, became Executive Director, National Commission on Libraries and Information Science (NCLIS). In this post she is responsible for providing leadership and direction to assure the optimum provision of library services in cooperation with regional, state, and local governments and with public and private agencies. Prior to coming to NCLIS, Martin was from 1979 to 1988, Director, Milton S. Eisenhower Library, Johns Hopkins University; from 1973 to 1979 she was Head, Library Systems Office, University of California, Berkeley. In 1977, she was coordinator, UCB/Stanford Research Library Program, and between 1965 and 1973, she was Systems Librarian, Harvard University Library.

Born in Cambridge, England, November 14, 1942. Susan K. Martin earned a B.A. in Romance Languages in 1963 from Tufts University, a 1965 M.S. in Library Science from Simmons College, and a Ph.D. in 1983 from the University of California, Berkeley, School of Library and Information Studies. She has taught at the University of Maryland, and has conducted workshops at the University of California, Berkeley, and Harvard University. She has also coordinated and taught at ALA's Reference and Adult Services and Library Information and Technology Association institutes. Martin serves on the library advisory council of universities, and she has been a consultant for numerous libraries and firms.

Susan K. Martin has broad writing and editing experience; she is a member of the Editorial Board of *Journal of Library Administration*, a member of the Board of Contributors for *Library Issues; Briefings for Faculty and Administrators*, a Consulting Board member for *Advanced Technology/Libraries*, and she edited the *Journal of Library Automation* for five years. She is a former *ALA Yearbook* author, and she has written approximately 75 professional journal articles.

MILLER, CHARLES EDMOND

Charles E. Miller, Director, University Libraries, Florida State University, was elected President of the Association of Research Libraries in 1988. He has held his position at Florida State since 1973. Prior to that he had served at Tulane University Library as Associate Director (1971-73); Assistant Director (1970-71); and Associate Librarian Medical Library (1969-70); and at Louisiana State University Library between 1966 and 1969 where he held successive posts as Cataloger, Humanities; Head, Order Department; and Head, Acquisitions Department.

Charles E. Miller was born August 3, 1938 in Bridgeport, Connecticut. In 1964, he earned a B.A. in English from McNeese State University and in 1966 he graduated from Louisiana State University with an M.S.L.S. Miller has been a member of the governing boards or an officer of the Association of Southeastern Research Libraries, SOLINET, the Center for Research Libraries, the Florida Library Association, and Research Libraries Group. He has served on the Editorial Board of *Research Libraries in OCLC: A Quarterly* and as Assistant Editor, *LLA Bulletin;* his writings include book reviews and a number of journal articles.

MILLER, FRANK WINSTON

Frank Winston Miller, Vice-President and Director of Marketing and Sales for The H.W. Wilson Company, was elected President of Friends of Libraries USA in 1988.

Born in Kokomo, Indiana, on October 7, 1940, Miller attended Indiana University at Bloomington and in 1966 he earned a B.S. During 1966-69 he worked as Business Manager at the Monroe County Public Library in Bloomington. He joined the Baker & Taylor Company in 1969 and held a variety of positions at that organization, the last of which was Director of School and Library Markets. In 1978 Miller began work at Birch Tree Group, Ltd. (a music publisher) in Princeton, New Jersey, and left that company as Senior Vice-President in 1982 when he joined The H.W. Wilson Company in his present position.

Miller has served on the ALA/AAP Joint Committee, and he currently serves on AAP's Professional and Scholarly Publishing Executive Council. He is one of New Jersey's lay delegates to the WCHLIST planning group and is a member of the New Jersey State Library and Archival Commission Advisory Board. Miller was a participant on the Library of Congress Management and Planning Committee as a representative of the Professional and Scholarly Publishing Committee. He is on the Advisory Board for The *ALA Yearbook of Library and Information Services* and is a member of the Bronx Arts Advisory Board.

MONTY, VIVIENNE
Vivienne Monty, Head, Government Documents/Administrative Studies, York University, Ontario, Canada, was elected President of the Canadian Library Association. (She held the post of Treasurer in 1980–81.) Monty, who was born in Budapest, Hungary on March 20, 1948, holds a 1971 B.A. in history and political science from the University of Toronto and a 1973 M.A. in library science from the same university. Before her promotion to her present post in 1982, she was Assistant Head from 1973 to 1982. In 1981, she became President, A & V Monty Investments, Ltd.

In 1987, Vivienne Monty received the Special Librarian of the Year Award from the Toronto chapter of the Special Libraries Association. Her recent writings include *Canadian Small Business Handbook*, Toronto, CCH (Canadian), 1985; "The Marketing Scene," *Ontario Business Magazine*, 1986; and with Mary Williamson "Canadian Art Documents/Documents Canadiens sur 1 'Art," *Art Documentation: Bulletin of the Art Libraries Society of North America*, v.2, no.1, 1983.

MOON, ILSE
Ilse Moon, researcher, writer, librarian, library educator, and information specialist, became Executive Secretary of the Association for Library and Information Science Education in July 1988. From 1979–1988, she was a regular contributor to *Current Biography*, and between 1985 and 1986 she wrote the column "Free and Inexpensive Materials for Library Collections" for *Collection Building*. Between 1976 and 1978 Moon was Director of Professional Development Studies and Lecturer at the Graduate School of Library and Information Studies at Rutgers University. She has also served at the Montclair (New Jersey) Public Library as Head of Technical and Supportive Services (1971–76); at Drew University Library as Reference Librarian (1970–71); at the College of William and Mary (Williamsburg, Virginia) as Chief and Assistant Catalog Librarian (1966-1970); at the University of Georgia Marine Institute as Librarian (1960–65); and at Ohio State University, Aviation Psychology Laboratory as Research Assistant (1953–60).

Ilse Moon earned an A.B. in sociology in 1952 at Antioch University, Yellow Springs, Ohio, and a M.S.L.S. concentrating on science reference work in 1966 at Columbia University's School of Library Service. Born October 7, 1932, in Nuremburg, Germany, she has written numerous articles on librarianship and book reviews. She is a member of the editorial board of *Collection Building* and *The Reference Librarian* and she is a consultant for Scarecrow Press.

Ilse Moon developed the Continuing Library Education Program for the Graduate School of Library and Information Studies at Rutgers, and she co-founded the 60th ALA's Independent Librarians Exchange and its Library and Information Literature Membership Group.

OTT, BILL
Bill Ott was named Editor-in-Chief of *Booklist* magazine, ALA's flagship review journal for school and public libraries. He came to *Booklist* in 1980 as Books for Adults Editor and was promoted to Managing Editor in June 1988.

Ott was born October 4, 1947, in Salem, Oregon. He studied at the University of Oregon (B.A. in English, 1969) and the University of Washington (M.A. in English, 1971 and M.L.S. in Librarianship, 1972).

In 1972 he became Serials Librarian at Timberland Regional Library, Olympia, Washington, and in 1975 he was promoted to Book Selection Coordinator. In 1980, Ott was appointed Head of Acquisitions at the King County Library System, Seattle. A regular contributor to numerous periodicals and newspapers, Ott has written book reviews and essays for *The New York Times Book Review*, the *Chicago Tribune*, the *San Francisco Review of Books*, the *Seattle Times*, and the *Seattle Weekly*. Since 1984, he has been the author of the new book column called "Quick Bibs" in *American Libraries*. From 1982 to 1987, he served as a contributing editor to the ALA newspaper, *Openers*, where his interview essays on such writers as Anthony Powell, P.D. James, and Bobbie Ann Mason appeared regularly. His publications include "The Death of Des Pereires: Possibilities for Compassion in Celine's World" in *Understanding Celine* (Genitron Press, 1984), and *What America Reads: Myth Making in Popular Fiction* (ALA, 1984), a booklet published as part of the ALA/NEH Let's Talk About It project.

Ott has also served as consultant to ALA's Notable Books Council (1980–present), as Materials Coordinator to the Let's Talk About It project (1986–87), and as judge for the Chicago Public Library's Carl Sandburg Awards (1985). He is a member of the National Book Critics Circle.

PENNIMAN, W. DAVID
W. David Penniman, Libraries and Information Systems Director, AT&T Bell Laboratories, Murray Hill, New Jersey, was elected President of the American Society of Information Science. He holds a 1975 Ph.D. in Communication Theory from Ohio State University, a 1962 M.S. from the School of Communication, University of Illinois, and a 1960 B.S. in Mechanical Engineering from the University of Illinois. Since 1960, Penniman has been active in the field of information systems development and research and information systems management. His proven expertise includes the areas of planning for information systems and services, corporate level strategic planning, senior-level management of information systems, services, and information research. He has also had direct research experience in human–computer interaction, computer networks, national information networking, international data flow, and information system evaluation.

At AT&T Bell Laboratories where he has been employed since 1984, Penniman manages the Bell Labs operated AT&T Library Network, which links libraries and information services at AT&T. Between 1978 and 1984, he was promoted at OCLC from Manager, Research Department (1978–80) to Director, Development Division (1980–82) to Vice-President, Offices of Planning and Research (1982–84). In 1977, he was Research Scholar, Computer Science Group, International Institute for

Biographies

Vivienne Monty

Ilse Moon

Bill Ott

W. D. Penniman

Biographies

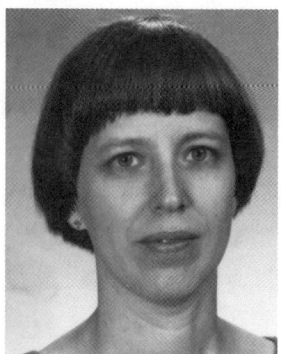
Judy M. Pitts

Marcia W. Posner

James Rettig

Ralph E. Ricardo

Applied Systems Analysis, Laxenburg, Austria. Between 1966 and 1977, he was Associate Manager, Information Systems Section, Batelle Columbus Laboratories; and from 1965 to 1966 Penniman was Associate Director, Engineering Publications Office at the University of Illinois.

Born December 19, 1937, in St. Louis, Missouri, Penniman is a member of the Board and Vice-Chairman, Engineering Information, and a member of the National Commission on Libraries Information Science Productivity Task Force, and he is on advisory boards of Syracuse University and Rutgers University. He is a prolific author, with more than 50 articles, reports, and papers to his credit. He has lectured and directed seminars on information systems and networks around the world.

PITTS, JUDY M.

Judy M. Pitts, Library/Media Specialist, Fayetteville (Arkansas) High School Library, was selected editor (with Barbara Stripling) of *School Library Media Quarterly*. Pitts' educational and experimental background commend her for the post. She received her B.A. in English and Education in 1969 from The College of the Ozarks, Clarksville Arkansas and her M.Ed. in 1979 from the University of Arkansas in Instructional Resources in Education. Her postmasters field is instructional resources.

Judy M. Pitts has held her current position since 1982. Prior to that she was Library/Media Specialist at Springdale (Arkansas) High School, and she taught English at the same school between 1976 and 1980. Between 1974 and 1976, she taught speech at the Subiaco (Arkansas) Academy, and from 1969 to 1974 she was an English teacher at Willow Springs (Missouri) Public Schools.

Pitts has broad experience as a writer and editor: *Brainstorms and Blueprints: Teaching Library Research As a Thinking Process* (with Barbara Stripling) Englewood,Colorado *Libraries Unlimited*, 1988); co-editor of *Arkansas Libraries*, 1985-1987; and author of numerous articles in *Arkansas Libraries, Arkansas Gazette, Springdale News, Bookreport, Arkansas Times, AAVA News and Views,* and *School Library Media Quarterly*. Pitts has also conducted a number of workshops, poster sessions, and staff development courses.

POSNER, MARCIA W.

Marcia W. Posner, children's library specialist, library educator, and authority in Judaica librarianship, was elected President of the Association of Jewish Libraries for the term 1988 to 1990. In 1951, she earned a B.S. in Education from the City College of New York, a 1967 M.L.S. from Queens College, and Ph.D. in Communications in Education from New York University in 1980. Posner established the Shelter Rock Jewish Center Library in 1967, and she remains its director. She was Children's Librarian and Assistant Director of the Hillside Public Library, Nassau County (New York) from 1967 to 1973. Between 1970 and 1980, she taught children's and young adult literature, public library programs, and reference and bibliography at Queens College library school. Posner has also taught Judaica librarianship at C.W. Post College, Bergen Community College, the UJA-Federation of New York, and at various Boards of Jewish Education and Federations throughout the U.S.

Born June 4, 1930 in Trenton, New Jersey, Marcia W. Posner is Library Consultant for JWB Jewish Book Council where she also coordinates National Jewish Book Awards and book-related publications and conferences. She has written a number of books: *Basic Sources for Jewish Libraries*, UJA Federation, 1980- ; *Jewish Children's Books: How to Choose Them; How to Use Them*, Haddasah Dept. of Education, 1986; *Juvenile Judaica: The Jewish Values Book-Finder*, AJL, 1984- ; *Selected Books for Jewish Children*, Jewish Book Council, 1984- ; *Selected Picture Books for Jewish Children*, JBC, 1984- ; and *Organizing a Jewish Women's Library Collection*, JBC, 1987. She has also written journal articles that were published in *Judaica Librarianship, School Library Journal, Jewish Book Annual,* and *AJL Bulletin*. Posner co-edits *Judaica Librarianship*.

RETTIG, JAMES ROBERT

James R. Rettig, reference librarian, author and editor, and teacher, is the youngest person to receive the Isadore Gilbert Mudge Citation awarded by ALA's Reference and Adult Services Division for "distinguished contribution to reference librarianship." Born November 11, 1950, in Chicago, he earned a B.A. in English in 1972 from Marquette University, and M.A. in English from the same institution in 1974, and an M.A. in Library Science from the University of Wisconsin at Madison in 1975.

Currently Rettig is Assistant University Librarian for Reference and Information Services, College of William and Mary, Williamsburg (Virginia). Between 1983 and the end of 1987, he served as Head Reference Librarian, University of Illinois at Chicago. He has also been Reference Librarian, Roesch Library, University of Dayton (Ohio) from 1978 to 1982; Head Reference Librarian, Murray State University in 1977 and 1978; and Assistant Reference Librarian at the same place in 1976 and 1977. He was a Teaching Assistant in the Department of English at Marquette University from 1972 to 1974, and he was Visiting Lecturer, University of Chicago Graduate Library School, where he taught Information Sources and Services for the Social Sciences and Humanities.

James Rettig has been author/editor of the "Current Reference Books" column in the *Wilson Library Bulletin*. He is editor of *Bibliographic Guides in the Humanities*, a series of guides to reference literature in the humanities (Libraries Unlimited). Volumes on music reference literature (1987), philosophy (1986), and screen (1986) have been published; other volumes are planned for religion, folklore, children's literature, science fiction, linguistics, journalism, and English and American literature. He is on the Editorial Board of *Reference Services Review*, a publication with which he has been involved as Assistant and Associate Editor since 1979. He has written articles on "Reference Services" and "Bibliographies, Indexes, and Other Reference Books" for *The ALA Yearbook of Library and Information Services* and *Reference and Information Service: A Reader for Today*, edited by Bill Katz (Scarecrow Press, 1986); *Library Serials Standards: Development, Implementation, Impact*, edited by Nancy Jean Melin (Meckler, 1984); *Serials and Microform: Patron-Oriented Management*, edited by Nancy Jean Melin (Meckler, 1983); *Online Searching Technique and Management*, edited by James J. Maloney (ALA, 1983); and *State-of-the-Art of Academic Library Instruction*, edited by Carolyn Kirkendall (ERIC document ED 171, 272), 79-113. Rettig is a prolific writer of journal articles for *Wilson Library Bulletin, Reference Services Review, The Reference Librarian, RQ, Journal of Academic Librarianship, Library Journal, Government Publications Review, Illinois Libraries*, and *ALA's Reference Books Bulletin*.

RICARDO, RALPH E.

Ralph E. Ricardo, Superintendent, Ascension Public Schools,

Donaldsville Louisiana, received the AASL/SIRS Distinguished Library Service Award for School Administrators at the ALA Annual Meeting in New Orleans. He began his career in education in 1957 as a mathematics and chemistry teacher at Lowery High School; he served as Assistant Principal and then Principal until 1970 when he went to Donaldsville Junior High as Principal. Between 1973 and 1975 Ricardo was Project Director and Supervisor, Ascension Parish School Board; from 1975 to 1981 he was Assistant Superintendent of Schools for Ascension Parish. He has held his present post since 1981.

Born December 21, 1931 in Donaldsville, Louisiana, Ricardo has a 1954 B.A. and 1962 M.S. from Southern University. His post-masters training in Educational Administration and Supervision has been at Louisiana State University. In 1960 he was awarded a National Science Foundation Fellowship for graduate study and research in mathematics. Ricardo has been both Secretary and President of the South Central Louisiana Association of School Librarians.

ROTHSTEIN, SAMUEL

Samuel Rothstein, librarian educator, and Professor Emeritus, School of Library, Archival, and Information Studies, University of British Columbia, received ALA's Beta Phi Mu award for distinguished service to education for librarianship. His distinguished professional career began in 1947 when he became a reference librarian at the University of British Columbia Library. He was subsequently promoted to Head of Acquisitions (1948); Assistant and Associate University Librarian (1954); Acting University Librarian and Director of the School of Librarianship (1961); Director and Professor of Librarianship (1961–70); Professor, School of Librarianship (1970–86); and Professor Emeritus (1986).

During the period between 1943 and 1982, Rothstein served with the Canadian Army Intelligence Corps (1943–46); he was a Board member and President of the Vancouver Jewish Community Centre (1962–72); he was consultant for the Science Secretariat of Canada (1969); he was Visiting Scholar, University of Hawaii (1969); he served as Visiting Professor, University of Toronto (1970); he taught at The Hebrew University of Jerusalem (1973); he was consultant for various university libraries (1970–77); he was Librarian in Residence, University of Toronto (1979); and he was Research Fellow at the University of Toronto Centre for Research in Librarianship (1981–82).

Born January 12, 1921, in Moscow (Russia), Samuel Rothstein came to Canada in 1922. He earned a B.A. in French and English from the University of British Columbia (U.B.C) in 1939, an M.A. in the same subjects from U.B.C. in 1940, a B.L.S. in 1947 from the University of California, and a Ph.D. in librarianship from the University of Illinois in 1954. Rothstein's publications include *The Development of Reference Services* (1955); *Training Professional Librarians for Western Canada* (1957); co-editor of *As We Remember It* (1970) and co-author of *The University— The Library*; contributions to several encyclopedias; and many articles and reviews in professional journals. He has also served on the editorial board of several journals and encyclopedias.

Rothstein's honors include the 1951–54 Carnegie Corporation Fellowship; the 1970 Helen Gordon Steward Award (British Columbia Library Association); the honorary D. Litt. degree from York University of Toronto (1971); the 1986 Canadian Library Association's Outstanding Service to Librarianship Award; and the 1988 ALISE Award for Outstanding Professional Contributions to Library and Information Science Education. He has been president of the American Association of Library Schools (the predecessor of ALISE), the British Columbia Library Association (BCLA), The Pacific Northwest Library Association (PNLA), and the Canadian Association of Library Schools (CALS). He has been an officer of the American Library Association, the Canadian Library Association, the Bibliographical Society of Canada, and the Canadian Council of Library Schools. He was elected to honorary life membership by BCLA, CLA, PNLA, and CALS. Four of his articles have been reprinted in the annual anthology *Library Lit.: The Best of...*

Samuel Rothstein considers his most significant achievement to have been that he was Founding Director of the University of British Columbia School of Librarianship.

SCHOENHERR, JOHN

John Schoenherr, winner of the 1988 Caldecott Medal as illustrator of the most distinguished picture book published in the United States, has illustrated 46 books. His Caldecott honor was for *Owl Moon*, Jane Yolen's long poem published by Philomel Books, a member of The Putnam and Grosset Group. Born July 5, 1935 in New York City the son of a Hungarian mother and a German father, he grew up in the ethnically mixed neighborhood of Sunnyside in Queens. Speaking only German, he learned as a young child to communicate with pictures. Recognizing Schoenherr's talent, his parents bought his first set of watercolors when he was eight and oil paints very soon after. By the time he was 13, he was attending Saturday classes at the Art Students League in Manhattan. As he developed his artistic skills, his interest in the world outside of New York City emerged, and he began an endless trek to the American Museum of Natural History and the Bronx and Central Park zoos, where he watched and sketched. His years of the study and illustration of wildlife have taken him to Alaska, to the hills of Iran, to the mountains of Utah, Wyoming, Montana, and California, and to the caves of Puerto Rico.

John Schoenherr holds a 1956 B.F.A. from Pratt Institute of Brooklyn, and he is a member of the American Society of Mammalogists, the Society of Illustrators, the Graphic Artists Guild, and the Society of Animal Artists. For Schoenherr, the Caldecott Medal is the latest in a series of awards including the 1965 Hugo (World Science Fiction) Award, the 1979 Society of Animal Artists Medal, the 1984 Philadelphia Academy of Natural Sciences Silver Medal and Best of Show, and the 1985 Society of Animal Artists Medal, and 13 awards from the Society of Illustrators.

Schoenherr's work has been exhibited at the New York Zoological Society, the Royal Ontario Museum, the Brandywine Museum, the California Academy of Sciences, the Denver Museum of Natural History Bratislava Biennale, and in many other locations.

SHAW, SPENCER GILBERT

Spencer G. Shaw, Professor Emeritus, Graduate School of Library and Information Science, University of Washington, library educator, children's and young adult specialist, folklorist, and premier storyteller, was given the highest honor of the American Library Association—honorary life member. He was born in Hartford, Connecticut, August 16, 1916. In 1940 he earned a B.S. in secondary education, English and social studies, and in 1941 he received a B.L.S. from the University of Wisconsin Library School. He pursued advanced studies in library science at the Graduate Library School, University of Chicago and in book illustration at Pratt Institute Library.

Shaw has a varied experiential background having served as

Biographies

Samuel Rothstein

John Schoenherr

Spencer G. Shaw

73

Biographies

John Steptoe

Barbara Stripling

Branch Librarian, Hartford (Connecticut) Public Library (1940–43 and 1945–48); Military Post Librarian, Ft. Devens (Massachusetts) 1943–44; Program Coordinator and Storytelling Specialist, Department of Work with Children, Brooklyn Public Library (1949–59); and Consultant, Library Service to Children, Nassau Library System, Garden City (New York) 1959–70. In 1970, he went to the Graduate Library School at the University of Washington as a Lecturer. He was progressively promoted to Associate Professor in 1971, to Professor in 1977, and to Professor Emeritus in 1986.

Spencer Shaw's research and teaching specializations include directed field work and directed field work seminars; children's materials, bibliographies, and indexes; the history of children's literature; ethnic and minority materials for children and young adults; the art and technique of storytelling; public library service for children; and library service to persons with special needs. He has been a library school visiting faculty member around the nation; Queens College Drexel University, Syracuse University, Virginia State University, Kent State University, University of Maryland, University of Hawaii, the University of Illinois, the University of Washington, and the University of Wisconsin–Madison. Shaw was also the first librarian member of the Editorial Advisory Board for *Childcraft: The How and Why Library*.

Spencer Shaw has written chapters in 14 monographs including *ALA World Encyclopedia of Library and Information Services*, 1985; *Arts in Cultural Diversity*, Sydney, Australia, Holt, 1980; and *Start Early for an Early Start: You and the Young Child*, ALA, 1976. His journal articles were published in *Children's Library* (Society of Children's Library, Tokyo), *Horn Book Magazine*, *School Library Journal*, *Public Libraries*, *Top of the News*, *Library Trends*, *Library Leads*, *Library Association of Alberta Bulletin*, *Library Journal*, *The New York Supervisor Library Quarterly*, *The Hartford (Connecticut) Courant*, and *The New York Times Book Review*. Shaw has narrated tapes for Westin Woods Studio and ACI Films, was featured on the U.S. State Department "Voice of America," and he wrote the script and narrated *Story on the Air: Let's Go to the Library*, a weekly radio broadcast for WHLI, Hempsted, Long Island, New York.

Among Spencer Shaw's numerous honors are the 1988 Distinguished Service Award of the ALA Black Caucus, the Arkansas Traveler Plaque from the Arkansas Library Association, the Grolier Foundation Award, establishment of the Spencer G. Shaw Research Storytelling Collection at the Invercartill (New Zealand) Public Library, Guest Narrator with the Sydney (Australia) Symphony Orchestra, Eminent American Designee in the Australia–American Festival, a Friends of the Library Award (Brooklyn Public Library), the President's Award of the Washington State Library Association, and the Spencer G. Shaw Honor Lecture Series (established by the Graduate School of Library and Information Science, University of Washington).

STEPTOE, JOHN LEWIS

John Lewis Steptoe painter, illustrator, and author of children's books, was recipient of the Coretta Scott King Award in New Orleans, July 12, 1988, for his illustrations in *Mufaro's Beautiful Daughters: An African Folktale* (Lothrop, Lee, & Shepard Books). The award, designed to commemorate the life, works, and dreams of the late Dr. Martin Luther King, Jr., and to honor Mrs. Coretta Scott King for her courage and determination to work for peace and world brotherhood, is presented to a black illustrator for "an understandingly inspirational and educational contribution designed to promote better understanding and appreciation of the culture and contribution of all peoples to the realization of the American dream."

John Steptoe was born in Brooklyn in 1950 and was reared in the Bedford–Stuyvesant section of that borough. He began making pictures on his own as a young child, and he received his only formal artistic training at the Manhattan School of Art and Design. While in school, Steptoe worked in HARYOU-ACT, an anti-poverty program in Harlem, and he studied with Norman Lewis, the painter. He began his first book, *Stevie*, at 16 and before the book was published three years later in 1969, it was reprinted in its entirety in *Life* magazine. *Stevie* was selected as an ALA Notable Book, and it received a Gold Medal from the society of Illustrators.

Steptoe is author–illustrator of nine books since *Stevie*; among them are *The Story of Jumping Mouse* (1984), a Caldecott Honor Book, and *My Best Words* (1974), whose illustrations have been described by Lena Sutherland in the *Bulletin of the Center for Children's Books* (University of Chicago) as "so brilliant in use of color, especially in outlining the children's faces, that the captivating Bwella and her brother are almost lost on most pages." Steptoe also illustrated Eloise Greenfield's *She Come Bringing Me That Baby Girl* (1974), a Boston Globe–Horn Book Honor Book for illustration and Rosa Guy's *Mother Crocodile* (1981), winner of the Coretta Scott King Award for Illustration.

John Steptoe states that "one of my incentives for getting into writing children's books was the great and disastrous need for books that black children could honestly relate to. I ignorantly created precedents by writing such a book. I was amazed to find that no one had successfully written a book in the dialogue which black children speak."

STRIPLING, BARBARA K.

Barbara K. Stripling, Library Media Specialist 10–12, Fayetteville (Arkansas) High School, was appointed co-editor (with Judy M. Pitts) of *School Library Media Quarterly*, the journal of the American Association of School Librarians in July 1988. Stripling comes well equipped for the assignment. She earned a B.A. in 1968 in Speech and Drama, Teaching Credentials at the University of Arizona in 1969, an M.A. in 1973 in communication and theatre from the University of Colorado and an M.Ed. in Instructional Resources in 1981 from the University of Arkansas.

Born October 4, 1946 in Topeka, Kansas, Stripling has held her present post since 1978. Prior to coming to Fayetteville, she was Library Media Specialist K–12 with the Greenland (Arkansas) Public School, a teacher of English, drama, and media at Chapel Hill-Carrboro (North Carolina) Guy B. Phillips, Jr. High School, a production and editorial assistant at Barbre Productions, Denver (Colorado), and a teacher of English and drama at Pueblo (Colorado) East High School.

Barbara K. Stripling has broad experience as an editor and author: co–author of *Brainstorms and Blueprints: Teaching Library Research As a Thinking Process* (with Judy M. Pitts), Englewood, Colorado, Libraries Unlimited, 1988; contributor to *The Emerging School Library Media Program: Readings*, compiled by Frances Beck McDonald, Englewood, Colorado, Libraries Unlimited, 1988; co-editor of *Arkansas Libraries*; and author of numerous articles in such professional journals as *AAVA News and Views*, *The Book Report*, *School Learning Resources*, *Catholic Library World*, *The Clearing House*, and *Arkansas Libraries*. Stripling has conducted a number of workshops at local, regional, and national conferences.

TAYLOR, MILDRED D.

Mildred D. Taylor, award-winning author of five books for Dial Books For Young Readers, was presented with the 1988 Coretta Scott King Award for her latest novel, *The Friendship*. This book also received the 1988 Boston Globe-Horn Book Award for fiction.

Taylor was born in Jackson, Mississippi and reared in Toledo, Ohio. Events that she recalls from her family history are the basis for her four "Cassie Logan" books that include *The Friendship, Let the Circle Be Unbroken, Song of the Trees*, and *Roll of Thunder, Hear My Cry*, the 1977 winner of the Newbery Medal. *The Gold Cadillac*, winner of the 1988 Christopher Award, was based on her childhood trips back to Mississippi to visit relatives.

Taylor received her B.A. in Education from the University of Toledo in 1965. Upon graduation, she entered the Peace Corps and taught history and English in Ethiopia for two years. She returned to the United States in 1967 and recruited volunteers for the Peace Corps until she enrolled in the University of Colorado School of Journalism, where she received her M.A. in 1969. As Study Skills Coordinator for the Black Education Program at the University of Colorado, she helped students who needed special background in reading, composition, study skills, and mathematics. Later Taylor interned at an International House.

During that period, Mildred D. Taylor wrote in her free time and was encouraged by her friends to submit her manuscripts for publication. When *Song of the Trees* won a first prize in the Council on Interracial Books Competition in 1973, Dial Books accepted the manuscript and published the book in 1975. Since then, she has devoted most of her time to writing books and is currently working on her sixth novel. About her writing Mildred D. Taylor says, "I wanted to show the Black person as heroic. In my own school days, a class of Black people in the United States always caused me painful embarrassment. This would not have been so if that history had been presented truly, showing the accomplishments of the Black race both in Africa and in this hemisphere . . . It is my hope that to children who read my books, the Logans will provide those heros missing from the schoolbooks of my childhood, Black men, women, and children of whom they can be proud."

THOMAS, LUCILLE COLE

Lucille C. Thomas, school library media specialist, library educator, and ALA Executive Board member, received the Grolier Foundation Award for her unusual contribution to the stimulation and guidance of reading by children and young people. Currently serving as adjunct Professor, Queens College of the City of New York, Department of Library and Information Science, she has been since 1973 a Consultant for the Board of Examiners, New York City Board of Education; for Blue Cross/Blue Shield Special Events; for Weston Woods Institute; and for Silver Burdett, Gale Publishers, World Book, and Putnams. From 1977 to 1983 when she retired, Thomas was Assistant Director, School Library Media Services, Office of Library, Media and Telecommunications, New York City Board of Education. She has been a Librarian at the New York City Public Schools and at Brooklyn Public Library, and she has been Adjunct Professor, Pratt Institute, Graduate School of Library and Information Science (1972-79), and at St. John's University, Division of Library and Information Science (1970-71).

Born in Dunn, North Carolina, Lucille C. Thomas earned a B.A. in English and Social Studies from Bennett College, a M.A. in English from New York University, and a M.S. in Library Science from Columbia University. She is Trustee of the Citizen's Library Council of New York State, of the Schomburg Center for Research, of the Women's City Club of New York, and of the American Reading Council. Thomas is also Secretary, School Libraries Section, International Federation of Library Associations and Coordinator, UNESCO/IASL Gift Book Program to school libraries in developing countries. Her writings include a chapter in Jovian P. Lang's *Unequal Access to Information Resources*, Pierian, 1988; a chapter in *Library Media Annual* 1985; a chapter in E. J. Josey's and Kenneth E. Peoples, Jr.'s *Opportunities for Minorities in Librarianship*, Scarecrow, 1977; and various articles in professional journals.

The Lucille C. Thomas Library at the Jessie Owens School (P.S. 26 in New York City) is named in her honor, and in 1982, she was one of five persons selected to spend two weeks in Paris as part of a cultural Exchange Program as guest of the French Ministry of Culture.

TUCKER, BEN R.

Ben R. Tucker, Chief, Office for Descriptive Cataloging Policy, the Library of Congress, received the 1988 Margaret Mann Citation as the cataloger with outstanding professional achievement in the areas of cataloging and classification through the publication of significant professional literature and the introduction of new techniques of recognized importance in the past five years. He began his career in 1957 as a Bookmobile Librarian at the Birmingham (Alabama) Public Library. Tucker came to the Library of Congress in 1959 as a Special Recruit. He was soon promoted to Descriptive Cataloger, Romance Languages Unit, Descriptive Cataloging Division. Between 1962 and 1966, he was a Descriptive Cataloger and Assistant Section Head, South Asian Languages Section, from 1967 to 1975 Deputy Principal Cataloger, Descriptive Cataloging Division, from 1975 to 1979 Principal Cataloger, and in 1979, he was elevated to his current post.

Born September 8, 1935 in Clanton, Alabama, Ben R. Tucker has a 1956 A.B. from Birmingham-Southern (Alabama) College; he pursued graduate studies in classics at Washington University (Saint Louis, Missouri) in 1956 and 1957, and in 1959 the University of North Carolina conferred a M.S.L.S. upon him. He received the Library of Congress 1978 Superior Service Award; in 1979 he was awarded Honorary Life Membership by the Music Library Association; and in 1983, the Library of Congress honored him with the Incentive Award.

Ben R. Tucker revised chapter 12 on audiovisual media and special instructional materials for the 1974-75 *Anglo-American Cataloging Rules*, North American Text. He has written numerous articles on professional meetings for *Library of Congress Information Bulletin* and on descriptive cataloging for *Cataloging Service Bulletin*.

WEIBEL, KATHLEEN

Kathleen Weibel, library educator and administrator and authority on continuing education, received the ALA Equality Award for her outstanding contribution towards promoting equality between women and men in librarianship. Since 1984 she has served as Director of Libraries, Ohio Wesleyan University. From 1982 to 1983, she was at the Library Learning Center and Office of the Assistant Chancellor for Educational Services, University of Wisconsin-Parkside as Reference/Instruction Librarian and Educational Services Administrative Interior. Weibel's other posts include Lecturer, School of Library and Information Studies, University of Wisconsin-Madison (1981-82, 1978, and 1974-76); Continuing Education Consultant Bureau of Specialist Library Ser-

Biographies

Mildred D. Taylor

Lucille C. Thomas

Kathleen Weibel

vices, Library Development, New York State Library (1978–80); and Project Coordinator, Continuing Library Education Planning and Coordination Project, University of Wisconsin Extension.

Kathleen Weibel, born February 28, 1945 in New York City, earned a B.S. in English in 1967 from Chestnut Hill College (Philadelphia) and a M.L.S. in 1969 from The School of Library Service at Columbia University. Since 1970 she has conducted approximately 100 workshops, colloquia, training sessions, and presentations on such widely diverse subjects as "I Work in a Library, but I'm Not a Librarian," "Managing College Libraries," and "Career Development." She has broad writing and publishing experience as editor of the *Wisconsin Women Library Workers Newsletter*, editor of *The RASS Newsletter* (Reference and Adult Services Section, New York Library Association), and contributing editor of *Collection Building*. Weibel has written book reviews; and has compiled bibliographies; her articles have been published in professional journals; and she wrote several *ALA Yearbook* articles on "The Status of Women." Her monographs include *Directory of Wisconsin Continuing Library Media Education Producers and Programs* (1977), *Women in Librarianship 1876–1976*, with Kathleen Heim (1978), *Library Lit. 12: The Best of 1981*, with Bill Katz (1982).

Black Caucus of ALA

When the American Library Association held its 1970 Midwinter Meeting in Chicago, E. J. Josey's vision for the founding of the Black Caucus of the American Library Association (BCALA) was transformed into an historical event. BCALA, as the organization was to become known, was founded to respond to the library profession's problems concerning black people and to the development of librarianship, studies, reports, and critical issues related to blacks and libraries.

Conferences. Meetings coincide with the Annual and Midwinter meetings of ALA and are devoted to business as well as to programs on timely topics. The New Orleans conference in 1988, where standing-room-only was available, featured Dr. Norman Francis, president of Xavier University of Louisiana, who spoke on "Excellence and Equality in Education—Librarians as Effective Partners."

Structure. BCALAs various committees include, but may not be limited to, Constitution and Bylaws, Program, Membership, Nominating, ALA Relations, Publications, Recruitment and Professional Development, Budget/Audit, and Awards. Periodically, however, task forces and ad hoc committees may be established to address specific short-term issues. As early as 1978, North Carolina Central University's School of Library Science, now School of Library and Information Sciences, accepted responsibility for the collection and maintenance of the caucus' permanent archives. Since 1974 BCALA has published a quarterly newsletter that apprises members of the caucus' activities and provides a variety of information of interest to the profession and to members.

Social and Ethical Issues. BCALA historically has taken a position on issues that affect blacks and other minorities. The caucus supported the Black Employees Association of the Library of Congress in its struggle, which began in 1971, to eliminate discrimination in employment and promotion at the Library of Congress. In 1988, a federal judge ruled in favor of 300 black plaintiffs involved in the suit and awarded them collectively $805,000. In the 1970s, the caucus instituted an exchange of librarians between African and American libraries. During the 1979–80 year, the caucus sponsored a booklift to the West Indies College Library that produced more than 16,000 volumes and $11,000. In 1988, the caucus donated $1,000 to the "Mountain of Books" (for Africa) Project of the Philadelphia-based African-American Heritage, Inc. The New Orleans conference in 1988 brought to light an issue of concern to BCALAers. The caucus found that *Childcraft: The How and Why Library—Freedom Stories* excluded essays on the struggles of black Americans for freedom and equality in the United States. An ALA Council resolution called for the editors and publishers of *Freedom Stories* to publish immediately either a revised edition or an addenda to portray accurately the freedom struggles of Afro-Americans and called upon individual members to express their concern by letter to the publishers.

One of the primary and continuing concerns of the caucus is the recruitment of blacks for the profession. Fellowships for study and positions available are announced in each issue of the newsletter.

Awards and Honors. Recognition of outstanding contributions of BCALA members has historical significance to the association. In 1988 Spencer Shaw, University of Washington SLIS Emeritus Professor, received the BCALA Distinguished Service Award for outstanding contribution to library education and to the profession.

The Profession and the Caucus. The caucus successfully supported the candidacy of two of its members who became president of ALA. Clara

Courtesy Orange County (California) Public Library.

BLACK CAUCUS OF THE AMERICAN
LIBRARY ASSOCIATION

CHAIR (July, 1988–June 30, 1990):
Edith M. Fisher, Ethnic Studies Bibliographer, Central Library, University of San Diego, La Jolla, California 92024

VICE-CHAIR/CHAIR-ELECT/PROGRAM CHAIR:
John Tyson, University Librarian, Richmond, Virginia 23173

SECRETARY:
E. Paulette Smith-Epps, Assistant, Office of Branches, Atlanta-Fulton Public Library, One Margaret Mitchell Square, Atlanta, Georgia 30303

TREASURER:
Mary Bilbo, Head Teacher Librarian, University of Chicago Laboratory School, Chicago, Illinois 60637

PAST CHAIR:
Marva L. DeLoach, Assistant to the University Librarian, Stanford University Libraries, Stanford, California 94305

Membership (November 1988): 500+
Publications: *BCALA Newsletter*, George C. Grant, editor, P.O. Box 2654, Rollins College, Winter Park, Florida 32789; *BCALA Membership Directory*, George C. Grant, editor.

Stanton Jones, the Association's first black president, held that office in 1976–77. For his election to the ALA presidency in 1984 and for service to the profession, E. J. Josey was presented a commemorative volume of approximately 200 cards, letters, and telegrams of congratulations. The candidacy and election of black ALA members to the ALA Executive Board, Council, divisions, various officers, boards and committees extend BCALAs interests and activities. It also endorses and supports selected other minorities for candidacy and election to such positions and memberships.

Support Activities. The Louise Giles Minority Scholarship Fund regularly receives financial support from BCALA. Charitable contributions have extended to other areas and activities, including continuing support for the Schomburg Center for Research in Black Culture in New York.

IFLA and the Caucus. Black librarians and several BCALA members attended the 1984 IFLA conference held in Nairobi in August of that year. The Kenya Library Association (KLA) and BCALA joined forces in a Preconference on African and Afro-American concerns. For its work, BCALA received awards and commendations from KLA.

JESSIE CARNEY SMITH

Blind and Physically Handicapped, Library Service to

Trends. In 1988 network libraries serving blind and physically handicapped readers throughout the United States continued to implement automated circulation systems and increased the use of technology to make libraries more responsive to handicapped patrons. Of 56 regional libraries, 41 are now automated and of the remaining 15, six are in the process of implementing an automated circulation system.

The National Library Service for the Blind and Physically Handicapped (NLS) expanded its use of automation in two ways. First, NLS nearly completed its NLSNET, which ties the 56 cooperating regional libraries together in an electronic data interchange. Network librarians can now communicate with NLS, with NLS' vendors, and with one another through electronic mail. Second, NLS implemented a new copy-allotment system that provides network libraries greater flexibility in the quantity of braille and recorded books they order for their readers.

Against this background, a number of states realigned their patterns of service to blind and physically handicapped readers to reflect changing priorities and to make more efficient use of state funding. In Illinois, the 15 subregional libraries were consolidated to five. Maine and Wisconsin decided to close subregional libraries, preferring a more centralized approach through a single statewide service point. Florida and Virginia, on the other hand, have each opened new subregional libraries, further decentralizing service in these states.

Technology. A communication center that produces braille on demand from paper and electronic sources was established at NLS. Used primarily to produce braille for staff who are blind, the center is a working model of how computer technology can be utilized to provide braille materials quickly and easily. The center is built around an IBM PC–XT utilizing WordPerfect for word processing and Duxbury Braille translation software. The computer is equipped with a Vert Plus speech synthesizer for audio output, a Totec optical character reader for imputing print material, and a VersaBraille II Plus paperless braille device for direct braille input. An Index Braille printer provides braille output.

The Washington Regional Library, administered by the Seattle Public Library, modified its automated circulation system to provide access by a blind staff member who now functions as a reader advisor at the library. Utilizing equipment provided as a job accommodation project with outside funding, this staff member has demonstrated how an automated circulation system can be made accessible to blind staff and patrons. The project uses a PC with an enhanced PC Talking Program and a PC–VT which allows it to function as a system terminal, a VersaBraille II, a Theil braille embosser, and a DECtalk speech synthesizer.

The Alexandria, Virginia, subregional library has the capability of coverting material on computer diskette into braille. The process, which utilizes a PC and a Romeo brailler, was made possible through a cooperative effort with Alexandria's Department of Human Services.

National Library Service. NLS, in cooperation with a consumer organization, the National Federation of the Blind (NFB), produced John Bartlett's *Familiar Quotations* in braille. The 105 volumes list some 22,500 sayings, quotations, and excerpts. NLS has provided one copy to each network braille-lending library, and the book is available for purchase from NFB.

NLS also began a series of leisure activity books. *Birding: An Introduction to Ornithological Delights for Blind and Physically Handicapped Individuals*, available in large print, introduces handicapped individuals to the joys of birdwatching. A second book in the series, *Fishing*, was also produced.

A new NLS monograph, *Talking Books: Pioneering and Beyond*, researched and written by former NLS staffer Marilyn Majeska, describes the role of recordings for this national service. Beginning with the invention of the tinfoil phonograph, it traces the development of recording from the $33\frac{1}{3}$ records and playback equipment to the current four-track $^{15}/_{16}$ ips cassettes and voice indexing.

NLS developed a tactile map collection that includes 350 braille maps from around the world available on loan directly from NLS.

Blind individuals visiting Washington, D.C., may obtain a tactile map of the metro subway system from their congressional representative. The subway map is the latest addition to the Tactile Capitol Project, funded by the Department of Education.

International. NLS has announced a world literature book club. The club, scheduled to run for two years on a trial basis, offers participants cassette books from other cooperating English-speaking countries such as Australia, Canada, Great Britain, Ireland, New Zealand, and South Africa.

The Royal National Institute for the Blind (RNIB), in a joint effort with the Inner-London Education Authority, has begun producing children's books with braille text on plastic laid over the print pages. Called clear-vision books, these books are part of RNIB's campaign to increase braille fluency in Great Britain.

The National Council for the Blind in Ireland (NCBI) moved into new national headquarters that include two recording studios, one for four-track talking books and one for magazines.

Outreach. NLS tested a pilot public relations campaign designed to alert senior citizens to the availability of Talking Book service. Customized media products including radio and television spots, billboard copy, posters for bus and subway, and localized articles for magazines and newspapers, were provided to six network libraries throughout the country.

The regional library administered by the Cleveland Public Library initiated a children's book club. Children receive a newsletter listing the selection of the month and an alternative title, and featuring guest columns by club members. The Cleveland Society for the Blind records these titles especially for the book club.

The Tennessee Regional Library arranged to have large-print copies of the *Concise Columbia Encyclopedia* and the *Merriam-Webster Dictionary* placed in each of Tennessee's county libraries.

The number of blind and physically handicapped individuals using library services continues to increase gradually. NLS and the network libraries are incorporating technology to streamline library service, to increase access for blind individuals for both employment and access to the collections in a non-print format and to expand the horizons of these individuals by offering additional and varied types of materials not otherwise available.

STEPHEN PRINE, JR.

Bookselling

General Economic Conditions. For the second consecutive year, most booksellers reported substantial increases in sales over the same period the year before. There continued to be "soft" spots around the country, especially in areas where economies had been dependent upon oil.

According to *Trends*, the annual publication produced by the Book Industry Study Group, market share of consumer expenditures on books in bookstores continues to increase. The rate is a little more than 1 percent a year. If this trend continues by 1990 or 1991, more than half of the books bought by consumers will have been bought in bookstores.

There are several theories about why this is happening. The most obvious is the ever-increasing number of bookstores in the United States, while the number of book clubs, schools, and libraries remains relatively fixed. During 1987 and 1988, an average of more than 400 people belonged to ABA in the prospective member category—that is, they intended to invest money in opening a bookstore of their own in the near future. Booksellers and publishers are promoting books and stores extensively, and advertising has picked up as a number of private, regional, and national catalogs, inserts, and newsletters now reach tens of millions of people annually. The ABA is studying how to generically heighten public awareness of books and bookstores, while booksellers continue to build, expand, and renovate their bookstore selling space at a steady pace.

It is estimated that about 20 percent of the bookstores that are members of the ABA have some form of computerized management information system that allows booksellers to have a better knowledge of what is selling and how frequently. This technology, when combined with databases on CD-ROM, electronic ordering, and more efficient wholesalers, likely will have an immediately positive impact on sales.

The 1988 Convention and Trade Show. The annual convention and trade show took place from May 28 to 31 in Anaheim, California. More than 25,000 people attended the event, which occupied more than 385,000 square feet to accommodate nearly 2,000 exhibits from more than 1,00 publishers. Innovations included the addition of reading rooms to the program where authors, such as Raymond Carver, Richard Ford, T. Coraghessan Boyle, Ishmael Reed, and Alice McDermott, read from their works in a place apart from the hectic pace of the convention floor. Among the many authors and celebrities who also appeared to talk about their work were Maurice Sendak, Judy Blume, William Kennedy, Clyde Edgerton, Carolyn Chute, David Brinkley, Lady Bird Johnson, Natan Scharansky, and Jonathon Kozol.

Censorship and First Amendment Concerns. The Supreme Court of the United States sent *Virginia v. ABA* (a case dealing with minor's access

> **AMERICAN BOOKSELLERS ASSOCIATION**
>
> PRESIDENT
> **J. Rhett Jackson,** The Happy Bookseller, Columbia, South Carolina
>
> VICE-PRESIDENT:
> **Kim Browning,** Dodds Bookshop, Long Beach, California
>
> SECRETARY:
> **Andy Ross,** Cody's Books, Berkeley, California
>
> TREASURER:
> **A. David Schwartz,** Harry W. Bookshops, 5623 North Lake Drive, Milwaukee, Wisconsin 53217
>
> EXECUTIVE DIRECTOR:
> **Bernard E. Rath**
>
> ANNUAL MEETING:
> June 3–6, 1989, Washington, D.C.; June 2–5, 1990, Las Vegas, Nevada.
>
> HEADQUARTERS:
> 137 W. 25th Street, New York 10001, 212-463-8450
>
> Membership (March 1988): 6,689 (4,138 main stores, 675 branches, 57 foreign, 37 institutional, 448 provisional, 252 individual, 1,082 associate)

legislation) back to the Virginia State Court. The Court was asked to evaluate the breadth of restrictions on minors' ability to view books deemed by the state to be harmful to them and the effect of the legislation on legitimate bookstores seeking to comply with the ordinance. When the Court concluded that the effect would be minimal, the U.S. Supreme Court told the state court to reconsider its initial decision in favor of ABA, given the changed circumstances.

ABA's members, through ABA's membership in both the Media Coalition and Americans for Constitutional Freedom (ACF), fought a drawn-out and emotional battle against one part of the Child Pornography and Obscenity Enforcement Act. The act passed with some minor modifications to protect legitimate booksellers from potential local law enforcement abuse and vigilantism, but for the most part is a serious setback to First Amendment advocates. It was passed virtually unnoticed as part of a sweeping drug enforcement bill, and it is expected that the new law will be challenged almost immediately as to the constitutionality of many of its parts. The act's primary goal seems to have been to equate dealing in pornography and/or obscenity with racketeering and to apply forfeiture provisions used in organized crime and drug laws to people and businesses that sell books.

ABA Membership. At the end of November 1988, full voting membership of the ABA stood at 4,280 businesses and 715 branches. All categories of membership, including non-voting, totaled 7,011.

BERNARD E. RATH

Buildings

Nineteen-eighty-eight brought progress on several major library building projects in the country. Two of the largest were new public library buildings planned for Chicago and Los Angeles.

Chicago Public Library (CPL) awarded the commission to build a new 500,000 net square foot central library to the SEBUS Group, following an international design competition. Ground was broken for the $140,000,000 building on October 13. This marked an important step toward resolving the long-standing problem of where and how to house the CPL central library, an issue that has faced Chicago Public since 1976 when the old central library was refurbished into the CPL Cultural Center and the main collections of the central library were moved into temporary storage.

The winning design was among five submitted in the competition. The SEBUS group represents a combination of design firms and developers, including Hammond Beeby & Babka, Inc. and Schal Associates. Construction on the new library, to be named the Harold Washington Library Center in honor of the late mayor, is scheduled to be completed in 1991.

Planning for an expanded main library for the Los Angeles Public Library (LAPL) was underway in 1986 when it was twice vandalized by major fires. The main library has been closed since that time, with plans proceeding simultaneously on temporary facilities and the renovation and expansion of the 1926 Bertam Goohue main library. A third fire (this one accidental) struck the main library in October 1988. No structural damage was done, and work on the main library was not expected to be delayed.

The temporary facility for the LAPL main library was expected to open in March 1989. At the same time, bids were to be opened for the construction of the expanded main library. The expansion will provide more than 360,000 net square feet to the main library; the project budget is $150,000,000. The building is expected to be finished in mid-1992.

A fire also figured in the destruction of more than 400,000 volumes at the National Academy of Sciences of the USSR Library in Leningrad. The fire broke out on February 14, evidently starting in the newspaper room, and burned for 19 hours. Of the 12,500,000 items in the library, 3,500,000 suffered water damage, 2,000,000 suffered heat and smoke damage, and 400,000 were destroyed.

Funding Library Construction. State funding for library construction was provided by a number of states, including Georgia and Illinois. Massachusetts passed a major library initiative that authorized, among other things, $35,000,000 for new library construction and renovation. Rhode Island voted just under $1,200,000 for public library construction. California authorized the issuance of $75,000,000 in state bonds to finance repair, renovation, and construction projects. New York proposed increased state funding for libraries, including $4,000,000 for library construction. Connecticut also advanced $4,000,000 for library construction.

Alternative funding sources were sought by a number of libraries. One such creative financing package was assembled in Sacramento, California, where a 140,000 square foot facility will also include a 6,000 square foot galleria containing a library bookstore and a cafe. Funding sources for

Buildings

On October 13, 1988, The Chicago Public Library held a festive groundbreaking ceremony for the new $144,000,000 Harold Washington Library Center, shown here in model. The neo-classical style and technologically advanced interior systems are the result of a highly-visible Design/Build Competition, won by the SEBUS Group. Scheduled for completion by March 1991, the Harold Washington Library Center will be the largest state-of-the-art public library in the country.

Arizona State University (Phoenix) Library atrium. [ASU Media Production]

a new building for the Johnson County Library (Buffalo, Wyoming) included a $250,000 grant from the state Farm Loan Board, a county appropriation, sales tax, the library's building reserve fund, and an LSCA Title II grant.

LSCA Title II continued to provide a boost to library construction. The FY1988 final allocation was $22,143,100, excluding carryover funding from previous years. States and localities were required to match those funds with at least $22,323,859. In practice, the state and local match has been much greater than the minimum required match.

Preliminary figures compiled on LSCA Title II projects for FY1987 indicated that at least 101 public library construction projects were completed as of December 5, 1988; another 25 LSCA Title II projects funded from the FY1988 allocation had been completed by that same date.

Trends/Notable Projects. Trends in library construction nationwide suggested at least a temporary leveling off in the number of public library projects; academic library projects experienced a notable increase over the past year. The annual buildings issue of *Library Journal* reported 98 new public library building projects and 140 additions, renovations, and remodelings for FY1988 (compared with FY1987's 101 new buildings and 149 additions, renovations, and remodelings). Total floor space added in 1988 projects was just under 2,700,000 square feet, down almost 10 percent from FY1987, but still significantly higher than the 1,000,000 square feet added five years earlier. There were 47 new academic library buildings reported to *Library Journal* for FY1988, a 42 percent increase over the previous year. The gross area of these 47 academic library building projects exceeded 2,800,000 square feet.

State library buildings were one particular focus of activity in 1988. The Library of Michigan moved into its new 312,000 square foot facility in the fall. The building will house the state library and museum, its collections, as well as the consulting staff. The design features limestone exterior walls and a central courtyard with copper-clad inner walls.

Work began in late 1987 on a new state library building for Illinois in Springfield. The 175,000 square foot structure will more than double the space now available in the Centennial Building. The new library located adjacent to the State Capitol and the Supreme Court Building, derives its design from the Beaux–Arts style of those neighboring structures.

The California State Library selected The Architects Collaborative, Inc. to manage the planning and development of the State Library Annex. The library's budget for FY1988–89 provides funding for design development, moving this project forward after a hiatus of three years.

Library construction in the South seems to be particularly productive. Florida libraries report a number of construction projects. The Pasco County Library System, headquartered in New Port Richie, Florida, announced a capital program that will build six new libraries at a cost of $10,000,000. Voters approved this program in a 1986 referendum. New libraries or branches were under construction for the Cape Canaveral Florida Public Library, the DeLand Area Library (Volusia County, Florida), Tampa–Hillsborough County (Florida) Public Library, the Collier County (Florida) Library, and the DeLand Area Library (Volusia County, Florida). The Volusia County Library Center also opened a new "International Children's Library and Discovery Center." This addition, more than three times the size of the original children's room, teaches children about foreign cultures through books, other library materials, and programs.

In New Mexico, an $11,000,000 addition to the library at New Mexico State University at Las Cruces was authorized. Voters in Phoenix approved a referendum for $55,000,000 to improve the city's libraries, with $44,000,000 earmarked for a new main library, still to be designed, and the balance will fund three new branches and expand a fourth. The main library will double in size, from 146,000 square feet to 300,000 square feet.

Oxnard (California) Public Library began work on an $11,000,000 72,000 square foot building, and a 4,000 square foot branch. The branch will be part of a neighborhood center that includes day-care facilities, an activity center for seniors and teens, and a small police office.

San Diego (California) Public Library continued to implement a long-range capital plan that has seen the construction of three new branches and the expansion of two others since 1984. Among the notable aspects of the implementation: in consecutive years, library branches received design awards from the local chapter of the AIA, first for their Otay Mesa Branch (a 10,000 square foot structure with a capacity of 50,000 volumes), then for their Linda Vista Branch (also 10,000 square feet, including two outdoor reading patios and a community meeting room). Future plans include a new LaJolla Branch and a new Scripps Ranch Branch, each to be 10,000 square feet in size.

A second compact storage building was opened by the University of California. Like the original, it is intended to house low-use material. The temperature is maintained at 65 degrees

Bibliotheca Alexandrina

The fame of Alexandria in the ancient world rested to a large extent on the great library believed to have been founded by Ptolemy I Soter in the likeness of Aristotle's library in Athens. It was originally conceived not as a library, but as a research center known as the temple of the Muses, or museum, that was to contain the collected wisdom and knowledge of the world at that time. With its holdings built up (within about two generations of its founding) to over half a million manuscripts, the library became a major center of science and art, and an intellectual meeting place for scholars of Mediterranean and Western Asian cultures. A second, subsidiary library (the daughter library) had to be built to house this large collection that comprised the world's first systematic storehouse of knowledge. The only surviving structure of the legendary Library is a dark cellar of the Serabium, the Library's annex, once a temple and later a sanctuary dedicated to knowledge.

The Greek kings of Egypt who succeeded Alexander were serious about learning. For centuries, they supported research and maintained in the library a working environment for the best minds of the age. It contained ten large research halls, each devoted to a separate subject; fountains and colonnades; botanical gardens; a zoo; dissecting rooms; an observatory; and a great dining hall where, at leisure, the great discussion of ideas was conducted.

Built on the side of the museum, the great library also served as a publications office. It had a catalog of all the works it possessed, an estimated 500,000 listed and classified manuscripts. It also enjoyed legal deposit rights and was entitled to make a copy of every book that entered the country or was reported on ships anchored in the harbor.

The New Bibliotheca Alexandrina. The New Alexandrian Library will be a public research library with holdings designed to enrich the cultural heritage of Egypt, the Mediterranean region, Africa, and the Arab world. The Library will provide a link to the world's major research libraries utilizing all modern forms of technology for the transfer and dissemination of information. Visitors and users of the Library will find not only the collections of books and manuscripts but also audiovisual and electronic media. When the Library opens in 1995, expectations are that there will be nearly 200,000 titles available, the ultimate target being 4,000,000 to 5,000,000 titles, with the possibility of an extension to 8,000,000 volumes.

On June 26, 1988, President Hosni Mubarak of Egypt laid the cornerstone on the 60,000 square meters allocated for the Library building. The site lies alongside the University of Alexandria campus and overlooks the Mediterranean sea along a substantial portion of its northern edge. The intention is to extend this new development into the peninsula that stretches out to the sea on the other side of the Corniche toward the old Mameluke citadel of Qait Bay. The citadel was built in 1480 on the site of the lighthouse which was one of the seven wonders of the world. From its beginning, the project has received the international support of UNESCO and the United Nations Development Program (UNDP), which have thus become co-promoters. UNESCO has launched an international appeal for this exceptional project in order to meet the cost of both the building itself and the collection.

Objectives of the Project. The main development objective of the New Alexandrian Library (Bibliotheca Alexandrina) is to establish a seat of learning with a public research library at its core, with particular attention given to branches of learning that relate directly to the historical, geographical, and cultural background of Alexandria, the Middle East, and the Mediterranean. It is anticipated that the Library will gradually emerge as the repository of all valuable materials on the history and culture of the region. It will also provide a safe place for valuable manuscripts and rare books gathered from other libraries in Egypt where environmental conditions are contributing to the rapid deterioration of these types of materials.

Architectural Competition. Because of the international interest the Library has generated, UNESCO and the government of Egypt have agreed to launch an international architectural competition for this building project. With the assistance of the International Union of Architects (IUA), a panel of jurors has been named to select the design and architect to be responsible for putting the idea into effect.

A total of U.S. $200,000 will be awarded as follows to the entrants submitting prizewinning designs: First prize: $60,000; Second prize: $35,000; Third prize: $25,000. The remaining $80,000 will be divided among the entrants who are awarded a Special Mention.

The International School of Information Studies. In reviving the long-established and glorified tradition of librarianship in the ancient civilization, the New Alexandrian Library will contain an autonomous graduate school of information studies, which will confer graduate degrees including the doctorate in various aspects of information and communication sciences.

Cost Estimates of the Project. On the basis of the feasibility studies conducted by UNESCO experts, it is estimated that the project will cost approximately $160,000,000, distributed as follows: $60,000,000 for construction; $40,000,000 for the purchase of books and other types of library materials, of which an initial amount of $12,000,000 will be needed to assemble the first collections; $1,000,000 for computerization of the Library; $3,000,000 for the establishment of the International School of Information Studies and staff training; $6,500,000 for the annual operating costs of the Library, to be paid from local resources and endowments.

Contributions to the project have already been made in two categories: $60,000,000 (the estimated value of the site), and $20,000,000 for the completed international conference center near the site, considered part of the facility.

The government of Egypt plans to open the Library in 1995 with 200,000 items and an adequate number of trained staff to meet operational requirements. A high-level national steering committee has been established under the chairmanship of the Minister of Education, by virtue of decree numbers 1319 and 1666 of 1987. Its membership includes the Ministers of Information, Culture, Tourism, the Governor of Alexandria, the President of the University of Alexandria, and two senior members of the University connected with library development. The development of the Library also figures in the Egyptian national Five-Year Development Plan.

References
1. Aman, Mohammed M. *Revival of the Ancient Alexandrian Library: A Study of Manpower Needs and Development and Establishment of a School of International Information Studies.* UNESCO, 1987.
2. Clavel, Jean-Pierre and Jacques Tocatlian. *Feasibility Study for the Revival of the Ancient Library of Alexandria: First Phase.* Paris, 1987.
3. Jackson, Sydney. "Alexandrian Library," in *ALA World Encyclopedia of Library and Information Services*, Chicago: ALA, 1980. p.32–33.
4. Parsons, Edward Alexander. *The Alexandrian Library: Glory of the Helenic World.* Amsterdam: Elsevier Press, 1952.
5. UNESCO. *Bibliotheca Alexandrina: Concours International d'Architecture/International Architectural Competition.* Paris, 1988.
6. UNESCO. *Bibliotheca Alexandrina: The Revival of the First Universal Library.* Paris, 1988.

MOHAMMED M. AMAN

---

and the relative humidity at 50 percent for material requiring special environmental conditions. The capacity of the structure is 3,500,000 volumes, with two planned additions that will take the total to 11,000,000 volumes. The campuses at Irvine, Los Angeles, Riverside, San Diego, and Santa Barbara are among the participants in this project.

Construction began on a new stack addition for the University of Wisconsin–Madison during 1988. This project will add 123,000 gross square feet at a cost of $44,900,000. Four of the eight floors are being designed for compact shelving. The addition will increase the capacity of the library by more than 2,300,000 volumes. A debate arose early in construction when it was discovered that part of the view of the State Capitol from Bascom Hill (a traditional symbolic link between the university and the legislature) would be obscured by the addition. The State Building Commission, however, voted to continue with the project as designed.

William and Mary College (Williamsburg, Virginia) celebrated its 295th anniversary with the dedication of a $3,000,000 addition to its Earl Gregg Swan Library.

The Cleveland (Ohio) Public Library announced a long-range capital plan that will update the central library's mechanical systems, convert long runs of periodical backfiles to optical disc formats, and improve electronic access to the library's holdings. A total of $67,500,000 is proposed for this project, including $46,000,000 for construction.

Boulder (Colorado) Public Library won approval for a $14,000,000 capital project including an expansion of the central building and construction of two new branches. The vote at referendum was 62 percent in favor of the library. The public library in Charlotte and Mecklenburg County, North Carolina likewise won voter approval of $2,900,000 for a new regional library. The 20,000 square foot building will provide space for 150,000 books, as well as other services.

LAMA Building and Equipment Section. The LAMA Building and Equipment Section had an active year in 1988. At the Annual conference in New Orleans the section sponsored a program titled "How to Get Your Money's Worth: A Client's Guide To Library Building Consultation." Featured speakers were Lee Brawner and David Kaser, who discussed the role of library building consultants in planning expanded facilities and the types of specialized knowledge and experience that a building consultant can bring to a project. Following their presentations, the audience divided into small groups to discuss working with building consultants in academic library settings and public library settings. These sessions were led by Kaser and Irene Hoadley (academic libraries) and Brawner and Betty Gay (public libraries).

Meetings of the Facilities Planning Discussion Group at the Midwinter and Annual conferences, chaired by Donald Kelsey, were well attended demonstrating that the discussion group has grown into a vital forum for exchanging information among librarians engaged in planning expanded facilities. The Architecture for Public Libraries Committee, chaired by Bill Sannwald, produced *Checklist of Library Building Design Considerations*. The Ad Hoc Committee on Physical Space Requirements for Libraries continued its efforts to develop nationally-recognized standards for library space needs.

ANDERS C. DAHLGREN

Canadian Library Association

Finances. Fiscal recovery, intellectual freedom and copyright legislation, and the development of improved services to members were the main issues driving the Canadian Library Association during 1988.

After suffering a disappointing fiscal year 1987 deficit of $350,000 (resulting from a combination of over-optimistic revenue projections, a substantial loss on Black Monday, and lack of timely and useful management accounting reports) all association units were forced to examine their priorities and to function through 1988 with severely reduced budgets. Spending was limited to activities that were revenue-producing and a new, more bottom line–oriented philosophy of service was established.

At the CLA Annual General Meeting in June in Halifax, Nova Scotia, the membership overwhelmingly supported a new dues schedule representing a staggered fee increase of 30 percent over a three-year period. Fiscal measures put in place for 1988 produced the desired results: CLA finished the year on target with its financial plan, membership revenue was up and a new fully automated financial reporting system was in place.

Legislative Issues

Intellectual Freedom. The Federal Government introduced its now infamous Bill C-54 on pornography May 5, 1987 (see *ALA Yearbook 1988*). After strong opposition from CLA and individual library boards across the country, Bill C-54 died on the order paper in the fall of 1988, when Parliament was dissolved for the federal election held on November 21. CLA presented its first intellectual freedom award to Les Fowlie and the Board of the Toronto Public Library for their strong stand against the bill. Toronto Public Library closed nearly all its branches for a day of protest and study sessions, gaining nationwide media attention for the detrimental effects of the bill on libraries.

In the fall of 1988 CLA appointed a Task Force chaired by Sheila Laidlaw, University of New Brunswick, to study the terms of reference of CLA's Intellectual Freedom Fund and to make recommendations about the most appropriate use of the fund. CLA has been active recently on related matters such as the importation of hate literature and censorship of "revisionist" history materials.

Copyright. After much debate and frequent legislative intervention by CLA, the first phase of Canada's copyright law amendments, Bill C-60, was passed in June. Phase one provides the enabling legislation for formation of copyright "collectives" in Canada, organizations similar to the U.S. Copyright Clearance Centre. CLA argued against the law's lack of a definition of fair dealing and warned against the possibility of the outflow of royalties for photocopying to countries such as the United States where, in certain circumstances, single copies of periodical articles are exempt from royalty payments. While the government argued that exemptions for libraries would appear in phase 2 in the fall of 1988, CLA feared that an election call would delay their introduction, leaving the library community working with half a bill. After some delays in the Senate, Bill C-60 passed, with promises from the government for consultation with CLA before phase 2 was introduced. CLA's fears about further delays were confirmed when the election was called. Introduction of phase 2 is not expected until some time in 1989.

Meanwhile, Canada's new English-language photocopy collective hired an executive director, and in the process of formation, has solicited copyright owners for membership.

Postal Subsidies. When the federal government threatened to eliminate postal subsidies for the library book rate, CLA went into action with a mail campaign from librarians across the country who pointed out to government officials the value of the library book rate for interlibrary loan and service to remote areas. As a result of this effort, the Minister of Communications announced in the spring that the library book rate would remain in place for another five years.

Member Services. Despite fiscal restraint during 1988, CLA beefed up its legislative activities and expanded membership services by arranging for online connect discounts for members on Wilsonline and Orbit in addition to discounts on Dialog offered in 1987. Through CLA's official travel agency, airline and car rental discounts have also been negotiated. An insurance package has been developed for introduction in 1989.

At its meeting of November 18, 1988, CLA Council enthusiastically endorsed the concept of CLA winter meetings to replace the fall Council meeting, and to be held in centers across the country that cannot host annual conferences. Beginning with winter 1990 CLA will hold its Winter Board, Council and Divisional executive meetings in a location outside of Ottawa. Meeting sites will alternate from East to West, depending on the location of the June annual conference. It is expected that a CLA presence in these areas will encourage more grassroots par-

---

CANADIAN LIBRARY ASSOCIATION

PRESIDENT (June 1988–June 1989):
Vivienne Monty, Head, Government and Business Library, York University, Downsview, Ontario

FIRST VICE-PRESIDENT/PRESIDENT-ELECT:
Beth Barlou, Head, Information Services, Saskatoon Public Library, Saskatoon, Saskatchewan

SECOND VICE-PRESIDENT:
Jean Dirksen, Head, Adult Services, Regina Public Library, Regina, Saskatchewan

EXECUTIVE DIRECTOR:
Jane Cooney

Membership (June 30, 1988): 4,500
Headquarters: 200 Elgin Street, Ottawa, Ontario K2P 1L5

Canadian Report

ticipation and provide an opportunity for more exchange among various units of CLA.

1988 Conference. More than 1,200 delegates attended CLA's 42nd annual conference in Halifax, Nova Scotia, June 16–20. Programming centered around the theme "Libraries in the Information Marketplace." The keynote speaker was Dian Cohen, a popular Canadian economics broadcaster who focused on the globalization of business and the movement from an industrial to an information economy. She warned the audience that the library community no longer has a monopoly on information.

Staff Changes. Two senior staff appointments were made in 1988. Ed Reed, CGA, was named Director of Finance and Administration in July and Barbara Zatlokal was appointed Director of Publishing in December.

JANE COONEY

Canadian Report

Legislative Issues. Federal legislation involving postal subsidies, copyright and pornography were the biggest issues on the Canadian library scene during the past year. The federal government passed phase one of Bill C-60 dealing with copyright in spite of strong representation by the Canadian Library Association, provincial associations, and other interested groups. Libraries are still concerned with the "fair dealing clauses," and how funds will be generated to pay reprography collectives. On the positive side, CLA will be consulted during phase two of the legislation. The library community is united in its stand for "single copy exemption" for the purposes of private study and research. There is opposition to this exemption by creators who are not happy with the "private study" clause. Although phase two has not been introduced, due to the fall federal election, reprography collectives are being established, and licensing agreements are being negotiated between authors and institutions such as provincial departments of education.

Edmonton Public Library. The Edmonton Public Library Board (Alberta) was attacked by a number of groups for its collection of revisionist materials, in particular material published by the Institute for Historic Review relating to the Holocaust. The EPS Board held three hearings at which eight groups submitted briefs. The hearings at times turned into political campaigning. Many discussions focussed on whether the library was collecting illegal material or whether it was dealing with a censorship issue. The final report of the Board listed ten recommendations in which current collection policies, cataloguing standards and intellectual freedom statements were maintained. The Board recommended staff training programs as well as public education programs on the role of the public library.

Funding Services. A controversial and complex financial arrangement was finalized this year between Canada Trust and the University of Ottawa. The university sold its library to Canada Trust for $38,000,000 then leased it back. This provided the university with much-needed funds which were distributed to its various departments. Canada Trust received a tax break because of the 100 percent depreciation of the collection in its first year. The university purchased a $35,000,000 annuity which allows it to buy back its own collection for 50 percent of its value in the 17th year of the 19-year lease. Shortly after the arrangement were finalized Ontario Provincial Treasurer, Robert Nixon, placed a moratorium on this "sale/leaseback" practice in the belief that it was inappropriate for publicly funded institutions to sell off their facilities. Reactions of librarians across the country varied: Some viewed leasebacks as an excellent means of generating much-needed funding, while others felt it was unethical.

Bill C-54, introduced in 1987 died a slow death, primarily due to efforts of civil libertarians, librarians, artists, and others worried about the stringent definition of pornography. Toronto Public Library closed 27 of 31 branches in December 1987 to protest the legislation and held a public information session to discuss concerns about this bill. Lew Fowlie, Chief Librarian at Toronto Public Library, was awarded CLA's first Intellectual Freedom Award for bringing the legislation to the attention of the public at large.

The Canadian Association of Research Libraries recently concluded a study that revealed that between 1978–88 libraries cancelled subscriptions valued at $4,200,000 and anticipate an additional $1,000,000 in cancellations.

The Ontario Library Association and the Ministry of Culture and communications have initiated an aggressive public library strategic planning process. "Planning Change Together—A strategic plan for Ontario Public Libraries" involves the entire library community.

The British Columbia's government report: "New Approaches: Ministerial Task Force on Public Libraries" reviewed the provision and delivery of service in British Columbia, in relation to the amount of provincial funding given to libraries.

Automation. Fraser Valley Regional Library System (British Columbia) continued with GEAC plans to link its 22 branches. Richmond Public Library (British Columbia) is upgrading its CLSI system. North Vancouver City Library (British Columbia) has initiated negotiations with CLSI. The Universite de Moncton Bibliotheque Champlain (New Brunswick) has purchased GEAC's System 9000. Parkland Regional Library (Manitoba) has the first online catalogue in public libraries in Manitoba; OCELOT will be used in all 16 branches.

Logo for Calgary, Alberta, Canada's October 1988 Association-Fest.

The University of Toronto and UTLAS celebrated the official implementation of the T/SERIES 50 Library System hardware and software designed by UTLAS for online circulation, cataloguing and networking.

CD-ROM is catching on across the country particularly in learning resource centres of two-year colleges.

Literacy. With 1990 looming as the International Year of Literacy, Prime Minister Brian Mulroney made a surprise announcement that $110,000,000 will be devoted to literacy projects over the next five years. Libraries are submitting proposals to ensure that they are at the forefront of the need to read campaign.

"READ UP ON IT," which premiered during the Seoul Olympics continues on selected programmes throughout the year. The book and Periodical Development Council's "Catalogue to Reader." It follows 50 English language Canadian trade books from publication to reviews to acquisitions by libraries.

Facilities. Vancouver Public Library survived a mini flood during the summer. A broken pipe caused water to rain down on some 4,000 books housed in basement storage. Quick action on the part of the staff and chief librarian Madge Aalto resulted in minimal damage.

Canadian Association of Small University Libraries, CASUL, is a new national library director's association organized by librarians not large enough to belong to CARL, Canadian Association of Research Libraries. There is a potential membership of 50-70 libraries. An Association-fest was sponsored by the Calgary Public Library and the University of Calgary Libraries to promote library associations. Two public libraries, Edmonton and Saskatoon, celebrated 75th anniversaries in 1988.

Facilities. The Moncton Public Library (New Brunswick), moved into its spacious new building with no increase in staff. Nepean Public Library (Ontario) moved into its new 30,000-square-foot central library in the new civic centre. Mississauga Public Library (Ontario) is planning a 150,000-square-foot building that will house a 200-seat theatre, a restaurant and patio, glass elevators and underground parking. Bibliothèque de St. Boniface (Manitoba), was opened by Winnipeg Mayor Bill Norrie. It is the only French language library in Western Canada. West Vancouver Library (British Columbia), is planning a $5,000,000 expansion. The Richmond Public Library (British Columbia), received approval on a referendum for $8,000,000 for an expansion that will include an art gallery, museum, and art centre.

The Faculty of Library Science, University of Alberta, is now called The Faculty of Library and Information Studies. Lakehead University (Ontario) announced a new undergraduate Bachelor of Arts degree in Library and Information Studies. The school was formerly known as the School of Library Technology. Faculty of Library and Information Science, University of Toronto, announced a Master of Information Science program, the first of its kind in Canada. The program's philosophy combines a foundation in computer and communication technology with an approach to computer-based information problems from the user's perspective. The University of King's College (Nova Scotia) is currently spread over three locations in one building and a fourth location in a second building, which results in paging for 90 percent of the collection. A new two-story building is in the planning stages; the final design will depend on the amount of money raised for the building fund.

Peter Freeman, Chief Librarian, University of Alberta Libraries, inspects a display of new science and technology journals deemed too expensive to order. [Randy Reichardt]

Appointments and Retirements. Madge Aalto was appointed Chief Librarian at Victoria (British Columbia) Public Library; Margaret Beckman was awarded the Honourary Doctor of Laws degree from the University of Waterloo; Sheila Bertram was appointed Dean, Faculty of Library and Information Studies, University of Alberta; Jean de Temple retired after 27 years as Assistant Director of Ottawa Public Library. de Temple was the head of OPL's Carlingwood Branch, the first branch in Canada to be located in a shopping mall; Gwenneth Evans, Director, External Relations, National Library of Canada, was appointed to ALA's Committee on Accreditation; Barbara Greeniaus was appointed Director, Library Services Branch, British Columbia; Frances Groen was elected President of the Medical Library Association. She is Life Sciences Librarian, Mcgill University (Quebec); Dean Halliwell retired as Chief Librarian, University of Victoria, after 28 years. He is a past president of British Columbia Library Association, Canadian Association of College and University Librarians, and the Canadian Library Association. Halliwell served two terms on the ALA Council. He was named University Librarian Emeritus. Judith Head was appointed Chief Librarian University College of Cape Breton, University of Sydney, Nova Scotia; Marjorie Kennedy was named to Library Education Honor Role of ALA, the only Canadian to be so recognized; Jean MacGregor retired from being chief, CISTI Document Delivery and Lending Service. MacGregor developed the service into what has become the largest document delivery operation in North America. Marnie Swanson was appointed Chief Librarian, University of Victoria, Victoria, British Columbia; Lee Teal was appointed Chief Librarian, Greater Victoria

(British Columbia) Public Library; Miriam Tees retired from associate professor McGill Graduate School of Library and Information Studies. An entrance scholarship has been established in her name; M. Eileen Travis received an honourary doctorate degree in Social Sciences from Université de Moncton, New Brunswick; and Morris Zbar was appointed Director, Libraries and Community Information Branch, Ministry of Culture and Communications. He served eight years as a trustee with the North York Public Library (Ontario) and was twice elected chair of the board.

In Memoriam. Nancy Bennett, Vice-President of the Canadian Library Trustees Association, was well-known in British Columbia libraries and with Canadian Library trustees.

Laurent G. Denis, Professor, University of Toronto, Faculty of Library and Information Science, was the first French Canadian to receive a Ph.D. in library science.

TERRI TOMCHYSHYN

Cataloging and Classification

Every few years cataloging goes through a special kind of upheaval as major codes and working tools are revised and reissued, and other new tools become available. The publication of the *Anglo-American Cataloging Rules, Second Edition (AACR2)*, in 1978 began the previous cycle. The publication of its 1988 revision began another.

Codes, Standards, Resources. The *Anglo American Cataloging Rules Second Edition, 1988 Revision* was carefully named to make its non-revolutionary nature clear. Its publication was welcomed with pleasure by most catalogers, and excited none of the fear and denunciation from administrators that greeted the original. Although its principles and major provisions remain intact, the publication differs substantially from the rules that were issued a decade ago. The 1988 revision incorporates all changes made to the rules in the past decade, including substantial revisions and additions for nonprint materials, both new (e.g. microcomputer software and digital sound recordings) and not so new (e.g. manuscripts, music, and cartographic materials). Though this version of the rules was not revolutionary, there are hints that the increasing presence and rapid evolution of nonprint information resources may necessitate a re-examination of even some of the most basic tenets of the present code. "Describe the item in hand" is not an easy instruction to follow for online databases, serially issued laser disks, and computer files. Since it was first implemented, libraries have used *AACR2* in conjunction with the Library of Congress' interpretations. It was therefore fitting that 1988 also brought publication of a consolidated version of *Library of Congress Rule Interpretations*.

The 11th edition of the *Library of Congress Subject Headings (LCSH)* also appeared. It is still red, but it now occupies three volumes. The most visible change from previous editions was that the old x, xx, and sa codes were replaced with tags such as UF, BT, NT, and RT (Unused Form, and Broader, Narrower, and Related Terms). As online catalog access becomes more common, the theoretical construct of LSCH, and the consistency with which it is followed, receive more frequent criticism, but LCSH is as widely used as ever. The appearance of new editions of the printed LCSH, however, is of decreasing significance because of the availability of alternative formats of the list, all of which are more up-to-date than the printed version. In addition to consulting the microfiche edition, librarians may also use LCSH from MARC tapes, either on local systems or through bibliographic networks, and this year LCSH appeared on CD-ROM as *CDMARC Subjects*. This version features a relatively friendly user interface, and provides various useful modes of access, including keyword and boolean searching capabilities. LC is sufficiently encouraged by the reception of this tool that it has announced the 1989 availability of *CDMARC Names*, the LC Name authority file on CD-ROM.

The *Dewey Decimal Classification, Twentieth Edition*, scheduled for publication in 1988, has been postponed until early 1989. In a significant departure from past practice, instructional information previously contained in a separate manual will be incorporated in the body of the schedule and tables. The year's biggest news for Dewey, however, was not the content of the schedules, but the sale of its publisher, Forest Press, to OCLC. The relationship is essentially commercial; the editorial process is to remain much as before.

The *USMARC Format for Bibliographic Data* was reorganized and reissued, with code lists (e.g. for geographic areas) sold separately. The proposal for Format Integration (creating a single format for all types of materials), was approved by MARBI (Committee on Representation in Machine- Readable Form of Bibliographic Information), the committee that governs the format. These changes should appear in 1989 updates, and should then begin to be reflected in network and system documentation. The *USMARC Authority Format* was reissued in a new, more elegant form, and like its bibliographic equivalent, is continuously revised through looseleaf updates.

Creation of yet another MARC format is under consideration. Detailed content analysis of the LC Classification schedules was undertaken as a first step toward designing a format for classification numbers. Although the work is being done with LC classification numbers, the need to make any format amenable to Dewey numbers has been recognized. The existence of such a format would not only serve as an editorial support system for maintenance of the LC classification system, and enable production of the schedules in a variety of formats, but enable creation of cataloging tools that would permit classifiers to classify online, and pave the way for using classification number searching to enhance subject access in online catalogs.

Of standards emanating from IFLA, the ISBD for Computer files has reached the second draft stage; a draft of a UNIMARC format for authorities is receiving comments; a manual of International Guidelines for Cataloging of Newspapers is in final review; and a document covering the application of ISBDs to cataloging component parts has been published.

Cooperative Cataloging. Progress continues on the Linked Systems Project (LSP). With OCLCs successful contribution of authority records to LC using a computer link, both RLIN and OCLC are now able to receive and send authority data to the Library of Congress through LSP. The next phase of development for LSP will be toward machine transfer of bibliographic records. In anticipation of that capability, the National Coordinated Cataloging Program (NCCP) Pilot Program was inaugurated. For the present, participating libraries contribute authority and bibliographic records online directly to LC. Eventually, these contributions will take place through the bibliographic networks, using LSP protocols.

Widening Horizons. The days when "loving books" was a sufficient reason to enter librarianship have long since passed, and the stereotypical view of a cataloger sitting alone at a desk surrounded by books is similarly out of date. Technological advances, shifts in attention and funding, and evolution of types of material have altered not only the means by which cataloging is performed, but the materials that are being handled and the ways in which information can be accessed through catalogs. Several events of last year exemplify these changes. Five years after its implementation of machine-readable cataloging in Chinese, Japanese, and Korean (CJK) characters, RLIN took non-Roman alphabet cataloging another step forward as it implemented Hebrew processing capabilities. Heightened awareness of preservation concerns and availability of funding for "reformating" vulnerable materials has had cataloging consequences, and provided the impetus toward beginning to establish standards for bibliographic control of preservation microfilms (both ALA and the Association of Research Libraries have begun work in this direction). Increased presence in libraries of materials in machine-readable form, as evidenced by the Library of Congress' opening a pilot reading room for digital-format materials, required additions and changes to the cataloging rules and added to the complexity of catalogers' work. It is beginning to cause reexamination of the place of nonbook cataloging instruction in library education programs.

A different sort of broadening perspective is being investigated at the Library of Congress. Organization of cataloging activities at LC has long differed from organization of those same activities at other libraries. Non-LC catalogers may perform all operations ranging from preliminary record creation through description, subject analysis, authority control, classification, shelflisting, MARC tagging, and catalog maintenance, while staff at the Library of Congress may perform only one or two segments of the process (such as description or shelflisting). One result of these different ranges of responsibility is that LC and non-LC catalogers sometimes have difficulty understanding the concerns of their fellow workers. While LC is by no means abandoning its current organization, it is in the process of designing an experiment in "whole book cataloging", in which volunteer catalogers would perform descriptive and subject cataloging and classification, plus shelflisting, and possibly other functions such as tagging and preliminary record creation. While the size, length, and exact parameters of the experiment are not yet set, it is tentatively scheduled to begin in 1989, and its results should be of interest to catalogers and administrators in all libraries.

Milestones. William J. Welsh, Deputy Librarian of Congress, retired in October, after more than 41 years at the Library, most of them in the former Processing Department, where he was Department director for eight years. Throughout his career, Mr. Welsh has been a firm supporter of library automation, and an effective advocate of bibliographic control. In September, his many contributions to bibliographic control were recognized as he received the IFLA Medal. Ben R. Tucker, Chief of the Library of Congress Office of Descriptive Cataloging Policy, was awarded the 1988 Margaret Mann citation in recognition of his contributions in the field of cataloging, including major roles in the creation and continuing revision of AACR2, as well as in its interpretation, and in articulation of the Library of Congress' application of the current code. Karen Markey, a member of the faculty of the University of Michigan School of Information and Library Studies, received the 1988 Esther J. Piercy award. This prize is given to recognize significant contributions and outstanding promise in the fields of technical services by a librarian with 10 or fewer years of professional experience. Ms. Markey is best known for her research into the possibilities of enhancing online catalog retrieval through call number access.

JANET SWAN HILL

Catholic Library Association

In 1988, the Catholic Library Association (CLA) established a chapter in Baton Rouge, Louisiana, began restructuring the Southern Florida chapter, and established a Bibliographic Instruction Round Table. The Association currently has 28 chapters, seven divisions, and two round tables.

Convention. The 67th Annual Catholic Library Association was held in New York City, April 4–7, 1988. This was the 12th joint meeting with the National Catholic Educational Association. Each Association sponsored programs during the four-day convention and an exhibit of more than 700 educational and library related materials and services shared by both groups. More than 15,000 educators and librarians attended the New York Convention for a discussion of the theme "Catholic Libraries/Education: Gift to the Nation." The 68th Annual Convention will be held in Chicago, Illinois, with a theme that expands upon the 1987 theme—"Catholic Libraries/Education: Gift to the Church."

Awards. Two scholarships are offered annually to foster professionalism and encourage promising talent to enter the library profession. The 1988 Andrew L. Bouwhuis Memorial Scholarship of $1,500 was awarded to Kathleen Hintz of Catskill, New York; she will attend the State University of New York at Albany. The World Book, Inc. Grant is provided for the continuing education of CLA members in children's librarianship. In 1988, the award of $1,500 was given to

CATHOLIC LIBRARY ASSOCIATION

PRESIDENT (April 1987–April 1989):
Irma C. Godfrey, St. Louis, Missouri

VICE-PRESIDENT/PRESIDENT-ELECT:
Brother Emmett Corry, OSF, St. John's University, Jamaica, New York

EXECUTIVE DIRECTOR:
John T. Corrigan, CFX

Membership (December 1987): 3,086
Official Journal: *Catholic Library World*
Headquarters: 461 W. Lancaster Avenue, Haverford, Pennsylvania 19041, 215-649-5251

Sister Margaret Golub, OSU and Mrs. Nancy Schmidtmann, both of New York.

The 1988 John Brubaker Memorial Award for an outstanding article appearing in 1986–1987 issues of *Catholic Library World* was presented to Rev. Roy M. Gasnick, OFM, Director of Communications for Franciscan Communications, Los Angeles, California. The Regina Medal Award was presented to Katherine Paterson for her "continued contribution to children's literature." The Parish and Community Libraries Section of CLA presented its 1988 Aggiornamento Award to Orbis Books for the "promotion of new visions and new awareness" of the Third World. The Neumann Chapter of CLA (Eastern Pennsylvania) received both the chapter Newsletter Award and the Membership Development Award. The High School Libraries Section presented its Certificate of Merit Award for contributions to the development of secondary school libraries to Rev. John Catoir, Director of The Christophers.

Publications. The CLA publications program specifically targets the needs of its unique membership in producing materials that respond to requests and surveys received and conducted by the Publications Committee. The two titles published by CLA in 1988 were *Young Adult Literature: Issues and Perspectives*, by Mary E. Gallagher, SSJ, and *Dewey Decimal Classification: 200 Schedules Expanded for Use*, by Mary Celia Bauer, SSND. Bibliographies of books for elementary and secondary Catholic schools are scheduled for publication in 1989.

The *Catholic Periodical and Literature Index*, a guide to Catholic literature and an extensive collection of Catholic periodicals, expanded its list of indexed periodicals to 157 during 1988. *Catholic Library World*, the Association's official journal, was produced by offset publication, having been done by letterpress since its inception in 1921.

Future. The CLA Ad Hoc Grants Committee completed its design of the CLA American Catholic Heritage Project in 1988. The purpose of the three–year project was to identify and describe significant accessible collections of pre–Vatican II, American Catholic popular literature. The product of this research will be entitled *American Catholic Popular Literature Collections: A Census and Descriptive Locator Guide to Significant Collections of American Catholic Pre–Vatican Council II Devotional, Liturgical, Apologetic, Historical, and Fictional Literature in Religious Houses and Libraries Affiliated with the Catholic Church in the United States*.

The seventh biennial CLA Leadership Institute was planned for August 1989. This meeting of all CLA elected local and national officers focuses on leadership skills, CLA organization and membership, and the development of goals.

JOHN T. CORRIGAN, CFX

Children's Book Council

National Children's Book Week. The Children's Book Council sponsored the 69th observance of National Children's Book Week in 1988. Book Week is the best-known of the Council's reading promotion activities. Chairman of the event was Marc Cheshire, formerly of Henry Holt and Company. His committee commissioned artists to create materials illustrating the theme "Wish upon a Book." Stephen Kellogg prepared the Book Week poster, while Jerry Pinkney's poster for older readers also appeared in a Spanish-language version. Bill Martin, Jr., and John Archambault wrote the 1988 Book Week poem. Others participating were Diane Stanley as the frieze artist, and Marylin Hafner and William Joyce, each creating streamers.

The Council's 1988 year-round reading promotion theme was "Any Place, Any Time, Reading Time," depicting perfect places and times for reading in eight funny posters by Nancy Carlson, Loreen Leedy, Emily Arnold McCully, and Rosemary Wells. Ann Grifalconi, a Caldecott Honor Book artist, created a large mural about the Bill of Rights, to encourage schools and libraries to develop programs and displays about the first ten amendments of the U.S. Constitution, as the 200th anniversary of the ratification of those amendments is commemorated. Four artists from as many countries created posters on the theme of Peace for the Council. They were Mitsumasa Anno (Japan), Leonard Baskin (U.S.), Felipe Davalos (Mexico), and Lisbeth Zwerger (Austria). Betsy Hearne, editor of the *Bulletin* of the Center for Children's Books at the University of Chicago, developed an outstanding list of books on peace themes; the list appeared in the

CHILDREN'S BOOK COUNCIL

CHAIRMAN (February 1988–January 1989):
Kate H. Briggs, Holiday House, New York

VICE-CHAIRMAN/CHAIRMAN-ELECT:
Doris Bass, Bantam/Doubleday/Dell, New York

SECRETARY:
Barbara Fenton, Crowell Junior Books, New York

TREASURER:
Paulette Kaufman, Morrow Junior Books, Lothrop & Lee, Greenwillow Books, New York

PRESIDENT:
John Donovan

VICE-PRESIDENT:
Paula Quint

ASSISTANT VICE-PRESIDENT:
Jeanette Brod

Membership (December 1988): 61 publishers
Headquarters: 67 Irving Place, P.O. Box 706, New York 10276-0706

Council's publication *CBC Features* and was reprinted for distribution with the peace posters.

The Council sponsored a conference in New York City on the theme "Social Responsibility and Children's and Young Adult Books." Approximately 40 speakers and discussion leaders examined aspects of the theme. The conference was covered by National Public Radio, with excerpts broadcast nationwide throughout Book Week, November 14-20. The Children's Book Council Honors Program was an important feature of this event. Honored for "a body of work that has examined significant social issues in outstanding books for young readers," Milton Meltzer and Mildred D. Taylor were singled out for the distinction by a selection panel that consisted of Jane Botham, Milwaukee Public Library; Rudine Sims Bishop, Ohio State University; and Sophie C. Silberberg, Fund for Free Expression, Chairman.

A major undertaking by the American Library Association-CBC Joint Committee was led by Floyd Dickman, Ohio State Library, who chaired a committee that selected a 200-title children's book exhibit at the request of the National Library of the Philippines. After being mounted in Manila in observance of U.S. Children's Book Week, the exhibit books—contributed by U.S. publisher—toured other cities in that country.

The Council's work with the American Booksellers Association (ABA) continued as the ABA-CBC Joint Committee mounted its popular "Children's Books Mean Business" exhibit for the tenth year. The International Reading Associa-

Children's Book Council Posters for Peace by Leonard Baskin (U.S.) on the left and Lisbeth Zwerger (Austria) on the right.

Children's Books Council Posters for Peace by Mitsumasa Anno (Japan) on the left and Felipe Davalos (Mexico) on the right.

Children's Library Services

tion-CBC Joint Committee sponsored its "Children's Choices" project for the fourteenth year. Ten thousand school children read new books in five different parts of the country and selected 115 "Children's Choices" for 1988. An annotated listing of the selections appeared in the October issue of *The Reading Teacher* and was widely distributed in reprint format. The National Science Teachers Association-CBC Joint Committee sponsored its annual "Outstanding Science Trade Books for Children" list. The National Council for the Social Studies-CBC Joint Committee's "Notable Children's Trade Books in the Field of Social Studies" appeared in the April/May issue of *Social Education* and was reprinted. The National Council of Teachers of English-CBC Joint Committee sponsored a national contest in which teachers were invited to describe creative ways in which children's books have been used in classrooms. There were eight winners, who received five hundred dollars' worth of new books from publishers, and whose winning entries were featured in the magazine *Learning*.

JOHN DONOVAN

Children's Library Services

Children's services in public libraries began 1988 in the center of the news. An Associated Press release touched off articles throughout the nation with headlines stating "Latchkey children take refuge in library." The concern was for children who are left unattended in the library by working parents who can't afford day care or who can't find adequate child care. The articles claimed that children as young as 2 or 3 years old are left unattended, that sometimes no adult appears to take them home at closing time.

Response from children's librarians and directors varied; some viewed the situation as a problem while others felt it was a situation to be welcomed. Larry Brandwein, director of the Brooklyn (New York) Public Library, in a letter to *The New York Times* said, "Our staff is alert to the needs and problems of all children whether accompanied by a parent or not. . . . It is up to us to show them that it's a good place to be; children must always know that they are welcome in the library."

The latchkey problem is not restricted to metropolitan libraries. Some parents in communities without adequate day care facilities look upon the library as a secure place to deposit children.

The Public Library Association Conference in Pittsburgh addressed the issue with a panel of the members who drafted a report on latchkey children. They advised that the library must be a part of the solution to the problem, and urged librarians not to penalize children for situations beyond their control. Libraries should be ready to offer information about child care centers and provide programs after school, the report said.

A model Intergenerational Library Assistance project was initiated in four public library systems (Dallas, Texas, Chicago, Los Angeles and Weber County/Ogden, Utah). The RSVP (Retired Senior Citizen Volunteers) in cooperation with the National Commission on Library and Information Services, plan and produce programs for the after-school crowd, assist libraries in providing community information and activities for children and conduct literacy and drug prevention activities. Houston, Texas, devoted the Harriet Dickson Reynolds Endowment Program to the issue.

The library in Rolling Meadows, Illinois initiated GASP, Great After School Programs, which enable children to choose among a variety of creative after-school activities.

The National Education Association urged communities to take advantage of the situation by providing resources to institutions to cope with the increasing numbers of latchkey children in their midst.

A recent survey of public libraries serving populations of at least 100,000 people found out fewer than one-third of the responding libraries have written policies or procedures that pertain to unattended children.

Reactions reported elsewhere have been extreme. *The Atlanta Journal Constitution* described a public library where children must have identification to be admitted and a permanent record is kept of every child who misbehaves. Children's librarians in New York, Milwaukee, Wisconsin, and elsewhere reported they were contacted by the media but their familiarity with the issue and positive comments were not considered newsworthy. For more on this

Milwaukee Public Library children with peace cranes for 1988 Lanterns for Peace project. (left) Chicago Public Library South Loop Elementary School children view a parakeet at the opening of the CPL Cultural Center Nature Connections. (right)

concern, see the special report in this volume on "Latchkey Children."

The shortage of children's librarians remains a top concerns for public libraries. Although the major reason cited is low salary, one director in Long Island could not find a qualified children's librarian for a salary exceeding $30,000. After a decrease in children's courses taught in library schools over the past few years, it is heartening to learn that Western Michigan University, Kalamazoo, Michigan, will open a library school in response to demand for children's librarians in both public and school libraries throughout the state and region.

The Free Library of Philadelphia has reinstituted a training program through which ten staff members are attending Drexel University for an M.L.S. Ten more staffers will enroll for the spring semester.

After a long struggle from the children's advocates in California libraries, a State Children's Consultant was appointed in late 1988. Gary Strong, State Librarian, will commit $3,000,000 to children's ethnic services. University of California already has a majority of minorities. Statistics from the California Department of Education indicate that by the year 2000, California's minorities will be the majority population.

Although libraries are clamoring for multicultural materials, the publishers are slow to respond, and 1988 saw an increase of books including multicultural neighborhoods and starring minority families, but the titles are far short of the demand.

The emphasis on early childhood education continues to be a major success in public library service to children. Next year the New York Public Library (NYPL) and New York University will sponsor a national conference on public library service to preschool children, celebrating the close of a three-year project that provided course work in early childhood education for New York Public Library children's librarians at NYU.

Public libraries all over the country are emulating successful programs like "Bright Beginnings" in Pittsburgh (book service in wellness clinics) and the Kentucky program "Catch 'Em in the Cradle." Arkansas initiated a program wherein pediatricians encourage their patients to get library cards and urge parents to read aloud to the child. The Junior League, in partnership with the Central Arkansas Library System, is funding a booklist to be distributed in the pediatricians' offices. Chicago instituted a "Parents as Teachers" program that involves toddlers and parents reading together two times a week, and continuing education classes for parents with topics such as interaction with toddlers, reading readiness skills, and observing children learn. The program includes one free book–and-field trip. Librarians at Prince George's County, Maryland, visit home day care providers to train the caregivers in storytelling techniques and reading readiness skills.

Milwaukee Public librarians Art Beaudry and Marceline Roberts (North Milwaukee folding a nine-foot paper crane for the city's Lanterns for Peace project. [Journal/Sentinel, Inc., Milwaukee]

In 1988 an emphasis on literacy for the adult prompted parent/child programs. The California Assembly passed a Literacy Services Act, which provided 20 libraries with funds to initiate programs that encouraged families to read together. In addition to individual programs for the functionally illiterate adult, the project included a program to introduce parents to books they could share with children up to 5 years of age. Milwaukee, Wisconsin, began a program in which parents read to children in neighborhood school and public library environments and are introduced to the literacy center in the public library by a volunteer tutor.

The Library Card Campaign, initiated by ALA in cooperation with NCLIS in the fall of 1987, brings increased registration in libraries around the nation. The Arizona Department of Education launched a Literacy Initiative for children, developed a "learning to read with literature" program, and began a reading recognition program, which will be linked to the Adult Literacy

LATCHKEY CHILDREN

"Here is an innovation that does honor to the sensibility of a people, and it is an American innovation: the libraries reserved for children.... They are better than a drawing room or a club. They are a home. And how many children, in these huge cities without tenderness, have none other one but that!

All respect is shown to the child. He is not asked if he is rich or poor, Catholic, Presbyterian or Quaker. He has complete freedom. From the hundreds or thousands of books within reach of his hand, he takes the one that pleases him. He may remain ten minutes or several hours."[1]

That spirit of public library service that children's librarians have worked so hard to provide remains alive and active in today's service to children. In hundreds of libraries across the country, thousands of children are active patrons. The majority come to savor books, while others arrive to attend programs and events. Many children visit libraries to do homework and research, while others unwind with friends after a long day at school. Some of today's children, however, use the library after school because their parents feel it is a safer alternative than being home alone. Some children choose the library themselves because it is

Children's Library Services

more fun or less frightening than being home on their own. Whatever the reason, the children's sections and rooms of today's public libraries are packed with children.

The after-school library population was the subject of much discussion and library action in 1988. Some libraries and librarians are overwhelmed by the sheer numbers of children arriving at 3 o'clock each afternoon—they are understaffed and unprepared to deal with the crowds. They see their role shifting from providing library service to providing day-care and a poor quality of day-care at that. "I did not become a librarian in order to baby-sit." "Half the children using the library after school are not there because they want to be, and they behave accordingly." "Is it possible to be effective as a children's librarian when there are 125 children in a space designed to seat 48?" "The other library staff, and even the director, seem to think library latchkey children are a problem I have created and expect me to solve alone!" These sentiments are real in many libraries.

Other librarians wonder what the fuss is all about. They have never seen more than a few children on any given day, or they have managed being so swamped for decades that they are surprised that anyone considers latchkey children a library problem. Even the term latchkey children[2] is offensive to some librarians who wonder if labeling intimates that we will be providing different service to the population so described. Different may imply less or more difficult service, and thus a strong potential for discrimination exists when labels are employed. Some children's librarians ask why large numbers of children in public libraries is not our goal.

Most public libraries believe that librarians strive to keep literacy, access to books, and promotion of children's literature at the core of their efforts to acquire material, plan programs, and reach out to the community. Librarians know where they stand when advocating literacy, but they are not clear about the rights of children to be in a safe, comfortable environment of their own choice.

Thus the element of choice is a pivotal issue in the latchkey debate. All children using the library need to be served. If the construction of a new middle school 100 yards down the block leads to a huge increase in public library use by middle school students, librarians must respond—perhaps in staffing patterns—part-time children's staff to bolster the "regulars" from 3 to 5. Perhaps the response should be in resources—special displays/events/materials/programs suited to that age group. Perhaps librarians' response must be in leadership—implementing an afterschool program in collaboration with school administration. Perhaps the response will involve the larger community and the local government—expanding the library. Whatever the choice, librarians must respond positively rather than reactively and they need support from library administrators. Overly large groups of children in a children's room are the sole responsibility of the entire staff and administration.

While providing library service we must also attempt to share the situation with the community. Perhaps decent child care is unaffordable or unavailable. Perhaps available care is inadequate to the specific needs of the work force. The Children's Defense Fund reports that 50 percent of all mothers with preschool children (9,500,000 women) are in the labor force; 71 percent of employed mothers with children younger than 18 work full time; by 1995 more than three-quarters of all school-age children (35,000,000) and two-thirds of all preschool children (15,000,000) will have mothers in the labor force; in the next decade, the need for child care will continue to rise. In 1979 there were 7,200,000 children younger than six with mothers in the labor force; by 1985 there were 9,600,000 and by 1995 the number will rise to almost 15,000,000; and in 1985, 68 percent of single mothers worked, the average annual income of a single mother being $10,076.[3]

The Service to Children Committee of ALA's Public Library Association in collaboration with the Library Service to Children with Special Needs Committee of ALA's Association for Library Service to Children took a hard look at these issues in 1988. The resulting position paper, "'Latchkey' Children in the Public Library," endorsed and approved by the two divisions' Boards is available from the American Library Association. The paper's executive summary, delineates "five specific demographic changes in the public library service population affecting library service to children: (1) increased labor force participation by women; (2) high divorce and teenage childbearing rates; (3) the declining number of adults available to children in neighborhoods; (4) an increase in the homeless, many of whom are families with children; and (5) the lack of easily available, affordable child care for working parents.

The result of these changes has been an increase in children using the public library for shelter, in lieu of supervised day-care after school, and an increase in children left in libraries at closing time. When coupled with fears of liability on the part of library administrators and trustees, the increasing presence of these children has produced a surge of policy development among public libraries. The resulting policies have frequently been overly strict and punitive, without clear problem definitions or carefully reasoned concern for either the welfare of children or for the public relations effect of such policies in the community."[4]

The position paper describes efforts of scores of libraries around the country facing increased populations of children using public libraries, but not by choice. Sections of the paper include a model policy development process with an important component on procedures for staff, program suggestions to meet the needs of this new clientele and their parents, and suggestions "to prevent public libraries from becoming part of the problem of unsupervised children. The position taken is that children should not be blamed for circumstances not of their own making and that public libraries risk destroying a long and noble history of serving children unless they treat the latchkey children issue as one that offers unparalleled opportunities for community networking and the provision of vital information services well within the historical mission of the institution."[5] That is, librarians must act as advocates in their communities to obtain the care children need.

Larry Brandwein, Director of the Brooklyn Public Library, in response to a *New York Times* article on latchkey children stated, "the concerns expressed (in the Times article) are very real ones. However, in addressing them we must not lose sight of the fact that children must always know that they are welcome in a library."[6]

STEVEN HERB

NOTES

1. Hazard, Paul, *Books, Children & Men,* Boston, Horn Book, 1944, p. 88–89.
2. From *The Random House Dictionary of the English Language,* 2d ed., a latchkey child is "a child who must spend at least part of the day alone and unsupervised, as when the parents are away at work. Also called door-key child. (1940-45) so called because such a child is provided with a key for getting into the home after school."
3. Children's Defense Fund, *A Call for Action to Make Our Nation Safe for Children: A Briefing Book on the Status of American Children in 1988,* Washington, Children's Defense Fund, 1988, p. 6.
4. "Latchkey Children in the Public Library: A Position Paper," Chicago, American Library Association, 1988, p. 2.
5. Ibid.
6. Brandwein, L., "Correspondance to Mr. Jack Rosenthal," *The New York Times,* cited in *Public Libraries,* 27, no. 2, Summer, 1988, p. 65.

program launched in 1987. The New York Public Library signed up 12,000 children the first week of the campaign; more than 10,000 children received cards in Louisville, Kentucky. Chicago Public Library launched a two-year effort in partnership with the Chicago Board of Education to ensure that every student has a library card during that period.

Libraries, in general, have received excellent press. San Francisco Public Library worked with ABC affiliate KGO-TV on a Summer Reading Program. KGO announced weekly the number of children enrolled in the program, spotlighting library activities throughout the Bay Area; two news stories a week were broadcast for nine weeks. San Francisco department stores featured storytellers as a boost for reading in a back-to-school segment. Milwaukee County, Wisconsin, libraries tied in with the Brewers baseball team and featured children from the county libraries in a pregame event with pitcher Juan Nieves. The county also participated in ceremonies at the Performing Arts Center to observe the anniversary of the Hiroshima bombing. More than 1,000 paper cranes crafted by children in the summer program were displayed at the event. Plans are under way to send the cranes to libraries in Japan.

Philadelphia is in its third year of a Read Together Coalition, which comprises the public library, three school systems, Temple University, the *Philadelphia Inquirer*, and more than 20 other organizations. Young Library Leaders, a coalition program, is in its third year.

The NBC affiliate in Philadelphia sponsored a "For Kids Sake" segment of the news, attended by more than 40,000 persons.

The Center for the Book, Library of Congress, has designated 1989 as the Year of the Young Reader. Broward County (Florida's) monthly celebrations will involve the symphony, jugglers, cooperative games, and nationally known children's authors and illustrators. The observance will include professional experts who will provide sessions in book talking, book reviewing, and other topics vital to quality library service for children.

Thirty Caldecott banners, created by children from around the United States, will tour the nation under the auspices of ALSC, a handsome celebration for the Year of the Young Reader. Nineteen eighty-nine will produce a variety of programs that will promote services to children in public libraries.

JANE BOTHAM

Children's Literature

Publishing. The publishing boom in children's literature continued in 1988, with an output of approximately 3,800 titles, including all hardbound and trade paperbacks. The three-year trends (1985–87) reported by the Association of American Publishers (AAP) and included in the 1988 *ALA Yearbook* revealed juvenile book title output at about the same level, while output in all categories dropped by about 10 percent. The 1988 *Bowker Annual* indicated a significant drop in imported titles over the three-year period, to 63 from 92 per year. Prices of children's books averaged $11.59; an average increase of 10

Winners!

First Prize

"Why I Love My Library Card"

Jumping Kangaroos, Prickly Porcupines,
Theodore Roosevelt and Teddy Bears,
Friendly Dinosaurs, Frogs and Princes,
 CHARGE IT!

Charlie and the Chocolate Factory,
Where the Sidewalk Ends,
Little House on the Prairie,
Tikki Tikki Tembo
Riddles, Giggles and Magic Tricks,
 CHARGE IT!

Rachel Carson, Benjamin Franklin,
Martin Luther King Jr., Louis Braille,
Helen Keller, Albert Einstein,
 CHARGE IT!

Revolution, Evolution, Pollution, Man on the moon,
Nuclear bombs, Extinction,
 CHARGE IT!

I love my library card because I can
charge forever and my payments are:
learning, laughter, and excitement. So I will
continue to use my card with the magic words:
 CHARGE IT!

Vivian L. Safrin, 3rd grade
Saguaro Branch Library
Phoenix, Ariz.

Second Prize

"Why I Love My Library Card"

With my number on the front,
My name on the back,
It helps me have a good book
In my school backpack.
Ramona, Beezus, Henry too,
All jump out at me when my reading's through.
The Great Brain's schemes,
Anne Shirley's dreams,
Miss Pickerell's adventures,
William's radio-receiving dentures.
And silly Mrs. Piggle-Wiggle
Who gives my funny bone a tickle.
Charlie's prize was a factory making candy,
But for me, a reward of books is just dandy.
For candy's gone in a week or a day.
But my library card is here to stay.
That's why I love my library card.

Sonja Engelsen, 4th grade
Issaquah Library
Issaquah, Wash.

Third Prize

"Why I Love My Library Card"

I have a special treasure
That takes me to far off places
I learn the customs and about the lands
Of all the different races.

Records, tapes, movies, and tools
Are some of the things you can borrow
If you don't find what you're looking for
It could be there tomorrow.

This treasure allows me to study in peace
Or to read just for pleasure and fun
I can copy from references on their machine
For a report that has to be done.

The clues I have given have helped you I'm sure
The puzzle was not very hard
The treasure that means so much to me
You've guessed it—my library card.

Marty Bogen, 6th grade
Grosse Pointe Park Library
Grosse Pointe Park, Mich.

Milwaukee Public librarians Art Beaudry and Marceline Roberts (North Milwaukee folding a nine-foot paper crane for the city's Lanterns for Peace project. [Journal/Sentinel, Inc., Milwaukee]

Readers as Writers

ALA Public Information Office poster celebrates The Year of the Young Reader and was designed by prize-winning illustrator Charles Van Allsburg.

percent per year. The average 12.3 percent increase reflected for all categories of books during 1985–87 was a slightly higher price increase than that for children's books.

Bowker Annual also revealed interesting trends in sales of juvenile books. Sales of juvenile hardbounds grew 15.4 percent and juvenile paperback sales grew 23.2 percent. The total sales in 1986 of $386,200,000 represented a 138.1 percent increase over the preceding 10 years.

Awards. Since the Newbery Award was first presented in 1922 in the United States, the number of awards given in the United States and elsewhere has grown steadily. The year 1988 was marked by an increase in awards presented by various state organizations. Table 1 lists selected major awards presented in the United States, the presenter, the rationale for presentation, and the award winners. Due to space limitations, honor books have not been included. Table 2 is a representative listing of major international awards.

Other News and Awards. The following items are also noteworthy: The Distinguished Service Awards of the National council of Teachers of English (NCTE) to Charlotte S. Hucki, author of one of the key texts in children's literature; The Zena Sutherland lecture by Paula Fox, and the Arbuthnot Lecture by Margaret Mahy; Children's Book Council Honors to Mildred Taylor and Milton Melzer; the YASD/*School Library Journal* Author Award to S.E. Hinton; the Kerlan Award to Jane Yolen; and the national Council of Teachers of English Award for Excellence in Poetry in Children's Literature to Arnold Adoff.

A review of the conferences and workshops posted in the news sections of *Horn Book* and *School Library Journal* indicates that the topics of most interest were writing for children, reading motivation, storytelling, humor in children's literature, social responsibility and children's books, evaluation of children's literature, picture books, and children's literature in the classroom.

Librarians interested in children's materials were prominently included among the 70 women honored by the Women's National Book Association: Maria Cimino, Mimi Kayden, Nancy Larrick, Margaret Melcher, Jean Mercier, Barbara Rollock, Isabel Schon, Anita Silvey, Peggy Sullivan, and Gioaia Timpanelli.

Activities. The theme of National Children's Book Week, November 14–20, 1988, was "Wish Upon a Book," an appropriate follow-up to the "Year of the Reader" and a lead-in to the premier in January 1989 of Public Broadcasting System's "Long Ago and Far Away," a series of productions of materials from children's literature.

The stuffed animals belonging to Christopher Robin Milne were given to the Central Children's Room at the Donnell Library Center of the New York Public Library. *Cricket Magazine* celebrated its 15th birthday.

ALA/Children's Book Council initiated a touring exhibit for the Philippines, which included 150 American titles (1980–87) based on cultural roots in the Philippines or Asia.

Trends and Issues. In preparation for writing this article, 30 experts in children's literature were asked what trends and issues they saw emerging during the past year. Five major journals

"Readers as Writers" packet for Ed Radlauer from the Association of Library Service to Children, ALA.

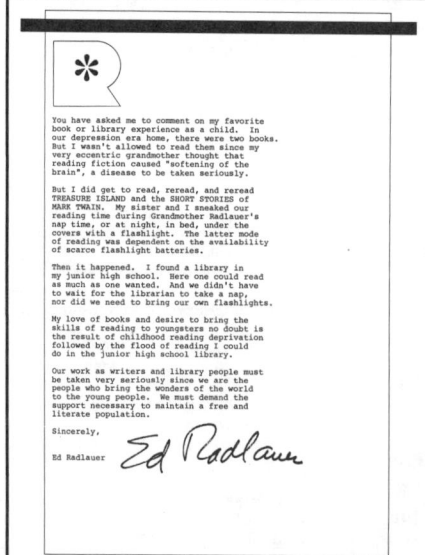
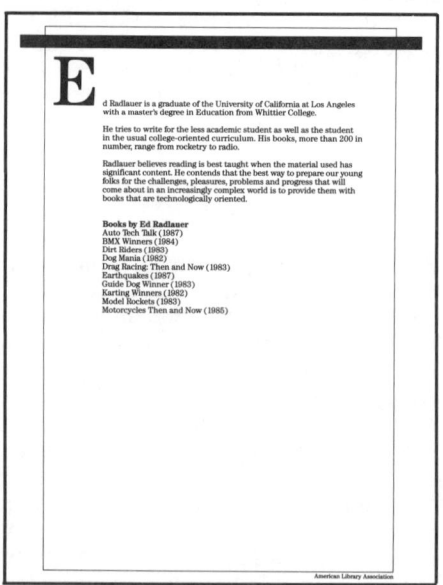

 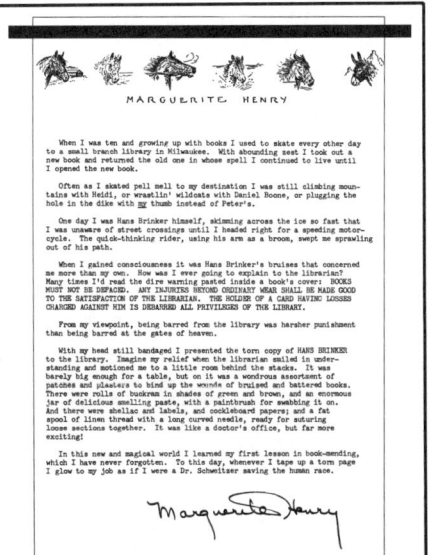 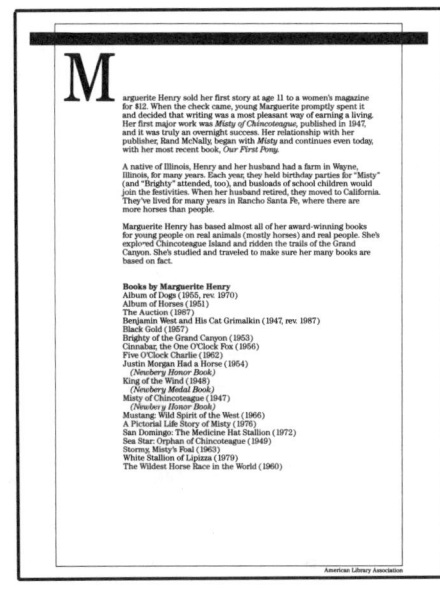

(*Horn Book, Bookbird, School Library Journal, School Library Media Quarterly,* and *Youth Services in Libraries*), were screened for further insights. The following trends and issues emerged: (1) Classroom use of children's literature as an important part of the curriculum continues to increase in several different areas. Literature-based reading programs are popular, with the trend away from controlled-vocabulary basals to "natural language" stories bound in trade children's books. The whole-language approach has stressed reading aloud and story-sharing as important activities with the young. These activities have major impacts on collections in public and school libraries. Cultural literacy is emphasized in elementary schools, with librarians playing a major role; (2) Increases in simultaneous publications of work in several countries has greatly improved the sharing of international literature. These efforts are encouraged by the Library of Congress Center of the Book Conference on Japanese Literature and the ALSC Preconference on International Juvenile Literature. Continued sensitivity to sharing of international literature is anticipated, with even more attention directed toward children's literature from emerging and Third World countries; (3) The care and planning devoted to production of fine picture books continues to produce an impressive quality of art work, with brighter and bolder colors and use of a wider range of media. This has led to a broader appeal of picture/storybooks and to an increase in the number and quality of board and manipulative books for preschoolers; (4) There has been a welcome increase in reissuing plays and classics appealing to today's children, with a trend toward lavish new editions and toward retelling adult-oriented tales (e.g., Chaucer) for younger audiences; (5) The line between juvenile and young adult books continues to blur; (6) More attention is being focused upon quality nonfiction informational books, with improved quality of photography and more concern for accuracy of information; (7) Works of poetry for children are increasing, while pop-up books seem to be on the decline; (8) Recognition of

Marguerite Henry "Readers as Writers" packet from the Association of Library Service to Children, ALA.

"Readers as Writers" packet for Evaline Ness from the Association of Library Service to Children, ALA.

 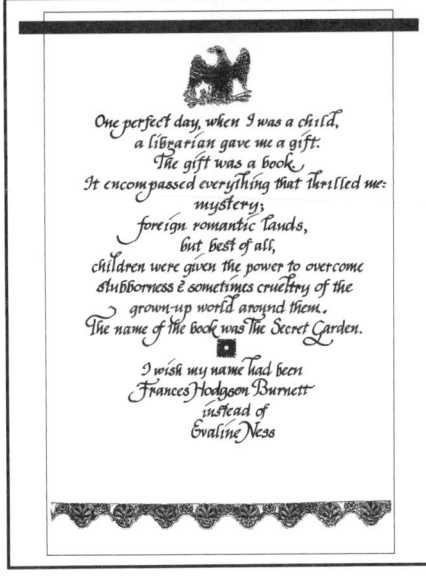 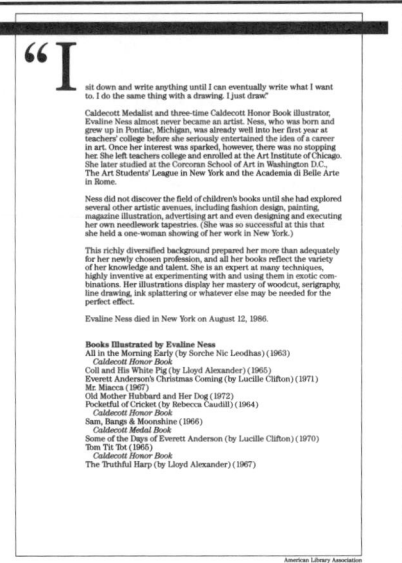

Children's Literature

small-press titles in the reviewing literature is apparently increasing, thus making them more available to selectors; (9) More books display an unfortunate return to didacticism; (10) The general increase in censorship of young adult literature is reflected in increased censorship of children's literature; (11) Young readers across the country are voting on more awards; (12) Acquisition of children's materials is becoming more difficult because of the shorter time between their publication and out-of-print or out-of-stock status; (13) Public library staff comment on the growth of services to infants and preschoolers, their concern for latchkey children and the shortage of children's service personnel.

In Memorium. The world of children's literature was saddened by the loss of Richard Chase, author, June 12, 1988; Adele DeLeeuw, author, June 12, 1988; Eleanor Estes, Newbery medalist, July 15, 1988; John D. Fitzgerald, author of the

Table 1. Selected Major Awards in the United States

Award	Presenter	Presented To/For	Winner
Jane Addams Award (since 1953)	Jane Addams Peace Association and the Women's International League for Peace and Freedom	The book that most effectively promotes peace, world community and social justice	To Sheila Gordon for *Waiting for the Rain*, in which two childhood friends in South Africa, one white and one black, move apart because of the pressures of living under apartheid (Orchard Books).
Mildred Batchelder Award (since 1968)	Association for Library Services to Children. American Library Association	The publisher of the most outstanding books originally issued in a foreign language	To Ulf Nilsson's *If You Didn't Have Me*, translated from the Swedish by Lone and George Bleecker, and illustrated by Eva Eriksson; about a little boy's experiences on his grandmother's farm and his introduction to the world of nature (Margaret K. McElderry).
Boston Globe/Horn Book Award (since 1967)	*Boston Globe* (newspaper)/*Horn Book* (journal)	An author of nonfiction, fiction and an illustrator	Fiction: To Mildred L. Taylor, for *The Friendship* (see Coretta Scott King Award); Nonfiction: To Virginia Hamilton, for *Anthony Burns: the Defeat and Triumph of a Fugitive Slave* (Knopf), a biography of an escaped slave who attained his freedom via the efforts of the Boston Abolitionists and others. Illustration: To Allen Say, for *The Boy of The Three Year Nap*, by Deanne Snyder (Houghton), a retelling of a Japanese folktale about a poor widow and her lazy son who becomes a responsible member of society.
Randolph Caldecott Medal (since 1938)	Association for Library Services to Children. American Library Association	Illustrators of the most distinguished picture books published in the U.S.	John Schoenherr, for Jane Yolen's *Owl Moon* (Putnam/Philomel), which creates an intense understanding of nature embedded in a story about the owling experiences of a little girl and her father.
Children's Book Award (since 1975)	International Reading Association	A children's author whose work shows unusual promise	To Philip Pullman, for *The Ruby in the Smoke* (Knopf), a Victorian mystery-thriller.
Coretta Scott King Award (since 1970)	Social Responsibilities Round Table. American Library Association	A black author and illustrator for outstanding inspirational contributions to children's literature	Illustration: To Ashley Bryan, for *What a Morning! The Christmas in Black Spirituals*, edited by John Langstaff, (Macmillan/McElderry). Fiction: To Mildred D. Taylor for *The Friendship*, illustrated by Max Ginsburg (Dial), a recounting of a 1930s story of four children viewing a black man's challenge to Southern tradition.
John Newbery Medal (since 1922)	Association for Library Services to Children. American Library Association	The most distinguished contribution to children's literature published in the United States.	Russell Freedman, for *Lincoln: A Photobiography* (Houghton/Clarion); a new biography for a longtime favorite for children's school reports.
Phoenix Award (since 1969)	Children's Literature Association	A book first published 20 years ago, of enduring quality and not an award winner	To Erik Christian Haugaard, for *The Rider and His Horse*; the book, published in 1968, deals with a teenage Jewish boy's adventures in Palestine during the Masada saga.
Regina Medal (since 1969)	Catholic Library Association	To an author of excellent books for children	To Katherine Paterson
Charles and Bertie G. Schwartz Award (since 1952)	National Jewish Welfare Board	To the book that combines literary merit with an affirmative expression of Jewish thought	Children's Literature: To Sonia Levitin, for *The Return* (Atheneum), the story of a Jewish Ethiopian family's flight to Israel; Illustration: To *Exodus*, retold by Miriam Chaikin, illustrated by Charles Mikolaycak (Holiday House).
Laura Ingalls Wilder Award (since 1954)	Association for Library Service to Children. American Library Association	To an author who has made a distinguished, enduring contribution to children's literature	Nominees for 1989 are Natalie Babbitt, David McCord, Elizabeth George Speare, and William Steig.

ALA Public Information Office poster celebrates The Year of the Young Reader and was designed by prize-winning illustrator Charles Van Allsburg.

The San Francisco Zoo sponsored a "Wild About Reading Festival" for San Francisco Bay children who completed the San Francisco Public Library's Summer Reading Programs.

Table 2. Selected Major Awards Presented Outside the United States

Award	Country	Winner
National Children's Book	Austria	Nonfiction: To Die Kinder von LaPacanda (The Children of LaPacanda), by Ernst A. Ekker, illustrated by Ulf Lofgren (Dachs). Illustration: To Eve Tharlet for Hans Christian Andersen's Die Prinzessin auf der Erhse (The Princess on the Pea) (Neugebauer); to Yoshi for Wer Versteckt Sich Hier? (Who's Hiding Here?) (Neugebauer). Translation: to Wolf Harranth, for Patricia Wrightson's Draussen in der Nacht (Night Outside), illustrated by Edith Adam (Jungbrunnen).
Filho	Brazil	Ponto de Tercer Poesia, by Sylvia Orthof, illustrated by Ge Orthof (EBAL Ed)
Carnegie	Britain	The Ghost Drum, by Susan Price (Farrar)
Greenaway	Britain	Crafty Chameleon, by Adrienne Kennaway (Little)
Howard–Gibbon	Canada	Moonbeam on a Cat's Ear, by Marie Louise Gay (Silver Burdett)
Canadian Library Association	Canada	Shadow in Hawthorn Bay, by Janet Lunn (Scribner)
Bratislava	International	To Hannu Tainu for illustration of Mister King, by Raya Siekkinen (Carolrhoda)
Hans Christian Andersen	International	Annie M. G. Schmidt, Dutch author; Susan Kallay, Slovak illustrator
Noma	Japan	Mamma no Kuroi Koza (Mom's Yellow Baby Elephant) by Akiko Sueyoshi, illustrated by Tomo Nakachi (Kodansha)
Sankei	Japan	Ryochan to Satochan no Ohanashi (The Tales of Ryo and Sato), by Masako Matsumura; illustrated by Hoko Kamata (Dainippon Tosho)

Great Brain Series, May 20, 1988; Miriam Gurko, biographer, July 3, 1988; Virginia Haviland, founder and long-time head of the Children's Literature Center of the Library of Congress, January 6, 1988; Robert Heinlein, science fiction author, May 10, 1988; Clement Hurd, illustrator, February 5, 1988; Charles Keeping, British illustrator, May 16, 1988; Arnold Lobel, illustrator/author, December 4, 1987; Ursula Nordstrom, editor–in–chief of juvenile books at Harper and Row, October 11, 1988; Harlow Rockwell, author/illustrator, April 7, 1988; Iris Vinton, author, February 6, 1988; and George Allan Woods, children's Book Editor of The New York Times, August 12, 1988.

JUNE SCHLESSINGER

Chinese-American Librarians Association (CALA)

Annual Conference. "Leadership: the Asian American Perspective," the CALA annual conference theme, complemented the theme of 1988 ALA Conference, "Visionary Leaders for 2020." Harry Lee, sheriff of Jefferson Parish, Louisiana, and Dr. Ching-chi Chen, Professor and Associate Dean of the Graduate School of Library and Information Science at Simmons College, were the speakers. In the second part of the conference, Dr. Chen presented "Project Emperor I," an interactive video disc demonstration project on the first emperor of China.

In 1988, in its role as an established national professional association, CALA was instrumental in urging ALA Council to adopt a resolution to support the use of the long form by the Bureau of the Census in the 1990 census. The Association also initiated an annual ALA Caucus Forum Breakfast at the ALA Conference. Through CALA, ALA Books & Electronic Products agreed to promote the sales of member Chiou-sen Chen's book, *How to Use Academic Libraries in the United States*, which was published in Chinese.

As an emerging international organization, CALA formed a sister relationship with the Library Association of Central Government Units and Scientific Research Networks in Beijing in January 1988, and with the Library Association of China in Taipei in July 1988. Four members, Daphne C. Hsueh, Susana J. Liu, Douglas Whitaker, and Irene Yeh, were selected to present papers in Taiwan and on the China mainland.

Organization. Five regional chapters were active in 1988—Northeast, Midwest, Mid-Atlantic, Southwest, and California. The themes of their meetings covered public library services to Asian Americans, Chinese medicine, Sino–U.S. cooperation in library development, networking, and university library collection development. The Association's 1988–89 committees included Awards, Books to China, Constitution and Bylaws, Finance, Foundation, Long-Range Planning, Membership, Nomination, Program, Public Relations, Publications, and Scholarship and Research Grants.

Awards. The annual Distinguished Service Award recipient of 1988 was Tze-chung Li, Dean and Professor of the Graduate School of Library and Information Science at Rosary College, River Forest, Illinois. Li was one of the founders of the Association.

Publications. In 1988, the Association, in cooperation with the National Taiwan Normal University, continued to publish the *Journal of Library and Information Science*, a semiannual publication in both English and Chinese. The journal is indexed or abstracted in *Index to Chinese Periodicals, Library Literature, PAIS, Information Science Abstracts*, and *Library and Information Science Abstracts*. CALA Newsletter is published three times a year.

Goals and Objectives. In 1988, the Chinese-American Librarians Association continued to promote better communication among Chinese-American librarians as well as between Chinese-American librarians and other librarians. Sino–American librarianship and library services were promoted and served as a vehicle whereby Chinese-American librarians cooperated with other organizations of similar or allied interests.

AMY SEETOO WILSON

CHINESE-AMERICAN LIBRARIANS ASSOCIATION

PRESIDENT (July 1988–June 1989):
Chan-chien Lee, University of Central Florida, Orlando, Florida

VICE-PRESIDENT/PRESIDENT-ELECT:
Peter R. Young, Faxon Company, Westwood, Massachusetts

TREASURER:
Sheila Lai, California State University, Sacramento, California

EXECUTIVE DIRECTOR:
Amy Seetoo Wilson, University Microfilms International, Ann Arbor, Michigan

JOURNAL EDITOR:
Nelson Chow, Rutgers University, New Bruswick, New Jersey

NEWLETTER EDITORS:
Diana Shih, American Museum of Natural History, New York; **Gladys Chaw,** College of San Mateo, San Mateo, California

MEMBERSHIP CHAIR:
Eveline L. Yang, University of Colorado, Denver, Colorado

Membership (December 1988): 350

Collection Building and Management

Money absorbed the attention of collection management and development practitioners and their library communities in 1988. Many libraries ended their fiscal years with acquisition budget deficits, although few were comparable to Princeton's announced $900,000 shortfall. While F. W. Faxon Company was predicting lower serials price increases for 1989 than those experienced during the previous three years, libraries continued to cancel subscriptions and standing orders. Faxon used its database to prepare two publications, *Library Profiles* and *Publisher Profiles*, to aid libraries in budget planning. Faxon also made available to its clients a software package, FISCAL, to be used with data downloaded from their files for managing local serials information. An Association of Research Libraries (ARL) Office of Management Services SPEC Kit illustrated 1980s versions of *Serials Control and Deselection Projects* (#147). The Research Libraries Group (RLG) Collection Management and Development Committee long-term serials project for chemistry journals provided a list of "level four plus" titles and inital commitments from member libraries were sought; similar lists were in preparation for mathematics and business.

Librarians, publishers, vendors and scholars addressed the issue in a multitude of forums and in print. The ALA Resources and Technical Services Division's (RTSD) Resources Section Library Materials Price Index Committee sponsored a program in New Orleans, "Trends and Tools: Managing the Crisis in the Library Materials Budget." The board of directors of the Medical Library Association passed a resolution deploring and protesting the effects of serials prices on the exchange and dissemination of information. The Society for Scholarly Publishing sponsored a seminar on the future of scholarly journals in Chapel Hill, North Carolina, on October 17-19. And the annual College of Charleston conference on acquisitions held on November 3-5 addressed all manner of book, serial, and scholarly publishing issues. ARL assessed members a $200 fee to fund an economic analysis of the effects of serials pricing on research libraries and their users via a contract with Economic Consulting Services, Inc. In August *ARL Briefing Package 1988-2: Rising Serials Prices and Research Libraries* was distributed to members for use in communicating with constituents about local problems.

RLG's Collection Management and Development Committee prepared to request members to document the effects of serials purchasing on their monographic collection building. American publishers reported an increase of 6.4 percent in the number of titles published in 1987 and a 6.2 percent increase in imported titles was documented. Average prices of hardcover books rose 11.9 percent in 1987 with most dramatic leaps in education, language, philosophy and psychology, poetry and drama, and sociology and economics. An ARL SPEC Kit (#141) explored how budget problems are influencing library use of approval plans. An ALA program jointly sponsored by the Association of American Publishers and RTSD; "Here Today, Gone Tomorrow: The Growing Out-of-Print Crisis," emphasized the effects of this phenomenon on reduced monograph budgets.

The effects of new non-print media on collection development were explored in an RTSD Collection Management and Development Committee preconference in New Orleans. "Collection Development in the Electronic Age" addressed a variety of issues such as copyright, preservation of electronically packaged information, and appropriate place for electronic information in library budgets. Hendrik Edelman offered what *Library Journal*'s review of the day (August 1988) termed a "bizarre scheme" for budgeting for information regardless of its packaging. The Public Library Association (PLA) presented another preconference, "Fast Forward: Video Collections and Public Libraries," treating collection development and other issues on this hot topic for public libraries. Young Adult Services Division Producers and Distributors Liaison Committee addressed "Plugging into Video: The Young Adult Collection." The American Association of School Librarians joined with the Library and Information Technology Association to discuss, among other topics, the impact of CD-ROM on collection development in its program, "CD-ROM Technology: Its Impact on Libraries and Education." The Map and Geography Round Table explored digitally accessed geographic information and its implications for map libraries. PLA's Multilingual Material and Library Service Committee and the Ethnic Materials Information Exchange Round Table talked about "Sounds-Pictures-Bytes-Multilingual Multimedia in Libraries."

Gifts of money and grants for collection building seemed fewer and smaller this year as reported in the library press. The most significant amounts were awarded by the National Endowment for the Humanities in the form of challenge grants to large libraries, such as Johns Hopkins University. The University of Texas, El Paso, received an endowment of $1,600,000 from the estate of a former faculty member and the New York Public Library received $1,000,000 from the Miriam and Harold Steinberg Foundation. Smaller amounts funded subject-specific collections, such as the University of Alabama's grant from the Network of Alabama Academic Libraries for Music score and sound recordings.

The most important monograph for collection development published this year is the third edition of *Books for College Libraries*. Its whopping $425 pre-publication price (for six volumes) sent librarians in all sizes of libraries scrambling for funding. *BCL3* is also available on magnetic tape or online; costs for these alternate formats are available from *Choice*. It will be interesting to learn how libraries make use of these offerings. Journal articles focussed heavily on serials pricing and allocation of acquisitions budgets, with Richard Hume Werking's "Allocating the Academic Library's Book Budget: Historical Perspectives and Current Reflections" (*Journal of Academic Librarianship*, 14(3):140-44, setting the stage for further work on this perennial issue. An RTSD Collection Management and Development Committee sub-committee continued its work on a *Guide to Budget Allocation*.

The issue of organizational structure for collection development was further explored in print in David G. Null's "Robbing Peter . . . Balancing Collection Development and Reference Responsibilties" (*College & Research Libraries* 49:448-52) and Karin E. Ford's "Interaction of Public and Technical Services: Collection Development as Common Ground" (*Journal of Library Administration* 9:41-53).

CODES (Collection Development and Evaluation Section of the ALA Reference and Adult Services Division [RASD]) held inaugural meetings at the annual ALA conference in New Orleans; chairs were announced for multiple committees and discussion groups, of which two focus on the organizational question: Staffing and Organization of CD/E Committee and Discussion Group on Dual Assignments.

Clearly, a revolution is aborning. Although Sheila Intner implored RASD not to duplicate RTSD efforts in collection development in her inaugural editorial in *Library Resources & Technical Services* (32:5-6), theory and practice have not reached a satisfactory conclusion to the "where does/should collection development fit in the library's organization chart?" question. Perhaps the better question is: "Where does collection development and management fit in ALA?"

Collection evaluation practices continue to focus on conspectus work. ARL produced a new edition of the North American Collections Inventory Project's *Manual*. The newest enhancement of the Conspectus Online is the implementation of Preservation Scope Notes. A microcomputer database for the Conspectus Online, which has potential for loading local data into the parent RLIN Conspectus Online, is under development at the University of North Carolina at Chapel Hill; eager potential users had hoped for its release for purchase by the end of the year to no avail. The Pacific Northwest Conspectus Database project communicates significant contributions to the conspectus process in its *Pacific Northwest Collection Assessment & Development Newsletter,* most notably in 1988 articles by Nancy Powell on assigning the 3a level (16:2–9) and on comparing publishing output statistics with collections and collecting (17:3–7). The Association of College and Research Libraries' (ACRL) Women's Studies Section reviewed a preliminary draft of a Women's Studies Conspectus, prepared by Sarah Pritchard of the Library of Congress.

Two international conferences highlighted collection development in 1988. Ninety members of the ACRL Western European Specialists Section met with 60 Western European librarians, publishers, and distributors in Florence, Italy, on April 4–8 to discuss "Shared Resources, Shared Responsibilities" in 19 90–minute sessions, each containing at least three short papers. Eighty-four representatives of ARL libraries joined 60 members of the Standing Conference of National and University Libraries (SCONUL) at a four-day conference in York, England, where five programs covered "Collections: Their Development, Management, Preservation, and Sharing." Those who could not attend these important meetings eagerly await publication of their proceedings.

The Center for Research Libraries was active on the collection development scene in 1988, issuing a revision of its *Collection and Services Policy Manual,* joining RLG, and offering a program in New Orleans entitled "The Center for Research Libraries' Programs and Services: What's There and How to Get It."

An important statement about collection management is found in "Standards for University Libraries: Evaluation of Performance (draft)," published in *College & Research Libraries News* (49:343–350) and discussed at hearings in New Orleans. It contains definitions and statements that should be useful and forceful tools for academic collection development librarians in the years ahead.

BONITA BRYANT

Continuing Library Education Network and Exchange Round Table

CLENE's primary goal is to encourage the sharing of information and to improve the quality of continuing education for all CE participants. During 1988 CLENE's efforts to incorporate elements of quality CE into its activities, provide continuity in program offerings and pursue cooperative efforts with other groups within ALA, resulted in an energetic, fiscally sound Round Table with continued growth in membership.

Publications. Additional training in newsletter design and the implementation of desktop publishing enhanced the attractiveness and readability of the quarterly *CLENExchange* newsletter. Streamlined procedures and use of first class postage improved mailing time. A new contract with the Medical Library Association to provide distribution of CLENE publications featured in *Library Journal*'s "Book Notes," enables the active sales promotion of *Continuing Education Needs Assessment: A Group Interview Technique* and the revised *Self Assessment Guides,* eight volumes covering librarians' knowledge and skills of such basic topics as budgeting and staff communications. Just prior to the ALA Annual Conference, CLENE RT published *Noteworthy Continuing Library Education in 1986 and 1987: A Source List of Topics and Providers."* Free copies were mailed to the membership and copies were sold at the ALA store. Input was solicited from state library agencies, state and regional library associations and graduate library schools. The list contains 163 noteworthy CE offerings of at least five contact hours arranged in 47 categories, including (1) Specific topic or title; (2) length of workshop; (3) target audience; (4) level of information; (5) sponsoring organization address; (6) contact for more information with telephone; (7) chief provider(s)/presenter(s); and (8) comments describing the offering or audience reaction. Response to this publication has been especially enthusiastic.

Annual Conference Programs. In New Orleans CLENE RT co-sponsored with LAMA, JMRT, LITA and ACRL Dr. Mary Broad's presentation, "Training that Sticks," building upon her previous ALA program and complimenting CLENE's conference program, "From Workshop to Worksite: Training Techniques That Assure Skill Transfer." Becky Schreiber, popular consultant and trainer, established an informal climate maximizing valuable audience participation to achieve four goals: (1) Improve human interaction skills: (2) effective working relationships; (3) internal staff development capabilities; and (4) specific problem solving. A checklist titled "Self Assessment for Transfer of Learning Skills" served as an overview of the session, prompting participants' input that was integrated into a list of practical tips to transfer training skills to the job. The large audience and follow-up evaluation indicate the tradition of building on previous programs linking related competencies is a CLENE characteristic appreciated by conference-goers.

Projects. Under the umbrella of CLENE RT,

CONTINUING LIBRARY EDUCATION NETWORK AND EXCHANGE ROUND TABLE

PRESIDENT (June 1988–July 1989):
Sherrie E. Snyder, Moline Public Library, Moline, Illinois

PRESIDENT-ELECT:
Mary Y. Moore, State Library, Olympia, Washington 98504

SECRETARY:
Blane K. Dessy, Public Library Service, 6030 Monticello Drive, Montgomery, Alabama 36130

Membership (August 31, 1988): 378

the National Council on Quality Continuing Education will mail packets containing copies of "Guidelines for Quality in Continuing Education for Information, Library and Media Personnel" which was adopted by ALA Council. Recipients will be asked to return a signed commitment to implement the guidelines in the development of CE offerings. Cost of the project will be split between a gift from Catholic University and CLENE. CLENE continued to sponsor one-to-one tutorials in which requesting participants receive an hour's free counseling from a continuing education or staff development expert specifically matched to the topic of their choice. Tutorials were offered for the first time at Midwinter in addition to Annual Conference. Both tutors and participants consistently rank their tutorial experience as a conference highlight. A joint proposal from CLENE and Chapter Relations to work with the ALA chapters to help them improve the planning and management of their annual conferences won the $5,000 ALA Goal Award. Objectives of "Improving Chapter Conferences" provide for an information-gathering and issue-identification process, a one-day conference at the 1989 Midwinter Meeting, a written guide on conference planning and a final report with recommendations for other ongoing activities to support conference planning to be added to the *ALA Chapter Handbook*. CLENE RT will sponsor training clinics for two years following the end of the project. Three CLENE representatives on the Project Advisory Committee will work with Project Coordinator Sandra Cooper.

Planning. The second annual planning retreat addressed two concerns: criteria for selection of future program topics and criteria for selection of future publications.

SHERRIE E. SNYDER

Copyright

For copyright, 1988 was an eventful year. The events were varied, and the implications should be of interest to information professionals now and in the future.

National Film Registry. Several individuals and organizations expressed their concern and objections, to certain recent alterations in old film classics (e.g., computer colorization of black-and-white films, panning and scanning, time compression), which in their opinion violate the artistic integrity of the work. The controversy led to the inclusion of the National Film Preservation Act of 1988, in the House-passed Interior and Related Agencies Appropriations bill (PL 100–446). The provision will establish a National Film Preservation Board in the Library of Congress. The Board will consist of 13 members, representing 13 named organizations, including film departments of New York University and the University of California at Los Angeles. The Librarian of Congress will appoint the Board, will establish a National Film Registry for films of cultural, historical, or aesthetic significance, and will provide a "seal" for such films. Archival copies of the registered films will be deposited at the Library of Congress and a collection of these films will be established. In consultation with the Board, the Librarian will also establish guidelines for films to be registered. The Act requires that the registered films must be at least ten years old and that the registration will be limited to 25 honored films a year.

The provision specifies language for labels for films on the registry if they are materially altered from the original or if they are colorized versions of black-and-white films. Such labels will be required before the altered versions could be distributed or exhibited to the public.

Record Rental. Congress approved an extension for eight years of the provisions of the Record Rental Amendment of 1984 and was signed into law on November 5, 1988 (now PL 100–617). The provision represents a compromise between the original senate bill (S2201) which made the Record Rental Amendment permanent and the House bill (HR4310) which extended it only for five years. Without the extension, the 1984 Act would expire in 1989.

The Act, aimed at commercial record rental establishments, prohibits the commercial rental, lease, or lending of audio recordings without the copyright owner's permission, continues to be needed because of the increasing sales for relatively indestructible compact disks and because of the high quality of copies obtainable from them. On the other hand, the Act extends an exemption for noncommercial rental, leasing or lending by nonprofit libraries and nonprofit educational institutions.

Computer Software Rental. The Record Rental provisions would be extended to Computer Software Rental Amendments Act of 1988, under S2727, which was introduced August 10, 1988 by Senator Orin Hatch. According to Senator Hatch, the common reason for renting a computer program is to make an unauthorized copy of it. The bill would prohibit the commercial rental, lease, or lending of a phonograph record or a particular copy of a computer program (e.g., on a tape, disk, or any other medium). The bill, however, does not extend the non-profit library and institutional exemption to computer software. A similar bill (HR1743) was introduced last year in the House by Representative Patricia Schroeder. No action had been taken on it at the end of 1988.

Berne Convention. The longstanding differences between the Berne Convention, a 102-year-old international agreement to promote improved copyright standards, and United States Copyright law, were initially reduced in 1976 by the passage of the revised copyright Act and later by the expiration of the Manufacting clause. On October 12, 1988, these differences were finally eliminated when the 100th Congress, after lengthy consideration, voted to join the Berne Convention for the Protection of Literary and Artistic Works. The legislation, which implements the Berne Convention in the United States, was signed into a law (PL100-658) on October 31, 1988.

Arguments against the Berne Convention centered on formalities and on the concept of "moral rights." The Berne Convention prohibits formality requirements for registration and deposit of the copyrighted works. It eliminates also use of the copyright notice on publications. The new

Copyright

legislation eliminated the mandatory notice of copyright(c) and replaced it with an incentive for voluntary notice. The joint House-Senate explanatory statement on the compromise amendment states that "the presence of voluntary notice affects only the ability of the defendant to seek mitigation of damages and not the ability of a literary, archives, or public broadcasting defendant to seek remission of damages under reasonable belief that "fair use" is present." Though copyright is now viewed as automatic, an author still cannot protect copyright ownership in a court action unless it has been registered.

Berne Convention signatories are required to recognize the author's "moral rights" to authorize or not authorize any alterations of his work or to prohibit a publisher from publishing or releasing his work if the author experienced a change of conviction or thoughts. Some U.S. publishers have expressed fear that adherence to the Berne Convention might confront the publishing industry with intolerable interference by authors during the publishing process. They also believe that this might lead to more litigation.

On the other hand, a majority of publishers, believe that adherence is an added advantage in their fight against growing international copyright piracy. U.S. trade deficits also added urgency to the adherence. Membership in the Berne convention will allow the United States to establish multilateral copyright relations with 24 countries in additional to the 79 member countries of the Universal Copyright Convention.

The Second Five-Year Review. According to section 108 (i) of the Copyright Act, the Register of copyright, after consulting with authors, publishers, librarians, and other users of copyrighted works, must submit to the Congress, every five years, a report on the statues of the intended statutory balance between the rights of the copyright owners and the needs of the users. The first report was submitted to the Congress in 1983 and the second on January 1, 1988.

The Register of Copyright concluded in the recent report that there is consensus among the interested parties that "a reasonable balance" exists between the computing interests concerning library photocopying. This was in variance from the 1983 report which found that "balance has not been achieved in practice." The same report suggested that the parties involved should get together to resolve their differences and that five specific changes in the copyright law should be considered.

The current report indicates that the above mentioned suggestions have been ignored in the interim five-year period and that "the general reaction to the publication of the 1983 report was far from earthshattering."

In specific, the current report rejected the "Umbrella Statute" that was suggested to the Congress in the 1983 report. Publishers were initially in support of its inclusion in the Copyright Law, but they since withdrew such support. Although few witnesses in public hearings, recommended its resurrection, the current report said the copyright office "cannot recommend it again." The rejection of the Statute by the general library community and the expanded scope of the copyright clearance center all mitigate against legislative enactment of the "Umbrella Statute" by Congress. Another recommendation from a few witnesses was to raise the ceiling on statutory damages for illegal photocopying to more than $100,000. (Section 504(c)). The current report, however, noted that "the range of statutory damages is already wide and adequate."

ALA and eight other organizations recommended a study of the effects of new technology on the intended statutory balance. Their concern is based on the fact that continued technological advancement could effect the future balance. Drawing on these recommendations, the copyright office in its current report asked the Congress to allow it to "study the effects of new technology on the balance" which now exists between the interested parties. Behind the concern regarding the new technology, is expansion of document delivery services, use of optical disks, and further development of networks and consorita. The copyright office indicated in the Report that if the scope of the next five-year review (due in 1993) is not expanded to include the effect of new technology, the Congress should either eliminate the mandated 5-year reviews or amend Section 108 (i) to increase the time between reviews to 10 years or more.

The 129-page (3-volume set) *Report of the Register or Copyrights, Library reproduction of Copyrighted Works (17 U.S.C. 108), Second Report*, January 1988, is available for $37 from GPO, Superintendent of Documents, Washington D.C. 20402. Stock No. 030-002-00162-4.

News with Implications. The Copyright office, in relation to registration of certain machine-readable copies, is considering requiring deposit of such works published in IBM or Macintosh formats, for use in collections of the Library of Congress. The Copyright Office asked for comments on the proposed regulations (deadline was October 11, 1988).

The American Council on Education (ACE); the National Associate of College and University Business Offices, and six other higher education groups signed agreement with the American Society of Composers, Authors and Publishers (ASCAP) and Broadcast Music Inc. (BMI). The new agreement replaces an expiring license and it, will allow institutions to continue to pay royalty fees for all copyrighted music in ASCAP/BMI repertory that are publicly performed at educational institutions. Under the new blanket royalty agreement, an educational institution should not pay fees to the performers and if there is no direct or indirect commercial purpose and no admission charge, or if an admission fee is charged and the proceeds are used exclusively for educational purposes, and provided the copyright owner does not object within a prescribed period.

Colleges and universities are not obliged to accept the new agreement, and they are free to negotiate directly with ASCAP and BMI if they believe they can get a better deal.

BV sued the University of California at Los Angeles, 657 F. Supp 1246 (cd Cal 1987), for copying seven of its computer software and associated documentation. In another case, Richard Anderson photography sued Redford University, 633 F. Supp 1154 (WD VA, 1986) for using without permission, photographs taken by the plaintiff of Radford University students for other publications. The plaintiffs lost in both cases because the court held that state universities could not be liable for copyright infringement under the sovereign immunity doctrine, regardless of their acts. The doctrine prohibits individuals from suing a state for violation of federal laws unless the later waived its immunity, or the Congress has taken it away.

In response to these decisions and a congressional request, the Copyright Office is seeking public comments on the issue of whether states should be immune for copyright liability under the Doctrine of Sovereign Immunity.

WILLIAM Z. NASRI

Databases, Computer-Readable

In 1988, most of the database industry's notable news was not about online databases themselves, but about the consolidation through merger of two major sets of vendors. Dialog joined Knight-Ridder in July and BRS joined Pergamon Orbit Infoline in December. As the growth of this innovation showed signs of slowing down and leveling off, online databases came out of the spotlight and yielded center stage to ancillary technologies. Gateways gained momentum, while CD-ROMs held their own. Videotex, still waiting for its big break, received some unexpected aid from Apple Computers and Judge Harold Greene.

Online databases might have been all but ignored if it were not for Dialog Information Services Inc., the world's most extensive electronic information retrieval company. Dialog changed hands in 1988. Gossip about the possibility of the sale, the sale itself and implications of the sale hogged industry publication headlines for much of the year. Arguably the biggest industry story of the year, it started with May rumors that the firm was on the market. Industry publications immediately began floating names of potential buyers and prices, but the purchase was not made public until July 11, when Knight-Ridder Inc. announced its purchase of Dialog from Lockheed Corporation for $353,000,000. Price was the most curious aspect of the sale. Though Dialog is huge—it offers data from more than 320 databases for access by more than 91,000 subscribers in 86 countries—its 1987 revenues of $98,100,000 and after tax income of $9,200,000 did not seem to justify the price tag. Instantly industry began to speculate, albeit inconclusively, on how Knight-Ridder intended to recoup its investment. (Knight-Ridder has made no substantial changes at Dialog, and Roger Summit remained President. Top management at neither company discussed future plans publicly.)

Knight-Ridder, however, is no neophyte in the electronic information industry. Its Vu/Text Information Sciences Inc. is the nation's largest database for regional newspapers. Industry analysts believe that combining certain Vu/Text and Dialog activities will reap economy of scale, and will result in more domestic international services in networking, marketing, and electronic information storage.

Dialog's sale overshadowed other mergers and acquisitions during the year. JPT Holdings Inc. formed a partnership with the Institute for Scientific Information (ISI) in June. Philadelphia-based ISI produces print and online indexes of scholarly literature in science and technology, arts and humanities, and social sciences; major databases included are SciSearch, Social SciSearch, and Arts and Humanities Search. In an intercompany transfer of Robert Maxwell holdings, the Maxwell Communications Corporation bought Orbit Infoline and Molecular Design from the Pergamon group. Depending upon whether performance targets are met, Maxwell will pay between £56,000,000 and £100,000,000 for the two businesses. By the year's end, the Maxwell conglomerate demanded industry attention with three additional purchases. First, Maxwell bought the U.S. publisher Macmillan for $2,600,000. In December, Maxwell's Pergamon Group Holdings purchased Dun & Bradstreet's Official Airlines Guide for $750,000,000 in cash. Maxwell scored another December coup by adding BRS, the New York-based online host, to its communciations fold. Full details were not available at press time.

The British information industry is in better shape now than it was in 1986, but investing in it is still risky. That was Phil Holmes' conclusion after he analyzed the results of Jordans' *The U.K. Information Industry: A Financial Survey of 240 Firms*. Companies that provide business data are the best prospects, Holmes said, but investments in the British industry are not secure. Results of the survey include statistics on net assets, turnover, profits, liquidity, and wages.

Statistics from Cuadra/Elsevier's *Directory of Online Databases* indicate that the long-expected slowdown in the American online database industry may be on its way. In 1987, 468 new databases went online, bringing the total number available to 3,700. But the number of new databases was down 20 percent from 1986, when 601 new databases went online. There was a net growth of 27 new online databases in 1987, but that only accounted for 36 percent of the growth in 1986 and 29 percent in 1985. The languid growth of online databases may be related to the increasing number of gateways (electronic connections from one database to another). During 1987, 15 new gateways were established, bringing the total to 59. Vendors of online services can use gateways to expand their database offerings without paying to mount the databases on their computers. This may make it increasingly difficult for new databases to make a dent in the market.

If that is the case, established databases like OCLC's Online Union Catalog may become rarer. The world's largest bibliographic database, the OCLC Online Union Catalog is flourishing: its 18,000,000th record was added in May. The Online Union Catalog has records in eight formats and contains more than 294,000,000 holdings/locations listings for the records.

OCLC's gateway, OCLC Link Service, however, has been less fortunate. Link Service was introduced in November 1986 and was discontinued in 1988 because of overall low usage and changing technology. The gateway offered ac-

Databases, Computer-Readable

cess to online databases from either an OCLC dedicated terminal or a dial-access terminal. But Link Service's failure is an exception. More gateways than ever, as Cuadra/Elsevier's statistics pointed out, are now springing up. New gateways added in 1987 include CA Online in Canada, inet America (the U.S. version of Canada's inet 2000), Intelligent Interface Facility in Western Europe, and CLIRS INTERNATIONAL, the first major Australian gateway to provide access to international online services. All Graphnet subscribers now have immediate online access to the National E-Mail Registry's nationwide directory of electronic mail users. The gateway will give Graphnet users access to the online addresses of other telex and E-mail users.

American Home Network Inc. added two new services to American/People Link, its national online network of clubs, conferences, mail, and forums in 1988. Via a gateway, People/Link subscribers can access the Passenger Airline Reservation System—also called Travelshopper—where they can view flight schedules and rates for all airlines, book reservations, and retrieve information on weather, currency conversions, and mileage between cities. Electronic Travel Agency—the second service—allows subscribers to purchase discounted cruises and tours, travel guides, gift items and other travel-related products.

The proliferation of gateways prompted the National Federation of Abstracting and Information Services to develop a Gateway Code of Practice. The Code was created to emphasize the weakness of historically sound contractual agreements in light of the recent growth of gateways and to promote discussion and understanding of the potential impact of the issues. In 1988, the Code was endorsed by Chemical Abstracts Service, Telebase Systems Inc., and Engineering Information Inc.

While gateways gained ground in 1988, the CD-ROM (Compact Disk Read-Only-Memory) surge that began in 1987 showed no signs of letting up. At the National Online Meeting, held in New York in May, 23 vendors set up presentations in a special CD-ROM gallery, and it was a popular attraction. The number of available CD-ROMs continues to grow, and their subject matter ranges from the arcane to the mundane. Tri Star Publishing's Master Search Bible CD-ROM, for example, contains several versions of the Bible with geographical, archaeological and historical works, Bible dictionaries, encyclopedias and histories of the Old and New Testaments on a single disk. The Information Access Company's InfoTrac II Academic Index CD-ROM, with references to more than 375 periodicals in myriad fields, is targeted at a more general audience: academic libraries.

Results of a 1987 survey suggest that libraries are ripe markets for CD-ROMs. The survey, conducted by Research Publications with the cooperation of ALA and 20 participating associations and societies, concluded that in survey results representative of the library marketplace, one out of every two professionals will be a CD-ROM user by 1990. In addition, the survey predicted that CD-ROM users will increase 54 percent by the end of 1988. More than 20,000 library and information professionals responded to the survey. Among the findings were: 2,956 already use CD-ROM technology, and 1,903 said they would be by the end of 1987.

Equally rosy predictions for the videotex industry came from Amin Rahme in 1988. Rahme, president of the International Videotex Industry Association, claimed that the year would finally see videotex take off in the U.S. on the Minitel model. US WEST Communications and Minitel USA, a New York City–based videotex firm formed by France Telecom, announced an agreement to work together to explore application of the French Minitel videotex concept and market development for a test city in the U.S.

Though 1988 saw no such videotex boom, the industry was bolstered by Apple Computer's entry into the field. In May at Boston's AppleFest, the company announced plans to market an electronic communications and information service especially designed for Apple owners. Apple-Link Personal Edition will have two main sections. The first will focus on information of interest to Apple users and third-party developers; the second will have more general information and communications services, such as electronic mail, synchronous and asynchronous messaging, news, weather, stock quotes, airline ticketing, and discount electronic shopping. Industry observers speculating on Apple's Johnny-come-lately entry into videotext conclude that the move makes sense. The service will allow Apple users to get more out of their computer, thus adding value to any Apple purchase.

There was more good news for videotex in 1988. On March 7, Judge Harold Greene released his ruling on gateway services following his mandated triennial review of the AT&T antitrust decision. To encourage growth of audiotex and videotex information services, Greene ruled that the RBOCs would be permitted to transmit such services. These include the electronic delivery of white-page listings searchable by name, address, and phone number; the development of gateways, single-entry points at the local level that provide users access to numerous local and national information services, for voice and data services; and provision of information to users on availability and usefulness of services.

But Greene's decision also places strict limitations on the RBOCs' involvement by refusing to allow them to generate or manipulate the content of those services. However, some observers say that the restrictive provision of electronic white pages limits the usefulness of this service to consumers because past videotex experience has shown that simply translating printed matter to electronic forms generates little consumer interest.

A 1988 Federal Communications Commission decision placated data communications users. The agency decided to drop its universally unpopular proposal to levy fees on service providers for access to the local telephone network.

The entire information industry was gratified by another Washington decision. On January 8, President Reagan signed into law the Computer Security Act of 1987, which prevents the U.S. Department of Defense (DOD) from controlling the content of unclassified data on government-created databases. The Act stipulates that the DOD's involvement be limited to data classified for national security or foreign policy reasons. The Department of Commerce will be responsible for all other information systems.

In a related regulatory matter, the Information Industry Association announced the formation of a Voice Information Services Technical Standards Committee, that will develop and promote uniform specifications for the voice information services industry for voluntary use in the areas of technical and human interfaces. This will be executed so that the industry will be encouraged to grow and so that these specifications will be recommended as standards to appropriate existing standards-making bodies.

MARJORIE M.K. HLAVA
GREG MACEWIAN

Education, Library

Library Schools. A positive note in 1988 was the absence of any reports on the actual closing of any library schools. The shortage of librarians and recruitment efforts was highlighted by a number of articles and programs throughout the year. While shortages of children's librarians, catalogers, and preservation specialists had received attention earlier, writers were noting and gathering evidence that the shortages are widely spread throughout the field.[1] Library recruiters are intensifying their efforts in a number of ways, including New York Public Library's staging of mock interviews for M.L.S. candidates and recruiters visiting library schools. Resources to guide recruiting efforts are one result of the California Library Recruitment Project, initiated by the California Society of Librarians and funded by the California State Library with LSCA funds.[2] The Office for Library Personnel Resources (OLPR) sponsored a preconference on "Recruiting for the Profession," where attendees had an opportunity to preview the 1989 National Library Campaign with its focus on librarians and the information function of libraries.[3] The attendees also heard about the findings of the OLPR sponsored project LISSADA "The Library and Information Science Student Attitudes, Demographics, and Aspirations Survey", which was later reported in American Libraries.[4]

In 1988, the American Library Association agreed to recognize two forms of accreditation: a master's degree from a program accredited by ALA for the first professional degree and a master's degree from an educational unit accredited by the National Council for the Accreditation of Teacher Education as appropriate for the first degree for school library media specialists.

Statistical Report.
Students. In the 1988 Library and Information Science Education Statistical Report published by ALISE, G. Glenn Sparks reported that 59 of the ALA accredited master's programs[5] had a Fall Term, 1987, enrollment of 14,754 (or 8,411.12 FTE), of which 3,465 were full-time students and 6,584 were part-time students.[6] Full-time students included 945 men and 2,520 women; part-time students 1,221 men and 5,363 women. Table 1 provides a comparison of FTE enrollment figures for master's, sixth-year, and doctoral programs for the past eight years. The ALA schools also reported 1,499 other graduates (502.17 FTE) and 1,781 undergraduate students (482.5 FTE). Twenty-five ALA schools reported off-campus enrollments of 4.25 to 71.25 FTE. The enrollment figures for the 8 non-accredited library schools[7] were 756 (401.06 FTE) master's students, 20 (1.86 FTE) post-master's; no doctoral students; 104 (41.58 FTE) other graduates; and 220 (82.63 FTE) undergraduates. The number of full-time equivalent master's students enrolled ranged from 26.34 to 239.4, with three schools reporting more than 200 FTE master's students. Table 1 provides a comparison of FTE enrollment figures for the past 7 years.

Tuition and required fees ranged from under $1,000 to $15,120, with 7 schools reporting more than $10,000. Among ALA accredited schools, 56 reported funding that ranged from $250 to $306,917, while 5 non-ALA accredited schools reported a range from $600 to $8,253. These figures are exclusive of funding obtained through loans or work/study programs.

Table 2 provides a comparison of the degrees awarded by accredited schools for the last eight years. The 59 ALA schools awarded 4,059 students (923 men, 3,135 women) the master's degree, an increase of 451 over 1986. Other graduates included 235 with bachelor's degrees, 68 with post-master's and 65 doctorates (24 men, 41 women). The seven non-ALA accredited schools reported granting 230 master's degrees (23 men, 207 women); 10 bachelor's degrees, one post-master's, and no doctorate degrees.

Placement and Salaries. The 37th annual report on placements and salaries of the 1987 graduates of ALA schools by Carol Learmont and Stephen Van Houten in Library Journal, has as its subtitle "The Upswing Continues."[8] Fifty-five of 60 eligible schools reported on 3,702 graduates who were awarded their first professional degrees. Among these, 2,477 were employed in professional or nonprofessional positions in libraries or information-related work; 2,122 (57 percent) in permanent professional positions; 279 in temporary positions and 76 in nonprofessional library placements. Of those who were employed, 594 (28 percent) found their permanent positions before graduation, 607 (29 percent) were employed within 90 days after graduation and 123 (6 percent) looked for three to four months. Others sought employment for periods up and more than six months while 421 individuals (20 percent) returned to their previous positions.

Salaries for men and women continue to differ. While the average beginning-level salary was $22,247 in 1987, the average for women was $22,046; for men it was $23,013. The median salary for all graduates was $21,116. The lowest salary, $9,500, was held by a public librarian; the highest $72,000 was in the category of "other library agencies." Public libraries accounted for 40 percent of the lowest salaries, down 4 percent from 1986. Individuals with prior relevant experience obtained an average salary of $24,018, up from $21,971 in 1986; for those without experience, the average salary of $20,402 was up from $19,458 in 1986.

Faculty. The ALISE statistical report on faculty by Timothy W. Sineath included data from 58 of the 60 ALA schools as of January 1, 1988, and from 8 of the non-ALA schools.[9] The number of faculty members decreased to 562 from 572 in 1987. This reflects fewer schools reporting in 1988 and excludes unfilled positions and persons on sabbatical. The number of full-time faculty members ranged from a low of 4 in one school to 33 in another, and the average faculty size was 10.21, an increase of .18 (from 10.03) in 1987. The trend toward decreasing faculty size had been noted from 1974.

Exclusive of deans and directors, 58 new faculty appointments were made in 1987. Of these, 43 percent were appointed at the assistant professor rank. Of the 5 new appointments at the rank of professor, all were males in United States schools.

On January 1, 1988, 45.3 percent of the faculty in all ranks (including deans and directors) were women, an increase of 3.8 percent from 1976, when the data were first collected. The largest increase (46 percent to 62.4 percent) was at the assistant professor level. A significant increase, 38.3 percent, was found in the number of female deans and directors. There were 23 female deans or directors in the academic year 1986–1987 and 1987–1988, compared with 12 during the 1975–76 academic year.

Based on 552 salaries at ALA school including those of deans and directors, the mean and median salaries for the 1987–88 fiscal year were: deans and directors, $65,262/$64,000; professors, $60,297/$63,592; associate professors, $49,706/$49,217; assistant professors, $39,154/$39,968; instructors, $35,218/$34,244; and lecturers $31,228/$34,047. Improvements in mean faculty salary were reported on the fiscal year basis as 6.5 percent for deans and directors, 2.4 percent for professors, 4.6 percent for associate professors, 3.7 percent for assistant professors, 14.2 percent for instructors, and 3.2 percent for lecturers. These figures are not based on comparisons of the same individuals shown in previous reports and do not reflect the influence of individual promotions, resignations, retirements, and new appointments.

Approximately 83 percent of the full-time faculty who taught in the 55 ALA schools had completed doctoral degrees prior to January 1, 1988. Of the 466 faculty members with doctorates, 68.4 percent had degrees in library and/or information science; 31.6 percent were in other fields. The percentage of faculty holding the doctoral degrees ranged from a low of 25 percent in one school to a high of 100 percent in 12 schools. Two schools reported half or less of their faculty holding doctorates.

Of the 560 full-time faculty members in ALA schools, 65.5 percent held tenure as of January 1, 1988. This is a slightly lower figure than the previous year's. Seven out of 10 faculty members in ALA schools have tenure.

A lost position was reported by 4 schools, lower than the 6 schools reporting such a loss in 1986–87. This is a sharp drop from the 17 schools that reported a loss of 21 faculty positions in 1982–83. Ten schools reported gaining 11.25 new positions, an increase over the 9.5 new positions reported last year.

Curriculum. Daniel D. Barron, writing on "Curriculum" for the ALISE *1988 Statistical Report*,[10] noted that of the 68 schools (60 ALA, 8 non-ALA), 13 have undergraduate majors in library and/or information science and 17 offer undergraduate minors.[11] Thirty-nine schools offer a post-master's degree, and 15 schools offer the doctoral degree program. Of the 60 ALA schools, 32 had one or more joint degree programs.

The minimum time for completion of the master's degree program in an ALA school ranged from 5 to 20 months, for the post-master's 5 to 12 months, and for the doctorate, 9 to 36 months. The maximum range is 2 to 10 years for the master's degree, 3 to 10 years for the post-master's and 3 to 14 years for the doctorate. For the master's degree, the ALA schools required from 6 to 44 semester hours of course work and 12 to 72 quarter hours, with the possibility of exemptions at 44 ALA and 6 non-ALA schools through transcript evidence, completed "approved" projects, a written examination, or approval from administrators and/or faculty members. Students could transfer from 3 to 27 hours for the master's degree and 6 to 30 hours for the doctorate degree.

Ten of the ALA schools required a master's thesis, 32 schools had this as an option. Three non-ALA schools required a master's thesis, one offered it as an option. Twelve schools require field work or work experience of all students, 60 offer it as an option. A comprehensive examination is required at 23 ALA and 6 non-ALA schools.

The most frequently required prerequisites for entering the master's program are the Graduate Record Examination (GRE) and Miller Analogies Test (MAT), along with the Test of English as a Foreign Language (TOEFL) for foreign students. Twenty-four ALA and 3 non-ALA schools require an interview.

Thirty-four ALA schools and 4 non-ALA schools offered one or more courses on an off-campus basis, for a total of 312 off-campus courses, an increase over last year's report of 289. Approximately 50 percent of these were required courses. No school offered a course at the doctoral level away from the main campus.

Twenty-nine ALA and two non-ALA schools added new courses. Sixteen ALA schools dropped courses, as did one of the non-ALA schools. Three ALA schools revised the total curriculum, 9 revised specific curriculum areas. Twenty-three schools had experimental or trial courses.

Financial Support. According to Fred Roper's report about 55 ALA schools in the "Income and Expenditure" section of the 1988 ALISE statistics,[12] the schools' average income was $861,179, an increase of 10.4 percent over the previous year, and 0.1 percent lower than in 1987. The 1987 increase was the largest percentage increase since 1978–79. Funding ranged from a low of $315,118 to a high of $3,955,761, with a median of $663,761 (1.7 decrease from 1985–86).[13] Roper observed that "this suggested that the significant increases are going to the schools with larger budgets and that schools with smaller budgets, while receiving increases, are not keeping pace with the larger schools."

Table 1. FTE Enrollments by Degree Programs As Reported by Schools with ALA-Accredited Programs

Year (Fall Term)	Master's		Sixth-Year		Doctoral	
	Schools Reporting	FTE	Schools Reporting	FTE	Schools Reporting	FTE
1979–80	63	6,234	35	145	25	312
1980–81	67	5,972	32	140	25	290
1981–82	69	5,820	37	149	24	304
1982–83	65	5,254	33	109	23	277
1983–84	64	5,515	30	122	23	290
1984–85	65	5,562	33	151	24	290
1985–86	56	5,756	29	88	20	309

Table 2. Degrees Awarded by Schools with ALA-Accredited Programs

Year	Master's		Sixth-Year		Doctoral	
	Schools Reporting	Degrees Granted	Schools Reporting	Degrees Granted	Schools Reporting	Degrees Granted
1978–79	58	4,804	20	158	22	77
1979–80	64	4,670	20	60	26	66
1980–81	69	4,717	26	105	13	67
1981–82	64	4,023	20	50	23	74
1982–83	64	3,784	23	51	21	61
1983–84	63	3,674	18	67	23	81
1984–85	55	3,596	21	75	17	56

The number of schools facing decreases doubled since 1987. The pattern of library schools being heavily dependent upon their parent institutions continued. The percentage of income from federal funds rose by almost one percent, while funding from other sources rose from 7.10 to 7.49 percent.

Continuing Education. M. Kent Mayfield in the "Continuing Professional Education" section of the 1988 ALISE statistics reported 500 events were held during 1986–87, a 4 percent increase over 1985–86. Approximately 18,830 people attended these events which included institutes, workshops, seminars, lectures, and short courses.

People, Organizations, and Activities.

Changes in Deans and Directors. Of 60 ALA schools reporting for the 1988 ALISE Statistical Report, there were 12 changes in appointments between 1987 and 1988. Four of these were "acting" or temporary appointments. The eight regular appointments included six males and two females.

Awards and Honors. F. William Summers was elected President of ALA; Leigh Estrabrook, President of ALISE. Recipients of ALA related awards included Spencer Shaw, ALA Honorary Life Membership, and Richard M. Dougherty, the Hugh C. Atkinson Memorial Award. For other awards to library educators see "ALA Awards Program," "Association for Library and Information Science Education," "Medical Library Association," and "Special Libraries Association." Library educators honored by their alma maters include: Margaret Mary Kimmel, Rosary College; Herbert S. White, Syracuse University; and Marilyn Miller, University of Michigan. The College of William and Mary awarded an honorary degree to Robert Wedgeworth. Fullbright winners included Darlene Weingand, Helen E. Williams, and Ira Harris.

Deaths. Mildred Lowe, the former Director of the Division of Library and Information Science, St. John's University, died on August 22.

REFERENCES

1. John Berry, "The Shortage of Librarians is Back," *Library Journal*, May 15, 1988, p.4 and Thomas M. Gaughan, "A Job Seeker's Market for Librarians," *American Libraries*, March 1988, p.180–81.
2. Katie Scarborough and Constance W. Nyhan, "Meeting the Need for Librarians: The California Library School Recruitment Project," *Library Journal*, October 15, 1988, p.44–49.
3. John Berry, Grace Anne DeCandido, and Nora Rawlings, "Leadership, Access, and Internal Politics," *Library Journal*, August 1988, p.33–42.
4. William E. Moen and Kathleen M. Heim, "The Class of 1988: Librarians for the New Millenium," *American Libraries*, November 1988, p.858–860, 885.
5. Hereafter, referred to as ALA Schools.
6. G. Glenn Sparks, "Students," p. 79–145 in *Library and Information Science Education Statistical Report, 1988*, ALISE, 1988.
7. Hereafter, referred to as non–ALA Schools.
8. Carol Learmont and Stephen Van Houten, "Placements and Salaries 1987: The Upswing Continues," *Library Journal*, October 15, 1988, p.29–36.
9. Timothy W. Sineath, "Faculty," p. 1–78 in *Library and Information Science Education Statistical Report, 1988*, ALISE, 1988.
10. Daniel D. Barron, "Curriculum," p. 147–193 in *Library and Information Science Education Statistical Report, 1988*, ALISE, 1988.
11. Fred Roper, "Income and Expenditure," p. 195–216 in *Library and Information Science Education Statistical Report, 1988*, ALISE, 1988.
12. Ibid, p.194.
13. M. Kent Mayfield, "Continuing Professional Education," p.217–241 in *Library and Information Science Education Statistical Report, 1988*, ALISE, 1988.

PHYLLIS J. VAN ORDEN

ERIC

The Educational Resources Information Center completed its 22nd year of service to education in 1988 with an additional 12,129 documents entered in the database and announced in *Resources in Education*, the monthly index of ERIC documents. An average of more than 1,010 new documents each month, this total brought the number of documents announced in RIE since the inception of the system in 1966 to 290,038 by the end of 1988. Full text copies of about 98 percent of these documents are available through the ERIC microfiche collection, which is available in about 780 libraries and information centers in the nation and 111 locations outside the United States.

ERIC Document Reproduction Service fills individual orders for any of the documents in the collection with microfiche copies or, for most of these documents, paper copies. Availability of the remaining documents is noted in *RIE* with the abstract for each citation. There were approximately 2,934 subscribers to *RIE* in 1988.

During the 1988 fiscal year, EDRS distributed 12,566,107 microfiche to their 783 standing-order customers, as well as approximately 17,475 microfiche and 2,306,311 pages of paper copy to individual customers.

An average of 1,414 journal articles were annotated and indexed each month during 1988 for *Current Index to Journals in Education*, the monthly index of the journal literature from ERIC, bringing the total for the year to 16,967. The total number of journal articles announced in *CIJE* since 1969, when this service was implemented, totaled 375,771 at the end of the year. Many of the more than 750 journals covered by *CIJE* are available through libraries, and reprints of individual indexed articles are available for about 65 percent of the journals from University Microfilms International. There were approximately 1,685 monthly subscribers to *CIJE* in 1988, of which 504 came from 62 countries around the world.

With the 29,096 documents and articles announced in *RIE* and *CIJE* in 1988, the total number of citations in the database was 665,809 at the end of the year.

Systems Activities. In 1988, SilverPlatter, one of the three companies that made the ERIC database available on CD-ROM with searching software for the IBM PC/XT and comparable microcomputers in 1986 and 1987, made available new software for searching the database on CD-ROM with the Apple Macintosh. This version takes advantage of the Macintosh user interface windowing capability. The three IBM versions—SilverPlatter, DIALOG OnDISC ERIC, and Search CD450 from OCLC—are still available with some enhancements.

Two new publication types were added to the authority list in 1988, Book Reviews (072), for use with lengthy substantive reviews of major works, and Machine-Readable Data Files (102), for use with the descriptions of education-related data files that were first announced in the January 1988 issue of *RIE*. Descriptions of about 30 data files were announced in *RIE* during the year.

The ERIC Document Reproduction Service improved its customer services in 1988 by extending hours for its toll free telephone number, and by instituting an order service via FAX machine, which accepts orders for individual copies of ERIC documents 24 hours a day. Transmission of copies of documents ordered directly to the client's FAX machine was tested with actual orders early in October 1988, and EDRS announced its standard new quick turnaround service for clients anywhere in the world in November.

A new reporting system for the ERIC Clearinghouses was implemented in 1988, with monthly statistical reports being transmitted online to Central ERIC in the Office of Educational Research and Improvement (OERI), U.S. Department of Education, using a standard spreadsheet format. The clearinghouses have been transmitting their weekly input for *RIE* and *CIJE* online to the ERIC Processing and Reference Facility since 1983 and monthly acquisition reports since 1985.

Status. Three clearinghouse contracts changed sponsors in 1988 as a result of systemwide competitions conducted in 1987. New host organizations, which were awarded five-year contracts to operate the clearinghouses, are Indiana University for the Clearinghouse on Reading and Communication Skills; Appalachia Educational Laboratory for the Clearinghouse on Rural Education and Small Schools; and American Institutes for Research for the Clearinghouse on Tests and Measurements. The sponsors of the remaining 13 clearinghouses were also awarded five year contracts.

Requests for Proposals for the ERIC Processing and Reference Facility contract and for a new system component, ACCESS ERIC, were sent out in 1988 and were under negotiation in November. ACCESS ERIC is intended to make the ERIC system more easily accessible to users by providing a central reference point and developing materials to assist users. It is expected that one of its functions will be to continue the ERIC Digests Online project, which was developed by the Clearinghouse on Elementary and Early Childhood Education.

BARBARA B. MINOR
JANE K. JANIS

Ethnic Materials and Information Exchange Round Table

The Ethnic Materials and Information Exchange Round Table (EMIERT) celebrated its fifth anniversary. Although it is one of the youngest ALA Round Tables, the roots of EMIE go back to 1967 when the American Association of School Librarians organized an Ad Hoc Committee on Treatment of Minorities in Library Materials. In 1972 the Social Responsibilities Round Table created an Ethnic Materials Information Exchange Task Force. A proposal to create an independent unit devoted to matters related to library services to ethnic and linguistic minorities was accepted in 1982 by the ALA Committee on Organization (COO) and approved by ALA Council in January 1983. The first chair of EMIERT was David Cohen whose dedication to the cause of library services to ethnic minorities was recognized by the Board, which presented him with an "Inaugural Executive Board Certificate of Appreciation" during the ALA Annual Conference in New Orleans.

A quarterly newsletter for the membership, *The EMIE Bulletin* has entered its sixth year of publication.

Organization. EMIERT has eight Committees and seven Task Forces. The Committees are: Conference Programming, Constitution and By-Laws, Membership, Nominating, Planning, Public Relations, Publications and *EMIE Bulletin*. The Task Forces concentrate on specific aspects of work, and are encouraged to present their own programs during annual conferences. Building Coalitions for Ethnicity, Children's Services, Collection Development, Ethnic Research, Jewish Librarians, Library Education, and Publishing and Minority Materials comprise the Task Forces.

1988 Conference. The Publishing and Minority Materials Task Force conducted a very successful program, "Publishing of Minority Materials, 1988 and Beyond," at the ALA Conference in New Orleans. There was a consensus among the participating editors and librarians that a special effort must be made to increase the availability of multiethnic quality titles. EMIERT presented a three-hour program "Is 'English-only' Enough?" Dr. Kamal K. Sridhar, of the Linguistics Department of Stony Brook University of New York, addressed the topic "Language and Culture Retention Patterns in the United States." Her research revealed a significant retention of the home language among the various ethnic groups. This is in sharp contrast with the tendencies of the immigrants of the early 20th century to forget their native languages and to concentrate on learning English. The thrust today supports the concept of bilingualism and reflects the current impact of ethnicity on our language patterns. Sridhar's speech was followed by a presentation of three library programs designed to promote and support retention of culture and languages. The principal co-sponsor of the presentation was REFORMA (National Association to Promote Library Services to the Spanish Speaking). It was also cosponsored by ALSC Committee on the Selection of Children's Books from Various Cultures, ALA Black Caucus, OLOS Advisory Council, PLA Multilingual Materials and Library Service Committee, and RASD Committee on Library Services to the Spanish Speaking. EMIERT cosponsored and participated in a number of other ALA programs such as "Librarians as Colleagues Across Racial Lines: Strategies for Action," "Equity in Information Services: The Nation's Minorities and the Leadership Challenge," "Developing Minority Leadership for the 1990's and Beyond," and "Sounds-Pictures-Bytes: Multilingual Multimedia in Libraries."

The Future. EMIERT is finishing the review of its bylaws. New goals are being prepared for the Collection Development Task Force to reflect the growing interest of libraries in providing services in languages other than English. The first draft of the Manual for EMIERT officers is under evaluation in preparation for the final edition. A first monographic publication and expansion of the *Bulletin* are also being considered.

MARIE F. ZIELINSKA

Federal Librarians Round Table

The FBI's Library Awareness Program is presented in other sections of this yearbook. Therefore, the Federal Librarians Round Table will update the library community on other, but no less significant issues. During 1988, the contracting out of federal libraries continues to be a major concern. The Office of Technology Assessment (OTA) reported on the urgent need to modernize the dissemination of federal information. Alternative salary scales for librarians were explored by the Department of Defense, and the National Institute of Standards and Technology.

Privatization

OMB Circular A-76 Refined. The contracting-out procedures, developed by the Office of Management and Budget and implemented through Circular A-76 were revised in 1988. When conducting cost comparison studies, an agency must now include all retirement benefits. The additional calculation of Social Security and thrift plans, which were previously excluded from contractor's costs, could make the difference for retaining some library libraries within the federal sector. David Muzio, OMB A-76 specialist, stated that vendors had an unfair advantage under the original procedures. This change was the result of an amendment to the Section 307 of the Federal Employees Retirement Act of 1986, which was signed into law on July 13, 1988. Did unfair cost-comparison procedures play a part in displacing federal library employees? Another change is an adjustment to the A-76 guideline that deleted the requirement for agencies to publish cost comparison reports in the *Commerce Business Daily* and the *Federal Register*. OMB will gather the information and be responsible for publishing it all at once in the above journals, a move that will cause delays in making this information publicly available. The watch-dog effect of public disclosure is considerably weakened. To add to last year's scenario of endangered libraries, the complete con-

---

ETHNIC MATERIALS AND INFORMATION EXCHANGE ROUND TABLE

CHAIR:
Marie Zielinska, National Library of Canada, Chief, Multilingual Biblioservice, 395 Wellington St., Ottawa, Ontario, K1A ON4

VICE-CHAIR/CHAIR-ELECT:
David Nieto, Library of Congress, Copyright Office, Washington, D.C. 20559

SECRETARY:
Jacquelyn Marie, Reference/Womans Studies Bibliographer, McHenry Library, University of California at Santa Cruz, Santa Cruz, California 95064

TREASURER:
Janice Beaudin, College Library, University of Wisconsin, 600 N. Park St., Madison, Wisconsin 53706

Membership (September 5, 1988): 545

tracting out of the National Oceanic and Atmospheric Administration occurred on May 1, 1988. After exhausting all appeals from employees and internal delays, the entire library staff was displaced. The Departments of the Interior, General Services Administration, and the Immigration and Naturalization Service are now under A–76 reviews and experiencing staff cutbacks. It should be noted, that when an A–76 review occurs, a hiring freeze happens as well. A loophole in the A–76 process states that staffs of fewer than 10 persons are exempt from the formal review process and can be contracted out immediately. The Health and Human Services Library is a classic example of how this loophole can affect federal library employment. Five years ago, when the library went under review, it was able to retain the services in-house. At that time, it was recommended that the staffing should be 13 persons. Through attrition and abolishing positions, only two people are running the HHS Library. With the staffing level under 10, the library is a prime candidate for contracting out without A–76 review.

It should be emphasized that the implications of contracting out is not simply the abolition of federal library positions. The long-term effect on access is controlled by the private sector whose primary motivation is profit.

On a happier note, Congressional intervention stopped the privatization of the National Technical Information Service. The Omnibus Trade and Competitiveness Act of 1988 (PL100–418), popularly known as the Trade Bill, was finally signed by President Reagan, following a veto and revision, on August 23, 1988. The Trade Bill included a provision prohibiting the contracting-out of work at NTIS for jobs in excess of $250,000. The National Institute of Standards and Technology Authorization Act for FY 1989 (HR 4417 and HR 5183) further limited any efforts to privatize NTIS "without the express approval of Congress." The bills enacted report procedures and Congressional oversight into major NTIS activities. Congressional efforts also took the lead in reshaping the National Bureau of Standards. The Trade Bill renamed the National Bureau of Standards to the National Institute of Standards and Technology (NIST). HR 4417 and 5183, now PL100-519, prescribed key innovations to modernize NIST to regain its "international pre–eminence as one of America's flagship R & D facilities." The NIST Research Information Center, headed by ALA President-elect Patricia Berger, was designated a governmental activity by the statute.

OTA Report: "Informing the Nation: Federal Information Dissemination in an Electronic Age." In October 1988, the Office of Technology Assessment (OTA), the analytical arm of the U.S. Congress, published a 333-page report that stressed the urgent need to modernize procedures at the Government Printing Office, NTIS, and the Depository Library Program. Technical advances in microcomputers, printers, scanners, compact disks, and online networks, to name but a few, could enable these programs to more cost-effectively distribute government information. OTA provided concrete suggestions and guidelines for each of these programs and agencies. Because electronic dissemination complicates the government's relationship with the commercial information industry, OTA emphasized the need for Congressional action to resolve federal information dissemination issues. This report is available from the Superintendent of Documents; the GPO stock number is 052-003-01130-1; price $14.00.

Alternative Salary Options for Federal Librarians. During the FLRT Membership meeting in New Orleans, Kenneth Hedman, Library Director of the U.S. Military Academy at West Point, described managing the civilian work force to budget (MCB). Library managers, having classification authorization and budgetary discretion, can reward productivity and efficiency. This two-year experimental program is being tested at 11 sites. Allen Cassady, Chief of the Personnel Demonstration Project at the National Bureau of Standards, discussed a five-year project in which flexible bands replaced the more rigid pay grades and schedules. One objective is to improve the quality of scientific and engineering staff by making salaries more competitive with the private sector.

Awards. Anne Heanue, ALA staff liaison, was the recipient of the third Federal Librarians Round Table Achievement Award. She was recognized for her significant contributions on access to federal government information, her activities in the Washington Office, and her efforts on Capitol Hill. Previous recipients are Patricia Berger, 1985, and Adelaide del Frate 1987.

DORIA BEACHELL GRIMES

FEDERAL LIBRARIANS ROUND TABLE

PRESIDENT (June 1988–July 1989):
Doria Beachell Grimes, National Technical Information Services, Annandale, Virginia 22003

VICE-PRESIDENT/PRESIDENT-ELECT:
Nancy Cummings Liston, U.S. Army Cold Regions Research and Engineering Laboratory Library, Hanover, New Hampshire 03755

SECRETARY/TREASURER:
Shirley Loo, Library of Congress, 606 Independence Avenue, SE, Washington, D.C. 20003

Membership (November 30, 1988): 472

Film and Video

Library Video Classics Project. The overwhelming success of the Library Video Classics project of the John D. and Catherine T. MacArthur Foundation stands out as the paramount media event in public libraries in 1988. Under the project, libraries have acquired collections of videocassettes at 10 percent of the listed price. More than 1,000 libraries (including some branches) participated, an astonishing number considering the fact that there are only about 1,000 public libraries serving communities of more than 25,000 population. The project was not without criticism since it unduly emphasized such mainstream British culture as *The Jewel in the Crown* or such blockbuster PBS television series as *Nova* at the expense of more innovative work, for example, videos produced by American independents. The plan also favored a few large distributors, leaving the small producers out in the cold. Criticism has, however, been muted in part because no one wished to alienate the MacArthur Foundation but mostly because librarians knew that they had been purchasing such Hollywood movies as old Doris Day favorites in quantity. Even the least of the MacArthur Project titles are many cuts above these. Moreover, MacArthur recently took some of the most important and best produced of such American independents as Fred Wiseman's *Missile*, Ira Wohl's *Best Boy*, and Christine Noschese's *Metropolitan Avenue* and placed them with libraries that accepted the titles in the original project—titles that would ordinarily never make it into smaller collections.

Festivals. The American Film and Video Festival (AFVF), sponsored by the American Film and Video Association (920 Barnsdale Road, La Grange Park, IL 60525) continues to be the most important film and video festival in the United States serving the needs of educators. Unlike other festivals that compete with it, AFVF has a nationwide membership of librarians, media specialists, distributors, and film and video makers, giving the festival a thrust lacked by other festivals. In the past AFVF was always held in New York, but in 1989 it will move into a hotel at Chicago's O'Hare Airport. It will be interesting to see if AFVF can maintain its preeminence in the new, somewhat isolated venue.

Two other festivals tried to take over the mantle of leadership from the American Film and Video Festival. The International Film and TV Festival of New York held in New York in November uses juries of leading educators and film specialists and closes with a black-tie awards banquet. Its 1988 Grand Award in the education category went to the outstanding art film *Paul Gaugin, The Savage Dream*, produced by The National Gallery of Art and distributed by Home Vision. National Educational Film and Video Festival (314 East Tenth Street, Oakland, CA 94606) is attempting to create a national presence. It also uses eminent juries, and in May 1988 gave its Best of Festival Award to *Fighting Back (1957-62)* from the PBS Series "Eyes on the Prize," on the civil rights struggle in America, produced by Henry Hampton and a landmark in television history.

The most prestigious award from all the festivals is the American Film and Video Festival's John Grierson Award named in honor of the pioneer British documentarian who founded the National Film Board of Canada. The 1988 Grierson winner, *Cane Toads*, was directed by Mark Lewis, an Australian; it is distributed in the U.S. by Icarus Films. *Cane Toads* uses humor to deal with serious ecological issues.

Outstanding Documentaries of 1988. The documentary field saw the entry of more films by Asian Americans than in previous years. These films often deal with the problems of parents and grandparents in assimilating into American life while facing racism. More women than ever entered documentary production. Their creations often dealt with feminist issues. A great many people worked with videotape, but a surprising number still worked with film. Many compromised by shooting in film and editing the final copy on videotape. Some of the significant productions of 1988 follow.

Drums of Winter. Color. 90 minutes. By Sarah Elder and Leonard Kamerling, distributed by Alaska Native Heritage Film Project, Box 81323, Fairbanks, AK 99708, this work explores in fascinating detail the ancient music and dance of an Eskimo people who live on the Yukon Delta on the Bering Sea.

Family Gathering. Color. 30 minutes. By Lise Yasui and Ann Tegnell, distributed by New Day Films, 853 Broadway, New York, NY 10003. The filmmaker, who is of Japanese ancestry, looks at the effect of the internment of her family by the U.S. Government in World War II following Pearl Harbor.

A House Divided. Color. 35 minutes. By Lyn Wright, distributed by the National Film Board of Canada, 1251 Avenue of the Americas, New York, NY 10020, this is perhaps the first film to deal with the tragedy of the abuse of the elderly.

How to Prevent Nuclear War. Color. 32 minutes. By Liane Brandon, distributed by New Day Films, 853 Broadway, New York, NY 10003, this is a positive, upbeat film about the activities anyone can engage in to lessen the threat of nuclear war.

Ika Hands. Color. 58 minutes. By Robert Gardner, distributed by the Museum of Modern Art, Circulating Film Library, 11 West 53rd St., New York, NY 10019, this is an intimate portrayal of the Ika, a native people of the highlands of the Sierra Nevadas of Northern Colombia who maintain their Pre-Colombian culture.

Inside Life Outside. Color. 60 minutes. *In video only*. By Sachiko Hamada and Scott Sinkler, distributed by Hamada and Sinkler, 185 East 3rd St., New York, NY 10009, it presents the harsh reality of a small group of homeless persons who live in a shantytown on a vacant lot in New York City.

Long Shadows. Color. 88 minutes. By Ross Spears, distributed by the James Agee project, 316 East Main St., Johnson City, TN 37601, this film examines the lasting impact of the American Civil War on American life and culture.

A Singing Stream. Color. 57 minutes. By Tom Davenport, distributed by Davenport Films, Box 527, Delaplane, VA 22025, it traces 20th-century black history through the music and cultural traditions of one Southern black family.

Young at Heart. Color. 28 minutes. By Sue Marx and Pamela Conn, distributed by New Dimension Films, 85895 Lorane Highway, Eugene, OR 97405, it is an inspiring, often amusing look at two elderly people who although in their eighties have a tremendous zest for life.

This is Our Home: It is Not For Sale. Color. 190 minutes. By Jon Schwartz, distributed by The Beacon Company, 205 Washington Avenue, Santa Monica, CA 90403, it chronicles the history of a Houston, Texas, neighborhood that went from all white to nearly all black and then became integrated. *This is Our Home* deals with the basic issues of racism in America.

WILLIAM J. SLOAN

Film and Video, Children's

American Film & Video Festival. The 30th American Film and Video Festival was held in New York City by the American Film and Video Association. Films of interest to children and young people that won awards included the following:

Animation—Red Ribbon—*Luxo Jr.* Director: John Lasseter. Distributor: Direct Cinema Ltd.

Original Works for Children—Blue Ribbon—*Words on a Page.* Director: Keith Leckie. Distributor: Beacon Films.

Red Ribbon—*Ready to Be a Wise Man.* Director: Robert Clem. Distributor: Direct Cinema Ltd.

Literary Adaptations for Children—Blue Ribbon—*In the Night Kitchen.* Director: Gene Deitch. Distributor: Weston Woods.

Red Ribbon—*Abel's Island.* Director: Michael Sporn. Distributor: Lucerne Media.

Documentaries for Young People—Blue Ribbon—*Children of Japan: Learning the New, Remembering the Old.* Director: Paula Heller. Distributor: Coronet/MTI Film & Video.

Red Ribbon—*They Look a Lot Like Us: A China Odyssey.* Director: Terry Woolf. Distributor: Kudlik Productions.

Original Works for Young Adults—Blue Ribbon—*Many Happy Returns.* Director: Joseph L. Butt Jr. Distributor: Coe Films.

Red Ribbon—*Seasonal Differences.* Director: Tom Robertson. Distributor: Coe Films.

Literary Adaptations for Young Adults—Blue Ribbon—*A Child's Christmas in Wales.* Director: Don McBrearty. Distributor: Beacon Films.

Red Ribbon—*Walking on Air.* Director: Ed Kaplan. Distributor: WQED/Pittsburgh.

Arts and Humanities—Red Ribbon—*Concerto Grosso Modo.* Director Francois Aubry. Distributor: Pyramid Film & Video.

Instructional Films: Language Arts—Blue Ribbon—*Living Poetry.* Director: Harvey Edwards. Distributor: Edwards Films Inc.

Red Ribbon—*The Cosby Show Episode #323-25 Shakespeare.* Director: Jay Sandrich. Distributor: VIACOM.

Instructional Films: Social Studies—Blue Ribbon—*China Since Mao.* (tie) Producer: BBC. Distributor: Films Inc. *Teedie.* (tie) Director: Edmund Levy. Distributor: Coronet/MTI Film and Video.

Guidance and Values—Blue Ribbon—*Degrassi Junior High: It's Late.* Director: Kit Hood. Distributor: Direct Cinema Ltd.

Red Ribbon—*Scared Straight: Ten Years Later.* Director: Arnold Shapiro. Distributor: Pyramid Film & Video.

Teenage Suicide—Blue Ribbon—*Dead Serious.* Director: Jerry Haislmaier. Distributor: Coronet/MTI Film & Video.

Red Ribbon—*It Begins with You.* Director: Susan Hughes. Distributor: Ramsey, Tanney, Tierney & Lang.

AIDS Education and Prevention—Blue Ribbon—*Young People and AIDS.* Producer and Distributor: Channing L. Bete Company, Inc.

Red Ribbon—*What is AIDS?* Director: J. Gary Mitchell. Distributor: Coronet/MTI Films & Video.

Music Video.—Blue Ribbon—*Women of the Calabash.* Director: Skip Blumberg. Distributor: Twin Cities Public Television.

Home Video for Children—Blue Ribbon—*Five Lionni Classics.* Director: Giulio Gianini. Distributor: Random House Home Video.

Red Ribbon—*The Tale of Mr. Jeremey Fisher and the Tale of Peter Rabbit.* Director: Mark Sottnick. Distributor: Sony Video Software Company.

Honorable Mention—*Shari Lewis Presents 101 Things for Kids to Do.* Director: Jack Regas. Distributor: Random House Home Video.

Instructional Films: The Sciences—Red Ribbon—*Solid, Liquid, Gas.* Director: David H. Gluck. Distributor: National Geographic.

Health/Sex Education—Red Ribbon—*Who Am I Now?* Director: Jon Leland. Distributor: Tambrands.

Parents' Choice Awards. In November, *Parents' Choice*, a review of children's media, named outstanding movies for children and families from the past 12 months. It passed over the highly visible *Who Framed Roger Rabbit?* and *Willow* as films with "great technical artistry and inventiveness in the service of screenplays that were hopelessly banal and occasionally tasteless."

The "few gems" recommended by Michael Medved, were, in alphabetical order, *Au Revoir les Enfants (Goodbye, Children)*, a "masterpiece . . . about the bittersweet pains of childhood" in an autobiographical film by Louis Malle about Jewish boys tracked down by Nazis; *Big*, an "unmitigated triumph" starring Tom Hanks as a 12-year-old in the body of a 30-year-old; *Big Top Pee Wee*, "a bizarre though pleasant concoction" starring Pee Wee Herman, which "is consistently amusing and inventive;" *Da*, in which Martin Sheen plays an Irish-born playwright interacting with the ghost of his difficult but loving adoptive father (Barnard Hughes); *The Grand Highway*, a French film in which a small boy is "sent to live with a group of endearing eccentrics in a rural town in the late 1950s; *Hope and Glory*, in which a seven-year-old boy "recalls his family's experiences during the darkest days of the Battle of Britain in World War II;" *Planes, Trains and Automobiles*, a "slapstick extravaganza," staring Steve Martin and John Candy, which "provides an underlying—and unexpected—sense of warmth and compassion;" *The Princess Bride*, "a radiant fairy tale" that "carries a valuable message about the joys of reading;" *Stand and Deliver*, with Edward James Olmos in "an Oscar-calibre performance as a Bolivian-born math teacher who burns with an intense determination to teach calculus to his impoverished barrio students;" and *Three Men and a Baby*, about "three playboy bachelors whose lives change overnight when a baby girl in a basket arrives on their doorstep."

Parents' Choice video awards were given to the following titles: *Pecos Bill* (Rabbit Ears Storybook Classics/Sony Video), *Family Circle Storyland Theater* (Paperback Visual Publishing), *Bach and Broccoli* (Family Home Entertainment/IVE), *Anne of Green Gables* (Walt Disney Video), *An American Tail* (MCA Video), *Abel's Island* (Random House Home Video), *Lady and the*

Tramp (Walt Disney Video), Sign-Me-A-Story (Random House Video), The Grizzlies (National Geographic/Vestron Video), Pee Wee's Playhouse, Volume 4, "Beauty Makeover," (High Tops Video), and The Glass Menagerie (MCA Video). Awards for group viewing, due to subject, content, or price, were Japan (Coronet/MTI Films), Luxo Jr./Red's Dream (Direct Cinema Ltd.), and Degrassi Jr. High, It's Late (Direct Cinema Ltd.) Honors went to the following titles: King Cole's Party/Wee Sing. (Price/Stern/Sloan), I'm a Three-Toed, Triple-Eyed, Double-Jointed Dinosaur (Rainbow Morning Music), Don't Eat the Pictures: Sesame Street at the Metropolitan Museum of Art (Random House), The Care Bears Adventures in Wonderland (MCA), Paddington Goes to the Movies (Kids Klassics), Snow White and the Seven Dwarfs (King Broadcasting), Maia; a Dinosaur Grows Up (Running Press Video), The Glory of Their Times (Vid-American), and Yellow Submarine/The Beatles (MGM/UA)

Parents' Choice awards for worthwhile television were the following: Preschool-5—Children's Storybook Classics (Showtime), Mister Rogers' Neighborhood (PBS), Muppet Babies (CBS), Sesame Street (PBS), The Brave Little Toaster (The Disney Channel), Duck Tales (Syndicated), Lyle, Lyle, Crocodile: The Musical (Home Box Office), Reading Rainbow (PBS), Square One Television (PBS). Ages 8-11—Alf (NBC), Don't Just Sit There (Nickelodeon), Mother's Day (Lifetime), The Wonder Years (ABC). Ages 12-up—Degrassi Junior High (PBS), Frank's Place (CBS), God Bless the Child (ABC), Main Street (NBC), Wonderworks (PBS). All Ages—Jim Henson's The Storyteller (NBC), Mighty Mouse: The New Adventures (CBS), Pee-Wee's Playhouse (CBS). Honors awards went to Everest in Winter (Arts and Entertainment), My Family and Other Animals (Arts and Entertainment), The Elephant Show (Nickelodeon), Head of the Class (ABC), The New Adventures of Winnie the Pooh (The Disney Channel), Pinwheel (Nickelodeon), Star Trek: The Next Generation (Syndicated), Tall Tales and Legends (Showtime). Awards for local television went to Home Turf (KRON, San Francisco), The New Explorers (WBBM, Chicago), Pick Up the Beat (WJLA, Washington, D.C.), Straight Talk: Rx for Safe Sex (KING, Seattle), Freedom Station (ITV, Owings Mills, Maryland), Ready To Go: AIDS Program (WNEV, Boston), Teen Times (KHJ, Los Angeles), Music Magic (KING, Seattle), Keep the Dream Alive, Children of the Dream (KING, Seattle).

Other Awards. Several films about young boys were highly honored this year. Academy Award nominations were given to Empire of the Sun (six), Hope and Glory (five, including best director) and Au Revoir les Enfants (two including best foreign film). Winners of interest to older children were The Man Who Planted Trees as best short animation and Innerspace for best visual effects. Directors Guild nominees for best movie director included My Life as a Dog and Empire of the Sun. Empire was also nominated for best drama. Winners were Hope and Glory as best comedy and My Life as a Dog for best foreign language film.

An Emmy Award for Best Comedy Series was won by The Wonder Years (ABC). A Humanitas TV Prize was given to The Flintstone Kids (ABC) for animation and to The Kid Who Wouldn't Quit: The Brad Silverman Story (ABC) for live action. This prize is given by a coalition of independent broadcast groups to writers of television programs that affirm human dignity and "probe the meaning of human life."

The Children's Film and Television Center of America, based in Los Angeles, presented The Ruby Slipper Awards in August. The winners, which are chosen by separate child and adult juries, were the following. Best Animated Short: Children's Jury—The Magic Quilt (National Film Board of Canada). Adult's Jury—Frog and Toad Together (Churchill Films). Best Live Action Short: Children's Jury—Harry the Dirty Dog (Barr Films) and The Legend of Firefly Marsh (Phoenix Films). Adult's Jury—Madi (Belgian Radio and Television). Best Episode from a Television Series: Children's Jury—Zoo Family (Nickelodeon) and Terrific Trips: A Trip to the Firehouse (Fisher Price). Adult's Jury—Ramona: Mystery Meal (Churchill Films) and Degrassi Junior High: What a Night! (Direct Cinema Ltd.). Best Television Special: Children's Jury—Blind Tom: The Story of Tom Bethune (KCET and the Beem Foundation). Adult's Jury—The Mouse and the Motorcycle (Churchill Films). Best Feature: Children's Jury—Bach and Broccoli (IVE) and Starlight (Michael Pochna). Adult's Jury—Bach and Broccoli. The Center also honored Jim Henson, creator of "The Muppets," with its Ruby slipper for "Outstanding Contribution to Children's Film and Television."

The Chicago International Festival of Children's Films, held for 10 days in October, marked its fifth year with an ambitious and imaginative program of films from 25 counties and a "Salute to Sweden" on opening night. The festival is organized by Facets Multimedia Inc., a not-for-profit, tax-exempt film and theatre organization involved in theatre development, film exhibition and distribution. The ballots of child viewers selected Tommy Tricker and the Stamp Traveller, a Canadian feature by Michael Rubbo, as "Most Popular Film" of the Festival. The adult jury presented First Prizes in a number of categories: Live Action/Feature—Princess Jasna and the Flying Cobbler (Zdenek Troska/Czechoslovakia), Animated Feature—Subway to Paradise (Jannik Hastrup/Denmark), Live Action Short—Soldier Jack (Tom Davenport/USA), Mixed Live Action and Animation—Runaway Ralph (John Matthews/USA), Animated Shorts—Little Sister Rabbit (Eva Eriksson and Jan Gustavsson/Sweden), Henry's Cat: Once Upon a Time (Bob Godfrey/England), The Cat Came Back (Cordell Barker/Canada), and The Dawning (Bergquist, Ekstrand, Odell, Ohlson/Sweden). First Prize awards were also given to video titles: Devil's Hill (Esben Storm/Australia), The Great Cheese Conspiracy (Vaclav Bedrich/West Germany) and Ramona: Siblingitis (Randy Bradshaw/Canada). First Prize for Best Director was given to Lasse Hallstrom, the Oscar-winning director of My Life As a Dog, for The Children of Bullerby Village and More About the Children of Bullerby Village, two

Films and Video, Children's

live-action features based on the Noisy Village books by Astrid Lindgren.

A special award, the Liv Ullmann Peace Prize, went to the film *The Man Who Planted Trees* (Frederic Back/Canada). John Matthews, who made *Runaway Ralph*, was given a Special Humanitarian Award in recognition of the humane nature of his films. Although many of the festival films did not have U.S. distribution at the time of the festival the number of buyers present for the programs means many titles will be becoming available, a goal of the festival.

The Council on International Non-Theatrical Events (CINE) submits winners of its Golden Eagle awards as U.S. entries to international film festivals. The 1988 children's films most frequently entered in international competitions were *How the Elephant Got His Trunk*, *The Mouse and the Motorcycle*, and *Red's Dream*, which was honored by a Diploma of Participation in Berlin and invitations to participate in São Paulo, Brazil, and Wellington, New Zealand. *Chicken Thing*, one of the most frequent winners, won the Grand Prize for Best Experimental Film in Algarve, Portugal.

Among the children's films named as Golden Eagle titles in 1988 were *Abel's Island*, *A Child's Christmas in Wales*, *Chuckie*, *Jonah and the Great Fish*, *Runaway Ralph*, *Soldier Jack*, and *There's a Nightmare in My Closet*.

Feature Films. Two of the most written-about films of the year were George Lucas' *Willow*, referred to by one critic as "The Empire Strikes Out," and Robert Zemeckis' *Who Framed Roger Rabbit*, an inventive but dark film combining live action and animation, which delighted adults. Other features were the extremely wooden *The New Adventures of Pippi Longstocking*; *The Lady in White*, a stylish and skillful but often terrifying ghost story seen through the eyes of a young boy; *Short Circuit 2*, an undistinguished sequel with a "singularly charmless" robot hero; *Little Nikita*, in which Sydney Poitier plays "The most conspicuous undercover agent in the annals of the F.B.I."; *Mac and Me*, a mildly amusing E.T. clone; and *The Rescue*, an unbelievable saga of young people who rescue the POW fathers from North Korea. In addition to *Big*, two other films, *Vice Versa* and *Eighteen Again*, featured adults switching bodies with young people, and sounded amiable, if undistinguished. At year's end two animated films were released to enthusiastic response. *The Land Before Time*, Don Bluth's tale of a band of young dinosaurs of different species joining together to find a safer place to live, drew high praise for its charm and animation. *Oliver and Company*, a new Disney film based loosely on *Oliver Twist* and featuring animals, was touted as the first in a series of animated features to use state-of-the-art computer techniques. One reviwer observed that its hip characters were often more interested in hustling than in whistling while they work. Disney's *Bambi* was reissued this year.

In addition to the highly acclaimed *Grand Highway* and *Au Revoir les Enfants*, there were other films featuring children and the problems of childhood which appealed to adults. *Pelle the Conqueror*, a Danish film that won the Golden Palm, the top prize, at the Cannes Festival is the story of an aging father and his young son. *Zelly and Me* was about an 11-year-old orphan raised by her possessive grandmother. *Salaam Bombay!* a drama about street children in India won a Golden Camera Award at Cannes for best feature by a new director. *The Wizard of Loneliness* portrayed a lonely young boy in a Vermont village in 1944, with actors who brought the film "to vibrant life."

Alice, a film based on *Alice in Wonderland* and made by Jan Svankmajer, Czechoslovak animator, was a surrealistic creation for adults. For *When the Wind Blows*, Raymond Briggs, an author/illustrator of children's books, wrote the screenplay based on his adult picture book, which portrayed a tidy little English couple trying to deal with nuclear holocaust.

Television. Network television continued its problem-of-the-month approach to afterschool specials with themes of date-rape, teenage gangs, illiteracy, AIDS, child abuse, and homelessness. Bright moments were *Runaway Ralph* (ABC), Jim Henson's *The Storyteller* (NBC), and *The Wonder Years* (ABC). *Mighty Mouse: The New Adventures* (CBS), by Ralph Bakshi, was called "clever, and hip and well-animated."

On public television and cable a wider range of interesting projects were seen. *A Friendship in Vienna* (Disney Channel), based on Doris Orgel's *The Devil in Vienna*, was called "profoundly sad and terribly moving." A miniseries based on Gerald Durrell's autobiographical book *My Family and Other Animals* appeared on Arts & Entertainment Network. Game shows for children were a fad; Nickelodeon presented *Double Dare* and syndicated it to the Fox stations to prevent imitators. Public television continued to present *Wonderworks*, celebrated *Sesame Street's* 20th anniversary, presented *Reading Rainbow* and added a new spring season for the program, hosted a ten-part series of programs about Ramona Quimby, *Ramona*, and presented *CE News Magazine*, a news series featuring Children's Express and its young reporters. Public television's Children's Television Workshop produced a new weekly series, *Encyclopedia*, for Home Box Office, using performance artists to convey alphabetical bits of information. Increasing sophistication of children, the range of viewing options, and the use of new people-meter ratings technology were seen as threatening advertising revenues on network television and endangering shows for children under age six who cannot or will not operate the ratings technology devices.

Action for Children's Television celebrated its 20th birthday and looked toward the passage of a bill to reimpose restrictions on television programming aimed at children. Although the measure was overwhelmingly approved by Congress, President Reagan exercised a pocket veto because he considered the bill an unconstitutional infringement of freedom of expression. The vaunted freedom of expression in broadcasting this year produced *Nightmare on Elm Street, Freddy's Nightmare*, an unsettling horror show, defended by its producers, Lorimar, on the grounds that no one under the age of 18 would be murdered, and the development of a Noids' cartoon series by CBS, based on a trademark character used in the advertising of Domino's Pizza and aimed at the possibilities for commercial tie-ins.

Video. Videocassette recorders were in 53 percent of American homes by early 1988. One of the biggest video successes has been children's videos because they are used as babysitters and children watch them over and over. Disney's *Sleeping Beauty* has sold a million copies. The best-selling cassette in videotape history at the beginning of 1988 was Disney's *The Lady and the Tramp*, which sold 3,200,000 copies in December 1987. Disney's *Cinderella*, available on video in 1988 for a limited time, sold 5,300,000 copies. *Benji the Hunted* made its appearance, as did *Bach and Broccoli*, one of the Family Home Entertainment/IVE titles from Canadian Rock Demers, which won good reviews but little screening time in commercial theaters in the United States. The biggest video event of the year was the availability of the most popular film of all time, *E.T. the Extraterrestrial*. Steven Spielberg's film reached video stores in October with advance sales of more than 11,000,000 cassettes, to become the top title in all time video cassette sales. Spielberg agreed to the deal with the lowest price yet for a major film and a $5 rebate from Pepsi-Cola to reduce the price still further, to $19.95, to guard against inferior pirated copies being released. MCA is taking extraordinary measure to guard against pirates and identify phony tapes. Sales were so high that MCA, which had expected a sales of 6,000,000 tapes, was unable to meet the immediate demand. *Cinderella* was in second place for best-selling tapes.

Ratings. According to a national poll by the Opinion Research Corporation of Princeton, N.J., 95 percent of parents with children under the age of 18 are aware of the rating system for commercial movies and videocassettes. Although 73 percent found the ratings "very useful" or "fairly useful," many expressed confusion about the meaning of the ratings—especially R, which applies to 60 percent of all rated films. It is estimated that by the time films reach video stores only 30 to 40 percent of the titles carry ratings on their jackets. Some have had footage added or deleted since theatrical distribution. Video retailers face pending legislation in 19 states over clearer labeling to regulate video rentals to minors. The labeling issue will have great impact on libraries.

Other Events. On November 18 Mickey Mouse celebrated his 60th birthday. In celebration of the 25th anniversary of Maurice Sendak's *Where the Wild Things Are* Weston Woods created a new musical score for the film version, with narration by Peter Schickele. For the 16mm films suitable for children that were named 1988 Notable Children's Films by the Association for Library Service to Children, see "Notables" in this yearbook.

MARILYN BERG IARUSSO

Foundations, Private

The American Association of Fund-Raising Counsel Trust for Philanthropy estimates that corporations and corporate foundations gave $4,500,000,000 and other private and community foundations gave $6,380,000,000 for charitable purposes in 1987. As significant as these dollars are, it is important to remember that bequests and gifts from living individuals contributed an additional $82,800,000,000.[1] Although the Foundation Center estimates there are 25,000 grant-making foundations, only 5,148 awarded nearly 92 percent of total foundation giving in 1985.

The competition for these precious dollars is very great. INDEPENDENT SECTOR estimates that there are 873,000 tax-exempt voluntary and philanthropic organizations which depend on charitable contributions. In addition, tax supported institutions (such as public universities, schools, hospitals, and police departments) have been turning more and more to the private sector for additional financial support.

The Foundation Center reports in its 1988 edition of *Foundation Grants Index* a total of 559 grants comprising $64,612,000 made to libraries in 1987. This figure represents 2.5 percent of grant dollars reported by private and community foundations in the United States. Table 1 shows the figures over the past 5 years.

The great majority of foundations have restrictions on their grant-making, most often geographic constraints, but in addition may restrict their giving in other ways (population served, type of organization, purpose). Table 2 shows the largest 20 grants to libraries as reported to The Foundation Center in the first ten months of 1988. Before sending any requests to these or other foundations, it is important for a library to do its homework in researching the fields of interest and any restrictions.

In 1984, the executive committee of American Library Association's Library Administration and Management Association approved the establishment of the "Fund Raising and Financial Development Section" (FRFDS). Barbara Fischler writes in the January 1987 issue of *Library Administration and Management* that 198 (out of 1,113 responding) libraries reported receiving grants from private foundations and 231 libraries reported receiving contributions from businesses, according to a survey conducted by FRFDS in the Spring of 1985. FRFDS is making plans to conduct another survey of fundraising by libraries. Looking at the Foundation Center figures, one would expect the survey to show that many more libraries are now receiving foundation grants.

Libraries have traditionally thought of foundations as possible sources of funding when trying to raise funds for building campaigns, despite the fact that many foundations exclude giving to capital campaigns. More and more libraries are beginning to recognize that many foundations prefer to make grants for pilot projects, or for one to three year programs that improve services but do not add to the library's overall costs unless the future funding is assured. Foundations that have never given to libraries may well be potential sources of funding for programs that serve particular demographic groups, or that fall in the subject field of interest of the foundation. For example, The Henry Luce Foundation Inc. made a grant of $50,000 to Harvard University's Fine Arts Library to support photographic exchange between American and Chinese art museums.

Freedom to Read Foundation

Table 1. Grants to Libraries as Reported 1983–1987

1983		1984		1985		1986		1987	
No.	Amount	No.	Amount	No.	Amount	No.	Amount	No.	Amount
378	36,940	421	24,621	493	63,078	570	68,196	559	64,612

All dollar figures expressed in thousands.
Source: Foundation Grants Index, © The Foundation Center, used with permission.

Table 2. 20 Largest Grants To Libraries In 1988 As Reported Through October 1988.

Recipient (State)	Amount	Foundation Donor (State)	Purpose
1. Indiana University Foundation	$12,000,000 (3 yrs.)	1. Lilly Endowment Inc. (Indiana)	For construction of campus library and statewide electronic information network
2. University of Zimbabwe	1,500,000 (4 yrs.)	2. The Ford Foundation (New York)	For staff and institutional development, specifically for Ph.D. training, to keep book and journal collections current, and to strengthen planning, budgeting, and fund-raising
3. Duke University (North Carolina)	785,000 (2 yrs.)	3. The Pew Charitable Trusts (Pennsylvania)	To expand remote storage capacity for library
4. Newberry Library (Illinois)	250,000 (5 yrs.)	4. The Chicago Community Trust (Illinois)	For general operating support
5. Online Computer Library Center (OCLC) (Ohio)	240,000 (3 yrs.)	5. The Henry Luce Foundation (New York)	For development of computer-based records at National Library of China in Beijing
6. Hawaii Pacific College	200,000	6. The Kresge Foundation (Michigan)	Toward renovation and expansion of library
7. Geneva College (Pennsylvania)	150,000 (3 yrs.)	7. The Buhl Foundation	For library automation
8. Long Island University (New York)	100,000	8. The Clark Foundation (New York)	For library computerization project
9. Wesley Theological Seminary (District of Columbia)	100,000	9. The Arthur Vining Davis Foundations (Florida)	To fund library renovations
10. Library of Congress (District of Columbia)	100,000	10. The Ford Foundation (New York)	For review of library's mission, strategies, and management practice
11. New York Public Library	100,000 (2 yrs.)	11. Helena Rubinstein Foundation, Inc. (New York)	For general support and for purchase of women's studies books and materials
12. Rochester Institute of Technology (New York)	75,000	12. The Clark Foundation (New York)	For library addition
13. Green Library (California)	75,000	13. Rockefeller Brothers Fund (New York)	For general budgetary needs of Green Library–Poland
14. Pierpont Morgan Library (New York)	68,000	14. Mary Flagler Cary Charitable Trust (New York)	Toward Mary Flagler Cary Music Collection 20th Anniversary exhibition
15. Albany Law School (New York)	50,000	15. The Clark Foundation (New York)	For new library
16. Georgetown University (District of Columbia)	50,000	16. The Clark Foundation (New York)	For new library study area for handicapped
17. New York Public Library	50,000	17. The Clark Foundation (New York)	For general support
18. Houston Academy of Medicine (Texas)	50,000	18. William Randolph Hearst Foundation (New York)	Toward development of Management Information System for Texas Medical Center Library
19. Concordia College (Wisconsin)	37,000	19. Siebert Lutheran Foundation (Wisconsin)	For purchase of library holdings and equipment
20. Amelia S. Givin Free Library (Pennsylvania)	25,000	20. The Whitaker Foundation (Pennsylvania)	For development campaign for construction of addition

Source: Custom printout from The Foundation Center, New York, used with permission.

New York Public Library received $25,000 from The Vincent Astor Foundation toward "A Visual Testimony: Judaica from the Vatican Library," a loan exhibition held in fall of 1988.

Foundation grants need not be large in order to make a significant difference. The San Francisco Foundation granted $5,000 to the Japanese American Library to promote understanding of Japanese-Americans and Japan through a diverse collection of library materials. The Fletcher Free Library in Burlington, Vermont received $6,000 from the Gannett Foundation, Inc. toward a program introducing senior citizens to library resources.[2]

The Foundation Center reports that only about 30 percent of the largest foundations publish brochures, reports or other documents to inform the public about their operations. Thus the public is in large part dependent upon the many published directories of foundations for its information. However, all private foundations are required under the tax law to file a tax return showing grants made, dollars awarded, officers, etc. These are photographed by the Internal Revenue Service and made available for sale in microfiche form. The Foundation Center purchases copies of these and makes them available for examination free of charge through its library network. In 1988 there are over 170 cooperating collections, with at least one in every state. (Call 1-800-424-9836 for more information.)

[1] Source: Giving USA, 1988 edition.
[2] The first three of these grants were made in late 1987, but not reported to The Foundation Center until 1988.

JEANNE L. BOHLEN

Freedom to Read Foundation

During 1988, The Freedom to Read Foundation (FTRF) continued as a strong voice for the protection of First Amendment rights. Founded in 1969 as a non-profit corporation committed to the legal defense of the library community when faced with censorship attacks by individuals, groups, or governments, The Freedom to Read Foundation was highly visible in 1988. Officers included Judith A. Sessions, President; R. Bruce Rich, Vice President, and Pamela G. Bonnel, Treasurer.

The most public and visible challenge to the freedom to read—and to have what one reads or views kept private—were the visits to libraries by agents of the Federal Bureau of Investigation under what was known as the Library Awareness Program.

The Freedom to Read Foundation in conjunction with the American Library Association filed a Freedom of Information Act suit regarding the FBI's "Library Awareness Program" and related activities; the suit appealed the vast amounts of deleted information in the documents ALA had received to date and attempted to force the Bureau to respond to ALA's second request.

The Foundation's Board carefully examined the possibility of suit for an injunction to force the Bureau to cease and desist. However, insufficient information forced FTRF to abandon such a step for the time being. (Insufficient information results from governmental activities. Where the governmental purpose is to suppress speech—the courts have almost always found that the government's activities violate the First Amendment. But if the governmental goal was to achieve some other purpose—for example, the clearly legitimate purpose of enforcing the criminal laws preventing espionage—any incidental suppression of speech that resulted from governmental efforts to achieve that other purpose do not violate the First Amendment, unless those governmental efforts were "wholly gratuitous" and were not reasonably related to achieving that other purpose.) The FBI has denied any purpose to suppress speech, and no compelling evidence existed to the contrary.

Thus, in order to win a suit against the FBI, the Foundation would have to prove either that FBI contacts with libraries are so unrelated to preventing espionage that such contacts are gratuitous and unreasonable; or that the FBI's real purpose was to deter patrons from using libraries or to deter librarians from providing information to patrons. Either proof would be fact–intensive, would require expensive and extensive depositions, and would result in a suit that would be very uncertain. The Board of Trustees directed staff and legal counsel to continue to monitor the FBI Library programs and to collect information toward a possible future suit.

In its ongoing legal casework, the Foundation filed amicus curiae briefs in two cases concerning censorship of optional curricular materials and worked to change a directive from the City Manager in Scottsdale, Arizona that potentially could have a disastrous impact on the public library there. There were also developments in two continuing cases.

In Scottsdale, Arizona, the City Manager ordered the Director of the public library not to make Playboy available to anyone under the age of 18, because he believed that, under Arizona's "Harmful to Minors" statute, the library staff might be liable for criminal prosecution for making "harmful materials" available to minors. The harmful material was thus far limited to *Playboy*, although in Casa Grande, Arizona, the City Manager directed that the book, *Truly Tasteless Jokes*, be kept from persons under 18. The Foundation considered the potential for escalation of titles deemed "harmful" to be enormous. FTRF wrote to the City Manager of Scottsdale urging that he rescind his directive. The letter made clear, however, the Foundation's firm intent to pursue this issue should the order not be rescinded.

FTRF was in court for several years in a "harmful to minors" case in the State of Virginia. *ABA v. Virginia* challenged Virginia's "harmful to minors" statute which, as written, prohibits the display of materials deemed harmful to minors. Display, under this statute, means in a manner that allows juveniles to view or peruse these allegedly harmful materials. This statute was declared unconstitutional in June 1985; the ruling was upheld in June, 1986. Virginia appealed the case to the U.S. Supreme Court, which in January, 1988, took the surprising step of sending the case back to the Virginia Supreme Court. The Virginia Court then ruled that none of the books submitted in evidence would be affected by the statute under the standard they decided was appropriate; namely, none of the books lacked serious literary, artistic, political, or scientific value for a legitimate minority of older normal adolescents. The court held that a bookseller who had a policy of not allowing juveniles to read books in the store that they are not allowed to buy, and prohibits such conduct when observed, complies with the statute. At the end of 1988, the case had been sent for reconsideration to the United States Court of Appeals for the Fourth District.

The Foundation was also involved in two cases concerned with curricular censorship. The first of these, *McCarthy v. Fletcher*, is ongoing. It concerns the censorship of two books in Lee McCarthy's English class at Wasco (California) Union High School. This case began in 1985. The principal–superintendent, Douglas Fletcher, restricted use of *Grendel*, by John Gardner, and later of *One Hundred Years of Solitude*, by Gabe Garcia Marquez, books on Lee McCarthy's assigned reading list, with other books as substitutes if parents or students objected to the two works. By late 1988, the case was before the Fifth Appellate District Court of the State of California. The Foundation filed an *amicus curiae* brief that carefully explicated the requirements of the First Amendment in regard to speech regulation in public schools and, also, distinguished regulation of speech in the curriculum and speech in school libraries.

In the second curriculum case, *Virgil v. School Board of Columbia County, Florida*, the Foundation joined the *amicus* brief of People for the American Way. This case concerned removal from the curriculum of Columbia High School in 1986, of volume I of *The Humanities: Cultural Roots and Continuities*, because of objections by parents of one student to Aristophanes' *Lysistrata* and *The Miller's Tale*, by Geoffrey Chaucer, neither of which were required or assigned reading. The parents objected to the sexual nature of

Friends of Libraries

the material and the "vulgarity." The School Board, acting on the Superintendent's recommendation, removed the book. A suit was filed by concerned parents in the U.S. District Court for the Middle District of Florida. The plaintiff parents lost. The case is on appeal to the U.S. Eleventh Circuit Court of Appeals. The Foundation joined in a brief which points out that the First Amendment's prohibition on the official suppression of ideas includes ideas concerning sexual relations, and, thus, the School Board's motives for suppressing these selections were improper.

Bullfrog Films v. *Wick*, the case brought by ten filmmakers against the U.S. Information Agency for its refusal to grant "certificates of education character" to documentaries has been in court several years. The suit charged that the United States Information Agency's (USIA) refusal was based on the content of the films which have to do with acid rain, the drug problems of America's youth, and U.S. policy towards Nicaragua, and which are generally not supportive of the Reagan administration's position on these issues. In October 1986, a U.S. District Court Judge ruled that the USIA's guidelines violated the First Amendment to the Constitution. On May 18th, Judge Tashima's 1986 ruling was upheld in the Ninth Circuit Court of Appeals. Judge Tashima also ordered the USIA to come up with "standards consistent" with the Constitution. On May 13, Judge Tashima ruled that USIA's new regulations are also unconstitutional. The Foundation participated early on as *amicus curiae*.

The Foundation's work covers the freedom to read in its many generic forms. It seeks to influence laws and practices that affect the interpretation of the First Amendment. The Foundation has been actively engaged in this work for 19 years.

JUDITH SESSIONS

Friends of Libraries

Friends of library groups concentrated on advocacy in 1988, as elections and tax initiatives focused attention on local library budgets. Friends groups in California, Texas, Oregon, Utah, and elsewhere attempted to bring library issues to the attention of the electorate, with varying success.

It is evident that funds raised by Friends of Libraries U.S.A. (FOLUSA) were increasingly applied to such budget items as video- and audio cassettes, compact disc collections, computers and associated software, and special books.

Awards. More than 400 persons attended FOLUSAs annual award luncheon at the ALA annual conference in New Orleans. Friends of Libraries U.S.A./Baker & Taylor awards included: Small Public Library to Friends of the Evanston Public Library for a "letters to the editor" campaign to heighten community awareness of library issues, purchasing books, purchasing computers for patrons' use, and for library acquisitions; Large Public Library to the Atlanta-Fulton (County, Georgia) Public Library Friends for their efforts to educate the funding bodies involved to the needs of the library, which resulted in salary increases for the 465 library employees, totaling $1.2 million; Friends of the Louisiana State University Library, Baton Rouge, won the Academic Library Friends award for promoting their book sale, which has become an annual community project.

Other conference highlights were: an address by author Rita Mae Brown and a panel discussion covering the most-asked questions of the year, Fundraising, Looking Good in Print, and Rural Friends. Richard Torbert handed the gavel to Frank W. Miller, H. W. Wilson Company, new FOLUSA president. Vice-president is Fred Philipp Ingram; Secretary, Robert Runyon, Librarian, University of Nebraska–Omaha, and Treasurer, Paul W. Karr, Deloitt, Haskins & Sells, Chicago.

Programs. In cooperation with Mellon Baule, Philadelphia, Pennsylvania, FOLUSA sponsored an appearance of Dr. James Billington at a legacies of Genius program held by a consortium of libraries in the Philadelphia area. Reprints of the address was published and distributed to members, in cooperation with The Center for the Book in the Library of Congress. FOLUSA programs highlighting Literary Landmarks, were held in San Antonio, and New Orleans.

Increased interest in FOLUSA spurred sales of its video, *Making Friends;* a videotape produced with the support of H. W. Wilson Company. FOLUSA provides members with special offers through the quarterly, *Idea Bank*, and with the cooperation of Taft Publishing Co. and Mellon Bank, respectively, who distributes a brochure, *Libraries: Getting into the Philanthropic Thick of Things* and *Discover Total Resources*. Other FOLUSA publications: fact sheets on how friends can help with literacy issues in their communities, how to stage a book and author event, and a revision of FOLUSAs most popular publication, the *National Notebook*.

FOLUSA urged its members to become involved in the White House Conference, and with the assistance of the H. W. Wilson Foundation, Cahner's Publishing Co., and World Book, to conduct a second, more comprehensive survey whose results are expected in early 1989.

FRANK W. MILLER

The Citizens for Library Excellence, a political action group formed out of the Friends for the Dallas Public Library, actively fought budget cuts in recession-riddled Dallas during 1988. Here Dallas Public Library Director and Citizens for Library Excellence supporters crowd City Council chambers.

Government Documents Round Table

Organization. The Government Documents Round Table (GODORT) addressed two areas of organization that provide membership with better access to information about the round table. The first area included the merger of the Constitution and Bylaws into one document, the GODORT Bylaws. This move eliminated duplicative language and brought together information that had been separated in the two former documents. Publication of the *GODORT Policies and Procedure Manual* in three versions (one for the general membership, one for officers, and one for executive officers) comprised the second area of organizational activity.

Response to Issues. As in previous years, the issues of privatization and of access to and distribution of government information in electronic formats formed the focus for much of the activity of the working units of GODORT. A measure of success for some of these activities was the signing of the Omnibus Trade and Competitiveness Act of 1988 that banned the complete contracting out of the National Technical Information Service. On January 9, 1988 GODORT, along with the Association of Research Libraries (ARL) Task Force on Government Information in Electronic Format, the American Association of Law Libraries, the ALA Legislation Committee, the Chief Officers of State Library Agencies (COSLA), and the Special Libraries Association, sponsored a forum on the GODORT Government Information Technology Committee's report, *Government Information Technology and Information Dissemination: A Discussion Paper* and the ARL Task Force Study, *Technology and U.S. Government Information Policies: Catalysts for New Partnerships*. During the Midwinter Conference, GODORT passed a resolution that ALA adopt the Government Information "Bill of Rights" included in the Government Information Technology Committee's discussion paper.

In addition, GODORT also responded to the plans for the 1990 Census as proposed by the Office of Management and Budget (OMB) by passing several resolutions directed to OMB asking that OMB reconsider its decisions on reduction of the long form sample size and on deletion of several questions used in the 1980 Census.

Programs Sponsored. The major GODORT program for the 1988 ALA Conference was "Finding the Answers to Some of Your Toughest Questions: Training the General Information Provider to Use Government Information." Featured speakers were Charles Seavey, University of Arizona; Karen Smith, State University of New York–Buffalo; Deborah Hollens, Southern Oregon State College; Mary Fetzer, Rutgers University; Barbara Hulyk, Detroit Public Library; Judy Fair-Spaulding, DIALOG; Lou Helen Sanders, University of Pittsburgh; and Gary Purcell, University of Tennessee, moderator. Additional programs co-sponsored or sponsored by GODORT were "Information Policies of International Organizations: Roadblocks to Access," "Information Access: Issues and Action," and "CD-ROM: Applications for Government Documents, 1990 Census."

GOVERNMENT DOCUMENTS ROUND TABLE

PRESIDENT (July 1988–June 1989):
Sandra S. McAninch, University of Kentucky, Lexington

ASSISTANT CHAIR/CHAIR-ELECT:
Susan Tulis, University of Virginia, Charlottesville

SECRETARY:
Timothy Byrne, University of Colorado, Boulder

Membership (May 31, 1988): 1,307
Expenditures (May 31, 1987): $40,104

Awards. GODORT honored two individuals in 1988. The James Bennett Childs Award, a tribute to an individual who has made a lifelong, significant contribution to documents librarianship, was presented to Patricia G. Reeling of Rutgers University. The CIS/GODORT/ALA Documents to the People Award, recognizing an individual who effectively encouraged the use of federal documents in support of library service, was presented to Agnes Ferruso of the Library of Congress.

Reeling was selected for her contribution as a library and information science educator with special concern for government information and for her distinguished publication record, including two regular columns on documents in *RQ* and *Documents to the People (DttP)*. Ferruso was chosen for her indefatigable abilities as a champion for documents and documents librarianship and for the vital role she played in initiating the Library of Congress U.S. federal depository documents collection and bringing together other collections of government publications to form a major research center for government information.

In 1988, the Readex/GODORT/ALA Catherine J. Reynolds Award went to Sheila Nollen, Western Illinois University and Steven Zink, University of Nevada–Reno. This award provides grants to documents librarians for travel and/or study in documents librarianship or in an area of study that would benefit directly their performance as documents librarians.

CAROLYN C. JAMISON

Government Publications and Depository System

Depository Library Access to Electronic Information. The depository library program entered the electronic age on September 6, 1988, when the first CD-ROM disc was distributed to 143 selected libraries. The disc was published by the Bureau of the Census, and contains data from the 1982 Censuses of Agriculture and Retail Trade. Following a test period, the disc will be distributed to all remaining depository libraries. This is one of five proposed pilot projects to test the feasibility of distributing information to depository libraries in electronic format. Two other projects are in CD-ROM format: the final edition of the *Congressional Record*, and the Environmental Protection Agency's *Toxic Release Inventory*. In the other two projects, 100 libraries will be ex-

Government Publications and Depository System

tended online access to the Department of Commerce *Economic Bulletin Board* for six months, and 18 to 22 libraries will have online access to the Department of Energy database for technical reports. The five projects were developed jointly by Government Printing Office (GPO) and the Joint Committee on Printing (JCP) staff. On July 11 JCP Chairman Representative Frank Annunzio (D-Ill.) inserted a notice in the *Congressional Record* (p. E 2322) asking for comments from members and constituents, and on July 13 sent a notice to executive branch agencies for comments. In a letter dated September 29, Office of Management and Budget (OMB) Director James C. Miller III stated that "executive branch agencies are providing electronic information products to Depository Libraries voluntarily and not as a legal obligation. Executive branch agencies are under no obligation to procure electronic information products, whether for their own or for the public's use, through GPO."

OTA Report on Electronic Dissemination. In early October, following a two-year study, the Office of Technology Assessment (OTA), a Congressional research unit, submitted its report, *Informing the Nation: Federal Information Dissemination in an Electronic Age*. The report focuses on the role of the Government Printing Office, National Technical Information Service (NTIS), and the Depository Library Program in an electronic age. It assesses three alternative futures for the Government Printing Office: a "traditional GPO-centralized" in which GPO would continue to provide centralized conventional printing services; a "traditional GPO-legislative branch only" under which GPO would provide printing services for the legislative branch only, while the printing procurement program would be transferred to the executive branch; and an "electronic GPO-decentralized" under which GPO would continue to provide centralized printing services, but would expand its range of electronic publishing services and disseminate selected electronic products though the sales and depository library programs. Mission agencies at their discretion would continue to disseminate their electronic products. The report also views closer cooperation or consolidation between the Superintendent of Documents sales program and NTIS as a viable alternative.

NTIS Privatization Thwarted. The Reagan administration has attempted since 1981 to privatize the National Technical Information Service. Five unsuccessful attempts had been made under OMB Circular No. A-76, "Policies for Acquiring Commercial or Industrial Products and Services Needed by the Government." Department of Commerce Task Forces in 1981 and 1986 rejected the idea. On January 6, 1988, the Department of Commerce, at the direction of OMB, announced in the *Federal Register* that it was planning to issue a request for proposals to privatize NTIS functions under the Federal Employee Direct Corporate Stock Ownership Plan. Under this plan, federal employees would exchange their government jobs for salaried positions with a contractor and be provided stock in the new firm. Opposition to privatization has come from the library community and Congress. In 1987 Representative Doug Walgren(D-Pa.) introduced H.R. 2159, which would establish NTIS as a wholly-owned government corporation. The text of H.R. 2159 was later incorporated into H.R. 4417, National Institute of Standards and Technology Authorization Act for Fiscal Year 1989. In a compromise between three committees a substitute version was enacted that would continue NTIS as a government agency. A floor amendment by Rep. Walgren that should discourage all further OMB attempts to privatize NTIS was accepted. It stated that NTIS "functions and activities . . . are permanent federal functions . . . and shall not be transferred . . . by contract or otherwise, to the private sector on a permanent or temporary basis without express approval of Congress." H.R. 4417 passed the House September 26, was passed by the Senate October 5, and approved by President Reagan October 24 as Public Law 100-519.

Administration Retreats on Challenge to JCP. On March 20, 1987, the Department of Defense (DoD), General Services Administration (GSA) and National Aeronautics and Space Administration (NASA) published in the *Federal Register* a change to section 8.802 of the *Federal Acquisition Regulation* (Title 48, *Code of Federal Regulations*) which would eliminate the role of the Joint Committee on Printing in the control of executive branch printing. It stated that, "the requirement in 44 U.S.C. 501(2) for the advance approval of the Congressional Joint Committee on Printing (JCP) prior to printing operations (or the acquisition of such printing) is unconstitutional under the Supreme Court's decision in *Immigration and Naturalization Service v. Chadha*, 103 S. Ct. 2764 (1983); therefore, the approval requirement neither binds the executive branch nor serves as the basis for any coverage in this subpart."

In response, Congress added section 309 to the FY 1988 Legislative Branch Appropriations Act which stated that "none of the funds appropriated for fiscal year 1988 by this Act or any other law may be obligated or expended by any entity of the executive branch for the procurement from commercial sources of any printing related to the production of Government publications (including forms) unless such procurement is by or through the Government Printing Office." The FY 1989 Legislative Branch Appropriations act included similar language in section 309. On August 29, 1988 DoD, GSA, and NASA published a proposed rule in the *Federal Register* that they are considering changes to delete the language in section 8.802 regarding JCP advance approval in response to "the fundamental congressional concern that gave rise to the enactment of section 309 of the (FY 1988) Legislative Branch Appropriations Act."

Depository Library Program. At the close of FY 1988 there were 1,394 designated depository libraries. Five libraries had been added, and six had voluntarily relinquished their designation. Three states remained unserved by a regional depository: Delaware, South Dakota, and Tennessee. The number of titles distributed to depository libraries in paper copy increased from 19,349 to 19,411 in FY 1988 and the number of copies distributed increased to 8,675,568 in FY 1988 from 8,343,996 in FY 1987. The number of titles distributed in microfiche decreased to 9,721 in FY 1988 from 21,970 in FY 1987 and the number of copies distributed decreased to 5,832,815 in FY 1988 from 11,152,989 in FY 1987. The decrease in microfiche was due to a default on the single microfiche contract on August 27, 1987. In order to prevent a reoccurrence, GPO broke the single contract into eight separate contracts. It was not until early summer 1988, following a series of appeals by the defaulting contractor and delays in awarding the new multiple contracts, that microfiche production was resumed on a steady basis.

LEROY C. SCHWARZKOPF

Health and Rehabilitation Library Services

The Decade of the Disabled (1983–1992) has reached its midpoint. Several trends continue to have impact on the fields of health and rehabilitation—the homeless, AIDS, aging. Business is assuming a more active role in "disability management" while growth in the labor force is projected to proceed at its slowest rate since the 1930s. A reduction in available young workers is expected to enhance employment opportunities for the aging and disabled population.

Technology continues to reduce the limitations imposed on a person with a disability—neuroelectronic hands allow double amputees to perform tasks; computer screen output is translated into voice or braille for the blind; and ultralight wheelchairs provide increased mobility.

"Shortchanging the Disabled," *U.S. News & World Report*, July 15, 1988, reports that for 37,000,000 disabled Americans, "access to assistive devices means independence, employment and leading a more independent life." The article states that "inventing the technology has been easy. But the people who need the devices aren't getting them." Money is a major factor.

Disabled policy: America's Programs for the Handicapped, A Twentieth-Century Fund Report, by Edward D. Berkowitz, discusses what the nation receives from its $100 billion investment in disability programs.

Listed below are a few of the ways the library community is continuing its advance toward seeing that the Decade of the Disabled is a successful one.

Awards. IBM's National Support Center for Persons with Disabilities, based in Atlanta, Georgia, received the President's Committee on Employment of the Handicapped, Large Employer of the Year award. The Center answered more than 19,000 calls for assistance, almost three times the rate of previous years.

James Chandler, retired Chief Librarian at the University of Maryland, received the 1988 Francis Joseph Campbell Award for inventing the Voice Indexing Technique used to index audiovisual tapes.

Programs. The Milwaukee (Wisconsin) Public Library, in cooperation with The Guest House Drop In Center, provides library, tutorial and job information services for the homeless.

The Topeka (Kansas) Public Library has a Red Carpet Service which delivers materials to homebound and institutionalized individuals. The Low Vision Center provides services for visually impaired library patrons.

The American Library Association headquarters, Chicago, Illinois, provides access to the hearing-impaired through its newly installed TTY/TDD link.

The Library of Congress, Washington, D.C., has organized an Eldercare Discussion Group for staff members who provide care for parents, spouses or other older persons.

The Chillicothe (Ohio) and Ross County Public Library processes 1,800-plus items delivered each month to 14 institutions and to homebound patrons, maintains three libraries at senior citizen residency centers, and visits patients in the hospital twice a week.

Phoenix (Arizona) Public Library has developed a Special Needs Center, a community resource for information for and about disabilities. Also included in the project is a Computer Workplace that provides electronic access to print for the blind or visually impaired.

The University of California, San Francisco, requires first-year medical students to take a course in Medical Informatics through which students learn how to perform online bibliographic searches.

Audiovisuals. To encourage fitness for special needs, 30-minute videos are provided by the National Handicapped Sports and Recreation Association for paraplegics, quadriplegics, amputees and people with cerebral palsy.

"Get Up and GO" is a 60-minute program developed to help Parkinson's patients strengthen their ability to sit, stand and move. Available from Health Tapes, Oak Park, Michigan.

"Read My Lips," from Speech Reading Lab, six videocassettes from 52 to 56 minutes, illustrate lipreading techniques.

Publications. *Disability Drama in Television and Film*, by Lauri E. Klobas, contains about 400 chronologically arranged entries of films in which the disabled are portrayed.

Financial Aid for the Disabled and Their Families, 1988–1989, by Gail Ann Schlacter and R. David Weber, provides more than 500 sources of educational financial aid for the disabled.

Information Technology and Health Care, by Barry Strickland–Hodge, Barbara Allan, and Brian Livesay, reviews medical information technology, various types of medical information, and the ways technology can improve information flow in structured health care services.

A Parent's Guide To Heart Disorders and *A Parent's Guide To Spina Bifida* initiate the University of Minnesota's new series of Guides to Birth and Childhood Disorders.

The Encyclopedia of Suicide, by Glen Evans and Normal L. Farberow, contains more than 500 entries examining the psychological, religious and philosophical aspect of suicide. Also provides information on methods, associations and hotlines employed in suicide prevention.

The Disabled Child and Child Abuse, by Donald F. Kline and Anne Kline, is a pamphlet that discusses why the disabled child may be at high risk for abuse. Available from the National Committee for Prevention of Child Abuse.

Library Without Walls, a booklet that describes the National Library of Medicine's Regional Library Network, is produced by the Medical Library Association.

Perspectives for Teachers of the Hearing Impaired and *World Around You* are two magazines available from Gallaudet University, Washington, D.C.

Worklife, formerly *Disabled U.S.A.*, is now the publication of the President's Committee on Employment of People With Disabilities, formerly the President's Committee on Employment of the Handicapped.

Access to Information Technology By Users With Disabilities: Initial Guidelines, issued by the U.S. Department of Education and the General Services Administration, provides information on insuring access to electronic equipment.

Databases. AIDSLINE, a new database covering the clinical and research aspects of AIDS, is now available through the National Library of Medicine (NLM) network.

GRATEFUL MED, a user friendly interface microcomputer software package, is also available by NLM.

SHARRON MCFARLAND

Information Technology

As in each of the past seven years, local library automation was the leading information technology in terms of library expenditures—an estimated $110 million of around $210,000,000 committed. While more than 8,500 libraries were using bibliographic utilities for online cataloging support and twice that many were doing remote database searching by the end of 1988, only 2,500 were using local automated systems larger than a personal computer. The average local library system procurement during 1988 appeared to be in excess of $220,000.

Online patron-access catalogs became the keystone of local library automation, displacing circulation control. Circulation was the priority of libraries that automated earlier because it was the most mature module of the "off-the-shelf" options available and was a relatively low-risk undertaking. Circulation systems control the movement of items in a library collection and facilitate the recovery of materials from borrowers. Most libraries are concerned with improving access to resources by providing author, title, and subject approaches, as well as key-word and boolean searching. They strive to make that access available to remote users, as well as those who come into the library. By becoming more fully automated, libraries can provide their patrons with a window on all of the files of the library: on order, in process, out in circulation, etc. The online patron-access catalog as one of the modules while only 75 percent required circulation. A substantially smaller percentage required acquisitions and serials control.

Turnkey vendors continued to dominate the local library systems market. Turnkey vendors provide hardware, software, installation, training, and ongoing support from a single source. More than a score of options were available, but only six turnkey vendors achieved sales of over $7,500,000 for the year: CLSI, Data Research Associates, Dynix, Geac Computers International, Innovative Interfaces, and OCLC Local Systems. Only one firm—CLSI—achieved sales of more than $35,000,000 for the year. Geac approached $20,000,000.

Supported software packages were available from more than a dozen vendors, but only Information Dimensions (formerly Batelle), NOTIS, Sydney, and VTLS appear to have achieved sales of more than $2,500,000.

Other major developments were: (1) the continuing interest on the part of most libraries in integrated library systems in which a number of functions share the same bibliographic file and command language, (2) growing emphasis on standard operating systems and programming languages, (3) the availability of a broader range of field-upgradable central processing units from supermicros to superminis, (4) increased interest in interfacing standards, (5) initial demand for interlibrary loan modules, (6) the renewal of interest in journal citation capabilities, (7) the increasing role of personal micros, and (8) the emergence of CD-ROM as a backup to patron access catalogs.

In 1988, most of the RFPs, even those which did not require delivery of several software modules, called for the provision of an integrated system that could be expanded. CLSI, which had been offering acquisitions and serials control on a separate processor, announced that it would migrate and fully interface these modules on the same processor as the circulation and patron access catalog modules by 1990. Innovative Interfaces also announced that it would integrate its highly successful Innovacq acquisitions and serials and control product to the same processor as its newly released circulation and patron access catalog modules.

The trend toward standard operating systems and programming languages gained momentum. CLSI rewrote its circulation and patron access catalog modules to UNIX and C, giving up its proprietary system software. Innovative Interfaces chose UNIX and C for its future development. In the third quarter, Geac purchased ALII, a firm which uses the UNIX-like Pick operating system—in part because it was becoming increasingly difficult to sell systems which rely on proprietary system software. Geac decided that a migration of its own product to another operating system and programming language was too costly.

There was a wider range of hardware available in 1988 than ever before. Some vendors offered options ranging from supermicros to superminis. Several offered systems configured around multiple machines, but more common were CPUs, which could be field-upgraded by adding boards, a more cost-effective expansion.

While minicomputer popularity continued, there was a sharp rise in the sale of smaller systems, with well over 100 supermicro-based systems sold. There were several complete system options for under $85,000.

Mainframe-based systems also proved popular, with at least 35 software packages sold. Northwestern's NOTIS was particularly popular with academic libraries and Information Dimension's TechLib with special libraries. The demand for NOTIS was so strong that the company was able to increase prices by 30 to 60 percent without adversely affecting sales. No other company undertook major price changes during the year.

A significant number of RFPs required conformity to emerging interfacing standards, primarily the Open System Interconnection (OSI) Reference Model standards developed under the auspices of the national Information Standards Organization. The record transfer standard had already been published by the beginning of the year, the interlibrary loan standard was completed during the year, the interlibrary loan standard was completed during the year, and the common command language standard was nearing completion. Several vendors accepted contractual provision for the delivery of software to support these new standards within 24 months of their publication. Implementation of OSI-based system will permit the linking of local library systems to one another, and to non-library systems.

Although vendors were still developing core functions of acquisitions, serials control, circulation, and patron access catalog, there was considerable interest in offering entirely new modules. The module that garnered the greatest amount of attention in 1988 was interlibrary loan. While relying heavily on the existing circulation module, the new module anticipates the linking of systems, which the introduction of the OSI software will facilitate. The typical price of $3,000 should make it attractive for libraries that handle at least 1,000 transactions a year. Delivery is generally slated for 1989 or 1990.

In mid-1985 several vendors had responded to the growing interest of medical libraries in Mini-Medline by offering to support the loading of journal citation files into local library systems. The initial Mini-Medline product was developed and marketed by the Georgetown University Medical Library, Washington, D.C. It facilitates the loading of several years of the most frequently cited medical sciences titles into the local system for searching in a manner similar to the online patron access catalog. The success of the product prompted CLSI, Data Research, and OCLC Local Systems to bid similar capabilities. CLSI installed two of the systems by the end of 1986, both using optical digital disk technology as the storage medium. While the initial emphasis was on medical literature, the potential existed to make the capability available in other subject areas. However, there was little demand in 1987—possibly due to the great interest in CD-ROM as an electronic publishing medium. In 1988, a number of RFPs reflected the desire of libraries to exercise an option to purchase the journal citation capability in the next two years. Several vendors committed to provide the necessary software and loader programs. The renewed interest in supporting journal citations files on local library systems appeared to reflect a recognition that CD-ROM is not an ideal medium when several concurrent users must have access to the same database.

PCs continued to play a major role in library automation, not only as standalones, but as components of larger systems. Both acquisitions and serials control were both popular as standalone packages, with Faxon's MicroLinx the most successful product. The popularity of circulation packages was surprising, although suitable for charging and discharging of library materials and the processing of overdues, these packages represent a dead end. They usually require the creation of a non-MARC database of the library's holdings that is unsuitable for patron access catalog and other functions. These databases, which represent a considerable investment, must subsequently be replaced.

Personal computers (PCs) continued to be successful backups for circulation control. Almost all turnkey vendors offered software for an IBM-PC clone to permit the collection of charges and discharges when the central site is down. The concept of the PC as a workstation also was more firmly established. As many as 20 percent of the devices on some systems were PCs that could function not only as terminals, but as access tools to various databases with the capability to download and manipulate data. The PCs also supported word processing, accounting, and electronic mail. Still missing, however, was the capability of transferring files back and forth to the local library system.

A number of libraries began to use CD-ROM as a backup for an online patron access catalog. In some cases, the backup was actually a CD-ROM union catalog displaying the holdings of several libraries. A few libraries implemented their entire patron access catalog on CD-ROM and hoped to interface it with circulation. The Library Corporation, developers of the highly successful Bibliofile cataloging support product, was the first to offer an interfaced circulation control module along with a CD-ROM-based patron access catalog.

Bibliographic utilities achieved only modest growth during the year. OCLCs revenues increased by just over $1,000,000 to $85,400,000. Retrospective conversion grew significantly, while RLIN, UTLAS, and WLN had relatively flat years. Brodart and Auto-Graphics continued to function as commercial bibliographic utilities in California, thus permitting state funds to be used for services supplied by them. While Brodart won a few accounts in Virginia, the growth was at the expense of The Computer Company, rather than at the expense of OCLC.

While commercial bibliographic services such as Brodart were of concern to the bibliographic utilities, the more serious threats were the CD-ROM-based cataloging support products. By the end of the year, Bibliofile had been installed in more than 1,000 libraries, including some that catalog more than 10,000 titles a year. General Research Corporation increased the threat by offering a product which contained not only LC MARC Records, but also 1,000,000 records drawn from the company's retrospective conversion database. This increased the hit rate substantially for all public and many academic libraries. OCLC responded just before the end of the year with its own CD-ROM-based cataloging support product, which would be available only to libraries that agree to add holdings for all of their cataloging to the online OCLC database.

Online searching continued to expand, but more slowly than in past years. More than 4,300 databases were available and more than 10 percent of North American libraries had searching accounts, but very few libraries spent more than $5,000 per year on searching. Special and academic libraries continued to be the primary users, with more than 40 percent of the libraries in each category maintaining accounts. They comprise due majority of libraries that more than $5,000 a year on remote database searching.

There was a growing interest in CD-ROM as an electronic publishing medium for databases and full-text publications. More than 250 products were available by the end of the year. At least one-fourth of the nation's 1,000 largest academic and public libraries had invested in the technology. Nevertheless, only Bibliofile, Disclosure, the Electronic Encyclopedia, and Microsoft Bookshelf passed the 1,000 sales mark. The majority of publishers continued to test the market, with no immediate prospects for profitability.

There were major increases in the number of digital telefacsimile installations in libraries in 1988. Libraries installed at least 600 new units during the year, as many as in the past four years combined. Two major factors were the dramatic drop in prices—with suitable machines costing well under $2,000—and the increasing willingness of state library agencies to provide grants for the purchase of the equipment. There was an increasing realization that building large online union catalogs and electronic message systems had not improved resource sharing as much as had been hoped. Delivery was cited as the weak link in resource sharing in a number of studies conducted during 1988. With more than half of all resource sharing consisting of exchanging photocopies of journal articles, telefacsimile can play a major role in speeding delivery.

While a large number of campuses and corporations were planning local area networks (LANs) in 1988, few library systems had yet been hooked up to the networks. Linking of PCs within the library constitutes most library experience with LANs.

RICHARD W. BOSS

Intellectual Freedom

Intellectual freedom issues grow more complex and challenging as a result of technological changes, legislative initiatives and court cases and the darkening trends in federal information policy increasingly threaten individual access to information and the free (and private) exercise of First Amendment rights.

One is struck by the need for increased sophistication within the profession if librarians are to continue to exercise their role as the guardians of free expression and as protectors of access to an unfettered and uncensored flow of all types of information within the country and around the world.

Library Awareness Program. 1988 was the Year of the FBI. The issue emerged in 1987 when an FBI visit to the Columbia University libraries seeking information about specific users alerted ALA and the NYLA to violations of library user confidentiality.

Laws in 38 states and the District of Columbia protect library user records from disclosure. Professional ethics require librarians to protect the privacy of library users in a manner similar to the doctor/patient or attorney/client privilege. ALA issued a nationwide alert in the fall of 1987 requesting librarians provide information of any such visits from FBI agents and received reports of about 20 such visits during the past 10 years, many of them from outside the New York area.

Thomas DuHadway, Deputy Assistant Director of the FBI's Intelligence Division, met in a closed meeting with the National Commission on Libraries and Information Science (NCLIS) following the ALA Midwinter meeting in San Antonio, Texas in January 1988. The meeting involved a briefing on the FBI's so-called "Library Awareness Program" which DuHadway said had been limited to the New York City area. DuHadway asserted that the program was vital to U.S. counterintelligence efforts in identifying and monitoring spies from hostile countries. He stated that a major emphasis of the program was warning library employees that they might be recruited or co-opted into assisting foreign intelligence agents and that the FBI was interested in knowing about suspicious behavior or contacts.

A number of NCLIS members were openly critical of the ALA Intellectual Freedom Committee and ALA Office for Intellectual Freedom staff members. A transcript of the meeting obtained by the Bureau of National Affairs revealed that the FBI had received a sympathetic hearing from NCLIS members and touched off a flurry of criticism of the Commission among librarians. Portions of the transcript were censored.

During the next several months national press coverage detailed a number of specific contacts between FBI agents and librarians. Protests from library organizations, media commentators and other concerned citizens increased. A request from the Intellectual Freedom Committee for a meeting with FBI representatives during the annual conference in New Orleans was declined.

Representative Don Edwards, a former FBI agent, held hearings on the FBI Library Awareness Program in July before his Subcommittee on Civil and Constitutional Rights in the U.S. House of Representatives. IFC Chair C. James Schmidt testified concerning ALA objection to the FBI program. In response to ALA FOIA requests, the FBI released 35 pages of heavily censored documents that provided little new information except that a "Library Awareness Program" initiated by the New York Office of the FBI sometime in the past had been criticized by the Washington headquarters of the agency as being a nonproductive use of manpower.

During the summer, the FBI agreed to a meeting with the Intellectual Freedom Committee, which was held at the Washington, D.C. Public Library September 9. During the two-hour meeting James Geer, Assistant Director of the FBI's Intelligence Division, DuHadway, James Fox, FBI New York Office, Terry Turchie, Chief, FBI Soviet Intentions Section, and Counsel Linda Reel defended the program and stated that they would continue it as necessary. They asserted that the last contact under the program had occured in December 1987, that the program was limited to the New York City area, and that other FBI contacts with librarians had been part of specific unrelated investigations. Conceding that

The FBI Library Awareness Program

On Thursday, June 4, 1987 two Federal Bureau of Investigation (FBI) agents visited the Math/Science Library at Columbia University and questioned the clerk on duty about the use of that library by foreigners. The librarian overheard the conversation, interrupted and referred the agents to the office of the University Librarian. Subsequently the Acting University Librarian, Paula Kaufman, reported the visit to the chair of the New York Library Association's Intellectual Freedom Committee who then reported the incident in ALAs Intellectual Freedom Committee. This single incident led to a series of disclosures, headlines, congressional hearings, and legislative attempts to secure federal protection for the privacy rights of library users.

During the 1987 Annual conference in San Francisco, ALAs Intellectual Freedom Committee (IFC) discussed the report of the visit at Columbia and decided to write to the Acting Director of the FBI to secure confirmation that the Bureau in fact had an active program of visiting libraries and inquiring about uses made of these libraries by foreigners. On July 31, the Bureau confirmed in writing that the "Library Awareness Program" was indeed active.

On September 18, 1987, *The New York Times* carried a front-page story in all its editions entitled "Libraries are Asked by FBI to Report on Foreign Agents." Subsequently, newspapers, magazines, television, and radio coverage of this program was extensive in all parts of the country and abroad, including a February 25, 1988 story titled "FBI Spying on Library Visitors" distributed to TASS, the telegraph agency of the Soviet Union.

After receiving confirmation from the FBI that such a program was active, the Intellectual Freedom Committee prepared and distributed on October 1, 1987 a statement advising libraries of all types that this program was "an unwarranted government intrusion upon personal privacy...that threatened the First Amendment right to receive information." The Bureau alleged that it "has documented instances, for more than a decade, of hostile intelligence officers who have exploited libraries by stealing proprietary, sensitive and other information and attempting to identify and recruit American and foreign students in American libraries." the IFCs advisory statement reminded libraries of ALAs 1970 policy statement on "Confidentiality of Library Records," and of the provision in ALAs 1981 "Statement on Professional Ethics" which protects library users' privacy "with respect to information sought or received, and materials consulted, borrowed, or acquired." The advisory statement concluded with a request that libraries visited by representatives of the FBI report all such visits to ALAs Office for Intellectual Freedom.

On January 14, 1988 at the conclusion of the ALA 1988 Midwinter Conference in San Antonio, the National Commission on Libraries and Information Science held a closed meeting during which its members and staff were briefed on the Library Awareness Program by Thomas DuHadway, Deputy Assistant Director of the Bureau's Intelligence Division. The transcript of this briefing, released under a Freedom of Information Act (FOIA) request to Toby Macintosh, a reporter for the Bureau of National Affairs, confirmed the existence of the program, provided more extensive justification for it, and indicated that the program was not limited to libraries in the greater New York City area.

The NCLIS transcript and reports received from libraries in response to IFCs advisory statement revealed that FBI representatives had visited libraries across the country during 1987 and had sought to acquire information about specific library patrons including their subject interests and the materials they had used or borrowed.

In May, 1988 Congressman Don Edwards, Chair of the House Judiciary Subcommittee on Constitutional and Civil Rights, scheduled hearings on the Library Awareness Program. On June 20, representatives of ALA, the Special Libraries Association, and the Association of Research Libraries testified along with librarians from Columbia University and the University of Maryland. On July 13, testimony taken from James Geer, Assistant Director of the FBIs Intelligence Division, repeated many of the allegations contained in the transcript of the NCLIS meeting and provided some additional facts. The Library Awareness Program was not the first such effort by the Bureau; there had been an earlier one in the 1970s. The latest Program was to be limited to libraries with scientific and technical materials in the New York City area while visits to libraries elsewhere in the country were related to specific investigations of specific individuals.

During ALAs 1988 Annual Conference in New Orleans, the IFC presented a status report to the Executive Board and to Council and requested and received approval to meet with representatives of the FBI in Washington to express the Association's concerns about the program and to take appropriate legal steps to compel disclosure of documents revealing the true extend of the Library Awareness Program. On September 9, members of the IFC and ALA staff and counsel met with Geer, DuHadway, and three other representatives of the FBI to express ALA's concerns and to hear the FBI's rationale for visiting libraries. Geer agreed to distribute to the Bureau's regional and district offices an IFC statement setting forth ALAs principles regarding open libraries and privacy rights for library users. At year's end, IFC was preparing the statement. Geer also indicated that needed future visits would begin with a library's administrative offices.

In addition to holding hearings on the Program, Congress began developing legislation to provide federal protection for the privacy rights of library patrons. Such a law would complement similar existing laws in 38 states and the District of Columbia by establishing a uniform standard for disclosure—a court order. The legislation (H.R. 4947/S. 2361) also contained protection from disclosure for video rental records. Staff from the Office for Intellectual Freedom worked with the ALA Washington Office, Congressional staff, and representatives from other associations to develop language for the legislation. In the closing days of the 100th Congress, under threat of an amendment that would have made the legislation unacceptable and would have negated the protection in the existing state laws, the support of ALA for the bill was withdrawn, and the legislation was adopted containing only the protection from disclosure of video rental records.

In the 18 months the Library Awareness Program has been monitored by the IFC, the larger context for it has become clear. FBI visits to libraries were part of a systematic, coordinated interagency effort to prevent access to UNCLASSIFIED information. This effort was organized by the interagency Technology Transfer Intelligence Committee—a group representing 22 federal agencies and hosted by the CIA—that produced a 1982 report on Soviet acquisition of western technology and published an updated version in 1985. The justification of the Program presented in Congressional testimony and in the meeting on the FBI with the IFC was contained in the report.

See "Soviet Acquisition of Western Technology" CIA, 1982, "Soviet Acquisition of Militarily Significant Western Technology," CIA, 1985, *Washington Post,* June 19, 1983, p. A-12, *New York Times* September 19, 1985, p. 14.

C. JAMES SCHMIDT

Intellectual Freedom

some of their agents' contacts with librarians "could have been more professional," the FBI representatives asserted that they had never asked library employees to either break state laws or violate professional ethics.

The FBI did acknowledge that in some instances their queries about library users may have preceded the adoption of some of those state laws. They also stated that the provision in all such statutes that library user records will be made available under a properly executed court order was too restrictive and not sufficiently flexible to meet FBI counterintelligence needs. They further acknowledged that librarians have the right to refuse to assist the FBI in queries that violate patron privacy. Despite a candid exchange of viewpoints during the meeting, committee Chair C. James Schmidt characterized the FBI's position as "not responsive to our concerns. The parties met, exchanged views, and agreed to disagree," he said.

Five days after the meeting, FBI Director William Sessions wrote to Rep. Edwards expressing the FBI's intention to continue to contact certain scientific and technical libraries in the New York City area (including university and public libraries) concerning hostile intelligence service activities in the libraries "when deemed necessary." He wrote that the FBI will ask for information about patrons "who identify themselves as Soviet or Soviet bloc nationals" who seek assistance in conducting library research, request referrals to students or faculty who might be willing to assist in research, remove materials without permission, or who seek certain biographical information, particularly on students and academicians. Sessions stated that the FBI will inquire further about what such persons are seeking from librarians; that the FBI will not attempt to circumvent local library management in contacts with employees; and that the Bureau is confident that librarians will cooperate in the program if it is explained to them.

The IFC offered to provide the FBI with a written statement for national distribution to FBI agents setting forth the role of libraries and the ethical and legal responsibilities of librarians and library staff. In exchange, the Committee offered to arrange distribution to the library community of a statement from the FBI concerning the structure, purpose, and goals of the Library Awareness Program. No response had been received from the FBI by the beginning of 1989.

ALA filed new FOIA requests seeking further information from the FBI about its library activities. The Intellectual Freedom Committee began planning a series of activities to increase librarian awareness of issues surrounding patron confidentiality and the ethical considerations of requests by the FBI and others for information about patron use of libraries.

Federal Legislation: Video and Library Privacy and Protection Act. Federal legislation to protect the privacy of video store customers and library users was introduced into Congress in 1988 following congressional outrage over a list of videotapes rented by the family of Supreme Court nominee Robert Bork reported during the battle over his nomination in the fall of 1987.

Librarians viewed the bill as a means of strengthening legal protection of library users' right to privacy and to extend such protection to the twelve states without confidentiality statutes. During September, ALA received information that the FBI was actively seeking to insert a "national security letter" disclosure process into the bill. The proposed amendment would have permitted the FBI to obtain records solely on the basis of a letter from a Bureau official asserting a national security need for the documents. In addition, it would have imposed a gag order on any librarian receiving such a request and mandated that the federal legislation override any conflicting protection of privacy contained in state statutes. Faced with this prospect of a major erosion of existing privacy rights, ALA withdrew its support from the library portions of the bill and they were stricken from the legislation.

Intellectual Freedom

American Library Association celebrates the Freedom to Read in Banned Book Week 1988 posters and bookmarks.

Child Protection and Obscenity Enforcement Act. The Child Protection and Obscenity Enforcement Act of 1988. finally passed in amended form as a part of an omnibus drug bill, raised grave concerns throughout the year because of broad and constitutionally troubling language applying to libraries. As originally drafted, the bill would have subjected entire library collections to seizure and forfeiture if a single item in circulation was later determined to be legally obscene. The difficulty in distinguishing between sexually explicit and obscene material, coupled with a provision that obscenity could be established on the basis of a ruling in any jurisdiction, was extremely worrisome. Despite some success at engaging congressional interest in the constitutional issues surrounding the legislation, the bill was a difficult issue during an election year. In final form, some of the more troubling sections concerning forfeiture and other issues were removed. Yet, along with Racketeer Influenced and Corrupt Organizations (RICO) prosecutions and expanding federal efforts to regulate the sexual content of telephone services and broadcasting, the bill represented another step in the federal assault on sexually frank speech and expression.

State Legislation. State legislatures addressed library user privacy with the passage of several new statutes and the strengthening of others during 1988. Another area of major intellectual freedom activity was in so-called "harmful to minors" statutes. A number of state legislatures attempted to limit access of people under 18 years to material dealing with sexual matters that would be legally protected if used by adults. Proposed legislation with similar wording—some of it broad enough to apply to the swimsuit issue of *Sports Illustrated*—was considered by many legislatures. Such bills passed in Nebraska and failed in Washington. Clearly this issue will continue to be problematical for librarians who are committed to the open access provision of the Library Bill of Rights.

Intellectual Freedom Leadership Development Institute. 52 participants from 38 states attended the first national Intellectual Freedom Leadership Development Institute, which was sponsored by ALA in Lisle, Illinois, May 5–7. Training sessions on the history of intellectual freedom illustrated how to recognize potential controversies, and examined legal issues and trends, lobbying, working with trustees, coalition building, working with the media and work-

Intellectual Freedom Round Table

shop planning. All participants pledged to organize an intellectual freedom workshop in their state or region by the end of 1989.

Actions. Despite the energy expended on FBI related matters, ALA's Intellectual Freedom Committee found time to address a variety of other issues. The Committee developed a resolution, which was adopted by ALA Council, affirming the rights of persons of all ages who have acquired immune deficiency syndrome (AIDS), AIDS-related complex (ARC) or who test positive for the human immune deficiency virus (HIV) to use libraries and access information without being subject to discrimination. The Committee revised the "Procedures for Implementing Policy on Confidentiality of Library Records." It also addressed the emerging problem of restrictions on access to databases required by vendors of on-line services and the implications for libraries asked to screen certain users from access to those services.

Intellectual freedom issues surrounding videotapes continue to plague librarians: widespread restrictions on access to videotapes on the basis of age were reported, with a distressing number of libraries and librarians defending the practice of charging fees for videotape circulations. The discrepancy between ALA policies on access to library services for minors and labeling, the tradition of fee-free service in public libraries, and the methods whereby libraries add videotapes to their services are certain to be one of the most challenging issues of the next decade. The conflict between long-cherished professional ideals and the practical requirements of their implementing them is an increasingly significant challenge.

Another mounting concern is the movement to establish English as the official language in a number of jurisdictions. Librarians anticipate repercussions and troubling implications regarding multicultural intellectual freedom.

Banned Books Week. "Open Books for Open Minds" was the popular theme of the 1988 Banned Books Week. ALA's resource book went into a second printing and an unprecedented number of requests were received for media interviews and other supporting information. Librarians and booksellers all over the country held programs and special events to celebrate the right to read and to heighten public consciousness of the dangers of censorship to the American way of life.

GORDON M. CONABLE

Intellectual Freedom Round Table

Membership. The Intellectual Freedom Round Table's (IFRT) 1988 membership stands at 1,554, a 10.4 percent increase over 1987. IFRT's commitment to supporting grass roots efforts to preserve freedom and to promote wide discussion of intellectual freedom issues is especially important during this time of continuing censorship activity.

Issues. The IFRT executive committee had useful, if sometimes heated, discussions on book commerce between the United States and South Africa. The issue was eventually defined within the broad context of freedom of access to information and ideas regardless of frontiers. To mark the 50th anniversary of the adoption of the *Library Bill of Rights* in 1989, a resolution drafted by Sue Kamm and John Swan was adopted unanimously by the executive committee and brought to the ALA membership at the annual conference in New Orleans. The resolution includes key statements from the *LBR* and Article 19 of the *Universal Declaration of Human Rights*; it reaffirms ALA's "support of the freedom of access to information and ideas and the freedom to communicate of all people, regardless of their origin, background, or views." The resolution was passed by membership after the elimination of the phrase "recognizing the difference between commerce in trade goods and commerce in ideas."

Programs. Approximately 800 people in New Orleans heard Helen Thomas address "How to Survive the 'Kill the Messenger' Syndrome." In this IFRT program co-sponsored with the IFC and IFC Divisions, UPI's senior White House Correspondent had the hall ringing with laughter as she described her personal experiences in and out of press conferences in Washington. Other lively and informative programs co-sponsored by IFRT included "Two Views of Intellectual Freedom," with IFRT's John Swan debating Noel Peattie, who represented the social responsibilities position, and "Building Bridges over Troubled Waters: Forming Alliances to Combat Censorship." The IFRT Roll Call of the States, held during the membership meeting, was an excellent opportunity to learn of intellectual freedom and censorship activities in many states. A handy packet of reports by state IFC chairs was made available to all attendees, and mailed to chairs unable to attend. The reports detail information on workshops, programs, and related activities; legislative activity; intellectual freedom incidents investigated; publications; surveys; coalition activities; helpful hints and ideas; and plans for the coming year.

Activities. Compilation of policies and procedures continues, while Martha Merrill and her committee were commended for their draft document. The development of a multimedia intellec-

---

INTELLECTUAL FREEDOM ROUND TABLE

CHAIR (July 1988–July 1989):
Laurence Miller, Library International University, Tamiami Campus, Miami, Florida

IMMEDIATE PAST CHAIR:
Dorothy M. Broderick, 1226 Cresthaven Drive, Silver Springs, Maryland 20903

VICE-CHAIR/CHAIR-ELECT:
Bill Davis, 218-A Brookdale Drive, Jefferson City, Missouri

SECRETARY:
Martha Merrill, Jacksonville State University, Houston Cole Library, Jacksonville, Alabama

TREASURER:
Thomas F. Budlong Jr., Hobgod Palmer Branch, Atlanta–Fulton Co. Public Library, Decatur, Georgia

Membership (August 31, 1988): 1,554

tual freedom kit is also progressing. A special form to facilitate information for the Roll Call of the States was developed and used successfully by state IFC chairs in 1988. The IFRT contributed $1,000 to the Freedom To Read Foundation for 1989. Lois Mills completed a survey of 60 library schools to ascertain whether they teach about the *Library Bill of Rights*, the *Freedom To Read Statement* and the ALA *Code of Ethics*. She found that 31 schools reported usage in multiple classes. The executive committee recognized, with gratitude, the assistance of Patrice McDermott of OIF and wished her good luck in her new position as a faculty member at Atlanta University. The committee also expressed deep appreciation to Dorothy Broderick for her outstanding leadership as IFRT chair.

Awards. The 1988 John Phillip Immroth Memorial Award in recognition of personal dedication to the cause of intellectual freedom was presented to Elliot and Barbara Goldstein of SIRS (Social Issues Resources Series). The award of $500 and a citation recognizes the impact that their financial support has had on raising the consciousness of many to the principles of intellectual freedom. The Goldsteins contributed their award money to the Freedom To Read Foundation. The 1988 State Program Award, funded by SIRS, went to the New York Library Association's Intellectual Freedom Committee and Intellectual Freedom Round Table. This award recognizes the most successful and creative statewide intellectual freedom project. The NYLAIFC and IFRT were chosen for their exemplary programs for professional and public information. They were cited for their outstanding intellectual freedom manual and newsletter and for an excellent IF pamphlet for the public. Their award was $1,000 and a plaque. The 1988 Eli Oboler Award for an outstanding intellectual freedom publication went to *Choosing Equality: The Case for Democratic Schooling*, edited by Ann Bastian and published by Temple University Press (1986). This award of $500 and a certificate is funded by HBW Associates Inc.

JUDITH SEREBNICK

IFLA

General Conference. "Living Together," the theme of IFLA's 1988 General Conference held in Sydney, Australia, celebrated the Bicentennial of Australia. The conference immediately followed that of the Library Association of Australia, and IFLA's sub-theme, "People, Libraries, Information" was reflected by more than 100 speakers and the 1,500 participants from 59 countries. His Excellency, the Right Honorable Sir Ninian Stephen, Governor-General of Australia opened the conference at the magnificent Sydney Opera House. Warren Horton, National Librarian of Australia, delivered the plenary address, "IFLA in the Antipodes: A Regional Perspective," urging IFLA to effectively encourage regional involvement in its work outside Europe and North America.

With more than 40 special interest groups, IFLA's program spanned many topics, including: problems of retrospective conversion in national and research libraries; networking potentialities and limitations for library networking in Europe and North America; library services for people with disabilities; cataloguing and classification of serials and the new technologies; improving the quality of continuing professional education; the information needs of the school community; standards in patent office publications; principles and practices of performance measurement; commercial and revenue-raising activities in national libraries; and strategic planning for library associations.

IFLA's Core Programs. IFLA's program for the Universal Availability of Publications (UAP) continued to focus on research and publicity. A contract was signed with UNESCO for the preparation of a document on *Measuring the Performance of Document Supply Systems*. A second contract was awarded by the Deutsche Forschungsgemeinshaft to update the 1984 publication on *The Impact of New Technology on the Availability of Publications*. Meetings between IFLA and GELC (Groupe d'Éditeurs de la Communauté Européene) continued to provide a forum for discussion between librarians and publishers on the availability of publications. The most recent product of these discussions was a joint statement of European librarians and publishers published as "The Use of Optical Media for Publication of Full Text: Cooperation Between Publishers and Librarians" in *IFLA Journal*, v.14, no.2.

IFLA's program for Universal Bibliographic Control International MARC (UBCIM), which promotes the exchange and use of compatible bibliographic records, completed the *Guidelines for the Application of the ISBDs to the Description of Component Parts*. Work also continued on the preparation of the new ISBD for computer files. A MARC-related publication, *The MINISIS/UNIMARC Final Report*, that appeared early in 1988, is the consultant's report of the investigation into producing bibliographic records in modified UNIMARC format using the MINISIS software package developed by IDRC, Canada.

The major emphasis of IFLA's program for Universal Dataflow and Telecommunications (UDT) was in accordance with the recommendations of the 1987 IFLA Preconference Seminar on OSI. With support from the British Library and the National Library of Canada, work has begun on a two-phase ILL Demonstration Project. The objectives of the project are to demonstrate the ability to interconnect library computer systems internationally using OSI standards, to demon-

---

INTERNATIONAL FEDERATION OF LIBRARY ASSOCIATIONS AND INSTITUTIONS

PRESIDENT (1985–89):
Hans-Peter Geh, Director, Württembergische Landesbibliothek, 7000 Stuttgart, FRG

FIRST VICE-PRESIDENT:
E. V. Pereslegina, Moscow, USSR

SECRETARY GENERAL:
Paul Nauta

Membership (1988): 1,213; affiliates in 123 countries
Headquarters: IFLA Secretariat, P.O. Box 95312, 2509 CH The Hague, Netherlands

strate the service benefits and constraints of such an interconnection, and to provide data needed for coordinating and planning of future ILL implementations and other OSI application protocols.

Working in cooperation with UNESCO, CDNL, and the Library of Congress, IFLA's program for Preservation and Conservation (PAC) has undertaken the coordination of an assistance program of recovery for the Library of the Academy of Sciences in Leningrad from the disastrous fire in February 1988. Progress has also been made on the production of educational materials and information. Copies of two slide/tape presentations originally produced by the Library of Congress have been placed in the PAC regional centers in Sablé, France; Leipzig, Germany; and Caracas, Venezuela. Under a UNESCO contract, work has begun on a slide/tape program on disaster preparedness to be issued in Spanish. Other UNESCO contracts were provided for a *Study on Insect Extermination in Libraries and Archives* and a *Study on Mass Conservation and Techniques for the Treatment of Library and Archive Materials*. CIDA support permitted the PAC program to hold a training seminar on preservation and conservation for francophone African librarians in October 1988. NCLIS has provided funding for the PAC international center to develop and update an online bibliographic database of information on library and archives preservation. Bibliographic information on non-English literature was also gathered.

Research Contracts. Other research undertaken by IFLA's professional groups with support from UNESCO included A Study on the Provision of Rural Community Information Services in Developing Countries; Guidelines for the Management of Professional Associations in the Fields of Archives, Library and Information Work; and National Library and Information Needs: Alternative Means of Fulfillment, Including the Role of National Libraries.

CLR. The Council on Library Resources had provided funding for a program development officer to develop IFLA's core programs on a firm international basis, scheduled for completion in March 1988. Just before the end of 1988 IFLA was notified that the CLR Board of Directors approved funding for a Robert Vosper IFLA Fellows program for $125,000 over a three-year period.

HANS-PETER GEH

International Relations

Activities. During 1988 American librarianship in particular and world librarianship in general benefited from Mikhail Gorbachev's *glastnost*. After eight years of cold war hostilities, relations between the two super powers approached some level of sanity, thanks to less antagonistic rhetoric and an announced withdrawal from Afghanistan. The second Soviet–American Library Seminar came as part of a larger package involving the American Council of Learned Societies, the International Research and Exchanges Board (IREX) and the USSR Ministry of Culture and the Library Council. Library representatives from the United States with expertise in preservation and technology met with 12 of their Soviet counterparts in Washington, D.C., on July 5–8 prior to the ALA annual conference. Topics discussed were relevant to the theme of the seminar, "Access to Library Resources through Technology and Preservation." Resolutions expressing the intent for future cooperation included a call for immediate exchange of "test" tapes in UNIMARC format between the Library of Congress and the Lenin State Library and the All-Union Book Chamber. The exchange will include an analysis of format and character set differences, of ISBD and a preliminary study of names and subject headings. In addition to bibliographic standards, resolutions dealt with online public access catalogs, networking and preservation were passed. Following the seminar, the delegation of 12 Soviet librarians and conservationists flew to New Orleans to attend the ALA annual conference, setting a precedent in the history of U.S.–USSR relations.

At the ALA conference in New Orleans, Lenin State Library Director Nokolai S. Kartashov presented 300 Soviet library books to ALA as a thank-you gift for hosting the USSR delegation. He also received preservation documents from the Resources and Technical Services Division. Also, in New Orleans, the co-chairs of the U.S.–U.S.S.R. Commission on Library Cooperation signed a protocol which calls for the possible exchange of current national bibliographies starting in 1989. In additional to seminar, several other cooperative projects between the two countries are planned for 1988–89. These include a seminar on library services to children planned for the Soviet Union in 1989, traveling book exhibits, the exchange of conservators and library educators, collaboration in art museum librarianship and facilitating access to the library materials of the respective nations.

Just three months after the Soviet delegation left the U.S., the Japanese delegation arrived in Racine, Wisconsin, for the fourth U.S.–Japan Binational Conference on Libraries and Information Science in Higher Education. The conference, held October 3–6, 1988, brought together 72 librarians and educators from the United States and Japan who have knowledge of an interest in policy, operations and technical matters of importance to libraries. Participants discussed computer applications, preservation and adaptation of ideographic language to the requirements of computerized bibliographic networks and database development.

International Relations Committee. The annual program of the International Relations Committee (IRC) which has gained popularity among the ALA conferees, had as its theme "Leadership in International Understanding: The Role of Libraries." Speakers were: Seymore Fersh, coordinator of curriculum development at Brevard Community College (Cocoa, Florida), who addressed the issue of removing international communication barriers, and Donald Sager, director of the Milwaukee Public Library, who discussed foreign exchanges from an administrator's point of view. Nikolai S. Kartashov, head of the Soviet Delegation, discussed the Soviet experience and described what is being done in the Soviet Union to prepare librarians and library science students

U.S./U.S.S.R. Seminar on Access to Library Resources Through Technology and Preservation

It was the Fourth of July, the sounds of high school bands from every state in the union filled the air. The faces and costumes of the band members reflected the incredible ethnic diversity of the U.S. Floats, colonial cavalcades, clowns, and jugglers assembled on the mall between the Washington Monument and the U.S. Capitol. Witnessing this annual display, was an especially animated group. Their gestures and delighted facial expressions were noticeable and contagious. And although their Russian words were not understood by most who observed them, it was clear that they were excited and fascinated by the festivities that surrounded them.

Later in the day, the visitors attended a typical Independence Day backyard barbecue in suburban Virginia—hamburgers, hot dogs, potato salad, and watermelon. At day's end, fireworks infused the night sky with color as the visitors watched from the roof of the Madison Building of The Library of Congress with the Librarian of Congress, who sported a Georgian cap.

The visitors were from the Soviet Union in the U.S. to participate in the U.S./U.S.S.R. Seminar on Access to Library Resources through Technology and Preservation, 5-8, July 1988. The seminar featured 12 Soviet participants and 30 U.S. participants discussing the state-of-the-art and future trends in networking, standardized approaches to bibliographic description, and preservation of deteriorating resources. The delegation was unusual because it included participants from several of the Soviet Republics—Estonia, Lithuania, and the Ukraine. Their attendance helped to create an awareness of the complexity of the USSR multinational library system and the role of republic libraries in preserving the national cultural heritage.

Background. Held at The Library of Congress, the seminar was an activity of the U.S./U.S.S.R Commission on Library Cooperation of the American Council of Learned Societies and the Library Council of the USSR. It was sponsored by the American Library Association (ALA), administered in the United States by the International Research and Exchanges Board (IREX), and held in cooperation with The Library of Congress.

The seminar was the first in a series of planned activities sponsored by IREX. ALA resumed cultural exchanges with the Soviet Union in July 1987 when a delegation of U.S. librarians, including Robert D. Stueart, Simmons College; Richard DeGennaro, The New York Public Library; Warren Tsuneishi, Library of Congress, and Marianna Tax Choldin, Slavic and East European Library, University of Illinois; went to the USSR to begin negotiations with the Ministry of Culture on behalf of ALA. James Billington, Librarian of Congress, and IREX's Wesley Fisher accompanied the delegation. The result of their visit was a draft Agreement and Protocol of the Commission on Library Cooperation between the American Council of Learned Societies and the Library Council of the USSR.

In August, at the 53rd International Federation of Library Associations and Institutions (IFLA) Council and General Conference in Brighton, several meetings were held to discuss practical concerns regarding the draft agreement and protocol. These discussions were very successful, and the agreement and protocol were signed later. The agreement provides for a renewed series of exchanges including the exchange conservators and library educators; a seminar on library services to youth planned for the Soviet Union in 1989; the exchange of traveling book exhibits; collaboration in art and museum librarianship; and holding a colloquium in the U.S. on library services to rural populations in 1989.

The Seminar. E.J. Josey, Chair of the ALA International Relations Committee (IRC) presided over the seminar. IRC committee member Warren Tsuneishi and Robert D. Stueart, Co-chair of the U.S./U.S.S.R. Commission on Library Cooperation, assisted in planning the seminar, which featured many prominent U.S. and U.S.S.R. librarians. The Soviet delegation was headed by Nikolai S. Kartashov, President of the U.S.S.R. Library Council and Director of the Lenin State Library. Kartashov is Co-chair of the U.S./U.S.S.R. Commission on Library Cooperation.

During the seminar, participants heard presentations on the automation of libraries and information services in the U.S. and U.S.S.R.; on database issues of bibliographic standards, online public access catalogs, and international issues in library networking; on regional conservation efforts in both countries; and on the Library of Congress deacidification project. Preprinted copies of all the formal papers were compiled, translated, and sent to the participants prior to the seminar. Tours were given of LC's rare book and special collections; motion picture, broadcasting, and recorded sound divisions; the Jefferson Building and the main reading room; geography and map division; optical disk project, and preservation research and testing laboratory.

Working groups met frequently to develop cooperative resolutions. In the process, U.S. participants learned through refreshingly frank and productive discussion how Soviet librarians were attempting to advance the cause of librarianship throughout the Soviet Socialist Republics. Aleksandr Sorokin, Director of the U.S.S.R. State Public Library for Science and Technology, described his country's new automated "information environment," pointing to a growing reliance on computer-based databanks, telecommunications modes of accessing information, and magnetic tape for information exchange. He admitted that his country lagged far behind the U.S. in library automation but added that Gorbachev's five-year plan for perestroika calls for a modernization of information technologies. Said Sorokin, a library user "has the right to demand that a library system should be as prompt and efficient in meeting his needs as

Robert D. Stueart, Dean, Graduate School of Library and Information Science, Simmons College, Boston (left), and Nikolai Kartashov, Director, Lenin State Library and President USSR Library Council (right), signing protocol for exchange of tapes in New Orleans at the 1988 ALA Annual Conference.

International Relations

modern computer-based information systems are in providing information service."

Nikolai S. Kartashov, Head of the Soviet delegation and Director of the Lenin State Library, summarized the activities of his institution—unifying resources, providing leadership in automation, centralizing networks, and offering standards for reading—and commented on the need for more up-to-date technology in the Soviet library system. Kartashov also called attention to the changes taking place in the Soviet Union, especially those easing restrictions on the flow of information. Thousands of mostly political and literary books repressed under Stalin are being returned from special shelves; access to copy machines in libraries in Estonia and Lithuania has become openly available; and censorship of religious literature is breaking down. He expressed his delegation's eagerness to learn from the experience of U.S. librarians in automating their libraries, add that "both the Soviet school of librarianship and the American school have their advantages and disadvantages. But the concerns we are addressing here can only be solved by the unified efforts of the whole library world."

Endorsing this view, F. William Summers, ALA President-elect and Dean of the Graduate School of Library and Information Science at Florida State University, spoke on the importance of and need for frequent exchanges and contacts between individual librarians from both countries. He further stated that "in the final analysis, technology doesn't solve problems, people do," thus underscoring the broader goal of cross-cultural information sharing and networking that was to highlight all the activities during the delegation's visit.

While most of the speakers adhered to their prepared texts, at times the discussion broadened to address the international ramifications of such issues as censorship, professionalism, and information distribution and preservation. Richard DeGennaro, Director of the New York Public Library, in explaining technology's democratization of access to library resources, stated that "technology is making the resources beyond its walls available within the library." Rowland C. W. Brown, President and Chief Executive Officer of the Online Computer Library Center (OCLC), commented on the importance of this statement and its special relevance to the seminar participants: "In a sense, we all going through a form of perestroika. . . . The important point for this conference is that these changes are worldwide in scope. It behooves us all to understand better than we have what is happening in other parts of the world— in this case the U.S.S.R. and U.S. Certainly the recent events in the U.S.S.R. which are gaining the attention of the entire Soviet citizenry as well as electrifying the world suggest new needs as well as new opportunities for collaboration. . . . Fortunately, technology enables us to . . .centralize and gain access to vast international information resources when decentralizing and distributing both processing and information. It need not be an either-or situation if we have the vision, the resources, and the will."

It was Iurii Torsuev, General Director of Research and Production at the All-Union Book Chamber of the USSR who made the most telling statement. "We are always arguing about cooperating with one another instead of just going ahead and cooperating," he said. "We must find ways of learning about each other," said Torsuev, and he cited with admiration the crowds of people he saw in the National Gallery of Art. "So many young people interested in art. Art everyone understands." Concluded Torsuev, "We must find a language in which to communicate. And we need an exchange with the U.S. in terms of our lifetime."

Protocol and Resolutions. During the four-day meeting, the participants attempted to find that "language," and in the end they signed a protocol calling for the exchange of current national bibliographies beginning in 1989. The Soviet specialists and staff from The Library of Congress Processing Services Department worked together to analyze a sample Soviet magnetic tape to determine cataloging and formatting differences. Their conclusion was that the differences are not insurmountable and future tape exchanges are feasible. Resolutions were passed on bibliographic standards, online public access catalogs, networking, and preservation. The resolutions were forwarded to the U.S./U.S.S.R. Commission on Library Cooperation for future action and are printed below.

New Orleans. Leaving hot and steamy Washington, D.C., the delegates headed to New Orleans to attend the 1988 ALA Annual Conference. This was the first Soviet delegation ever to attend an ALA Annual Conference and fortunately, they not only observed, but also participated in programs. Kartashov spoke at the IRC program, "Leadership in International Understanding: The Role of Libraries." He focused on the Soviet Union's efforts to develop programs, services and collections which promote cross-cultural appreciation and international understanding. Sorokin participated in the International Relations Assembly, enumerating some of the latest developments in Soviet librarianship. The Soviets also participated in the social side of the conference, at an IRRT reception aboard the riverboat *Delta Queen,* at the Newbery/Caldecott banquet and at the Mardi Gras-emulating reception. They enjoyed the Southern hospitality of New Orleans Public Library board member Susan Ormond at her home for dinner, and they were the honored guests at ALA's Inaugural banquet. Throughout the conference Russian-speaking ALA members were available as hosts/mentors for the delegates.

In the exhibit hall, the Soviets showcased a collection of 300 publications individually selected to represent a cross section of Soviet society and interests and the best in Soviet librarianship. Kartashov later presented the entire collection to the ALA's Executive Board as a gift that was made a part of the permanent collection at the Association's headquarters library and, in the words of ALA's President Margaret E. Chisholm, "remains forever as a symbol of cooperation and friendship between ALA and the USSR."

This first step in reestablishing relations with our Soviet colleagues was an important first step. Considering the language, cultural, and political barriers, our language is still stiff, our actions ponderous, our formal papers sometimes obscure and difficult to read, and our behavior hesitant. The proposals presented by our Soviet colleagues were encouraging, and their remarks refreshingly frank, and a genuine desire to cooperate was obvious. It is a remarkable period in Soviet history and the challenge to the U.S. library community is to embrace enthusiastically their requests for cooperative activities, to start working today to discover that universal language for librarianship.

ROBERT P. DOYLE

PROTOCOL
In connection with the U.S./U.S.S.R. Seminar on Access to Library Resources through Technology and Preservation, held at The Library of Congress 5-8 July 1988, the Scientific-Production Firm "The All-Union Book Chamber" held working sessions with staff of the Processing Services department, Library of Congress. The goal of the meeting was the analysis of a magnetic tape provided by the Soviet delegation to resolve differences in cataloging and formatting practices leading to the possible exchange of current national bibliographies beginning in 1989. This analysis indicated that the differences are not insurmountable and that tape exchange would be feasible.

As a next step, The Library of Congress supplied to the All-Union Book Chamber a test tape of US-MARC records. After analysis of this tape, the sides will exchange letters concerning any remaining problems.

It is proposed that collaboration of this working group consisting of

American and Soviet specialists be continued. Tentative agreement was reached on the desirability of an exchange of visits by specialists (two or three persons annually on a non-foreign currency basis) between the All-Union Book Chamber and The Library of Congress to further prepare for the possible exchange of tapes and subsequently for improvement of this work.

Wednesday, 6 July 1988

RESOLUTIONS FROM WORKING GROUP 1 ON DATABASES: BIBLIOGRAPHIC STANDARDS

1. Immediate exchange of "test" tapes in UNIMARC format between The Library of Congress and Lenin State Library and the All-Union Book Chamber and analysis of format differences, character set differences, ISBD, and preliminary investigation of names and subject headings.
2. Establish bilateral working group to study results of this analysis to identify means to accommodate the differences with the goal to establish permanent exchange relations for machine-readable data files.
3. When Lenin State Library has access to an X.25 network, a working group should be established to investigate remote (online) access to U.S./U.S.S.R. bibliographic resources.
4. Establish a working group to identify opportunities for joint research in library and bibliographical automation and a continuing exchange program for specialists in these areas.

Wednesday, 6 July 1988

RESOLUTIONS FROM WORKING GROUP 2 ON DATABASES: ONLINE PUBLIC ACCESS CATALOGS

1. Endorse adherence to the use of international standards where they exist and to identify jointly areas where standards are needed to further the development of Online Public Access Catalogs.
2. Establish a test environment wherein institutions in both countries can have access to a variety of U.S./U.S.S.R. Online Public Access Catalogs installations and evaluate the services provided.
3. Establish a joint study group to enunciate design principles for the development of Online Public Access Catalogs. These would include jointly designing user studies and specifying mechanisms for the automatic monitoring of patterns of use.
4. Create a joint study group to establish the principles and processes that ensure control of quality when creating bibliographic data.

Thursday, 7 July 1988

RESOLUTION FROM WORKING GROUP 3: NETWORKING

1. Establish a specific Subcommission on Networking and Technical Exchange under the existing U.S./U.S.S.R. Commission on Library Cooperation. This broad oversight committee could help promote and recommend exchanges and projects in what will be a complex and multifaceted development. This Subcommission will cooperate with the scholarly community of both countries in regards to international computer networking. The Subcommission should help review, facilitate, and promote specific projects, pilot demonstrations, and exchanges of mutual interest.
2. Some specific areas for which working groups could begin initial exploration include: (a) Exchange of information on emerging and adopted information standards; (b) Explore potential of developing a CONSER type relationship to facilitate bibliographic control of serial titles in the U.S./U.S.S.R. (c) Analysis and recommendations concerning machine-readable data tapes to promote increased compatibility and usefulness; (d) Explore ongoing exchange of tapes; and (e) Explore pilot demonstrations of online access to U.S./U.S.S.R. network databases including suggestions for training and documentation.

Friday, 8 July 1988

RESOLUTIONS FROM WORKING GROUP 4: PRESERVATION

1. Continue the international effort spearheaded by the International Federation of Library Associations and Institutions (IFLA) to develop cooperative programs to preserve library materials.
2. Support the binational effort to improve microcopying facilities which facilitate the preservation and exchange of library materials.
3. Support the international effort to assist libraries to recover from damages by natural disasters to their collections.
4. Collaborate on developing mutually agreeable technical standards for preservation microfilm.
5. Exchange technical information related to preservation, conservation, and microfilming via conferences, translations of technical papers, and exchange of conservators between the countries.
6. Explore methods of providing information about what has been microfilmed within each country and is available for purchase.
7. Activate joint efforts on the part of U.S./U.S.S.R libraries in developing standards and exchanging information technologies insuring the preservation of library resources in both countries.

to develop international understanding and support programs, services and collections that promote cross-cultural appreciation and awareness. Bertha Chandler, Librarian at the Second Air Division Memorial, Norwich Central Library, England, described her experiences working and living overseas.

A number of important resolutions were approved by the ALA. They were: (a) endorsement of the "Glenerin Declaration," a by-product of a series of tri-national meetings sponsored by NCLIS, the British Library, and the Canadian Institute for Research on Policy; (b) support of the international efforts to rebuild the Alexandrian Library; (c) endorsement of the concept to establish "U.S. Friends of the Alexandrian Library"; (d) approval of the IRC affiliation with the American Association for the Advancement of Science-Science and Human Rights Program; and (e) contributions of books by American libraries and publishers to developing countries. In other actions, the IRC requested the ALA Executive Director to send a telegram to Federico Mayor congratulating him on his election as Director General of UNESCO.

The International Relations Round Table. The program of the International Relations Round Table (IRRT) in New Orleans provided American librarians with the valuable opportunity to exchange their international experiences. "International Experiences of American Librarians" provided the conferees with the opportunity to explore some ways that American librarians can go abroad for professional experiences. Speakers were: Tanja Lorkovic, Charles Baldwin and Jean Straub who described their experiences.

Librarians interested in exchanges should find helpful the newly published *Going International; Librarians' Preparation Guide for a Work Experience/Job Exchange Abroad* (ALA, 1988). This how-to manual, a product of the Joint IRC/

IRRT Subcommittee on Exchanges, was compiled by Linda E. Williamson and offers sound advice and a useful checklist.

Other Associations and Organizations. The International Association for School Librarians, with assistance from the American Association of School Librarians, held its 17th annual international conference in Kalamazoo, Michigan, from July 24 to 29, 1988. The theme of the Conference was "Great Expectations: Standards, Innovative Programs and New Technologies." Four keynote speakers highlighted these areas, interspersed with presentations on various aspects of the topic by participants from 12 countries. Sessions on school library research at the international level and on needs which participants felt important for school library education programs were held. The 1989 conference will be in Kuala Lumpur, Malaysia, July 22–26. It will emphasize "School Libraries: Centers for Life Long Learning."

The Association for Library Service to Children sponsored the 1988 ALSC Preconference entitled "Going Global: Celebrating International Children's Books." The Association for College and Research Libraries (ACRL) organized ACRL's first overseas conference on "Shared Responsibilities: Librarians and Western European Studies in North America and Western Europe," in Florence, Italy, April 4–8, 1988. Plans are underway for another international conference to be held in September, 1989 in Cambridge, England. The 1989 ACRL conference on April 2 will have an international component. The Public Library Association (PLA) provided an international focus to its conference in Pittsburgh last April. PLA is also cooperating with its counterpart in England by providing opportunities for exchange. An international scholarship entitled the PLA/CLSI International Study Award has been established in the amount of $5,000 for public librarians to go overseas on an exchange basis.

Other notable events of the year included the establishment of Article 19 in April, at the Annual Awards Dinner for the Overseas Press Club, modeled in part after Amnesty International. The name of the organization and its book, which was published under the title *Article 19 World Report: Information, Freedom and Censorship*, compiled by Kevin Boyle (Times Books), derived from Article 19 of the United Nations' Universal Declaration of Human Rights, which was adopted in 1948 and ratified by 80 nations. The publication date, October 1988, coincides with the 40th anniversary of the adoption of the United Nations' Universal Declaration of Human Rights.

The American Society for Information Science. The American Society for Information Science (ASIS) continued to expand its international activities through programs at the annual conference international outreach activities. The October 1988 program featured four technical sessions, three of which were organized by the Special Interest Group/International Information Issues (SIG/III) in cooperation with the Automated Language Processing (ALP). Topics were: "Machine–Aided Translation: A Global View"; "Information Technology in the Caribbean"; and "Chinese Library and Information Systems: Looking Ahead." The fourth technical program was an "International Geoshere/Bioshere Programme of Global Change: Research Developing New Scientific Databases for Action." The Student Chapter of the Year Award went to the ASIS Student Chapter at the University of Taiwan's Department of Library and Information Science.

U.S. Support to International Programs. The National Commission on Library and Information Science (NCLIS), was an important part of U.S. efforts to further its objectives in the international arena and to support and strengthen U.S. participation in international organizations to compensate for the loss of direct participation in UNESCO programs. NCLIS spent $216,500 on the following activities: FID Clearinghouse on Education and Training, $25,000; IFLA program for preservation, conservation and a reading promotion campaign in Africa, $40,000; NISO's international information standards activities, $20,000; ISCTI's program for consolidating and strengthening the U.S. presence in ICSTI, $20,000; U.S. National Committee for FID, $20,000; U.S. National Archives and Records Administration for preservation and conservation activities to enhance the development of archival programs in Latin America, $50,000; Preconference activities for the second European Conference on Archives, $21,500; and conference on Textbooks and Translations Standards in Latin America, $20,000. The State Department provided the ALA with $6,000 for two American librarians, Sara Fine and Roger Parent, to attend the UNESCO General Information Program (PGI) Intergovernmental Council Meeting in Paris November 21 to 25, 1988.

Library/Book Fellows Program. The USIA–funded ALA Library/Book Fellows Program is in its third year, thanks to a grant of $295,410 awarded by the agency to the ALA to continue administration of the program. The program places U.S. library and publishing professionals in working situations overseas for periods of several months to one year. Last September, the program placed fellows in posts in Argentina, Egypt, France, Liberia, Malawi, North Yemen, Sweden, Thailand, Uganda, and Venezuela.

MOHAMMED M. AMAN
MARY JO AMAN

International Relations Round Table

A variety of concerns comprised the agenda for the year (July 1987–July 1988): (1) annual program and planning meetings, (2) reception and hospitality for foreign guests, (3) bylaws and procedures revision, and (4) area reports to the membership. The issues considered reflect the overall mission of the International Relations Round Table (IRRT), which since 1956, has been:

> To develop the interests of librarians in activities and problems in the field of international relations; to serve as a channel of communication and counsel between the International Relations Committee and the members of the Association; and to provide hospitality and information to visitors from abroad. The IRRT

arranges programs in business meetings and appoints representatives to attend meetings of other professional groups.

In addition, the IRRT serves as an ALA membership forum for the introduction, exchange, discussion, and dissemination of ideas and information relating to international librarianship. Open to all ALA members, the Round Table serves the interests of generalists who enjoy providing hospitality for and meeting with foreign librarians and library school students as well as those interested in specific international concerns and projects. Reflecting a broad cross section of ALA constituencies, IRRT includes public, school, academic, and special librarians as well as information specialists.

During the year, IRRT Chair, Theodore F. Welch, presided over meetings. Other officers for the year were Vice Chair/Chair Elect, Miles M. Jackson; Past Chair Henriette D. Avram; Secretary-Treasurer, Corinne Nyquist; Member-at-large Chair, David L. Easterbrook; *International Leads* Editor, Carroll H. Varner; Membership Chair, Meseratch Zecharias; and Area Committee Chairs, Hwa-wei Lee and Tze-Chung Li (East Asia); R.N. Sharma (South Asia); Joanne Zellers (Africa); Louella V. Wetherbee (Latin America); Michael W. Albin (Middle East and North Africa); and Kent Mulliner and Lian The-Mulliner (Co-Chairs) (Southeast Asia). Elaine K. Wingate served as ALA staff liaison.

The Membership Chair discussed a new membership form that was adopted by IRRT. The Executive Committee met in San Antonio on January 10 and on July 10 in New Orleans. Several meetings were held in conjunction with the ALA Annual Conference in New Orleans. The program, followed by the membership meeting, was held on July 10. The Executive Committee met on Monday July 11, and the IRRT reception took place that evening. On July 12, IRRT cosponsored a program with the International Relations Committee on "The Role of Libraries in Increasing International Understanding."

The theme for the IRRT program in New Orleans was "International Experiences of American Librarians." The three main speakers were Jean Straub, Adult Services Librarian, Milwaukee Public Library, who was on exchange to Dublin, Ireland; Tanja Lorkovic, Head of Cataloging, University of Iowa Library, who spent a year as a consultant at the University of North Sumatra, Medan, Indonesia; and Charlene Baldwin, Reference Librarian, Science-Technology Engineering Library, University of Arizona, who spent three months setting up a library in Niamy, Niger. Bruce Bonta served again as Chair for the Program.

The Chair of the Reception Committee was Elizabeth Sarkodie Mensah of the Loyola (New Orleans) University Library. Hospitality Chair was Connie Machado. Xavier University Library (New Orleans). More than 200 librarians, more than half of whom were from at least 45 countries, attended the reception at the Docking Wharf for the New Orleans *Delta Queen*. Plenty of food and drinks, dancing to the Cajun band, and an indoor/outdoor atmosphere was the setting for this grand event.

Nominations Chair, Allen B. Veaner, nominated Hideo Kaneko, Curator of the East Asian Collection, Yale University and former IRRT Area Chair, as the next Vice Chair/Chair Elect. The motion was then passed and accepted by the membership. Another motion was passed that the current Secretary-Treasurer, Membership Chair, and Member-at-large Chair be nominated for a second term each. All area chairs made either written or oral reports for the year. These reports are summarized in *International Leads*. The Executive Committee supported several IRC resolutions, including one to call on state library associations to "adopt" a developing country library association by paying the adopted country's IFLA dues. Two other motions passed, one that addresses the concept of the "Friends of the Alexandrian Library (USA)" and one that encourages libraries to donate books to developing countries. The work of the Ad Hoc Committee on the Bylaws and the Procedures Manual Revision continued, but the rewrite process was not completed in time for submission to the membership for a vote.

THEODORE F. WELCH

INTERNATIONAL RELATIONS ROUND TABLE

CHAIRPERSON (July 1988–July 1989):
Theodore Welch, Director of Libraries, Northern Illinois University, DeKalb

VICE-CHAIRPERSON:
Miles M. Jackson, Dean, Graduate School of Library Studies, Honolulu, Hawaii

PAST CHAIRPERSON:
Henriette Avram, Assistant Librarian for Processing Services, Library of Congress, Washington, D.C.

SECRETARY-TREASURER:
Corinne Nyquist, Librarian, State University of New York at New Paltz

Membership (August 31, 1988): 739

Junior Members Round Table

The 1987–88 year was one of stability and maintenance for the Junior Members Round Table. The organization continued to grow, and persevered in its attempts to attract new members to ALA, especially among library school students.

Annual Conferences. JMRT focused its efforts in 1988 on providing a particularly strong group of programs at the ALA conference in New Orleans. Among these was an orientation highlighted by Library of Congress Deputy Library Bill Welch, ALA Executive Board member Liz Futas, and poet/"All Things Considered" commentator Andrei Codrescu. The President's program featured a variety of speakers addressing the issues of job hunting for the recent graduate as well as the more seasoned seeker. The membership meeting included Herb White and Judith Bardwick speaking on the problem of career plateauing. JMRT activities at the conference concluded with the All-Conference Social, JMRT's fundraising event. Club 4141 was the site of the 1988 soiree, which featured the live rhythm and blues sounds of Deacon John and the Ivories and champagne, and turned a nice profit for the Round Table. The 1988–89 fiscal year started out on sound financial and administrative footing.

> **JUNIOR MEMBERS ROUND TABLE**
>
> PRESIDENT (July 1988–July 1989):
> **Karin E. Ford,** State Library, 325 W. State St., Boise, Idaho
>
> VICE-PRESIDENT/PRESIDENT-ELECT:
> **Myrtis C. Collins,** Collection Development/Reference Services, University of California, Berkeley, California
>
> SECRETARY:
> **Laura Sullivan,** Steely Library, Northern Kentucky University, Highland Heights, Kentucky
>
> TREASURER:
> **James Moun,** University of Illinois/Chicago, Chicago, Illinois
>
> Expenditures (August 31, 1988): $15,893

Awards. JMRT'S awards programs, including the JMRT 3M Professional Development Grant, the Shirley Olofson Memorial Award, and the EBSCO scholarship, continued to attract qualified applicants. This year's 3M Grant award winners included: Joan Dobson, Nancy Palma, and Linda Scott. The EBSCO scholarship went to Janice Pardoe, and the Shirley Olofson award was granted to Judy Jeng and James Huesmann. All were recognized at an Awards Recognition reception in the JMRT suite.

Affiliations. The JMRT Liaisons program, through which JMRT members represent the Round Table in other ALA units and divisions, developed quickly, as 10 new liaison positions were added. Most of these were positions on the membership committees of ALA divisions, but some divisions, most notably, the Library Administration and Management Association (LAMA), have used the JMRT liaisons program to identify and attract strong new leadership within the library profession.

DIANE J. CIMBALA

Law and Law Libraries

Privacy Legislation. In 1988, the Subcommittee on Civil and Constitutional Rights of the House Judiciary Committee of Congress held hearings on the FBI's Library Awareness Program, which seeks to obtain library patrons' circulation records and librarians' cooperation to report suspicious behavior by library patrons. Sponsors of H.R. 4947, designed to protect the privacy rights of library users, noted that 38 states and the District of Columbia already have library privacy laws of some sort. Section 4509 of the *New York Civil Practice Laws and Rules* was amended to enlarge the scope of library privacy legislation to include not only circulation records but computer data base searches, interlibrary loan transactions, reference queries, requests for photo copies of library materials, title reserve requests and usage of audio-visual materials, films or sound recordings.

Lexis v. Westlaw. With the intervention and encouragement of two federal judges, West Publishing Company (West) St. Paul, Minnesota, and Mead Data Central Inc. (MDC), Dayton, Ohio, agreed July 18, 1988 to a settlement that ended the much-publicized legal and legislative copyright disputes between the two companies. (See "LEXIS v. WESTLAW," *ALA Yearbook of Library and Information Services, 1988.*)

Under the terms of the settlement MDC will pay West license fees for the use of the National Reporter System on MDC's computer-assisted legal research service, LEXIS. MDC was also granted the right to add West's compilations of the statutes of certain states to LEXIS.

Copyright Development. The Berne Convention Implementation Act of 1988, was signed into law on Oct. 31, 1988, by President Reagan. When the United States becomes the 78th member of the Berne Convention, it will extend its multilateral copyright relations to 24 additional countries. U.S. copyright experts anticipate that adherence to Berne will enhance U.S. efforts to protect copyright works and combat copyright piracy throughout the world. Although neutral in intent, how the courts will view the Berne Implementation Amendments may be cause for future legislative activity.

The Berne Convention provides for protection of an author's moral rights. Congress, however, in the legislative history and final text of the Act specifically declared that the Berne Convention was not "self-executing" and hence the legal situation in the U.S. as it pertained to an author's moral rights was similar to the status quo before the Act. As stated in Sect 3(b) of the Berne Implementation Amendments: "(b) Certain Rights not affected—The provisions of the Berne Convention, the adherence of the U.S. thereto, and the satisfaction of the U.S. obligations thereunder, do not expand or reduce any right of an author of a work, whether claimed under Federal, State or the common law—(1) to claim authorship of the work; or (2) to object to any distortion, imitation of, or other derogatory action in relation to, the work that would prejudice the author's honor or reputation."

Academic Law Library Directors. An article by Michael J. Slinger, Associate Director for Public Services, University of Notre Dame Law Library, "The Career Paths and Education of Current Academic Law Library Directors," *Law Library Journal*, v. 80, p. 217–239, 1988, is the first comprehensive study of the qualifications, experiences and accomplishments that characterize today's academic law library directors. Slinger's study was based on responses from 160 academic law library directors. Ninety-eight (61 percent) of the directors were male, and sixty-two (39 percent) were female; 92 percent of all directors hold the M.L.S. degree, while 88 percent of the directors hold both a law and library degree; the average age upon attainment of the first directorship is 32; on the average, directors spend eight years at their first directorship; the average age for a director is 45, and average experience as a director is 12 years.

Slinger notes, "unquestionably, the statistic that stands out more than any other in [the] study is the tremendous disparity between faculty rank for male directors in comparison with female directors...while 65 percent of male directors are full professors, only 29 percent of females hold that rank; of the 13 directors who hold no faculty rank, 12 are females. Slinger adds: "I do not believe these disparities are explainable from any of the information I analyzed. These differences in rank appear to be evidence of serious inequities, which should be clearly examined in the near future."

Annual Conference. Under the leadership of President Albert O. Brecht, the 81st Annual Meeting of the AALL held in Atlanta, Georgia, June 26–29, 1988, set a record as the second largest in the history of the association. Paid registrations of 1,849 were augmented by guests and staff, for a grand total of 2,501. Margaret A. Leary was elected President of the AALL and Richard A. Danner was elected Vice-President/President Elect. Kay Moller Todd and Kathleen T. Larson are new members of the Executive Board. William H. Jepson resigned as Executive Director of the AALL and he was replaced by William D. Murphy, as acting Executive Director on September 1, 1988. The exhibit hall was filled to capacity with 174 booths representing 124 firms and organizations. The new Virginia Association of Law Libraries petition for chapter status was approved as the 28th chapter of the AALL. The executive Board selected Howe and Hutton, a law firm with a practice limited to non-profit organizations as legal counsel for AALL.

The Guide to International Legal Research was the 1988 winner of the Joseph L. Andrews Bibliographical Award. Four AALL members of the received the 1988 Distinguished Service Awards: Earl Borgeson, Forrest Drummoned, Frank Lukes and Bethany Ochal. The Executive Board approved a resolution urging the U.S. Congress to fund public access to the on-line index of Latin American official gazettes by the Hispanic Law Division of the Library of Congress.

American Bar Association Academic Law Library Statistics. Among requirements for accredation by the American Bar Association of law school libraries is the completion of extensive annual questionnaires requesting information on their budgets, collections and staff. The 1988 questionnaire contained 136 numbered questions with subparts distributed in machine-readable format, on floppy diskettes. The law libraries were requested to complete the questionnaire on an IBM compatible microcomputer, retaining a hard copy print-out of the results for their own records. Results were reported in the *Law Library Journal;* a more comprehensive version is available for purchase from the Statistics Coordinator of the American Association of Law Libraries. Problems relating to

Table 1. Monographs
(Law and Law-related Texts and Treatises Published in English)

	Mean Cost per Title	Percentage Increase over Previous Year	Index	No. of Titles Indexed
1973/74	$11.16	—	100.00	2,534
1986/87	$60.84	37.49%	545.16	2,695

Table 2. All Serials Included in Other Price Indexes
(Legal Periodicals, Looseleaf Services, Commercially-published Court Reporters and Legal Continuations)

	Mean Cost per Title	Percentage Increase over Previous Year	Index	No. of Titles Indexed
1973/74	$ 50.08	—	100.00	719
1986/87	$176.40	11.91%	352.24	1,202

Table 3. Legal Periodicals

	Mean Cost per Title	Percentage Increase over Previous Year	Index	No. of Titles Indexed
1973/74	$11.95	—	100.00	345
1986/87	$29.27	8.97%	244.94	497

Table 4. Looseleaf Services

	Mean Cost per Title	Percentage Increase over Previous Year	Index	No. of Titles Indexed
1973/74	$181.80	—	100.00	92
1986/87	$659.08	6.80%	362.53	143

Table 5. Commercially Published Court Reporters
(Law and Law-related Texts and Treatises Published in English)

	Mean Cost per Title	Percentage Increase over Previous Year	Index	No. of Titles Indexed
1973/74	$173.63	—	100.00	14
1986/87	$526.61	4.22%	303.29	16

Table 6. Legal Continuations

	Mean Cost per Title	Percentage Increase over Previous Year	Index	No. of Titles Indexed
1973/74	$ 44.67	—	100.00	268
1986/87	$173.65	-16.43%	394.03	546

copyright, data ownership and confidentiality must be resolved before ABA distributes survey results.

1986/87 Statistical Survey of Law School Libraries and Librarians. David A. Thomas, Statistics Coordinator, American Association of Law Libraries and Professor of Law and Law Librarian, Brigham Young University, in his annual summary of American Bar Association reported in *Law Library Journal*, v. 80, 485, 1988, proposed new statistical form and self-evaluation form for measuring law library quality. Thomas notes, many law school librarians believe that the statistical emphasis on size of collection, staff and budget provide an incomplete picture of a library, and that facilities, services and resources must be measured with less emphasis on comparisons among libraries and more attention to library self-evaluation.

The 1986-87 Statistical Survey of Law School Libraries reveals that the mean total budget of the 175 ABA-accredited law libraries was $1,015,813.90 and the median $934,745.00. For law libraries with collections of 100,000 to 200,000 volumes the mean was $680,911.60 and the median $632,937. For law libraries with collections of 200,000 to 300,000 volumes, the mean was $970,399.30 and the median $940,040. For law libraries with collections of 300,000 or more volumes, the mean was $1,477,533.30 and the median $1,264,780.

Harvard Law School Library ranked first, with a total budget of $4,497,479; New York University ranked second, with a total budget of $3,729,325; Georgetown ranked third with a total budget of $3,637,588; Columbia University was fourth with a budget of $2,614,361 and the University of Michigan was fifth with a budget of $2,326,591.

Price Index for Legal Publications 1986/87. In the words of Bettie Scott, (*Law Library Journal*, v. 80, p. 139, 1988, the cost of monographs in 1986/87 "went up a whopping 37.49 percent and all categories of serials increased 11.91 percent." It is interesting to note that while the overall cost of serials increased once again, the cost of legal continuations declined to 16.43 percent. Scott attributed the decrease to "the significant increase in the number of serial titles—the category nearly doubled—and the fact that many of these titles are small sets or single volumes supplemented by pocket parts, the expensive forms of supplementation."

College Library Technology. The Department of Education published final regulations implementing the College Library Technology and Cooperation Grants Program, 53 *Federal Register* 27114 (7/18/88). The purpose of the program is "to encourage resource sharing projects among the libraries of institutions of higher education through the use of technology and networking and to improve library and information services provided to them by public and nonprofit private organizations."

Career Hotline. The Career Hotline is now in operation at the AALL headquarters in Chicago: 312-939-7877. A recorded message will give descriptions of positions available, along with the necessary information to respond to a prospective employer. Any employer—AAL member or non-member—can use the Career Hotline Service to publicize an opening. Announcements should be sent to the Chicago headquarters and include job title, qualifications, basic duties, salary range and specifics, and the individual to be contacted to apply. To insure accuracy, listings cannot be taken over the telephone, but AALL's Telefax 312-431-1097 can be used for this purpose. Listings will be run for a two-week period and will be invoiced at the rate of $25 for the first 60 words, $5 additional for every 10 words over 60. Renewals for another two weeks are at the same rate.

Self-Help Law Bibliography. Single copies of the *Self-Help Law Bibliography* are available free from the New Jersey State Library, Law Section, 185 W. State St., CN520, Trenton, NJ 08625-0520, Att: Nola Crawford. Requesting libraries should include a mailing label if possible.

JULIUS J. MARKE

Libraries and Literacy

The American Library Association is still a leader in literacy awareness efforts. At the Annual Conference in New Orleans President Bill Summers called for three major commitments by librarians: to intellectual freedom, to freedom of access and to professionalism. Pollster Lou Harris, and former Speaker of the House Tip O'Neill echoed the literacy theme. A sense of urgency to capitalize on the cresting awareness campaign, the need to study and evaluate efforts to date and a strong move toward institutionalization of literacy services seems to pervade the library profession. The extent of literacy activities is discussed in a recent publication, *Libraries and Literacy Education: Comprehensive Survey Report*, by Deborah Wilcox Johnson, Jane Robbins, and Douglas Zweizig. *Libraries Improve Florida's Education: A Report on the Role of Public Libraries in the Education of Florida's*

On September 14, 1988 more than 500 persons attended the Oklahoma County Literacy Breakfast and gave a standing ovation to guest speaker John Corcoran, the California millionaire who told of his experience as a new reader. Corcoran's story has been covered on Phil Donahue's talk show, ABC's "20/20," and in People magazine.

Children and Illiterate Adults was written by E. Walter Terrie and F. William Summers for the Division of Library and Information Services in Florida in 1987.

The National Coalition for Literacy. The National Coalition for Literacy meets several times a year to share information, to raise funds to support the telephone information and referral service (1-800-228-8813), and to coordinate national activities. The major media awareness campaign has been carried forward by Project Literacy U.S. (PLUS) sponsored by PBS/ABC. In 1988, the focus turned to youth in an attempt to break the cycle of illiteracy. The high point of Coalition activity was the "Literacy Honors" celebration held in Washington, D.C. in November. A symposium entitled "Needs for the 1900s: The Next Steps for Literacy" cosponsored by the Coalition and Project Literacy U.S., was hosted by Barbara Bush. Papers were presented on "State of the Art in the Literacy Movement," "Foundation Perspectives," "The Role of the Media," and "The Impact and Potential of Technology" during the first segment. The second segment focused on "Business and Labor" and what state and local governments can do to improve literacy. Congress responded to the needs of the illiterate population by declaring July 2 as "National Literacy Day." Two longstanding sources of funding were reallocated. The FY'89 Adult Education Act provided $136,000,000 for state grants, $12,000,000 for workplace literacy, $5,000,000 for English training, $2,000,000 for national scope programs, $7,000,000 for homeless adult programs, $15,000,000 for a new Even Start program for parents and children, and $5,000,000 for a new student literacy corps. The Library Literacy Program, Title VI of the Library Services and Construction Act, awarded $4,787,000 in FY'88 grants. Congress also included basic education and literacy training as

ALA Public Information Office poster promotes reading.

part of the new Welfare Reform Act and reemphasized the need for literacy components in job training programs with an eight percent set aside that amounted to more than $144,000,000. The *Intergenerational Library Literacy Act* introduced in October, 1988 proposed to reallocate, from Title II of the Library Services and Construction Act, $5,000,000 in unobligated funds which

The American Academy of Advertising and International Advertising student competition winner on literacy.

have been carried over from past years. Congress took no action before closing in December 1988. Funds were to be spent for demonstration programs that would match older volunteers with libraries interested in developing after-school literacy and reading skills programs for latchkey children.

While these are scattered approaches providing a band-aid solution to the problem at best, an ad hoc committee called "The Working Group on Adult Literacy," has taken a broader and more far-reaching position.

Publications. Among the many literacy publications of 1988 the following may be useful to librarians: *Guidelines: Writing for Adults with Limited Reading Skills*, published by the U.S. Department of Agriculture; *Youth Indicators 1988: Trends in the Well-being of American Youth*, recently released by the Office of Educational Research and Improvement of the U.S. Department of Education; and *The Bottom Line: Basic Skills in the Workplace*, a joint publication of the U.S. Department of Education and U.S. Department of Labor.

The Future. In discussions and writings within the profession there is an awareness of the increasing gap between the haves and the have nots caused by technology and the barriers caused by illiteracy, an awareness also occuring in adult education. The public library was established to insure access to education and information for all. The library profession must use the coming year to capitalize on the current awareness to define and promote our role, establish the philosophy that literacy "projects" are ongoing library services, and secure continuous funding within the library budget. In doing so, we will carry out the mission of the library and improve the quality of life of those we serve.

JANE C. HEISER

Library Administration and Management Association

The Library Administration and Management Association (LAMA) had an active and effective year in which its membership grew 4.8 percent for a total of just over 5,000; it passed (by a margin of two to one) a $10 dues increase in two steps; it absorbed its total adjustment to accrual accounting; and it expanded the Executive Committee to include the chair of the Budget and Finance Committee and LAMA's Councilor. Here are some highlights.

(1) Because membership continues to grow and interest in LAMA is high, the 1987–88 and 1988–89 presidents received far more requests for committee appointments than the Association could provide. One of LAMA's strengths is the commitment and energy members bring to their assignments: the alacrity and ability with which people have taken on work, and completed it, is unique.

(2) *Library Administration and Management* (*LA&M*), our new magazine, has taken off: we have more than 500 paid subscriptions and expect to be in the black much sooner than anticipated. Much of the credit goes to the founding editor, Donald E. Riggs, Director of Libraries at Arizona State University. With the advice and help of the *LA&M* Editorial Board, chaired by Jennifer Cargill, Associate Librarian, Rice University, he identified individuals to write articles on middle management, organizational structure, information futures and access, and managing human resources. The fall 1988 magazine on Legal Issues was produced by the first guest editor. In 1989 the themes will be Leadership: Nature and Nurture; Financial Resources Innovations; Tinker, Taylor, Librarian, Business Officer; and Crunching Numbers Creatively. Associate Editor Charles Lowry, Director of Libraries at the University of Texas at Arlington, will become Editor after the January 1989 issue, and a new Associate Editor, Fred M. Heath, Texas Christian University, was selected at the 1989 Midwinter meeting.

(3) The quality of conference programming continued to draw enthusiastic crowds, at least half of them not division members. The Program Committee, chaired by Jim Neal, Assistant Dean at Penn State University Libraries, and Robert F. Moran, Jr., Indiana University Northwest Libraries, held the number of conference programs at 12, applying carefully developed criteria to each program proposal. In New Orleans, the division offered three preconferences: Automating Acquisitions: Managing Change; A Leadership Survival Kit; and Managing Employee Turnover. Programs in New Orleans ranged from Using Microcomputers for Graphic Presentations of Statistics to Training That Sticks, Hiring The Right Person, Mentor/Protege: Librarians Helping Librarians, Swap 'n Shop for PR and All That Jazz, Getting Your Money's Worth from Library Building Consultants, a Fund Fare Exchange, and Now That You've Got the Grant: Establishing a Good Track Record in Financial Administration.

(4) LAMA's regional institute program, administered by the Special Conferences and Programs Committee, chaired by William Gosling, Assistant Director for Technical Services at the University of Michigan, approved three new institutes in San Antonio: The Bottom Line in Financial Management, Patricia G. Schuman and Betty J. Turock, presenters; The Library Building Planning Process: A Practical Approach, Donald G. Kelsey, presenter; and The Communication Roles of Supervisors: Talking with Employees, Suellyn Hunt, Donald W. Lewis, and Maureen Sullivan, presenters, which was offered October 17–18 in Minneapolis. A recent addition to the list of seven existing institutes, on leadership survival, was offered for the first time at the Virginia Library Association and then in Alabama in fall 1987, twice in Pennsylvania in early June, in New Orleans, and October 4–5 in Phoenix, Arizona.

Mary R. Somerville, 1987–88 President of the Association for Library Service to Children, and Vivian R. Wynn, 1987–88 President of the Young Adult Services Division, agreed to do the LAMA/ALSC/YASD regional institute on managing youth services. They have developed the content and format for a one and one-half to two-day institute.

(5) John H. Martin, Jr., Head, Division of Technical Support, Orlando Public Library, presided over the tremendous workload moving

through the Publications Committee. The committee progressed in converting from a reactive to a proactive group. It continued the tradition of "circuit riding," visiting with section executive committees to answer questions and to stimulate new publications.

Publications produced in 1988 include *Automation Projects: The Evaluation Stage, Checklist of Library Building Design Considerations, Library Buildings Consultants List (1989)*, and *Staff Development: A Practical Guide*.

The Publications Committee continued to be concerned about serious delays in publishing papers from preconferences and conference programs. The committee urged the LAMA Program Committee to require that papers be submitted at the time of a program or within a specified period thereafter. In New Orleans and Washington (1989), the Committee devoted time to brainstorming about new publishing projects.

Kay Ann Cassell's *Knowing Your Community and Its Needs*, no. 14 in the "Small Libraries Publications Series" (SLPS), was published in January; in the summer *Great Library Promotion Ideas IV* will be published. GLPI I—III were sold successfully at the annual conference as a unit for a special price.

Anders Dahlgren recommended to the Board that the merged positions of Small Libraries Publications series editor and committee chair be separated. He continues to chair "SLPS" and Richard A. Matzek, Director of Libraries at Nazareth College in Rochester, New York, edits the series. *Working with Government Authority* by Deborah Miller and *Preservation and the Small Library*, by Marcia Lowry are in process. Topics assigned are collection development, genealogy/local history and the small library, literacy and the small library, the nonprint collection and the small library, and young adult services.

(6) LAMA is planning a Leadership Issues Forum to be held in 1990. The forum will focus on issues significantly affecting current and rising leaders in the profession. Joining a Committee chaired by Donald E. Riggs are Charles M. Brown, Richard M. Dougherty, Ann Heidbreder Eastman, Rodney M. Hersberger, Carol F.L. Liu, James G. Neal, Kay K. Runge, Hans Rütimann, Gary M. Shirk, Carolyn A. Snyder, and Karen A. Whitney. Neal chairs the Program Subcommittee and Shirk the Site Selection and Finance Subcommittee.

(7) With ACRL, LITA, and RTSD, LAMA cosponsors the new Hugh C. Atkinson Memorial Award, which was given for the first time at the 1988 annual conference to Richard M. Dougherty, Professor, Information and Library Studies, the University of Michigan in Ann Arbor.

(8) With the executive committees of most of the other divisions, LAMA participated in the first joint session in Lisle, Illinois, October 21–23. LAMA participated in preliminary discussions about the operating agreement, discussed two new joint projects: a PLA/LAMA/ASCLA proposal for the World Book—ALA Goal Award to develop a plan for consensus on the reauthorized Library Services and Construction Act, and a PLA/LAMA regional institute for new directors of public libraries. The operating agree-

Library Administration and Management Association

Library Administration and Management Association annual breakfast honored Betty Bender (left) 1986–87 LAMA president. Ann Eastman, 1987–88 president (right) presented Bender with the LAMA T-shirt.

ment was the sole topic of the November 11–13 meeting of the divisions, COPES, and ALA management at which LAMA President Maureen Sullivan represented the division.

(9) The International Federation of Library Associations (IFLA) suggested that LAMA assist in developing a management round table. Some groundwork has been done, because an ad hoc task force has investigated the division's need for a group focusing on international issues.

(10) Dallas Young Shaffer, Monterey County Librarian, Salinas, California, was elected President–elect.

President's Program. A special task force on Leadership and Communication, chaired by Nancy Davenport, Assistant Director for Special Programs of the Congressional Research Service, Library of Congress, helped plan that part of the presidential program that focused on "the language of leadership." Louis I. Middleman, Research Associate, Management Systems Laboratories at Virginia Tech, facilitated a midwinter planning session. The San Antonio session and the President's program in New Orleans maintained President Margaret Chisholm's focus on leadership. LAMA's 1988–89 President Sullivan sharpened that focus by selecting leadership development as her theme.

LAMA also asked all ALA divisions and appropriate round tables to identify one or more conference programs in New Orleans that dealt with some aspect of access to library service and information. The list was featured in the conference program. On July 10, William J. Welsh, Deputy Librarian of Congress, addressed the topic of "Access and the Style of Leadership." The access portion of the President's program was assisted by a task force chaired by Robert W. Oram, Director of Libraries, Southern Methodist University. LAMA's major response to the *Report of the Commission on Freedom and Equality of Access to Information* (the Lacy Commission Report) was that the division lead in keeping the important topic of access before ALA member-

Library Administration and Management Association

ship. Dennis Day, Chair of the ALA Committee on the Commission Report, brought important current ideas to the Oram task force at several conferences.

The LAMA President's theme was "The Language of Leadership." Almost 30 people proposed to write papers, and 23 were microfiched and given away at the President's Dinner. Don Riggs will edit a book *Communication: The Language of Library Leadership,* derived from these papers and it will be published in 1989 by ALA.

Don Riggs and Gordon A. Sabine, Special Assistant for Oral History to the University Librarian at Arizona State University, edited *Libraries in the 90's: What the Leaders Expect,* an Oryx Press book of interviews with 25 library and information science leaders. Among those interviewed were active LAMA members—Patricia W. Berger, Richard M. Dougherty, Ann Heidbreder Eastman, Joseph A. Rosenthal, and Gary Strong.

Other LAMA Committees. Budget and Finance Committee. Like other ALA units, LAMA and its staff spent more time than usual on financial matters as the Association shifted to accrual accounting and put up a new system for handling financial data. Rodney M. Hersberger, Director of Libraries at California State University in Bakersfield, and John Vasi, Assistant University Librarian, University of California/Santa Barbara, and their committees analyzed numbers, trends, and implications for LAMA units. LAMA member Robert W. Frase was recognized by the ALA Council in January 1989 for his work on this matter.

Governmental Affairs Committee. Chaired by Nancy Bolt, State Librarian of Colorado, the Committee sponsored the resolution passed by Council in January on permanent, acid-free paper for books. It is this language that prompted Senator Pell in October to introduce a Senate joint resolution to establish a national policy on permanent papers.

Membership Committee. Chaired by Carol Liu and Judith A. Adams, this committee's effort to increase LAMA's racial and ethnic diversity produced excellent results. Fourteen representatives of ethnic organizations made recommendations for improving LAMA's services to ethnic librarians and library supporters. A new membership brochure was published, the activity interest form was revised; and Liu wrote a helpful "Get Involved" information sheet for potential LAMA members.

Winston A. Walden, Director of Tennessee Tech University Library, was the division's representative to the Junior Members Round Table. Chaired by William Jones, Assistant University Librarian at the University of Illinois–Chicago, the Membership Services Representatives (MSR) Network Task Force completed its charge of recommending a support group for the Membership Committee and specified how MRSs should function at the state and regional levels.

Sections. Highlights of the Building and Equipment Section's activities were an annual conference program, "Getting Your Money's Worth: A Client's Guide to Library Building Consultants"; pre-production was underway for several prospective programs for the 1989 Dallas conference, including an important preconference on library lighting; solicitation of entries for the new edition of the *Library Building Consultants List;* solicitation of applicants for the AIA/ALA Library Buildings Award to be made at the 1989 Dallas conference; and submission of a manuscript to the Publications Committee for a *Checklist of Library Building Design Considerations.*

The Fund Raising and Financial Development Section looked within as it reorganized and revised some committee charges. A preconference on advanced fundraising is planned for Dallas. A new survey of fundraising organizations in public and academic libraries is planned. The proposal for a joint (with ACRL) fundraising clearing house has been approved. An instrument to survey alternative resources to support libraries will be considered at the annual conference with the actual survey to be conducted in 1989.

The Library Organization and Management Section prepared final guidelines for a library management consultants list. In addition to planning conference programs, the Planning and Evaluation of Library Services Committee held an information exchange in San Antonio on "the aesthetics of information," which addressed the effectiveness of evaluating library programs. The Risk Management and Insurance Committee agreed to undertake revision and updating of the ALA's *Insurance Manual for Librarians (1977).* The section organized two new discussion groups: Research on Library Organization and Management and Leadership.

Making final plans for a regional institute on the communication role of supervisors was a major accomplishment for the Personal Administration Section in 1988. The section worked closely with *LA&M* editor Donald Riggs on the June 1988, issue on Managing Human Resources. The Publications Committee is reviewing activity in this area across the section, and two members of the Economic Status and Welfare Committee, Sue Webreck Alman and Bill Jones, wrote a *Library Journal* article on organizational health testing. A resolution on that subject was passed by Council in Washington. In New Orleans, Council passed an important resolution on freedom from mandatory drug testing for library employees, that was written by the PAS Economic Status and Staff Welfare Committee.

The Public Relations Section also emerged from reorganization. It continued to sponsor strong programs, including Swap 'n Shop, and turn its attention to public relations education for librarians at or through library schools; to issues and trends that have implications for library public relations; to the need for polishing lobbying skills; and to regional institutes. The section annually co-sponsors with the H.W. Wilson Company the John Cotton Dana Library Public Relations Awards.

The Statistics Section characterized its year as one of "growing awareness of the central importance of library statistics for ALA and the federal government." The highlight of activity was the drafting of a *Report on United States Library Statistics.* This report provides ALA with background on the major issues on library statistics over the last 25 years and recommends a role for the Association in the future.

Maureen Sullivan, Yale University Libraries.

The NISO Z39.7 library statistics standard is due for a five-year ballot in May 1989. The section recommended that a small ad hoc task force of knowledgeable individuals be appointed to coordinate this review. Two section members attended both 1987 meetings on statistics of the National Commission on Libraries and Information Science/Center for Education Statistics. The chair, Peter R. Young, was appointed to a task force created by an inter-agency memorandum of understanding between CES and the National Commission on Library and Information Science (NCLIS) to continue work with the states and libraries to develop a federal/state cooperative system of gathering public library statistics.

The Acquisition Systems Committee of the Systems and Services Section, its youngest Committee, presented a preconference in New Orleans on the wide range of issues related to the management of such systems. It will be reported out in a 1989 publication. The Management practices Committee developed a brief, annotated bibliography on stress management resulting from its discussion of "technostress." The Circulation Services Committee plans its first conference program for Dallas; it will address new circulation services and traditional services that have changed or been enhanced through automation. The Committee is also considering a way of sharing information with colleagues—short bibliographies or checklists, or a "how to" series on such topics as bar code labeling, system selection, stacks maintenance and materials preservation, document delivery, and copyright problems. By way of putting closure on the era of systems devoted solely to circulation, the section Publications and Bibliography Committee will produce a ten-year cumulative bibliography. It will devote more attention to publications arising from other Committees and to requests from the LAMA Publications Committee.

Discussion Groups. LAMA discussion groups are less formally constituted than committees and sections. The Middle Management Discussion Group program in 1987 on "The Problem Boss," drew an overflow crowd of about 600 for a three-hour program, and was cited by *Library Journal* as "best of the conference." More than 60 percent of the audience was not LAMA members. This discussion group has a tradition of holding a session at the Midwinter conference to review and discuss topics from the Annual conference program. More than 100 people attended the session in San Antonio. Appropriate materials, especially bibliographies, were prepared and distributed.

Conclusion. LAMA began as a federation, one might say, of the old Library Administration Division and several other groups and it has developed into a mature division of ALA. Over the years, committees and sections have found common ground and learned to work together effectively within LAMA and ALA. In 1988 LAMA advanced its agenda by focusing on the importance of effective communication in leadership, on access as a major issue facing the profession today, and on drawing attention to LAMA itself. An ad hoc task force on Marketing was established. LAMA was among the divisions that asked ASCLA to reconsider the wording of a library networking statement because the January document did not appear to accomplish the anticipated goal. Hearings were held July 11. LAMA was delighted that 1988–89 ALA President William Summers continued to emphasize access, and that LAMA President Sullivan will emphasize leadership skills development.

LAMA is one of the divisions with members who are professionals but who do not hold library degrees: public relations, fundraising, proposal writing, building design, personnel, and automation experts. LAMA offers its members a wide variety of options and entre to several nontraditional groups whose work benefits libraries.

LAMA's Work Related to ALA's Priority Areas. Access to Information. In addition to LAMA's response to the Lacy Commission *Report* and identification of New Orleans programs on access, numerous division activities and publications of the FRFDS and PRS help inform the public about library materials and services.

Legislation/Funding. In addition to the work of FRFDS, the Statistics Section has been represented at numerous meetings where data in support of ALA's lobbying efforts have been discussed and generated. When Congress suddenly grew interested in putting library construction money back into LSCA, SS had the necessary data at hand. The Governmental Affairs Committee moved the resolution on permanent, durable paper in January, and it is dealing with the FBI library awareness program. LAMA is offering a new institute on financial management, and has developed institutes on fundraising and grantsmanship.

Intellectual Freedom. The Governmental Affair Committee work on the FBI library awareness program was a major 1988 effort. LAMA's representative to the Freedom To Read Foundation, Martha B. Gould, Director of the Washoe County Library in Reno, Nevada, has been an intellectual freedom activist for many years.

Public Awareness. Bringing libraries to the attention of their several publics is the focus of PRS's work. Individual library efforts are widely promoted at the Fund Fare Exchange, Swap 'n Shop, and other programs at each conference.

Personnel Resources is handled successfully by the Personnel Administration Section which offers sellout programs and offered its first regional institute—on the communication role of supervisors—in Minneapolis in October. Programs offered by other groups often focus on personnel matters.

LIBRARY ADMINISTRATION AND MANAGEMENT ASSOCIATION

PRESIDENT (July 1988–June 1989):
Maureen Sullivan, Head, Library Personnel Services, Yale University Libraries, New Haven, Connecticut

VICE-PRESIDENT/PRESIDENT-ELECT:
Dallas Y. Shaffer, County Librarian, Monterey County Library, Salinas, California

EXECUTIVE DIRECTOR:
John W. Berry

Membership (August 31, 1988): 5,074
Expenditures (August 1988): $237,112

Library Services, Development, and Technology. The Buildings and Equipment, Library Organization and Management, and Systems and Services sections are active in this area. Automating Acquisitions and A Leadership Survival Kit were topics for 1988 preconferences; programs included Managing Shared Systems and Getting Your Money's Worth from Library Building Consultants. Several new publications fall in this priority area, as do many titles in the Small Libraries Publications series.

LAMA thinks that in dealing with ALA's mission, priorities, and goals, the substantive work of all the divisions must not be overlooked. It is at that level that most members have access to ideas—not on the floor of Council or in the Executive Board room.

Irene E. Moran, formerly of the Brooklyn (New York) Public Library who now lives in California, received the LAMA Certificate of Appreciation at the President's Dinner on July 10 at the Plimsoll Club. She has chaired the Public Relations Section and was a founding member of the Fund Raising and Financial Development Section.

ANN HEIDBREDER EASTMAN

Library and Information Technology Association

Sherrie Schmidt, Texas A & M University

During 1988 the Library and Information Technology Association (LITA) demonstrated a renewed dedication to addressing many of the problems raised by the rapid pace of technological innovation. In 1987 at the annual conference LITA formed a new committee on access to information and the potential barriers that technology might impose. In addition to the detailed technical programs for which LITA is well known, programs at the annual 1988 conference in New Orleans focused on the use of technology to battle illiteracy and the undemocratic potential of certain innovations. Through its committees, programs, and publications, LITA serves ALA and the profession as an advocate for the traditional ideals of librarianship as well as an illuminator of technological advances.

Organization. Several years ago, LITA reorganized around an interest group structure with a minimal number of administrative committees. Interest groups are initiated through a petition process and must be renewed periodically. These interest groups have been very successful in promoting discussion and presenting programs on a variety of topics and issues including online catalogs, expert systems, authority control, retrospective conversion, telecommunications, and distributed systems. The newest interest group will discuss concerns relating to library consortia that share automated systems.

Planning. The reorganization of LITA was motivated by an attempt to involve more of the membership in programming and other Association activities. LITA has instituted a bottom-up planning process that is driven largely by the interest groups and other committees rather than by the officers and board. A planning breakfast is held at each ALA conference that assembles all the interest group chairs, all chairs of committees, the officers, the boards, and staff to discuss current activity and future directions for LITA. The information gathered at this meeting is vital to an effective planning process. A planning committee, chaired by the vice-president, is charged with using the results of this meeting to formulate ideas for programs, publications, and other activities.

Publications. The two periodical publications of LITA are thriving. The *LITA Newsletter*, under the editorship of Walt Crawford, has become an important source of information on LITA activities and for continuing education. It is notable in that it is the only ALA periodical that is prepared using desktop publishing. *Information Technology and Libraries*, the learned journal of LITA, celebrated its 20th year of publication, the first 13, under the title *Journal of Library Automation*.

Programs. LITA programs at ALA conferences are well-attended and provide valuable opportunities for learning for all ALA members. LITA held two preconferences, one before the 1988 annual conference on screen design and one on expert systems. During the annual conference, LITA programs featured the impact of CD-ROM, using the online catalog for interlibrary loan, library applications of electronic mail, project management, and the use of technology to promote adult literacy. The president's program, "Whose Revolution Is It Anyway?", focused on the effect of technology upon freedom of access. Because of the LITA National Conference, scheduled for October 2-6, 1988, no institutes or programs were held outside of the ALA conferences.

Awards. The 1988 LITA/Gaylord Award for Achievement in Library and Information Technology was presented to Barbara E. Markuson in recognition of her leadership in shaping the development of library automation over the past two decades.

The first Hugh C. Atkinson Memorial award was presented to Richard M. Dougherty. This award is sponsored jointly by LITA, LAMA, and ACRL.

In all, 1988 was a year of gathering force for LITA. The new organization and the planning process have taken root and are producing splendid programs and exciting ideas for the future. LITA is also beginning to delineate its role in defining issues of information policy that go beyond the technical areas that many associate with the division.

WILLIAM GRAY POTTER

LIBRARY AND INFORMATION TECHNOLOGY ASSOCIATION

PRESIDENT (July 1987-June 1988):
Sherrie Schmidt, Sterling C. Evans Library, Texas A & M University, College Station 77843

VICE-PRESIDENT/PRESIDENT-ELECT:
Carol A. Parkhurst, University Library, University of Nevada, Reno 89557

EXECUTIVE DIRECTOR:
Linda J. Knutson

Membership (August 31, 1989): 3,904 personal and 925 organizational
Expenditures (Estimated 1988/89): $455,741

The Library Association (of the United Kingdom of Great Britain and Northern Ireland)

The Library Association is the professional body for all persons working in library and information services in the United Kingdom. It was formed in 1877 and received a Royal Charter in 1898. The functions and structure of the Library Association are similar to but not identical with those of the American Library Association. The Library Association has approximately 24,000 members, including nearly 2,000 residents outside the United Kingdom. Members work in all kinds of libraries and information services.

The President of the Association for 1989 is A.G.D. White, Deputy Librarian of the City of Edinburgh. The Chief Executive is George Cunningham. The Association's Head Office is at 7 Ridgmount Street, London WC1E 7AE.

Charging for Library Services. During 1988 the Association was deeply engaged in controversial proposals from the British Government calling for the levying of charges for some public library services which are now provided free. In February, the government published a consultation document "Financing Our Public Library Service: Four Subjects for Debate." The document proposed, among other things, that local authorities in charge of public library services should consider establishing premium book services so that the public could obtain the most popular works more quickly but for a fee. It also suggested that a fee should be charged when a public library had to obtain a book for a reader from a library in another part of the country and should charge when clients seek information from a computer-based source or obtain help with an inquiry from specially expert librarians.

These and other proposals in the consultation document prompted considerable controversy, and the Library Association took the lead in making the case for the traditional British practice of providing all book loans free and making only modest charges for obtaining books on the library interlending system. The Association's response to the Green Paper was sent to the government in June. The government will consider all the comments made on the Paper and is expected to propose new legislation to come into effect around 1990.

Libraries in Parliament. Meanwhile, during the parliamentary session 1987/88, the Association has been active in connection with a number of pieces of legislation passing through parliament. The Education Reform Act transfers the control of schools from local authorities to boards of governors and head teachers. The Association was concerned that this might result in a lowering of standards for school library services. Its attempt to achieve an amendment to the Bill was unsuccessful, but in the course of debate assurances were obtained from government.

New Copyright Act. A major concern of the Association during 1987 was the proposed new copyright legislation now embodied in the Copyright, Designs, and Patents Act 1988. Among other things, the Act established a legal framework within which copyright owners and publishers can establish licensing schemes to permit photocopying of copyrighted materials. The Act also established a Copyright Tribunal to exercise oversight and to protect the public interest. The principle of "fair dealing" (equivalent to "fair usage" in American law) is retained, but the Association had to mount a major effort to ensure that the copying of material for commercial purposes could be covered by "fair dealing" as well as copying for private study. On this point, the Association's efforts were successful in achieving an amendment of the Bill as it passed through parliament.

The European Community. A growing number of initiatives on library and information matters are coming from the European community (better known to some as "The Common Market"). The community, through its Council of Ministers drawn from all 12 member states, has the power to impose laws overriding the domestic legislation of member states. One proposal being actively considered during 1988 was that it should become compulsory throughout the Community to impose a Value Added Tax (VAT) on books and other forms of literature. The Library Association successfully resisted a similar proposal when it emanated from the British Government in 1984 and has joined with publishing, bookselling and other interests to oppose the new proposal emanating from the European Commission. The outcome is uncertain, but there is reason to hope that the Association's efforts will result in member states remaining free to charge no VAT on books and other literature if they do not wish to do so.

Another major initiative from the European Community in 1988 was the publication of a consultation document on cooperation between European libraries. The document presages community support for speeding up the introduction of computerized cataloging in library systems throughout the community. At present, there is a wide variation in the use of such facilities. A major motivation in the new initiative is to encourage high technology in the European Community and thereby to facilitate greater exchange of information between the vast treasure houses of European libraries. For this purpose, the Council of Europe, a different body with lesser powers but wider membership than the European Community, is also encouraging the computerization of catalogs of old stock in the main European library systems. Meanwhile, new Community programs in the cultural field are being prepared. In brief, it seems clear that the European Community will be an increasingly important forum for activity on library and information matters, closely affecting services provided in member states and the interests of other countries. The Library Association is producing a major report on library and information activities within the European Community and the Council of Europe, to be published early in 1989.

GEORGE CUNNINGHAM

Library History

Although the major or special events of 1988 in library history appeared fewer in number when

Library History

compared to the previous year, they are representative of conferences, anniversary celebrations, publications, and other activities.

Conferences. The two association meetings that regularly included programs on library history continued in 1988. At the meeting of the Association of Library and Information Science Education, held in San Antonio, Texas, January 7, Donald C. Dickinson and Margaret F. Maxwell (both of the University of Arizona) presented papers to the library history interest group of professional educators. Dickinson's paper, "Henry E. Huntington: The Early Years of His Book Collecting Career," was a biographical study, while Maxwell in "Libraries on the Last Frontier: Bringing Books to Arizona" dealt with the Arizona State Library and the critical year of 1956.

At the annual conference in New Orleans, the Library History Round Table of the American Library Association, along with the Library Research Round Table, devoted a program to the implications for librarianship and its history of Gerda Lerner's recent book, *Creation of Patriarchy*. (This session is reported at greater length in the Library History Round Table report in this volume.)

The International Symposium on Library History in the International Context convened on April 14–15 at the Herzog August Bibliothek, Wolfenbüttel, Federal Republic of Germany. The meeting was arranged by the Round Table on Library History of the International Federation of Library Associations and Institutions in close cooperation with the Wolfenbütteler Arbeitskreis für Bibliotheksgeschichte. Among the 13 speakers who represented as many countries and gave reports on the status of library history research in their respective nations was Wayne A. Wiegand (University of Wisconsin–Madison), who represented the United States. His paper, along with others of this significant meeting, will appear in the summer 1989 issue of *Libraries & Culture*.

The seventh annual Texas Library History Colloquium, sponsored by the Graduate School of Library and Information Science of the University of Texas at Austin, the Lyndon B. Johnson Presidential Library, and the Texas Center for the Book, was held on May 6 at the Johnson library in Austin. It focused on "Federal Legislation and Texas Libraries: The Enduring Legacy of the Yarborough Years," featuring a paper on U.S. Senator Ralph Yarborough's contributions to modern library history by Lottie Simpkins Meador (Texas Christian University). Robert W. Tissing, Jr. (Lyndon B. Johnson Presidential Library) described "Library Legislative Archives in the LBJ Library." Other presentations included Will Howard (Houston Public Library) on "Directions in the Library History of Texas: Patterns and Prospects" and Wayne Gray (Dallas Public Library) on the Texas Center for the Book. The annual event is intended for librarians, archivists, historians, and others who have a research or personal interest in the history of libraries and archival collections in Texas.

Anniversaries. The Jewish Theological Seminary of America celebrated its centennial with *Of Learning and Libraries: The Seminary Library at One Hundred*. The Riverside City and County Public Library (California) issued a publication by Ronald J. Baker entitled *Serving Through Partnership: A Centennial History of the Riverside City and County Public Library, 1888–1988*. Among other anniversaries were those of the Ellsworth (Maine) City Library (90 years), the Edmonton (Canada) Public Library, the Multnomah County (Oregon) Central Library, and the San Diego County (California) Library celebrated 75th anniversaries. The American Society for Information Science continued its year long celebration of 50 years and released an anniversary issue of its *Bulletin* (June/July). The graduate schools at Rosary College (River Forest, Illinois) and the University of Texas at Austin celebrated their 40th anniversaries.

Publications. The number of major publications dealing with American library history did not increase substantially in 1988. The long-awaited reference work—Arthur P. Young's *American Library History: A Bibliography of Dissertations and Theses*, 3d ed. rev. (Scarecrow), which includes more than 1,100 entries—appeared. Entries for dissertations and theses were accompanied by an informative abstract.

Another achievement of the year was *The Harvard University Library: A Documentary History*, prepared by Kenneth E. Carpenter (CIS Academic Editions, Congressional Information Service). It consists of some 29,000 pages of material reproduced on approximately 375 microfiche that document the pioneering and significant practices and historical evolution of one of the most esteemed research libraries of the world. A hard-copy guide provides a classification and index to the material.

Other publications in 1988 included *My Harvard Library Years*, the second, posthumously published, volume of Keyes D. Metcalf's memoirs (Harvard College Library) and *Jesse Shera, Librarianship, and Information Science* by H. Curtis Wright (School of Library and Information Science, Brigham Young University).

Two periodical articles in particular stirred interest in library history. The proposal of George S. Bobinski (State University of New York at Buffalo) to preserve a Carnegie library building as a permanent memorial and a public museum of the early American public library appeared in the May *Wilson Library Bulletin*. A letter from Wayne A. Wiegand in the September *American Libraries* solicited responses from a small public library that possessed substantial local archival records that might be studied in some detail. Both appeals have attracted attention to public library history projects in a brand of library history that has been neglected in recent years.

Other Historical Activities. The journal for those concerned with library history changed its name at the beginning of the year to *Libraries & Culture* from the *Journal of Library History* and continues to be published quarterly by the University of Texas Press and under the auspices of the University's Graduate School of Library and Information Science. A call for papers went out for Library History Seminar VIII, "Reading and Libraries," to be held at Bloomington, Indiana on May 9–11, 1990. The national seminar is sponsored every five years by the Library History Round Table of the American Library Association and *Libraries & Culture*. The 1990 meeting is co-sponsored by the School of Library and Information Science, Indiana University.

DONALD G. DAVIS, JR.

Library History Round Table

Organization and Structure. Although the Library History Round Table spent much of 1988 adjusting to structural and functional changes enacted in 1987, it also expanded the scope of its activities. For example, LHRT's membership agreed to establish standing committees for Research, Publications, and the Library History Seminar series. The Research Committee will be responsible for encouraging research in library history, for serving as liaison with other ALA units and professional organizations engaged in relevant historical research, and for administering the Justin Winsor Award. The Publications Committee will be responsible for promoting and encouraging publications reporting the results of research in library history, for serving as liaison with publishing units of ALA to encourage the incorporation of historical perspective into their publications, and for overseeing the publications of the Round Table. The Library History Seminar Committee will be responsible for planning, developing and executing quinquennially held meetings which have become known as the Library History Seminar Series. The current committee is planning for Library History Seminar VIII, which will be held May 9–11, 1990, at Indiana University in Bloomington. In the future the Round Table will also consider the establishment of an Education Committee, which will foster and encourage the teaching of library history in schools of library and information science. At its Summer 1988, meeting, the LHRT Executive Board appointed an ad hoc committee to draft an LHRT position paper on the role of library history in library education.

Publications. The semiannual LHRT Newsletter, now under the able editorship of Joanne E. Passet of UCLA's Graduate School of Library and Information Science, completed another year as LHRT's chief communications organ for reporting current research topics and events of interest in library history. The Round Table continues its relationship with Libraries & Culture: A Journal of Library History, which officially changed its title from The Journal of Library History upon publication of the Winter issue of 1988. Finally, The Round Table is also taking steps to become an active participant in future efforts to preserve documentation of library history; several members are engaged in planning a survey of archival records pertaining to library history, with a view to publishing a guide to American public library archives in the near future.

Program. The LHRT Program at the 1988 Annual Conference in New Orleans, co-sponsored by ten other ALA divisions and round tables, was titled "The Creation of Patriarchy:" Its Implications for Librarianship." It featured Dr. Gerda Lerner, Robinson–Edwards Professor of History at the University of Wisconsin—Madison and author of The Creation of Patriarchy (1985). Lerner's keynote address was followed by perceptive commentaries from Rebecca Bingham, Director of Media Services for Jefferson County, Kentucky; and Sharon Hogan, Director of Libraries at Louisiana State University. An audience of 350 joined in a lively post-presentation question and answer period.

For the fourth successive year LHRT joined with the Library Research Round Table to sponsor a joint Research Awards Program, at which LHRT and LRRT award winners summarize the findings of their papers. Winner of the 1988 Justin Winsor Prize (awarded exclusively by the Library History Round Table) was Brother Thomas O'Connor of Manhattan College in New York City, whose paper was entitled "Library Service to the American Commission to Negotiate Peace and to the Preparatory Inquiry, 1917–1919."

WAYNE A. WIEGAND

Library Instruction Round Table

Professional development, interlibrary cooperation, and teaching exceptional patrons were key thematic elements of work in the Library Instruction Round Table in 1988.

Annual Conference. Sharon Stewart chaired the 1988 Conference Program Committee and moderated the Program: "A-LIRT! Teaching Exceptional Patrons." Three speakers focused on the disabled, the adult illiterate, the adult intimidated literate, and international learners that make up over a third of our national population. Marsha Broadway highlighted progress toward the goal of eliminating physical and intellectual barriers for disabled library users and encouraged librarians to be aware of their attitudes toward the disabled. Kathleen O'Gorman asked "How libraries might educate adults more effectively in the personal, social, and environmental dimensions of their lives." She suggested that libraries best serve adult learners when librarians (1) are conscious of the transforming nature of library resources; (2) implement programs that foster and facilitate both oral and silent reading; (3) provide opportunities for informed discussions about learners' interests and concerns; (4) encourage collaborative learning in social and global dimensions; and (5) are proactive catalysts to felt needs of adult learners. Doreitha Madden made recommendations for improving user education services to international patrons. She encouraged librarians to evaluate their library instruction programs and implement improvements regularly, by developing a knowledge base for multicultural or non-English speaking patrons in the communities to be served.

Committees. Louise Greenfield and Abigail Loomis chaired the Affiliates Committee that designed an information packet for a data–gather-

---

LIBRARY HISTORY ROUND TABLE

CHAIRPERSON (July 1988–July 1989):
G. Barry Weavill, Graduate School of Library Service, University of Alabama

VICE-CHAIRPERSON/CHAIRPERSON-ELECT:
Suzanne Hildenbrand, School of Information and Library Studies, State University, Buffalo

SECRETARY-TREASURER:
Charles A. Seavey, Graduate Library School, University of Arizona

Membership (August 31, 1988): 341 (282 personal; 59 organizations)

Library Instruction Round Table

ing network training program. The committee established an Affiliates Information Database and Network that will form the bedrock for information gathering, professional mentoring, and networking with Librarians in all types of libraries. Doris Miller and the Public Relations/Membership Committee expanded the number of LIRT Bites (informal luncheons) at both midwinter and annual conferences, to provide greater opportunities for librarians to discuss user education issues. Eileen Liebeskind and Rae Haws led the Continuing Education Committee that developed a joint working relationship with the Library Orientation Exchange Organization, authored two excellent bibliographies: "LIRT Top Twenty for 1987," and "Library Instruction for Nontraditional Clientele."

The Research Committee, chaired by Patricia Vanderberg developed an instrument: "Aims of User Education Survey" and collected data from 500 libraries across the nation. Results will be published in the organization's LIRT News in 1989. Published articles: "Role of Library Instruction within the Educational Process," by Patricia Vanderberg; "How To Do Research In Library Instruction," by Emily Bergman; "How to Read Research," by Mary Gouke; "How To Market Library Instruction," by Sharon Goad; and "A Bibliography on CD-ROM Technology as Used in Library Instruction Application," by Julia Gelfand.

J. Randolph Call spearheaded the Handbook Publications Task Force that acquired a publisher for the ALA Goals Award Library Instruction Planner Handbook Manuscript." Contractual details have been completed and editorial work is in progress. Charles Dintrone and the Liaison Committee compiled lists of programs related to library instruction and distributed them to several thousand attendees at Midwinter and Annual Conferences. As chairperson of the Publications Committee and editor of the LIRT News, respectively, Elizabeth Dailey and Emily Okada published four issues during one of the most prolific periods of manuscript presentations in the history of the Round Table. The Elections Committee, chaired by Mary P. Popp, developed an excellent slate of candidates for election to official positions in the Library Instruction Round Table: Fay Golden, Vice-President/President Elect; Nel Ward, Secretary; and Pamela Engelbrecht, Treasurer, were elected. The committee developed a procedure to expedite the work of the vice-president in appointment of committee members, and is continuing the Leadership Skills Development Project.

Tobeylynn Birch chaired the Long-Range Planning Committee that revised the "Planning and Goal Progress Evaluation Form," and drafted a membership survey questionnaire. The CAI Task Force, chaired by Robert Kuhner, prepared a list of commercially available software and completed a survey of library publications that review software dealing with CAI library skills. Three committee members authored research on the topic during the year: Julie Bobay summarized the survey in "Computer Assisted Instruction for Library Skills: Review Sources;" Wilfred Fong wrote "Authoring Languages;" and Martin Kesselman published "Hypercard, CAI." Having already served for several years as excellent chairperson of the CAI Task Force, Robert Kuhner was appointed to chair the newly established Computer Applications Committee.

Under the leadership of Marilyn Barr, the Organization and Bylaws Committee completed revisions to the Organizational Manual and the Committee Notebooks. The following bylaw changes were prepared by the committee and approved by membership at the Annual Conference; (1) Publications Committee to have the LIRT Newsletter Editor and Assistant Editor as voting ex officio members and to have a separate committee chair; (2) CAI Task Force to become the Computer Applications Committee; (3) Elections Committee to expand and include Elections/Nominations, with added responsibilities of assisting the Vice-President in committee selections; and (4) the formulation of an ad hoc committee on guidelines to assist the Vice President in the orientation of new committee chairs.

Discussion Group Forums. Planning and cooperation among librarians in all types of libraries impact positively on the education of library users and enable librarians to: clarify collegial expectations and goals for teaching library users in the public, private, and academic communities; define critical thinking and research skills necessary for successful educational development at each academic level in the learning process; to explore problems of transferability of library skills between academic levels or stages of development; and to develop plans of action that complement the educational process.

Tobeylynn Birch, Vice-President/President elect, sponsored and led the LIRT Discussion Group forums that focused on these issues at both the Midwinter and Annual Conferences.

Mary P. Popp and Lois Pausch conducted interviews of leading Bibliographic Instruction Librarians as part of research and long-range planning of the organization, and will chair the Fifteenth Anniversary Task Force to continue this work. Thelma Tate represented the Round Table at the International Federation of Library Associations and Institutions (IFLA) 154th Conference that was held in Sydney, Australia. Discussions focused on cooperative research and planning to improve communication technologies, resources, and user education in the global community.

THELMA H. TATE

LIBRARY INSTRUCTION ROUND TABLE

PRESIDENT (June 1988–July 1989):
Tobeylynn Birch, Library Director, California School of Professional Psychology, Los Angeles

VICE-PRESIDENT/PRESIDENT-ELECT:
Fay A. Golden, Liverpool (New York) Public Library

SECRETARY:
Nellie C. Ward, Phoenix, Arizona

TREASURER:
Pamela N. Engelbrecht, Virginia Polytechnic Institute and State University Library, Blacksburg

Membership (August 31, 1988): 1,118

Library of Congress

Resolving to find ways "to get the champagne out of the bottle," Librarian of Congress James H. Billington initiated a year of transition at the Library of Congress with an open invitation to the Library's staff and constituents to begin a yearlong process of examining the institution, defining its mission, and envisioning ways that the Library can better serve the nation now and in the 21st century.

Billington created the Management and Planning (MAP) Committee, consisting of 28 Library staff members; sought advice from a blue-ribbon National Advisory Committee (NAC), consisting of leaders in the library, academic, legislative, judicial, business, and information communities; listened to library partners at forums scheduled throughout the country; and hired the Arthur Young, Inc., management consultant firm to work with staff to review the Library's internal organization and functions.

By the end of 1988, the MAP Committee had considered more than 900 written suggestions from staff members and patrons, identified issues to be addressed, drafted vision statements for shaping the Library's future, and articulated a mission for the Library in the year 2000 and beyond. Five new pilot projects were announced.

National Advisory Committee. Three overriding concerns emerged from the National Advisory Committee (NAC) meetings, subgroup reports, and members' letters: access, collaboration, and leadership. Although NAC members advocated nationwide access to the Library's online card catalog, there was no consensus as to whether the database should be retailed through other libraries or be made available directly to end users. NAC members observed that the marketing of Library services and products raises questions of intellectual property rights, fair competition with the private sector, competitiveness in international markets, and national security interests.

NAC members encouraged greater collaboration and cooperation with other libraries. Members attending a May meeting agreed that the Library of Congress should participate with the American Library Association as *a* national library and not as *the* national voice for libraries.

Regional Forums. Librarians at regional forums from Pittsburgh, Pennsylvania, to Sacramento, California, and at ALA meetings in New Orleans expressed a variety of concerns relating to the Library. They indicated a desire for the Library to assist in developing and articulating a national information policy; to allow direct access to its databases; to support local and regional preservation efforts; to seek ways of using television to deliver the Library's message about the importance of books and reading; to serve a growing multilingual population; and to aggressively collect and disseminate foreign publications, especially those relating to Japanese scientific and technological developments.

The Library Collections and the Congress. Congressional appropriations for the Library in 1988 totaled $247,950,000, which exceeded the 1987 appropriation by approximately $8,600,000—a gain of 3.6 percent. In March,

Howard Nemerov was appointed the third Poet Laureate of the U.S. He succeeded Richard Wilbur in September. Nemerov received the Pulitzer Prize in poetry and the National Book Award in poetry in 1978, the Theodore Roetke Memorial Prize for Poetry in 1968, and the Bollingen Prize for Poetry in 1981. He also will occupy the position of consultant in Poetry to the Library of Congress, created in 1936.

James Billington and other Library officials testified before Legislative Branch Appropriations subcommittees of the House and Senate appropriations committees to request $274,198,000 for the 1989 budget.

Funds appropriated for the purchase of general and law materials decreased by $75,000, or 1.6 percent. Although this decline continues a trend of the past three years, the decrease was not as drastic as the previous 14 percent reduction in book-purchasing funds, from $5,200,000 in 1985 to $4,510,000 in 1987. Overseas blanket-order receipts declined 15 percent in 1987 and the number of serial receipts decreased by 20 percent in 1987 but increased slightly during the first half of 1988.

In February the Collections Development Office held a Pacific Island seminar, the 18th in a series on foreign acquisitions, to complete a world survey begun in 1983 to identify collection needs. Library representatives also met in San Francisco to join in a review with other libraries of materials available on Southeast Asia through field offices in Jakarta and New Delhi.

In addition to the acquisition of music, microform, and print materials, the Library began developing a special collection of high-tech media and in November opened "The Library of Tomorrow," a pilot Machine-Readable Collections Reading Room. By the year 2000, the Library will have the most comprehensive software collection in the world. The reading room is equipped with IBM-compatible and Macintosh hardware, including CD-ROM and laser videodisk drives.

Processing and Accessing the Collections. Highlights for the year in the Processing Services Department include addition of the two-millionth name authority record to the Library's online Authority File, the release of new bibliographic products in machine-readable format, the publication of new aids for catalogers, developments in overseas cataloging, and some cooperative projects.

The Library's Cataloging Distribution Service

Library of Congress

Librarian of Congress James H. Billington meets with librarians at the 1988 Annual Conference in New Orleans. Here he speaks with Congresswoman Lindy Boggs (D–La.). In the background is William A. Moffett, director, Oberlin College Library.

(CDS) attained a milestone with Release 2.0 of the National Union Catalog, which enables participating institutions to submit bibliographic records in machine-readable format. In the first half of the year, the NUC database had grown 12 percent to a total 393,631 records. CDS also released COMARC subjects, the library's entire subject authority file on CD-ROM.

Preserving and Housing the Collections. In its efforts to save books from embrittlement caused by the deterioration of acidic paper, the Library of Congress entered the engineering test phase of a pilot deacidification facility at the Texas Alkyls Chemical Company near Houston, Texas. Planning is under way to design and construct a full-scale facility for the treatment of some 1,000,000 books a year.

Phase I of the renovation and restoration of the Thomas Jefferson and John Adams buildings progressed with the upgrading of electrical, mechanical, fire-protection, and security systems.

The Library continued its endeavors to preserve the nation's record of culture and history and to share this legacy through recordings, exhibits, publications that in 1988 included ten major bibliographies, and films shown at the Mary Pickford Theater.

Outreach. The Library of Congress strives to stimulate public interest in the nation's culture and heritage through a variety of special services and activities. It also engaged in several outreach projects for the nation. The Librarian of Congress and the Library's Center for the Book and Children's Literature Center successfully initiated congressional action to proclaim 1989 "The Year of the Young Reader." The President signed legislation issuing the proclamation on November 15. The campaign encourages parents, educators, librarians, government officials, corporations, and associations to join in a nationwide effort to spark the interest of young persons in reading. Supporters include the Congress, regional statewide centers for the book (which grew to 17 with the addition of Colorado and Arizona centers), the American Library Association, publishers, and the media. The Center for the Book also celebrated National Book Week November 28 to December 5, 1988, with a lecture by Richard Rhodes, whose book, *The Making of the Atomic Bomb*, won the National Book Award in 1987.

American Folklife Center. The American Folklife Center continued to document American folk history and culture. Publications in 1988 included *The Grouse Creek Cultural Survey; Integrating Folklife and Historic Preservation Field Research*, and *Quilt Collections: A Directory for the United States and Canada*. The Center also sponsored a series of folk concerts.

National Library Service for the Blind and Physically Handicapped (NLS/BPH). Highlights for the year included the publication of a new monograph, *Talking Books: Pioneering and Beyond*, which traces the development of recorded books and playback equipment for use by the blind and physically handicapped. NLS/BPH launched its most ambitious outreach program with a campaign directed to seniors. NLS/BPH also established a World Literature Book Club to circulate cassette recordings of best-sellers and long-time favorites from English-speaking nations other than the U.S.

Copyright Office. Capping a century-long effort to bring the United States into the Berne Union, the oldest and most elaborate international arrangement governing the protection of copyrights, the U.S. House of Representatives and the U.S. Senate in 1988 approved U.S. adherence to the Berne Convention for the Protection of Literary and Artistic Works. The Copyright Office also announced copyright regulations pertaining to colorized versions of motion pictures. It also decided to require a single registration of all copyrightable expression embodied in a computer program, as well as computer screen displays, owned by the same claimant. The office delivered to the Congress a second five-year *Report of the Register of Copyrights on Library Reproduction of Copyrighted Works*, which studies the balancing of scholars' needs and claimants' rights.

Congressional Research Service. Providing in-depth analyses, information and reports exclusively for the Congress, the Congressional Research Service (CRS) responded to 235,000 research requests in the first half of the year—the highest number for any six-month period.

Federal Library and Information Center Committee (FLICC). The Federal Library and Information Center Committee (FLICC) supports more than 2,500 federal libraries and information centers in the United States and abroad. Contractual services brokered to the federal sector by the committee's operating arm, the Federal Library and Information Network (FEDLINK) grew to approximately $97,100,000 by the close of fiscal year 1988 from nearly $47,900,000 in fiscal year 1987.

Information Office. In 1988 the Library's Information Office began distributing the weekly *Library of Congress Information Bulletin* (LCIB) electronically with the assistance of the FEDLINK electronic bulletin board to more than 1,200 libraries and other subscribers, including federal libraries overseas. The Information Office annually distributes some 14,000 print copies of *LCIB*, the Library's official newsletter, and publishes a monthly "Calendar of Events."

Law Library. With more than 1,700,000 volumes, the Law Library serves as the foreign law research arm of the Congress and as a comprehensive reference and referral service for the Executive and Judicial Branches. The Law Library continued a project to make the text and amendments to the U.S. Constitution available in 14 foreign languages.

Conferences and Seminars. Several of the Library's symposia and conferences in 1988 were international in scope, focusing on Soviet and Hispanic subjects. Scholars, art historians, musicologists, theologians, and librarians from around the world were convened at the Library for a major conference, "The Millennium of the Baptism of Rus': The Impact of Christianity on the Culture of the Eastern Slavs." Librarian of Congress James H. Billington, a noted scholar of Russian cultural history, opened the conference. In commemoration of the millennium, the Library prepared an exhibit of approximately 50 items from its extensive collections of Russian, Ukrainian, and Byelorussian materials. The Library also was the site for a "Seminar on Access to Library Resources Through Technology and Preservation," the first project of the U.S./U.S.S.R. Commission on Library Cooperation. The Library of Congress and the Embassy of the Argentine Republic cosponsored a symposium, "Domingo F. Sarmiento: Nation-Builder, 1811–1988," to commemorate one of the outstanding intellectuals and statesmen of 19th-century Argentina. Another symposium, "Padre Felix Varela: Cuban Philosopher, Priest, Patriot," was conducted in Spanish at the Library.

The Library celebrated National Hispanic Heritage Week, September 11–17, with a talk by Jaime Escalante, an award-winning mathematics teacher featured in a film, "Stand and Deliver," also shown at the Library; with a panel discussion of the upcoming celebration of the Christopher Columbus Quincentenary, 1492–1992; and with a concert by the Mariachi San Cristobal from Mexico.

Black History Month. Andrew Young, mayor of Atlanta, was the keynote speaker for the Library's observance of Black History Month in February. Other events included a performance by the Howard University Jazz Ensemble, a symposium on "Writing and Teaching Black History," and a series of films.

Celebrating Music and Literature. The Music Division of the Library presented two ambitious concert seasons, plus a Summer Chamber Festival. Featured were the Library's resident ensembles—the Juilliard String Quartet and Beaux Arts Trio, playing the Library's Stradivarii—as well as several established and promising young performers. Programing ranged from familiar baroque and classical pieces to contemporary works commissioned from special endowments and funds for premiere performances in the Library's Coolidge Auditorium.

Highlighting a series of literary events at the Library was the appointment of Howard Nemerov as the third Poet Laureate of the United

Sandra Day O'Connor, Associate Justice, U.S. Supreme Court, served as a member of the National Advisory Committee, appointed by Librarian of Congress James H. Billington to assist in a year-long review of the Library.

States, who succeeded Richard Wilbur in September. Other events included a reception for Mexican author Carlos Fuentes and a one-man dramatic performance of "Byron in Hell" by British actor Ian Frost.

GAIL M. FINEBERG

Library Press

Major reference tools for the profession, a change in ownership of a historic publishing house, several reviews of the library press, and key changes in editorial positions were principal features of the library press in 1988.

New publications. We continue to witness the imaginative combination of computer technology and traditional print on paper in preparation of reference tools. Two important examples during the year are a new biographical directory of librarians and the new edition of *Books for College Libraries*.

The mammoth two-volume *Directory of Library & Information Professionals*, published in collaboration with ALA by Research Publications, gives biographical information on about 43,000 individuals. It replaces *Who's Who in Library and Information Services*, published in 1982, which was much more selective in the 12,000 individuals it included. The first volume of the new work includes an alphabetical listing of the biographees with considerable biographical data from those willing to complete questionnaires and briefer information on other individuals as compiled from different sources. The second volume includes several indexes for those represented by biographies in the first volume. The major print resource is supplemented by a CD–ROM.

The third edition of *Books for College Libraries* was published by the American Library Association as a project of its Association of College and Research Libraries (ACRL). Including some 10,000 more titles than were listed in the second edition in 1975, the 50,000-title entry publication is arranged in six volumes bound in handsome green cloth. This valuable list of recommended titles can be searched online through the bibliographic utility Utlas.

In 1988 Bowker completed publication of the 13th edition of *The Reader's Adviser*, expanded to six volumes. Bowker complements this basic print set with its *Books in Print Plus*, an enhanced version on CD–ROM of available and forthcoming publications.

The Library of Congress issued the 11th edition of its *Library of Congress Subject Headings*. Published in three large volumes, the new edition lists 163,000 records.

OCLC and Forest Press. In 1988 OCLC Inc., the manager of the world's largest bibliographic utility, announced its purchase of the Forest Press from the Lake Placid Foundation. The Forest Press, historic publisher of the Decimal Classification, was founded by American library pioneer Melvil Dewey. OCLC reported it will explore publication of the Dewey classification in electronic format. As OCLC announced its new acquisition, Forest Press announced that in January 1989 it will release the 20th edition of the Dewey Decimal Classification.

Periodical Prices. The high cost of periodical publications remains a continuing concern in library literature. *American Libraries* featured Charles Hamaker's complaint that prices of European-produced journals "continue to gut U.S. research libraries" ("The Least Reading for the Smallest Number at the Highest Price," October 1988, p. 764-768). Richard M. Dougherty and Brenda L. Johnson in *Library Journal* wrote that libraries must "look at any other options they have—whether that means resource sharing or alternative forms of publication." They admit that "it becomes ever more appealing for scholars, bibliographic utilities, and university libraries to become more directly involved in the communication, publication, and distribution of scholarly information" ("Periodical Price Escalation: A Library Response," *Library Journal*, May 15, 1988, p. 27-29).

Libraries as Publishers. The concept of libraries as publishers is echoed in a publication from the Association of Research Libraries (ARL) System and Procedures Exchange Center, a unit in the Office of Management Services (formerly Management Studies). SPEC Kit 145, released in June 1988, described "Library Publications Programs." Of the 118 ARL libraries surveyed for this study, 105 report they operate publishing programs, although most do not actively market their products.

To provide guidelines for library publishers, Sylverna Ford describes Carnegie Mellon University's production of its newsletter in her article, 'The Library Newsletter: Is It for You?" (*College & Research Libraries News*, November 1988, p. 678-682). ACRL issued as CLIP Note 10, a survey of such documents in its *Annual Reports for College Libraries*, compiled by Kenneth J. Oberembt.

Review of the Press. Libraries Unlimited issued the fourth volume in its series, *Library and Information Science Annual*. Coverage of professional literature in this publication continues to grow, with the fourth edition reviewing 549 titles issued by U.S., Canadian, British, and Australian firms and agencies—a 50 percent increase since the first volume in 1985. The new edition also includes reviews of 48 library periodicals and abstracts of recent doctoral dissertations in library science.

Library Journal and Booklist. Judith L. Palmer's lengthy study comparing fiction reviews in *Library Journal* and *Booklist* appeared in volume 7 of *Advances in Library Administration and Organization*. Palmer focuses on 1964 to 1984, and presents numerous findings on coverage of fiction titles and promptness of reviews. She concludes that "*Library Journal* has done a better overall job of reviewing new fiction."

Library Trends. The library press received a lengthy review and analysis in the Spring 1988 issue of *Library Trends*, "Library Literature in the 1980s." The issue concludes with Lawrence W. S. Auld's descriptive account of the *Library Trends* for its first 34 years, 1952–1986. He demonstrates that the general approach used successfully in the first issues has been continued in the present (p.868).

Library Quarterly. Whereas Auld presents an impersonal summary of *Library Trends*' history, Steve Norman provides a much more lively account of "The *Library Quarterly* in the 1930s: A Journal of Discussion's Early Years" (*Library Quarterly*, October 1988, p. 327–351). The conflicts in the profession at the journal's founding, the faculty of the University of Chicago's Graduate Library School's disagreements on objectives, and the disputes arising from an unfavorable book review or a rejected manuscript give a realistic view of problems involved in the communication of scholarly information.

Library Periodicals. New periodicals and newsletters include the *Library Personnel News*, a quarterly publication from ALA's Office of Library Personnel Resources, and *MLS: Marketing Library Services*, a newsletter issued eight times a year by Riverside Data Inc., Sudbury, Massachusetts. *MLS* is designed to provide libraries with practical, useful tips on marketing techniques. One basic library computer periodical, *Small Computers in Libraries*, evidently felt it should expand its scope and at year's end announced that in 1989 the journal will be known as *Computers in Libraries*.

In the last few years, ALA and PBS (The Public Broadcasting System) have worked together with ALA preparing and mailing announcements and brochures about PBS specials to libraries. In 1988 the relationship developed further with the introduction of a newsletter, *PBS/Library Pipeline*, that will call attention regularly to PBS offerings. Late in 1988, *The Journal of Academic Librarianship* announced publication of a new monthly reviewing tool, *Preview*, to cover reference and professional literature. The "Guide to Professional Literature" in the journal will henceforth restrict itself to literature of interest to academic librarians.

Authorship. *Library Journal*, September 1, 1988 p. 125–131, included John Budd's investigation on "Publication in Library & Information Science: The State of the Literature." Updating and expanding upon a 1979 study by Daniel O'Connor and Phyllis Van Orden, Budd presents information on manuscripts submitted to 48 journals and determines a rejection rate of approximately 60 to 70 percent.

Stuart Glogoff examines the editorial review process in his study for the *Journal of the American Society for Information Science*, November 1988, p. 400–407: "Reviewing the Gatekeepers: A Survey of Referees of Library Journals."

Personnel. Karl Nygren, long associated with *Library Journal* and the founding editor of *Library Hotline*, died in August. Paul H. Brawley, editor of *Booklist* since 1973, died in October. Lois R. Pearson retired from her post as associate editor of *American Libraries*. Paul Kobasa, assistant director for marketing in ALA Publishing Services, accepted a position with World Book. Joel M. Lee, senior manager of ALA's Information Technology Publishing, took a position with Auto-Graphics. Milo Nelson announced his resignation as editor of *Wilson Library Bulletin*. New professionals arriving on the library publishing scene include Thomas M. Gaughan as managing editor for *American Libraries* in February, and Leonard Kniffel as associate editor in October. Earlier in the year at *American Libraries* Edith McCormick was promoted to production editor and Gordon Flagg to senior editor, articles.

Cahners Publications, parent organization for *Library Journal*, named Fred Ciporen publisher of *Library Journal* and *School Library Journal*. Susan DiMattia was appointed editor of *Library Hotline*, and Nora Rawlinson was named editor of *LJ Book Review*. At ALA Bill Ott became editor of *Booklist*. Among divisional journals Judy Pitts and Barbara Stripling were named editors of *School Library Media Quarterly (SLMQ)*; Kathleen Heim editor of *Public Libraries*; and Josette Anne Lyders editor of *Journal of Youth Services in Libraries (JOYS)*.

Awards. The *California State Library Foundation Bulletin* received the H. W. Wilson Library Periodical Award. Wayne A. Wiegand received the G. K. Hall Library Literature Award for *The Politics of an Emerging Profession: the American Library Association, 1876-1917* (Greenwood Press, 1986). Peter Hernon and Charles R. McClure received the Best Information Science Book Award from the American Society for Information Science for their volume *Federal Information Policies in the 1980s: Conflicts and Issues* (Ablex Publishing, 1987). The 1988 Winners of Blackwell/North America Scholarship Award, presented by the Resources Section of ALA's Resources & Technical Services Division, were Joe A. Hewitt and John S. Shipman for "Cooperative Collection Development among Research Libraries in the Age of Networking," *Advances in Library Automation and Networking*, a new annual publication from JAI Press. A new award, funded by K. G. Saur and presented by ACRL for the best article during the year in *College & Research Libraries*, was presented to Robert Boice, Jordan M. Scepanski, and Wayne Wilson for their article, "Librarians and Faculty members: Coping with Pressures to Publish," in the November 1987 issue of that journal.

RICHARD D. JOHNSON

Library Programs, Department of Education

During the past three years, the Office of Library Programs (LP) in the Department of Education's Office of Educational Research and Improvement (OERI) continued to provide national leadership in administering nine library grant programs totaling more than $135,000,000 in FY 1988. The state formula grant programs funded under the Library Services and Construction Act (LSCA) were managed by Robert Klassen and the discretionary grants programs under LSCA and the Higher Education Act (HEA) were headed up by Frank Stevens.

A number of new initiatives were begun to strengthen the Office's leadership role. In December 1987 LP cosponsored with the Library of Congress' Center for the Book the "Leaders Are Readers" symposium featuring the Secretary of Education, William J. Bennett, and the Librarian of Congress, James Billington, as major speakers. The program provided an opportunity for more than 200 high school student government presidents and their sponsors to interact with these federal officials. It represented the Department's major contribution for the Bicentennial of the Constitution and the Year of the Reader.

LP has focused on implementing the collection and dissemination of library statistics. In 1985 the former Division of Library Programs took the lead in co-funding with the National Center for Educational Statistics (NCES) an ALA pilot project to develop a Federal-State cooperative system for the collection of public library statistics. LP engaged a consultant on library statistics to advise the office and NCES about the range of statistics for public, academic, and school libraries. LP also strongly supported the development of public library statistics on services and resources for children and young adults. LP took the lead in originating, designing, and monitoring these two projects funded by NCES. The Young Adult Survey was completed in 1988 and the Children's Survey is underway. These two Fast Response Surveys give us the first national data in these critical areas of public library service.

The Library Improvement Act of 1988 was the Department's first request for funding for library programs in seven years. Although there has been no action on the legislation, the concepts it contains are worth consideration as the reauthorization of LSCA is addressed in 1989.

Another LP effort has been the identification of the "Issues in Library Research-Proposals for the Nineties." More than 200 field experts have identified nine major issues confronting the profession and have defined priorities based on these issues. The essays explore and expand the issues and were published under the title *Rethinking the Library in the Information Age, Issues in Library Research: Proposals for the 1990s*. (Available from OERI, Education Information Branch, Information Services, 555 New Jersey Avenue, NW, Washington D.C. 20208, 800-424-1616.)

LP also worked with the Department's National Diffusion Network to identify exemplary library and media center programs. *Check This*

Library Research Round Table

Out: Library Program Models details 62 such programs (available from the Superintendent of Documents, U.S. Government Printing Office, Washington, D.C. 20402 for $15). More than 5,000 copies of Check This Out have been distributed. Its popularity led to the publication of Check This Out: Highlights of Model Library Programs, which features 14 programs representative of the 62 original entries. (Both titles are available from OERI, Education Information Branch, Information Services, 555 New Jersey, Avenue NW, Washington, D.C. 20208, 800-424-1616, free of charge.) LP continues to publish its priority report on LSCA State grant activities under Titles I, II, and III. LSCA Programs: An Action Report highlights the uses of state funding for literacy, the handicapped, the institutionalized, public library construction, interlibrary cooperation and resource sharing, and for library services through urban and metropolitan public libraries. This report, along with the abstracts and reports for each discretionary HEA and LSCA IV and VI programs, is available from the LP office at the address listed for OERI.

Program Accomplishments. Under Anne Mathews' leadership, the Office of Library Programs has seen the successful implementation of two new grant programs, HEA, Title II-D, (Library Technology and Cooperation Program for Academic Libraries) and LSCA, Title VI, (Library Literacy Program). To date more than 700 projects have been funded under Title VI of LSCA. In FY 1988, 21 grants went to state libraries and 203 to local public libraries from the appropriation of $4,787,000. Also, during its first year of operation in FY 1988, the HEA II-D program funded 46 library technology and cooperation projects with its $3,590,000.

Library Services and Construction Act. More than $118,000,000 was available to the stataes for the FY 1988 appropriation from Titles I ($77,406,208), II ($22,143,100), and III ($18,295,620) in support of 3,000 library projects.

More than 25 percent of the Title I project funds were spent directly to improve public library services for such special groups as the functionally illiterate, the handicapped, and the elderly. In addition, Title II project funds were used to stimulate more than 200 local public library construction projects. Title III funds provided incentive support to 500 regional, state, and local cooperative projects. A tremendous turnover in State LSCA coordinators during the past few years, prompted the Office to launch a series of five regional technical assistance workshops (Jefferson City, Missouri, Baltimore, Atlanta, Denver, and Boston). Through these workshops, the Office was able to reach all states with updated information about LSCA State formula grant program management.

Under LSCA IV, 17 special projects for $1,156,857 and 175 basic grants amounting to $646,893 were awarded in FY 1988 to improve public library services for Indian tribes. An additional $601,250 went to support library services for Hawaiian natives.

Higher Education Act. After several years of funding only fellowships under HEA Title II-B, LP re-established the funding of institutes with

Table 1. Library Programs Department of Education
Funding for FY 1989 Programs

Title No.	Topic	Funds Granted
LSCA I	(Public Library Services)	$79,388,820
LSCA II	(Public Library Constuction)	21,877,520
LSCA III	(Interlibrary Cooperation and Resource Sharing)	18,719,960
LSCA IV	(Library Services for Indian Tribes and Hawaiian Natives)	2,448,700
LSCA VI	(Library Literacy)	4,730,000
HEA II-B	(Library Career Training)	400,000
HEA II-B	(Library Research and Demonstration)	309,000
HEA II-C	(Strengthening Research Library Resources)	5,675,000
HEA II-D	(Library Technology and Cooperation)	3,651,000
	TOTAL	$137,200,000

$409,000 available for library career training in FY 1988; 3 institutes and 14 master's and 9 doctoral fellowships were funded. A dramatic increase in the funding demand for institutes reflects the driving need for continuing education.

Although funding for research is very limited, LP continues to support several significant projects that have great potential for influencing national library development. The most visionary of these resulted in Rethinking the Library in the Information Age referred to earlier.

Of the recent research funded under HEA, Title II-B, Drexel University, Philadelphia, Pennsylvania, received a grant to develop criteria for determining "What is a good public library?" Rutgers State University, New Brunswick, New Jersey, was funded to develop a cognitive model for the search process and determine the information needs of information seekers. The University of Wisconsin–Madison received a grant to develop an evaluation model of library literacy programs in public libraries.

Research projects funded under the $309,000 FY 1988 appropriation include Clarion State University of Pennsylvania for assessment of the information needs of rural Americans and an Indiana University Foundation study to determine factors that facilitate or inhibit the development, evaluation, refinement, and dissemination of an innovation.

The $5,744,000 appropriation for FY 1988 under HEA, Title II-C, strengthening Research Library Resources, supported 37 bibliographic control projects, 20 preservation and conservation projects, and 4 collection development projects. Table 1 shows FY 1989 funding approved for nine programs.

ROBERT KLASSEN

Library Research Round Table

Activities. In 1988 the Library Research Round Table (LRRT) held a special reception to honor

Jesse H. Shera for outstanding leadership in promoting the importance of research to the effective development of the theory and practice of library and information service and to celebrate the establishment of an endowment to fund the Jesse H. Shera Award for Research. The reception was held during the ALA Midwinter meeting on January 9 at the Holiday Inn River Walk in San Antonio, Texas. Ann Prentice, in charge of the reception, was assisted by Mike Marchant, Gary Purcell, and Mary Jo Lynch. The program included introductory remarks by Ann Prentice and Barbara Immroth, LRRT Chair; Gary Purcell, a 1975 Case Western Reserve graduate, was host of the program that included excerpts from the writing of John S. Millis, Chancellor of Case Western Reserve, 1949–67, a letter from Conrad Rawski, Dean, School of Library Science 1977–80, Case Western Reserve, remembrances from Thomas J. Galvin, readings from a biography of Jesse Shera by Curtis Wright, and presentation of Shera's *Introduction to Library Science,* translated into Chinese in 1986 by Sha Li Zhang.

LRRT cooperated with the ALA Committee on Research by commenting on the Committee's "ALA Goals: Research Questions/Issues" and with the ALA Planning Committee by suggesting strategies related to research for additions to ALA's Strategic Long-Range Plan. The Steering Committee decided to discontinue the Information Suite because of other opportunities to present research during the Annual Conference and recent low attendance at the suite.

At the 1988 New Orleans ALA Annual Conference LRRT sponsored a program on "The Role of the U.S. Department of Education (USDE) in Developing a Core of Library Science Research" in which Anne Mathews of the U.S. Department of Education provided an overview of USDE programs for funding library research. Mathews distributed two documents, "Office of Library Programs: Research Agenda" and "Chronological History of Library Research and Demonstration Grants Under HEA Title II–B (1977–87 inclusive.") Tom Childers, Betty Turock, and Doug Zweizig, who had received USDE funding, responded to Mathews; Danny Wallace was program chair and moderator of the panel.

Lisa deGruyter, Austin (Texas) Public Library chaired the Research Forums. In the first forum on July 10, there were three presentations. Jim M. Choi, University of South Carolina discussed "Learning Styles of University Librarians and Implications for Professional Development." Ray N. Larson, University of California, Berkeley discussed "The Decline of Subject Searching in Online Public Access Catalogs," and Jo Bell Whitlatch, San Jose State University, discussed "Client/Service Provider Perceptions of Service Outcomes in Academic Libraries." In the second forum on July 11, there were two presentations, "Alternatives in Information Delivery in Rural Areas: An Experiment in Social Engineering," by Jack Glazier, University of Missouri, Columbia and "The Effectiveness of Libraries: The Public Library," by Nancy Van House, University of California, Berkeley and Tom Childers, Drexel University. In the third forum on July 12, two papers were presented, "Comparing Bradford Type Scatter: A Bibliometric Problem," by OCLC's Chandra Prabha and "Statistical Validity and Reliability of the Research Libraries Group *Conspectus for Music*" by William E. McGrath State University of New York, Buffalo, and Nancy Nuzzo.

Beth Paskoff, Louisiana State University, chair of the Information Exchange Suite, was assisted by Michael Carpenter. The suite was open for the three information exchange sessions, informal discussions of research with eleven different presenters, and a doctoral discussion group covened by Dean Evelyn Daniel of the University of North Carolina.

Awards. George Whitbeck, Indiana University, chaired the Shera Award Committee. Danny Wallace, Indiana University and Bert Boyce, Louisiana State University, received the 1988 Jesse H. Shera Award for Research for their paper, "Holdings as a Measure of Journal Value," delivered at the awards program co-sponsored with the Library History Round Table on July 10. Wallace and Boyce, the first recipients of the newly named award received awards certificates and checks for $250 each.

BARBARA FROLING IMMROTH

Library Service to Older Adults

The surge in the older population continues to have increasing impact on society and public policy. The older population demonstrates great vitality, growing power and economic influence, especially in Florida, Arizona, the Carolinas, New Mexico, Utah, Nevada, Alaska, Hawaii and Washington where the over–65 population increased by 20 percent or more between 1980 and 1986.

Like other societal institutions, libraries face challenges to serve this population. The number of older adults using the library has been relatively small. Some estimate that only 10 to 15 percent of persons over 60 years of age are library users. However, this is changing as the educational level of older persons increases.

Educational Levels. A comparison of the 55 to 64 age group with the over–75 group demonstrates the changes in educational level. A U.S. Census Bureau study indicated that 15.5 percent of Americans age 75 or older had attended college while 19.7 percent completed high school. Among the 55 to 64 age group, 24 percent had attended or graduated from college and an additional 39 percent had graduated from high

---

LIBRARY RESEARCH ROUND TABLE

CHAIRPERSON (July 1988–July 1989):
Joe A. Hewitt, University of North Carolina

VICE-CHAIRPERSON/CHAIRPERSON-ELECT:
Nancy A. Van House, University of California, Berkeley

PAST CHAIRPERSON:
Barbara Immroth, University of Texas at Austin

SECRETARY-TREASURER:
Nancy Koller, University of California, Riverside

Membership: 769 (670 personal; 99 organization)
Expenditures: $3,568

Library Service to Older Adults

school. Thus, 65 percent of citizens 75 years or older had less than a high school diploma. Clearly, there are challenges for libraries to serve the growing older adult population who will be more likely to consider libraries as an important part of their lives.

The New York State Board of Regents prepared a policy statement: "Educational Elements of a Comprehensive State Policy on Aging." The six major policy directions provide opportunities for libraries to be a part of the educational plan of older adults: provide education and training opportunities for older persons; enhance the coordination of services for the elderly; involve the elderly as active participants in society; educate students at all levels about aging; train needed professional, paraprofessional and informal service providers for older persons; and increase the research potential of the postsecondary institutions to address the needs of the elderly. In each of the recommendations the library can be a facilitating agency to meet needs for materials, offer information services, promote volunteer opportunities, promote aging education, and work collaboratively with other agencies.

The Regents' policy statement delineates one role for libraries: "Neighborhood institutions, such as libraries, that are easily accessible during the day should increase opportunities for personal development and resource sharing by expanding their programs for the elderly." There are tasks to be undertaken to serve older adults, either singly or in cooperation with agencies such as senior centers, community agencies, and area aging agencies. The selection of materials, planning of appropriate environments, staff selection and training, and service delivery will be influenced by the growing older population.

We are fast becoming a nation that requires regular training or education for a changing work place. The tremendous resources committed to inservice activities and professional development herald a society that recognizes the need to retool on a regular basis. Older workers are among the persons most needing skills to cope with a changing work place and new expectations for employees. Libraries have a role in this educational phase through materials selection in collaboration with other community agencies, economic development programming, and listings of job opportunities.

Educational Needs of Older Adults. The educational needs of older adults are pertinent as libraries consider their potential roles in the educational progress of older adults. Organizers of 13 forums held in Illinois communities in 1988 to gather data about the educational and information needs of older adults solicited participation by older adults as well as from educators and service providers. The forum report has implications for library programming and services. The informational needs recommended by the forums included how to maintain independence, physical fitness, nutrition, health, memory and mental alertness, survival skills and financial management. The educational needs included basic education, job retraining, non-credit courses, special degrees for older persons, as well as more specific requests for programs or courses related to communication, music, religious studies, sociology, theatre, art, and computers.

The barriers to providing these needs, reported from the forums, are pertinent for planning library services for older adults. Attention to transportation, sensitivity of staff to a special clientele, adequate information about programming, rewarding participants for their interest and participation, keeping costs low and building confidence are highly recommended to overcome barriers that may preclude utilization of libraries and other educational institutions. Gender differences in utilization of information are being studied at the University of Minnesota. The American Association of Retired Persons, employing a Commonwealth Fund grant, is examining information dissemination methods targeted at SSI users. The information needs of older adults are being investigated at Southern Illinois University at Carbondale.

Older Adults as Library Resources. The shift in the educational background of older people will be coupled with other changes in our society, such as an increasing amount of leisure time for retirees. This not only provides opportunities for library programming but also presents a valuable source of volunteers.

Librarians around the country have discovered that services to old and young can be accomplished through intergenerational programming. Years ago people spent more time with their extended families, grandparents enjoyed long hours with their grandchildren, and family get-togethers often included relatives from at least three generations. Today Americans find they have to work at bringing the young and old together. This is the reason such programs as "Share the Magic" in Pekin, Illinois, have been so successful. "Share the Magic" is a special Christmas program for grandparents and grandchildren who may not be related. The "grandparents and grandchildren" gather at the Pekin Public Library to give parents an opportunity for Christmas shopping. The evening includes a picture-taking session, sharing of wishes, and a holiday gift. The South Bay Cooperative Library System in Santa Clara, California, a pioneer in establishing intergenerational library programs, has older volunteers who help children select books, listen to them read, lead story hours, demonstrate crafts, and play games. The RSVP Intergenerational Library Assistance Project helps public libraries in Dallas, Texas; Chicago, Illinois; Los Angeles, California; and Ogden, Utah; provide assistance to children who use libraries after school. The Retired Senior Volunteer Program (RSVP), composed of 400,000 elders throughout the nation who are 60 years of age and older, serve in 750 community projects. Through the Library Assistance Project, individual libraries work with RSVP to identify the needs of local children and develop plans to use volunteers in literacy improvement, drug education, homework assistance, and other areas. Other sites will be chosen in 1989.

Another indication of the interest and value of intergenerational programming is House Resolution 5486, passed October 6, 1988. The bill establishes funding for "demonstration projects using older adult volunteers to provide intergenerational library literacy programs to children during after-school hours." $5,000,000 has been appropriated for fiscal year 1989.

Library Developments. There is considerable interest in researching and writing about the burgeoning older adult population and its impact on libraries. The *Library Outreach Reporter*, a bimonthly newsletter, provides an important information source for librarians interested in writing and reading about special programs for older adults.

A scarcity of resources hinders expansion of library programs for older adults in many communities. Now is the time to plan for the future as the changing demographics of American society demand attention to older citizens as we approach the 21st Century.

JANE ANGELIS
DOUGLAS BEDIENT

Map and Geography Round Table

Since its beginning in 1980, the Map and Geography Round Table (MAGERT) has grown to be the world's largest map library organization with more than 400 personal and institutional members. Providing a forum for the exchange of ideas, MAGERT is meeting its goals by fostering communication among not only map librarians but also among all library professionals. Joint programs with the Government Documents Round Table and ACRL's Rare Books and Manuscript Section have traditionally raised awareness among participants to the problems, opportunities, and responsibilities shared in respective areas of librarianship.

Publications. Published since 1980, MAGERT's bimonthly newsletter, *base line* (edited by Carol Collier, University of Wyoming), the most timely publication produced for map librarians, provides current information on new cartographic materials and other publications of interest to map and geography librarians, reviews, and news of meetings, government activities, and recent events in the field. Beginning in January 1989, *base line* will have a sister publication, *Meridian*, a semiannual journal whose articles will explore the value of maps in libraries and their significance as reference materials; Philip Hoehn, map librarian at the University of California at Berkeley, is the editor.

The *Guide to U.S. Map Resources*, first published by ALA in 1986, is undergoing its first revision, with work in process for the next edition, to be published in 1990 or 1991.

MAGERT's first occasional paper, *Exploration and Mapping of the American West: Selected Essays* was published in 1987 by Speculum Orbis Press. It was followed in 1988 by Jeffrey A. Kroessler's *A Guide to Historical Map Resources for Greater New York*, also published by Speculum Orbis Press.

Honors Award. The 1988 Honors Award was given to Ralph Ehrenberg, Library of Congress, for outstanding contributions to map librarianship. Previous winners are Elizabeth Manpen, Library of Congress (1987), David A. Cobb, University of Illinois (1986), Gary W. North, USGS National Mapping Program (1985), Jeremiah B. Post, Free Library of Philadelphia (1984), and Mary L. Larsgaard, University of California at Santa Barbara (1983).

Hammond Inc./MAGERT Award. The Round Table established a new ALA award in 1986. The Hammond Inc./MAGERT Award consists of a scroll and prize of $300. The award, sponsored by Hammond Inc., honors the best essay or article on map librarianship published in the calender year preceding its presentation. The award was not presented in 1988.

Activities. Through representation on the Cartographic Users Advisory Council, MAGERT continues to work with government map-producing agencies for broader distribution and more effective use of their products. Annual meetings in Washington, D.C., provide an opportunity for updates on new government programs, educational presentations, and continuing dialogue between these agencies and librarians representing map users.

Officially formed and recognized in 1987, the joint RBMS–GODORT–MAGERT Committee on Rare Government Documents began to explore the problems and concerns associated with government documents and maps as rare materials. Identification, evaluation, and preservation are current topics of discussion.

MAGERT annual conferences traditionally have a pre-conference workshop and a tour; the successful 1987 workshop, "Map Librarianship for the Government Documents Librarian," was repeated by Donna Koepp and David A. Cobb in New Orleans in 1988. Sessions sponsored or co-sponsored by the Round Table were, "Government Documents as Rare Books" (RBMS/GODORT/MAGERT co-sponsors), "Map Records on NOTIS" (NOTIS/MAGERT co-sponsors), "Mapping of the National Parks," "Women in Cartography," and "Contributions to Cartographic History," with the last mentioned being held at the Historic New Orleans Collection. The Round Table has 13 committees and 12 liaisons to other organizations; the committees and liaisons report at the annual business meeting.

MARY L. LARSGAARD

MAP AND GEOGRAPHY ROUND TABLE

CHAIR (July 1988–June 1989):
Mary Anne L. Waltz, Area Studies Department, Bird Library, Syracuse University, Syracuse, New York 13210

VICE-CHAIR/CHAIR-ELECT:
Brent Allison, Map Library, University of Minnesota, Minneapolis 55455

SECRETARY:
Heather Rex, University of New Mexico, Albuquerque 87131

TREASURER:
Suzanne Clark, Documents/Maps Department, Bailey/Howe Librry, University of Vermont, Burlington 05405

Membership (August 31, 1988): 415

Medical Libraries

Year of Reaction. Nineteen eighty-eight was a year of reaction for medical libraries as they watched their purchasing power diminished for yet another year. It was a year when all the indexes that measure average changes in prices of

Medical Libraries

goods and services purchased by colleges and universities reported that book and periodical prices increased more than such other expenses as salaries, fringe benefits, equipment, and utilities. The trend, for the second consecutive year, was to turn to technology, to cancel even more periodicals, and to purchase fewer books. It was a time to look in a different direction for more substantial, long-term solutions to a national problem. With recurring financial problems in medical libraries as a backdrop, the Medical Library Association conducted an environmental scan during the year as part of its strategic planning initiative. In summary, the results were that the Association, the profession, and its libraries will require innovative ways to address the information needs of the future.

In keeping with its own strategic planning initiative, the Medical Library Association also accepted an invitation from the Special Libraries Association to participate on a task force to determine perceptions of the profession's image and to develop and implement a plan to enhance that image.

Quality assurance programs received considerable attention in the hospital library community during the year as the Joint Commission on Accreditation of Hospitals (JCAH) announced that the cornerstone of its accreditation process will continue to be quality assurance. While JCAH does not currently mandate quality assurance programs for hospital libraries, all such libraries are encouraged to develop a program on their own prior to 1990 when the JCAH process is due to be amended.

Legislation. In previous years medical libraries stressed the urgent need for investigation into the issues surrounding the impact of new devices and technologies on the application of copyright law. Overall testimony from libraries during 1987 reflected a general feeling that Section 108 of the Copyright Law should be expanded to include audiovisual works, art works, and machine-readable works. There was also general support for frequent reviews, particularly as related to developing technology and changes in copying practices. During 1988, a federal appeals court in California held that state governments, including universities, can reproduce copyrighted works without permission and avoid liability for money damages. The case involved commercial software and is expected to be appealed to the U.S. Supreme Court. As medical libraries revised their collection development policies to include commercially-produced software for public use, such challenges to the Copyright Law have again risen to the legislative forefront.

The FBI's Awareness Program gained high visibility during 1988, particularly among libraries with collections related to any area of science. This FBI program attempted to enlist librarians in a surveillance effort aimed at "suspicious behavior" by foreign users of U.S. technical libraries. Libraries, including the Medical Library Association, passed strongly worded resolutions in opposition to this program throughout the year. The main thrust of the opposition centered on the fact that librarians serve as professional facilitators to First Amendment access to information versus the FBI's view that librarians should serve as regulators of information—the antithesis of the library professional code of ethics that protects each user's right to privacy with respect to information sought or received and to materials consulted, borrowed, or acquired.

During 1987 the officers of the Medical Library Association and the Association of Academic Health Science Library Directors formed the MLA/AAHSLD Legislative Task Force. In 1988 the Task Force continued educating congressional staff about the group's legislative agenda and the entire realm of biomedical information and knowledge management. The Task Force also established three funding priorities for the legislative agenda over a five-year period: (1) retooling/renovation of medical library facilities; (2) library school curriculum/mid-career training; and (3) funding for basic and applied research in medical information science.

Publishing. Medical libraries reeled at increases in periodical subscription rates that topped 38 percent in some cases. These increases were due in part to: currency fluctuation; increased publishing costs—paper, postage, staff; profit motive; differential pricing between commercial and individual subscriptions; and a good library market. Prices charged by foreign publishers reflected the weakened U.S. dollar. And, the fact that a large amount of medical scholarly information published abroad has been created in the U.S. at public expense added a note of irony to the situation. The higher prices reflect, however, the real cost of restructuring an information industry that also competes for information resources while developing and marketing scholarly information in new machine-readable databases. Likewise, competition for resources at the local level is a part of the problem of medical libraries, with reduced federal support for higher education resulting in increased competition for funding from state and private agencies.

The Medical Library Association passed a resolution deploring and protesting market-based discriminatory pricing of foreign subscriptions. On the heels of such resolutions were many sessions between publishers and medical librarians. These sessions generally pointed to the need for joint research projects to help individual libraries and publishers improve decisions.

In response to serial inflation issues in general, the Association of Research Libraries (ARL) contracted with an economic consulting firm during 1988 to carry out analyses of serials prices and the cost of serials publishing as part of a study of the feasibility of alternative sources of serials publishing. This study should clarify the economics of the journals industry and lead to further consideration of strategies for influencing costs and availability of the scholarly record.

Preservation During 1988. The National Library of Medicine awarded a four-year contract to microfilm 35,000,000 pages of brittle monographs and serials; the records of these materials will appear in NLM's *SERLINE*, a database containing bibliographic information for approximately 70,000 medical serials. Through this project NLM will borrow missing volumes and issues from throughout the world and incorporate the borrowed pieces into the microfilming process.

The Technical Association of the Paper and

Pulp Industry (TAPPI) held a symposium to provide an opportunity for exchanging information on paper manufacturing and trends in the paper industry and to focus on increasing awareness of the magnitude of the brittle books problem and the importance of alkaline, permanent paper. The Director of the National Library of Medicine, a major speaker at this symposium, outlined the challenges facing research libraries and the preeminent role of permanent paper in reducing the need for future preservation treatment. There was general agreement that manufacture of alkaline paper is expanding substantially in the U.S. and Western Europe, while alkaline paper remains a small portion of the total paper market. Unfortunately, there was also considerable divergence among paper industry representatives as to their role in alleviating the problems caused by acidic paper.

The National Library of Medicine (NLM) also convened its Permanent Paper Task Force during 1988 with members including commercial, academic, and professional society publishers, paper manufacturers, printers, editors, librarians, and preservationists. The NLM Task Force expects that the proportion of publications on acid-free paper will double over the next five years. The Medical Library Association passed a resolution during 1988 supporting NLM's campaign to encourage medical publishers' use of acid-free paper.

National Library of Medicine. The most exciting work at NLM during 1988 was in the field of medical informatics. The research staff developed systems focused on the creation of information for a given subject on everything that science "knows."

Meetings. The Medical Library Association held its 88th annual meeting in New Orleans, Louisiana in May. The meeting centered on forces affecting information creation, distribution, and management; federal controls; privatized databases; current social issues and their impact on health and health information services; and, changing technology in the workplace.

At the 54th General Conference of IFLA in Sydney, Australia in August, the Section on Biological Medical Sciences Libraries held sessions on ten major areas of library services.

Plans were underway for the 6th International Congress on Medical Librarianship to be held in New Delhi, India in 1990.

The Association of Academic Health Science Library Directors held its meeting during the 99th annual meeting of the Association of American Medical Colleges in Chicago, Illinois in November.

JAMES F. WILLIAMS

Medical Library Association

The Medical Library Association (MLA) continues its commitment to serve society by improving health through the provision of health care information, the education of health professionals, the conduct of research, and the improvement of the public's understanding of health. MLA is committed to improving the knowledge and skills of its membership, to developing and maintaining information systems and resources, and to promoting a legislative agenda that supports access to the world's health sciences information.

A Year of Implementation. Nineteen eighty-seven was a year of intense strategic planning for MLA with the development and approval of a new mission and a set of goals. Nineteen eighty-eight was a year of implementation. The Board of Directors developed strategic priorities to give focus to the work of 1989. The Executive Director negotiated a ten-year lease and moved MLA's headquarters to larger, less expensive space in Chicago's Loop. MLA members approved a new credentialing and career recognition program that established an Academy of Health Information Professionals.

The Academy recognizes four categories of membership, each with more rigorous requirements. All members are certified as medical librarians. Admission to the Academy is based on educational requirements, documented knowledge in core areas of health sciences librarianship, and professional experience. Membership is extended for a period of five years and can be renewed by completing a flexible program of professional development.

Organizational planning necessarily involves assessing the environment in which the organization exists. Such current trends in the health care industry as rising insurance costs for health care providers and decreased federal funding for health care programs are having a serious, negative impact on hospital budgets. This downturn is leading to the restructuring, downsizing, and closing of many institutions. Among the first services affected in financially distressed hospitals are those provided by the library. MLA is currently analyzing trends and developing strategies for dealing with these and related problems affecting its hospital library members.

Information Issues and Policy. During 1988, MLA joined with other library associations in opposing the Federal Bureau of Investigation's Library Awareness Program. In a resolution condemning the program, the Medical Library Association confirmed its endorsement of the Library Bill of Rights and the American Library Association's Code of Ethics, which state that information available to the general public should be provided to all on an equal and confidential basis.

A legislative task force composed of members of MLA and the Association of Academic Health Sciences Library Directors continued its efforts to educate congressional staff and officers at the National Institutes of Health (NIH) regarding the need to retool and renovate medical libraries, to revise library school curricula and provide training for mid-career health sciences librarians, and to fund basic and applied research in health information science. MLA, along with a number of other library associations, spoke out against the discriminatory journal pricing policies of a number of foreign publishers.

MLA member Trudy Gardner testified at a National Institutes of Health (NIH) regional meeting regarding the present means of funding biomedical research as if information access, management, and dissemination were tangential to the research effort rather than an integral part of the research process. Valerie Florance, Chair, MLA

Medical Library Association

Governmental Relations Committee, also presented public witness testimony on behalf of the National Library of Medicine's budget.

Continuing Education. In keeping with a direction established by MLA's planning process to increase member involvement in program design, the Board of Directors restructured the Continuing Education Committee to include four subcommittees with responsibilities for developing continuing education courses, establishing criteria for quality control of courses, evaluating and assisting instructors, and providing support to chapters, sections, and other regional groups in developing and presenting courses. MLA's educational programs provide members with the knowledge and skills needed to keep pace with changes within the profession. The Continuing Education Committee and staff presented 31 courses at the 1988 annual meeting. New courses relevant to the changing work environment covered such topics as preserving endangered collections, designing expert systems, managing microcomputers, writing procedures manuals, and presenting workshops.

Publications. During 1988, the Medical Library Association published *Personal Filing Systems: Creating Information Retrieval Systems on Microcomputers*, by Sherri McCarthy and *Drug Information: A Guide to Current Resources*, by Bonnie Snow. *Health Sciences Librarianship and Administration*, the third volume of the encyclopedic *Handbook of Medical Library Practice*, edited by Louise Darling with David Bishop and Lois Ann Colaianni, also bears a 1988 imprint.

President Eloise C. Foster appointed Julie Kesti of the University of New Mexico editor of the *MLA News* effective with the March 1989 issue. Kesti replaced Nancy Fabrizio who served in that position since 1985. Foster also named Janet Fisher of East Tennessee State University to succeed Mitsuko Williams as the newsletter's international news editor. Recommended by a search committee of MLA members and staff, Irwin H. Pizer began his term as editor of the *Bulletin of the Medical Library Association* effective with the January 1989 issue. Pizer replaced Susan Crawford who had served in the position since 1983.

Beginning with the January 1989 issue, the *Bulletin of the Medical Library Association* had a new format. The journal moved to a completely redesigned 8½ by 11 inch format with a four-color cover. The editor also planned changes that will enhance the scholarly quality and appeal of the journal.

In keeping with MLA's commitment to encouraging the use of acid-free paper by publishers of scientific literature, all major MLA publications are printed on paper that conforms to paper permanence standards established by the American National Standards Institute.

Annual Meeting. The 88th Annual Meeting of the Medical Library Association was held May 20-26 in New Orleans, Louisiana. More than 1,700 registrants attended the plenary sessions, the exhibits, the continuing education courses, the annual awards ceremony, the official association business meetings, the committee meetings, and many other programs as well as various social events.

Plenary Session I focused on "Strategic Management of Libraries: Stewardship versus Competitive Strategy," the debate on differing approaches to obtaining the resources necessary to accomplish library goals. Speakers Nina Matheson, Director of the Welch Medical Library, The Johns Hopkins University; Donald Marchand, Dean of the School of Information Studies at Syracuse University; and Patricia Battin, President of the Commission on Preservation and Access, Council on Library Resources, debated the economic and intellectual value of information in terms of the strategic management of libraries. Eugene S. Mayer, Associate Dean and Area Health Education Center Program Director, School of Medicine, University of North Carolina at Chapel Hill, and Sara Fine, Associate Professor, School of Library and Information Science at the University of Pittsburgh, spoke on "Managing Transformation: Internal and External" at Plenary Session II. Mayer discussed the role of information professionals as generalists involved in maintaining an awareness of the larger whole. Fine addressed the challenges of managing people in light of technological advances.

Robert Wedgeworth, Dean, School of Library Services, Columbia University, delivered the John P. McGovern Award Lecture, the keynote address. His talk, "Access to Intellectual Property: The Foundation of Biomedical Communication Systems for the 21st Century," provided the opportunity for reflection on the contributions of the medical library community to broadening access to the work of researchers and scholars and the implications of access questions for future biomedical communications systems on the tenth anniversary of the new copyright law.

Gerald J. Oppenheimer, Director Emeritus, University of Washington Health Sciences Library and Information Center, delivered the Janet Doe Lecture. Oppenheimer's speech "Domus or Polis? The Location of Value" addressed how difficult transitions are for professional associations, MLA in particular. He described MLA's inward-looking, library–oriented perspective during the first half of the century. He then examined "the gradual development, within [MLA], of a consciousness of its place in society as an organization of professionals holding certain values, the reflection of these values in association attitudes, and their expression in what might broadly be called political activity." That expression is manifest in MLA's new mission statement.

In her inaugural address, incoming President Eloise C. Foster, Director, American Hospital Association Resource Center, provided insight into the challenges that lie ahead for MLA as it bridges the gap from strategic planning to action. She expressed the view that implementation is more difficult than planning because of the necessity to assess the impact of each potential action. Implementation also requires adequate monitoring of the environment and, when needed, appropriate modifications to preconceived plans. As a result, implementation needs to proceed in a careful, step–by–step fashion.

Honors and Awards. Alison Bunting was presented with the 1988 President's Award for her outstanding work as principal investigator for "The Nation's Health Information Network: His-

> **MEDICAL LIBRARY ASSOCIATION**
>
> PRESIDENT (May 1988–May 1989):
> **Eloise Foster,** Director, Resource Center, American Hospital Association, 840 N. Lake Shore Drive, Chicago 60611
>
> PRESIDENT-ELECT:
> **Frances Goen,** Medical Library, McIntyre Medical Services Building, McGill University, 3655 Drummond Street, Montreal, PQ H36 1Y6 Canada
>
> IMMEDIATE PAST PRESIDENT:
> **Holly Shipp Buchanan,** Corporate Information Resources, NKC Hospitals, Inc., Louisville, KY 40232
>
> EXECUTIVE DIRECTOR:
> **Raymond A. Palmer**
>
> Headquarters: Suite 300, Six North Michigan Avenue, Chicago, Illinois 60602

tory of the Regional Medical Library Program, 1965–1985." The President's Award is given by the Board of Directors only on special occasions when a member has made an outstanding contribution in the profession during an MLA year.

Three awards were presented for the first time at MLA's 1988 annual meeting. Dorothy Hill was named first recipient of the Louise Darling Medal for Distinguished Achievement in Collection Development in the Health Sciences. Support for the Darling Medal is provided by an endowment fund established with a gift from Ballen Booksellers International, Inc., to honor individuals, institutions, or groups of individuals who are members of MLA and who have made significant contributions to health sciences librarianship in collection development. Audrey Powderly Newcomer received the Estelle Brodman Award for the Academic Medical Librarian of the Year. This award, recently established with a gift from Irwin H. Pizer, recognizes significant achievement at mid–career in academic health sciences librarianship and potential for leadership and continuing excellence. The MLA Award for Distinguished Public Service was conferred upon Congressman Claude D. Pepper for his support of biomedical research as a member of the U.S. House of Representatives, and especially for his efforts in establishing a Center for Biotechnology at the National Library of Medicine. The award recognizes outstanding contributions to the public good through the advancement of health, welfare, and intellectual freedom.

MLA's highest professional distinction, the Marcia C. Noyes Award, was presented to Trudy Lamb for advancing the profession with her many innovative contributions to hospital librarianship, and in particular for the establishment of the first Regional Medical Library program. The Ida and George Eliot Prize, sponsored by Login Brothers Book Company for a work judged most effective in furthering medical librarianship, was given to Thomas J. Galvin and Ellen Gay Detlefsen for "Education for Health Sciences/Biomedical Librarianship: Past, Present, Future," which was published as part of the "Special Report on Education for Health Sciences Librarianship" in the April 1988 *Bulletin of the Medical Library Association*. The Frank Bradway Rogers Information Advancement Award,

sponsored by the Institute for Scientific Information for outstanding contributions to the application of technology to the delivery of health sciences information, went to Charles Goldstein for the development of an integrated library system which was the basis for LS2000.

A special award was given to Susan Crawford in recognition of the completion of her second term as editor of the *Bulletin of the Medical Library Association*.

Other award recipients included: Beth Paskoff, MLA Doctoral Fellowship sponsored by the Institute for Scientific Information; Sitsofe Dzansi, Cunningham Memorial International Fellowship; Rick B. Forsman, Continuing Education Grant; Colleen Marty, MLA Scholarship; and Jacquelyn Cenacveira, MLA Scholarship for Minority Students.

RAYMOND A. PALMER

Mountain Plains Library Association

The Mountain Plains Library Association (MPLA) celebrated its 40th anniversary in 1988 as an organization focused on creating opportunities for professional development for the membership. Strengthening of standards for certification for media specialists and providing support for member-state association activities received renewed emphasis from the organization.

Awards. The association's Professional Development Committee, chaired by Bonnie Campbell, Topeka (Kansas) Public Library, awarded 14 professional development grants. Elnora Mercado, Denver, Colorado, received the largest grant to support her participation in the "International Symposium on New Technologies and Applications in Libraries," Xi'an Shaanxi Province, China. Other grants supported training in the use of computer applications, study of antiquarian bookmanship, study of approaches to library data gathering and analysis, research in children's literature and participation in a variety of seminars and institutes. MPLA awarded a grant to the North Dakota Library Association to complete the initial compilation of the North Dakota Periodical Index. The index is expected to be continued as an annual, published with local resources.

Annual Conference. The 1988 annual conference, held in Omaha, October 19–22, was a joint meeting with the Nebraska Library Association

> **MOUNTAIN PLAINS LIBRARY ASSOCIATION**
>
> PRESIDENT (Unexpired term, June–August 1988; and October 1988–October 1989)):
> **Jerry Kaup,** Minot Public Library, Minot, North Dakota
>
> VICE-PRESIDENT/PRESIDENT-ELECT:
> **Duane F. Johnson,** University of South Dakota Library, Vermillion
>
> EXECUTIVE SECRETARY:
> **Joseph R. Edelen, Jr.,** University of South Dakota Library, Vermillion
>
> Membership (September 1988): 854

and the Nebraska Educational Media Association. The conference focused on librarians and libraries as "Preservers of the Past, Shapers of the Future." More than 800 conferees comprised a record-setting attendance. Preconference sessions included, "I Win—You Win Negotiations," "Basics in Desktop Publications," "Space Planning and Evaluation for Libraries and Information Centers," and "Managing Change for Positive Personal Growth."

Dr. James H. Billington, Librarian of Congress, conference keynote speaker, also led a discussion on "The Library of Congress in the 21st Century." Session topics included "Booktalks as Book Bait," "Cooperative Preservation Measures for Libraries," "From Idea to Published Young Adult Novel," "Writing and Illustrating Children's Books," and "Fiction as Enhanced Truth." A post-conference seminar featured authors of books for children and young adults.

DUANE F. JOHNSON

Music Library Association

The Music Library Association serves the community of music librarians and works together with the other organizations to achieve mutual goals. The work of MLA is carried out by its committees and by 12 regional chapters. The Association publishes a quarterly journal *Notes*, a quarterly newsletter, and two occasional series of indexes and technical reports. Membership is open to anyone interested in this aspect of librarianship.

Annual Meeting. The 1988 annual meeting in Minneapolis, Minnesota was attended by more than 400 members despite the sub-zero temperatures of early February. A pre-conference workshop on Music Manuscripts, Archives, and Special Collections, held February 9–10, combined professional archivists and curators of nonmusical collections with MLA respondents who related the general principles and concerns to the specific needs of music librarians.

Among the most popular sessions in the meeting proper was "Planning for Library Audio Facilities," chaired by James Cassaro. MLA will publish the papers from this session, which should be of interest to many kinds of libraries, as a part of its Technical Reports Series. Other plenary programs included "Subject Access to Popular Music," "Copyright: Ten Years After," and "Special Resources in Music," which focused on relevant resources in areas such as business and government documents. As usual one session—"Music in Minnesota: Past and Present"—acquainted MLA members with local musical events. A lively program on career paths, "Deadends and Open Doors," confronted the question of when and why music librarians leave the profession—and why they stay. More than 40 smaller sessions—roundtables, committee meetings, and interest groups—many of them open to any interested members, were enthusiastically attended.

The 1989 annual meeting of MLA will take place March 15 through 18 at the Stouffer Inn in Cleveland, Ohio, and will be preceded by a workshop: "Music in an On-line Environment." Future meetings are scheduled in Tucson, Arizona (1990), Indianapolis, Indiana (1991), and Baltimore, Maryland (1992).

Awards. Professor Donald W. Krummel from the University of Illinois, distinguished scholar of the music trade, bibliographer of American music, and educator of countless librarians, was presented with a citation for his significant contributions to music librarianship in all of these fields. The Vincent H. Duckles Award for the best book-length music reference work of the year went to the monumental *New Grove Dictionary of American Music*, edited by H. Wiley Hitchcock and Stanley Sadie. The award for the best article on music librarianship went to Carol June Bradley for "Notes of Some Pioneers," a description of America's first music librarians appearing in *Notes* December, 1986. The Association's award for the best review in *Notes* was given to Richard Taruskin for his discussion of the book *Early Music* in the June, 1986 issue. David A. Day, music librarian at Brigham Young University, won the Walter Gerboth Award, given for support for a bibliographic project undertaken by a young librarian, to work on a catalog of opera materials from the Theatre de la Monnaie in Brussels.

Board of Directors. During the past few years MLA has been moving from a comparatively casual, largely volunteer group toward an organization with a more highly structured budget and a nucleus of invested capital. Appointed officers with substantial responsibilities such as the treasurer, executive secretary, convention manager, the placement and publicity officers, and the publications editors—all MLA members—receive honoraria. Other committees and officers submit detailed budgets that are approved by the Finance Committee and the Board of Directors. Subscriptions and membership are handled by a commercial management service. Formulating this structure has not been accomplished without growing pains, but the process is largely accomplished, thanks to the considerable efforts of the past two MLA administrations. The Association is in good financial health and most operating procedures are outlined in a regularly updated *Handbook*. Work is progressing on a similar manual of convention procedures.

Newly elected MLA Board Directors are Laura

MUSIC LIBRARY ASSOCIATION

PRESIDENT (March 1987–March 1989):
Lenore Coral, Cornell University

VICE-PRESIDENT/PRESIDENT ELECT:
Susan T. Somer, The New York Public Library

TREASURER:
Sherry Vellucci, Westminster Choir College, Princeton, New Jersey

RECORDING SECRETARY:
Jean Geil, University of Illinois, Urbana

EXECUTIVE SECRETARY:
A. Ralph Papekhiew, Indiana University

Membership (1988): 2,050
Notes circulation: 2,976
Headquarters: P.O. Box 487, Canton, Massachusetts 02021

Dankner, Richard Griscom, and Diane P. Walker. A. Ralph Papakhian was appointed Executive Secretary; Paula Matthews, Placement Officer; and Dawn Thistle, Publicity Officer. Susan Dearborn is the Advertising Manager for *Notes*; James Farrington assumed the editorship of the *MLA Newsletter* in the fall of 1988.

Committees. As a result of meetings of the joint committee of music librarians and music publishers, the Music Publishers' Association has agreed to start printing scores for libraries on durable acid-free paper. New music available in this format will be identified in the Music Received section of *Notes* by the standard infinity symbol, which will also appear in the scores.

Hours of stimulating discussion among music catalogers and other concerned librarians are a regular feature of the meetings of the Bibliographic Control Committee at MLA conferences. The subcommittees on MARC formats and Subject Access have been particularly active, addressing aspects of these fields unique to the cataloging of music materials. In 1988 the Subcommittee on Descriptive Cataloging also reviewed the final draft of the second edition of *ISBD(PM): the International Standard Bibliographic Description for Printed Music*.

As befits performing artists, the MLA Committee on Reference and Public Service is exploring possibilities for describing reference work in theatrical rather than militaristic metaphors. Experience in managing stage fright, encouraging ensemble performance, and dealing with audience hecklers, the Committee suggests, may help bring reference librarians out of the trenches and into the spotlight.

Music librarians share many concerns with librarians throughout the world. Uses of the new technology, refinements in bibliographic access, and resource sharing and collection development occupy prominent roles in MLA committee work. At a time when the number of positions available for music librarians seems to be larger than the pool of good applicants, the Association is looking at ways to recruit and educate qualified people for music librarianship.

SUSAN T. SOMMER

National Agricultural Library

As the nation's chief resource and service for agricultural information, the National Agricultural Library (NAL) has a mission to provide access to and use of information. Specialized centers, cooperative endeavors and use of new media are augmenting services and products to clientele ranging from agricultural researchers and regulators to consumers of agricultural products and the public at large.

Collection. One of NAL's primary resources, its collection of books, journals, reports, audiovisuals, and now including software and laser disks, has increased to almost 2,000,000 volumes. The collection policy guiding the selection of agricultural information materials, reflecting current needs and interests of the USDA and the agricultural community, was updated in September, 1988.

Collection evaluation studies have been under way: a study of NAL holdings in the subjects of soil and water conservation has been completed; studies in agricultural trade and marketing and in robotics in agriculture are in process.

Preservation and Projects. The NAL, with assistance from the Association of Research Libraries (ARL), began a preservation planning project involving a consultant-assisted self-study.

Two cataloging projects assist in providing access to publications in a standard format. Land-grant university libraries from 43 states are participating in a project to assure coverage of state agricultural publications, an underutilized source of valuable information. Records for these documents are incorporated into the AGRICOLA database of NAL and are also contributed to the AGRIS (Agricultural Resources Information System) database of the Food and Agriculture Organization (FAO) of the United Nations, further increasing their worldwide access. In the other program NAL has established a network of libraries to participate in a cooperative cataloging project of agricultural monographs using OCLC as the host bibliographic utility.

Information Centers. A 13th specialized information center was established in 1988. The Youth Development Information Center (YDIC), a joint project of the USDA Extension Service and NAL, provides information services to development professionals who plan, develop, implement and evaluate educational programs designed to meet the changing needs of America's youth. The Rural Information Center (RIC) now actively involves state and extension agents serving as coordinators in 35 states. Forty-eight states, 4 trust territories and 3 foreign countries used RIC services in fiscal year 1988, its first full year of operation.

Supplemental funding from a number of cooperating agencies allowed the Aquaculture Information Center to improve services and produce a wide variety of information resources. Major accomplishments include the creation of a full-text aquaculture CD-ROM as part of the National Agricultural Text Digitizing Project at NAL, the receipt of an expert advisory system on Louisiana State aquaculture for inclusion in the center's AquaRef Advisor and an international project with the FAO to create an expert system on African aquaculture.

The Animal Welfare Information Center is working with several agencies and institutions: Texas Tech University of the Health Sciences, Lubbock, Texas, for production of an audio visual on alternatives in research; the Scientist Center for Animal Welfare, Bethesda, Maryland, for the publication of their proceedings; the Institute of Laboratory Animal Resources, National Academy of Sciences, Washington, D.C., for update of guidelines for the management of laboratory dogs and rodents and for a guide to pain recognition and alleviation in laboratory animals; Princeton Scientific Publishing Company, for publication of two books on toxicology; and the University of Maryland for production of an expert system for determining proper anesthesia and analgesia for a variety of laboratory animals in different conditions.

The National Alternative Farming Systems Information Center is part of a Congressionally

National Agricultural Library

mandated program on low-input farming systems coordinated by the Cooperative State Research Service of the U.S. Department of Agriculture.

Technology. NAL's AGRICOLA database, with 2,600,000 citations to the agricultural literature, is available on CD-ROM from two commercial vendors, SilverPlatter Information Inc. and OCLC Online Computer Library Center Inc. Silver Platter offers the complete database from 1970 to the present on four disks: 1970-76, 1977-80, 1981-84 and 1984-present. CRIS (Current Research Information System) is planned for inclusion on disks issued in 1989. OCLC has issued AGRICOLA on CD-ROM as part of its *Search CD450* Agriculture Series, which includes AGRICOLA, CRIS and AgMIL (a selected database of agricultural citations compiled from OCLC's Online Union Catalog). OCLC offers the database on three discs covering 1979-82, 1983-85 and 1986-present (AGRICOLA/CRIS). AGRICOLA is available online with the BRS and DIALOG database vending services.

Twelve-inch laser optical disks have been the focus of a project to evaluate their potential to store and disseminate agriculturally-related full-text databases. In the first phase, the *Pork Industry Handbook* and 200,000 records from NAL's AGRICOLA database were placed on an optical disk. In the second phase, photocomposition tapes and word processing files as well as printed text were chosen as sources for material to test further the conversion and mastering process. Sixteen institutions have been participating in phase two and will help evaluate the disc containing the full text (in digital form) and related illustrations (in analog form) of 13 USDA and State Extension publications.

The National Agricultural Text Digitizing Project is testing a new method of capturing full-text and images in digital format for publication on CD-ROM discs. Four thousand pages of text and images of noncopyrighted publications are being scanned, converted, edited, and indexed. Other materials will be added later. The purpose is to provide in-depth access.

With the cooperation of the Forest Service and the University of Maryland, NAL has completed a 12-inch videodisc containing 34,000 photos from the USDA Forest Service Historical Photograph Collection. Other USDA photos are being put on a WORM (Write Once, Read Many) laser disk.

NAL, working with the University of Maryland (University College, Center for Instructional Design and Evaluation), has designed and produced a system using a computer coupled with laser videodisc to provide instruction in searching the AGRICOLA database. This interactive system, called ARGRICOLearn, incorporates text, graphics, motion pictures, animation and sound.

The staff at NAL are creating small-scale microcomputer systems to mimic advisory work done by human experts, in particular to guide users to appropriate references—books, articles, laws, etc.—or in some instances, to the answer to specific questions.

A new integrated library information system, ISIS (Integrated System for Information Ser-

Statistical Summary of Primary NAL Activities

Types of Activity	FY 1988 Actual	Productivity FY 1989 Estimate	FY 1990 Estimate
Serial Issues Added	142,709	165,000	166,000
Number of Titles Cataloged	22,729	23,000	23,500
Articles Indexed	88,599	90,000	95,000
Pages Preserved	1,661,000	1,712,000	8,235,000
Document Requests Filled	195,352	224,655	248,353
Reference Inquiries Answered	27,156	28,514	29,968
Automated Searches Conducted	5,849	6,141	6,448
Current Awareness (CALS) Searches	98,110	107,921	118,713
Current Awareness (CALS) Profiles	17,588	19,347	20,310

vices), is replacing fragmented, multiple computer operations as NAL. The system was provided by the Virginia Tech Library System (VTLS), Virginia Polytechnic Institute and State University.

The NAL has inaugurated an electronic bulletin board system called ALF (Agricultural Library Forum). The system provides a convenient, low-cost tool for electronically accessing information about NAL products and services and for exchanging agricultural information and resources among libraries, information centers, and other information users. ALF, open to anyone interested in agricultural information, is available 24 hours per day, 7 days per week.

Information Network. Individuals from several land-grant libraries have been selected by ballot as officers of the newly formed "Agricultural Libraries Information Network." Plans call for participation by agricultural industry libraries, 1890 land-grant institutions, the National Association of State University and Land Grant Colleges, Public Libraries Association, Special Libraries Association, state libraries, and other agriculturally related professional associations.

Outreach. A dedication ceremony opened an exhibit of photographs, books and artifacts entitled "Agriculture in China: A Visual Landscape." The exhibit consisted of 40 large color photographs and miscellaneous photographs loaned by the Chinese Embassy and from NAL's Forest Service Photographs Collection, herbarium specimens, farm tools, rare books and other artifacts. The keynote address at the dedication ceremony was given by His Excellency Han Xu, Ambassador from The People's Republic of China. U.S. Secretary of Agriculture, Richard Lyng welcomed the large assembly of visitors and USDA staff and introduced Ambassador Han.

A new 16-minute videotape, "The National Agricultural Library—For Your Information," describes the NAL, its collections and services. Another new videotape, "AGRIS/CARIS, Sharing of the World's Agricultural Information," documents the activities of the AGRIS and CARIS databases of the FAO.

AGRIS and CARIS are cooperative international systems established on the concept of having each country participating in providing the information produced within its territory. There are 120 national and 14 regional centers contributing data to be included in the AGRIS database of agricultural literature citations. NAL provides 50,000 citations from U.S. publications to AGRIS annually. The database contains more than 1,000,000 records, and is accessible through the multilingual thesaurus AGROVOC (AGRicultural VOCabulary). The U.S. version of AGRIS, without the U.S. contributions, is available online on DIALOG; in printed form the database is titled AGRINDEX. NAL and the AGRIS Coordinating Centre have been working together to ensure that the AGROVOC thesaurus and the CABI (Commonwealth Agricultural Bureaux International, United Kingdom) thesaurus, used by NAL for its AGRICOLA database, are increasingly compatible. NAL has also been cooperating with AGRIS to eliminate overlap between the two databases.

JOSEPH H. HOWARD

National Commission on Libraries and Information Science

For the U.S. National Commission on Libraries and Information Science (NCLIS), 1988 was a year marked by program accomplishments, internal changes, and controversy. Highlights of the year include enactment of the law calling for a second White House Conference on Library and Information Services, presentation of the first NCLIS Recognition Award, establishment of a Federal-State Cooperative System for Public Library Data, publication of the NCLIS hearings on Sensitive But Not Classified Information, and progress on the governance, information age, and information literacy and education programs. A closed session of the year's first Commission meeting, at which a representative of the FBI explained the FBI Library Awareness Program, engendered controversy that reflected on the Commission and mobilized large segments of the library profession.

Commissioners and Staff. Vice-Chairman, Bessie Boehm Moore, who has served on the Commission since its creation by Congress in 1971, was replaced by Charles E. Reid of New Jersey. Subsequently, Moore was voted the unique title of Vice-Chairman Emeritus. Elinor H. Swaim of North Carolina was appointed to complete the term of Patricia Barbour, who resigned. Both Raymond J. Petersen of Connecticut and Commissioner Julia Li Wu were confirmed by the Senate. Margaret Phelan and Wanda L. Forbes were reappointed and await confirmation by the Senate. George H. Nash, scholar-in-residence at the Hoover Institution, saw publication of the second volume of his biography of Herbert Hoover.

Early in 1988 Executive Director Vivian J. Arterbery resigned to return to the Rand Corporation. Dr. Susan K. Martin, the new Executive Director, joined the Commission in August. Formerly director of the Milton S. Eisenhower Library of Johns Hopkins University, Dr. Martin brings a background in academic librarianship, library networking, and information technologies to NCLIS. Deputy Director David Hoyt and longtime staff members Dorothy Pollet Gray and Marti Quigley left the Commission during 1988.

FBI Library Awareness Program. At its January 14 meeting in the San Antonio Public Library, NCLIS heard a presentation in closed session by Thomas DuHadway about the FBI Library Awareness Program. As described by the FBI, this program deploys agents to various academic and scientific and technical libraries to question and elict the cooperation of library staff members in observing suspicious behavior on the part of potential foreign intelligence operatives. The transcript of this presentation was released, with some portions excised, under a Freedom of Information Act request. Opposition to this program and NCLIS' perceived tolerance of it mounted in the library and other communities. In response NCLIS adopted a resolution reaffirming its commitment to open access to information for all, the right of privacy for all library users, and unequivocal support of First Amendment rights.

WHCLIS II. On August 8, President Reagan signed PL 100-382, authorizing and requesting the President to call and conduct a White House Conference on Library and Information Services (WHCLIS) between September 1, 1989 and September 30, 1991. The law authorizes a $6,000,000 appropriation to provide states and territories with matching funds for their preconferences and to support the national Conference.

Recognition Award. The first annual NCLIS Recognition Award, established to honor initiative in improving and promoting the nation's library and information services, was presented to Pizza Hut, Inc. for its "BOOK IT" National Reading Incentive Program. The program, which involves more than 14,000,000 children and their parents and teachers nationwide, provides incentives and rewards for children's reading accomplishments.

Federal-State Cooperative System for Public Library Data. The National Center for Education Statistics and NCLIS have signed a memorandum of understanding to continue joint development of the Federal-State Cooperative System for Public Library Data (FSCS), which expands the 1987 12-state pilot project conducted by the American Library Association under contract to the Department of Education. When fully developed, this system will collect and publish public library statistics annually and fill a gap in statistical information which has existed since 1982. NCES will transfer $225,000 to NCLIS in fiscal year 1989.

Other Programs. The Commission received $5,000 from Gaylord and a commitment of $20,000 from the Council on Library Resources for an invitational symposium of school librarians, teachers, school administrators, curriculum specialists, and others to suggest improvements in the education system by incorporating information resources and librarians fully into the teaching process. In the international arena, NCLIS published the previously adopted trilat-

The National Endowment for the Humanities

eral Glenerin Declaration and served as the intermediary in securing $216,000 in State Department grants for 12 projects sponsored by various organizations. NCLIS also adopted a policy of adhering to the permanent paper standard by publishing the Hearing on Sensitive but Not Classified Information and its Annual Report 1986-87 on alkaline paper stock.

SANDRA N. MILEVSKI

The National Endowment for the Humanities

The National Endowment for the Humanities is an independent grantmaking agency created by Congress in 1965. The Endowment supports research, education, and public understanding of the humanities through grants to individuals, organizations, and institutions. Many of the grants to institutions are made to libraries. The Endowment's grantmaking operations are conducted through five major divisions: (1) The Division of General Programs endeavors to fulfill the Endowment's mandate to foster public appreciation and understanding of the humanities. The division includes programs that assist institutions and organizations in developing projects for presentation to general audiences. The division is composed of programs for Museums and Historical Organizations, Media, Public Humanities Projects, and Humanities Projects in Libraries. Applications must meet published deadlines and criteria in the guidelines for each of the programs in the division. (2) The Division of Research Programs provides support for basic research projects in the humanities, for research resources, for the preparation of important research tools, for editing of significant texts in the humanities, and for the publication of scholarship in the humanities; all work important for library collections. (3) The Division of Fellowships and Seminars, through several programs, provides stipends that enable individual scholars, teachers, and members of nonacademic professions to undertake study and research in the humanities that will enhance their capacity as teachers, scholars, or interpreters of the humanities and that will enable them to make significant contributions to thought and knowledge in the humanities. Many of the fellows travel to the collections found in libraries, and many of the seminars are held in some of the nation's research libraries. (4) The Division of Education Programs supports projects and programs through which institutions endeavor to renew and strengthen the impact of teaching in the humanities at all levels, including nontraditional ways that could be conducted through libraries. (5) The Division of State Programs makes grants to citizens' committees in each state and to three territories to provide support for local humanities projects, primarily directed at general audiences.

In additional to support through each of the five divisions, support is also available to libraries through two offices. The Office of Challenge Grants aims to help institutions to develop new and increased nonfederal, long-range sources of support in order to improve the quality of their humanities resources and activities and to strengthen their financial stability. The Office of Preservation offers grant support for a sustained and coherent attack on the problem of deteriorating resources in the humanities. Grants from the Office of Preservation focus on saving informational content, improving research collection maintenance, and developing preventive care practices.

Examples of grants made to libraries by the various NEH Divisions and Offices during the fiscal year, 1987, include:

Division of General Programs. (1) The American Library Association was awarded $358,000 to support a nationwide series of programs in public libraries about the work and lives of 13 major American poets. (2) Another award to the ALA for $374,839 was made to support a traveling exhibition, interpretive materials, and reading and discussion programs on the history and significance of the French Revolution at more than 30 public libraries throughout the country.

Professor Robert Stepto of Yale University leads a discussion of Russell Baker's memoir Growing Up *at the Hamden Miller Library in Hamden, Connecticut. This program was one of 120 scholar-led book discussions in "American Lives," a project taking place in 30 Connecticut libraries between September 1988 and May 1989. Sponsored by the Southern Connecticut Library Council and funded by a grant from the National Endowment for the Humanities, "American Lives" focuses on American biographies and autobiographies and how the lives of celebrated and ordinary Americans reflect or challenge the dominant values in our society.*

(3) The Delaware Library Association was awarded $147,860 to support scholar-led reading and discussion programs on six themes in 40 libraries on the Delmarva Peninsula of Delaware, Maryland and Virginia. (4) The John Carter Brown Library received an award of $10,500 to support planning for an exhibition with interpretive catalog, an international conference, and public lecture series on how New World discoveries influenced European ideas about civilization. The lectures will be part of the Columbian Quincentenary.

Division Of Research Programs. (1) The Huntington Library was awarded $10,000 to support the publication of a two-volume guide to the medieval and Renaissance manuscripts held by the Library. (2) An award of $15,000 was made to the University of Arizona to support preparation of a bilingual dictionary of the Hopi Language. (3) Columbia University received an award of $100,000 to support cataloguing on the RLIN and selective preservation of Avery Library's architectural drawings and the development of a database/videodisc interface. (4) The Research Libraries Group, Inc. (Stanford) received an award of $39,000 to support the addition of 13,000 machine-readable records for Chinese rare books of the National Center Library, Taipei, Tiawan, onto RLIN.

Office Of Challenge Grants. (1) John Hopkins University Library was awarded $248,000 to support an endowment that will provide long-term support for the selection, acquisition, and preservation of library materials in the humanities. (2) An award of $650,000 was made to the Newberry Library, Chicago, to support an endowment that will support cataloguing and staff positions in reader services, preservation, and technical services. (3) The San Antonio (Texas) Public Library received an award of $90,000 to strengthen its humanities collection and create an endowment for humanities materials in the future.

Office Of Preservation. (1) The American Theological Library Association received an award of $110,000 to support a nationwide, cooperative effort that will preserve on microfiche 8,000 monographs on the history of religious thought published between 1850 and 1910. (2) An award of $145,167 was awarded to ARL to support the implementation of preservation planning programs in 10 U.S. research libraries. (3) The Idaho State Library received a $63,616 award to support Idaho's participation in the U.S. Newspaper Program. (4) The Center for Research Libraries received $90,642 to support the microfiching of Civilian Conservation Corps newspapers.

NEH Guidelines And Information. The Public Affairs Offices at NEH supplies guidelines, deadlines, and other information about any Division, Program, or Office at the National Endowment. Further information is available on request from the Endowment at 1100 Pennsylvania Avenue N.W., Washington, D.C. 20506; (202) 786-0438.

THOMAS C. PHELPS

National Library of Canada

In 1988, the National Library of Canada (NLC) celebrated its 35th anniversary. During the year, it sponsored a number of events to promote and advance its three-fold mission: to preserve Canada's published heritage; to promote the development of libraries and library service throughout Canada; and to support resource sharing among libraries.

Canadiana. All aspects of the Canadiana collections received attention during 1988. The legal deposit regulations were extended to include microforms, in addition to the monographs, periodicals, sheet music, musical scores, sound recordings of Canadian interest, looseleaf services and educational kits already subject to the National Library Act (1969). The National Library receives two copies of every work under $50 and one copy of works over $50, offered for public distribution and sale in Canada. In 1988, it made a commitment to protect one copy by creating a formal Preservation Collection of Canadiana. One of the two copies is designated "the preservation copy". The second or "service copy" is available to researchers and libraries through interlibrary loan. This decision required a policy to ensure the purchase of second copies for those items that cost more than $50.

In addition to acquiring and preserving works published in Canada that are written by and about Canada and Canadians, the National Library is responsible for providing bibliographic records of these items. In 1988 the Cataloguing-in-Publication program, coordinated by the Library, was extended to include publications of the federal government. Another initiative has led to the production of BiblioDisc, a CD–ROM product developed by the Book and Periodical Development Council, the Canadian Telebook Agency and the Library. BiblioDisc contains bibliographic and ordering information on current Canadian publications and supplements the national bibliography *Canadiana*, available on microfiche, tape, in paper copy, online and through the file transfer option of the MARC Records Distribution Service and DOBIS Search Service.

The National Library also demonstrated its interest in supporting retrospective bibliography by co-publishing Patricia Lockhart Fleming's *Upper Canadian Imprints, 1801-1840: A Bibliography* with the University of Toronto Press.

In an agreement with the International Council

The April 13, 1988 Glenn Gould Exhibition ribbon-cutting ceremony (left to right) Dr. M. Scott, National Librarian of Canada, Mr. and Mrs. R.H. Gould, and the Honorable Flora MacDonald, Minister of Communications.

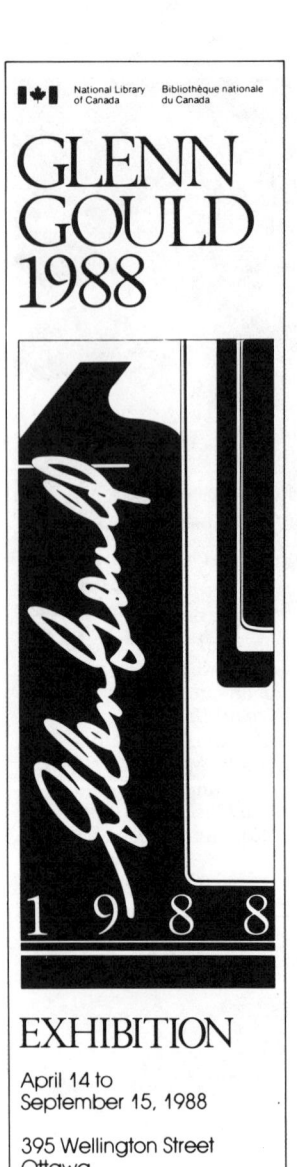

for Canadian Studies, the Library is strengthening its ties with Canadian Studies centres abroad and ensuring that materials produced by Canadianists are acquired and recorded. Those items which fall within the guidelines of the national bibliography will be recorded in *Canadiana*. Other materials such papers and articles will be included in a bibliography produced by the International Council.

Programs. The Cultural Events Program is an important vehicle for promoting Canada's musical and literary heritage. "Glenn Gould 1988," an exhibition dedicated to one of Canada's best-known musicians, attracted thousands of visitors from Canada, the United States and abroad, and received extensive media coverage. An exhibition catalogue and a calendar complemented the audiovisual experience.

"The Secret Self: an Exploration of Canadian Children's Literature" was designed to attract children, parents, authors, librarians, publishers and illustrators to the magical quality of books. A series of events based on the celebration of works for children: readings, workshops, illustrated lectures, storytelling, brought people of every age into the Library. A poster, catalogue and quiz produced by the Library promoted the exhibit to a wider audience.

"Read Up on It" was launched during the Olympics in Seoul, Korea. Similar to "Read More about It," the program is sponsored by the Canadian Broadcasting Corporation, the Book and Periodical Development Council and the Library. It aims to bring contemporary Canadian books and magazines on subjects related to the television program to the attention of Canadian viewers.

Library Development. In 1988, the National Library concentrated its standards development, based on Open Systems Interconnection, on the Interlibrary Loan (ILL) Protocol Project, conformance testing and the National Directory Service. The Library contracted with six commercial firms and one library to produce reports on the implementation and testing of the interlibrary loan protocol. An international version of the protocol, already accepted as a Canadian standard, has been defined for consideration by the International Organization for Standardization. In 1988, the National Library appointed Leigh Swain director of the IFLA Universal Dataflow and Telecommunications Core Program, which has been its responsibility since 1986. The main focus of the Program in 1988 was a project to demonstrate the feasibility of using the interlibrary loan protocol for the international exchange of ILL messages.

Resource Sharing. Two seminars on resource sharing were held within the context of the annual conferences of the Canadian Library Association and the Association des sciences et techniques de la documentation. Representatives from the different types of libraries and from various parts of Canada made presentations and stimulated discussion on the issues related to the borrowing of materials from one library for the use of readers and researchers of another library: philosophy, lending policies and practices, location tools, costs and document delivery.

The potential for resource sharing among libraries was enhanced through a six-month trial interlibrary loan referral project, jointly sponsored by the National Library and OCLC. During the trial, the National Library provided new services to the Canadian and U.S. members of the Northwest Group Access Program by searching the complete OCLC data base in those instances where a library had not found the required document. An online referral was then made to the library where the item was located. OCLC member libraries were also able to use the National Library as a last resort for supplying or locating items likely to be held in Canada.

National Librarian's Report. In April 1988, the National Librarian, Marianne Scott, presented *Orientations: A Planning Framework for the 1990s* to the National Library Advisory Board. The report, the result of a two-year process of organizational renewal and planning, was the basis for discussion, consultation and planning with the Canadian library community in preparation for the complex and rapidly changing information age of the '90s.

GWYNNETH EVANS

National Library of Medicine

On November 4, 1988, Congress passed Public Law 100-607 directing that a National Center for Biotechnology Information be established at the National Library of Medicine. A sum of $8,000,000 was authorized for fiscal year 1989 to carry out the functions of the Center. Earlier in 1988, Congress had appropriated $3,800,000 for the Library to carry out biotechnology-related programs.

The Center is given the responsibility to create automated systems for knowledge about molecular biology, to conduct research into advanced methods on how to handle biotechnology information, and to coordinate the gathering of biotechnology information worldwide.

Online services. The legislation that created the National Center for Biotechnology Information also directed the Library to work closely with other federal agencies to establish a databank of information on the results of AIDS research conducted in the United States and abroad. Earlier in the year, the Library had created a database—AIDSLINE—that was essentially a subset of MEDLINE.

The number of user access codes issued by the NLM for its online MEDLINE network grew by 50 percent for the second successive year. There are now more than 20,000 codes. Individual health professionals represent the fastest growing segment of the NLM online network. This is the result of the continuing popularity of the Grateful Med "front-end" software for microcomputers. Version 3.0 was announced in January and, by the end of the year, the number of copies of Grateful Med sold by the National Technical Information Service since its introduction in 1986 reached 13,000. Another improvement in 1988 was to increase the frequency of MEDLINE updating—from monthly to twice a month. More than 4,000,000 searches of the MEDLINE and other databases were conducted on the NLM computers in 1988.

A number of the agreements signed by NLM and private companies to produce compact disks (CD-ROM) containing MEDLINE came to fruition in 1988. There are now at least a half-dozen such products on the market. In September, the Library sponsored a one-day "evaluation forum" to hear from both the producers and the users of the new products.

A new committee, the Literature Selection Technical Review Committee, met for the first time in 1988. This Committee provides policy advice to the NLM about the literature covered in NLM bibliographic products and reviews and recommends specific journals for indexing in NLM publications (such as *Index Medicus*) and the electronic databases.

Preservation. The emphasis on preservation continued in 1988. The "National Preservation Plan for the Biomedical Literature" was distributed throughout the Regional Medical Library Network. Several newspaper columns about the peril to library materials printed on acid-based paper were distributed nationwide. The Permanent Paper Task Force, established by the Library on the recommendation of the Board of Regents, met twice in 1988. The Task Force is formulating standards for the making and use of permanent (non-acid) paper and is encouraging major medical publishers to use this paper in their books and journals.

Outreach. Early in 1988, Congress added a new responsibility to the Library's basic mandate to publicize the services of the NLM. There is a concern that the Library's online and other information services are not being used to maximum benefit, especially by health professionals in rural and remote areas of the nation. As a first step in this direction, the Library will update several sections of the Long Range Plan (published in 1986), including those pertaining to education/outreach. An Outreach Planning Panel, chaired by Dr. Michael DeBakey, met at the Library in November to review the NLM's outreach program and make recommendations for improvement. The Panel will meet twice more early in 1989.

The Medical Library Assistance Act was reauthorized by the Congress in 1988 at a level of $14,000,000 in fiscal year 1989 and "such sums as may be necessary for fiscal year 1990." At the same time the Congress raised the current maximum that the Library can award for a resource grant to $750,000 from $500,000.

ROBERT MEHNERT

National Technical Information Service

NTIS Function. NTIS collects, organizes, and markets technical information generated by U.S. and foreign governments in all areas of science and technology. Its mission is to provide both the U.S. private and public sectors with government-produced scientific and technical information to maximize the return on Federal R & D investments as well as to provide foreign technical information to increase U.S. competitiveness in the global economy. NTIS is a relatively small Government organization of about 330 employees that is required to price its products and services to fully recover its costs of providing them to users.

When Government agencies, their contractors, and grantees forward their reports to NTIS, they are cataloged, indexed, abstracted into a computer system, and microfilmed for an archival system. The citations are computerized so that the resulting NTIS Bibliographic Database can be accessed by the public through the major commercial online information vendors. Portions of the database are also available on CD-ROM.

Additions to Inventory. The NTIS collection includes material from the National Aeronautics and Space Administration (NASA), the Departments of Defense, Energy, Commerce, Health and Human Services, the Environmental Protection Agency, and more than 200 other Federal agencies. In 1988, more than 66,000 information items (technical reports, software, numeric databases, patent applications, published searches, and other items) were added to the collection. This included approximately 22,000 reports from foreign sources, one-third of the total. Nearly 2,000,000 different technical publications are now available, none of which is ever out of print. The online NTIS Bibliographic Database contains 1,300,000 records, dating back

National Technical Information Service

to 1964. But NTIS is more than a secondary source of technical reports: it has a variety of announcement and dissemination products and services to serve the user community.

Technology Applications. NTIS operates the Center for the Utilization of Federal Technology (CUFT) to alert industry and government to technology resulting from U.S. Government R&D considered to have real potential for commercial or practical use. CUFT's Office of Federal Patent Licensing (OFPL) conducts the most active licensing program in the Federal Government. Licensable properties come primarily from the Departments of Health, Agriculture, Interior and Commerce. The yearly number of licenses granted increased from 20 in FY 1981 to 66 in FY 1988 for a total for those years of 336. Revenues from these licenses have increased each year. Private sector sales of products covered by the granted licenses exceed $200,000,000 of which $70–$90,000,000 represents exports protected by some of the 1,200 or so foreign patents obtained by OFPL during FY 1981 through FY 1988. Recently, more emphasis has been placed on increasing exclusivity in new licenses so that companies can have maximum incentive to invest their own funds in rapid commercialization.

In addition to the Office of Federal Patent Licensing, CUFT contains the Office of Applied Technology which handles specialized information products to aid in transferring technology to the private sector. One product, the Federal Applied Technology Database, provides public access to selected results of U.S. Government R&D and engineering activities. *Federal Technology Catalog* contains carefully evaluated summaries of selected processes, instruments, materials, equipment, software, services, and techniques, and a *Directory of Federal Laboratory and Technology Resources—A Guide to Services, Facilities, and Expertise* has been published.

Foreign Technology. In this era of global competition, many U.S. innovators are discovering the value in foreign-source technical information. NTIS input from abroad is now one-third of the total. There are acquisition agreements with government or private sector organizations in more than 60 countries, including Canada, Western Europe, India, the Peoples Republic of China, and Japan. In 1986, Congress passed the Japanese Technical Literature Act, which included coordination of U.S. Government activities in collecting and disseminating information, cataloging and analyzing government and nongovernment activities, and consulting with industry on its Japanese information needs. NTIS, assisting with this activity, produced the second edition of a directory of Japanese information activities in the U.S. and a bibliography of Japanese technical information translated into English at U.S. Government expense.

In 1988, NTIS improved the "Foreign Technology Newsletter" giving it a new front section with reviews and syntheses of major research programs, activities of specific organizations and laboratories, conference summaries, and descriptions of specific new technologies, processes, and discoveries. Contributing sources include the Office of Naval Research, the Foreign Broadcast Information Service, and embassies.

The newsletter also covers foreign research and development reports in such fields as advanced microelectronics, structural ceramics, and superconductivity.

NTIS supplies access to the Japanese Online Information System, consisting of many technical databases in English and Japanese. The databases are mounted in Tokyo at the Japan Information Center for Science and Technology (JICST). The JICST/NTIS cooperative agreement allows any interested party in the U.S. to access the latest Japanese research results.

Library Ordering Program. The VPI and State University Library in Virginia and the University of Texas at Austin Library signed agreements to participate in the NTIS Library Ordering Program. These libraries handle orders for NTIS documents as an extension of their services to patrons. Other participants are the University of Colorado/Boulder Government Publications Library, the Detroit Public Library, the Newark Public Library, and the St. Louis Public Library. NTIS wishes to add more libraries to this program.

Service Improvements. There were a number of service improvements during 1988 including a new telephone system that permits answering calls more promptly; more workshops and seminars co-sponsored by library groups, universities, and vendors of the NTIS Database to instruct users in efficient and effective online searching of the NTIS Bibliographic Database; monthly updates to the Federal Research in Progress Database; and the ability to order NTIS reports on the OCLC system online.

Joint Ventures. One primary strategy of NTIS to improve dissemination is to increase the number of joint ventures with private information enterprises so that particular market niches will be well served. Such alliances draw on mutual strengths to improve access, timeliness, quality, and ease-of-use of government information. Joint ventures improve NTIS' ability to disseminate scientific and technical information by creating a product or service which gives added value to the information user.

Privatization. During the year, two laws containing language prohibiting the contracting out of NTIS were enacted by the Congress; the Omnibus Trade and Competitiveness Act, P.L. 100–418, signed August 23, and the National Institute of Standards and Technology Authorization Act for FY 1989, P.L. 100–519, signed October 24. The Authorization Act states that, "The functions and activities of the Service [NTIS] . . . are permanent Federal functions to be carried out by the Secretary [of Commerce] through the Service and its employees, and shall not be transferred from the Service . . . without the express approval of the Congress." The new laws also call for improvements in NTIS facilities.

Goals. Within recent years, NTIS goals have been directed at assisting the private sector in benefiting from Government R & D, thereby helping America to remain competitive. The goal is still to provide access to more technology and business information generated by the Federal Government—in all formats—to undergird R & D programs, encourage innovation, and stimulate productivity in the U.S.   ALAN R. WENBERG

Networks

Each year we look for new trends and major changes in networking at the state, regional, and national levels. There were no dramatic breakthroughs or major developments in networking in 1988. Three continuing developments of importance to networking are worth noting. They are (1) CD-ROM (Compact Disc-Read-Only Memory), (2) the increasing use of "FAX" (telefacsimile), and (3) international networking.

In the case of the latter, the Library of Congress (LC), OCLC, and WLN have been most active. To contribute to the standards efforts, LC is represented on an international CD-ROM working group sponsored by the International MARC Advisory Committee of IFLA (International Federation of Library Associations and Institutions). The group is working to coordinate efforts of national libraries as they proceed to develop prototype CD-ROMs with their respective bibliographic records. The British Library, the Bibliothèque Nationale, the National Library of Canada, and LC have engaged the same contractor to develop prototype CD-ROMs. The Federal Republic of Germany and Japan are also working independently with the same contractor to develop their respective national books-in-print on CD-ROM.

Libraries in 22 foreign countries contribute to and/or use information in the OCLC Online Union Catalog. Some of the countries participating are Australia, Canada, People's Republic of China, Federal Republic of Germany, France, Spain, and the United Kingdom. WLN has software licensees in the national libraries in Australia, New Zealand, People's Republic of China, and the United Kingdom.

The impact of CD-ROM technology in resource sharing and reference continues to present a challenge. One 5 1/4 CD-ROM disk can store 275,000 printed pages or 1,500 floppy disks. The medium is durable and reliable but presently limited to storing information. Master disks are expensive to make, though replication is inexpensive. A bewildering array of formats and access software and a lack of currency exists. Each CD requires an individual work station, and currently there is no mechanism for multiple access to disks. Some libraries are experimenting with stringing together or networking up to 20 individual CD-ROM readers. It works as long as the CD-ROM products share the same access software. The use of CD-ROM is limited to off-line retrospective data with updating usually on a quarterly basis and in some cases monthly. WLN's LaserCat, a union catalog of holdings of 380 U.S. and Canadian libraries, contains more than 2,400,000 MARC records. It is updated quarterly (the use of WLN network online provides the current information), and can be tailored to the library's specification—it can access only the libraries holdings or the entire union list.

The "Reference by GammaFax" project involving ten multi-type libraries, and coordinated by the Illinois DuPage Library System combines the technologies of CD-ROM searching and telefacsimile transmission providing an opportunity for testing the feasibility of sharing database resources among libraries in a network configuration.

Seven states, Arizona (72 locations), Georgia (6 locations), Illinois (192 installations), Maryland, Michigan (81 sites), New Jersey, and Pennsylvania have statewide FAX networks and Connecticut, Florida, and New Mexico are currently developing FAX networks.

National Libraries. Two Library of Congress MARC distribution services will be inaugurated in 1989—one will be an expanded service for distribution of records in the Chinese, Japanese, and Korean vernacular. The second will constitute the first distribution by LC of the National Union Catalog records in machine-readable form. These two new services are being launched with the cooperation of RLG-RLIN.

The National Agricultural Library (NAL) agreed to the creation of a board for its Agricultural Libraries Information Network. Land-grant university library directors elected the first board in mid-1988. NAL and 42 land-grant libraries have entered into a cooperative project to test a new method of capturing full-text and images in a digital format for publication on CD-ROM laser disks. The project will evaluate a turnkey scanning system to determine whether it is now possible to provide in-depth access to the literature of agriculture while at the same time preserving it from rapid deterioration.

The National Library of Medicine (NLM) Regional Medical Library (RML) Network, now in its 21st year, has begun a program to register members formally. This will give NLM and the RMLs a more accurate picture of the network. By the end of 1988, the RML network expects to complete a follow-up to the 1984 interlibrary loan (ILL) cost study that was used as the basis for setting the current national maximum charge of $8.00 for filling an ILL request. The 1988 study will determine the current average cost of an ILL.

National Utilities/Networks. FLICC/FEDLINK members and participants' service dollars for riding network contracts approximately doubled in comparison with the $50,000,000 expended in 1987. This reflects the network's ongoing success brokering services for the federal sector.

OCLC continues to grow and expand its services. There are more than 9,400 participating libraries, 8,481 dedicated terminals/workstations online, 22,000,000 records online, 300,000,000 location listings, and 3,800,000 ILL transactions. At year's end OCLC acquired the rights to the Dewey Decimal Classification and the assets of its publisher, Forest Press. More than 200,000 libraries in 135 countries use DDC, the world's most widely used classification system for library materials.

WLN in 1988 was working toward a major change in its governance structure in order to increase its operational flexibility and broaden the scope of participation on its governing board. WLN is seeking legislation allowing it to be reformed as a private, nonprofit corporation.

States. The central networking source in all states is resource sharing through ILL. The three necessary stages are identification of the resource, location, hopefully in the immediate area or within the state, and timely delivery. The U.S. Mail and UPS are still the mainstays, but some states use courier services between libraries in geographic proximity. During 1988, more states were utilizing telefacsimile both to transmit requests and in a limited way, to transmit textual material.

A second major network service provided at the state level is reference and research. States like Arizona, Connecticut, Illinois, and New York based their state networks on designated centers for supporting both ILL and reference and research services. Some states, such as North Carolina, Florida, and Georgia utilize OCLC as the basis of their bibliographic and resource sharing network.

The development of multitype systems/networks continues to be the major goal of states as they move toward full participation in resource sharing by all types of libraries. By the end of 1988, Illinois completed conversion of 16 of its 18 systems from single type to multitype. In September 1988, California sponsored four statewide conferences followed by a retreat in October with the goal of defining the parameters of network development and a strategy for developing the statewide planning process and resolution of network issues by the entire library community. Florida has two multitype library consortia and anticipates that the majority of the state will be served by multitype consortia within the next five years. Oregon has six systems funded basically from local sources.

A multitype library study completed for New York does not recommend developing multitype systems/networks. It suggests that the current structure of systems and 3Rs continue and that closer cooperation and planning of services will serve in place of multitype networking.

Conversion of records continues at a rapid pace in Florida for public institutions and in Indiana and Kentucky for private institutions. COM catalogs are now used in Delaware and Kentucky. Connecticut and Maine are providing CD-ROM catalogs.

At the end of the year, it is again clear the leadership role of state library agencies with access to and use of LSCA Title I and III funds and state funding in support of systems and networks is paramount. Statewide multitype network development in the various states is at various stages: statewide in Illinois and New Jersey, for example, and limited in Colorado, Connecticut, Florida, Kentucky, Minnesota, and Oregon. Most of the other states are in the study or early developmental phase.

With all the major bibliographic conversion projects to machine-readable records by academic and public libraries, the increasing development of online public access catalogs and online union catalogs and the constantly changing and improving technology like CD-ROM, the outlook for networking at the state and national level in 1989 is bright.

ALPHONSE F. TREZZA

Notables

This article lists notable books for general readers; notable books, recordings, films, filmstrips and videos for children; and notable books, films, and videos for young adults. (See also articles on *Young Adult Literature, Children's Literature,* and *Film and Video, Children's* in this volume.)

The 1988 Notable Books list was compiled by the Notable Books Council of the Reference and Adult Services Division, American Library Association. The titles were selected for general appeal and literary merit as well as for their significant contribution to the expansion of knowledge and the pleasure they can provide to adult readers.

The members of the Notable Books Council for 1988 were William Gargan, Chair, Brooklyn College Library (Brooklyn, New York); Kay Ann Cassell, New York Public Library; Mary H. Daniel, Christopher Newport College (Newport News, Virginia); Suzanne E. Druehl, Central Arkansas Library System (Little Rock, Arkansas); Jack Forman, Mesa College Library (San Diego, California); Michele M. Leber, Fairfax County (Virginia) Public Library; Abby Schor, Evanston (Illinois) Public Library; Marilyn Shackelford, Tulsa (Oklahoma) City–County Library System; Beth Sibley, Moffett Library, University of California at Berkeley; Phyllis Z. Singer, Bayside (New York) High School; Marilyn Souders, *Newsweek* Library (New York); and Bill Ott, *Booklist,* consultant.

Notable Books of 1988
Fiction

Allende, Isabel. *Eva Luna.* Translated from the Spanish by Margaret Sayers Reden. Knopf.

Carver, Raymond. *Where I'm Calling From: New and Selected Stories.* Atlantic Monthly Press.

Delillo, Don. *Libra.* Knopf.

Dexter, Pete. *Paris Trout.* Random.

Dubus, Andre. *Selected Stories.* David Godine.

Erdrich, Louise. *Tracks.* Holt.

Garcia Marquez, Gabriel. *Love in the Time of Cholera.* Translated from the Spanish by Edith Grossman. Knopf.

Greenberg, Joanne. *Of Such Small Differences.* Holt.

Lessing, Doris. *The Fifth Child.* Knopf.

Mukherjee, Bharati. *The Middleman and Other Stories.* Grove.

Naylor, Gloria. *Mama Day.* Ticknor & Fields.

Powers, J.F. *Wheat That Springeth Green.* Knopf.

Sexton, Linda Gray. *Points of Light.* Little, Brown.

Smith, Lee. *Fair and Tender Ladies.* Putnam.

Spark, Muriel. *A Far Cry from Kensington.* Houghton.

Tyler, Anne. *Breathing Lessons.* Knopf.

Nonfiction

Berton, Pierre. *The Arctic Grail: The Quest for the Northwest Passage and the North Pole, 1818-1909.* Viking.

Cagin, Seth, and Philip Dray. *We Are Not Afraid: The Murder of Goodman, Schwerner, and Chaney and the Civil Rights Campaign for Mississippi.* Macmillan.

Ellmann, Richard. *Oscar Wilde.* Knopf.

Gay, Peter. *Freud: A Life for Our Time.* Norton.

Goodwin, Richard N. *Remembering America: A Voice from the Sixties.* Little, Brown.

Hansen, Eric. *Stranger in the Forest: On Foot across Borneo.* Houghton.

Lester, Julius. *Lovesong: Becoming a Jew.* Holt.

Maddox, Brenda. *Nora: The Real Life of Molly Bloom.* Houghton.

McPherson, James M. *Battle Cry of Freedom: The Civil War Era.* Oxford.

Pagels, Elaine. *Adam, Eve, and the Serpent.* Random.

Sharansky, Natan. *Fear No Evil.* Translated by Stefani Hoffmann. Random.

Notable Children's Books of 1988

Notable Children's Books of 1988 were selected by the Notable Children's Books Committee of the Association for Library Service to Children, American Library Association.

The list is composed of children's books published in the United States during 1988 that are of especially commendable quality and outstanding literary merit and that reflect children's interests in exemplary ways. The list includes books of various genres for children of all ages.

Members of the 1988 committee were Grace W. Ruth, Chair, San Francisco (California) Public Library; Patricia A. Bakula, Shunk Library (Menomonee Falls, Wisconsin); Christine Behrmann, (New York City); Therese G. Bigelow, Hampton (Virginia) Public Library; Joanna R. Long (Madison, New Jersey); Carole J. McCollough (Southfield, Michigan); Alice P. Naylor, Appalachian State University (Boone, North Carolina); Debra E. J. Robertson (Pittsburgh, Pennsylvania); Zena Sutherland, University of Chicago.

Ackerman, Karen. *Song and Dance Man.* Illustrated by Stephen Gammell. Knopf.

Agee, Jon. *The Incredible Painting of Felix Clousseau.* Farrar, Strauss, & Giroux.

Alcock, Vivien. *The Monster Garden.* Delacorte.

Arnosky, Jim. *Sketching Outdoors in Winter.* Lothrop, Lee & Shepard.

Ashabrenner, Brent. *Always to Remember: The Story of the Vietnam Veterans Memorial.* Dodd, Mead.

Barton, Byron. *I Want to Be an Astronaut.* Crowell.

Bawden, Nina. *Henry.* Illustrated by Joyce Powzyk. Lothrop, Lee & Shepard.

Berry, James. *A Thief in the Village and Other Stories.* Orchard.

Bjork, Christina. *Linnea's Windowsill Garden.* Translated by Joan Sandin. Illustrated by Lena Anderson. R & S Books/Farrar, Strauss, & Giroux.

Booth, Jerry. *The Big Beast Book.* Illustrated by Martha Weston. Little, Brown.

Cleary, Beverly. *A Girl from Yamhill: A Memoir.* Morrow.

Colman, Warren. *Understanding and Preventing AIDS.* Children's Press.

de Regniers, Beatrice Schenk and others, eds. *Sing a Song of Popcorn: Every Child's Book of Poems.* Illustrated by Marcia Brown and eight other Caldecott Medalists. Scholastic.

Dickinson, Peter. *Merlin Dreams.* Illustrated by Alan Lee. Delacorte.

Ellis, Sarah. *A Family Project.* McElderry.

Fleischman, Paul. *Joyful Noise: Poems for Two Voices.* Illustrated by Eric Bellows. Harper & Row.

Fox, Paula. *The Village by the Sea.* Orchard.

Freedman, Russell. *Buffalo Hunt.* Holiday.

Fritz, Jean. *China's Long March.* Putnam.

Giblin, James Cross. *Let There Be Light: A Book about Windows.* Crowell.

Goble, Paul. *Iktomi and the Boulder: A Plains Indian Story.* Orchard.

Greenfield, Eloise. *Grandpa's Face.* Illustrated by Floyd Cooper. Philomel.

———. *Under the Sunday Tree.* Paintings by Mr. Amos Ferguson. Harper & Row.

Haldane, Suzanne. *Painting Faces.* Dutton.

Hamilton, Virginia. *Anthony Burns.* Knopf.

———. *In the Beginning: Creation Stories from around the World.* Illustrated by Barry Moser. Harcourt Brace Jovanovich.

Hansen, Joyce. *Out from this Place.* Walker.

Hartling, Peter. *Crutches.* Translated by Elizabeth D. Crawford. Lothrop, Lee & Shepard.

Henkes, Kevin. *Chester's Way.* Greenwillow.

Hughes, Shirley. *Out and About.* Lothrop, Lee & Shepard.

Jones, Diana Wynne. *The Lives of Christopher Chant.* Greenwillow.

Larrick, Nancy, compiler. *Cats Are Cats.* Illustrated by Ed Young. Philomel.

Lester, Julius. *More Tales of Uncle Remus: Further Adventures of Brer Rabbit, His Friends, Enemies and Others.* Illustrated by Jerry Pinkney. Dial.

Little, Jean. *Little by Little: A Writer's Education.* Viking Kestral.

Loh, Morag. *Tucking Mommy In.* Illustrated by Donna Rawlins. Orchard.

Macaulay, David. *The Way Things Work.* Houghton.

MacLachlan, Patricia. *The Facts and Fictions of Minna Pratt.* Harper & Row.

Marshall, James, adapter. *Goldilocks and the Three Bears.* Dial.

McKinley, Robin. *The Outlaws of Sherwood.* Greenwillow.

McKissack, Patricia. *Mirandy and Brother Wind.* Illustrated by Jerry Pinkney. Knopf.

Meltzer, Milton. *Benjamin Franklin: The New American.* Watts.

———. *Rescue: The Story of How Gentiles Saved Jews in the Holocaust.* Harper & Row.

Morrison, Lillian, selector. *Rhythm Road: Poems to Move To.* Lothrop, Lee & Shepard.

Myers, Walter Dean. *Me, Mop, and the Moondance Kid.* Delacorte.

———. *Scorpions.* Harper & Row.

The Nativity. Illustrated by Julie Vivas. Harcourt Brace Jovanovich.

Opie, Iona and Peter Opie, eds. *Tail Feathers from Mother Goose.* Little, Brown.

Owens, Mary Beth. *A Caribou Alphabet.* Dog Ear Press.

Parker, Steve. *Skeleton.* Knopf.

Rogasky, Barbara. *Smoke and Ashes: The Story of the Holocaust.* Holiday.

Roth-Hano, Renee. *Touch Wood: A Girlhood in Occupied France.* Four Winds.

Sattler, Helen R. *Hominids: A Look Back at Our Ancestors.* Illustrated by Christopher Santoro. Lothrop, Lee & Shepard.

Schwartz, Amy. *Annabelle Swift, Kindergartner.* Orchard.

Scott, Elaine. *Ramona: Behind the Scenes of a Television Show.* Morrow.

Snyder, Dianne, adapter. *The Boy of the Three-Year Nap.* Illustrated by Allen Say. Houghton.

Steig, William. *Spinky Sulks.* Farrar, Strauss, & Giroux.

Thiele, Colin. *Farmer Schulz's Ducks.* Harper & Row.

———. *Shadow Shark.* Harper.

Thomas, Jane Resh. *Saying Goodbye to Grandma.* Illustrated by Marcia Sewell. Clarion.

Trezise, Percy and Dick Roughsey. *Turramulli the Giant Quinkin.* Gareth Stevens.

White, Ruth. *Sweet Creek Holler.* Farrar, Strauss, & Giroux.

Wiesner, David. *Free Fall.* Lothrop, Lee & Shepard.

Williams, Vera B. *Stringbean's Trip to the Shining Sea.* Illustrated by Vera B. and Jennifer Williams. Greenwillow.

Yorinks, Arthur. *Company's Coming.* Illustrated by David Small. Crown.

Notables

Notable Children's Recordings of 1988

The 1988 Notable Children's Recordings were selected by the Recording Evaluation Committee of the Association for Library Service to Children, a division of the American Library Association. The annual list covers children's recordings released in the United States during 1988.

Members of the 1988 Recording Evaluation Committee were Sarah McCarville, Chair, Oshkosh (Wisconsin) Public Library; Kristi Thomas Beavin, Arlington County (Virginia) Public Library; Mary Ann Brown, Mangum Primary School (Bahama, North Carolina); Gretchen Furber, King County Library System (Bellevue, Washington); Marcia Hupp (Mamaroneck, New York); Grace O'Connor (Chicago, Illinois); Patricia Patrick, Albany (New York) Public Library; Karen Stanley (Galveston, Texas); and Lila Wisotzki, Baltimore County (Maryland) Public Library.

A Chair for My Mother. Mulberry Books/William Morrow.
A Child's Gift of Lullabyes. J. Aaron Brown & Associates.
Daddy-Long-Legs. Audio Book Contractors.
Family Tree. Sundance Music, Inc. Distributed by A & M Records.
Flying Africans. Earwig Music.
Free to Be a Family. A & M Records.
Happy Birthday. Elephant Records. Distributed by A & M Records.
I Wish I Was a Dinosaur. Silo/Alcazar Records.
Jerusalem Shining Still. Caedmon.
Joseph the Tailor and Other Jewish Tales. Syd Lieberman.
Mail Myself to You. Rounder.
Mr. Bach Comes to Call. Classical Kids.
Mufaro's Beautiful Daughters. Weston Woods.
Owl Moon. Weston Woods.
Pecos Bill. Windham Hill.
Peter Ustinov Reads the Orchestra. Mark Rubin Productions. Distributed by Silo/Alcazar, Inc.
The Sandman: Lullabies and Night Time Songs. Marlboro Records.
The Secret Garden. Spoken Arts, Inc.
Shake Sugaree. Music for Little People.
Star Dreamer. Alacasam! Records.
The Tale of Tom Kitten. Spoken Arts, Inc.
The Titanic: Lost and Found. Random.
Treasure Island. Cover to Cover Cassettes.

Notable Children's Films and Videos of 1988

The 1988 Notable Children's Films and Videos were selected by the Film and Video Evaluation Committee of the Association for Library Service to Children, a division of the American Library Association. The list is composed of children's films, videotapes and videodisc recordings available for use in homes and libraries and copyrighted or released during 1988. Among criteria used by the Film and Video Evaluation Committee are the effective use of the special techniques of the media and clear and appropriate use of visuals, voices, music, language and sound effects to create a unified artistic whole. Adaptations of materials originally produced in other mediums must remain true to, expand upon, or complement the original work in some way, in addition to meeting general criteria for excellence.

Members of the 1988 selection committee were Rita Hoffmann, Chair, Chicago (Illinois) Public Library; Mary Rinato Berman (Valley Cottage, New York); Marsha Huddleston, Chicago (Illinois) Public Library; Kelly Jennings, Tulsa (Oklahoma) City-County Library System; Marina Starr LaTronica (Berkeley, California); Kathie Meizner, Montgomery County (Maryland) Department of Public Libraries; Marilyn P. Phillips (University City, Missouri); Marion A. Sisson, Milwaukee (Wisconsin) Public Library; Julia M. Smith, Akron–Summit County (Ohio) Public Library; Kathryn Weisman, Glencoe (Illinois) Public Schools; Judy Zuckerman, New York Public Library.

Abel's Island. Random House Home Video.
Banana, Banana...Banana Slugs! Bullfrog Films.
A Child's Christmas in Wales. Beacon/Journal Films.
Concerto Grosso Modo. Pyramid Film & Video.
Frog and Toad Together. Churchill Films.
In the Night Kitchen. Weston Woods.
Luxo Jr. Direct Cinema.
Ramona Series: *Ramona's Bad Day; The Great Hair Argument; New Pajamas; Squeakerfoot; Mystery Meal; Ramona the Patient; Rainy Sunday; Goodbye, Hello; The Perfect Day;* and *Siblingitis.* Churchill Films.
Red's Dream. Direct Cinema.
Runaway Ralph. Churchill Films.
Soldier Jack. Davenport Films.

Notable Children's Filmstrips of 1988

The 1988 Notable Children's Filmstrips were chosen by the Filmstrip Evaluation Committee of the Association for Library Service to Children, a division of the American Library Association. The list presents notable filmstrips (with cassettes) for young people through age 14. Included are filmstrips of especially commendable quality that reflect respect for a child's intelligence and imagination, exhibit venturesome creativity, and, in exemplary ways, reflect and encourage a child's interest. In making selections, the committee considered aesthetic and technical aspects, including the effective use of visuals, voices, music, language, and sound effects that together create a unified whole. If adaptations, the filmstrips must remain true to, expand upon, or complement the original work while meeting the general criteria for excellence.

Committee members for 1988 were Jane Kuntsler, Chair, New York Public Library; Ione S. Cowen, Akron–Summit County (Ohio) Public Library; Dorothy J. Evans (Chicago, Illinois); Carole Fiore (Dunedin, Florida); Ellen Loughran, Brooklyn (New York City) Public Library;

Frances J. McCurdy, Pittsburg (Kansas) Public Library; Shelley G. McNamara, University of Maine (Farmington, Maine); Susan Reisner, Northbrook (Illinois) Public Library; Nancy Seiner (Pittsburgh, Pennsylvania); Civia M. Tuteur, Chicago (Illinois) Public Library; Barbara D. Widem, Montgomery County (Maryland) Department of Public Libraries.

Alphabatics. Random House/Miller Brody.
Arthur's Teacher Trouble. Random House/Miller Brody.
Hot Hippo. Weston Woods.
The Iran Contra Arms Affair. Random House.
Meet the Author: Betty Miles. Random House.
New Coat for Anna. Random House.
The Paper Crane. Random House/Miller Brody.
Rumpelstiltskin. Random House/Miller Brody.
The Seal Mother. Random House.
Selkie Girl. Random House.
Teeny Tiny. Listening Library.
The Village of Round and Square Houses. Weston Woods.
Town Mouse and Country Mouse. Weston Woods.
The World of Crabs. Clearvue, Inc.

Films and Videos for Young Adults 1988

The 1988 Films and Videos for Young Adults were chosen by the Selected Films and Videos for Young Adults Committee of the Young Adult Services Division, American Library Association. The films and videos were selected from titles released in the United States in 1987 and 1988 and suggested by school and public librarians and media specialists across the country. The titles were chosen on the basis of young adult appeal, technical quality, subject content, and potential utilization with young adult audiences.

The 1988 committee included Catherine Charvat, Chair, Sherwood Regional Library (Fairfax County, Virginia); Hyonah Ahn, Chicago (Illinois) Public Library; Donna Barkman, Columbia University (New York City); Juanita Foster, Hennepin County (Minnesota) Library; Paulette Goodman, School District #102 (LaGrange Park, Illinois); Ralph Huntzinger, King County Library System (Seattle, Washington); Jo Ann Kingston, Flint (Michigan) Public Library; and Irene Wood, *Booklist*, consultant.

AIDS-Wise, No Lies. New Day.
Cat Who Drank and Used Too Much. FMS Productions.
Confessions of a Read-a-holic. Pyramid.
The Day They Came to Arrest the Book. Filmfair.
Five Out of Five. Women Make Movies.
Gullah Tales: The Fight. Direct Cinema.
The Man Who Planted Trees. Direct Cinema.
Martin Luther King, Jr.: Letter from Birmingham Jail. Coronet/MTI.
Not Just Any Flower. Phoenix.
Quitter. Pyramid.
Red's Dream. Direct Cinema.
Shoeshine. Direct Cinema.
Snookles. Pyramid.
Soldier Jack. Film Ideas.
'Til Death Do Us Part. New Day.
Tin Toy. Direct Cinema.
Waltzing Matilda. AIMS Media.
Warm Reception in L.A.. Pyramid.

Best Books for Young Adults

The books on this list, all published between September 1987 and December 1988, were selected by the Best Books for Young Adults Committee of the Young Adult Services Division, American Library Association. The 1988 committee members were Eugene E. La Faille, Jr., Chair, Brunswick School (Greenwich, Connecticut); Catherine Clancy, Boston Public Library; Audrey Eaglen, Cuyahoga County (Ohio) Public Library; Matthew Kollasch, Fort Dodge (Iowa) Public Library; Marjorie Lewis, Scarsdale (New York) Junior High School; Barbara A. Lynn, Econo-Clad Books (Topeka, Kansas); Colleen Macklin, Milwaukee (Wisconsin) Public Library; Margaret H. Miller (Sherman Oaks, California); Hazel Moore, New Orleans City Schools; Carlos Najera, Houston (Texas) Public Library; Judy T. Nelson, Bellevue (Washington) Public Library; Donald B. Reynolds, Jr., Central Kansas Library System (Great Bend, Kansas); Sallie H. Roberts, College of Education, Ohio University (Athens, Ohio); Karlan Sick, New York Public Library; Rebecca S. Taylor, New Hanover County (North Carolina) Public Library; and Sally Estes, *Booklist*, consultant.

Ashabrenner, Brent. *Always to Remember: The Story of the Vietnam Veterans Memorial.* Dodd, Mead.
Bova, Ben. *Welcome to Moonbase.* Ballantine.
Brown, Rita Mae. *Starting from Scratch: A Different Kind of Writer's Manual.* Bantam.
Cable, Mary. *The Blizzard of '88.* Atheneum.
Cagin, Seth and Philip Dray. *We Are Not Afraid: The Murder of Goodman, Schwerner and Chaney and the Civil Rights Campaign for Mississippi.* Macmillan.
Cleary, Beverly. *A Girl from Yamhill: A Memoir.* Morrow.
Coman, Carolyn and Judy Dater. *Body and Soul: Ten American Women.* Hill.
Cormier, Robert. *Fade.* Delacorte.
Deaver, Julie Reece. *Say Goodnight, Gracie.* Harper & Row.
Edgerton, Clyde. *The Floatplane Notebooks.* Algonquin Books.
Feldbaum, Carl B. and Ronald J. Bee. *Looking the Tiger in the Eye.* Harper & Row.
Flanigan, Sara. *Alice.* St. Martin's.
Fleischman, Paul. *Joyful Noise: Poems for Two Voices.* Harper & Row.
Freedman, Russell. *Lincoln: A Photobiography.* Clarion.
Gelman, Rita Golden. *Inside Nicaragua: Young People's Dreams and Fears.* Watts.
Giddings, Robert. *The War Poets.* Crown.
Gordon, Jacquie. *Give Me One Wish: A True Story of Courage and Love.* Norton.
Greenberg, Joanne. *Of Such Small Differences.* Henry Holt.
Greene, Marilyn. *Finder.* Crown.
Hailey, Kendall. *The Day I Became an Autodidact.* Delacorte.
Hambly, Barbara. *Those Who Hunt the Night.* Ballantine.
Hamilton, Virginia. *Anthony Burns: The Defeat and Triumph of a Fugitive Slave.* Knopf.
_____. *In the Beginning: Creation Stories from Around the*

Obituaries

Haskins, James and Kathleen Benson. *The 60s Reader.* Viking Kestral.
Hillerman, Tony. *A Thief of Time.* Harper & Row.
Hinton, S.E. *Taming the Star Runner.* Delacorte.
Hoffman, Alice. *At Risk.* Putnam.
Hoover, H.M. *The Dawn Palace: The Story of Medea.* Dutton.
Hotze, Sollace. *A Circle Unbroken.* Clarion.
Janeczko, Paul, selector. *The Music of What Happens: Poems That Tell Stories.* Orchard.
Jens, Inge, editor. *At the Heart of the White Rose: Letters and Diaries of Hans and Sophie Scholl.* Harper & Row.
Kennedy, William P. *Toy Soldiers.* St. Martin's.
Kingsolver, Barbara. *The Bean Trees.* Harper & Row.
Knudson, R.R. and May Swenson, selectors. *American Sports Poems.* Orchard.
Koertge, Ron. *The Arizona Kid.* Little, Brown.
Komunyakaa, Yusef. *Dien Cai Dau.* Harper & Row.
Kozol, Jonathan. *Rachel and Her Children: Homeless Families in America.* Crown.
Langone, John. *AIDS: The Facts.* Little, Brown.
Lopes, Sal, editor. *The Wall: Images and Offerings from the Vietnam Veterans Memorial.* Collins. World. Harcourt Brace Jovanovich.
Mackay, Donald A. *The Building of Manhattan: How Manhattan Was Built Over Ground and Underground from the Dutch Settlers to the Skyscraper.* Harper & Row.
Madaras, Lynn. *Lynn Madaras Talks to Teens about AIDS: An Essential Guide for Parents, Teachers, and Young People.* Newmarket: Harper & Row.
Mahy, Margaret. *Memory.* McElderry.
Mazer, Norma Fox. *Silver.* Morrow.
McKinley, Robin. *The Outlaws of Sherwood.* Greenwillow.
Meltzer, Milton. *Rescue: The Story of How Gentiles Saved Jews in the Holocaust.* Harper & Row.
Mills, Judie. *John F. Kennedy.* Watts.
Morrison, Lillian, selector. *Rhythm Road: Poems to Move To.* Lothrop, Lee & Shepard.
Myers, Walter Dean. *Fallen Angels.* Scholastic.
———. *Scorpions.* Harper & Row.
Ngor, Haing. *Haing Ngor: A Cambodian Odyssey.* Macmillan.
Noonan, Michael. *McKenzie's Boots.* Orchard.
Paulsen, Gary. *The Island.* Orchard.
Pringle, Terry. *The Preacher's Boy.* Algonquin.
Pullman, Philip. *Shadow in the North.* Knopf.
Riddles, Libby and Tim Jones. *Race Across Alaska: First Woman to Win the Iditarod Tells Her Story.* Stackpole.
Rinaldi, Ann. *The Last Silk Dress.* Holiday.
Ritter, Lawrence S. *The Babe: A Life in Pictures.* Ticknor & Fields.
Rochman, Hazel, collector. *Somehow Tenderness Survives: Stories of Southern Africa.* Harper & Row.
Rogasky, Barbara. *Smoke and Ashes: The Story of the Holocaust.* Holiday.
Ruskin, Cindy. *The Quilt: Stories from the NAMES Project.* Pocket Books.
Rylant, Cynthia. *A Kindness.* Orchard.
Severin, Tim. *The Ulysses Voyage: Sea Search for the Odyssey.* Dutton.
Sleator, William. *The Duplicate.* Dutton.
Vare, Ethlie Ann and Greg Ptacek. *Mothers of Invention: From the Bra to the Bomb: Forgotten Women and Their Unforgettable Ideas.* Morrow.
Willeford, Charles. *I Was Looking for a Street.* Countryman.
Wolff, Virginia E. *Probably Still Nick Swansen.* Henry Holt.
Wyss, Thelma Hatch. *Here at the Scenic-Vu Motel.* Harper & Row.
Xiyang, Tang. *Living Treasures: An Odyssey Through China's Extraordinary Nature Reserves.* Bantam.

Obituaries

Paul Holm Brawley

BRAWLEY, PAUL HOLM (1942–1988)

Paul Holm Brawley, Editor of *Booklist*, ALA's review journal for public and school libraries, died on October 2, 1988. Before becoming *Booklist* Editor-in-Chief in 1973, he served as the magazine's first Nonprint Materials Editor (1969–73).

Born September 27, 1942, Brawley received a B.A. in English from Southern Illinois University in 1965 and an M.S. in L.S. from Simmons College in 1968. Before coming to *Booklist*, he worked as Recordings Librarian (1965–66) and Audiovisual Librarian (1966–68) at Boston Public Library.

During the Brawley years there were many changes in *Booklist*. Reviews became longer, more critical, more imaginative, more varied in tone, and much more timely. Innovations begun under his direction include printing of cataloging information with every review, use of free-lance subject specialists to complement staff reviewers, publication of special bibliographies and columns, introduction of the "Upfront" section devoted to reviews of high-demand adult books, and publication of the annual Editors' Choice lists. More recently, Brawley was instrumental in overseeing the magazine's transition to an in-house automated prepress system. He also saw *Booklist* develop into one of ALA's leading sources of revenue.

It was perhaps in the design of the magazine that Brawley made his most lasting impression. In 1974, he introduced four-color design, along with a new and attractive page design; since that time, *Booklist* covers—all of which he personally selected—have become the magazine's hallmark.

In addition to his *Booklist* responsibilities, Brawley served as guest lecturer in library science at Kent State University, Dalhousie University, Syracuse University, and the University of Washington.

CORY, JOHN MACKENZIE (1914–1988)

John Mackenzie Cory, seventh Director of the New York Public Library (NYPL), died suddenly on April 11 at the age of 74. At the time of his death, he was Director Emeritus of NYPL. Cory's career at the Library spanned 27 years and covered all facets of Library endeavor. As Director NYPL from 1970–78, he was responsible for administering the operations, collections, and services of the entire system. Before 1970, John Cory was Deputy Director of the institution for seven years, and Chief of its Branch Libraries for 12 years.

Prior to joining NYPL, he was the Executive Director of the American Library Association (1948–51, Associate Librarian at the University of California at Berkeley (1945–48), a Senior Public Librarian Specialist at the U.S. Office of Education (1942–43), and Director of Libraries at the University of Alabama at Tuscaloosa (1940–42).

John Cory's contributions to librarianship were far-reaching. He was an Adjunct Professor of library administration at Columbia University for more than 30 years. Between 1966 and 1970, he serves as Executive Director of METRO (New York Metropolitan Reference and Research Library Agency, a cooperative agency with research library service in New York City and surrounding areas). In 1956 he was

Obituaries

President of the New York Library Association. Cory was a frequent contributor to professional library periodicals.

Between 1984 and 1988, he was a part-time consultant with Gossage Regan Associates, Inc., a library personnel services and consulting firm. Before his death, Cory assisted Boards of Trustees in public library systems in nationwide searches for new directors.

Born January 13, 1914, in Asheville, North Carolina, he was a 1936 graduate of the University of California at Berkeley with a B.A. in history. In 1937 he received a Certificate in Librarianship from the same institution, and he received a law degree from Hastings College of Law (Hastings, Nebraska) in 1934.

The New York Public Library Newsletter retirement tribute to Cory observed, "No task has been too large or small to attract his full attention. His tenure as Director has covered a crucial period of the Library's development. John Cory's flexibility and imagination have helped steady the institution through rough times of financial restriction . . . .We salute his range of knowledge, his integrity, his loyalty, his stick-to-it-iveness. We particularly salute his encyclopedic grasp of the library world, his vision and sense of theory about his profession."

DEMPSEY, FRANK J.
(1926–1988)

Frank J. Dempsey, library administrator and library public relations consultant, died September 11 just months after his retirement in April from the Arlington Heights Memorial Library, Arlington Heights, Illinois.

Dempsey had been Executive Librarian at Arlington Heights for 15 years. He was Reference Librarian at New Public Library (New Jersey) from 1953 to 1955 and Head Librarian, Oakland Naval Supply Center, from 1955 to 1957. He became Assistant Director in 1957 and Director between 1962 and 1972 of the Berkeley (California) Public Library before moving to the Midwest.

A native of San Francisco, Dempsey received a 1950 B.A. in history and education and a 1953 M.L.S. from the University of California, Berkeley, after serving on active duty in the U.S. Navy. Dempsey was Chair, Public Relations Section, Library Administration and Management Association of ALA and Chair of the Regional Library Advisory Council of the North Suburban (Illinois) Library System. He had been President of the Illinois Library Association and co-chaired the local arrangements group for the 1985 annual ALA meeting in Chicago. Dempsey was also a past President of the Chicago Library Club and of the Pro Musica organization in Arlington Heights. He founded Suburban Libraries United for United Planning, a group of nine neighboring libraries that won grants for literacy activities, Night Owl after-hours reference service, and special services for the Spanish-speaking. From this group grew the Library Cable Network Consortium, a pioneer in cable television for libraries.

At Arlington Heights, Dempsey managed a 1978 building program that doubled the size of the library from 30,000 to 60,000 square feet. In 1976 this library was one of the first to install a CLSI computerized checkout system. A new Community Services Department that included a bookmobile that brought a multiphased outreach program to the community was established. Dempsey also helped revitalize the Friends of the Library until in 1988 there were 1,000 members, who had contributed more than $100,000 in gifts to the Arlington Heights library.

Frank J. Dempsey was an avid reader; he wrote numerous book reviews, a monthly column, "Executive Desk," for Arlington's monthly *Readout*; he spoke frequently at library and civic meetings; and he wrote a chapter in *The Library in the Political Process* (Oryx).

On his retirement, Dempsey said, "Because I am public relations minded, I felt it was important to inform the community of the many services available to them. Tied in directly with this is the fact that our circulation has increased dramatically—from 860,000 to 1,369,000 since 1973, up 84 percent. Arlington Heights has been rated as one of 50 outstanding libraries in the U.S."

After his retirement in April 1988, Dempsey had worked as a library public relations consultant, working from his home in Chicago and from his vacation home in Barbados, West Indies.

EDWARDS, MARGARET ALEXANDER
(1902–1988)

Margaret Alexander Edwards, teacher, librarian, library educator, humanitarian and director of one of the most innovative and successful young adult programs in the history of public libraries, died on April 19 at the age of 85. Known to many as Alex, she was born October 23, 1902, in Childress, Texas. Margaret Alexander was reared in a home where books were not abundant, but where reading and learning were valued. She earned an A.B. degree from Trinity College in San Antonio, Texas, in 1922, where she studied to become an English teacher. After a few years of teaching in Texas high schools, she left for New York City where she received a Master's degree in Latin from Columbia University in 1928.

She became a Latin teacher at Towson High School in Baltimore County, Maryland, the following year. However, in 1932, Joseph L. Wheeler, renowned Director of the Enoch Pratt Free Library in Baltimore, Maryland, invited her to join the Enoch Pratt staff to establish a program for young adults. During her tenure at Pratt, she received her library degree from Columbia University (1940). She remained at Pratt for 30 years. Her influence on young people and the many librarians who trained and worked with her can never be measured adequately.

Her philosophy of work with young adults is beautifully and ofter entertainingly related in her book, *The Fair Garden and the Swarm of Beasts*, which was published in 1969. Dozens of librarians developed their theory of public service under her demanding yet exhilarating tutelage. She also reached hundreds of other librarians through her writing, speeches, workshops, and summer courses in library schools in Canada and in mose regions of the U.S.

Margaret Edwards retired in 1962 to live with her husband, Dr. Philip Edwards, on their farm in Harford County, Maryland. She became active in the League of Women Voters in her community; and she sought opportunities to assist young persons, especially through books and reading.

On May 22, many friends and colleagues gathered at Pratt Library for a memorial service for Margaret Alexander Edwards. At the conclusion of the service, Maryland Senator Julian Lapides, her attorney and close friend, announced that she had bequeathed her estate to three trustees who are to use the funds to further the personal reading of young adults. Margaret Edwards had expressed in her will that her worldly goods be used to experiment with ways of effectively promoting young adults reading and of inspiring young adult librarians to perfect themselves as readers' advisers.

LOWE, MILDRED
(1921–1988)

Mildred Lowe, well-known library educator and government docu-

John Mackenzie Cory

Frank J. Dempsey

Margaret Alexander Edwards

Mildred Lowe

Karl Nyren

ments expert, died in an automobile accident on August 22. A professor at St. John's University, Jamaica, New York, for 17 years, Mildred Lowe retired as Director of the Division of Library and Information Science in 1987. Her recent professional activities included recruiting new members to the library profession and lobbying for improved funding for libraries in New York State. She was a Councilor-at-Large of the New York Library Association, and she was active in METRO. At the Spring 1988 Long Island Library Conference she received the Librarian of the Year Award.

Mildred Lowe was born in New York City on April 4, 1927. She earned a B.A. in Sociology from Brooklyn College in 1960, an M.L.S. from Pratt Institute in 1965, and a Doctor of Library Science degree from Columbia University in 1972. Before coming to St. John's, she was the Government Serials Librarian at the State University of New York in Farmingdale between 1965 and 1968.

In honor of her memory, St. John's University has created The Dr. Mildred Lowe Memorial Scholarship Fund to benefit needy students of the Division of Library and Information Science at St. John's.

NYREN, KARL
(1921–1988)

Karl Nyren, former library administrator and editor since 1972 of R. R. Bowker's *Library Hotline*, died on August 13. He was internationally known as the feisty, honest editor of the most fiery newsletter on librarians and librarianship. Nyren came to Bowker in 1966 as a senior editor. Between 1960 and 1966, he had been Director, Cary Memorial Library, Lexington, Massachusetts; he was Director for a year of the Peabody Institute Library in Danvers, Massachusetts; and he began his library career in 1955 as Fine Arts Department Assistant, Boston Public Library.

Born November 25, 1921, in Boston, Karl Nyren received an A.B. in English in 1949 and an M.A. in English literature in 1950 from Boston University. He was a premier journalist whose motto was integrity.

Oral History Association

Annual Meeting. The theme of the 1988 Annual Meeting of the Oral History Association (OHA), held in Baltimore, Maryland, October 13–16, was "Community History, Multiculturality, and People of Color." The major speakers were: Bernice Johnson Reagon, director of the program in Black American Culture at the Smithsonian Institution, who spoke on "Oral Transmission and Information Technology; A Twentieth Century Union"; John Kuo Wei Tchen, whose presentation was titled "Oral History, Counter-Hegemony and the year 2000"; and Sidney Mintz, professor of Anthropology at Johns Hopkins University, who spoke on "History Within History: Memory and Enactment." Other panels and sessions explored oral history in multi-ethnic and multi-racial communities, ethics of interviewing, and the political dimensions of historical consciousness in the interview situation. A number of tours into Baltimore neighborhoods and to the Smithsonian in Washington D.C. were available to conferees, who numbered more than 375.

Publications. The Association has embarked on an ambitious publications program. *The Oral History Review*, edited by Michael Frisch, has been expanded to two issues a year, available with a membership in the organization. A pamphlet on oral history and the classroom written by Barry Lanman and George Mehaffy, will be available through the Association. Another pamphlet is being prepared on oral history and family history, and one on community history is under consideration. OHA continues to publish a quarterly association newsletter, Annual Report, and Membership Directory.

Major activities of the Association over the past year centered on three areas. The Association has moved to establish an endowment. To date almost $10,000 has been donated by members and friends, or contributed in the form of life memberships. Thomas Charleton of Baylor University heads the Endowment Committee. The Association has begun discussions with the Organization of American Historians, the American Historical Association and other concerned professional organizations, on the problems relating to the accumulation of oral history interview tapes in the hands of unaffiliated scholars. The goal of these discussions is preparation of a statement to encourage such scholars to make their tapes and interviews available through deposit arrangements with various collections. The statement would contain advice on legal rights, processing, and tape maintenance. The Association has formed a committee on multiculturality to encourage participation at all levels by people of color. The Committee is charged with advising all other OHA committees on various steps to take to make the organization more open to multicultural participation. Co-Chairpersons of the committee are Rena Benmayor of the Puerto Rican Studies Center at Hunter College in New York and Warren Nishimoto of the Oral History Program at the University of Hawaii at Manoa.

Committee Actions. The International Committee was most successful in devising programs to bring more international scholars to the Baltimore meeting. A grant from the Institute for International Education was used to underwrite the participation of several international graduate students. The State and Regional Committee, after meeting with the representatives of various state and regional oral history organizations, has recommended that the committee structure be so amended that seats on the committee be reserved for representatives of the various local organizations.

The Publications Committee also has embarked on an ambitious plan to solicit advertising for all OHA publications. Margot Knight of

---

ORAL HISTORY ASSOCIATION

PRESIDENT (October 1988–October 1989):
Ronald E. Marcello, University of North Texas

PRESIDENT-ELECT:
Lila Johnson Goff, Minnesota Historical Society, St. Paul, Minnesota

EXECUTIVE SECRETARY:
Richard C. Smith, Oral History Program, University of California, Los Angeles

Headquarters: 1093 Broxton Avenue, #720, Los Angeles, California 90024

Washington, D.C., is the new advertising representative. The Site Selection Committee has selected the following locations for forthcoming meetings: 1989, Galveston, Texas; 1990, Cambridge, Massachusetts; 1991, Salt Lake City, Utah; 1992, Cleveland, Ohio.

Information on these sites and on all OHA activities can be obtained from the Executive Secretary, Richard C. Smith, Oral History Program, University of California, Los Angeles, 90024.

RONALD J. GRELE

Pacific Northwest Library Association

Annual Conference. The 1988 annual conference was held in Juneau, Alaska, August 10–13. The conference theme was "Forging the Future; Preserving the Past" and featured Lynn Johnston, noted cartoonist of "For Better or Worse," as keynote speaker. Attendance was good at the three pre-conference and 20 conference presentations. For the second year in a row, the Management Interest Group sponsored a pre-conference workshop by Susan and Peter Glaser of Glaser and Associates, Eugene, Oregon. This Year's topic was "Team Building and Team Management" and was enthusiastically received. Other highlights included presentations by Marilyn Jones, University of California, Berkeley, "Disaster Preparedness"; Henry Bates, "Local Cooperative Collecting Agreements"; Linda Wallace and Patricia Scarry, ALA, "Marketing for Small Libraries"; Bridget Lamont, Illinois State Library, "The Right Stuff—Do We Have It?"; and Spencer Shaw, Professor Emeritus of the University of Washington, GSLIS, "The Best of Oral Tradition—In Touch With Today."

The membership passed two resolutions at the general meeting, one urging publishers to use permanent paper in publishing materials of enduring value, the other urging libraries to oppose spiraling serial subscription rates by every means possible. Plans are well underway for the August 16–19, 1989, conference in Coeur d'Alene, Idaho, and the August 1990 conference in Portland, Oregon. The 1989 theme is "One Person Can Make a Difference."

Interest Groups. In 1985, PNLA restructured the organization around interest groups. While it has been a challenge to effectively integrate these interest groups into the life of the association, they have found a valuable place in conference programming. At the Juneau conference, seven interest groups proposed and planned 13 of the 20 sessions and one sponsored a pre-conference. Several interest groups completed special projects during 1988. The Academic interest group (Rosemary Ross, Chair) published and distributed the biennial *Library Statistics of Colleges and Universities in the Pacific Northwest*. The Intellectual Freedom Interest Group (June Pinnell-Stephens, Chair) completed the *PNLA Intellectual Freedom Handbook* under the direction of Mary Lauderbach.

Committees. PNLA's structure also includes four standing committees: Bibliography, Continuing Education, Nominations, and Young Readers' Choice Award. The Young Readers' Choice Award formed in 1940, is notable for the fact that children in grades 4 through 8 elect the annual award winner. The committee selects the nominees from authors who published children's books three years earlier. This year's winner was Barth Clements, author of *Sixth Grade Can Really Kill You*. She received her silver medal at the YRCA luncheon in Juneau and spoke about how and why she writes.

The Bibliography Committee compiled the "PNLA Checklist of Books and Pamphlets Relating to the Pacific Northwest," its 30th Checklist, which appeared in the summer issue 1988 of the *PNLA Quarterly*. The Continuing Education Committee sponsored a pre-conference "Workshop on Workshops," presented by Judith Frey, Continuing Library Education coordinator for the University of Washington GSLIS.

Other Activities. The President's Distinguished Service Award, inaugurated in 1987 by Peggy Forcier to honor individuals who have given exceptional and long-standing service to PNLA, was awarded to Anna Green in 1988. Green, Director of the Portneuf District Library, has served as PNLA's Conference Exhibits Chair for the past ten years.

The PNLA Quarterly completed its 52nd year of publication and remains the lifeblood of information for Pacific Northwest librarians. In 1988, issues focused on library construction and disaster planning. Fearless editor Kappy Eaton appears to have finally subdued the U.S. Postal Service's regulations for second class mailing permits.

GEORGE V. SMITH

PACIFIC NORTHWEST LIBRARY ASSOCIATION

PRESIDENT (October 1988–September 1989):
George Smith, Alaska State Library, Juneau, 99801

FIRST VICE-PRESIDENT/PRESIDENT-ELECT:
Carol Hildebrand, Eugene Public Library, Oregon

SECOND VICE-PRESIDENT:
Ann Joslin, Idaho State Library, Boise, 83702

SECRETARY:
Jane Pinnell-Stephens, Fairbanks North Star Public Library, Alaska

TREASURER:
Adrien Taylor, Boise State University Library, Boise, Idaho 83705

Membership (September 1988): 852

Personnel and Employment: Compensation and Pay Equity

Beginning level salaries. *Library Journal*'s 1987 survey of placements and salaries for graduates of ALA–accredited library school program revealed an average beginning level salary of $22,247. This figure represents a 7 percent increase over 1986's average beginning level salary of $20,874 and is the largest increase since 1981. For new library school graduates with relevant prior experience, the 1987 average beginning salary was $24,018, an increase above the 1986 figure of $21,971. For the fifth continuing year

Personnel and Employment: Compensation and Pay Equity

the increase in the average beginning level salary was higher than the year's cost of living increase.

The average beginning salary for women was $22,045, a 6 percent increase from 1986. For men, the average beginning salary was $23,013, a 7 percent increase. Only in the survey category "Special Libraries" do women receive a higher average salary.

The median, or middle figure in a list of all salaries reported, was $21,116 for all graduates; $21,000 for women, and $22,000 for men. The lowest beginning level salary reported was $9,500 for a position in a public library; the highest $72,000 in the category "Other" (excluding public, school, college and university, and special libraries). Of the 60 eligible library schools, 55 responded to the survey, LJ's 37th annual report.

Academic Libraries. Preliminary data from the 1988 Association of Research Libraries *ARL Annual Salary Survey* cited beginning professional salaries ranging from $17,288 to $27,606. Median professional salaries for 1988/89 ranged from $23,506 to $47,315. For ARL libraries reporting a director's salary, the combined average was $79,807; for men $80,456; for women $78,146. Department heads average salaries in ARL libraries ranged from $33,517 for Head of Circulation to $44,259 for Head, Computer Applications.

The College and University Personnel Association provides salary data for academic librarians in its annual *Administrative Compensation Survey*. The 1987–88 survey includes the responses of 1564 higher education institutions. For all universities, the median salary for Director of Library Services was $52,044; for all four-year colleges the median was $32,370; for all two-year colleges responding, the median director's salary was $35,000. The CUPA survey also reports salary figures for five "senior positions" in academic libraries. For all universities, the median salary for Circulation Librarian was $27,500; for Acquisitions Librarian $30,570; for Technical Services Librarian $33,117; for Public Services Librarian $36,384; and for Reference Librarian, $29,800.

Public Libraries. The *ALA Survey of Librarian Salaries 1988* reports an all-region median salary of $47,184 for Director of a large public library serving a population of 100,000 or more. For a medium-sized public library serving a population of 25,000 to 99,999 the all-region median Director's salary was $25,723. Reported salaries are highest in the West and Southwest and lowest in the Southeast. The all-region median salary reported for Department Heads or Branch Heads was $28,260 in large public libraries and $23,401 in medium-sized public libraries.

The *ALA Survey* also reports a median salary for a beginning librarian with no professional experience of $20,436 in large public libraries and $19,500 in small public libraries across all regions. For Children's and/or Young Adult Services Librarian, a median salary for all regions was reported as $22,962 for large public libraries and $20,541 for small public libraries.

The Memphis, Tennessee Public Library publishes an annual statistical report for southern public libraries with budgets of $700,000 or more. The report includes salary figures for beginning librarian, department head, assistant librarian, and librarian, as well as library clerk and paraprofessional staff. Salaries reported for department heads in 1988 ranged from $19,596 to $55,123; for librarian from $30,326 to $78,043.

School Libraries. The Educational Research Service publishes a three-part report of the *National Survey of Salaries and Wages in Public Schools*. The survey conducted in the fall of 1987 collected data on salaries paid from 979 public school systems throughout the U.S. The average salary paid school librarians in all geographic ar-

As Director of the Petersburg Public Library in Virginia, Wayne manages a half million dollar budget, oversees a staff of twenty-five and develops innovative library programs for over forty thousand people. If you want to get your hands on some big bucks, maybe you should get a Master's Degree in Library and Information Science, too.

THE FUTURE IS INFORMATION. TAKE CHARGE OF THE FUTURE.

For more information, write to "Library Careers", American Library Association, 50 E. Huron St., Chicago, IL 60611.

eas was $30,046. The Southeast region reported the lowest average salary of $26,472; the Far West reported the highest average salary of $35,671.

Special Libraries. The Special Libraries Association conducts an in-depth salary survey of its members every three years. The comprehensive 1988 survey had 4,089 respondents. The full results will appear as the *SLA Triennial Salary Survey 1989*. Preliminary data were reported in the fall 1988 issue of *Special Libraries*. For the overall U.S., median salary was $32,000 with an average low salary of $19,528 and an average high of $57,943.

Pay Equity. ALA's Pay Equity Committee continued its high level of activity by sponsoring U.S. Representative Lindy Boggs to speak on pay equity at the annual conference in New Orleans. An ALA publication, *Pay Equity: An Action Manual for Library Workers* by Carolyn Kenady, was completed. Helen Lewis, Vice-President of the Connecticut affiliate of the American Federation of Teachers reports successful pay equity negotiations for library employees at the University of Connecticut and the Connecticut State Library. Almost all library employees received significant equity pay increases. Connecticut law now mandates that all inequities between state job titles must be eliminated by 1990. Librarians in Colorado won pay equity settlements by comparing their salaries to those at peer institutions and to teaching faculty at their own institutions. Over $30,000 was added to the base salary pool for academic librarians in Denver and $27,000 to those at Colorado Springs. In Montgomery County, Maryland, librarians' classification was raised one to two pay grades, while library desk assistants were raised three pay grades. Farmington, Connecticut, added $100,000 to the 1988 library payroll in an effort to have library workers salaries in parity with other town employees within three years.

Trends. ALA Council passed a resolution on minimum salaries which calls for the publication of state minimum salaries in ALA publications and established a task force whose charge is to recommend ways by which ALA can support state initiatives to set minimum salaries. Sixteen state associations have set minimum salary levels, with Wisconsin setting the highest minimum level of $23,700. ALA Placement again reported fewer job seekers than positions at our Midwinter and Annual conferences. Graduates of library schools nationwide increased by only 200 individuals over last year's number, for a total of 3,702. The decline in the number of available librarians apparently is affecting salaries. Should this trend continue, pay equity for librarians may be an attainable goal.

PAUL M. GHERMAN
FRANCES O. PAINTER

Personnel and Employment: Continuing Education and Staff Development

In 1988 a nine-question survey was sent to 50 Chief officers of State Library Agencies regarding the status of Continuing Professional Education (CPE) in library and information science in their states. Thirty state librarians responded.

In reply to what the respondent considered the major trends in CPE in 1988, 30 percent listed improved coordination of efforts among providers; 26 percent said more use of distance learning methodologies; 20 percent indicated greater demand for automation courses in small and medium-sized libraries.

In reply to what the respondents viewed as the major issues in the field of CPE that should be faced and acted on by the profession, 17 percent wrote of appropriate recognition for participation in CPE; and 13 percent listed each of the following—more funding for CPE, improved CPE quality (especially at local levels), lack of advanced CPE opportunities for MLS degree holders, lack of CPE for non-professionals, and need for management CPE.

In answer to the third question of whether there was a state CPE plan, 33 percent indicated that they operated such a plan and 47 percent of those who said there was no state plan now indicated one was in the process of development (or redevelopment).

In response to what the state librarians thought the most effective delivery system for CPE, 80 percent listed workshops.

In answer to the question concerning distance learning systems, 37 percent said they were using some type of distance learning, chiefly teleconferencing; 58 percent of those not using distance learning modes were not planning to do so in 1989.

Wisconsin Educational Television Network (ETN) students participating in a teleconferencing class at the University of Wisconsin–Madison as part of their continuing education services training.

In response to the most effective ways of assuring quality of CPE opportunities, 47 percent suggested qualified leaders with training in adult education methodologies; 30 percent listed the use of only state-approved providers. Twenty percent said they used the ALA 1988 approved *Guidelines for Quality in Continuing Education for Information, Library and Media Personnel.*

In answer to the question on the demand for certain type of content in CPE, 67 percent indicated that the information in greatest demand today relates to automation; 27 percent cited the need for training in basic library skills; 23 percent listed personnel issued (especially human resource development).

In response to "What kind of effort and/or support by the following groups do you believe would be of greatest help in strengthening CPE in your state," 50 percent listed cooperation between associations and with the state library; 27 percent stated more cooperation was needed between schools, the associations, and the state agency. Other suggestions ranged from greater flexibility in scheduling CPE, to holding special events featuring CPE, to offering advanced courses for MLS degree holders. The chief suggestion for government agencies was more funding (30 percent); next was advocacy of CPE (17 percent); 47 percent of the respondents offered no suggestions for government agencies. Relative to library support, 30 percent listed promotion of CPE events, 20 percent said released time for CPE; ten other suggestions were mentioned from paying for staff to attend CPE, to opening in-house CPE events to all who might be interested and qualified to attend.

Turning to suggestions for corporations 30 percent suggested funding, including scholarships for CPE; 23 percent listed the sharing of their CPE programs with librarians at reduced charges. Relative to the public, the only help on which there was agreement was that 23 percent thought the public should be active in demanding trained professional librarians. Relative to the individual librarian, 33 percent listed personal involvement and commitment to participate in CPE opportunities; 13 percent stated that librarians should make their needs known to providers.

When asked about *CE Activities at the State Level,* 30% of the state librarians listed coordinated, long-range planning; and 27 percent listed various workshops. A wide array of activities were mentioned: literacy training for librarians and trustees; statewide database training on the new CD-ROM statewide database, followed by individual assistance as required; completion of plans for paraprofessional certification; encouraging non-MLS library employees to attend a week-long class at library school; holding one major CPE event per month; formal evaluation of the state's certification program for public librarians; and development of CPE study circles.

Graduate Library Education CE Programs. Perhaps the most telling sign of the lack of importance placed on CPE by the library schools is the statistic presented in the *1988 Library and Information Science Education Statistical Report* published by the Association for Library and Information Science Education (State College, PA: p. 252 ALISE,) which indicates that only 1 percent of the average income per school ($872,000) was spent on CPE—the lowest amount for any of the budget categories listed, of the 65 schools participating in the ALISE survey, only 49 (75 percent) schools reported any CPE activities.

On the positive side, the 1988 ALISE report indicates that 500 CPE activities were offered—20 more events than in the 1987 report with a 3,000 rise in attendees.

Professional Associations. The Special Libraries Association (SLA) reported three new CPE offerings: the executive Development Academy was developed as an intensive seven-day program to be conducted by Carnegie Mellon graduate school faculty starting in March 1989; SLA's first self-study program, "Time Management in the Small Library," is available on floppy disk for IBM and Apple Computers as well as in a manual workbook format; the Resume Referral Service is the newest addition to SLA's professional growth offerings—and the first of its kind in the library profession. Using a computer program to sort pertinent variables, the Service matches job applicants to available positions by salary, geographic preference, area of specialization and education. It is available to both SLA Members and non-members as well as all those who employ library/information professionals. Two regional programs offered in ten locations drew more than 600 participants. At the SLA Annual Conference in Denver 23 courses attracted more than 1,100 participants; at the 1988 Winter Conference, three courses, four workshops and a unit of the Middle Management Institute were offered. The 1988 State-of-the-Art Institute on "Global Ties Through Information" was co-sponsored by SLA and international library associations: the Japan Special Libraries Association, the Canadian Library Association, the Library Association (U.K.), Aslib, the Library Association of Australia, and IFLA.

On January 12, 1988, the ALA Council in a major action adopted "Guidelines for Quality in Continuing Education for Information, Library and Media Personnel." The Guidelines response to the profession's need since 1973 for quality assurance in continuing education. The *Guidelines* are an adaptation of the 1976–77 Program for Quality in Continuing Education for Information, Library, and Media Personnel developed, with funding from the U.S. Office of Education, by the Continuing Library Education Network and Exchange (CLENE).

In 1988, *CLENE* (Continuing Library Education Network and Exchange) Round Table issued a list of 163 noteworthy CPE offerings in 47 board categories as submitted by 26 state library agencies, 27 graduate library schools, and 11 library associations.

American Association of Law Libraries (AALL). AALL took a major step forward in 1988 when it hired its first professional continuing education staff member with the title Professional Development Officer and charged with providing administrative support its CPE programs. In 1988 AALL sponsored three summer institutes and four workshops.

Medical Library Association (MLA). The MLA Course Roster has a Foundations Series and a Dimensions of Current Practice Series. Courses in the Foundation Series stress basic skills and concepts for the entering health sciences librarian or the librarian who wishes a refresher course on the basics of a particular topic. Three Foundation courses are now available as self-study courses.

Canadian Library Association (CLA). CLA Seminars grow in popularity each year with 1988 attendance surpassing 1,000 participants at 18 sites across Canada. Topics included "Career Self-Management Strategies: Enhancing Career and Life Satisfaction," "Technology Update: Practical Systems for Today," and "AACR2: Practice and Practicality."

IFLA Continuing Professional Education Round Table (CPE RT). During the 1988 IFLA Conference in Sidney, Australia, the Round Table convened a professional paper meeting focusing on "Continuing Education Quality Assurance"; a workshop with the theme "Distance Learning Techniques"; a planning meeting for the IFLA Paris Conference in August 1989 and the development of a proposal for an *IFLA Continuing Professional Education Guidebook*; participated in a workshop given by the Kuring-gai College of Advanced Education; made a presentation at the combined meeting of the Library Association of Australia Education for Librarianship Section and the Distance Education Special Interest Group; and participated in the IFLA all-conference Poster Session.

A major accomplishment of the year was the initiation of the *IFLA CPE NEWS Letter* which has a computerized mailing list of 500 people representing 61 nations. The chief special project was the sponsorship of a Continuing Professional Education Seminar in Martin, Czechoslovakia, in October, on the 10th Anniversary of the Center of Continuing Education for Slovak Librarians and the 125th anniversary of the Slovak National Library. It was recommended that similar seminars sponsored by the Round Table, be held regularly worldwide; that each country hold regular CPE conferences; that guidelines be developed for quality assurance in CPE; that each country designate a reporter for CPE activities; and recommendations relative to methodologies of CPE.

Finding. In 1988 more than $128,000 of Higher Education Act (HEA) Title II-B (Library Career Training Program) funds supported three training institutes.

Although the total amount of Library Services and Construction Act (LSCA) Title I (Public Library Services) and Title III (Interlibrary Cooperation and Resource Sharing) funds used for continuing education is not know, reports indicate that state library agencies, local public libraries, and library cooperatives provide a variety of CPE opportunities to support the purpose of LSCA. For example, the Delaware Division of Libraries held workshops on reference skills and business resources, and collection development. The Ohio State Library contracted with Case Western Reserve to provide a series of workshops designed to train their library staff in management, organizational development, and local area network assessment, focusing on managing in a union environment. In 1988 more than $461,000 in LSCA Title VI (Library Literacy Program) funds were used for 21 projects that trained librarians, tutors, and trainers.

ELIZABETH W. STONE

Preservation of Library Materials

To review the year in preservation is no longer a simple task. Libraries regard preservation as actions taken to retard or prevent deterioration or damage to library materials by controling the environment and/or by direct treatment. The increasing scope of media in most library collections presents great technical challenges to curators of collections. In major research libraries in particular, the greatest impetus for action continues to be the widespread and well-documented problem of brittle paper, in both the current immensity of the problem and the continued increase in each year's production of materials on acid stock. With progress from technical investigations, shared practical experience, newly-forged alliances, and the continued growth of awareness of the problem, it is difficult to summarize activities.

Technical Developments. Preservation administrators are constantly immersed in chemical study and evaluation projects as fumigation, deacidification, and mass treatment of library materials in both commercial and nonprofit institutions become priority considerations. Fumigants in the form of sulfuryl fluoride (trade name VIKANE) from Dow Chemical are being investigated by the Getty Conservation Center as a resource for insect eradication in library materials. Parylene, a product of Union Carbide, will be evaluated for its potential as a gas phase polymer technology specifically for strengthening brittle, bound materials; tests indicate that the process strengthens brittle or weakened cellulose materials, but future focus will be on increasing the scope of treatment to allow efficient widespread library applications. The U.S. Office of Technology Assessment (OTA) presented its report Book Preservation Technologies in May, examining the three leading deacidification processes currently available: DEZ (diethyl zinc), Wei T'o and the bookkeeper process. The report concluded that no one option was the ultimate solution and indicates that all three should continue to be explored, since each has unique weaknesses and strengths. As follow-up to the OTA report, the House Appropriations Committee review of Library of Congress (LC) operations agreed that for LC to contract out for deacidification services (both research/design and eventual operation of a facility) is appropriate, but that deacidification is not a sole source technology, and competition is appropriate for the final decision on the technology used at LC. LCs backing of research related to the DEZ process may be due to the slow development of the other processes. Even as the OTA report and legislative recommendation were making news, a new technology for deacidification based on ammonia and ethylene oxide was announced as a service offered by a commercial binder.

Different types of technological developments were noted in microfilming; in 1988 the Image Permanence Institute (IPI) announced several research results which promise to continue impacting for some time. A new photographic activity test was developed—a standard test procedure which will more accurately indicate the changes in photographic materials. Using the new test, IPI explored issues confronting all collection managers: the stability of black-and-white photographic images (especially microfilm) and of photographic enclosure materials. One especially important conclusion was that although many silver images have been ruined by poor processing (the problem of residual chemicals), a more important deterioration mechanism is image oxidation. Currently IPI is extending its research into methods of protecting images. Contracts for study let by the Commission on Preservation and Access confront the issue of scaling up microfiling production; the Mid Atlantic Preservation Service (MAPS) will investigate archival standards for microfiche, high-speed density checking capacity, and, working with Xerox Corporation, will work on developing a composing/reducing camera for digitization of 35 millimeter film, to then become the source of a variety of products and formats.

Practical Experience. The Northeast Document Conservation Center (NEDCC) has since its beginnings been providing survey services to institutions wanting to begin preservation activity. Now NEDCC, with partial funding from the Institute of Museum Services, will train additional paper conservators to do general conservation survey work, relieving their backlog of survey work and also providing more qualified surveyors to the field. NEDCC also announced plans based on the experience of their inhouse filming operations to train microfilm camera operators. The common experience of "yellow snow" covering the aisles of stacks loaded with brittle books led to innovation by the Harvard Law Library, and perhaps earned the "preservation whimsey of the year award." Small sealed bags of crumbs of brittle paper were gathered and tagged with a ditty "knowledge written for the ages—food for the scholar; knowledge on this crumbling paper—yours for a dollar." The Mid-Atlantic Regional Archives Conference (MARAC), responding to needs of its members, held a disaster recovery workshop. The practical experience and concern of Ellen McCrady, publisher of the *Abbey Newsletter,* led to a new title in library (and related trades) literature: the *Alkaline Paper Advocate* began publication in January. Its chief function will be to provide a forum for alkaline paper producers and consumers who now find communication difficult because of the complexity of the marketplace.

Growing Awareness of Preservation Problems and Solutions. As author Baraba Goldsmith worked on newspapers from the collections of the New York Public Library (NYPL), she became concerned about the brittle materials disintegrating, even under careful use. As a trustee and donor to NYPL, she was concerned about preservation. Her work includes support of two NYPL initiatives dealing with paper; NYPL created a clearing house for information called the Center for Paper Permanency and a related group called Authors and Publishers in Support of Preservation of the Printed Word. The latter solicits commitments from authors and publishers that first printings of works will be on alkaline paper. Likewise in Washington, D.C. alkaline and permanence were emerging issues; on May 19 an interim specification on paper permanence was made available to government agencies and the Government Printing Office. The document uses many of the requirements of ANSI Z39.48–1984, but it does not require a symbol or statement of compliance. In the waning days of the 1988 congressional session, Senator Claiborn Pell (Democrat, Rhode Island) introduced a sample resolution to establish a national policy on permanent paper. Although this late introduction received no congressional action, Pell announced his intention to reintroduce the legislation in January 1989 and to hold subsequent public hearings. The resolution recommends that federal agencies require the use of permanent paper "for publications of enduring value," that archival quality paper be used for federal records, and that American publishers use permanent paper and indicate such in advertisements, catalogs, and bibliographic lists. Also in Congress, Sidney Yates (Democrat, Illinois) held hearings on the budgets of the Institute for Museum Services (IMS) and National Endowments for Arts and Humanities. A half day on preservation of books and paper focused on microfilming, deacidification, and use of alkaline paper.

In October, another group gathered in Washington, D.C. to discuss paper: a symposium on paper permanence was held by TAPPI, the Technical Association for the Pulp and Paper Industry. Brought together for the first time were leading representatives of all groups interested in paper permanence; Congress, standards organizations, research laboratories, paper industry, librarians and archivists, and government paper and printing personnel. In addition to technical sessions on alkaline papermaking and lobbying concerns, a strategy session for people actively working for alkaline paper in their own sectors (Libraries, archives, and publishers) was organized.

The Commission on Preservation and Access established a series of Scholarly Advisory Committees that will develop a strategy for preservation and priorities for selection in each major field of scholarship. There are committees for philosophy, art history, modern languages, and literature. The Getty Grant program also brought together a September seminar in Minnesota on preservation issues for scholarly resources for art history. Invited representatives from a wide range of associations discussed the typical problems of brittleness in materials not immediately suitable for microfilming, a replacement option for most collections.

Late October saw a meeting of 60 liberal arts college library directors comprising the "Oberlin Group," to discuss the role of major liberal arts colleges in the emerging national preservation program. The Commission on Preservation and Access formed a similar group to explore the role of mid-sized libraries in the national brittle book preservation program.

The Committee for Institution Cooperation (CIC), consisting of the libraries of the Big Ten Universities and the University of Chicago, received funding for more than $1,000,000 for microfilming materials in Western European literature and history, African studies, Slavic and Eastern European Studies, and the history of science and technology. It was the first major effort in preservation for this group that has existed for many years. Of particular note is the fact that this is the first major cooperative undertaking by institutions using RLIN, OCLC, and local online databases for shared bibliographic catalog and queuing information.

State and National Activity. The New Hampshire State Library began a modest grant program to encourage public libraries to have surveys done by NEDCC, preliminary to preparing a comprehensive preservation plan. New Jersey continued its preservation grant program. New York and Florida initiated disaster response educational programs to lead eventually to statewide coordinated, cooperative efforts for disaster response. Connecticut introduced legislation that will require use of alkaline paper; this action came through lobbying by the state's new preservation advocacy group.

The Office of Presidential Libraries of the National Archives and Records Administration completed a third year of a systematic preservation program documenting the conditions of papers and/or record materials (and their containers) held by repositories. Materials seem to be surprisingly stable, but they are not expected to stay that way without severe restrictions on future use and attention to storage environments.

The National Library of Medicine (NLM) commissioned an assessment survey of preservation needs of the biomedical literature and the capabilities of repositories to contribute to preservation. At the conclusion of the survey, undertaken by the New York Academy of Medicine, it is expected that a national agenda for preservation of biomedical literature, including grants for microfilming and other preservation projects, will be coordinated through NLM's Regional Medical Library network.

The biggest news in 1988 in preservation was undoubtably the increase in the budget of the National Endowment for the Humanities (NEH) Office of Preservation, from $4,500,000 to $12,330,000. There are five primary areas of support for funds: the U.S. Newspaper Program (USNP), special humanities collections; resources for the education and training of preservation personnel; state and regional information and consultant services; and basic research and development as well as general work and promotion on the preservation of brittle books, serials, and other types of library materials. This initiative and the planning efforts to achieve and expend it will be a chief force in preservation into the 21st century.

ANN G. SWARTZELL

Public Libraries

The media's rediscovery of latchkey children in public libraries, the Public Library Association's (PLA'S) third national conference, OCLC's Conference on the Future of Public Libraries, funding and financial alternatives, and the dramatic growth of telefacsimile mark some of the major trends in public libraries during 1988.

Stimulated by major wire service articles and televised interviews, libraries of all sizes in virtually every region of the nation re-examined their policies and programs for helping unsupervised children and their parents. The Cooperating Libraries of Central Maryland made available a video produced by Baltimore Gas and Electric, which was designed for children and parents. Queensborough Public Library greatly expanded its programs on parenting with the help of special grants. The Brooklyn (New York) Public Library widely welcomed latchkey children, to counter the impression that some public libraries discouraged their presence. The Houston (Texas) Public Library drew upon its Harriet Dickson Reynolds Endowment to fund a workshop on the latchkey child, while professional conference programs featured several sessions on the topic.

National Conference. PLA's third national conference in Pittsburgh April 27–30 used "Bridges to the 21st Century" as its theme, and attracted record attendance to a wide range of pre- and postconferences, tours, talk tables and programs, Historian Barbara Tuchman served as the keynoter, but "Mr. Rogers" stole the show with an emotion-loaded overview of his neighborhood. Probably the most overlooked program featured an unveiling of the Reagan Administration's new library program. After seven years of zero funding for libraries, the new package proposed funding for services to the disadvantaged, networking and research, and an end to the Library Services and Construction Act.

It was no coincidence that a larger-than-life Andrew Carnegie greeted conference attendees at the opening reception at the Carnegie Institute. The third national conference offered a very large selection of programs on philanthropy and fund raising and attracted standing-room-only crowds. Mary Jo Lynch reported on the results of the H.W. Wilson Foundation funded survey on nontax revenues to public libraries. This was summarized in last year's *Yearbook*, and the final report was published by ALA during 1988.[1]

A growing interest in collection development was evidenced in the programs. "Public Library Involvement in Adult Literacy," a report of a U.S. Department of Education funded study, was presented by Debra Johnson and Douglas

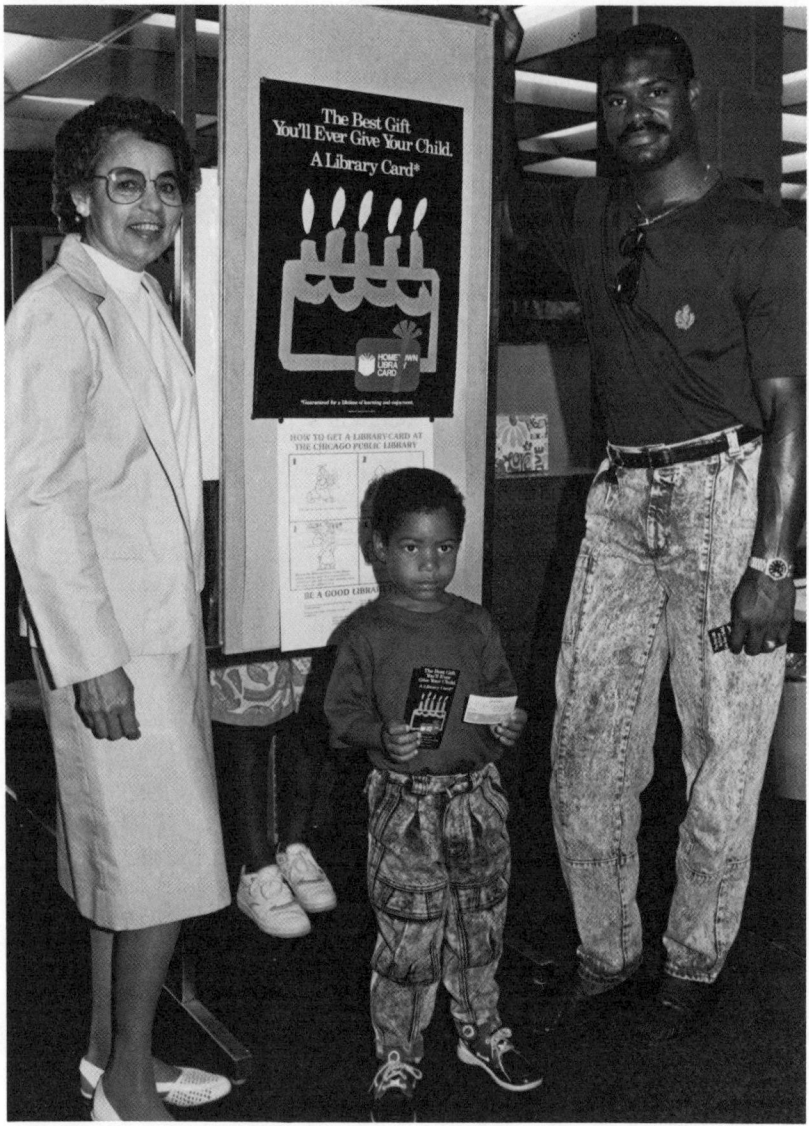

Chicago Bear Dave Duerson (right) and children's librarian Annie Carroll look on as Chase Duerson proudly displays the library card he just got at The Chicago Public Library in July. CPL joined the American Library Association in encouraging all parents to give their children "The Best Gift You'll Ever Give Your Child ... A Library Card." [Phil Moloitis]

Zweizig. It documented some of the more successful models developed by public libraries and the growing involvement of the institution in literacy efforts. Services to special users were reviewed in a wide range of other conference programs. Besides the latchkey child, the aged, the young adult, the deaf and hearing impaired, the business community—even snowbirds—were featured.

Earlier in the year, OCLC held an invitation–only Conference of the Future of the Public Library. 54 library trustees, administrators, educators and state library agency administrators were assembled in Dublin, Ohio, at OCLC's headquarters from March 20–22. Futurist Robert Olson of the Institute for Alternative Futures provided the keynote presentation on the accelerating changes in society, particularly relating to technology. The balance of the conference was based on three papers. Thomas Ballard predicted that public libraries will transcend traditional methods to provide improved services and resources and advocated decentralized larger collections. Linda Crismond projected how public librarians will need to interact more effectively with users, and the skills they will need. Crismond expressed concern about increasingly bi-modal society, the information "haves" and "have nots". Various strategies were discussed, including tiered services that extract fees to support their higher cost.

The third speaker was Kathryn Stephanoff, whose assignment was the projection of interlibrary cooperation and resource sharing. Stephanoff assessed the impact of technology upon the ability to serve two "neighborhoods," which she described as those with needs and those with money. While praising the application of computers to allow libraries to stretch limited resources, Stephanoff cautioned against being a pioneer in their use. Each of the speakers faced a series of panel reactors, followed by a small group discussions. Rowland Brown concluded by noting the role that the technology can play in reducing the risks involved in extending library leadership. A videotape and published conference proceedings were produced by OCLC.[2]

Public Library Finance. A fairly large number of public libraries held successful referenda during the past year. The Toledo & Lucas County (Ohio) Public Library gained 64 percent approval for a 10-year levy that will facilitate expanded collections, programs and hours. The St. Louis (Missouri) Public Library raised tax revenue from $400,700,000 to $8,700,000 with a 60 percent margin of public approval. The Miami–Dade County (Florida) Library gained $47,000,000 in new taxes to pay for new books over the next decade. The Cleveland (Ohio) Public Library will receive an additional $7,800,000 as a result of a 2-mill, five-year levy approved by taxpayers. Sixty-four percent of the voters in Spokane, Washington, approved a $5,000,000 capital improvements levy for their library, and Kalamazoo, Michigan, voters approved tax increases for library service by a 62 percent margin.

Not every effort was successful. The voters in Shasta County, California, rejected a tax increase of 0.5 percent and their public libraries were closed. The Multnomah County Library (Portland, Oregon) lost a two-year battle to create a new library district when the Portland City Council backed off granting their support to the transition.

1988 brought major public library construction. Architects were selected and a design approved for the new Harold Washington Library, which will serve as the Central Chicago Public Library. The Public Library of Columbus and Franklin County (Ohio) broke ground for a $37,000,000 expansion of its central library while the Cuyahoga County Public Library (Cleveland, Ohio) opened the first of four kiosks in major shopping malls in suburban areas. The Los Angeles Public Library reopened two of the three branch libraries that were closed due to earthquake damage; a third will be replaced with a new building. The central Los Angeles Public Library experienced a third fire, this time due to a construction accident; damage was limited to recently restored murals. The Baltimore County Public Library (Towson, Maryland) opened two branches during 1988. Its White Marsh Library features neon signs to highlight service areas, reference kiosks and a small business information section in a 15,000-square-foot leased facil-

Retail Shops in Public Libraries: A Survey

Libraries are getting into the retail business. In increasing numbers, libraries are opening stores to sell merchandise to library visitors. Reasons for opening a library store range from extending and complementing library services, to recycling discarded materials, to promoting public relations for libraries, to making money.

To learn more about library stores, ALA in November 1988 mailed questionnaires to 24 libraries with retail stores. Of the 20 libraries that responded, 17 reported having library stores; one reported that its store closed in 1986; one sponsors annual book sales but has not established a retail outlet; and one plans to open a store within the next 18 to 24 months. This special report is a summary of the responses.

A Recent Phenomenon. As with many innovations in library service, the Library of Congress led the way in the development of retail shops. The "Jefferson Sales Shop" opened as a visitor service on the ground floor lobby of the original Library of Congress building in 1976. Many visitors to the library wanted a souvenir to take home. A private donation of $500 allowed the library to produce its first postcard products.

The earliest public library store reported in the survey is "The Book Shop," which opened January 1980 at the Ann Arbor (Michigan) Public Library. An extension of the library's successful biannual used book sales, The Book Shop continues to stock only used materials—library discards, donations, books from local university teachers and students.

The New Orleans Public Library has the newest store, which opened in September 1988. Within the next two years, Boston Public Library plans to have a store in its newly renovated main library.

No Typical Store. Library stores come in all shapes and sizes, from a mere 48 square feet for the free-standing "Friendshop" at Seattle Public Library to a generous 3,700 square feet for "Friends of the Library Bookstore" at Orlando Public Library. About a third of the stores fall within a 200- to 500-square-foot range; another third are between 500 to 1,000 square feet.

First floor of the central library, near the circulation desk or a main entrance is, by far, the most popular store location. An exception is "Secondhand Prose" at Chicago Public Library, located on the first floor of a building that previously was a regional library and now is being renovated as a community cultural center. The store may move.

Some stores were included in new building plans. Architects for the Broward County (Florida) Main Library planned a glass-enclosed space for the "Friends of the Library Gift Shop" in a well-traveled area across from the auditorium and the popular library. Library architects designed a free-standing store space for The Library Store at Dallas Public Library. (For two years, store staff set up and took down the store every day until portable gates were installed in 1984.)

Other stores have been tied to renovation projects. "The Library Shop" at The New York Public Library is located in a restored room noted for its Old English charm and architecture. "Pratt Place" is in a glass-enclosed room built during renovation at Enoch Pratt Free Library in Baltimore.

Most often, however, existing space has been modified to make do. The Ann Arbor shop is in a multi-use basement room lined with bookshelves. Long tables are set up during store hours. When the library is remodeled, store staff hopes to have its own space. "Books Plus," the District of Columbia Library store, used to be a public locker room, and "Andrew's Alcove" at the Carnegie Library of Pittsburgh was an office.

Glass walls and windows are popular features, allowing library and street traffic to see into the stores. Typical furnishings include bookshelves, display cases, tables, and floor and countertop racks. Wall space often is used to display posters and framed pictures.

Business hours vary widely. Most stores are open five weekdays and Saturday. Four are open everyday; Orlando is planning to add three hours on Sunday. The Dallas store is open the most hours, 58 a week. The average business week is 38 hours.

Merchandise. More than half of all the stores carry new books, bookbags, cards and stationery, postcards, and various supplies, e.g., pens, pencils, paper. Other popular items are used books, educational toys, museum store items, mugs, jewelry and such book-related accessories as bookmarks, bookplates, bookcovers and bookends.

The Friends at the Minneapolis Public Library operate the Minneapolis Planetarium as well as the library book shop; so they stock planetarium-related items. Seattle, of course, does a brisk business in umbrellas and rain hats.

All but one shop sell books. Four (Ann Arbor, Chicago, New Orleans, and Pittsburgh) sell only used books and magazines—although New Orleans soon will carry bookbags, souvenir items, and supplies. Seven shops sell new books; five sell new and used.

The "Friends of the Library Gift Shop" in Anchorage sells autographed books from author receptions at the library. "Books Plus" sells books on Dr. Martin Luther King, Jr. and other black leaders. New York carries books about research, writing, book design, and printing. High-demand study books for standardized tests, e.g., GED, SAT, GRE, are on order in Orlando.

Friends of the Library Gift Shop, Z.J. Loussac Library, Anchorage, Alaska. Friends advertise their Russian lacquerware and Alaskan crafts in a local visitors' guide.

Public Libraries

Other areas of new book sales include regional titles, local authors, children's books, library publications, cookbooks, art books, genealogy, works, and books related to library exhibits. The Friends of the Cincinnati and Hamilton County Public Library published a coloring book of Cincinnati, one of the products at "The Friends Shop." "Shhh! The Library Gift Shop" in Cleveland sells several gift items with the library identification.

Materials most often are purchased through catalogs and trade publications and from local vendors. About half of the store managers also attend local and national gift shows, including the Museum Store Association annual meeting. Other sources of store merchandise are local craftspeople and artists, library withdrawals, and donations.

Sales. The survey asked stores to report their gross and net sales for their first year of operation and for the current year. First-year sales ranged from $400 (Seattle) to $523,000 (New York). Typical first-year sales, however, fell between $20,0000 and $40,000, and typical current-year sales averaged $68,000, a substantial increase over first-year sales.

Formulas for calculating net sales were too varied to compare. Fourteen of the 16 stores, however, reported that they are profitable. Eleven characterize store traffic as moderate; four report heavy traffic.

Most often store revenues go to Friends groups for library projects or are reinvested in the store for inventory and staff. The Friends who manage "The Book Shop" in Ann Arbor give store revenue to the library to support staff development—for attending professional meetings or taking classes. They also fund the children's storyhour and print the library newsletter. Three stores contribute to the library's general fund and materials budget.

At the Library of Congress, two-thirds of the profits are reinvested in the shop; one-third is returned to the library to support programs.

Who's Minding the Store? Oversight of store operations is evenly split between Friends groups (9) and library administration (8). Typically, the store manager is either a library staff member who has job responsibilities other than the store or an unpaid member of the Friends group. A few Friends managers are paid; most are not. "Friendshop" at the Virginia Beach Public Library is managed by a Friends committee.

In Baltimore and New York, the store managers are full-time library staff members with no additional responsibilities.

Staffing during store hours ranges from two to six, often with a mix of paid personnel and volunteers. Stores report volunteer staff pools of from 10 to 60.

Publicity and Public Opinion. Library newsletters and free coverage in local media are the most common vehicles for store publicity—and in some cases the only vehicles. Some stores have developed direct mail fliers.

In Anchorage, the Friends took out a paid ad in the local visitors guide. The Ann Arbor and Cincinnati stores promote sales through coupon offers.

Library stores enjoy universal acceptance in their communities. Library users are enthusiastic, surprised and appreciative. Library staff is supportive, cooperative and ecstatic. Stores report no complaints from local bookstores or other related businesses. In fact, booksellers are buyers and have co-sponsored author appearances. "The Friends Shop" in Cincinnati reports good relationships with local booksellers, because "we send customers to them, and they know it!"

Museum Store Association. More than half of all library stores are members of the Museum Store Association (MSA). A group of representatives of library stores meets regularly at the annual MSA convention, and many library store personnel attend regional MSA meetings held twice a year.

The Museum Store Association and its members are excellent resources for libraries operating stores. Membership information is available from: Museum Store Association, 501 S. Cherry Street, Suite 460, Denver, CO 80222.

A few stores are members of the American Booksellers Association, and several intend to join.

Other Retail Outlets. In addition to library stores, some libraries also report having restaurants. The New York Public Library franchises a seasonal cafe. The Broward County Library has a restaurant on its second floor operated by a local caterer who has a contract with the county. A tea shop is part of the library renovation plan in Boston.

Since 1985, the Dallas Public Library has operated "BookEnds," a used book store that is completely separate from The Library Store. Other entrepreneurial activities libraries report are T-shirt and tote-bag sales from the circulation desk and a video rental service.

Future Plans. Expansion, remodeling, additional merchandise, and increased marketing efforts are in the works for library stores. Just about every store reports plans for growth and development.

The future for retail outlets in libraries is promising. The success stories of the stores reported in the survey indicate libraries have much to gain in converting borrowers into buyers.

A list of library stores and a complete tally of survey results is available from Marcia Kuszmaul, Public Information Office, ALA.

MARCIA J. KUSZMAUL

---

ity. BCPL's new Hereford Branch is a mini-facility staffed by 32 volunteers in a rural area of the county, which is connected by hotline to a larger regional center for reference assistance.

Monroe Township (New Jersey) received $2,000,000 and 10 acres from a local developer to construct a public library. Public libraries throughout the nation reported similar major gifts to support services or construction. The Free Library of Philadelphia received $861,430 from the William Penn Foundation for books to aid children and their parents. The Louisville (Kentucky) Public Library received $500,000 for its science and business collection from the Capitol Holding Company, and topped off its $6,000,000 endowment drive. The Los Angeles Public Library went over the top of its $10 million "Save the Books" drive. The Pasadena (California) Public Library held a $300-a-plate, black-tie dinner as part of its effort to raise $2,400,000 to restore its central library, and was more than halfway to its goal by midyear. Not so fortunate was the New York Public Library, which was notified that the National Endowment for the Humanities would reduce its $2,000,000 annual subsidy to $1,000,000 and eliminate it entirely by 1990.

Personnel. Some major personnel changes took place during 1988. Vartan Gregorian resigned as president of the New York Public Library to assume a similar position at Brown University, ending an unparalleled period of growth for NYPL. Bernard Margolis succeeded Ed Dowlin as the director of the Pikes Peak (Colorado) Library District. Eileen Longsworth replaced Guy Schuurman as director of the Salt Lake County (Utah) Public Library. Elizabeth Stroup left the Library of Congress to become Librarian at the Seattle (Washington) Public Library. Dale Thompson moved from Assistant Director to Director of the Providence (Rhode Island) Public Library. Betty Bender retired from the Spokane (Washington) Public Library, and Sharon Hammer assumed responsibilities as director of the Fort Vancouver (Washington) Public Library. Frank Dempsey, who retired from the Arlington Heights (Illinois) Public Library, died during the year. Rachel Wayne Nelson ended her distinguished library career by retiring from the Cleveland Heights-University Heights (Ohio) Public Library.

Stephen Whitney resigned from the San Bernardino (California) Public Library under charges of embezzlement. Keith Reville, who was fired from the Anchorage (Alaska) Public Library, was replaced by Faye Alexiev, a management consultant who had aided the new mayor's campaign. Jim Gosier was fired from the Harford (Maryland) County Department of Public Libraries. Cleveland (Ohio) Public Library staff picketed for higher pay and protested a proposed reduction in annual sick leave to 9 days from 15 days. The Denver (Colorado) Public Library reported continued growth of its volunteer program, noting that 32,000 hours had been contributed to 637 persons at their institution.

Collections and Services. Public library collections continued to increase through a variety of means. The Brooklyn Public Library auctioned off its Bobby Fisher Chess Collection, and used the $14,025 it gained for purchase of more popular titles. The Thousand Oaks (California) Public Library received the Rudy Vallee collection, valued at $275,000. The Duluth (Minnesota) Public Library launched an adaptive toy collection for the benefit of handicapped children. The Memphis-Shelby County (Tennessee) Public Library began a program of book deposits in shelters for the homeless. The John D. and Catherine MacArthur Foundation reported that 600 public libraries throughout the nation had taken advantage of its offer to furnish collections of PBS video classics at substantially reduced cost. The Los Angeles (California) City Council released $2,800,000 to restore 700,000 books which have been kept in cold storage since their library's disasterous fires.

The literature abounded with reports of use and purchase of telefacsimile equipment by public libraries throughout the nation. Nassau County (New York) for example, purchased 54 fax machines for all the member libraries of that system. The Montana State Library's FAXNET won an award from *Administration Magazine* for its innovative use of this technology. As the cost of this equipment decreased, and the quality and speed of transmission improved, more local libraries installed equipment to complement their photocopy service. A $2,500,000 Dynix System replaced the CLSI system used by the Multnomah County Library (Portland, Oregon). A $5,300,000 contract was awarded to DRA to install a 550 terminal system at the Los Angeles County Public Library.

A rich array of programs and exhibits characterized 1988. The Free Library of Philadelphia scheduled an exhibit and programs on black life in Philadelphia during the late 1700s and early 1800s. The Chicago Public Library arranged a major exhibition and programs on Author Nelson Algren. Libraries around the nation honored Dr. Martin Luthur King, Jr. in January and Black History Month in February. The Enoch Pratt Free Library, Baltimore, Maryland, scheduled more than 100 hours of public programs. The Public Library of Columbus and Franklin County (Ohio) held an "African Dreams" bedtime story sequence and demonstrations on "Food in the Black American Tradition." The Milwaukee (Wisconsin) Public Library announced a massive read-in involving 100 schools and 750 volunteers during the week preceding Martin Luther King, Jr.'s birthday. The Atlanta-Fulton County (Georgia) Library announced a "Youth Showcase" spotlighting young persons in dance, drama and music. The Brooklyn (New York) Public Library planned a series of programs on famous black performers. Prince George's County (Maryland) Public Library won an achievement award from the National Association of Counties for Wee Care, an outreach program to family day care centers. The Orange County (California) Public Library won an award of merit from the Association of State and Local History for its program on local archives.

Two survey results concerning public libraries were announced. The Urban Library Council revealed that major urban libraries identified maintenance of local library funding and deterioration of book budgets as chief concerns for the present and immediate future. The U.S. Department of Education conducted a survey of services and resources for young adults in public libraries during 1987. The results reported in 1988 indicated that one out of every four patrons in public libraries was between 12 and 18 years of age. Eleven percent of all public libraries reported having a position designated as Young Adult Librarian, while 84 percent reported having a young adult collection. The National Commission of Libraries and Information Science and the National Center for Educational Statistics reached an agreement to work in cooperation with state library agencies to ensure more timely

"Bozo the Clown" encourages Chicago children to use the library as he receives his own library card from Chicago Public Library Commissioner John B. Duff and "The Cat in the Hat."

publication of statistics on public libraries. Meantime, the PLA published *Public Library Data Service Statistics Report '88*,[3] its first effort at cooperative data collection on public library trends.

NOTES

1. Lynch, Mary Jo. *Non-Tax Sources of Revenue for Public Libraries.* Chicago, American Library Association, 1988.
2. Brown, Roland C. W., ed. *Conference on the Future of the Public Library.* Dublin, Ohio, OCLC Inc., 1988.
3. Public Library Association. *Public Library Data Service Statistical Report '88.* Chicago, American Library Association, 1988.

DONALD J. SAGER

Public Library Association

Under the leadership of President Susan Goldberg, the Public Library Association (PLA) provided diverse continuing education opportunities, an expanded publications program, and a forum for debate on issues of concern to the profession.

Membership, "The Very Best PLAce To Be!". PLA's new membership recruitment slogan reflected positive findings of a member survey completed with the help of the ALA Communications Department. More than 90 percent of the respondents valued PLA membership, stating that the division is responsive to their needs and addresses important concerns. 71 percent indicated they attend PLA programs at ALA Annual Conferences, 59 percent have attended PLA's national conferences, and 54 percent sought PLA publications in addition to *Public Libraries.* PLA membership grew to 6,298, making the division the second largest within ALA. The Public Library Affiliates Network was formally established with voting rights on the PLA Board. Charter state association members were Colorado, Delaware, Florida, Illinois, Iowa, Kansas, Massachusetts, Michigan, Minnesota, Mississippi, Missouri, Montana, Nebraska, Ohio, Oklahoma, Pennsylvania, Texas, Washington, Wisconsin and Wyoming.

Support of the division's goals was shown in another tangible way when members passed a $10 dues increase on the 1988 ballot. The additional funding was earmarked for further development of the Public Library Data Service, an expansion of *Public Libraries* and a staff editor for the publication, enhanced support of membership services, public relations and other division publications, supplemental funding for conference programs and incentive grants for sections and committees.

Conferences and Workshops. An extraordinary array of programs was provided by PLA during the year. At the ALA Annual Conference in New Orleans, the division's sections and committees sponsored programs reflecting the diverse interests of members. PLA President's Programs: "A Sense of Place: The Value of Cultural Institutions to the Community" with architect and planning consultant Robert McNulty; "The Presidential Election and the Future of the Library Industry" with pollster Louis Harris. Alternative Education Program Section: "Getting It Together: Networking for Lifelong Learning," "The Kellogg Foundation and Education and Job Information Centers," and "Intergenerational Approaches to Literacy." Armed Forces Library Section: "Creative Coping II: Upgrading Our Image and Supplementing our Resources." Community Information Section: "Community Information and Referral: Essentials for Success." Public Library Systems Section: "Managing Trends in System Services." Small and Medium-sized Libraries Section: "Roles of Small Public Libraries," "Doing Rural Economic Development," "The Doctors Are In: Group Therapy Sessions for Branch Coordinators, Managers and Librarians." PLA Committees provided programs on gaining political clout through alliances, using focus groups to sample public opinion, developing multilingual audio-visual collections, recruiting children's librarians, and mastering desktop publishing. Three special interest preconferences were sponsored by PLA in New Orleans: "Fast Forward: Video Collections and Public Libraries," "Managing Work Relationships: Moving from Conflict to Collaboration," and "Design and Construction Administration for New and Remodeled Libraries."

PLA's 1988 National Conference far exceeded all attendance goals with 3,948 registrants (up 1,415 from 1986) and 241 exhibits (up from 191). Conference Chair Donald Sager, Milwaukee (Wisconsin) Public Library, Program Chair Sarah A. Long, Multnomah County (Oregon) Library and PLA Program Officer Bridget Bradley aided scores of members in designing the conference with featured programs for practitioners, trustees and educators, nationally noted speakers, quality exhibits, and a splendid reception at the Carnegie Library. The 1991 conference is scheduled for San Diego, California. Charles Robinson, Baltimore (Maryland) County Public Library, will chair the planning committee. Proceeds from the Pittsburgh conference will be used to underwrite the conference in San Diego.

Publications. The newly established PLA Publications Assembly, chaired by Kathleen Balcom of Downers Grove (Illinois) Public Library, fulfilled its charge to evaluate and unify the publication efforts of the division. Yearlong efforts of assembly members resulted in a decision by the PLA Board of Directors to increase publication of *Public Libraries* to six issues per year. The *Public Libraries* Advisory Board, chaired by Carolyn Anthony of the Skokie (Illinois) Public Library, developed specifications for extensive format changes and provided guidance to Kathleen

Melissa Buckingham, Free Library of Philadelphia.

PUBLIC LIBRARY ASSOCIATION

PRESIDENT (July 1988–July 1989):
Melissa Buckingham, Free Library of Philadelphia, Philadelphia, Pennsylvania

VICE-PRESIDENT/PRESIDENT-ELECT:
Sara A. Long, Multoonah County Library, Portland, Oregon

EXECUTIVE DIRECTOR:
Eleanor Jo Rodger

Membership (August 31, 1988): 6,298 (5,577 personal; and 721 organizational)
Expenditures (August 31, 1988): $472,441

Heim, Louisiana State University, the new editor of the journal.

The PLA Publications Committee chaired by Karen Krueger, Janesville (Wisconsin) Public Library, prepared an attractive annotated checklist of PLA publications and developed strategies to encourage members to submit manuscripts. The committee's efforts resulted in publication revenues exceeding budget projections by more than 100 percent.

Publications introduced during the year include *Information and Referral Promotional Samples*, *Public Library Data Service Statistical Report, 1988*, and *Materials Availability Study, 1987*, from the Fairfax County (Virginia) Public Library. Also introduced during the year was the *EIC Linkletter*, a newsletter produced by the PLA Education Information Project with support from the W.K. Kellogg Foundation.

Awards. The 1988 Allie Beth Martin Award was given to Daniel O. Robles, director of the Blanchard Community Library in Santa Paula, California. The citation and an honorarium of $3,000 were donated by the Baker & Taylor Company in recognition of the librarian's knowledge of books and his ability to share that knowledge with the community. The 1988 Advancement of Literacy Award was given to the Gannett Foundation. The recipient was selected by the PLA Alternative Education Program Section and the award was sponsored by RHC Spacemaster.

Key Issues. After more than a year of discussion, the PLA Board of Directors did not endorse a proposal from an independent group of educators and practitioners to accredit public libraries. Citing philosophical concerns about the value and the process of the proposed accreditation, the Board withdrew its liaison and directed that its position be distributed to the library press. The Board also endorsed a call for a Fast Response Survey on children's services in public libraries to be conducted by the U.S. Department of Education and approved a project to develop output measures for children's services.

Services to Children Committee Chair Mary K. Chelton, Montgomery, Maryland County Department of Libraries, won publication approval for the committee's position paper, *Latchkey Children in the Public Library*, completed in collaboration with ALA's Association for Service to Children.

Considerable effort by the membership was required to fulfill the Association's goal for 1988, but success would not be possible without the talent and dedication of the PLA staff. Led by Eleanor Jo Rodger, the innovative Executive Director, the PLA staff coordinated the programs and services that resulted in high-satisfaction ratings by members and in a strengthened division. With this foundation PLA will continue to contribute to the vitality of the American Library Association. KATHLEEN MEHAFFEY BALCOM

Public Relations and Marketing

There truly has never been a better time to be involved in library marketing and public relations (PR). Nearly the entire profession now advocates utilization of these management techniques.

Groundbreaking for Holdenville (Oklahoma) Public Library's expansion project was a media event with homeowner T. Boone Pickens, Jr. on hand for the ceremony. Pickens, Chairman of Mesa Limited Partnership, an energy company, pledged to match local fundraising efforts up to $62,500. The Holdenville addition is to be partially funded by a federal grant award.

The 1988 ALA *Planning Document: Observations and Strategies* designated "Public Awareness" as one of the organization's top four priorities. The Associations Annual Conference in New Orleans reflected this goal with eleven programs, a poster session, and a workshop on marketing or public relations. The Annual Conference of the Special Libraries Association (SLA) in Denver offered two continuing education courses and three programs on library promotion. The Medical Library Association (MLA) once again sponsored a marketing continuing education course at its Annual conference.

The Library Administration and Management Association's Public Relations Section was completely reorganized in a new structure consisting of nine committees and a discussion group that would increase the section's responsiveness to membership needs.

The Public Library Association (PLA Marketing of Library Services Committee enjoyed a particularly productive year when it sponsored the PLA Conference program on marketing libraries to the business community in Pittsburgh. In New Orleans the Committee presented a well-attended program on utilizing focus groups.

The Association of College and Research Libraries (ACRL) provided an exciting forum for public relations interests. The ACRL Public Relations in Academic Libraries discussion group (PRIAL) sponsored "Desktop Publishing as a Public Relations Tool" at ALA Mid-winter in San Antonio. Its Annual Conference program presented a new paradigm for approaching academic library public relations. This program was summarized i the *Catalyst*. Seven journal articles described various PR applications in academic libraries.

Marketing or Public Relations? Inclusion of the term "Marketing" in the title of this yearbook's essay reflects a growing recognition of this approach by library managers. Public relations advocates normally subsume marketing under their own banner, citing the limited applicability of this business world specialty to the public sector. On the other hand, marketers tend to subsume public relations into the framework

National Library Week 1988 posters continued to focus on library cards.

of their own large-scale marketing plans.

This lively debate extends far beyond librarianship into other professions with non-profit organizations. The two concepts often are used interchangeably, unfortunately producing great confusion. This essay noes *not* equate public relations and marketing. Rather, it acknowledges the many similar techniques shared by both specialties while respecting the philosophies unique to each approach.

LAMA Public Relations Section. Years of planning came to fruition at ALA Midwinter 1988 when PRS began operating under its newly-reorganized structure, with PRS Chair Marg Chartrand and PRS Chair-elect Jon Eldredge overseeing the implementation phase of the reorganization. The Chair-elect also sought to create greater diversity within the section's leadership through 47 committee appointments and 14 re-appointments. Table 1 depicts the increasing representation of different library types on PRS committees.

Three new PRS committees began planning to realize PRS goals within the larger LAMA organization. For example, the PRS Education & Training Committee employed a "Preferred Futures" technique for reaching group consensus on goals. This process resulted in a proposal to sponsor a two-day PR institute at a library school. The PRS State and Regional Programs Committee and the PRS Committee on Recognition sought to define their roles in ways that would complement the goals of existing LAMA committees.

The PRS Public Affairs Committee immediately began developing techniques for predicting future social, economic, and political trends that might affect libraries. This trends analysis intended to alert the profession about emerging issues so that librarians might respond rapidly and effectively through their public relations programs. The Lockheed Corporation donated online time and expertise to the Committee by performing DIALOG database searches. The PRS Public Affairs Committee also proposed sponsoring a conference program on PR evaluation.

The PRS Legislative Skills Committee surveyed state library associations with legislative PR activities. Information gathered was to be organized into a clearinghouse for PRS members. The Committee also discussed with the PRS Publications Committee the possibility of jointly revising *Getting It Passed: Lobbying for Libraries* (1984). The Publications Committee planned a preconference on the PR applications of desktop publishing.

The PRS Swap and Shop Committee's annual program in New Orleans greatly exceeded planners' expectations by shattering previous attendance records with more than 2,500 conferees at the Swap and Shop program "Library PR and All That Jazz." Mini-sessions on winning a John Cotton Dana Library PR Award, executing local level campaigns for National Library Week, and employment of PR techniques for building political support were presented to overflow audiences.

More than 300 entries representing 29 states competed in the Swap and Shop "Best of Show" contest. Judges selected 13 winners and 25 honorable mentions. "Best of Show" winning entries were displayed along the Library Public Relations Council awards and John Cotton Dana Library Public Relations Award winning entries.

JCD Public Relations Contest. This annual contest serves as a living memorial to librarianship's greatest PR pioneer: John Cotton Data (JCD) (1856-1929). A panel of ten judges reviewed 121 entries during the week of March 7-11 in New York City. Table 2 summarizes results for award categories by library type. Judges' reports confirmed a long-term trend of steadily improving quality of contest entries.

Great Library Promotion Ideas came out in its fifth edition which described the salient features of each winning entry and reviewed non-winning entries that contained noteworthy PR ideas.

The JCD Judging Committee continued its ongoing education program designed to increase entrants' chances for winning awards. Michael Haeuser wrote an article on the contest in *College & Research Libraries News*; Marian Karpisek co-

The Year of the Librarian: Ask a Professional. Ask Your Librarian

National Library Week April 9–15, 1989 made history with the theme "Ask A Professional. Ask Your Librarian." The theme was the first to spotlight library professionals and the focus for an ongoing public awareness campaign during what was called the American Library Association's "Year of the Librarian."

The campaign reflected long-standing concern about the public image of librarians, also new and growing concerns about respect and visibility of the profession in the Information Age, and the need to attract bright young people to the field.

Surveys done as part of ALA's strategic long-range planning process show that the image of the librarian ranks among the top five concerns of the profession along with library finances, access to information, intellectual freedom, and library personnel resources.

John Berry III, editor-in-chief of *Library Journal* voiced frustration about appointment of non-librarians to top-level library posts, in his editorial "The Unknown Librarian," May 15, 1987. "It is a signal failure of librarianship that so little is known about what it takes to be a top librarian," Berry said in urging a public awareness effort.

Margaret Slater, writing in *Library Review*, August, 1981, concluded that there is reason to believe the public image of the library professional is changing for the better but added, "in the noisy marketing of information technology...the librarian as the human intermediary has vanished."

As part of her focus on developing "Visionary Leaders for 2020," 1987–1988 ALA President Margaret E. Chisholm called on librarians to take a leadership role in promoting their profession. Librarians are not alone in their concern about professional image, according to Dr. William A. Mindak, author, consultant, and professor of marketing at Tulane University in New Orleans. Mindak, who has advised professional groups, including accountants, lawyers, funeral directors, orthodontists, and florists, was keynote speaker at the National Library Week workshop during the 1988 ALA Annual Conference in New Orleans. "Librarians must overcome any reluctance about promoting themselves if they are to achieve the respect and recognition they deserve," Mindak told an audience of more than 500. "We all went into a profession so we wouldn't have to promote ourselves," Mindak said. "But there is too much competition today for the individual's attention, so everyone must promote."

Mindak said that he applauds the shift from promoting libraries and books to librarians. He said that "high touch"—the people element—is more important than "high tech." Marketing and selling a professional means building and maintaining a mutually beneficial relationship, Mindak explained. "Don't be preoccupied with your professional skill," he cautioned. "Show your users what they will get out of your relationship. Focusing attention on yourselves can be a double-edged sword," he added. "You will get attention from your wonderful new campaign, but you will also be raising expectations. You are promising your users they will meet dynamic, assertive and benefit-oriented librarians."

The "Ask A Professional" campaign spotlighted the people behind the service with a simple, consumer-directed message easily adapted for local use. The ALA Public Information Office (PIO) led the way at the national level by placing articles and public service messages in magazines and on television throughout 1989. The first ad appeared in the January 1989 *Good Housekeeping*.

To encourage similar efforts by local libraries, PIO sponsored a "Librarians in the Media" contest with *American Libraries* magazine and NBC television. A grand prize of $1,000 is to be awarded for the best year around coverage of librarians in local media during 1989.

Campaign promotional materials were introduced in a special videotape preview, produced by the ALA's Public Information Office and underwritten by Baker & Taylor, at the opening session of the 1988 ALA Annual Conference. These included a series of four boldly designed posters, bookmark, sticker, and print and telephone public service advertisements.

The television spot began by noting that there are questions anybody can answer ("Who's buried in Grant's Tomb?") and questions nobody can answer ("What's the meaning of life?"). It goes on to cite a range of questions that librarians can help answer: "How much is my old car worth?" "What was Bogart's first movie?" "Who's my state representative?" The print ads are adapted from the posters, each featuring a different message with the "Ask A Professional" theme line. On one, the word "Answer" is surrounded by a maze with the headline "Find the Answer Fast." Another, with "The Ans" in bold type, advises "Don't Settle For Half An Answer." An out-of-focus "ANSWER" carries the message, "Get A Clear Answer." A large question mark carries the reminder: "Get Answers To All Your Little Questions Too."

The public service ads, sample press releases, and ideas for how to adapt the campaign locally were included in the *1989 Library Publicity Campaign Book*. Special sections focus on special, academic, school, and public libraries. All materials can

Don't Settle For Half An Answer.
Ask A Professional. Ask Your Librarian.

Find The Answer Fast.
Ask A Professional. Ask Your Librarian.

Public Relations and Marketing

be purchased for local use through the ALA Graphics Catalog. Creative services for the campaign were donated by Martin Williams Advertising of Minneapolis. Design was by Richard Page, formerly with the Indianhead Library System, in Eau Claire, Wisconsin and now with the McCool & Company in Minneapolis. Copy was written by Christopher J. Wilson, of Martin Williams. In explaining the team's approach, Page said: "This campaign says librarians are *the* people to ask for information. It makes people better realize and appreciate their expertise. And we feel it quickly and eloquently positions librarians the way they should be positioned."

Page noted that the campaign intentionally avoided stereotypes, citing Pauline Wilson's *Stereotype and Status: Librarians in the United States* in which she states that "the real solution to the stereotype has to come from within. . . .librarians must acquire a better perspective on the stereotype and learn to take it in stride." According to Page, "any advertising that tries to dispel the stereotype would probably be ineffective and could inadvertently contribute to the stereotype; it's the idea that the more you shout there's no problem, the more you plant the idea that there is a problem. Plus, our own gut feeling is that the average consumer isn't particularly interested in hearing how important librarians are to a community, or how misunderstood librarians are and that they should be appreciated for the expertise they provide. . . . We do think consumers will respond to a real benefit, namely getting information."

The "Ask A Professional" campaign continues a National Library Week tradition of colorful, eye-catching promotional materials even as it breaks new ground. The first observance was celebrated in 1958 with the theme "Wake Up and Read." Succeeding themes continued the emphasis on reading under sponsorship of the National Book Committee, a nonprofit group composed of publishers, librarians, teachers, and citizens. ALA took over sponsorship when the committee disbanded in 1974.

In addition to the "Ask A Professional" campaign, the ALA Public Information Office worked with the Office for Library Personnel Resources to develop a new campaign promoting careers in library and information science. The campaign responds to current and projected shortages in the library field. The theme for the recruitment campaign is "The Future Is Information. Take Charge Of The Future." Materials include a brochure, print public service ads, and posters illustrated with photographs of real library science diplomas.

The *1988–89 Occupational Outlook Handbook* noted that the number of graduates of master's degree programs in library science dropped to less than half the level of the mid–1970s, while a larger-than-average proportion of librarians will reach retirement age through the year 2000. Library associations in some states have reported acute shortages of children's librarians and school library media specialists. A survey of cataloging positions open in 1985 found that 56 percent of the positions were vacant seven months or more.

"After Mary Got One Of These, The Magazines And Newspapers Wouldn't Leave Her Alone." is the theme for one recruitment poster explaining that, as head of the Serials Department at Northwestern University Library, in Evanston, Illinois, Mary Margaret Case is responsible for the acquisition and inventory control of every journal, magazine and newspaper in the library collection. Wayne Crocker, director of the Petersburg Public Library in Virginia, is featured on another poster with the headline "After Wayne Got One Of These, He Was Given Half A Million Dollars." Another poster featuring Steve Herb, Coordinator, Children's Services, Dauphin County (Pennsylvania) Library System, states: "After Steve Got One Of These, He Became The Star Of A Popular Children's Program." The posters served as the basis for print public service advertisements distributed to selected national publications. A 13–page brochure gives an overview of opportunities in the profession, including education requirements and salary considerations. Campaign materials were available from ALA Graphics for use on college campuses.

Speaking at a preconference "Each One, Recruit One" at the 1988 ALA Annual Conference, Vartan Gregorian, president of the New York Public Library, spoke frankly. "Librarians should not consider themselves passive actors on the stage of humanity," he said. "You are not followers of the Age of Information but leaders. This is your specialty. Unless you eliminate your inferiority complex, this profession is going to suffer. You as professionals must end your squabbles. Downgrading of each other leads to downgrading of the profession." Referring to the new campaign materials, Gregorian said: "This is Madison Avenue. It is your passion and your pride that will sell this profession."

LINDA WALLACE

authored an article on a specific winning entry in *School Library Media Quarterly*; and Marilyn Shuman summarized 1988 winners' entries in *Library Administration and Management*.

Contest judges were available at an annual conference exhibit booth and at a table during the Swap and Shop program to discuss winning entries. They also distributed star-shaped stickers to publicize the contest, and they presented a videotape of winning media entries. Outreach activities were extended with presentations at state conferences by Judge Michael Haeuser at the Minnesota Library Association and Laurie Sabol at the Ohio Library Association.

ALA Public Information Office. The ALA Public Information Office (PIO) continued to play a central role in the National Library Card Sign-up Campaign launched in 1987 with the theme "The Best Gift You'll Ever Give Your Child. . .A Library Card." More than 10,000 posters and 1,500,000 bookmarks were distributed for the campaign.

The Reader's Digest Foundation contributed an additional $138,000 to develop new campaign materials directed at older children and teens. These included television and radio spots.

The National Library Week April 17–23 theme "The Card with a Charge" reinforced the library card campaign message. National Library Week Partners—63 national education and literacy associations—promoted the message with their members. The winner of the nationwide contest

Table 1. Committee Membership By Type of Library, LAMA Public Relations Section, 1985–1988

Library Type	1985	1986	1987	1988
Academic	15	12	20	26
Association	1	0	0	0
Consortium	4	9	9	5
Consultants	4	1	3	3
Library School	0	0	1	2
Military	1	1	0	3
Public	54	49	57	61
School	3	3	2	7
Special	3	3	3	5
State	14	8	7	8
Annual Totals	99	86	102	120

Source: *LAMA Roster of Officers and Committees,* 1985–1988

Table 2. John Cotton Dana Library PR Award Contest 1988

Library Type	Number of Entries	Special Award	JCD Award
Academic	12	2	0
Association	1	1	0
Consortium	8	1	0
Military	8	0	1
Public	81	9	1
School	7	1	0
Special	2	0	1
State	2	0	0
Totals	121	14	3

Source: John Cotton Dana Award Judging Committee
Note: The ALA Awards section in this volume lists names of winners.

"Why I Love My Library Card" received first prize for a poem that compared a library card to a charge card with an endless line of credit. More than 750 libraries participated in the contest. The summer 1988 issue of PIOs *PR Activity Report* described the contest. The National Library Week Committee awarded the Kentucky Library Association a $1,000 Grolier Grant for its statewide library card sign-up campaign.

During National Library Week former librarian Congressperson Major Owens (Democrat–New York) and U.S. Senator Alfonse D'Amato (Republican–New York) introduced joint resolutions declaring September as "National Library Card Sign-up Month." The Sears "Back to School" catalog, sent to nearly half of all U.S. households, encouraged children to sign up for library cards. Macy's and The Company Store catalogs also promoted library card ownership and 25,000,000 Happy Meals boxes at McDonald's restaurants carried library card messages.

The 1989 National Library Week theme "Ask a Professional: Ask a Librarian" was unveiled at the ALA Annual Conference, 1988 *Yearbook* essay by Linda Wallace described the campaign. Academic librarians particularly thought the graphics would appeal to college and university audiences.

PIO assisted ALA units and officers in using mass media effectively for telling the library story. Topics such as the FBI Library Awareness Program, the shortage of librarians, latchkey children in libraries, and the implications of reduced access to government information drew considerable media attention. The FBI Library Awareness Program was featured on ABC's "Nightline" and "Good Morning America," and in such newspapers as *USA Today*.

The ALA Public Information Office placed public service advertisements in a diverse array of national publications including *Learning, Working Mother, Seventeen,* and *Better Homes and Gardens*. The popular year-end issue of *Rolling Stone* carried a full-page for the teen library card campaign with a commercial value of $40,000.

A new PIO brochure, *America's Libraries: New Views,* presented noteworthy statistics about public, school, and academic libraries. This colorful brochure was distributed to members of Congress and the mass media, serving as the catalyst for a comprehensive feature story about innovative library services in *The New York Times* of September 21. The brochure was also used by libraries for generating political and/or financial support.

Major entertainment stars again contributed support for ALAs celebrity "READ" poster series. Included among them were Michael J. Fox, Oprah Winfrey, and Phil Collins. Singer/actor Ruben Blades appeared on the first Spanish-language celebrity poster "LEER ES PODER" (Reading is Power); Keshia Pulliam Knight of the "Bill Cosby Show" appeared on a library card campaign poster with the message "I Got Carded at the Library."

JON ELDREDGE

Publishing, Book

Merger mania continued in 1988 with fewer, but larger, deals. According to *BP Report*, there were 49 mergers and acquisitions through November 21, 1988, compared with 58 the previous year. However, Robert Maxwell's $2,500,000,000 acquisition of Macmillan set a record for the publishing industry. Maxwell was not the only foreigner to buy a U.S. publishing house in 1988; Pearson, Hachette, Elsevier, International Thompson, and Taylor & Francis also acquired U.S. houses.

Statistics. According to the Association of American Publishers, total book sales were up to 9.2 percent in 1987, as compared with 5.8 percent in 1986. The biggest gains were seen in trade books (18.1 percent) and juvenile paperbacks (19.6 percent). Overall, sales totaled $11,400,000,000. Thanks to the weak dollar, books exports were up 22 percent in 1987 and up 30.8 percent during the first half of 1988, according to the Commerce Department. The publishing trade deficit (imports minus exports) was reduced from $100,000,000 in 1986 to $4,500,000 in 1987. A record high of 124 hardcover books had reported sales of more than 100,000 copies in 1987, and 17 of the best-sellers sold more than 500,000 copies. Everyone seemed to be publishing children's books, but 1989 is expected to be the peak year of the baby boomlet, and the birth rate should then start to decline as the baby boom generation ages. This means sales of children's books should remain strong through the end of the century. The Library of Congress declared 1989 to be the Year of the Young Reader.

Advances to writers continued to soar—$10,000,000 to Mary Higgins Clark for a four-book deal, $4,900,000 for the sequel to *Gone With The Wind* and $3,000,000 for the paperback rights to Scott Turow's *Presumed Innocent*.

Library Market. Librarians continued to express dismay over the rising cost of books and serials—an increase rate much higher than the Consumer Price Index. While the largest increases were seen in foreign journals and impacted academic libraries, concern was widespread enough for ALA's Resources and Technical Services Division to establish a Task Force on Economics of Access to Library Materials, chaired by Robert Wedgeworth, Dean of Columbia University School of Library Service.

Takeovers. British Publishing magnate Robert Maxwell, who had failed to take over Harcourt Brace Jovanovich in 1987, succeeded in buying Macmillan in 1988 after a lengthy fight. In May an unsolicited offer for Macmillan was made by the Robert Bass Group. In July, Maxwell entered the bidding. In September Macmillan agreed to a leveraged buyout by Kohlberg Kravis Roberts (KKR). Shortly thereafter Bass withdrew his offer, leaving KKR and Maxwell to take the issue to court. The deal, finally resolved in November, ended with Maxwell paying Macmillan $90.25 a share—considerably more than Bass's original offer of $64. This makes Macmillan the largest acquisition in book publishing history at about $2,500,000,000. Maxwell also purchased Science Research Associates in 1988. Even before these purchases, *BP Report* estimated that foreign publishers own 25 percent of the U.S. book publishing business. Publishing houses owned by foreign companies generated sales of approximately $2,800,000,000 in 1987 out of total U.S. sales of $11,400,000,000.

Hachette, the French publisher, bought Grolier, encyclopedia publisher and direct mail marketing, for $450,000,000. Funk & Wagnalls, another encyclopedia publisher, was bought by the Field Corporation, former owner of World Book. McGraw-Hill, in an effort to define its business better, put its trade division up for sale and bought the school and college divisions of Random House. Random House bought Crown and Vanguard Press, making Random House the nation's largest publisher of general books. Macmillan sold its science list to Wiley and Harper & Row bought Zondervan. Addison-Wesley was bought by the British firm, Pearson, and Lyle Stuart was sold to a privately-held real estate company. Dodd, Mead sold rights to its children's books, Agatha Christie titles, and others to Putnam. Times Mirror bought Richard D. Irwin, publisher of college texts. Robert Bell & Co. bought Bell & Howell, the parent company of Charles Merrill. At least a dozen more buyouts took place during the year.

Fairs. The 40th postwar Frankfurt Book Fair was held in October with more then 7,500 exhibitors, an increase of nearly 10 percent. The fair was described by many as being quieter than usual, perhaps because the growing use of FAX machines is replacing some face-to-face negotiations that were formerly necessary in signing book contracts. Visitors to the 1988 London Book Fair were up by 31 percent.

Copyright. After a three-year effort, the U.S. finally joined the century-old Berne Copyright Convention. Congress passed the necessary legislation making membership effective early in 1989. The Copyright Office asked Congress to amend the Copyright Act so that states cannot claim immunity from copyright suits brought against state institutions on the basis of the 11th Amendment. As it now stands, state universities, for instance, may claim that their photocopying could not be restrained by the Copyright Act. The Association for Copyright Enforcement was formed to press copyright suits against offending corporations. To be funded from income to the Copyright Clearance Center, the Association will initially pursue the Texaco case.

AAP. Membership statistics and financial situation for the Association of American Publishers continued to improve. AAP has been successful in pursuing pirates. A Taiwan court fined copyright enfringers of the *Concise Encyclopaedia Britannica*. A government survey estimated that American publishers are losing about $427,000,000 to book pirates in 10 nations, most of them in Southeast Asia. Nat Wartels, founder of the Crown Publishing Group, won the AAP's Curtis Benjamin Award for Creative Publishing.

AAUP. A new executive director, Tim Phillips, was appointed by the American Association of University Presses, and suppliers exhibited at the annual meeting for the first time. Another first was the attendance of a top-level delegation of Soviet publishers.

Court Cases. A legal suit was brought by John Cheever's heirs over the proposed publication of a Cheever short story collection by Academy Chicago. The publishers of J. D. Salinger, L. Ron Hubbard, and Robert Maxwell biographies were taken to court. The Supreme Court refused to hear an appeal in the Tennessee textbook case where Christian fundamentalists sought to keep their children from reading books that violated their religious beliefs in school.

Awards. Walker Percy was named the National Endowment for the Humanities Jefferson lecturer. Random House made a clean sweep at the 1988 National Book Awards (NBA): the fiction award went to Pete Dexter for *Paris Trout*, and the nonfiction award to Neil Sheehan for *A Bright Shining Lie: John Paul Vann and America in Vietnam*. Random House's editorial director Jason Epstein was awarded a special NBA medal for a distinguished contribution to American letters. Pulitzer Prizes were awarded to Toni Morrison for *Beloved*, William Meredith for *Partial Accounts: New and Selected Poems*, and Robert V. Bruce for *The Launching of Modern American Science 1846-1876*. All three books were published by Knopf. Other winning books were Richard Rhodes' *The Making of the Atomic Bomb* (Simon & Schuster) and David Herbert Donald's *Look Homeward: A Life of Thomas Wolfe* (Little, Brown.) The 1988 Nobel Prize for Literature went to Egyptian novelist Naguib Mahfouz. (For Newbery and Caldecott medal winners, see American Library Association and Awards in this volume.

Table 1. Estimated Book Publishing Industry Sales, 1972, 1977, 1982, 1986-87

	1972	1977	1982		1986		1987			
	$	$	$	% chg from 77	$	% chg from 82	$	% chg from 86	% chg from 82	% chg from 77
Trade (Total)	444.8	887.2	1355.5	52.8	2095.5	54.6	2428.5	15.9	79.2	173.7
Adult Hardbound	251.5	501.3	671.6	34.3	1025.8	52.7	1211.5	18.1	80.4	141.7
Adult Paperbound$	82.4	223.7	452.0	102.1	683.5	51.2	767.6	12.3	69.8	243.1
Juvenile Hardbound	106.5	136.1	180.3	32.5	290.1	60.9	334.5	15.3	85.5	145.8
Juvenile Paperbound	4.4	26.1	51.5	97.3	96.1	86.6	114.9	19.6	123.1	340.2
Religious (Total)	117.5	250.6	390.0	55.6	475.5	21.9	539.3	13.4	38.3	115.2
Bibles, Testaments, Hymnals, and Prayerbooks	61.6	116.3	163.7	40.8	182.9	11.7	210.7	15.2	28.7	81.2
Other Religious	55.9	134.3	226.2	68.4	292.6	29.4	328.6	12.3	45.3	144.7
Professional (Total)	381.0	698.2	1230.5	76.2	1722.5	40.0	1845.2	7.1	50.0	164.3
Technical & Scientific	131.8	249.3	431.4	73.0	579.1	34.2	635.9	9.8	47.4	155.1
Business & Other Professional	192.2	286.3	530.6	85.3	747.5	40.9	796.8	6.6	50.2	178.3
Medical	57.0	162.6	268.5	65.1	395.9	47.4	412.5	4.2	53.6	153.7
Book Clubs	240.5	406.7	590.0	45.1	698.4	18.4	779.4	11.6	32.1	91.6
Mail Order Publications	198.9	396.4	604.6	52.5	620.6	2.6	627.4	1.1	3.8	58.3
Mass Market Paperback Rack-Sized*	250.0	487.7	685.5	40.6	792.3	15.6	893.7	12.8	30.4	83.2
University Presses	41.4	56.1	122.9	119.1	160.5	30.6	172.1	7.2	40.0	206.8
Elementary & Secondary Text	497.6	755.9	1051.5	39.1	1604.0	52.5	1705.1	6.3	62.2	125.6
College Text**	375.3	649.7	1142.4	75.8	1409.8	23.4	1521.2	7.9	33.2	134.2
Standardized Tests	26.5	44.6	69.7	56.3	96.6	38.6	101.9	5.5	46.2	128.5
Subscription Reference	278.9	294.4	396.6	34.7	501.2	26.4	516.2	3.0	30.2	75.3
AV and Other Media (Total)	116.2	151.3	148.0	-2.2	211.1	42.6	213.0	0.9	43.9	40.8
Elementary and High School	101.2	131.4	130.1	-1.0	177.4	36.4	174.7	-1.5	34.3	33.0
College	9.2	11.6	7.9	-31.9	13.5	70.9	15.1	11.5	91.1	30.2
Other	5.8	8.3	10.0	20.5	20.2	102.0	23.2	14.9	132.0	179.5
Other Sales	49.2	63.4	77.1	21.6	96.5	25.2	104.2	8.0	35.1	64.4
Total	3017.8	5142.2	7864.3	52.9	10484.5	33.3	11447.2	9.2	45.6	122.6

$ Includes Non-Rack-Sized Sales by Mass Market Publishers of $113.5 million in 1982; $172.9 million in 1986; and $200.0 million in 1987.

* The added reporting of certain mass market publishers in 1985 and 1986 has given this survey data from all major MMPB publishers. Based on this information, it would seem that our estimates of the industry sales were virtually "on the mark." However, to allow for the few small non-reporting MMPB publishers, we have increased our 1982 estimate by $20 million, and our 1986 estimate by $30 million.

**The Higher Education Division of AAP has requested the Statistical Service Center to conduct an independent survey of college publishers. For 1987, this survey of 50 college publishers, which in the opinion of the Higher Education Division Statistics Committee represents the majority of known college publishers, reported sales of $1,249.1 million. The results of this Survey, and a list of the participants, are presented as Table G1.

Source: Association of American Publishers, Inc.

Best-sellers. Among the bestselling books of 1988 were Tom Clancy's *Cardinal of the Kremlin* and *A Brief History of Time*, by British astronomer Stephen W. Hawking. Donald Trump's *Trump: Art of the Deal* and Tom Wolfe's *Bonfire of the Vanities* both enjoyed many weeks on best-seller lists. The newest Sidney Sheldon (*The Sands of Time*) and James Michener (*Alaska*) sold well. Following on the success of his 1987 book, *Cultural Literacy*, E. D. Hirsch compiled *The Dictionary of Cultural Literacy* which defines the terms that every American ought to know.

Miscellaneous. The University of Scranton closed its Center for the Study of the Book, which had been headed by book industry analyst John Dessauer. Transaction Periodicals Consortium plans to continue to publish *Book Research Quarterly*, now edited by Beth Luey and which it had co-sponsored with the Center. Congress voted to exempt writers and artists from an IRS regulation that deductions for the expense of a work in progress must be deferred until the work produced income. Authors can now deduct business expenses in the year in which they were incurred. Congress also agreed to continue an appropriation to the U.S. Postal Service that will allow it to continue the subsidy that allows books to be mailed to libraries below cost.

Deaths. Frederick Ungar, founder in 1940 of the New York publishing house that bore his name died in 1988.

SANDY WHITELEY

Publishing, Electronic

The year 1988 did not see any slowdown in technology changes. If 1987 was the "Year of CD-ROM," then 1988 was the "Year of Connectivity," and 1989 promises to be the "Year of Gateways." Regardless of what year it was, the quality of our research tools and the ability to access and manipulate information improve with each new change in technology.

Communications and Connectivity: Networking. Private network systems are proliferating. Ranging in size from small local area networks (LANs) within single buildings to larger networks, like that run by the Colorado Alliance of Research Libraries (CARL), networks are connecting users at multiple sites for the purpose of sharing both equipment and information resources.

The CARL system offers an online catalog, circulation and acquisition control, and Grolier's Online Encyclopedia for numerous research li-

The Library of Congress issued its first compact disk read-only memory (CD-ROM) subject. Issued by the Cataloging Distribution Service, the compact disk CDMARK Subjects, contains the complete subject authority file of the library.

braries in the state, including the Colorado School of Mines, the Denver Public Library, and the University of Denver. Similar systems are being used at other locations such as the one at Carnegie Mellon in Pennsylvania, which not only offers a variety of locally stored databases but also provides gateway access to larger commercial services such as Dialog.

LANs, usually restricted to a single building or site, offer similar advantages. Montclair Public Library in New Jersey is automating its catalog and will shortly be able to supplement or replace its card catalogues with workstations that will also show patrons whether a book is "in" or "out." By expanding access to this local network from other libraries in neighboring towns, patrons at any location will have access to a larger collection than would otherwise be possible.

Online Services. The year 1988 was another year of consolidation within the online database industry, with the most notable event being the sale of Dialog to Knight-Ridder. Another significant event was the addition of real-time services by several professional research services. For example, Dialog now offers real-time news from a variety of sources, and Mead Data acquired Dataline, a Canadian stock-quote vendor.

While overall growth of the online industry was almost 20 percent during 1987, some impact to future online usage is expected from the growth of CD-ROM products. Dialog and BRS, anticipating a decline in per-user revenue, have both started marketing CD-ROM titles of their own. While these titles are more expensive to a single user than online costs would be, they are effective search tools for high-frequency usage.

Online vendors tend to control pricing of their services, but one publisher this year instituted a change that could have far-reaching implications for both end-users and other database publishers. Taking the position that changes in communications and retrieval technology have made connect-time no longer feasible as a pricing mechanism, Chemical Abstracts Service (CAS) has insisted its vendors now charge for the information actually retrieved rather than for the time used to access it. Under its new rate schedule, the average cost to an end-user will be about 10% higher for an average search of CAS material.

Gateways. Gateways connect one online service to another, allowing a user to access files from many sources without having to subscribe to multiple vendors. Some of the more popular gateway services include those offered by Telebase Systems (Easynet) and Western Union (Easylink). However, with recent changes in federal laws, regional Bell operating companies (RBOCs) are now allowed to offer gateway services and are already running experimental services in serval areas. Nynex, in the New York State area, is testing a gateway service in Burlington, Vermont. Other, similar tests are now underway by BellSouth and Southwestern Bell in other parts of the country.

Telefacsimile and Telephone Voice Services. By the end of 1988 there will be more than 2,000,000 telefacsimile (fax) machines in use in the United States, and fax networks are growing rapidly. The advantage of fax is that a copy of an original document may be sent from one location to another in less than 30 seconds for the average cost of $1 per page.

Library-specific applications have not yet emerged, but the use of fax technology use by interlibrary lending networks is growing rapidly. A notable example of this is Kanfax, a fax network established this year through a series of grants made by the Kansas Library Network Board. By the end of 1988, there will be 17 public and school libraries throughout the state participating in the network.

Telephone service, using specialized voice lines designated as "976" and "900" networks, proliferated in 1988. Services vary from teenage party lines to daily horoscopes, and charges average between $2 and $3 per minute of use. In Denver, General Electric Information Service (GEnie) will offer a subset of its online service, including the *Grolier Online Encyclopedia*, through the Mountain Bell "976" network. Even though GEnie's computers are located in Maryland, Denver residents will be able to access the service through this unique network for as little as $3 per hour.

Optical Storage. CD-ROM. There are about 300 CD-ROM titles that are commercially available, with about one-third of the total identified as library reference or automation tools. According to a survey by Research Publications, almost a third of all librarians now use CD-ROM products, and more than half of all librarians expect to use them by 1991.

Clearly, CD-ROM has found a home in libraries. Some predict that more than 75,000 librarians will be using CD-ROM by the year 1991. Aside from the obvious benefits of space, cost-effectiveness versus other technologies, and ease of use, CD-ROM provides a durable and long-lasting medium for storing information. This can be as compelling a reason to use CD-ROM as the sophisticated retrieval software it includes.

CD-ROM and Networking. CD-ROM traditionally has been cast as a single-user device, but this is starting to change. The benefits of allowing multiple users to access a single disk are obvious, and the growth of local area networks is beginning to make this possible. A CD-ROM laser driver, compared to a magnetic hard disk, is a relatively slow machine, and simultaneous use by more than five to six users causes a dramatic deterioration in performance. Interestingly, the solution to this problem has not come from boosting the driver performance, but by unique "traffic control" methods by network software.

Several companies have either released or are developing networking products for CD-ROMs. These include Meridian Data, Custom Design Technology, and Online Incorporated. Online, working with Grolier Electronic Publishing, is developing a network software product that will allow any and all users on a local area network to access the *Grolier Electronic Encyclopedia*.

Again, changing technology offers solutions to problems—in this case issues like the arrangement and administration of electronic workstations within the library itself. No longer will it be necessary to set up and monitor schedules for users to access a CD-ROM, since many patrons will be able to use a single device.

New Optical Formats and Multimedia Databases. As another example of how one technology change will foster many others, new formats of optical discs continue to be introduced. During 1987, Philips and Sony announced a multimedia disc format called Compact Disc Interactive (CD-I), which allows the use of sound and graphics along with text. Shortly after that, RCA announced a format called Digital Video Interactive (DVI), which encompasses sound, graphics, text, and motion.

Desktop Publishing and Its Applications for Libraries

Librarians are keepers of the printed word, but they are a creative lot, and these days they are also prolific producers of a wide variety of printed materials. Their creations range from simple "Out Of Order" signs to bookmarks, program fliers, bibliographies, calendars, banners, certificates, maps and guides to buildings, pamphlets, newsletters, and directories, to the usual letters and memoranda of bureaucratic library organizations. Having recognized that effectiveness depends on appearance as well as content, libraries were long faced with the trade-off of quality versus time, cost, and effort. On one end of the scale was the hand-lettered sign: cheap, fast, and easy. At the other end of the scale was the document produced by professional graphic designers and typesetters: very expensive and time consuming. In the middle ground, librarians learned to cope with the limitations of typewriters, scissors, paste, and self-adhesive letters; this was definitely not easy.

Then, a couple of years ago, librarians discovered that a microcomputer with a word-processing program helped to manipulate text effectively. Library staffers learned that corrections need not be made at the price of retyping and that once entered, text almost never had to be typed again. Some of the pain was taken out of creativity. But that left two problems: the integration of graphics and text onto a controlled layout and the quality of the printing process. Dot-matrix printers were improved, but resolution of around 150 dots per inch still did not look legible enough. Text could be printed on "letter-quality" daisy-wheel impact printers, but these printers could not do graphics. Besides, they were horrendously slow and noisy.

The solutions to these problems are at hand, and they have come to be called "desktop publishing" (DTP). In the last year or so librarians have been discovering joyfully that this new technology has freed them to be more productive than ever before. They are finding that, without the services of outside professionals, they can produce documents in final form, ready for readers or camera-ready for duplication. With equipment compact enough to fit on a desktop, and costing under $8,000, library staffers now have full command over the creative process, with the power to control the position, size, and shape of text, graphics, and other page elements of all kinds. With "What-You-See-Is-What-You-Get" (WYSIWYG) displays, library personnel can have immediate feedback on the results of changes. As they discovered before with word processing, they can have it just the way they want it. Although the artistic instinct certainly has not been given equally to everyone, at least the labor involved in editing now has little inhibiting effect on the creative urge.

Integration of graphics and text has been achieved by more powerful personal computers, matched with graphically oriented, easy-to-learn page layout programs. Print quality came with the introduction of reasonably priced laser printers capable of quietly and speedily generating text and graphics at twice the resolution of a typical dot-matrix printer. The typical model uses technology similar to that of a photocopy machine and produces 300 dots-per-inch output at eight pages a minute. This is still far less than commercial typesetting equipment at 1,200 to 2,500 dots-per-inch, but the average reader will not know the difference. The paradigm setup consisted of the Apple Macintosh microcomputer, Aldus Pagemaker software, and the Apple Laserwriter printer, which came into use in 1984. Since that time, Apple has introduced several new models of computers and laser printers with greatly improved capabilities. Although Apple's prices are considered high by many, they also maintain a special sales program for schools and libraries, with substantial discounts.

Major page layout programs now competing with Pagemaker include Ready, Set, Go! (Letraset) and QuarkXPress (Quark). Other products are also proving useful to desktop publishers. Scanners sold by Apple and other companies add the ability to convert printed graphics, including halftone photographs, to digital form. They may then be stored on disk, modified in whole or in part for size, contrast, brightness, etc., by programs such as Image Studio (Letraset) and included in document layouts. Frame-grabbers can similarly capture and manipulate video signals from a camera. Scanners can work with optical character recognition programs to convert printed text into digital form which may then be modified and used in exactly the same manner as the product of any word processor, thus eliminating keyboard labor in many cases. Graphics programs ranging from MacPaint and MacDraw (Claris) to Aldus Freehand and Illustrator 88 (Adobe) make it easier to create art or modify someone else's. Collections of clip-art images are available on disk for librarians less blessed with artistic ability or time. Full-page monitors are available, which are particularly useful for Macintosh models that come with nine-inch screens. These provide the ability to easily view an entire page of a document at one time. Although this can be done on a smaller screen by sizing the image of the page to fit the screen, the text is generally too small to read.

Printers using ink-jet technology that match the 300 dots-per-inch resolution of the typical laser printer are available but are much cheaper than the laser. There are also high-end laser printers sold by Apple and others. Both kinds lack the Postscript page-description language interpreter that enables the better laser printers to provide full control of position, size, and shape of both graphics and text. A printer with a Postscript interpreter is needed to take advantage of the capabilities of current page layout and graphics programs.

Libraries that are locked into the IBM-compatible world of equipment either by choice or because of rigid purchasing policies are not left out. A variety of good equipment and software available for MS-DOS users exists. Well-regarded page layout programs include Ventura Publisher (Xerox) and the MS-DOS version of Pagemaker. Purchase and installation of such a system may be more complicated, however. This is partly due to the fact that while the Macintosh comes with a mouse and a graphic operating system, the owner of an IBM-compatible may have to install separately a mouse and a graphic environment system, such as Microsoft's Windows or Digital Research's GEM interface. Existing systems may require the addition of costly high-resolution graphics cards and monitors. Although most libraries will not find it necessary to produce color documents, many users already have low-resolution color monitors and are addicted to the color, but high-resolution color monitors are particularly expensive. Adding a hard disk drive and more memory may also be required, and a faster microprocessor may be desired.

Compared to straight text, graphics demands more memory, disk space, and processing power. This is true, regardless of the brand of computer. Macintosh owners will find that life without a hard disk is like getting to work on a motorbike. What's more, a 20 megabyte drive was once satisfactory, but many users will now want at least 40 megabytes. No less than one megabyte of memory will also be highly desirable, if not necessary. Unfortunately, although the cost of hard drives has steadily dropped, at the present time memory chips are in short supply and prices are high, due to high demand and international market conditions. This shortage may ease in 1989 as manufacturing capacities increase, and the price of memory chips may resume its long-term downward trend.

Another kind of microcomputer already in place in many libraries is the underrated Apple II series. These machines have been used for several years in many places for a kind of desk-top publishing. Word-processed text printed on a good dot-matrix printer has been merged with computer-generated clip art or other graphics using cut-and-paste methods to produce usable results. Programs such as the ubiquitous Print Shop and Newsroom have long been used to produce fliers, signs, banners, and newsletters with computer integrated text and graphics. The economics of such methods are hard to beat, when the equipment is already owned, and the software prices are a very small fraction of the cost of Macintosh programs, and an even smaller fraction of MS-DOS prices. Newer programs, such as Springboard Publisher (Springboard Software), Publish It! (Timeworks), or GEOS (Berkeley), provide a Macintosh-like graphic interface on the Apple II, with page layout, word-processing, and graphics creation capability. In addition, some of these programs now claim the ability to print on a laser printer.

The technology of desk-top publishing, like the microcomputers upon which it is based, has been developing rapidly. Significant developments are seen each year. There is always the temptation to wait for next year's model. But the promise of better things tomorrow does not compensate for the lost opportunity to accomplish things today. The opportunity for libraries to produce their own high-quality documents economically is here now.

MARVIN I. GARBER

In 1988, Microsoft, Philips, and Sony announced CD-ROM Extended Architecture (CD-ROM XA), which allows the use of sound, graphics, text, and full-motion video. To further confuse the issue, Tandy has also announced that it is working on a compact disk that can be erased and reused.

While all these different disk formats seem confusing, what they represent is an opening up of new tools for publishers to use. For example, Facts on File has developed a French-English dictionary on optical disc that provides not only text and pictures, but also recorded pronunciations of words. Grolier has under development a *Multimedia Encyclopedia* that provides text, pictures, maps, and audiovisual essays, in addition to learning tools using text, graphics, and sound.

Summary. While technology is improving the way that we deal with information, the quality of the information exchange itself is also improving. A plain text database, once considered state of the art merely by virtue of the fact that it came in electronic form, is now likely to include such enhancements as sophisticated indexing and cross-referencing, graphics, and audio. Regardless of what form this combination of data takes, the consumer is the one who ultimately benefits—it is an enriched and enriching experience of seeking and finding information.

Bibliography

Bowers, R. A. ed. *Optical Publishing Directory, 1987*, Learned Information, 1987, Medford, N.J.

"Computers in Higher Education," 1988, *Chronicle of Higher Education*, Washington, D.C.

Information Industry Factbook: The Information Industry's Annual Report, 1988, Stamford, Connecticut. Digital Information Group.

Nelson, N. M., ed. *CD-ROM's in Print 1987*, 1988, Westport, Connecticut. Meckler Publishing.

Pitkin, Gary M. "Serials on OPACs/Access to Articles through CARL and the Online Catalogue," *American Libraries*, 19, no.9 (October 1988): 769–70.

Reese, Jean. "Surveying the CD-ROM Scene: What's Out There?" Conference paper. Online meeting, New York City, 1988.

Shanks, Linda C. "Information on the Line," *Presstime*, September 1988.

Tiampo, Janet M. "Evaluating the CD-ROM Industry." *CD-ROM Review* 3, no.2 (April 1988): 21–23.

Travis Nicholls, Paul. "Statistical Profile of Currently Available CD-ROM Database Products," *The Laserdisk Professional* 1, no.4 (November 1988): 38–45.

Way, Harold E. "Telefacsimile in a Library Network." Conference paper. Online meeting, New York City, 1988.

FRANK J. FARRELL
RICHARD TOWNLEY

Publishing, Serials

It started a decade or so ago as a fire fight against the increasing cost of periodicals. By 1988, the fight had developed into a battle, but a battle without victory in sight.

Periodicals have doubled, tripled, and even quadrupled in price. According to the annual ALA report (*Library Journal*, April 15, 1988, p. 37), "Serial prices continue to climb . . . . The average subscription price of a U.S. periodical in 1988 is $77.93 . . . . This year's average percentage increase is 9.1 percent."

Any relief in sight is shattered by prospects of more inflation. The magazine trade journal *Folio* in its March 1988 issue states that subscription prices are going up. "More than 20 percent of magazines plan to increase basic subscription prices this year—compared to 11 percent in 1987. Small and regional titles are leading the way." Publishers' justification includes increased costs, inflation, and the necessity to meet a recent postal hike. For example, *Newsweek* boosted its basic subscription price 10 percent because postal increases cost an added $2,400,000 in 1988.

What's the librarian's solution to all of this? Nothing much except conferences and numerous articles. Is anything else possible? Probably not, at least as long as certain periodicals are required for libraries and publishers are less than sympathetic with library budgetary limitations.

Meanwhile, the not-so-necessary titles are acting as a brake and the only practical approach is to cancel subscriptions, even long-standing ones. If there is a common picture of the serials librarian these days it is of that individual attempting to determine what *can* be cut, what *probably can* be cut, and what *cannot* be cut. Formulas, methods, and even software programs abound in offering help, but none is worth much when it comes to the final decision.

Stanford University Libraries is typical. With a projected 1988–1989 budget shortfall of more than $200,000, $100,000 worth in science journals will be dropped. The story is repeated in library after library, regardless of type, size, or location.

Of course that is scarcely any solution. Future research will pay for today's lack of money. And the money is lacking. It simply is no show to request more funds for periodicals. The Reagan years have broken the backs of the budget experts and, at least for the time being, there is no hope. Libraries will continue to suffer until periodicals publishers realize that they are killing themselves off and/or until library budgets increase. Plans from threatening publishers to national cooperation serve only to fill space in magazines. One example is almost the entire May 15, 1988 issue of *Library Journal*.

The often heard solution of stemming the flood of new journals runs against all past and present experience, i.e., the number of titles will continue to increase, not decrease. Scholarly publishing, once confined to a few well-known journals in each academic field is now booming. Narrow interest publications are emerging by the thousands. While there is no official tally, publishers and librarians estimate that the number of American scientific journals has doubled since 1970, to perhaps 5,000 titles. And at Harvard, annual subscriptions for periodicals in the humanities and social sciences alone have jumped nearly 20 percent in the last five years, to nearly 20,000 titles.

The international figure is even more impressive—some 70,000 periodicals. At least 40,000 scientific journals are now estimated to roll off presses around the world. And in sociology alone approximately 2,400 scholarly articles are generated each year. From time to time conferences, congresses, and hearings attempt to decrease the birthrate of journals. For example, the American Medical Association is planning an international meeting on peer review in biomedical publications. Quality control may cause control over numbers, but skeptics doubt that the results will differ from those of previous gatherings—more papers about the meeting published in more journals.

The revolution in production is cited as a basic reason for the proliferation of new periodicals. The British *Observer*, June 19, 1988, p. 11 describes it as "a media empire in your back bedroom." Translated, this is the age of desktop publishing. Only in the past 12 months have professional publishers become convinced that there is something in microcomputers for them. Desktop publishing means that with less than $30,000 (for the purchase of software, printers, microcomputers, etc.) one can publish from camera ready copy to be sent directly to commercial printers.

The start-up cost of a magazine being a fraction of what it was only a year ago reduces the amount of risk capital needed to get into print. A new title called *Desktop Publishing* which explains to laypersons how it is all done, and increasingly more regular computer journals carry stories and features on what has come to be known as DTP.

With that, what are the best new magazines of 1,000 or so published in 1988? Some 20 such titles see "Magazine Madness" (*Library Journal*, April 1, 1988). Among them are *American Visions*, a tribute to Black History and culture; *Big Times*, for those with vision problems who want to read encouraging news about the U.S.; and *Spy*, a humor magazine out of New York City. Most newcomers are little poetry and literary magazines. Others are specialized for business, e.g., *Decorative Rug* which caters to rug merchants. Then there are a few for librarians, e.g., *The Acquisitions Librarian*, *CD Review Digest*, and *CD-ROM Librarian*. The only certainty about new magazines is that each year brings more of them.

Reviews are few, appearing regularly in *Library Journal* "Magazines," and periodically in *American Libraries* and *Wilson Library Bulletin*. Regrettably, *Choice* gave up its regular column on magazines in early January 1988, the reviews now being integrated with the subjects. This questionable approach in when more, not fewer reviews are needed, seems most unfair to academic libraries that relied on *Choice* for selection of new journals.

European and Japanese firms continue to buy American publishing houses. In 1988, Hachette S.A. of France agreed to pay $47,200,000 for

Dianandis Communications. This means that numerous library/newstand favorites are now French owned, among these: *Woman's Day, Audio, Stereo Review, Popular Photography, Flying, Road and Truck, Car and Driver,* and *Boating.* In another purchase, *Reader's Digest,* which for 60 years published only the one magazine, agreed to acquire *Family Handyman,* one of the largest home improvement magazines. In 1987, the *Digest* bought *Travel Holiday* and the company hopes to procure several special interest magazines in the next several years.

After numerous owners, the popular literary magazine, *Saturday Review* (founded in 1924), became the property of Bob Guccione's *Penthouse* group. The troubled title was rumored to have been purchased from Manhattan Media for $3,500,000. The new publisher hopes to boost the circulation from 150,000 to more than 500,000 by giving readers more viable information on the arts.

One of the world's most popular magazines, and certainly the one found most in doctors' offices, celebrated a 100th anniversary in 1988. The familiar yellow and white cover *National Geographic,* created in 1888 at a meeting of 33 men intent upon organizing a society for increasing and diffusing geographical knowledge, claims a membership of more than 10,000,000.

Concomitantly with the continuing success for *Discover* and *Scientific American, Science Digest,* defunct since 1987, reappeared in the spring of 1988 with an initial newsstand distribution of 400,000 copies. The magazine was purchased by Family Media when it bought *Discover* from Time Inc. for $26,000,000. Unlike *Discover,* the new magazine will target specialists rather than novices.

When a newspaper refers to the bombing of Libya as "coercive diplomacy," and Colonel North states that he is careful not "to infect other people with unnecessary knowledge," there is suspicion of double speak, and the English Department at Rutgers University celebrates the language pollution in its *Quarterly Review of Doublespeak.* Since 1974, the journal has made annual awards to people who perpetrate grossly unfactual language. Winners in 1988 included Colonel North, the National Aeronautics and Space Administration, and Ed Meese.

In the "can it be true department," the British version of *Reader's Digest* (circulation 1,600,000 is to toughen its image by moving into investigative journalism. According to the editor, the magazine is a bastion of conservative, middle-of-the-road editorial policy, but his purpose is to make it more lively. Whether or not this journal will come to America remains to be seen.

Celebrating the change in the Soviet Union's liberated publishing policy, *Glasnost Magazine* arrived. Available both in the USSR and the U.S. (in translations) the 65 pages reports on cultural, economic, and political change. On May 9, the publisher was sentenced to seven days in jail, but later released. The magazine continues to be issued, its longevity being dependent on authority in the USSR. In another demonstration of Glasnost, *PC World USSR* is now on Soviet newsstands. The Russian language quarterly originates in the U.S., and the first issue included 30 ad pages. Incidentally, one of the few British-based magazines to triple its circulation in the 1980s is *Marxism Today* (available in the U.S., too) and published by Britain's Communist Party.

While subscriptions carry the cost of scholarly journals, advertising makes the 200 or so general, newstand magazines profitable. Who spends the most ad dollars? At the top is Philip Morris with close to a $245,000,000 budget, followed by General Motors, Ford, Nabisco, Chrysler, Procter & Gamble, AT&T, and Time.

Saturated with youth, American publishers are now turning the other direction. With a predicted boom in the over 50 population during the next decade or so, the new interest is in so-called "mature" magazines such as *Modern Maturity, Golden Years,* and *50 plus.* Among the new titles, *Lears* is directed to older women, in spite of the fact that it features advertisements with much younger types. Incidentally, *The Nation* published a cartoon satirizing France Lear, the founder of *Lear's* magazine. The cartoon appeared despite protest of 34 *Nation* staff members who "are outraged that sexism is still prejudice, especially in a left magazine."

Such standard dental and doctor office reading material as battered copies of *Reader's Digest, Time,* or *Good Housekeeping* are giving way to titles such as *Doctor's Orders, Heart Beat, Healthy Heart, Special Report,* and about a half dozen others of a similar nature. All of these are free; they carry attractive advertising and are a delight to salespeople who think magazine reading in public places can be persuasive for their products. So far there is a real debate whether an individual with sick kids, a bad tooth, or a finicky heart is all that involved with reading anything.

There were too many readers of *Business Week* in 1988. In one of the most extensive insider information investigations in years, various people were found supplying brokers and investors with copies of the magazines one to two days before publication. Using the tips, i.e. the stocks mentioned as good buys in the magazine, the transgressors had an uncharacteristic chance to buy before the information became general knowledge.

All of this scrambling about for money is not due to vastly underpaid editorial workers. According to a *Folio* survey (August, 1988, p. 103–121) the average salary of an editorial director is now $58,774. The top one third are paid close to $100,000 while the lower one third average $28,000. Experience (more than 20 years) and sex (male) are two major factors in higher salaries.

WILLIAM A. KATZ

Reference and Adult Services Division

To meet the intellectual, professional, and vocational interests of librarians and their allies in the information field, the Reference and Adult Services Division (RASD) focused on four areas of activity in 1988: *organizational development,* to meet more effectively the needs of its members; *publication activities,* to stimulate and disseminate information on reference and adult services;

conference programming, to contribute to the professional development of librarians interested in these areas; and *awards*, to encourage and recognize outstanding contribution to the field.

Organizational Developments. Organizationally, RASD consists of four sections, 88 committees and subcommittees, 12 discussion groups, and the Council of State and Regional Groups.

In 1988, there were a number of organizational "firsts" within RASD. With the help of the Executive Committee, RASD Executive Director Andrew Hansen drafted the division's first financial plan. The Executive Committee held its first retreat, meeting in Lisle, Illinois, with other ALA divisional Executive Committees. Near the end of the year, the first program officer, Margaret M. Monsour, was hired for the division; she will concentrate on publishing, programming, and special projects. The first elections were held for the two new RASD sections established in 1987; the elected chairs are David Kohl for the Collection Development Section (CODES) and Mark Leggett for the Business Reference and Services Section (BRASS). In less than one year, both sections have attracted sizeable memberships. At the end of 1988, CODES had registered more than 1,000 personal members and BRASS had enrolled more than 750.

The divisional planning process, initiated in 1984, moved ahead in 1988. To operationalize the RASD mission statement, the division's board of directors approved seven priority and goal areas: information sources, personnel, user needs, physical facilities, divisional effectiveness, service patterns, and reference management. Under the direction of immediate past presidents Elizabeth Stroup and Charles Bunge, the planning committee developed a specific process for continuous planning for the division.

Publications. A number of RASD's basic publishing components were unchanged in 1988. "Notable Books for 1987"—with its annotations of 27 outstanding works of fiction, nonfiction, and poetry—was issued as a leaflet in *Booklist* and in camera-ready sheets. The annotated list of "Reference Sources of 1987," selected by RASD's Outstanding Reference Sources Committee, appears in *American Libraries* and unannotated in *Booklist*; titles in the list were displayed at the Annual Conference and at local meetings. RASD's quarterly newsletter, *RASD Update*, remained under the editorship of Connie Miller.

However, a major change took place in the editorship of *RQ*, the division's official journal. After completing two consecutive terms as editor, Kathleen Heim turned over the assignment to Elizabeth Futus, who became the ninth editor in the journal's 28-year history.(For more on Futus, see her biography in this volume.) Heim left behind a journal that had grown to more than 600 pages in 1987–88 and that had adopted a commitment to the refereeing process for journal article selection. Futus began tenure by instituting a new design for the cover and interior logos and by initiating a new column, "The Alert Collector," in volume 28.

Several new publications were introduced by RASD in 1988. "A Consumer's Guide to the Current Bibliography of Historical Literature," prepared by the History Section's Bibliography and Indexes Committee, was issued simultaneously as the second in RASD's Occasional Papers series and as the first in RASD's Consumer Guides to Reference Works in History series. "Guidelines for Use of Information Request Form," prepared by the Cooperative Reference Service Committee, and "Guidelines for Library Services to Hispanics," prepared by the Committee on Library Services to the Spanish Speaking, were both published in Summer *RQ*. "Remote Access to Library–Based Information Systems: A MARS Checklist," prepared by the Machine–Assisted Reference Section (MARS) Patron Access to Computer-Based Reference Systems Committee, was released in the October–December issue of *Update*. As a one-year special project, members of the BRASS steering committee prepared a monthly "Quick Biz" column in *American Libraries* that targeted different business and economics topics and cited recent books.

Conference activities. Reflecting the diverse interests of its membership, RASD sponsored eight programs on topics that ranged from genealogical research to optical disk catalogs at the 1988 Annual Conference in New Orleans.

The major program, "Twelve Years Till 2000: Prepared for the 21st Century," speculated on the future of reference issues in three major areas: Florence Skelley, President of Telematics, addressed patron expectations; James Neil, Assistant Dean at Pennsylvania State University, focused on library staff; and Peter Watson, Library Director at Idaho State University, considered reference sources. Then, a panel of three librarians working in academic and public library settings (Patricia Swanson, University of Chicago Science Library; Judith Drescher, Memphis–Shelby (Tennessee) County Public Library; and Louise Berry, Darien (Connecticut) Public Library) applied the speakers' forecasts to the reality of their institutions. In another program sponsored by RASD (and co-sponsored by ALA Publishing and the Reference Books Bulletin Editorial Board), four publishers discussed developing major subject encyclopedias and dictionaries.

Three RASD sections and three committees also had programs at the annual conference. BRASS discussed the best sources for researching stocks, bonds, and IRAs and distributed an annotated bibliography of useful reference works. The History Section examined southern genealogical and local historical sources and re-

Gail A. Schlachter, Reference Services Press.

REFERENCE AND ADULT SERVICES DIVISION

PRESIDENT (July 1987–July 1988):
Gail A. Schlachter, Reference Services Press, San Carlos, California

VICE-PRESIDENT/PRESIDENT-ELECT:
Arthur S. Meyers, Hammond Public Library

EXECUTIVE DIRECTOR:
Andrew M. Hansen

Membership (August 31, 1988): 5,217 (4,227 personal; 990 organizational)
Expenditures (August 31, 1988): $177,456

search institutions, and MARS drew on the experience of practitioners to look at automated reference desks. RASD committee programs concentrated on databases and services to labor, selecting and promoting small presses/literary magazines in libraries, and optical disk library catalogs.

In addition, RASD co-sponsored a number of conference programs with other ALA units, including resources for the ethical dilemmas of health care (with the Association of Specialized and Cooperative Library Agencies), trends in library services to the aging (with ASCLA), and the collection of core statistics (with the Library Administration and Management Association).

In a different type of conference activity, MARS members supplied the technical backup in ALA's experiment of providing computer equipment to personal members and staff at the 1988 Midwinter and Annual conferences.

Awards. In 1988, RASD sponsored six awards to honor individuals or institutions making outstanding contributions to reference or adult services librarianship. The Dartmouth Medal, which recognizes achievement in creating reference books of quality and significance, was presented for the second year in a row to Macmillan Press, this time for publication of its 16-volume *Encyclopedia of Religion*. The Southern Labor Archives at Georgia State University received the John R. Sessions Memorial Award, which is designed to recognize a public library or library system's outstanding contribution to the labor community. The Margaret E. Monroe Library Adult Services Award, established to recognize significant contributions to the profession's understanding and practice of service to adults, was given to Jane K. Hirsch. In recognition of his high standards for reviewing and evaluating reference sources, James R. Rettig received the Isadore Gilbert Mudge Award, which honors distinguished contributions to reference librarianship. (For more on Rettig, see his biography in this volume.) Elfreda A. Chapman won the Reference Service Press Award of $500 presented to the author of the most outstanding article published in RQ during the preceding two volume years. RASD's newest award, the $1,000 Facts on File Grant, replaced the seven-year-old Facts On File Award and was presented for the first time in 1988. The grant was established to encourage imaginative library programming that makes current affairs more meaningful to adults. Chicago Public Library won this award; it will support CPL's NOONLINE forum, in which experts explore the various immigration issues facing the United States.

BRASS is planning an award that will honor outstanding individual contributions to business reference services. RASD expects to formalize and approve the award in 1989.

GAIL A. SCHLACHTER

Reference Services

The library world is filled with speculation and scenarios about the role of libraries in the future of information delivery. Already new technologies are having an impact on reference work: news, issues, and activities of 1988 reflect the increasing use of electronic media for information retrieval in coexistence with traditional sources and services.

Automated Reference Environment. The degree of automation in libraries varies widely. Still, it is not unusual for a reference desk in the late 1980s to include access to some combination of a local online catalog, possibly also a local network, a bibliographic utility like OCLC, such in-house machine-readable databases as information and referral files, and dial-up access to commercial databases for ready reference. Frequently electronic mail, telefacsimile equipment, and microcomputers are also present. In the reference room itself, users may need assistance with the online public access catalog, reference sources in such optical media formats as CD-ROM, and online searching in commercial databases. Computer-assisted instruction and other new technologies may provide directional information or point-of-use instruction. At the 1988 annual ALA conference, the Reference and Adult Services Division (RASD) Machine Assisted Reference Section looked at "Automation and the Reference Desk" in a panel discussion which surveyed automation in reference service, its impact on personnel, physical environment issues, equipment, and formats.

In addition to the effects of technology on the provision of information, the widespread availability of microcomputers is enhancing the function and management of reference services. Librarians are using software to create scheduling programs for the reference desk, to computerize reference files, and assist in collection management. In many libraries desktop publishing systems produce bibliographies, user aids, and brochures of outstanding quality.

The next dramatic focus will clearly be in the area of expert systems for reference and also in hypertext/hypermedia. These systems began to capture wide attention in 1988, in good part because of Apple's new HyperCard software. Expert systems (computer-based presentations that provide problem-solving advice incorporating the skills of a human expert) have been used in manufacturing, in medical diagnosis, and in libraries for descriptive cataloging. A 1988 preconference at ALA's annual meeting on planning the development of a library expert system explored wider applications. While the dynamics of question negotiation need more research, there are already a few current reference applications. The Answerman system developed at the National Library of Agriculture helps users find answers to agricultural questions. An interactive computer presentation can provide directions and also guide users through such topics as "Finding Books" or "Finding Journals." The advantages of such microcomputer-based presentations is that they are always available, they siphon off routine questions, and they may help those who prefer not to ask. Among recently developed computer-assisted instruction programs using Apple MacIntosh and HyperCard software are Infomaster and HyperCard programming that includes sound, animation, and graphics as well as options for linking and searching for information.

CD-ROM. Finishing its fourth year on the

scene, CD-ROM technology continues to have an impact on collections and services. While it is clear that libraries are in the midst of another information storage and retrieval revolution, librarians are not sure whether CD-ROM is "the new papyrus" or a passing moment in technology's time-line, as other optical media are in development. The benefits and the present drawbacks of this technology have been copiously noted in library literature and earlier *ALA Yearbook* articles. So has the tremendous enthusiasm which library users show for CD-ROM. New products, industry developments and refinements in hardware and software and extensive reporting on how CD-ROM has been integrated into reference services were widely evident in 1988. The annual ALA conference offered nearly 20 programs or poster sessions on optical media. Nor was the topic neglected at national online meetings. The September CD-ROM Expo in Chicago was oriented toward users rather than producers, providing librarians with the opportunity to see new equipment and products. TECHNO-COM:CD-ROM, a national teleconference, was broadcast from studios in Illinois to many sites all around the country. The literature was again replete with articles on CD-ROM. Online, Inc. (*Online* and *Database*) introduced a new journal, *The Laserdisk Professional*, with practical, informative articles; news; and product reviews.

Several developments in industry promise somewhat smoother use of CD-ROM. New releases of retrieval software show response to comments and suggestions from librarians. While the differences in commands and databases still pose a problem for users if several systems are present, "online" tutorials and help windows now assist with user training. Many systems support "daisy-chaining" drives together. One of the exciting developments in 1988 was in the area of networking and the potential of multiple workstations capable of accessing a single CD-ROM drive or a bank of drives. Meridian Data, Silver Platter, and Information Access announced network systems. Early in the year Apple unveiled its CD drive, which should expand use in school and public libraries.

"Vaporware" products, announced and promoted but never produced, have been a problem in the past, but in 1988 more than 200 titles were commercially available. While about 10 percent are for cataloging support, the rest are indexes, general reference works, and other texts. *Laser-Disclosure*, a much-discussed new product at the Special Libraries Association meeting, has disks that contain not only the index but also the full text of the Securities and Exchange Commission filings, thereby replacing the microfiche collection. *Science Citation Index* on CD-ROM was winner of the *Laserdisk Professional* product of the year award with features not available online. New indexes include *Newspaper Abstracts* and *Periodical Abstracts* from University Microfilms. Directory sources such as *Peterson's College Databank* (Silver Platter) are also being published.

The *ALA Yearbook* for 1987 queried whether "this marriage (of libraries and CD-ROM) could be saved." But 1988 saw libraries experimenting even more with the technology and integrating it philosophically and physically into reference services. In 1988, libraries reply, "we are working on the relationship."

Online Services. Lockheed's midyear sale of Dialog Information Services for a hefty price of $353,000,000 indicates the strength of an industry which, while growing more slowly, now offers more than 3,800 databases through 576 services. The National Online Meeting, sponsored by Learned Information Inc. in the spring and Online '88 in October showcased new products and services and offered searching tips and techniques. Applications of other emerging technologies such as desktop publishing and hypertext to online searching were also presented. One new enhancement is cross-file searching of a topic with a single set of search terms. Dialog's OneSearch won the 1988 *Online* magazine award for this feature now also available on Vu-Text and Dow Jones. Graphic images became retrievable online in 1988 in the Trademarkscan database on Dialog. An enhancement from BRS, "treeword explode" will facilitate searching in medical databases.

While several new databases appeared in 1988, certain trends from the previous year continued in force. More full text and more "real-time," or newswire databases are offered. *Chemical Abstracts* tested its new pricing structure for the databanks that mount its service. In response to lowered connect-time revenues resulting from high-speed data transmission, use of personal computers, host system enhancements (and increased skill of online searchers), new revenues are to be derived from the number of search terms used rather than online time. "Winds of change" are in the air as Jeff Pemberton notes in his March editorial in *Online* with the "potential for fundamental changes in the way the business is structured and conducted." He notes that declining revenue from printed indexes will cause producers to place less importance on print and increasing emphasis on electronic distribution, a step toward the publishing future that clearly has an effect on reference services.

Into its second decade, online searching is a staple of library service and is to some degree available in all types of libraries, even innovative school media centers. However, penetration is still strongest in special and larger academic libraries. According to ALA's Office for Research, public library online service is common (61 percent) only in communities over 500,000. It is offered in only 25 percent of libraries serving communities with populations between 25,000 and 100,000. Access to end-user searching or a different pricing structure may help to broaden the opportunities.

While other buzz words dominated discussions in 1988, training library users to search online was still an issue. *End-user Searching: Services and Providers* (Martin Kesselman and Sarah Watstein, ALA, 1988) reviews the literature, discusses gateways, front-end software and laserdisk products. The Online '88 conference had a special session for end-user searchers. Perhaps in response to the attractive fixed cost feature of optical disk searching, several fee options were introduced by online vendors in 1988. BRS announced "After Dark Unlimited" with unlimited use of this end-user option for six months at $13,500. Another alternative for school, academic or public libraries is the Answer Machine, a product from the developers of the Easynet gateway. Several options allow unlimited access from a secure workstation or through an online catalog. The Biosis Connection, aimed at life science researchers, was also introduced.

Familiar Concerns. Reference librarians must deal with the vocabulary (modem, Boolean, CD-ROM, FAX, hyper-media) and the technology while still remembering old faithfuls like the *Dictionary of Anonymous and Pseudonymous English Literature*. Although little is untouched by those changes in the recording and delivery of information, there are familiar activities and abiding concerns in reference work. Charles Anderson's "Exchange" column in *RQ* remains a forum for elusive reference answers.

However, when reference librarians note the number of "half-right" answers reported in surveys of information service, and reference librarians remain concerned about the quality of reference services. The annual conference in 1988 was silent on the accuracy issue in terms of major programs, but RASD has re-instituted the Performance Standards for Reference/Information Librarians Discussion Group. Gail Schlacter, new president of RASD, in the Fall issue of *RQ* reminds that outdated materials present a hazard for accurate reference service, calling for written policies for selection/deselection in reference.

James Rettig, who once compared obsolescence in reference collections to Love Canal in fallout potential, received the 1988 Mudge award for distinguished contributions to reference librarianship and his work in setting high standards in reviewing and evaluating reference sources.

While exciting sources in CD-ROM have become important, reference materials in traditional book formats continue to be a staple for collections. The 1988 Dartmouth Medal for an outstanding reference work was awarded to a subject encyclopedia, the 16-volume *Encyclopedia of Religion* edited by Mircea Eliade and published by Macmillan. The Reference Sources Committee of RASD considered 2,000 new print titles before selecting the 26 outstanding sources announced in *American Libraries* (May 1988).

Many current topics in reference really concern problems of management rather than professional knowledge. An issue of *The Reference Librarian* (no.19, 1987) was devoted to finance, budgets, and management in reference. A 1988 ALA annual meeting presentation of a national model for the collection of core reference statistics was crowded with attendees. Planning and decisions necessitated by new formats and changing services ensure continued interest in sharing ideas.

Library conferences and the reference press in 1988 reflected not only interest in automation and technology but also the concern of reference librarians for reaching more users: the aged, those of multicultures, and the disabled.

Instruction. Reflecting the impact of an increasingly automated environment, the Bibliographic Instruction section of ACRL's preconference in New Orleans on "The Future of BI: Approaches in the Electronic Age" featured Sharon Hogan, recipient of the current Miriam Dudley award for bibliographic instruction, as a keynote speaker. Another session on "Teaching CD-ROM" addressed major instructional issues as well as practical approaches and materials. Online public access catalogs pose new roles for reference librarians in instruction and training.

A program at the October Library Information and Technology Association conference "Training Users and Training Staff For and with Technology" addressed an issue vital to the success of library automation. Teaching critical thinking skills and reaching diverse groups were also emphasized by Bibliographic Instruction in 1988.

Interlibrary Loan and Cooperative Reference. The Information Standards Organization's (NISO) standard for data elements necessary to successfully complete an interlibrary loan (ILL) request sent via any medium was approved in July. The interlibrary loan community hopes that the terminology of the ILL subsystems of bibliographic utilities will also be updated. Telefacsimile for sending and filling requests still interests the interlibrary loan librarians. The University of Alaska Library is experimenting with transmitting text material via broadcast signal, using the statewide television channel. Of more immediate significance, a University of Illinois at Chicago study demonstrated that current conventional methods of interlibrary loan document delivery are just as efficient as commercial services.

Conclusion. Richard DeGennaro, Director of the New York Public Library, aptly characterized the transformations in libraries brought about by computer and communications technology. "The principal effect... has been to bring about a revolution in access to library resources by users. Technology is making the resources within the library available beyond its walls, and the resources beyond its walls available within the library."

Online databases and large bibliographic utilities like OCLC brought tremendous resources for reference into the library. Local online catalogs and networks greatly improve access to collections and resource sharing. The other side of this picture is that electronic information and telecommunications also allow patrons to use library resources and other information sources from home, offices, dorms and laboratories. The "wired campus" with networks of personal workstations such as those of Lehigh University or Indiana University are models. Public libraries also increasingly offer dial-up access to online catalogs and electronic bulletin boards. Clients of special libraries are the targeted end-users of the databank services. This is the environment in which reference and information librarians must examine their role and services.

MARGARET C. POWER

REFORMA

Nineteen eighty-eight was a year of continued growth, development and achievement for REFORMA. Membership increased by 23% to include members in 32 states, South and Central

SEPTEMBER — HISPANIC MONTH

DESIGNS FROM PRE-COLUMBIAN MEXICO
ORANGE COUNTY PUBLIC LIBRARY

Orange County (California) Public Library honors Spanish Americans.

America, Puerto Rico, Spain and Canada. REFORMA is governed by an Executive Board which includes officers, committee chairs and the presidents of local chapters. Currently there are eight REFORMA chapters: Arizona; El Paso, Texas; Pennsylvania; New Jersey; New York; Orange County, California; Santa Barbara/Ventura, California; Washington, D.C.; Los Angeles, California; LIBROS/San Diego California; and one affiliate, Bibliotecas Para La Gente, in the San Francisco area.

Strategic Planning. The association entered the second stage of its long-range planning process in 1988. In 1987 the REFORMA Long Range Planning Task Force surveyed the membership regarding issues of concern, priorities and future direction. At the 1988 ALA Conference in New Orleans the Task Force presented its final report, targeting five areas for strategic planning, and making specific recommendations to the Executive Board. As a result, a blue-ribbon committee was appointed by the president to devise a plan of action and set long- and short-term goals and objectives for the organization. This second stage will chart REFORMA's direction well into the next decade.

ALA Program. REFORMA continues to strengthen ties with ALA by working closely with the various divisions, round tables, committees and caucuses. "Is English-Only Enough?: Cultural Heritage, Language and Libraries" was the title of a jointly sponsored REFORMA–EMIERT program presented in New Orleans. This activity was co-sponsored by five other ALA groups. The program opened with a timely, informative and lively debate on the controversial "English-Only" issue featuring Arnold Torres, consultant on Hispanic affairs and former executive director of the League of United Latin American Citizens, and Tom Olsen, Director of Public Affairs for U.S. English. The second part, presented by Dr. Kamal Sridhar, professor of Linguistics at SUNY, addressed the question of why some immigrant groups retain their native language longer than others. The program closed with a panel presentation on practical approaches to cultural heritage and language promotion in libraries. On a lighter side in the Big Easy, REFORMA and SALALM co-sponsored a festive and well-attended reception organized by FIL (Guadalara Book Fair) and the Mexican Publishers Association.

Mentor Program. The lack of bilingual/bicultural librarians remains one of the most pressing concerns for the association. As a result, two years ago the REFORMA Education Committee began to develop an exciting Mentor Program with the University of California at Los Angeles (UCLA). As of the spring of 1988, 12 successful mentor/mentee relationships had been established. Mentees have graduated and become mentors themselves. UCLA reports that Latino student applications have doubled from previous years. In 1988 a $5,000 grant was awarded by the California State Library to enable the program to reach a wider audience, organize quarterly workshops and design a Mentor Training Manual.

To build on the success at UCLA the Education Committee has joined forces with Bibliotecas Para La Gente to expand the program to California's other two library schools. Led by Adelia Lines, the committee's goals this year include the establishment of mentor programs at San Jose and Berkeley, and publication of a guide to the establishment of mentor programs with library schools.

Chapter Activities. From coast to coast, Reformistas have been active in local and professional activities. The Los Angeles chapter participated in a variety of events this year. Among them: the Greater East Los Angeles Voter Registration Proj-

---

REFORMA

PRESIDENT (July 1988–June 1989):
Ingrid Betancourt, Newark Public Library, Newark, New Jersey

SECRETARY:
Rhonda Ries Kravitz, California State Library, Sacramento, California

TREASURER:
Rene Amaya, Los Angeles County Library, Compton Library, Atedna, California

NEWSLETTER EDITOR:
Elaine Valenzuela, Tucson Public Library, Arizona (1989); **Elena Tscherny,** Washington, D.C. (1989)

Mailing address: REFORMA, c/o Liz Rodriguez Miller, Library Administration, Tucson Public Library, P.O. Box 27470, Tucson, Arizona 85726

Membership (February 1989): 658; 8 local chapters; 1 affiliate

ect, the Children's Film Festival in Long Beach, and the first Latino Literacy Conference. Several REFORMA members have worked on the policy agenda being developed in California as a result of the statewide invitational conference, "A State of Change: California's Ethnic Future and Libraries. Recognizing the need to publicize and market the library in Hispanic communities, where a tradition of library service often does not exist, the Northeast Chapter once again this year organized a series of library awareness programs on a popular Spanish-language radio station during National Library Week. Conversely, in an effort to create an awareness of the particular library needs of urban ethnic communities, the chapter is holding all its meetings this year at northeast area library schools. After a successful meeting at the Palmer School of Library Science in New York, the chapter was invited to develop a curriculum for a course in library service to ethnic communities. The course is scheduled to be taught in the summer of 1989. The president of the chapter, Mario Gonzalez, was invited to teach this course.

REFORMA Scholarships. Two $1,000 scholarships were awarded by REFORMA in 1988 to deserving library students interested in pursuing a career in library service to the Spanish-speaking. Janet Goitia from San Jose, California, and Marie Alexandra Salinas from Austin, Texas, were selected from a pool of 17 applicants to receive awards.

INGRID BETANCOURT

Research

Research represents an investigation characterized by certain activities: (1) reflective inquiry (identification of a problem, conducting a literature search to place the problem in proper perspective, and formulation of a logical or theoretical framework, objectives, and hypotheses/research questions); (2) adoption of appropriate procedures (research design and methodologies); (3) the collection of data; (4) data analysis; and (5) presentation of findings and recommendations for future study. Presumably, attempts to ensure reliability and validity guide steps 2 and 3.

Few published studies include all five components, however. A weak link in any component may invalidate or negate the value of a particular study. One component that enhances the overall utility of the study is the presentation of findings—effective writing and the potential use of graphics. Writing, directed to a specific audience and shaped by the nature of the study, is a major determinant to the ultimate success of a study. Graphics reinforce a thesis and enable authors "to make their cases more compelling." The "graphic representation of data can also clarify whether or not inferential statistics are appropriate."[1]

In the social sciences, there are different types of research. *Basic* research concerns the pursuit of knowledge for its own sake and may or may not immediately contribute to a theoretical base of knowledge. *Applied* research validates theory and initiates the revision of theory. *Action* research is usually applied research directed to an immediate problem. Librarians often conduct action research to generate data useful strictly for local decision making. The potential danger of *action* research, therefore, is that it tends to focus on local problems to the exclusion of a broader context—theory building.

The literature of library and information science for 1988 comprises articles that address the definition and purpose of research, discuss trends, advocate the formulation of a research agenda, and question the impact of research findings. The year also saw the continuance of research miniconferences. This essay examines the developments in these areas that emerged during 1988.

Definition of Research. Martell defines research by noting six components of the process: statement of the problem, setting hypotheses, development of a methodology, the conduct of the study and the generation of findings, analysis of the findings, and the drawing of conclusions that do not exceed study findings and data. Martell's components are more selective than those enumerated in the previous section and focus on one type of research—hypothesis testing. His definition omits the context in which the hypotheses are set and the role of research design. He suggests "the provision of data is often the primary product of research."[2] Such is true for action research, but not necessarily for basic and applied research.

Martell recognizes that published research might "enlighten the reader." Research should provide "information, guidelines, or recommendations that might reasonably allow the reader to do something different, in an improved way."[3] The statement of the problem should address an issue that has "broad implications for the profession."[4] In that context, action research may become "applying and utilizing research methodology to implement social change." As Altman and Antieau observed, such research was conducted in the 1970s to the detriment of basic and applied research.[5]

Research and Management Studies. The exchange of viewpoints between D'Elia and Van House represents disagreement over the purpose of data collection and the practical goals of research.[6] Van House argues that the collection of data valuable to management need not be evaluated strictly from a research perspective. D'Elia's argument is that management studies should demonstrate the same rigor as research studies. He maintains that librarians could easily draw incorrect inferences from management studies.

D'Elia questions the utility, application, and discriminatory powers of fill rates as performance measures. Van House does not share the same level of concern and calls for further research and the review of data collection on a larger scale. Library managers, she points out, must realize "the possible consequences of making a decision based on imperfect data."[7] D'Elia suggests that fill rates do not warrant further testing. Such testing, in his opinion, should have occurred before the implementation of performance measures.

The exchange between D'Elia and Van House raises questions about the statistical expertise of library managers. One weakness in the exchange is that neither evaluates performance measures in the contest of basic and applied research,[8] nor discusses the reliability and validity of the data from which they draw their conclusions. Lack of knowledge about the data, and the data collection process itself, complicates independent verification of their assertions.

Murfin and Bunge offer an excellent example of action research on reference service.[9] Their perception study neither chose the sample of libraries randomly nor controlled for educational background of paraprofessional staff. They gathered data to answer specific management questions, but the underlying assumptions of their data set are unclear.

Their study contradicts at least one portion of a much more finely crafted study, which suggested that, "... reference administrators should consider mechanisms for assigning untrained staff members responsibilities for answering at least factual reference questions."[10] In action research, the precision of analysis often exceeds the precision of the data.

Trends in Research. Atkins' analysis of subject trends for 1975–1984 in nine library and information science journals "shows the eclectic nature of publishing in the library profession." He states:

the fifty-eight subjects identified for this study range from the most popular subject—library management—to the least popular—library fund raising. . . . In between these extremes, there is a heavy concentration on such automation-related subjects as information retrieval, databases, cataloging, library automation, technology, and research methods.[11]

"Evidence of original research, or manipulation of data in a scholarly fashion" comprise the key elements for the inclusion of an article in his analysis. Such vague criteria detract from the study's reliability and validity. Analysis limited to subject content does not address the design and methodology employed. However, Atkins' study provides a benchmark from which other researchers can build and compare.

Impact of Research. Impact is the effect of use or "of. . . an output on some process or activity." Impact and use differ but their linkage has "not received adequate attention."[12] Researchers employ specific methods to assess impact. Citations, or references to works that authors include in their writings, constitute one general measure of impact, assuming a definable relationship between citing and cited works exists.

Altman and Antieau drew a random sample of projects funded by the Library Research and Demonstration Branch (LRDB), U.S. Department of Education (DOE), to determine impact using citations. The sample of 163 projects received more than $18,000,000 in funding. Approximately half of the projects funded from 1965 to 1980 "made no impact in the literature."[13] Further, "citations tended to cluster in a small number of library-related serials. The citations themselves clustered around a handful of funded projects."[14]

During the 1970s, the LRDB program "was directed to pursue a social policy as well as a research agenda. What improves social policy does not necessarily enhance research."[15] The implications of their findings assume added importance when noting that Martell, the Association of Research Libraries, the Council for Library Resources, and the Department of Education all advocate the development of a research agenda to identify funding priorities and the projects presumed to make a potential impact.

Library Statistics: A Current Review

This report is the sixth in a series that updates Sources of Library Statistics, 1972–1982 *(ALA, December 1983). Like that pamphlet, the update describes published statistics about libraries as well as statistics on related topics. The focus is on national statistics that are published periodically and that are expected to continue.*

The most important happening in 1988 related to the future of such statistics was the April passage of the Hawkins-Stafford Elementary and Secondary School Improvement Amendments of 1988 that became Public Law 100-297. The new law gave greater power and responsibility to the National Center for Education Statistics (NCES) and also restored "National" to its name. Libraries are mentioned six times in the law. Although it had always been assumed that libraries were part of education, and statistics about libraries had been collected by NCES, the new law specifically mandates library statistics for the first time.

Public Libraries. Even before the new law was passed, NCES began to increase its activity in the area of public library statistics. In February, a Memorandum of Understanding was signed whereby the National Commission on Libraries and Information Science (NCLIS) would organize a Task Force to plan the development of what was later named the Federal-State Cooperative System (FSCS). Serving on the Task Force were Daniel Carter, Commissioner, NCLIS; Eileen Cooke, ALA Washington Office; Ray Fry, Library Programs, U.S. Department of Education; Carol Henderson, ALA Washington Office; Mary Jo Lynch, ALA Office for Research; Anne Mathews, Director of Library Programs, U.S. Department of Education; Amy Owen, Director, Utah State Library; Richard Palmer, Ohio State Library; Margaret Phelan, Commissioner, NCLIS; Charlie Robinson, Director, Baltimore County Library; Joseph Shubert, State Librarian of New York; Jan Feye-Stukas, Minnesota Department of Education, Library Development and Services; Peter Young, Chair, LAMA Statistics Section and Director of Academic Information Services at Faxon; and Barratt Wilkins, Florida State Librarian.

The Task Force met seven times between March and November to draft an action plan based on groundwork done by the ALA Office for Research in a 1985–87 pilot project. The pilot project had examined the feasibility of a system that would combine the annual collection of statistics from public libraries in the 50 states with the periodic reporting of national statistics on public libraries by NCES. By the end of 1987, data in machine-readable form for Fiscal Year 1986 had been received from 12 states and transferred to the NCES mainframe. Early in 1988 NCES analyzed the data, sent reports back to participating states, and met with state data coordinators to discuss ways to improve subsequent data collection and reporting.

In November, the Task Force approved a final draft of the technical report of its work prepared by Richard Palmer of Ohio State Library and critiqued the first draft of a popular version. The technical report, in draft form, had been presented to the Chief Officers of State Library Agencies (COSLA) at an October meeting and COSLA had agreed to begin acting as the coordinating agency for the system in late 1989. Also in November, NCES and NCLIS signed a

Research

second Memorandum of Understanding whereby NCLIS would begin implementation of the plan while COSLA was setting up procedures. The first step was a Training Workshop for state data coordinators held in Annapolis, Maryland, in early December.

A second project involving public library statistics was implemented by the Public Library Association (PLA). The design for a Public Library Data Service (PLDS), the statistical component of PLA's Public Library Development Program, was tested during 1987. Early in 1988, PLA sent a questionnaire to all public libraries serving populations of 100,000 or more, all libraries that contributed to the Public Library Development Program, and any others requesting participation. The first annual report published by PLA in July 1988 contains statistics for 422 individual public libraries on their resources, services, and expenditures plus summary statistics on these variables and graphs of the summary statistics.

School Libraries. No new national data were published on school libraries in 1988, but steps were taken to ensure the availability of such data in 1989 and beyond. NCES began negotiations with the ALA Office for Research regarding a contract to design several new components of the biennial School and Staffing Survey (SAS) conducted by the Elementary and Secondary Education Division of NCES. Existing questionnaires will be modified and new instruments will be developed to collect data about various aspects of school library media centers and their staffs. The NCES data eventually will provide a regular and comprehensive view of school library media centers. A very valuable but more limited view has been provided in the biennial report on "Budgeting and Expenditures for Materials in School Library Media Centers" based on data gathered by Marilyn Miller in a survey of subscribers to *School Library Journal* (*SLJ*). Questionnaires were sent out in late 1988 for the fourth report to be published in the June-July 1989 issue of *SLJ*.

Academic Libraries. For many years NCES has conducted a periodic survey of academic libraries as part of the Higher Education General Information Survey (HEGIS). HEGIS which has now been replaced by IPEDS (Integrated Postsecondary Education Data System) will collect data on many topics from all postsecondary institutions, those offering accredited degrees (the HEGIS universe), and any others offering education beyond the baccalaureate degree. A library survey will continue to be part of IPEDS and questionnaires for the first survey were mailed in the summer of 1988. A report is expected in late 1989.

Special Libraries. Historically, statistics on this component of the library field have been sadly lacking. In 1988, however, the Special Libraries Association (SLA) took the first steps toward filling the gap. The staff position of Director, Research and Information Resources, approved in October 1987 was filled in January 1988 by Tobi Brimsek. The report of SLA's Special Committee on Research, accepted by the SLA Board in June, recommended a research agenda that included "developing baseline demographic data" on special libraries and librarians.

NISO Standard on Library Statistics. All of these efforts in the area of national periodic statistical reports on libraries will be influenced by work that began in 1988 to revise the 1983 standard on library statistics established by Committee Z39 of the American National Standards Institute. Committee Z39 was the forerunner of the National Information Standards Organization (NISO). All NISO standards must be either reaffirmed, revised, or withdrawn every five years. When the library statistics standard came up for review in 1988, it was determined that revision was necessary. A revision committee, co-chaired by Mary Jo Lynch, Director of ALA's Office for Research, and Peter Young, Director of Academic Information Services at Faxon and current Chair of the ALA Library Administration and Management Association's Statistics Section, met for the first time in November. Also serving on the committee are Tobi Brimsek, Special Libraries Association; Jan Feye-Stukas, Minnesota Department of Education, Library Development and Services; Dean Hollister, R. R. Bowker Company; Richard Lyders, Executive Director, HAM-TMC Library; Marilyn Miller, Chair, Department of Library and Information Studies, University of North Carolina at Greensboro; and Kendon Stubbs, Associate Librarian, University of Virginia. The Committee hopes to complete its work within a year.

MARY JO LYNCH

A Research Agenda. "The Agenda for the Nineties," championed in Anne Matthews' impassioned editorial, is a politically sensitive document.[16] The central issue in the agenda debate is funding for research.

Lost in the deliberation is the realization that any agenda for research is essentially political. Those who decry the agenda as a stricture on unfettered research miss the point that funding agencies have always defined funding agendas. DOE has a mandate to form priorities and to translate these priorities into an agenda for funding.

Matthews confuses funding with research when she declares, "but goals have to be set if research is not to be aimless. . . ."[17]

The agenda debate is an example of reinvention of the wheel, when examined from a larger perspective. Price documented the change from "little science" to "big science" 25 years ago.[18] Just 21 years ago, Greenberg's analysis of scientific inquiry under federal government aegis delineated the compromises and opportunities for governmentally funded research.[19] The question is not whether we should have basic research and a research agenda, or assign priorities for funding, but "in what ways and for what purposes should research in library and information science be expanded?" The answer to the question must be supplied by all of us involved in research.

Research Miniconferences.[20,21] Jeffrey Katzer, who chaired the ASIS Research Committee in 1986, acted upon a proposal initiated by Christine Borgman (UCLA) to initiate a series of student miniconferences on research. The Research Committee and the ASIS Board of Directors supported the idea with the stipulation that the miniconferences be operated locally and that ASIS would not provide any resources other than its name and encouragement.

Several interesting features that emerged from the miniconferences may become regular components of future conferences. First, the call for papers often elicits more responses than can be presented in one day; therefore, the host school must carefully select the *best* papers for presentation. Second, the conference usually has a keynote address by a renowned information scientist. Third, the best paper presented at the conference receives a cash prize. The purpose of the prize is to offset the travel costs of the winner attending the next ASIS annual meeting to present the paper. Fourth, the Research Committee sponsors a full panel session at the ASIS annual meeting, whereby research award winners present their work to a broader community.

Table 1. National Science Foundation, Knowledge Models and Cognitive Systems Program Awards, FY 88

Author	Institution	Title of Project	Amount
		Formal Models	
Wyllis Bandler	Florida State University	Fuzzy Extension for Information Science	$5,000
Andrew U. Frank	University of Maine, Orono	A Formal Model for Representation and Manipulation of Spatial Subdivisions in Information Systems	5,000
John A. Hartigan	Yale University	Clustering Algorithms	76,500
Thomas Imielinski	Rutgers University, New Brunswick	Complexity Tailored Information Systems	149,996
Paris Kanellakis	Brown University	Logic, Databases and Parallel Computation	105,961
Donald W. Loveland	Duke University	Extending the Domain of Logic Programming	91,033
R. Duncan Luce	Harvard University	Axiomatic and Meaningfulness Studies	83,881
David McAllester	Massachusetts Institute of Technology	Knowledge Representation for Mathematics	120,135
Nils J. Nilsson	Stanford University	Multi-valued Logics	120,728
Robert M. Oliver	University of California, Berkeley	Conference on Influence Diagrams for Decision Analysis, Inference, and Prediction at UC Berkeley, April 1988	19,877
Judea Pearl	University of California, Los Angeles	Graphoids: A Representation for Dependence and Relevance in Automated Reasoning	120,044
Fred S. Roberts	Rutgers University, New Brunswick	Scales of Measurement and the Limitations They Place on Information Processing	49,712
John S. Schlipf	University of Cincinnati	The Effectiveness of Non-Motonic Inference	20,937
Glenn R. Shafer	University of Kansas	Belief Functions in Artificial Intelligence	89,078
Yoav Shoham	Stanford University	Nonmonotonic Temporal Reasoning	120,816
Edward Shortliffe	Stanford University	Pragmatic Approaches to Reasoning Under Uncertainty	141,325
Richard H. Thomason David S. Touretzky	Mellon-Pitt-Carnegie Corporation	Logical Foundations for Inheritance Theory and Knowledge Update	106,394
T. Toffoli	Massachusetts Institute of Technology	Information Mechanics	77,000
Moshe Y. Vardi	IBM Corporation	Conference on Theoretical Aspects of Reasoning About Knowledge	21,500
Robert T. Winkler	Duke University	Combining Dependent Information: Models and Issues	96,554
		Natural Language Systems	
Robert C. Berwick	Massachusetts Institute of Technology	Learnability and Parsability	20,762
Gail A. Bruder	State University of New York, Buffalo	Cognitive and Computer Systems for Understanding Narrative Text	189,751
Eugene Charniak	Brown University	Single-Semantic-Process Theory of Parsing	134,250
Richard H. Granger	University of California, Irvine	Unification of Lexical, Syntactic, and Fragmatic Inference in Understanding	114,800
Hans Kamp	University of Texas, Austin	The Logic and Representation of Properties and Propositions for Computer Natural Language Processing	75,000
George P. Lakoff	University of California, Berkeley	Lexical Network Theory	100,278
Douglas P. Metzler	University of Pittsburgh	An Expert System Approach to Syntactic Parsing and Information	76,122
Sergei Nirenburg	Carnegie Mellon University	Acquisition and Maintenance for Knowledge Bases for Natural Language Processing Systems	97,621
Victor Raskin	Purdue University	Acquisition and Maintenance for Knowledge Bases for Natural Language Processing Systems	96,506
Yorick Wilks	New Mexico State University	The Development of Collative Semantics Including a Parallel Processing Implementation	99,929
Yorick Wilks	New Mexico State University	Machine Tractable Dictionaries as Tools and Resources for Natural Language Processing	127,990
		Cognitive Systems	
James A. Anderson	Brown University	Cognitive Application of Matrix Memory Models	43,432
Thomas L. Dean	Brown University	Time-Dependent Planning for Autonomous Systems	69,850
Donald W. Dearholt	New Mexico State University	Properties of Networks Derived from Proximities	62,730
Gerald F. DeJong	University of Illinois, Urbana	Explanation-Based Learning	75,000
Simon Kasif	Johns Hopkins University	Parallel Logic Programming	59,986
Benjamin J. Kuipers	University of Texas, Austin	Deep and Shallow Models in the Knowledge Base	91,230
Amy L. Lansky	SRI International	Localized Planning for Parallel Domains Using Temporal Logic Constraints	128,497
Daniel Osherson	Massachusetts Institute of Technology	A Computational Approach to Decision Making	52,041
Leonard Pitt	University of Illinois, Urbana	Reductions and the Complexity of Learning Problems	60,000
Leonard Pitt	University of Illinois, Urbana	A Workshop on Computational Learning Theory	15,000
Lynne M. Reder	Carnegie Mellon University	Components of Initial Skill Learning; Development of Effective Examples and Training Procedures	125,000
Charles Rich Richard C. Waters	Massachusetts Institute of Technology	Toward a Requirements Apprentice: On the Boundary Between Informal and Formal Specifications	114,642
James Schmolze	Tufts University	Parallel Algorithms for Knowledge Representations	100,000
Lokendra Shastri	University of Pennsylvania	The Design Analysis and Evaluation of a Connectionist System for Representing Structured Knowledge	124,155
Paul E. Utgoff Andrew G. Barto	University of Massachusetts, Amherst	Learning Efficient Recognizers for Analytically Derived Concepts	480,499
Susan Wiedenbeck	University of Nebraska, Lincoln	Beacons in Computer Program Comprehension	11,989

Table 2. National Science Foundation, Robotics and Machine Intelligence Program Awards, FY 88

Author	Institution	Title of Project	Amount
		Speech Recognition	
James F. Allen	University of Rochester	Basic Research in Representing Plans Occurring in Natural Language Discourse	$25,000
Mary E. Beckman	The Ohio State University Research Foundation	Modeling Prosodic Patterns for Automatic Speech	25,000
Mary E. Beckman	The Ohio State University Research Foundation	Informational Structure in Articulator Movement and Acoustic-Duration Patterns	60,460
Robert C. Berwick	Massachusetts Institute of Technology	Computational Properties of Natural Languages	62,500
Robert C. Berwick	Massachusetts Institute of Technology	Computational Properties of Natural Languages	15,500
John W. Chowning Bernard Mont-Reynaud	Stanford University	Intelligent Analysis of Composite Acoustic Signals	130,776
Ronald A. Cole Richard M. Stern	Carnegie-Mellon University	Phonetic Classification of Continuous Speech	150,000
Jan Edwards	City University of New York, Hunter College	Informational Structure in Articulator Movement and Acoustic-Duration Patterns	40,398
David Lunney Robert C. Morrison	East Carolina University	Functional Group Analysis of Infrared Spectra Using Auditory Pattern Recognition	10,000
Mitchell Weintraub	SRI International	Development and Evaluation of Auditory Models	65,023
Stephen A. Zahorian	Old Dominion University	Spectral Shape Factors as Acoustic Invariants for Speech Perception	60,000
		Image Understanding	
Terrance Boult	Columbia University	Acquisition of Three-Dimensional Information	61,493
David B. Cooper	Brown University	A Bayesian Approach to Computer Vision	86,502
John G. Daugman	Harvard University	Computer Vision and Biological Vision	35,000
Charles R. Dyer	University of Wisconsin	Parallel Vision Algorithms for Shared-Memory and Pipeline Multiprocessors	80,795
Kie-Bum Eom	Syracuse University	Robust Random-Field Models for Images with Long- and Short-Term Dependencies	28,685
F. Alberto Grunbaum	University of California, Berkeley	Mathematical Tools for Image Reconstruction	65,000
Robert Hummel	New York University	Solving Ill-Conditioned Problems in Computer Vision	55,000
Robert Hummel	New York University	The Visual Hierachy of Model-Based Recognition	6,442
Russ Miller	State University of New York, Buffalo	Parallel Algorithms for Image Analysis, Computational Geometry, and Graphs	54,111
Robert A. Morris	University of Massachusetts, Boston	Image Processing and Digital Typography	43,217
Prasanna Mulgaonkar Robert C. Bolles	SRI International	Vision-System Programming	149,906
Theodosius Pavlidis	State University of New York, Stony Brook	Regularization Techniques in Image Analysis	85,845
Alexander P. Pentland	Massachusetts Institute	Learning and Recognition in Natural Environments	65,000
V. K. Prasanna-Kumar	University of Southern California	Parallel Processing of Computer Vision Problems	31,556
Azriel Rosenfeld	University of Maryland	Perceptual Organization in Computer Vision: Pyramid-Based Approaches	182,052
Jayant Shah	Northeastern University	Segmentation of Images	33,066
Mihran Tuceryan Anil K. Jain	Michigan State University	Perceptual Grouping in Computer Vision	81,241
Deborah K. Walters	State University of New York, Buffalo	Representation of Visual-Feature Variables in Connectionist Networks	85,421
Matthew O. Ward	Worcester Polytechnic Institute	Image Segmentation Using Domain Constraint Knowledge	31,809
Terry E. Weymouth	University of Michigan at Ann Arbor	Knowledge-Guided Detection of Inner-Ear Hair Cells in Digital Images	60,078
		Pattern Analysis	
Arthur W. Burks John H. Holland	University of Michigan at Ann Arbor	Classifier-System Algorithms and Architectures for Learning and Discovery	102,044
Jamie Carbonell	Carnegie-Mellon University	U.S. Japan AI Symposium	40,967
Michael Conrad Roberto R. Kampfner	Wayne State University	Evolutionary Programming and Neural Computation	65,000
Michael Conrad Roberto R. Kampfner	Wayne State University	Evolutionary Programming and Neural Computation	3,500
Robert P. Daley	University of Pittsburgh	Research in Inductive Inference	20,000
Michael J. Flynn	Stanford University	Performance Evaluation of Parallel Logic Programming	9,586
Stephen I. Gallant	Northeastern University	Connectionist Learning Algorithms Suitable for Expert Systems	60,000
Stephen Grossberg	Boston University	Meeting of the International Neural Network Society	10,000
Moshe Kam	Drexel University	State-Space Analysis and Design for Neural Networks	30,000
David Kirsh	Massachusetts Institute of Technology	Workshop on Foundations of Artificial Intelligence	5,000

Table 2. National Science Foundation, Robotics and Machine Intelligence Program Awards, FY 88, *Continued*

Author	Institution	Title of Project	Amount
		Speech Recognition	
Benjamin J. Kuipers	University of Texas, Austin	Deep and Shallow Models in the Knowledge Base	45,615
Victor R. Lesser	University of Massachusetts, Amherst	A Research Facility for Cooperative Distributed Computing	431,000
Drew V. McDermott	Yale University	Theory of Learning Algorithms	41,118
		Robotic Perception	
Ronald J. Williams	Northeastern University	Reinforcement-Learning Connectionist Systems	80,000
Narendra Ahuja	University of Illinois, Urbana	Computer Vision	62,500
Dana H. Ballard	University of Rochester	Parameter Networks and Spatial Cognition	85,521
Ramalingnam R. Chellappa	University of Southern California	Kinematics and Structure of a 3-D Rigid Object from a Sequence of Noisy Images	86,455
Su-shing Chen	University of North Carolina	Computer Vision and Image Understanding	56,710
Earnest Davis	New York University	Perception and Planning	55,000
Hon-Son Don	State University of New York, Stony Brook	A Machine Vision Architecture for Passive Depth Perception and Scene Analysis	29,998
Ronald Fearing	University of California, Berkeley	Shape Interpretation Using Tactile Sensing	35,000
Ernest L. Hall	University of Cincinnati	Three-Dimension Measurements for Robot Vision	40,939
Ellen C. Hildreth	Massachusetts Institute of Technology	Recovering Environmental Layout from Visual Motion	62,500
Anil K. Jain Ramesh Jain	Michigan State University	Workshop on Range-Image Understanding	14,949
Ramesh Jain	University of Michigan, Ann Arbor	Motion Detection and Segmentation in Spatio-Temporal Space	53,510
Takeo Kanade Charles Thorpe	Carnegie Mellon University	Understanding 3-D Dynamic Natural Scenes with Range Data	87,719
Chia-Hoang Lee	Purdue University	Motion and Correspondence Studies for Computer Vision	39,739
Tom M. Mitchell	Carnegie Mellon University	Artificial Intelligence and Machine Learning	62,500
George Nagy	Rensselaer Polytechnic Institute	Visibility-Oriented Algorithms for Digital Terrain Models	69,168
Nasser M. Nasrabadi	Worcester Polytechnic Institute	A Stereo Vision Technique Using Curve Segments and Relaxation Matching	32,267
Tomaso Poggio Ellen C. Hildreth Edward H. Adelson	Massachusetts Institute of Technology	Motion Analysis in Biological and Computer Vision Systems	167,131
Anca L. Ralescu	University of Cincinnati	Modeling Imprecision with Support-Logic Programming	22,304
Hanan Samet	University of Maryland	Spatial Data: Representations and Problems	141,662
Neelina Shrikhande	Central Michigan University	Recognition of 3-D Objects Via Structured Light and Color Textures	32,785
Shin-Min S. Song	University of Illinois	Gait and Mobility Study for the Design of an All-Terrain Walking Machine	50,475
Steven L. Tanimoto	University of Washington	Integrated Systems for High-Speed Vision	110,758
William B. Thompson	University of Minnesota	Moving-Object Detection	61,500
		Robotic Reasoning	
Peter K. Allen	Columbia University	Extending the Capabilities of Robotic Systems	62,500
Christopher Atkeson	Massachusetts Institute of Technology	Computational and Experimental Studies of Motor Learning in Humans and Robots	25,000
Bruce R. Donald	Cornell University	Towards Task-Level Robot Programming	65,996
Stephen Grossberg	Boston University	Adaptive Sensory-Motor Planning by Humans and Machine	154,558
Thomas C. Henderson	University of Utah	Dexterous Manipulation	49,119
John E. Hopcroft	Cornell University	A Program of Research in Robotics and Automation	119,970
Thomas G. Huang	University of Illinois, Urbana	Three-Dimensional Motion Analysis	66,698
Joseph K. Kearney	University of Iowa	Programming with Articulated Objects	34,009
Michael Kuperstein	Neurogen	Neutral-Network Controller for Adaptive Hand-Eye-Coordination Robots	41,300
Gin McCollum	Good Samaritan Hospital and Medical Center	Structure of Human Posture Control	68,024
Drew V. McDermott	Yale University	Spatial Reasoning for Problem Solving	88,736
Thomas W. Miller Filon H. Glanz L. Gordon Kraft	University of New Hampshire, Durham	Control of Robotic Manipulators Using a Neural-Network-Based Learning Controller	61,758
Joseph S. Mitchell	Cornell University	Computational Geometry Problems in Robotics	30,072
Leona Morgenstern	Brown University	Perception and Planning	55,562
Colm O'Dunlaing Chee-Keng Yap	New York University	Motion-Planning Problems in Robotics: Algorithmic Issues	80,637
Robin J. Popplestone	University of Massachusetts, Amherst	Robotic Plan Formulation as the Design of Behavior	80,490
Mark W. Spong	University of Illinois, Urbana	Nonlinear Methods in Robotic Control	4,000
Joe Warren	Rice University	Algorithmic Algebraic Geometry for Geometric Modeling	28,959

Table 3. National Science Foundation, Information Technology and Organizations Program Awards, FY 88

Author	Institution	Title of Project	Amount
Coordination Theory and Technology			
Tora K. Bikson	Rand Corporation	User Modifiable Interfaces: A Field-Experimental Assessment of Effects	$199,435
Bernard P. Cohen	Stanford University	Status and Information Transfer in Face-to-Face and Computer-Mediated Problem Solving	82,080
Jolene Galegher	University of Arizona	Conference on Technology and Cooperative Work Computer Information	13,107
Itzhak Gilboa	Northwestern University	Bounded Rationality and the Role of History in Decision Under Uncertainty	44,907
James S. Jordan	University of Minnesota	Information Processing in Interactive Organization	109,340
Ronald Lee	University of Texas	Bureaucracy and Artificial Intelligence Logic Modeling of Bureaucracy	46,222
Thomas W. Malone	Massachusetts Institute of Technology	Coordination Theory Workshop	24,978
Stanley Reiter	Northwestern University	Collaborative Research on Informational Aspects of Distributed Computing and Decentralized Resource Allocation	110,732
Donald G. Saari	Northwestern University	Toward a Mathematical Foundation for Information and Decision Sciences	43,887
Information Technology Impacts and Policy			
William J. Baumol	New York University	The Role of Computers and Scientific and Technical Information in Comparative Economic Development	171,476
Stanley Besen	Rand Corporation	Standard Setting in the Telecommunications and Computer Industries	106,575
Paul A. David	Stanford University	Informational and Organizational Impacts on Productivity: The Economics of Control and Reliability in Complex Production Processes	302,180
Paul A. David	Stanford University	The Political Economy of Information Technology Standards: Towards a Framework for Policy Research	25,467
Paul A. David	Stanford University	The Economic Impact of Technological Advances in Information Processing Equipment: A Quantitative Study	25,000
John L. King	University of California, Irvine	Information Technology and New Economic Growth Opportunities for the 90s	14,800
Rob Kling	University of California, Irvine	Social Dimensions of Desktop Computing	100,000
Kenneth L. Kraemer	University of California, Irvine	The Evolution of Computing in Local Governments	125,000
Edwin Mansfield	University of Pennsylvania	Flexible Manufacturing System in Japan, Europe, and the United States: Diffusion and Economic Impact	101,175
James B. Rule	Bank Street College of Education	The New Uses of Information: Impact in Organizations	14,088
Garth Saloner	Massachusetts Institute of Technology	Economic Issues in Standardization	127,557
Information Theory			
Kenneth B. Dunn / Chester S. Spatt	Carnegie Mellon University	The Effects of Information, Transaction Costs and Uncertainty on Debt Contracts and Pricing	46,450
Daniel Friedman	University of California, Santa Cruz	Market Mechanisms in Electronic Asset Markets: An Experimental Investigation	143,984
John H. Kagel	University of Houston	Information Impact and Information Processing in Common Value Auctions: Experimental and Theoretical Investigations	37,500
Richard E. Kihlstrom / Andrew Postlewaite	University of Pennsylvania	Studies in the Economic Theory of Asymetric Information	54,489
Jean Tirole	Massachusetts Institute of Technology	Contract Design Under Asymmetric Information	35,577

Table 4. National Science Foundation, Database and Expert Systems Program Awards, FY 88

Author	Institution	Title of Project	Amount
Databases			
Amr El Abbadi	University of California, Santa Barbara	Fault-Tolerant Algorithms for Distributed Databases	$60,000
Don S. Batory	University of Texas, Austin	Genesis: A Project to Develop a Reconfigurable Database Management System	119,097
Peter Buneman	University of Pennsylvania	Combining Object-Oriented and Relational Database Programming	117,882
Shashi Gadia	Iowa State University of Science and Technology	An Investigation of Temporal Databases from Foundation to Implementation	53,686
Seymour Ginsburg	University of Southern California	Mathematical Foundations of Databases	10,000
Goetz Graefe	Oregon Graduate Center	Expert Systems for Database Query Optimization	45,377
Richard B. Hull	University of Southern California	Theoretical Investigation of Access Mechanisms for Semantically Motivated Database Models	49,729
Lawrence J. Henschen / Jiawei Han	Northeastern University	Logic and Databases	102,858
Fred Maryanski	University of Connecticut	Generation of Conceptual Data Models: Production of Model-Specific Software	15,000
Jack Minker	University of Maryland, College Park	Artificial Intelligence, Parallel Logic Programming and Deductive Databases	57,955

Table 4. National Science Foundation, Database and Expert Systems Program Awards, FY 88 *Continued*

Author	Institution	Title of Project	Amount
		Databases	
Shamkant B. Navathe	University of Florida	Methodologies for Distributed Database Design	53,746
Raghuanth Ramakrishnan	University of Wisconsin, Madison	Theory and Compilation of Data Intensive Logic Programs	73,588
Edward Sciore Sharon C. Salveter	Boston University	Deriving and Maintenance of Rules in an Intelligent DBMS	158,000
Timoleon Sellis	University of Maryland, College Park	Multiple-Query Processing and Caching in Deductive Database Systems	49,632
Abraham Silberschatz	University of Texas, Austin	Theory and Compilation of Data Intensive Logic Programs	101,628
Frederick N. Springsteel	University of Missouri, Columbia	Entity-Relationship Design of Information Systems	58,435
David W. Stemple Tim Sheard	University of Massachusetts, Amherst	Recursive Queries and Abstract Data Types in Databases	73,992
Susan D. Urban	University of Miami	The Active Use of Constraints in the Design of Object-Oriented Database Applications	59,855
	Knowledge Based Systems		
Dik Lun Lee	Ohio State University Research Foundations	Software and Hardware Techniques in Knowledge Base Machines	60,000
Phillip Chen-Yu Shen	Purdue University	Object-Oriented Knowledge Base Management Systems	60,000
Leon Sterling	Case Western Reserve	Meta-Interpreters for Expert Systems	149,229
Stanley Y. W. Su	University of Florida	Research on Object-Oriented Knowledge Base Management Technology for Improving Productivity and Competitiveness in Manufacturing	23,929
William B. Thompson James R. Slagel	University of Minnesota	Knowledge-Based Justification	43,961
Jeffrey D. Ullman	Stanford University	Research into the Design and Implementation of Knowledge-Based Systems	205,443
	Information Retrieval Systems		
Christos Faloutsos	University of Maryland, College Park	Signature File Methods for Text Databases	3,880
Edward A. Fox Jane T. Nutter	Virginia Polytechnic Institute and State University	Organized Lexical Knowledge for Information Retrieval	4,284
Richard S. Marcus	Massachusetts Institute of Technology	Advanced Models and Techniques for Expert Interactive Retrieval Assistance	55,044
Vijay Raghavan Jitender S. Deogun	University of Southwestern Louisiana	Cluster-Based Adaptive Information Retrieval System	69,013
William M. Shaw Judith B. Wood	University of North Carolina, Chapel Hill	An Evaluation and Comparison of Term and Citation Indexing	75,487
	Fundamental Research		
Richard E. Korf	University of California, Los Angeles	Realtime, Parallel Heuristic Search	60,032

Table 5. National Science Foundation, Interactive Systems Awards, FY 88

Author	Institution	Title of Project	Amount
Norman Badler	University of Pennsylvania	A Representation for Natural Human Movement	$42,533
Alan Biermann	Duke University	An Architecture for Voice-Dialogue Systems	96,428
Richard Bolt	Massachusetts Institute of Technology	Eye Movements in Multi-Modal Human Computer Dialogue	170,611
Alan H. Borning	University of Washington	Generating Interactive Displays from Declarative Specifications	166,000
Michael Drillings	U.S. Army Research Institute	Committee on Human Factors	27,510
Gerhard Fischer	University of Colorado, Boulder	Design Principles for Comprehensive Systems	356,726
Bradley Goodman	Bolt Beranek & Newman, Inc.	Plan Recognition and Miscommunication	64,476
Max Henrion M. Granger Morgan	Carnegie Mellon University	Qualitative Interfaces for Quantitive Models	150,000
Donald D. Hoffman	University of California, Irvine	A Formal Investigation of Perceptual Information Processing	66,166
Scott E. Hudson	University of Arizona	A General Purpose Program Visualization Support Tool	171,086
David Maier	Oregon Computing Center	Generating Interactive Display from Declarative Specifications	175,281
Gary Marchionini	University of Maryland, College Park	Mental Models for Adaptive Search Systems: A Theory for Information Seeking	70,732
Arthur Melmed	New York University	Multimedia Display Environments	56,600
David B. Pisoni	Indiana University, Bloomington	Perception of Synthetic Speech Generated by Rule	3,500
Robert D. Rodman	North Carolina State University	Dialogue Processing for Voice Interactive System	53,559
Gerard Salton	Cornell University	Interface Tools and User-System Interaction in Automatic Information Retrieval	139,553
Paul Smolensky	University of Colorado, Boulder	Computer-Aided Reasoned Discourse	167,866
Barry L. Vercoe	Massachusetts Institute of Technology	A Portable Language for Audio Processing and Psychoacoustic	113,373
Robert C. Williges Beverly H. Williges	Virginia Polytechnic Institute	Paradigm for Experimental Research on Computer-User Interaction	166,337
David Zeltzer	Massachusetts Institute of Technology	Modeling Motor Behavior and Virtual Environments for Three-Dimensional Computer Animation	87,222

Students, host schools, and ASIS consider miniconferences worthwhile vehicles for promoting student research, encouraging students to meet with their future colleagues, and enabling ASIS members to meet students who have a promising future as information scientists.

Conclusion. Disciplines and professions are molded by, and mold, their literature. One element raised from a review of trends in, and examples of, research reported in 1988 is that there is much discussion but little synergy. Although the literature includes all types of research, librarians most often conduct management-oriented, action research. Kobasa reports that "of ALAs best-sellers, 7 percent fall into the philosophical and theoretical foundations category; in contrast, approximately 21 percent of the catalog titles and 20 percent of ALA titles overall are in this category."[22] Such findings indicate a duality in the profession with respect to research—we want it, but only as a utilitarian aid to decision making. This duality may also be one of the causes of the furor over research agendas.

Any brief analysis of available research studies must acknowledge the large quantity of work which is submitted for publication. Budd notes that library and information science journals claim they reject "approximately 60 to 70 percent of [the] manuscripts" received.[23] Editorial policies and practices attempt to separate quality, from quantity, research. If there is one research agenda we all can agree to it surely must be that we need to improve the quality of research (with greater demonstration of a study's reliability and validity) and the access to this research. At the same time, we must focus and hone our research directions and skills.

PETER HERNON
C.D. HURT

REFERENCES AND NOTES

1. Charles H. Davis, "Editorial," *Library & Information Science Research*, 10:1 (January–March 1988).
2. Charles Martell, "Editorial: What is Research?" *College & Research Libraries*, 49:183 (May 1988).
3. Ibid.
4. Ibid., p. 184.
5. Ellen Altman and Kim Antieau, "Dissemination and Impact of U.S. Department of Education's Library Research and Demonstration Projects: A Citation Analysis," *Government Information Quarterly*, 5:53–55 (1988).
6. George D'Elia, "Materials Availability Fill Rates: Additional Data Addressing the Questions of the Usefulness of the Measures," *Public Libraries*, 27 (Spring 1988): 15–23; Nancy Van House, "In Defense of Fill Rates," *Public Libraries*, 27 (Spring 1988): 25–27; D'Elia, "A Response to Van House," *Public Libraries*, 27 (Spring 1988): 28–31; and Van House, "A Response to D'Elia," *Public Libraries*, 27:32 Spring 1988).
7. Nancy Van House, "In Defense of Fill Rates," p. 27.
8. Peter Hernon, "Utility Measures, Not Performance Measures, for Library Reference Service?," *RQ*, 26:453–57 (Summer 1987).
9. Marjorie E. Murfin and Charles A. Bunge, "Paraprofessionals at the Reference Desk," *Journal of Academic Librarianship*, 14:10–14 (March 1988).
10. Charles A. Bunge, "Professional Education and Reference Efficiency," Dissertation, University of Illinois, 1967, p. 146–47.
11. Stephen E. Atkins, "Subject Trends in Library and Information Science Research, 1975–1984," *Library Trends*, 36:633–58 (Spring 1988).
12. Charles R. McClure, "The Federal Technical Report Literature: Research Needs and Issues," *Government Information Quarterly*, 5:37–38 (1988).
13. Altman and Antieau, "Dissemination and Impact of U.S. Department of Education's Library Research and Demonstration Projects," p. 53.
14. Ibid.
15. Ibid. p. 55.
16. Anne J. Matthews, "D.O.E. Responds to the 'Another Research Agenda' Editorial," *Library & Information Science Research*, 10:119–20 (April–June 1988).
17. Ibid., p. 119.
18. Derek Price, *Little Science, Big Science* (New York: Columbia University Press, 1963).
19. Daniel S. Greenberg, *The Politics of Pure Science* (New York: New American Library, 1967).
20. Jeffrey Katzer, Syracuse University, supplied the information upon which this section is based.
21. See Sharon L. Baker and Ronald R. Powell, "The Research Efforts of Major Library Organizations," in *Library and Information Science Annual*, vol. 4 (Englewood, CO: Libraries Unlimited, 1988), pp. 46–50. This article discusses the programs of national associations "to stimulate research for the profession and for introspection."
22. Paul Kobasa, "Synergy, Not Cause and Effect: The Library Profession and Its Literature," *Library Trends*, 36:695–708 (Spring 1988).
23. John M. Budd, "Publication in Library & Information Science: The State of the Literature," *Library Journal*, 113:126 (September 1, 1988).

Resources and Technical Services Division

During the 1987/88 year Resources and Technical Services Division (RTSD) management focused on staff training, fiscal control and increased visibility within the larger ALA organization. Member activities concentrated on improving existing programs and establishing several new ones.

STAFFING

By the end of the year, RTSD enjoyed a full complement of staff. Executive Director Karen Muller, who had joined RTSD in June 1987, trained new staff members Darryl T. Howell (Administrative Secretary, who arrived in August), Yvonne McLean (Secretary II, who came on board in September), and JoAnn C. King (Program Officer, who joined the staff in June).

BUDGET

RTSD entered the 1987/88 year with a $17,671 deficit (cash accounting basis), or $60,642 (accrual basis). All areas of the organization, under the guidance of the Directors Board with advice from the Budget and Finance Committee, continued to exercise fiscal vigilance, so that RTSD ended the year with a positive balance, on an accrual basis, of $79,818. The fiscal goal is to achieve by 1992 a fund balance totalling 25 percent of the average of the operating budgets for the three prior fiscal years.

INCREASED VISIBILITY

RTSD provided requested information for both the ALA Committee on Program Evaluation and Support and the ALA Planning Committee. The

Planning & Research Committee gathered information on research within RTSD for the ALA Committee on Research. RSTD appointed a liaison to the ALA Committee on Ethics.

Planning. In January 1988 RTSD held a planning session attended by the Directors Board, the section executive committees and Planning/Research Committee members. Council member Sharon A. Hogan served as facilitator. Participants generated ideas for action for all facets of the "ALA Mission, Priority Areas and Goals" statement, and the Directors Board created an ad hoc Task Force to coordinate and disseminate the information gathered at the planning session and to recommend an ongoing planning framework.

PROGRAMS

With more than 500 members actively participating in 165 working groups, RTSD continued existing programs and initiated new efforts.

Continuing Education. In 1987/88 RTSD conducted four institutes, two serials cataloging workshops, a classification institute and a preservation microfilming institute. At the ALA annual conference in New Orleans in July RTSD sponsored preconferences on collection development in the electronic age and on management strategies for disasters which jeopardize library collections. In New Orleans RTSD also mounted programs on optical disk technology, out-of-print books, the escalation of serials costs, preservation microfilming, the revised version of Anglo-American Cataloguing Rules, 2d edition, linked systems, microcomputer software and U.S. copyright.

Publications. *LRTS* and the *RTSD Newsletter* made adjustments in frequency during 1988. Two new RTSD publications appeared: *Guide for Writing a Bibliographer's Manual*, by the Resources Section Collection Management and Development Committee, as the first issue in the "Collection Development Guidelines" series; and *Cataloging Correctly for Kids*, published jointly with the American Association of School Librarians and the Association for Library Service to Children. The Directors Board approved the Publications Committee's operating guidelines and empowered the Committee to act with discretion between association conferences on approval of publication manuscripts under an urgent deadline.

Ongoing Activities. The following list of actions in a sample of the panoply of topics addressed by RTSD working groups.

- The Publisher/Vendor Library Relations Committee distributed draft documents on "Non-Receipt of Prepared Orders" and "Unsolicited Receipts with Services." They continue to update and distribute a list of Gille imprints.
- The Audiovisual Committee distributed more than 700 copies of its brochure entitled "Happiness Is Having One Title" to producers and distributors of AV materials.
- RTSD joined the Freedom to Read Foundation.
- The Directors Board authorized an evaluation of the RTSD awards system and methods for presenting awards.
- The Membership Committee created a membership application form and customized brochures for public librarians and Junior Members Round Table members. As a result of its recommendations, RTSD sponsored a booth at the Public Library Association national conference in April. To encourage new institutional members, RTSD now offers for the first three years of institutional membership a ten percent discount on the registration fee for each representative from that institution attending an RTSD workshop.
- At the Midwinter meeting RTSD supported the legislation which ALA Council approved advocating the greater production and use of alkaline paper for printing.
- RTSD supplied ALA Executive Director Thomas J. Galvin with comment on the draft proposal for the revised operating agreement among partners to AACR, which was discussed at the meeting of AACR Principals at the 1987 IFLA. RTSD subsequently commented on the new draft agreement and Executive Director Karen Muller assisted at the meeting of Principals at the 1988 IFLA meeting.
- RTSD contributed to standards development through its representatives to organizations that develop standards, such as the National Information Standards Organization (NISO), Cooperative Online Serials (CONSER), the National Institution for Conservation (NIC) and the Association for Image and Information Management (AIIM).
- The Duplicates Exchange Union distributed an exchange list to cooperating members, facilitating their exchange of duplicates.
- The Planning and Research Committee initiated its review of RTSD units, beginning with division-level discussion groups.

New Directions. In 1987/88 RTSD established several new directions.

- The Directors Board voted to appoint a task force to develop a strategy for ALA's participation on national and international levels in discussion, investigation, and actions relating to the availability, economics, and distribution of library materials.
- In July, RTSD President Marion T. Reid and RTSD International Relations Committee Chair Merrily A. Smith presented notebooks to members of the Russian delegation of librarians attending the ALA annual conference. The materials—copies of the docu-

Resources and Technical Services Division

Carolyn L. Harris, Columbia University.

RESOURCES AND TECHNICAL SERVICES DIVISION

PRESIDENT (July 1988–June 1989):
Carolyn L. Harris, Columbia University Assistant of Library Service, New York

VICE-PRESIDENT/PRESIDENT-ELECT:
Nancy R. John, University of Illinois, Chicago

EXECUTIVE DIRECTOR:
Karen Muller

Membership (August 31, 1988): 6,037 (4,979 personal; 1,058 organizational)
Expenditures (August 31, 1988): $288,702

mentation created for the 1988 RTSD/PLMS Preconference on Management Strategies for Disaster Preparedness, were officially received by Nikolai Semenovich Kartashov, president of the USSR Library Council, director of the Lenin State Library of the USSR, professor and head of the delegation; and Iuliia Petrovna Niuksha, head of the Document Conservation Department of the Saltykov-Shchedrin State Public Library in Leningrad.
- The Directors Board established two additional thrusts: creation of a group to develop national guidelines for the bibliographic control of master microfilm catalog records and exploration of the feasibility of sponsoring a study on the costs, availability, and distribution of scholarly information.

AWARDS

Five individuals during the annual membership meeting in July received special recognition. Karen Markey, University of Michigan School of Information and Library Studies, received the Esther J. Piercy Award for contributions to technical services in her first decade as a librarian. Ben R. Tucker, Chief of the Office for Descriptive Cataloging Policy at the Library of Congress, received the Margaret Mann Citation for his outstanding professional achievement in cataloging. University of North Carolina at Chapel Hill librarians Joe A. Hewitt and John S. Shipman received the Blackwell/North America Scholarship award for their article "Cooperative Collection Development among Research Libraries in the Age of Networking" (*Advances in Library Automation and Networking*, 1, 1987). The Bowker/Ulrich's Serials Librarianship Award was given to OCLC Manager of Resource Sharing Marjorie E. Bloss.

In 1987/88 the Resources and Technical Division achieved a full complement of office staff, re-established a firm financial footing, increased its visibility within the ALA arena, initiated a long range planning effort, continued existing services and expanded in new directions.

MARION T. REID

Risk Management for Libraries

Libraries of all types and sizes are becoming increasingly aware of the need to protect themselves from the risks of loss due to all sorts of disasters—theft and employee dishonesty, liability claims, and legal actions resulting from mishandled personnel matters. The first feature article in this book expounds in more detail on management of natural disasters.

To be protected fully and to be ready to respond to dangers, libraries must develop comprehensive risk management programs consisting of a combination of insurance, preventive safety and security measures, disaster plans, and a thorough knowledge of personnel policies. Risk management is an ongoing responsibility. The following summary of events and issues for 1988 illustrates the variety of concerns that faced risk managers.

Insurance. The continued liability insurance crisis was further illustrated by a survey of public libraries conducted by the Peru (Indiana) Public Library which revealed that the cost of insurance continued to rise steadily and sometimes drastically in Indiana. Nevertheless, libraries made progress in meeting the high cost of liability insurance. For example, the New York Library Association announced availability of reasonably priced professional liability insurance (up to $500,000 for each claim) for its individual and institutional members.

Antitrust actions charging conspiracy to cancel off or make prohibitively expensive certain types of liability insurance were filed in eight states against several major insurance firms including Allstate, Aetna Casualty, Hartford Fire Insurance, and Cigma Corporation. The American Library Association offered a preferred group automobile policy from GEICO. This benefit, along with an ALA/GEICO Preferred Home Insurance Plan, was made available to ALA members as a money saver for personal insurance.

Disasters. Adequate disaster planning, including prevention, preparedness, and recovery, remains a critical element of a sound risk management program. Compared to the previous two years, 1988 was a relatively quiet year for major library disasters. Unfortunately, one of the disasters was a very tragic fire in the Soviet Union which destroyed thousands of priceless rare books and other historical documents.

Natural Disasters. On April 19 a tornado destroyed the soon-to-be-opened Madison Branch of the Suwanee River Regional Library in rural north Florida. But for a delay in delivery of the library's refinished shelving that postponed moving the collection and furnishings from the old library, the damage would have been worse. The storm, the worst in Florida in 22 years, killed four and damaged property extensively, ripping large holes in the roof of the nearby junior college library where heavy rain destroyed equipment and more than 1,000 books.

Natural disasters also have indirect but tangible effects on libraries. In North Dakota, for example, falling oil prices and the disastrous summer drought drastically reduced the state tax base resulting in a two percent cut in all state agency budgets for the last 10 months of the biennium. As a result, the North Dakota State Library was forced to cancel one-third of its standing book orders.

In Southern California, three branches of the Los Angeles Public Library damaged in the Whittier Narrows earthquake of October 1987 reopened in temporary quarters on July 28; two of the libraries were undergoing repairs and renovations; and the third branch will require a new building. In the aftermath of recent earthquakes, the California State Library specified recommendations for replacing older bookstacks that do not meet current earthquake standards. Because earthquakes can rupture overhead pipes, it was suggested that standard joints be replaced with flexible plumbing connections to reduce water damage to collections.

A September 15 *Library Journal* article described a different type of library involvement for disaster preparedness. A small branch of the Orange County Public Library serves as headquarters for a citizen group established to provide disaster information to the town of Silverado (pop. 1,200) in the Santa Ana Mountains. The story told of the involvement of a Residents Emergency Action Committee and the library in successfully fighting a September 1987 forest fire that threatened the town.

Humanmade Disasters. One of the most tragic library disasters of this century occurred when fire broke out on Sunday evening, February 14, in the Library of USSR Academy of Sciences in Leningrad. The Library, founded in 1714, was among the world's largest and most unique collections. Of the 12,000,000 items in the collections, 400,000 were consumed by fire; 3,600,000 sustained water damage; 10,000 were infected with mold; and 7,500,000 volumes needed preventive care to block the spread of fungus. Losses in the rare book and manuscript collections were extensive: 188,000 foreign-language editions of the 18th, 19th, and 20th centuries from the world-renowned Baer Fund, a quarter of the library's unique newspaper collection, and many rare volumes collected over two centuries.

Preservation experts from around the globe, including the U.S., were dispatched to the Soviet Union to assist in the assessment of damage and to provide advice on recovery. Soviet newspapers not only carried detailed accounts of the tragedy, but criticized library officials for neglect and failure to respond to reporters and academy fellows who warned of an impending disaster. Faulty wiring in the newspaper department was blamed for the tragedy. Soviet citizens who scaled a fence to stop bulldozers from clearing away rare materials mixed in with the ashes and who volunteered daily to help dry out water-damaged materials kept the loss from being completely devastating.

A large, rich collection of materials on orthodox Jewry in the 20th century that emphasized materials on the Holocaust was destroyed by a fire in May at the New York offices of the National Orthodox Jewish Archives in the Wall Street area. A campaign has begun to replace the collection.

The Central Public Library of Los Angeles, closed since 1986 after being struck by two disastrous fires, remained in the news throughout 1988. In late 1987 the City Council approved a $152,400,000 package for rehabilitation and expansion of the building. In February, the city filed a $23,600,000 lawsuit against Harry Peak, a part-time actor suspected of starting the blaze. Peak, who was arrested in February 1987 and later released without charges, sued the city and fire department employees for $15,000,000 in damages for false imprisonment, slander, and other charges. Although there was insufficient evidence for a criminal charge, the city felt it had substantial evidence to win a civil case.

Ground was broken for the new library on June 3, and on September 13, the City Council approved spending $2,800,000 to restore the 700,000 water-damaged books that had been in deep freeze since 1986. Incredibly, on October 11, a third fire caused by ignition of debris by a cutting torch broke out in the basement of the building where renovation and expansion were in progress. By the end of February, the "Save the Books" Campaign had achieved its original goal of $10,000,000. Unfortunately, a $90,000,000 ten-year bond issue for the Los Angeles library system fell just short of receiving voter approval in October. The bond issue would have funded repairs to four earthquake-damaged libraries, would have done seismic work on eight others, would have expanded several libraries, and would have built three new branches.

Theft and Mutilation of Library Materials. A thought-provoking article in the March *American Libraries* by Lawrence W. Towner, President and Librarian-Emeritus of the Newberry Library in Chicago, decried the plague of theft, especially of rare materials, in libraries. Towner noted that "the real victim of book theft is far greater than the disappearance, temporary or permanent, of materials for study and research. The real victim is trust—that fragile net that for so long and so lovingly has held the library, its staff, the scholarly user, the book collector, and the bookseller together." He blamed the problem primarily on "indifference compounded by innocence, ignorance, and complacency." His concern is aptly illustrated by the following descriptions of some of the more significant incidents of library theft in 1988.

A man was arrested on April 18 after being discovered twice by a custodian in the closed special collections area of the University of California-Riverside Library. The suspect, Stephen C. Blumberg, who had burglary tools in his possession when apprehended, posed as a University of Minnesota professor in order to gain access to the area. He was subsequently found guilty, fined $1,000, and given three years probation and a suspended sentence. He remained under investigation by Los Angeles police for thefts of more than $1,400,000 of books and manuscripts from a number of West Coast university libraries.

Gustav Hasford, a screenwriter nominated for an Academy Award in 1988 for his work on the screenplay *Full Metal Jacket*, was charged with grand theft and possession of stolen property in San Luis Obispo County Municipal Court (California) in June. Nearly 10,000 books, including more than 800 from 62 libraries all over the world, were found in two self-storage lockers in San Luis Obispo by police using a warrant to look for books taken from the library at Cal Polytechnic University. In many cases, Hasford had checked the books out legally but never returned them. He was scheduled to go to court on August 18.

In Austin, Texas, a page from a rare document in Albert Einstein's own handwriting was stolen from a display case in the Flawn Academic Center on the University of Texas campus in March. The page, one of several on exhibit from the Harry Ransom Humanities Research Center, was recovered a week later and Samuel Royal, 18, was arrested and charged with the theft.

Other reported cases of significant thefts of library materials included a former Kentucky State University professor arrested for allegedly stealing some 2,000 books from libraries in Kentucky and Virginia and a University of North Carolina/Greensboro student who confessed to the theft of 700 books from the university library.

Risk Management for Libraries

Robert M. Willingham, Jr., former rare book curator of the University of Georgia Library, was found guilty on September 8 of stealing manuscripts, rare books, and prints from the university. His sentence of 15 years in prison, 15 years probation, and $45,000 in fines will be appealed. In a related story, art scholar Charles Merrill Mount was convicted and sentenced to three years in prison for transporting historic documents stolen from the Library of Congress and the National Archives.

In Oklahoma, Governor Henry Bellmon signed into law a bill which provided for fines of up to $1,000 for theft or destruction of materials worth up to $500 and up to $10,000 for more expensive items.

Dishonesty and Fraud. In San Bernadino, California, Stephen Whitney was charged with embezzlement for allegedly buying college textbooks for his wife with public library funds.

Security and Related Problems. Library security personnel are responsible for protecting collections, buildings, staff, and users from such threats as fire, physical attack, verbal abuse, theft, and mutilation of library materials. Individual or group protests, peaceful or violent, also pose potential security problems. In January a University of Maine at Orono student staged an act of civil disobedience by refusing to allow his book bag to be searched and by refusing to identify himself to a library staff member. The student, who was protesting the library's policy of searching bags for food and drink as users enter the building, was arrested and charged with criminal trespassing.

In February students on two college campuses staged library-related protests. At Fordham University, a "study-in" in the Rose Hill campus library protested a nine percent tuition hike. At Oregon State University students rallied in front of the library to protest overcrowded student study areas and insufficient numbers of books. Students, administrators, and faculty thus united to obtain additional funding for a new library wing and more books.

Late in 1987, the Minnesota Library Association went on record in support of alternative bookstores and information sources in the Twin Cities area—many of these outlets had been harassed, threatened, and robbed over a several-month period.

Liability and Related Legal Issues. Today's risk manager's responsibilities go far beyond the realm of insurance, fraud, and security matters and extend to lawsuits and other legal actions resulting from liability claims, mishandling of personnel matters, and health and safety issues. The growing awareness of the need to deal with legal issues was underscored by a number of articles in library literature for 1988. *American Libraries* ran a series on "Legal Issues Affecting Libraries and Librarians"; the September issue of *Library Administration & Management* focused on such legal topics as comparable worth, confidentiality of library records, and changes in laws related to personnel matters.

In El Paso, Texas, local television and newspaper librarians were subpoenaed to testify in a pretrial hearing for accused rape and kidnapping suspect David Leonard Wood. Defense attorneys wanted to prove that pre-trial publicity, supported by news stories brought by the media librarians, prevented their client from getting a fair trial. The U.S. Supreme Court ruled in November 1987 that prison inmates researching their own legal cases may not be denied access to libraries.

In New Jersey, legislation was proposed that would levy heavy fines and jail terms for persons illegally holding historic state documents stolen from the Statehouse basement in the thirties and forties: a six-month amnesty period was proposed before penalties would go into effect. The Ohio Attorney General ruled that a local taxing authority could not refuse to place a bond issue proposed by a local public library board on the ballot.

Late in 1987, Coretta Scott King, widow of Martin Luther King Jr., sued Boston University for the return of King's personal papers so that they can be kept at the King Center for Nonviolent Social Change in Atlanta. King deposited his papers at the university in 1968, but the suit maintained that they belong to his estate rather than to the institution where he earned his doctoral degree.

Health and Safety. Library and information professionals continued to demonstrate a strong commitment to educating the public about the problem of AIDS. As a result, several libraries and library systems developed programs aimed at broad dissemination of information. Among them were Memphis Shelby County Public Library and Information Center; the New York State Library; Clinton-Essex-Franklin Library System (upstate New York); and the Capitol Region Library Council (Connecticut). Programs include information packets, television programs, databases, videos, training for librarians, and printed materials. The library at the University of California, Berkeley, published *AIDS: A Guide to Research Sources*. The annual New York Library Association conference in October in Buffalo held a conference-within-a-conference on dissemination of AIDS information.

Little progress was made on the project (announced in March 1987) to study the air quality of the Madison Building of the Library of Congress. It was not until summer 1988 that the National Institute of Safety and Health, which is conducting the study, sent invitations to participate in a pilot project to test the methods to be used in the main study.

The Akron-Summit County Ohio (ASCPL) Public Library Board approved a new nonsmoking policy for all library buildings and vehicles. ASCPL also encouraged (and reimbursed) employees who participate in stop-smoking, weight loss, stress management, cardiovascular improvement, and lifestyle assessment screening programs.

Personnel Matters. Since library managers and library boards are exposed to the risk of lawsuits due to improper hiring, firing and disciplinary matters, it is imperative that they be thoroughly versed in proper personnel procedures and that they know current personnel law.

In January 1988, Keith Revelle, Director of the Anchorage Municipal Library for more than a decade, was terminated by new Mayor Tom Fink on recommendation of the Library Advisory Board. Revelle sued the Mayor, some Board members, and others to get his job and back pay as well as punitive damages. James Gosier, Director of the Hartford County, Maryland, Library was fired by his library board which cited "personnel problems" in its report.

In Hawaii, John Penebacker, a non-librarian and "well-known and well-respected Board of Education member," was named Deputy State Librarian in early January. The appointment spurred many letters of protest to local newspapers by displeased librarians.

In two separate incidents, school librarians became the center of controversy after making remarks which resulted in temporarily losing their jobs. In Chicago, librarian Kay Thompson was one of three teachers ordered transferred out of Roberto Clemente High School following an interview in which she and two other teachers "detailed the difficulties of teaching in an inner-city high school"; students and community members charged that many of the remarks were racist. Thompson was temporarily re-instated following a lawsuit claiming that her First Amendment rights had been violated.

In Gould, Arkansas, school librarian Lois Bostic resigned her job following a parental protest over an allegedly racist remark she had made to her all-black sixth grade class. Subsequently, the students sent a petition requesting her reinstatement, and the Board agreed.

An employee of the Illinois State Library, Margaret Collins, was awarded $15,000 in punitive damages and $10,000 in compensatory damages following a suit in which she claimed that she had been retaliated against for filing race discrimination complaints in 1982 and 1983. In Cleveland, the 1986 sex discrimination suit filed by Linda R. Silver against the Cuyahoga County Public Library Board of Trustees was settled out of court. Silver, an unsuccessful candidate for the position of director in 1986, had charged sex discrimination.

Issues of pay equity continued to concern library professionals. Deborah J. Leather's article "Comparable Worth: The Limitations of Federal Legislation and Litigation" in the September issue of *Library Administration & Management* provided a good overview of the topic. ALA began compiling a manual to "provide background, direction, and tools for working on pay equity in the library setting."

The Windsor (Connecticut) Public Library discovered that state laws regarding employment of minors as library pages do not take precedence over federal laws. The law of the land requires that the student workers be paid minimum wage and that they work only a certain number of hours each week. Connecticut libraries had paid pages 15 percent below minimum wage.

In July the Library of Congress was ordered to pay $805,000 to several hundred black employees who had been passed over for promotion during 1973 to 1987. The award was later reduced to just over $200,000 after the library admitted its liability and disputed the original amount of the award.

Speaking at the ALA Midwinter Conference in San Antonio, James Harrington of the Texas Civil Liberties Union decried drug testing in the workplace as "Chemical McCarthyism" and "urged ALA to develop a strong, official position to protect its members."

ROBERT A. SEAL

School Library Media Programs

Information Power. The most important event in 1988 was the publication of *Information Power: Guidelines for School Library Media Programs*. Some members of the profession speculate that this will be THE event of the decade for the profession; some suggest that it is the most important event since the publication of *Standards for School Library Programs* in 1960. Whatever verdict history will accord it, the publication of *Information Power* has signaled a renewed commitment and enthusiasm among the profession. There is little room for doubt that the profession has accepted the publication as a manifesto for the positive recognition of school library media specialists and programs in the educational community.[1]

The document was researched and a rough draft developed by an ad hoc committee made up of representatives of the American Association of School Librarians (AASL) and the Association for Educational Communications and Technology (AECT). Chaired by James Liesener, the members of the committee were Ruth Bell, Diane de Cordova Biesel, Rebecca Bingham, Carolyn Cain, Judith Davie, Bernard Franckowiak, Bob Hale, Winona Jones, Addie Kinsinger, Jane Love, and Jeanette Smith. The text was based on a thorough review of the available research and literature, and the best professional judgment of the Committee, and was written with significant input and feedback from many others in the profession.

Information Power describes an ideal library media program in qualitative terms. That program must have a strong commitment to technology and innovation, but must also be based on the strong foundations that traditional media and services offer the school. It requires that the school library media specialist work in a partnership with teachers and administrators to fully integrate the school library media program into the curriculum of the school. One of the most important statements in the document is that every school should have at least one full-time library media professional and that the minimal education required for that person to enter the profession is the master's degree. *Information Power* places an emphasis on the building-level school library media program, but speaks also to the importance of district and state library media programs.

AASL and AECT have joined forces do everything possible to see that *Information Power* is implemented in the nation's schools. Each has appointed a guidelines implementation task force that has worked and continues to work cooperatively on a number of projects. The first project was *Information Power: A National Teleconference*, produced by the associations in cooperation with the Instructional Services Center

School Library Media Programs

of the University of South Carolina. More than 10,000 persons viewed the two-hour teleconference and phoned in more than 170 questions from down link sites in every state in the United States and many provinces in Canada. The teleconference was made possible through the corporate sponsorship of the Bound to Stay Bound Book Company, the Follett Book and Software Companies, the Highsmith Company, and the Social Issues Resources Series (SIRS).

Other activities in the implementation effort to date include a pre-conference at ALA in New Orleans; the AASL President's Program in New Orleans that focused on the document and introduced The *Information Power Video* regional workshops to train state implementation teams in Park City, Utah, Chicago, Illinois, Washington, D.C., and Dallas, Texas; a newsletter called "I to the P power" that provides news and is a forum for sharing ideas; and articles and presentations for related teacher, administrator, and parent associations. A second national teleconference will be developed in cooperation with the National Association of Elementary School Principals (NAESP) and the National Association of Secondary School Principals (NASSP) that will be produced in February, 1989.

AASL and AECT have developed a *Discussion Guide to Information Power* and *A Planning Guide for Information Power*. Encyclopaedia Britannica Corporation, in cooperation with AASL and AECT, contracted Frank Frost Productions to develop *The Information Power Video*. This 20-minute piece features John Goodlad and a number of exemplary school library media programs that introduce the basic concepts described in the *Information Power*. ALA Video also produced a 30-minute edited version of the *Information Power* teleconference.[2]

ALA and NCATE. At ALA Midwinter Meeting in San Antonio, Texas, Council agreed for ALA to become a member of the National Council for the Accreditation of Teacher Education (NCATE). AASL was instructed to develop a list of competencies to be used by institutions seeking accreditation for school library media specialist preparation programs and provide names for visitation teams and review boards. The Committee, chaired by Marilyn Miller, presented the committee's report to Council at the Annual Meeting in New Orleans and it was approved. Approval, however, did not come without a great deal of discussion. The Standing Committee on Library Education (SCOLE) presented the following statement to Council: "The Master's Degree from a program accredited by the American Library Association, or its foreign equivalent, is the appropriate professional degree for librarians." The AASL committee presented the following statement: "The Master's Degree in Librarianship from a program accredited by the American Library Association or a Master's Degree with a specialty in school library media from an educational unit accredited by NCATE is the appropriate first professional degree for school library media specialists." Both statements were approved by Council, but were referred to the ALA, Policy Monitoring Committee for recommendation on terminology and to determine the extent to which they were consistent with existing policy related to library and information science education.

AASL accepted *NCATE Guidelines for the Preparation of School Library Media Specialists* in New Orleans and NCATE accepted them in August. Previously, the only guidelines available for institutions preparing for NCATE accreditation were those prepared by AECT. AECT guidelines are more strongly focused on the production and use of media rather than a more holistic or generalist view of the school library media specialist as the first professional position in the school. For the time being, an institution can elect to follow either or both sets of guidelines as they seek NCATE accreditation.

Distance Education. One of the most exciting events in the education community during 1988 was the funding of Star Schools, a federal program that is providing $20,000,000 to stimulate educators to make broader use of available and developing telecommunications systems. The initial funding involves four cooperative projects that have just gotten under way this spring. The Midlands Consortium, the Satellite Educational Resources Consortium (SERC), the TI-IN Network, and the Technical Education Research Center Project (TERC). The first three primarily involve the development and delivery of specific programs for students in rural areas by way of satellite and television. TERC is a computer-based project that involves the student as a participant in a network of other students and scientists in an experimental learning environment.[3] As this awareness and the implementation of distance learning spreads, school library media specialists will, no doubt, have some very important roles to play.

Shortage of Professionals. A number of writers continued this year to describe the growing shortage of professionals to fill youth services jobs in libraries.[4] This number includes real and projected shortages for school library media specialists. To combat this problem, the profession has been urged to develop a strong recruiting effort. One of the suggested recruitment strategies is the use of distance education via telecommunications.[5]

AASL CE Coordinator. On a more positive note, AASL has made a major commitment to continuing education with the appointment of Ann-Terese Costello. Costello serves as the Coordinator for Professional Development and Continuing Education and will be working with library schools, state affiliates, other professional associations, and other units in ALA to encourage the development of quality continuing education programming.

Intellectual Freedom. During 1988 there were the usual efforts to censor *The Chocolate War* and *Forever*, among other materials in school library media programs, reported by the ALA, Office for Intellectual Freedom. Some were met with successful resistance from school library media specialists. The most disturbing event in this area, and one that has the potential of impacting school library media programs is the *Hazelwood School District v. Kuhlmeier*. Although the decision was related to the principal having the "right" to censor school newspapers, it also included in the list "other school-sponsored expressive activities" that are "part of the school curriculum." With the increased emphasis that the profession is placing on the school library media program as an integral part of the curriculum, this decision could be interpreted in many ways, some of which could become very oppressive to the collections developed by the school library media specialist.

Federal Funding. Some light at the end of the tunnel may be flickering as PL 100-297 offers some new opportunities for funding of school library media programs and new opportunities for school library media specialists to participate in the allocations process. PL 100-297 supersedes the Education Consolidation Improvement Act of 1981 and offers as one of its purposes "to provide a continuing source of innovation, educational improvement, and support for library and instructional materials." It also "targets" for assistance, programs for acquiring library and library related materials and the training, of "librarians." It also requires that representatives from elementary and secondary school librarians be appointed to state advisory committees by governors in states that wish to participate in the funding program.

Issues and Concerns. In addition to the events and activities previously discussed, the literature provides a number of issues of concern to the profession. These center primarily on flexible scheduling, the role of the school library media specialist, the potential for the school library media program and specialist in a literature-based curriculum, the definition and implementation of information management curricula to replace "library skills," the few pieces of research that have been completed during the year, the reality of old collections that date back to NDEA and ESEA funding days, and lack of funding for collections and programs. One person described the latter two situations well at the Public Library Association conference as the "impoverishment of school libraries."[6]

REFERENCES AND NOTES

1. The complete list of school library media program standards to date are
   Certain, C.C. (1917)."A standard high school library organization for accredited secondary schools of different sizes," *Journal of Educational Administration and Supervision* 3p. 317-338.
   Certain, C.C. (1925). *Elementary School Library Standards*, 19 Chicago, American Library Association.
   American Library Association Committee on Post-War Planning. (1945). *School Libraries for Today and Tomorrow*, American Library Association, Chicago, Illinois.
   American Association of School Librarians. (1960). *Standards for School Library Programs*, Chicago, ALA.
   American Association of School Librarians and Department of Audio-visual Instruction, National Education Association. (1969). *Standards for School Media Programs*. Chicago, ALA.
   American Association of School Librarians and Association for Educational Communications and Technology. (1975). *Media Programs: District and School*. Chicago, ALA.
   American Association of School Librarians and Association for Educational Communications and Technology. (1988). *Information Power: Guidelines for School Library Media Programs*. Chicago, ALA.
2. For additional ordering information, contact Ann Weeks at AASL.
3. The funded Star Schools Projects include: Midlands Consortium, 470 Student Union Building, Oklahoma State University, Stillwater, OK 74078;
   Satellite Educational Resources Consortium, Southern Educational Communications Association (SECA), Post Office Box 50,008, Columbia, SC 29250;
   Technical Education Research Centers, 1696 Massachusetts Ave., Cambridge, MA 02138
   TI-IN, 1000 Central Parkway North, Suite 190, San Antonio, TX 78232.
4. *Future Scan*, 572, March 21, 1988;
   William Moen and Kathleen Heim, "The Class of 1988: Librarians for the new millennium," *American Libraries* (November 1988);
   Stanley Zenor, "For Starters," *Tech Trends* (September 1988).
5. Phil Turner, "Recruiting School Library Media Specialists," in *Librarians for the New Millennium*, William Moen and Kathleen Heim, eds., Chicago, ALA.
6. *American Libraries*, June 1988, p. 431.

DANIEL D. BARRON

Seminar on the Acquisition of Latin American Library Materials

Annual Conference. Annual conferences are devoted to a specific aspect of the acquisition of Latin American library materials, of Latin American bibliography, or of related matters, and consideration of the progress made, and further action necessary, by SALALM and its committees and cooperating organizations in solving problems related to its concerns. Approximately 200 registrants from the United States, Latin America, Europe, and the Caribbean participated in SALALM XXXIII, held at the University of California-Berkeley and Stanford University, June 6-10, 1988. The theme of the conference was "Frontiers, Borders and Hinterlands: Research Needs and Resources."

The José Toribio Medina award for outstand-

SALALM

PRESIDENT (June 1988-June 1989):
Barbara Robinson, University of Southern California

VICE-PRESIDENT/PRESIDENT-ELECT:
Ann Hartness, Library of Congress, Rio De Janeiro, Brazil

TREASURER:
Jane Garner, University of Texas at Austin

EXECUTIVE SECRETARY:
Suzanne Hodgman, University of Wisconsin-Madison

Membership: 473 (30 percent outside U.S.)

ing contribution by a SALALM member to scholarship in Latin American studies was presented to George Elmendorf for "Nicaraguan National Bibliography, 1800–1978/Bibliografía Nacional Nicaragüense, 1800–1978."

Membership. The SALALM membership year runs from September 1 to August 31. Membership in 1987–1988 reached 473—320 personal members and 153 institutional members. More than 30 percent of the membership is from outside the United States.

Most of SALALMs accomplishments are effected through its 28 committees and subcommittees, in which more than 40 percent of the personal membership participates.

Publications. Publications issued in 1988 include *An Acquisitions Manual/Manual de Adquisiciones/Manual de Aquisições*, by William Ilgen and Deborah Jakubs (Bibliography and Reference Series, 21); *Directory of Vendors of Latin American Library Materials*, by Howard Karno and David Block. 3d Ed. (Bibliography and Reference Series, 22); *Bibliography of Latin American and Caribbean Bibliographies, 1987–88*, by Lionel Loroña (Bibliography and Reference Series, 23). *Intellectual Migrations: The Transcultural Contributions of European and Latin American Emigrés* (Papers of the Thirty-First Seminar on the Acquisition of Latin American Library Materials), edited by Iliana Sonntag. Other publications are the quarterly *SALALM Newsletter* and the annual *Microfilming Projects Newsletter*.

Founded in 1956, and incorporated in 1968, the Seminar on the Acquisition of Latin American Library Materials is an international organization of libraries, librarians, book dealers, and scholars interested in the control and dissemination of bibliographical information about all types of Latin American publications and also in the development of library collections in support of Latin American studies. Its primary activities are the annual conference and the publications program. The SALALM Secretariat is located at the Memorial Library, University of Wisconsin-Madison.

SUZANNE HODGMAN

Serials

Data gathered by the Association of Research Libraries (ARL) indicates that median 1986/87 expenditures for serials by its "106 university library members were 18.2 percent higher than in 1985/86 while the number of titles received grew by only 2 percent." Data published by L. Knapp and R. Lenzini in April 1988 indicated that the increase in 1988 prices of U. S. titles was but slightly higher than that of 1987: 9.1 percent vs. 9.9 percent respectively (*Library Journal*, April 15, 1988). During 1988 the journal pricing issue, as in previous years, continued for good reason to dominate discussion within the academic serials community.

Several professional associations have been active in investigating and publicizing the problem of rising prices. ALA/RTSD established a blue-ribbon commission, headed by Robert Wedgworth, to investigate the issue. RTSD's Publisher/Vendor/Library Relations Committee established a special pricing subcommittee to coordinate statistic gathering, identify trends, and disseminate findings. The Research Libraries Group's (RLG) Collection Management and Development Committee launched a short-term initiative to identify expensive titles that at least one RLG member would commit *not* to cancel. They also began a longer-term project aimed at identifying serials in chemistry, mathematics, and business that form the core of a research-level collection. During 1988 ARL launched a two-part "Serials Project" comprised of two parts. In part one, the Association produced and mailed to its members a document titled *ARL Briefing Package 1988-2: Rising Serial Prices and Research Libraries*. The packet was a compilation of selected articles that described and analyzed the problem, along with a brief question-and-answer overview. A second, longer-term objective is the development "of an analytical project intended to produce a report using statistical analysis of increases in serial prices aimed at determining causes among factors such as currency fluctuation, production and distribution costs, and profit motivations." Economic Consulting Services, Inc. (ESC) will conduct the economic analysis. Anne Okerson, author of a fine overview of the issue "Periodical Prices: A History and Discussion," *Advances in Serials Management* 1:101-134, will work with ARL staff on the final report. ECS will develop cost indices for production and distribution of U.S. and West European journals. Staff is gathering 1973–1988 price-per-page data for a sample of 165 journals. "A strategic emphasis of the study will be to determine the potential for introducing elements of competition into the technical and scientific journal market in an attempt to moderate the rate of price increases."

David Farrell, Associate Dean of Libraries for Collection Management, (Indiana University) produced a very useful publication for ARL on the price problem. "Serials Control and Deselection Projects," *SpecKit* 147, September 1988 draws together documents from a dozen university libraries that detail local efforts to deal with the immediate budget problems caused by spiraling prices.

Much of the debate over the issue continues to be conducted at regional meetings as well as in meetings of state and regional associations. The North American Serials Interest Group (NASIG), in particular, is the premier forum for discussion among librarians, publishers and vendors. At NASIG's third annual meeting (held in Atlanta, June 1988) publishers' representative—who at earlier meetings had felt under-represented on programs—offered spirited and documented defenses of their side of the issue. During 1988 Elsevier in particular made special efforts to send senior-level staff to association meetings to address the concerns of the library community.

One of the key 1988 regional meetings took place in October at Chapel Hill, North Carolina. Sponsored jointly by the Society for Scholarly Publishing and the University of North Carolina Library, a small group of librarians, publishers, vendors and scholars discussed the future of scholarly journals. Several key issues were identified: the need to differentiate more precisely among the various subdisciplines within the sciences and to sort out the informational needs and use patterns of each community; the need to focus on the impact of price rises not only on the sciences, but on the humanities and social sciences as well; the large number of resources expended on campuses outside of the library system and the bearing of those expenditures on the role of the library in the day-to-day research process. The conference was noteworthy because organizers made a special effort to include working scholars in its deliberations.

In order to speed the distribution of research and information on the pricing issue, a group of librarians—Chuck Hamaker (Louisiana State University), Gayle Garlock (University of Toronto), Michael Keller (Yale University) and Mark Sandler (University of Michigan)— began to collect data and distribute it through the various electronic mail networks. For many librarians, publishers and vendors electronic distribution is underlining the limitation of even the fastest modes of paper distribution. Newsletters are a rich source for citations to articles and letters from a wide range of publications. For example, a table that may have eluded many librarians appeared in *Bulletin of the American Society for Information Science* (October–November 1988, p.11–15) illustrates the "internationalization of the U.S. information scene." The table lists parent firms and the various information producers in their "stables": publishers, database services, online hosts, support services, media and entertainment outlets and representative publications.

Both vendors and publishers have been responding to the growing demand within the library community for help in anticipating price increases and in managing their serials budgets. Major U.S. and foreign vendors, as a part of their regular services, are providing customers with predictions of serial prices and with analyses of their particular serial lists. They also began to offer various special deals to trim or eliminate service charges. Gordon & Breach introduced a plan designed to trim 1989 prices and to forestall cancellations by North American customers.

In addition to its relatively new CD-ROM product, *Ulrich's Plus*, Bowker has begun to distribute *Ulrich's News*, a useful newsletter. The April issue (v.1, no.3) includes a number of pie charts that illustrate the explosion in science journal publishing, in the aggregate and by broad discipline. In 1978, *Ulrich's News* listed 8,062 science titles in their database; today, that database lists 29,621 entries. New journal launches have been greatest in the medical and biological sciences.

The Institute for Scientific Information introduced several products designed to enhance the use of the journal literature: a CD-ROM version of *Science Citation Index*; and *Current Contents on Diskette*. The latter, a weekly version of the *Current Contents/Life Sciences* edition, covers 300 journals. The initial release is designed to run on Apple Macintosh machines; an IBM version will follow.

The Colorado Alliance of Research Libraries during 1988 released *Uncover*, "a database of article information taken from the contests page of over 10,000 multi-disciplinary journals." The database includes abstracts and can be searched by key word. Vendors and individual campuses are exploiting the possibilities of the electronic networks that are now in place and are exploring development of a table-of-contests type of services. In 1989 we are likely to see more such efforts to provide users with enhanced access to our increasingly expensive journal literature.

The CONSER (Cooperative Online Serials) Program continues to serve as a model for cooperative bibliographic projects. While awaiting effective linked system development, project members designed and began to test procedures that would allow RLG non-OCLC members to actively contribute records to the CONSER database, which resides within OCLC. Cornell University and the University of Michigan were the first RLG members to begin active contribution during 1988. Also during 1988, the Library Services Department of Chemical Abstracts Service became the first affiliate member to join the Program.

ROBERT L. HOUBECK, JR.

Social Responsibilities

The social responsibility of libraries and librarians became a focal issue within the profession some two decades ago, and has remained a top priority for the American Library Association. In response to social issues, libraries have covered a wide spectrum in service patterns and programming. Social issues have remained intentionally paramount, although the focus periodically shifts in emphasis.

Libraries are responding to such educational and informational societal issues as Acquired Immune Deficiency Syndrome (AIDS), alcoholism, apartheid, the blind and physically handicapped, child abuse, children and young adult problems and adjustments, day care centers, drugs, English as a second language, employment and career information, environmental issues, ethnicity, Gay Rights, housing conditions and the homeless, illiteracy and aliterates, the incarcerated, latchkey children, lifelong learning and continuing education, mental and physical health issues of the younger and older citizenry, missing children, Native Americans, nuclear energy, nursing and senior citizens homes, outreach and referral services, peace, services to shut-ins, stress and hypertension, voter rights and voter registration, women's issues, working mothers, and world relief.

All of these programs continue throughout libraries in the United States, but during 1988, major thrusts revolved around the proliferation of information and the role of the library in the information age. With the profusion of information and libraries' ability to cope and meet the needs of all constituencies, concerns have centered on access to information and assisting patrons in using information, literacy and adapting to technological applications, latchkey children, child abuse, civil rights, teen-age suicide, and serving the elderly in the dissemination and interpretation of information relative to these crucial areas.

Access. A standing Committee on Freedom and Access to Information was formed within ALA to collect information on the many facets of

Social Responsibilities

access and to provide oversight for divisions, round tables, and committees of council.

The urgency for libraries to provide materials in native languages portends to increase in magnitude with the current trend in the United States to declare English the official language. If this trend expands, the responsibility to provide materials in native languages will transfer to the library community where requests are increasing rapidly. Voters in Arizona, Colorado, and Florida declared English their state official language in the 1988 elections.

The Denver Public Library has formed "Library Focus Groups" with representatives from the Black, Southeast Asian, and Hispanic communities to increase dialogue and get a better understanding of how the library can better meet their specific needs. Service to children, books in native languages, and materials and programming indigenous to blacks have been requested.

The Eastern Shore Regional Library in Maryland has instituted a program "Project ACCESS," to increase access to the deaf and hearing impaired in eight rural county library systems. Initial difficulties were encountered in securing videotapes with closed captions. The library profession is asked to emphasize the need for close-captioned video materials when dealing with vendors.

Children and Young Adults. Senator Christopher J. Dodd and Representative Claude Pepper introduced legislation to create a Young Americans Act (S.476/H.R.1003), modeled after the Older American Act, seeking to fill the gaps created by the wide and diverse distribution of children and youth services now scattered throughout more than 100 federal cabinet-level departments, to increase the visibility of children's issues and to supply children, youth, and their families with better coordinated prevention and intervention services. The American Library Association, in July 1988 adopted a resolution (CD #72) in support of the Young Americans Act recognizing "that youth are the nation's most valuable resource for the strong, dynamic future of our democracy, ". . . that "school and public libraries across the United States provide valuable and essential informational, recreational, and enrichment services for youth," . . . and that "it is critical [for] the library community [to] participate in [the] planning and development of [a] national youth policy."

The "Latchkey Child" is not a new problem for libraries, but it is one that has accelerated throughout libraries in the country within the past ten years. A noticeable increase began during the period of the Atlanta children's murders in the early eighties. With more mothers entering the work place, libraries have been viewed as safe havens for children after school. Although many libraries are making program adjustments through story hours, reading and film programs, and organized tutorial services, the unattended child has become a library issue of serious concern and one to be dealt with. Children remain on the premises after closing hours with no other place to go, and some create discipline problems and must be evicted from the premises during open service hours. Often there is no way to reach the parents. At library conferences and workshops, it is being clearly articulated that libraries should establish policies relative to library staff and library liability. The Public Library Association and the Association for Library Services to Children have published *Latchkey Children in the Public Library*. This 60-page guidebook outlines a process for developing policy and programs, with suggestions to librarians on how to circumvent exacerbating the problem. The publication can be purchased from ALA's Order Department.

Civil Rights and Ethnicity. Varied and unique programs were produced during Black History Month. The Enoch Pratt Library exhibited a collection of photographs entitled "But Now When I Look Back," highlighting the postwar transformation of rural black culture in southern Maryland. The New Orleans Public Library programmed the narration of black folktales, held a symposium on "An Agenda for Black Progress: Education, Leadership, and Self Help Programs," and scheduled the performance of a black history play, while the Oklahoma City Metropolitan Library sponsored a soul food luncheon.

Members of the ALA Black Caucus raised questions about affirmative action hiring policies at ALA headquarters and questioned whether aggressive action was being taken to recruit minority staff for middle management and higher positions.

The University of Michigan Library addressed the re-emergence of racism in academia by sponsoring a week-long seminar, "Overcoming Racism: Exploring the Value of Diversity," in response to charges of institutional racism levied against the University. *American Libraries* reported that among the most popular programs at the ALA's 1988 Annual Conference were those focusing on services to special groups. Reviewing the program listings for minorities was de ja vu. Programs focused on "Equity in Information Services: The Nation's Minorities and the Leadership Challenge"; "Educational Excellence of Asian Americans: Myth or Reality"; "Developing Minority Leadership for the 1990's and Beyond"; "Sexual Orientation: Library Employment Practices"; and "Librarians as Colleagues across Racial Lines." Contributed articles appearing in library media indicate that all is not equitable within the profession in 1988.

The Elderly. It is predicted that the decline in population will mean an older work force by the year 2000, and that one person in seven will be age 65. Libraries face an increasing challenge to provide access and information services to meet the special needs of this distinct group. The Arkansas State Library and the Arkansas Department of Human Services have collaborated on a Wellness Program for Older Persons to display and circulate materials on health care for the aging in all public libraries in the state. The Brooklyn Public Library and the Brooklyn Area Agency on Aging collaborate in the Services to the Aging (SAGE) program for bookmobile delivery of materials. A comprehensive driver retraining course, geared to the needs of older Americans, has been developed by the American Association of Retired Persons (AARP). The Putnam Valley Free Library in New York sponsored the course for persons 50 years or older under the title "55 Alive/Mature Driving." Those who complete the course receive cost reductions on insurance and a reduction in moving violation points.

The Homeless. The Memphis/Shelby County Public Library and Information Center is working with the Metropolitan Interfaith Association in placing book packs in temporary housing facilities for the homeless. The book packs include magazines, books for children and adults, and information about the library. The Milwaukee Public Library is conducting a project which operates out of "The Drop-in Center", a day shelter for the homeless; it maintains a browsing collection of library materials, a library sponsored peer tutoring program, and a jobs services component. GED information, local newspapers, and high interest reading materials are provided at the "Guest House," a local shelter, and at the Central Library where many of the homeless spend their days. The Montgomery County Department of Public Libraries in Maryland developed cards listing services provided to the homeless in four regions of Montgomery County. The cards are available in all library branches and they provide information on where to receive emergency food and shelter. The Multnomah County Public Library in Oregon, established a reading room in an inner city center for the homeless. The New York Public Library operates projects for the homeless in some welfare hotels, motels, and daytime shelters providing book collections, story hours for children, programs, workshops, and volunteer training. San Diego's central library provides information on social service agencies that assist the homeless. Tulsa City–County Library assisted in setting up a day shelter for the homeless, and maintains a depository collection of books and magazines. The downtown library provides assistance to job seekers.

Institutional Library Service. The Washington State Library provides library services directly to adult corrections, juvenile rehabilitation, mental health, developmental disabilities, and veterans residential institutional throughout Washington state. This Institutional Library Service (ILS) is provided by staff from branches, stations, and deposit collections in 61 locations in 37 state residential institutions. Collections provide materials in varied formats and media, and special programming is designed to meet indigenous institutional needs.

Literacy. Illiteracy is not a recently recognized problem in the United States as federal programs in literacy date back to the period of the Works Progress Administration (WPA). The Atlanta-Fulton Public Library was one of the first libraries in the nation to receive federal funding for literacy and continuing education under the WPA. These programs were designed for citizens who had been deprived of a formal education, those who had no reading skills, and those who were in need of basic skills to enter the labor market at levels above basic subservience. Literacy, however, has now become a national campaign. Libraries are addressing the broad range of literacy problems that face the nation, working independently; with other established literacy, community, business, and church groups; or providing teaching and meeting facilities. In response to joint efforts in building a literacy agenda, Mrs. Jeannie Bailies, the first lady of Virginia (1986–1990), established an Office of State Adult Literacy that seeks to coordinate the state government's fragmented literacy programs and a Virginia Literacy Foundation that recognizes the need to ensure a viable work force for the future. An estimated 22 percent of the population in Virginia, does not read or write well enough to function adequately. The Virginia State Library and Archives in association with The Virginia Literacy Foundation and the Office of State Adult Literacy presented a two day Statewide Literacy Conference on "Building a More Literate Virginia." The broad-based training conference had more than 300 in attendance. The participants were librarians, literacy volunteers, business representatives, and educators. The conference covered the following areas: Virginia's public and private groups working together; motivating students and volunteers; urban-centered, community-based literacy programs; teaching basic reading skills; tutoring learning disabled students/adults; student recruitment; rural/urban viewpoints; family literacy; utilizing computers in literacy programs; college-based literacy programs; literacy in the work place; and collection building. Ernest L. Boyer, President of the Carnegie Foundation for the Advancement of Teaching, gave the keynote address; and Dan M. Lacy, Vice President of the Business Council for Effective Literacy, gave a major address on public and private groups working together for a more literate society. Other coalition building literacy projects involving libraries, literacy groups, businesses, service organizations, educational agencies and/or churches are being conducted in Jonesboro, Arkansas, to assist a ten-county network of library systems in developing volunteer literacy councils; in the Morris-Reeves Library Richmond, Indiana, to operate jointly a program for recruitment and training, and to establish a public awareness program; and in the Eugene (Oregon) Public Library, to establish sub-coalitions in rural areas of the county using public libraries as the organizational centers. More than 23 Massachusetts libraries are providing basic reading/writing and ESL instructions. In new York, the Mid-Hudson Library System conducted a literacy project, "Reading Together," for families at risk. Six libraries conducted programs, with the balance of a grant used for programs and resources that could be merged with regular library services. A media campaign encouraged families at risk to register at the library. Mid-Hudson bought 274 radio commercials with 54 spots donated by the stations. Quarter-page advertisements were placed in publications reaching 242,912 households. Each library received 24 carefully selected books for use by parents with poor reading skills. Workshops were held on the Illiterate Parent and Outreach to Families at Risk with a group called the Musical Munchkins presenting musical activities for use in programming for children and their parents. Twenty-six libraries reported that 1,253 children up to age 8, and 1,292 other family members registered for new library cards between June and September, 1988.

ELLA GAINES YATES

Social Responsibilities Round Table

The Social Responsibilities Round Table (SRRT) invited the candidates for ALA president and treasurer to a meeting of Actin Council during the Midwinter Meeting in Chicago. The candidates discussed their views and answered questions relating to social responsibilities and libraries. Neither of the presidential nominees, Patricia Berger and Rebecca Bingham, won an endorsement from SRRT Action Council, but Carla Stoffle was endorsed for treasurer.

Task Forces. The Feminist Task Force sponsored a program at the Annual Conference in New Orleans called "Librarians as Colleagues across Racial Lines: Strategies for Action." The program grew out of a preconference held in 1987. Keynote speakers were Aileen Hernandez, former president of NOW, and Elizabeth Martinez-Smith, director the Orange County (California Library System. Others on the program included Clara Stanton Jones, E.J. Josey, Susan Hinojosa, and Betty-Carol Sellen.

The Coretta Scott King Awards Task Force honored Mildred Taylor, author of *The Friendship*, and John Steptoe, illustrator of *Mufaro's Beautiful Daughters: An African Tale* for outstanding contributions to children's literature.

SRRT co-sponsored with the Intellectual Freedom Round Table a debate called "Two Views of Intellectual Freedom" in New Orleans. John Swan of the Intellectual Freedom Round Table debated SRRT's Noel Peattie; each vigorously and articulately defended his point of view. The debate was followed by questions from the audience, after which it appeared that a majority of those present favored Swan's more absolutist First Amendment approach.

A number of other programs were presented by SRRT task forces at the Annual Conference. A program titled "Southern Voices: Alternative Literary and Political Publishing in the South" was sponsored by the Alternatives in Print Task Force. Speakers included Andrei Codrescu, John Guidry, Tom Dent, and Robert Sullivan. The Feminist Task Force presented a program called "Introducing Women's Groups in ALA," and they co-sponsored the program "The Creation of Hierarchy: Its Implications for Librarianship." The Gay and Lesbian Task Force sponsored a panel discussion called "Sexual Orientation: Library Employment Practices."

The Peace Information Exchange Task Force received approval for an annual Peace Award to honor a library or librarian for contributions to the advancement of knowledge related to issues of international peace and security. The award is supported financially by SIRS.

Action Council members for 1988-89 included John Hostage, Carol Davies-Nador, Diedre Conkling, Christine Jenkins, Jody Bush, Chris Sokol (*Newsletter* editor), Denise Botto, James Danky, Cal Gough, Bethany Lawton, Jackie Eubanks, and Gail Warner. Task force coordinators were Daniel Tsang (Alternatives in Print), Donnarae MacCann (Civil Rights), David Searcy (Coretta Scott King Award), Polly Thistlethwaite (Feminist), Helen K. Hill and Vince Menotti (Gay and Lesbian), Jim Byrnes (Homeless), Corinne Nyquist (International Human Rights), Jeanene McNair (Library Union), and Stephen Stillwell (Peace Information Exchange).

JOHN HOSTAGE

Sound Recordings

In 1988, all three sound recording configurations—CD, cassette, and LP—experienced a paroxysm of production. Most major companies dug deep into their vaults to resurrect and digitalize landmark recordings dating as far back as 1932. And there were outpourings of freshly minted recordings for children. CBS and Polygram denied reported plans to desert vinyl in favor of CDs but insiders continued to predict the early demise of LPs. It was anticipated that the U.S. market would follow in the wake of Japan, where CDs have dominated for several years: CDs were introduced in Japan earlier than in the U.S. and were offered from the outset to Japanese consumers at prices comparable to those set for LPs. This policy, combined with the availability of Japanese CD recorders, could soon spread to the U.S. and could further hasten the slide of LPs into oblivion. In this country, most new classical releases were on CDs, stimulating upscale consumers to acquire CD hardware and upgrade their hi-fi components to take advantage of the superb tonal power of the new medium.

Laws, Illegal Listening, and Lewd Lyrics. RIAA, which had threatened to launch a lawsuit against the first manufacturer to bring DAT records to the U.S., joined forces with the International Federation of Phonogram & Videogram Producers (IFPI) in a war on the recordable compact disk, an even greater threat to copyright owners than the DAT. Mass production of the dreaded record-once disks (CD-R) could commence as early as 1989. Motivated by concern that hogwild copying would discourage creative output, leading European and Japanese consumer electronic companies and IFPI representatives met in London on November 30. This was the first meeting between hardware and software interests since their abortive, acrimonious get-together in Vancouver in December 1986. The long-standing dissension between the two segments of the home entertainment industry showed signs of abating with both sides acknowledging a shared need to achieve a technological solution to a home copying problem precipitated by digital recordings, DATs, and reusable CDs. The delegates resolved to consider

---

SOCIAL RESPONSIBILITIES ROUND TABLE

ACTION COUNCIL COORDINATOR:
John Hostage, Harvard Law School Library, Cambridge, Massachusetts

SECRETARY:
Carol Davies-Nador, United Nations Library, New York, New York

TREASURER:
Diedre Conkling, Weber County Library, Ray, Utah

Membership (August 31, 1988): 990 (895 personal; 95 organizational)

formation of a small joint working group to look into various technical solutions of the problem and to address the need to protect artists' intellectual property rights. Legislative and other government authorities would be consulted by the working group.

Directly related to the "piracy in the home" problem was the determination of the National Bureau of Standards that the proposed CBS Copy-Code was an abysmal failure. Engineers confirmed that the system to inhibit DAT players' copying of CDs: (1) degraded musical quality, (2) could be easily bypassed, (3) failed to forestall illicit taping, and (4) often issued false alarms, i.e., prevented recording even when no encoding was present. A simple circuit, buildable by an amateur and costing about $100, could circumvent the Copy-Code. The NBS ruling, in effect, removed a major obstacle to DAT's eventual entrance onto the American market.

In November, affiliation of the U.S. with the Berne Copyright Convention was signed into law by President Reagan. Membership will benefit the U.S. in its efforts to combat record and video piracy worldwide and will improve standards of protection for U.S. works in participating nations. Because notices must be mailed to the 75 Berne signatories three months in advance of formal ratification, it will be mid-1989 before the U.S. becomes a full member. Current U.S. copyright law will be changed in two ways: the copyright notice requirement will be eliminated so works lacking the notice will not move into the public domain and civil penalties will become more severe. For ordinary infringement, the minimum fine will be increased from $250 to $500, the maximum fine from $10,000 to $20,000 per count, and for willful infringement, the maximum will jump from $50,000 to $100,000. In line with the trend towards stringent enforcement was California's enactment of landmark legislation. Piracy, counterfeiting, and bootlegging penalties were stiffened, and California became the first state to enact a statute providing for penalties comparable to those imposed by federal law. This legislation is strategically important because more than 40 percent of the illicit sound recordings distributed in the U.S. originate in California.

At the federal level, the 100th Congress authorized extension of the Record Rental Bill. This prolongs through 1997 a law granting owners of a sound recording and its songs exclusive rights to authorize record rentals. Originally enacted in 1984, this law had been due to expire in 1989.

Of growing concern to advocates of privacy rights is the rapid improvement of electronic devices for both receiving and recording conversations. Use of such equipment in schools to eavesdrop on drug deals and to impose discipline has worried lawyers because of the possible infraction of students' personal right to privacy. Such "sneak" recording is limited in 14 states (California, Delaware, Florida, Georgia, Kansas, Louisiana, Maryland, Massachusetts, Michigan, Montana, New Hampshire, Oregon, Pennsylvania, and Washington) to instances when interception of oral conversations is consented to by all parties. Accordingly, taping should be limited to the private refreshing of recollection (oral history compilation), and recordings should not be released to third parties without a very careful consideration of the content and the legal consequences of unauthorized dissemination.

In a year of generally good legislation, the Child Protection and Obscenity Enforcement Act was passed by Congress as part of a mammoth omnibus drug bill—a bad and probably unconstitutional bill. The obscenity section in itself is more than 50,000 words long, and its provisions could enable anyone to go after a person or business merely suspected of purveying pornography. The definition of porn is ambiguous, i.e., whatever is perceived by the local community as obscene. Books, magazines, video, and sound recordings are now vulnerable to attack. The bill's anti-obscenity provisions are buried in a piece of very popular, untouchable anti-drug legislation, so this section's constitutionality must be tested in the courts. As it stands, the law states that "it is illegal to knowingly receive or possess obscene material with an intent to distribute." Conviction carries a prison charge and fine. The law sets a chilling precedent for federal intervention and adds further confusion to the existing maze of state and local anti-obscenity laws and ordinances.

Inspired by this legislation, Parents Music Resource Center (PMRC) founders Susan Baker and Tipper Gore leveled charges against the recording industry in a November 28 "Op Ed" article in the *Washington Post*. The two PMRC leaders cited the lyric from the song "Anything Goes" contained in the best-selling album "Appetite for Destruction" produced by Guns N' Roses. The offending lyric, "Panties round your knees, with your ass in debris, doin' dat bump and grind with a push and squeeze" was accompanied by a graphic depicting a raped, semi-nude woman. The producers responded by pointing out that the graphic, a painting by Robert Williams, had been exhibited widely and reproduced in *Art Forum* and other reputable journals, and that the woman represented a sobering world view of the condition of all humankind.

Sonic Solutions Restores and Purifies Golden Oldies. Before 1988, there had been justifiable reluctance to convert old analog master tapes onto CDs because the result could only underplay the potential of the new medium. The noise, cracks, pops, and glitches in the original only became more prominent on the CD. Therefore, 30 years of LP production appeared destined for premature and permanent retirement—too bad, because in earlier times, many great performers had postponed placing their legacy on LP until they felt emotionally, technically, and philosophically "ready," to take the step. Now, thanks to the NoNoise process developed by Sonic Solutions, a San Francisco-based firm, it had become feasible to reach into the vaults and transfer the heritage of the LP period onto CDs. The newly devised restoration process elicits sonic revelations from older recordings and improves the original. Artificial intelligence is employed to identify clicks and pops. The process involves reconstruction and not removal and elimination of anomalies without adversely affecting the original music. More than 2,000 points of sound are measured to yield an accurate assessment of the

Sound Recordings

whereabouts and distribution of unwanted noise. A special computer program involving more than 53,000,000 calculations for each second of playing time is used, and the denoised version is then rerecorded on new digital tape which in turn serves as master for the final CD product. As a result, we can now hear Maurice Ravel conducting a performance of the *Bolero* with the Lamoureux Orchestra (1932) and Serge Prokofiev leading the Moscow Philharmonic in a 1938 performance of the *Romeo and Juliet Suite no. 2*. Also available are revivified vintage CBS recordings of Bruno Walter, George Szell, Sir Thomas Beecham, Elisabeth Schwarzkopf, Fritz Reiner, Arthur Schnabel, and many others. The technique also makes it possible to insert machine-composed short passages of music in places where there is insufficient material for audio reconstruction.

The back catalog release bonanza of 1988 is mostly attributable to the astounding effectiveness of the process of Sonic Solutions combined with the lure of profit to be gained by reissuing deceased performers' output. As might be expected, this same technique can be used by forensics experts and psychiatrists, for example, making taped murder dialogues or cockpit-controller conversations audible above background noise.

Subliminal Sound Recordings. Random House marketed two new subliminal series, "For Women Only" and "The Refresher." The first title released in the "For Women Only" series was "Greater Energy." Planned for future release are "PMS Relief," "Weight Loss," and "Greater Beauty." "The Refresher" series will hit the stores in May 1989 and will include "Traveler's Refresher," "Smoker's Refresher," "5:00 Refresher" and "Wake-up Refresher." The intent is to arm listeners with techniques for tapping greater personal energy at times of the day when many people feel run down or tired.

Two Simon & Schuster lines produced by Enhanced Audio Systems of Emeryville, California, were distributed in conjunction with the Acupressure Institute of America in Berkeley and Founder Michael Reed Gach. One side of each tape includes instruction in self-acupressure, on how to relieve stress and increase blood circulation. Acupressure is purportedly older than acupuncture and easier to administer. A card inside the cassette box has diagrams and instructions on acupressure, which can be consulted without dependence on the tape. Subliminal persuasion and New Age music is offered on the other side of this tape. Waldenbooks stocks between 8 and 16 subliminal titles in their typical store; these tapes have been one of their most popular nonfiction items for some time. Random House has developed its own special consumer come-on, an adjustable listening threshold, set just below the audible level. This permits users to watch television, read, knit, cook, or carpenter while being subliminally massaged by the tape's message. Favorite items provide advice on weight loss, memory improvement, getting organized, speed learning, money making, along with myriad titles on the art of love, self-esteem, ESP, and smoking cessation. In 1988 these tapes moved into Musicland outlets in special packages resembling long boxes used for many CDs.

Children's Recording Upswing. Inspired by the baby boomlet, producers recorded unprecedented numbers of recordings for children. Added to standard storytelling and musical genres were some offbeat products. Records for parents as listening partners, educational, "fun to listen to," and audio-therapeutic categories, along with sleep inducing tapes produced by psychiatrists and enhanced by natural sounds, appeared in record and book stores. RCA and other formerly aloof big labels moved into the kiddy market. New labels such as High Windy (storytelling), MZA, and Youngheart joined such established names as Caedmon, Sine Qua Non, and Spoken Arts. In addition, new avenues such as SongLine were built, cleverly bridging the gap between parents, educators, recording artists, and merchandisers. SongLine is a computer program that plays taped selections of music that can be called up either from a standard telephone outside the retail outlet or from a dedicated line in the store. The caller has one of two options; she/he can press numbers on the phone that correspond to a child's age and pre-audit several age-matching selections, each followed by the song's title, artist's name, and album number OR (for ordering by mail) press numbers of letters on the phone that match the catalog order code. This foretaste option has been a boon for busy working parents in northern California. As expected, the highest number of calls has been between 5 and 10 p.m. on weekday evenings.

Spoken word audio for children provided in book/cassette packages has been another small but steady and significant segment of the audio publications business. Viking Penguin and William Morrow added book/cassette lines in fall 1988. Those who worry about children's literacy development prefer the combination format to stand-alone cassettes because the tapes reinforce rather than replace the reading experience. Parents often buy book/cassettes for children just learning to read, because the cassettes add audio dimension and incidentally encourage reading. When both parents are working, this format can complement the brief time they spend with their children and in cars, tapes with headphones become one great way to keep otherwise unruly passengers occupied constructively. This pacification cum learning process has been bolstered by recent introduction of cheap sturdy cassette players for tots by such toymakers as Fisher-Price. To date, sales of *Make Way For Ducklings* and *Madeleine* have outstripped all other titles. In 1988, celebrity readers were signed on for a new series of book/cassette packages that should appeal to upscale, highly educated parents as well as their children distributed by Rabbit Ears Jack Nicholson reads Kipling; Robin Williams reads the story of Pecos Bill; Meryl Streep reads Beatrix Potter, and Glenn Close reads Hans Christian Andersen.

All's Quiet on the Classical Front. A shakeout of CD manufacturers commenced in mid-1988 and threatened to continue through 1989 because of an oversupply on retailers' shelves. The MCA classics division dismissed Vice-President Tom Shepard after he had been on the job for little more than two years. Recording projects begun with pianist Ruth Laredo and the two-piano team of John and Richard Contiguglia were aborted and rumors of classical cutbacks elsewhere in the industry abounded in December. The main activity of the year was the reissuance of revered performances out of the past and their conversion onto CDs. Top classical artists of 1988 were Vladimir Horowitz (Mozart) and Wynton Marsalis (Baroque music for trumpets). Beethoven retained his perennial status as favored composer with the Emperor Concerto and Fifth Symphony staying on the top 40 classical charts. The single most unusual repertoire happening of the year was the dual appearance of new operas by American composers: John Adam's *Nixon in China* and Philip Glass's *Akhnaten*, both of which earned almost universally favorable reviews.

Finally, Philips announced that it would begin releasing a comprehensive Mozart retrospective on disk as part of the 1991 bicentennial celebration of this composer's death. Mozart freaks should reserve at least eight feet of free shelf space for this ambitious project comprising 180 CDs of music in 45 volumes.

Changing Keys to the Sound Recordings Literature. The *CD Review Digest Annual, v. 1: 1983-1987*, bound in two parts (part 1: Classical Recordings and part 2: Jazz, Popular, Soundtrack, Cast and Video Recordings) was published in 1988. The *Annual* cumulates the first volume of the paperbound *CD Review Digest* (1987) and provides retrospective coverage of reviews published between 1983 (the first year of the CD) to 1986. Citations to more than 19,000 reviews of approximately 8,000 recordings are presented. Thirty-nine journals published in the U.S., Canada, U.K., and Australia are scanned in a compilation that has developed into an absolutely essential companion for any serious CD buyer. Excerpts from reviews provide the gist of critical assessments and often give two or more quotations airing consensus judgments or revealing meaningful differences of opinion amongst critics. Performer, label number, reviewer, and title indexes add to the reference value of this already superfine publication.

Greene CD Catalog ceased publishing its bimonthly book in June, and decided instead to issue an annual catalog.

Phonolog now includes a new-releases section that lists titles for records, CDs, and tapes appearing during the previous week. Each update incudes an entire replacement section for new releases. Published by Trade Service Corporation since 1948, *Phonolog* now has more than 1,000,000 listings.

Schwann experienced a change of management in 1988. It is now being run by NILS (National Insurance Law Service), an ABC publishing agent. As of January 1989, three separate catalogs were produced: (1) the *Schwann CD Catalog* (monthly), sporting a new cover with four-color graphics; (2) the *Schwann Catalog* (a quarterly, replacing the former *Super Schwann*; and (3) the *Artists Issue* (an annual for classical recordings only, arranged by performer).

Hardware and Format Developments. The industry's experiment with 3-inch compact disks continued in 1988. As of October, CBS, A&M, MCA, Motown, PolyGram, WEA, and at least 16 other labels had issued a total of 220 titles. Industry spokespersons were betting on the 3-inchers' success because they represent a bargain for the consumer who desires high quality sound, convenience, and durability at an affordable price. The format appeals to the 18 to 24 year old consumer and the less affluent older music lover. Manufacturers' releases have catered to this bimodal audience, including pop and rock but also offering a wide array of classical, jazz, folk, and golden oldies. The 3-inchers were being packaged in three different ways: (1) CD-3 singles featuring current hit singles with a "B side," as (2) CD-3 maxi-singles, containing long play dance mixes, and as (3) CD-3 mini-albums consisting of compilations or samplers with up to four cuts. Prices were in the $3.98 to $5.98 range. The future of the format is tied to sales of pocket, portable, and full-size CD players, capable of accommodating the 3-inch format. At year's end, at least 15 companies were producing new models including single disk players and changers, multi-disk players, portables, and a car player, enhancing the format's chances of gaining a long term foothold.

In April, Tandy Corporation announced development of their THOR-CD (Tandy High-Intensity Optical Recording), which they expect to price somewhat below the range anticipated for DATs. Philips and other companies are expected to also develop their own reusable CDs. The CD will probably blow the DATs out of the water because the blank medium will likely remain less expensive than the DAT, and CD playback equipment and recordings are well entrenched in the market. Meanwhile, the production flow of DAT players and recordings is still a dribble, not a torrent. Optical disks are extraordinarily durable; they allow space for liner notes, and disks are the medium of choice for interactive, computer driven data manipulation and access.

The LP lost ground again in 1988 as major classical labels phased out this format in their full, mid, and budget price lines. In January 1989 DGG started to issue new topline recordings only on CD. In the first of half of 1988 LPs slipped again with unit sales falling 22.4 percent while unit shipments of CDs increased as they have each year since their introduction in 1983. This time, they shot up by 64 percent. In early 1987, LPs had accounted for 17 percent of the total market; a year later their share had shrunk to 12 percent.

DAT software was bogged down in a gray and pricey market with supportive hardware failing to catch on because major labels remained reluctant to create necessary repertoires. Only a trickle of prerecorded DAT software was reaching the marketplace so there was very little incentive to invest in system development. The complexity of the technology and litigatious atmosphere generated by announcements of its arrival in the U.S. made it more difficult to achieve price reductions than had been the case with CD players. Prices in the $1,200 to $1,600 range have not inspired a headlong rush to buy hardware. At the same time CD players were flying out hi-fi salon doors in late 1988 with sales up 50 percent over the same period in the previous year. As of June, the Electronics Industry Association of America

Sound Recordings

was projecting 1988 sales of 4,800,000 players compared with 3,300,000 in 1987 and 1989 projections of 5,600,000.

In summary, 1988 was an innovative transition year—a time to stop, look, listen, compare, sit back, and savor. Institutional and personal collectors of sound recordings were well advised to take careful stock, to review the growing universe of choices offered by the industry, and to gather their breath, wits, and dollars before making any major hardware or software purchase decisions.

RICHARD SWEENEY HALSEY

Southeastern Library Association

Southeastern Library Association continued as an organization of people working together to promote library and information services in the Southeastern region of the United States, stimulating professional interest and providing interesting and exciting ideas through its journal and biennial conference.

Conference. SELA capped off the 1986–88 biennium with a successful conference in Norfolk, Virginia, October 24–29. Co-sponsored with Virginia Library Association, the preconferences and conference were attended by 1,894 people. Authors Pat Conroy, Rita Mae Brown, and Pulitzer poet Henry Taylor were the main speakers highlighting the theme, "The Creative Spirit: Writers, Words, Readers." Other authors featured included Alf Mapp, Jr., Newberry winner Russell Freedman, and Ernest Gaines. A variety of programs included PR campaigns; fund raising for libraries; CD-ROM Technology; mentoring; videos in libraries; poetry; creativity techniques for improving the mind; discussions both critical and supportive of networking in the Southeast; problems with the FBI; and teaching children the joy of reading. The Interlibrary Loan Meeting included resolutions adapted by the 50-plus participants in favor of: interlibrary lending of returnable materials within the Southeast free of any charges to the borrowing institution; Southeastern libraries establishing reasonable and consistent interlibrary loan photocopy charges and supplying photocopies at no charge within the region; OCLC participant libraries in the Southeast entering their interlibrary loan policies in the OCLC Name/Address Directory; and Southeastern libraries participating in the OCLC union list of serials holdings for the entire region.

Awards. The 1988 Outstanding Southeastern Author Award went to Ernest J. Gaines for *A Gathering of Old Men*. The Outstanding Southeastern Library Program Award was presented to Iberia Parish Library, New Iberia, Louisiana, for its summer workshops in natural science, drama, art and archaeology for young people between the ages of four and seventeen. David E. Estes received the Rothrock Award, which honors a librarian who has made an exceptional contribution to library development in the Southeast. The first SELA President's Award, presented for outstanding contributions to the library field by a lay person, went to Barbara Cooper of Ft. Lauderdale, Florida.

Honorary life memberships were received by Rebecca Bingham; Cora Paul Bomar; Dr. A. Lawson; Helen D. Lockhart; and David Estes.

The Wilson Award for the best article published in *The Southeastern Librarian* during the biennium went to Dr. Jim Carmichael of North Carolina for "A School for Southern Conditions: The Library School in Atlanta, 1905–1988."

Activities. Much that was accomplished during the biennium took place during the 1988 year. A revised handbook was published under the direction of Savan Wilson and the Handbook Committee, with input from all Section and Committee chairs. Changes in the Association's Constitution and Bylaws were implemented and approved by the membership in time to be included in the 1988 revised *Handbook*. The 1988 Southern Books Competition received more than 50 entries; the winners will become part of a traveling display coordinated by the Southern Books Competition Committee.

A new editor of *The Southeastern Librarian* was chosen to begin duties with the 1989 issues. The Intellectual Freedom Committee requested an update on censorship activities in the region from each member state's committee representative. The Public Relations Committee's active year included sponsoring a library public relations contest as well as arranging conference media opportunities and issuing press releases. SELA enjoyed a membership increase of 368 for the year.

Biennium conference. Representatives from all Sections and Committees will meet in the spring of 1989 to plan for activities in the biennium. Emphasis will be on proposing well-designed programs for the next conference; setting up regional workshops; resuming efforts to bring Arkansas into the Association; increasing membership; and continuing the increasing mutual support of SELA and SOLINET.

Dates and cities for the next three conferences, jointly sponsored with state library associations, are 1990—December 4–8, Nashville, Tennessee, Opryland Hotel; 1992—March 17–21; New Orleans, Louisiana, New Orleans Hyatt; and 1994—May 3–7, Orlando, Florida, Hyatt Orlando.

CLAUDIA H. MEDORI

SOUTHEASTERN LIBRARY ASSOCIATION

PRESIDENT (November 1988–November 1990):
George R. Stewart, Birmingham Public Library, Birmingham, Alabama

VICE-PRESIDENT/PRESIDENT-ELECT:
James E. Ward, David Lipscomb College, Nashville, Tennessee

SECRETARY:
Gail R. Lazenby, Cobb County Public Library, Marietta, Georgia

TREASURER:
James E. Ward, David Lipscomb College, Nashville, Tennessee

EXECUTIVE SECRETARY:
Claudia Medori, P.O. Box 987, Tucker, Georgia 30085

Membership (November 1988): 2,096

Special Libraries Association

The Special Libraries Association (SLA) is an international organization of librarians and information professionals who work in special libraries and information centers serving user communities of corporate, research, government, technical, and academic institutions that utilize or create specialized information. SLA provides a variety of services to increase the professional skills and leadership roles of those in the special library sector of the profession.

In its efforts to serve and put knowledge to work, SLA spent $1,612,703 on services and programs for its membership. Allotment of funds to chapters, divisions, and committees accounted for 18 percent, program services 14 percent, cost of non-service publications 6 percent, and Association office operations and occupancy cost 47.1 percent.

The Association has 55 chapters and 28 divisions which interact with one another and with other Association units such as the Board of Directors, committees, organization representatives, and the Executive Director and staff.

Chapters. The 1988 theme for the Chapter Cabinet was "Managing the Chapter Like A Business." It was acknowledged that such management issues as fiscal responsibility, personnel, administration, and operations must be addressed and managed by each chapter and that each chapter needs a business plan to handle current problems and to plan for the future.

Divisions. Regional meetings were conducted by the Pharmaceutical, News, Business and Finance, and Library Management. Two Divisions are working on the international aspect of special libraries. The Museums, Arts and Humanities division participated in the Association's Art/Museum Arts and Humanities Exchange Program; SLA representatives visited Soviet art libraries. The international colloquium on Library and Information Services in Astronomy in Washington, D.C. will include participants from the Physics, Astronomy, and Mathematics Division. The Newspaper Division name was changed to News, and the Environmental and National Resources Divisions merged.

Annual Conference. The Annual Conference in Denver, Colorado, June 11–16 had the theme of "Expanding Horizons: Strategies for Information Managers. The two hundred programs and events and the numerous exhibits held the interest of the 4,635 attendees.

The two general session speakers, Keynoter Michael Annison, President of Westrends and Roger van Oech, President of Creative Think did an excellent job of covering the theme. Annison spoke on "Expanding Horizons," and van Oech addressed "Strategies for Information Managers."

The Divisions scheduled an outstanding number of programs on a variety of topics.

Awards. The following awards were presented at the Awards Banquet: Honorary Member, W. Kenneth Lowry and William J. Welsh; SLA Professional Award, Evelyn Butler and Elizabeth W. Stone; SLA President's Award presented to members of the President's Task Force on the Value of the Information Professional appointed by SLA Past President Frank Spaulding, James M. Matarazzo, Chair, Miriam Drake, Helen Manning, Ann W. Talcott, James B. Tchobanoff, Allen B. Veaner, and H. Spaulding, SLA President 1986/1987; SLA John Cotton Dana Award, Beryl L. Anderson, Ron Coplen (posthumously), Paul Klinefelter; and Enid Thompson; SLA Hall of Fame, Robert W. Gibson, Jr., Edythe Moore, Ruth S. Smith, and Miriam Tees; Fellows of the Special Libraries Association, Vivian Arterbery, Bernard Basch, Laura N. Gasaway, H. Robert Malinowsky, and James M. Matartazzo, and H. W. Wilson Award, Herbert White.

Professional Development. SLA continues to provide high caliber continuing education programs and related services to the membership and other information professionals. Two regional education programs, "New Technology and its Impact on You" and "Managing the One-Person Library" were offered throughout the U.S. The Winter Education Conference, held in conjunction with the SLA Winter Meeting in Colonial Williamsburg, Virginia, attracted a record number of continuing education attendees. This conference offered three full-day courses, four half-day workshops, and the "Analytical Tools" unit of the Middle Management Institute.

Fund Development Activities. Two Special Programs were funded in 1988. James Matarazzo received $3,200 for further study on the "Value of the Information Professional," and Robert V. Williams and Fred W. Roper received $2,200 for a "Study of the Management and Services of Special Libraries in the U.S. and Canada." A silent auction at the Education Conference raised $3,800 to support the Special Programs Fund Grant.

Government Relations. The Association's Government Relations Program has established SLA as a valuable resource of information on library legislation and activities. The Association presented testimony on proposed privatization of NTIS; changes in the Federal Librarians' Register; reduction in 1990 Census data; imposition of FCC access charges; and the FBI Library Awareness Program.

SLA was a co-sponsor of Legislative Day during National Library Week, and by action of the Board of Directors, contributed $10,000 to the Canadian Library Association to support legislative changes to the Canadian Copyright Law.

Adding to the SLA government relations network, the Board approved the recommendation of the Government Relations Committee to approve government relations representatives in divisions to supplement the work of chapter representatives.

Publishing services. SLA's serial publications, the *Specialist* and *Special Libraries* continue to excel. Other serials include *Who's Who in Special Libraries, SLA Triennial Salary Survey, SLA Guide Series,* and *SLA Research Series.* Seven new titles were completed in 1988: *The Information Profession: Facing Future Challenges,* the proceedings for the 1987 State-of-the-Art Institute; *Library Management in Review,* V. II; *U.S. Government Publications Catalog,* 2d. ed.; *Libraries and Information centers within Women's Studies Research Centers; Managerial Competencies of Twelve Corporate Librarians; Survey of SLA Software Users;* and *Tools of the Profession.*

State of the Art Institute. The topic for the 1988

Institute October 17–19 in Washington, D.C., at the Washington Hilton was "Global Ties Through Information." The Institute was cosponsored by SLA and six international library associations: Aslib (Association for Information Management); the Canadian Library Association; IFLA; the Japan Special Libraries Association; the Library Association, United Kingdom; and the Library Association of Australia.

The diverse program covered many applicable subjects, and the speakers were well versed in their areas of expertise—they stimulated and involved the audience. Proceedings of the Institute were published at the end of the year. The quality and success of the first three Institutes undoubtedly guarantee this as a continuing member benefit.

Students. Emphasis on SLA Student Groups included a Student Group Newsletter (a first in 1988) and a reception and program for the students at the Annual Conference. Three new Student Groups were formed at Catholic University, The University of California at Berkley, and at Rutgers University.

Recruitment Aids. The Association published two new membership brochures to assist in recruitment. One provides comprehensive information to members on Association programs and services. The other gives information on SLA member benefits to non-member information professionals.

Public Relations. The Public Relations program gained greater recognition for SLA's membership both inside and outside the profession. At the annual meeting the Association gave its first award recognizing the journalist who published an outstanding feature article on special libraries to David Holmstrom, feature editor for *The Christian Science Monitor*, for "Christine Maxwell; The Business of Information" (*Inflight Magazine*, an American Airlines publication).

Scholarships. Scholarships for $6,000 were awarded to Debra Kay Barnes and Christopher Durane Forney. The Plenum Scholarship for $1,000 was received by Beth Paskoff, who is working on her Ph.D. at Florida State University.

Research. The Research Committee established four categories of research: basic and applied research, education for special librarianship, survey and data collections, and research on professional issues.

Additional Services and Products Offered by SLA. SLA has initiated a new computer assist program on "Time Management in the Small Library." It will be in floppy disk format and accompanied by a workbook, additional reading, and exercises. SpeciaLine is SLA's 24-hour jobline, serving both job seekers and employers. It handled 184 jobs in 1988. Resume referral service were offered to members and non-members as well as organizations seeking to hire information professionals beginning January 1989. The Executive Development Academy, a collaborative effort between SLA and Carnegie Mellon University, was available in March 1989. Middle Management Institute, a program designed for middle-level professionals consisting of 75 hours of instruction was well received.

Presidential Projects for 1988–89. SLA President, Joe Ann Clifton, selected two special projects to be accomplished during her presidential year. The first was an invitational meeting scheduled for April 1989 in Washington, D.C., to discuss and plan how SLA can urge and assist the government in developing needed information policy. Clifton's second presidential goal, "Enhancing the Image of the Librarian/Information Professional," is an inter-society project with representatives on the SLA Presidential Task Force from the American Library Association, the American Society for Information Science, and the American Association of Law Librarians. Also cooperating without representation on the Task Force are the Canadian Library Association, the Association of College and Research Libraries, the Art Libraries Society, the American Association of School Librarians, and the Medical Library Association.

A survey instrument will be utilized to determine the image of librarians in selected societal groups. A public relations program with a television, radio, newspaper, and journal blitz will be implemented if the image of librarians requires improvement. Kaycee Hale will chair the Task Force.

To achieve a successful, fiscally sound association that is responsive to its members' professional needs requires an informed membership that furnishes input and responds to issues, supported by a Board of Directors dedicated to leadership and effective management working with an outstanding Executive Director such as Dr. David Bender and his creative staff. SLA is fortunate to have such a superb team.

JOE ANN CLIFTON

SPECIAL LIBRARIES ASSOCIATION

PRESIDENT (June 1987–June 1988):
Joe Ann Clifton, Litton Industries, Woodland Hills, California

PRESIDENT-ELECT:
Muriel B. Regan, Gossage Regan Associates, New York

SECRETARY:
James B. Tchobanoff, Pillsbury Company, Minneapolis, Minnesota

TREASURER:
Catherine A. Jones, Library of Congress, Washington, D.C.

EXECUTIVE DIRECTOR:
David R. Bender

Membership (September 30, 1988): 11,618
Headquarters: 1700 Eighteenth Street, N.W. Washington, D.C. 20009

Standards

The National Information Standards Organization Z39 (NISO), is the voluntary standards body in the U.S. responsible for library, information service, publishing, and specialized library equipment standards. NISO is the organization designated by the American National Standards Institute (ANSI) to develop standards within the above scope. All NISO standards are developed according to consensus procedures stipulated by ANSI and receive final approval from the ANSI Board of Standards Review. Thus they become joint ANSI and NISO standards when they are completed and are designated ANSI Z39.[number] or ANSI/NISO Z39.[number], by which numbering they are commonly known.

ANSI is the U.S. national body member of the International Organization for Standardization (ISO). Accordingly, ANSI delegates to NISO the responsibility of advising on ISO work and of representing the U.S. on ISO committees for ISO standards relating to the NISO scope.

New Standards Approved by NISO. Five standards were approved by the NISO voting members and the ANSI Board of Standards Review in 1988. One was an older standard, ANSI/NISO Z39.21, *Book Numbering*, the national standard for the International Standard Book Number (ISBN) which had been undergoing revision. The new ISBN standard has an expanded scope that includes all media, not just book format material. The name of the standard and the identification number will retain the word "book" because it is widely known. The same changes were introduced into the international counterpart of this ANSI standard (ISO 2108) at a May 1988 meeting of ISO.

Approval of ANSI/NISO Z39.59, *Electronic Manuscript: Preparation and Markup*, is a major step forward in setting standards for published manuscripts. This standard could lead to more efficient publisher/author and publisher/printer interactions. It could also widen options for printer hardware and software if equipment manufacturers can offer generalized products based on the standard. This standard is a specific implementation of the general structure standard for markup languages developed by the ISO Technical Committee for computer standards: *Standard Generalized Markup Language (SGML)*, ISO 8879.

Another standard that builds on ISO computer industry standards received final approval in 1988: ANSI/NISO Z39.50, *Information Retrieval Service Definition and Protocol Specification for Library Applications*. This standard defines the protocol at the application level for interactions between information retrieval systems running on different computer hardware and software. It is a library-specific part of the general Open Systems Interconnection (OSI) model developed in ISO.

ANSI/NISO Z39.63, *Interlibrary Loan Data Elements*, was approved for publication in late 1988. This standard specifies data elements that identify both the item requested and the requesting institution in interlibrary loan transactions. It is based on the ALA paper interlibrary loan form, but the NISO standard is intended to be independent of the transmission medium.

The fifth standard finalized in 1988 was ANSI/NISO Z39.64, *East Asian Character Codes (EACC)*. This standard establishes the computer codes for characters in the Chinese, Japanese, and Korean scripts. The set is currently used in the U.S. by the systems at the Research Library Information Network (RLIN) and Online Computer Library Center (OCLC) and on the bibliographic records for Chinese, Japanese, and Korean material distributed on tape by the Library of Congress.

New Printer. The above standards and ANSI/NISO Z39.61, *Recording, Use, and Display of Patent Application Data* (completed in 1987), will be the first six to be issued by Transaction Publishers, Inc. In 1988 NISO signed a three-year contract with Transaction for publishing and marketing American National Standards developed by NISO. By working with its own publisher, NISO will be able to control the design of the standards documents and to pursue new avenues in marketing the standards. The latter is critical to wider use and adoption of NISO standards. The standards will also continue to be available through ANSI in New York.

Work in Progress. The following standards work was in progress during 1988. Under each topical category, the scope of new standards under development is briefly described and existing standards undergoing revision are listed. All new development is handled by a Standards Committee (SC) established for the specific standard. Every five years, existing standards are reviewed by NISO voting members and recommendations to reaffirm them as they are, revise them, or withdraw them are made. A recommendation to revise may result in the formation of an SC to handle the revision, if it is major, or appointment of an editor to incorporate the suggestion.

Automation and Data Interchange. SC G, Common Command Language for Use in Interactive Information Retrieval, chaired by Margaret Morrison, finished revision of the draft standard after balloting ended in early 1988. Following correspondence with those who submitted negative ballots and comments, the new draft was to be submitted for ballot in early 1989. This new draft standard specifies the vocabulary, syntax, and operational meaning of commands in a command language for use with online interactive retrieval systems.

SC LL, Circulation Systems Data, held its first meetings in 1988. This standard, which is to be based on work by the Automation Vendor Interface Advisory Committee (AVIAC), will be a dictionary of data elements required in a circulation system and will specify the communications format for the data. In order to avoid privacy concerns, NISO has been careful to clarify that standardizing data does not imply that private data will be made available outside a system.

SC DD, Computerized Serials Orders and Claims, sent a draft standard for ballot and subsequently revised it in 1988. The draft will be circulated to NISO members again in 1989. This standard is a companion to ANSI Z39.45, *Computerized Book Ordering*. The serial standard includes, in addition to ordering, the order response, claim, and claim response messages.

Publishing Practices. Two new standards affecting the physical packaging of nonbook forms of material were under development in 1988. SC FF, Computer Software Description, chaired by Ed Swanson, is working on a standard that specifies the information that should appear on software packaging and in advertisements for software. SC Z, Eye-Legible Information on Microfilm Leaders, Trailers, and Containers, is chaired by Louis Willard. Both of these standards are especially important to libraries because the information in these items is not eye-legible without equipment. Thus they are difficult for staff to catalog and for users to as-

Five existing standards of special interest to publishers were undergoing revision during 1988. Review of ANSI Z39.10, *Directories of Libraries and Information Centers*, ANSI Z39.32, *Information on Microfiche Headings*, and ANSI Z39.22, *Proof Corrections*, indicated that major revision was not needed. Editors are incorporating suggestions, and the revised standards will be balloted in 1989. Standards Committees have been formed to revise two current standards that had been reviewed and for which more extensive revision was needed. SC VV will revise ANSI Z39.6, *Trade Catalogs*, which specifies the content and format of trade catalogs. SC NN has been charged with the revision of ANSI Z39.41, *Book Spine Formats*.

Preservation. Three new standards that will assist in the preservation of library materials are under development. SC GG, Hard Cover Case Bindings, chaired by Carolyn Morrow, completed a first draft standard that will be circulated to NISO members in 1989. The draft standard describes methods and materials compatible with reasonable permanence and durability. It includes specifications for such aspects as grain direction of text paper, inside margin size, endpaper construction, leaf attachment, rounding, backing and spine lining operations, casemaking and casing-in, and materials used.

Work began on two other preservation standards by new committees: SC R, Environmental Conditions for Storage of Paper-based Library and Archive Collections, and SC MM, Environmental Conditions for the Exhibition of Library and Archival Material.

SC II continued to work on an addition to the current standard ANSI Z39.48, *Permanence of Paper for Printed Library Materials*, that would extend the standard to coated papers.

The standard for *Permanent and Durable Library Catalog Cards* (currently numbered ANSI Z85.1) was reviewed in 1988, and ballots that recommended revision were received. Voters requested that the permanence requirement pertaining to acidity and durability be enhanced. The standard will be revised and balloted in 1989.

Control of Materials. SC CC continued work on a standard serial issue and article identifier to be used in automated systems for serial check in and ordering and for transmission of serial and article data between systems. A new draft will be ready for circulation in early 1989.

A second SC working in the area of control is SC W, Holdings Statements for Non-Serial Items, chaired by Stephen Davis. A new draft, which is more closely aligned with ANSI Z39.44, *Serial Holdings Statements*, was circulated for ballot in late 1988. The committee anticipates that this ballot will be successful and the standard will be completed in 1989.

Three existing NISO standards are also undergoing revision: ANSI Z39.19, *Guidelines for Thesaurus Structure, Construction, and Use*, ANSI Z39.29, *Bibliographic References*, and ANSI Z39.1, *Periodicals: Format and Arrangement*. The revision work of SC Q on ANSI Z39.1 progressed to ballot in late 1988. Several negative votes were received which the committee will work to resolve in early 1989. Committees were also organized to handle the revisions of the thesaurus and reference standards.

Romanization. NISO has a number of standards for romanization which were reviewed during 1987–88. ANSI Z39.11, *Romanization of Japanese*, and ANSI Z39.12, *Romanization of Arabic*, were both reaffirmed without change. Minor changes were recommended for four standards, largely to bring them closer to the ALA/LC romanization tables. Editors for these four were appointed in 1988 and work should be completed by early 1989. These standards are ANSI Z39.24, *Romanization of Slavic Cyrillic Characters*, ANSI Z39.25, *Romanization of Hebrew*, ANSI Z39.35, *Romanization of Lao, Khmer, and Pali*, and ANSI Z39.37, *Romanization of Armenian*.

Statistics. Three existing NISO standards for statistics are undergoing revision. ANSI Z39.7, *Library Statistics*, will be revised by SC UU, co-chaired by Mary Jo Lynch of ALA and Peter Young of Faxon, Inc. Comments on ANSI Z39.8, *Compiling Book Publishing Statistics*, were not major so the text was edited and the standard will be recirculated for approval in 1989.

ANSI Z39.20, *Library Materials—Criteria for Price Indexes*, was reviewed for reaffirmation in 1988, and NISO voting members called for revision. A committee will be formed to revise that standard.

Other Standards Reviewed. Two additional NISO standards were reviewed and reaffirmed in 1988: ANSI Z39.33, *Identification Codes for Use by the Bibliographic Community*, and ANSI Z39.30, *Order Form for Single Titles*.

Negative reaffirmation ballots were received on five standards for which editors or committees will be appointed to revise the standards in 1989: ANSI Z39.23, *Standard Technical Report Number*; ANSI Z39.46, *Patent Documents–Identification of Bibliographic Data*; ANSI Z39.45, *Claims for Missing Issues of Serials*; ANSI Z39.31, *Format for Scientific and Technical Translations*; and ANSI Z39.34, *Synoptics*.

New Standards Work Approved in 1988. SC QQ will develop a standard for the physical preparation and binding of theses and dissertations. The purpose of this standard is to assure long–term retention of the documents by the academic institutions involved. The standard will include specifications for paper, inks, duplication, illustrations, inclusion of oversized material, and bindings.

SC RR was charged with development of a standard specifying adhesives for affixing identification and security labels to library materials. The standard should specify adhesives that remain permanently bonded without damaging the label, the item, or adjacent items.

SC SS will be formed to develop a standard that specifies basic information that should be provided by vendors when advertising products used to store, rehouse, contain, bind, or repair library materials, including books, pamphlets, sound recordings, videotapes, manuscripts, maps, and photographs. The standard will also specify information that should be used in advertisements for such products.

SC TT was established, with Dan Iddings as

chair, to develop standards for several groups of data elements that are included on CD-ROM and other optical media. These data element sets, called files on the optical media, include publisher file, data preparer file, copyright file, abstract file, and bibliographic file.

NISO Structure. Since NISO became incorporated in 1983, it has been administered by a Board of Directors following bylaws and operating procedures of the organization. Patricia R. Harris serves as the Executive Director of NISO, maintaining the NISO office that occupies guest worker space at the National Bureau of Standards.

NISO has two types of memberships: voting member and information associate. At the end of 1988, NISO had 65 voting members.

Nineteen eighty-eight was the last year for publication of the newsletter of NISO under the old name, *Voice of Z39*. In 1989, reports on NISO activities will be expanded in content and will be issued in a new publication titled *Information Standards Quarterly (ISQ)*. A subscription to *ISQ* will be available from the NISO office.

Standards Information. Approved ANSI standards developed by NISO may be obtained from Transaction Publishers, Inc., Rutgers University, New Brunswick, NJ 08903; telephone (201) 932-2280. Standing orders for ANSI Z39 standards are available. The same address may be contacted to be placed on a mailing list for information on newly published standards. Information on the NISO program, membership applications, and subscriptions to *ISQ* are available from the NISO office: National Information Standards Organization, P.O. Box 1056, Bethesda, MD 20817; telephone (301) 975-2814.

SALLY H. MC CALLUM

State Libraries

State libraries have been concerned with a variety of issues and engaged in numerous programs and activities to further their statewide library leadership role and to encourage citizens' access to resources and services. While there is considerable diversity among the states in terms of library service needs and demands, funding, enabling legislation, and even state library organizational patterns, there were issues and concerns in common among the vast majority of the states. Several of these issues were of major importance in 1988.

Literacy. Many state libraries initiated or continued statewide library literacy programs during the year. State libraries were also instrumental in providing financial assistance to local public libraries and literacy coalitions for programs addressing community literacy needs. The California State Library has made literacy a major program goal since 1984. The state's literacy campaign has reached 77 of the 169 jurisdictions. In fiscal year 1987-88, $4,500,000 in state funds was available to support local library literacy efforts. In addition, funds were made available to establish the "Families for Literacy" program aimed at breaking patterns whereby illiteracy is passed from generation to generation. Twenty-one local library jurisdictions participated in the initial year of this program.

The Alabama Public Library Service continued to support the Alabama Literacy Coalition and sponsored the first statewide literacy public awareness campaign patterned after the successful Florida campaign "Illiteracy. We Can't Afford It."

Since the Secretary of State Literacy Grant Program was signed into law three years ago, Illinois has awarded a total of $14,000,000 to literacy programs throughout the state. A special State Literacy Advisory Board was appointed by the Illinois Secretary of State Jim Edgar to oversee distribution of funds allocated to support statewide literacy efforts. In FY88, $4,000,000 was distributed to 89 literacy programs. Other activities during 1988 included an ongoing statewide public awareness campaign, a literacy hotline, and hosting and planning assistance by the Illinois State Library of a national conference on State Literacy Initiatives in April.

The Oklahoma Department of Libraries launched a major program to organize literacy councils in cities across the state, with the ultimate goal of making literacy instruction available to 95 percent of the population within 25 miles of their homes. The State Library committed to and sponsored the state's first successful statewide literacy program and public awareness campaign, "Oklahoma . . . Do You READ Me?" A statewide literacy conference was held in the fall to convene literacy volunteers, students, and service organizations. An Oklahoma project that established literacy programs in the state's correctional facilities won the 1988 national Laubauch Literacy Action Award. The Oklahoma Department of Libraries was one of three state agencies cooperating in this project.

Many state libraries took leadership and cooperative roles in statewide literacy efforts. Important long-range planning efforts have resulted in programs in Indiana and Kentucky. Cooperation with literacy coalitions has been the foundation for state library efforts in Florida, Massachusetts, Mississippi, New Jersey, and Virginia. Many state libraries received funding under LSCA Title VI for literacy programs and activities.

White House Conference on Library and Information Services. Since efforts began to have a second White House Conference on Library and Information Services (WHCLIS), state librarians and staff have encouraged, supported, and closely monitored developments toward that end. In 1988, President Reagan signed Public Law 100-382 authorizing and requesting the President to call and conduct a White House Conference on Library and Information Services to be held not earlier than September 1, 1989, and not later than September 30, 1991. The National Commission on Libraries and Information Science is the federal agency responsible for the White House Conference, and states will be developing plans and strategies for participating in pre-White House Conference activities. Minnesota State Librarian William Asp chaired the National Commission-sponsored Preliminary Design Group. Three themes were proposed by this group for the second WHCLIS: literacy, productivity, and democracy. State librarians, state library staff, and others representing 38 states at-

State Libraries

tended the WHCLIS Task Force annual planning meeting in Minneapolis August 24–27. Recommendations and strategies for the second White House Conference were developed. Indications are that most states will be planning preconferences, and state libraries have been leading in this effort.

LSCA Reauthorization. The Library Services and Construction Act (LSCA) is the major program for federal assistance in the development of library services. State libraries have utilized LSCA funds to support a wide range of public library services, services to special clientele and institutionalized persons, to support library-based literacy programs, to strengthen resource sharing and cooperative endeavors, and to stimulate the improvement of access to information through technology. Funds have also been available for the construction and renovation of public library facilities.

In considering the LSCA reauthorization process, the Chief Officers of State Library Agencies (COSLA) indicated that the following issues should be explored prior to drafting the reauthorization language: adequate funding for literacy programs and for services to the disadvantaged, elderly, limited-English speaking, blind and physically handicapped, and institutionalized; adequate funding for resource sharing and interlibrary cooperation; greater access to new information technology; preservation and conservation of library materials; increased authorization levels and base grants to provide adequately for service needs; and greater coordination between federal and state governments in the administration of Titles IV, V, and VI.

Preservation/Conservation. A growing number of state libraries are providing statewide leadership in the preservation and conservation of library and historical materials. Such efforts typically have been in close cooperation with other state and local archival, library, and historical organizations and agencies. The trend appears to include libraries of all types and often includes the private sector in planning and implementation of preservation and conservation programs. Priority was given to such programs at the state libraries of Connecticut, New Hampshire, New Jersey, South Carolina, and Virginia. State needs assessment studies previously conducted in Illinois and New York led to numerous appraisal, training, and technical support activities in those states during 1988. The State Library of Florida completed a yearlong disaster preparedness assessment and training program, resulting in a strong statewide disaster preparedness network of public and academic libraries. The Texas State Library and the Nebraska Library Commission began the preservation needs assessment process with the goal of developing a statewide preservation plan.

Plans, Studies, and Standards. Planning for library development was a major activity of many state libraries during 1988. Several states completed plans or reviews of plans for public library and library systems development. The review of the 1986 study of the future of Illinois library systems was completed and recommendations were presented to the Illinois State Library. The Missouri State Library presented its long-range plan for library development in a series of public hearings. The State Library of North Carolina completed its working plan for aiding the development of library and information services. Studies and planning efforts were initiated or under way for public library development in Georgia, Michigan, Nebraska, and New York.

Resource sharing and multitype library cooperation was the subject of studies and planning efforts initiated in California, Iowa, Utah, and Washington. Task forces in California and Iowa addressed the issues, needs, and technology related to multitype library cooperative activities and programs in their states. In those states, meetings and forums were held to secure input from librarians and others interested in cooperative partnerships and services. The State Library Division in Utah participated in a study of the state's academic libraries, library technology, and interlibrary cooperation. The Washington State Library commissioned two studies, the first to examine the feasibility of building a statewide automated union list of serials, and the second to study present resource sharing patterns in the state.

Of importance to state libraries were two other nationwide study and planning projects. The School of Information Studies and the Maxwell School of Citizenship and Public Affairs at Syracuse University, with the National Association for State Information Systems, Inc., conducted a National Study of Information Resources Management in State Government. Based on the need for state government to manage both information resources and information technology effectively if information is to have value and be a strategic resource for government, the study reviewed the effects of information resource management on both central state and functional agencies. Policy within the states was reviewed; a survey collected data on information resource management practices and strategies; and selected states received site visits. State libraries were important contributors to the study and expect that the results will guide some planning at the state level for information resources management and information technology in the future.

The second study on federally generated public library statistics was the focus of planning by the National Commission on Libraries and Information Science (NCLIS) and the National Center for Education Statistics (NCES). State Librarians Amy Owen (Utah), Joseph Shubert (New York), Barratt Wilkins (Florida), and Public Library Specialist Janice Feye-Stukas (Minnesota) served on a joint NCLIS and NCES task force to develop a system for the collection of statistical data on public libraries and the timely publication of the statistics. State libraries will be the locus for coordination of data gathering activities in the states.

Facilitating the development and revision of library standards continued to be an important activity for state libraries. The Illinois State Library appointed a task force to address the issues of standards for system services and evaluation methods for these services. Public library standards were adopted in Alabama as a result of work by a joint committee of the Alabama Library Association and the Alabama Public Library Service. The State Library of Kansas also issued a new edition of the Kansas public library standards. Extensive assistance was received from the Kansas Library Association in compiling the standards. Utah continued the implementation of its *Upgrade Process* for planning, evaluation, and goal setting for the state's public libraries. The goal of the state library is to have implementation of public library standards identified through this process by 1990.

Cooperative Endeavors. The most popular networking venture within the states during 1988 was the installation of a telefacsimile machines and the creation or enhancement of telefacsimile networks. Some variation of a FAX networking approach occurred in nearly half the states, with significant programs being boasted in Florida, Kansas, Montana, New York, Pennsylvania, Virginia, and Wyoming. Montana State Library's FAXNET Project received a national award for outstanding achievement in its innovative use of facsimile technology by the *Administrative Magazine of New York*.

The South Dakota Project for Automated Libraries System became a reality after five years of planning. The computerized card catalog program, known as South Dakota P.A.L.A. (Public Access Library System), provides information on ten state-owned libraries and additional public, school and private college libraries are expected to participate in the future.

New interlibrary loan codes were released in Illinois and Florida. Significant within the new Illinois code is the policy that libraries may not charge for specific classes of materials loaned within the network. The Florida code emphasizes a new series of borrowing and lending protocols which accommodate the addition of medium- and small-sized public libraries and private academic and special libraries to the network.

Legislation and Funding. Statutory changes in Alabama increased the size and representation of the executive board members of the Alabama Public Library Service from five to seven members representing congressional districts instead of being at-large. The new Mississippi Statewide Library Development Systems Act of 1988 clarifies the role of library boards of trustees, increases the millage levy limit for both cities and counties, and exempts libraries from the state's ten percent annual increase cap. The law also makes provision for accreditation standards and distribution of state funds based on level of service provided to the community.

Confidentiality of library records laws were enacted in Massachusetts, New York, and Rhode Island. The New York law includes computer database searches and reference requests in addition to circulation records. The Massachusetts law provides broader protection for the library user's right to confidentiality and privacy and provides libraries who are network members the legal authority to exchange information regarding patrons and loaned materials without violating the user's confidentiality rights. The Rhode Island law includes businesses as well as libraries in its right of privacy provisions. Video stores and bookstores have the same prohibitions as libraries.

Oklahoma passed a library theft bill aimed at saving taxpayers money and improving patron access to information. Persons convicted of stealing or destroying materials are subject to fines, restitution, penalities, or both.

California secured matching funds for repair and construction of libraries through the Construction and Renovation Board Act.

Budget increases of significance achieved during 1988 include a 21 percent increase in the Rhode Island Department of State Library Services budget, especially in the areas of per capita grants to public libraries and public library construction funds. The Oklahoma Department of Libraries received a 39 percent increase for 1989. Increases include ten new positions, increased materials budget and a 54 percent increase for the development and expansion of public library service. Alabama Public Library Service received a $3,900,000 increase in the FY89 budget over its FY88 budget of $5,200,000. The Virginia State Library and Archives had a 24 percent increase in its 1988–89 appropriation over its previous two-year appropriation.

New Buildings and Renovations. New state library buildings were planned or under construction in Illinois, Michigan, and Virginia. In early 1989, the Library of Michigan will open the second-largest state library in the U.S., ranking behind only New York. The Illinois State Library will be housed in a five-story, 164,000-square-foot building which was estimated for completion in September, 1989. The Virginia State Library and Archives received $750,000 for a preplanning study for its new facility.

People. New state library heads were named in Maryland, Nebraska, Pennsylvania, and Rhode Island. In Maryland, Maurice Travillian was named Assistant State Superintendent for Libraries replacing Nettie Taylor who retired after 28 years in the position. Sara Parker, State Librarian of Montana, was named Pennsylvania State Librarian, replacing Elliot Shelkrot. Rod Wagner, Deputy Director of the Nebraska Library Commission, was named to replace John Kopischke as Director. Bruce Daniels was named Director of the Rhode Island Department of State Library Services after having served in that position on an acting basis during the leave of absence of Fay Zipkowitz.

LORRAINE SCHAEFFER SUMMERS

Theatre Library Association

Awards. As the Theatre Library Association (TLA) entered its 51st year in 1988, the annual presentation of the George Freedley Memorial Awards and the Theatre Library Association Awards was again the highlight of the year's events. The awards were presented at a reception on May 18, in the Vincent Astor Gallery at The New York Public Library at Lincoln Center. The Freedley Award, for the best book of 1987 on live theatre, was presented by Estelle Parsons to Charles Shattuck for *Shakespeare on the American Stage, II: From Booth and Barrett to Sothern and Marlowe* (Folger Books/Associated University Presses). Shattuck also received the Bernard

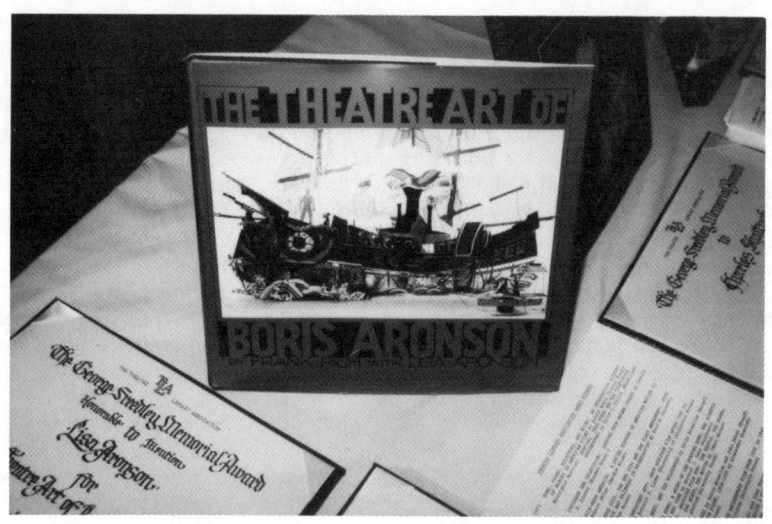

The Theater Arts of Boris Aronson.

Hewitt Award from the American Society for Theatre Research for the best book of 1987 on theatre history at the Society's annual combined meeting with TLA. The Theatre Library Association Award for the best book in the field of film, radio or television was presented by Barbara Goldsmith to John Canemaker for *Winsor McCay: His Life and Art* (Abbeville Press). The Freedley Award Honorable Mention was presented to Frank Rich and Lisa Aronson by Tony Walton for their study *The Theatre Art of Boris Aronson* (Knopf). The Theatre Library Association Award Honorable Mention was presented by Frank Perry to John Sayles, in absentia, for his *Thinking in Pictures: The Making of the Movie "MATEWAN"* (Houghton-Mifflin). Each award winner received a check for $250; each honorable mention, a check for $100. The large number of nominations and the high attendance at the ceremonies indicated the increasing significance of the awards in the field of performing arts publishing.

Activities. On July 11 in New Orleans, TLA conducted its annual summer program meeting and tour in conjunction with the ALA Annual Conference. During the morning, more than 50 conferees visited the Saenger Performing Arts Center, then proceeded to the French Quarter for a private tour of the Historic New Orleans Collection housed in what was once a private home. A well-attended luncheon at Antoine's was followed by a program at Le Pétit Théâtre du Vieux Carre, where the group heard talks on the history of theatre in New Orleans and on theatre holdings in the area, including the historic New Orleans Collection, the Howard-Tilton Library at Tulane University, and the Amistad Research Centre; and the history and importance of the Library and Archive of Le Pétit Théâtre itself. A reception followed the program.

The annual meeting of the Theatre Library Association was held at the Museum of the City of New York October 21, 1988. Louis A Rachow, former Curator of the Hampden-Booth Library at the Players in New York, was named official historian of the Association. It was also announced that Madeleine Nichols, recently appointed Curator of the Dance Collection of The New York Public Library, had been retained as TLA's legal counsel. Four new members were elected to the Executive Board for three-year terms. The members of the current Board are Susan Brady, Archivist, Manuscripts and Archives, Sterling Memorial Library, Yale University (1989-91); Maryann Chach, Archivist, Shubert Archive, New York (1989-91); John W. Frick, Department of Drama, Culbreth Theatre, University of Virginia, Charlottesville (1989-91); Wendy Warnken, Consultant, Ontario Arts Council, Canada (1989-91); Walter Zvonchenko, Theatre Reference Librarian, Library of Congress Performing Arts Library, John F. Kennedy Center, Washington, D.C. (1989-91); Elizabeth Burdick, Librarian, International Theatre Institute of the U.S. (1986-89); Geraldine Duclow, Curator, Theatre Collection, Free Library of Philadelphia (1987-89); Brigitte Kueppers, Theatre Arts Librarian, UCLA (1986-89); Richard C. Lynch, private collector (1987-90); Louis A. Rachow (1986-89); Bob Taylor, Assistant Curator, Billy Rose Theatre Collection, The New York Public Library at Lincoln Center (1987-90); and Richard

---

THEATRE LIBRARY ASSOCIATION

PRESIDENT (1988-1989):
Mary Ann Jensen, Curator, William Seymour Theatre Collection, Princeton University Library

VICE-PRESIDENT:
James Poteat, Manager, Research Services, Television Information Office, New York

SECRETARY-TREASURER:
Richard M. Buck, Assistant to the Chief, Performing Arts Research Center, The New York Public Library at Lincoln Center

RECORDING SECRETARY:
Lois Erickson McDonald, Associate Curator, The Eugene O'Neill Theater Center, New London, Connecticut

Membership (October 1988): 526 (274 personal; 252 institutional)
Dues (calendar year): personal, $20; institutional, $25. U.S. currency only
Headquarters: 111 Amsterdam Avenue, New York 10023, Attn.: Richard M. Buck, Secretary-Treasurer

Wall, Theatre Librarian, Benjamin S. Rosenthal Library, Queens College (New York) (1986–89).

The program meeting was a celebration of the 100th Anniversary of the birth of Eugene O'Neill. TLA members visited an exhibition prepared by Patrick Hoffman, Acting Curator of the Theatre Collection at the Museum of the City of New York, called "AMERICAN LINES: Manuscripts of Eugene O'Neill," and heard several TLA members discuss their association with the life of O'Neill. They were joined on the panel by actress Geraldine Fitzgerald and moderator George C. White, the President of the Eugene O'Neill Theatre Center in Waterford, Connecticut.

The American Society for Theatre Research and the Theatre Library Association held their annual combined meeting in Columbus on the campus of The Ohio State University November 10–13. Some 80 registrants heard and discussed 27 papers on topics ranging from "The Phenomonology of Applause" to "Alternative Visions of Blanche DuBois: Uta Hagen and Jessica Tandy in *A Streetcar Named Desire*." The featured speaker was playwright Jerome Lawrence, cosponsor of the Jerome Lawrence and Robert E. Lee Theatre Institute at OSU, which hosted the meeting. Highlights of the weekend were tours of the Martin Luther King, Jr. Performing Arts Center, which carries out a very active program in a restored church building, and of the Ohio Theatre, a restored, landmarked, Loew's motion picture palace.

Publications. The 13th volume of *Performing Arts Resources*, the TLA annual, published in October, was edited by Barbara Naomi Cohen-Stratyner. It contains the proceedings of a 1985 conference held in Rutherford, New Jersey, on the Drew/Barrymore acting dynasty. Included are six provocative essays and the first full text of Maurice Barrymore's play *Nadjezda*. The Theatre Library Association also publishes *Broadside*, a quarterly newsletter, edited by Alan J. Pally.

RICHARD M. BUCK

Trustees

The traditional role of the trustee is undergoing redefinition, according to the American Library Trustee Association and trustee leaders in a number of states. In Iowa and California there have been efforts to change or abolish library boards, while in Georgia trustees have found a "whole new life" helping directors build new libraries financed by bond issues they worked to pass.

A concern that some librarians and city administrators feel boards are no longer needed has often surfaced at trustee workshops and annual meetings in California. When the Monterey Park library board was abolished, the Friends of the Library brought suit on behalf of city residents maintaining that the action was illegal. Final action is pending.

The League of Municipalities in Iowa has circulated a draft of proposed state legislation to be introduced early in 1989 which would put all funding for public libraries under city or county government, making the boards advisory and not administrative, and reducing trustee terms from six to four years.

The role of trustees defies generalization. The history of library development in each state is different, and within a state there is usually great variety in statutory authority and duties. Volunteer service today is said to require more than on-the-job training to function effectively. Ideally there should be a local board orientation and manual of duties and policies. Board members should also attend training sessions at state workshops and conventions. The role of the trustee is delineated through this educational process. Leadership from the state library agency, and commitment from directors and trustee leaders is essential.

Manuals Define Role. A group of trustees in California supervised the publication in 1987 of the *Trustee Tool Kit for Library Leadership*, in cooperation with the California State Library (California State Library Foundation, P. O. Box 942837, Sacramento, CA 94237-0001). Significant changes had occurred since issuance of the previous manual. The preparation and dissemination of this invaluable manual promoted clarification of the roles and duties of California trustees throughout the state. The manual describes: (1) the variety of statutory authorities for boards in the state; (2) sources of funding and ways of obtaining funds; (3) legal duties, liabilities and rights; (4) effective board organization and operation; (5) planning, policy setting, and other responsibilities; (6) public relations; and (7) advocacy.

Friends' Role. This manual also covers the distinction between trustees and Friends of the Library, valuable in any state where Friends are proving their worth through public awareness activities and fund-raising. Trustee leader Marilyn Stevenson of Palos Verdes Estates, California, says that "the Friends of the Library serve a role, but it is a very different role from that of trustee." Friends are separate, independent organizations while advisory or administrative boards have legal responsibilities. There should be a "mutually communicative, cooperative and supportive relationship between board and Friends," according to the *Tool Kit*.

Many Friends groups are being formed in Louisiana, where trustees may serve as chairs of special projects but cannot be officers due to conflict of interest. By law, trustees cannot ask for voter support of bonds or taxes, but Friends are free to do so.

The relationship between trustees and library foundations is also addressed by the California manual. In many states trustees generally take active roles in getting such foundations established. Ruth Kampa, a former California state trustee president, was determined to leave the San Jose Public Library Foundation as a lasting contribution to her library. In Oklahoma, where 30 new library buildings are being constructed throughout the state, some libraries have developed foundations with the building program as the impetus.

Pat Reynolds, recent chair of the Southeastern Library Association trustees and Friends of the Library section, speaks enthusiastically of the role of trustees in DeKalb County, Georgia. After passage of a $29,000,000 bond issue, Director Barbara Loar created committees and assigned

241

each board member specific and communal tasks. Reynolds describes library headquarters as "an open door" and her director "in total command and very fair. When she calls, we listen."

Georgia public library directors, who have a statewide political action committee, assign trustees an important role in advocacy. A dinner arranged by directors and trustees for the Governor of Georgia, at which the Governor received a special award, afforded a more powerful presentation than either group could accomplish alone.

Leaders Define Role. The role of the trustee is being redefined in many states through educational programs and manuals, new legislation, and leadership development with increased responsibilities. The trustees who compose the Mississippi Library Commission have strong statutory authority and define their role as critical in serving the state's illiterate, blind, and physically handicapped and other special populations through outreach programs. Trustees set policy and do not overlap activities of the Friends, who have a statewide organization and support trustee activities.

Tennessee State Librarian Edwin Gleaves tapped a trustee as leader of the committee that prepared a long-range plan that addresses the role of trustees. Colonel Joseph W. Jones, Jr., Newbern, was given a substantial role in conducting research and securing input during public hearings. After this experience he declared that "a dynamic state library agency makes a difference."

Mary Beth Long, incoming chair of Southeastern Library Association trustees and Friends of the Library, feels baby boomers coming of age are showing that it is "becoming the thing to do to give back. The library is the perfect place to work on solving current problems concerning literacy, education and employment."

Long, of Counce, Tennessee, sees trustees working alongside library professionals and using their career talents to help the library. She feels the role of the trustee is: one, to secure money, because without money people can't be helped; and two, to serve with integrity and without compensation or personal gain. She sees the trustee/staff relationship as "a balancing act but one which takes the pressure off by making a decision collectively."

Trustees and White House Conference. In late 1988 three trustees were appointed by Congress to the advisory committee that will assist the National Commission on Libraries and Information Science in planning and conducting the second White House Conference. They are Joan Reeves of Rhode Island, Nelwyn Murphy of Mississippi, and Virginia Young of Missouri. Continuing enhancement of the role of the trustee should result from their activities.

BARBARA COOPER

United States Board on Books for Young People

The United States Board on Books for Young People (USBBY) was established in 1984 as one of the 45 national sections of the International Board on Books for Young People (IBBY) which was founded in 1953, with a secretariat in Geneva, Switzerland. The objectives of the USBBY, a non-profit organization, are to encourage the provision of reading materials of merit for young people throughout the world; to cooperate with the other national sections of IBBY whose objectives are similar to those of USBBY; and to facilitate the exchange of information internationally on aspects of books and reading for children and young people.

Organization. The Board of Directors of USBBY includes the officers (president, vice-president and president-elect, and treasurer), two directors elected by the membership at large, and two directors appointed by each of the patron organizations: American Library Association (ALA), Children's Book Council (CBC), International Reading Association (IRA), and National Council of Teacher's of English (NCTE). Headquarters for the USBBY secretariat is the IRA in Newark, Delaware.

Activities. Programs for the membership and for others who wish to attend are held during the annual conferences of the patron members. In addition there is an annual business meeting. In 1988 this was held in November in New York City during a one-day conference sponsored by the Children's Book Council, with Katherine Paterson as the speaker. Dianne Monson was installed as President, Margaret McElderry was elected Vice-President and President-elect, and Divna Todorova was elected to the Board.

During the year a number of committees were at work selecting: the United States entry for the Rising Sun Award sponsored by the Japanese section of IBBY; the U.S. entries for the Janusz Korczak Literature Prize given by the Polish Section of IBBY; suggestion for books that might be used in a set of films to be made by Alan Sloan featuring books of many countries; the U.S. entries for the next Biannale D'Illustrations Bratislava (BIB) and books to be sent to a documentation center in Norway that draws together books for both children and adults on children with disabilities.

A committee considered the possibility of preparing in the United States a work that would discuss all of the winners of the international Hans Christian Andersen Award, which is presented by IBBY to an author and an illustrator every two years. A USBBY committee selects the U.S. nominees for this award. The most recent committee, under the leadership of Barbara Elleman, not only selected the U.S. entries for the 1988 award, which was given in Oslo, but also arranged for certificates to be prepared for current and previous U.S. winners. Certificates will be presented to all future U.S. authors and illustrators who represent the United States in this international competition.

USBBY presented its second Ezra Jack Keats Award in 1988. This award, co-sponsored with UNICEF and funded by the Ezra Jack Keats Foundation, goes to a young illustrator, who has not illustrated more than five children's books or worked in the field for more than five years. Barbara Reed of Canada, the 1988 winner, recieved the $5,000 prize. The U.S. entrant, Leslie Baker, whose first book *The Third Story Cat* was published in 1987, received one of the three honor awards. Twenty-two sections of the *IBBY* participated in the 1988 competition.

USBBY publishes a newsletter twice a year that updates the membership on both USBBY and IBBY activities. IBBY publishes a quarterly journal, *Bookbird*, which is available in the United States through EBSCO.

Biennial Congress. "Children's Literature and the New Media" was the theme of the 1988 biennial congress, which was held in Oslo, Norway. The United States will host the IBBY congress for the first time in Williamsburg, Virginia, September 2–7, 1990. The general theme of the congress will be "Literacy Through Literature; Children's Books Make a Difference."

For further information about USBBY, write the USBBY Secretariat, International Reading Association, P.O. Box 8139, Newark, Delaware 19714.

JEAN E. KARL

Universal Bibliographic Control

Core Programs. Through its Core Programmes, IFLA (International Federation of Library Associations and Institutions) seeks to provide practical means for the advancement of international library cooperation. In 1988, IFLA's Universal Bibliographic Control and International MARC [UBCIM] Programme continued to be managed by the British Library (London) under the professional guidance of IFLA. It is funded by contributions from national libraries and by sales of its publications, and it is advised by a committee composed of representatives of IFLA and the Conference of Directors of National Libraries [CDNL]. The concept of UBC is closely linked to that of UAP (Universal Availability of Publications), which is also promoted by IFLA.

In 1988, Universal Bibliographic Control continued to be concerned with standardization of bibliographic description and authority control in catalog systems. It promoted cataloging-in-publication, legal deposit, and standard numbering (ISBNs for books and ISSNs for serials). It also promoted the cause of national bibliographic agencies and networks in all countries. By the establishment of standards and guidelines for professional practice, it worked to facilitate the free exchange and interpretation of bibliographic information among countries and across language barriers. In 1988, the increasing pace of automation in libraries, and the growth and falling costs of new information media, permitted libraries in both the industrialized and developing world to benefit from technological decentralization and to gain local access to more stored knowledge than before. Universal Bibliographic Control took account of the telecommunications revolution.

International MARC [Machine-Readable Cataloguing] activities in 1988 were concerned with promoting applications of the UNIMARC format. This was originally developed (on the initiative of CDNL) for the exchange of machine-readable bibliographic records between national bibliographic agencies, but during 1988 it was increasingly adopted by national libraries as a national format, and by smaller special libraries. Records in UNIMARC format can now be output by various software packages, and are available on many CD-ROM products. The UBCIM Programme held a well-attended UNIMARC Workshop during the 1988 IFLA Conference in Sydney, Australia.

Publications. The Programme's long-established journal, *International Cataloguing & Bibliographic Control* [ICBC] continued during 1988 to report on developments in bibliographic control and MARC networks from an international perspective, by means of news items and authoritative articles. The new revised edition of the *International Standard Bibliographic Description for Serials* was published in 1988. It was prepared by members of a review committee chaired by Lucia Rather of the Library of Congress. The long-awaited publication *Guidelines for the Application of the ISBDs to the Description of Component Parts* aims to meet the needs of libraries and A&I [abstracting and indexing] services. It covers the analytical description of a chapter, article, track of a record, or part of any whole unit for which a bibliographic record would ordinarily be made. Prepared by an IFLA Committee chaired by Tom Delsey of the National Library of Canada, *Component Parts* gives makers of analytical descriptions a degree of flexibility as to descriptive elements and punctuation. In 1982, IFLA began discussions with the International Development Research Centre [IDRC] on ways in which the IDRC's MINISIS software might be enhanced to allow it to generate bibliographic records in modified UNIMARC format. The result was the *MINISIS/UNIMARC Project: Final Report* by the consultant, Elaine W. Woods, published by the UBCIM Programme in 1988, in its Occasional Papers series. The interface given in this document aroused worldwide interest. A major publication during 1988 was the *Proceedings of the National Bibliographies Seminar*," edited by W.D. Roberts. This seminar was held during the 1987 IFLA Conference in Brighton, United Kingdom, to mark the tenth anniversary of the 1977 UNESCO-sponsored International Congress on National Bibliographies. The contributors to the Seminar analysed the progress made in the production of national bibliographies in both the industrialized and the developing countries, and point the way forward.

OTHER PROJECTS

UNIMARC Authorities. The UNIMARC Format for Authorities, a project sponsored by the IFLA Section on Cataloguing and the Section on Information Technology, has developed a UNIMARC format specifying a record structure and data element definitions for the exchange of machine-readable authority records for personal and corporate names, and uniform titles. In 1988, the project Steering Group, chaired by Christine Bossmeyer of the Deutsche Bibliothek (FRG), circulated a final draft for public comment. The final text will be published by the UBCIM Programme early in 1989.

Subject Authorities. An international working group of the IFLA Section on Classification and Indexing is developing draft Guidelines for Subject Authority Files, based on the 1984 UBCIM publication *Guidelines for Authority and Reference Entries*. Work continued in 1988,

Universal Serials and Book Exchange

chaired by Barbara Kelm of the Deutsche Bibliothek. A progress report will be made to the 1989 IFLA Conference in Paris.

ISBD(PM). Review of the 1980 edition of the ISBD(PM) (printed music) continued in 1988. Heinz Lanzke of the Deutsche Bibliothek was chairperson of the joint IAML/IFLA review group. A final draft was prepared for publication by the UBCIM Programme in 1989.

ISBD(A). Work on a revision of the 1980 edition of the ISBD(A) (antiquarian) continued under a review group chaired by Richard Christophers of the British Library. A draft text was circulated for public comment. The final text is expected to be published in 1989.

ISBD(CF). At the same time as well-established ISBD texts were being reviewed, the appearance of new types of material in library collections led to a demand for descriptive guidelines. Collections of published machine-readable products, both data files and software, presented their own special problems of description and identification. A working group, under John Byrum of the Library of Congress, which had studied existing proposals and drawn up a draft ISBD text, continued work on this during 1988 with the assistance of the UBCIM office. Publication of the new ISBD(CF) for computer files is expected in mid-1989.

Standard Practices. The UBCIM Programme commissioned Dorothy Anderson, formerly Director of the Programme, to prepare a revised and updated version of her 1982 book *Standard Practices in the Preparation of Bibliographic Records*. This was completed and will be published early in 1989 in the series of UBCIM Occasional Papers.

Authority Files Survey. With the approval of the Coordinating Board of the IFLA Division of Bibliographic Control, a major survey of the current international provision and use of name authority files was launched in 1988. It is being conducted by Marcelle Beaudiquez and Françoise Bourdon of the Bibliothèque Nationale, Paris, with the assistance of the UBCIM Programme Officer, W.D. Roberts. A questionnaire was drawn up for circulation to national bibliographic agencies, and an interim report will be presented at the 1989 IFLA Conference in Paris.

In addition to the above projects, further discussions took place on the future direction and role of the UBCIM Programme, in the context of the development of OPACs (online public access catalogs) and OSI (open systems interconnection).

The Programme Officer will answer queries on the professional content of the UBCIM Programme. Continuing emphasis will be placed on the Programme's coordination and publishing role. Current publications may be obtained from the Publications Officer, UBCIM Programme, c/o British Library Bibliographic Services, 2 Sheraton Street, London W1V 4BH, United Kingdom.

WINSTON D. ROBERTS

Universal Serials and Book Exchange

USEB's 40th year. In 1988, the Universal Serials and Book Exchange Inc. (USBE), marked its 40th year of service to the library community. The success of USBE as a reliable and cost-effective clearinghouse and redistribution center for periodicals and books is reflected in the approximately 16,000,000 items redistributed since 1948.

Responding to the changing needs of its membership, USBE has continued to develop in new directions and provide new services. New emphasis has been placed on USBE's potential role as a document delivery service. Increased contact with corporate libraries and research institutions have been designed to develop awareness of the USBE collection as a service of "on demand" documents. Also, in 1988, some progress was made toward a long-held goal of developing a machine-readable holdings record of a select portion of the USBE collection. Next year promises to provide more development in this area. Two new services were offered to USBE members in 1988. A "Bulletin Board" service provides members with an opportunity to list collections they wish to sell in the USBE newsletter (*USBE/NEWS*). USBE now has a toll-free number for telephone rush requests.

Membership. USBE membership in 1988 consisted of 902 libraries and educational organizations around the world. There were 769 members in the United States and 133 members in 37 other countries. Consortiums, which account for 107 members, provides an opportunity for smaller or more specialized libraries to receive the benefits of USBE membership and access to the 4,000,000 items in the collection. New consortium groups joining USBE in 1988 included: Capital District Library Council (17 members), Research Triangle Park Consortium (4 members), and the Consortium of Universities of the Washington Metropolitan Area (11 members). USBE's marketing endeavors continued to emphasize personal contact with members and potential members through exhibiting at the ALA Annual Conference and Midwinter Meeting and the SLA and MLA meetings. Dr. Howard Rovelstadt represented USBE at the IFLA Conference in Sydney, Australia.

Management. Claude L. Hooker, Managing Director; H. Gerald Phillips, Director of Membership Services, and Robert L. Hodges, Business Manager, directed USBE through a sometimes difficult 1988. This stability in management was especially important in a year in which changing library purchasing patterns resulted in reduced income and tighter budgetary restrictions for USBE. The active participation of the Board of Directors was again essential to USBE operations. President Pat Molholt, Vice-President Agnes M. Griffen, and Treasurer Sharon Rogers worked closely with the USBE staff to develop policies necessary for the future of the organization. Particularly important was their assistance in negotiating a new lease agreement for USBE's warehouse space, thereby insuring a smooth continuation of operations for the near future.

Board of Directors. Under the leadership of Pat Molholt, Associate Director of Libraries, Rensselaer Institute of Technology, the 1988 USBE Board of Directors comprised Past-President Martin Runkle, Director, University of Chicago Library; Vice-President/President-elect Agnes

M. Griffen, Director, Department of Libraries, Montgomery County Maryland Government; Treasurer Sharon J. Rogers University Librarian, George Washington University; and Secretary Helen C. Wiltse Associate Director of Libraries, Georgia Institute of Technology. Members of the Board were Peter Bridge, Chief, Cataloging in Publications Division, Library of Congress; Joyce D. Gartrell, Head, Serials Cataloging, Columbia University Library; Charlota C. Hensley, Assistant Director for Research and Development, University of Colorado at Boulder Libraries; Sharon A. Hogan, Director of Libraries, Louisiana State University; Ellen Hoffman, Director of Libraries, York University; Susan J. Cote, Library Director, Case Western Reserve University. Members of the Executive Committee and Board of Directors are elected annually for two-year terms by USBE member institutions.

CLAUDE L. HOOKER

Urban Libraries Council

A capacity audience attended the annual meeting of the Urban Libraries Council in New Orleans July 9, to hear a panel of outstanding public library administrators address the subject, "An Agenda for Urban Public Libraries for the Nineties."

Marilyn G. Mason, director, Cleveland Public Library, considered the Federal role in funding urban public libraries; Richard De Gennaro, director, New York Public Library, presented an overview of library technology; Thomas E. Alford, assistant city librarian, Los Angeles Public Library, reviewed urban populations' service problems; and Clarence R. Walters, OCLC program officer for State and Public Libraries, discussed relationships between urban public libraries and state library agencies.

Ronald A. Dubberly, director, Atlanta-Fulton Public Library, and chair, ULC Planning Committee, moderated the program and summarized the results of a recent ULC survey on major problems and successes of urban public libraries.

As an outcome of the panel discussion, audience interaction and survey results, the Executive Board of ULC established a Legislative Committee to prepare recommendations for the Urban Libraries Council in anticipation of the mandated forthcoming White House Conference. Robert C. Wilburn, President, Board of Trustees, Carnegie Library of Pittsburgh, was appointed Committee Chair.

Complimentary copies of *Statistical Report '88* were distributed during the year to Urban Libraries Council members in appreciation for their cooperation in making possible the publication of urban libraries statistics. This new publication, to be compiled and published annually by the Public Library Association, is a result of the Public Library Project, a cooperative venture of the Public Library Association, the Chief Officers of State Library Agencies, and the Urban Libraries Council.

As in previous years, a meeting of the ULC Board of Directors was held in Washington D.C. during National Library Week, permitting members of the Board to visit their elected representatives in support of increased funding for the Library Services and Construction Act.

New Directors elected by the membership at the Annual Meeting included James R. Dawe, trustee, San Diego Public Library; Ronald A. Dubberly, director, Atlanta-Fulton Public Library; Kenneth F. Duchac, Ellicott City, Maryland; Stephanie Tubbs Jones, trustee, Cleveland Public Library; Joseph W. Lippincott, Jr., Nokomis, Florida; Samuel F. Morrison, assistant commissioner, Chicago Public Library; and Patricia F. Turner, trustee, Baltimore County Public Library.

The Urban Libraries Council is an affiliated member of the American Library Association.

KEITH DOMS

Video in Libraries

In many ways, 1988 was a watershed year for video in libraries. As VCR penetration hit the 60 percent mark in our nation's homes, more than 60 percent of our libraries offered videos to their patrons; and in libraries that served populations of 25,000 or above, the percentage carrying video broached 80 percent. Clearly, video in libraries has arrived.

But with that arrival has come a host of new problems and concerns for librarians. And, with the "newness" of video beginning to erode, 1988 brought a steady barrage of questions from all corners about issues as practical as processing and as far-reaching in their philosophical implications as access by minors.

The Outside Challenge. One brief skirmish during the first quarter of the year resulted in the subject of video in libraries making headlines across the country. On March 31, the Heartland Institute, an independent think-tank group out of Chicago, released a 27-page report entitled: *The Private Video Library: A Bright Beginning, An Uncertain Future.* Written by William B. Irvine, an assistant professor of philosophy at Wright State College (Dayton, Ohio), the brief monograph charged that the video store owner's livelihood was being threatened by the growing number of public libraries who were offering videos to their patrons. Poorly reasoned, and rather absurd in a number of its charges, the report was picked up by the Scripps Howard national wire service.

Responses came from Eleanor Jo Rodger, Executive Director of the Public Library Association (PLA), Sally Mason, Director of the ALA-Carnegie Video Project; and Randy Pitman, Edi-

---

URBAN LIBRARIES COUNCIL

PRESIDENT (June 1987–June 1989):
Paulette H. Holahan, New Orleans, Louisiana

VICE-PRESIDENT:
Phil Dessauer, Tulsa, Oklahoma

SECRETARY:
Donald J. Sager, Milwaukee, Wisconsin

TREASURER:
Roslyn S. Kurland, Hollywood, Florida

EXECUTIVE DIRECTOR:
Keith Doms

Membership (December 1988): 183 public libraries
Headquarters: 3101 W. Coulter St., Philadelphia, Pennsylvania 19129

tor of Video Librarian. Although the furor died down rather quickly, the article was read by a number of video store owners nationwide, and ill feelings were exacerbated between video stores and libraries.

The ALA-Carnegie Video Project. In post- and preconferences at PLA and ALA, the workshop "Fast Forward: Video Collections and Public Libraries" addressed standing-room only crowds of librarians. Headed by Sally Mason, the other workshop speakers included: Irene Wood, Non-Print Editor of Booklist; James C. Scholtz, General Consultant/AV Services at the Northern Illinois Library System and author of Developing and Maintaining Video Collections in Libraries; and Randy Pitman, Editor of Video Librarian. The agenda included talks on selection standards and sources, acquisitions, collection development, circulation and security, access by minors, censorship, copyright, budgeting, and new technology.

Two ALA-Carnegie Video Project videocassettes premiered: The Librarian's Video Primer: Establishing and Maintaining Your Video Collection (written by Randy Pitman, and produced by the Georgia Library Video Association) and Fast Forward: Libraries and the Video Revolution (written by Kathy Coster and produced by the Library Video Network).

In addition to the talks, three mini-sessions were held on the subjects of charging for video, blanket licensing, and marketing the library video collection. During the conferences, Baker & Taylor provided continuous video screenings for attendees.

The other major contribution of the ALA-Carnegie Video Project appeared at year's end: Video For Libraries: Special Interest Videos for Small and Medium-sized Public Libraries. This book, edited by Sally Mason and James C. Scholtz, had the distinction of being the first book dealing with the subject of video in libraries to appear in print. Developing and Maintaining Video Collections in Libraries by James C. Scholtz would be the second, appearing in December.

Selection Tools. The amount of space devoted to audiovisual material reviews, in general, continued to be disproportionate to the space allotted to print material reviews—though steps are now being taken to close the gap. The primary review sources continue to be Booklist, Library Journal, and School Library Journal in the general library literature. Booklist, with its "Home Video for Libraries" column has been the frontrunner in responding to the need for more reviews of videocassettes. Library Journal has announced plans to increase its coverage for 1989.

In the area of specialized literature, the monthly newsletter Video Librarian entered its third year of publication with an expanded review section; and Librarians' Video Review, a quarterly edited by James C. Scholtz, continued to offer more reviews per issue than any other publication.

At library conferences around the country, the consensus has been that a new library periodical devoted to the whole range of audiovisual materials was sorely needed, and 1989 might well see such a publication.

Vendors. Any new service brings a host of new vendors into the library market, and video has been no exception. Numerous fly-by-night distributors have sprung up to sell videocassettes to libraries at anywheres from full retail to full retail plus 400 percent.

Earlier, libraries did quite a bit of business with Commtron, the largest supplier of prerecorded videocassettes to the commercial market. But, recently, librarians have looked to the traditional library vendors who are more receptive to and conscious of the special requirements of the library market. Two vendors that have garnered the lion's share of public library video business, and were actively involved in supporting the ALA-Carnegie Video Project were: Baker & Taylor and Ingram.

Both companies maintain large stocks of special-interest videos which non-traditional library suppliers, such as Commtron, do not ordinarily stock. Both companies have also been very helpful with setting up defective returns policies.

The Marketplace. The library market, with its share of more than $20,000,000 in video purchases, is slowly but surely coming to the attention of video manufacturers who are becoming aware of libraries as a lucrative, and largely untapped, market. With the increased interest on the part of home video producers, educational video producers had to revise their marketing strategies to be able to compete with the growing number of "low-priced" videos on the market.

Prices continue to plummet from an average of $400 per program in 1988 to under $100. The CPB/Annenburg Project, working in conjunction with ALA under the guidance of Sally Mason, released the highly-acclaimed Voices and Visions series on American poets at the rock-bottom price of $29.95 per episode. Included in the price were full public performance rights.

And, in a major promotion, PBS Video dropped prices on a number of excellent programs, including such renowned series as "This Old House," "Spaceflight," "Out of the Fiery Furnace," and "The Ring of Truth." Prices ranged anywhere from $39.95 to $79.95. Libraries purchasing more than 100 titles were charged $30 per title. According to Laura Browse, at PBS, the library response was overwhelming. PBS plans to release more titles at lowered prices in the coming year.

On the home video front, several distributors continued to branch out into the special-interest market, providing librarians with an increased range of programming choices. Vestron Video added the NOVA series to its highly successful National Geographic video line, and by year's end were planning to release programming from the National Audobon Society. Mystic Fire Video, another independent, acquired the rights to Bill Moyers' series of interviews with Joseph Campbell: "The Power of Myth," which they're selling at $29.95 per episode. And LCA video continued to release high-quality children's educational programming in the $14.95 to $19.95 price range.

Issues in Video Librarianship. The PLA and ALA video workshops presented the first opportunity for librarians to get together and discuss issues that have arisen with the addition of video to libraries. Primary among those concerns were whether to charge for video, whether to open the entire collection to minors, and mass confusion over what is meant by "public performance" as it relates to libraries.

The "fee vs. free" debate is neither new nor specifically limited to videocassettes, but it has come to the fore in this area (rather than, say, copy machines) because of several factors: (1) high visibility, (2) the similarity to video stores, and (3) the occasionally staggering amount of money involved. Library patrons, by and large, are not terribly concerned about paying for checking out videos; they've become accustomed to doing so at the video stores. But armchair philosophers in libraryland have turned a skeptical eye towards the fee issue and raised some pretty unsettling questions.

The main fear is that a $100,000 shot in the budgetary arm from videocassette rentals could very well have an effect on materials selection. If the public is primarily interested in popular feature films (and these titles generate the most revenue), would it not be possible for librarians to focus their attention on providing the hits, while passing over some of the less saleable titles? Many libraries have discontinued charging for videos, but a number still charge, and the controversy continues.

Another hot topic is whether to let minors have unregulated access to the entire video collection. The arguing camps, as on many other issues, have split into the idealistic and the practical. Idealists quote the Library Bill of Rights and the ALA Freedom to View Statement as their backing for total access by everyone. The practical camp points out that the MPAA ratings system is understood and accepted by everyone, and that many local legislatures have forced commercial video stores to tighten up on their access to R-rated movies by young children.

The real issue, of course, revolves around the unique nature of visual media as compared to print materials. Print offers a natural barrier—language—to children. Visual media, on the other hand, requires no special training to decode. Children may not understand what's being shown on the screen, but they are able to process the images, for better or worse. (Unless a child can read, words are merely squiggles and carry no meaning.)

In many cases, the battle has resulted in libraries that bar access but buy across the whole range of video materials available; or libraries who have open access, but are very selective about the video titles they purchase. Neither of these situations is ideal.

A relatively recent, but already highly charged, issue to appear on the library front is the question of public performances in a library. Several libraries with study carrels and/or viewing rooms have received cease-and-desist letters from Hollywood studios, concerning the showings of copyrighted feature films in public libraries. The question is not so much whether a library can show a Disney video and invite the general public, but whether a patron can watch a video on the library premises. A small but powerful cottage industry exists in order to sell to libraries, among other institutions, blanket or umbrella licenses that allow libraries to show feature videos for an annual fee. Representatives of both Films Inc. and the MPLC spoke at PLA and ALA this year to a group of suspicious and confused librarians. It is uncertain whether any real questions were answered, but there's no question that the "public performance" issue will become a major one in 1989.

Video Saga. Several strong developments emerged in the video in libraries saga in 1988, including the publication of the first books on the subject and the appearance of seminars and workshops at both PLA and ALA, where in previous years there had been only silence.

Prices on video materials continued to decline as the range of programming grew wider. With the novelty of video beginning to fade, librarians began to focus more attention on building video collections that did not duplicate what was already available on the corner store. Controversial issues, such as "fee vs. free," access by minors, and public performance, came out of the closet into the arena of open discussion.

If 1988 proved to be an eventful year, 1989 promises to be even more volatile as more libraries become involved in the most exciting new service in public libraries since the introduction of the paperback book.

RANDY PITMAN

Washington Report

The 100th Congress adjourned on October 22, two months earlier than last year and reflecting a last-minute urgency with the national election a little more than two weeks away. Altogether 11,282 legislative measures were introduced during the two sessions of this Congress, but only 713 became public law, and of those only a couple dozen held implications or direct benefits for libraries and librarians.

For the first time since 1977, Congress completed action on all 13 appropriations bills before the beginning of the new fiscal year, October 1. This was due mainly to the two-year budget summit agreement made between the White House and Congress in the fall of 1987. Funds for the two categorical federal library grant programs, the Library Services and Construction Act and the Higher Education Act (HEA) Title II activities, amounted to $137,200,000, 1.6 percent above last year's $135,089,000. Unfortunately, the combination of lack of grass roots support for the HEA II-B library training and research program and the complicated budget allocation compromises has taken its toll. HEA II-B funds slipped in the last two years from $1,000,000 to $709,000. Back in the late '60s, $8,250,000 was appropriated for training alone.

Despite passage of a new elementary-secondary education law (PL 100-297) in the spring, with more emphasis on the school library program, it still remains part of the Chapter 2 block grant which provides no guarantees that any federal funds will actually be spent for local school library purposes. Exacerbating the situation and demonstrating the vulnerability of block grants was the Senate's consideration of FY 1989 education appropriations. The House had approved $517,430,000 for chapter 2, but by the

Washington Report

time the Senate finished siphoning funds from it and earmarking the dollars to pay for other favored programs, $41,000,000 had been taken away. Conference negotiations and later budget cuts finally settled on $491,728,000—$12,400,000 less than the FY 1988 appropriation.

Even though action on appropriations advanced at a relatively fast pace, the various stages between House and Senate consideration were tortuous, requiring a constant balancing act between the provisions of the Gramm-Rudman-Hollings deficit reduction law and the Congressional-White House budget summit agreement. Especially noteworthy among appropriations was the $8,000,000 increase for the preservation program at the National Endowment for the Humanities, which prevailed due to the strong leadership of Representative Sid Yates (D-IL) on the Appropriations Committee backed up by Representative Pat Williams (D-MT) on the Budget Committee.

WHCLIS II. At last—after three and a half years of cliff-hanging—legislation calling for a second White House Conference on Library and Information Services (H.J.Res. 90) finally had the differences between House and Senate versions resolved, was signed by President Reagan on August 8, 1988, and is now Public Law 100-382. However, the law surfaced too late to obtain funding for its $6,000,000 authorization. So, winning an appropriation to implement the conference process was a high priority after the 101st Congress convened in 1989. Meanwhile, those who are interested in participating in the process wrote to their U.S. Representative or Senators, indicating their concern for libraries and the need for greater public awareness and support, in order to serve their respective clienteles better.

The purpose of WHCLIS is to develop recommendations for the further improvement of library and information services of the nation. The "whereas" clauses set forth ideas to indicate a possible range of issues to be considered during

Table 1. Fiscal Year 1989 Budget Appropriations for Library and Related Programs (Dollars in thousands)

Library Programs	FY 1988 Appropriation	FY 1989 Budget	FY 1989 House	FY 1989 Senate	FY 1989 Appropriation
Elementary and Secondary Education Act I					
Chapter 2 (includes school libraries)	$ 504,131	$ 567,500[1]	$ 517,430	$ 476,000	$ 491,728
GPO Superintendent of Documents	24,662	26,800	25,155	25,155	25,155
Higher Education Act	10,052	0[2]	10,262	10,052	10,079
Title II-A, College Libraries	0	0	0	0	0
II-B, Training and Research	718	0	718	718	709
II-C, Research Libraries	5,744	0	5,744	5,744	5,675
II-D, Technology	3,590	0	3,800	3,590	3,651
Library of Congress	247,971	274,198	256,883	257,278	257,278
Library Services and Construction Act	125,037	0[2]	132,382	125,037	127,165
Title I, Public Library Services	78,986	0	85,000	78,986	81,009
II, Public Library Construction	22,595	0	22,595	22,595	22,324
III, Interlibrary Cooperation	18,669	0	20,000	18,669	19,102
IV, Indian Library Services		(funded at 2%	of appropriations	for LSCA I, II & III)	
V, Foreign Language Materials	0	0	0	0	0
VI, Library Literacy Programs	4,787	0	4,787	4,787	4,730
Medical Library Assistance Act	9,414	9,790	deferred	9,790	9,673
National Agricultural Library	12,194	13,599	13,446	14,682	13,268[3]
National Commission on Libraries and Information Science	718	755	750	750	741
National Library of Medicine	58,496	60,836	64,836	60,836	64,058
Library Related Programs					
Adult Education Act	134,036	150,000	166,754	167,180	162,210
Bilingual, Immigrant, Refugee Education	191,751	200,504	201,782	197,009	199,791
ESEA Ch. 1 (Disadvantaged Students)	4,327,927	4,566,084	4,663,719	4,589,800	4,570,246
Educationally Handicapped Children (state grants)	1,431,737	1,474,239	1,478,539	1,508,200	1,475,449
Educational Research	46,573	51,531	50,343	44,960	47,079
HEA title III, Developing Institutions	152,370	136,978	180,000	169,978	174,577
IV-C, College Work Study	588,249	600,014	635,000	600,014	610,097
VI, International Education	25,419	25,419	25,419	25,419	25,114
National Archives and Records Administration	112,000	117,862	121,962	113,862	117,900
National Center for Education Statistics	20,953	32,869[1]	33,169	29,500	31,122
National Endowment for the Arts	167,731	167,731	169,000	168,631	169,090
National Endowment for the Humanities	140,435	140,435	153,700	144,235	153,000
National Historical Publication and Records Commission	4,000	0	4,000	4,000	4,000
Postal revenue forgone subsidy	517,001	19,023[4]	436,417	436,417	436,417
Postsecondary Education Improvement Fund	11,645	13,645	13,645	11,645	11,856
Science and Math Education	119,675	119,675	119,675	139,000	137,332
Star Schools	19,148	0	19,148	10,000	14,399
VISTA Literacy Corps	2,872	0	2,872	2,872	2,838
Women's Educational Equity	3,351	0	3,351	2,620	2,985

[1]Request revised following enactment of School Improvement Act.
[2]Administration proposed $76,000,000 Library Improvement Act to replace LSCA and HEA II.
[3]Congress approved $14,268,000, but by error, the amount signed into law was $13,268,000.
[4]Free mail for blind and overseas voters only.

the Conference which is to be held between September 1, 1989 and September 30, 1991. In order to give the States sufficient time to carry on their own Governors' conferences and/or other meetings to gain maximum attention for their respective services, resources, and needs and to provide input for the national Conference, it is most likely that, the White House Conference will not be held before the fall of 1991.

Participants in WHCLIS, according to the law, are to be one-fourth library and information professionals, one-fourth active library and information supporters (including trustees and friends groups), one-fourth government officials, and one-fourth general public.

The conference is to be planned and carried out under the direction of the National Commission on Libraries and Information Science (NCLIS) which is to be assisted and advised in planning and conducting the Conference by a 30-member advisory committee broadly representative of all areas of the United States. In addition to the Secretary of Education and the Librarian of Congress, eight members are to be designated by the NCLIS Chairman; five by the Speaker of the House; five by the President pro tempore of the Senate; and ten by the President.

By the end of the year, more than 20 of the 30 appointments had been made. The first three were Senate designees: Joan Ress Reeves of Rhode Island, an ALA and American Library Trustees Association (ALTA) member and the new Chair of the White House Conference on Library and Information Services Taskforce (WHCLIST); Rebecca Ann Floyd, a lawyer from Jackson, Mississippi, Executive Director of MS Protection and Advocacy System, Director of Client Assistance Program for the Blind, and past Chair, Friends of Handicapped Readers; and Richard G. Akeroyd, Jr., Connecticut State Librarian and ALA member. House appointments were Representatives William Ford (Democrat–Michigan), Pat Williams (Democrat–Montana), and Major Owens (Democrat–New York); Nelwyn Murphy, mayor of Booneville, Mississippi, and a library trustee; and Virginia Young of Columbia, Missouri, an honorary ALA member, trustee, and current member of the ALA Legislation Committee. NCLIS appointees include three members of the Commission: Chairman Jerald Newman, Daniel Casey, and Daniel Carter, plus Margaret Chisholm, ALA Immediate Past President; Carmencita Leon, WHCLIST member from Puerto Rico; Hugh Mahoney, Office of the County Executive, Mineola, New York, and Kenneth Tomlinson, Executive Editor of *Reader's Digest* and former NCLIS Chair. President Reagan named half of his appointees: Louis Barnett of California, Director of Citizens for the Republic; William Cassell, President of Heidelberg College, Tiffin, Ohio; Gloria Hom, Chair of the Economics Department, Mission College, Santa Clara, California; Mary Jane Martinez, First Lady of Florida and former School media specialist; James C. Roberts of Virginia, President of the American Studies Center in Washington, D.C.; and Eileen Schouweiler of Nevada, representing the general public.

The White House announced two more appointments on January 18, 1989: Stuart Forth, Director Emeritus of Libraries, Pennsylvania State University, and Jerry Parr, former Secret Service Agent now in private security.

Year of the Young Reader. On December 5, President Reagan proclaimed 1989 as Year of the Young Reader and called upon parents and educators, librarians and publishers, and all Americans to observe the year with appropriate programs, ceremonies, and activities. Among other things, he said

> We can all help young readers discover the blessings and the enjoyment that reading offers. Parents can read aloud to their children. Families and schools can make reading materials a familiar part of youngsters' surroundings and can suggest regular visits to libraries. Educators and concerned citizens can re-double their efforts to ensure that students remain in school and that literacy programs for people of all ages are available in their areas. Each of us can give young people the good example of reading ourselves. We can explain the freedom we Americans enjoy to read and write and study as we like.

The entire text of the proclamation is on page 49291 of the December 7, 1988, *Federal Register*.

EILEEN D. COOKE

Women in Librarianship

COSWL. For COSWL, ALA's standing Committee on the Status of Women in Librarianship, 1988 was a noteworthy year. The Committee was awarded a 1988/89 World Book/ALA Goal Award to gather oral histories of minority women librarians. *Minority Women Librarians' Personal Perspectives on Librarianship* aims to identify, interview, and compile for publication the personal experiences, reminiscences, and perspectives of minority women and the impact these experiences have had on librarianship. During 1988 COSWL members also produced a new edition of *Sexual Harassment on the Job*, the *Directory of Library and Information Profession's Women's Groups*, and a sequel (1982–86) to *On Account of Sex: An Annotated Bibliography on the Status of Women in Librarianship 1977–81*.

Salary Surveys. In their annual report on placements and salaries, Carol Learmont and Stephen Van Houten (*Library Journal*, October 15, 1987) reported that an upswing in salaries continued during 1987 with the average beginning salary increasing $1,373 or 7 percent over 1986. 1987 was the fifth year that the increase in the average beginning salary was higher than the increase in the cost of living. The average beginning salary for women was $22,045, a 6 percent increase over 1986; for men, $23,013, a 7 percent increase, for a difference of $968. The average beginning salary was higher for men in all types of libraries (difference ranging from $722 to $4,056) but special libraries where women's average beginning salary was $110 more than men's. In 1987, the range of starting salaries was greater for men ($13,000–$72,000), a difference of $59,000, than for women ($9,500–$44,000), a difference of $34,500. The median salary for all 1987 graduates was $21,116, an increase of $1,116 over the

Pay Equity in Minnesota

During the past few years, the State of Minnesota has made giant strides toward achieving pay equity for public employees, including library personnel. Late in the 1970s, the job classes in state government were evaluated to determine if job classes with predominantly female incumbents were paid less than job classes with predominantly male incumbents. The results of the evaluation when plotted on a graph (see Figure 1) showed clearly that female-dominated job classes in state government were consistently paid less than male-dominated job classes that were of a comparable value. (Job values had been determined earlier through a state-contracted study conducted by Hay Associates.)

Based on these findings, the Minnesota Legislature, in 1980, passed laws to eliminate sex bias in salaries for state government jobs and authorized supplementary salary funds to implement pay equity, i.e., raise the lower paid predominantly female job classes to the same level as comparably valued predominantly male jobs. It was estimated that elimination of pay disparities would cost ap-

FIGURE 1

Job Classes by Hay Point & Salary

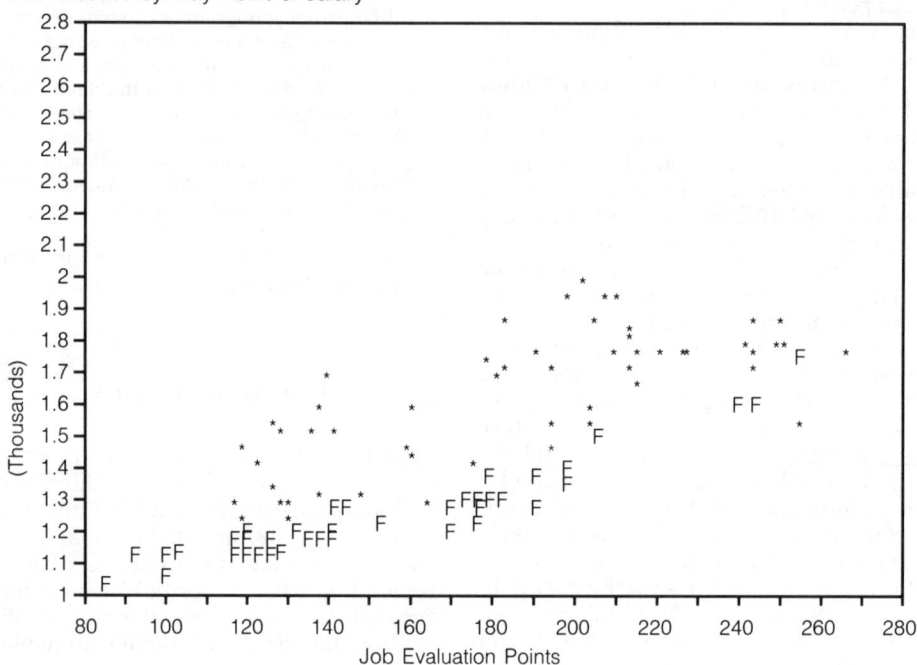

FIGURE 2

Job Classes by Hay Point & Salary

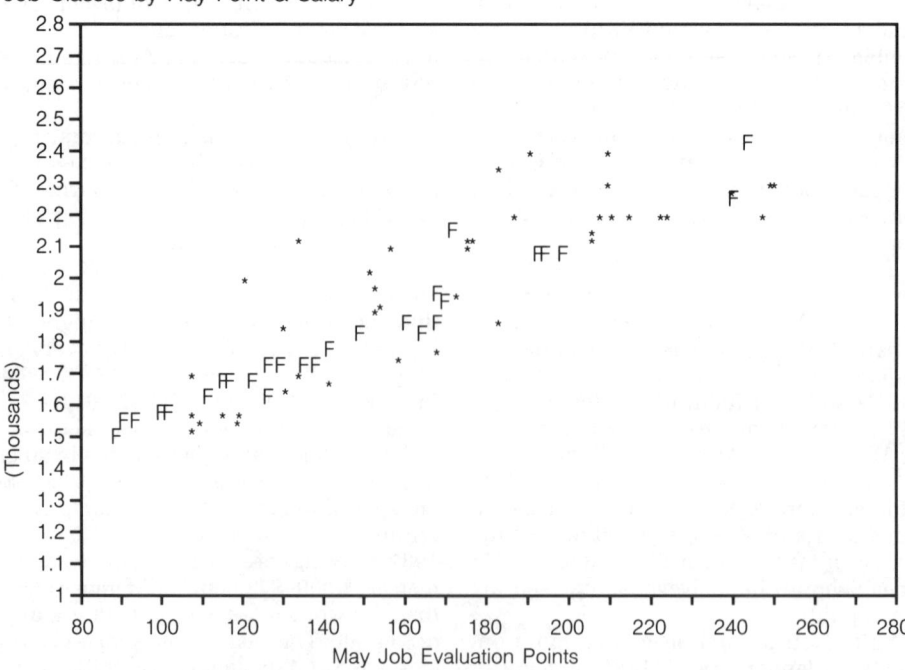

FIGURE 3

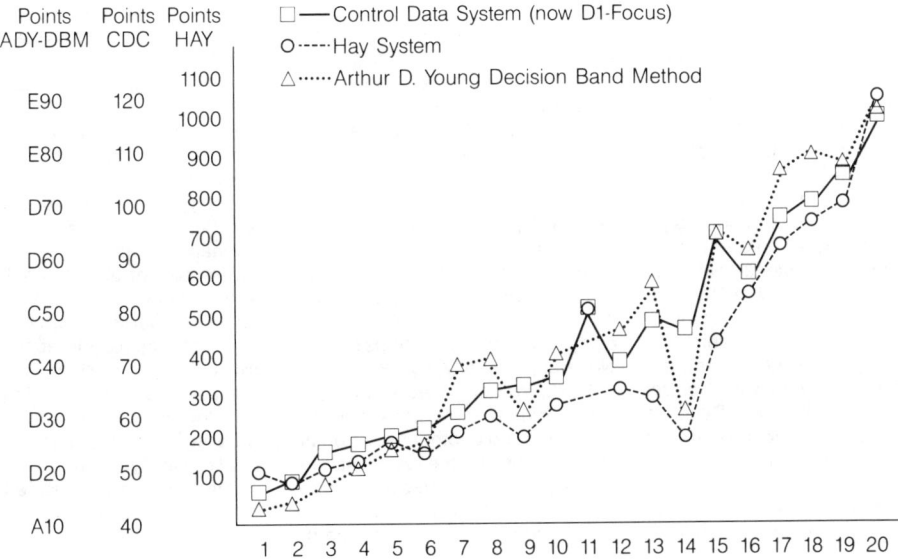

FIGURE 4

Average Points and Recommended Pay as Percent of Library Director Job

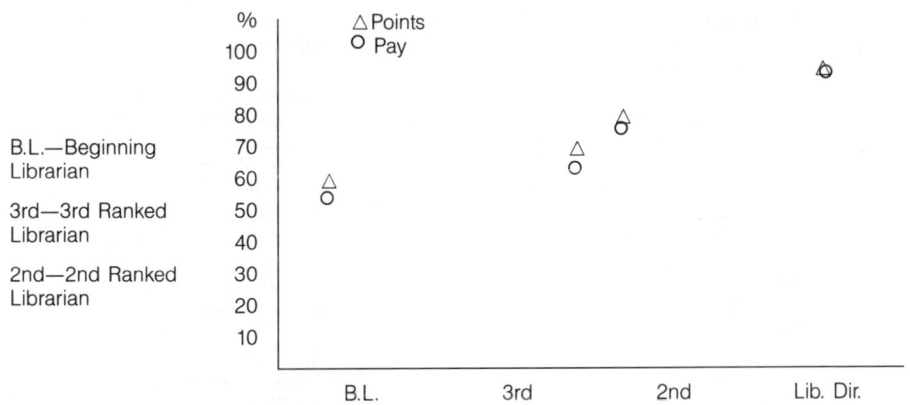

proximately 4 percent of the state's annual payroll. The legislation was implemented and as a result, by 1985, when state jobs were again plotted on a graph (see Figure 2), male and female job classes both followed a similar pattern. The pay disparities noted now are presumed to be a result of market forces or union negotiations rather than sex bias.

Because almost all library jobs in state government were female dominated and underpaid, librarians and other library staff in state agencies all received increases. Since professional librarian jobs in the state universities and community colleges are classified as faculty, a "balanced" class, persons in those job classes did not receive pay equity adjustments. Library support staff in job classes that were predominantly female did receive pay equity increases. The University of Minnesota was not included in the original state study and it subsequently conducted its own evaluation using its own originally designed system. All library positions that were nonfaculty, civil service were found to be underpaid. The plan to establish an equitable salary structure at the University is still being implemented.

As a result of the finding of disparities in pay based on sex in state government employment and the relatively low cost to correct the disparities successfully, the Minnesota Legislature in 1984 passed the Local Government Pay Equity Act. That Act required all political subdivisions of the state (e.g., cities, counties, school districts) to establish equitable compensation relationships between female-dominated, male-dominated, and balanced classes of employees. The law further required each political subdivision to file a report with the State Commissioner of Employee Relations. This report was to include information about job classes, the percentage of females in each class, the comparable work value of each job as determined under a system chosen by the local political subdivisions, the minimum and maximum monthly salary for each class, and the plan for establishing equitable compensation. The reports were to be filed by October 1, 1985. The law also provided that the information in the reports was to be considered private data until July 31, 1987.

In the spring of 1988, staff at the Minnesota Office of Library Development and Services studied the pay equity reports that had been filed by

Women in Librarianship

the political subdivisions that operated public libraries. The purpose of the study was to find out how library jobs had been valued by the various job evaluation systems, to identify inequities in pay, and to determine how library jobs were ranked in relationship to one another.

The study was very difficult to conduct because of the variance in quality of the reports and because many of the largest cities and counties still had not completed their studies. At the time, reports from 67 political subdivisions were analyzed: 52 from cities, 7 from counties, and 8 from regional libraries. These reporting jurisdictions had used different types of job evaluation systems, but most used either the State Job Match (a list of sample city and county job titles, job descriptions, and point values based on the Hay system), the Focus System (created by Control Data Corporation), or the Decision Band Method (developed by Arthur D. Young & Company).

The first finding of the study was that overall the major evaluation systems used by the political subdivisions did appear to value library jobs appropriately. In addition, when the results from the three major job evaluation systems used by cities were listed and plotted on a graph, they all portrayed relatively similar values for similar jobs. (See Figures 3 and 5.)

The second major finding was that the female-dominated library jobs across the board were inadequately compensated in relation to comparably valued male-dominated jobs within the same jurisdiction. The percentage of each inequity identified ranged from 10 percent to over 200 percent. The average cost to the cities and counties to correct their identified pay inequities was only 3.9 percent of payroll. Most jurisdictions planned to establish fully equitable compensation relationships (i.e., implement pay equity) by 1991.

The third finding concerned examination of how library jobs ranked in relation to one another based on the value of jobs and the recommended pay. Again, the universe used to look at this question was small—fewer than 20 libraries. And, because the various job evaluation systems used different methods to determine job values, the only way to compare the different systems was to convert job values into percentages. Figure 4 shows that when the library director job and recommended pay were computed to be 100 percent, the second ranked library position was usually identified to be valued at 80–85 percent of the top job, the third ranked library position was valued at 60–70 percent, and the beginning librarian job was valued at 50 percent.

The process of eliminating pay inequities of public library positions in Minnesota continues and vigilance on the part of all policymakers and employees will be needed for many years in order to assure that equitable compensation is achieved and maintained. It is clear that without the Local Government Pay Equity Act, the effort to identify and eliminate sex-based pay inequities for public employees in Minnesota, especially those in libraries, would have taken decades.

JANICE FEYE-STUKAS

Figure 5. Comparison of Three Job Evaluation Systems

SAMPLE NO.	SAMPLE OF ADY-DBM SYSTEM		SAMPLE OF HAY SYSTEM		CDC FOCUS SYSTEM BENCHMARK JOBS	
1	A12	Clerk Typist	102	Clerk Typist II	47	Clerk Typist (Entry)
2	A11	Laborer	86	Caretaker	51	Laborer
3	A13	Equipment Operator I	136	Maintenance I	53	Light Equipment Operator
4	B21	Accounting Clerk	173	Accounting Clerk II	55	Accounts Payable Clerk
5	B22	Secretary to General Manager	194	Secretary City Manager	56	Department Secretary
6	B22	Bldg. Maintenance II	157	Maintenance II	57	Heavy Equipment Operator
7	C42	Fire Fighter	263	Fire Fighter	64	Fire Fighter
8	C42	Librarian III	275	Branch Librarian	64	Branch Librarian
9	B31	Engineering Technician	150	Engineering Technician II	65	Engineering Technician
10	C42	Police Officer	274	Police Officer	65	Patrol Officer
11	N.A.	Liquor Store Manager	505	Liquor Store Manager	77	Liquor Store Manager
12	C51	Chief Inspector	360	Building Inspector	78	Building Inspector
13	D62	Recreation Director	343	Assistant Director of Recreation	81	Recreation Supervisor
14	B32	Foreman	213	Working Foreman	82	Streets Foreman
15	D62	City Engineer	450	Public Work Superintendent	94	Public Works Supervisor (2nd Level)
16	D64	Library Director	611	Library Director	90	Library Director
17	E81	Fire Chief	716	Fire Chief	99	Fire Chief
18	E82	Police Chief	742	Police Chief	101	Police Chief
19	E81	Finance Director	805	Finance Director	107	Finance Officer
20	E92	City Administrator	1192	City Administrator	124	City Administrator

1986 figure of $20,000. The 1987 median for female graduates without previous experience was $19,486, and for men $23,278; the 1987 median for female graduates with experience (work of a professional and/or subject nature of a year or more) was $24,757 and for men was $24,420. Some of these salary differences may be explained by the types of libraries in which women are employed. Women accounted for 81 percent of the placements in public libraries where 40 percent (44 percent in 1986) of the lowest starting salaries were reported. But they also accounted for 90 percent of the placements in school libraries where 41 percent (39 percent in 1986) of the highest starting salaries were reported. A total of 61,063 positions were listed in 1987, compared with 60,807 in 1986; the demand for children's and young adult specialists continues to be strong as does that for technical service specialists, especially catalogers.

SLA. The Special Library Association has conducted a triennial salary survey since 1967. The survey of SLA members taken in 1988 reported that mean annual salary for Canadian members as $37,079 and for United States members as $34,110 (*SLA Triennial Salary Survey 1989*, November 1988). Females comprised 83 percent of the total responses (2,793) from the United States and 85 percent (356) of the total Canadian responses. Salary data is reported by 25, 50 and 75th percentiles with 50th percentile as the median. Instead of highest and lowest salaries, SLA reports an average of the lowest 10 percent and an average of the highest 10 percent. In every percentile, the salaries reported by women were lower than those reported by men. The mean annual female salary in the United States was $33,374, in Canada, $36,357; the mean annual male salary in the U.S. was $37,766, in Canada $41,286. The U.S. salary differential ranged from $1,806 in the lowest 10 percent to $11,478 in the highest 10 percent while in Canada the differential was $2,767 in the lowest 10 percent and $15,621 in the highest 10 percent. Although salaries in every percentile were lower for women than for men, women experienced the greatest percentage increases. Since 1976 U.S. female salaries have increased 115 percent, compared with 93 percent for males, and in Canada, female salaries have increased 142 percent compared to 112 percent for males. In Canada, the median salary for women with 1–5 years experience exceeds that of men by $3,000; with 6–10 years experience, women's median salary is $428 more than men's. But with 11 or more years experience the median salary for women falls below that of men. In the U.S. the median male salary exceeds that of the median female salary at all levels of experience although the differential is less at the lower end of the experience range.

ALISE. The January 1, 1988 report from 60 library and information science programs accredited by ALA (*Library and Information Science Education Report 1988*, 1988) noted 562 full-time faculty members in 55 schools, down from 572 in 57 schools in 1987. Of the 562 full-time faculty, 307 or 54.6 percent were male and 255 or 45.3 percent were female. Although the 1988 ratio of female to male faculty members is the highest of any year since 1976, the percentage of female faculty members has increased by only 3.8 percent, from 41.5 percent in 1976 to 45.3 percent in 1988. Since 1976 the greatest percentage increase has occurred in the assistant professor rank, from 46 percent female to 60.2 percent female. There was also a significant increase in both the percentage and number of female deans, from 19.7 percent (12) in 1975/76 to 38.3 percent (23) in 1987/88. But the salary differential between male and female deans/directors not only continues but has increased in the last year. Of the 49 deans/directors who had fiscal year appointments and who reported salaries, 30 were male and 19 were female. The mean male salary for deans/directors was $69,655 (median, $66,991), and increase of 10.2 percent over 1987; the mean female salary for deans/directors was $60,167 (median, $56,468), and increase of 7.1 percent over 1987. However the salary differential between male and female deans/directors in 1988 was $9,489. While this differential was less than the high of $11,253 in 1985, it was $1,503 more than in 1987.

Fifty-eight new faculty appointments were made in 1987/88, 24 males, 34 females. The greatest number of new appointments (43) was at the assistant professor rank. Of the 43 new assistant professors, 26 were female and 17 were male. Thirty-one (13 male, 18 female) of these new appointments were for the academic year; the mean salary for the 13 males was $29,365 (median $25,000); the mean salary for the 18 females was $28,895 (median $29,895). The male/female salary differential for new academic year appointments at the assistant professor rank in 1986/87 was $1,951; in 1987/88, the differential had decreased to $470, both favoring men. However, when those persons without doctoral degrees were removed from the comparison the difference was only $76, still favoring men. When both academic and fiscal year assistant professor appointments were considered, the male mean salary was $30,051, while the female mean salary was $31,884, the $1,833 difference favoring women.

Other Salary Surveys. For the second year the New England Chapter of the Association of College and Research Libraries conducted a salary survey of general, four-year undergraduate institutions in the New England region. Seventy libraries reported usable data for 749 professional positions; 56 libraries reported data for both 1986/87 and 1987/88. The mean salary in the 56 libraries was $28,679 in 1986/87 and $30,656 in 1987/88, an increase of 6.9 percent. The composition of the staff changed very little; in 1986/87 35.1 percent were male, 64.9 percent female; in 1987/88, 33.8 percent were male and 66.2 percent female. While the overall average salary increase in 1987/88 was 6.9 percent, the increase for women was 7.7 percent and for men 5.6 percent. In 1988 of the 749 professional positions in 70 libraries, 253 were filled by men, 496 by women. The average male salary for all positions was $33,121, the average female salary for all positions $28,797. The salary differential in 1987/88 based on years of experience ranged from $672 for 0–3 years of experience to $10,302 for 32–35 years of experience, all favoring men.

Other Studies. Nancy A. Van House studied four classes of University of California, Berkeley, MLS students between 1982 and 1984 on their decisions to enter librarianship (*Library and Information Science Research* 10, 1988). The study examined whether men and women differed on four questions: (1) do they differ in two job–related characteristics, educational qualifications and geographical mobility? (2) do they differ on the values they place on career outcomes? (3) do they express different preferences for the type of library in which they wish to be employed? and (4) do men and women have different salary expectations? Van House's study showed that men and women do differ in educational backgrounds; more men than women had social science degrees, although more women than men had science/math degrees. Forty-one percent of the men had advanced degrees but only 21 percent of the women did. Also, women were more than twice as likely to report that they were limited to one geographical area. Although the reasons for entering librarianship differed somewhat between men and women, the relative rankings of reasons and the factors that were considered in the decision were not dissimilar. Public and special libraries or nonlibrary employment were most often the preference of women while men preferred academic library employment. Only in the class of 1985 did men and women expect comparable salaries, in all other classes women expected to receive lower salaries than men. Van House concluded that male and female respondents differed little on their reasons for wanting an MLS or in their evaluation of the costs and benefits. But the study indicated that the sex segregation by type of library has already begun among MLS students; the differences in the distribution of men and women among types of libraries can be explained at least in part by differences in preferences. More research is needed to see what determines those preferences.

SANDRA K. PETERSON

Women's National Book Association

Activities. The annual WNBA breakfast during the ALA conference was held July 9 in New Orleans. Betty Carter, who teaches children's literature at the School of Library and Information Studies, Texas Woman's University, Denton, Texas, was the featured speaker. Her topic was nonfiction for children, specifically how dinosaur books demonstrate publishers' growing recognition that children are as interested in the wonder of the real world as they are in fiction. The attention to format, use of specialists as authors and multiple offerings on the same topic for different age groups were documented by the titles Carter brought to illustrate her talk.

The Women's National Book Association and Women in Scholarly Publishing jointly sponsor a panel at the Modern Language Association convention each year. The topic for the December 1987 meeting was "The Changing World of Publishing—Its Effect on Scholars." The panel focused on women's studies at the 1988 convention in New Orleans.

Local chapters of WNBA presented a wide range of programs in 1988, reflecting the diversity of their membership. Topics included independent bookstores (Boston), university presses (New York), the Meese Commission on Pornography (Detroit), publishing mergers (Washington), and magazine editing (San Francisco), among others. The San Francisco Chapter presents a book purchase award each year to a college student sponsored by a faculty member who writes an essay on what books mean to him or her. Binghamton Chapter President Margiana Benza was recognized by the Broome County Status of Women Council as a "Woman of Achievement."

National and chapter activities are reported in The Bookwoman, WNBA's national newsletter. The Bookwoman also includes book reviews and such feature articles as the scholarship evolving around women's issues and the National Women's History Project.

Awards. The sixth annual Lucile Michels Pannell Award was presented at the ABA convention in Anaheim, California, to Marilyn Dugan and Sheilah Egan of A Likely Story Children's Bookstore in Alexandria, Virginia. Dugan and Egan programmed a year of creative events that included themed story hours, author appearances, Saturday morning vocational sessions, and a sensational "Week Without TV" project. The Pannell Award is endowed by the estate of the Chicago educator and librarian who was also a bookseller at Carson Pirie Scott's Hobby Horse Bookshop. Dugan and Egan received a $2,500 check and a page of original art from Mordicai Gerstein's Arnold of the Ducks, hand-colored by the illustrator.

The biennial WNBA Award was presented in late October to Claire Friedland at a cocktail reception in New York. The WNBA Award honors an American bookwoman "for an outstanding contribution to the world of books and, through books, to the society in which we live." Now owner of Friedland Enterprises, a book production consulting firm, Friedland was one of the first women in a management position in book production. A long-time active member, Friedland served a term as National Vice-President and represented WNBA at United Nations international conferences on women in Mexico City in 1975 and in Copenhagen in 1981. Tributes to Friedland were presented by Cathy Rentschler, Past President of WNBA; Jane Isay, Editorial director, General Publishing Group, Addison-Wesley; and Elizabeth A. Geiser, senior vice-president, Gale Research Company. In her acceptance speech, Friedland said that while she was awed to join the ranks of notable women who had been honored in the past, she was especially pleased to be able to call attention to the production side of publishing, which is filled with people who are rarely visible to the public, but are nonetheless essential to the industry.

Annual Meeting. President Cathy Rentschler presided at the Board of Directors' annual meeting in Los Angeles in May. Representatives from the Boston, Detroit, Los Angeles, Nashville, New York and Washington chapters attended, along with national officers and committee chairs. New national officers were inducted at the close of the two-day meeting.

WNBA, founded in 1917, is the only organization in the book world open to women and men in all occupations allied to the publishing industry. Since it represents no special interest group, WNBA offers educational and literary programs for all. Publishers, wholesalers, and other organizations support the work of WNBA as sustaining members.

CATHY RENTSCHLER

WOMEN'S NATIONAL BOOK ASSOCIATION, INC.

PRESIDENT (1988–89):
Cathy Rentschler, Editor, Library Literature, The H. W. Wilson Company, Bronx, New York

VICE-PRESIDENT/PRESIDENT-ELECT:
Marie Cantlon, President, Proseworks, Boston

SECRETARY:
Suzanne Lavoie, Writer, Mill Valley, California

TREASURER:
Susan B. Trowbridge, Addison-Wesley Publishing Co., Reading, Massachusetts

EDITOR OF THE BOOKWOMAN:
Nancy Musorafite-Lutz, Arthur Sackler Gallery, Washington, D.C.

Membership (1988): 900

Young Adult Library Services

Major Concerns and Directions. AIDS and sex, suicide, and abuse of drugs, alcohol, and children are topics of concern to youth and the professionals who work with them. Young adults are also interested in materials on music, teen pregnancy, abortion, the occult, homelessness, and history, especially the Vietnam War and World War II. In most areas of the country, young adult tastes in fiction leaned toward horror novels, romance series (Sweet Valley High), humor, and the classics. Problem novels and SF/fantasy fiction had varied popularity.

Library policy on teen access to videos and on reference services and materials for young adults continued to evolve, while recruitment and salary levels of YA librarians were ongoing concerns of the profession.

Most libraries assessed attempts at censorship to be about the same as last year. Mesa, Arizona, reported an increase of verbal complaints (rather than formally written). A public library system in Massachusetts reported that a school library system did not purchase *Lynda Madaras Talks to Teens About AIDS* for fear of censorship attacks. For titles of censor targets see the *Newsletter on Intellectual Freedom*. Several libraries received objections to audio recordings such as the Santa Clara, California, complaint about the graphics of the "Guns and Roses" album. Heavy metal music, recordings by Twisted Sister, Ice-T and 2 Live Crew were also singled out.

The landmark U.S. Supreme Court ruling in *Hazelwood School District v. Kuhlmeier* narrowed the view of the constitutional rights of public school students by affirming that public school officials have broad power to censor school newspapers, plays, and other "school-sponsored expressive activities." According to the July 1988 *Newsletter on Intellectual Freedom*, the decision had immediate effect on court decisions in Florida, California, and Nebraska and a number of schools nationwide.

Collection Development. Lillian Gerhardt, editor-in-chief of *School Library Journal*, reported the average price of spring 1988 children's and young adult titles was $13.15, an increase of about four percent. Fewer than 15 percent of the libraries replying to a survey for this article reported slight increases in budgets and there were no reports of significant cuts to YA collection development funds.

Most libraries continued to devote the majority of the YA collection budgets to purchasing hardcover titles, but libraries such as Elsie Quirk and Collier County in Florida and Sno-Isle Regional in Washington spent 80–90 percent on paperbacks. Allocations for videos in no way reflected the popularity of the format. The Fairport Public and Upper Hudson Library System in New York spent 12 percent and 20 percent, respectively; other respondents spent less than 12 percent. Posters were modestly supported in some collections and compact disks made inroads.

Programs and Teen Publications. Summer reading clubs, contests, exhibitions, book promotions, and academic improvement programs were the most popular types of YA programs in public libraries. At least one library sponsored a summer reading program that revolved around a movie theme; others were patterned on TV game show formats. Allen County Indiana capitalized on the Olympics for a "Summer of Champions" YA reading program in which more than 1,500 enrolled. Poetry and photography contests and exhibitions were featured elsewhere. Winning designs of a T-shirt contest were reproduced on shirts and were sold by the Friends of the Library at Broward County Florida. "The Write Stuff" creative writing contest for middle schoolers in Northport Public, New York, was a cooperative effort of classroom teachers and local writers. Active teen volunteer groups at Orange County (California), Lafayette (Louisiana), Clearwater (Florida), and Fairport (New York) assisted with a number of activities in several libraries. "Computer Pix," a database developed by Wayne Oakland Library Federation (Michigan), matched teen interests with book titles. "Live . . . It's the Groton Public Library" is a video tour of the library produced through the cooperative efforts of

Patt Behler, children's and young adults' consultant at the Missouri State Library, sorts through some of the 50,000 cards returned to the State Library during the "Every Child . . . a Library Card" campaign. [Madeline Matson, Missouri State Library]

a 7th grade English class in Groton Library (Colorado). The Venice Area Public (Florida) production of "The Reluctant Dragon" dramatized by 30 young adults in the cast and crew, was performed for children and in area nursing homes. In "Books Come Alive" (East Baton Rouge, Louisiana) students created original portrayals of characters from adolescent fiction using oral interpretation and improvisation.

Academic improvement programs covered the ever-present term paper and science fair projects. There were some programs just for fun, such as "Heartstoppers: A Festival of Ghost Stories" (Franklin Avenue, Iowa) where ghost stories were read in a park shelter for Halloween; a skateboarding exhibition at Broward County (Florida); and a "Sherlock Holmes Festival." Ventura County (California) had a packed house for a two-day workshop offered by a free-lance cartoonist.

Publications by young people, generally supported as in-house publications included art exhibition catalogs, poetry compilations, reviews, literary magazines, bookmarks, flyers, and news-

255

Young Adult Library Services

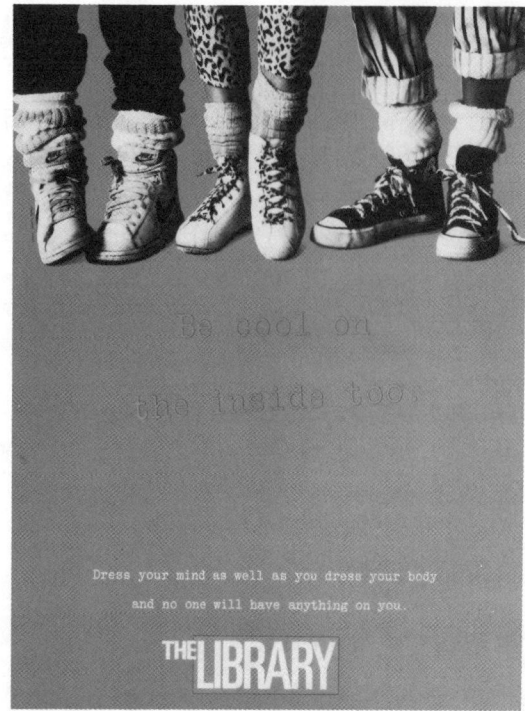

letters. General news publications often included art, puzzles, reviews, and literary compositions by teens. Artwork by teenager Chris Thompson from Sno-Isle Regional Library System (Washington) was selected for the ALA/YASD "Best Books for Young Adults 1987" booklist.

Community Cooperation. Young adult library services forged links with various organizations in local communities for projects such as sexuality workshops, teen tutoring, talk shows on teen issues, and posting job openings. Mesa, Arizona, enlisted juvenile court offenders for community service and provided space for meetings with probation officers. Other cooperative efforts: providing books to a home for runaways, and a battered wives shelter, establishing a peer counseling group, to present a peer counseling workshop for area high schools, and producing a Teen Helpcard with names and telephone numbers of local agencies.

Continuing Education: Publications and Programs. Young adult librarians consistently identified VOYA as the most significant journal in the field, followed by School Library Journal, Booklist, and Journal of Youth Services in Libraries. Wilson Library Bulletin, Kliatt Young Adult Paperback Book Guide, and Horn Book were also highly regarded. Emergency Librarian, ALAN Review and Bulletin of the Center for Children's Books round out the top 10 journals cited by librarians serving young adults.

Joni Bodart's Booktalk! 3 was most often mentioned as the outstanding book of 1988. Two 1987 ALA videos have been used for continuing education: Hazel Rochman's "Tales of Love and Terror: Booktalking the Classics, Old and New" (based on a book by the same title) and "The Facts of Love in the Library: Making Sexuality Information Relevant and Accessible to Young People" by Patty Campbell with an introduction by Dr. Ruth Westheimer.

The results of a nationwide survey of 846 libraries were released in July by the U.S. Department of Education's National Center for Education Statistics in Services and Resources for Young Adults in Public Libraries. Findings indicated that while young adults comprise a major component of public library users, only 11 percent of public libraries employ librarians to serve young adults. Another US/DOE publication is "Youth Indicators 1988" a compilation of data from 1950–1988 on the status and trends of youth ages 14 to 24.

Booklists and guides popular with librarians included The Second Young Adult Program Guidebook, prepared by members of the Youth Services Section of the New York Library Association, the 59th edition of NYPL's Books for the Teen Age, 1988 and "Nothin' But the Best: Best of the Best Books for Young Adults, 1966–1986," titles selected by participants in a 1988 YASD pre-conference program. Guidelines for Young Adult Services in Public Libraries of New Jersey (1987) and Standard for Youth Services in Public Libraries of New York State (1984) were still influential documents. A revision of Pat Scales' ever-popular "Communicate Through Literature" is available as "Communicating Through Young Adult Books."

Publications generated by a region, state, or local area include the newsletter of Southwest Florida Young Adult Network; YA Minutes and Newsletter (Monroe County, New York); BAYA Book Reviews by the Bay Area Young Adult Librarians in California; and "The Go-Between: A Newsletter for Educators About Services and Programs for Teens at Mesa (Arizona) Public Library." A brochure of the Allen County (Indiana) Public Library "Young Adults' Services" described the collection, services and programs offered to middle- and high-school students.

In addition to the wide range of programs offered at the ALA Annual Conference in New Orleans, a national conference that made an impact in 1988 was "Social Responsibility and Children's and Young Adult Books," sponsored by the Children's Book Council. Librarians attending the YASD/National Endowment for the Humanities institutes "Courtly Love in the Shopping Mall" explored program planning and promotion, interagency networking, and grant writing.

A number of state library associations scheduled programs focusing on young adult topics. Locally sponsored programs emphasizing reference materials, latchkey children, storytelling, cablevision for libraries, reaching vulnerable youth, youth networks, psychology of young adults, and reviewing of sex education books.

Leaders and Models. Numerous individuals and library systems provided inspiration for library service to young adults, including: Susan Madden, King County Library System (Washington); Vivian Wynn and Audrey Eaglen, Cuyahoga County (Ohio); Colleen Macklin, Milwaukee Public Library (Wisconsin); and Christy Tyson, formerly at Spokane Public Library (Washington) and now Youth Services Consultant for the Alabama Public Library Service. Among libraries recognized for outstanding services were Mesa Public Library (Arizona); Miami-Dade Public Library System (Florida);

Monroe County Library System (New York); and New York Public Library (New York). Individuals influencing the direction of YA library services in 1988 included Evelyn Shaevel, Jack Forman, Joni Bodart-Talbot, Hazel Rochman, Roger Sutton, Patty Campbell, Dorothy Broderick, Gerald Hodges, Barbara W. Razzano, and Mary K. Chelton.

PATSY H. PERRITT

Young Adult Literature

Young Adult Author Award. Every year a variety of "firsts" is recorded, including such events as a first book or a first speaking engagement, but in 1988 a special "first" occurred in the field of young adult literature. *School Library Journal* and the Young Adult Services Division of the American Library Association awarded the first YASD/*School Library Journal* Author Award to S. E. Hinton. Sponsored by *School Library Journal*, this award of a $1000 cash prize and citation is presented to an author "whose book or books, over a period of time, have been accepted by young adults as an authentic voice that continues to illuminate their experiences and emotions, giving insight into their lives."

Beginning work on *The Outsiders* (Viking/Dell) at the age of 15, using characters based on teens whom she knew, signaled the start of her writing career. She continued her writing for young adults with *That was then, this is now* (Viking/Dell), *Rumble Fish* (Delacorte and Dell) and *Tex* (Delacorte and Dell). Susan Tait, Award Committee Chair said that, Hinton's work "has had enormous impact on the kinds of books written for young adults." Thus it is most appropriate that S. E. Hinton was the first recipient of the SLJ/YASD Young Adult Author Award.

Reading Habits. Teenagers' reading habits are described in a July 23, 1988 *Publisher's Weekly* survey that was based on telephone interviews of a national representative sample of 503 teenagers, aged 13–17. The teens were asked how much time they spent the previous day watching television, listening to radio and reading newspapers, magazines, and books. The disheartening responses reveal that electronic media, television and radio are much more important in the lives of young adults than reading materials. This may explain why book stores realize only 17 percent of their total sales from this young adult market.

Graphic Novels. A type of literature that is appearing more often in the United States, after years of popularity in Europe and Asia, is the graphic novel. *When the Wind Blows,* by Raymond Briggs (Schocken, 1982) and *Maus: A Survivor's Tale,* by Art Spligelman (Pantheon, 1986), are two graphic novels that received attention when they were named to the YASD Best Books for Young Adults (BBYA) list. In 1988, another graphic novel, *Barefoot Gen: the day after,* a cartoon story of Hiroshima, by Keiji Nakazawa (New Society Publishers), was among the nominees for the 1988 BBYA list. Modern comic books are not limited to entertainment value, they are also a means of using words and graphics to illuminate all sorts of subjects —from fiscal reports in Japan to novels in Europe.

Problem Novels. Two well-known young adult authors released new works in the fall. Robert Cormier's *Fade* is more autobiographical, than any of his previous works. S. E. Hinton returned to young adult writing with *Taming the Star Runner,* another story of a handsome, tough yet sensitive male.

Many 1988 books dealt with coping with grief. Perhaps one of the finest crafted was *Say Goodnight, Gracie* a first novel by Julie Deaver. Hadley Irwin's *So Long at the Fair* involves the death of a best friend, Ashley, who commits suicide. Livvie Sinclair's year-long ordeal in a psychiatric hospital trying to cope with the death of her friend David, is compassionately handled in *Sex Education,* by Jenny Davis.

The technique of journal keeping was used by several authors including Thelma Hatch Wyss in her hilarious *Here at the Scenic-Vu Motel.* Ouida Sebestyen's tale of terror, *Girl in the Box,* finds Jackie McGee kidnapped and locked in a dark, damp room with only a typewriter for companionship, writing notes to her parents, to maintain her sanity.

The 1960s. The number of books released in 1988 that center around the 1960s is symbolic of the continued fascination with the time period. Walter Dean Myers' Vietnam War novel *Fallen Angels* is dedicated to his brother, Thomas Wayne "Sonny" Myers, who was killed in action on May 7, 1968.

Continued interest in the 1960s because of the 25th anniversary of the November 22, 1963 assassination of John F. Kennedy was reflected in Robert MacNeil's *1963: The Year Kennedy was Shot,* a prose and photograph collection. Judie Mills wrote an outstanding, well–documented biography, *John F. Kennedy,* which goes beyond surface charm and charisma, to expose Kennedy's underlying multifaceted character.

Adult Books for Young Adults. Every year sees an increase in adult books that are well–received by young adults; the trend continued in 1988. Joanne Greenberg's *Of Such Small Differences,* a poignant, realistic novel brings readers into the world of the deaf–blind. On a humorous note, Terry Pringel's *The Preacher's Boy,* reveals the tribulations of Michael Page in his relationship with his Baptist minister father, from the time he gets the giggles as he tries to deliver a sermon at his father's church, to the graphic retelling of his amorous activities with Amy Hardin. In a different vein, Peter Abrahams wrote a chillingly terrifying novel, *Hard Rain,* a 1980s kidnapping, Russian espionage, and sinister deals narrative that originated because of a previously unknown happening at the late 1960s Woodstock Music Festival. The return of long–dead wolves who savage the townspeople of Steel Harbor, Maine confounds journalist Fran Thomas in a horrifying novel, by Earle Wescott, *Winter Wolves.* Tony Hillerman's *A Thief of Time,* offers a mystery within a mystery, as Chee and Leaphorn track a missing archaeologist, who is trying to decipher the code of the vanished Anasazi Indian tribe.

Science Fiction and Fantasy. Science fiction and fantasy, remain the favorite of young adult readers. Anne McCaffrey fans delighted in *Dragonsdawn,* the story of the first colonization of Pern. John Christopher's *When the Tripods Came* offered an explanation of how the world re-

Young Adult Services Division

acted to the first landing of Tripods; Greg Bear's *Eternity* was a sequel to *Eon*; Piers Anthony continued his Incarnations of Immortality series with a sixth offering, *For Love of Evil*; and Terry Brooks added *Wizard at Large* to the Magical Kingdom of Landover series. Shirley Rousseau Murphy concluded her Dragonbard trilogy with *Dragonbards* the account of the final battle against the evil Quazelzeg, Lord of the Dark.

PAMELA G. SPENCER

Young Adult Services Division

Susan B. Madden, King County, Washington.

The Young Adult Services Division (YASD) has shown exceptional growth with the second largest percentage increase of all divisions in ALA in 1988 (7.8 percent, 188 members). This exciting increase reflects what is occurring nationally. There is a resurgence of interest in and support for young adult needs and concerns. Increased library staffing, programs, materials, and public support for adolescent needs and concerns are developing throughout the U.S. This is readily apparent at a variety of levels: national and local legislation; state and regional conference programs and speakers; in-house and professional continuing education workshops; library school curriculums; and professional recruitment efforts for youth specialists. Within the ALA priority areas, YASD has been highly visible and productive.

Access to Information/Intellectual Freedom. The YASD Intellectual Freedom Committee provided a major program in New Orleans: Building Bridges over Troubled Waters: Successful Coalition Building. *You Are Not Alone: Intellectual Freedom Issues and Library Service to Youth* publication sold more than 500 copies. The Teen Pregnancy Task Force's packet, *Teen Pregnancy Crisis: Libraries Can Help*, sold out and it was revised and reprinted to meet demand. The YASD Intellectual Freedom Committee developed offense and defense strategies for those under censorship fire by the creation of the very useful "Hit List," which cites 20 frequently challenged young adult titles with reviews and justifications to counter censorship attempts. YASD's Dallas program: "Teenagers, They Ain't Cute Anymore," dealt with the societal disenfranchisement of young adults, especially in conjunction with information. "AIDS and Teenagers," another Dallas program, was designed to provide information on materials and programming in this sensitive and vitally important area.

Legislation and Funding. A resolution supporting the Young American Act of 1987, sponsored by YASD/ALSC/AASL, was adopted by ALA Council in July 1988. This legislation will result in each state receiving no less than $300,000 for "the planning and advocacy of services in order to assure young individuals (24 and under) the availability of (1) the best possible physical and mental health; (2) adequate and safe physical shelter; (3) the highest quality of educational opportunity; (4) effective training apprenticeship and productive employment; (5) the widest range of civic, cultural and recreational activities, which promote self-esteem and a sense of community; and (6) genuine participation in decisions concerning the planning and managing of their lives. Items 3, 5 and 6 are particularly pertinent to school and public librarians, and the sponsoring divisions will work with their legislative committees to provide information for implementation at the state and local level. Lobbying suggestions, appropriate programs, liaison how-to's with other youth-serving agencies, and youth participation techniques are some anticipated areas to be developed.

YASD/ALSC/AASL, working on methods of implementing the Young American Act of 1987, are also planning the 1990 White House Conference on Youth which, as part of the legislative requirement, specifies that at least one-fifth of the public members of each committee shall be 24 years old or younger!

A Dallas YASD program, "Youth Participation and Youth Issues, White House Conference II" was developed to aid librarians in planning involvement strategies for this second White House Conference.

Public Awareness. YASD worked with the ALA Public Information Office for a continuation of the "Library Card Campaign" with new and special emphasis on young adults. A written "how-to" piece for getting young adults into the library was done by former YASD Board Member Christy Tyson (Spokane Public Library/Alabama State Library) and printed on the back of an eye-catching poster.

Public awareness was heightened at the local level by programs developed as a consequence of the YASD/NEH series, "Library Programming in the Humanities for Young Adults." For example, the Multnomah County Library System of Portland, Oregon with the Beaverton City Library and the Oregon Committee for the Humanities, scheduled four very successful programs in a series called, "The Horror of It All." YASD and ALSC hosted a reception in honor of the "Year of the Young Reader" at the 1989 Midwinter meeting to facilitate networking with members of other national organizations serving youth.

The *School Library Journal*/YASD Author Achievement Award's first recipient, S. E. Hinton, gained professional and popular press coverage as "an author whose book or books have provided young adults with a window through which they can view their world and which will help them to grow and to understand themselves and their role in society." Hinton received the Award at the YASD luncheon in New Orleans attended by 480 people. The ever popular and heavily used *Best Books for Young Adults*, due to improved ALA marketing, increased 1987-88 sales. The *Recommended Books for Reluctant*

YOUNG ADULT SERVICES DIVISION

PRESIDENT (July 1988–July 1989):
Susan B. Madden, King County Library System, Seattle, Washington

VICE-PRESIDENT/PRESIDENT-ELECT:
Gerald Hodges, School of Library and Information Science, University of Iowa, Iowa City

EXECUTIVE DIRECTOR:
Evelyn Shaevel

Membership (August 31, 1988): 2,488
Expenditures (August 31, 1988): $100,366

Young Adult Readers list and the New Orleans program resulted in wide press coverage. The New Orleans YASD preconference, "Still Great in '88," increased *Best Books* readership and awareness. The resulting pamphlet entitled "Nothin' but the Best: Best Books for Young Adults, 1966-86" was published jointly by YASD and the ALA Public Information Office. The *Outstanding Books for the College Bound* lists continued to rate highly with the profession and the public. Work began on new editions with 1990 publication dates for *Biographies*, *Fiction*, *Fine and Performing Arts*, *Nonfiction* and *Theater*. Frequent requests from libraries of all types and the public revealed a need for genre lists; YASD is responding in: *Mystery*, *Romance*, *Horror*, *Science Fiction*, and *Sports*. Exciting promotional work with genre "book dumps" and other innovative approaches are being developed by YASD and ALA's Public Information Office and is supported by a $5,500 grant from the Carnegie Reading List Fund.

Personnel Resources. YASD is joining with the Library Administration and Management Association and the Association of Library Service to Children to develop a series of regional institutes on "Managing Youth Services"—a spin-off of the New Orleans program, "Money and Power," with Mary Somerville and Vivian Wynn. Responding to members' stated needs, YASD also began developing a regional workshop curriculum for those who work with young adults but have no training in young adult services or materials. The planned institute, "Doing YA Services without Training: What You Need to Know," will probably hit the road in the spring of 1990. The *Journal of Youth Services in Libraries*, the jointly-supported journal of YASD and ALSC, named a new editor, Josette Lyders. At a joint meeting of the ALSC and YASD boards in New Orleans, a decision was made to make the *Journal* refereed on a trial, three-year basis. It is hoped that this will increase research-related articles and will broaden the author submissions from academia, while retaining the popular and useful style for which the *Journal* is noted.

The YASD's President's Programs in New Orleans and Dallas address two sides of services delivery: "Money and Power" and "Sharing the Wealth: How to Transmogrify Your Daily Experience into Trainer/Speaker/Consultant Experience." "Demystifying Best Books: How Do You Select Best Books," a Dallas program, will aid librarians in selection techniques and offer promotion and programming tie-ins. A manual on "Youth Participation in Libraries" is being developed to help librarians plan, develop, and implement youth participation programs in their libraries. "Training Librarians and Youth = Success," a Dallas program which will offer implementation techniques for librarians wanting to set up youth participation programs.

Library Services Delivery and Technology. A continuation of the YASD/NEH project, "Library Programming in the Humanities for Young Adults" occurred with workshops in St. Augustine, Florida (September 1988) and Philadelphia, Pennsylvania (November 1988); a final presentation is planned for AASL's Salt Lake City conference in October 1989. YASD, pleased with the NEH partnership, is developing a new proposal, "Helping 17-year-old's to Know—Cultural Literacy. . . .Libraries and YA's," designed to aid youth librarians and administrators working with scholars on improving ways and means of enriching young adult education and societal awareness. It obviously works well as an implementation tool for the Young Americans Act of 1987. YASD is working with the Department of Education's survey report, "Services and Resources for Young Adults in Public Libraries." Some of the report's staggering implications include 25 percent public library use is by young adults, and 11 percent of public libraries have young adult librarians.

A YASD preconference in Dallas, chaired by Mary K. Chelton, will train participants in "Tough Talk: Booktalking and Beyond." It is designed to offer the basics to inexperienced librarians and to incorporate new and creative ways for experienced librarians to motivate young adult readers with such promotional techniques as videos, public address systems, and audiocassettes. "Showcase of Selected Films," a Dallas program designed not just to show outstanding young adult films, but also to offer promotion and programming techniques that librarians can readily use at the local level, should be well attended.

People. Margaret Edward's death was mourned, and her extraordinary contributions were recognized by the Young Adult Services Division in a resolution which commended her as a pioneer in the establishment of services to young adults in public libraries. For more on Margaret Edwards, see her obituary in this volume.

SUSAN B. MADDEN

State Reports

On the following pages state correspondents report on events of general interest during 1988. They provide systematic coverage on state library associations and state agencies. Data are given as of the end of 1988. ALA membership is given for state associations reporting it.

ALABAMA

Alabama Library Association (founded 1905)

Membership: 1,388; *annual budget:* $62,571.

President: Mary Maude McCain, Tarrant Elementary School, Tarrant 35217.

Vice-President/President-elect: Regina Cooper, Huntsville-Madison County Public Library, Huntsville 35804.

Executive Secretary: Sandra K. Sutton, Box 601, Helena 35080.

Annual meeting: April 11–14, 1989, Birmingham; April 24–27, 1990, Perdido Hilton.

Publication: Alabama Librarian (10 times-a-year).

Alabama Public Library Service (The State Agency)

Blane K. Dessy, Director
6030 Monticello Drive
Montgomery 36130

Alabama Department of Education

Jane Bandy Smith, Educational Specialist in Library Media
Library Media Unit
 111 Coliseum Building
 Montgomery 36109

Major News. The Alabama Public Library Service (APLS) received a 75 percent budget increase for the fiscal year that began October 1, 1988. The Legislature appropriates funds to APLS from the Alabama Special Education Trust Fund. State Aid to public libraries, which is included in the APLS budget, jumped to $1.121 per capita from $0.885 per capita. APLS Director Blane K. Dessy credited Governor Guy Hunt and the Legislature, which passed the budget unanimously.

March 2, 1988, marked the first Legislative Day in Alabama. Sponsored by a coalition of library-related organizations, the event was attended by over 200 librarians and trustees. A delegation of 35 attended ALA Legislative Day in Washington, D.C.

In April the Gannett Foundation awarded APLS a $75,000 Literacy Challenge Grant to create the Alabama Literacy Coalition. An advisory council headed by Governor Hunt was formed and a director hired. The Coalition has held a conference of literacy providers from throughout the state, and is producing a monthly newsletter.

A joint committee of the Alabama Library Association (AlaLA) and APLS completed *Standards for Public Library Service in Alabama*. The standards, in part funded with LSCA Title I, were developed with the assistance of consultants Debra W. Johnson, Karen J. Krueger and Douglas L. Zweizig. The standards document was adopted by the association in April and by the APLS Executive Board in July.

Alabama Library Association (AlaLA). The Association held its annual conference in Montgomery, April 12–15, 1988, with "Libraries in the Center Ring: A Celebration" as the theme. Dr. Ferrol Sams, Georgia novelist and physician, was the keynote speaker. Among the conference highlights were addresses by Emily Mobley, President of the Special Libraries Association; Judith Krug, Director of the Office for Intellectual Freedom; Will Manley, Director of the Tempe, Arizona, Public Library; and Judith Drescher, Director, Memphis/Shelby County (Tennessee) Public Library and Information Center.

The Association honored authors James Haskins for his series of children's books *Count Your Way Through . . .*; Andrew Hudgins for *Saints and Strangers* and Robert Inman for *Home Fires Burning*. Other awards presented were the Citation of Exceptional Service Award to Betty D. Beal, the Distinguished Service Award to Arlo Becklund and the Citation of Merit Award to the Friends of Alabama Libraries (FOAL).

In March, *THE ALABAMA LIBRARIAN*, The AlaLA monthly publication, changed to a slickly illustrated production in magazine format.

AlaLA implemented a group Health Insurance Program as a new service for membership. Open enrollment was set to begin December 1, 1988. AlaLA Council has also appointed an Ad Hoc Task Force to investigate an Alabama Jobline.

State Library. The APLS Executive Board was increased to a seven-member board appointed by the Governor comprising one representative from each of the state's Congressional Districts.

The Regional Library for the Blind and Physically Handicapped, a division of APLS, celebrated its 10th Anniversary at a rededication of services ceremony on June 15th. Attended by 128 guests including state government officials, the celebration included an old fashioned barbecue with country and western entertainment. The event focused media attention on the services of the regional and the 263 volunteers who devoted 3,074 hours to audio production and equipment repairs. Three new consultants joined the APLS Library Development staff: Mary Alice Fields, Margaret Murray, and Christy Tyson. The development staff conducted 23 continuing education workshops during 1988, 15 of them using the new *Standards for Public Library Service in Alabama*. Artwork for the 1988 Statewide Summer Reading Program, "Summer Safari," was developed in cooperation with the Art Department at the University of Alabama. Students submitted camera-ready material for posters, reading certificates, reading records and bookmarks, which were judged by a committee of children's specialists from Alabama public libraries. The summer program reached 37,314 young people through the 1,852 programs conducted by public libraries and public library systems; reading certificates were earned by 21,590 youngsters. Participants were 77 percent school children, 17 percent preschoolers and 6 percent young adults. APLS coordinated a special TDD project which was funded by the Alabama Legislature. A $10,000 appropriation was used to distribute 28 TDDs to public libraries and sponsor a workshop with Alice Hagemeyer on Library Services for Hearing Impaired Patrons.

Public Libraries. George Stewart, Director of Birmingham Public Library, began his term as

President of the Southeastern Library Association (SELA) at the close of the joint SELA/Virginia Library Association meeting in Norfolk, October 29. The City of Gulf Shores dedicated its new Thomas B. Norton Public Library September 25. Designed by architect Carleton McCurry, the library serves a year-round community of 2,500, and expands service during the winter months to meet the needs of over 10,000 residents.

School Libraries and Media Centers. School funding is on a consistent basis, following two years of prorated budgets. The effect of proration on personnel may have far-reaching impact: Alabama's shortage of school library media personnel could be exacerbated if personnel assigned two roles continue to leave the library media center for the classroom. Many persons are considering retirement since the Alabama Legislature approved a 25-year retirement with full benefits. Along with other professionals across the nation, Alabama's school library media personnel are promoting the new guidelines that have been published jointly by the American Association of School Librarians and the Association of Educational Communication and Technology. School library media coordinators, university and college educators, and the state professional leaders met in Birmingham to revise state guidelines to correlate with *Information Power: Guidelines for School Library Media Programs*. Library and Media Professionals (LAMP) Workshops, held on five consecutive days across the state, combined a materials exhibit with professional development programs. Keynote speaker for the workshops was the Lieutenant Governor's wife, Marsha Folsom, who is serving as Honorary Chairperson for the Alabama Reading Incentive Council.

Academic Libraries. The National Endowment for the Humanities (NEH) awarded the Auburn University Center for the Arts and Humanities $246,514 to coordinate a project titled "Read Alabama!" The program will unite patrons of 40 public libraries and scholars in studies of Alabama's best books from 1840 to the present. Phil Turner was named Dean of the Graduate School of Library Service after a yearlong national search. Turner had been the Acting Dean since the Retirement of Dr. James D. Ramer in 1987. The Graduate School of Library Service to the University of Alabama (GSLS) officially began its Ph.D. program with the enrollment of six students selected from an impressive array of applicants. GSLS, in partnership, with JVC Discover America, completed the production of a demonstration CD-ROM. The Ralph Brown Draughon Library, Auburn University, began construction of a 207,000-square-foot addition in May 1988. Currently the library is housed in 172,000 square feet, which will be totally renovated as part of the approximately $23,000,000 project that includes a 425-vehicle parking ramp.

The Mervin H. Sterne Library, University of Alabama, Birmingham (UAB), dedicated its new 105,000-square-foot addition and renovation. The Sterne Library at UAB coordinated an art exhibit, "Fin-de-Siecle Faces: Portraiture in the Age of Proust," and provided an in library exhibit, "Remembrance of Proustian Places: Photographs of Proustian Sites by Contemporary French Photographer Francois-Xavier Bouchart." The University of Alabama (UA) received an HEA Title II D grant to demonstrate an "electronic classroom." The project will evaluate two methods of bibliographic instruction provided to undergraduate engineering students.

Networks and Interlibrary Cooperation. The Network of Alabama Academic Libraries (NAAL) published *Major Microform Sets in Alabama Libraries*. The union list and guide completes efforts to identify microform sets, finding guides, bibliographies and library holdings. An HEA Title II C grant was awarded to UA to catalog individual holdings in two microform sets, *Confederate Imprints and French Revolutionary Pamphlets*. This compliments the NAAL efforts to provide an online catalog of materials held in all member libraries. NAAL received an HEA TITLE II D grant to implement document delivery by telefacsimile among members; 29 OCLC member libraries will receive equipment and partial support for operating costs.

People. Appointments: Virginia Algermissen to Director, Lister Hill Library of Health Sciences, University of Alabama, Birmingham; Dr. Alice Bahr to Director of Library, Springhill College; William Hubbard to Director of Libraries, Jacksonville State University; Lee Pike to Director, Business Library, University of Alabama; Bob Schremser to Director, Alabama Library Exchange; Mary Francis Tipton to Library Director, University of Montevallo. Retirement: Ruth Estes after 23 years as Director, Oneonta Public Library and Pat Blalock retired from Selma/Dallas County Public Library in May 1988.

FRED D. NEIGHBORS

ALASKA

Alaska Library Association (founded 1960)

Membership: 344; *annual budget:* $70,380.

President: Mark C. Goniwiecha, University of Alaska, Fairbanks (October–March 1989).

Vice-President/President-elect: Jacqueline Lauren Barker, B.P. America, Anchorage (March 1988–September 1988).

Annual meeting: March 4–7, Homer.

Publications: Sourdough (quarterly).

Division of State Libraries

Karen Crane, Director
Pouch G
Juneau 99811

School Library Media Coordinator

Jo Morse
Alaska State Library
3600 Denali
Anchorage 99503

During 1988 Alaskan libraries, at the request of the State Library, undertook an intense review of the state's use of WLN, the Western Library Network. Early in the process libraries agreed that any decision regarding the network would be made by consensus and that all libraries would either stay with WLN or transfer to OCLC. Both networks were invited to make formal structured presentations at the Alaska Library Association's annual conference. In mid-September, libraries across the state were polled for a decision regarding WLN. The directors of the state's research and resource libraries met in September and decided to stay with WLN if a number of requirements are met. The benchmark would be passage of WLN legislation during the 1989 legislature. If legislation is not passed and signed by the governor, Alaskan libraries will migrate to OCLC. The decision was difficult for Alaskan librarians, but the process of working as a network to come to consensus again demonstrated the strength and uniqueness of the Alaska Library Network.

State Association. The theme of the annual conference, held in Fairbanks in March, was "Building Library Support with Creative Marketing." ALA President Margaret Chisholm welcomed members and gave a program on Visionary Leaders for 2020. Kaycee Hale, Fashion Institute of Design & Merchandising, Los Angeles, was the keynote speaker. OCLC and WLN both made formal presentations to members. Other presenters included Brooke Sheldon, Susan Hirschman and Susan B. Madden. The membership passed a dues increase. Phyllis DeMuth and Isabelle Mudd were both presented with lifetime honorary membership in AkLA; Bev Moore, of Delta, was awarded the AkLA travel grant; the Baker and Taylor Grass Roots Award went to Sandra Muise from Whittier. Members passed a resolution opposing HB 449, an act relating to obscenity. State Librarian Karen Crane and immediate Past President Diane Brenner represented Alaska in Washington, D.C. for ALA's fourth annual Legislative Day. In October, Mark Goniwiecha resigned his position as President to accept a position at the University of Guam Library. Past-President M. Diane Brenner was appointed interim president. Local chapters participated in fund raising activities as means to share the lobbyist costs. AkLA's top legislative priority—full funding for Public Library Assistance grants—was achieved.

State Library. The State Library awarded a contract to HBW Associates, a national library consulting firm, to assist in the development of a new statewide library plan. A final report is due in June of 1989. Executive Order 70 transferred the State Archives and Records Management from the Department of Administration to the Division of State Libraries. The transfer will promote better access to records, historical documents and papers, both public and private. The State Library awarded a total of $1,500,945 in grants for FY 1989, $874,695 of which was given to 91 public libraries for assistance and matching grants. The regional services program provided monthly library services by mail to over 3,000 patrons who live in remote areas without public libraries. New operating money will fund, for the first time, the Southeast Region coordinator position that has been an AkLA priority for the past 10 years. *A Manual for Small Libraries in Alaska*, written and compiled by Audrey Kolb, was distributed to public and depository libraries. The State Library received $200,000 in new capital funding, which was used to transfer telecommunications traffic to the State Data Network. This transfer reduced annual telecommunication connection charges to WLN to $51,192 from $178,000, a 71 percent reduction.

Public Libraries. Following a series of secret and allegedly illegal personnel actions, longtime Anchorage Municipal Libraries Director Keith Revelle was fired by the mayor of Anchorage. Revelle later filed suit against Mayor Tom Fink and library advisory board chairwoman Wilda Marston. Faye Alexiev, a management consultant and mayoral election campaign researcher, was appointed as interim director. In a letter to Mayor Fink, AkLA protested the appointment of Ms. Alexiev who does not hold an M.L.S. and who has no prior library experience. A search for a new director is currently under way. The public library in Fairbanks had hours and dollars restored after a year of reduction. This came from a very conservative Assembly. Sue Sherif was elected the Public Libraries Representative for the Governors Advisory Council. Kenai Wasilla, Homer, Petersberg and Soldotna automated in 1988. The 1987 All Alaska Radio and Television Goldie Award went to Kegoayah Kozga Library in Nome and to a local radio station, KNOM, for public service announcements on General Amnesty Month, which encouraged the return of overdue items.

School Libraries/Media Centers. Eight school libraries were validated under the Department of Education's "Promising Practices, Criteria for Excellence" program. Battle of the Books continued to be AASL's most visible program with 43 Alaska school districts participating. The State Library helped fund teleconference costs for final battles. AASL/Alaska was invited to become a member of the Department of Education's Literature Panel, as well as an affiliate member of the DOE Cabinet of Professional Associations. Roz Goodman, AASL/Alaska president, was one of four members of the Fine Arts Curriculum Committee of the Bering Straight School District, which received the 1988 Governor's Art Award. Many authors visited Alaska in 1988 through the Authors to Alaska, AASL/Alaska, Authors to Fairbanks, and the Anchorage and Ketchikan School District programs. Judy Arteaga, Ketchikan School District middle school librarian, was named Alaska's School Librarian of the Year. Mollie Bynum, Anchorage School District, was presented the AASL/Alaska Service Award.

Academic Libraries and Special Libraries. One of AkLA's legislative priorities was full funding of the university budget request for libraries. The University of Alaska Southeast received $2,500,000 for construction of its library addition. The City and Borough of Juneau contributed $500,000 in capital money to help construct the UAS Library. In exchange, UAS donated some of its waterfront property to the Borough, which will use the land to develop commercial fisheries. Funding of $612,000 was provided to the University of Alaska Anchorage for Phase I library renovations, handicap access and consortium library purchases. The first new professional position in many years was added to the library's budget. California's gain is Alaska's loss as University of Alaska Fairbanks (UAF) Librarian Bob Geiman accepted a position in Newhall, California. Paul McCarthy was selected as the new director. UAF Library also faired well in the legislative budget process, obtaining additional money for acquisition of materials. AkLA's Special Libraries Round Table was responsible for the summer issue of Sourdough, reporting on specialized collections in and about Alaska. Martha Shepard was elected as the Special Libraries Representative for the Governor's Advisory Council.

Buildings. Juneau will soon be the home of two new libraries. The long-awaited Juneau Public Library, on a prime waterfront location, was accepted from the contractor in late December. Work progresses on the University of Southeast multimillion-dollar facility. In 1988 Tenakee Springs and Delta Junction public libraries celebrated opening of new buildings with state grants.

Networks, Interlibrary Cooperation. The 1988/89 Alaska Library Network microfiche catalogs, a major resource for most Alaskan libraries and the largest state union catalog produced by WLN, has 886,959 titles. Three college libraries are using the circulation component of the University of Alaska's Gnossis system. Ketchikan and Sitka are working on legislative appropriations to implement automated community library systems comparable to Juneau's Capital City Libraries project. Juneau-Douglas High School came on-line with Capital City Libraries. Interlibrary cooperation grants totaling $212,323 were given by the State Library to 12 libraries.

Intellectual Freedom. Mark Goniwiecha, AkLA President and member of ALA's Intellectual Freedom Committee, wrote editorials on the FBI Library Awareness Program and on Banned Books Week that were published in several of Alaska's major papers. AkLA's IFC Committee continues to circulate its lending library of materials and sell its popular "I Read Banned Books" pin. A formal complaint about *Our Bodies, Our Selves* has been filed by parents at a Juneau middle school. Action is pending on several other challenges.

AkLA Conference. The AkLA Continuing Education Committee offered a series of teleconferences by Brooke Sheldon, former ALA President, entitled "Management, A Learned Skill." The follow-up session was held at the ALA New Orleans Conference. The Basic Reference workshop was offered throughout the state. Juneau hosted more than 200 participants at the Pacific Northwest Library Association conference, "Forging the Future, Preserving the Past."

People. George Smith, Alaska State Library assumed the presidency of PNLA. Fairbanks librarian June Pinnell-Stephens begins a two-year term as secretary of PNLA. Virginia Cheney, Ft. Richardson base librarian, retired recently. One of AkLA's founders, she served as its first president 1961-62. Sherry Taber was appointed new Southeast Coordinator of the Alaska State Library. Palmer Public Library welcomed David Zavortink, formerly with Fairbanks North Star Borough Library, as its new director. John Carlson, former mayor of the Fairbanks North Star Borough, died in March. During his tenure as mayor, Fairbanks North Star Borough built two new libraries. Carlson served for a number of years as a member of the Governor's Advisory Council on Libraries.

ANN K. SYMONS

ARIZONA

State Association. The Arizona State Library Association continued to present outstanding conferences and continuing education programs for its members during 1988. MIDCON V, a one-day, midyear conference, focused on legislative issues. Keynote speakers were Eileen Cooke, Director of ALA Washington Office, and F. W. Summers, President-Elect of ALA. More than 1,300 people attended the annual conference in Phoenix in October, and more than 50 out-of-state speakers joined the many talented Arizona speakers for a total of 220 people who gave their time and expertise. Notable authors included Rosemary Wells, Lois Duncan, Celia Halas, and Sue Grafton. Librarian speakers included David Kaser, Judy Krug, Peter Hernon, Charles Bunge, and Christy Tyson.

State Library. On April 18 the Library of Congress gave formal approval to creation of the Arizona Center for the Book, the sixteenth national center. In cooperation with the Arizona State Library Association (ASLA), the *Statewide Plan for Arizona Libraries* was completed. The plan has implications for all types of libraries and will be updated annually. Every three years, an outside consultant will be engaged to evaluate progress and develop a new three- to five-year plan. The SOLAR (Serials OnLine in Arizona) Project moved to the Department from Arizona State University in July.

"Empowering, exhilarating, upbeat"— these were words used by participants to describe the first annual ASLA/Department Fall Forum, held in September as a major outcome of a June retreat on mutual concerns of the two organizations. Forum participants included both seated and newly elected ASLA Board members along with key members of the Department's management staff, advisory boards, and commissions. While the topic of this first Forum was responsibilities for implementation of the new state plan, the spirit of camaraderie and shared enthusiasm was of equal benefit.

The Legislature appropriated $800,000 in planning monies for a new archives building. The state agency filled several key positions. Ray Tevis is now Research Library Division Director; Terese Varga is SOLAR Project Coordinator; Robin Cabot is a new Public Library Development Consultant in the Library Extension Division; and Beth Ellen Woodard is the new Public Library Program Consultant in the same division.

Networking and Cooperation. The Arizona Interlibrary Loan Center (AILLC), funded by the State and LSCA, operates from the Phoenix

---

Arizona State Library Association (founded 1926)

Membership: 1,148; *annual budget:* $200,000.

President: Linda Saferite, Scottsdale Public Library (November 7, 1987–October 8, 1988).

President-elect: Dora Biblarz, Hayden Library, Arizona State Library (October 8, 1988–November 4, 1989).

Annual meeting: October 4-8, 1988, Tucson.

Publication: ASLA Newsletter (ten times a year).

Editor: David Paxton, University of Arizona.

Executive Secretary: Jim Johnson, Arizona State Library Association, P.O. Box 26187, Phoenix, AZ 85068, 602-691-3885
Arizona Job Hotline: 602-278-1327

Department of Library, Archives and Public Records

Sharon Womack, Director
State Capitol
1700 W. Washington
Phoenix 85007

Public Library and provides interlibrary loan services for book and photocopy requests from all types of libraries throughout the state. AILLC staff processed 54,353 requests during 1987, up 29.2 percent from 1986. The Arizona Research Information Center (ARIC), funded by LSCA and located at the Tucson Public Library, provides in-depth reference service to public libraries. In 1987, 3,161 referrals were sent to ARIC, up 10.5 percent from 1986.

Buildings. On March 30, 1988, 400 people gathered at Arizona State University's new West Campus to dedicate the $8,000,000 Fletcher Library, the first permanent building on the 300-acre campus in northwest Phoenix. Among the dignitaries attending and participating in the ceremony was Acting Governor Rose Mofford, who spoke of her involvement with the progress of the West Campus, an idea conceived as long as 20 years ago. The library has a seating capacity of 900, will hold 300,000 volumes, and covers 95,000 square feet. As the center of the campus, the brick and limestone building is designed with its desert environment in mind. A copper dome, a central skylight, lightwells, a brick screen wall to create a shaded arcade, and a 45-foot bowed glass window in front of the building take special advantage of the light, and at the same time protect inhabitants from the heat. The library will be the focal point for the campus; no other building will stand taller. Designed by architects Anderson DeBartelo Pan Inc., the library is wired and cabled to provide electronic communication and access throughout the building. An electronic information center, the Fletcher library utilizes the ASU online catalog, which, in combination with a rapid document delivery system, provides West Campus students with access to the 2,200,000-volume collection on the Tempe campus.

On April 29, 1988, the citizens of Phoenix passed a record $55,000,000 bond proposal for a new 250,000-square-foot central library, construction of three new branch libraries, and expansion of an existing branch. The projects will be completed over the next six years.

Intellectual Freedom. The Intellectual Freedom and Legislation Committees of the Arizona State Library Association, unsuccessful at persuading State Legislative Committees to defeat a major detrimental change to Arizona's obscenity statutes, waged a successful campaign with the Motion Picture Theater Association, the Video Store Owner's Association, the Newspaper Publisher's Association, and others to persuade the Governor of the State to veto the legislation.

Awards. Arizona State Library Association awards, presented during the annual conference, went to Nancy Cummings, Director, Yuma City-County Library, as Librarian of the Year; W. David Laird, University Librarian, University of Arizona, received the Distinguished Service Award; C. Diane Bishop, Superintendent of the Arizona Department of Education, was given the Rosenzweig Award; Michael Goyer, City Manager, Sierra Vista, won the Outstanding Decision Maker Award; Betty Baker was cited as Outstanding Arizona Author; and Sharon Womack, Director, Department of Library, Archives and Public Records, received the ASLA President's Award.

Transitions. Gretchen Whitney joined the faculty of the University of Arizona Graduate Library School. Donna Taxco Tang was selected to participate in the 1988/89 ALA/USIA International Library Book Fellows program.

She will assist the Argentina National Commission for Popular Libraries in conducting a community survey of needs and resources, and in establishing a library network in Patagonia.

JUNE GARCIA

ARKANSAS

Arkansas Library Association (founded 1911)

Membership: 850; *annual budget:* $62,000.

President: Stephen Dew, University of Arkansas Library, Fayetteville 72701 (October 1988–October 1989).

Vice-President/President-elect: Terri Sypolt, Arkansas State Library, Jonesboro 72401.

Executive Director: Sherry Walker, P.O. Box 21883, Little Rock, AR 72221.

Annual meeting: October 30–November 1, 1988, Little Rock.

Publications: Arkansas Libraries (quarterly); *Newsletter* (six times a year).

Arkansas State Library

John A. Murphy, Librarian
One Capitol Mall
Little Rock 72201

Arkansas State Department of Education

Mary Gillespie
One Capitol Mall
Little Rock 72201

The year 1988 was one of analysis and planning for the Arkansas Library Association as librarians across the state took steps to revitalize the Association and to increase its effectiveness. The impetus for this review was the Association's selection as one of three Arkansas nonprofit groups to participate in a six-month institute directed at improving the management of nonprofit associations.

Funded by the Winthrop Rockefeller Foundation and Systematics, Inc., the Nonprofit Management Institute was conducted by consultants experienced in the nonprofit sector. Each participating agency selected a planning team and four two-day sessions were held with the teams meeting together. Each session was divided into group meetings and individual team meetings so that specific Association problems could be addressed. Additionally, each group met with a consultant between the two-day sessions to individualize further the Institute for the Association. Topics covered included long-range planning, leadership and executive board development, executive board/staff relationships, resource development, financial management, and organizational accountability.

ALA's Executive Board viewed the Institute as an important opportunity to evaluate present activities and to plan for the state Association's future. ALA's commitment to the program was demonstrated by the personnel appointed to the planning team. Collectively, the five librarians on the team had 30 years ALA Executive Board experience. The team included former Presidents, the President-Elect, the Chapter Councilor, and persons heavily involved in the work of ALA divisions and committees during the past decade. ALA's general membership also voiced support for a frank analysis of the Association and its work.

The planning team agreed that the review and planning process should be a two-year commitment, so the six-month Institute was seen only as a beginning. Membership opinions were gathered through two surveys conducted at membership meetings during the year. Most changes made to date were procedural in nature. A few structural changes were adopted by the membership at the annual conference. Additional structural changes remained under discussion as options for recommendation at the conclusion of the second year of planning.

The major action taken was to no longer employ an association management firm as support staff and Executive Director for the Association. The firm had been employed as ALA staff for the past four years, but the decision was made to return to the association's earlier staff configuration—to employ a part-time employee who would work solely for ALA. Planning team members and the general membership alike thought that such a change would improve the delivery of services to the general membership and would also increase support services for the Executive Board and officers of the Association.

State Association. Review of the state association's services and planning for future development dominated the year. Remaining efforts were devoted to the annual conference which was centered on the theme that in Arkansas libraries, "Literacy Is Our Business." For the first time, a part of the annual conference was opened at no charge to the general public. This open session was devoted to the literacy theme and featured Jim Trelease, author of *The Read Aloud Handbook*, as the primary speaker. Though the first program of the conference, this session attracted the conference's largest audience as non-librarians joined Arkansas Library Association members in attendance.

Other popular programs included local writer Gene Lyons who has been a former editor for *Newsweek* and other magazines and a feature writer for numerous national publications. Lyons discussed the ethical and political decisions made by journalists and editors that determine what is reported to the public as "news." ALA trustee members heard from one of the consultants working with the Association in the Institute discuss the roles and responsibilities of a nonprofit agency board member. Many librarians and support staff participated in a visit to a local bindery to see firsthand how that work is done. Conferences are never without their social highlights, and the evening buffet held in the galleries of the Arkansas Arts Center provided a memorable setting for an enjoyable evening during the 1988 conference.

State Library. The Arkansas State Library continued its efforts to increase library cooperation in the state and to encourage resource sharing. A preliminary statewide fax network was established during the year with the assistance from the state library, and plans were developed for further expansion of the network in the coming year. The library provided continued technical and financial support for the microfiche *Arkansas Union Catalog*.

School Libraries. School librarians continued to be an active group during 1988. Susan and Franco Pagnucci presented a workshop at

ALA's conference on how to use poetry and puppetry effectively with children. The annual summer workshop sponsored by the Arkansas Association of School Librarians and Media Educators division of ALA proved to be particularly popular due to a changed format that encouraged presentation of numerous and different topics. Three time blocks for the day permitted simultaneous presentation of five topics. The resulting 15 programs ranged from the theoretical to the practical.

The Charlie May Simon Award, voted by students in the fourth, fifth, and sixth grades, went to Patricia MacLachlan for *Sarah, Plain and Tall*. Honor books were Larry Callen's *Who Kidnapped the Sheriff?*, Eth Clifford's *The Remembering Box*, and Margery Evernden's *The Dream Keeper*.

Arkansas school librarians were selected by AASL for national leadership positions in 1988. Retta Patrick was elected President–Elect of the division, and Barbara Stripling and Judy Pitts were named editors of *School Library Media Quarterly*.

Public. The Sixth Annual Author Symposium brought to Little Rock authors, illustrators, and editors of children's books for two days to speak to librarians and parents about their crafts. Speakers were Byrd Baylor, Bruce Brooks, Larry Callen, Esther Hautzig, Susan Hirschman, Otto Salassie, and Mildred Pitts Walter.

Academic. Academic librarians enjoyed exceptional programming in 1988. The College and University Division's workshop in April featured Richard Dougherty as principal speaker. He spoke on the serials crisis facing academic libraries. The first day of the meeting featured panels of Arkansas librarians presenting information on key issues in public and technical service. Tom Dillard, the evening banquet speaker, spoke on the growing Arkansas photography archives at the University of Central Arkansas. His talk was accompanied by a slide presentation drawn from those collections. ACRL Executive Director Jo Ann Segal addressed academic librarians at ALA's annual conference.

Representatives from each campus in the University of Arkansas (UA) system formed a group to develop a system–wide plan for UA library development. It was hoped that a unified approach to library development would result in increased academic library financial support from the state legislature.

The University of Central Arkansas (UCA) added several special collections of note. The library acquired the library of Edgar Chesnutt—more than 600 volumes—considered one of the finest private collections of Trans–Mississippi West Civil War materials available. UCA also acquired the records of Rose Publishing Company, the first major publisher of Arkansas materials in the state, and Lee Spencer's papers related to the WPA Writers' Project in Arkansas. Spencer, a former UCA librarian, spent many years collecting material related to the Arkansas project.

Awards. Arkansans were the recipients of several national and local library awards during 1988. Fred Darragh received ALTA's Major Benefactor Award for his matching grants to each county seat public library for the purchase of Arkansas materials. Darragh contributed more than $33,000 to the project. The award was presented to Darragh at the ALA Annual Conference where he was honored at a reception at the Governor's Mansion following the presentation.

Bessie Moore was named the Outstanding Citizen of the Year by WHCLIS Task Force. Cleotta Mullen received the Robert S. Bray Award from the National Library Service for the Blind and Physically Handicapped. The Gannett Foundation, the foundation arm of Gannett Newspapers, owner and publisher of the *Arkansas Gazette* among other newspapers, received PLA's Advancement of Literacy Award.

State association awards were presented at the annual conference. Lucille Lucas Murphy received the Frances Neal Award for lifetime contributions to Arkansas librarianship. The Distinguished Service Award was presented to Rose Hogan, Director of the University of Arkansas for Medical Sciences Library. Hogan is one of only four members to have served the Association as both President and Chapter Councilor. Bob Razer received the LaNell Compton Award for the best article published in *Arkansas Libraries* during the previous two years. Razer won the award, which is named for a librarian who edited the journal for 25 years, for a series of four articles about Arkansas' library history which were published during ALA's 75th anniversary in 1986. Lee Gordon, a trustee at the Central Arkansas Library System in Little Rock, was named the year's outstanding trustee.

ALA's $1,000 scholarship to a library school was won by Frances Hager, an employee in the Special Collections Department at the University of Central Arkansas (Conway). She will attend North Texas State University (Denton). Kay Barnes, winner of the Association's 1987 scholarship, won a $6,000 scholarship in 1988 from the Special Libraries Association. Barnes will use the SLA award to continue her studies at Texas Woman's University (Denton) toward a career in special libraries.

BOB RAZER

CALIFORNIA

California Library Association (founded 1895)

Membership: 2,588; *annual budget:* $364,000.

President: Halbert Watson, Pomona Public Library (November 1988–1989).

Vice-President/President-elect: Janice T. Koyama, Moffitt Undergraduate Library, University of California, Berkeley 94720.

Executive Director: Mary Sue Ferrell, Suite 300, 717 K Street, Sacramento, CA 95814–3477.

Annual Meeting: November 12–14, 1988, Fresno.

Publication: CLA Newsletter (monthly).

California State Library

Gary E. Strong, State Librarian
P.O. Box 942837
Sacramento 94237-0001

California's public libraries continue to face problems in funding, but librarians, library supporters, and the general citizenry have determined that libraries will survive. County libraries have been hit particularly hard with closures and continual decreases in local funding. The library community rallied to influence passage of state and local bonds. The Public Library Construction and Renovation Bond Act, Proposition 85, which evolved from a three-year struggle and passage of SB 181 authored by Senator Bill Keene, will provide $75,000,000. Additional lobbying will most likely be necessary to insure that Proposition 98 intended for K-12 schools and community colleges also provides funds for school libraries and media centers. Some fear Proposition 98 may adversely affect the level of funding for California's four-year colleges and universities. Voters also approved Proposition 78, the Higher Education Facilities Bond Act, which will provide funding for construction and renovation of some academic libraries.

Local initiatives passed in Modoc County, and the cities of Berkeley, San Francisco, Santa Monica, and Vacaville. Shasta County citizens voted against additional taxes in March and again in September. Their libraries are closed! Los Angeles voter support fell short of the necessary two-thirds.

The crisis in California's public libraries united the library community. Campaigns were carefully planned; volunteers played a big part, and so did the professional community. Friends of the California Library Association formed an alliance, Californians for Community Libraries, to support Proposition 85. Funds were raised to create, with the help of experts, a quiet media blitz in communities across the state. Volunteers assisted libraries in getting support and endorsements from legislators, newspapers, and other sympathetic groups to achieve local success.

California Library Association. "Libraries Uniting Cultures Through Knowledge" was the theme chosen by President Halbert Watson for the 90th Annual Conference of the California Library Association (CLA) held in Fresno, November 12–16. Total registered attendance was 1,920, with 145 company exhibitors and 182 booths and tables. A partnership was formed with school librarians when, for the first time, their conference was held back-to-back with CLA's. Aside from having an opportunity to bring both sets of officers together and to attend each other's meetings, there was the added advantage of drawing exhibitors who would not have otherwise displayed at both conferences.

CLA Council and its members achieved a number of goals in 1988, most notably the progress made toward the long-range planning begun in 1987. In 1988, Councilors and invited guests began exploring issues, developed a mission statement, identified strengths and weaknesses, and drafted a list of goals and objectives. A very capable long-range planning committee was established, and data were collected from CLA members and non-members.

Five regional forums were also held to provide additional input. The final activity was a Pre-Conference On the Long-Range Plan in which invited participants reviewed and refined five major goals to be implemented in the coming months. Emphasis was to be on improving ethnic and cultural diversity within CLA; stengthening CLA, its structure and the services it offers members; and improving its leadership role.

State Library. California was acknowledged and honored nationally for its achievement in the California Literacy Campaign. Leadership comes from Gary E. Strong, State Librarian, and his staff, all of whom continue to strengthen the program.

Strong reported that more than 16,300 adult learners received instruction, and more than 12,500 volunteer tutors participated during the year. In addition, the California Alliance for Literacy received $100,000 from the Gannett Foundation to conduct training, to improve coordination of its referral program, and to support the Family for Literacy program designed to combat illiteracy which spreads from generation to generation.

Two major events occurred during the year for which the State Librarian, his staff, volunteer librarians who helped carry out supporting activities, and other participants deserve a great deal of praise. One was the state of change conference; the other was the conferences on multitype library networking.

The conference, "A State of Change: California's Ethnic Future and Libraries," was held in May, in response to a recommendation from a small group of concerned ethnic minority librarians that the State Librarian sponsor a conference to address the needs of the state's fast-growing ethnic minority and racial populations, and to explore implications for public libraries of a perceived disparity in adequate services for such groups. Strong accepted the challenge, and the concerned group became the conference planning group.

Background for the conference came from a study, *Public Libraries Face California's Ethnic and Racial Diversity*, conducted by Rand Corporation researcher, Judith E. Payne. The conference, attended by 115 invited participants, included key officials and policymakers from government, business, industry, educators, community leaders, and librarians. They addressed public library issues and how well these libraries serve Black, Asian-Pacific, American Indian, and Hispanic communities.

Henry G. Cisneros, Mayor of San Antonio, gave a provocative keynote address. He stated that "there is a national imperative to educate our people for the future. Part of the American ideal is to enlighten and inform, and our libraries are part of that continuing process."

Recommendations from the conference resulted in eight regional informational awareness forums that were attended by more than 600 people. Additional comments were gathered and published in November as *Conference and Awareness Forum Proceedings, 1988: A State of Change: California's Ethnic Future and Libraries.* In 1989/90, $3,000,000 from LSCA funds will be appropriated to implement recommendations from the State of Change Conference.

The California Conferences on Networking were held to acquaint librarians with ongoing activities. More than 700 California librarians and library users met in September to discuss multitype library networking and addressed the question, What should be done next.

The California Library Networking Task Force planned a three-day retreat involving key resource people and leaders to review concerns, benefits, and barriers to networking. Participants were charged with developing a planning methodology and preparing and documenting necessary services. Recommendations will eventually be translated into action.

School Libraries and Media Centers. Fresno was also the setting for the California Media Library Educators Association (CMLEA) annual conference held November 16–19. A variety of meetings centered on the theme, "Libraries, Learning, Literacy, the Heart of the Matter." There were 1,200 in attendance, including exhibitors. The Association focused on three goals: (1) to maintain close relationship with the curriculum; (2) to concentrate on the 1988 guide *Information Power: Guidelines for School Media Programs*; and (3) to direct its energies toward securing improved state support.

Funds from Proposition 98 are intended for K–14 but President Kessler was concerned that school libraries might be overlooked. CLA resolved to remind public school and governmental officials that the children of California deserve access to adequate libraries and that the school library media centers should receive funds as well as the school districts.

CMLEA has 1,400 members and a Board of six: President, Janis Kessler (May 1988–May 1989); Director, Instructional Resources, Bakersfield City School District; President-Elect, Jim Fryer; and four Vice Presidents: Rick Nupoll, Penny Kastinus, Tom Eulert, and Kay Kniemeyer. The Association also publishes *CMLEA Journal* (semi-annual) and *CMLEA Newsletter* (quarterly).

Appointments, Deaths, Retirements. Major appointments include Michael Gorman, University Librarian, California State University, Fresno; Susan (Firestein) Hildreth, Assistant County Librarian of Auburn–Placer County Library; Carol Keator, Director, Santa Barbara Public Library; Judith Segal, Director of Black Gold Cooperative Library System; Elizabeth Talbot Silvia, Alameda County Library Community Relations Coordinator; and Sue Soy, Director, South State Cooperative Library System.

The 1989 officers of CLA include President, Janice T. Koyama; Vice-President/President-Elect, Catherine Lucas; Treasurer, Linda D. Crowe; for California Institute of Libraries: President, Shula Monroe; Vice-President/President-Elect, Catherine Lucas; Marilyn McDonald; for California Society of Librarians: President, Sandra A. Vella; Vice-President/President-Elect, Al Milo; for California Library Employees Association: President, Barbara Lerma; Vice-President/President-Elect, Leslie JoAnn Williams.

Everett T. Moore, Associate University Librarian Emeritus, University of California at Los Angeles, died on January 5, 1988. Moore was known and honored nationally for his outstanding contributions on intellectual freedom. Patrick Barkley, Director of Claremont Colleges Libraries died in May 1988. Barkley founded and formerly directed the OCLC Pacific Network.

California retirees include Robert Hart, Director of Santa Barbara Public Library, and from the State Library, Ann E. Kirkland, Consultant, and Nancy Percy, Assistant State Librarian.

Awards. Four libraries won the John Cotton Dana Award. Sierra Madre Public Library won the major award for its yearlong public relations program. Special Categories were won by (1) Alameda County Library for its local support project; (2) Orange Public Library for using Friends to publicize a Homebound Delivery Service; and (3) San Francisco Public Library for a Book Buddies Program for hospitalized children. The first Californian to win the Allie Beth Martin Award was Daniel O. Robles, Director of Library Services for Blanchard Community Library, Santa Paula. ACRL's K. G. Saur Award for Best Article in *College and Research Libraries* was won by Jordon M. Scepanski, Director, Library/Learning Resources, California State University, Long Beach. The article, "Librarians and Faculty Members: Coping with Pressures to Publish," was co-authored by Scepanski, Robert Boice, and Wayne Wilson. The Justin Winsor Prize Essay Award was given to Brother Thomas O'Connor, Saint Mary's College of California, Moraga. The essay, "Library Service to the American Committee to Negotiate Peace and to the Preparatory Inquiry, 1917–1919," was judged outstanding by ALA's Library History Round Table as noted in *American Libraries*, September 1988. The State Library received the H. W. Wilson Library Periodical Award. Gary E. Strong, State Librarian, edited the winning title: *California State Library Foundation Bulletin*. Strong and the State Library were also recognized and honored by Laubach Literacy Action.

BETTY J. BLACKMAN

COLORADO

Colorado Library Association (founded 1892)

Membership: 770; *annual budget:* $60,000.

President: Charles Hendricksen, Director, Mesa College Library, Grand Junction, 81502.

Vice-President/President-elect: Donna Jones, Director, Arkansas Valley Regional Library Service, Pueblo, 81004.

Executive Director: Judy Votisek

Annual meeting: October 8–11, 1988, Breckenridge.

Publications: Colorado Libraries (quarterly); *CLA News.*

Colorado Office of Library and Adult Services, Colorado Department of Education

Assistant Commissioner: Nancy Bolt
Colorado Department of Education
201 East Colfax Avenue
Denver 80203

Colorado State Library. If a single major hot topic emerged in Colorado Library land during 1988, it was probably resource sharing. Two major studies sponsored by the Colorado State Library focused on Colorado's existing resource-sharing mechanisms. In addition, the state saw a substantial increase in state funding for two elements of the statewide resource-sharing picture. An in-house study, authored by Virginia Boucher, on sabbatical from the University of Colorado at Boulder, and Susan Fayad, State Library Network Consultant, focused on interlibrary loan at the state's seven regional library service systems and Denver Public Library, which receives state funding as the Colorado Resource Center (CRC). The study produced 38 recommendations, which cluster around collections, participation and protocols, verification and location, subject requests and reference referral, staffing, reciprocal borrowing, and administration. The seemingly most controversial recommendations involve equipping the state's libraries with microcomputers and modems to tap into bibliographic databases and perform their own interlibrary loans directly.

The second study, into which the above study fed, was undertaken by Library Planning Associates. Commissioned with LSCA funds, the "Systems/CRC Study" incorporated other cooperative activities and interlibrary loan performed by the regional systems. The final report will be released to the libraries for discussion during 1989, pending final discussion by the Systems' governing boards, and acceptance by the State Board of Education.

The two major performers in the statewide interlibrary loan picture, the seven regional library service systems, and the Denver Public Library as Colorado Resource Center received substantial increases in funding from the state legislature in 1988. Systems received an additional $300,816 for cooperative services, and Denver Public received an additional $200,000 for enhanced statewide reference referral. Increasing these two line items in the State Library's budget for distribution programs was of highest priority to the state's libraries. Another distribution program, County Equalization, which provides funds to libraries in the state's poorest counties, received a 12 percent funding increase. Offsetting these legislative successes was the failure to convince funding authorities to fund a new building for the State's Library for the Blind and Physically Handicapped, which for six months was so overcrowded that new acquisitions could not be organized or distributed to patrons.

State Association. The Colorado Library Association met in Breckenridge, October 8-11, with the conference theme "Challenge 1988." Major speakers included Margaret Chisholm, Guy St. Clair, William Randolph, and Charles Hamaker.

Public Libraries. A series of day-and-a-half Trustee Workshops, sponsored by the Colorado State Library and funded with LSCA funds, took place across the state in the spring and fall. The workshops featured Alice Ihrig and members of the Colorado State Library staff, including State Librarian Nancy Bolt.

Fifty public library directors, staff, system directors, and State Library staff attended a workshop on the Public Library Planning Process, also sponsored by the State Library and funded with LSCA monies. The workshop leader was Sandy Cooper.

A dedicated committee worked throughout the year investigating and making recommendations toward revising the state's Library Law.

After 1987's sales tax increase for Boulder's public library, earmarked for a new central library building, voters went to the polls again to decide whether to build a new building two miles away or on the present site in the downtown government complex. Boulder's library came under fire during the year, being charged with censorship and sequestering of children's books by zealous library staff members.

Estes Park voters approved formation of a library district and taxation at 2.5 mills to support it. This resulted in a budget increase of approximately one third.

"Read-A-World" was the theme for the statewide Summer Reading Program, coordinated by the Colorado State Library and a statewide advisory committee.

School Libraries. The culmination of two years of lively discussion concerning Colorado media endorsement was reached in March when the State Board of Education passed new regulations for school library media endorsement. The new rules, which go into effect in 1991 and were eventually supported by The Colorado Educational Media Association (CEMA) board, require applicants to complete all of the courses necessary to earn a master's degree but do not require the degree.

Colorado Information Power, updated guidelines for Colorado's library media centers, was worked on by CEMA members and the State Library staff during the year. The guidelines were published early in 1989. Teleconferencing of ALA's "Information Power" was well received in Colorado.

Keith Lance of the Colorado State Library began conducting a building level survey of library media centers.

Academic and Special Libraries. A new edition of *Colorado Academic Libraries Master Plan* was completed. The Colorado Commission on Higher Education (CCHE) prepared to end a two-year freeze on approval of academic library construction or remodeling projects. A special committee submitted its report to CCHE, recommending that construction projects be considered again and that the requests show careful examination of compact and off-site storage, alternative methods of information transfer (including document delivery, facsimile, and expanded interlibrary loan), and the role of the library in the campus curriculum and environment. Complete collection development policies (including deselection) must also be submitted with the request for construction funds.

Building Programs. Two libraries in the southwest corner of the state opened new facilities in 1988. The Dolores Public Library remodeled a fire station with LSCA Title II funds and opened during National Library Week. The Archuleta County Library in Pagosa Springs opened a totally new building, the Ruby M. Sisson Memorial Library, in December. The latter was financed, in part, with proceeds from a benefit performance by singer Dan Fogelberg, who is a resident of the area.

The Kremmling Branch of the Grand County Library opened its renovated and expanded building in the summer. The Bailey Branch of the Park County Library opened a new building. Colorado Mountain College in Leadville completed a remodeling project. The Pueblo Library District's main facility underwent an asbestos removal and handicapped access project.

Colorado Center for the Book. During 1988 Colorado formed its Center for the Book, housed in the Colorado State Library but privately funded.

Networks and Cooperation. The Colorado Alliance of Research Libraries (CARL) formed an affiliate, CARL Systems, Inc. Its first new service, a serials access and control system called UnCover, made its appearance in November.

Libraries in the MARMOT Project, a consortium of 17 libraries and regional systems in western Colorado, opted to join CARL as Associate Members, along with Regis College, the State Community College System, and Pikes Peak Library District in Colorado Springs. MARMOT members also voted to expand their hardware, making addition of new libraries a possibility in 1989.

The Central Colorado Library System contracted to take over project management of the IRVING Library Network. LSCA grants continued funding retrospective conversion to add to the statewide database, including such collections of national interest as Mesa Verde National Park Library and Great Sand Dunes National Monument Library.

Awards. The CLA Librarian of the Year award went to Lynda Welborn, Senior Librarian in the Children's Library of Denver Public Library. She has worked in all types of libraries and has been particularly active as the CLA legislative liaison. Welborn's efforts were largely responsible for obtaining the large increases in funding for the seven regional systems, the County Equalization program, and the Colorado Resource Center.

The CLA Lifetime Achievement Award was given to Bea Malchow, recently retired as Director of the Longmont Public Library, a position she held for 20 years.

For the first time, CLA made an award to an outstanding paraprofessional, awarding the Lucy Schweers Award to its namesake, Lucy Schweers of the University of Northern Colorado, a former CLA President.

Major Appointments. Bernard Margolis was appointed the new director at Pikes Peak Library District in Colorado Springs. James Williams is the new University Library Director at the University of Colorado at Boulder. William Randall was appointed new Commissioner of Education by the Colorado State Board of Education; as such, he also has the official title of "Colorado State Librarian."

Deaths. Anne Marie Falsone, former Assistant Commissioner of Education for Library and Adult Services, and State Librarian from 1976 to 1986, died in a plane crash near Durango on January 19, 1988.

S. JANE ULRICH
DANIEL W. LESTER

CONNECTICUT

Connecticut Library Association (founded 1891)

Membership: 995; *annual budget:* $111,100 (1988-1989).

President: Virginia Vocelli, Avon Public Library (July 1988-June 1989).

Vice-President/President-elect: Laura Kahkonen, Windsor Public Library.

Executive Secretary: Vacant.

Annual meeting: March 1989, Cromwell.

Publications: Connecticut Libraries (11 issues per year).

Connecticut State Library

Richard G. Akeroyd, State Librarian
231 Capitol Avenue
Hartford 06106

Instructional Media Consultant

Betty Goyette
Connecticut State Department of Education
Hartford 06106

Connecticut State Library. Governor William O'Neill has proclaimed 1989 as "The Year of the Library." In order to take full advantage of this declaration, State Librarian Richard Akeroyd formed a statewide committee to coordinate public relations and promotional events of the year.

The Connecticut State Library (CSL) fully implemented the reorganization which began in 1987. The functions of the State Library are in four areas: Administration, Historical Services, Patron Services and Library Services. In 1988 the new Advisory Council for Connecticut Library Planning and Development, which replaced four separate advisory groups, was also formed. Several planning groups began examination of the state's interlibrary loan policies and practices and the relationship of the State Library to the Cooperating Library Service Units. The State Library also has established a Connecticut Center for the Book.

Legislative Action. The 1988 legislative campaign of the Connecticut Library Association again demonstrated the effectiveness of a strong community network of librarian lobbyists. The campaign yielded fourth year bonding of $2,000,000 for the Connecticut Library and Information Network and $4,000,000 for the library construction. The Legislature also approved full funding of the new formulas for the funding of the state's academic libraries. The Board of Governors of Higher Education adopted a strategic plan *Investing in Connecticut's Future*, which called for the revision of formulas and guidelines by which needed growth and development of state academic libraries are measured and funded. To implement the new formula models in the 1988–89 budget, a total of 57.5 new positions, additional automation funds and a $4.47 million increase in acquisitions budgets were all added for a total of $5,760,448 in new appropriations.

Moderate success was achieved in the requested increases for Cooperating Library Services Units with a $100,000 increase appropriated rather than the requested $510,000. CLA also had supported the State Library's request for two additional positions, a preservation and conservation officer and a rural library consultant, but only partial funding for the conservation position was achieved.

Early in fiscal year 1988–89 it became clear that state revenues would not meet expected expenditures. After enjoying several years of surplus the Governor ordered all state agencies to cut 3 percent from their current year's budget. This was especially disappointing after having achieved such long-awaited increases in support of the state academic libraries. The Governor also has requested all agencies to submit a 10 percent reduction plan for the 1989–90 fiscal year. CLA's 1989 legislative agenda will again include an increase in funding for CLSUs, increased reference acquisitions for the state library and increased funding for C-Car, the state's library materials delivery system. Bonding will be requested for automation and public library construction.

Library Association. During 1988 the Connecticut Library Association continued its efforts toward improving librarians' salaries. The Connecticut Library Association's Executive Board voted to raise the recommended minimum entry level salary to $23,310, effective July 1, 1989. CLA continues its policy of not advertising positions whose salaries fall below the recommended minimum on either its *Jobline* or in *Connecticut Libraries*. As follow-up to the report of the Blue Ribbon Panel on Librarians' Salaries, the Executive Board of CLA addressed each area of concern in the report and appropriate sections and committees of the association were given responsibility for implementing the recommendations. A press packet prepared by the Public Relations Section included ideas for promoting libraries and librarians, information on how to gain local support and funding, and information on the difficulty of filling positions because of low salaries. The Development Committee will establish a Speakers Bureau of librarians and others willing to speak to library trustees and other groups about the importance of salary increases. The Public Relations and Publicity Sections are organizing a major statewide promotion of libraries to be timed during National Library Week in 1989. Former CLA President Susan Bullock, Meriden Public Library, was appointed salary ombudsman to act as the chief contact for salary related questions.

Improving salaries and the public image of librarians was the theme of the Connecticut Library Association's Annual Conference in April 1988. Programs included "Taking Responsibility for Equitable Sales," "From Nanny to Dynamo: Real and Unreal Images of Children's Librarians" and "Professional Image: Technical Services Librarians." Speakers included Bernie Segal, author of *Love, Medicine, and Miracles*, Arthur Curley, and Herbert S. White.

CLA, funded by a grant from Grolier, Inc., organized a major publicity campaign for National Library Week in 1989. Scheduled events include a newspaper supplement, billboards, and booths in shopping malls. Cochairs for NLW Committee are Susan Smayda and Marcia Trotta.

Connecticut Library and Information Network. In 1988 the state legislature approved $2,000,000 to fund statewide automation development. These funds will be used to complete conversion of the Connecticut Union List of Serials to OCLC, allow additional libraries to join automated networks, assist cooperative systems to upgrade current hardware, upgrade telecommunications, support automation projects in unautomated regions of the state, place telefacsimile machines in libraries to speed ILL and fund the development of a statewide CD-ROM database. The new Advisory Council for Connecticut Library Planning and Development replaces the Connlinet Council, previously charged with formulating statewide automation policy. One of the most exciting automation developments that is sure to have long-range impact is the production of the statewide CD-ROM database. The first disks, undergoing a name change from "Project Amoeba" to "reQuest," were due to be distributed to libraries in January 1989. Coordinating its development with the State Library, the Capitol Region Library Council began reQuest as a component of their CircCess public online catalog. Shortly after their planning began for CD-ROM, Connlinet became interested in applying CD-ROM technology as a method of linking disparate databases for resource sharing. CRLC was asked to administer the project on a statewide basis. Having received first-year funding of $200,000 from Connlinet, the goal of reQuest is to explore using Autographics CD-ROM technology as a viable method of linking a variety of databases already in existence in Connecticut and to use this information to augment interlibrary loan activities. Funding will include a mastering of the database and distribution of workstations. There are 30 hardware test sites and 30 software test sites. The database for the test phase will include 1,000,000 records from CircCess libraries, the Connecticut State Library, University of Connecticut Health Center, and the libraries in LEAP, LION, and Groton-Waterford databases. Second-year funding of $475,000 will expand the database and fund additional workstations for participating libraries.

Cooperating Library Service Units. The six cooperating library service units (CLSUs) in cooperation with the State Library are developing regional projects to upgrade reference service within the regions using LSCA funds. The CLSUs are also administering cooperative adult book discussions funded through grants from the Connecticut Humanities Council, LSCA and the National Endowment for the Humanities. Topics include "American Lives: Reflections on Our Values and Ourselves"; "Contemporary American Short Stories"; "Celebrating Lives: An Intergenerational Exploration of Life After 65"; "Science Fiction Literature"; "Common Ground"; and "Worldview." The Southeastern Connecticut Library Association developed an information project titled *AIDS: The Best Defense Is Information* that placed a basic collection of books and brochures on the medical, social, and public policy aspects of the epidemic in 25 public, school and academic libraries. The Capitol Region Library Council implemented the project in 33 libraries in the Hartford area as did the Eastern Connecticut Library Association for the Willimantic Public Library. In 1989 the remaining CLSUs will be implementing an expanded version of the project, incorporating public programming components.

Awards and Prizes. The Connecticut Library Association honored four librarians at their annual conference in April 1988. Barbara Bryan, Director of the Nyselius Library, Fairfield University, was named CLA's 1988 Librarian of the Year for "outstanding service given to the library profession, for knowledge and wise judgment generously shared, for unassuming leadership offered to your library and to the State of Connecticut." Laurel Goodgion, Director of the Portland Public Library, and Louise Blalock, Director of the New Canaan Library, shared the CLA Special Achievement Award for their "leadership of the Connecticut Service Measures Task Force, Planning for Excellence Committee." Betsy Wilkens, head of children's services at the Windsor Public Library, received the 1988 Faith Hektoen Award "in recognition of the significant impact she has had on library services to children in Connecticut."

People. James Benn, former Director of the Southeastern Connecticut Library Association was named Director of Planning and Network Services at the State Library. Susan Draper Cormier was named children's consultant, Division of Library Services, Connecticut State Library. Zena Koss Friedman joined the State Library as Associate State Librarian for Programs. She is the former Director of the Research Library Division, Arizona State Library, Archives and Public Records. Beth Mainiero, formerly Director of the Hamden Library, accepted the position of director of the Greenwich Library. Virginia Vocelli was named Director of the Avon Free Public Library. She was formerly head of the Faxon Branch of the West Hartford Public Library and is currently serving as CLA's President.

SHARON BRETTSCHNEIDER

DELAWARE

Delaware Library Association (founded 1934)

Membership: 188; *annual budget:* $12,310.

President: Grace S. Husted, New Castle County Department of Libraries.

Vice-President/President-elect: Mary Gise, Claymont Library.

Annual meeting: April 22–23, Rehoboth.

Publication: Delaware Library Association Bulletin (3 issues a year).

Division of Libraries

Louise Wyche, State Librarian
48 S. DuPont Highway
Dover 19901

State Aid to Libraries. The Delaware Legislature gave a much-needed boost to the state's public library budgets by doubling the state's contribution from $.66 per capital to $1.32 for a total of $791,000. The increase in state aid was spearheaded by Representative Ada Leigh Soles, a member of the Joint Finance Committee and a long-time supporter and friend of libraries. The additional funds will be used to help libraries meet state standards for number of operating hours, staff and book collections.

State Library. King Research Inc. of Rockville, Maryland, completed its needs assessment of Delaware libraries and developed a five-year plan for public library development. The plan identified essential goals and included recommended actions for the entire Delaware library community. Some of the key recommendations are to: expand and strengthen state-wide services and county library systems; upgrade and develop adequate facilities throughout the state; adopt and implement new technology; upgrade staff in libraries through hiring practices and continuing education; and establish better communication between the Division of Libraries and the library community of the state. The King Research Report is the basis for the Division's new LSCA Long-range Plan for 1989 to 1993. All state library staff positions were reclassified and upgraded by the state Personnel Department to new minimum entry levels.

Public Libraries. In 1988 New Castle County (the northernmost of our three counties) chose to change its status from a federated system to become a member the New Castle County Department of Libraries. In July 1989, the Hockessin Public Library will come under the full administrative jurisdiction of the county, ending the contractual status begun in 1977. This will bring to five the number of libraries in the New Castle County Department of Libraries (Concord Pike, Kirkwood Highway, Newark, Claymont and Hockessin). The remaining five continue on a contractual basis (New Castle, Appoquinimink, Corbit-Calloway, Delaware City and Wilmington).

The State of Delaware, New Castle County, and the Hockessin Public Library Board of Trustees are cooperating building a new library facility in Hockessin. In a funding package negotiated this summer, New Castle County donated a portion of land in Swift Park for the building site and agreed to provide funds to update the library's current Needs Assessment Report. Delaware, with the support of Hockessin-area legislators, included $300,000 in the bond bill as seed money for the project. The Hockessin Board will provide funds for a professional fundraiser and establish a Fund-raising Committee to secure private funding for the remainder of the project.

On the other side of the county, the Claymont Library, housed in a historic, one-room schoolhouse, was forced to abandon services. Renovation of part of the local Community Center was already under way and the library, after a three-month interruption of service, opened to the public in April in a facility doubled in size. A much-needed Children's Librarian Denise Macaluso from Pittsburg was added to the staff in December.

Mark Titus, DLA past president and director of the Concord Pike Library, resigned in April 1988 to pursue a financial career with Merrill Lynch. His replacement was in place in early 1989. Mary Ann Uitto, formerly with the University of Delaware, joined the staff as Children's Librarian.

The Friends of the Concord Pike Library successfully solicited matching funds from ICI Inc. in order to donate a personal computer to the library.

The New Castle County Department of Libraries is working with RMG Consultants to update requirements for automating nine libraries in the county. Wilmington Library, as a result of its capital projects fund-raising campaign, signed a contract with CLSI for an integrated system of library automation. Site preparation for the computer has begun.

Librarians in the New Castle County public library system have engaged in a great deal of committee work. A public awareness campaign is being organized, a formula for more equitable funding is being developed, the long-range plan has been updated, and statistical reporting methods are being examined.

In Kent County, the Dover Public Library experienced the growth expected after their 1987 expansion. Circulation increased 27 percent over the previous year, the number of borrowers increased 7 percent and children's services and program attendance increased a phenomenal 63 percent. The library began three LSCA Tile I projects that run through December 1988. UPDATE is a collection development project for nonfiction books, PLUG is a public relations campaign, and the third project is a cooperative venture with Smyrna and Harrington libraries for a large print book circuit.

In Sussex County, the southernmost county, increased building activity was welcomed. Seaford District Library doubled its space to 7,500 square feet to provide a meeting room, offices, and staff space. The building was made accessible to the handicapped.

Lewes Public Library built a 7,916 square foot building on land provided by the city. State Bicentennial funds as well as other grants were combined with funds raised locally to pay for this facility.

Milton Library renovated a portion of the second floor of its building for a meeting room for library programs and activities. Shelbyville Library began construction of an addition to house book stacks and made the building accessible to the handicapped. The library is located in an old home, which will be renovated in FY 1989 to provide staff space, meeting space and a reading room. Greenwood Library began construction of a modular building to replace the trailer that has housed the library since 1978.

Delaware Library Association. The Delaware Library Association Spring Conference at Rehoboth Beach Country Club in Sussex County April 22–23 provided good programs as well as a stunning view of the ocean. Successful interaction with state and local legislators was achieved with a panel discussion focusing on funding, state vs. local control, and the need for library advocacy. Discussion was followed by lunch with a legislator at each table, providing an opportunity for individual communication. Other programs included CD-ROM, public domain software, and computers for adult literacy. The dinner speaker was John N. Berry, editor of *Library Journal*, who spoke on the inherent "goodness" of and need for libraries. The second day's programs addressed censorship in Delaware and program ideas for children. Members of a panel discussed fundraising and provided an excellent overview of the roles of Friends, trustees, foundations, and development officers, as well as the possibility of a library establishing a library foundation. The conference ended with lunch and a dynamic speaker Charles Brandt, a Wilmington lawyer who had just published his first novel.

The fall meeting in Dover on October 28 featured Don King of King Research in Maryland, who provided a summary of the needs assessment and long-range plan prepared by his consulting firm for the state library.

College and Research Libraries. The College and Research Libraries Division worked to heighten the awareness and knowledge of the gathering, indexing, and dissemination of State government publications. CRLD sponsored a workshop entitled "Delaware Documentation" to clarify the responsibilities of state agencies and to discuss accessibility of state publications. The Division also established a Committee on State Government Documents, which is charged with identifying problems and making suggestions to the appropriate organizations and agencies.

Delaware School Library Media Association. Thirty-five Delaware School Library Media Association (DSLMA) members attended the April national teleconference on Information Power, which addressed new National School Library Media Program guidelines. These new national guidelines are a major item on the DSLMA's agenda for 1988–89. The other major thrust is the restoration of a library media specialist position in the Department of Public Instruction to represent school libraries.

The Public Library Division became a charter member of the Public Library Association Affiliates Network. The Children's Services Division sponsored the Summer Reading Club program in conjunction with the Division of Libraries and had the largest participation to date—5,510 registered children, a 48 percent increase over 1987.

GRACE S. HUSTED

DISTRICT OF COLUMBIA

DCLA. The District of Columbia Library Association, unlike most state associations, offers programs and activities throughout the year because it serves a relatively small geographical area. Although the Association does not hold an annual conference, it does hold at least two association-wide activities. In May 1988,

District of Columbia Library Association
(founded 1894)

Membership: 843; *annual budget:* $28,050.

President: William R. Gordon, Prince George's County Memorial Library System, 6532 Adelphi Road, Hyattsville, MD 20782 (September 1988–August 1989).

Vice President/President-elect: Shirley Loo, Library of Congress, CRS #LM221, Washington, D.C. 20540.

Secretary: Carol Henderson, ALA Washington Office, 110 Maryland Avenue, N.W., Washington, D.C. 20002.

Treasurer: Elizabeth Warren, Arlington County Public Library, 1015 N. Quincy Street, Arlington, VA 22201.

Annual Meeting: (banquet) May 1988.

Publication: Intercom (monthly).

State Library of the District of Columbia

Hardy R. Franklin, State Librarian

School Library Media Services

Bester D. Bonner
D. C. Public Schools
Washington, D.C. 20001

---

the Association had James Billington, the newly installed Librarian of Congress, as its banquet speaker. He described his view of the role of the Library of Congress (LC) and his efforts to provide a clearer definition of LC's various roles.

An awards program was initiated by DCLA in 1988. After review of types of awards established by other state library associations, DCLA inaugurated a Distinguished Service Award "to recognize a member of the Association who has made an outstanding contribution to the Association through distinguished service." Murray Howder was presented with the first award. Also presented at the banquet was a rare Honorary Life Membership to Mary K. Feldman, longtime editor and co-editor of Intercom, the Association's newsletter.

The other annual event is a New Members Reception usually held in November. The one in 1988 for the current membership year was held at the Cosmos Club which was, until spring of 1988, a men-only club, which finally opened its membership to women after years of pressure. DCLA passed an opportunity to use the Club for an event several years earlier because of its exclusionary policy but had a well-attended gathering under the new regime.

DCLA interest groups and committees once again offered a host of varied programs throughout the year. Programs were organized by the following interest groups and committees: Children and Young Adults; Local History, Genealogy and Folklore; Government Documents; Management; Microcomputer (a new interest group in 1988); Reference; Technical Services; and Intellectual Freedom. In addition, the DCLA National Library Legislative Day Committee, which organizes and plans Legislative Day during National Library Week with the ALA Washington Office, again coordinated a highly successful day of visits to Congressional offices from library supporters from all over the country. In 1988, the Special Libraries Association joined with DCLA and the ALA Washington Office in sponsoring this important event.

DCSLA. The Washington Chapter of the Special Libraries Association (DCSLA) offered programing and activities throughout the year in the same manner as DCLA. In 1988 the Washington Chapter had eight interest groups including Biological Sciences, Geography and Map, Information Technology, Military, News, Picture, Social Science, and Student. In addition, a group of environmental/natural resources librarians met throughout the year and explored the idea of chapter affiliation. A sampling of program topics included AIDS information sources; collection development for cartographic collections; automated systems for translating foreign information; escalating prices of science and technology journals; a tour of National Public Radio; "West–East Technology Transfer: The National Security Implication"; and preservation of library materials.

Joint Spring Workshop. The annual Joint Spring Workshop was sponsored by DCLA, DCSLA, the Law Librarians Society of Washington, D.C., ASIS-Potomac Valley Chapter, the Council of Library Technicians, and the Federal Library and Information Center Committee. The theme, "Library Automation: Hype vs. Humanity," focused on how people in a library setting manage and interact with the technology available to them.

District of Columbia Association of School Librarians (DCASL). In 1988, DCASL used its annual spring luncheon to offer the two candidates for ALA President-elect a forum to present their points of view. The two candidates both had a connection with DCASL: Rebecca Bingham had chosen a career in school librarianship and Patricia Berger had been an active member of the D.C. library community. DCASL also co-sponsored a program in May with the Children and Young Adult Interest Group of DCLA entitled "The Visual Experience: A Film Workshop."

District of Columbia Public Library (DCPL). Library use continued to climb in 1988. During the fiscal year circulation rose 6 percent resulting in the highest per capita circulation in 14 years. All other use indicators also showed gratifying increases. Two major contributing factors to these increases were the continuing increases in the book fund and experiencing the first full year of extended hours in all branch libraries.

DCPL completed a project of reclassifying all professional library positions creating, for the first time, career ladders for entry level librarians. This reclassification project, postponed for many years because of budget reductions and then the need to fund the restoration of basic services, received the needed support for funding from the Mayor and City Council. The results not only provide librarians with a fairer wage for their work but also improve DCPL's ability to attract good applicants for professional positions in a tight marketplace.

Online information services became an integral part of the reference service offered by DCPL. The service includes DIALOG, DATATIMES (daily newspaper database), and DC DOCKET (local legislative database). In addition, CD-ROM technology for accessing periodical literature was extended to regional branch libraries.

The adult basic education (ABE) project providing easy-to-read materials for adults and coordinating literacy efforts throughout the District continued to grow and expand. In December a Family Literacy Conference was offered to encourage reading as a family activity.

Library programs, with the goal of encouraging reading, provided a wide variety of activities. "Summer Quest 88" was highly successful again at motivating children to read. A series of five reading and discussion programs based on the "Let's Talk About It" model was offered in the autumn on the theme, "The Journey Inward: Women's Autobiography." Other major programs included co-sponsorship of the annual D.C. Historical Studies Conference, observance of the 15th annual Deaf Heritage Week, working with the National council on the Aging to present a series of programs in senior citizen centers called "Silver Editions," co-sponsoring an annual program and reception for local authors, and many others.

The Library also was the inaugural stop for the first traveling exhibition of books from the Soviet Union, a major exchange organized by the U.S. Information Agency. The exhibition displayed 1,000 books published in the Soviet Union on a wide range of topics. Most of the publications were donated to DCPL and other libraries in the area.

In the early fall, ground was broken for the new Shepherd Park Branch Library. The new facility is expected to open in early 1990 and will be the 21st full service branch library in the DCPL System.

DCPL embarked on a new venture of offering a program for cable television carried on the new city government channel. Each program is about 15 minutes in length and offers information on library materials, services, and programs.

Academic Libraries. In 1988 the Washington Research Library Consortium (WRLC), a nonprofit corporation formed by eight universities, took a series of steps toward several objectives: implementation of an online catalog, construction of a central facility for storage of seldom used materials, a coordinated collection development program, a preservation program, and an advanced delivery and communication system. An agreement was signed with NOTIS for the purchase of software. WRLC has replaced the Library Council of the Consortium of Universities in coordinating the collection development and resource sharing programs previously managed by the Library Council.

The Lauinger Library of Georgetown University acquired additional space and completed a major renovation of its first floor. The Divinity Library at Howard University was moved to a new building. The University of the District of Columbia reoccupied its Mount Vernon Campus Library after a year of work to repair serious water damage suffered in 1987.

Several major grants were received by universities including a $100,000 grant from the National Endowment for the Humanities to Georgetown for indexing Jesuit historical records; a $55,000 grant from the National Historical Publications and Records Commission to George Washington University to develop a university archives and records management program; a $50,000 grant from Our Sunday Visitor Foundation to Catholic University for the conservation of nineteenth-century canon law materials; and the continuation of an HEA Title II-C grant to identify and bring under bibliographic control collections on the history and culture of Washington, D.C.

CAPCON, a regional library network which

includes academic libraries as well as other types, expanded its membership to more than 100 libraries. CAPCON continued to offer numerous networking services and continuing education programs.

Federal libraries. Contracting out of federal libraries and the ramifications of A-76 continued to be of major concern.

People. Patricia Wilson Berger was elected Vice-President/President-elect of the American Library Association. Cathy A. Jones was elected Treasurer of the Special Libraries Association. Paul Vassallo was appointed Executive Director of the Washington Research Library Consortium. Donald Dennis retired from the position of American University Librarian. Bester D. Bonner was appointed Director of Library Media Services for the D.C. Public Schools. Charmaine Stander Boyd, a librarian who founded the D.C. Citizen Advocates for Libraries which lobbied successfully for better support for the publicly funded libraries in the District, died from a brain tumor.

MARY E. RAPHAEL

FLORIDA

Florida Library Association (founded 1920)

Membership: 1,100; *annual budget:* $142,753.

President: Dr. Althea H. Jenkins, University of South Florida Library, Sarasota 34243 (May 1988–May 1989).

Vice-President/President-elect: Thomas L. Reitz, Seminole Community College Library, Sanford 32771

Annual meeting: May 9–13, Jacksonville.

Publication: FLASH (monthly).

Division of Library and Information Services

Barratt Wilkins, State Librarian
R. A. Gray Building
Tallahassee 32399-0250

State School Library Media Supervisor

Sandra Ulm, Administrator
School Library Media Services
303 Winchester Building A
Tallahassee 32399

Major News. A statewide Library Public Awareness Campaign titled "The Best Gift You'll Ever Give: A Florida Library Card" was successfully conducted during the past year. The LSCA-funded program, administered by the Florida Library Association, included television promotions, free bookmarks, posters, stickers, and clip art to assist all types of libraries in the state to share "The Best Gift."

F. William Summers, Dean of the Graduate School of Library and Information Studies, Florida State University, was installed as President of the American Library Association.

Charles E. Miller, Director of University Libraries at Florida State University, was installed as President of the Association of Research Libraries.

Florida was the site of one of the series of national forums on the future of the Library of Congress held by the Librarian of Congress, James Billington, and the Management and Planning Committee (MAP). The forums gave local librarians an opportunity for input on the direction the Library of Congress should take to provide a leadership role for libraries in the future.

State Association. The 19th annual Library Day attracted more than 600 library Friends, trustees, librarians, and local government officials. The highlight of the event was the launching of the Library Public Awareness Campaign. Florida's First Lady, Mary Jane Martinez, a librarian, joined attendees at lunch and cut a cake decorated to symbolize a library card. The 1987 Legislator of the Year Award was presented to State Senator W. D. Childers of Pensacola.

More than 650 registrants viewed 85 exhibits and participated in 71 programs at the 65th annual conference of the Florida Library Association in Miami Beach. President John D. Hales chose the theme "Quest for Quality." Conference speakers included U.S. Representative Major R. Owens, a librarian; Dr. James Billington, Librarian of Congress; Dr. Herbert White, Dean of the Library School of Indiana University; Florida Secretary of State Jim Smith; and author Richard Peck. Awards presented were Corporate Award to Winn Dixie-Davis Brothers Foundation of Jacksonville; Library Service Enhancement Award to Palm Harbor Junior Women's Club; Outstanding Citizen Award to Alice Skinger, the Chair of Monroe County Library Board; and the Trustee and Friends Award to Merhl and Emily Shoemaker of Flagler County. The Young Adult Caucus and Children's Caucus of the Florida Library Association gave its first Betty Davis Miller Award to the Miami-Dade Library System for its youth outreach project to 500 Dade County schools, parks, and day-care centers. The annual award, named after the State Library's recently retired Youth Services Consultant, will honor outstanding programs in Youth Services.

State Library. A series of Grants Writing Workshops that covered the spectrum of processes, procedures, and concerns involved in applying for and managing Library Services and Construction Act (LSCA) projects was held in three locations around the state. The workshops were open to librarians or representatives of organizations eligible to receive federal Library Services and Construction Act funds. Each participant received a manual that will be updated by the Federal Programs Office.

A statewide disaster assistance information and referral center was established in the State Library to aid academic and public libraries that experience materials-related emergencies. As a part of Florida's newly developed Library Disaster Preparedness and Recovery program, the center networks with libraries across the state as a central repository for local library disaster plans and provides information on available resources. Six regional workshops trained more than 149 people from 119 libraries in the techniques of disaster preparedness and recovery. A final report describing the LSCA-funded program is available from the State Library.

In 1988, the State Library of Florida initiated a three-year project to provide machine-readable records and bibliographic control for Florida state government documents. The project is being funded through an LSCA Title I grant. The Florida Documents Collection is the most complete in the state, with some documents dating to the territorial period (1821–1845). Comprehensive cataloging of the collection, both current and retrospective, into the OCLC system will provide cataloging records for the state depository libraries and will promote documents resources to libraries statewide through identification and access of OCLC records.

The annual Project Librarians' Conference explored the theme "Ethnic Diversity: Impact on Public Library Service in Florida." The three-day workshop attracted 110 participants from across the state. Dr. Hardy Franklin, Director of the Martin Luther King, Jr. Public Library in Washington, D.C., was one of the workshop presenters.

A special four-day Institute on the Fundamentals of Children's Services was held at Florida State University. Sponsored by both the University's School of Library and Information Studies and the State Library of Florida, this intensive in-service training was aimed at paraprofessionals and newcomers in the field of children's services. The Florida Summer Library Program, which used the ALA promotional materials and theme "There's Magic in Books," accounted for a statewide program attendance of 360,687.

Friends and trustee workshops on "Funding Strategies and Planning for Public Libraries" attracted 250 participants in four locations around the state. John Buchner Winfield, an Atlanta-based financial consultant, conducted the daylong workshops. The State Library also produced the publication *Florida Public Library Board Manual, 1988.* The manual provides a basic reference on the responsibilities of library board members and a current source of legal and general information for practicing and potential board members.

Plans were initiated for a Governor's Conference to be held in anticipation of the second White House Conference on Library and Information Services.

Institution Libraries. The annual continuing education conference for 60 state institution and jail librarians was held at the University of Florida. Conference presentations included: a grants management seminar; an overview of adult programming; and a session on repairing, selecting, and using videocassettes and compact discs.

"Making a Difference: Florida's Institution Libraries" is a videocassette produced to give librarians, students, boards, and policymakers a picture of library development in Florida's correctional, mental health, and retardation facility libraries. The North Florida Evaluation and Treatment Center was awarded an LSCA grant to produce the video that was filmed at nine North Florida institutions. The 28-minute video may be borrowed from the State Library's audiovisual section.

Public Libraries. Statewide library development continued to increase with the addition of Union County to those 62 counties already providing countywide library service. Twenty libraries reported foundation or endowment programs in 1988 totaling $567,435. Nine public libraries were awarded $221,983 in Title VI Library Services and Construction Act grants for literacy programs.

The Council for Florida Libraries continues to support the Florida Center for the Book, the Key West Literary Seminar, and planning for the second White House Conference. The Council also works closely with Friends and trustee groups throughout the state and encourages them to hold book and author events, a concept begun in 1980.

Seven of Florida's nine subregional libraries for the blind and physically handicapped have been automated using the READS system developed for the Library of Congress/National Library Service. All subregionals have now been linked by computer to the regional library in Daytona Beach (the Division of Blind Services Bureau of Library and Information Services). BLS/NET is the name for this new network that provides subregional libraries with access to the regional library's computer for updating patron records, requesting interlibrary loans, and reviewing transaction records.

Public libraries in Florida continue to maintain active involvement in literacy initiatives statewide. During 1988 alone, LSCA funds were used to expand literacy projects in 13 systems which serve 25 counties. These 13 systems served more than 2,000 adult students.

School Libraries and Media Centers. The Sunshine State Young Readers Award Program, a reading motivation program for students in grades 3–8, is cosponsored by the Florida Association for Media in Education and the School Library Media Services Office of the Florida Department of Education. Now in its sixth year, the program continues to grow. In 1987–88, 902 schools participated in the program, with 83,343 students reading enough books to vote in the statewide balloting. Barthe De'Clement's *6th Grade Can Really Kill You* won in both grade categories, 3–5 and 6–8.

Building Programs. Fifteen public libraries were awarded a total of $2,150,000 in state and federal funds for construction projects. To assure greater equity for public library grant applicants, several amendments were made to Florida's construction grant administrative code.

A devastating tornado struck Madison County in north central Florida and destroyed the new, unoccupied public library. Construction of the 3,500-square-foot building had just been completed, but furnishings and books had not yet been moved when the tornado struck. The new facility was funded through an LSCA construction grant and $90,000 raised by the community. However, the building was insured and work has begun on rebuilding the library.

Two major building renovations at the State Library building occurred this year. The Bureau of Archives and Records Management remodeled its research rooms and staff office areas, and the Bureau of Library Services and the Bureau of Interlibrary Cooperation areas were remodeled to create more efficient use of workspace.

Networking and Interlibrary Cooperation. The Florida Library Network operates, with the State Library as its administrative host, under a council appointed by the Secretary of State and a smaller policy board elected by members of the council. General policy for network development is put forth in the *Florida Long-Range Plan for Interlibrary Cooperation.* In addition, committees are appointed for special purposes, such as the FLN Interlibrary Loan and Delivery Systems Committee, which was active in 1988.

A major component of the Florida Library Network is a statewide, multitype library network for interlibrary loan (FLIN). In 1988, FLIN adopted a statement of "Resource Sharing Philosophy and Policies," which incorporated the LC Network Advisory Committee's "Library Networking: A Statement of a Common Vision." The Network is based on the principles of mutual benefit and reciprocity, with no fees or charges for properly referred requests. A system of protocols provides for equalization of workload among the 53 library members of FLIN. In addition, 80 other libraries may use the resources of FLIN through direct transmission of requests over OCLC. All other libraries in the state may obtain free interlibrary loan by referring hard-copy requests through the State Library, which then relays them to holding libraries through OCLC.

In 1988, two multitype library consortia (first funded in 1984) moved into new stages of maturity. The Southeast Florida Library Information Network (SEFLIN) hired its first director and established a firm financial basis from local sources through the establishment of membership fees which will provide over $200,000 per year toward ongoing costs of support of administration and program costs. Membership was expanded in 1988 from the original seven large libraries to include four additional major libraries in the area. The Tampa Bay Library Consortium (TBLC) instituted new membership fees and also established a centralized automated library support system for members who do not have local systems. Membership in TBLC, which is broad-based and includes many smaller libraries, has increased to more than 60.

Florida Center for Library Automation (FCLA), established and operated with specific legislative appropriations since 1984, provides automated library support systems to the nine state universities and their various campuses. Services include online public access catalogs, circulation, and acquisitions. The nine databases currently contain over 5,000,000 bibliographic records. FCLA continues to be a pivotal point of concern in developing statewide automation, and in 1987/88 the legislature ordered special studies of the future role of FCLA by the Postsecondary Education Planning Commission and the Florida Information Resources Network.

Awards. The Library Education Centennial Honor Roll recognized 18 individuals for outstanding service to library education. Harold Goldstein, Professor and former Dean, Florida State University School of Library and Information Studies, was honored posthumously. Dr. Goldstein created the first doctoral program in the Southeast and served as president of both the Association for Library and Information Science Education and the Florida Library Association.

ETHEL A. HUGHES

GEORGIA

Events. The Georgia Library Trustees and Friends Association and the Georgia Council of Public Libraries sponsored the fifth annual Georgia Library Legislative Day in Atlanta on February 4, 1988. Georgia's First Lady, Elizabeth Harris, presented the Georgia Library Trustees and Friends Association's 1987 Honor Award to State Representative Terry L. Coleman of District 118 in Eastman. The award is presented annually to a state legislator who displayed leadership and outstanding support for the libraries and educational concerns during the preceding year.

Georgia Library Association (founded 1898)

Membership: 813; annual budget: $41,000.

President: James E. Dorsey, Director, Chestate Regional Library System, 127 N. Main St., Gainesville 30505-2399.

Vice-President/President-elect: Robert Richardson, Director, Duckworth Libraries, Young Harris College, Young Harris 30582.

Secretary: Laura Lewis, Assistant Director, Troup–Harris–Coweta Regional Library, 500 Broome St., LaGrange 30240.

Treasurer: Irma Harlan, Chatham–Effingham–Liberty Regional Library, Savannah 31499.

Biennial meeting: October 25–27, 1989, Jekyll Island.

Executive Secretary: Ann W. Morton, P.O. Box 833, Tucker 30084.

State Department of Education, Division of Public Libraries Services

Joe Forsee, Director
156 Trinity Avenue, S.W.
Atlanta 30303

Division of Instructional Media Services

Nancy Hove, Director of Media Services Unit
Twin Towers, 20th Floor
Atlanta 30334

Members of the Metro Atlanta Library Association were hosted by the Canadian Consulate during the Association's winter social. On display was a sample collection of books by Canadian authors. Collections were presented to public libraries in the metro area by the consul.

Academic Libraries. Materials documenting the life of former U.S. Secretary of State and University of Georgia Law Professor Dean Rusk have been made available for research at the Richard B. Russell Memorial Library in Athens. When complete, the collection will consist of oral histories of Rusk and his associates in the Kennedy and Johnson administrations; copies of documents drawn from the files of the Kennedy and Johnson presidential libraries, the State Department, and the National Archives; a collection of films, photographs, books and articles, and personal papers and files during his 17 years at the University of Georgia.

The Emory University Division of Library and Information Management held a gala program in April to honor its alumni and faculty and to celebrate its history that dates back to 1905. The library school, the oldest in the Southeast, formally closed in August 1988.

Georgia State University joined Yale and Harvard universities in the spring as the owner of one of approximately 14 copies of the first edition of political economist Adam Smith's *Wealth of Nations.*

Former United States Senator Herman E. Talmadge and D. W. Brooks, Chairman of the Board Emeritus of Gold Kist, Inc., donated their personal papers to the Richard B. Russell Memorial Library at the University of Georgia. The Talmadge Collection provides a comprehensive view of Georgia and national politics and government from the 1920s to the present by documenting the political career and legacy of this Georgia native. The Brooks Collection spans the 40 years of Mr. Brooks' prestigious career in agribusiness, advisory positions with U.S. presidents, and his work with the Methodist Church and numerous colleges and universities.

The Medical College of Georgia named the Library in honor of Robert B. Greenblatt. An endowment in his memory has been established by the Greenblatt family. The Bainbridge College Library placed most of the books on Circulation Plus.

The library at the Southern College of Technology in Marietta put four new bells in the bell tower atop the newly expanded library. Commenting that he wishes to support the "heart of learning" at the university, head football coach Vince Dooley has donated $100,000 to strengthen the university's libraries.

Public Libraries. DeKalb County Public Library and Ketchum Public Relations received an award for television sports produced in 1986 as part of their library bond referendum campaign. The Atlanta Chapter of the International Association of Business Communicators awarded their Gold Flame Award for the Campagne Edition of the Orvrall Communications Program to the series of five 30-second television spots which were used to express the importance of public libraries, the range of services offered, and the resources available for community use. The television spots helped the DeKalb County Public Library see the passage of the $29,000,000 bond referendum which will double the size of the system in the next three years.

Athens Regional Library was awarded a grant from the Georgia Endowment for the Humanities for "The Sense of Place in American Thought and Literature." The program consists of a series of radio presentations, film showings, lectures, and public discussions.

On June 5, 1988, the Clayton County Library System celebrated the dedication and grand opening of its new headquarters library in Jonesboro. The $3,200,000 facility was designed by Scogin Elam and Bray Architects of Atlanta and was built by M. G. Engineering and Construction Company on 3.75 acres donated by Needham B. Bateman, a local physician.

DeKalb County Public Library received the 1988 National Association of Counties Achievement Award for its Avondale/MARTA rapid transit branch library.

The R. J. Taylor, Jr. Foundation awarded the East Central Georgia Regional Library a grant to publish the second volume of the *Personal Name Index to the Augusta Chronicle*. Compiled by librarian Alice Walker, this volume lists more than 30,000 names and covers the years 1800–1810.

School Media Centers. The Georgia Library/Media Department declared April 1988 as Media Month in Georgia. The theme selected was "Helping Georgia Read." This theme ties in with the state's emphasis on literacy.

The Media Services Department of the Fulton County School System installed online bibliographic database searching in 13 high school media centers and the Paul D. West Professional Library. The high schools are using the Classroom Instruction Program of DIALOG Information Services, Inc. Curriculum-related online searches are available at no cost to students and teachers in the high schools.

The Glynn County School System and Griffin High School in Spalding County were honored by the State Board of Education as 1987–88 Recognition of Excellence recipients for exemplary media services.

People. Gordon Baker, Kemp Elementary School, Hampton; Grace Bellamy, Lumpkin County Middle School; and Helen Miller, Henry County Senior High School, McDonough, were honored with the 1988 Media Specialist of the Year Awards. Thomas G. Basler, Medical College of Georgia, is Chairman-Elect of the Friends of the Library Information System, a consortium of 20 medical libraries which use integrated library systems based on the Georgetown University Medical Library System. Melvin McKinney Bowie, a member of the College of Education faculty at the University of Georgia in the Department of Instructional Technology, received the Carroll Preston Baber Research Award at the 1988 American Library Association Annual Conference. Elizabeth Collins, Director of the Sara Hightower Regional Library, received the Award of Excellence in Public Library Services from the State School Superintendent, Werner Rogers, at the Georgia Board of Education's May meeting in Atlanta. Ann Curry, a former national board member of the League of Women Voters and active community volunteer in metro Atlanta, was elected the 1987–88 chairman of the Atlanta–Fulton Public Library Board of Trustees.

Jane M. Norcross, a trustee of the DeKalb County Public Library for 21 years, received the American Library Association Trustee Citation for the outstanding manner in which she has served library development for more than 25 years. Mary Jean Sloan received the 1988 Walter Bell Award presented by the Georgia Association for Instructional Technology. Nancy F. Williams, former head of Reader Services and Collection Development at Mercer University, Atlanta, was named Director of the university's library. Frank Winstead, Director of Educational Media for the DeKalb County Schools, was the first recipient of the GLMA/SIRS Freedom of Information Award.

Deaths. Josephine F. Thompson, retired professor of the School of Library and Information Studies of Atlanta University, died July 25, 1988, in Atlanta.

HELEN CITRON WILTSE

HAWAII

State Association. A Tri-Conference of the Hawaii Library Association, the Hawaii Association of School Librarians and the Pacific Association for Communications and Technology was held on March 18 and 19 at the Ilikai Hotel in Waikiki. The theme was "Current Issues: Literacy, Leadership, Technology" and the featured speaker was Emily Mobley, President of the Special Libraries Association.

Public Libraries. The 1988 Hawaii State Legislature provided full support to almost every legislative and budget request sought by the Board of Education and the Hawaii State Public Library System and endorsed by the Friends of the Library of Hawaii. The Legislature appropriated $5,000,000 for repair and maintenance of Hawaii's 49 public libraries, beginning July 1, 1988, which represents more money spent than in all the years since 1962 when the public library system was established. Expanded, renovated or new public libraries have been designed or constructed at 10 locations throughout the state. A

Hawaii Library Association (founded 1922)

Membership: 400; *annual budget:* $16,000.

President: Donna Marie Garcia, 4156 Rice St., Lihue, Hawaii 96766. BYU–Hawaii, Laie, 96762 (March 1988–March 1989).

Vice-President/President-elect: Sandra Akana, Waimaudo Public & School Library.

Annual meeting: March, Honolulu.

Publications: HLA Newsletter (4–6 times a year); *HLA Journal* (annual).

Hawaii State Library, State Librarian

Bartholemew A. Kane
State Librarian's Office
Kekuanaoa Building
465 S. King St., B–1
Honolulu 96813

State School Library Supervisor

Patsy Izumo
641 18th Avenue
Honolulu 96816

$1,000,000 increase in the public libraries' operating budget translates into wage increases for 177 student helpers, new positions for public service, more security service, more money for magazines, an increase in library automation, new and replacement equipment throughout the system, and a consultant study of the classification and compensation of public librarians.

The Hawaii State Library System's Online Public Access Catalog (OPAC), implemented in 1987–88, is the fourth stage of an automation program that began in 1973. The Hawaii State Public Library System automation program is unique in the world because it is the only completely automated statewide system in the nation, as well as the largest, with 254 terminals in 49 branches.

The Hawaii State Public Library System continues to provide "people programs" for the promotion of library service. Among the most recent are a library card campaign that resulted in 36,000 new card holders; a public awareness ad campaign promoting library usage and a career as a librarian; children's summer reading programs; a young adults' humanities program; book talk teams; and a teen library council.

School Libraries and Media Centers. Planning for the next decade of school media programs statewide includes implementation of revised standards, utilization of technologies to provide and expand services and development of a school library network.

The Hawaii Association of School Librarians and State School Library Services Office will submit the revised standards or guidelines for school library media center programs for approval in early 1989. These local standards are in consonance with the national *Information Power* guidelines.

The Computer Review Center and Clearinghouse, originally founded as an Education Consolidation and Improvement Act (ECIA) Chapter 2 project, is an ongoing state funded program. The Center coordinates the review of computer resources, acts as a clearinghouse of evaluation information and coordinates the site license activities for Minnesota Educational Computing Consortium (MECC) for Hawaii's public schools.

The School Library Network (SLN) project, funded by ECIA Chapter 2, is in its second year. The project objectives include establishing a computer database of school library holdings (using *Bibliophile* as a resource), providing for circulation automation functions of school libraries, facilitating interlibrary loan procedures and a document delivery system. Twelve school libraries will be included in the SLN pilot by June 1989.

Ten school libraries (elementary, intermediate and secondary), in conjunction with the Department of Education Multimedia Services Branch, are currently piloting a Distance Learning Technology project utilizing the ITV-based national consortium operated by WNET/New York, LEARNING LINK. This project, funded by the Hawaii State Legislature, is an interactive telecommunications system that has a national core content and the tools/utilities to customize local databases.

Improvement in instruction through the integration of library and content area instruction continues to be a major focus. The successful *Children As Authors* program is implemented in all districts; literature-based learning activities are being expanded as is a three-part in-service program on collection development.

Academic, and Other Special Libraries. The University of Hawaii at Manoa Library, in partnership with the University Computing Center, opened the Computerized Learning and Information Center (CLIC) at Sinclair Library in early 1988. The Center, used by students, faculty and staff, provides 80 workstations to access commercial software, faculty-developed software and "reserve" software. Emphasis is on CAI programs, programs that aid instruction and skill development and that enhance learning and teaching. Access to the library's on-line public catalog and to PLATO are also provided.

The Science and Technology Reference Department, in cooperation with the University of Hawaii Center for Tropical and Subtropical Aquaculture, established a Library Aquaculture Workstation with funding from the USDA. The workstation includes the CD-ROM Aquatic Sciences and Fisheries Abstracts.

Hamilton Library, the research library on the University of Hawaii at Manoa campus, will be closed during the Summer of 1989 to remove material containing asbestos from the second floor of the building. Microform and periodical services at the Library have been reorganized and moved into a physically remodelled and expanded space on the first floor of Hamilton. Modern reader/printer equipment and a fully staffed service desk enhance access to these important collections.

Implementation of on-line circulation was completed at the University of Hawaii at Manoa Library. Conversion to online circulation for the Hawaiian/Pacific, Government Documents and Audiovisual Services Collections was begun. Remote dial-in access to the Library's online public catalog is also now available to UH students, faculty and staff from their home or office terminals. Access is provided by terminal and modem through the UH Computing Center. More than 250 users have taken advantage of this new service.

Two HEA Title II-C grants were received by the University of Hawaii at Manoa Library. The first, in the amount of $45,000, was received to microfilm the Pacific area newspapers. Another grant for $64,000 provides bibliographic access to the Tsuzaki/Reinecke Creole (Pidgin) Collection.

The second phase of automation was implemented at the University of Hawaii at Hilo Library in August when the automated circulation system was initiated.

Networks and Interlibrary Cooperation. Grant funding for $27,000 from LSDA, established HEALTHFAX, an interlibrary cooperative program between the Hawaii State Library System, the Hawaii Medical Library and the University of Hawaii Library Science/Technology Reference Department to facilitate document delivery of health-related reference questions to public library patrons.

Year of the Young Reader activities are coordinated by the School Library Services office, the Hawaii State Public Library, the Hawaii Association of School Librarians, the local council of the International Reading Association, and other organizations.

Professional Interests. The appointment of a non-librarian to the post of deputy state librarian in January sparked controversy across the state. Protests against the State Librarian's selection of a Board of Education member, John Penebacker, to the post, subsequently ratified by the Board, were made by librarians and non-librarians, including a Hawaii State Senate's Women's Caucus. The appointment was later ruled to be improper by the State Ethics Commission and the State Attorney General advised that the position was not exempt from civil service hiring rules, invalidating the hiring procedure. Mr. Penebacker accepted a lower-paying position, exempt from civil service rules, as special assistant to the State Librarian which was created by the Governor. Opposition to the appointment focused primarily on the conflict of interest, since the State Librarian reports to the Board of Education; Mr. Penebacker's lack of formal training or experience in librarianship, as specified in the original job advertisement; and charges of discrimination against women. The position of deputy state librarian is undergoing the process of civil service classification and recruitment by the Department of Personnel Services, which may take seven or more months. The Board of Education, meanwhile, will seek an exemption from civil service for the deputy position from the 1989 Legislature.

Awards. The 1988 Nene Award winner was *You Shouldn't Have to Say Goodbye* by Patricia Hearmes. The runner-up was *Dear Mr. Henshaw* by Beverly Cleary.

Appointments. John R. Penebacker was appointed Special Assistant to the State Librarian. Martin J. Faigel, formerly with the University of Alabama, was appointed Collection Development Officer for the University of Hawaii at Manoa Libraries. Terry Webb, formerly of the Joseph F. Smith Library at Brigham Young University-Hawaii was appointed as Library Director at Kapiolani Community College.

Deaths. David Kittelson, former Head Librarian of the Hilo College Library, and longtime Curator of the Hawaiian Collection and former University Archivist, died March 1, 1988.

SUSAN F. MAESATO
KENNETH R. HERRICK

IDAHO

Idaho Library Association (founded 1915)

Membership: 494; *annual budget:* $32,971.

President: Margaret McNamara, Director, American Falls District Library, American Falls 83211 (October 1988–October 1989).

Vice-President/President-elect: David Case, Lewis and Clark State College, Lewiston 83501.

Annual meeting: August 11–19, 1989, Coeur d'Alene.

Publication: The *Idaho Librarian* (quarterly).

Idaho State Library

Charles Bolles, State Librarian
325 West State Street
Boise 83702-6072

State School Library Media Supervisor

Rudy Leverett, Consultant
State Department of Education
Boise 83702

"Reflections, or Back to the Future," was the theme of the Idaho Library Association's (ILA) 1988 conference that attracted more than 300 attendees to Boise October 6–8. The keynote address by Jim Trelease was "Reading Aloud: Motivating Children to Make Books Into Friends, Not Enemies."

Favorite books—for adults, young adults, and children—held an honored place in the conference. The 1989 conference, scheduled for August 16–19 in Coeur d'Alene, will be the first combined meeting of the ILA and the Pacific Northwest Library Association.

State Library Activities. Frank Nelson, formerly director of the Sheldon (Washington) Public Library, headed the Eastern Idaho field office November 15, 1988. Individual consultants were in place in Southeastern Idaho: Marj Shelby, director, maintains her office in the State Library in Boise, and in Northern Idaho, Karen Strege, formerly director of the East Bonner District and who took office in November after the resignation in July of Janet Crowther, maintains her office in Moscow.

The State Library appointed a District Law Revision Task Force in April 1988 to conduct a complete review of district library law in Idaho. The Task Force will introduce a measure in the 1989 session of the Idaho Legislature to bring the Library District Law into conformity with other sections of the *Idaho Code* and to clarify several areas that have come into question. Task Force members will also consider legislation to simplify the establishment, consolidation, and expansion of library districts, as well as issues related to the funding of library districts.

As a follow-up to the Strategy Study completed in 1987, the State Library engaged The Consulting Librarians Group, Sandra Cooper, Managing Consultant, to work with the Continuing Education Task Force to prepare a Statewide Continuing Library Education Plan for 1989–1991. A mission statement, roles and responsibilities, and goals and objectives were formulated for review by the Idaho library community. The final plan was delivered to the Idaho State Library in December 1988 for implementation beginning in 1989.

Another extension of the results of the Strategy Study was the appointment of the Idaho Library Automation Task Force, which was asked to provide statewide automation planning for libraries in Idaho. Among their recommendations to the State Library were coordination of automation development, investigation of various means of funding library automation in Idaho, establishment of efficient and inexpensive telecommunications transmission, and commissioning of a study to determine whether library automation development should be centralized or distributed.

The State Librarian convened the Idaho Collection Development Committee in the fall of 1987. This committee, supported by funds from the Pacific Northwest Conspectus Database Project, has been investigating various means of maximizing Idaho's library materials resources. Among the activities of the committee is cooperative collection development, development of collection development policies at the local level, and better methods of exchanging information about resources. The committee is also looking at ways to promote programs of the PNCD in Idaho.

Staff changes at ISL include the retirement of Evva Larson as Blind and Physically Handicapped Services Librarian. In her time at the State Library, she served 16 years as Assistant State Librarian. Her position at the State Library has not been filled. Carol Silvers was promoted by the State Library to fill a newly established position as State Documents Coordinator in July of 1988. Also in July, Luan Knospe was employed to coordinate Idaho's participation in the National Endowment for the Humanities United States Newspaper Project.

Academic Libraries. The University of Idaho is reviewing journal subscriptions with campus departments, targeting $100,000 in cancellations in the current year. "The University of Idaho Library: A Centennial History," compiled by Karen A. Buxton, was recently distributed. This illustrated booklet was based on an unpublished manuscript by Robert D. Hook and Richard J. Beck.

The Idaho State University Library will receive a $60,000 gift from the Idaho First National Bank which will fund the purchase of the INNOVACQ automated serials control system. Also, a library endowment fund is being started with the proceeds from the sale of a house in Lava Hot Springs.

Boise State University Library Special Collections Department published *The Frank Church Papers: A Summary Guide* by Ralph W. Hansen and Deborah J. Roberts. Northwest Nazarene College is moving into an endowment drive and has targeted $500,000 for library collection development and the conversion of periodical holdings to microforms.

VALNET, a multilibrary automated catalog and circulation system with courier service, opened last April. Lewis-Clark State College library houses the host processor. VALNET serves five libraries in seven locations. Paul Kraus, Director of Lewis-Clark State College, announced a $64,000 grant which will allow expansion to new locations including Walla Walla Community College, Grangeville, Orofino, LCSC branch campus in Coeur d'Alene, Clarkston High School, and others.

Building Programs. LSCA II grants for remodeling were awarded to Preston Carnegie Council District Library and Filer Public Library. The Blackfoot Public Library moved into a remodeled store in the downtown area.

Awards and Honors. Keith Peterson's *This Crested Hill* won the Idaho Book Award. A silver medal was presented to the author of this centennial history of the University of Idaho. Honorable mentions went to Keith Peterson for *Company Town*, Rae Ellen Moore for *Just West of Yellowstone* and Leslie Leek Durham for *Heart of a Western Woman*.

Joanne Sutton was honored as Idaho's Librarian of the Year at the ILA Awards Banquet. She chairs the Intellectual Freedom Committee for ILA and is a school librarian.

PAUL HOLLAND

ILLINOIS

Illinois Library Association (founded 1896)

Membership: 3,320; *annual budget:* $538,585.

President: Marlene Deuel, Illinois State Library, Springfield 62756 (January 1988–June, 1989).

Vice-President/President-elect: Fred Peterson, Illinois State University, Normal, 61761.

Executive Director: Willine C. Mahony, 33 W. Grand, Suite 301, Chicago 60610.

Annual meeting: May 11–13, Chicago.

Publication: ILA Reporter (quarterly).

Illinois State Library
Bridget Lamont, Director
Centennial Building
Springfield 62756

School Library Media Supervisor
Marie Sivak
Illinois Office of Education
Springfield 62702

State Association. On May 11–13, 1988, the Illinois Library Association (ILA) held its annual conference in Chicago. The theme, "Illinois: Building Strategies for Services," attracted some 1,817 attendees, the largest in ILA's history. The opening session, co-sponsored by the Illinois State Library (ISL) and ILA, featured Allan Bloom, author of the best-seller *The Closing of the American Mind*. The membership on May 12, 1988, considered by-law revisions and a restructuring of ILA recommended by the ILA Executive Board, which was based on a Strategic Plan adopted in 1987. The membership failed to pass the bylaws by a two-thirds majority. Subsequently, the ILA Board that unanimously endorsed the strategic plan and bylaws sent a mail vote, which was approved, 919 to 280, and provided for reorganization of the association with changes effective July 1, 1989. The Association has begun its long-range planning for the new structure, with changes from units to special interest groups and in the fiscal and organizational year.

The Illinois Authors' Luncheon, co-sponsored by READ Illinois and the office of the Secretary of State, featured Scott Turow, author of the best-seller *Presumed Innocent* and a Chicago lawyer. Twenty-five libraries sponsored Illinois guest authors under the Take an Author to Lunch program.

State Library Activities. The ISL Automation Committee's discussion draft of the statewide automation plan, "Cooperative Long Range Automation Plan for Illinois Libraries," addressed automation in the State in the context of cooperative resources sharing. Initiatives included development of a library telecommunications network and implementation of workable interface linking ILLINET/ONLINE (IO) with other major automated systems.

State Library Building. On April 13, 1988, more than 300 guests attended a "beam" signing ceremony in Springfield for the new state library. The event initiated the construction phase of the five-story, 164,000-square-foot structure, to be located east of the state capitol. Total cost of the project, including land and construction, is $36,000,000.

Advances in Networking Online 1988. Illinet On-line consists of the statewide Library Computer System (LCS) and the Full Bibliographic Record (FBR). About 800 terminals are placed in 29 colleges and university libraries, as well as in the headquarters building of each library system and the Illinois State Library (ISL). LCS contains records representing 10,200,000 titles and 17,800,000 million volumes. The FBR database, with 3,400,000 bibliographic records, held more than 4,000,000 unique MARC records by the end of 1988. The long-range plan for IO, "Expansion and Enhancement of Library Computer Systems in Illinois," suggests a member of initiatives.

NILRC (Northern Illinois Learning Resources Cooperative), a consortium of 44 institutions of higher learning including community colleges as well as universities, has received a $40,030 LSCA Title III grant to prepare a statement on technical needs. The document will serve as the framework for the Illinois Library Telecommunications Network. An earlier LSCA grant funded the gathering of data for the functional report for this project.

Public Libraries. The PLS' "Avenues to Excellence" Review Committee analyzed the results of a survey completed by 376 of the 610 public libraries in Illinois on the state per capita grant requirements. The committee prepared a 'hearings' draft, which was introduced at the 1988 ILA Conference. After four statewide hearings, the final document, "Avenues to Excellence II," was prepared and adopted by the PLS Board (9/13/88) and by the ILA Board (11/4/88). The Section also is preparing workshops for administrators of small public libraries serving fewer than 10,000 patrons.

Illinois Library Trustees Association (ILTA). ILTA and PLS co-sponsored two workshops on long-range planning, in partial fulfillment of the per capita grant requirements. Approximately 200 trustees and librarians attended the meetings, which were held in October in Mount Vernon and in Naperville.

School Librarians, Media Centers, and Youth Services. IAME, the Illinois Association for Media in Education, and the Illinois Reading Council were among co-sponsors of the Rebecca Caudill Young Readers' Book Award. Lynne Reid Banks, author of *The Indian in the Cupboard*, was the first recipient of the award, which was presented at the Illinois School Library Media Association Conference in October 1988.

The annual IAME Honor Award was presented at Triple I 1988 to Carole Morrison, DuPage Library System. Triple I is sponsored by IAME, the Illinois Association for Educational Communications and Technology, and the Illinois Association for Supervision and Curriculum Development.

Academic Libraries. The Illinois Association of College and Research Libraries (IACRL) with the Resources and Technical Services Section co-sponsored a conference to inform professionals involved in using, interpreting, acquiring, and organizing new formats in a variety of settings. The conference was held October 27–29 in Bloomington, Illinois.

At the 1988 ILA Conference, IACRL sponsored three discussion group sessions: "Conservation at the Circulation Desk: Saving Our Materials," "Technology and BI: What Works and What Doesn't," and "Education and Training for Acquisitions: What Makes a Successful Acquisitions Librarian."

Resources and Technical Services Section (RTSS). The joint RTSS/IACRL Conference, held October 27–28, 1988, in Bloomington, Illinois, featured Peter Simon of R. R. Bowker as keynote speaker. Other sessions focused on such topics as the librarian-software-publisher-relations, the librarian-publisher-vendor interface, desk-top publishing, copyright, telefacsimile, and OCLC enhancements.

Youth Services Section (YSS). YSS held programs and workshops in various locations on different subjects. A panel discussion featured six speakers from areas of library service that focus upon and influence youth services; a professional skills workshop addressed rights and restrictions of child patrons and youth services staff. YSS also sponsored the annual Storytelling activity at the ILA Spring Conference. The Fall Workshop featured young people's author Phyllis Reynolds Naylor.

District Library Section (DILS). In its efforts to provide information about district libraries, DILS plans to videotape its traveling slide road show on how to become a district library. DILS also continued its conference scholarship to the ILA Annual Conference.

Government Documents Round Table (GODORT). GODORT's program at the 1988 ILA Conference featured Michael Stevens of the Department of Defense Information Analysis Center for Manufacturing Technology, Illinois Institute of Technology, Chicago, who explained what happens in a DOD Information Analysis Center and, specifically, at his center. Plans were made for a fall workshop.

Specialized Library Services Section (SLSS). Two hundred thirty disks were copied at the SLSS microcomputer freeware exchange booth at the 1988 ILA Annual Conference. Of these, 75 percent were requests for IBM programs and the balance were for Apple programs. Five free SLSS memberships were given away at the Conference.

Junior Members Round Table (JMRT). JMRT sponsored four $100 scholarships and one $250 scholarship at the 1988 ILA Conference. JMRT also initiated a paper competition on the topic "Life After Library School: Were You Prepared for the Real World?" The four winners presented their papers at the annual conference, and a panel discussion followed the presentations. The Crosman Award honored an active younger/newer member of the profession who has made a significant contribution to the community.

Library Assistants Section (LAS). In October 1988 LAS presented a miniconference: "The Library: A Stressful Environment" on new technologies and how they affect reference/information services—reaching out to patrons, time management, staff evaluations, and correct telephone techniques. The Awards and Recognition Committee presented the Jane O'Brien Award at the 1988 ILA Conference to Elvera Hinkle, Addison Library.

Librarians for Social Responsibility (LSR). The theme of LSR's program at the ILA Conference was "Libraries and Latchkeys: The Escalating Problem of Unattended Children in Public Libraries." Research reports, latchkey policies from libraries throughout the U.S., and definitions of terms ("unattended child," "vulnerable child") were offered. A LSR bibliography was distributed to those attending the session.

Intellectual Freedom Committee. IFC's programs for the 1988 ILA Annual Conference included "Coping When the Censor Comes," "Writing Intellectual Freedom Policies," and "Freedom of Information Act: Nuts and Bolts." The Committee also worked to establish an intellectual freedom network through the library systems.

I READ (Illinois Reading Enrichment and Development). More than 588 libraries, schools, reading centers, and military bases in Illinois and 15 other states sponsored I READ's DEVOUR A BOOK as their summer reading program theme. They reached approximately 145,000 young people during 1988. The statistics for the Devour a Book program were impressive: workshops for five library systems in Illinois and 125 libraries; more than three hours of programs at the 1988 ILA Annual Conference in Chicago; four library recipients of the I READ Award; and more than 200 attendees at the I READ Showcase.

The Legislative Library Development Committee (LLDC). LLDC's efforts in 1988 resulted in an increase of approximately three percent in funding of Illinois library systems that are totally reliant on the state for their funding. The section also was instrumental in securing first-time funding for the new HEA Title II-D. The LLDC conducted a series of successful "Road Shows" to provide the "hows" and "whys" of legislative advocacy. Their efforts prompted approximately 80 people to go to Washington for ALA Legislative Day and more than 200 participants in ILA Legislative Day in Springfield.

Awards. Awards presented at the ILA Conference included the Hugh T. Atkinson Award, which was given to the Illinois Valley Library System (IVLS). The YSS Davis Cup, awarded to individuals who have made an outstanding contribution to work with children, went to Mary Ann Sarver, Rockford Public Library.

Building Programs. Chicago Public Library broke ground in October 1988 for the new $144 million Harold Washington Center, to be completed in 1991 and to be located on State Street, between Congress and Van Buren. The building will contain 750,000 square feet and rise ten stories above the ground level.

Deaths. Charles Herrick, administrator, Helen Plum Memorial Library, Lombard, and a past PLS president, died September 6, 1988.

Frank Dempsey, a past president of ILA and administrator of the Arlington Heights Memorial Library, died September 11, 1988.

PATRICIA M. HOGAN

INDIANA

Indiana Library Association (founded 1891)

Indiana Trustee Library Association (founded 1902)

Membership: 960 (ILA), 1,700 (ILTA); annual budget: $163,000.

President ILA: William F. Bolte, Jeffersonville Twp. Public Library, 211 E. Court Ave., Jeffersonville 47131 (May 1988–May 1989).

Vice-President/President-elect ILA: Betty C. Martin, Vigo County, Public Library, One Library Square, Terre Haute 47807.

President ILTA: Sandra Sawyer, Fulton County Public Library, 320 W. 7th, Rochester 46975.

Vice-President/President-elect ITLA: Roena Rand, Gary Public Library, 220 West 5th Avenue, Gary 48402.

Annual meeting: May 10–13, Ft. Wayne.

Publications: Focus on Indiana Libraries (11 per year); *Indiana Libraries* (occasional).

Indiana State Library

C. Ray Ewick, Director
140 N. Senate Avenue
Indianapolis 46204

School Library Media Supervisor

Jacqueline G. Morris
Indiana Department of Education
Room 229, State House
Indianapolis 46204

As a result of a study conducted by the Resource Sharing Technologies subcommittee of the Indiana State Library Advisory Council, CD-ROM and telefacsimile technology will be introduced into 54 of the state's 238 public libraries for the first time. LSCA funds are being used to purchase equipment, and software. Training and equipment procurement will be handled by the Indiana Cooperative Library Services Authority. Each of the nine Area Library Service Authorities will receive equal grants that will allow placement of equipment, and software in all areas of Indiana. Selection of sites, equipment, and software will be completed in early 1989. The project will move Indiana libraries forward into utilization of technology for the delivery of information.

State Legislation. The 1988 session of the Indiana General Assembly produced minor achievement in actual bill passage for libraries in Indiana. Only one Association-sponsored measure, a revision of the Library Service Authority law allowing the LSAs to use proxy votes to achieve a quorum, received the Governor's signature.

The Indiana Library Association–Indiana Library Trustee Association (ILA–ILTA) Legislative Committee hosted a statewide Legislative Forum to solicit membership input into the formulation of the annual legislative program. State Senator Louis Mahern inspired Forum participants with marketing tips on how to lobby legislators. To assure that all state legislators were contacted, the Committee again sponsored Regional Library Days. The program encouraged local contacts by librarians and trustees of all legislators.

State Associations. In response to suggestions made by the membership in a survey conducted during 1987, the ILA–ILTA Strategic Planning Committee presented a final report for the Five-Year Plan to the Joint Boards of the Association. A new Legislative Advocate was selected by the Associations. Kathy Dinsborn, Indianapolis, succeeded Ann Moreau; Ann had been the Advocate since 1981.

The Association of Indiana Media Educators (AIME) held its 10th annual conference in Indianapolis, March 3–5, "Targeting: Techniques, Technology, Tradition." Featured guests included Blanche Woolls, keynote, School of Library and Information Science, University of Pittsburgh; and Doris Epler, Pennsylvania Department of Education, speaking on "Access Pennsylvania."

The statewide Summer Reading Program sponsored by the ILA Children's and Young People's Division used the theme "Summer of Champions."

State Library. The Continuing Education and Orientation Committee (CEOC) of the State Library Advisory Council (ISLAC) and the State Library sponsored a two-day workshop on training trainers. Charlaine Ezell, Continuing Education Specialist, State Library of Michigan, was the presenter.

A statewide workshop was held for public library trustees in April. Topics included effective administration of modern organizations, legal responsibilities of trustees, planning, standards, personnel issues and policies for public libraries.

The Indiana Center for the Book, with Satellite Centers in ten cities, opened at the State Library in March; Jean Jose, Assistant Director of the State Library, is the project coordinator.

Output measures for public libraries were published for the first time. Seven of the 12 measures defined and recommended for public libraries by the American Library Association were included in the report. LSCA Title II Construction Grants for renovation were awarded to four public libraries: Hammond, Hagerstown, Peru, and Thorntown. Twenty-four public libraries and eight institutional libraries received LSCA grants for literacy projects. Seven public libraries were awarded LSCA Title VI Library Literacy grants. Approximately 125 out of 238 public libraries now offer formal literacy programs. An LSCA VI Prison Literacy Project increased literacy training resources available to the state's correctional institutions and convened a planning council representing state agencies, prisons, and community groups.

Videotapes were produced with the cooperation of the State Boards of Accounts and Tax Commissioners on the public library budget process, bookkeeping procedures, and the state retirement program. The Libraries and Business Development Committee was formed as a subgroup of the State Library Advisory Council to investigate ways Indiana libraries can improve communication with the business community and increase usage of libraries by that community. The State Library and the School of Library and Information Science, Indiana University, co-sponsored a study of the educational role and services of public libraries in Indiana.

Public Libraries. Six previously unserved townships approved joining existing public library districts, leaving 249 townships with 325,000 residents unserved. Participating libraries in the state's reciprocal borrowing increased to 230 out of 238.

School Libraries and Media Centers. The Learning Resources Unit of the Center for School Improvement and Performance (Indiana Department of Education) provided leadership in the implementation of the new *Information Power* guidelines for school library media programs. Lilly Endowment funded Project REAP (Reading Excitement and Paperbacks) which is designed to encourage recreational reading, to involve parents, and to ensure that appealing books are available to children in grades 4–6. Forty schools participate in the project.

Academic Libraries. The Lilly Foundation awarded a $2,900,000 grant to the Indiana Commission for Higher Education to automate catalog records of the state universities and private colleges. The Commission is also asking for an additional grant from the state government for $27,000,000 to be allocated over the next five years to further fund the project.

Building Programs. Public libraries involved in planning for new and/or expanded facilities included: Auburn, Bloomfield, Bluffton–Wells County, Delphi, Evansville, Greensburg, Indianapolis–Marion County (branches), Jasper, Kokomo, and Marion. Public libraries starting building/remodeling projects: Alexandria, Attica, Frankfort, Ellettsville Branch of Monroe County (Bloomington), Tippecanoe County (Lafayette), Hagerstown, Hartford City, Middletown, Winchester, South Bend, LaPorte, Morgan County (Martinsville), Peru, Rockport, Rushville (remodeling), Knox County (Vincennes), and Waterloo.

Public library projects completed expansions at Angola and Batesville; new buildings at Columbus, Dunkirk, Franklin, Lawrenceburg, Middlebury, Mooresville, and Newburgh (Chandler Branch); remodeling buildings at Morrisson-Reeves (Richmond), North Webster, Princeton, and Union City.

Academic libraries that completed projects in 1988 were DePauw, Indiana University at South Bend, and University of Notre Dame Law School. Anderson University started a building project.

Networks and Interlibrary Cooperation. The nine ALSAs offered 105 continuing education programs for 3,400 library staff members and trustees. The Indiana Electronic Mail Hotline Network sponsored by the ALSAs and the State Library includes a statewide continuing education calendar and library jobline. The Take Home Education program was again offered by the ALSAs and Indiana University School of Library and Information Science.

INCOLSA (Indiana Cooperative Library Services Authority) moved its headquarters and added a microcomputer lab, online training facility (OCLC and information retrieval), and computer room. INCOLSA participated in a National Science Foundation Grant along with Purdue University, Eli Lilly, and local school systems to introduce online searching in middle schools. Software was redesigned for a community information project, IYRIN, in which retrieval capabilities were added along with other new features.

Two statewide INCOLSA workshops featured information retrieval and new technology. *Tools for the Mind* featured Miriam Drake (Georgia Institute of Technology) and a panel of Indiana experts who explored the expansion of information retrieval and related technology for user accessibility. A second workshop, *Catch the Wave*, was co-sponsored with the ILA Library Automation and Technology Division on the impact of telefacsimile and CD-ROM in the delivery of library service.

Awards. Librarians, trustees, and libraries honored by ILA–ILTA in 1988 included Outstanding Trustee: James E. Freeman, Jr., Anderson Public Library; Intellectual Freedom: Shirley McCartney, Goshen Public Library; Outstanding Library: Anderson Public Library; Outstanding Librarians: Donald C. Johnson, Porter County Public Library System; and Barbara Fischler, University Library, IUPUI; Outstanding Library Assistant: Kay Martin, Lebanon Public Library; Citizens Award: John Chapin, Plainfield. Other awards went to Barbara E. Markuson, Library and Information Technology Association/Gaylord Award for Achievement in Library and Information Technology; AIME Awards: Peggy L. Pfeiffer Service Award to Jacqueline Morris; Sena Kautz Merit Award to Ted R. Thomson; Edgar Dale Award to Janie Whaley.

Appointments. Carolyn A. Snyder was named acting Dean for Indiana University Libraries; Kathy Dinsborn was appointed Lobbyist, ILA–ILTA; Linda Yoder was named Director, Nappanee Public Library; Mary J. Snider was appointed Librarian in ISL Genealogy; Evelyn Walker became Director, Alexandrian Library, Mt. Vernon; Emily Cooper-Bunyan was named Director, Washington Carnegie Public Library; Joyce Misner became Manager, Allen County Public Library Reader Services Department; Thomas E. Nisonger and Debora Shaw became professors at Indiana University SLIS, Bloomington; Marla Baden became Tri-ALSA Reference Center Director, Ft. Wayne; Connie Patsiner became Executive Director, Indiana Library Film & Video Service; Jackie Nytes became Associate Director for Management Services, Indianapolis–Marion County Public Library; Ann Moreau went to Indiana School for the Deaf Library; Emily I. Melton became Head of Public Services, IUPUI Library; Virginia Andis became Planning Consultant, State Library; Brenda Blackburn-Foster became Executive Director, Southeastern Indiana Area Library Services Authority; Jeff Propps went to INCOLSA as Microcomputer Specialist; Margaret Hamilton became Director, Greenwood Public Library; and Krystal Smith became Director, Fulton County Public Library.

Retirements. Martha Hoffman (Flora–Monroe Public Library); Jane Sandburg (Bloomfield–Eastern Greene Public Library); Ruth Fuson (Coatesville Public Library); Mary McMillan (Plainfield Public Library); Lawrence Downey (Indianapolis–Marion County Public Library); Clara Palm (Michigan City Public Library); Bill Richardson (Allison Gas Turbine, GMC); and Hugh Warren (South Bend Public Library).

Deaths. Ruth Kellogg and Mary Kay (Henning) Kirschner expired.

MARTHA E. (CATT) FEDERSPIEL

IOWA

Major News. For the first time in the history of the state, the Iowa Legislature approved funds for local library support. The approved sum of $100,000 was designated for open access pilot projects, a blue-ribbon task force on multitype library cooperation and state grants for multitype cooperation projects.

Iowa Library Association (founded 1890)

Membership: 1,785; *annual budget:* $86,480.

President: Patricia Coffie, Waverly Public Library, Waverly (January 1988–January 1989).

Vice-President/President-elect: Cynthia Dyer, Dun Library, Simpson College, Indianola 50125.

Executive Secretary: Naomi Stovall, 823 Insurance Exchange Building, Des Moines 50309.

Annual meeting: November 2–4, 1988, Ames.

Publication: CATALYST (bimonthly).

State Library of Iowa

Shirley George, State Librarian
Historical Building, Des Moines 50319

School Library Media Supervisor

Betty Jo Buckingham
Department of Education
Des Moines 50319

Other budget news was not so pleasant: Waterloo Public Library reduced hours to 48 (39 in summer) and staff declined a negotiated salary increase, to maintain positions; Bettendorf Public Library reduced its budget by $70,000; even though a special state allocation increased Iowa State University Library's materials budget by 8.2 percent in 1988, a cutback of 1,200 journal subscription was necessary.

State Association. ILA President Pat Coffie directed the annual conference at the Scheman Center in Ames, with the theme "Iowa Libraries: Changes? Changes!" General session speakers included Herbert White, Dean, School of Library & Information Science, Indiana University; Jim May, Storyteller, Woodstock, Illinois; and author, Howard Mohr, Cottonwood, Minnesota. Norman Horrocks, Scarecrow Press; and David Wooters, International Museum of Photography, were among sessions speakers. Two excellent workshops, one on dealing with inappropriate patron behavior, and the other on exploring interlibrary cooperation, were conducted at the five spring meetings across the state. The Iowa Chapter took part in the Five State Conference of Academic Librarians at La Crosse, Wisconsin, in April.

The Governmental Affairs Committee reported passage of several bills by the state legislature: special tax levies for libraries binding on city governments; confidentiality of patron information requests; restriction of library revenue-producing activities; and other competition with private enterprise.

State Library Activities. Thousands of visitors to the World Ag Expo held in Amana September 7–10 visited the "Library Country" booth, a cooperative production of several Midwestern library agencies. The State Library celebrated its sesquicentennial with an open house on June 30, 1988. Final results of a study of the volunteer certification program for public librarians will be available early in 1989. Grant writing workshops held in six locations were cosponsored by the State Library and the Regional Library System.

Public Libraries. In 1988 the Iowa City Public Library returned to full hours on July 1, after receiving 2.5 additional positions. The Library completed its second five-year plan in June 1988. Iowa City was the first library to incorporate role setting into its long-range plan.

The Davenport Public Library also restored hours of opening to 69, and celebrated 20 years in its building designed by Edward Durell Stone. Ames Public realized a 52.6 percent permanent increase in its materials budgets, to $171,000. The Mason City Public Library became the first installation site for the Library Corporation's Bibliofile Circulation System, a personal computer-based network system. The Cedar Rapids Public Library which relocated a branch to a shopping mall, is participating in a new reciprocal borrowing agreement with Iowa City Public Library and libraries in Linn and Johnson counties.

As 1988, came to a close the Iowa library community sought answers to the concerns of the Iowa League of Muncipalities for greater uniformity of city policies in the areas of budget, accounting, purchasing, mode of compensation, and personnel actions.

School Libraries and Media Centers. University of Northern Iowa Department of Library Science held its Fall 1988 Conference on the new national school library media guidelines, *Information Power*. Southeast Regional Library System and the River Bend AEA jointly sponsored a conference on issues of concern to school and public librarians. The Department of Education is revising the state guidelines for school library media programs.

Academic and Special Libraries. The University of Iowa Libraries received a special appropriation of $341,000 from the state Legislature and the Governor to enhance its acquisitions budget. The University of Iowa Men's Intercollegiate Athletics Department announced a gift of $200,000 for the University Libraries; a number of CD-ROM products, were purchased with the first instalment. The Law Library is providing multiple computerized resources to the law school community. In addition to LEXIS and Westlaw, Computer Assisted Legal Instruction (CALI) lessons are available in 20 areas of the law. NEXIS and electronic access to indexing of legal periodicals are receiving heavy use. PCs for student use are in increasing demand.

Iowa State and its sister Regent's university libraries are engaged in cooperative resource sharing. ISU is also planning such activities with the Mid-America State Universities Association.

Since 1984, Iowa State University Library has been actively strengthening its ties with university libraries in the People's Republic of China. Among new manuscript collections acquired were the papers of Congressmen Berkley Bedell and Cooper Evans whose service in the U.S. Congress covered activity in House committees on agriculture, world hunger and technology assessment. The Herbert Hoover Presidential Library set a new record for visitors during 1988. More than 115,000 individuals had visited the library through its doors by the end of 1988. The University of Northern Iowa Library signed a contract with Innovative Interfaces, Inc. for the installation of an automated system. The first components of the online, public access catalog are scheduled to be installed in mid-1989, Sen. Charles E. Grassley designated the University of Northern Iowa Library as the official repository of his papers.

Buildings Programs. The State Library awarded LSCA Title II grants totaling $300,180 in 1988.

Networks and Interlibrary Cooperation. The State Library sponsored the production of the third edition of the "Iowa Locator," a CD-ROM compact disk that currently lists the location of approximately 5,000,000 library items in Iowa. The Blue Bear Group of Central City, Colorado, is the vendor responsible for receiving, sorting, and resending the 78,000 ILL and reference files generated annually by Iowa libraries.

Intellectual Freedom. November 21, 1988 marked the 50th Anniversary of the Library Bill of Rights, a fundamental statement concerning open access to information and ideas. The first Library Bill of Rights was approved by the Des Moines library's board of trustees November 21, 1938. The document was later adopted by the American Library Association and by libraries throughout the nation.

Awards. Gerald Hodges was elected Vice-President/President-elect of the Young Adult Services division of ALA and will assume the office of President in July 1989. Norman Kelinson was elected Vice-President/President-elect of the American Library Trustees Association and will assume the office of President in July 1989. Edwin J. Zastrow of Iowa City, was given an Outstanding Trustee Award by the Iowa Library Trustee Association (ILTA).

The Iowa Educational Media Association presents four service awards annually, the newest which is the Media Professional of the Year Award went to Jean Donham, District Coordinator Media Programs for the Iowa City Community Schools. The Iowa Library Association Foundation awarded two scholarships at the the ILA fall conference: Aileen F. Maddox, a student at the University of Iowa School of Library and Information Science received the first Jack E. Tillson Scholarship; the 1988 ILA Foundation Scholarship was awarded to Kathreen Pisarik, a student in the University of Northern Iowa Department of Library Science.

Appointments. Timothy Walch to Assistant Director of the Hoover Presidential Library; Carol French Johnson to Director of Cedar Falls Public Library; Nicky Stanke to Director of Dubuque Carnegie-Stout Public Library; Matthew Kollasch, Director of the Fort Dodge Public Library; Norma Hervey, Head Librarian at Luther College. Also Linda Robertson, to Director of Information Services for the State Library, William Cochran to Director of Library Development, Nancy Harvey to Head of Reference; Nancy Lee, etc. Head of the Documents Depository; and Dennis Peterson, to Director of Library at Palmer College of Chiropractic.

Deaths. Hazel Westgate, Children's Librarian at the Iowa City Public Library for nearly 40 years, died May 17, 1988.

CARL F. ORGREN

KANSAS

Legislation. Increase of state general fund support for the grants-in-aid program, for the blind and physically handicapped program and for the Interlibrary Loan Development Program was high on the list of legislative priorities in Kansas for 1988. The publication of the Kansas Library Catalog (formerly the Kansas Union Catalog) the index of statewide library holdings, at least biannually was also identified as a major legislative issue during 1988.

State Association. "Humanizing the Infor-

Kansas Library Association (founded 1900)

Membership: 854; *annual budget:* $33,740.

President: Marlene Hendrick, Director of Special Community Services Division, Topeka Public Library, 1515 W. Tenth St., Topeka 66604.

Vice-President/President-elect: Karen Cole, Director, Forsyth Library, Fort Hays State University, Hays 67601.

Annual Tri-Conference: March 23-26, Kansas City, Hilton Plaza.

1988 Tri-Conference: April 5-8, Topeka, Ramada Inn.

Publication: KLA Newsletter (three times a year).

Kansas State Library

Duane F. Johnson, State Librarian
3rd Floor, Capitol Building
Topeka 66612

School Library Media Supervisor

June Saine Level
State Department of Education
Topeka 66612

---

mation Age" was the theme of the triconference of the Kansas Library Association (KLA), the Kansas Association of School Librarians (KASL) and the Kansas Association of Educational Communication and Technology (KAECT). Major speakers for the March meeting held in Kansas City, Missouri included futurist Harold Pluimer; Kansas native Bill Kurtis who formerly co-anchored the "CBS Morning News"; Pulitzer Prize winner Richard Rhodes, a native of Kansas City; Gary Paulsen, author of numerous children's books; and Tom Ballard, controversial library personality and author of *The Failure of Resource Sharing in Public Libraries and Alternative Sources* (ALA 1986). The Public Library and Trustee sections combined on September 28-29, 1988 to present their second separate conference, "Economic Vitality: Challenge and Opportunity." Dr. Tony Redwood, executive director of the Institute for Public Policy and Business Research at the University of Kansas, was a featured speaker. The College and University Section of KLA held its annual conference October 6-7, 1988, at Emporia State University; the theme was the "Role of Academic Libraries in Economic Development."

The final draft of *Measurements of Quality: Public Library Standards for Kansas, 1988* was accepted at the Public Library Section meeting at the triconference in March 1988, and was published and mailed to all public libraries in August 1988.

STATE LIBRARY ACTIVITIES

Physically Handicapped. Reader Enrollment and Distribution System (READS), an inventory control and circulation automated system developed by the Library for the Blind and Physically Handicapped Division of the Library of Congress, was implemented. READS is expected to be operational at all sites by mid-1989. The Regional Library for the Blind and Physically Handicapped received one of the 25 Voices and Visions Poetry grants jointly sponsored by ALA and the National Endowment for the Humanities.

Library Development. The Library Employment Education Plan (LEEP), the continuing education program of the State Library, continued to grow during 1988. By the end of 1988, LEEP had enrolled 1,292 librarians from all types of libraries, as well as numerous library trustees.

Literacy. The library literacy project maintained its high quality during 1988. The literacy coordinator, in addition to regular duties, now supervises 14 volunteers under the VISTA Literacy Corps. With the assistance of LSCA Title I funds, a second LSCA Title VI grant and administrative funds awarded under ACTION, the State Library assumed the leadership responsibility for the state's literacy efforts in Kansas.

Older Americans. During 1988 the State Library's contributions to older Kansans moved toward networking the State Library, the seven regional systems of cooperating libraries and the 13 Area Agencies on Agency. LSCA Title I grants were awarded to 14 individual projects under the Services to the Elderly program. Topeka Public Library's Red Carpet service was recognized as the premier service provider to older Americans in the U.S.

Buildings. Kansas library building projects during 1988 ranged from simple remodeling to construction of new facilities. However, only the libraries at Humboldt, Colwich, Americus, Independence, McCracken, Sharon Springs and Sterling received LSCA Title II assistance. The libraries at El Dorado, St. Francis, Central Kansas Library System, Mulvane and Parker completed Title II public library construction projects begun in FY 1986 and FY 1987.

Networks & Interlibrary Cooperation. "Library Cooperation in Kansas, 1988-1992"—the long-range plan developed in 1987 by the administrators of the seven regional systems of cooperating libraries, the Kansas Library Network Board and representatives of the State Library—was implemented during 1988. The Interlibrary Loan Development Program (ILDP), in its fourth year of operation, provided collection development grants for all types of libraries based on a statewide collection development plan. The Network Board agreed to use LSCA Title III funds to purchase telefacsimile units for eight Kansas libraries early in 1988. This program is intended to improve the document delivery between Kansas libraries and to demonstrate the potentials and problems of using telefax document delivery for multitype resource sharing in Kansas. In 1988 for the first time, the Network Board also awarded federal funds to provide grants to school libraries for online searching services.

School Libraries. About 83 percent of the state's schools have some kind of library service. There are 347 high school libraries, 82 junior or middle schools with libraries, and about 800 elementary schools with enrollments of more than 100 that have school libraries.

Awards and Honors. The William Allen White Children's Book Award for 1988 went to Betsy Byars for her book, *Cracker Jackson*. Byars won her first in 1980 for *The Pinballs*.

Lori Heller received a White Service Award for her contributions as the Administrative Assistant to the White Award Program from 1982 to 1987. Barbara Herrin received a White Service Award for ten years of service on the White Award Book Selection Committee. On March 22, 1988, the Kansas Center for the Book, headquartered at Topeka Public Library, became one of only 15 affiliates of the National Center for the Book at the Library of Congress. Affiliate centers are responsible for developing and coordinating activities that celebrate the literary heritage and ongoing book related activities of their respective localities.

Appointments and Retirements. Kathleen Ruth Bradt, Associate Director of the Baker University Library at Baldwin, was named chair of the Kansas Library Network Board. Winifred Lichtenwalter, Director of the Leavenworth Public Library was named to the Board, and Nil Whittington, Associate Academic Affairs Director of the Kansas Board of Regents, assumed her post on that Board during 1988. Mona Carmack was named director of the Johnson County Library. Charles Perdue became director of Kansas City, Kansas, Public Library, and Kent Oliver became director at Olathe Public Library. Ann Ide married and changed her name to Ann Bailey shortly after becoming the director of Bradford Memorial Library at El Dorado. Leslie Bell assumed Ann's responsibilities at the Northwest Kansas Library System. Marcia Ransom became the director of the Winfield Public Library, and Janice Hoyt was named Director of Pratt Public Library during 1988. Rev. Paul Jackson, formerly director at Winfield Public Library, now directs a seminary library in Indiana while working toward his Ph.D. in theology.

Richard Neuman, Director of Salina Public Library, announced his retirement effective August 1989. Dr. Neysa Eberhardt, Director of Newton Public Library, Bev Oberle, Director of McPherson Public Library, and Jane Williams, Director of Larned Public Library, also announced their retirements during 1988. Oneita Johnson, former Director of Pratt Public Library officially retired during 1988.

ROY BIRD

KENTUCKY

Kentucky Library Association (founded 1907)

Membership: 1,312; *annual budget:* $71,475.

President: Linda Perkins, 9707 Holliday Drive, Louisville 40272.

Vice-President/President-elect: Jean Almand, Library Services, Western Kentucky University, Bowling Green 42101.

Secretary: Charles King, Kenton County Public Library, 5th and Scott, Covington 41011.

Executive Secretary: Mary Underwood, Kentucky Library Association, 1501 Twilight Trail, Covington, 41011.

Annual meeting: October 11-13, 1989.

Publication: Kentucky Libraries (quarterly)

Department of Library and Archives

James A. Nelson, State Librarian and Commissioner of the Department for Libraries and Archives
Box 537
Frankfort 40602

Program Consultant for School Media Services

Judy Cooper
State Department of Education
1830 Capital Plaza Tower
Frankfort 40601

Kentucky voters elected Wallace Wilkinson governor and approved a statewide lottery in November 1988. The new governor called a special session to address implementation of the lottery and to consider funding for education.

State Library. The Department for Libraries and Archives issued a comprehensive plan for the development of public libraries in the state. *Public Library Development in Kentucky*, published in 1988, addresses four major areas of need: planning, services, personnel, and physical facilities. The Department concentrates on the areas of highest priority: planning, continuing education, and interlibrary cooperation.

LSCA MURL money funded the Louisville Free Public Library's acquisition of a patent collection and enhancement of the Lexington Public Library's business collection to support Lexington's World Trade Center.

Title I funding established the READ's computer system in the Louisville Free Public Library's Subregional Library for the Blind and Physically Handicapped. Projects awarded to Calloway, Hancock, Muhlenberg, and Washington Counties included building a database of community services for older adults developing a video collection of this clientele, and promoting general library services to seniors. Projects for young adults funded for Owsley and Christian counties included establishing a homework laboratory complete with computer and engaging young adults to compose an oral history of the county. KDLA's Division of State Library Services established Kentucky Library Information Centers to provide such services as ready reference, research, interlibrary loan for periodical requests and continuing education workshops related to reference and information retrieval

Volume 1 of the *Guide to Kentucky Archival and Manuscript Collections* was published, along with *Connexions: A Plan to Establish a Coordinated Continuing Education Program for Public Library Personnel in Kentucky; Public Library Trustee Orientation Manual; The Selection of a Public Library Trustee; Statistical Report of Bookmobile Service, Fiscal Year 1987; Statistical Report of Kentucky Public Libraries, Fiscal Year 1986-87* and *Register of Vietnam War Casualties From Kentucky*.

State Association. The Kentucky Library Association's Public Relations Committee received the 1988 Grolier Grant for promoting National Library Week. A variety of businesses and organizations assisted KLA's promotion, particularly the Foodtown and Houchen grocery chains, which donated more than 1,000,000 grocery bags. The Kentucky Library Trustee Association became a Section of KLA in October. Betty Daniels received the Outstanding Public Library Service Award; the Floyd County Public Library received the Outstanding Trustee Award.

Public Libraries. State aid to public libraries increased to 38¢ per capita in 1988; 114 of the 120 counties provide county-wide library service. The Lexington Public Library, the Logan Helm-Woodford County Library, the Campbell County Public Library, and the Pennyrile Regional office participated in a nationwide survey to test guidelines and standards for quality bookmobile service.

The Louisville Public Library received a John Cotton Dana Special Award for mobilizing the community and creating a successful Library Foundation with the campaign "Support for the Library is Overdue."

The Logan Helm Woodford County Public Library joined 24 other libraries in the United States as demonstration sites for the "Voices & Visions: Reading Viewing and Discussion programs in America's Libraries," a cooperative effort from the National Endowment for the Humanities and the American Library Association. The John D. and Catherine T. MacArthur Foundation awarded videocassette collections to several libraries and regional consortia in Kentucky. Public libraries and the Kentucky Educational Television received a $25,000 grant from the Annenberg/CPB (Corporation for Public Broadcasting) Project.

School Libraries and Media Centers. Kentucky state accreditation standards required that every elementary and secondary school have a school library media center. In 1988 1,079 certified school media librarians administered programs in 1,399 public schools. The minimum funding requirement for the 1988-89 school year was $7.20 per pupil, which included $4.20 for print materials and $3.00 for nonprint materials. The Legislature mandated library/research/reference skills instruction for all grade levels. The Kentucky School Media Association presented the 1988 Outstanding School Media Librarian Award to Linda Perkins, an elementary media librarian from Kenwood Elementary in Louisville. Gary Tatum, principal at Kenwood Elementary, received the Outstanding School Administrator Award.

Academic and Other Libraries. The University of Louisville's Library acquired its 1,000,000th volume, *Vocabularius Breviloquus*, published in 1482 by Catholic scholar Johann Reuchlin. The University also unveiled its automated card catalog MINERVA. The University of Kentucky Libraries was awarded a grant from the National Endowment for the Humanities to continue the Kentucky Newspaper Project. The Kentucky Department for Libraries and Archives awarded public library construction grants to Boone, Henry, Russell, Breathitt and Pike counties.

Networks and Interlibrary Cooperation. The Kentucky Department for Libraries and Archives awarded data conversion grants to: Oldham County Public Library (general collection conversion), Bell County Public Library (general collection conversion), University of Kentucky M.L. King Library (state government document collection), Murray State University (general collection) and Cornhouser Medical Center Library at the University of Louisville (medical materials). These records will be made available on a statewide union database maintained by the Kentucky Library Network Inc. The network distributed the first edition of its union database microfiche catalog in February 1988; 193 multitype library members will utilize it for resource sharing. The second edition, in production, will contain the records of 55 members libraries and approximately 1,750,000 unique records. Plans include putting the database on compact disk and obtaining funding to help members acquire CD workstations.

The Council of Independent Kentucky Colleges and Universities (CIKCU) a voluntary consortium of 21 privately funded academic institutions has undertaken a project to convert bibliographic records into machine-readable form. Auto Graphics of Pomona, California, was selected to convert the shelflists online; Christie Robinson was employed as project director.

Intellectual Freedom. A bill dubbed the "obsenity bill" or "censorship bill" received attention during Kentucky's 1988 General Assembly. Investigation disclosed that the probable target of the bill was "adult movies" rented by video stores. However, due to the broad nature of the bill and First Amendment principles, Kentucky Library Association's Intellectual Freedom Committee, as well as the librarians in the state, were alerted and an organization of video retailers employed an attorney to represent their interests. The bill was sent back to committee, where it died. The American Civil Liberties Union became involved in an incident relating to a book entitled *Witches and Witchcraft*. The book was again placed. Other titles questioned during the year were: books by Judy Blume, *Teenage Romance, Pornography and Silence, Lonesome Dove, Deenie, Blue Skies, No Candy, I Am the Cheese, LeBaron Secret, Destiny, Homer the Hunter, It Can't be Helped, and Slaughterhouse Five*. The inclusion of *As I Lay Dying* by William Faulkner and Malory's *Le Morte D'Arthur* in School library collections was challenged.

People. University of Kentucky's professor for Library and Information Science Robert E. Cazden was elected to the American Antiquarian Society. Professor Anne McConnell retired from the University of Kentucky's College of Library and Information Science. Dr. Thomas Waldhart, professor at the University of Kentucky's College of Library and Information Science is acting Dean for the college.

Anne Kearney, University of Louisville, was awarded a grant from the Academic Library Professional Development Committee of the Kentucky Library Association to the effects of the 1976 Copyright Act on libraries and teaching faculty.

A resolution was read at the ALA New Orleans Conference in honor of Margaret Willis, former State Librarian of Kentucky who died September 9, 1987. State Law Librarian Wesley Gilmer, Jr. died March 7, 1988.

EDWARD KLEE

MAINE

State Association. A record number of librarians and book people, 630, attended the Maine Library Association/Maine Educational Media Association annual conference, held May 15-17 at the University of Maine in Orono. Speakers included psychologists Mardy Grothe and Peter Wylie; whole language advocate Bill Martin; Guy St. Clair of the "One Person Library"; novelist Robert Cormier; and language columnist Richard Lederer. A traditional feature of the conference is the auction to benefit the scholarship and student loan funds of the two associations. Auction proceeds were $2,869. Another annual benefit for the scholarship and loan funds is the raffle of a quilt composed of blocks designed and sewn by librarians from across the state. This year's raffle netted $1,800.

State Library Activities. "Vision 2000" is the title of the cooperative long-range plan developed, at the request of the state commissioner of education, by the Maine State Library and its fellows within the Department of Education and Cultural Services, the Maine His-

Maine Library Association (founded 1893)

Membership: 800; *annual budget:* $32,000.

President: Reta Schreiber, Bangor Public Library.

Vice-President/President-elect: Nann Blaine, Hilyard, Auburn Public Library.

Executive Secretary: Cathy Callahan, Maine Municipal Association, Community Drive, Augusta 04330.

Annual meeting: May 21-23, 1989, Orono (joint with Maine Educational Media Association; May 20-22, 1990, Orono).

Publications: Downeast Libraries (quarterly); *Maine Memo* (10 issues a year).

Maine State Library

J. Gary Nichols, State Librarian
State House Station 64
Augusta 04333

School Library Media Supervisor

Walter Taranko
Maine State Library
State House Station 64
Augusta 04333

---

toric Preservation Commission, the Maine Arts Commission, and the Maine State Museum. This document identifies the statutory mandates of the four agencies and their organizational and program needs for the next decade. The long-range plan led to a new approach to funding requests through the Legislature, the Community Cultural Services Initiative. The agency directors and the commissioner anticipate that this cooperative approach will more clearly identify the services provided and the constituents toward whom the services are directed.

Public Libraries. A $10,550 grant from the Maine Humanities Council to the Maine Literacy Coalition is being used by seven public libraries in the state for an innovative reading and discussion program for adult new readers who are enrolled in literacy courses. Called "Reflections," the program involves humanities scholars and adult new readers in discussing the major issues in selected children's books. Each site is using one of three themes: American history, family relationships, or other cultures. The goals of the project are to: (1) stimulate adult new readers to explore children's literature; (2) enhance cooperation and communication between local libraries and literacy providers; (3) develop a model for family literacy; (4) create an awareness among new readers about the enjoyment of sharing literature and ideas; (5) encourage adult new readers to read to their children; and (6) encourage adult new readers to use their public libraries. The seven participating libraries are in Bangor, Lewiston, Machias, N. Berwick, Norway, Portland, and Presque Isle.

School Libraries and Media Centers. "Bridging the Gap to Lifelong Information Skills" is an initiative of the Maine Educational Media Association (MEMA). The project began with workshops in each of the state's three library districts to identify the ways in which library skills instruction traditionally limited to the school library could be transferred to bibliographic instruction in public and academic libraries. The workshops were followed by a session at the annual conference, and a MEMA task force has been formed to continue to identify strategies and programs.

Academic Libraries. The University of Maine system has signed contracts for systemwide online public access catalog and circulation services with Innovative Interfaces, Inc., and Digital Equipment Corporation. This is the first installation of INNOPAC software on DEC equipment. Database loading began in late June and the circulation module began in September. On November 8 voters approved a $36,800,000 bond issue for the University of Maine system. Among the capital improvements funded by the bond will be a $9,200,000 addition to the University of Southern Maine library in Portland.

Networks and Interlibrary Cooperation. On July 1 the Talking Books program was centralized at the Maine State Library. The program previously had been operated from five public libraries serving as subregional centers—Bangor, Houlton, Lewiston, Portland, and Waterville. The move was made because operating costs had increased beyond the State Library's subsidy to each subregional center and demands for collection and staff space at the local libraries had crowded the Talking Books collections.

Professional Concerns. The first statewide survey of public library staff salaries was published in November under the auspices of the Maine Library Association. The survey includes professional, nonprofessional, and custodial salaries.

Intellectual Freedom. Author Stephen King accepted the first MLA/MEMA-SIRS Intellectual Freedom Award at the MLA/MEMA spring conference in May. The award consists of $500 to the recipient, $500 in materials to the library of the recipient's choice, and a commemorative plaque from SIRS. King chose Old Town Public Library to receive the materials portion of the award. King was selected from several nominees in recognition of his strong public stand and considerable personal efforts to defeat the Maine Obscenity Referendum in 1986. Deborah Locke and Elaine Albright participated in the Leadership Training Institute on Intellectual Freedom sponsored by ALA, May 5-7. Locke is librarian at Westbrook High School and chairman of the MLA/MEMA Intellectual Freedom Committee. Albright is director of libraries at the University of Maine and a member of ALA Council.

NANN BLAINE HILYARD

MARYLAND

State Library Network. The statewide library bibliographic database was expanded during 1988. This database includes 2,100,000 records from more than 100 public, academic, special libraries and school library media centers. It is available to libraries in three forms: MILNET, an online database including direct interlibrary loan; MICROCAT-on-CD including all records on two compact discs; and MICROCAT XII which includes the same records on microfiche.

User Fees Issue. Maryland public librarians divided sharply over the issue of charging user fees for services leading to a battle in the Maryland General Assembly during 1988. After extensive lobbying by both sides on the issue, the General Assembly passed legislation authorizing Baltimore County Public Library and Prince George's County Public Library to charge fees for the circulation of videocassettes.

Citizens for Maryland Libraries. The Citizens for Maryland Libraries held their annual meeting in Baltimore on October 29. They presented their highest honor—the Marion Satterthwaite Award for outstanding contribution to libraries by a lay person—to Offie Clark, Chair of the Maryland Advisory Council on Libraries and a former trustee of the Harford County Public Library. The group also gave a special recognition award to the recently retired Assistant State Superintendent for Libraries, Nettie B. Taylor.

Trustees. The Trustee Division of the Maryland Library Association joined the Department of Education and the Maryland Advisory Council on Libraries in sponsoring a training session for trustees June 11. The Division also held their annual conference in Denton on November 19. This meeting featured Kare Anderson as speaker on "Selling the Public Library" and a review of a model electronic information project in the Caroline County Public Library.

Task Forces. A Task Force on Networking was named by State Superintendent David Hornbeck. This group was assigned to develop a plan for the improvement of the State Library Network by February 1989. Agnes Griffen of the Montgomery County Public Library was named as chair. A Task Force on Law Review was appointed to examine all State laws relating to public libraries. This group studied the need for revision in the State Aid formula, personnel laws, and the governance of the Regional Library Resource Centers.

People. Joseph Shilling was named as State Superintendent of Schools following the resignation of David Hornbeck, who had served in that position since 1976. Rosa Presberry was appointed Chief of the School Library Media Services Branch in the Division of Library De-

---

Maryland Library Association (founded 1932)

Membership: 900; *annual budget:* $25,000.

President: Nadia P. Taran, Southern Maryland Regional Library Association, Box 10609, LaPlata 20646.

Vice-President/President-elect: Mary Landry, Librarian, Dundalk Community College Library, Baltimore 21222.

Executive Secretary: Robert Greenfield, 115 West Franklin Street, Baltimore 21201.

Annual Meeting: May 5-6, 1989, Towson.

Publication: CRAB (bimonthly).

Maryland State Department of Education

J. Maurice Trevillian,
Assistant State Superintendent for Libraries,
Division of Library Development and Services,
200 W. Baltimore St.,
Baltimore 21201

School Library Media Supervisor

Rose Presberry, Chief,
School Library Media Services Branch,
Division of Library Development and Services,
200 W. Baltimore St.,
Baltimore 21201

velopment and Services following the resignation of Paula Montgomery. Barbara Smith was named as Chief of Network and Information Services Section of the Division of Library Development and Services. She replaced Diana Cunningham, who had resigned to take a position at the Health Sciences Library and the University of Maryland. Paula Miller was appointed Regional Librarian of the Eastern Shore Regional Library Resource Center. She replaced Annette Milliron who resigned to accept a position in California.

Nettie B. Taylor retired as Assistant State Superintendent for Libraries after forty years of service to the Maryland State Department of Education. Taylor, who held the position of Assistant State Superintendent since 1960, provided leadership on such issues as the development of State Aid Program and the coordination of a statewide library network. She also pushed for the adoption of Standards for School Library Media Programs by the State Board of Education which were put into place shortly before her retirement. J. Maurice Travillian was appointed to fill the position.

J. MAURICE TRAVILLIAN

MASSACHUSETTS

Massachusetts Library Association (founded 1890)

Membership: 1,000; *annual budget:* $75,000.

President: Louise R. Brown, Wayland Public Library, 5 Concord Road, Wayland 01778 (July 1987–June 1989).

Vice-President: Anne O'Brien, Pollard Memorial Library, Lowell 01852.

Executive Secretary: Paula Bozoian, P.O. Box 556, Wakefield 01880.

Annual meeting: May 8–9, Sturbridge.

Publications: Bay State Librarian (3 issues per year); *Bay State Letter* (8 times per year).

Board of Library Commissioners

Roland Piggford, Director
648 Beacon Street
Boston 02215

Major News. The high impact activity for the Massachusetts public library scene in 1988 may well have been a $100,000 state grant and its results. The Massachusetts Library Association (MLA) received the grant for a "statewide public relations campaign in cooperation with a professional marketing/public relations agency . . . to build public confidence in libraries as sources of the kind of accurate, current information people need every day to make informed decisions." The campaign, conducted by the Clarendon Group, a Boston public relations firm, is called "Breaking the Silence." Jeff Katz, chair of the PR Campaign Committee, reported: "The goals of the campaign were to position libraries as contemporary providers of information on a practical scale; to challenge the prevailing image of libraries as oriented toward the past, as quaint but irrelevant, as the friend of students, scholars, and children, but not of the community member in the role of consumer, homeowner, or parent. Accordingly, we pitched our campaign toward breaking the traditional stereotypes of libraries, toward the library as a down-to-earth provider of practical information at no charge. We were aiming at information provided in a way that would be perceived to be as friendly as leaning over the backyard fence, but more accurate, more complete. In each of the 10-second spots we tried to show a situation in which a question or problem arose, or was implied, and a solution was found at the library. In other words, work got done, questions were answered, people were made happy as a result of using their libraries."

The specific situations used required information on parenting, home repair, travel, consumer issues, and personal finance. Ads were effective in video, audio, and print formats.

Katz observed that "as the campaign unfolded, our print ads, our TV psa's, our radio psa's and the outdoor advertising we did, all received an amount of daytime airplay that exceeded our most optimistic expectations. In a particularly ferocious market like television, our materials have appeared during "60 Minutes," Red Sox baseball, and prime-time movies in the Boston area. Our series of four 10-second television spots are still receiving significant air play in the Boston, Worcester, and Springfield markets. Our print ads are still making regular appearances in a variety of weekly and daily papers, and we expect these ads to break in regional editions of national magazines like *Time* and *Newsweek* soon."

The media value of the air time and the print and billboard space provided is calculated at an impressive $977,100 for the $100,000 spent. The television ads alone ran on stations with potential viewing in over 3,000,000 households. MLA considers it an excellent return for the funding agency—the Massachusetts Board of Library Commissioners.

State Association. The Massachusetts Library Association approved the "Standards for Public Library Services to Children in Massachusetts" during 1988. The standards were developed by an ad hoc committee representing children's librarians, public library directors, regional systems, and library education. The recommended standards were reviewed in public meetings across the state prior to the MLA vote, and follow the current trend toward qualitative from quantitative standards. They, in the words of the committee, "describe the philosophy and principles underlying good library service to children and define essential characteristics of such service." Published standards are available for $5 a copy from MLA.

Two new units—the Children's Issues Section and the Corporation Libraries Round-Table—were formed in 1988. The latter group is targeted toward public libraries whose trustees boards are also nonprofit corporations. Both units will be collecting dues and offering programs and services to their members.

MLA adopted $22,000 as the recommended minimum salary for beginning professional librarians for 1988.

The MLA Executive Board has adopted three priorities for 1988–89: (1) Membership—MLA will seek to increase the number of members through a broader representation of the several levels of library staff and from a variety of library types. MLA will work toward higher participation in programs and other activities and encourage increased awareness of MLA and what it can do. (2) Public Relations—Building on the FY88 Public Relations grant, MLA will work to expand public understanding of the library profession. MLA will work to improve the image of librarians and will encourage individuals to join the profession. (3) Access—Noting many recent instances where information has been seriously restricted, MLA will focus on access issues. This may mean monitoring federal and state legislation, keeping abreast of ALA communications, and being aware of occurrences in our society which endanger the individual's right to information.

MLA's annual conference was held in Springfield in May. Program topics included information access, automation of serials, moving the library, lobbying skills, "Fireworks, Brass Bands & Elephants" (PR techniques,) CD-ROM products for reference work, AIDS information sources, personnel skills, literacy, and human relations skills.

State Library Activities. The Massachusetts Board of Library Commissioners has undergone significant staff changes. Robert Dugan, formerly head of Library Development, has taken a position in the federal service. Tom Ploeg, formerly Consultant for Library Construction, joined Eastern Library Interiors. New staff include Patience Jackson, Consultant on Library Construction; and Gregor Trinkaus-Randall, Consultant for Preservation and Collection Development.

The Commissioners have adopted administrative regulations for construction projects to be funded under the new Staate allocation of $35 million for public libraries. The more than 120 intents filed for the funds represent some $138 million in requests. Competition will be fierce for the funding.

Networks and Interlibrary Cooperation. Twenty-four libraries have joined with the Boston Public Library in creating a statewide telefax network for public libraries. Locations in all three regional systems are connected to Boston primarily for journal articles and directory information. The network was started with grant support from the Board of Library Commissioners.

The librarians in public higher education institutions across the state, with financial support from the State Board of Regents, are also connecting through telefax. The state library at the University of Lowell is the initial site with fourth-generation machines and flat bed scanners. All the state college libraries eventually will be connected through telefacsimile.

MARGO CRIST

MINNESOTA

Minnesota Library Association (founded 1891)

President: Michael Haeuser, Folke Bernadotte Memorial Library, Gustavas Adolphus College, St. Peter 56082.

President-elect: Ms. M. J. Rossman, S–33 Wilson Library, 309 19th Avenue South, University of Minnesota, Minneapolis 55455-0414.

Executive Director: Joanne Kelty, c/o North Regional Library System, 1315 Lowery Avenue North, Minneapolis 55411-1398.

Annual meeting: October 5–7, 1988, Rochester; October 11–13, 1989, Mankato.

Publication: MLA Newsletter (10 times a year).

281

Department of Education, Office of Library Development and Services
William G. Asp, Director
440 Capitol Square Building
550 Cedar Street
St. Paul 55101

State School Library Media Supervisor
Mary Dalbotten
State Department of Education
St. Paul 55101

The first Minnesota Festival of the Book, a week-long series of events sponsored by the Friends of the Saint Paul Public Library and corporate, foundation, and individual sponsors in Minnesota, was held September 10-18. The purposes of the festival were to spotlight groups that promote reading, literacy, books, and the written word, by gathering forces and planning together; to expand and reinforce the joy of reading; and to join together as a community in celebrating reading and books. More than 60 organizations participated in the festival. The closing event was held at the World Theater in Saint Paul (home of "A Prairie Home Companion") and featured the presentation of the first Minnesota Book Awards. Winners were Tom McGrath (poetry); Patricia Hampl (nonfiction); Kathleen Coskran (first book); Barbara Juster Esbensen (younger children); Gary Paulsen (older children); and Garrison Keillor (fiction). Also honored was Kay Sexton, retired buyer for B. Dalton Bookseller, for distinguished service to readers, writers, and publishers.

Legislation. An attempt to repeal extension of access of library services to all 87 Minnesota counties or to make it optional, died in a Senate committee. Funding for public library services as a special levy, thereby being exempt from levy limits, passed on the last night of the session, after a valiant effort by Minnesota librarians to encourage support from their legislators. A provision, passed as a part of the omnibus education aids bill, requires the Department of Education to make recommendations about the organization, financing, and formation of regional public library districts. A task force was formed to work on the issue and to report December 1. Volunteers in libraries and other municipal organizations were provided the same protection against lawsuits as granted to municipal employees.

Associations. The Minnesota Library Association (MLA) held its annual conference October 5-8 at Rochester on the theme "Leadership: You Can Make a Difference." Keynote speaker was David Jennings, former speaker of the Minnesota House of Representatives. Programs included sessions on "Serving Older Library Patrons," "Hunger, Homelessness, and Libraries," "Leadership in Information Policy," "Bibliographic Triage," "Library Services for the Disabled," "Security for Now and the Future: Socially Conscious Investing," "Linking Systems for Resource Sharing," "How do Librarians Lead?" "Pay Equity," "Children's Librarians as Leaders," "Leadership in Academia," and "War and Peace in Children's Media." Featured speakers included Nancy Steigmeyer, editor of the *ALTA Newsletter*; Kathleen Stack, Director, Department of Community Services, Saint Paul; D. Kay Gapen, Director, General Library System, University of Wisconsin-Madison; Sheila Intner, Simmons College; and Margaret Preska, President, Mankato State University.

Mona Carmack, 1988 president of MLA, resigned in July when she moved out of state. She was succeeded by Vice-President Mike Haeuser, Gustavus Adolphus College. Newly elected officers for 1989 include M. J. Dustin, MINITEX, Vice-President/President-elect; Robbie LaFleur, Legislative Reference Library, Secretary; Jim Newsome, College of St. Catherine, member-at-large for intellectual freedom.

The Minnesota Educational Media Organization (MEMO) held its annual Upper Mississippi Media Conference October 27-29. Keynote speaker was Roger Taylor, gifted education specialist, speaking on "Meeting the Media Needs of the Gifted." Session included programs on technology in education, emerging disk technology, collection mapping, and the Kerlan Collection. MEMO officers for 1988 include Shirley Christenson, Anoka-Hennepin Independent School District, President; Gail Juba, Proctor Public Schools, President-elect; and Tim Eklund, Park Rapids Public Schools, Past-President.

Buildings. New York Mills opened its new 3,300 square foot public library building on February 28. Rush City held the grand opening of its new public library on May 7. Hennepin County Library opened its new Maple Grove Library during National Library Week, and Anoka County Library opened new libraries in Ramsey and Andover.

Macalester College dedicated its new $15,000,000 library in September. Dedication speaker was Vartan Gregorian, New York Public Library. Several sessions related to books also were held during the week of the dedication, which coincided with the Minnesota Festival of the Book.

Awards. The Minnesota Library Association presented certificates of merit to Carolyn Stanson in recognition of her energy, enthusiasm, and abilities in support of quality children's programing in libraries and to the city of New York Mills for its extraordinary effort in providing a new public library facility for the community and for the example set for other small towns in Minnesota. The President's Award was presented to Barbara Byers, Washington County Library, and the Distinguished Achievement Award to Don Pearce, University of Minnesota, Duluth. Peace also received the first award from the North Country Library Cooperative. The 1988 Maud Hart Lovelace Book Award was presented to *Night of the Twisters*, by Ivy Ruckman. Hennepin County Library received an Achievement Award from the National Association of Counties for its literary awareness program.

People. David Dorman was appointed Automation and New Technology Specialist in the Office of Library Development and Services. On March 1 Trish Conroy, formerly Children's Librarian and Assistant Director of the Alexandria Public Library, was named Director. Bona Carol Enstrom was named Director of the Bemidji Public Library. Barbara Jones, former Director of the University of Northern Iowa Library, became Head of Reference at the Minnesota Historical Society in October.

Mary Sund retired in April after 38 years of service to the Virginia Public Library, the last ten years as Director.

Russell J. Schunk, former Director of the Library Division of the State Department of Education, died in November 1987. Mary Meyer, former Supervisor of Media Services for the Duluth Public Schools, died April 27. Marilyn Brunton, Youth Services Coordinator at the Lake Agassiz Regional Library, died in 1988.
EDWARD SWANSON

MISSISSIPPI

Mississippi Library Association (founded 1909)

Membership: 1,100; *annual budget:* $108,000.

President: Jane C. Bryan, Jackson-George Regional Library, 3214 Pascagoula St., Pascagoula 39567.

Vice-President/President-elect: Sid Graves, Carnegie Public Library, Clarksdale 38614.

Executive Secretary: Bernice L. Bell, P.O. Box 20418, Jackson 39209-1448.

Publication: Mississippi Libraries (quarterly).

Mississippi Library Commission
David Woodburn, Director
1221 Ellis Ave.
P.O. Box 10700
Jackson 39209-0700
Publication: The Packet (Newsletter).

State Department of Education
Joan P. Haynie, Educational
  Media Consultant
P.O. Box 771
Jackson 39205

State Association. "The Best Reading, For the Largest Number, At the Least Cost" was the theme reiterated at the annual conference of the Mississippi Library Association (MLA). The October meeting, held in Jackson, feautured Lea Wells, library consultant, who led an ACRL-sponsored workshop on "Improving Job Performance: Strategies for Supervisors." General session speakers included Charles Robinson, director of the Baltimore (Maryland) County Library, and Marvin Scilken, director of the Orange (New Jersey) Public Library. Robinson spoke on "What is the 'Best Reading' and Who Is to Say What It Is?" Scilken's topic was "Libraries and the Least Cost Factor." Linton Weeks, founding editor of *Southern Magazine*, spoke on "The Real South," to a session sponsored by public library and junior member groups. Dan Iddings, of RMG Consultants, spoke on CD-ROM implications for libraries and Phil Turner, dean of the library school at the University of Alabama, at a school librarians session, discussed his book, "Helping Teachers Teach." Other topics explored were "Liability and the Librarian," "I'll Get There: It's Going to be Worth the Trip: Young Adult Services in Mississippi," and "Where am I?: Signs in the Library."

MLA and the Mississippi Library Commission (MLC) co-sponsored an annual NLW Workshop and Legislative Luncheon. More than 350 legislators, librarians, trustees and friends attended the February meeting where "communication" was the operative word. Publicity methods and a presentation by Eileen Cooke, ALA's Washington Office chief, were featured.

State Library and Public Libraries. MLC and public libraries dominated library activity in the state for 1988: Major legislation for the administration of the state's public libraries and a threatened reorganization of the state library agency, along with initial work toward standards for public libraries, progressed throughout 1988.

The Mississippi Statewide Library Development System Act of 1988 grew out of a 1987 Public Library Task Force. Designed to provide better financing and administration, the law was signed by Governor Ray Mabus in May. Areas covered included a definition of the duties and terms of library trustees, funding at a level of three mills for cities and four mills for counties, and greater flexibility of governments to fund libraries. Also called for is the development of standard for public libraries. A 15–member committee was established to compose standards. The composition of the committee will include seven trustees, five library directors and three at-large members.

Many librarians perceive a broad-based reorganization of state government, proposed by the governor, as a threat to the operation of the Library Commission and to public libraries generally. A series of public hearings attracted numerous librarians, trustees, and patrons who spoke against merging MLC with the state's education department. Speakers against the proposal cited erroneous assumptions by the accountant-based proposal. One example held that book orders for public libraries could be merged with textbook orders—a "myth," according to one witness. MLC's newsletter, *The Packet* reported deep support for MLC as an independent agency.

The Shelby Public Library was recently designated a Mississippi Landmark. This branch of the Bolivar County Library is housed in the old Shelby railroad depot that dates to the late 19th century, whose history follows the rise and decline of railway traffic in the region. Closed as a station in 1968, the depot was converted into a library in 1977.

Clarksdale's Carnegie Library sponsors the Delta Blues Museum, which was the beneficiary of a fund-raiser by ZZ Top, the rock group. The city hopes to raise $1,000,000 to establish a Muddy Waters exhibit and become a center for blues music. The Jackson/Hinds Library System opened a new branch named for Mississippi author Margaret Walker Alexander who wrote *Jubilee* and *For My People*.

School Libraries. A survey sponsored by MLC indicates that school-age children constitute a sizable patronage of public libraries in the state: MLC officials noted the purpose of the study was to demonstrate the importance of the public library to the school-age population. For example, during one week in January the Elizabeth Jones Library in Grenada, with a population of 10,000, served 541 students. The public library of Warren County-Vicksburg (population of more than 25,000) served 1,249 students that week.

Academic and Special Libraries. Motivated by special funds allocated by the state Legislature in 1987, eight publicly supported universities joined in a cooperative automation project. Participating institutions were Alcorn State University, Delta State University, Jackson State University, Mississippi State University, Mississippi University for Women, Mississippi Valley State University, University of Southern Mississippi and the University of Mississippi. Coordinated by the institutions' Library Directors' Council, the libraries engaged a consultant, reviewed alternatives and mutually recommended a vendor for turnkey systems.

The University of Southern Mississippi hosted its 21st Children's Book Festival in March, honoring author Jean Fritz with its annual Silver Medallion. Fritz, who spoke at the Festival, was recognized for her historical fiction. She is the author of more than 40 children's books. Also on the program were Steven Kellogg and William Joyce. The Ezra Jack Keats Foundation hosted the Ezra Jack Keats Lecture that featured Nancy Hands, Dr. and Mrs. Martin Pope and Florence B. Freedman.

Awards. MLA sponsors several annual awards; the newest is the Mississippi Authors Award. The 1988 winners were Felder Rushing for *Gardening Southern Style* and Terry Cline for *Quarry*, a novel.

The Peggy May Award, a memorial to a young MLC assistant director, was given to Lora Long, Associate Professor Emeritus of the University of Southern Mississippi. The Outstanding Achievement Award, given to a librarian or trustee for contributions to the profession, went to Bette Nelson, trustee of the Iuka Public Library. The Past Presidents' Award, voted by previous MLA presidents to an outstanding newcomer to the profession, was awarded to Sean A. Ferrell, director of the Laurel-Jones County Library. The Ed Ransdell Award, which recognizes the role of instructional television and media personnel, was given to Bonnie Sullivan, librarian at Lanier High School in Jackson and to Carl Thach, principal at Bassfield High School.

Appointments. Jean Major was appointed director of the University of Mississippi Library; James R. Martin became director of the library of the University of Southern Mississippi. Sean Ferrell was appointed director of the Laurel-Jones County Library; Linda Crawford was appointed director of South Delta Library Services (Yazoo City); Sarah Pannell is now director of Union County Library; and Virginia Holtcamp was appointed director of the Oktibbeha County Library.

JAMES F. PARKS, JR.

MISSOURI

Major News. During October, the Missouri State Library distributed the first edition of the statewide database on CD-ROM. More than 200 Missouri libraries are participating in the database project, including public, academic, school, and special libraries. Brodart Automation Company produced the database; users will search the database with the LePac software. The first edition of the database contains some 3,000,000 records representing more than 6,000,000 holdings. The database will be updated three times a year, with complete recompilation each fall.

As part of the automation project, the State Library offered LSCA grants to all tax-supported public libraries to enable them to purchase microcomputers with CD-ROM drives, modems, and bibliofile systems for in-house retrospective conversion. In addition, 90 academic libraries were offered grants to purchase CD-ROM drives. The next phase of the statewide automation project will be the implemen-

Missouri Library Association (founded 1900)

Membership: 1,100; *annual budget:* $81,000.

President: Dorothy Sanborn Elliott, St. Joseph Public Library, 10th & Felix St., St. Joseph 64501. (October 1988–October 1989).

Vice-President/President-elect: Ronald G. Boley, Curtis Laws Wilson Library, University of Missouri-Rolla, Rolla 65401.

Executive Coordinator: Jean McCartney, Missouri Library Association, 1015 East Broadway, Suite 215, Columbia 65201.

Annual meeting: October 4-6, 1989, Osage Beach.

Publication: MO INFO: *The Newsletter of the Missouri Library Association* (bimonthly).

Missouri State Library

Monteria Hightower
Associate Commissioner for
Libraries and State Librarian
P.O. Box 387
Jefferson City 65102

State School Library Media Supervisor

Missouri Department of Elementary
and Secondary Education
P.O. Box 480
Jefferson City 65102

---

tation of an interlibrary loan telecommunications system.

The University of Missouri-Columbia School of Library and Informational Science, in cooperation with the State Library, conducted a continuing education needs assessment.

Governor John Ashcroft organized LIFT-Literacy Investment for Tomorrow, a nonprofit foundation established to improve the reading, writing, speaking and mathematical skills of more than 1,000,000 Missourians.

State Association. The Missouri Library Association (MLA) sponsored its first Legislative Day in April. The event attracted 125 librarians, library trustees and friends to Jefferson City for meetings with their legislators regarding funding for libraries and the importance of libraries to the educational and economic health of the state.

The MLA held its 88th annual conference in Springfield with the theme "Libraries and Continuing Education: The Emerging Environment." Keynote speaker was F. William Summers, president of the American Library Association, who spoke on "Continuing Education: Our Unmet Professional Commitment."

State Library Activities. Missouri's involvement in the national library card campaign was a great success. More than 275 public libraries and branches participated in the "Every Child a Library Card" campaign with approximately 50,000 children returning postcards to the State Library indicating that they use their public library and the name of their favorite book.

The State Library has strengthened its continuing education efforts by hiring new consultant staff, and sponsoring several workshops and training programs throughout the state in 1988.

"Make Tracks to Your Library" was the theme of the 1988 Missouri Youth Summer Library Program, now in its sixth year.

State Librarian Monteria Hightower appointed a Strategic Planning Committee that drafted a five-year plan for the direction and improvement of library services in Missouri.

The State Library staff conducted 10 training workshops at which copies of the statewide database, training manuals for the database and telecommunications system, and ILL guidelines and directory were distributed. The State Library hosted a regional meeting that brought 10 LSCA coordinators to Jefferson City.

Wolfner Library for the Blind and Physically Handicapped, a division of the State Library, mounted an extensive promotional campaign to inform service providers and potential users about its special reading materials. Wolfner staff developed a new brochure and mailings that were sent to health care and eye care specialists statewide.

The Missouri State Census Data Center, part of the State Library, signed a contract with the University of Missouri–Columbia and the University of Missouri–St. Louis for support services for dissemination and promotion of 1990 census data and other census products.

Public Libraries. Springfield–Greene County Library has a new mobile learning center that travels through the county providing service to individuals who want to improve their reading and writing skills.

St. Louis Public Library, one of 62 patent depository libraries in the nation, was selected as one of ten test sites for a CD-ROM version of Classification and Search Support Information System (CASSIS), the U.S. Patent Office database. Citizens voted tax increases for St. Louis Public Library.

St. Charles City–County Library, Webb City Public Library, Sweet Springs Public Library and Carthage Public Library.

The Daviess County Library established a small business and tourism development center for county residents. St. Louis County Library and the Pattonville School District formed a "business partnership" for the purpose of motivating young children to read. The Cape Girardeau Public Library is involved in a unique volunteer program whereby first-time offenders, sentenced by local courts to 20–30 hours of public service, work in various capacities at the library. Kansas Citians voted overwhelmingly to separate the public library from the public school system. Kansas City had been the largest metropolitan public library in the Nation that was still governed by a school board, and the only such case in the state of Missouri.

Mexico–Audrain County Library and St. Louis Public Library received grants from the U.S. Office of Education for further development of their literacy programs.

Daniel Boone Regional Library has created "baby bags" for expectant parents. The white canvas bags with "baby blue" trim contain books, audio-cassettes and brochures on topics related to pregnancy and parenting as well as a catalog of services provided for parents by nonprofit agencies, organizations and interest groups in the three–county area served by the library. The bags are checked out as a regular library item, but patrons are allowed to keep the nonbook materials.

St. Joseph Public and Rolling Hills Consolidated Library, also headquartered in St. Joseph and serving two counties, have merged their technical services departments. Kansas City Public Library has established five learning centers to help adults with limited reading skills. A community attitude survey conducted in Cape Girardeau showed 80 percent of the residents rating the public library as a high–quality community service. Eight out of 10 residents use the library at least once a month. St. Louis Public Library has set up homework centers for children at three of its branches.

School Libraries, Media Centers. "Focus on the Future" was the theme of the Missouri Association of School Librarians' spring conference held in Kansas City.

Baby-Sitting is a Dangerous Job by Willo Davis Roberts, won the 1988 Mark Twain Award, which will be presented at the annual Missouri Association of School Librarians conference in 1989.

Academic Libraries, Special Libraries. Westminster College and William Woods College, both in Fulton, received a joint technology grant from the U.S. Office of Education to strengthen and expand their interlibrary lending system.

The University of Missouri–Columbia Libraries have been designated an Early English Books Research Center by University Microfilms Inc. The libraries received the honor for their support of the company's Early English Books Series, which began 50 years ago.

Ward Edwards Library at Central Missouri State University is disposing of its card catalog by contributing the cards to a local boy scout paper drive. The library has a new online catalog called LUIS, Library User Information System.

The Missouri Botanical Garden Library was awarded a $253,320 grant from the U.S. Office of Education to continue its project of reclassifying and recataloging its collections into the OCLC database.

The Harry S. Truman Library, Independence, is making major changes in its exhibit program. St. Louis Mercantile Library began a year-long oral history project with individuals who were involved in the waterways industry and with the Mississippi River. The project will help to preserve significant information about the history of river transportation in the United States.

Building Programs. Kansas City Public Library opened the Lucile H. Bluford Branch, the first branch to be constructed in 25 years. Named after a local civil rights leader and newspaperwoman, the branch was made possible by a 1986 tax levy increase. The library will build three full–service branches in the next few years. Nine public libraries received LSCA Title II grants for construction, renovation, handicapped access, energy conservation and additions. The three libraries in Kirksville were involved in major construction projects in 1988.

Maryville College in St. Louis opened a new library in the spring. St. Louis County Library embarked on a major building project to remodel and enlarge its headquarters facility. The county library is the largest public library in the state, with an annual circulation of 7,500,000. The Walter C. McCanse Memorial Library, located in Mount Vernon, was dedicated during National Library Week. Mid-Continent Public Library is in the midst of an eight–year building program, having constructed 11 new branches.

Awards. Aileen Helmick received the Special Service Award of the Missouri Association of School Librarians. She is on the library science faculty at Central Missouri State University. Gene Martin, director of Daniel Boone Regional Library, received the 1988 Beta Phi Mu Award. Susie Donnelly, trustee of Thomas Jefferson Library System, active in MLA and former chair of the Missouri Governor's Conference on Library and Information Services, received the MLA Meritorious Achievement Award. Jan Tonsing, librarian at Parkway Central High School, was named Teacher of the Year by the school. Diane L. Smith was elected secretary of the White House Conference on Library and Information Services Task Force.

Deaths. Jill Franklin, director of Cass County Public Library; J. Parker Stokes, director of Macon Public Library, and Vivian S. Meier, first librarian at Clayton Public Library.

Appointments. Library directors appointed in 1988 include: Sally Galbraith Pierce, Jackson Public Library; Sue Ann Schlosser, Webster Groves Public Library; Mildred Seboldt, Riverside Regional Library; Patricia Andermann, Kinderhook Regional Library; Sharon Willey, Cass County Public Library; Cheryl Goltz, Rolla Public Library; Linda L. Carder, Missouri Valley College; Neoma Techau, Brookfield Carnegie Library; Michelle Lahey, Midwest Research Institute; Lynn Crites, Farmington Public Library; Mark Daganaar, Three Rivers Community College; Glenda Driggs, Tarkio College; Sally Closson, Kansas City Art Institute; Joan Rapp, University of Missouri–St. Louis; Paladugu V. Rao, Central Missouri St. University; Dr. Jerrold Lee Brooks, St. Louis Mercantile Library; Dr. Burton M. Wheeler (interim director), Washington University; and Carolyn Trout, Joplin Public Library.

Richard T. Miller, assistant state librarian and a State Library staff member for 14 years, resigned in December to become the Montana state librarian.

Paul White was named assistant director of Mid–Continent Public Library.

Retirements. Library directors retiring in 1988 were: Helen Burns, Brookfield Carnegie Library; Christine Steele, Willow Springs Public Library; Helen Keith, Caruthersville Public Library; Annie Rae Gray, Hillsboro College, and Catheryn Higdon, Grundy County–Jewett Norris Library.

MADELINE MATSON

MONTANA

Major News. If one word must be used to characterize the Montana library landscape in 1988, that word would be CHANGE. School libraries reshaped their accreditation standards into competency–based outcomes. University system, school, and public libraries alike reeled under budget cuts necessitated by a tax freeze coupled with a poor economy. One change welcome as a chinook was that no new or old "tax revolt" initiatives qualified for the November ballot. The change with the most far–reaching implications of all did not take place, and a majority of Montana librarians hoped that it never would.

The Western Library Network (WLN) has served as the state's primary bibliographic utility and resource sharing mechanism since

Montana Library Association (founded 1914)

Membership: 521; *annual budget:* $52,311.

President: Georgia L. Lomax, Flathead County Free Library, 247 First Avenue, East, Kalispell 59901 (June 1988–May 1989).

Vice-President/President-elect: Karen Hatcher, Mansfield Library, University of Montana, Missoula 59812.

Annual meeting: April 29–May 2, 1987, Butte; April 26–29, 1989, Billings; May 2–5, 1990, Great Falls.

Publication: Library Focus (4–6 issues a year).

Montana State Library

Richard Miller, State Librarian
1515 E. 6th Ave.
Helena 59620

School Library Media Supervisor

Margaret (Margy) Rolando
Room 106, State Capitol
Helena 59620

the early 1980s. Montanans greatly value the duplication-free database and WLN's powerful searching capabilities. LaserCat, which makes the database available to the smallest libraries via CD-ROM technology, has expanded the horizons of dozens of communities. Therefore, it was with great concern that the Montana library community monitored WLN's proposed transition from state agency status to that of a private, non-profit corporation. Montanans, valuing the quality services available only from WLN, drafted resolutions of support and recommended that scarce resources be allocated to fund its Network resource sharing responsibilities. At year's end, however, a Technology Contingency Planning Team had been appointed and was researching alternatives to address a situation they fervently hoped would never materialize.

State Association. The 75th annual conference was held in Helena April 27–30. Attended by 403 registrants, it featured ALA President Margaret Chisholm as keynote speaker, OCLC Vice-President for Library Planning Mary Ellen Jacob, and computer whiz kids Eric Anderson and Bob Skapura. A raffle, complete with diamond ring to commemorate the diamond jubilee, raised funds for travel grants and legislative activities. Judy Meadows (Helena) served as Conference Chair.

Additional Association activities included publication of a membership booklet describing the Montana Library Association (MLA), compilation of a children's bibliography featuring Montana subjects and authors, and solicitation of position papers by gubernatorial candidates on selected library issues.

State Library Activities. FY 1989 LSCA projects approved during 1988 included $10,000 for a materials delivery demonstration project; $12,500 for collection development meetings; $10,000 for a voluntary certification program for public library staffs; $15,000 each for WLN recon of selected titles from the Montana Last Copy Fiction Depository (Billings) and the Montana Historical Society collections; and $87,500 for a two-year automation consultant program.

Projects completed in 1988 included an interlibrary loan study and a long-range plan for library continuing education. *Core Collection Guidelines for Smaller Libraries*, a publication giving detailed information for libraries to consider when developing collections, was sent to all public and school libraries.

Two collection development workshops were presented in three locations each. "Looking Around: Planning for your Library Community" emphasized the role of community analysis in the collection development process. "Treasure or Albatross" offered assistance to library staffs and policy makers on gifts, weeding, and care of library materials.

The Law Revision Committee, which reviewed all Montana statutes regarding libraries, distributed a final report at the state conference in April. Top priorities were assigned to "Information Access Montana," a state aid bill; revision of State Library Commission powers and federation law; and removal of the State Librarian's position from the state classification system.

Public Libraries. Funding problems were serious enough that two of the state's major newspapers ran feature articles on both the causes and the cutbacks. The property tax freeze, lower coal severance taxes, and loss of federal revenue sharing have left many libraries in a serious financial bind.

The good news was that both Missoula and Great Falls passed bond issues for automation funding. Parmly Billings Library migrated from CLSI to DYNIX, and Livingston became the first small library with a fully automated circulation desk. Parmly Billings Library also received $87,000 to remodel its Montana Room during the state's centennial year.

School Libraries, Media Centers. An electronic bulletin board named GOLIATH strengthened school librarians' ability to communicate across Montana's huge distances in 1988.

Project Excellence, a Board of Public Education program designed to meet the 1987 Legislature's call for a definition of basic education, resulted in new, proposed accreditation standards for Montana library media programs. "Student Outcomes, the Policies, Processes, and Resources Needed to Achieve These Outcomes" are competency-based student performance criteria for primary, intermediate, and graduating students.

Academic Libraries, Special, and Others. As Montana's academic libraries faced cutbacks and University of Montana students sold L.U.S.T. (Library Under Stressed Times) buttons to raise money, library use fees were considered by the Board of Regents as a way to provide revenue. Outcries from the library community were not only predictable but loud, and resulted in indefinite deferral of the proposal.

Montana Tech's library established a Patent Depository Center, the only one in a multistate area. Montana medical libraries hosted more than 70 librarians at the Pacific Northwest chapter of the Medical Library Association (PNC/MLA) in Bozeman, October 5–8.

Shodair Hospital in Helena, one of 15 key genetics centers in the world, was asked to demonstrate and test a microcomputer and video disc-based system called POSSUM (Pictures of Standard Syndromes and Undiagnosed Malformations) from Australia.

Building Programs. The Montana State Library Commission approved $159,832 in 1988 LSCA Title II construction matching funds for a new public library in Belgrade, for an addition to the Lincoln Community Library, for a handicap access parking lot for the Bitterroot Public Library (Hamilton), for handicap access to the Chouteau County Free Library (Ft. Benton), and for an energy efficiency remodel of the Plains Public Library entrance.

Dedications commemorated completion of highly successful remodeling and expansion projects at the Big Horn County (Hardin) and Bitterroot Public (Hamilton) Libraries, while the Laurel Public and Polson City Libraries moved into new buildings.

Networks, Interlibrary Cooperation. The Montana Faxnet Project continued to provide telecommunications leadership in the Big Sky Country, permanently placing fax machines in 16 public libraries and publishing a fax directory and resource guide.

Five of the six regional federations contracted with the Lewis & Clark Library (Helena) for centralized interlibrary loan and reference backup services in an effort to cut down on overhead costs and to increase efficiency in the face of ever-decreasing networking revenues.

Intellectual Freedom. The most comprehensive anti-pornography ordinance in the state was passed in June by Lincoln County (Libby) voters. Placed on the ballot by county commissioners at the request of Citizens for Decency Through Law, the three ordinances address display of materials harmful to minors, distribution and sales of hard-core pornography, and nude performance in a public place. Proponents have pledged to promote adoption of the ordinances in Billings and Great Falls.

Professional Interests. Marilyn LeBlond, Sidney Public Library, assumed responsibility for editing the Association newsletter, *Library Focus*. Ellen Newberg (Billings), Montana Councilor, completed the second of two years as chair of the ALA Chapter Relations booth. Darlene Staffeldt, Montana State Library, served as State Agency Section Representative on the Mountain Plains Library Association board. Karen Hatcher, University of Montana, completed a two-year term as Pacific Northwest Library Association secretary.

Awards. "Mindflight," a statewide public relations program sponsored by the federations, won a John Cotton Dana Special Award. The Montana Faxnet Project received the 1987 Silver Office Automation Award for outstanding achievement in its innovative use of telefacsimile technology.

Five Montana libraries qualified for a series of Library Services and Construction Act Title IV grants totalling over $120,000 to further literacy efforts in the state. They are Sidney Public Library, Flathead County Library (Kalispell), Bitterroot Public Library (Hamilton), Polson City Library, and Montana State Library.

Eight members of the library community were honored by the Montana Library Association for their contributions. Don Wetzel, Superintendent of the Corvallis Public Schools, received the School Administrator of the Year Award, while Trustee of the Year went to Lawrence Johnson of the Bitterroot Public Library (Hamilton).

Honorary Life Memberships were presented to E. Al Blockey (Bozeman), Edna Berg (Bozeman) and Glenda Bell (Billings). Special Friend to Libraries Award went to Peggy Muñoz (Hamilton) and Vonnie Voth (Ronan). Friends of Montana Libraries presented Sue

Nissan (Butte) its first annual Top Shelf Award for her work with the organization.

Appointments and Retirements. New appointments to key public library positions in the state included Jim Heckel as Director of the Great Falls Public Library, succeeding Richard Gercken; Jim Jondrow as Director of the Glasgow Public Library; Julie Shepard as Head Librarian of the Hearst Free Library (Anaconda), succeeding Natalie Sliepcevich who retired after 50 years of service; and Sandra Watts as director of the Big Horn County Library (Hardin), succeeding Jean Miller who retired.

Glenda Bell, library enthusiast and activist, retired from School District 2 (Billings) after a full and productive career.

At the State Library, Richard Miller succeeded State Librarian Sara Parker. Deborah Schlesinger served as interim State Librarian from August through December. Barbara Ridgway succeeded retiring 22-year veteran Darlene Tiensvold as Director of Services for the Blind and Physically Handicapped, and Jon Sesso became Director of the Natural Resource Information System. Mary Hudspeth (Libby) and C.E. Abramson (Missoula) were reappointed to the Montana State Library Commission for terms extending through 1991.

Deaths. Larry Thompson, program manager for the National Resource and Information System at the Montana State Library since 1985, died February 11th. Marie MacDonald, Glendive Public Library Director from 1964 to 1974, died July 25th.

ELLEN NEWBERG

NEBRASKA

Nebraska Library Association (founded 1895)

President: Laureen Riedesel, Beatrice (November 1988–November 1989).

Vice-President/President-elect: Dorothy B. Willis, Omaha.

Executive Secretary: Raymond B. Means, Creighton University, Omaha 68178.

Annual meeting: October 26–27, 1989, Lincoln (joint with the Nebraska Educational Media Association).

Publication: NLA Quarterly.

Nebraska Library Commission

Rod Wagner, Director
1420 P Street
Lincoln 68508–1683

School Library Media Supervisor

Jack Baille
Department of Education
Lincoln 68509

Nebraska Educational Media Association

President: Alan Wibbels, Central City.
Vice-President/President-elect: Bonnie Zetterman, Lincoln.
Publication: NEMA News.

Major News. At the urging of the Nebraska Library Association's (NLA) lobbyist and Legislative Committee and the Nebraska Library Commission (NLC), members expressed their opposition to Legislative Bills 117, 181, and 1020. Provisions of the bills would likely place unreasonable burdens on libraries and interfere with local governance functions as they deal with the effects of obscene materials on children.

LB1117 established an Educational Technology Center within the Department of Education; its purpose is to introduce and integrate technology and innovation in schools.

State Association. Legislative Day activities included librarians visiting and having lunch with state legislators. Of primary concern this year were the bills dealing with censorship.

Spring meetings of the NLA centered on a variety of themes: "Your Library Serving Your Community" was the theme of NLA's Public Library, Trustees, and School, Children, and Young People's sections.

"The Effective Librarian: Educator Politician, or Practitioner" was the theme of the College and University and Special Institutional sections. Herbert White, Dean of Indiana University School of Library and Information Science, was the theme speaker.

The 1988 Tri-Conference theme, "Preservers of the Past, Shapers of the Future," involved the Mountain Plains Library Association (MPLA), the Nebraska Educational Media Association (NEMA), and NLA as they met in Omaha, October 19–22. James Billington, Librarian of Congress, was the keynote speaker. Pre-conferences focused on negotiations, desktop publishing, space planning, and personal growth. "Meet the Author" was the subject of the post-conference on adolescent literature. Authors were Gary Paulsen, Gloria Miklowitz, Alden Carter, Bruce Degen, and Eve Bunting.

Executive boards of NEMA and NLA appointed members to a committee to study the feasibility of a merger of the two associations (Chair Joie Taylor, Columbus). NLA elected officers; Dorothy Willis, President-elect; Clara Hoover, Secretary; and Dick Allen, MPLA representative. NEMA elected officers: Bonnie Zetterman, President-elect, Eunice Parrish, Secretary; Board members, Bill Beck and Marilyn Sampson.

State Library Activities. The Nebraska Publications Clearinghouse, marking its 15th anniversary, announced that it houses more than 50,000 state documents and 250,000 federal publications. The Clearinghouse is charged with developing and maintaining a system to collect, catalog, and loan official state government publications.

Guidelines for public library accreditation and librarian certification were implemented. The guidelines were created to support and encourage development of public library services, to promote voluntary accreditation of public libraries and certification of public librarians, and possibly to affect state aid grants to public libraries. More than 435 librarians have taken advantage of the certification and 180 libraries have been accredited, representing 63 percent of the public libraries in Nebraska.

The Commission approved continuation of the OCLC retrospective conversion grant program and offered a new grant program for library automation planning; both were funded with Library Services and Construction Act monies. After receipt of the final report presenting alternatives for the future of the Nebraska State Database, by RMG, Inc., the Commission elected to use the OCLC state database function and Group Access Capability. The Commission will continue to administer Nebraska's OCLC network, NEBASE. It was approved by OCLC as a full-service network.

Governor Kay Orr reappointed Sandra Riley of Columbus, and appointed Donna Trueblood of Lexington, Lucille Vannoy of North Platte, and Norma Young of Lincoln, as Commissioners. The Commission initiated a strategic planning process involving Nebraska libraries in determining long-term goals and objectives. A steering committee with representation from a variety of libraries and communities are helping to guide the planning process. Consultants from Hanna:Keelan Associates will assist with process design and implementation.

Publication of *Guidelines for Young People's Library Service in Nebraska* was a cooperative effort between NLC and the School, Children's and Young People's Sections of NLA.

A new database was added to those offered by the Nebraska Online Database Service. The Nebraska Education Information Center Directory is a statewide directory of community service organizations which assist patrons making career decisions, re-entering the job market, starting a new business, or returning to school. This Information and Referral Library resource was funded through the Nebraska Education Information Center Network grant from the W. K. Kellogg Foundation.

Public Libraries. Twenty-six libraries received videocassette recorders as part of the ALA-Carnegie Video Project. Made possible by a grant from the Nebraska Committee for the Humanities, Cooper Foundation, the Woods Charitable Fund, and the Andrew W. Mellon Foundation, 40 libraries acquired the Library of America series. Omaha's Wired Library (OWL) is Omaha Public Library's new electronic bulletin board. WILL Workshops (Workshop in Library Leadership) continued to be a successful activity in which trustees focused on the development of leadership responsibilities. Through a cooperative arrangement of the Omaha Public Library and Cox Cable Television the Library received $8,000—the matching donation of Cox with that of library patrons. The Union Pacific Foundation contributed $40,000 and the Friends of the Library gave $25,000 to the Omaha Public Library Foundation to help match a grant from the Kiewit Foundation to purchase an automated circulation and catalog system. Omaha Public Library's Milton R. Abrahams Branch Library, which opened in April, won the Honor Award form the Nebraska Society of Architects and the City Beautification Award from the Omaha Women's Chamber of Commerce. Abrahams served for many years on the Library Board and is currently president of the Omaha Public Library Foundation.

School Libraries and Media Centers. Several groups of library media specialists participated in the teleconference on the library/media guidelines, *Information Power*, on April 12. Donna Peterson, Lincoln, is coordinating implementation of the new guidelines.

Networks and Interlibrary Cooperation. Sponsored by the Eastern Library System with major funding by the Nebraska Committee for the Humanities, Jim Trelease spoke to librarians and educators on the value of reading aloud to children. A conference sponsored by NLC and the Postsecondary Educational Libraries and Resource Centers of Nebraska (PELARCON) included 90 librarians to explore the possibility of cooperative collection development.

Pete Hamon, Director of the South Central Library System, Madison, Wisconsin, spoke to the State Advisory Council Systems Committee as they met to plan for Systems activities.

Intellectual Freedom. Ron Norman, Editor of the *NLAQ (Nebraska Library Association Quarterly)* devoted the Summer 1988 issue to "Censorship and Intellectual Freedom," in which Judith Krug, ALA Office for Intellectual Freedom, authored an article, "The impact of the Reagan Years on Intellectual Freedom."

An Academic Freedom Coalition of Nebraska has been formed with representatives from several organizations, including NLA.

Professional Interests. Results of a survey conducted by an NLA Ad Hoc Committee on Comparable Worth (Chair, Janice Boyer, Omaha) revealed that NLA's membership is primarily white (97.4 percent), female (87.7 percent), and between the ages of 39-59 (79 percent). Full-time employees have a mean salary of $22,699; the mean for women was $21,496 and for men it was $29,773.

Awards. NLA's 1988 Meritorious Service Award was presented to Ruth Lenser, Tilden. Thelma L. Lang was selected to receive the 1988 Trustee Citation for her outstanding contributions to library service in Litchfield. NEMA awarded a meritorious award to Hope Weaver, Neligh. The School, Children's and Young People's Section of NLA awarded the 1988 Mad Hatter Youth Service Award to Kay Paulsen, media specialist for the Scottsbluff Public Schools. Mollie Ferguson, nominated by the children at Ravenna Elementary School, received the "Sunshine Award" presented by Channel 13. Sharon Borden, Metropolitan Technical Community College, Omaha, received an award from the Hobby Industries of America and the Public Information Office of ALA, for her innovative "Adopt a School" project. Bette Keefe, Bellevue library media specialist, received Nebraska's "Celebrate Literacy" Award. Mary Nash, Creighton University Library, received the 1988 Distinguished Service Award from the NLA College and University section. Thelma Hamilton received the Geneva Chamber of Commerce's Outstanding Service Award for her service to the community's children. The McGoogan Library of Medicine, University of Nebraska Medical Center, received a John Cotton Dana Special Award given for exceptional library public relations. McGoogan Librarian, Audrey Powderly Newcomer, received the Medical Library Association's first Estelle Brodman Award given for achievement at mid-career and potential for future leadership. Golden Sower Awards were presented to Patricia Lakin and Patience Brewster for their book, *Don't Touch My Room* and to Barthe DeClements for her *Sixth Grade Can Really Kill You.*

Appointments. Rod Wagner was appointed Director of the Nebraska Library Commission. He served as Deputy Director from 1974 to 1988. Nancy Busch was appointed Deputy Director. Janice Boyer was named Assistant Director for Administrative Services, University of Nebraska at Omaha. Verda Bialac was appointed assistant director, Omaha Public Libraries.

Deaths. Marian Wagner, former reference/interlibrary loan librarian, Columbus Public Library died February 28. Marion Playfoot, former serials librarian at the University of Nebraska at Omaha, died November 24.

Other. The first OOPS' Annual Storytelling Festival/Workshop (Omaha Organization for the Purpose of Storytelling) convened June 23, at the Omaha Metro Community College.

E. LAVERNE HASELWOOD

NEVADA

Nevada Library Association (founded 1946)

Membership: 183; *annual budget:* $26,000.

President: Carol Madsen, Elko County Library (January 1988–January 1989).

Vice-President/President-elect: Lynn Ossolinski, Incline High School, Incline 89450.

EXECUTIVE SECRETARY: Susan L. Conway, Getchall Library, University of Neveda/Reno, Reno 89557

Annual meeting: October 12–14, 1989, Boulder City.

Nevada State Library and Archives

Joan Kerschner, State Librarian
Capitol Complex
Carson City 89710

Nineteen eighty-eight was proclaimed "Year of the Library" in Nevada by Governor Richard H. Bryan in celebration of the more than 30 new or expanded facilities that have been constructed as a result of two bond issues. Construction documents were completed for a 119,000-square-foot facility in the heart of the capitol complex for the Nevada State Library and Archives, and incoming Governor Bob Miller included a recommendation of $20,299,000 for construction to begin March 1990.

State Library Activities. The State Library and Archives funded production of the statewide database on CD-ROM. The catalog of nearly 1,500,000 holdings is available in the public, community college, and university libraries around the state. Small libraries use the CD-ROM database as their only catalog while larger libraries whose catalogs are online use the database as a backup catalog and for interlibrary loan. This is in addition to the statewide network that links all six regional computer systems. Automation in rural libraries has been a priority effort resulting in even the smallest, most remote Nevada libraries making use of state-of-the-art automation. Very remote locations are dialing into the statewide network to search catalog and circulation databases, and utilizing software that permits online ordering from vendors and participation in the statewide union catalog on CD-ROM. A statewide library card is in use in most locations throughout the state.

Second-year funding for the Nevada Literacy Coalition was obtained from the Gannett Foundation, the Job Training Partnership Act, and Library Services and Construction Act (LSCA) Title VI. The Governor's biennial budget proposes two positions for literacy at the Nevada State Library and Archives (NSLA). The number of literacy volunteer programs grew from nine to thirteen in 1988 with the assistance of the Coalition, with seven more on the drawing boards. Students being tutored by volunteers increased 84 percent while number of tutors trained increased 46 percent.

Grants were obtained to purchase energy materials for local libraries, to activate humanities programming, and to arrange and describe 480 cubic feet of Nevada's state and territorial records, dating from 1855 to 1945. A bill is pending in the Legislature to establish a regrant program for local records management programs with $50,000 state and $150,000 NHPRC funds. The Governor has recommended additional office staff and program funds to complete records schedules for all state agencies within four years.

Public Libraries. Business and buildings were booming in Nevada in 1988. Las Vegas/Clark County Library District opened several new or expanded facilities and circulation topped 2,000,000 items for the first time. Literacy programs in Las Vegas received national recognition when Coordinator Lee Green and volunteer Margaret Mounton spoke on their specialty, computer-assisted literacy instruction, at the Laubach International Conference in San Diego and the Adult Literacy and Technology Conference in Pittsburgh. Library District fund-raisers included $70,000 raised for the annual "Bucks for Books" campaign, and the district was the first to install CLSI's new sequent computer.

The Washoe County Library obtained property for two new branches while negotiation continued for a third site. The firm of Professional Library Consultants, Inc., was retained to develop the building program for these sites. In addition, the Washoe County Library budget received a dramatic increase of $1,200,000 including 24 new staff positions. A new children's wing was opened at Sparks Branch and the main library was renovated. Hours increased at all branches. In Elko, the main library was renovated, and a new branch was constructed at West Wendover. Civic Crown, a special community planning committee, began long-range plans for Elko Public Library.

All public librarians were trained in the planning process and will make use of this training in updating their statutorily required master plans and in developing a new statewide plan in 1989.

Academic Libraries. It was a good year for private funding in Nevada's academic libraries. The library at the University of Nevada, Reno, received $117,000 from the Robert Z. Hawkins foundation to purchase seven CD-ROM products. The University of Nevada, Las Vegas (UNLV), received $100,000 from the W. M. Keck Foundation to enhance its online public catalog. The money was used primarily for retrospective conversion and quality control of their database. The library began cooperating in an exciting new program with the required freshman composition classes at UNLV to provide a library skills laboratory for all students entering the university.

School Libraries. School libraries made strides in automation and funding with assistance of a new position for school library coordinator at the Department of Education. The Department and the State Library teamed up to bring schools into the automation system and to create and strengthen several school/public libraries in rural areas.

Intellectual Freedom. Following in the wake of the challenges to books by Jack Prelutsky, *Witches, Witches, Witches* was challenged in a rural school library in Nevada. The fate of the book was left undecided.

Nevada Library Association. Judith Krug, Director, ALA Intellectual Freedom Office, was keynote speaker for the conference, which highlighted intellectual freedom issues from beginning to the final program. A panel of the state librarian, local media celebrities, and a local author participated.

People. State Librarian Joan Kerschner received the Council of State Governments Charles McCarthy Award for Leadership in Information Services. Washoe County Librarian Martha Gould was named Civil Libertarian of the Year in Nevada. Charles Hunsberger, Clark County Library District, was named Librarian of the Year by the Nevada Library Association, was featured in the *Nevada Today* newspaper, and received an award from the Nevada Council on the Arts for promotion of galleries and public places arts projects in Las Vegas libraries. Bonnie Buckley, State Library and Archives, received a special citation for her work on literacy funding.

Cookie Mouton, Las Vegas/Clark County Library District, received the ALA trustees award for Literacy, and Mr. and Mrs. Hank Greenspun were given the award for private donations based on their donation of prime development land for the new, 22,000-square-foot Green Valley Library in Clark County. Marilyn Davenport, Las Vegas/Clark County Library District, received the *Bronze Quill* and several other awards for her work as a graphic artist from the International Association of Business Communicators.

Longtime Nevada librarian Carroll Gardner moved from the directorship of Boulder City District Library to become Director of Henderson District Public Library. Henderson is the third-largest city in the state and has a new facility under construction.

JOAN G. KERSCHNER

NEW HAMPSHIRE

New Hampshire Library Association (founded 1889)

Membership: 555; *annual budget:* $29,989.

President: Kathy E. Richardson, Nashua Public Library, 2 Court St., Nashua 03060 (June 1988–June 1989).

Vice-President/President-elect: Patricia M. Topham, Plymouth Public Library, Plymouth.

Secretary: Barbara Young, Exeter Public Library, Exeter.

Treasurer: Ellen L. Hardsog, Derry Public Library, Derry.

Annual meeting: May 1–3, 1989, Manchester.

Publication: NHLA Newsletter (bimonthly), Amy Bahr, editor, Abbie Greenleaf Library, Franconia.

Department of Libraries, Arts and Historical Resources

Shirley Gray Adamovich, Commissioner
Matthew J. Higgins, Director of the
Division of Libraries (State Librarian)
20 Park Street
Concord 03301-6303

The major efforts of librarians throughout New Hampshire in 1988 focused on the New Hampshire Automated Information System (NHAIS). At present, in addition to the Capital Area Library Network (CAPNET), there are four regional systems, each using OCLC's LS/2000 software with each system in a different stage of development. Regional systems were developed to address the need of larger public and academic libraries for automated circulation systems. And, because of telecommunication costs and the large number of titles and holdings involved, it was decided to set up regional systems to serve the needs of larger libraries while providing libraries with regional online union catalogs.

Each system will also be part of a telecommunications network. Utilizing Codex telecommunications equipment and a combination of State Police microwave and telephone lines, all systems will be connected via dial-up access to the nearest regional system. At that point the library will choose the regional system it wishes to search. Thus, with one telephone call, a library will have access to all systems.

Some Codex telecommunications equipment has already been installed, and the rest was in place early in 1989. With the network in place and all regional systems in operation, libraries will have access to approximately 1,000,000 titles owned by all types of libraries throughout New Hampshire.

Annual Conferences. The 99th Annual Conference of the New Hampshire Library Association (NHLA) was held at Franklin Pierce College in Rindge, June 13–15, with the theme of "Images of the 80's and Beyond." Programs dealt with librarians' personal images as well as the library's image. Topics for discussion included computers, mime, occupational hazards, videos, fashion, young adult space planning and other pertinent subjects. Canoeing on the lake, new library songs, and the annual talent show provided lighter moments.

The Fall Meeting was held on November 10, at the Lake Shore Farm Resort in Northwood with the main topic of discussion "The Grey Panther Explosion: Library Services for the Older American." Betty Turock of Rutgers University, one of the nation's leading authorities on older Americans, was to have been the speaker, but she could not be present because of illness. Her paper was read to the group and discussed.

Frank J. Williams, President of the Abraham Lincoln Society, Springfield, Illinois, spoke on "Abraham Lincoln, Friend of Librarians and the Book." At the business meeting the treasurer announced receipt of the bequest to NHLA under the will of Rosalie Norris, librarian at the Amherst Town Library in the 1940s of one-third of her estate ($37,270) to establish a scholarship fund. The annual auction raised almost $1,000 to support the Association's activities. Frances Wiggin, Bedford Public Library, again served as auctioneer.

The New Hampshire Library Association will celebrate its centennial in 1989. One of the highlights of the 100th Annual Conference to be held in Manchester May 1–3 will be the publication of *The Road Taken*. NHLA was the first state library association to be incorporated in the U.S. The Centennial Committee collected pictures and information (enough material was received for two books): the result will be a second book to be published in late 1989.

State Library. The New Hampshire State Library took the first step in combating deteriorating library materials by inviting all public libraries to apply for preservation surveys to be conducted by the Northeast Document Conservation Center. Support for the surveys was received from the National Endowment for the Humanities and LSCA Title I funds. Public libraries in Charlestown, Conway, Farmington, Jaffrey, Laconia, Manchester, Rochester, and Temple were selected.

Cooperation. Many New Hampshire librarians recognize the lack of formal young adult service in the state's public libraries, and they are creating a grassroots group to investigate the matter. The Young Adult Services Interest Group received its impetus from the CONNECTING Institutes on the young adult and reading held at the University of New Hampshire in 1985 and 1987. In July, school and public librarians and trustees met in Franklin to hear Marilee Foglesong, New York Public Library's Coordinator for Young Adult Services, report on what other states, individual libraries, and library systems are doing for young adults. A panel then presented various aspects of young adult (YA) service that might be incorporated in New Hampshire libraries.

As a result, the Merri–Hill–Rock (Merrimack, Hillsborough, and Rockingham Counties) Cooperative in November initiated a *YA Newsletter* containing information on articles and resources available through the COOP. The *Newsletter* Committee, chaired by Elizabeth O'Donnell, ALA Young Adult Services Division Committee member and Supervisor of Circulation Services at the Manchester City Library, hopes to expand the *Newsletter* into a statewide publication.

Intellectual Freedom. The Intellectual Freedom Committee joined the fight to kill passage of State House Bill 981–FN on restricting access by minors to videocassettes and requiring proof of age for attending movies. Librarians were concerned about the language of the bill and about how it might apply to library activities and programs. Gary McCool of Lamson Library, Plymouth State College, testified on behalf of NHLA before the Senate's Internal Affairs Committee hearing on the bill. His testimony helped slow progress of the bill but did not convince the Committee to vote it "inexpedient to legislate." Instead the bill was sent to a study committee where it may or may not die.

Professional Interests. The New Hampshire Writers & Publishers Project (NHWPP), located in Portsmouth, is a newly-formed nonprofit organization committed to supporting New Hampshire writing and publishing. Its goals are to increase public awareness and appreciation of the state's literary efforts, to make New Hampshire literature more easily available, to provide quality programing and to act as a literary resource center for the state. The first issue of NHWPP's monthly newsletter was published in November; the publication will serve as a statewide informational resource linking writers to writers and writers to audiences. The Project will provide libraries with assistance and information on books, authors, and programs previously difficult to track.

Awards. Shirley Gray Adamovich, Commissioner of Libraries, Arts, and Historical Resources, received the Granite State Award at the 7th annual commencement exercises of the University of New Hampshire's School for Lifelong Learning on June 5. The award recognizes people who have made exceptional contributions to the community and the state. Adamovich was cited for her dedication to the education of all New Hampshire citizens, especially to adult learners. She has been involved in teaching and designing courses for more than 30 years, including courses in American and English literature and in library and information science at both the undergraduate and graduate levels.

At the New England Library Association's Silver Jubilee Banquet on October 23, in Sturbridge, Massachusetts, Emerson Greenaway, of New London, was awarded the first "Great Librarian Award" honoring outstanding service to New England libraries.

Appointments. Ruth Katz was named University Librarian at the University of New Hampshire (UNH) and assumed the duties of that position on August 1. She replaced Donald Vincent who retired in May after 26 years of service. Katz came to UNH from East Carolina University where she was Director of Academic Library Services.

Deaths. Arthur E. Porter of Manchester died May 21, 1988. An attorney, he served on the New Hampshire State Library Commission from 1968 until he retired as Chairman of that body in 1985.

Dorothy M. Little of Hampton died August 24, 1988. Active in the New Hampshire Library Trustees Association for many years, Dorothy Little served as its President from 1982 to 1984. She had been a trustee of the Lane Memorial Library in Hampton for many years and had recently retired as librarian of the Instructional Material Center of Supervisory School Union No. 21 in Hampton.

LOUISE C. PRICE

NEW JERSEY

New Jersey Library Association (founded 1890)

Membership: 1,558; *annual budget:* $165,600.

President: Norma Yueh, Ramapo College Library (May 1989–April 1990).

Vice-President/President-elect: Irene Cakowski, Director, Monroe Township Library.

Executive Director: Danilo H. Figueredo, P.O. Box 1534, Trenton 08007.

Annual meeting: May 3–5, Atlantic City.

Publications: New Jersey Libraries (quarterly); *New Jersey Libraries Newsletter* (monthly).

Division of State Library, State Department of Education

Barbara Weaver, State Librarian
185 West State Street, CN 520
Trenton 08625

Local and Community Services

Christine Keresztury,
Assistant Coordinator,
New Jersey State Library,
185 W. State Street, CN 520,
Trenton 08625

State School Library Media Supervisor

Jean Harris
New Jersey State Library
185 West State St., CN 520
Trenton 08625

The big news in the state was the "Jobs, Education, and Competitiveness Bond Act" on the November ballot was approved by the voters by a margin of 2-to-1. This act, actively supported by Governor Thomas H. Kean, allocates $350,000,000 for the development, improvement, and expansion of technical and scientific research centers in the state. About $60,000,000 will be used to construct additional library space. As the Governor noted, "The last time we spent money on building labs and libraries was in 1971. We still paid 35 cents a gallon for gasoline back then. The Giants were still playing in New York. And who knew what a VCR was?"

Library Association. VCRs and the new information technology was very much on the mind of New Jersey librarians. The State Library contracted King Research Inc. to conduct a study on library automation. Their report, published in the spring and distributed by the State Library, made numerous recommendations for the improvement of online bibliographic work, communications, and resource sharing, emphasizing the importance of continuing education and of matching the needs of local libraries, regional cooperatives, and the State Library. The report pointed out to librarians where New Jersey is on automation and where it should be in the future.

The future of library leadership was a statewide concern. To address the issue, the State Library offered a three-weekend seminar on the subject of leadership. Candidates were sought and 30 librarians, representing public and academic libraries, large and small institutions, were selected. When the seminar was over, the participants were matched with mentors who will introduce the new leaders to diverse aspects of librarianship and administration.

No doubt some of these new leaders will be studying the role of performance measure as a tool to improve library service, another project undertaken by the State Library and supported, in its initial stage, by the New Jersey Library Association. The proposal is to develop guidelines that will encourage excellence and provide better services to patrons, making the library more responsive to the community.

As the state continues to attract New Yorkers and other residents of the tri-state area, libraries find themselves providing more and more service. To satisfy the needs of these growing communities, library buildings are being repaired and expanded, and new facilities are being erected. Anywhere you look in the state, from the rural communities of South Jersey to the crowded suburbs 10 miles from Manhattan, from the Jersey shore to the mountains bordering upstate New York, you see new buildings opening their facilities to new patrons, and old libraries adding new wings.

Legislation. To facilitate funds for this growth, a bill will be introduced at the New Jersey Assembly calling for a bond issue of $50,000,000 for library construction. The sponsor of this bill is Assemblyman Robert Smith.

The library construction bill is endorsed by the New Jersey Library Association. The Association, through its Government Relations Committee, is working closely with the Assemblyman. This represents yet another effort taken by the New Jersey Library Association (NJLA) on behalf of New Jersey libraries. In 1988, NJLA saw one of its bills become law. In the spring, the governor signed into law a bill that clarified the status of joint libraries and included them under the laws and regulations pertaining to municipal libraries. These libraries had not been included in the municipal budget.

Late in the year, public libraries received an increase in the per capita state aid given to public library (an increase of 25¢ per capita). This came as a result of legislation proposed and supported by NJLA, assisted by its Government Relations Consultant, Roger McDonough, former State Librarian and past ALA president.

Legislation was not the only area of interest to NJLA. Other topics addressed through its programs were latch-key children in public libraries, conservation, automation, and the FBI and its "Library Awareness Program," affirming, once again, NJLA's support of the confidentiality act.

People. The year ended with the death of David Weill, Director of the East Brunswick Public Library, and the appointment of Alex Boyd as Director of the Newark Public Library, the largest public library in the state. The previous director, Thomas J. Alrtuz, past president of NJLA, is now an Associate Director of the New York Public Library. Roger McDonough retired. In his honor, a Senate proclamation was signed, listing his many achievements as State Librarian and NJLA's Government Consultant. In May, Danilo H. Figueredo, formerly of the Research Libraries of New York Public Library, was appointed Government Consultant and Executive Director of the New Jersey Library Association.

DANILO H. FIGUEREDO

NEW MEXICO

New Mexico Library Association (founded 1924)

Membership: 518; *annual budget:* $28,300.

President: Karen J. Watkins, New Mexico State Library, Santa Fe.

Vice-President/President-elect: Gloria Trujilo, Fairview Elementary School, Espanola.

Annual meeting: April 13–15, 1988, Las Cruces; April 26–28, 1989, Santa Fe.

Publication: NMLA Newsletter (five issues per year).

New Mexico State Library

Virginia Hendley, State Librarian
325 Don Gaspar
Santa Fe 87503

School Library Media Supervisor

Mary Jane Vinella
State Department of Education
300 Don Gaspar
Santa Fe 87503

Awards. The following awards were made in 1988: Librarian of the Year–Dolores Padilla, Belen Public Library; Trustee of the Year–William Racoosin, Alamogordo Public Library; Community Achievement Award–Elizabeth Wacondo, Laguan Pueblo, Celsa Quintana, Espanola; Distinguished Service Award–Javier Vargas, Las Cruces; Marion Dorroh Memorial Scholarship–Susan Veltfor, Santa Fe. F. William Summers, Sylvia Bender-Lamb, Louella Wetherbee, Paul Erdman, and Alice B. Ihrig were among the speakers at the 1988 conference in Las Cruces from April 13 to 15.

Library Education. Northern New Mexico Community College in Espanola will establish an AAS degree program in Library Technology. Plans are formulating to offer all or part of the MLS degree from the University of Arizona at the University of New Mexico. North Texas University will do the same at the University of Texas, El Paso.

Legislation. A statewide group of concerned library advocates called Library Book '88 worked toward the passage of several pieces of legislation on the November 1988 ballot. Chaired by Carol King of Albuquerque, the activist group mailed hundreds of thousands of fliers promoting library issues and made speeches and presentations around the state. Affiliated groups such as a Las Cruces organization made thousands of telephone calls prior to the election. Their efforts were successful: $1,500,000 was allocated for the purchase of books and other library materials for public libraries in New Mexico; a $45 million issue was passed to fund academic and public school projects throughout the state including $11,100,000 for library construction at New Mexico State University; and adoption of an amendment to the state constitution that would add "the purchase of books and other library resources" to the list of purposes for which a county could raise money through a general obligation bond.

Buildings. Now in its Centennial Year, the University of New Mexico in Albuquerque opened two new branch libraries—the Parish Memorial Library (business administration and economics) and the Centennial Science and Engineering Library. The city of Truth or Consequences dedicated its new public library in the fall of 1988. New Mexico State University completed extensive renovation of its facility in preparation for new construction, which was approved by the New Mexico voters. The Las Cruces Public Library completed the addition of a second floor.

Academic Libraries. Both the University of New Mexico and the New Mexico State University Libraries implemented the INNOVACQ online acquisitions and serials check-in system. The UNM General Library contracted with Carlyle for an online public access catalog. New Mexico State implemented the circulation function of its VTLS online catalog.

Legislation and Intellectual Freedom. The New Mexico Legislature passed Senate Memorial 45, which "requires the elimination in the state's schools of the teaching of and/or counseling by certain psychological techniques, e.g. transcendental meditation, altered states of consciousness or the occult." This measure caused considerable difficulty for school libraries throughout the state. A bill relating to obscenity died in adjournment.

School Libraries. A high level of standards survived despite a campaign to greatly reduce requirements for school library personnel, which was aggressively opposed by the library profession.

Public Libraries. The continuing decline in severance tax revenues from the petroleum and mining industries sustained severe pressure on library appropriations. State aid to public libraries, which reached a high of $240,000 in the early 1980s, was reduced for the third consecutive year, to $136,294 or nine cents per capita.

Deaths. Chester Linshied, former director at New Mexico State University and former president of NMLA, died in Kerrville, Texas.

Retirements. James Dyke, former director of the New Mexico State University Library, Texas A & M Library, and Eastern New Mexico University Library, and past president of NMLA; Lois Godfrey, past president of NMLSA and Assistant Head Librarian of the Los Alamos National Laboratory Library; and Mary Ferguson, former Head of Cataloging, New Mexico State University.

LOWELL R. DUHRSEN

NEW YORK

New York Library Association (founded 1890)

Membership: 3,112; *annual budget:* $390,160.

President: Julie Cummins, Coordinator of Children's Services, New York Public Library, New York (October 1987–October 1988); Janet E.Steiner, Excecutive Director, South Central Research Library Council, Ithaca (October 1988–October 1989).

Vice-President/President-elect: Frances R. Roscello, Associates Bureau of School Library Media Programs, New York State Education Department, Albany.

Executive Director: Nancy W. Lian, 15 Park Row, Suite 434, New York 10038.

Annual meeting: October 12–16, Buffalo.

Publication: NYLA Bulletin (10 issues a year).

New York State Library

Joseph F. Shubert, State Librarian and Assistant Commissioner for Libraries
State Education Department
Cultural Education Center
Empire State Plaza
Albany 12230

School Library Media Supervisor

Robert E. Barron, Chief
Bureau of School Library Media Programs
State Education Department
Albany 12234

State Association. The Association's highest priority, the passage of a library omnibus bill, was not met in 1988. In spite of a lot of legislative assurances that 1988 would be the year of the library, legislators failed to make good on their promises when the state budget was finally adopted in time for the state fiscal year April 1-March 31. 1988 was the third consecutive year with no increase in library funding.

The 95th annual conference was held in Buffalo with the theme "Breaking the Information Barrier: Librarians on the Frontier." Conference attendance hovered over the 2,000 mark. Author Judy Blume started the conference with her stirring and poignant keynote address; and Scott Armstrong, National Security Archive made a strong case for free access to government information at the send-off breakfast.

The Outstanding Services to Libraries Award went to Richard Panz, director of the Finger Lakes Library System. Harold Hacker of Rochester, received the Outstanding Advocate of Libraries Award.

An innovation in 1988 was a conference-within-a-conference on AIDS. Several sections joined together in a series of programs on AIDS. NYLA Council approved a statement on AIDS related materials in school libraries in support of the State's initiative to provide instructional programs on AIDS and encourage school library media centers to acquire and provide unrestricted access to materials dealing with AIDS.

At the annual business meeting, membership approved two Bylaws amendments: to change the makeup of Council by extending the length of term for Councilors-at-large from two to three years, increase the number of seats from two to three, and eliminate the position of second vice-president; and to facilitate the submission of petitions for elected officers of the association and ease the time requirements.

The School Library Media Section Executive Board developed a leadership program that won the AASL/ABC-CLIO Leadership Development Award of $1,750. Membership approved extensive changes that have streamlined the structure of the organization at the 1988 Spring Conference in Rochester.

The Public Library Section began publication of a newsletter "Public Library Synergy" and awarded 12 grants to public library systems to conduct workshops on "Measuring Up To Standards." Reference and Adult Services Section published four issues of its newsletter "Rassmatazz," prepared a membership recruitment brochure, awarded a continuing education grant of $150 and created two committees. Academic and Special Libraries Section initiated planning for a statewide conference involving other academic and special library organizations. The Round Table on the Concerns of Women published two issues of their expanded newsletter and sponsored or -o-sponsored three programs at the NYLA conference. Ethnic Services Round Table produced its first newsletter. They plan to issue two or three issues per year. They presented two programs and co-sponsored two others at NYLA annual conference. The Government Documents Round Table submitted its final recommendations for redesign of the New York State document depository program to the State Library. Two issues of Documents to the People of New York State were produced. *Government Publications for School Libraries: A Bibliographic Guide and Recommended Core Collection*, by Donald Voorhees was published. The first issue of an index to New York State government document serials will be completed soon.

Junior Members Round Table voted to change its name to New Members Round Table. The Library and Information Science Educators Round Table was revived, and two programs were planned for the NYLA conference. The Continuing Education Committee offered three workshops at the conference. The Public Awareness Committee began a year-long promotion to raise the public's consciousness of New York library resources and services.

At its May 20, 1988, meeting NYLA adopted a policy statement on the confidentiality of library records that should be submitted to the policy-setting board of each library for approval.

On June 13 Governor Cuomo signed into law as Chapter 112 of the Laws of 1988 that classified *all* types of library records as confidential.

State Library. The New York State Library contracted with King Research Inc. of Rockville, Maryland, to conduct a study of the 22 public library systems, nine reference and research library resources systems, and the 46 school library systems.

Two colloquiums on Technology and the Research Environment of the Future were sponsored by the State Library. On February 12, Manuscripts and Special Collections entered the State Library's first of 20,000 musical scores into RLIN in the Scores Format.

The State Library was designated an Early English books Research Center by Universities Microfilms International. The State Library was one of 30 libraries added to OCLC's Enhance program.

Jerome Yavarkovsky, Director of the State Library, chairs a task force to make recommendations on a permanent infrastructure for research in library and information, one of four created by the U.S. Department of Education's Office of Library Programs.

Public Libraries. Vartan Gregorian resigned as president and chief executive officer of The New York Public Library to become the 16th president of Brown University. Ten libraries in New York were among 224 libraries nationwide to receive federal grants to combat illiteracy. Michael F. Bocamazo was appointed chief of the branch administration at the Brooklyn Public Library, and is responsible for the library's 58 branches. Herke Kordish, former Assistant University Librarian for Planning and Financial Services at Columbia University, is the new Deputy Director of the Research Libraries, The New York Public Library. The New York Public Library announced that the extensive collection of Robert Moses papers is now open to scholars. Robert Omer, AV consultant since 1971 for the Upper Hudson Library Federation, retired in January 1988. The Buffalo and Erie County Library acquired at an auction an 1885 letter from Mark Twain to James Fraser Gluck to add to its major collection of Twain material.

The New York Public Library dedicated its new Goldsmith-Perry Preservation Laboratory on February 11. The laboratory will preserve books, newspapers and maps on microfilm at the rate of 2,000,000 frames per year. Marcia Lane Purcell has been appointed coordinator of adult services for The New York Public Library and its 81 branches. Julia J. Brady, Associate director for Central Library Services, The New York Public Library, retired after 41 years of service.

Jeanette Knapp, adult services/reference coordinator who has been with the Southern Adirondack Library System since 1974, retired in January. Ruth Ann Carr was appointed Chief of the United States History, Local History, and Genealogy Division of the Research Libraries of The New York Public Library. Ruth Jones, Head of Circulation, Rochester Public Library, retired after 30 years of service.

The New York Public Library launched its library card campaign on April 21. The slick red-and-white cards, which should last a lifetime, are part of a $3,800,000 effort to computerize the circulation at branches in Manhattan, the Bronx, and on Staten Island. The goal is to register more than 500,000 school children in the three boroughs; more than 60,000 new borrowers were signed up in the first six weeks. The Buffalo and Erie County Public Library opened a collection of materials on alcohol and substance abuse in its central library on May 13. The collection was made possible through a $59,100 grant from the State Division on Alcoholism and Alcohol Abuse.

On August 3 Governor Cuomo signed into law a bill authorizing financing of a new $16,000,000 library for the Blind and Physically Handicapped in New York City.

School Libraries. Rose Mary Tobiassen of the Riccardi Elementary School in Saugerties received the School Library Media Specialists of Southeastern New York Beatrice Griggs Memorial Incentive Grant of $1,000 for her special project, EZ2C, of large print and read-along materials for visually impaired children. Lucille Cole Thomas, formerly Assistant Director of New York City School Libraries, was the 1988 recipient of the ALA/Grolier Foundation Award of $1,000 for the stimulation of reading by children and young people over a distinguished career spanning more than 30 years. School Library Media Specialists were included for the first time as an eligible area of teachers for Empire State Challenger Scholarships and Fellowships. The Greater Rochester Area School Media Specialists established a scholarship to provide financial assistance to a person working towards certification as a school library media specialist and who intends to work in one of the seven counties represented by GRASMS.

Academic and Special Libraries. The new Benjamin S. Rosenthal Library of Queens College was dedicated on September 15. Located at the heart of the Flushing campus, the $60,000,000 library will house 65 different collections encompassing more than 2,000,000 items. The Onondaga County Public Library opened its new Central Library in June in The Galleries of Syracuse. The Elmer Holmes Bobst Library at New York University announced a $1,000,000 gift from the Elmer and Mamdouha Bobst Foundation. Kenneth Furst, assistant director for science libraries, SUNY Stone Brook, retired January 1. William B. Martin is the new head librarian at the Adirondack Community College, Glens Falls. Elaine F. Sloan, formerly dean of university libraries, Indiana University, was appointed Vice-President for Information Services and University Librarian, Columbia University. Joseph F. Shubert became president of the Association of Specialized and Cooperative Library Agencies. Muriel B. Regan, principal of Gossage-Regan Associates, New York, was voted president-elect of the Special Libraries Association. Emmett Corry has been named director of the Division of Library and Information Science, St. John's University, Jamaica. Kate Storms has been appointed principal law librarian, New York State Appelate Division 4th, Department Law Library, Rochester.

Deaths. Jacqueline Enequist died December 1, 1987 in Asheville, North Carolina. She was with the State Library from June 1964 until her retirement in October, 1981.

Henry J. McCormick, Director of the Syracuse Public Library 1961-74 and Assistant Director for Administrative Services, Onondaga County Public Library from 1975 until his retirement in 1977, died September 27, 1987.

W. Mercedes Riley, retired Director of Library Services, Arlington Central School District, died in June 1987.

Jane Stevens, retired Associate Professor, Columbia University School of Library Services, died December 1, 1987. Associated with Columbia since the mid-1960s, she was editor of *Library Literature* for ten years.

Majorie J. Benzinger, Associate Librarian and Coordinator of Branch Libraries, Science and Engineering Library, SUNY Buffalo, died December 26, 1987, just prior to her planned retirement.

Peter McCann Gillard, Director, Smithtown Library since 1979, died January 6.

Gladys E. Love died October 6, 1987 at the age of 98. She joined the Rochester Public Library in 1914 and retired in 1958.

Marion Mullen, longtime Head of Reference, Syracuse University Library, died December 13, 1987.

Bruce J. Bergman, Library Director, New York City Campus, Pace University until his retirement in October 1987, died on January 3. He had been on the Pace Library staff since 1962.

Margherite Hall Girard, librarian at the Canajoharie Library and Art Gallery for 40 years until her retirement in 1968, died December 2, 1987.

John Mackenzie Cory, former Executive Secretary, the American Library Association and Director of The New York Public Library 1970-78, died April 11.

Karl Nyren, former Senior Editor of *Library Journal* and Editor *Library Hotline* died August 13.

Gussie Gaskill, Curator, Wason Collection and President White Historical Library, Cornell University until her retirement in 1963, died in March 1988.

James K. Webster, Manager, Earthquake Center Information Service, SUNY Buffalo, was killed in an automobile collision May 1.

Thor E. Wood, Chief of the Performing Arts Research Center, New York Public Library, died April 28.

Mildred Lowe, Director of the Division of Library and Information Science at St. John's University from 1979 until her retirement in 1987, was killed in an automobile accident August 22.

Barbara R. Donovan, Library Media Specialist, Marlboro High School, died March 1988.

Jack Spear died in November 1988. He retired from the Division of Library Development, New York State Library, in 1985 after 33 years of service.

ROBERT E. BARRON

NORTH CAROLINA

Issues. Networking, the new state documents depository system, and continued public library construction dominated state activities during 1988. Two of the state's five graduate library science programs changed their names. The program at the University of North Carolina at Greensboro was renamed the Department of Library and Information Studies; the School of Library Science at the University of North Carolina at Chapel Hill was renamed the School of Information and Library Science. ALA also announced continued accreditation of the School of Library and Information Sciences at North Carolina Central University in Durham. *Library Quarterly* once again ranked the School of Information and Library Science at the University of North Carolina at Chapel Hill as the number one school in the United States.

In November State Librarian Jane Williams announced plans to resign in the Spring of

North Carolina Library Association (founded 1904)

Membership: 2,200; *biennial budget (1988-1990):* $114,600.

President: Patsy J. Hansel, Cumberland County Public Library and Information Center, 300 Maiden Lane, Fayetteville 28302 (October 1987–October 1989).

Vice-President/President-elect: Barbara A. Baker, Durham Technical College, 1627 Lawson St., Durham 27703.

Biennial meeting: October 10–13, 1989, Charlotte; November 13–15, 1991, High Point.

Publication: North Carolina Libraries (quarterly).

Division of State Library, Department of Cultural Resources

M. Jane Williams, State Librarian
109 East Jones Street
Raleigh 27611

School Library Media Supervisor

Elsie L. Brumback, Assistant State Superintendent
Department of Public Instruction
Raleigh 27602

1989. Secretary of Cultural Resources, Patric Dorsey, appointed Assistant State Librarian Howard F. McGinn to succeed Williams. President Ronald Reagan nominated State Library Commission Chair, Elinor H. Swaim of Salisbury, to the National Commission on Library and Information Science. Congress adjourned before her nomination could be approved by the full Senate. It is expected that President Bush will renominate her. Mary Kit Dunn of Greensboro served a second term as Chair of the White House Conference on Library and Information Services Task Force (WHCLIST).

State Association. North Carolina Library Association (NCLA) President Patsy Hansel of Fayetteville named two new Association committees. The Ethics Committee is chaired by Dr. Jerry Campbell, University Librarian and Vice-Provost, Duke University; the Marketing Committee is chaired by Assistant State Librarian Howard F. McGinn. The Association added a new Round Table on Special Collections. It also began investigating creation of a new round table for paraprofessional concerns. The 1991 Biennial Conference will be held in High Point. The Association remained in good financial health and announced that $20,000 would be made available to sections, round tables, and committees to support programs at the 1989 Biennial Conference in Charlotte.

The North Carolina Association of School Librarians (NCASL), a constituent association of NCLA, held a very successful conference in Winston-Salem October 27-28. NCASL President Carol Southerland chose the convention theme "Information Power: Building Partnerships for Tomorrow" to tie the conference into INFORMATION POWER, the new AASL/AECT guidelines for school media programs. The Public Library Trustees Association held its annual conference at the Research Triangle Park May 12-13. Guest speaker was ALA President F. William Summers. Successful workshops were conducted by all sections. The Governmental Relations Committee organized the State's representation at National Library Legislative Day and the North Carolina State Assembly Legislative Day.

State Library. As noted above, State Librarian Jane Williams will resign early in 1989. Assistant State Librarian Howard F. McGinn will succeed her. In other State Library appointments, Denise Sigmon was named Chief of the Technical Services Section and Gary Harden, Assistant Chief of Technical Services.

The State Library hosted the semi-annual meeting of the Chief Officers of State Library Agencies (COSLA) and a joint COSLA–Council of State Governments Workshop in October in Raleigh. The annual Quiz Bowl competition was conducted. Mount Tabor High School in Forsyth County won the 1988 competition. The State Library continued its funding of the North Carolina Literacy Association. The summer reading program was conducted in more than 200 libraries across the state and carried the theme: "Take a Ride on the Reading Railroad."

The North Carolina State Documents Depository System, created by the General Assembly in 1987, began operations. Marjorie Lindsey directed the start-up of the program; Sally Ensor was named Clearinghouse Coordinator. A steering committee will serve as an advisory body to the clearinghouse. The requirements for participating libraries were completed and the first microfiche produced for distribution. Liaison was also established with all state agencies to facilitate document collection. The first depositories were the State Library; the North Carolina Collection at the Davis Library of the University of North Carolina at Chapel Hill; Robeson County Public Library, Lumberton; Forsyth County Public Library, Winston-Salem; Joyner Library, East Carolina University, Greenville; Atkins Library, University of North Carolina at Charlotte; and Randall Library, University of North Carolina at Wilmington.

Public Libraries. Plans for the construction of new headquarters and branch libraries were begun in Duplin County, Pender County, Charlotte-Mecklenburg, Cumberland County, Sheppard Memorial Library, Greenville, Pettigrew Regional, Onslow County, Johnston County, East Albemarle Region, Neuse Regional, Caldwell County, Appalachian Regional, Sampson-Clinton, Cleveland County, Davidson County, Forsyth County, and BHM Regional.

Buildings. New buildings were dedicated by Harnett County Public Library, Lillington; Burke County Public Library, Valdese; and Ashe County Public Library, West Jefferson. The state's first dual-purpose library building was dedicated in Creedmore. The building is a joint public library and community college library and serves as a branch of the Granville County Public Library and Vance-Granville Community College.

Networks/Interlibrary Cooperation. Development of the North Carolina Information Network continued. The North Carolina Online Union Catalog at OCLC continued to grow through tapeloading and the daily contributions of OCLC members. More than 8,500,000 holdings are now listed. More than 800,000 holdings have been tapeloaded into the Online Catalog since the project's inception in 1985. The State Library began the manual data entry of holdings into the North Carolina Online Union List of Serials also at OCLC. This database already contains more than 42,000 serials holdings locations. Initial data entry efforts have concentrated on the holdings of libraries in the Metrolina Library Association based in Charlotte and the holdings of health science libraries. The number of dial access selective users of the OCLC databases increased to 85, and the number of interlibrary loan transactions by these dial access users alone increased to 2,000 a month. The State Library increased the number of electronic bulletin boards maintained on Western Union's Infomaster System to 18. Several of these bulletin boards are produced in conjunction with the North Carolina Department of Commerce, the North Carolina Biotechnology Center, the North Carolina Division of Travel and Tourism, the State Data Center, and the State's Office of Purchase and Contract. One hundred thirty-seven libraries of all types had access to Western Union using LSCA Title III funding. The State Library placed 32 additional telefax machines in libraries, bringing the total number of FAX machines in libraries to more than 100. In conjunction with the North Carolina Department of Commerce, the State Library assumed responsibility for offering the services of Commerce's Business Information Reference Center. This program provides information on all state government programs dealing with businesses and also serves as a comprehensive online directory to state government.

Installation of the OCLC LS2000 systems on 15 campuses of the University of North Carolina neared completion. The Western North Carolina Library Network went online. An LS2000, housed at Appalachian State University in Boone, serves as the host for the online catalogs of Western Carolina University in Cullowhee and the University of North Carolina at Asheville. The Triangle Research Libraries Network (TRLN) continued to enhance interinstitutional searching programs and circulation systems were brought online. TRLN serves libraries at North Carolina State University, University of North Carolina at Chapel Hill, and Duke University. The University of North Carolina's Educational Computing Service continued to develop its packet switching network, LINCNET, to serve the needs of all types of libraries in the state. LINCNET node installation began at 30 community colleges.

Professional Interest. The statewide North Carolina Library Staff Development Program, based at the School of Library and Information Sciences at North Carolina Central University, entered its fourth year of operation. The program is a joint program of the library schools at the University of North Carolina at Chapel Hill, the University of North Carolina at Greensboro, Appalachian State University, East Carolina University, and North Carolina Central University. The library school at Appalachian State University celebrated its 50th anniversary.

Awards. Christopher Forney, President of the student Special Libraries Association (SLA) Chapter at North Carolina Central University, received a $6,000 scholarship from SLA. Laura Gasaway, Director of the Law Library at UNC–Chapel Hill, was elected a Fellow of SLA. Joe A. Hewitt and John S. Shipman of the Davis Library at UNC–Chapel Hill won the 1988 Blackwell/North American Scholarship Award. Barbara L. Anderson, Forsyth County Public Library in Winston-Salem, was honored by the National Bicentennial Leadership Project for the development of programs promoting the U.S. Constitution. Janet L. Freeman, Director of the Library at Meredith College in Raleigh, was elected Executive Secretary of the Southern Baptist Library Association. Cumberland County Public Library and Information Center won two Library Administration and Management Association awards at ALA annual conference in New Orleans. Ridley R. Kessler, Federal Documents Librarian at Davis Library, UNC–Chapel Hill, was elected Chair-Elect of GPO's Depository Library Council. State Librarian Jane Williams and Susan K. Nutter, Director of Libraries at North Carolina State University, were elected to the SOLINET Board of Directors. Edward G. Holley, Professor at the School of Information and Library Science at UNC–Chapel Hill, won the 1988 ACRL Academic or Research Librarian of the Year Award. The Henderson County Public Library, Waynesville, won the Friends of North Carolina Public Libraries Outstanding Library Friends Group Award. Perry White of Sanford was re-elected Vice-President for Government Affairs of FOLUSA. Richard Danner, Director of the Law Library, Duke University, was elected Vice-President/President-Elect of the American Association of Law Librarians. Ted Waller, Meredith College, served as President of the North Carolina SLA chapter. Irene Hairston, Winston-Salem, served as President of the North Carolina Public Library Trustee Association. Wayne Modlin, Director of Fontana Regional Library System, Bryson City, served as President of the North Carolina Public Library Directors Association.

Deaths. Charles C. Dean, retired director of the library at North Carolina A & T University, died January 20. Ethel K. Smith, retired director of the library of Wingate College, Monroe, died February 7. Mattie U. Russell, retired Curator of Manuscripts at Duke University, died May 4. Annie L. Yates, retired ILL Director at the State Library, died in April. Mildred C. Herring, retired professor of library science at North Carolina Central University, Appalachian State University, and Western Carolina University, died June 21. Norma Womack, director of the library at Methodist College, Fayetteville, died in July. Myra Champion, founder and curator of the Thomas Wolfe and North Carolina Collections at the Pack Library, Asheville, died April 20.

HOWARD F. MCGINN

NORTH DAKOTA

State Library Association. The North Dakota Library Association (NDLA) held its annual meeting at Dickinson in September with the theme "Kaleidoscope: Our Ever Changing Libraries!" Preconference programing included a workshop on problems of the one person/small library; DIALS—Direct Individual Access Library System; and AIDS: Can you get it from a book? (sponsored by the health science information section). Keynote speaker was Will Manley, Director of the Tempe (Arizona) Public Library. A credit workshop on reference materials for small and medium-sized libraries was conducted by Dr. David Loertscher, Senior Acquisitions Editor, Libraries Unlimited, Englewood, Colorado. Sectional programs at the conference included pay equity in North Dakota (academic library section) and state government information materials (government documents round table). The banquet speaker was Bill Lowman, cowboy poet and humorist.

North Dakota Library Association (founded 1908)

Membership: 423; *annual budget:* $56,300.
President: Diane Caley, Ward County Public Library, Minot (September 1988–September 1989).
Vice-President: Dolores Vyzralek, State Historical Society of North Dakota, Bismarck.
Annual meeting: September 21–23, 1989, Grand Forks.
Publication: Good Stuff (quarterly).

North Dakota State Library

Patricia L. Harris, State Librarian
Liberty Memorial Building
Capitol Grounds
Bismarck 58505

School Library Media Supervisor

Patricia Herbel
Department of Public Instruction
Capitol Building
Bismarck 58505

The NDLA Trustees Section presented three awards: Major Benefactor Award to Mayor Lonny Alder of Hazen; Literacy Award to Ronald Spanel of Wahpeton; and Trustee Citation Award to Irma Remboldt of Gackle.

NDLA President Betty Gard, recognized the following members for their service to the Association: Lorraine Ettl (outgoing secretary of the Association); David Boilard (Chair of the Constitution and Policies Committee); Paulette Nelson (Chair of the Intellectual Freedom Committee); and Susan Podrygula (former Editor of *The Good Stuff*). Marilyn Hadberg (Minot) received the Baker & Taylor Grassroots Grant Award through the Junior Members.

The 1989 North Dakota Centennial Conference theme for the annual meeting to be held in Grand Forks is "North Dakota Libraries: Continuing a Century of Pride and Progress."

Academic Libraries. Library Excellence for North Dakota (LEND) a proposal submitted to a North Dakota State Board of Higher Education, PEAQ (Partnerships to Enhance Academic Quality) steering committee aims to obtain resources to improve academic quality in higher education and to build partnerships between colleges and universities and between higher education and such other interests as elementary and secondary education, economic development, minority groups, business, industry, and agriculture.

This proposal was selected as one of six for consideration by the Board of Higher Education. It was to be included in the legislative budget request for 1989–91 submitted by the governor.

Two projects funded by the U.S. Department of Education, College Library Technology and Cooperation Grants program (HEA, Title II-D) provides $110,000 to Bismarck State College and Library Excellence for North Dakota to automate the 1,600,000 record database of North Dakota college and university library holdings through the development of a statewide, online library catalog that will link the North Dakota State University catalog, the Minnesota State University library system, and the South Dakota State system. Mayville State University was awarded $35,757 to develop the first stage of a statewide online library catalog by a cooperative effort with the University of North Dakota (Grand Forks) libraries to create an online, shared library catalog between the two universities. This project will provide the base for future library automation and will permit the universities to link with databases in Minnesota, South Dakota, and Manitoba.

The Chester Fritz Library at the University of North Dakota (Grand Forks), through money from the Chester Fritz endowment, will install 70 terminals and personal computers in the public reference area, the Harley E. French Library of the Health Sciences, and the Thormondsgard Law Library. Eventually, UND and the State Board of Higher Education Computer Network in Bismarck hope to link 20 libraries by computer. The first phase of the state library computer system will cost about $1,000,000. Approximately half of this amount comes from UND funds.

Public Libraries. The Public Library Planning Committee completed the *North Dakota Public Library Manual* and distributed it at the annual conference of NDLA in September. The *Manual* brings together, in one source, information pertaining to public library planning and development that the Committee initiated and developed over the past several years. It includes public library job descriptions, public library salary survey, trustee manual (revised), intellectual freedom manual for North Dakota libraries, disaster preparedness manual, interlibrary loan manual, guidelines for North Dakota school library media centers, library services for young adults and children in North Dakota, relevant statewide library automation materials, membership directories, and ALA/MPLA/NDLA promotional and membership information.

Four North Dakota public libraries (Grand Forks, Minot, Dickinson and Devils Lake) received one of 600 videocassette recorders presented to Carnegie libraries throughout the United States. The VCR gift program was established by the Carnegie Corporation of New York to commemorate its 75th anniversary.

The Grand Forks Public Library acquired a collection of toys and developed a circulation system to lend the toys to children with special needs. The collection was initiated through LSCA, Title II funding received through a grant proposal submitted to the North Dakota State Library.

Angie Dickinson, a well-known Hollywood actress from North Dakota, was a surprise visitor at the Edgeley Public Library on June 18, 1988. Her secretary, born in Edgeley, brought her to the library to surprise Ruth Evert, the librarian.

School Libraries. The annual School Administrator of the Year Award was presented to Wayne Granfor, principal of Pioneer and Lincoln Elementary Schools in Bismarck, at the annual NDLA convention in Dickinson. School library media specialists throughout the state attended seminars to implement *Information Power: Guidelines for School Library Media Centers* released in the spring. A Bismarck Public Schools Library Task Force, formed under the direction of the Assistant Superintendent of Instruction, presented a plan for library excellence to the School Board. The five-year strategic plan provided for district-wide library development and centralization of all library technical services. It was a package of possible enhancements that was supported but was not funded by the School Board because of other budget demands.

State Library. The North Dakota State Library sponsored an Executive Institute funded by LSCA, Title I to provide management training for public library administrators, July 31–August 3 in Bismarck. In implementing the July 1 directive of the Governor for a two percent reduction in general funds, the State Library discontinued purchasing materials, except for those in demand and immediately necessary, and equipment. Travel funds and postage were also reduced. The monthly newsletter, *The Flickertale,* was suspended for three months.

The budget reduction placed the State Library, for the first time, in the position of falling below the federal minimum dollar amount to qualify for 1989 Library Services and Construction Act funds. Subsequently the State office of Management and Budget included the State Library in its deficiency payment bill for reinstating the funds necessary to remain qualified for federal funds. The Governor's 1989–91 budget recommendations for the State Library, including state aid to public libraries, were released on December 15, 1988.

The Governor's Advisory Council on Libraries, chaired by David Boilard, formulated a resolution and sent a plaque thanking Cyndy Schaff for her dedication as a member and Chair of the Council for the past several years. The Council began reviewing procedures to formalize its own means of conducting business. A section that compiles LSCA policy decisions will be included. The Council met several times during the year to conduct business and consider grant applications. The Council received $573,376 in LSCA grant applications and $247,060 was awarded. Members of the Council were Sheila Cofer, Claryce Erickson, Bernard Ibes, Helen Jacobs, Jerry Lamb, Dean Lenaberg, Beverly J. Quamme (Vice-Chair), Joy Wezelman, David W. Boilard (Chair), and Patricia L. Harris, State Librarian (ex officio).

David Boilard and Beverly Quamme attended ALA Legislative Day in Washington, D.C. to discuss federal funding of library services and their impact on North Dakota Libraries.

A Governor's Library Planning Task Force, chaired by Ed Warner, Director of Libraries, University of North Dakota (Grand Forks), was directed to "create a strategic plan for the development and improvement of library services in North Dakota." The Task Force met several times between September 1987 and May 1988. The final report was released to the Governor on July 1, 1988. The plan was termed DIALS—Direct Individual Access Library System. It proposed a fairly comprehensive approach and emphasizes individual citizen access to all library resources in the state with a minimum of impediments. The plan seeks to involve in a linked system all types of libraries—school, public, academic, and special. The estimated costs for implementation of DIALS was $973,030; it will be new State funding (1989–91). Members of the Task Force were Kyle Patterson Cross, Marilyn Guttromson, Sally Oremland, Barb Satran, Cynthia Schaff, Gary Schultz, Les Snavely, Larry Spears, Raymond Stewart, Ed Warner (Chairperson), and Joy Wezelman.

Summer Reading Program. The NDLA Children's Round Table conducted its 1988 summer reading theme "Devour a Book." This program was developed by a group of librarians in Illinois and included a book of ideas and promotional materials. More than 3,000 children voted on the nominations for the annual Flicker Tale children's book award. Winners were *Miss Nelson has a Field Day,* by Harry Allard for the primary book category and *Nothing's Fair in Fifth Grade,* by Barthe DeClements for the juvenile book category. The Children's Round Table is compiling a bibliography of juvenile materials about North Dakota or books written by North Dakota authors. It will be released during National Library Week and School Library Media Month (April 1989). "Roughriders Read" was selected as the 1989 North Dakota Centennial theme for the summer reading program. A promotional booklet that includes artwork and ideas for bulletin boards, fun activities, speakers, and puppets or easy costumes, is being developed for public and school librarians throughout the state.

North Dakota Periodicals Index. For the first time ever, an index that provides access to information in North Dakota's magazines was available. The indexing project was one of the first to receive official status as a Centennial project and the North Dakota Centennial Commission provided a $17,150 centennial grant. It is sponsored by the North Dakota Library Association. Michael Miller, Project Director, and a librarian at the North Dakota State University Library indicated that close to $60,000 public and private grants and donations was raised to support the project. It is also estimated that $75,000 of volunteered indexing service has been donated by 35 North Dakota librarians during one year of indexing. Presentations about the indexing project were conducted at the Mountain Plains Library Association Conference and the ACRL Regional Conference in LaCrosse, Wisconsin. The 1986 and 1987 editions have already been released; the Centennial edition (1981–85) will be released during the summer or fall of 1989, and the 1988 edition will be available in early 1989.

People. Appointments to libraries in the state during 1988 include Eric Halvorson, North Dakota State Library; Mark Bowman, North Dakota State Library; Kathy Trana, North Dakota State Library; Amy Christianson, Chester Fritz Library (UND); Michael Hurley, Chester Fritz Library (UND); and Kelly Harrison Hall (Williston). Jerry Kaup, Director of the Minot Public Library is currently serving as President of the Mountain Plains Library Association.

NEIL V. PRICE

OHIO

Nineteen eighty-eight was a year of celebration for a number of library organizations in Ohio. The Ohio Library Foundation celebrated its 25th anniversary; the Ohio Friends of the Library celebrated its 15th anniversary; and the Junior Members Round Table of the Ohio Library Association (OLA) celebrated its 10th anniversary.

Emphasis was placed in 1988 on strengthening the political influence of Ohio libraries. The Legislation Committee of OLA held seven forums around the state to discuss the legislative issues most important to the membership. From these forums and a survey of the membership, a plan for an "Educational Campaign for the Increased Political Effectiveness of Ohio Libraries" was adopted. Also the "OLA Legislative Policy 1989–1990" was approved by the OLA Board as was a position paper on the confidentiality of library records. OLA had supported a bill on confidentiality of library records until amendments backed by the Ohio Association of Chiefs of Police and the Ohio Prosecuting Attorneys Association made the bill unacceptable. The bill was allowed to die in committee. Confidentiality of library records is a priority with the library community in the state and work will continue to get an acceptable bill passed by the Legislature.

Ohio Library Association (founded 1895)

Membership: 2,297; *annual budget:* $187,775.

President: Kathy East, Wood County District Library, Bowling Green 43402.

Vice-President/President-elect: J. Riegel, Wagnall's Memorial Library, Lithopolis, 43136.

Executive Director: Bonnie Beth Mitchell, 40 South Third Street, Suite 230, Columbus 43215.

Annual meeting: October 26–28, 1989, Toledo (with OELMA); October 11–13, 1990, Dayton.

Publications: OLA Bulletin (triannually); *Ohio Libraries* (6 issues a year).

State Library of Ohio

Richard Cheski, State Librarian
Columbus.

School Library Media Supervisor

Jackie Wagner
Division of Elementary and Secondary Education
Columbus.

State Association. The president's theme for the year was "Ohio Libraries—We Have a Story to Tell." The Ohio Library Association joined with the Academic Library Association of Ohio (ALAO) and the Ohio Educational Library Media Association (OELMA) for their first concurrent conference, November 3–5, 1988, in Columbus. More than 2,600 attended the conference whose theme was "Growing Into the Future Together."

In the Spring, OLA held six highly successful chapter conferences around the state with a record-breaking attendance of 1,901. Each division of the Association contributed programs and the Ohio Friends of the Library participated in the conferences. The Loyalty to the Ohio Library Association (LOLA) awards were reinstated and were presented during the chapter conferences. The Ohio Library Trustee Association also held six well-attended regional conferences.

A reorganization of the publishing program brought together three journals—the journals of the Ohio Library Association, the Ohio Library Trustee Association, and the Ohio Friends of the Library—under one title *Ohio Libraries.*

Nineteen eighty-eight saw an outpouring of publications. The two major publications were *Accounting Handbook* and *Ohio Public Library Administrators Handbook,* both by Task Forces of the Management and Administration Division. Other publications were *Elder-Berries: Library Programs for Older Adults,* by the Task Force on Services to Older Adults of the Outreach and Special Services Division; *Directory of Microcomputers* by the Automation and Technology Division; a children's services recruitment brochure by the Children's Services Division; *Have You Been to Your Institution Lately?—Libraries Serving People in Institutions*, a brochure by the Round Table for Library Services to the Institutionalized; and *Video—Especially for Children*, a selected list of videotapes recommended by the Audio Visual Round Table and the Children's Services Division.

Three well-attended workshops were held throughout the year: "The Ohio Automation Challenge," sponsored by the Automation and Technology Division; "Library Building: Start to Finish," sponsored by the Management and Administration Division; and back by popular demand, "Reference Services for Small and Medium-sized Libraries," sponsored by the Reference and Information Services Division.

Dorothy Spencer, Administrative Assistant, OLA, retired after 20 years of service. Merly Gunderman was hired by OLA to fill the new position of Director of Communication.

State Library 1988. LOAN, a statewide access program, was introduced to libraries and the public in 1988. LOAN, Libraries of Ohio Access Network, is a voluntary, cooperative program which allows any Ohio resident to borrow print materials from any participating library regardless of whether or not that resident lives within the participating library's local service area. LOAN responds to recently enacted state legislation that changed public library funding from county collected intangibles tax to a statewide funding source based on the state income tax, and is sponsored by the State Library of Ohio, the Ohio Library Association, and the Ohio Library Trustee Association. To date, 122 of 250 public libraries voluntarily participate in LOAN. OLA provided participating libraries with publicity materials including brochures, posters, and window decals for use in their communities.

A year ago the Library of Congress announced that Ohio was chosen for a Center for the Book which had as its mission to foster an appreciation of the aesthetic and practical value of books and to promote the use of books and reading. Initially, the State Library administered the Center until a Board of Trustees was formed in July. Bylaws were passed and Articles of Incorporation were filed. Attention was then turned to programming. Programming ideas for the Center will be drawn from results of a statewide survey.

In June, National Bookmobile Guidelines for Bookmobile Services were adopted by the 150 librarians attending the State Library's Fourth National Bookmobile Conference in Columbus. Bookmobile librarians and administrators from 31 states and Canada attended the Conference.

Ohio's FAX network was greatly expanded by the addition of 25 new telefacsimile machines purchased by the Ohio State Library and distributed to the regional library systems and various Ohio libraries. A working document for librarians titled "The Authoritative Guide on the Use of Telefacsimile in Libraries: An Occasional Paper" was published and distributed statewide.

The Talking Book program revived the volunteer program by sponsoring two day-long repair marathons in Columbus. New groups of the Telephone Pioneers, the principal group volunteering to fix talking book machines, were started in Columbus, Bridgeport, Toledo, Lancaster, and Cleveland. Approximately 25,000 Ohio residents use the Talking Book Program; more than 37,000 pieces of equipment are controlled and maintained by the State Library. In 1988, 56 sublending agencies helped provide equipment to users with two additional agencies to be operational in 1989.

Residents in southwestern Ohio were better served by the Southwest Bookmobile Center's new 28-foot bookmobile which was built to shelve approximately 3,000 books.

The State Library Circulation Department and Media Center strengthened services and met growing demands of state government employees. Interlibrary loans increased by 18 percent in 1988 while film and videotape circulation increased by seven percent. Reference librarians answered 15,179 questions. Database searches increased by 17 percent. The State Government Specialist assisted more than 800 state employees with their information needs by meeting with and helping them.

SLOLine, the Ohio State Library electronic mail system, expanded its membership to include all types of libraries. By the end of 1988, 67 public, 21 academic, 9 special, and 23 other libraries were members of the SLOLine network.

In fiscal year 1988, the State Library awarded 48 Library Services Construction Act (LSCA) Title I, 3 Title II, and 23 Title III grants. In all, $4,564,309 in LSCA funds was awarded.

Library Statistics. A statistical report issued in 1988 (with statistics for 1987) indicated that Ohio had 250 public libraries holding 32,763,160 volumes, with 6,262 total staff including 1,314 professionals. Total operating budget was $208,641,711. School library media centers numbered 3,675 holding 28,943,053 volumes. They were directed by 1,670 professionals with a total operating budget of $27,942,313. Ohio had 132 academic libraries holding 27,217,123 volumes and directed by a staff of 2,364, including 922 professionals, and a total operating budget of $111,053,034. Institution libraries numbered 46 holding 200,104 volumes with a staff of 36, including 21 professionals, and a budget of $954,868. Special libraries numbered 135 holding 1,630,614 volumes with a staff of 451, including 138 professionals, and a budget of $8,772,513. The Ohio State Library and three field units had 2,158,738 volumes with a staff of 132, including 38 professionals, and an operating budget of $5,467,154.

Awards. The Ohio Library Association selected Robert F. Cayton of Marietta College to join the OLA Hall of Fame. Nancy Wareham, Cleveland Area Metropolitan Library System, was named Librarian of the Year; Sue McCleaf, Newton Falls Public Library, received the Diana Vescelius Memorial Award, and Dorothy Baker received the Citizen of the Year Award.

The Ohio Library Trustees Association presented the Award of Achievement to the Portage County District Library and the Ohio Friends of the Library presented an Award of Achievement to the Kirtland Public Library.

The Academic Library Association of Ohio named Charles Maurer, Denison University, Librarian of the Year, and the Ohio Educational Library Media Association presented the Edgar Dale Award to Betty Cleaver of Ohio State University.

Appointments. Library administrators appointed in 1988 included Don Barlow, Director, Westerville Public Library; Frances Black, Director, Grove City Public Library; Ralph Holibaugh, Director, Kenyon College Library; John Montag, Director, Wittenberg University Library; Judith Sessions, Director, Miami University Library; and Stephen Wood, Director, Cleveland Heights–University Heights Public Library.

Retirements. Library administrators retiring in 1988 were Jane Bradford, Director, Westerville Public Library; Rachel Nelson, Director, Cleveland Heights–University Heights Public Library; and Frank Steer, Jr., longtime member of the Akron–Summit County Public Library Board of Trustees.

Deaths. Deaths of prominent Ohioans in 1988 included Donna Chin, Instructor, Kent State University School of Library Sciences, Columbus program; and Jane Small, Director of the Defiance Public Library.

HANNAH V. MCCAULEY

OKLAHOMA

Oklahoma Library Association (founded 1907)

Membership: 999; *annual budget:* $47,927.

President: Steve Skidmore, Director, Ponca City Library, 515 E.Grand, Ponca City 74601 (July 1988–June 1989).

Vice-President/President-elect: Marilyn Hinshaw, Director, Eastern Oklahoma District Library System, 801 W. Okmulgee, Muskogee 74401.

Executive Secretary: Kay Boies, 300 Hardy Drive, Edmond 73013.

Annual meeting: May 3–6, 1989, Oklahoma City; April 18–21, 1990, Tulsa.

Publication: Oklahoma Librarian.

Oklahoma Department of Libraries

Robert L. Clark, Jr., Director
200 North East 18th St.
Oklahoma City 73105

State School Library Media Supervisor

Barbara Spriestersbach
Oklahoma Department of Education
Oliver Hodge Building
Oklahoma City 73105

The year 1988 brought good news to Oklahoma's library community. An improved state budget picture meant increased state aid to public and academic libraries. Cooperative programs drew upon new technologies to improve performance and add services. Literacy programs continued to grow. Several libraries responded to the state's call for economic diversification by becoming active players in the economic development of their communities.

State Association. Successful lobbying efforts by the Oklahoma Library Association (OLA) played a major role in obtaining increases in state aid to public and academic libraries and lead the way to legislative passage of the state's first Library Theft Bill. The new law makes it a misdemeanor to steal or deface library materials, and imposes monetary fines for breaking the law.

OLA received grant funds from the Oklahoma Foundation for the Humanities and the National Endowment for the Humanities to develop reading and discussion programs in conjunction with the centennial of Oklahoma's 1889 land runs. The programs, titled "The Oklahoma Experience," will feature the works of writers who have had a significant impact on people and events in the state.

Working with the Oklahoma Coalition Against Censorship, OLA members monitored censorship cases in Stillwater and Yukon schools. In both cases, the books in question remained on the shelves and reading lists.

An OLA committee of school and public librarians awarded the first Sequoyah Young Adult Book Award to Iowa authors Lee Hadley and Ann Irwin. Their book, *Abby, My Love*, was voted favorite young adult novel by Oklahoma students.

State Library. Controversy over special interest projects and prison funding slowed down the 41st Oklahoma Legislature, and came within several hours of shutting down the Oklahoma Department of Libraries (ODL). But by the time lawmakers adjourned on June 30, the state library had received a 39 percent budget increase for Fiscal Year 1989, "the largest increase this department has ever received," according to ODL Director Robert L. Clark, Jr. The department's appropriation bill included a 54 percent funding increase for the development and expansion of public library service. After years of no-growth budgets, this was good news to the state's public libraries. Per capita state aid rose from an average of 0.41 to 0.56 cents.

During the year, the Department's interlibrary loan referral center reported a 12 percent increase in interlibrary loan requests across the state. The Records Center Division, in charge of assisting state agencies with records management, offered a series of outreach workshops to help city and county officials manage local government records. ODL began the second year of its successful Library VCR Project, which helps public libraries expand their video collections. And more than 29,000 children discovered their country through participation in ODL's Summer Reading Program, "Movin' On U.S.A."

ODL, the Oklahoma Department of Corrections and the State Department of Education shared 1988's national Laubach Literacy Action Award for a project which established literacy programs in all of the state's correctional institutions. September 14 was Literacy Breakfast Day all across Oklahoma. Thousands of literacy volunteers, students, business leaders and government officials attended more than 90 local breakfasts to hear about the problems and solutions to adult functional illiteracy. Organized by ODL with assistance from local libraries, literacy councils and businesses, the event was one of the largest literacy awareness campaigns conducted in the nation.

Children's author Peter Spier, and John Y. Cole, Executive Director of the Center for the Book in the Library of Congress, visited the state in September to help the Oklahoma Center for the Book kickoff "1989 The Year of the Young Reader." Working with other state agencies and a special task force of teachers and child care specialists, ODL and the Oklahoma Center for the Book prepared programming manuals to assist librarians and educators during the year-long reading celebration. A special television series on Oklahoma authors will be shown during 1989 as part of the celebration. The Oklahoma Center for the Book also joined forces with Friends of Libraries in Oklahoma to sponsor an Oklahoma Authors Read-A-Thon during Library Legislative Day.

Public Libraries. Twelve Oklahoma public libraries capitalized on their role as information providers to meet the particular employment and business needs of their cities. Funded by federal dollars from ODL, the libraries set up individualized programs, ranging from job training to small business assistance to market data collection. Participating libraries were Anadarko, Bartlesville, Eastern Oklahoma District Library System, Frederick, Pioneer Library System, Ponca City, Southern Prairie Library System, Tulsa City–County Libraries, Tonkawa, Watonga, Western Plains Library System, and Wewoka.

Tulsa County voters passed an ad valorem tax increase along with a $4,200,000 bond issue during 1988. New funding will help the Tulsa City–County Library System operate at present levels, computerize public access catalogs and build four new branch libraries.

At Eastern Oklahoma District Library System, a "taxing" situation has delayed planned improvements at Muskogee County branches. A voter-approved ad valorem tax increase was inadvertently left off the Muskogee County tax bills. The system will recover the lost revenue over a three-year period.

Jefferson County voters rejected establishment of a library millage that would have provided citizens with service through the Chickasaw Library System (CLS). Meanwhile, CLS moved ahead with improvements in its five-county service area, establishing a computerized catalog system which links the collections of all branches and the bookmobile.

Midwest City Public Library was one of 30 libraries that hosted the "Are We to be a Nation" exhibit on the U.S. Constitution. Bristow Public Library aired children's book reviews each weekday morning on a local radio station. Inspired by a renovation and expansion project, Ponca City Public Library developed its first comprehensive public relations campaign. El Reno Carnegie Public Library received national recognition for its special archival collection.

School Libraries/Media Centers. Funding for the State Department of Education's Library Media Improvement Grants was maintained, and 221 school sites received funds for equipment and programs. Over 1,700 librarians and educators attended the 1988 Encyclo-Media workshop which featured the theme "Information Power." The Oklahoma School Video Consortium, a program to enhance school video collections, expanded to include 250 districts, with 309 video titles available for duplication.

The Oklahoma Association of School Library Media Specialists awarded the first Polly Clarke Award to a library media specialist who has been instrumental in the establishment of an exemplary library media program. The first awardee was Shan Glandon from Jenks West Elementary School.

Academic and Special Libraries. Oklahoma's academic libraries received a 25 percent increase in funding from the state legislature.

Increases in salary and material budgets at Oklahoma State University's Library were "the biggest increases in the last several years," according to Director Edward R. Johnson.

A $130,000 gift from the Kerr Foundation to the University of Oklahoma Law Center and Health Sciences Center libraries will help fund a prototype CD–ROM of the two collections. A grant from the National Endowment for the Humanities will help O.U.'s Western History Collections produce a computerized guide to the collections. A $100,000 endowment has also been established to support Western History's acquisition and preservation programs.

The Oklahoma Chapter of the Special Libraries Association was recognized with a special proclamation by Governor Henry Bellmon during National Library Week. The association offered programs for library school students, sponsored continuing education workshops for members, and continued to contact librarians in "unique" settings.

Networking/Interlibrary Cooperation. The Oklahoma Network for Continuing Higher Education (ONCHE), funded by state funds and a 1985 grant from the W. K. Kellogg Foundation, began preparing 14 public libraries around the state to serve as links in continuing adult education programs. The libraries received computers, career guidance software, telefacsimile machines and teleconference equipment during 1988. Participating libraries were Ada, Altus, Bartlesville, Duncan, Elk City, Enid, Lawton, McAlester, Muskogee, Norman, Seminole, Woodward, Oklahoma County's Metropolitan Library System and Tulsa City-County Libraries. ONCHE is working to develop a statewide network of educational services through colleges, universities, public libraries and the state public television authority. ONCHE grant funds have also provided the Tulsa Area Library Cooperative (TALC) with group access capabilities to OCLC interlibrary loan. The one-year project will allow all TALC libraries to access OCLC interlibrary subsystems through other member libraries.

Buildings. Federal grants through the State Library, private funds and public fund-raising helped improve library facilities across the state. Construction and renovation projects completed, planned or underway in 1988 included facilities in Miami, Kingfisher, Holdenville, Durant, Woodward, Wewoka, Inola, Stilwell, The Village, Yale, Sallisaw, Barnsdall, Anadarko, Grove, Waurika, Warner, Hominy and Tryon.

Awards. Oklahoma author S. E. Hinton was the first recipient of the Young Adult Author Achievement Award, given by ALA's Young Adult Services Division. The $1,000 award is funded by School Library Journal.

Oklahoma Library Association Awards went to Judy Moody, Barbara Spriestersbach and Duane Meyers. Moody was honored for her work with Friends groups. Spriestersbach was presented with a Distinguished Service Award for her leadership and contributions to Oklahoma's school libraries. Meyers was recognized for his efforts to establish the Oklahoma Coalition Against Censorship.

Dee Ann Ray, Director of the Western Plains Library System, was inducted into the Western Oklahoma Hall of Fame for her work with the Oklahoma Historical Society and her contribution to the production of slide/tape shows on the history of four western Oklahoma counties.

People. Robert Swisher is new Director of the University of Oklahoma School of Library and Information Studies. Swisher replaces the retiring Sylvia Faibisoff. Stephen Thomas is new Director of the Southeastern Public Library System of Oklahoma.

Angie Debo, leading Oklahoma author and historian, died February 21, 1988, at her home in Marshall, Oklahoma. The author's nine books serve as a cornerstone of American Indian and Oklahoma scholarship. Debo's struggle to publish the truth about Oklahoma's early days, and America's treatment of the Indian was the subject of an episode of the PBS series "The American Experience."

WILLIAM R. YOUNG

OREGON

Oregon Library Association (founded 1941)

Membership: 840; *annual budget:* $43,400.

President: Michael Gaston, Siuslaw Public Library, Box A, Florence 97439.

Annual Meeting: March 28–31, 1990, Portland Marriott.

Publication: Oregon Library News (monthly).

Oregon State Library

Wesley A. Doak, State Librarian
State Library Building
Salem 97310

School Library Media Supervisor

James Sanner
Oregon Department of Education
Salem 97310

Major News. Automation of Oregon's libraries took a giant step forward in 1988 with installation of a system at the University of Oregon, and initial planning for automation at Jackson County Library system, the Coos Cooperative Library Service, Clackamas County Libraries, and the Umatilla Library District. One of the largest automated systems in the country will be installed in 1989 following signing of a contract in 1988 with Dynix by the Multnomah County Library.

Elections in Oregon had a major impact on the operation of several public libraries. Some library districts received approval for stable funding measures bringing the number of districts now funded and operating to nine out of eleven districts formed. Seven of the districts obtained voter-approved tax bases and two have serial operating levies.

Of statewide significance was passage of the first tax base for Baker County Library District, the first special library district formed in Oregon to serve an entire county. Thirteen library funding measures were approved in 1988. In May, the Jackson County Library System won support for $2,100,000 in operating funds each year for three years. The Tillamook County Library levy was passed overwhelmingly in March. The Sweet Home Public Library passed a three-year serial levy, its sole source of revenue. The Tualatin Public Library will substantially improve services due to passage of a tax base for the City of Tualatin.

Several library funding measures did not win voter approval, resulting in the closure of two libraries. The Sherwood Public Library failed to get funds in May; a one-year levy was turned down in June; the library closed in September and will remain closed indefinitely.

Failure of a levy for the Lane County Library in June meant the end of more than eleven years of bookmobile service to 90,000 rural residents and a cut of 10-15 percent in operating revenues for seven city libraries. County Commissioners are seeking ways to revive the county library program and agreed to lend the bookmobile's 18,000-volume collection and the two librarians to the Eugene Library during the interim.

As several public libraries consider forming special districts or other governance alternatives, libraries in Deschutes County were consolidating into a county library system with Deschutes County headquarters library in Bend and a branch in La Pine. In July 1989, the county will also assume responsibility for libraries in Redmond and Sisters.

State Association. The Oregon Library Association (OLA) continued its efforts to establish one strong and unified library organization. Representatives of Oregon's library groups (the Oregon Coalition of Libraries) met in January, when OLA invited all Oregon library groups to form divisions of a new state organization restructured on the ALA model. Support for joint activities already accomplished include joint membership for OLA and the Oregon Educational Media Association (OEMA), some joint legislative activities, and coordinated intellectual freedom and continuing education activities. It was decided not to hold the joint OLA–OEMA conference, previously planned for October 1989.

Formation of a Public Library Division in OLA in 1987 had opened the door to establishment of additional divisions. During 1988, members of both the ACRL/Oregon Chapter the Oregon Health Sciences Libraries Association (OHSLA) decided to pursue OLA division status. Jim Hayden, past president to OEMA intends to form an OLA school library division. Both young adult and technical services librarians are seeking round table status in OLA.

OLA spent the 1988 non-legislative year developing a study calendar in preparation for the 1989 legislative session. OLA's legislative priorities were (1) increased state per capita funding with service criteria as a phased-in eligibility requirement; (2) funding of resource-sharing programs that would include continuation of a statewide periodicals union list database, reimbursement for interlibrary lending, a statewide library card, a delivery and communications system, an Oregon database of library holdings, and provision of Ed-Net, a hybrid telecommunications educational service via microwave direct broadcast satellite, low-power television, or other methods; (3) state library consultant services for libraries of rural library development, continuing education and children's services; and (4) encouragement to replace federal funds currently used for State Library operations with state monies, thus freeing the federal funds for grants to libraries.

The Legislative and Library Development Committee began to build coalitions of library supporters for the 1989 legislative package by establishing a Legislative Network. A Political Action Committee continues to support Oregon Library Legislative activities.

The 1988 OLA conference, "Libraries: Windows to the World," drew nearly 500 librarians in April. Highlights included crime writer Ann Rule speaking on "A Writer's Life," a talk by syndicated Oregon political columnist, Russell Sadler, and Evergreen State College President Joe Olander on the "Madness of Ill-Literacy." Keynote speaker was John Y. Cole Director of the Center for the Book at the Library of Congress.

Senator Mark Hatfield was presented with an Honorary Life Membership in OLA for his long support of libraries.

Conferees debated proposed quantitative "Standards for Public Libraries." The standards as adopted at the 1988 conference deal with resources necessary to provide "adequate" and "excellent" local library services. Use of the standards will be voluntary.

A special OLA task force had been appointed in late 1987 to explore methods for maintaining the flow of free telephone directories into Oregon libraries following the telephone companies' decision to charge libraries for the books. A media campaign and letter-writing defense fought the action of the companies and a draft proposal for free distribution of generic phone books was sent to U.S. West Company for consideration.

OLA divisions and round tables sponsored several workshops and special events. "Picture Books in the Context of Literacy" was the subject of the Children's Division fall workshop, and "Be a Super Sleuth—Solve It All at Your Library" was the theme for the 1988 statewide Summer Reading Program.

A statewide workshop in providing library service to county jails and state adult correctional facilities, sponsored by OLA's Outreach Round Table in September, culminated a yearlong LSCA project.

State Library. In June the State Library Talking Book and Braille Services (TBABS) dedicated a new state-of-the-art Reading Room for the Blind, the first of its kind for the blind and physically handicapped in the nation. The reading room was financed with an LSCA grant, donations, and volunteers.

Ruth Kratochvil, former director of the Douglas County Library System, was named Director of the TBABS, replacing Kathleen McHarg, who was appointed to the position of Assistant State Librarian. McHarg had been TBABS director for three years. She was recipient of the Governor's Management Recognition award for outstanding achievement in government service. The Partners of Americas sent her to Costa Rica in September to help establish library services to blind and physically impaired Costa Ricans.

The Oregon State Library celebrated the 50th anniversary of its building on December 9 and festivities were held during National Book Week.

Public Libraries. An innovative partnership between Oregon public libraries and the Oregon Museum of Science and Industry (OMSI), a leading science/technology center, was initiated with LSCA grant funding. The Oregon Library Exhibits Network, a cooperative venture to add interactive exhibits to library collections of books and services permits libraries to accommodate a broader spectrum of citizens with limited access to museum facilities. Four public libraries participated in the first phase of the project; future expansion will include additional libraries and exhibits.

Members of the Oregon Young Adult Network (OYAN), librarians and others interested in working with young adults, share program ideas and book discussions; the group held its quarterly meeting in July.

Several Oregon public libraries planned activities in 1988. The Jackson County Library System credits success of its operating levy at the polls to a public opinion survey completed by students from the Southern Oregon State College School of Business. The Washington County Cooperative Library Service worked with consultant Raymond Holt to develop a library facilities plan through the year 2005. Holt also assisted Salem Public Library with planning. Library consultants HBW Associates conducted a planning study for the Cooperative Library Network of Clackamas County.

The report made recommendations on future buildings needed and for overall governance and funding of library services. HBW also assisted Eugene Public Library plan a library facility, and worked with the Corvallis-Benton County Public Library to develop a long-range plan for library growth.

The Multnomah County Library received LSCA grants to establish a reading room in the Old Town area of Portland for use by low-income hotel and transient population and to develop a "Reaching for Reading" project to build links between the library and more than 100 day-care centers in the county. In March, the Multnomah County Library opened "The Title Wave," a store that sells discarded library books and is staffed by volunteers.

Two departing public librarians were recognized by resolutions of the OLA board citing their significant contributions to the state. Donna Selle, Director of the Washington County Cooperative Library Service and an active member of OLA, left her position to become Director of the Jefferson-Madison Regional Library at Charlottesville, Virginia. Mary Louderback, Head of Adult Services at Eugene Public Library since 1983, left for a position at the Gallagher Law Library at the University of Washington. Louderback was a charter member of OLA's Outreach Round Table and has been active in conference planning and as Chairman of the OLA Telephone Book Task Force.

School Libraries and Media Centers. "A Bridge to New Ideas" was the theme for a joint October and Washington library media professionals in Portland. More than 100 sessions covering print and electronic forms of communication were presented. Judith Krug of ALA's Intellectual Freedom Office was a key speaker, and Zacharie Clements, nationally-known motivational expert, was banquet speaker.

Academic Libraries, Special Libraries and Others. The annual joint conference of the Oregon and Washington chapters of ACRL was held in October with the theme "Scholarship for Academic Libraries." Featured speakers were Kathleen Heim, Dean of the School of Library and Information Science, Louisiana State University, Baton Rouge, and editor of RQ, and Jay Poole, Assistant University Librarian, the University of California, Irvine, and former editor of Choice and Texas Library Journal.

Linfield College (McMinnville) received an LSCA grant to continue updating an online conversion of the Oregon Regional Union List of Serials (ORULS) that contains the serials holdings of 160 Oregon and regional libraries. The seventh and last microfiche edition of ORULS was published in September. Efforts are underway to continue funding of ORULS through the State Library budget.

The Lewis and Clark College Northwest Writing Institute received an LSCA grant for a ten-month project to link writing, reading, and talking in Oregon libraries. "Writers at Home in Oregon Libraries" brought working authors to 16 remote locations for three-day residencies. The program was designed as a pilot for establishing an ongoing state Writer-In-Residence position.

The annual information retrieval conference sponsored by the Interinstitutional Library Council of the Oregon State System of Higher Education, "Online Northwest '88," was held in January at Oregon State University (Corvallis). The two-day session included twelve workshops on various online searching topics.

Building Programs. Public library buildings were completed or under construction in Wilsonville, North Bend, West Linn, Hermiston, and the Gresham branch of the Multnomah County Library. An existing building will be remodeled into a library and police station in Sandy following passage in June of a $300,000 bond issue. Two other construction projects will not be funded due to defeat at the polls in March. One unsuccessful bond measure would have funded a new headquarters facility for the Douglas County Library System and purchased books and equipment for the headquarters library and ten branches. A new bookmobile would have been assured for the Chemeketa Cooperative Regional Library Service if a five-year capital construction levy for Chemeketa Community College had been approved. The levy would also have provided some money for the tri-county, multi-type cooperative's automated system.

Intellectual Freedom. Mary Ginnane, Coordinator of the Oregon Intellectual Freedom Clearinghouse reported that the clearinghouse dealt with 13 formal challenges in 1988, five in school libraries and eight in public libraries. Two challenges were not decided before the end of the year, but the other eleven final decisions were to retain the challenged material. All contested items were books, and according to Ginnane, objections concerned either "sex, violence, or the occult."

Awards. The 1988 Evelyn Sibley Lampman Award recipient was noted children's and young adult author Irene Bennett Brown of Jefferson. Presented at the April OLA conference, the award is given annually to an Oregonian who has made a significant contribution to children in the fields of literature and/or library service.

CAROL VENTGEN

PENNSYLVANIA

Pennsylvania Library Association (founded 1901)

Membership: 1,757; annual budget: $200,000.

President: James Hollinger, Lancaster County Library, Lancaster.

Vice-President/President-elect: Peter Deekle, Blough-Weis Library, Susquehanna University, Selinsgrove.

Executive Director: Margaret D. Bauer, PLA Headquarters, 3107 North Front Street, Harrisburg 17110.

Annual meeting: October 9-12, King of Prussia.

Publication: PLA Bulletin (eight times per year).

State Library of Pennsylvania

Sara A. Parker, Acting State Librarian
Box 1601
Harrisburg 17126

The ACCESS PENNSYLVANIA Statewide Library Card System became truly statewide for the first time in this its third year of operation. A total of 389 public libraries in 67 counties are now participating. It is estimated that 6,000,000 books will be borrowed through this program during FY 1988-89.

The 1988-89 budget of the Commonwealth of Pennsylvania included the following increases directly related to libraries: a raise in funds for adult literacy to $7,000,000, more than tripling state support for adult learners over two years; support for the statewide Library Card System component of ACCESS PENNSYLVANIA was increased from $2,000,000 to $3,000,000, and the school library catalog program was expanded to $500,000 from $350,000.

State Association. The Pennsylvania Library Association's (PLA) annual conference was held at the Holiday Inn, King of Prussia, October 9-12. Highlights of the gathering included an inspiring address by former U.S. Attorney General, Ramsey Clark, a panel of deans from the three ALA-accredited library schools, moderated by Library Journal editor, John Berry, on the future of library education, and a series of thought-provoking programs centering on children's librarianship.

PLA increased membership to 1,757 in 1988 from 1,650 in 1987. A Library Administration and Management Round Table was organized and charged with implementation of the minimum starting professional salary standard of $20,000. In cooperation with the State Library, a Youth Services Taskforce was convened to recommend actions to improve library service to children. The Pennsylvania Citizens for Better Libraries celebrated its tenth birthday in 1988. PCBL was created as a statewide Friends of Libraries to foster and promote public awareness programs for all libraries and to serve as a sounding board for the citizens of Pennsylvania in matters pertaining to local and statewide information.

PLA and PCBL work together on Library Legislative Day. The 1988 event, held in Harrisburg March 15, saw more than 400 citizens and librarians lobbying their legislators for full state funding for the ACCESS PENNSYLVANIA Statewide Library Card System.

State Library of Pennsylvania. During 1988, the third edition of the ACCESS PENNSYLVANIA database on CD-ROM laser disk was issued. The union catalog now contains more than 4,000,000 records from 300 school, public, and academic libraries. The State Library also convened an 18-member committee to develop an application for a National Endowment for the Humanities grant to begin a statewide preservation program; disbursed $21,500,000 in state aid to 207 public libraries and library systems, which benefited 574 individual libraries, branches, and bookmobiles; awarded federal LSCA grants to more than 100 libraries; continued funding of the Pennsylvania Public Libraries Film Center; strengthened WORKPLACE, a project to provide career and education counseling to adults in public libraries; and coordinated exhibits of public library service at local government officials conferences across the state.

Public Libraries. Library tax referenda were passed in Marshall and Bethlehem townships and in West Chester Borough in the May primary election.

Awards. Thomas Childers, professor in the College of Information Studies, Drexel University, was awarded a $132,000 grant by the Office of Educational Technology and Innovation, U.S. Department of Education. Margaret S. Bauer, PLA Executive Director, was designated as a Certified Association Executive (CAE) by the American Society of Association Executives. Dauphin County Library System, Harrisburg, won its third John Cotton Dana National Library Public Relations Award in five years during ALA New Orleans. Among awards presented by PLA at its annual conference in 1988 were the Elected Official Award, which went to John H. Broujos and Jon D. Fox of the House of Representatives of the Pennsylvania General Assembly for their work as co-chairs of the Legislative Coalition for Libraries and the Distinguished Service Award to Stuart Forth.

People. Sara A. Parker, former State Librarian of Montana, became Pennsylvania's State Librarian August 15. Stuart Forth, first Dean of Pennsylvania State University Libraries, since 1973, retired in October. ALA Council saw Pennsylvanians in the spotlight. Toni Carbo Bearman and E. J. Josey from the University of Pittsburgh School of Library and Information Science were elected Councilors-at-Large with terms beginning at Midwinter 1989. Amy Kellman, Carnegie Library of Pittsburgh, was elected to Council's 1988–89 Committee on Committees. Susan Cady, Lehigh University, was appointed to serve a two-year term on the Council Resolutions Committee.

Diane L. Ambrose was named Director, Beaver County Federated Library System. Peter Deekle became the Director of the Blough-Weis Library, Susquehanna University, Selinsgrove. Nancy Cline, Assistant Dean and Head of Bibliographic Resources and Services Division of the Pennsylvania State University Libraries since 1984 became Dean of University Libraries. Sally Felix, Coordinator of Advisory Services and Continuing Education, Library Development Division, State Library of Pennsylvania, was named Director, Lackawanna County Library System, Scranton. Carolyn Hale, former Regional Librarian at the Northwest Regional Library, Philadelphia, was appointed Public Relations Director for the Free Library of Philadelphia. Roberta Greene became Director, West Shore Public Library, Camp Hill. Janis M. Lee was named District Consultant, Delaware County Library System, Media. Charles R. Peguese left his fourteen year post at the Library Development Division of the State Library to become Assistant Dean of Academic Affairs, Harrisburg Area Community College. Marnie Rees retired as Director, Lackawanna County Library System, Scranton. Kim Spanos-Telsing joined the York County Library System as Children's Coordinator.

Deaths. Alma Winton, former Head Librarian, Shippensburg State College Library, died December 10, 1987. Winton went to Shippensburg in 1941 and was the head planner for the Ezra Lehman Memorial Library built in 1968. Since her retirement in 1970 she had been an avid birdwatcher. May Virginia Kunz Valencik, PLA President, 1950–51, and director Allentown Public Library, 1942–63, died June 7.

PRISCILLA GRECO MCFERREN

RHODE ISLAND

The most significant event for Rhode Island libraries is that the Rhode Island Library Study conducted with Peat, Marwick, Main & Company was completed in August 1988. The study recommended changing three major ar-

Rhode Island Library Association (founded 1928)

Membership: 534; *annual budget,* $23,350.

President: Douglas Pearce, Warwick Public Library (November 1988–November 1989).

Vice-President/President-elect: Carol DiPrete, Roger Williams College, Bristol.

Annual meeting: November 5–7, 1989.

Publication: RILA Bulletin (monthly, except August).

Rhode Island Department of State Library Services

Bruce Daniels, Director
300 Richmond Street
Providence 02908-4322

eas of library development in the state—governance, funding and networking. Since the study was a joint effort between the Department of Library Services and the Rhode Island Library Association, both participated as members of the Legislative Commission. Once legislation is completed, librarians around the state will be lobbying for passage. Legislation was to be ready for the General Assembly by the January 1989 session. Depending upon action of the Legislative Commission, a 50–50 funding (state–local) for public libraries and a change in the present network from a regional to a statewide system could be recommended. A Legislative Commission, headed by Providence (Rhode Island) Senator Victoria Lederberg, began developing legislation for the 1989 session.

Networking and Interlibrary Cooperation. Obviously legislation coming out of the Rhode Island Library Study will have an impact on the structure of networking in the state if, indeed, there is a change from a regional to a statewide system. However, the Rhode Island Library Information Network (RHILINET), the group advising the Department of State Library Services, has been very active. Recommendations for standards for Principal Public Library and Special Research and Regional Centers were promulgated and approved by the Advisory Board of Library Commissioners. In addition, a revised Interlibrary Loan Code was approved. A special task force of RHILINET examining statewide databases was released in early 1989. Even though the network may be changed structurally, the activities of RHILINET will continue to assure high quality services.

Rhode Island Library Association (RILA). RILA is participating with the Department of State Library Services in the library study referred to earlier. Once legislation is introduced, Association members will be actively lobbying for its passage.

At the spring business meeting, discussion centered on dues increases and whether the association should hire permanent staff and if so, whether there would be sufficient funds to support staff.

The annual conference held at the Providence Marriott November 13–15 was successful. Approximately 250 persons attended; programs ranged from image building to hearing F. Williams Summers, President of ALA, speak on the national library perspective on automation programs. The conference ended with a tour of the newly renovated Providence Public Library and the Providence Atheneum. Two programs relating to the Peat, Marwick, Main Library Study drew large groups to discuss the study's implications for different types of libraries and for general library development in the state. At the business meeting a salary resolution passed relating salaries to situations, but with a final outcome of a minimum salary recommended of $21,000 a year. The gavel was passed from President Catherine Mello Alves to President-elect Douglas Pearce.

Department of State Library Services (DSLS). The Governor appointed Bruce Daniels Director of the Department after serving as Acting Director. The Department also moved to new quarters with more space and an optimal functional facility. A statewide program sponsored and funded by the Department was the Charlestown String Quartet Concerts, which traveled to several public libraries. Other statewide programs funded and sponsored were a "Ticket to Read"—a summer reading program—and the "Closing of the American Mind" series. The Department also participated with other organizations in sponsoring statewide public issues forums in public libraries. With an NEH grant, Newport Public Library developed a program titled "Common Ground: The Migration of the Yankee Culture," which was presented to various audiences.

The Regional Library for the Blind and Physically Handicapped was automated after several years of planning to facilitate access and control of materials.

Public Libraries. The Public Library Standards, established by the Department of State Library Services and approved by the Advisory Board of Library Commissioners, went into effect July 1, 1988. The standards set minimum staffing and funding levels as well as requirements for long-range planning. Libraries must comply by July 1989 to be eligible to receive state funding.

CLAN & RIALC, the two major public library automated systems, were merged into one statewide system, thus networking 29 public libraries into the CLSI circulation system at Providence Public Library. Plans are to have an online catalog of all networked libraries within the foreseeable future. In the interim, the Champlain Foundation and the Department of State Library Services provided funding for the database to be available through CD-ROM to all networked libraries and to the 13 higher education special research centers in the Rhode Island Interrelated Network.

School and Academic Libraries. School library standards were being revised for the first time since 1968. Revision for school libraries is part of a comprehensive state Basic Education Plan (BEP).

In January, Troy Earhart, Commissioner of Elementary and Secondary Education, appointed a School Library Standards Group that helped develop a document on improving education in the state. In April, a teleconference relating to Information Power was held at two sites so that many school librarians could attend. In March the Rhode Island Educational Media Association (RIEMA) held its annual conference on "We Are the Keys to the Information Age." Other topics covered were literacy, copyright, AIDS education, and teaching library skills.

On the academic front the legislature passed a bill funding a union list of serials of the academic and research libraries in Rhode Island. Online access to the union list will be made in 1989 by Faxon Company.

The Higher Education Library Information Network increased its membership to include Roger Williams College. The four institutions (University of Rhode Island, Rhode Island College, the Community College of Rhode Island, and Roger Williams College) investigated integrated library systems. An online catalog is anticipated for 1990 if funding is available.

A 100,000-square-foot addition to the University of Rhode Island Library referendum was passed in the general election. Brown University's online catalog became operational with WLN as vendor. The Naval War College in Newport has begun its automation project and installed a ULISYS-based catalog.

Buildings. The Providence Public Library completed its three-year renovation project with a grand opening on November 13. North Smithfield Public Library continues expansion of its present facilities. After a long delay, the South Kingstown, Peace Dale Library began renovation of its historic building. Other major renovations begun include the William Hall and Oaklawn branches of the Cranston Public Library. Brown University's Music Library, Orwig, opened for the fall semester.

University of Rhode Island, Graduate School of Library and Information Studies (URI-GSLIS). At the ALA Annual Conference in New Orleans, it was announced that the URI-GSLIS had been accredited. Under Elisabeth Futas' able leadership, the school began to regain strength after a rather painful period.

Coalition of Library Advocates (COLA). COLA, a group of librarian and citizen advocates, had an active year. The annual meeting in the Governor's Executive Chambers at the State House heard local storyteller Lenny Cabral. In October, James Billington, Librarian of Congress, gave an inspiring talk to approximately some 200 people. Joan Ress Reeves continued to guide the group.

People. There were a number of important changes in personnel in Rhode Island. Dale Thompson was named Director of the Providence Public Library. At the Department of State Library Services Bruce Daniels was named Director; Dorothy Frechette has been named Deputy Director; Howard Boksenbaum was appointed Chief of Library Planning, Development and Information Services; and Beth Perry was named head of the Regional Library for the Blind and Physically Handicapped. Catherine Mello Alves was appointed Coordinator of the Island Interrelated Library System. New public library directors were Kathy Bullock at Woonsocket, Virginia Taken at Johnston, and Dolores Tansey at Tiverton. Richard Olsen, Director of Rhode Island College, was elected Vice-President/President-elect of the New England Library Association. Joan Ress Reeves was elected Chair of the White House Conference on Library and Information Services Task Force and was appointed to the White House Conference Committee.

CAROL K. DIPRETE

SOUTH CAROLINA

Major News. The major news of 1988 was the restoration of State Aid for public libraries to $1 per capita, with a minimum of $10,000.00 total to the smallest counties. A one-time, five-cent-per-capita grant was included in the legislation. The successful campaign was led by the Association of Public Library Administrators, and the South Carolina State Library. This is the first time in four years that state aid attained $1 per capita.

State Association. The South Carolina Library Association held its 62nd Annual Conference in Myrtle Beach in November. The conference was entitled "PRO PUBLICUS BONUM: Libraries and Information for the Public Good." Keynote speaker, Deborah Miller, Director of Governmental Services for the Illinois Library Association, spoke on "You can make a difference: Library advocacy in the public arena." Lieutenant Governor Nick Theodore addressed the Commission on the Future of South Carolina and Library roles in that future. Gloria Glaser, Past President of the American Library Trustee Association, and Perry White, Southeastern board member of Friends of Libraries, USA took part in a discussion on the need for friends, trustees, and librarians to work together for better libraries.

State Library. The South Carolina State Library and the Southeastern Library Network are cooperating on a project that examines the potential of SOLINET consultation services for libraries requiring assistance on various aspects of library automation. The pilot project will target small and medium-sized public libraries. The SOLINET staff will provide assistance in the production of specifications for the local system, assist in reviewing and evaluating vendor proposals, present recommendations to library boards, provide training, and planning for conversion. The state library will fund consultation costs for ten libraries for two years. Local libraries will pay travel and per diem costs for SOLINET staff. The state library has placed all the bibliographic records of state documents into its online database. It ceased the publication of its *Checklist of South Carolina State Publications*, because access to the documents is available through the South Carolina Library Network and through OCLC.

Public Libraries. The Greenville County Library won a John Cotton Dana "Certificate of Merit" its publication of the New Readers Booklist in Spanish. The list was prepared in English by Pat Gilleland and translated into Spanish by Maria del Pilar Agnar-Riddle. The Oconee County Council approved $60,000.00 for the first phase of a countywide online system for the Oconee County Library. The Friends of the Greenville County Library held a statewide Friends of Libraries workshop in September. Representatives from about ten county library systems across the state attended.

School Libraries and Media Centers. The two South Carolina school districts selected for the Public School Library Media Center Demonstration Project funded by the South Carolina State Library selected their software vendors. Lexington County School District Five selected the PCemas program produced by Scholar-Chips Software, Inc. The School District of Oconee County selected Winnebago Software. Oconee completed automation of its participating schools and is using the software. The South Carolina "ADOPT A LIBRARY" program raised more than $124,000 for school libraries in 1988.

Academic Libraries. Columbia Bible College in Columbia, S.C. has added the Ridderhoff Center, which connects with the Library to form a Learning Resource Center. Media and music facilities are the focus of this $3,300,000 addition. The state Legislature passed the Capital Improvement Bond Bill, which includes assistance for academic libraries in the state. The University of South Carolina is receiving $2,144,000 for a library/administration building for its Salkahatchee campus and $300,000 for a library addition to its Sumter facility. The Technical Education System will receive $3,044,500 for improvements to library facilities Piedmont Tech, Tri County Tech, and Trident Tech. The state is also funding $11,000 to the Commission on Higher Education for the Formula Distribution of Books and $1,000,000 to the University of South Carolina (Columbia campus) for library automation.

Building Programs. The Darlington County Library received a new 15,000-square-foot main library building at a cost of $1,097,000. James Decker of the Charleston County Library announced plans for the construction of a $3,200,000 branch library building in Mount Pleasant. The facility is part of a countywide building program which will see other branches constructed in the northern and western areas of the county. Renovations are scheduled for the main library as well. The Laurens County Library received word that the Laurens County Council agreed to underwrite $125,000 for the building fund. The library also received $25,000 from the new Wal-Mart Distribution Center. The Myrtle Beach City Council approved expansion of the Chapin Memorial Library to 27,000 square feet by adding two new wings to the present building at a projected cost of about $2,000,000. Chapin Memorial Library is the only municipal library in the state.

Networks and Interlibrary Cooperation. The State Library awarded an LSCA grant to the University of South Carolina School of Medicine for the creation of the Charleston Area Union List of Serials. The list being added to the library's serials database and includes the holdings of the College of Charleston, the Citadel, Baptist College, Trident Technical College, Medical University of South Carolina, and the Charleston County Library. The South Carolina Association of Public Library Administrators, in cooperation with the

---

South Carolina Library Association (founded 1915)

President: Betty E. Callaham, Director, South Carolina State Library, P.O. Box 11469, Columbia 29211 (October 1988–October 1989).

Vice-President/President-elect: Joseph Boykin, Director, Clemson University Libraries (1990–1991).

Annual meeting: November 9–11, 1989, Hilton Head Island.

Publications: South Carolina Librarian (Semi-annual); *News and Views* (bimonthly).

South Carolina State Library

Betty E. Callaham, Director
P.O. Box 11469
Columbia 29211

State School Library Media Consultant

Pamela Pritchard
South Carolina Department of Education
Columbia 29201

State Library, received an NEH grant of $100,000 for a two-year "Let's Talk About It" project and hired Frannie Ashburn to coordinate the project. The State Library is housing materials and providing staff assistance. Larry Freeman, Field Services Librarian, and Ashburn conducted a one-day workshop in Columbia to familiarize scholars, discussion leaders, and librarians with the project. The meeting featured Elizabeth Baer, Dean of the College, Washington College, Chestertown, Maryland, National LTAI scholar; Pat Bates, project director for Howard County Public Library-Miller Branch Library in Ellicott City, Maryland, the originator of the concept; and Sandra Cooper, former ALA project director for the national program. Anderson, Greenville, Marion, Clarendon, Fairfield, and Lancaster were the first county library systems to participate in the program.

Intellectual Freedom. Betty Callaham, Director, South Carolina State Library, participated in ALA's Intellectual Freedom Leadership Development Institute. Callaham was also interviewed by the head of the Columbia office of the Federal Bureau of Investigation, who was seeking information about the status of confidentiality legislation in regard to libraries. Callaham gave the agent copies of the South Carolina law and of publicity on the FBI Awareness Program.

Professional Interests. The Public Library Section of the South Carolina Library Association voted to increase the state salary scale to $22,000 per year from $20,000 per year for a beginning professional librarian. Though not binding, the scale is usually adopted by the State Library as a basis for paying salary supplements to public libraries.

Awards. Evelyn Welborn, former trustee, and a member of the Friends of the Anderson County Library, received the South Carolina State Library's Distinguished Service Award for raising more than $500,000 for the library over a period of years. Patricia Doyle, Chair, Georgetown County Library, received a Distinguished Service Award for spearheading a drive for a new main library for the system. She was so successful that the library will receive the main library and two branches. The Friends of the Library Award of the South Carolina Library Association was presented to "King" Dixon, Athletic Director, University of South Carolina, who chaired the fund-raising drive for the Laurens County Library.

Retirements. Kenneth Toombs, long-time Director of Libraries of the University of South Carolina and Deputy Director Davy Jo Stribling Ridge, retired in the summer of 1988. Annie Francis Blackman, Director of the Olin D. Johnston Library, Anderson College, retired in July.

CARL STONE

SOUTH DAKOTA

South Dakota librarians will remember 1988 as a banner year—especially for funding and implementation of the South Dakota Library Network's (SDLN) online catalog in the ten state-supported libraries. Other good news included a growing harmony between small libraries and the State Library and the initial members of SDLN, receipt of several sizable gifts and grants, completion of the largest building project in several years, and burgeoning circulation figures in several public libraries.

The crucial event in the success of the seven-year drive to create a joint integrated online library automation system occurred in October 1987, when Governor George Mickelson, after consulting legislative leaders, accepted UNISYS Corporation's offer to begin immediate expansion of its PALS system at Black Hills State College to the other nine state-supported libraries. The state was obligated to pay for the system in July 1988 at the start of its new fiscal year, or UNISYS could repossess the hardware and software. From that agreement the legislative appropriation proceeded without controversy to the inclusion of SDLN in the general appropriation bill that passed in March.

The appropriation was formally made to the State Library, which perforce became the manager of SDLN, while the former planning committee was transformed into an advisory committee. Later in the year, user-interest groups were created to broaden participation in further development of SDLN.

The expanded system was operational by the end of April; the governor spoke at a ribbon-cutting ceremony at the State Library on June 22; and individual libraries held their own ceremonies in September. The nine new participants hoped to implement the online circulation system early in 1989.

South Dakota librarians envisioned SDLN as a system open ultimately to any South Dakota library wanting to join and able to pay its share of the costs. At year's end six private colleges, a native American tribal college, and two public libraries had applied to join SDLN during 1989, and Sioux Falls Public Library had indicated it would support inclusion of its holdings in the catalog for other libraries to be able to access. The additional members will bring SDLN close to realization of the claim by library and political supporters that it is the first statewide, multitype integrated online library system in the nation.

Legislation. Nearly as significant for libraries as the legislative funding of SDLN was the defeat of two legislative proposals that would have potentially harmed libraries. Senate Bill 181 would have applied to adults the very extensive restrictions currently in South Dakota law on distributing to minors materials and performances depicting nudity and sexual activity. After the South Dakota Library Association utilized its "phone tree" to generate librarian contacts with their legislators, the bill was narrowly defeated in two votes in the Senate.

An initiated referendum, called Dakota Proposition II, that would have rolled back and capped local property taxes without providing replacement revenues was opposed by a formal membership resolution at the SDLA convention. It was defeated by a 60-40 margin in the November election.

State Association. More than 200 gathered in Rapid City in September for the annual convention, whose theme was "Your Library—The KNOW Place." Highlights included preconferences on professional communications skills and on the MARC format for small libraries; several sessions relating to computer applications in libraries; a luncheon at Storm Mountain featuring South Dakota's resident Caldecott Award winner, Paul Goble; and the Awards Luncheon with mystery author William Reynolds as speaker.

The second South Dakota Children's Book Award, now named the Prairie Pasque Award after the official state flower, was given by vote of South Dakota children to Lois Lowry's *Switcharound*. In honor of the upcoming centennial of statehood, South Dakota Library Association organized a statewide Centennial Summer Reading Program for children for 1989.

State Library. The State Library (SDSL) did not receive its requested staffing increase and got only a minor improvement in its budget, excluding the sum allocated for SDLN. Nevertheless, SDSL responded positively to the insistent requests from small public and school libraries that the service cuts imposed in 1986 should be softened. In the first full year of the restrictions, the State Library experienced a one-third drop in requests.

State Librarian Jane Kolbe announced at the end of 1987 that the State Library Board had directed the State Library to be generous in granting exceptions to the ban on subject requests. In response to a suggestion from the Public Library Section of SDLA, the State Library supplied *Subject Guide to Books in Print* to 35 small public libraries, which pledged to share use with local school libraries.

The State Library decided to mandate subscriptions to a list of only 20 popular periodicals for small libraries to be eligible to request photocopies of periodicals articles from the SDSL. The original requirement had been subscriptions by 1988 to all periodicals indexed in *Abridged Readers' Guide*.

Kolbe concluded an agreement with the University of Minnesota for its library's federal documents regional depository to act as the regional depository for the state's selective depositories. Then began discard procedures for unneeded federal documents.

The strategic planning process started two years earlier produced a draft "Long-Range Plan, 1989-1993," which also serves as the five-year plan required by LSCA. The plan projects development of stronger standards for public libraries, sets a goal for all public libraries in communities more than 5,000 to have plans by 1992 to join SDLN, promotes the 16 largest schools entering SDLN, plans grants

---

South Dakota Library Association (founded 1907)

Membership: 540; *annual budget:* $23,735.

President: Nancy Sabbe, Madison Public Library, 209 East Center, Madison 57042 (September 1988-September 1989).

Vice-President/President-elect: Ethelle Bean, Dakota State College, Mundt Library, Madison 57042.

Annual meeting: October 5-8, 1988, Rapid City; October 11-14, 1989, Aberdeen.

Publication: Book Marks (bimonthly).

South Dakota State Library

Jane Kolbe, State Librarian
State Library Building
800 Governors Drive
Pierre 57501

School Library Media Supervisor

Donna Gilliland
South Dakota State Library
State Library Building
800 Governors Drive
Pierre 57501

of LSCA money to aid retrospective conversion of catalog records by these libraries, and projects a trial cooperative borrowing program in one region of the state.

Public Libraries. In January, Sioux Falls Public Library added an online catalog to the Dynex online circulation system it acquired in 1987. In the fall the first branch, constructed and stocked with materials funded from the estate of Ruth Kennedy Caille, a former head of the library, was opened. Sioux Falls also became the first public library in the state with telefacsimile capacities.

A new public library opened mainly with the aid of donations in Java in March. Most remarkable was Larry and Jo Dobson's gift of a microcomputer to hold the library's online catalog, which the community hoped would soon have dial-up access. Dewey County Library moved into a new building using fund-raising to match an LSCA grant.

School Libraries. A task force of educators and representatives from SDLA developed revisions of the state administrative rules for school libraries and librarians. Adopted changes are requirements that among the 18 hours of credit required for school librarian certification must be courses in reference, cataloging, book selection, and library administration and that each school system must adopt and then update a comprehensive library plan prior to an accreditation review.

Academic Libraries. Augustana College's Mikkelsen Library received a gift of $300,000 from alumni Helmer R. Myklebust and his deceased spouse, M. Helen Myklebust, to aid library automation, climate control, and a rare book room. The donors also established a trust fund of about $1,000,000 for an endowment to support library and related programs. Oglala Lakota College acquired a $450,000 grant from the Pew Trust to finish the design and start construction of a new library.

The libraries of Augustana College, Sioux Falls College, and North American Baptist Seminary, all located in Sioux Falls, and Sioux Falls Public Library were awarded a challenge grant of $120,000 by the Bush Foundation for a joint automation project that will permit the college libraries to join SDLN and the public library's catalog records to be added to the SDLN database to enhance local resource sharing.

The family of former professor of printing Windsor Straw donated his collection of fine printing and antiquarian books to South Dakota State University's Briggs Library.

Networks and Interlibrary Cooperation. The school and small public library representatives organized as SDLN/ACCESS continued to push not to be excluded from the benefits of shared online catalogs and the resulting ease of resource sharing, and SDLN made access to its database available by contract. Any library with a microcomputer can receive a password and use of a toll-free line to SDLN's database for a nominal fee, training in the system, and agreeing to interlibrary loan rules that make the State Library the first source for needed materials and thereafter "the smallest library geographically closest." More than 100 attended workshops.

Members of SDLN/ACCESS, in cooperation with the State Library, began exploring the possibilities of shared lines to reduce telecommunications costs and a statewide plan for retrospective conversion of catalog records for school and small public libraries which are not OCLC members. These problems must be overcome for full participation in SDLN.

Professional Interests. Education for librarianship has become an increasing concern in recent years as several ALA-accredited master's programs in nearby states closed, the University of South Dakota ended its limited library science program, and librarians in small libraries perceived the need to upgrade skills to participate in shared cataloging and automated systems.

The South Dakota State Library–sponsored institute at Northern State College held its third annual two-week session in July. The SDLA-sponsored Task Force on Continuing Education conducted an extensive survey of continuing education needs and filed a report at the annual SDLA convention. The agreement of Emporia State University with a consortium of northwest Iowa libraries to provide library science courses in Sioux City, Iowa, was greeted as helpful in filling the gap in professional education services regionally.

Awards. Patricia Kougl, librarian of Dewey County Library, was named SDLA's Librarian of the Year. SDLA also recognized Marg Tabbert, head of Hyde County Library, as New Librarian of the Year; Governor George Mickelson as Friend of the Library for his crucial support of SDLN; Helmer Myklebust also as Friend of the Library for his $1,300,000 in donations to Augustana College's library and his longtime interest in library service; and Frances Storm, trustee of Tripp County Library for more than a decade and fund-raiser for its move to new quarters, as Trustee of the Year.

Appointments. Robert Paustian was appointed Director of Libraries, University of South Dakota.

PHILIP BROWN

TENNESSEE

Tennessee Library Association (founded 1902)

Membership: 1,161; *annual budget:* $66,988 (FY 1988).

President: David A. Kearley, DuPont Library University of the South (July 1, 1988–June 1989).

President-elect: Carolyn Stark, Public Library of Nashville/Davidson County.

Executive Secretary: Betty Nance, Nashville.

Annual meeting: April 21–22, 1989, Knoxville.

Publications: Tennessee Librarian (quarterly); TLA Newsletter (bimonthly).

Tennessee State Library

Betty Lature,
Library Media Specialist
Nashville

State Library and Archives. On August 11, 1988, the Tennessee Advisory Council on Libraries unanimously endorsed the *Tennessee Long-Range Program for Library Services and Development, 1988/89–1992/93*, which had been prepared by a committee of the Council over a period of 18 months. The committee, chaired by a library trustee, Col. Joseph Jones, had created 15 drafts of the program, two of them distributed to more than 1,000 Tennessee librarians, trustees, government officials and interested lay persons. The first general distribution draft included two evaluation forms, one that addressed the nine goals and objectives, the other that encouraged suggested plans of action. The Long-Range Planning Committee completely revised the draft document based on the more than 300 responses received and a second mailing to all interested Tennesseans was completed. Following the second mailing, seven open hearings were held across the state to allow a final review of the program. More than 350 people attended the hearings and the response to the final draft was overwhelmingly positive. The final long-range program provides a blueprint for the growth and development of Tennessee libraries.

Among activities derived from the Long-Range Program are plans for a Tennessee Governor's Conference on Library and Information Services in 1990 (preliminary to the White House Conference II); the development of standards for public libraries; the coordination of statewide summer reading programs; and development of recommendations concerning the future of government publications in the state's libraries. The State Library and Archives continued with its direct service grants to public libraries including funding of a retrospective conversion project at Memphis State University for serial publications held in Tennessee libraries.

Tennessee Library Association. The Tennessee Library Association (TLA) held its 1988 convention in Nashville in April with more than 590 librarians, friends and trustees in attendance. The conference theme, "Libraries for Today and Tomorrow," was a good description of the many programs presented. Keynote Speaker Frank P. Grisham, Executive Director of SOLINET and former TLA President, challenged librarians to prepare themselves for a future as "knowledge navigators," masters of the lifelong learning process. Other featured speakers included Kathleen Imhoff of the Broward County Public Library, who discussed networks using telefacsimile transmission to deliver journal articles; Anne A. Heanue, Associate Director of The ALA Washington Office, who discussed government restrictions on information; Mary Berghaus Levering, Chief, Network Division of the Library of Congress' National Library Service for the Blind and Physically Handicapped, who urged librarians to rethink services for senior citizens; and Congressman Major Owens of New York, who encouraged librarians to work together for stronger legislation and emphasized the need for all library-related groups to work together. Tennessee Governor Ned McWherter spoke to the Trustees and Friends Luncheon about the importance of libraries and his commitment to literacy work. The star of the conference was author Alex Haley who held an overflow, standing audience spellbound for nearly two hours as he told how he began his writing career and shared stories about his family.

In June TLA held its second Orientation and Planning Workshop to provide an opportunity for outgoing chairs to turn over files to incoming chairs, to acquaint members of the TLA Board with their responsibilities, and to begin planning for the next TLA convention.

At the August 13 meeting, the TLA Board of Directors approved the establishment of a bimonthly newsletter to provide members with current, up-to-date information about association activities. The first issue was published in October.

Legislation. The TLA Intellectual Freedom

Committee, chaired by Bill Prince working with the TLA Legislation Committee chaired by Claudia Schauman, convinced the Tennessee House Judiciary Committee to sponsor Confidentiality of Library Records Legislation. When Governor McWherter signed the bill on May 2, 1988, Tennessee became the 38th state to enact a law protecting the confidentiality of circulation records in libraries. Representative Bill Purcell of the House Judiciary Committee was very supportive in helping get the legislation passed.

Tennessee had a very successful Legislative Day on March 16 in Nashville with many librarians from across the state participating. Five Tennesseans represented the state during National Library Legislative Day in Washington, D.C., on April 19th. Carol Hewlett, Claudia Schauman, Judy Greeson, Edwin Gleaves, and trustee Jonas Kisber visited with Tennessee legislators to talk about libraries and about literacy.

Academic Libraries. "Academic Library Education in Tennessee" was the program topic at the Fall meeting of the TLA College and University Libraries Section at Austin Peay State University. Program speakers included Wil Clouse (Vanderbilt), Gary Purcell, University of Tennessee, Knoxville (UTK), and Jill Keally (UTK).

The Medical Center Library at Vanderbilt University celebrated the acquisition of its 150,000th bound volume in April. Johnson Bible College began an $800,000 library addition that will add 14,000 square feet to the present facility. The State Legislature appropriated $200,000 toward plans for a new library facility at Memphis State University.

The Projects Committee of the Memphis Library Council worked with the Graduate School of Library and Information Science at the University of Tennessee Knoxville to begin an MLS program in Memphis. Coursework began in the fall.

Peabody College of Vanderbilt University in Nashville established a Master's level program to prepare school library media specialists, with emphasis on instructional technology and information management.

Public Libraries. A recently appointed Joint Tennessee Library Association/Tennessee State Library and Archives Committee on Public Library Standards has begun work on developing public library standards. The committee developed a working statement on the role and scope of the Interim Tennessee Minimum Standards for Public Libraries and is currently collecting data.

Recent anniversary celebrations include the Chattanooga-Hamilton County Bicentennial Library, which celebrated its 100th anniversary on October 16, 1988, and the Lebanon-Wilson County Public Library, which celebrated its 50th anniversary on February 14, 1988.

Memphis was one of 30 cities selected to house the touring exhibit "Are We to Be a Nation?" which focuses on the people, politics, and events that shaped a revolutionary new government. The exhibit was at the Main Library of the Memphis/Shelby County Public Library and Information Center for five weeks.

School Libraries. School librarians used petitions and a committee to lobby the State Department of Education for a library media supervisor. In July Betty Latture was named Library Media Specialist in the Division of Curriculum and Instruction. Attention was also focused on the new national guidelines.

Tennessee's *Information Power* Implementation Team was chaired by Carolyn Daniel. The team co-sponsored with the State Department of Education a series of drive-in conferences around the state highlighting the partnerships concept emphasized in *Information Power*. Additional presentations were made at several meetings and conferences.

Buildings. The General Assembly appropriated $906,000 for library construction projects at 28 eligible locations in Tennessee. These state funds will be used with local funds to get matching funds under Title II of the LSCA. Communities with new or remodeled facilities include Clinton, Coffee County, Crockett County, Jasper, Johnson County, Lenoir City, Loretto, Martin, Petros, South Chetham County, and Springfield.

Awards. The Tennessee Library Association made the following awards in 1988: Louise Meredith School Library Media Service Award to Catherine Bruner, Librarian at Brown Middle School, Harrison, Tennessee; TLA Honor Award to Diane N. Baird, Senior Librarian, Warioto Regional Library, Clarksville; Tennessee History Book Award to Fred A. Bailey for *Class and Tennessee's Confederate Generation*; a special citation to Paul Clements for *A Past Remembered: a Collection of Antebellum Homes in Davidson County*; Outstanding Trustee Award to Anne Lowe of Putnam County.

Rosie Phillips, a student at the Graduate School of Library and Information Science, University of Tennessee, Knoxville, won the 1988 Baker and Taylor/Junior Members Roundtable Grassroots Grant. The $250 grant paid her expenses to the 1988 TLA convention.

The Tennessee Children's Choice Book Award was renamed the Volunteer State Book Award. Four awards will be given for the most popular books in grades K-3, 4-6, 7-9, and 10-12. Children in these age ranges will vote for their favorite titles from the list developed by 15-member subcommittees for each grade level. The first awards will be made in 1989.

Appointments. Betty Latture was appointed Library Media Specialist, Tennessee Department of Education in July. Mary King Givens was named Acting Director, University of Tennessee-Memphis Health Sciences Library. Jess A. Martin, Director, UT Memphis Health Sciences Library since 1971, retired May 31. Scarlett G. Graham is the new Director, Vanderbilt Television News Archive. Nancy Norton was named Director, Information Services Division, Martin Marietta Energy Systems. James E. Ward, Director, Crisman Memorial Library, David Lipscomb College, was elected Vice-President/President-elect of the Southeastern Library Association.

Deaths. Mildred L. Iddins, Carson Newman College Librarian Emeritus, for whom the college's special collection and archives are named, died in March. Dr. Joe Morgan, trustee for Houston County, died May 30. Timothy Eatherly Dail, former Lebanon/Wilson County Library Board and Highland Rim Regional Library Board member died during 1988.

CAROLYN C. DANIEL

TEXAS

Texas Library Association (founded 1902)

Membership: 4,472; *annual budget:* $435,000

President: Gretchen Staas, Garland Independent School District, Garland 75040 (April 1988-April 1989).

Vice-President/President-elect: Patricia L. Doyle, McKinney Memorial Public Library, McKinney, 75069.

Executive Director: Patricia H. Smith, 3355 Bee Cave Road, Suite 603, Austin 78746.

Annual meeting: April 11-15, 1989, Houston.

Publications: Texas Library Journal (quarterly); *TLACast* (Newsletter, eight issues per year).

Texas State Library

William D. Goach, Director and Librarian
Box 12927/Capitol Station
Austin 78711

Library Media Program

Mary Boyvey, Program Director,
1701 North Congress Avenue
Austin 78701

Despite the downturn in the Texas economy since 1984, 1988 was a good year for the state's libraries. Activities included numerous successful and well-attended conferences, progress in cooperative efforts such as union catalogs, an increase in services available to more than 17,000,000 citizens, and completion of a number of new or improved library buildings. On the negative side, Texas, along with other states, felt the impact of the increased cost of serial publications. This hindered the dissemination of information, especially in the academic community.

State Library Association. More than 110 programs, business meetings, and other events constituted the Texas Library Association's (TLA) 75th annual conference, dedicated to the memory of Jerre Hetherington, Executive Director, 1954-1983. Featured speakers included Jamie Gilson, popular children's author; Sid Fleischman, Newbery Medal winner; Liz Carpenter, author and raconteur; and Cactus Pryor, humorist and widely known media personality, who depicted Texas' colorful folklorist-professor J. Frank Dobie in excerpts from a two-act play. Program topics focused on such current issues as literacy, pay equity, time management, problem bosses, the impact of automation, and CD-ROMs.

Frank D. Hankins received the Distinguished Service Award, given only ten times in the Association's 85-year history. S. Joe McCord was named Librarian of the Year, and Linda Hetherington Claytor, daughter of TLA's revered Jerre Hetherington, received the Outstanding Service to Libraries Award, which recognizes the contribution of laypersons. The Briscoe Library, University of Texas Health Science Center at San Antonio, won the Library Project of the Year Award for its drug information program. Betty Ren Wright, author of *Christina's Ghost*, received the Texas Bluebonnet Award. This award, for which

303

children in grades 3–6 vote for their favorite book from a master list of titles, is sponsored by the Texas Association of School Librarians and the Children's Round Table, both units of TLA. The Association also presented nine Benefactor Awards.

The Association, in cooperation with its districts, sent ten representatives to the ALA Legislative Day, April 19, in Washington. Half of TLA's ten districts held eight legislative breakfasts during the year at various locations around the State. At the third biennial Legislative Day, scheduled for February 15, 1989, librarians and laypersons will seek support for appropriate funding for state university, public, and school libraries, the inclusion of school librarians on the career ladder with classroom teachers, and other important matters. The Texas Association of School Librarians surveyed its members in 1988 to learn if they want to be added to the career ladder. School librarians substantially endorsed the proposal. This is the third attempt to get the legislature to approve this long-overdue reform.

In other activities, nearly 300 members of committees and boards of the Association attended the Annual Leadership Assembly in Austin, July 21–23. E. Dale Cluff and Mary Kay Snell are the new Representatives-at-large to the Executive Board, and Margaret Irby Nichols was elected ALA Chapter Councilor.

Texas Education Agency. The Texas Education Agency's (TEA) program to accredit school libraries has helped improve services within many school districts. Current standards require libraries to hold a minimum of ten books and two audiovisuals per student and to remain open at least half of every instructional day. Requirements also emphasize weeding obsolete materials. TEA produced nine publications during the year, including *Attracting Students to the Library Media Center*, *Library/Information Skills for Quality Education*, and *Library Learning Resources Facilities—New and Renovated*. The Agency also produced nine videotapes on school library administration and three on authors. The Texas Education Agency Library Media Program maintains a complete price list of these publications.

Texas State Library. The State Library reported that the 412 public libraries that are members of the ten systems serve more than 14,000,000 Texans, 86 percent of the total population. Only 43 public libraries in the state fail to meet minimum criteria for system membership. When Foard County (population 1,912) received the first of three annual $20,000 grants to establish library service for its residents, the number of Texas counties without service was reduced to 14 (of 254). Eleven public libraries received Library Services and Construction Act Title II grants totaling $1,221,668.

The State Library awarded $2,868,051 to ten large metropolitan libraries and $160,600 to 30 academic libraries to fill interlibrary loan requests through the Texas State Library Communications Network. Almost 400,000 requests were filled during 1987–88, an increase of 20 percent over the previous period. Some 400,000 children participated in the 1988 Reading Club, "Trailblazers, Stargazers," co-sponsored by the Texas State Library and local libraries. Seventy Kurzweil Reading Machines were placed in public and academic libraries throughout Texas, allowing visually impaired people, many for the first time, to use locally available resources.

An 80,000-square-foot building expansion at the State Library's Record Center resolved space problems for both Records Management and the Division of the Blind and Physically Handicapped. Removal of materials to the new facility allows the Archives Division to gain necessary stack space which also is secure.

A task force appointed jointly by the Texas State Library and the Texas Library Association will study the preservation needs of Texas libraries. The group is charged with developing a state preservation plan.

Awards and Grants. The J. Frank Dobie Trust gave grants totaling $4,750 to nine public libraries which serve communities of less than 25,000, plus a special award of $1,000 to the Texline Public Library. The awards were presented in April at the Texas Library Association's annual conference.

Houston Endowment, Inc., donated $760,000 to the Clayton Library, Center for Genealogical Research, Houston Public Library. The grant will provide furnishings and equipment for the Center's new addition.

The National Endowment for the Humanities and the U.S. Department of Education awarded grants to six major libraries, including the General Libraries of the University of Texas at Austin, to support a multiyear cooperative project to make Latin American library materials more available to the scholarly community. During the first year alone, the $200,555 grant to the University of Texas at Austin will fund the addition of 21,000 new records to the national bibliographic database and add holding symbols to 28,500 more records in the OCLC online national catalog. Plans exist to extend the funding and increase the list of participating libraries in order to bring the project to a successful conclusion in 1992, the 500th anniversary of Christopher Columbus' discovery of the Western Hemisphere.

Academic Libraries. At the end of July 1988, the General Libraries of the University of Texas at Austin finished the first phase of its retrospective conversion project. Slightly more than 102,000 bibliographic records were converted into machine-readable form by OCLC. The holding symbol for the General Libraries also was attached to the OCLC online record.

The Association of Higher Education began the development of a union catalog of the holdings of five north Texas libraries by inviting proposals from major vendors of optical disk library cataloging products. AMIGOS Bibliographic Council, Inc., in conjunction with the Library Corporation, was chosen as vendor. The project will integrate into one database more than 1,000,000 unique titles held by five libraries: Baylor University, Dallas County Community College District, Dallas Public Library, University of North Texas, and University of Texas at Arlington.

Other events in academic libraries during the year include the appointment of B. Donald Grose as Director of Libraries at the University of North Texas and the completion of new library facilities at Texas Wesleyan College, Prairie View A & M University, and Southwest Texas State University. The latter university also announced the establishment of the Southwestern Writers Collection, which focuses on regional writers, songwriters, and musicians.

Robert R. Douglass, Dean Emeritus, Graduate School of Library and Information Science (GSLIS), University of Texas at Austin, died in October 1988. Douglass founded GSLIS in 1948 and served as dean until his retirement in 1968.

Other Events. In addition to the Texas Library Association's annual conference and Annual Leadership Assembly, there were a number of other meetings during the year: the 6th Texas Conference on Library Automation, Houston; the AMIGOS spring and fall Technical Sessions, "Effective Database Management: Issues and Strategies"; and "People, Machines, and Change: The Impact of Automation on the Organization Chart"; a mini-conference, "The Cost of Cooperation in Academic and Research Libraries," sponsored jointly by AMIGOS and the School of Library and Information Sciences, University of North Texas, Denton; and the 7th Annual Texas Library History Colloquium, held at the Lyndon B. Johnson Presidential Library, Austin, which focused on Senator Ralph Yarborough's contributions to federal legislation designed to improve libraries and education.

The Book Club of Texas, founded in 1929 by Stanley Marcus and others, was reestablished. The purpose of the group is to publish books that "typify the best standards of bookmaking, in regard to subject matter, printing, binding, and typographical design." Before ceasing in 1941, the Club produced seven noteworthy books, now avidly sought by collectors. At its first annual meeting, held in Austin on November 12, the membership decided to publish *Goodbye to a River*, by John Graves; *My First Thirty Years*, by Gertrude Beasley, with an introduction by Larry McMurtry; and *Glorious News! An Enquiry into the Nature of Certain Nineteenth-Century Texas Broadsides*, by W. Thomas Taylor.

MARGARET IRBY NICHOLS

UTAH

Utah Library Association (founded 1912)

Membership: 580; *annual budget:* $16,000.

President: Paul Mogren, Mariott Library, University of Utah (April 1988–February 1989).

First Vice-President: Carolyn Dickenson, Salt Lake City Public Library.

Executive Secretary: Gerald A. Buttars, Utah State Library.

Annual meeting: April 27–29, Ogden, Utah.

Publication: Utah Libraries/News (bimonthly).

Utah State Library Commission

Amy Owen, Director
2150 South 300 West, Suite #16
Salt Lake City 84115

State Association. The Utah Library Association held its annual convention in April 27–29 in Ogden, Utah. The conference theme was "Librarians in a Diverse Society." The program featured Charles Bourne, Director of the General Information Division at DIALOG Information Services, as the keynote speaker. Linda Sillitoe, author of *Salamander: The Story of the Mormon Forgery Murders*, spoke at the President's Luncheon.

The Continuing Education Committee developed a workshop titled, "Operational Policies for a Public Library," presented at Snow College in Ephraim October 8, Utah State University in Logan March 30, and at the ULA Conference April 27th. On November 13th ULA co-sponsored, with the Children's Literature Association of Utah a seminar with Patricia MacLachlin, author of the Newbery Award for *Sarah Plain and Tall*.

The Association faced a big hurdle when a tax roll-back initiative was placed on the November ballot. The tireless efforts of Eileen Longsworth, chairman of the Association's legislative committee, helped defeat the initiative, which would have dealt a devastating setback to library services in Utah.

State Library Activities. Utah State Library renamed their newsletter "Directions for Utah Libraries." The attractive graphics and design have increased the appeal of this important resource to librarians in Utah. The Third Annual Utah Public Library Institute for Training (Project UPLIFT) was held on the University of Utah campus in August. Dr. Brenda Branyon-Broadbent, Associate Professor of Instructional Technology at Utah State University, taught the core course. Mary Bushing of Montana State Library conducted a course on collection development. Mary Jackson, the Children's Consultant for the Nebraska State Library Commission, presented a series of workshops on library services to children.

The UPLIFT-T (Utah Public Library Institute for Trustee Training) sponsored a meeting for all Utah public library trustees and library directors August 26 at the University of Utah. State Library Director Amy Owen gave a progress report on the Upgrade Process, Utah's standards and the public library development grants package. Communication and public relations was the subject of a panel discussion, and the featured luncheon speaker was Jon Memmott of Taxpayers for Utah, who discussed the tax limitation initiatives on the November ballot and their possible effect on Utah's libraries.

The Project Literacy/Utah public relations campaign occurred during January, February, and March. Advisors for the campaign included Governor Norman Bangeter, Senator Orrin Hatch, Congressman Wayne Owens, U.S. Secretary of Education T. H. Bell, and State Superintendent of Public Instruction James Moss. The purpose of the campaign was to heighten public awareness of literacy and to enhance the work of literary organizations in Utah and ACCESS, the Governor's Commission on Literacy.

Public Libraries. The Nephi Public Libraries literacy program is in its second year of operation.

Salt Lake Public Library System has received a tax hike of $246,900 yearly in order to improve libraries within the next 10 years. It was also chosen by the national RIF (Reading is FUNdamental) to host a workshop designed to teach people who work with children how to instill in them a love of books and reading. Spencer Shaw, nationally popular storyteller, was the featured speaker.

Palmer DePaulis, mayor of Salt Lake City, signed a proclamation declaring September "Library Card Sign-Up Month" in Salt Lake City. The city library system participated in the national library card sign-up campaign sponsored by the American Library Association and the National Commission on Libraries and Information Science.

Logan Public Library is one of 25 public libraries selected to participate in the "Voices and Visions" project funded by ALA and NEH. Based on the "Let's Talk About it" reading and discussion project, "Voices and Visions" incorporates video programs from the series on American poetry by the same name. From March to June, libraries will host an eight-to 10-week series of poetry discussion programs.

As a result of a unique agreement between American Fork and Highland residents, library circulation by Highland patrons increased more than 200 percent and three-fourths of Highland households have active library cards. American Fork moved to a $20 non-resident fee, causing Highland residents to revolt and demand some kind of city block payment. The American Fork Library Board presented a proposal to the Highland City Council that required allowing Highland to pay $3 per capita in 1988 for library services. Both cities were pleased with the results: as Highland citizens obtain library services more cheaply than they could have on their own, and American Fork welcomes additional revenue.

Utah State University announced plans to hold courses in several outlying communities. Price City Library and Uintah County Library in Vernal are the two pilot sites in Utah for the Kellogg-funded courses.

Academic and Special Libraries. In celebration of the University of Utah Marriott Library's first 20 years, the Friends of the University of Utah Libraries declared 1988-1989 the "Year of the Library." Sunday afternoon "Books and Authors" series featured outstanding Utah authors from October 1988 through April, 1989. Other special events include films, panel discussions and social gatherings. Exhibits planned highlight the Marriott's unique holdings, which illustrate the history of the library, the University, Utah arts, and Salt Lake City architecture.

The Marriott Library also received a $41,340 grant from the U.S. Department of Education to make social science data files more accessible to researchers at 300 U.S. and foreign universities. The project involves cataloging data to enable social scientists to use existing information to test new hypotheses and draw new conclusions.

A few changes in the automation program occurred at the Harold B. Lee Library at Brigham Young University. The library installed a number of CD-ROM products including eight from Wilsondisc, ERIC from SilverPlatter, InfroTrac II, Books in Print Plus, Ulrich's Plus, Dissertation Abstracts, Newspaper Abstracts, ABI/Inform, and Periodical Abstracts. Keyword and boolean logic capabilities were added to the patron-access catalog at the Lee Library.

The Genealogical Library in Salt Lake was renamed The Family History Library of The Church of Jesus Christ of Latter-day Saints. The number of patrons increased by 30 percent to approximately 2,700 per day, possibly due to the availability of a few new automated research tools such as the Family History Library Catalog on compact disk, the U.S. International Genealogical Index online and the online evaluation model of the Ancestral File. A series of research outlines for the United States was completed by the staff of the Family History Library.

Buildings. Groundbreaking ceremonies for the Provo City Library was held on April 18th. The cost of the entire project is estimated at $1,500,000.

Ribbon-cutting ceremonies at the new Pleasant Grove Library and Senior Citizen Center took place June 6. The groundbreaking for Lehi's new library occurred on June 25. LSCA Title II funds are being used to convert the old senior/junior high building to a spacious new library facility.

Networks and Interlibrary Cooperation. Provo City Library and Provo School District have formed a library computer network, Project IMPACT, one of two programs of this type in the nation. Provo City Library and the media centers at Provo and Timpview High, Farrar and Dixon Middle, and Sunset View and Westridge Elementary Schools share an online common database for interlibrary loan at no charge for students. The cost of the project has been minimal because the computer hardware and software was funded by grants from the Utah State Board of Education, the Ultimate Corporation, and the Eyring Research Foundation. Other schools in the district will be added to the network as funding allows.

Awards and Grants. The Utah Endowment for the Humanities (Salt Lake City) and The Library of America (New York) made a joint effort to help Utah public libraries with limited resources acquire The Library of America series, a definitive collection of America's greatest writers. The Andrew W. Mellon Foundation, The Utah State Library, and the Utah Library Association matched the grant.

The Division of State History received a grant of $116,000 from National Historical Publications and the Research Commission to fund the Utah Historical Records Information System project to survey historical records repositories in the state and enter their descriptions into RLIN. The project, beginning July 1, was a joint effort of the Historical Society and State Archives of Utah.

People. Eileen Longsworth was appointed Director of the Salt Lake County System. Donna Slusher, Murray Library Director, and Mary Petterson, Assistant Director, Weber County Library, retired in 1988.

NATHAN M. SMITH

VERMONT

The General Assembly enacted a reform of the Open Meeting Law to clarify the conduct of meetings of local boards and commissions, including boards of trustees of public libraries.

The Vermont Board of Libraries approved the draft of a planning document, "Envisioning Excellence: Planning the Library's Future," based on the premise that good library service is an evolutionary, community-based process.

The Department of Libraries is now planning on how to provide community and state information to library users by bringing local libraries online with the statewide automated library system over the next five years.

State Association. A major accomplishment during 1988 was the formulation of revisions to Vermont's Public Library Laws. Membership approved new Annual Conference fiscal and planning policies. Three bylaw changes were approved: the Personnel Com-

Vermont Library Association (founded 1892)

Membership: 362; *annual budget:* $6,625.

President: Michael Price, Bennington Free Library, Bennington (January 1988–January 1989).

Vice-President/President-elect: Penny Pillsbury, Brownell Library, 6 Lincoln Street, Essex Junction 05452.

Secretary: Claire Buckley, South Burlington.

Annual meeting: May 24–25, 1989, Poultney.

Publication: VLA News (10 issues a year).

Vermont Department of Libraries

Patricia E. Klinck, State Librarian
Montpelier 05602

School Library Media Consultant

Leda Schubert
State Department of Education
Montpelier 05602

---

mittee was made a standing committee; the immediate past-president becomes the chair of the Government Relations Committee; the Executive Board may appoint a Section Chair (Public Library Section, etc.) to the office of Vice-President/President-Elect should a vacancy occur. Membership also approved a new minimum salary ($19,500) for beginning librarians.

The National Library Week Committee organized a Legislative Day to facilitate information exchange between librarians and their state representatives. About 416 people attended the Annual Conference at Norwich University. The 1988 district meetings centered on intellectual freedom, legal issues, service to unaffiliated students, personnel, and service issues. Each section held successful fall meetings.

Registration information revealed that 84 members of the Vermont Library Association (VLA) earn less than $5,000 a year; 51 earn between $5,000 and $10,000; 38 earn between $10,001 and $15,000; 45 between $15,001 and $20,000; 42 between $20,001 and $25,000; 42 more than $25,001.

State Library. The Department of Libraries (DOL) received a 12.5 percent increase in its FY 88/89 budget. All five regional libraries automated their circulation system and 45 public libraries participated in DOL's touring artists program. Summer activities for children centered around the theme "Summer Feast" with programs devoted to edible plants, nature walks, gardening. DOL's tenth annual film festival was scheduled in two locations in 1988 and attendance justified this first dual program. Beginning this year, DOL began to purchase more videos than film.

Public Libraries. Of the 80 public libraries that met the Minimum Standards for Vermont Public Libraries in 1988, the Rutland and Burlington libraries met all of the criteria for the first time in a number of years. Ten libraries participated in the "Silver Editions," a humanities reading/discussion program developed by the National Council on the Aging and funded by the National Endowment for the Humanities. Vermont is one of six states to offer these programs.

School Libraries and Media Centers. School libraries continue many resource-sharing network activities, but lack of funding is preventing many of them from full participation. Only 50 of the state's 450 schools are contributing to the Union Catalog and fully participating in the Vermont Interlibrary Loan Network. DOL is not in a position to fund terminal placement and/or telecommunication charges.

Academic Libraries. The University of Vermont is participating in a national program sponsored by the U.S. National Agricultural Library to locate, catalog, digitize and index documents important to agriculture. The University Library has acquired over 700 Canadian and provincial documents (70,000 pages) concerning acid rain. Norwich University has completed plans for a new library building but no construction date has been set. Increased use of public and organized college libraries by nonaffiliated college students continues to pose service problems for many of the state's underfunded and understaffed libraries.

Building Programs. The DOL moved from its former location within the Supreme Court Building to a new structure attached to the Vermont Historical Society Library and the museum. The Vermont Board of Libraries awarded LSCA, Title II grants to public libraries in Colchester and Burlington. Montpelier's Kellogg–Hubbard Library remodeled its facility after a fire caused by an arsonist.

Networks and Interlibrary Cooperation. The Union Catalog continues to be the basis for the statewide resource-sharing network; 80 percent of the requests generated in Vermont are filled in-state. The number of ILL requests has risen to more than 100,000 a year. Only one public library has converted its collection to standardized machine-readable format, and DOL is offering challenge grants to public libraries to encourage conversion.

Intellectual Freedom. As Chair of the Senate Judiciary Committee, Vermont's Senator Leahy has been a key figure in hearings on both the FBI library program and the Child Protection and Obscenity Enforcement Act of 1988 (S.2033, H.R. 3889). Another Vermont figure, American Booksellers Association President Ed Morrow has testified strongly against the vague definitions and the penalties in the Act.

Professional Interests. The Vermont Reading Project has for three years, continued to coordinate high-quality adult reading discussion programs. To date, 16,000 people have taken part in 33 different reading programs offered at 116 public libraries. This year, residents of state hospitals and correctional facilities participated in a reading project entitled "Survivors." Fourteen public libraries conducted a series for adult new readers funded by the Vermont Council on the Humanities. Patricia MacLachlan, the Newbery Award-Winning author of *Sarah Plain and Tall*, presented the 11th annual Smith Lecture sponsored by DOL. A Task Force on Children's Services organized by DOL has prepared "Recommendations for Public Library Service to Children in Vermont," an update of a 1979 publication.

Awards. DOL's statewide automation project received one of ten Innovations in State and Local Government Awards Programs grants sponsored by the Ford Foundation and the John F. Kennedy School of Government, Harvard University. The grant was for $100,000. Burlington's Fletcher Free Library received large-print books valued at $300 from G.K. Hall Publishers. The St. Johnsbury Athenaeum received a grant from the State Division of Historic Preservation. DOL awarded Elva Sophronia Smith grants to Greensboro Free, Hartland Public, Cobleigh Library in Lyndonville, and the Orwell Free Library to enable them to improve service to children.

Appointments. In 1988, DOL arranged its first shared position: Deanna Held and Amy Howlett are each responsible for administering the Southeast Regional Library for half a year. Margene F. Fennell joined the DOL staff to direct operations at the Northwest Regional Library in Georgia, Vermont. Linda McSweeney resigned her position in DOL's Reference Services Unit to become library director at the Vermont Technical College. Katherine Reichert is the new library director at Green Mountain College.

Deaths. George Lindsey, a staff member of Brattleboro's Brooks Memorial Library and an active member of VLA, died May 24.

MILTON H. CROUCH

VIRGINIA

Virginia Library Association (founded 1905)

Membership: 1,300; *annual budget:* $85,151.

President: Patricia M. Paine, Deputy Director, Fairfax County Public Library, Fairfax 22030

President-elect: Wendell Barbour, Director, Captain John Smith Library, Christopher Newport College, Newport News 23606.

Executive Director: Deborah Trocchi, 80 S. Early St., Alexandria 22304.

Annual meeting: November 16–18, 1989, Hot Springs.

Publications: Virginia Librarian (quarterly). VLA Newsletter (10 times a year).

Virginia State Library

Ella Gaines Yates, State Librarian
11th Street at Capitol Square
Richmond 23219

Supervisor of School Libraries & Information Technology

Gloria K. Barber
101 North 14th Street
James Madison Building, 18th Floor
Richmond 23216

State Association Report. The Virginia Library Association and the Southeastern Library Association held a joint conference in Norfolk, Virginia, October 26–29, which attracted more than 1,800 librarians, trustees, friends, writers and exhibitors. The conference theme was "The Creative Spirit: Writers, Words, Readers." Authors Pat Conroy, Henry Taylor, Russell Freedman and Rita Mae Brown spoke of their craft and read from their works.

Programming throughout the conference was varied. Jesse L. White, Jr., Executive Director of the Southern Growth Policies Board, and Howard F. McGinn, Jr., Assistant State Librarian, North Carolina Department of Resources, presented a program on the analysis of demographic megatrends affecting the southeastern states and the effect these trends have on libraries. Other programs included "The Future of the Federal Document Depository System," sponsored by the VLA Public Documents Forum, "Needs of Researchers in a Technological Age," "Hands on Mentoring: Myths and Realities," and "Poetry Alive."

Russell Freedman, author of *Lincoln, A Photobiography*, received the Jefferson Cup Award, presented by the Children/Young Adult Round Table of VLA to the author of the best book in the field of U.S. history written especially for young people. The VLA College and University Section and Yankee Book Peddler awarded Katherine McKenzie of the College of William and Mary and Julie Still of the University of Richmond, the Professional Development Grant to assist them in attending the annual conference. Virginia Kelly of Pulaski County and Sara V. Kyle of Carroll County shared the VLA Trustee Award which recognizes distinguished service to libraries or a library in the state. The Friends of the Handley Library in Winchester received the VLA Friends Award. Teresa Bernier received the Junior Members Round Table Grassroots Award which is funded by Baker and Taylor.

The Association continued to progress towards the goals of the strategic plan that had been developed in the previous year. A major reorganization of the Association was proposed and passed by the membership. A continuing education committee was also established to "provide continuing educational opportunities for library personnel and support groups."

The FBI Awareness program caused concern among Virginia librarians. The VLA Council voted unanimous support of the VLA Intellectual Freedom Committee's resolution decrying the FBI's program. A letter of support to ALA's Intellectual Freedom Committee stated VLA's opposition based on the grounds that it (the FBI program) threatens, among other things, the First Amendment right to receive information.

The Virginia Library Association acted as a non-partisan intermediary in facilitating a meeting between the staff of the State Library and public library directors in the state. Among the major concerns of those who called for the meeting was a lack of communication with the State Librarian, Ella Gaines Yates, and curtailment of support services to small and medium-sized public libraries because of the high percentage of career-level employee turnover in the State Library. After the meeting, a statewide Public Library Directors Association was formed.

1988 VEMA Conference. "Literacy and Technology . . . Preparing for the 21st Century" was the theme of the 14th Annual Virginia Educational Media Association Conference. Held in Virginia Beach on November 3-5, conference speakers included Ida Hill, State Department of Education; James Mecklenberger, Director of the Institute for the Transfer of Technology to Education; and authors, Elliott Engel and Robert Newton Peck.

VEMA also sponsored an annual Leadership Conference in June at Hampton University in Hampton, Virginia. "More Than Survival Skills" was attended by 65 members, spouses, and friends of VEMA. The keynote speaker was James Mecklenberger. Vera Williams of Longwood College addressed "Valuing Self: Where a Leader Begins," and Mary Miller of the Virginia Cooperative Extension Service spoke on "High Tech and a Kellogg Grant—A Community View."

Networking. The Virginia State Library and Archives requested $2,700,000 for networking in its budget for 1988-90 that was to go before the General Assembly for approval.

The State Networking Users Advisory Board (SNUAB) organized an ad hoc networking committee to aid in obtaining a grassroots consensus about networking priorities in Virginia. To this end, a Networking Conference sponsored by SNUAB, the Virginia Library Association, the Virginia State Library and Archives, the Virginia Educational Media Association, and the Virginia Chapter of the Special Libraries Association was held in Lynchburg on September 16. Speakers for the conference, "Networking: What's In It for Me?" were Louella V. Wetherbee, Executive Director of Amigos Bibliographic Council, Inc., and Ella Gaines Yates, State Librarian, who was the luncheon speaker.

The Virginia Library Networking Task Force, appointed by Virginia Secretary of Education Dr. Donald J. Finley, began to identify projects that [would] address the issues of access to the library resources of the Commonwealth and the equitable distribution of responsibilities and costs of that access." Major project proposals are (1) a statewide bibliographic database; (2) a statewide union list of serials, maintained in electronic format and retrievable either electronically or in hard copy; (3) a backup reference and referral service provided by one or more research libraries within the Commonwealth; (4) telefacsimile transmission capability by each library in the state to send and receive information; (5) a formal interlibrary Loan Code to regulate and coordinate the sharing of resources among network members; (6) a document delivery system for the movement among network members of materials that cannot be transmitted electronically; (7) reimbursement of costs incurred by net lenders of materials; (8) a telecommunications network to which all network member libraries have access; and (9) identification and support of major resource collections.

Literacy. The Virginia State Library and Archives in association with The Virginia Literacy Foundation and The Office of State Adult Literacy sponsored a conference, "Building a More Literate Virginia," in Richmond on September 12 to 13. The keynote address was given by Ernest Boyer, President of the Carnegie Foundation for the Advancement of Teaching. Boyer called the literacy campaign "a crusade to affirm the dignity of every human being," and urged the more than 400 attendees towards "increased and earlier efforts to get to the roots of illiteracy." Dan M. Lacy, vice president of the Business Council for Effective Literacy, told conference participants that "the health of our economy and society as a whole" depends on conquering illiteracy.

Seven libraries in the Commonwealth received LSCA Title VI grants to support local literacy programs. Grants ranged in size from $6,544 to $25,000. Libraries receiving support were Fauquier County Public Library (Warrenton); Jefferson-Madison Regional Library (Charlottesville), Lonesome Pino Regional Library (Wise); Newport News Public Library System; Rappahannock County Library (Washington); Washington County Public Library (Abingdon); and the Virginia State Library and Archives (for support of the second statewide literacy conference). The Virginia Library Board awarded $300,403 to 17 libraries for literacy programs under Title I.

State Library and Archives. Lisa Fox, Preservation Director, SOLINET, studied the condition of the Virginia State Library and Archives Building in regard to preservation for the benefit of architects and the state's General Services Division of Buildings and Grounds. In the first phase of her report, Fox stated that the building was not only failing to preserve the library's collections but in fact was contributing to further deterioration due to uncontrolled temperature and humidity. Steps were being taken to rectify the situation.

The State Library received a $44,851,197 appropriation from the state legislature for a two-year period covering 1988-90. This is a 24 percent increase over the 1986-88 appropriation. Of that amount, $750,000 was set aside for a pre-planning study for a new library building. The present facility is 280,000 square feet and is inadequate to accommodate the growing service needs of Virginia.

The summer reading program was coordinated by the State Library with Garfield the Cat as the "centerpiece" for the program. Posters, bookmarks, miniature Garfield pencil toppers, reading logs, and certificates were provided those libraries that chose to participate and a series of workshops were held in April to share program ideas.

Cooperative Programs. Two telefax projects were awarded Title III funding by the Virginia State Library Board. One, submitted by the Virginia State Library and Archives, included ten public and academic libraries throughout the state. The other, submitted by the Lynchburg Area Libraries Consortium, included six public libraries and community college and private academic libraries in the area. These projects were merged and focus on linking libraries through the combination of telefacsimile machines, microcomputers, and CD-ROM readers. The proposed configuration would allow the transmission of data, documents, pictures, and graphics from fax to fax, PC to PC, and CD-ROM to PC to FAX.

The Lexington Area Conservation Cooperative (LEXACON) completed a three-phase library project which involved six libraries in Lexington. The project provided the libraries of Washington and Lee University's undergraduate and law schools, George C. Marshall, Virginia Military Institute, Rockbridge Regional, and Southern Seminary with basic information concerning preservation of their respective circulating collections. Phase I focused on building surveys; phase II was a workshop on book repair; and phase III was the creation of a disaster plan.

The Southside Virginia Library Network under the leadership of the staff of Lancaster Library, Longwood College, received an LSCA grant to provide hardware and some software for high school libraries and some public libraries in 12 counties in Southside Virginia to interface with Longwood's VTLS system. Twenty-five libraries can now dial into Longwood's online system.

Certification. The 1988 Virginia General Assembly enacted legislation to take effect January 1989 (House Bill 438) to exempt college and university librarians from certification and licensure and to transfer the certification of Virginia public librarians from the Department of Commerce to the Virginia State Library Board. This followed a year long debate on licensing and certification in which the Virginia Library Association was heavily involved in trying to determine the opinions of librarians from all types of libraries around the state.

Buildings. Three Title II LSCA grants were awarded by the Virginia State Library Board for building projects. The Central Rappahannock Regional Library received $200,000 for renovations; the Pittsylvania Public Library also received $200,000 for renovations; and the Pulaski County Library received $76,192 for construction of a branch in Dublin.

Awards. James R. Retting, Assistant University Librarian for Reference and Information Services, the College of William and Mary, received the Isadore Gilbert Mudge Citation for distinguished contributions to reference librarianship. (See Rettig's biography in this volume.)

Nancy Anne Hill, Head Cataloger, Hollins College, was chosen to represent the American Library Association and U.S. librarianship as a Library/Book Fellow. Hill will assist Sanaa University in North Yemen with the development of the library's technical services departments by designing more efficient procedures, cleaning up cataloging backlogs, and coordinating the work of the departments within technical services.

Appointments. Appointed to head public libraries around the state were Brian Armentrout, Appomattox County Public Library; Sarah Crigler, Madison County Library; Bradley Green, Wythe-Grayson Regional Library; David Hulvey, Farmville-Prince Edward Community Library; William A. Muller, Bristol Public Library; Donna Selle, Jefferson-Madison Regional Library; and Lillie Tuttle, Fluvanna County Library.

Deaths. Donald R. Haynes, State Librarian for 14 years, died on January 30 in Richmond after a brief illness. Haynes was Director of the Virginia Historical Society at the time of his death. Richard P. Gravely, Jr., a member of the Virginia State Library Board since 1986, died on October 4. Gravely was a native of Martinsville, Virginia.

SANDRA WOOD HEINEMANN

WASHINGTON

State Library Activities. The State Library continued to provide high-quality library services within increasingly limited fiscal resources by utilizing various automated systems and developing cooperative arrangements. The Washington State Library (WSL) pioneered the concept of shared remote database subscriptions in its innovative approach to the federal legislative database LEGISLATE. Through cooperative negotiations with branch agency libraries and the vendor, a subscription is shared for these services with training coordinated by WSL.

In 1988, WSL maximized the use of the CD-ROM version of the WLN bibliographic database by placing it in the major public service departments of reference and government publications and by providing it for the Cataloging Department in Technical Services. Microcomputers equipped with word processing and spreadsheet software were placed in each major operating department, and a LAN was installed with additional graphics software in the administrative area.

The Serials Department was equipped with a PC-based automated serials control system. As the database of serials is built, labor intensive activities such as claiming and check in are being automated. The 5,000 title serials

Washington Library Association (founded 1905)

Membership: 1,250; *annual budget:* $100,000.

President: Thomas R. Mayer, Sno-Isle Regional Library, Marysville 98270 (August 1987–August 1989).

First Vice-President/President-elect: Mary M. Carr, Crosby Library, Gonzaga University, E. 502 Boone Ave., Spokane 99258.

Corresponding Secretary: Marjorie Burns, Bellevue.

Annual meeting: April 26–29, 1989, Seattle; April 18–22, 1990, Pasco.

Publications: Highlights (5 times per year); *Washington Library Advocate* (4 times per year); *ALKI*, library journal.

Washington State Library

Nancy Zussy, State Librarian
AJ-11
Olympia 98504

Superintendent of Public Instruction

Bobbie J. Patterson
Coordinator of Information Center Resource
Office of Superintendent of Public Instruction
FG-11
Olympia 98504

database will provide increasingly useful information for collection development, as well as collection management decision making.

In 1988, WSL made a significant effort to enhance its services and collections through establishment in 1987 of The Friends of the Washington State Library and by application for private and federal grants. By 1988 the Friends Board of Directors had been appointed.

Private and federal grants made several major projects possible in 1988: a major grant of $265,762 from the National Endowment for the Humanities to complete the microfilming portion of the Washington Newspaper Project. Several Washington foundations contributed to raising matching funds from the private sector. In 1987, administration of a major private grant for $748,000 from the Kellogg Foundation to establish and administer Education Job Information Centers in four public libraries in Washington was given to the State Library. In 1988, the second year of the three-year project, communities experiencing high unemployment and rapidly changing economic conditions used the centers extensively. The four centers established to date are in Raymond (the Timberland Regional Library District), Spokane, Everett, and Longview.

In recognition of Washington's Centennial year, 1988–89, the State Library received a $35,000 grant to support "Washington's Libraries Celebrate the Centennial." The award supports writing and publication of an annotated bibliography of Washington authors who have won the Governor's Writers Award since 1967 and a week of activities to recognize Washington's authors planned for May 14–19, 1989.

In order to increase access to its collections, the State Library has embarked on an ambitious project to finish retrospective conversion of its circulating collections in 1988. By year's end 95 percent of the circulating collection was in the database. Collection assessment, weeding, and inventory are an integral part of the retrospective conversion project. WSL also increased access to resources beyond the Pacific Northwest. In January 1988, when the University of Washington ended a Resource Sharing program which had provided interlibrary loan referral and verification services for libraries throughout the region, it became necessary for WSL to access collections beyond its region. Because membership in the Northwest Group Access Project provided that access, WSL became a referral library for libraries in Washington that had joined the Northwest Group Access project thereby permitting search of the OCLC database.

Grant funds were received to support several programing efforts for the institutionalized population in 1988. Eight program sessions were held at three state residential institutions. WSL also received a Title VI literacy grant to plan and develop peer literacy tutoring at the Western State Reformatory. The Department of Corrections and the Department of Health and Human Services also contributed support to this project called "Read to Succeed." The project developed tutoring skills among inmates, who then taught literacy skills to their peers. The program was so successful that the institution continued to support the program after the grant ended.

Goals, objectives, and activities for the next five-year cycle of LSCA funds were developed and filed as the WSL Long-Range Plan for 1989–93. The plan's development required effort from the Washington State Advisory Council on Libraries, the Library Planning and Development staff, and the Public and Technical Services State Library staff.

The Washington State Library received a $25,000 LSCA Title VI grant from the U.S. Department of Education for a special project titled "Literacy Assessment for Washington State." The goal of the project is to develop a responsive and appropriate program of adult literacy state library service.

WSL instituted a multi-year cooperative collection development project funded by LSCA Title III whose goal is to increase the access to information resources throughout the state and region for Washington's citizens.

Public Libraries. The percentage of the state served by public libraries increased from 96.47 percent to 96.74 percent in 1987. Library districts spent $14.90 per capital while municipal libraries spent $25.63 per capita and 8.53 items were circulated per capita.

The state legislature again provided only "band-aid" measures to cope with the adverse effect of prorationing when the sum of all junior taxing districts' levies exceeds $9.15 per $1,000 assessed valuation of property. During the legislative session, House Bill 886, which would have repealed the library exemption from the Moral Nuisance Law and would have revised the definition of materials which are "harmful to minors," was introduced. Although the bill was killed in committee, public libraries were concerned about its introduction in 1989.

The Spokane County Library District won a ten-year bond issue election by 64.13 percent. Provided was $4,975,000 to be used for the expansion of two buildings, construction of one new 5,000 square foot building, consolidation of support services into a single building, expansion of the computer system, and purchase of library materials. The King County Library System's $67,000,000 bond issue passed with 64.4 percent approval. The system will build new libraries in Woodinville, Pine Lake, Upper Snoqualmie Valley, Shoreline, Carnation/Duvall, two library buildings each in East Kent and Federal Way. Also planned are libraries in Algona/Pacific, Juanita, Overlake/Crossroads and Richmond Beach and a new service center for the district. The bonds will also enable expansion and renovation of the existing libraries in Bellevue, where major changes are planned, and in Newport Way, Redmond, Maple Valley, and Burien. Expansion is also planned for the Traveling Library Center, which serves retirement and nursing homes, community centers, and children's day-care facilities. The building program will cost an average of $.13 per $1,000 assessed valuation a year for 20 years. North Bend residents voted on March 15 to annex to the King County Library System.

The Hoquiam branch of the Timberland Regional Library System building bond issue for $1,900,000 for renovation and expansion of its 1911 Carnegie building passed with 68 percent approval. Three Washington public libraries received LSCA Title VI awards from the U.S. Department of Education for literacy programs: Asotin County Library, Kitsap Regional Library, and Pend Oreille County Library. Five public libraries continued to provide Education and Job Information Centers under grants from the Washington State Library funded with a Kellogg Foundation grant: Longview Public Library, Everett Public Library, Raymond Branch of the Timberland Regional Library, Spokane Public Library, and the Pend Oreille County Library.

Two workshops for public library trustees were sponsored by the Washington State Library and the Washington Library Friends and Trustees Association: the role of the board chair in the management of the Board and relationships with the library director, and the role of the board chair in the management of board meetings. A third workshop, Library Leadership (WILL), in Yakima in October focused on roles, funding, and marketing, and was attended by more than 130 trustees and staff.

School Libraries and Media Centers. The Washington Library Media Association (WLMA) combined efforts with the Oregon Education Media Association to present a joint conference, "A Bridge to New Ideas." More than 1,300 people attended the two-day event in Portland, Oregon in October. Sessions included investigation of new technologies, personal growth, information skills instruction, and a variety of literature-related events.

A pre-conference workshop and several conference sessions focused on the 1987 Washington *Information Skills Curriculum Guide*, which offered a fresh approach to instruction related use of information resources and it moved beyond the limits of the library calling for a partnership with teachers in this important area of learning.

Information Power: Guidelines for School Library Media Programs (AECT/ALA, 1988) parallels closely some of the work already in progress in the state. In response to these new guidelines and a need to incorporate new technologies, WLMA and the State Superintendent of Public Instruction office began revising the 1981 state guidelines for library media programs. The update committee hopes to complete its work by fall 1989.

A change in certification requirements for library media specialists in 1987 and retirement of a growing number of people in the field caused increased enrollment in school library media classes. While the number of institutions in the state offering such courses diminished to five during the past 15 years, the new growth coupled with improving continuing education efforts bring hope for the future.

In October, a statewide task force published a report calling for major developmental efforts in providing instructional opportunities through telecommunications technologies. Separate groups address K-12 and higher education needs and propose joint uses of major facilities in a statewide network.

Academic Libraries. The 1988 Summer Institute on East Asian Librarianship was held at the University of Washington, July 18–29. Joining members of the University of Washington faculty were people from 27 institutions in the U.S. and East Asia. The Washington State Chapter of the Association of College and Research Libraries held a joint fall conference on "Scholarship for Academic Libraries" on October 15–16.

University libraries continued to participate in international development projects by sending librarians to work with project teams in such countries as Yemen, Malawai, and India. In a joint project with the University of Washington, The Evergreen State College Library hosted a series of activities on "Connections: Linking Library Instruction to Innovations in Undergraduate Education." The project was funded by the Washington Center for the Improvement of Undergraduate Education.

Western Washington University completed a $35,000 renovation of its science reference and stack area; also funded was $250,000 for compact shelving. The University of Washington Libraries (UWL) received $10,000,000 from Paul Allen, co-founder of Microsoft Corporation. In recognition of the gift, the new library addition currently under construction will be named in honor of Allen's deceased father, Kenneth S. Allen. The University of Washington also continued installation of a Geac Library Information System with a database with 1,300,000 unique titles in full MARC format. UWL was also awarded a U.S. Department of Education Title II-C grant of $179,378 to catalog maps of the Pacific Northwest held in its libraries and in those of the University of Oregon Library. The grant will enable original cataloging on OCLC for 6,200 map titles.

Building Programs. The Cheney Library of Spokane County Library District broke ground for its new building in late February; some 360 people surrounded the library site, celebrating the community effort to raise $610,000 towards a new building; the new library was dedicated in November. The Des Moines Public Library, a branch of the King County Library System, opened its new $1,300,000 building in October. The George B. Brain Education Library was formally dedicated during ceremonies in Cleveland Hall at Washington State University. The Mountlake Terrace Public Library, a branch of the Sno-Isle Regional Library, celebrated its ground breaking in November 1987 and opened the doors to the new library in August 1988.

The Everett Community College Library in the multimillion dollar John Terry Library Media Center and the Gary Parks Student Union opened on the first day of fall quarter classes—just 19 months after the tragic President's Day arson fire that destroyed the library and took the life of Everett fire fighter Gary Parks. Tacoma Public Library's remodeled and enlarged McCormick Branch and its Moore Branch opened in September. Seattle Public Library's renovated Fremont and Douglass-Truth branches were reopened in 1988. The expanded and renovated Winlock Public Library, a branch of the Timberland Regional Library, was dedicated on June 18. The grand opening of the new Coupeville Public Library, a branch of the Sno-Isle Regional Library, was held in June; the new construction of 2,000 square feet included plans for expansion.

Networks and Interlibrary Cooperation. The Western Library Network (WLN) again sought private, non-profit status to increase flexibility in making sound business decisions, to broaden authority over and responsibility for WLN by extending governance to all state participants in the Network, and to open more avenues for long-range funding beyond user fees and charges. Approval of change in status will be sought in the 1989 session of the state legislature. The end of fiscal year 1987 marked the first anniversary of WLN's online Interlibrary Loan Subsystem (ILL), a state-of-the-art module to which almost all WLN members have signed up.

Intellectual Freedom. Efforts in 1988 to remove materials from school and public libraries prompted active and effective response from librarians, teachers, parents, students, and others concerned with supporting intellectual freedom principles. Materials challenged in Washington school and public libraries during 1988 included *Annie On My Mind*, by Nancy Garden; *The Girl*, by Robbie Branscum; *Uncle Shelby's ABZ Book: A Primer for Tender Young Minds*, by Shel Silverstein; *Breakthrough—Emerging New Thinking*, by Elena Loshchenkova and Harold Sandler; *Say: What You Should Know About Homosexuality*, by Morton Hunt; *Wilted*, by Paul Kropp; *The Shining*, by Stephen King; and *How We Are Born; How We Grow*, by Joe Kaufman. Thanks to concerted action by individuals concerned with protecting first amendment freedoms, most challenged materials were successfully retained on library shelves.

Librarians statewide united to oppose legislation that would have rewritten state obscenity laws to repeal the long-standing exemption for libraries. Definitions of harmful materials in all versions of the legislation were so broad and ambiguous that they could apply to numerous materials in public library collections. Special credit goes to a small group of legislators who worked hard and effectively to protect library interests. In another legislative matter, the Washington Library Association jointed the American Civil Liberties Union and booksellers as plaintiffs in a suit to block enforcement of a new anti-pornography ordinance that was overwhelmingly approved by voters in Bellingham, Washington.

The Intellectual Freedom Committee of the Washington Library Association surveyed public libraries on current videotape collections and circulation policies. The survey revealed numerous policy variations and several apparent departures from principles enumerated in the Library Bill of Rights. Results of the survey prompted the Association to adopt "Guidelines for the Use and Circulation of Videotapes in Washington State Libraries." WLA membership also adopted a resolution on

"Intellectual Freedom and Apartheid," which opposes economic policies directed against South Africa that interfere with the flow of information between the two countries.

Awards. The Certificate of Achievement for Excellence in Financial Reporting was awarded to the Fort Vancouver Regional Library by the Government Finance Officers Association of the United States and Canada (GFOA) for the Library's Comprehensive Annual Financial Report for Year Ended December 31, 1986. Fort Vancouver Regional Library is the first library in the nation to receive the certificate. The Documents Department in the Central Washington University Library (CWU) received a Government Printing Office "Certificate of Excellence" award after official inspection by a representative of the Superintendent of Documents Office in Washington, D.C. This is the first time the CWU Library had received the prestigious award, and it is also the only one in the Pacific Northwest in the last ten years to be so honored. ALA Executive Board member Lucille C. Thomas announced Spencer Shaw's Honorary Membership with the following words "For his active and creative career as a children's librarian, storyteller par excellence, lecturer, library educator and for his service to the American Library Association, we hereby confer upon Spencer Shaw the highest ALA Award, Honorary Membership." (For more on Shaw, see his biography in this volume.) Rodney Askelson, Librarian for the Washington State Library Institutional Library Services Program Northwest Module, received the Washington Correctional Association's 1988 Academic Achievement Award. He was cited for "getting results that make a difference in his fellow humans' lives, and for his contribution to furthering the goals of corrections." Susan Madden, King County Library System Coordinator of Young Adult Services, was honored as a "Woman of Achievement" during the 57th Matrix Table Awards Dinner sponsored by Women in Communications, Inc. Kathryn Trump, a student at the University of Washington Graduate School of Library and Information Science, was awarded the Washington Library Association scholarship for academic year 1988-89. Her specialty is technical services.

Appointments. Richard Ostrander, Director of the Yakima Valley Regional Library, was appointed to the Washington State Library Commission. Bruce Zeigman was appointed Executive Director of the Western Library Network. Sarah Pederson, who had been Acting Director, was appointed Director at the Evergreen State College. Elizabeth Stroup was appointed Seattle City Librarian. Stroup, a native of the Pacific Northwest, most recently held the position of Director of General Reference at the Library of Congress. Sharon Hammer from Marin County Library (California) was appointed as the Library Director of the Fort Vancouver Regional Library; she is a graduate of the University of Washington and has previous library experience with the Seattle Public Library, and the King County Library System. Victoria Parker was named Director of the Orcas Island Library District, and Shirley Hake was named Director of the Lopez Island Library District. Sherrylynne Fuller, previously Director of the University of Minnesota Biomedical Library, became Director of the University of Washington Health Sciences Library and Information Center and the Director of the Pacific Northwest Regional Health Sciences Library Service. Gerald Oppenheimer was appointed Director Emeritus, University of Washington Health Sciences Library and Information Center.

Deaths. Alta Grim, a former State Librarian, passed away in Olympia in 1988. Thelma Jonish, who was Director of the Walla Walla County Rural Library District from 1977 to 1985, died in Walla Walla in May, 1988.

MARGARET CHISHOLM

WEST VIRGINIA

West Virginia Library Association (founded 1914)

Membership: 664; *annual budget:* $48,608.

President: Rebecca D'Annunzio, Liberty High School Library, Clarksburg (December 1988–November 1989).

Vice-President/President-elect: Tom Brown, Blacfield/Concord Colleges, Beckley and Athers.

Annual meeting: October 13-15, 1989, Huntington.

Publications: West Virginia Libraries (quarterly); *Friend to Friend* (quarterly).

West Virginia Library Commission

Frederic J. Glazer, Executive Director
Cultural Center
Charleston 25305

Coordinator of School Library Media/Technical

Jeanne Moellendick
State Department of Education
Building B, Capitol Complex
Charleston 25305

Major Issues. "A Day in the Life of West Virginia Libraries" established proof positive that library service is an important educational component in the lives of all citizens. Fifty-four percent of our population are card–carrying library users. During the first week of February each of the 179 public libraries designated a day to measure the services the library provided to the community. A count was taken of every person. The number of persons who entered the library was recorded, as were the number of materials returned and checked out; questions asked; reference assistances given; materials used in-house; computers, typewriters, copy machines utilized, and programs offered. In sum, every possible function of a public library was quantified , including sheltering the homeless. More than 20,000 people use libraries during one day; the weekly total is 125,000. Annual transactions total 17,000,000.

Library resources and usage continued to improve during 1988. Public libraries in West Virginia attained a long–sought standard of two volumes per capita. There has been a leveling pattern of financial support through modest improvements of funding by local entities. More than 70 Friends groups raised more than $80,000 for support of their libraries.

West Virginia led the nation in the national campaign to sign up all school children as card–carrying library users. Through the "Library Cards for Fun and Profit," 105,905 students obtained library cards, 97 libraries enrolled 100 percent of the students in 368 schools in 45 counties.

State Association. At the 15th annual Library Appreciation Day Dinner, held at the Charleston Civic Center February 16, 800 librarians, trustees, Friends and library workers acquainted the 80 percent of legislators in attendance with the needs of libraries. Guest speaker was *Fortune* magazine managing editor Marshall Loeb, author of *Marshall Loeb's 1988 Money Guide.*

"United We stand" was the theme of the 71st annual meeting of the Association in October. Carol Henderson of the ALA Washington Office gave a legislative update at the First General Session. Trustees held sessions to discuss "Trustees and Librarians: Who Does What?" and "Problem Solving for Libraries Statewide." The West Virginia Library Automation Network met to discuss common problems as did the Library Directors Interest Group and OCLC Users Group. Gubernatorial candidates, state representatives and chairs of Senate and House Finance Committees composed a panel on "Ask the Politicians."

Speakers included Beverly Van Hook, author of Supergranny; Dr. Dale Nitzschke, President of Marshall University; Dr. Jerry Mallett, Findlay College, who spoke on "Motivating Children to Read Through Humor"; Pamela Makricosta, Literacy Coordinator at Mary H. Weir Library; Rich Sowash who addressed the question of "Looking for Mr. Goodbook: How Will I Choose the 2,500 Books I Will Read During the Rest of My Life?"; Dr. Michael Harris, University of Kentucky professor, spoke on "Librarians in the Post-Industrial Age: Crisis and Controversy"; Dr. David Butt, Pennsylvania State University, gave an address titled "Communicating Non-Verbally: You Are Your Message."

Other programs presented included Awards banquet speaker Gail Galloway Adams; FAX; desk-top publishing; endowments and retirements. Meetings included the State Advisory Council, Intellectual Freedom Organizational Meeting, Section business meetings; and discussions of programming for children and young adults.

State Library Activities. The 15th annual Marshall Library Skills Institute graduated 79 students in 1988. After the first-year course in Basic Management, advanced students could elect Production of Audiovisual Aids, Children's Literature, Orientation to Educational Media, and West Virginia Source Materials for college credit. A salary survey conducted in 1988 revealed that the average salary for a professional librarian is $19,017. Nonprofessional salaries (for other library employees) average $5.31 per hour.

The Library Commission received a $25,000 LSCA title VI Literacy grant to train local literacy boards and to provide a library in every county with a set of training tapes. The Commission received a grant in 1987 to establish and train 21 literacy groups statewide.

The statewide automation network became more cost–effective through the establishment of the northern tier in Morgantown. By eliminating three direct lines to Charleston and using the West Virginia Network of Educational Telecommunications (WVNET) trunk line, the Commission is saving $10,000 annually.

Public Libraries. The Public Library Section (PLS) co–sponsored a spring workshop with the Junior Members Round Table (JMRT) and the Special Libraries Section at Cedar Lakes. An Interest Group for Youth (IGY) has been formed.

School Libraries/Media Centers. A joint

conference with the West Virginia Media Association was held in April in Morgantown. Schools and public libraries celebrated the third "Great West Virginia READ OUT" November 15, 1988, when 500,000 "READ OUT" buttons were distributed to library staffs and to the public. Statewide, the time between 1:30 and 2:00 p.m. was set aside for everyone from the Governor on down to stop whatever they were doing and read. The event was co-sponsored by the Department of Education and the Library Commission.

Academic Libraries. The Section's spring workshop was on the topic "Research, Writing and Publishing for Academic Libraries." The Section directory was updated.

Building Programs. The Library Commission began the year with $222,203 in carryover federal funds, no state appropriation (the first year since 1982 that no appropriation was made) and a backlog of 38 projects totaling $8,616,250. An allotment of $234,588 in federal funds brought the total available funds to $456,791 and allowed the approval of five projects.

Awards. At its annual conference, the West Virginia Library Association presented the Dora Ruth Parks Award to Merle Moore, Director of the Clarksburg-Harrison County Public Library. The Literary Award was given to Denise Giardina. The Junior Members Round Table presented the Outstanding Library Service Award to Judy Wallen. The Baker & Taylor Grassroots Award went to Rebecca VanDerMerr. The E. Frances Jones Memorial Award for the outstanding student was presented to Kathy Cummings of the Alum Creek Library.

The Friends Section presented awards to Friends of Marion County Public Library, Mannington Public Library, and Fairview Public Library for their countywide efforts toward passage of a tax levy. Debbie Hanlin from the Allegheny Mountaintop Public Library received the Friends outstanding individual award.

People. Memorial resolutions were passed at the annual conference honoring E. Sid Allen, Charles T. Burdiss, James B. Deck, James K. Jordon, and Elizabeth McKenzie Wood. Retirements included James R. Glenn and John E. Scott.

SHIRLEY A. SMITH

WISCONSIN

State Association. The Wisconsin Library Association (WLA) is healthy and flourishing. Membership grew by 5 percent with the special and public library units representing the largest increases. The budget process was revamped: a finance committee was formed, a contingency account was established, and the association has computerized its budget process.

The Literary Awards Committee will be overseeing WLA's involvement in Discover Wisconsin Writer's Week as an annual event, and the Legislative Day Committee has been made a standing Committee of the organization. The Wisconsin Center for the Book (the only such center operating under the aegis of a state library association) will be overseeing the "Let's Talk About It" project. The WLA Foundation Committee met its fund-raising goals and established the Centennial Club to recognize the 100th anniversary of WLA. The Cen-

Wisconsin Library Association (founded 1891)

Membership: 1,600; *annual budget:* $145,000.

President: Heather Eldred, Wisconsin Valley Library Services, Wausau (January 1988–January 1989).

Vice-President/President-elect: Joann Carr, Director, University of Wisconsin–Madison/School of Education–IMC., Madison.

Executive Director: Faith B. Miracle, 1922 University Avenue, Madison 53705.

Annual meeting: October 25–27, 1989, Americana Resort, Lake Geneva.

Publications: WLA Newsletter (bimonthly); *ACRL/WAAL Newsletter; CYASS Newsletter;* Documents Section Newsletter, *Eagle Press, The Wisconsin Library Media Skills Guide K-12.*

Wisconsin Department of Public Instruction, Division for Library Services

Leslyn Shires, Administrator
125 S. Webster, P.O. Box 7841
Madison 53707

tennial Club is seeking 100 persons who will each pledge $500 toward the Foundation; approximately one-third of their goal has been reached. The Centennial Planning Committee made strides in planning the 100th anniversary of WLA in 1991. The membership committee had a logo pin designed and produced, and sales were brisk at the WLA store during the annual conference. The year ended with a very successful conference which had as its theme, "CONNECTIONS . . . Libraries Linking."

State Library Activities. In Wisconsin, the Division for Library Services, as part of the Department of Public Instruction, serves as the state library agency. A Task Force on Public Library Legislation and Funding and the Council on Library and Network Development (COLAND) submitted reports to the state Superintendent of Public Instruction in August. The Task Force recommended that a Public Library Foundation Program be included in the Superintendent's 1989-91 budget request. The Task Force sees the foundation option as a means for property tax relief and proposes to guarantee a minimum level of state funding for public library service at $12 per capita statewide. COLAND submitted proposals on multitype library cooperation and statewide library automation funding for the WISCAT database, an automation consultant, retrospective conversion and CD-ROM equipment.

Public Libraries. Opportunities for professional growth and development characterized the year's activities of the Wisconsin Association of Public Librarians (WAPL) in 1988. A successful spring conference, co-sponsored with four other units, was organized around the theme of "Don't Sell Yourself Short: Marketing Your Product and Your Profession." WAPL continued its Personnel Networking Program, which provides funds for public library staff members to work in other public libraries to broaden their perspective and to strengthen networking in Wisconsin's public libraries. The Burlington Public Library Board donated $1,000 from its trust fund to provide

five WLA conference grants to deserving librarians. The WAPL Executive Board enthusiastically supported Wisconsin's participation in the Public Library Association Affiliates Network and became one of its charter members.

Trustees. The trustees, too, had a busy year of educational opportunities, culminating at the WLA annual conference where one day was designated "Trustee Day" with a full slate of special programs.

Academic Libraries. The high point of the year for academic librarians came in April at a five-state conference held in LaCrosse. A grant from ACRL allowed the Wisconsin Association of Academic Librarians (WAAL) and four other state chapters to sponsor the conference, which was attended by more than 450 people from North and South Dakota, Minnesota, Iowa and Wisconsin. The keynote speaker was the Librarian of Congress, James Billington. A full day CD-ROM fair provided opportunities for seeing and using the latest CD-ROM products.

Jean Thompson, chair of the Library Development and Legislation Committee proposed a resolution opposing the efforts of the FBI to violate the privacy of library users and urging the Wisconsin Congressional delegation to seek legislation requiring the FBI to abide by state laws on the confidentiality of library records. The resolution was passed by the WLA membership at its annual meeting.

School Libraries and Media Centers. The *Skills Manual*, prepared by the Wisconsin Association of School Librarians (WASL), was revised and continues to be a very popular item; it is now listed in the Highsmith catalog. A Task Force on Leadership, Training and Licensure appointed by the state Superintendent of Schools recommended that the current Instructional Library Media Supervisory license be eliminated. WASL, along with other school organizations, expressed dissatisfaction with this recommendation by writing letters, speaking at open forums and presenting a compromise proposal to the Task Force.

Special Libraries. During its second year as a Division of WLA, the Association of Wisconsin Special Librarians (AWSL) spent 1988 in developing its bylaws and in planning. Membership in the division rose dramatically; 42 members were added in 1988.

Building Programs. Waukesha Public Library completed a major addition, adding 40,000 square feet to a 20,000-square-foot building. Dodgeville, Verona, Galesville and Bloomer completed building programs, and an addition was constructed at Cross Plains. Wisconsin Lutheran College Library dedicated its new building in September, and University of Wisconsin–Madison Memorial Library has begun expansion of its facility.

Networks and Interlibrary Cooperation. Changes in resource sharing patterns in the state interlibrary loan structure were a primary topic of study and discussion in 1988. Interest in preservation through the year-old Wisconsin Preservation Program (WISPPR) is building slowly. Participation in the Council of Wisconsin Libraries New Technologies Information Service continued to grow and now reaches beyond the traditional network membership and even beyond state boundaries. Other highlights include cooperative automation planning among the private academic libraries in the southeast part of the state and a highly successful countywide multitype CD-ROM catalog for resource sharing.

Professional Interests. The WLA Careers Committee is studying the library education programs in the state. The WLA Ad Hoc Committee for the Study of Minimum Salaries presented a resolution at the annual WLA conference recommending $23,700 for entry-level, fulltime librarians who possess an ALA-accredited MLS degree. The resolution was accepted by the membership.

Awards. The 1988 Banta Award was given to Ellen Hunnicutt for her novel *Suite for Calliope*. Wayne Wiegand received the 1988 G. K. Hall Award for Library Literature for *Politics of an Emerging Profession: The American Library Association 1876-1917*. WLA awards: Trustee of the Year: Ann DeSwarte, Joseph Mann Public Library, Two Rivers; Librarian of the Year: Jane Robbins, Director, School of Library and Information Studies, U.W.-Madison; Library of the Year: Elisha D. Smith Public Library, Menasha; Citation of Merit: League of Women Voters, Ozaukee County; WLA Board of Directors Memorial Citation: Wayne Bassett, Marathon County Public Library and Wisconsin Valley Library Services.

Appointments. Mohammed M. Aman, Dean of the U.W.-Milwaukee School of Library and Information Science, was appointed to an international team that will advise the Egyptian government on rebuilding the ancient Library of Alexandria at a site near the location of the original library.

Deaths. Wayne Bassett, Marathon County Public Library and Wisconsin Valley Library Service; Lucy Beck, Kenosha Public Library; Gladys Cavanaugh, retired publisher of the *Subject Index to Children's Magazine*, former librarian with Madison Metropolitan School District and former professor with the U.W.-Madison library school; Shirley Knodle, former director of Verona Public Library; Margaret Moss, former Director of Libraries for the Madison School System, assistant professor at the U.W.-Madison library school and ALA Councilor.

SARAH M. MCGOWAN

WYOMING

For most libraries in Wyoming, 1988 was a quiet year. Though the worst forest fires in the state's history may well have an indirect impact on libraries because of their adverse effects on the economy, no library was ever directly threatened by the flames. Most libraries did not suffer budget cuts as severe as those of 1986 and 1987, but funding continued to be a problem; maintaining the quality of existing services generally took precedence over developing new or expanded programs. The 1988 Legislature did not consider any important library measures. Even the censors were quiescent, as there were no serious intellectual freedom battles involving libraries.

Wyoming Library Association. Attendance at the 1988 annual conference in Cody was the lowest in a decade, with only 138 registrants, yet the spirit of the meeting was optimistic and a session on long-term goals for the Association drew vigorous participation. The Association approved the creation of a new Health Science Section, which held its first meeting during the conference. The keynote speaker was ALA's Judith Krug, surveying current intellectual freedom issues. Other speakers dealt with such diverse topics as library volunteers, literacy programs, library displays and the

Wyoming Library Association (founded 1914)

Membership: 440; *annual budget:* $30,000.

President: Jerome W. Krois, Wyoming State Library, Cheyenne 82002 (September 1988-September 1989).

Vice-President/President-elect: Susan Simpson, Albany County Public Library, Laramie 82070.

Executive Secretary: Kay Nord, P.O. Box 304, Laramie 82070.

Annual meeting: October 4-7, 1989, Laramie.

Publication: Wyoming Library Roundup (three times a year); *WLA Newsletter* (bimonthly).

Wyoming State Library

Wayne H. Johnson, State Librarian
Supreme Court Building
Cheyenne 82002
Publication: The Outrider (10 times a year)

State School Library Media Supervisor

Jack Prince, Coordinator of
 Instructional Resources
Wyoming Department of Education
Hathaway Building
Cheyenne 82002

---

place of comic books in library collections.

September saw the debut of the *WLA Newsletter*, a bimonthly publication designed to heighten membership awareness of Association activities on a more timely basis than the *Roundup*, the principal WLA journal. Initial response from the members was favorable.

There were two sectional meetings this year, both at Casper in May. The Public Library Section held a seminar on library marketing; a joint meeting of the Children/Young Adult and School Library/Media Sections included workshops on a variety of mutual concerns.

Wyoming State Library. In an unprecedented (and never publicly explained) action, the Legislature chose to fund some State Library programs for the entire 1988-90 fiscal period and other programs for only the first year of the biennium. Consultant services, bibliographic services, the statewide online circulation system and LSCA-funded pass-through programs were fully funded; the remainder of the Library's operations were not. Restoration of appropriations for the full operation of the Library will be a critical issue in the 1989 legislative session.

The Legislature also directed that a study be undertaken of apparent duplication between federal document depository programs at the State Library and the University of Wyoming Libraries. In November the Task Force on the Federal Depository recommended consolidating the programs at the university. If the recommendation is approved by state and federal officials, it likely will be effective in 1990.

In September the Library published *Cowboy and Rodeo Books for Young Buckaroos*, a very well-received bibliography compiled and illustrated by staff member Kathleen Keating.

Public Libraries. LSCA Title VI literacy grants went to the Albany County Public Library, the Natrona County Library, and the Riverton Branch of the Fremont County Library.

At the end of January Bess Sheller retired after almost 37 years of service to the Carbon County Library, 13 of them as Director.

Academic Libraries. Reduced public funding for the University of Wyoming Libraries may be offset by the activities of the Library Associates, a volunteer organization of alumni and other concerned citizens, which became a reality in 1988 after several years of planning. The Associates program includes issuing a newsletter.

In order to make optimum use of personnel in the face of budget cuts, the University Libraries put a major staff reorganization into effect at midyear. The Libraries' acquisitions operation was automated with INNOVACQ, replacing an obsolete in-house system.

Librarian of Congress James Billington was guest of the University Libraries in October; he gave a public address and conducted a colloquium for library staff.

Representatives of the University of Wyoming and the state's seven community colleges met at Douglas for an intensive two-day Articulation Conference in May. A major concern of the session was cooperative collection development among the institutions' libraries.

School Libraries. The Wyoming Educational Media Association's spring workshop was held in Casper April 23; computers and television production were the principal topics. The fall meeting was held jointly with the International Reading Association, also in Casper, October 6-8; the program featured popular authors Eve Bunting, Tomie de Paola and Tasha Tudor.

The Wyoming State Library plans to expand its services to school libraries. Alice Farris, Cheyenne Central High School librarian, is the chair of the Task Force examining this issue.

Interlibrary Cooperation. A potentially important program, the creation of a statewide library telefacsimile network, was getting underway as 1988 ended. With State Library leadership and LSCA funding, the program initially will link academic and public libraries, and may expand to include other publicly funded libraries. The system utilizes existing telephone links.

A pilot project exploring means of making OCLC's cataloging and interlibrary loan systems available to smaller libraries that cannot justify individual installations was begun in November. Initial participants were the libraries of Casper College, the University of Wyoming Casper Center, Carbon County and Converse County. Other libraries may join later. Financial support is primarily from an LSCA Title III grant.

Awards. Major awards presented by the Wyoming Library Association during its annual conference in 1988 were: Distinguished Service Award, Bess Sheller, Carbon County Library; Media Support Award, *Cody Enterprise*; Trustee Award, Norma Prevedel, Sweetwater County Library; Milstead Award for service to children and/or young adults, Clare Johnson, Johnson County School System; and Indian Paintbrush Children's Book Award, Betty Ren Wright for *The Dollhouse Murders*.

Charles Levendosky, Casper journalist, poet and intellectual freedom fighter, acquired another distinction in 1988: he was named Poet Laureate of Wyoming.

Deaths. Agnes Wright Spring, historian, author and former Wyoming State Librarian, died March 20 at the age of 94. Spring had served both Wyoming and Colorado as State Historian.

PAUL B. CORS

Index

This index to the 1989 *ALA Yearbook of Library and Information Services* is based on the protocols established in the 1988 index, which paid careful attention to balance, by identifying, classifying, and clarifying all possible entries and yet holding the index to a manageable size that would not add an overwhelming amount to the cost of *The Yearbook*. In the interests of cost effectiveness it was decided: (1) Not to provide cross-references from initialisms to full names of organizations, institutions, and groups. In most cases, full names are used, but some initialisms will be found. Users are referred to the partial list of intitialisms and acroynyms at the end of this index for help in identifying the appropriate full name; (2) Not to provide "see" and "see also" cross-references, but instead to depend upon the sophisticated searching skills of the users to locate the proper heading(s).

The basic criteria for selection of entries from an indexed article included the following: **Persons** were indexed if they won awards; if they were officers or major components of associations; if they assumed directorships of large libraries; if they died; if their biography is included; or if they wrote an article in *The Yearbook*.

Institutions, including the named libraries, were indexed if they won an award; if they received a grant; if there had been a major change in buildings, location, goals, and objectives; or if there was other substantive interest. **Associations** and **Subjects** are indexed where quantity of relevant information so dictates.

The indexers wish to express their appreciation for the help of indexing students at Clarion University of Pennsylvania, Texas Woman's University, and the University of North Texas in the compilation of this index.

Aalto, Madge, 85
ABC-CLIO, 32, 290
Abid, Ann, 97
Abstracting and Indexing Services, 13
Academic Librarian of the Year Award, ACRL, 18, 32, 53, 292
Academic libraries, 119
 in Alabama, 261
 buildings and, 80
 Choice and, 52
 in Colorado, 265
 in Connecticut, 267
 in Delaware, 268
 in Florida, 271
 in Georgia, 271
 in Idaho, 271
 in Illinois, 274
 in Indiana, 276
 in Iowa, 277
 in Kentucky, 279
 in Maine, 280
 in Massachusetts, 281
 in Mississippi, 283
 in Missouri, 283
 in Montana, 285
 in Nevada, 288
 in New Mexico, 290
 in New York, 291
 in North Dakota, 293
 in Oklahoma, 295
 in Oregon, 298
 paraprofessionals, 54
 preservation and, 185
 in Rhode Island, 300
 salaries and, 180, 253
 in South Carolina, 300
 in South Dakota, 302
 statistics and, 210
 in Tennessee, 303
 in Texas, 304
 in Utah, 305
 in Vermont, 306
 in Washington, 309
 in Washington, D.C., 269
 in West Virginia, 311
 in Wisconsin, 311
 in Wyoming, 312
Academic Library Friends Award, 312
Academy Awards, 309
Academy Chicago, 196
Academy of Certified Archivists, 45
Accreditation, 18, 105
 Montana and, 76
 Nebraska and, 286
 of public libraries, 191

 of school libraries, 23, 302, 304
Achievement Award (Minnesota), 282
Acquisitions, 235
Action for Children's Television, 114
Adamovich, Shirley Gray, 288
Adams, John, 230
Addison-Wesley, 196
Adhesives,
 standards, 236
Adle, David, 54
Administration Magazine Award, 189
Adoff, Arnold, 94
Adult Services, 19, 147, 226
 in Connecticut, 267
 public libraries and, 185
 in Vermont, 306
Adult Services in the Eighties, 20
Adults, Library Services to, 19
Advancement of Literacy Award, 176, 191
Affiliation Subscription Program, 42
Affirmative action, 28
AFL/CIO, 37
Africa, 76
Aggiornamento Award, 87
AGRICOLA, 165
AGRIS, 163
AIDS, 50, 121, 128, 169, 220, 308
Air force libraries, 46
Air Force Library (Belgium), 46
Air Force Outstanding Librarian Award, 46
Akana, Sandra, 272
Akeroyd, Richard G., 249, 266
ALA/AASL and NCATE, 23
Alabama, 260
Alabama Department of Education, 260
Alabama Library Association, 260
Alabama Literacy Coalition, 260
Alabama Public Library Service, 238, 260
Alabama (University), 99, 261
Alabama (University, Birmingham), 261
Alameda County (California) Library, 33, 265
Alaska, 261
Alaska Association of School Libraries, 262
Alaska Division of State Libraries, 261
Alaska Library Association, 261
Alaska Library Networks, 261
Alaska State Library, 261

Alaska (University, Fairbanks), 262
Alaska (University) Library, 262
Albany County (Wyoming) Public Library, 312
Alberta (Canada) University, 85
Alcohol Abuse, 291
Alder, Lonny, 293
Alexandrian Library, 130
Algermissen, Virginia, 261
Alkaline Paper Advocate, 184
All Alaska Radio and Television Goldie Award, 262
All-Union Book Chamber, 130
Allard, Harry, 294
Allen, E. Sid, 311
Allen, Paul, 309
Allison, Brent, 157
Almand, Jean, 278
ALOHA, 16
Altman, Ellen, 209
Alves, Catherine Mello, 300
Aman, Mohammed M., 82, 49, 134, 312
Aman, Mary Jo, 134
Ambrose, Diane L., 299
American Association of Law Librarians, 18, 21, 22, 183, 292
American Association of School Libraries, 23, 27, 32, 50, 262, 290
American Association of University Presses, 196
American Booksellers Association, 78, 89, 117
American Council of Learned Societies, 50, 130, 131
American Film and Video Association, 110
American Film and Video Festival, 110
American Home Networks, Inc., 104
American Indian Library Association, 26
American Indians, 25
American Library Association, 18, 20, 23, 27, 32, 50, 51, 62, 85, 89, 102, 105, 116, 119, 121, 124, 128, 131, 138, 166, 172, 193, 207, 209, 249, 278, 279, 291
American Library Trustee Association, 32, 41
American National Standards Institute, 234
American Society for Information Science, 18, 42, 134, 146, 216
American Society for Theater Research, 239

313

Index

American Theological Library Association, 44, 167
Ames (Iowa) Public Library, 277
Anadarko (Oklahoma) Public Library, 296
Anchorage (Alaska) Public Library, 187, 188
Andermann, Patricia, 284
Anderson, Barbara L., 294
Anderson, Beryl L., 233
Anderson (Indiana) Public Library, 276
Angelis, Jane, 156
Anglo-American Cataloging Rules, 2nd Edition, 1988 Revision, 86
Angola (Indiana) Public Library, 276
Animal Welfare Information Center, 163
Ann Arbor (Michigan) Public Library, 187
Anneberg ICPB Project, 279
Anno, Mitsumasa, 89
Anoka County (Minnesota) Public Library, 282
Antieau, Kim, 209
Apple Computers, 103, 199
Aquaculture Information Center, 163
Arabic, 236
Arbuthnot Lecture, 51, 94
Archives, 44, 262
Archives of the United States, 44
Archulete County (Colorado) Library, 266
AGRICOLearn, 164
Argentina, 119
Arizona, 262
Arizona Department of Library, Archives, and Public Records, 262
Arizona State Library Association, 262
Arizona State University, 17, 80, 262
Arizona (University), 167, 262
Arkansas, 263
Arkansas Arts Center, 263
Arkansas Library Association, 263
Arkansas State Department of Education, 263
Arkansas State Library, 226, 264
Arkansas (University) Library, 264
Armed Forces Libraries, 46
Armed Forces Libraries Section, 47
Armenia, 236
Armentrout, Brian, 308
Army libraries, 46
Aronson, Boris, 240
Art Libraries, 47
Art Libraries Society/Australia-New Zealand, 47
Art Libraries Society/Norge, 47
Art Libraries Society/North America, 47
Arteager, Judy, 262
Arterbery, Vivian, 233
Artificial intelligence, 43
Artists Issue, 231
Asbury Theological Seminary (Kentucky), 44
Ashe County (North Carolina) Public Library, 292
Asian-Americans, service, 7
Asian/Pacific American Librarians Association, 48
Askelson, Rodney, 310
Asotin County (Washington) Library, 309
Asp, William J., 61, 281
Association for Copyright Enforcement, 196
Association for Educational Communications and Technology, 22, 27
Association for Library and Information Science Education, 18, 49, 253
Association for Library Services to Children, 33, 50, 92, 173, 259

Association of Academic Health Science Library Directors, 158
Association of American Publishers, 195
Association of College and Research Libraries, 27, 32, 51, 52, 125, 144, 191, 253, 292
Association of Indiana Media Educators, 276
Association of Jewish Libraries, 54
Association of Research Libraries, 58, 59, 163, 167
Association of Special Libraries and Information Bureau, 233
Association of Specialized and Cooperative Library Agencies, 33, 61, 291
Association of State and Local History (California), 189
Astor (Vincent) Foundation, 115
Athens (Georgia) Regional Library, 272
Atkins, Stephen E., 209
Atkinson (Hugh C.) Award, 14, 32, 51, 107, 141, 144, 275
Atlanta-Fulton County (Georgia) Public Library, 227
Atlanta-Fulton County (Georgia) Public Library Friends, 118
Auburn University (Alabama), 261
Augustana College (South Dakota), 302
Author Achievement Award, YASD, 258
Automation, 44, 122, 181
 Armed Forces Libraries, 46
 in Canada, 85
 in Connecticut, 267
 in Idaho, 274
 in Illinois, 274
 in Indiana, 276
 in Missouri, 283
 in Montana, 285
 in Nebraska, 286
 in Nevada, 287
 in New Hampshire, 288
 in New Jersey, 289
 in North Carolina, 292
 in North Dakota, 293
 in Oregon, 297
 in South Dakota, 301
 standards, 235
 theological libraries and, 44
 US-USSR relations and, 131
 in Vermont, 306
 in Washington, 308
 in Wisconsin, 311
Avram, Henriette D., 36, 63
Award for Achievement in Library and Information Technology, 144, 276
Award for Distinguished Public Service, MLA, 161
Award for Library Literature, 311
Award of Achievement (Ohio), 295
Award of Excellence in Public Library Services (Georgia), 272
Award of Merit, American Society for Information Science, 43
Awards, 18, 20, 32, 42, 43, 48, 49, 51, 53, 54, 61, 63, 77, 83, 87, 93, 99, 101, 107, 110, 112, 118, 119, 121, 129, 134, 135, 138, 141, 144, 147, 153, 155, 157, 161, 162, 191, 196, 202, 218, 223, 232, 233, 249, 254, 258, 260, 264, 265, 266, 273, 275, 276, 277, 278, 279, 280, 282, 283, 284, 285, 286, 288, 289, 292, 293, 295, 296, 298, 299, 300, 302, 303, 305, 306, 310, 311, 312
Baber (Carroll Preston) Research Award, 33, 272
Bahr, Alice, 261
Bailey, Fred A., 303
Baille, Jack, 286

Bainbridge College (Georgia), 272
Baird, Diane N., 303
Baker and Taylor Company, 32, 118, 191, 193, 246, 261, 303, 306, 311
Baker, Barbara A., 291
Baker, Betty, 263
Baker, Dorothy, 295
Baker, Gordon, 272
Balcom, Kathleen Mehaffy, 191
Ballen Booksellers, International, 161
Banks, Lynne Reid, 275
Banned Book Week, 126
Banta Award, 311
Barber, Gloria K., 306
Barbour, Wendell, 306
Barker, Jacqueline Lauren, 261
Barkley, Patrick, 265
Barley, Ann, 278
Barlou, Beth, 83
Barlow, Don, 295
Barnes, Kay, 234, 264
Barnett, Louis, 249
Barnette, Nancy, 45
Barnsdall (Oklahoma) Public Library, 296
Barron, Daniel D., 223
Barron, Robert E., 291
Basch, Bernard, 233
Baskin, Leonard, 89
Basler, Thomas G., 272
Bass, Doris, 88
Bassett, Wayne, 312
Bastian, Ann, 37, 129
Batchelder (Mildred L.) Award, 33
Batesville (Indiana) Public Library, 276
Battelle, 14
Bauer, Margaret D., 298
Beal, Betty D., 260
Bean, Ethelle, 301
Bearman, Toni Carbo, 42
Beaudin, Jane, 25
Beaudry, Art, 93 (photo)
Beck, Lucy, 312
Becklund, Arlo, 260
Bedell, Berkley, 277
Bedient, Douglas, 156
Behler, Pat, 256 (photo)
Beilstein, 13
Bell & Howell, 196
Bell, Bernice L., 282
Bell, Glenda, 286
Bell (Walter) Award, 272
Bellamy, Grace, 272
Bender, Betty, 141 (photo), 189
Bender, David, 232
Benjamin (Curtis) Award for Creative Publishing, 196
Bennett, Nancy, 86
Benza, Margiana, 254
Benzinger, Majorie, 291
Berg, Edna, 286
Berger, Patricia, ix, 27, 64 (biog., photo), 270
Bergman, Bruce J., 291
Bering Straight (Alaska) School District, 262
Berne Convention, 101, 136, 150, 196
Bernier, Teresa, 307
Berry, John, 140, 193
Bertram, Sheila, 85
Best Information Science Books Award, 43, 153
Best JASIS Paper, 43
Best of Festival Award, 111
Beta Phi Mu, 33, 62
Beta Phi Mu Award, 33, 62
Beta Phi Mu Award (Missouri), 284
Betancourt, Ingrid, 65 (biog., photo), 208
Bettendorf (Iowa) Public Library, 276
Biblarz, Dora, 262
Bibliographic control, 154, 243

314

Index

Bibliographic instruction, 15, 47
Bibliographic utilities, 123
Bibliographies, 63
Bibliographies and Indexes in *American Book Publishing Record: 1983-1987* (table), 64
Bibliographies, Indexes, and Other Reference Books, 63
Bibliotecas Para La Gente, 207
Bibliotheca Alexandrina, 81
Bibliotheque de St. Boniface (Canada) Library, 85
Bierhorst, John, 51
Big Horn County (Montana) Library, 285
Billington, James H., 150 (photo)
BIOSIS, 14
Biotechnology, 169
Birch, Tobeylynn, 148
Bird, Roy, 278
BIS Infomat, Ltd., 13
Bishop, C. Diane, 263
Bismarck State College (North Dakota), 293
Bitterroot (Montana) Public Library, 285
Black Caucus of ALA, 76
Black, Frances, 295
Black librarians, 76
Blackburn-Foster, Brenda, 276
Blackfoot (Idaho) Public Library, 274
Blackman, Betty, 265
Blacks, service, 7
Blackwell/North America, 39, 292
Blackwell/North America Scholarship Award, 39, 153, 218, 292
Blades, Ruben, 195
Blaine, Nann, 279
Blalock, Louise, 267
Blind and Physically Handicapped Library Services, 77
Blockley, E. Al, 286
Bloomer (Wisconsin) Public Library, 311
Bloss, Marjorie E., 18, 37, 65 (biog., photo), 218
Blumberg, Stephen C., 219
Bobinski, George S., 146
Bobst (Elmer and Mamdouha) Foundation, 291
Bodart-Talbot, Joni, 40
Boggs, Lindy, 150 (photo)
Bogle International Travel Fund Grants, 39
Bohlen, Jeanne L., 116
Boice, Robert, 18, 32, 53, 153
Boies, Kay, 295
Boise State University (Idaho), 274
Boisse, Joseph, 18, 54 (photo)
Boley, Ronald G., 283
Bolles, Charles, 273
Bolt, Nancy, 265
Bolte, William F., 275
Bonner, Bester D., 128
Book Club of Texas, 304
Bookmobiles, 295
Books,
 exchange, 244
 notable, 172
 prices, 195
 sales of, 78
 standards, 236
Books for College Libraries, 51, 99, 151
Booksellers, 78
Bookselling, 78
Bookstores, 187
Boomgaard, Jan, 45
Borden, Sharon, 287
Borko, Harold, 43
Boss, Richard W., 123
Bostic, Lois, 221
Boston Globe/Horn Book Award, 96
Boston (Massachusetts) Public Library, 187, 281

Boston University (Massachusetts), 220
Botham, Jane, 93
Boulder (Colorado) Public Library, 82
Bound to Stay Bound Books, Inc., 38, 197
Bound to Stay Bound Books Scholarships, 38
Bowhuis (Andrew L.) Memorial Scholarship, 87
Bowie, Melvin M., 33, 272
Bowker (R. R.) Company, 14, 18, 35, 63, 218
Boyce, Bert, 37, 155
Boyd, Alex, 289
Boyd, Charmaine Standard, 270
Boykin, Joseph, 300
Boyvey, Mary, 303
Bozolan, Paula, 281
Bradley, Carol June, 162
Bradt, Kathleen Ruth, 278
Brain (George B.) Education (Washington) Library, 309
Bratislava Award, 97
Brawley, Paul H., 152, 176 (obit., photo)
Bray (Robert S.) Award, 264
Brecht, Albert O., 136
Brenner, M. Diane, 261
Brettschneider, Sharon, 267
Brevard Community College (Florida), 130
Brewster, Patience, 287
Briggs, Kate H., 88
Brisman, Shimeon, 54
Broadman (Estelle) Award, 161, 287
Bronze Quill Award, 288
Brooklyn (New York) Public Library, 20, 90, 226
Brooks, D. W., 272
Brooks, Jerrold Lee, 284
Broujas, John H., 299
Broward County (Florida) Public Library, 187
Brown, Irene Bennett, 298
Brown (John Carter) Library (Rhode Island), 166
Brown, Louise R., 281
Brown, Philip, 302
Brown, Tom, 310
Brown University (Rhode Island), 300
Browning, Kim, 78
BRS, 13
Brubaker (John) Memorial Award, 87
Bruce, Robert K., 39
Bruce, Robert V., 196
Bruk, Mellon, 118
Brumback, Elsie L., 291
Brunton, Marilyn, 282
Bryan, Ashley, 96
Bryan, Barbara, 267
Bryan, Jane C., 282
Bryant, Bonita, 110
Bryant, Tyrone, 32
Buck, Richard M. 241
Buckingham, Betty Jo, 276
Buckingham, Melissa, 190 (photo)
Buckley, Bonnie, 288
Buffalo and Erie County (New York) Public Library, 291
Buildings, 17, 79, 186
Bullfrog Films, 118
Bullock, Kathy, 300
Bunge, Charles A., 209
Bunting, Aleson, 161
Burdess, Charles T., 311
Burke County (North Carolina) Public Library, 292
Burke, Joe, 46
Burlington (Vermont) Free Library, 306
Bush Foundation, 302
Business services, 15, 276, 292, 296
Business Week, 202
Butler, Evelyn, 233

Buttars, Gerald A., 304
Buzan, Norma, 42 (photo)
Byars, Barbara, 282
Byars, Betsy, 278
Bynum, Mollie, 262
C. L. Systems, Inc., 38
Cahner's Publishing Co., 118
Cakowski, Irene, 289
Caldecott (Randolph) Medal, 33, 51
Caley, Diane, 293
Calgary (Canada) Association Fest, 85
California, 79, 264
California Alliance for Literacy, 265
California Institute of Libraries, 265
California Library Association, 264
California Library Employees Association, 265
California Media Library Educators Association, 265
California Society of Librarians, 265
California State Library, 80, 207, 238, 264
California State Library Foundation Bulletin, 38, 153
California (University), 82
California University (San Francisco), 264
Callaham, Betty, 301
Callahan, Cathy, 279
Campbell (Francis Joseph) Citation, 33, 61, 121
Canadian Association of Library Schools, 18
Canadian Association of Research Libraries, 84
Canadian Association of Small University Libraries, 85
Canadian Library Association, 18, 83, 84, 183, 233
Canadian Library Association Award, 97
Canadian Report, 84
Canadian Trust, 84
Cane Toads, 111
Canemaker, John, 239
Cantlon, Marie, 239
Cape Canaveral (Florida) Public Library, 80
Cape Girardeau (Missouri) Public Library, 284
Capitol Holding Company, 188
Carder, Linda L., 284
Careers, 135
 development of, 193
 Hotline, 138
 Washington and, 308
Cargill Information Center (Minnesota), 33
CARLYLE, 16
Carmack, Mona, 278
Carmichael, Jim, 232
Carmody, Barbara A., 40
Carnegie (Britain) Award, 97
Carnegie Library of Pittsburgh (Pennsylvania), 259
Carnegie Reading List Awards, 39
Carnegie Reading List Fund, 259
Carnegie Video Project, 246, 286, 293
Carpenter, Kenneth E., 146
Carr, Joann, 311
Carr, Mary M., 308
Carroll, Annie, 186 (photo)
Carroll, Bonnie C., 43
Carter, Daniel, 249
Carthage (Missouri) Public Library, 284
Case, David, 273
Case, Donald O., 49
Case Western Reserve University (Ohio), 16
Casey, Daniel, 249
Casper, Dale E., 17
Cassell, Kay Ann, 17
Cassell, William, 249
Cataloging, 86, 163

315

Index

of agricultural information, 163
Holocaust and, 55
Library of Congress and, 86
Music Library Association and, 163
standards for, 243
US-USSR relations and, 131
Catalogs, online, 16, 88, 145
Catholic collections, 88
Catholic libraries, 87
Catholic Library Association, 87
Catholic University (District of Columbia), 101, 269
Catoir, John, 87
Caudill (Rebecca) Young Readers Book Award, 275
Cavanaugh, Gladys, 312
Cayton, Robert F., 295
CD-ROM, 13, 52, 63, 103, 119, 170, 198, 205, 225
in academic libraries, 17
Connecticut and, 267
Indiana and, 276
international technology and, 123
Library of Congress and, 86
Nevada and, 237
networks and, 171, 198
reviewing of, 53
Cedar Rapids (Iowa) Public Library, 277
Celebrate Literacy Award (Nebraska), 287
Cenacveira, Jacquelyn, 161
Censorship, 84, 126, 134, 196, 223, 262, 266
booksellers and, 79
Canada and, 83
Freedom to Read Foundation and, 116
IFRT and, 128
Kentucky and, 279
Nebraska and, 286
Nevada and, 288
Oklahoma and, 295
Oregon and, 298
videos and, 247
Washington and, 309
young adults and, 255, 258
Census, 119
Arizona and, 262
Connecticut and, 266
Indiana and, 276
Kansas and, 278
Missouri and, 284
Ohio and, 295
Oklahoma and, 296
sound recordings and, 229
Center for Research Libraries, 100
Center for the Book, 93, 311
Center for the Study of the Book, 197
Center for the Utilization of Federal Technology, 170
Central Arkansas Library System, 264
Central Arkansas (University) Library, 264
Central Colorado Library System, 266
Central Kansas Library System, 278
Central Washington University Library, 310
Certificate of Achievement for Excellence in Financial Reporting, 310
Certificate of Appreciation, LAMA, 144
Certificate of Merit Award, Catholic Library Association, 87
Certificate of Merit (Minnesota), 282
Certification,
Iowa and, 277
Montana and, 285
Nebraska and, 286
of school librarians, 199
Society of American Archivists and, 45
Chaikin, Miriam, 96

Champaign (Illinois) Public Library, 19
Champion, Myra, 292
Champlain Foundation, 299
Chandler, James G., 33, 61, 121
Chapin, John, 276
Chapter Relations Committee, 40
Chapter Relations Office, 40
Charlotte and Mecklenburg County (North Carolina) Regional Library, 82
Chartrand, Marg, 192
Chase, Richard, 96
Chatman, Elfreda A., 38, 204
Chattanooga-Hamilton County (Tennessee) Bicentennial Library, 303
Chemical Abstracts Services, 14, 198
Cher, Donna, 38
Cheshire, Mark, 88
Cheski, Richard, 294
Chesnutt (Edgar) Library (Arkansas), 264
Chicago (Illinois) Public Library, 7, 34, 79, 80, 90, 204, 275
Chicago International Festival of Children's Films, 113
Childers, Thomas, 299
Childers, W. D., 270
Children, services, 91, 50, 90, 130, 185, 225
in Florida, 270
in Massachusetts, 281
in Nebraska, 286
in North Dakota, 294
output measures for, 191
in Vermont, 306
Children's Book Award, 96
Children's Book Council, 88, 94
Children's Book Council Honors Program, 88, 94
Children's Choices for 1988, 89
Children's Film and Television Center of America, 113
Children's Library Services, 90
Children's literature, 88, 96-97 (tables), 242
film and video, 112
notable, 172
Children's Television Workshop, 114
Childs (James Bennett) Award, 33, 119
Chillicothe (Ohio) Public Library, 121
Chin, Donna, 295
China, 277
Chinese, 235
Chinese-American Librarians Association, 98
Chinese Library Association, 98
Chisholm, Margaret, 193, 310
Choice, 52
Choosing Equality, 129
Christenson, Shirley, 282
Church, Frank, 274
Cimgala, Diane J., 136
Cimino, Maria, 94
Cincinnati and Hamilton County (Ohio) Public Library, 188
Ciporen, Fred, 150
Circulation,
online, 272
standards, 235
Citation of Exceptional Service Award (Alabama), 260
Citation of Merit (Wisconsin), 311
Citation of Merit Award (Alabama), 260
Cited Trustee Award, 42
Citizen of the Year Award (Ohio), 295
Citizens Award (Indiana), 276
Citizens for Maryland Libraries, 280
City Beautification Award (Nebraska), 286
Civil Libertarian of the Year (Nevada), 288

Civil Rights, 226
Clarion State University (Pennsylvania), 154
Clark, Robert L., 295
Clarke (Polly) Award, 296
Clarksdale (Mississippi) Carnegie Library, 283
Claymont (Delaware) Library, 268
Clayton County (Georgia) Library System, 272
Clayton, Linda Hetherington, 303
Cleaver, Betty, 295
Clements, Barth, 179
Clements, Paul, 303
CLENE Round Table, 40
Clerk, Office, 280
Cleveland (Ohio) Public Library, 78, 82
Clift (David H.) Scholarships, 38
Clifton, Joe Ann, 66 (biog., photo), 234
Cline, Nancy, 299
Cline, Terry, 283
Clinton (Tennessee) Public Library, 303
Closson, Sally, 284
CLSI, 122
Coalition of Library Advocates, 300
Cobleigh (Vermont) Public Library, 306
Cody Enterprise, 312
Coffee County (Tennessee) Public Library, 303
Coffie, Patricia, 276
Coker (C. F. W.) Prize, 45
Colby-Sawyer College (New Hampshire), 17
Cole, Karen, 17, 277
Coleman, Terry L., 271
Collantes, Augurio, 49
Collection Building and Management, 98
Collection development, 98, 149, 154, 163, 266
in academic libraries, 15
ARL and, 57
in Canada, 167
in Idaho, 274
in Kansas, 278
minorities and, 10, 109
in Montana, 285
at National Agricultural Library, 163
public libraries and, 185
video and, 246
in Washington, 308
in Wyoming, 312
young adult materials and, 255
College and Research Libraries Award, 153
Collier County (Florida) Library, 81
Collins, Elizabeth, 272
Collins, Margaret, 221
Collins, Myrtes C., 135
Collins, Phil, 195
Colonial Dames Scholarship, 45
Colorado, 265
Colorado Alliance of Research Libraries, 266
Colorado Center for the Book, 266
Colorado Department of Education, 265
Colorado Educational Media Association, 266
Colorado Library Association, 266
Colorado Mountain College, 266
Colorado Resource Center, 265
Colorado State Library, 265
Columbia University (New York), 16, 125, 167
Commission of Library Cooperation, 130
Committee for Institution Cooperation, 185
Committee on Accreditation, ALA, 18
Committee on the Status of Women in Librarianship, 40

316

Community Achievement Award
  (New Mexico), 289
Compact disk, sound, 228
Competencies,
  Montana and, 284
  of school librarians, 23
Compton (La Nell) Award, 264
Computer assisted instruction, 148
Computer in Libraries, 152
Computers, standards, 235
Conable, Gordon M., 128
Conference Grants (Wisconsin), 311
Conference Grants, YASD/Baker and
  Taylor, 40
Congressional Information Service,
  13, 34, 119
Congressional Research Service, 150
Connecticut, 79, 190, 266
Connecticut Humanities Council,
  267
Connecticut Library Association, 267
Connecticut State Library, 238, 266
Connecticut (University), 267
Conroy, Trish, 282
Conservation, 130, 235
Consulting, 61
Continuing education, 52, 100, 107,
  147, 181
  AASL and, 24
  in Alabama, 260
  in Alaska, 262
  in Arizona, 262
  in Idaho, 274
  in Indiana, 276
  in Kansas, 278
  in Kentucky, 278
  Medical Library Association and,
    160
  in Missouri, 283
  in Montana, 285
  personnel and, 154
  Public Library Association and,
    190
  Resources and Technical Services
    Division and, 217
  in South Dakota, 302
  Special Libraries Association and,
    233
  theological libraries and, 44
  in Virginia, 307
  young adult services and, 256
Continuing Education Grant, MLA,
  161
Continuing Library Education
  Network and Exchange Round
  Table, 100
Conway, Susan L., 287
Cooke, Eileen D., 249
Cooney, Jane, 84
Cooper, Barbara, 232, 242
Cooper, Judy, 278
Cooper, Regina, 260
Cooper-Bunyan, Emily, 276
Cooper Foundation, 286
Coplen, Ron, 233
Copyright, 14, 83, 84, 101, 136, 145,
  150, 196, 228
Copyright Clearance Center, 196
Coral, Lenore, 162
Corcoran, John, 138 (photo)
Corporate Award (Florida), 270
Correctional institution libraries, 61
Coretta Scott King Award, 96
Corrigan, John T., 88
Corry, Emmett, 87, 291
Cors, Paul B., 312
Cory, John Mackenzie, 176 (obit.,
  photo), 291
Coskran, Kathleen, 281
Council of Postsecondary
  Accreditation, 19
Council on Library Resources, 21,
  50, 52, 130, 165
Cox Cable Television, 286
Crane, Karen, 261
Crawford, Linda, 283
Crawford, Susan, 161

Credentials, 22, 105
  ALA and, 28
  for law library directors, 136
  of medical librarians, 159
  of school librarians, 23, 302
Creedmore (North Carolina) Public
  Library, 291
Cricket Magazine, 94
Criger, Sarah, 308
Crist, Margo, 281
Crites, Lynn, 284
Crockett County (Tennessee) Library,
  303
Crosman Award, 275
Cross Plains (Wisconsin) Public
  Library, 311
Crouch, Milton H., 306
Crowe, Linda D., 265
Crown, 196
Cuesta, Yolanda J., vii, 125
Cumberland County (North Carolina)
  Public Library, 292
Cummings, Kathy, 311
Cummings, Nancy, 263
Cunningham, George, 145
Cunningham Memorial International
  Fellowship, 161
*Current Index to Journals in
  Education (CIJE)*, 108
Curriculum, 54, 106
Cyrillic, alphabet, 236
D'Annunzio, Rebecca, 310
Daganaar, Mark, 284
Dahlgren, Anders C., 83
Dahlstrom, Joe, 17
Dail, Timothy Eatherly, 303
Dakan, Tony, 47
Dale (Edgar) Award, 276, 295
Dallas (Texas) Public Library, 118, 187
Dalrymple, Prudence, 50
Daly, Simeon, 44
Dana (John Cotton) Certificate of
  Merit, 300
Dana (John Cotton) Public Relations
  Award, 33, 46, 195 (table), 233,
  265, 279, 299
Dana (John Cotton) Special Award,
  285, 287
Daniel, Carolyn C., 303
Daniels, Betty, 279
Daniels, Bruce E., 62, 239, 299
Danner, Richard, 21, 292
Darling (Louise) Medal, 161
Darlington County (South Carolina)
  Library, 300
Darrah, Fred K., 33, 42, 264
Dartmouth Medal, 34, 63, 204, 206
Data, transfer, 129, 235
Databases, 52, 64, 103, 122, 128
Databases, Computer-Readable, 103
Dauphin County (Pennsylvania)
  Library System, 33, 299
Daval, Nicola, 61
Davalos, Felipe, 89
Davenport (Iowa) Public Library, 277
Davenport, Marilyn, 288
Davis, Bill, 128
Davis Cup Award, 175
Davis, Donald G., Jr., 146
Davis, Sheryl, 38
Davis (Watson) Award, 43
Day, David A., 162
D'Elia, George, 208
De'Clements, Barthe, 271, 287
De Kalb County (Florida) Public
  Library, 272
De Swarte, Ann, 311
Dean, Charles C., 292
Dearstyne, Bruce, 45
Debo, Angil, 296
Decade of the Disabled, 121
Deck, James B., 311
Deekle, Peter V., 17, 299
Delaware, 268
Delaware Division of Libraries, 268
Delaware Library Association, 166,
  268

Delaware School Library Media
  Association, 268
DeLeeuw, Adele, 96
Dempsey, Frank J., 177 (obit.,
  photo), 189, 275
Demuth, Phyllis, 261
Dendy, Adele S., 17
Denis, Laurent, 86
Denver (Colorado) Public Library,
  225, 265
Department of Commerce, 105
Department of Defense, 104
Department of Education, 50, 78,
  209, 293, 304, 305, 308
Department of State, 165
Depauw University (Indiana), 276
Depository libraries, 110, 119
Derwent, 14
Desktop Publishing, 199, 201
Desktop Publishing and its
  Applications in Libraries, 199
Dessauer, Phil, 245
Dessy, Blane K., 100, 260
Detlefsen, Ellen Gay, 161
Devel, Marlene, 274
Devils Lake (North Dakota) Public
  Library, 293
Dew, Stephen, 263
Dewey County (South Dakota)
  Library, 302
Dewey Decimal Classification,
  Twentieth Edition, 86
Dewey (Melvil) Medal, 34,
Dexter, Pete, 196
Di Prete, Carol K., 300
Dialog, 13, 103, 197
Dianandis Communications, 201
Dickenson, Carolyn, 304
Dickinson (North Dakota) Public
  Library, 293
Diffendal, Anne, 45
*Directory of Library and Information
  Science Professionals*, 151
Disasters, 130
  Florida and, 270
  management of, 1, 218
Dissertations, standards, 236
Distinguished Achievement Award
  (Minnesota), 282
Distinguished Library Service Award
  for School Administrators, 34
Distinguished Service Awards, 45
  Alabama, 260
  Arizona, 263
  Arkansas, 264
  Black Caucus, 77
  Chinese American Library
    Association, 98
  District of Columbia, 268
  National Council of Teachers of
    English, 94
  Nebraska, 287
  New Mexico, 289
  Oklahoma, 296
  South Carolina, 301
  Texas, 303
  Wyoming, 312
District of Columbia, 268
District of Columbia Association of
  School Librarians, 269
District of Columbia Library
  Association, 268
District of Columbia Public Library,
  187, 269
District of Columbia State Library,
  268
District of Columbia (University), 269
Dixon, King, 301
Doak, Wesley A., 297
Dobson, Jo, 302
Dobson, Joan, 136
Dobson, Larry, 302
Dobie (J. Frank) Trust, 304
Doctoral Dissertation Competition
  Award, 50
Doctoral Dissertation Fellowship,
  ACRL, 18, 38, 53

Index

317

Index

Doctoral Dissertation Scholarship, ISI, 43
Doctoral Fellowship, MLA, 161
Doctoral Forum Award, 43
Document delivery,
    Montana and, 285
    Universal Serials and Book Exchange and, 244
Documentary films, 111
Documents to the People, 34
Documents to the People Award, 34, 119
Dodd, Mead, 196
Dodgerville (Wisconsin) Public Library, 311
Doe (Janet) Lecture, 161
Dolores (Colorado) Public Library, 266
Doms, Keith, 245
Donald, David Herbert, 196
Donham, Jean, 277
Donnelly, Susie, 284
Donovan, Barbara R., 291
Donovan, John, 89
Dooley, Vince, 272
Dorroh (Marion) Memorial Scholarship, 289
Dorsey, James E., 271
Dougherty, Richard M., 14, 32, 53, 66 (biog., photo), 107, 141, 144
Douglas, Robert R., 304
Dover (Delaware) Public Library, 268
Dowler, Lawrence, 45
Downing, Joel C., 35
Doyle, Patricia, 301
Doyle, Patricia L., 303
Doyle, Robert P., 132
Drake, Miriam, 233
Drexel University (Pennsylvania), 154
Driggs, Glenda, 284
DuMont, Rosemary, 50
Duckles (Vincent H.) Award, 162
Dudley (Miriam) Bibliographic Instruction Librarian of the Year, 18, 34, 53
Duerson, Chase, 186 (photo)
Duerson, Dave, 186 (photo)
Duff, John B., 191 (photo)
Dufty, Jeffrey, 39
Dugan, Marilyn, 254
Duhrsen, Lowell R., 290
Duke University (North Carolina), 17
Dunkirk (Indiana) Public Library, 276
Dunn, Mary Kit, 291
Durant (Oklahoma) Public Library, 296
Dustin, M.J., 282
Dyer, Cynthia, 276
Dzansi, Sitsofe, 161
East, Kathy, 294
East Asia, 309
East Brunswick (New Jersey) Public Libraries, 33
East Central Georgia Regional Library, 118
Eastern Shore Regional Library (Maryland), 225
Eastman, Ann Heidbreder, 144
EBSCO, 38
EBSCO Scholarship, 38, 136
Econo-Clad, 50
Edelen, Joseph R., 161
Edmonton (Canada) Public Library, 146
Education, Library, 107 (tables)
Educational Information Center, 20
Edwards, Margaret Alexander, 177 (obit., photo), 259
Egan, Sheilah, 254
Egypt, 81
Ehrenberg, Ralph E., 36, 157
EIC/Intelligence, 14
EIC Newsletter, 191
Ekker, Ernst A., 97
El Dorado (Kansas) Public Library, 278

El Reno (Oklahoma) Carnegie Public Library, 296
Eldred, Heather, 311
Eldredge, Jon, 192
Elected Official Award (Pennsylvania), 299
Electronic mail, 295
Electronic publishing, 99, 123, 151, 197
    Federal Information and, 110
    government, 57, 120
    standards, 235
Eliot (Ida and George) Prize, 161
Elliott, Dorothy Sanborn, 283
Ellsworth City (Maine) Library, 146
Ellsworth, Ralph E., 66 (biog., photo)
Elmendorf, George, 223
Elsevier, 195
Emmy Award, 113
Emory University (Georgia), 272
Employment, 130
Employment Quick Start Program (Oklahoma), 20
Emporia State University (Kansas), 302
Encyclopaedia Britannica Corporation, 37, 222
Encyclopedia of Religion, 34, 63, 206
Enequist, Jacqueline, 291
Enoch Pratt Library, 226
Enstrom, Bona Carol, 282
Epstein, Jason, 196
Equal Opportunity Act, 7
Equality Award, 34
ERIC, 108
ESA-IRS, 14
Esbensen, Barbara Juster, 281
Estabrook, Leigh Stewart, 50, 67 (biog., photo), 107
Estes, David E., 232
Estes, Ruth, 261
Ethnic Materials and Information Exchange Round Table, 108
Eugene (Oregon) Public Library, 227
European Common Market, 145
Euster, Joanne, 54
Evaluation, 54
Evans, Cooper, 277
Evans, Gwynneth, 168
Evans, Frank B., 44
Everett Community College (Washington) Library, 309
Everett (Washington) Public Library, 309
Evergreen State College (Washington) Library, 309
Everhart, Nancy, 36
Evrick, C. Ray, 275
Exhibits, 191
Exhibits Round Table, 35
Expert systems, 43
Eyring Research Foundation, 305
Facts on File, 34
Facts on File Award, 34
Facts on File Grant, 204
Faculty, 106
Fairfax County (Virginia) Public Library, 8
Fairview (West Virginia) Public Library, 311
Falsone, Anne Marie, 266
Family Handyman, 201
Family History Library (Utah), 305
Famous Amos Cookies, 35
Fantasy, 258
Farmers Branch (Texas) Library, 33
Farrell, Frank J., 200
FAXNET, 189
Faxon (F. W.) Company, 98
Faxon (Frederich Winthrop) Scholarship, 38
Faye, Alexiev, 262
FBI Library Awareness Program, 125
Federal Bureau of Investigation, 125, 14, 27, 116, 136, 158, 165, 301
Federal Communications Commission, 104

Federal Librarians Achievement Award, 34, 110
Federal Librarians Round Table, 34, 109
Federal libraries, 270
    funding of, 109
    networks and, 171
Federal Library and Information Center Committee, 150
Federspiel, Martha E., 276
Fees for service, 128, 145, 280, 305
    Montana and, 285
    video and, 246
Feldman, Mary K., 268
Felix, Sally, 299
Fellow, Society of American Archivists, 45
Fellows Award, Special Libraries Association, 233, 292
Fellows Posner Prize, 45
Fellows Program, 130
Fennell, Margene F., 306
Fenway Libraries Online, 16
Ferguson, Molly, 287
Ferrell, Mary Sue, 264
Ferrell, Sean A., 283
Ferrier, Douglas M., 18
Ferruso, Agnes, 34, 119
Feye-Stukas, Janice, 252
Field Corporation, 196
Fighting Back, 111
Figueredo, Danilo H., 289
Filer (Idaho) Public Library, 274
Filho (Brazil) Award, 97
Film and Video, 110, 112
Films, 110
    handicapped, 121
    notable, 172
Filmstrips, notable, 172
Financial Development Award, Gale Research Company, 34
Fineberg, Gail M., 151
Fink, Eleanor, 48
Fires, 1, 219
First Amendment Rights, 125, 78, 116
Fiscal Year 1989 Budget Appropriations, 248 (table)
Fischler, Barbara, 276
Fisher, Edith Maureen, 67 (biog., photo), 76
Flathead County (Montana) Library, 285
Fleckner, John A., 44
Fletcher Free Library (Vermont), 116
Flicker Tale Children's Book Award, 294
Floods, 1
Florida, 185, 270
Florida Library Association, 270
Florida State Division of Library and Information Services, 238, 270
Floyd County (Kentucky) Public Library, 279
Floyd, Rebecca Ann, 249
Foard County (Texas) Library, 304
Fogerty, James, 45
Folger Shakespeare Library, 35, 53
Folklife Center, 150
Follet Book Company, 221
Follet Microcomputer Award, 36
Follet Software Company, 36, 221
Foodtown, 279
Forbes, Wanda, 165
Ford Foundation, 306
Ford, Karen, E., 135
Ford, William, 249
Foreign technology, 170
Forest Press, 34, 152, 171
Forest Press Award, 35
Forney, Christopher Durane, 234, 292
Forsee, Joe, 271
Forsman, Rick B., 161
Fort Vancouver (Washington) Regional Library, 310
Foster, Eloise Cantzon, 67 (biog., photo), 160

Index

Foundations,
  grants by (tables), 116
  private, 115
Fowlie, Les, 83, 84
Fox, Jon D., 299
Fox, Lisa L., vii, 1
Fox, Michael J., 195
Fox, Paula, 94
Frankfurt Book Fair, 196
Frankie, Suzanne O., 18
Franklin (Indiana) Public Library, 276
Franklin, Hardy, 268
Franklin, Jill, 284
Freedley (George) Memorial Award, 239
Freedman, Russell, 37, 51, 67 (biog., photo), 96, 306
Freedom of Information, 225
Freedom of Information Act, 116
Freedom of Information Award (Georgia), 272
Freedom to Read Foundation, 116, 128
Freeman, James E., 276
Freeman, Janet L., 292
Freeman, Peter, 85 (photo)
Fremont County (Wyoming) Library, 312
Friedland, Claire, 254
Friend of the Library (South Dakota), 302
Friends groups, 188
Friends of Alabama Libraries, 260
Friends of Libraries, 118, 241
  in Oklahoma, 296
  in Montana, 286
  in West Virginia, 310
Friends of Marion County (West Virginia) Public Library, 311
Friends of North Carolina Public Libraries, 292
Friends of the Concord Pike (Delaware) Library, 268
Friends of the Evanston Public Library, 118
Friends of the Greenville County (South Carolina) Library, 300
Friends of the Handley (Virginia) Library, 307
Friends of the Library Awards,
  in Montana, 286
  in South Carolina, 301
Friends of the Louisiana State University Library, 118
Friends of the St. Paul (Minnesota) Public Library, 281
Friends of the University of Utah Libraries, 305
Fritz (Chester) Endowment, 293
Fryer, Jim, 265
Fuller, Sherrylynne, 310
Fumigants, 183
Funding, 22, 51, 149, 153
  of academic libraries, 16
  accreditation and, 19
  in Alabama, 260
  in California, 264
  in Colorado, 265
  in Connecticut, 266
  of continuing education, 183
  of federal libraries, 109
  in Florida, 270
  of government information, 120
  in Hawaii, 272
  in Illinois, 275
  in Iowa, 276
  of library construction, 79
  of library education, 106
  of literacy programs, 139
  in Maine, 279
  in Minnesota, 281
  in Montana, 285
  in New York, 308
  in North Dakota, 293
  in Oklahoma, 295
  of Oral History Association, 178

  in Oregon, 297
  in Pennsylvania, 298
  of public libraries, 185
  for research, 216
  in Rhode Island, 299
  in South Dakota, 301
  state libraries and, 239
  statistics, 209
  in Utah, 304
  in Vermont, 306
  in Washington, 308
  in West Virginia, 310
  in Wyoming, 312
  of young adult services, 258
Fundraising and Financial Development, 115
Funk & Wagnalls, 196
Futas, Elizabeth, 67 (biog., photo), 203
Gaines, Ernest J., 232
Gale Research Company, 34, 63
Galesville (Wisconsin) Public Library, 311
Galvin, Thomas, 27, 161
Gannett Foundation, 32, 116, 191, 260, 264, 265
Gannett Newspapers, 264
Garber, Marvin I., 200
Garcia, Donna Marie, 272
Garcia, June, 263
Gard, Betty, 293
Gardner, Carroll, 288
Gardner, Richard K., 52
Gasaway, Laura, 233, 292
Gaskill, Gussie, 291
Gasnick, Roy M., 87
Gaston, Michael, 297
Gateways, 14, 103, 198
Gay and Lesbian Book Award, 34
Gay, Mary Louise, 97
Gaylord, 36, 144, 165, 276
Gaylord Award for Achievement in Library and Information Technology, 36
GEAC, 16, 122
Geh, Hans-Peter, 130
GELC, 129
Genealogical Library (Utah), 305
General Research Corporation, 123
Geneva (Nebraska) Chamber of Commerce, 287
Geography, 157
George, Shirley, 276
George Washington (District of Columbia) University, 269
Georgetown University (District of Columbia), 123, 269
Georgia, 79, 271
Georgia Council of Public Libraries, 271
Georgia Endowment of the Humanities, 272
Georgia Libraries Media Association, 272
Georgia Library Association, 271
Georgia Library Trustees and Friends Association, 271
Georgia State Department of Education, 238, 271
Georgia State University, 37, 204, 272
Georgia University, 271
Gerboth (Walter) Award, 162
Getty (J. Paul) Foundation, 185
Getty (J. Paul) Trust, 48
Gherman, Paul M., 181
Giardena, Denise, 311
Gibson, Robert W., Jr., 233
Giles (Louise) Minority Scholarships, 38
Gillard, Peter McCann, 291
Gillespie, Mary, 263
Gilliland, Donna, 301
Gilmer, Wesley, 279
Girard, Margherite Hall, 291
Gise, Mary, 268
Givens, Mary King, 303

Glandon, Shan, 296
Glasnost Magazine, 202
Glass, Phillip, 231
Glazer, Frederic J., 310
Glenerin Declaration, 130
Glyn County (Georgia) School System, 272
Goach, William D., 303
Goals Award, ALA, 101, 249
Godfrey, Irma C., 87
Goff, Lila Johnson, 178
Goitia, Janet, 208
Gold Flame Award, 272
Goldberg, Susan, 190
Golden, Fay, 148
Golden Sower Award (Nebraska), 287
Goldhor, Herbert, 34, 68 (biog., photo)
Goldsmith, Barbara, 184
Goldstein, Barbara, 129
Goldstein, Charles, 161
Goldstein, Elliot, 129
Goldstein, Elliot and Eleanor, 35
Goldstein, Harold, 271
Goltz, Cheryl, 284
Golub, Wister Margaret, 87
Goniwiecha, Mark, 262
Gonzales, Mario, 208
Goodgion, Laurel, 267
Gordon, Lee, 264
Gordon, Sheila, 96
Gordon, William R., 268
Gorman, Michael, 18, 265
Gosier, James, 220
Gotivals, Joan, 18
Gould, Martha, 288
Gould, R. H., 167 (photo)
Government documents, 119
  Florida and, 270
  Nebraska and, 286
  North Carolina and, 291
  rare, 157
  South Dakota and, 302
  Wyoming and, 312
Government Documents Round Table, 33, 118
Government Finance Officers Association of the United States and Canada, 310
Government Printing Office, 110, 120, 310
Government Publications and Depository System, 119
Governor's Art Award, 262
Goyer, Michael, 263
Goyette, Betty, 266
Graham, Scarlett G., 303
Grand Award in Educational Film, 111
Grand County (Colorado) Library, 266
Grand Forks (North Dakota) Public Library, 293
Granfor, Wayne, 293
Granite State Award, 288
Grants, 16, 20, 25, 44, 50, 52, 56, 138, 153, 166, 179, 185, 194, 204, 207, 222, 260, 265, 270, 272, 273, S274, 276, 277, 278, 279, 283, 286, 287, 290, 293, 295, 297, 298, 299, 300, 301, 302, 304, 305, 306, 307, 308, 311, 312
Graphics, 199
Grassley, Charles E., 277
Grassroots Grant, 261, 303, 311
Gravely, Richard P., 308
Graves, Sid, 282
Great Librarian Award (New Hampshire), 289
Green, Anna, 179
Green, Bradley, 308
Greenaus, Barbara, 85
Greenaway (Britain) Award, 97
Greenaway, Emerson, 288
Greene, Roberta, 299

319

Index

Greenfield, Robert, 280
Greensboro (Vermont) Free Library, 306
Greenspun, Hank, 288
Greenville County (South Carolina) Library, 33, 300
Greenwood (Delaware) Library, 268
Gregorian, Vartan, 188
Grele, Ronald J., 68 (biog., photo), 179
Grierson (John) Award, 111
Griest, Lisa, 39
Griffin, Agnes M., 245, 280
Griffin High School (Georgia), 272
Griggs (Beatrice) Memorial Incentive Grant, 291
Grim, Alta, 310
Grimes, Doria Beachell, 110
Groen, Frances, 85
Grolier Education Corporation, 39, 196
Grolier Foundation, 35
Grolier Foundation Award, 35, 291
Grolier National Library Week Grant, 39, 195, 279
Grose, B. Donald, 18, 304
Grove (Oklahoma) Public Library, 296
Gulf States (Alabama) Public Library, 260
Gundermann, Merly, 295
Gwinn, Nancy, 45
Haas, Stephanie W., 43
Hachette S.A. of France, 195, 201
Hacker, Harold, 289
Haddely, Lee, 295
Haeuser, Mike, 282
Hager, Frances, 264
Hairston, Irene, 292
Hake, Shirley, 310
Hall (G. K.) Award for Library Literature, 35, 153
Hall (G. K.) Company, Inc., 35, 306, 311
Hall of Fame Award, Special Libraries Association, 233
Hall of Fame (Ohio), 295
Halliwell, Dean, 85
Hallstrom, Casse, 113
Halsey, Richard Sweeney, 232
Hamden (Connecticut) Public Library, 166
Hamer (Philip M. and Elizabeth Hamer Kegan) Award, 45
Hamilton, Margaret, 276
Hamilton, Thelma, 287
Hamilton, Virginia, 96
Hamlin, Debbie, 311
Hammer, Sharon, 189, 310
Hampl, Patricia, 281
Handicapped, services, 77, 121, 147, 149, 225
  in Alabama, 260
  in Florida, 270
  in Missouri, 283
  in Ohio, 295
  in Texas, 283
Hankins, Frank, 303
Hans Christian Andersen Award, 97
Hansel, Patsy, 292
Hansen, Andrew M., 202
Hardware, 122
Harnett County (North Carolina) Public Library, 292
Harper & Row, 196
Harranth, Wolf, 97
Harris, Carolyn L., 216, 217 (photo)
Harris, Jean, 298
Harris, Patricia L., 293
Harris, Patricia R., 237
Hart, C. D., 216
Hart (John C.) (New York) Public Library, 33
Hartland (Vermont) Public Library, 306
Hartman, Linda Carol, 36
Hartness, Ann, 42

Harvard University (Massachusetts), 35, 53, 115, 306
Harvey, Norma, 277
Haselwood, E. Laverne, 287
Hasford, Gustav, 219
Haskins, James, 260
Hatcher, Karen, 284
Hatfield, Mark, 297
Haugaard, Erik Christian, 96
Hawaii, 272
Hawaii Library Association, 272
Hawaii-Manoa (University), 273
Hawaii natives, 25
Hawaii State Library, 262, 272
Hawkins (Robert Z.) Foundation, 288
Haynes, Donald R., 308
Haynie, Joan P., 282
HBW Associates, 37
Head, Judith, 85
Health, 220
Health and Human Services Library, 110
Health and Rehabilitation Library Services, 121
Health information services, 158
Health sciences, 169
Heanue, Anne A., 34, 110
Hearmes, Patricia, 273
Hebrew, 236
Heckel, Jim, 286
Heim, Kathleen, 50, 153
Heinemann, Sandra Wood, 308
Heiser, Jane C., 140
Heishman, Eleanor L., 18
Hektoen (Faith) Award, 267
Held, Deanna, 306
Heller, Lori, 278
Helmick, Aileen, 284
Henderson County (North Carolina) Public Library, 292
Hendley, Virginia, 289
Hendrick, Marlene, 277
Hendricksen, Charles, 265
Henne (Francis) Award, 35
Hennepin County (Minnesota) Public Library, 8, 282
Henry, Marguerite, 95
Hensen, Jim, 113
Henshaw, Rod, 40
Herb, Steven, 92
Herbel, Patricia, 293
Hermiston (Oregon) Public Library, 298
Hernon, Peter, 43, 153, 216
Herrick, Charles, 275
Herrick, Kenneth R., 273
Herrin, Barbara, 278
Herring, Mildred C., 292
Hervey, Norma J., 18
Hetherington, Jerre, 303
Hewitt (Bernard) Award, 239
Hewitt, Joe A., 39, 153, 154, 218, 292
High Windy, 230
Higher Education Act, 7, 247, 270
Highsmith Company, 221
Hightower, Monteria, 283
Hildebrand, Carol, 179
Hildenbrand, Suzanne, 147
Hill, Dorothy, 161
Hill, Janet Swan, 87
Hilton, Linda, 38
Hilyard, Nan Blaine, 280
Hinkle, Elvera, 275
Hinshaw, Marilyn, 295
Hinton, S. E., 94, 257, 258, 296
Hintz, Kathleen, 87
Hirsch, James R., 204
Hirsch, Jane K., 21, 36
Hispanics, service, 7
Historical Society of Pennsylvania, 53
Historically Black Colleges and Universities (NBCU) Project, 52
History, 43, 147
Hlava, Marjorie M. K., 105
Ho, May Lien, 33

Hobby Industries of America, 287
Hodges, Gerald, 258, 277
Hodgman, Suzanne, 224
Hogan, Patricia M., 275
Hogan, Rose, 264
Hogan, Sharon A., 18, 34, 53
Holahan, Paulette H., 245
Holdenville (Oklahoma) Public Library, 296
Holibaugh, Ralph W., 18, 295
Holland, Paul, 273
Holley, Edward G., 18, 32, 53, 63, 68 (biog., photo), 292
Hollinger, James, 298
Holmes (Oliver Wendell) Award, 45
Holmstrom, David, 234
Holtcamp, Virginia, 283
Hom, Gloria, 249
Hominy (Oklahoma) Public Library, 296
Honhart, Frederick, 45
Honor Awards,
  Illinois, 275
  Nebraska, 286
  Tennessee, 303
Honors Award, MAGERT, 36, 157
Hooker, Claude L., 245
Hoover (Herbert) Presidential Library, 277
Hopi Language, 167
Hostage, John, 228
Houbeck, Robert L., 225
Houchen, 279
Houghton-Mifflin, 50
Houston Endowment, Inc., 304
Houston (Texas) Public Library, 304
Hove, Nancy, 271
Howard-Gibbon (Canada) Award, 97
Howard, Joseph, 165
Howard University (District of Columbia), 269
Howder, Murray, 268
Howlett, Amy, 306
Hoyt, Janice, 278
Hubbard, William, 261
Huck, Charlotte S., 94
Hudgins, Andrew, 260
Huesmann, James L., 39, 136
Hughes, Ethel A., 271
Hughes (Langston) Community Library (New York), 7
Hulvey, David, 308
Humanities, 259
Humphry, John Ames, 35
Humphrey, Susanne M., 43
Hunnicutt, Ellen, 311
Hunsberger, Charles, 288
Huntington Library, 167
Husted, Grace S., 268
Iarusso, Marilyn Berg, 50, 51 (photo), 115
Iberia Parish (Louisiana) Library, 232
IBM, 200
IBM National Support Center for Persons with Disabilities, 121
ICI, Inc., 268
Idaho, 17, 273
Idaho Book Award, 273
Idaho First National Bank, 274
Idaho Library Association, 273
Idaho State Library, 167, 273
Idaho State University, 274
Idaho (University), 274
Iddins, Mildred L., 303
Illinois, 274
Illinois Association for Media in Education, 275
Illinois Library Association, 274
Illinois Library Trustees Association, 275
Illinois Reading Council, 275
Illinois School Library Media Association, 275
Illinois State Library, 80, 238, 275
Illinois (University), 16
Illinois (University, Chicago), 57
Illinois Valley Library System, 275

Index

Image, 234
  ALA and, 193
  Connecticut and, 267
  New Hampshire and, 288
Immroth, Barbara F., 155
Immroth (John Phillip) Award for Intellectual Freedom, 35, 129
Indexes, 63
Indexing,
  of art and architecture, 47
  of periodicals in North Dakota, 294
Indian Paintbrush Children's Book Award, 312
Indiana, 275
Indiana Library Association, 275
Indiana Library Trustees Association, 275
Indiana State Library, 238, 276
Indiana University, 16
Indiana University (South Bend), 276
Indiana University Foundation, 154
Indians, Library services, 7, 25
Information, access,
  ASIS and, 42
  future of, ix
  GODORT and, 119
  government sources, 57
  IFRT and, 128
  LITA and, 144
  Massachusetts and, 281
  Ohio and, 295
  students and, 22
  Virginia and, 307
Information Access Corporation, 63, 104
Information Access in the 1990s, ix
Information Power, 22, 27, 221
Information policy, 149, 234
  on government documents, 120
  law librarians and, 21
  state libraries and, 238
Information Technology, 43, 122
INFOTRAC, 14
Ingram, 246
Inman, Robert, 260
Innovative Interfaces, 122
Inola (Oklahoma) Public Library, 296
INOVAQUE, 16
Insects, 183
INSPEC, 13
Institute for International Education, 179
Institute for Museum Services, 184
Institute for Scientific Information, 38, 43, 103, 161
Institutional libraries,
  Florida, 270
  Indiana, 276
  Oklahoma, 296
Institutional services, 308
Insurance, 218
Integrated library systems, 122
Intellectual freedom, 124, 128, 223
  in Arizona, 263
  in Canada, 83
  FBI and, 125
  in Kentucky, 279
  in Maine, 280
  in Montana, 285
  in New Hampshire, 288
  in New Mexico, 290
  in Oregon, 298
  in South Carolina, 303
  in South Dakota, 301
  in Vermont, 306
  videos and, 247
  in Washington, 309
  young adults and, 258
Intellectual Freedom Award, 32
Intellectual Freedom Award (Canada), 83, 84
Intellectual Freedom Award (Indiana), 276
Intellectual Freedom Award (Maine), 280
Intellectual Freedom Committee, ALA, 125, 27

Intellectual Freedom Round Table, 35, 128, 228
Intellectual Freedom Round Table State Program Award, 35
Intergenerational Library Assistance Project, 90
Interlibrary loan, 129, 186
  in Arizona, 262
  in Canada, 83, 168
  in Colorado, 265
  in Florida, 271
  in Montana, 285
  networking and, 171
  in South Dakota, 302
  Southeastern libraries and, 232
  standards, 235
  state libraries and, 239
  in Texas, 304
Internal Revenue Service, 197
International Association of Business Communicators, 43, 129, 168, 183, 233, 288
International Federation of Library Associations and Institutions, 47, 129
International Federation of Libraries, 47
International Film and TV Festival, 111
International Library Book Fellows Program, 119
International Organization for Standardization, 234
International Reading Association, 89
International relations, 130, 134
  handicapped services and, 78
  oral history and, 179
  with Russia, 131
International Relations Committee, 130
International Relations Round Table, 262, 130
International Research and Exchange Board, 130
International Standard Book Number, 234
International Thompson, 195
Iowa, 276
Iowa City Public Library, 277
Iowa Educational Media Association, 277
Iowa Library Association, 276
Iowa Library Association Foundation, 277
Iowa State Library, 238, 277
Iowa State University, 276
Iowa (University), 16
Irwin, Ann, 295
Irwin (Richard D.), 196
Ives, Alan, 45
Izumi, Patsy, 272
Jackson, J. Rhett, 78
Jackson, Mary E., 40
Jackson, Miles, 49, 134
Jane Addams Award, 96
Janis, Jane K., 108
Jamison, Carolyn C., 119
Japan, 170
Japan Special Libraries Association, 233
Japanese American Library, 116
Japanese standards, 235
Jasper (Tennessee) Public Library, 303
Java (South Dakota) Public Library, 302
Jefferson Cup Award, 306
Jeng, Judy, 39, 136
Jenkins, Althea H., 270
Jensen, Mary Anne, 239
Jescke, Channing R., 44
Jewish Theological Seminary of America, 146
Jimenez, Rita, 38
Jobson, Joan, 39
John, Nancy, 216

John Newbery Medal, 96
Johns Hopkins University (Maryland), 16, 99, 167
Johnson Bible College (Tennessee), 303
Johnson, Carol French, 277
Johnson, Clare, 312
Johnson County (Tennessee) Library, 303
Johnson County (Wyoming) Library, 80
Johnson, Donald C., 276
Johnson, Duane F., 162, 277
Johnson, Lawrence, 286
Johnson, Jim, 262
Johnson, Margaret, 18
Johnson Publications, 35
Johnson, Richard D., 153
Johnson, Wayne H., 312
Joint Commission on Accreditation of Hospitals, 158
Joint Committee on Publishing, 120
Jondrow, Jim, 286
Jones, Donna, 265
Jones (E. Francis) Memorial Award, 311
Jonish, Thelma, 310
Jordan, James K., 311
Jordan, Sharon L., 42
Josey, E. J., 131
Journal of Youth Services, 50
JPT Holdings, 103
Juba, Gail, 282
Junior Members Round Table, 38, 135, 303
Kahkoven, Laura, 266
Kallay, Susan, 97
Kan, Katherine Louise, 39
Kane, Bartholemew A., 272
Kaneko, Hideo, 135
Kansas, 277
Kansas Association of Educational Communications and Technology, 277
Kansas Association of School Librarians, 277
Kansas City (Missouri) Public Library, 284
Kansas Library Association, 277
Kansas State Library, 238, 278
Kaplan, Lesly Ann, 39
Kaplan, Wendy, 48
Karl, Jean E., 243
Kartashov, Nikolai Semenovich, 131 (photo), 217
Katz, Ruth, 18, 289
Katz, William A., 202
Kaufman, Paula, 125, 18
Kaup, Jerry, 161, 294
Kautz (Sena) Merit Award, 276
Kayden, Mimi, 94
Kearley, David A., 302
Kearney, Anne, 279
Keator, Carol, 265
Keats (Ezra Jack) Award, 242
Keats (Ezra Jack) Lecture, 283
Keck (W. M.) Foundation, 288
Keefe, Bette, 287
Keillor, Garrison, 281
Kelinson, Norman, 41, 277
Kellogg, Ruth, 276
Kellogg (W. K.) Foundation, 20, 191, 296, 305, 308
Kelly, Carol M., 18, 38, 53
Kelly, Virginia, 307
Kelsey, Ann, 39
Kenmore West High School (New York) Library, 33
Kennaway, Adrienne, 97
Kennedy, Marjorie, 85
Kentucky, 278
Kentucky Library Association, 39, 194, 279
Kentucky Library Trustee Association, 279
Kentucky School Media Association, 279

321

Index

Kentucky State Department of Library and Archives, 238, 278
Kentucky (University), 279
Kerlan Award, 94
Kerr Foundation, 296
Kerschner, Joan G., 288
Kessler, James, 265
Kessler, Ridley R., 292
Kesti, Julie, 160
Kiewit Foundation, 286
Kindlen, Jean, 18
King, Coretta Scott, 220
King (Coretta Scott) Award, 35, 228
King County (Washington) Library System, 308
King, Stephen, 280
Kingfisher (Oklahoma) Public Library, 296
Kinney, Gregory, 45
Kirschner, Mary Kay, 276
Kirtland (Oklahoma) Public Library, 295
Kitsap (Washington) Regional Library, 309
Klassen, Robert, 154
Klee, Edward, 279
Kleine Brogel Library (Belgium), 46
Klinck, Patricia E., 305
Klinefelter, Paul, 233
Knight, Keshia Pulliam, 195
Knight-Ridder, 14, 103
Knodle, Shirley, 312
Knopf, 196
Knutson, Linda, 144
Kobasa, Paul, 28
Kohler, Kathleen, 45
Kohlstedt Exhibit Awards, 35
Kolb, Audrey, 261
Kolbe, Jane, 301
Kollasch, Matthew, 277
Korean standards, 235
Kouge, Patricia, 302
Krasner, Rhoda, 33, 42
Kratochvil, Ruth, 297
Krois, Jerome W., 312
Krug, Judith, 27
Krummel, Donald W., 162
Kuszmaul, Marcia J., 188
Kyle, Sara V., 307
Lahey, Michelle, 284
Lakin, Patricia, 287
Lamb, Trudy, 161
Lamont, Bridget, 274
Lampman (Evelyn Sibley) Award, 298
Lancaster, F. Wilfrid, 43
Lancour (Harold) Scholarship, 63
Landry, Mary, 280
Lane (Sister M. Claude) Award, 45
Lang, Thelma L., 287
Languages,
  programming, 122
  standards, 235
LANs, 123
Lao, standards, 236
Large Public Library Friends Award, 118
Larrick, Nancy, 94
Larsgaard, Mary L., 157
Las Vegas/Clark County (Nevada) Library District, 287
Latchkey children, 91, 50, 90, 185, 191
Latin America, 223, 304
Lature, Betty, 303
Laubach Literacy Action Award, 265, 296
Laura Ingalls Wilder Award, 96
Law and Law Libraries, 136
Law libraries, 21
Lawrenceburg (Indiana) Public Library, 276
Laws and legislation, 170
  ALTA and, 41
  Arizona and, 262
  ARL and, 56
  Britain and, 145
  California and, 264
  Canada and, 84
  Connecticut and, 266
  copyright and, 101
  Georgia and, 271
  Idaho and, 273
  Indiana and, 275
  Iowa and, 276
  Kansas and, 277
  Maryland and, 280
  medical libraries and, 158
  Minnesota and, 281
  Mississippi and, 282
  Montana and, 285
  Nebraska and, 286
  New Jersey and, 289
  New Mexico and, 289
  Ohio and, 294
  older adults and, 156
  Oregon and, 297
  South Dakota and, 301
  Special Libraries Association and, 233
  state libraries and, 239
  Tennessee and, 303
  Texas and, 146, 304
  Washington, D.C. and, 269
  young adult services and, 258
Lazerow (Samuel) Fellowship, 18, 38, 53
Leab (Daniel J. and Katharine) American Book Prices Current Exhibition Catalogue Awards, 35, 53
Leab, Katherine Kyes and Daniel J., 35
Leadership, 141
  academic libraries and, 14
  Library of Congress and, 149
  Minnesota and, 282
  Nebraska and, 286
  New Jersey and, 289
Leadership Development Award, 32, 290
Leary, Margaret A., 22, 69 (biog., photo), 136
Lebanon-Wilson County (Tennessee) Public Library, 303
Lee, Chang C., 69 (biog., photo), 98
Lee, Joel, 28
Lee, Michael M., 18
Legal issues, 220
Legislator of the Year Award (Florida), 270
Lenoir City (Tennessee) Public Library, 303
Lenser, Ruth, 287
Leon, Carmencita, 249
Lerma, Barbara, 265
Lerman, Linda P., 55
Lester, Daniel W., 266
Level, June Saine, 277
Levendosky, Charles, 312
Leverett, Rudy, 273
Levitin, Sonia, 54, 97
Lewes (Delaware) Public Library, 268
Lewis and Clark College (Oregon), 298
Lewis and Clark (Montana) Library, 285
Lewis-Clark State College (Idaho), 274
LEXIS, 136
Li, Tze-Chung, 98
Liability, 220
Lian, Nancy W., 290
Librarian of the Year (Arizona), 263
Librarian of the Year (Colorado), 266
Librarian of the Year (Connecticut), 267
Librarian of the Year (Idaho), 273
Librarian of the Year (New Mexico), 289
Librarian of the Year (Nevada), 288
Librarian of the Year (Ohio), 295
Librarian of the Year (South Dakota), 302
Librarian of the Year (Texas), 303
Librarian of the Year (Wisconsin), 311
Librarians, status, 193
Libraries and Culture, 146
Libraries and Literacy, 138
Libraries Serving Special Populations Section, 33
Library Administration and Management Association, 32, 53, 82, 140, 144, 259, 292
Library and Information Science Education Award, 49
Library and Information Technology Association, 32, 53, 144, 276
Library Association, 145, 233
Library Association, Australia, 129, 233
Library Association, China (Beijing), 98
Library Awareness Program, 125
Library Bill of Rights, 128
Library Book Fellows Program, 134
Library cards, 94
  ALA and, 194
  children's services and, 51
  Missouri and, 283
  New York and, 309
  Pennsylvania and, 298
  Utah and, 305
  West Virginia and, 310
  young adults and, 258
Library Company of Philadelphia (Pennsylvania), 35
Library cooperation, 133, 145, 148, 206
  in academic libraries, 16
  in Arizona, 262
  Association of Specialized and Cooperative Libraries and, 61
  in Canada, 167
  in Connecticut, 267
  in European Common Market, 145
  disasters and, 6
  in Florida, 271
  in Iowa, 276
  in Kentucky, 278
  in New Hampshire, 288
  in Oklahoma, 295
  in Pennsylvania, 298
  state libraries and, 238
  U.S.-USSR, 131
  in Wisconsin, 311
  in Wyoming, 312
Library education, 83, 107 (tables), 156, 253
  ARL and, 56
  Continuing Education and, 182
  distance, 222
  in Egypt, 82
  honor awards, 271
  law librarians and, 21
  minorities and, 207
  in New Mexico, 289
  in North Carolina, 291
  school library programs, 23
  in South Dakota, 302
  in Tennessee, 303
  U.S.-USSR, 131
Library history, 145
Library History Round Table, 38, 147
Library Instruction Round Table, 147
Library management, 233
  disasters and, 1
  risk, 218
Library of America, 286, 305
Library of Congress, 14, 17, 51, 64, 121, 130, 131, 149, 171, 184, 195
Library of Congress Rule Interpretations, 86
Library of Congress Subject Headings, 152
Library of Congress Subject Headings, 11th Edition, 86
Library of the Year (Wisconsin), 311
Library Periodical Award, Wilson (H. W.) Company, 38

Library Press, 151
Library Programs, Department of Education, 153
Library Project of the Year Award (Texas), 303
Library Research Round Table, 37, 154
Library Schools, 104 (tables)
Library Service Enhancement Award (Florida), 270
Library Services & Construction Act, 7, 17, 25, 80, 139, 154, 183, 185, 237, 247, 265, 267, 270, 274, 275, 277, 278, 283, 286, 287, 288, 291, 293, 295, 297, 298, 300, 302, 303, 304, 305, 306, 307, 308, 311, 312
Library Service to Older Adults, 155
Library Staff Development Grant, Wilson (H. W.) Company, 40
Library Statistics: A Current Review, 209
Liddy, Elizabeth DuRoss, 43
Lifetime Achievement Award (Colorado), 266
Lifetime Honorary Membership Award (Alaska), 262
Lilly Endowment, 276
Lindsey, George, 306
Linfield (Oregon) College, 298
Linked Systems Project, 87
Linshied, Chester, 290
Lippincott (Joseph W.) Award, 36
Lippincott, Joseph W., Jr., 36
Liston, Nancy Cummings, 109
Literacy,
  Arkansas and, 263
  Nevada and, 287
  North Carolina and, 292
  state libraries and, 237
  Utah and, 305
  Virginia and, 307
  Washington and, 308
  West Virginia and, 311
  Wyoming and, 312
Literacy Award, ALTA, 32, 42
Literacy Award (North Dakota), 293
Literacy Challenge Grant, 260
Literacy, Illiteracy, 22, 138, 139, 147, 227
  Alabama and, 260
  California and, 265
  Canada and, 85
  children's services and, 91
  continuing education and, 283
  Florida and, 270
  Indiana and, 276
  Kansas and, 278
  LITA and, 144
  Maine and, 280
  Montana and, 285
  New York and, 291
  Oklahoma and, 296
  Pennsylvania and, 298
Literary Award (West Virginia), 311
Little Brown, 196
Little, Dorothy M., 289
Loertscher, David V., 33
Logan Helm Woodford County (Kentucky) Public Library, 279
Login Brothers Book Company, 161
Lomax, Georgia L., 284
London Book Fair, 196
Long, Lora, 283
Long, Sara A., 190
Long-range planning, 264
Longsworth, Eileen, 188, 305
Longview (Washington) Public Library, 309
Loo, Shirley, 268
Loretto (Tennessee) Public Library, 303
Los Angeles (California) Public Library, 7, 79, 218
Los Cruces (New Mexico) Public Library, 290
Louderback, Mary, 298

Louisiana State University, 20
Louisville (Kentucky) Free Public Library, 33, 278, 279
Louisville (University, Kentucky), 16, 279
Love, Gladys E., 291
Lovelace (Maud Hart) Book Award, 282
Lowe, Anne, 303
Lowe, Mildred, 107, 177 (obit., photo), 291
Lowell (University, Massachusetts), 61
Lowry, Charles, 140
Lowry, Lois, 301
Lowry, Kenneth W., 233
Luce (Henry) Foundation, 44, 115
Lui, Victor, 38, 63
Lunn, Janet, 97
Lyders, Josette, 50, 69 (biog., photo), 153, 259
Lyle Street, 196
Lynch, Clifford A., 43
Lynch, Mary Jo, 210
Lyons, Gene, 263
McAninch, Sandra S., 119
MacArthur (John D. and Catherine T.) Foundation, 20, 50, 110, 189, 279
McCallum, Sally H., 237
McCarthy (Charles) Award, 288
McCartney, Jean, 283
McCartney, Shirley, 276
McCauley, Hannah V., 295
McCleaf, Sue, 295
McClure, Charles R., 43, 153
McCord, Stanley Joe, 18, 303
McCormick, Henry J., 291
MacDonald, Flora, 167 (photo)
MacDonald, Marie, 286
MacDonald, Marilyn, 265
McDonald's Restaurants, 195
McElderry, Margaret, 96, 242
McElderry (Margaret) Books, 33
Macewian, Greg, 105
McFarland, Sharron, 122
McFerren, Priscilla Greco, 299
McGinn, Howard F., 192
McGoogan (Nebraska) Library of Medicine, 33
McGovern (John P.) Award Lecture, 161
McGowan, Sarah M., 312
McGrath, Tom, 281
McGraw-Hill, 196
McKenzie, Katherine, 306
MacLachlan, Patricia, 19
McLaughlin, Lee, 46
McLeod, H. Eugene, 44
McLeon, Stuart, 43
McNamara, Margaret, 273
McSweeney, Linda, 306
Macalester College (Minnesota), 15, 17, 282
Macmillan, 63, 103, 195, 203
Macy's, 195
Mad Hatter Youth Service Award, 287
Madden, Susan B., 258 (photo), 259, 310
Maddox, Aileen F., 277
Madison County (Florida) Public Library, 271
Madsen, Carol, 287
Maesato, Susan F., 273
Mahfouz, Naguib, 196
Mahnert, Robert, 169
Mahoney, Hugh, 249
Mahony, Willine C., 274
Mahy, Margaret, 94
Maine, 279
Maine Educational Media Association, 279
Maine Humanities Council, 279
Maine Library Association, 279
Maine State Library, 279
Maine (University), 16, 280

Mainiero, Beth, 267
Major Benefactors Award, ALTA, 32, 42, 264, 293
Major, Jean, 283
Malchow, Bea, 266
Malinowsky, Robert H., 233
The Man Who Planted Trees, 113
Management Strategies for Disaster Preparedness, 1
Manhart, Marcia, 48
Manhart, Tom, 48
Mann (Margaret) Citation in Cataloging and Classification, 36, 87, 218
Manning, Helen, 233
Mannington (West Virginia) Public Library, 311
Manuscripts, standards, 235
Manzo, Bettina J., 40
Map and Geography Round Table, 36, 157
Maps, 157, 309
MARC, 243
MARC (UBCIM), 129
Marcello, Ronald E., 179
Margolis, Bernard, 188, 266
Marke, Julius J., 138
Marketing, 191
Markey, Karen, 37, 70 (biog., photo), 87, 218
Markuson, Barbara E., 36, 144, 276
MARMOT project, 266
Martell, Charles, 208
Martin (Allie Beth) Award, 36, 191, 265
Martin, Betty C., 275
Martin, James R., 18, 283
Martin, Jane, 284
Martin, Kay, 276
Martin, Susan Katherine, 70 (biog., photo), 165
Martin (Tennessee) Public Library, 303
Martinez, Mary Jane, 249
Martinson, Doris, 45
Marty, Colleen, 161
Maryland, 280
Maryland Library Association, 280
Maryland State Department of Education, 280
Maryland (University), 125
Maryville College (Missouri), 284
Mason City (Iowa) Public Library, 277
Mason (Harold) Judaica Reference Book Award, 54
Massachusetts, 79, 281
Massachusetts Board of Library Commissioners, 281
Massachusetts Library Association, 281
Massachusetts State Library, 238
Matarazzo, James M., 233
Mathews, Virginia H., 26
Matson, Madeline, 284
Matsumura, Masako, 97
Matthews, John, 113
Maurer, Charles, 295
Maxwell Communications Corporation, 103
Maxwell, Robert, 195
May (Peggy) Award, 283
Mayer, Thomas R., 308
Mayville (South Dakota) State University, 293
Mead Data Central, 136
Means, Raymond B., 286
Meckler Publishing, 64
Media Professional of the Year Award (Iowa), 277
Media Specialist of the Year Award (Georgia), 272
Media Support Awards, 312
Medical College of Georgia, 272
Medical libraries, 157, 159
Medical Library Association, 18, 157, 161, 182, 191

Index

323

Index

Medina (Jose Toribio) Award, 223
MEDLINE, 169
Medori, Claudia H., 232
Meese, Ed, 202
Meier, Vivian S., 284
Meissner, Aroland, 18
Melcher, Daniel, 33
Melcher (Frederic G.) Scholarship, 39
Melcher, Margaret, 94
Mellon (Andrew W.) Foundation, 16, 56, 286, 305
Melton, Emily, 28, 40, 176
Meltzer, Milton, 89, 94
Membership, (table) 30
Memphis/Shelby County (Tennessee) Public Library, 226
Memphis State University (Tennessee), 302
Mercado, Elnora, 161
Mercier, Jean, 94
Meredith (Louise) School Library Media Service Award, 303
Meredith, William, 196
Meritorious Achievement Award (Missouri), 284
Meritorious Service Award (Delaware), 287
Merrill (Charles Company), 196
Metcalf, Keyes D., 146
Mexican Publishers Association, 207
Mexico-Audrain Country (Missouri) Library, 284
Meyer, Mary, 282
Meyers, Arthur S., 202
Meyers, Duane, 296
Miami (Oklahoma) Public Library, 296
Miami-Dade (Florida) Library System, 270
Michelson, Avra, 45
Michigan State Library, 79, 238
Michigan (University), 16, 45, 226
Mickelson, George, 302
Mickey Mouse, 115
Microcomputers,
  desktop publishing and, 199
  information technology and, 123
Microfilming, 184
Microform, 44, 121
Microsoft, 14
Mid-Continent (Missouri) Public Library, 284
Middle County (New York) Public Library, 33
Middlebury (Indiana) Public Library, 276
Miessner, Jan, 80 (photo)
Mika, Joseph J., 62
Mildred Batchelder Award, 96
Milevski, Sandra N., 166
Miller (Betty Davis) Award, 270
Miller, Charles Edmond, 55, 70 (biog., photo), 270
Miller, Frank Winston, 70 (biog.), 118
Miller, Helen, 272
Miller, Laurence, 128
Miller, Marilyn L., 23, 210
Miller, Nancy E., 43
Miller, Paula, 280
Miller, Richard, 286
Miller, Robert H., 281
Milo, Al, 265
Milstead Award, 312
Milwaukee (Wisconsin) Public Library, 7, 90, 121, 134, 192, 226
Mini-Medline, 123
Minneapolis (Minnesota) Public Library, 188
Minnesota, 250, 281
Minnesota Book Awards, 281
Minnesota Department of Education, 281
Minnesota Educational Media Organization, 282

Minnesota Festival of the Book, 281
Minnesota Library Association, 281
Minnesota Mining and Manufacturing Company, 136
Minnesota State University System, 293
Minnesota (University), 250
Minor, Barbara, 108
Minorities,
  Asian/Pacific, 49
  blacks, 76
  in California libraries, 265
  children's services and, 91
  Hispanics, services to, 207
  law librarians and, 21
  libraries and, 108
  recruitment, 54
  service to, 7
  women, 249
Minot (North Dakota) Public Library, 293
Minudri, Regina, vii
Miracle, Faith B., 311
Mississauga (Canada) Public Library, 85
Mississippi, 282
Mississippi Authors Award, 283
Mississippi Library Association, 282
Mississippi Library Commission, 238, 282
Missouri, 283
Missouri Association of School Librarians, 284
Missouri Botanical Garden Library, 284
Missouri Library Association, 283
Missouri State Library, 238, 283
Missouri (University, Columbia), 16, 284
Mitchell, Bonnie Beth, 294
Mitchell, Marilyn, 18
Model Cities Act, 7
Modlin, Wayne, 292
Moellendick, Jeanne, 310
Moffet, William, 18, 51, 150 (photo)
Mogren, Paul, 304
Molholt, Pat, 244
Moncton (Canada) Public Library, 85
Monographs, law, (table), 138
Monroe (Margaret E.) Adult Services Award, 20, 36, 204
Monroe, Shula, 265
Monson, Dianne, 242
Monsour, Margaret M., 202
Montag, John, 295
Montana, 284
Montana Faxnet Project, 285
Montana Library Association, 285
Montana State Library, 189, 285
Montana Tech, 285
Montpelier College (Vermont), 306
Monty, Vivienne, 71 (biog., photo), 83
Moody, Judy, 296
Moon, Ilse, 49, 71 (biog., photo)
Moore, Bessie, 165, 264
Moore, Beverly, 261
Moore, Edythe, 233
Moore, Everett T., 265
Moore, Mary Y., 100
Moore, Merle, 311
Moore, Thomas J., 18
Mooresville (Indiana) Public Library, 276
Moran, Irene E., 144
Moreno, Nancy Quesada, 32
Morgan, Joe, 303
Morita, Ichiko, 48
Morongo Band of Mission Indians Library (California), 26
Morris, Jacqueline S., 24 (photo), 48, 276
Morrison, Carole, 275
Morrison, Toni, 196
Morton, Ann W., 271
Mosher, Paul H., 18
Moss, Margaret, 312

Mount, Charles Merrill, 220
Mount Vernon (Missouri) Public Library, 284
Mountain Plains Library Association, 161, 286, 294
Mountainside Publishing Company, 34
Mountlake Terrace (Washington) Public Library, 309
Mouton, Cookie, 288
Mudge (Isadore Gilbert) Award, 204, 206
Mudge (Isadore Gilbert) Citation, 36, 308
Mullen, Cleotta, 264
Mullen, Marion, 291
Muller, Karen, 216
Muller, William A., 308
Multnomah County (Oregon) Public Library, 146, 226, 298
Mulvane (Kansas) Public Library, 278
Munoz, Peggy, 286
Murfin, Marjorie E., 209
Murgar, Sarla R., 18, 38, 53
Murphy, John A., 263
Murphy, Lucille Lucas, 264
Murphy, Nelwyn, 242, 249
Murphy, William, 21, 138
Museum Computer Network, 47
Museum Store Association, 188
Music, cataloging, 244
Music Library Association, 162
Music Publishers' Association, 162
Mutilation, 219
Myers, Sara J., 44
Myklebust, Helmer R., 302
Myklebust, M. Helen, 302
Mysterious Press, 35
MZA, 230
Nach, Mary, 287
Naftalin, Francis H., 37, 42
Nance, Betty, 302
Nasri, William Z., 103
National Advisory Committee, 149
National Aeronautics and Space Administration, 202
National Agricultural Library, 163, 171
National Agricultural Library Statistics, 163 (table)
National Alternative Farming Systems Information Center, 163
National Archives and Records Administration, 44, 185
National Association of Counties, 189, 282
National Association of Counties Achievement Award, 272
National Book Award, 150, 196
National Center for Education Statistics, 209, 238
National Children's Book Award (Austria), 97
National Children's Book Week, 88, 94
National Coalition for Literacy, 138
National Commission on Library and Information Science, 27, 90, 124, 125, 134, 165, 209
National Council for Social Studies, 89
National Council for the Accreditation of Teacher Education, 23, 90, 105
National Council of Teachers of English, 89
National Council of Teachers of English Award for Excellence in Poetry in Children's Literature, 94
National Council on Quality Continuing Education, 100
National Educational Film and Video Festival, 111
National Endowment for the Arts, 184

National Endowment for the
Humanities, 16, 20, 44, 52, 56,
64, 99, 166, 184, 188, 196, 259,
261, 267, 268, 278, 279, 295,
298, 299, 301, 304, 306, 308
National Geographic, 202
National Historical Publications, 305
National Historical Publications and
Records Commission, 269
National Indian Education
Association, 7
National Information Standards
Organization, 210, 234
National Institutes of Health, 160
National libraries, 171
National Library Card Campaign, 27
National Library Legislative Day, 24
National Library of Canada, 167
National Library of Medicine, 14,
121, 159, 160, 169, 171, 185
National Library Service for the
Blind and Physically
Handicapped Award, 77, 264
National Library Week, 193, 194
National Library Week, 192
National Oceanic and Atmospheric
Administration Library, 110
National Orthodox Jewish Archives,
219
National School Library Media
Program of the Year Award, 37
National Science Foundation, 204
(table), 276
National Science Teachers
Association, 89
National Technical Information
Service, 56, 110, 119, 120, 169
Natrona County (Wyoming) Library,
312
Navy libraries, 47
NCLIS Recognition Award, 165
Neal, Donn C., 45
Neal (Frances) Award, 264
Nebraska, 286
Nebraska Committee for the
Humanities, 286
Nebraska Educational Media
Association, 162, 286
Nebraska Library Association, 162,
286
Nebraska Library Commission, 238,
286
Nebraska Society of Architects, 286
Nebraska (University), 287
Neighbors, Fred D., 261
Nelson, Beete, 283
Nelson, James A., 278
Nelson, Margaret, 45
Nelson, Rachel Wayne, 189
Nemerov, Howard, 149 (photo), 151
Nene Award, 273
Nepean (Canada) Public Library, 85
Ness, Evaline, 94
Nestle, Joan, 34
Network of Alabama Academic
Libraries, 99
Networks, Networking, 61, 147, 165,
197, 225, 261
in Arizona, 262
in Arkansas, 263
in California, 265
in Colorado, 265
in Florida, 271
in Hawaii, 273
in Illinois, 275
in Indiana, 276
in Iowa, 277
in Kentucky, 279
in Maine, 280
in Massachusetts, 281
in Montana, 285
in Nebraska, 286
in Nevada, 287
in New Hampshire, 288
in North Carolina, 291
in Oklahoma, 296
in Rhode Island, 299

in South Carolina, 300
in South Dakota, 301
state libraries and, 239
US-USSR relations and, 131
in Utah, 305
in Vermont, 306
in Virginia, 307
in Washington, 309
in Wisconsin, 311
Neumann Chapter, Catholic Library
Association, 87
Nevada, 287
Nevada Council on the Arts, 288
Nevada Library Association, 288
Nevada State Library and Archives,
287
Nevada (University, Las Vegas), 288
Nevada (University, Reno), 288
New Castle County (Delaware)
Department of Libraries, 268
New England Library Association,
288
*New Grove Dictionary of American
Music*, 162
New Hampshire, 288
New Hampshire Library Association,
288
New Hampshire State Department of
Libraries, Arts and Historical
Resources, 185, 235, 288
New Jersey, 185, 289
New Jersey Library Association, 289
New Jersey State Library, 238, 289
New Librarian of the Year (South
Dakota), 302
New Mexico, 289
New Mexico Library Association,
289
New Mexico State Library, 289
New Mexico State University, 81,
290
New Mexico (University), 289
New Orleans (Louisiana) Public
Library, 187, 226
New York, 79, 185, 290
New York Library Association, 32,
129, 290, 308
New York Mills (Minnesota) Public
Library, 282
New York Public Library, 7, 187, 91,
99, 115, 184, 226, 291
New York State Library, 238, 291
New York University, 16, 291
Newberg, Ellen, 286
Newberg (Indiana) Public Library,
276
Newbery (John) Medal, 37, 51
Newberry (Illinois) Library, 167
Newcomer, Audrey Powderly, 161,
287
Newport (Rhode Island) Public
Library, 299
Nichols, J. Gary, 279, 308
Nichols, Margaret Irby, 304
Nicolaisen, Birgit, 38
Nieto, David, 109
Nilsson, Ulf, 96
Nissan, Sue, 286
Niuksha, Iuliia Petrovna, 217
Nobel Prize, 196
Nollen, Sheila H., 37, 119
Noma (Japan) Award, 97
Nonprint materials, 53
Norcross, Jane, 37, 42, 272
Nord, Kay, 312
Norris, Rosalie, 288
North America Collections Inventory
Project, 56
North American Baptist Seminary
(South Dakota), 302
North Bend (Oregon) Public Library,
298
North Carolina, 291
North Carolina Association of School
Librarians, 292
North Carolina Central University,
291

North Carolina Library Association,
291
North Carolina State Library, 238,
292
North Carolina (University), 224, 291
North Carolina (University,
Greensboro), 291
North, Colonel Oliver, 202
North Dakota, 293
North Dakota Centennial
Commission, 294
North Dakota Library Association,
161, 293
North Dakota State Library, 293
North Dakota State University, 293
North Dakota (University, Grand
Forks), 293
North Texas (University), 289
Northeast Document Conservation
Center, 184
Northern Illinois Learning Resources
Cooperative, 274
Northern Iowa (University), 277
Northern New Mexico Community
College, 289
Northwest Nazarene College (Idaho),
274
Norton, Nancy, 303
Norwich Central Library (England),
134
Notables, 172
NOTIS, 122
Notre Dame (University, Indiana),
276
Noyes (Marcia C.) Award, 161
Nyren, Karl, 16, 152, 177 (obit,
photo), 291
Oakland (California) Latin American
Library, 8
Oberlin College (Ohio), 17
Oberman, Cerise, 18
Oboler (Eli M.) Memorial Award, 37,
129
O'Brien, Anne, 281
O'Brien (Jane) Award, 275
OCLC, 17, 64, 86, 103, 164, 171,
185, 225, 261
O'Connor, Sandra Day, 151 (photo)
O'Connor, Thomas, 38, 147, 265
Office for Library Outreach Services,
39
Office of Education, 284
Office of Library Personnel
Resources, 50, 193
Official Airlines Guide, 103
Oglala Lakota College (South
Dakota), 302
Ohio, 294
Ohio Educational Library-Media
Association, 294
Ohio Friends of the Library, 294
Ohio Library Association, 294
Ohio Library Foundation, 294
Ohio Library Trustees Association,
295
Ohio State Library, 295
Ohio State University, 295
Oklahoma, 295
Oklahoma City (Oklahoma)
Metropolitan Library, 226
Oklahoma County (Oklahoma)
Public Library System, 20
Oklahoma Department of
Corrections, 296
Oklahoma Department of Libraries,
296
Oklahoma Foundation for the
Humanities, 295
Oklahoma Library Association, 295
Oklahoma Library Association
Awards, 296
Oklahoma State Department of
Education, 296
Oklahoma State University, 238, 296
Oklahoma (University), 296
Olden, Edward A., 50
Older adults, services, 155, 277, 288

325

Index

Index

Oliver, Kent, 278
Olofson (Shirley) Memorial Award, 39, 136
Olsen, Cynthia M., 39
Olsen, Richard, 300
Omaha (Nebraska) Public Library, 286
Online catalogs, 16, 88, 145
Online, Inc., 64
Online Magazine Award, 205
Online services, 14, 205
  health science, 169
  Iowa and, 277
Onodaga (New York) County Public Library, 291
Ontario Library Association, 85
Oppenheimer, Gerald J., 161
Optical disc, 200
Oral history, 178
Oral History Association, 178
Orange County (California) Public Library, 26, 33, 49, 97, 189, 207, 219, 265
Orbis Books, 87
Orbit Infoline, 83, 103
Oregon, 297
Oregon Education Media Association, 297, 309
Oregon Library Association, 297
Oregon Library Exhibits Network, 298
Oregon Museum of Science and Industry, 297
Oregon State Library, 297
Oregon State University, 297
Orgren, Carl F., 277
Orlando (Florida) Public Library, 187
Orthof, Sylvia, 97
Orwell (Vermont) Free Library, 306
Ostrander, Richard, 310
Otero-Boisvert, Maria, 39
Ott, Bill, 71 (biog., photo), 153
Ottowa (University, Canada), 84
Our Sunday Visitor Foundation, 269
Outstanding Achievement Award (Mississippi), 283
Outstanding Advocate of Libraries Award, 290
Outstanding Arizona Author, 263
Outstanding Citizen Award (Florida), 270
Outstanding Citizen of the Year Award (Arkansas), 264
Outstanding Decision Maker Award (Arizona), 263
Outstanding Individual Award (West Virginia), 311
Outstanding Information Science Teacher, 43
Outstanding Librarians Award (Indiana), 276
Outstanding Library Assistant Award (Indiana), 276
Outstanding Library Award (Indiana), 276
Outstanding Library Friends Group Award (North Carolina), 292
Outstanding Library Service Award (West Virginia), 311
Outstanding Public Library Service Award (Kentucky), 279
Outstanding School Administrator Award (Kentucky), 279
Outstanding School Media Librarian Award (Kentucky), 279
Outstanding Service Award (Nebraska), 287
Outstanding Service to Libraries Award (New York), 290
Outstanding Service to Libraries Award (Texas), 303
Outstanding Southeastern Author Award, 232
Outstanding Southeastern Library Program Award, 232
Outstanding Trustee Award (Iowa), 277

Outstanding Trustee Award (Indiana), 276
Outstanding Trustee Award (Kentucky), 279
Outstanding Trustee Award (Tennessee), 303
Outstanding Trustee of the Year Award (Arizona), 264
Owen, Amy, 305
Owens, Major, 249
Oxnard (California) Public Library, 81
Ozaukee County (Wisconsin) League of Women Voters, 311
Pacific Association for Communications and Technology, 272
Pacific Northwest Library Association, 179
Packaging, standards, 235
Padilla, Dolores, 289
Pages, 221
Pagnucci, Franco, 263
Pagnucci, Susan, 263
Paine, Patricia M., 306
Painter, Francis O., 181
Pali, standards, 236
Palm Harbor (Florida) Junior Women's Club, 270
Palma, Nancy, 39, 136
Palmer, Raymond A., 161
Palmer, Richard, 209
Pannell (Lucile Micheals) Award, 254
Pannell, Sarah, 283
Panz, Richard, 290
Papalhiew, A. Ralph, 162
Paper, standards, 236
Pardoe, Janice, 38, 136
Parent, Roger H., viii
Parents' Choice Awards, 112
Park County (Colorado) Library, 266
Parker (Kansas) Public Library, 278
Parker, Sara A., 239, 299
Parker, Victoria, 310
Parkhurst, Carol A., 144
Parks (Dora Ruth) Award, 311
Parks, James F., 283
Parmly Billings (Montana) Library, 285
Parry, Pamela J., 97
Pasco County (Florida) Library System, 80
Paskoff, Beth, 161, 234
Past Presidents' Award, 283
Patents, 14
  Missouri and, 284
  standards, 235
Paterson, Katherine, 87, 96
Pathchogue-Medford (New York) Public Library, 19
Patrick, Retta, 22, 264
Patsiner, Connie, 276
Patterson, Bobbie J., 308
Paul Gaugin, The Savage Dream, 111
Paulsen, Gary, 281
Paulsen, Kay, 287
Paustian, Robert, 302
Pay equity, 179
  in Minnesota, 250
  risk management and, 221
Pearce, Don, 282
Pearce, Douglas, 299
Pearson, 195
Pease (Theodore Calvin) Award, 45
Pedersen, Sarah, 18, 113
Pederson, Ann, 45
Pend Oreille (Washington) County Library, 309
Penebacker, John, 220, 273
Penn (William) Foundation, 188
Penniman, W. David, 43, 71 (biog., photo)
Pennsylvania, 298
Pennsylvania Citizens for Better Libraries, 298

Pennsylvania Library Association, 298
Pennsylvania State Library, 298
Penthouse, 202
People for the American Way, 117
Pepper, Claude D., 161
Percy, Walker, 196
Perdue, Charles, 278
Pereslegina, E. V., 129
Periodicals, 55, 98, 152, 224
  ALA, 30 (table)
  costs, 54, 160, 179, 195
  exchange, 244
  indexing, in North Dakota, 294
  law (table), 138
  online, in Arizona, 289
  reviewing of, 53
  standards, 236
Perritt, Patsy H., 257
Personnel, 138, 179, 181
  in academic libraries, 17
  ALA and, 193
  Kentucky and, 278
  North Carolina and, 292
  risk management and, 220
  Wisconsin and, 292
Personnel and Employment: Compensation and Pay Equity, 179
Personnel and Equipment: Continuing Education and Staff Development, 181
Peterson, Fred, 274
Peterson, Keith, 273
Peterson, Raymond J., 165
Peterson, Sandra K., 253
Petroleum Abstracts, 13
Petros (Tennessee) Public Library, 303
Pew Charitable Trust, 17, 302
Pfeiffer (Peggy L.) Service Award, 276
Phelps, Thomas C., 167
Philippines, 89
Phillips, Beulah, 46
Phillips, Rosie, 303
Philpot, Clive, 47
Phoenix Award, 96
Phoenix (Arizona) Public Library, 81, 121, 263
Phonolog, 231
Photocopying, 102, 196
Pickens, T. Boone, 192 (photo)
Pierce, Sally Galbraith, 284
Piercy (Esther J.) Award, 37, 87, 218
Piggford, Roland, 281
Pillow, Lucille B., 16
Pillsbury, Penny, 305
Pineda, Conchita J., 49
Pisarek, Kathreen, 277
Pitman, Randy, 247
Pitts, Judy M., 25, 71 (biog., photo), 153
Pizer, Irwin H., 160
Pizza Hut, Inc., 165
PLA Advancement of Literacy Award, 264
Planning, 44, 51, 149, 168, 203
  American Library Trustee Association and, 42
  in Arizona, 262
  in Arkansas, 263
  ARL and, 55
  by Association for Library and Information Science Education, 49
  in Canada, 85
  by CLENE, 101
  in Connecticut, 266
  in Delaware, 268
  disasters and, 2
  in Illinois, 274
  in Indiana, 276
  in Kentucky, 278
  by LITA, 144
  in Maine, 279

Index

by medical libraries, 159
in Missouri, 283
by National Archives and Records Administration, 44
by National Library of Canada, 168
in Nebraska, 286
in Nevada, 288
in North Dakota, 293
by REFORMA, 206
by Resources and Technical Services Division, 217
in Rhode Island, 299
in South Dakota, 302
by state libraries, 238
in Tennessee, 302
by theological libraries, 44
in Vermont, 305
in Virginia, 307
in Washington, 308
Playboy, 117
Playfoot, Marion, 287
Pleasant Grove (Vermont) Library, 305
Plenum Scholarship, 234
Poetry, 19
Pollard, Richard C., 18
Polson City (Montana) Library, 285
Popular Culture and Libraries, 54
Portage County (Ohio) District Library, 295
Porter, Arthur E., 289
Posner, Marcia W., 54, 72 (biog., photo)
Postal rates, 83, 197
Poteat, James, 239
Potter, William Gray, 144
Power, Margaret C., 206
Prairie Pasque Award, 301
Prairie View A & M University (Texas), 304
Predicasts, 14
Prentice, Ann E., 18
Presberry, Rose, 280
Preservation, 45, 130, 150, 154, 162, 167, 183
in academic libraries, 14
in art publications, 47
disasters and, 1
law librarians and, 21
medical libraries and, 159, 169
National Endowment for the Humanities and, 248
by National Library of Canada, 168
New Hampshire and, 288
New York and, 291
paper, 179
Pennsylvania and, 298
of periodicals, 48
Society of American Archivists and, 45
standards, 236
state libraries and, 238
in theological libraries, 44
US-USSR relations and, 131
Virginia and, 307
Preservation of Library Materials, 183
Presidential Projects, 234
President's Award, AASL/Baker and Taylor, 32
President's Award (Arizona), 119
President's Award, MLA, 161
President's Award (Minnesota), 282
President's Award, SELA, 232
President's Award, SLA, 233
President's Distinguished Service Award, Pacific Northwest, 179
Preston-Carnegie Council District Library, 274
Prevedel, Norma, 312
Price, Louise C., 289
Price, Michael, 305
Price, Neil V., 294
Price, Susan, 97
Price (Waldo Gifford Leland) Award, 45
Prince George's County (Maryland) Public Library, 189

Prince, Jack, 311
Prine, Stephen, 78
Printers, desktop publishing, 200
Professional Award, Special Libraries Association, 233
Professional Development Grant, 3M/JMRT, 39, 136, 306
Professional Development Grants, Mountain Plains Library Association, 161
Project REAP, 276
Providence (Rhode Island) Public Library, 300
Public Awareness,
Florida and, 270
librarians and, 193
Massachusetts and, 281
young adult services and, 258
Public Broadcasting System, 20
Public Information Office, ALA, 138, 193, 194, 287
Public libraries, 185, 190
in Alabama, 260
in Alaska, 262
book stores in, 187
buildings, 80
in California, 264
children's services and, 90
in Colorado, 266
in Connecticut, 267
in Delaware, 268
in Florida, 270
in Hawaii, 272
in Georgia, 272
in Illinois, 274
in Indiana, 276
in Iowa, 277
in Kansas, 278
in Kentucky, 278
latchkey children in, 91
literacy and, 140
in Maine, 279
in Maryland, 280
in Massachusetts, 281
in Minnesota, 281
minority service in, 7
in Mississippi, 281
in Missouri, 284
in Montana, 285
in Nebraska, 286
in Nevada, 287
in New Jersey, 289
in New Mexico, 290
in New York, 290
in North Carolina, 292
in North Dakota, 293
in Oklahoma, 296
in Oregon, 297
in Pennsylvania, 298
in Rhode Island, 299
salaries and, 180
in South Carolina, 300
in South Dakota, 302
state libraries and, 237
statistics, 209, 165
in Tennessee, 303
in Utah, 305
in Vermont, 305
video and, 110
in Washington, 308
in West Virginia, 310
in Wisconsin, 311
in Wyoming, 312
Public Library Association, 27, 32, 92, 185, 190, 191, 209
Public Library Data Service, 209
Public relations, 191, 234, 264
librarians and, 193
library stores and, 187
Massachusetts and, 281
Montana and, 285
Public Relations and Marketing, 191
Publishers, 64
Publishing, 129, 151, 195, 201
adult services and, 19
of children's literature, 93
of research, 216

medical libraries and, 158
Publishing, Book, 195
Publishing, Serials, 201
Publishing Services, ALA (table), 30
Pueblo (Colorado) Library District, 266
Pulitzer Prize, 196
Pullman, Philip, 96
Pungitore, Verna L., 50
Purdue University (Indiana), 276
Putnam, 196
Putnam and Grosset Group, 39
Putnam and Grosset Group Award, 39
Putnam (Herbert W.) Honor Award, 39
Putnam (Herbert W.) Honor Fund, 39
Putnam Valley (New York) Free Library, 226
Queens College (New York), 16
Queens College (New York) Library, 17, 291
Queensborough (New York) Public Library, 20
Racoosin, William, 289
Radlauer, Ed, 95
RAF Upper Heyford Base (England) Library, 33
Rand, Roena, 275
Randall, William, 266
Randolph Caldecott Medal, 96
Random House, 196
Ransdell (Ed) Award, 283
Ransom, Marsha, 278
Rao, Paladugu V., 284
Raphael, Mary E., 270
Rapp, Joan, 284
Rare books, cataloging, 244
Rath, Bernard E., 79
Ray, Dee Ann, 285
READ Illinois Project, 19
Reader's Adviser, 152
"Readers as Writers," 94
Reader's Digest, 201
Reader's Digest Foundation, 194
Readex Corporation, 37, 119
Reading,
adult services and, 19
Mississippi and, 282
public libraries and, 91
Recognition of Excellence Award (Georgia), 272
Recordings,
notable, 172
rental and, 101
Records, 136
New York and, 291
privacy of, 125, 239, 303
Recruitment,
ALA and, 194
of minorities, 9
Reed, Barbara, 243
Reed, Mary Hutchings, 27
Reed (Sarah Rebecca) Scholarship, 63
Reeling, Patricia, 33, 119
Reeves, Joan Ress, 242, 249, 300
Reeves (Morris) Library, (West Virginia), 227
Reference,
in academic libraries, 15
books, 63
networks and, 172
Reference and Adult Services Division, 1, 19, 36, 63, 172, 202
Reference Service Press Award, 37, 204
Reference Service Press, Inc., 37
REFORMA, 109, 206
Regan, Muriel B., 232, 291
Regina Medal, 87, 96
Reichert, Katherine, 306
Reid, Charles E., 165
Reid, Marion T., 218
Reitz, Thomas L., 270
Religion Index, 44
Remboldt, Irma, 293
Rentschler, Cathy, 254

327

Index

Research, 153, 208
 academic libraries and, 14
 LRRT and, 76
 on minority service, 9
 SALALM and, 223
 Special Libraries Association and, 234
Research libraries, Alexandrian, 81
Research Libraries Group, 48, 98, 167
Research Paper Competition Award, 50
Research Publications, 63
Resnik, Linda, 44
Resource sharing, 100, 168
 in academic libraries, 15
 in Illinois, 274
 in Iowa, 277
 state libraries and, 236
Resources and Technical Services Division, 32, 53, 216
Resources in Education (RIE), 108
Restaurants, 188
Retail Shops in Public Libraries: A Survey, 187
Retired Senior Volunteer Program, 156
Rettig, James R., 36, 64, 72 (biog., photo), 204, 206, 308
Revelle, Keith, 220
Reviewing, 52, 201
Reynolds (Catherine J.) Award, 37, 119
Reza, Bob, 264
RHC Spacemaster, 191
Rhode Island, 79, 299
Rhode Island Department of State Library Services, 299
Rhode Island Library Association, 299
Rhode Island (University), 300
Rhodes, Gloria L., 40
Rhodes, Richard, 150, 196
Ricardo, Ralph E., 34, 72 (biog., photo)
Richards, Pamela S., 50, 63
Richardson, John V., 49
Richardson, Kathy E., 288
Richardson, Robert, 271
Richmond (Canada) Public Library, 85
Riedesel, Laureen, 286
Riegel, J., 294
Riley, W. Mercedes, 291
Risk Management for Libraries, 218
Risks, management, 218
Riverside City and County (California) Public Library, 146
RLIN, 16, 87
Robbins, Jane, 311
Robert Bell & Co., 196
Roberts, James C., 249
Roberts, Marceline, 91 (photo)
Roberts, Willo Davis, 284
Roberts, Winston D., 244
Robinson, Barbara, 42
Robles, Daniel O., 37, 191, 265
Rochester Institute of Technology (New York), 16
Rockefeller (Winthrop) Foundation and Systematics, Inc., 263
Rodger, Eleanor Jo, 190
Rogers (Frank Bradway) Information Advancement Award, 161
Rolando, Margaret, 284
Rolling Meadows (Illinois) Public Library, 90
Rollock, Barbara, 94
Rolstead, Gary O., 21
Roman, Susan, 50
Rosary College (Illinois), 146
Roscello, Frances R., 290
Rose Publishing Company, 264
Rosenbach Museum and Library, 35, 53
Rosenzweig Award, 263
Ross County (Ohio) Public Library, 121

Rossman, M. J., 281
Rothrock Award, 232
Rothstein, Samuel, 33, 49, 62, 73 (biog., photo)
Round Rock (Texas) Independent School District, 37
Royal, Samuel, 219
Ruby Slipper Awards, 113
Ruckman, Ivy, 282
Rufsvold, Margaret I., 32
Runkle, Martin D., 55
Rural Information Center, 163
Rural libraries, 131
Rush City (Minnesota) Public Library, 282
Rushing, Felder, 283
Rusk, Dean, 271
Russell, Mattie U., 292
Rutgers University (New Jersey), 154
Sabbe, Nancy, 301
Sabosik, Patricia E., 53
Sacramento (California) Public Library, 80
Saferite, Linda, 262
Safety, 220
Sager, Donald J., 189
St. Charles City-County (Missouri) Library, 284
St. Francis (Kansas) Public Library, 278
St. Johnsbury Atheneum (Vermont), 306
St. Louis County (Missouri) Library, 284
St. Louis (Missouri) Public Library, 170, 284
Salaries, 105, 179, 249
 Connecticut and, 267
 in federal libraries, 110
 Maine and, 280
 Massachusetts and, 281
 pay equity, 250
 Pennsylvania and, 298
 Rhode Island and, 299
 South Carolina and, 301
 statistics, 165
 in Vermont, 305
 in Wisconsin, 311
Salinas, Marie Alexandra, 208
Sallisaw (Oklahoma) Public Library, 296
Salt Lake (Utah) Public Library System, 305
San Antonio (Texas) Public Library, 167
San Diego (California) Public Library, 81
San Francisco (California) Public Library, 8, 33, 93, 94, 265
San Francisco Foundation, 116
San Jose (California) Biblioteca Latinoamericana, 8
Sandy (Oregon) Public Library, 298
Sankei Award, 97
Sanner, James, 297
Sarver, Mary Ann, 275
Satterthwaite (Marion) Award, 280
Saturday Review, 202
Saur, K. G., 32, 153
Saur (K. G.) Award, 18, 32, 53, 265
Sawyer, Sandra, 276
Say, Allen, 96
Scarecrow Press, 34
Scepanski, Jordan M., 18, 32, 53, 153, 265
Schlachter, Gail A., 203 (photo), 206
Schlesinger, Deborah, 286
Schlessinger, Bernard S., viii
Schlessinger, June H., 96
Schlosser, Sue Ann, 284
Schmidt, Annie M.G., 97
Schmidt, C. James, 27, 124, 125
Schmidt, Sherrie, 144
Schmidtmann, Nancy, 87
Schoenherr, John, 33, 51, 73 (biog., photo), 96
Scholarship in Library and Information Technology, 38

Scholarships, 21, 54, 63, 87, 135, 161, 208, 234, 264, 277, 278, 288, 292, 310
Schon, Isabel, 94
School Administrator of the Year Award (Montana), 286
School Administrator of the Year Award (North Dakota), 293
School Libraries, 145, 181
 in Alabama, 260
 in Alaska, 262
 in Arkansas, 263
 in Britain, 145
 in California, 264
 in Colorado, 266
 credentials, 23
 in Florida, 270
 funding of, 248
 in Georgia, 272
 in Hawaii, 272
 in Illinois, 275
 in Iowa, 277
 in Kansas, 278
 in Kentucky, 279
 in Maine, 280
 in Mississippi, 283
 in Missouri, 284
 in Montana, 284
 in Nebraska, 286
 in Nevada, 288
 in New Mexico, 290
 in New York, 291
 in North Dakota, 293
 in Oklahoma, 295
 in Oregon, 298
 in Pennsylvania, 298
 in Rhode Island, 300
 in South Carolina, 300
 in South Dakota, 302
 statistics, 210
 in Tennessee, 303
 in Texas, 304
 in Vermont, 306
 in Washington, 309
 in West Virginia, 311
 in Wyoming, 312
School Library Media Programs, 221
School Library Journal, 258, 296
School Library Media Quarterly, 25
Schouweiler, Eileen, 249
Schreiber, Reta, 279
Schremser, Bob, 261
Schreyer, Alice, 52
Schubert, Leda, 305
Schuman, Patricia, 28
Schunk, Russell J., 282
Schwann Catalog, 231
Schwann CD Catalog, 231
Schwartz, Charles and Bertie G. Award, 96
Schwarzkopf, Leroy C., 121
Schweers, Lucy, 266
Schweers (Lucy) Award, 266
Science, 89
Science Digest, 202
Science fiction, 258
Science Research Associates, 196
Scott, Linda, 39, 136
Scott, Marianne, 168
Scottsdale (Arizona) Public Library, 117
Scranton (University, Pennsylvania), 197
Seaford (Delaware) District Library, 268
Seal, Robert A., 221
Searching, online, 123
Sears, 195
Seattle (Washington) Public Library, 187, 77, 309
Seavey, Charles A., 39, 62
Seboldt, Mildred, 284
Security, 219
 in academic libraries, 16
 Oklahoma and, 295
Segal, JoAn S., 51
Segal, Judith, 265
Selle, Donna, 298, 308

Index

Seminar on the Acquisition of Latin American Library Materials, 223
Sendak, Maurice, 115
Sennett, Brother Denis, 45
Sequoyah Youth Adult Book Award, 295
Serebnick, Judith, 129
Serials, 224
Serials Librarianship Award, 18, 37, 218
Series, 129, 272, 280
Service Award (Alaska), 262
Service Award, ALISE, 49
Service to Diverse Populations, 7
Sessions (John) Memorial Award, 37, 204
Sessions, Judith A., 18, 116, 295
Sexton, Kay, 281
Shaevel, Evelyn, 61, 258
Shaffer, Dallas Young, 141
Shattuck, Charles, 239
Shaw, Margaret, 47
Shaw, Spencer, 73 (biog., photo), 77, 107, 310
Sheehan, Neil, 196
Shelby (Mississippi) Public Library, 283
Shelbyville (Delaware) Library, 268
Sheller, Bess, 312
Shepard, Julie, 286
Shera, Jesse H., 154
Shera (Jesse H.) Award for Research, 37, 154
Shilling, Joseph, 280
Shilts, Randy, 34
Shipman, John S., 39, 153, 218, 292
Shires, Leslyn, 311
Shodasir Hospital (Montana), 285
Shoemaker, Emily, 270
Shoemaker, Merhl, 270
Shubert, Joseph F., 62 (photo), 291
Sidney (Montana) Public Library, 285
Siekkinen, Raya, 97
Sierra Madre (California) Public Library, 33, 265
Silver, Linda R., 221
Silver Medallion (Mississippi), 283
Silver Office Automation Award, 285
Silver Platter, 14, 63, 108, 164
Silvey, Anita, 94
Simon & Schuster, 196
Simon (Charlie May) Award, 264
Simpson, Susan, 312
Sineath, Timothy, 50
Sioux Falls College (South Dakota), 302
Sioux Falls (South Dakota) Public Library, 302
Sivak, Maine, 274
Skidmore, Steve, 295
Skinger, Alice, 270
Slater, Margaret, 193
Sloan, Elaine F., 18, 291
Sloan, Mary Jean, 272
Sloan, William J., 111
Small, Jane, 295
Small Public Library Friends Award, 118
Smith, Diane L., 284
Smith (Elisha D.) Public Library, 311
Smith (Elva Sophronia) Grants, 306
Smith, Ethel F., 292
Smith, George V., 179
Smith, Jane Bandy, 260
Smith, Jessie Carney, 77
Smith, Krystal, 276
Smith, Nathan M., 305
Smith, Patricia H., 303
Smith, Ruth S., 233
Smith, Shirley A., 311
Sno-Isle (Washington) Regional Library, 309
Snyder, Carolyn A.W., 39, 276
Snyder, Sherrie E., 100
Social Issues Resources Series, Inc., 32

Social responsibilities, 88, 225, 228
Social Responsibilities Round Table, 34, 228
Social studies, 89
Society for Scholarly Publishing, 99
Society of American Archivists, 18, 45
Sociological Abstracts, 13
Software, 199, 14
  evaluation of, 123
  cataloging of, 244
  for desktop publishing, 199
  rental of, 101
  reviewing of, 53
  standards, 235
Somerville, Mary R., 51
Sommer, Susan T., 163
Songline, 230
Sound recordings, 228
South Africa, 128
South Carolina, 300
South Carolina Association of Public Library Administrators, 301
South Carolina Library Association, 300
South Carolina State Library, 238, 300
South Carolina (University), 221, 300
South Chetham County (Tennessee) Library, 303
South Dakota, 301
South Dakota Library Association, 301
South Dakota State Library, 238, 301
South Dakota State University, 293, 302
Southeast Florida Library Network, 16
Southeastern Library Association, 232, 260, 306
Southeastern Library Network, 300
Southern California (University), 17
Southern College of Technology (Georgia), 272
Southern Illinois University, 16
Southern Mississippi (University), 283
Southwest Texas State University, 304
Soy, Sue, 265
Spanel, Ronald, 293
Spaulding, H., 233
Spawn, Carol M., 18
Special Achievement Award (Connecticut), 267
Special collections, 264, 189
  in academic libraries, 16
  in Arkansas, 264
  in Canada, 167
  in Georgia, 271
  in Idaho, 274
  in Iowa, 277
  in New York, 291
  in Oklahoma, 295
  in South Dakota, 302
  in Texas, 304
Special libraries,
  in Alaska, 262
  in Hawaii, 273
  in Illinois, 275
  in Iowa, 277
  in Mississippi, 283
  in Missouri, 283
  in Oklahoma, 296
  salaries and, 181, 252
  statistics, 210
  in Utah, 305
  in Washington, D.C., 269
  in Wisconsin, 311
Special Libraries Association, 18, 47, 125, 182, 191, 210, 232, 252, 269, 292
Special Libraries Association Award, 20
Special Service Award (Missouri), 284
Spencer, Lee, 264

Spencer, Pamela G., 258
Spokane County (Washington) Library District, 308
Spokane (Washington) Public Library, 309
Spriesterbach, Barbara, 296
Spring, Agnes Wright, 312
Springfield (Tennessee) Public Library, 303
Staas, Gretchen, 303
Stam, Diedre, 47
Standards, 210, 54, 234
  Alabama, 260
  Association of Specialized and Cooperative Libraries and, 61
  for bibliographic control, 243
  cataloging and, 86
  information technology and, 123
  interlibrary loan and, 168
  Massachusetts and, 281
  Montana and, 284
  Oregon and, 297
  public libraries and, 278
  Rhode Island and, 299
  Texas and, 304
  Vermont and, 306
  for voice information, 105
Standards for Accreditation, 18
Stanke, Nicky, 277
Stanley, Thomas F., 18
Stark, Carolyn, 302
State aid,
  in Alaska, 262
  in Delaware, 268
  in Iowa, 276
  in Kentucky, 279
  in New Jersey, 289
  in New Mexico, 290
  in Oklahoma, 295
  to public libraries, 260
  in South Carolina, 300
State Data Networks, 61, 300
State libraries, 237
  Association of Specialized and Cooperative Libraries and, 61
  buildings, 80
  networking and, 172
State of the Art Institute, 233
State Program Award for Intellectual Freedom, 129
Statistics, 50, 61, 138, 143, 153, 165, 189, 209, 236, 238, 245, 249, 295, 310
Steadman, Susan, 40
Steinberg (Myriam and Harold) Foundation, 99
Steiner, Janet E., 290
Stepto, Robert, 166 (photo)
Steptoe, John Lewis, 35, 74 (biog., photo), 228
Sterling, Stephanie, 38
Stevens, Jane, 291
Stewart, George, 232, 260
Still, Julie, 306
Stilwell (Oklahoma) Public Library, 296
Stine, Walter, 38
Stokes, J. Parker, 284
Stone, Carl, 301
Stone, Elizabeth W., 183, 233
Stores, 187
Storm, Frances, 302
Stormline Press, 19
Storms, Kate, 291
Storytelling, 287
Stovall, Naomi, 276
Straw, Windsor, 302
Stripling, Barbara K., 25, 74 (biog., photo), 153
Strong, Gary E., 264
Stroup, Elizabeth, 188, 310
Student Paper Award, ASIS, 43
Students, 105
Stueart, Robert D., 131 (photo)
Sturm, Danna, 287
Stussy, Susan A., 18
Sueyoshi, Akiko, 97

329

Index

Suffolk County (New York) Library System, 19
Sullivan, Bonnie, 283
Sullivan, Maureen, 140, 142 (photo)
Sullivan, Peggy, 94
Summers, F. William, 27, 107, 270
Summers, Lorraine Schaeffer, 239
Sunshine Award (Nebraska), 287
Sunshine State Young Readers Award, 270
Sussex County (Delaware) Libraries, 268
Sutherland (Zena) Lecture, 94
Suwanee River (Florida) Regional Library, 218
Swain, Elinor H., 165, 291
Swanson, Edward, 282
Swanson, Marnie, 85
Swartzell, Ann G., 185
Sweet, Donald G., 18
Sweet Springs (Missouri) Public Library, 284
Swisher, Robert, 296
Symons, Ann K., 262
Synoptics, standards, 236
Sypolt, Terri, 263
Tabbert, Marg, 302
Tacoma (Washington) Public Library, 309
Taft Publishing Company, 118
Taiwan (University), 134
Taken, Virginia, 300
Talcott, Ann W., 233
Talmadge, Herman E., 272
Tampa-Hillsborough County (Florida) Public Library, 81
Tang, Donna Taxco, 263
Tansey, Dolores, 300
Taran, Nadia P., 280
Taranko, Walter, 279
Taruskin, Richard, 162
Tate, Thelma, 148
Tatus, Gary, 279
Taylor & Francis, 195
Taylor, Mildred D., 35, 75 (biog., photo), 89, 94, 96, 228
Taylor, Neetie B., 280
Taylor, (R. J.) Foundation, 272
Taylor, (Sydney) Awards, 54
Tchobanoff, James B., 233
Teacher of the Year (Missouri), 284
Teal, Lee, 85
Techau, Neoma, 284
Technical Association for the Pulp and Paper Industry, 184
Technical Education Research Center Project, 222
Technical reports, standards, 236
Technology, 121, 130
  in academic libraries, 16
  handicapped services and, 77
  Nebraska and, 286
  New Jersey and, 289
  Oklahoma and, 295
  public libraries and, 185
  US-USSR relations and, 131
Tees, Miriam, 233
Telecommunications, 129, 199
Telefacsimile, 123, 198
  in academic libraries, 17
  in Alabama, 261
  in Indiana, 275
  in Kansas, 278
  in Massachusetts, 281
  in Montana, 284
  networking and, 171
  in North Carolina, 292
  in Ohio, 295
  public libraries and, 185
  state libraries and, 239
  in Virginia, 307
Telephone Pioneers, 295
Television, children's, 113
Tennessee, 302
Tennessee History Book Award, 303
Tennessee Library Association, 302
Tennessee State Library and Archives, 302
Tennessee (University), 302
Texas, 303
Texas A & M University, 34
Texas Association of School Librarians, 304
Texas Bluebonnet Award, 303
Texas Education Agency, 304
Texas Library Association, 303
Texas State Library, 238, 304
Texas (University), 146, 170, 304
Texas (University, Arlington), 33
Texas (University, El Paso), 16, 99, 289
Texas (University, San Antonio), 303
Texas Wesleyan College, 304
Texline (Texas) Public Library, 304
Tharlet, Eve, 97
Theatre Library Association, 239
Theatre Library Association Award, 239
Theft, 219
Thesauri, 165, 236
Theses, standards, 236
Thomas, Jane Louise, 35
Thomas, Lucille Cole, 35, 75 (biog., photo), 291
Thomas, Stephen, 296
Thompson, Dale, 189, 300
Thompson, Enid, 233
Thompson, Kay, 221
Thompson, Larry, 286
Thomson, Ted R., 276
Tillson (Jack E.) Scholarship, 277
Timberland (Washington) Public Library, 309
Times Mirror, 196
Timpanelli, Gloria, 94
Tipton, Mary Frances, 261
Tobiassen, Rose Mary, 291
Tomchyshyn, Terri, 86
Tome Associates, Ltd., 14
Tomlinson, Kenneth, 249
Tonsing, Jan, 284
Toomer, Clarence, 18
Top Shelf Award (Montana), 286
Topeka (Kansas) Public Library, 121
Topham, Patricia M., 288
Torbert, Richard, 32, 42
Tornados, 218
Toronto (Canada) Public Library, 83, 84
Toronto (University, Canada), 85
Torsuev, Iurii Vladimirovich, 133
Totten, Herman L., 18
Towne, Pamela, 281
TRADEMARKSCAN, 13
Transaction Publishers, Inc., 237
Translations, 236
Travel Grant Award (Alaska), 261
Travic, Eileen M., 85
Travillian, J. Maurice, 239, 281
Trelease, Jim, 263
Trezza, Alphonse F., 172
Trocchi, Deborah, 306
Trout, Carolyn, 284
Trujillo, Gloria, 289
Trujillo, Roberto G., vii, 7
Trump, Kathryn, 310
Trustee and Friends Award (Florida), 270
Trustee Award (Virginia), 307
Trustee Award (Wyoming), 312
Trustee Citation, ALA, 272
Trustee Citation (Nebraska), 287
Trustee Citation Award (North Dakota), 293
Trustee Citations, 37
Trustee of the Year (Montana), 286
Trustee of the Year (New Mexico), 289
Trustee of the Year (South Dakota), 302
Trustee of the Year (Wisconsin), 311
Trustees, 241
  in Florida, 270
  in Wisconsin, 311
Trustees Award for Literacy, 288
Trustees Honor Award (Georgia), 271
Truth or Consequences (New Mexico) Public Library, 290
Tryon (Oklahoma) Public Library, 296
Tsia, Betty L., 39
Tucker, Ben R., 36, 75 (biog.), 87, 218
Tules, Susan, 119
Tulsa (Oklahoma) City-County Library, 226
Tulsa (University, Oklahoma), 16
Turner, Phil, 261
Tuttle, Lillie, 308
Twain (Mark) Award, 284
Twenty-fifth Anniversary of *Choice*, 52
Tyson, John, 76
Ullmann (Liv) Peace Prize, 113
Ulm, Sandra, 270
Ulrich, S. Jane, 266
Ultimate Corporation, 305
Underwood, Mary, 278
Unger, Fred, 197
Union City (California) Library, 8
Union lists, 267
  in Iowa, 277
  in Kentucky, 279
  in Maryland, 280
  in Missouri, 283
  in Nevada, 287
  in North Carolina, 291
  in Oregon, 298
  in Pennsylvania, 298
  in Rhode Island, 300
  in South Carolina, 300
  in South Dakota, 301
  in Texas, 304
  in Washington, 308
Union Pacific Foundation, 286
UNISYS, 16
United Nations, 81, 129, 134
United States Board on Books for Young People, 242
United States Information Agency, 118, 263
Universal Availability of Publications (UAP), 129
Universal Bibliographic Control, 243
Universal Serials and Book Exchange, 244
University Microfilms, 16, 35
University of Hawaii Center for Tropical and Subtropical Aquaculture, 273
UNIX, 122
Unruh, Elizabeth L., 14
Urban Libraries, 189, 245
Urban Libraries Council, 245
UTLAS, 85
USMARC Authority Format, 86
USMARC Format for Bibliographic Data, 86
U.S./USSR Seminar on Access to Library Resources Through Technology and Preservation, 131
USSR, 79, 131, 151
USSR Academy of Sciences, 219
Utah, 304
Utah Division of State History, 305
Utah Endowment for the Humanities, 305
Utah Library Association, 304
Utah State Board of Education, 305
Utah State Library Commission, 238, 304
Utah (University), 305
Valencik, May Virginia Kunz, 299
Vallee (Rudy) Collection, 189
Valtfort, Susan, 38
Value Added Tax, 145
Van Allsburg, Charles, 93
Van DerMerr, Rebecca, 311
Van Doren, Phyllis, 107
Van House, Nancy, 154, 208, 253
Vanderbilt University (Tennessee), 303

Index

Vann, J. Daniel, 18
Vargas, Javier, 289
Vassallo, Paul, 270
Veaner, Allen B., 233
Vella, Sandra A., 265
Veltfor, Susan, 289
Vendors, 122, 246
Ventgen, Carol, 298
Vermont, 305
Vermont Board of Libraries, 305
Vermont Council on the Humanities, 306
Vermont Department of Libraries, 305
Vermont Division of Historic Preservation, 306
Vermont Library Association, 306
Vermont (University), 306
Verona (Wisconsin) Public Library, 311
Vescelius (Diana) Memorial Award, 295
Video, 14, 99
  adult services and, 20
  children's, 112
  copyright and, 101
  handicapped, 121
  Kentucky and, 279
  in libraries, 245
  Nebraska and, 286
  New Hampshire and, 288
  notable, 172
  Oklahoma and, 296
  Vermont and, 306
  Washington and, 309
Videotex, 103
Village (Oklahoma) Public Library, 296
Vinella, Mary Jane, 289
Virginia, 306
Virginia Beach Public Library, 188
Virginia Educational Media Association, 307
Virginia Library Association, 232, 306
Virginia State Library, 170, 227, 238, 307
Virginia (University), 16
Vocelli, Virginia, 267
Volunteer State Book Award, 303
Volunteers, 156, 189, 260, 265
Volusia County (Florida) Library Center, 81
Voth, Vonnie, 286
Votisek, Judy, 265
Vu Text, 103
Vyzralek, Dolores, 293
Wacondo, William, 289
Wadham, Timothy R., 39
Wagner, Jackie, 294
Wagner, Marian, 287
Wagner, Rod, 239, 287
Waldhart, Thomas, 279
Walker, Evelyn, 276
Walker, Sherry, 263
Wallace, Danny P., 37, 155
Wallace, Linda, 194
Walter, Bob, 18
Waltz, Mary Anne L., 157
Ward, James E., 232, 303
Wareham, Nancy, 295
Warner (Oklahoma) Public Library, 296
Wartels, Nat, 196
Washington, 308
Washington Centennial, 308
Washington Correctional Association Academic Achievement Award, 310
Washington Library Association, 308
Washington Library Media Association, 309
Washington Newspaper Project, 308
Washington Office, ALA, 269
Washington Report, 247
Washington State Library, 226, 238, 308

Washington State University, 309
Washington (University), 309
Washoe County (Nevada) Library, 287
Wasser, Mary E., viii
Waterloo (Iowa) Public Library, 276
Watkins, Karen J., 289
Watson, Halbert, 264
Watson, Peter, 18
Watts, Sandra, 286
Waukesha (Wisconsin) Public Libraries, 311
Waurika (Oklahoma) Public Library, 296
Weaver, Barbara, 289
Weaver, Hope, 287
Weavill, G. Barry, 147
Webb City (Missouri) Public Library, 284
Webster, Duane, 18, 55
Webster, James K., 291
Wedgeworth, Robert, 161
Weeks, Ann Carlson, 265
Weibel, Kathleen, 34, 75 (biog., photo)
Weill, David, 289
Weise, Charlotte, 43
Welborn, Evelyn, 301
Welborn, Lynda, 266
Welch, Theodore F., 135
Welles, Margaret, 279
Welsh, William J., 87, 233
Wenberg, Alan R., 170
West Bloomfield (Michigan) Schools, 37
West Linn (Oregon) Public Library, 298
West Publishing Company, 136
West Vancouver (Canada) Library, 85
West Virginia, 310
West Virginia Library Association, 310
West Virginia Media Association, 311
West Virginia State Library Commission, 311
Western Library Network, 171, 284, 308
Western Oklahoma Hall of Fame, 296
Western Washington University, 309
Westgate, Hazel, 277
WESTLAW, 14, 136
Westminster College (Missouri), 284
Wetzel, Don, 286
Wewoka (Oklahoma) Public Library, 296
Whaley, Janie, 276
Whallen, Judy, 311
Wheeler, Burton M., 284
Where the Wild Things Are, 115
Whetzel, Michael, 38
White, A. G. D., 145
White, Herbert, 233
White House Conference on Libraries and Information Services, 24, 25, 41, 165, 237, 242, 248, 258, 270, 264, 284, 291, 302
White Service Award, 278
White (William Allen) Children's Book Award, 278
Whiteley, Sandy, 197
Whitney-Carnegie Fund, 50
Whitney-Carnegie Fund Grants, 39
Whitney, Karen A., 25
Whitney, Stephen, 220
Wibbels, Alan, 286
Wick, Robert L., 40
Wiegand, Wayne A., 35, 146, 147, 153, 311
Wiley, 196
Wilkens, Betsy, 267
Wilkins, Barratt, 270
Willey, Sharon, 284
William and Mary (College, Virginia), 17, 82
Williams, James, 18, 159, 266
Williams, Leslie JoAnn, 265

Williams, M. Jane, 291
Williams, Martha E., 43
Williams, Nancy F., 272
Williams, Pat, 249
Williams, Robert V., 233
Willingham, Robert M., 220
Willis, Dorothy, 286
Wilson, Amy Seetoo, 98
Wilson, Don W., 44
Wilson (H. W.) Award, 232, 233
Wilson (H. W.) Company, 33, 63
Wilson (H. W.) Foundation, 118
Wilson (H. W.) Library Periodical Award, 153, 265
Wilson, Wayne, 18, 32, 53, 153
Wilsonline, 83
Wilsonville (Oregon) Public Library, 298
Wiltse, Helen Citron, 272
Winfrey, Oprah, 195
Winn Dixie-Davis Brothers Foundation, 270
Winsor (Justin) Prize Essay, 38, 147, 265
Winstead, Frank, 272
Winton, Alma, 299
Wisconsin, 311
Wisconsin Association of School Librarians, 311
Wisconsin Centennial, 311
Wisconsin Division for Library Services, 311
Wisconsin Library Association, 311
Wisconsin Lutheran College, 311
Wisconsin (University), 82, 154, 180
Wissenberg, Frances, 54
Wittenborn (George) Memorial Award, 48
Womack, Norma, 292
Womack, Sharon, 263
Woman of Achievement, 310
Women, 249, 250
Women in Librarianship, 249
Women's National Book Association, 254
Women's National Book Association Award, 254
Women's National Book Association Honors, 94
Wood, Elizabeth McKenzie, 311
Wood, Stephen, 295
Wood, Thor E., 291
Woodburn, David, 282
Woods Charitable Fund, 286
Woodward (Oklahoma) Public Library, 296
Woodward, Ward M., 18
Woods (William) College (Missouri), 284
Woolls, Blanche, 40, 62
World Book ALA Goals Awards, 40
World Book, Inc. Grant, 87
World Book, Incorporated, 40, 118, 249
WPA Writers' Project, 264
Wright, Betty Ren, 303, 312
Wright, Curtis H., 146
Wright, Helen K., viii, 75, 177
Wu, Julia Li, 165
Wyche, Louise, 268
Wyoming, 312
Wyoming Educational Media Association, 312
Wyoming Library Association, 312
Wyoming State Library, 312
Wyoming (University), 312
Yale (Oklahoma) Public Library, 296
Yale University (Connecticut), 16
Yamachika, Ray, 46
Yates, Annie L., 292
Yates, Ella Gaines, 227, 307
Year of the Librarian, 193
The Year of the Librarian: Ask a Professional. Ask a Librarian, 193
Year of the Young Reader, 51, 93, 150, 195, 249, 296

331

Index

Yoder, Linda, 276
Yoshi, 97
Young Adult Author Award, 257, 296
Young Adult Library Services, 255
Young Adult Literature, 257
  notable, 172
  social responsibility and, 88
Young adult services, 189, 222, 225, 255, 258
  Nebraska and, 286
  New Hampshire and, 288
Young Adult Services Division, 39, 50, 175, 257, 296
Young American Act, 258
Young, Arthur P., 146
Young, Peter, 98, 210
Young Readers' Choice Award, 179
Young, Virginia, 242, 249
Young, William R., 297
Youngheart, 230
Youth Development Information Center, 163
Yueh, Norma, 289
Zastrow, Edwin J., 277
Zbar, Morris, 85
Zeigman, Bruce, 310
Zetterman, Bonnie, 286
Zielinska, Marie F., 109
Zink, Steven, 37, 119
Zondervan, 196
Zussy, Nancy, 308
Zwerger, Lisbeth, 89

Cumulative Index to Biographies and Obituaries in ALA Yearbook, (1976-1989).

References are to year and page.

Abell, Millicent D., 82:64 (biog., photo)
Adams, Scott, 83:199 (obit.)
Aiken, George D., 83:54 (biog., photo)
Akers, Susan Grey, 85:16 (obit., photo)
Alexander, Lloyd, 87:75 (biog., photo)
Alexander, Mary Louise, 77:221 (obit.)
Alison, William Andres Greig, 80:73 (biog.)
Allain, Alex P., 76:101 (biog., photo)
Anderson, Florence, 77:53 (biog., photo)
Arterbery, Vivian J., 85:7 (biog., photo); 87:75 (biog., photo)
Asheim, Lester Eugene, 77:53 (biog., photo); 85:7 (biog., photo)
Atkinson, Hugh, 87:227 (obit., photo)
Aveney, Brian Henry, 81:73 (biog., photo)
Avram, Henriette D., 82:64 (biog., photo); 89:64 (biog., photo)
Axford, H. William, 81:213 (obit., photo)
Baer, Mark H., 77:53 (biog., photo)
Baker, Augusta, 76:101 (biog., photo); 82:64 (biog., photo)
Baker, Dale Burdette, 76:101 (biog.)
Barber, Margaret Ellen, 85:7 (biog., photo)
Barker, Tommie Dora, 79:193 (obit., photo)
Barnstead, Winefred Glen, 86:232 (obit., photo)
Batchelor, Lillian L., 78:207 (obit.)
Battin, Patricia Meyer, 79:48 (biog., photo); 88:70 (biog., photo)
Beard, Sarah Allen, 85:16 (obit.)
Bearman, Toni Carbo, 78:59 (biog., photo); 81:73 (biog., photo); 87:75 (biog., photo)
Belpre-White, Pura, 83:199 (obit., photo)
Bender, David Ray, 80:73 (biog., photo)
Benton, Charles, 79:48 (biog., photo)
Berger, Mary C., 81:73 (biog., photo)
Berger, Patricia Wilson, 89:64 (biog., photo)
Berninghausen, David K., 83:54 (biog., photo)
Berring, Robert C., 86:81 (biog.); 87:75 (biog., photo)
Berry, John, 86:81 (biog., photo)
Betancourt, Ingrid, 89:65 (biog., photo)
Betancourt, Virginia, 82:64 (biog.)
Bewley, Lois M., 84:15 (biog., photo)
Bidlack, Russell Eugene, 78:59 (biog., photo)
Billington, James H., 88:70 (biog., photo)
Bloss, Joan W., 81:73 (biog.)
Bloss, Meredith, 83:199 (obit., photo)
Bloss, Marjorie E., 89:65 (biog., photo)
Bodart, Joni, 86:81 (biog.)
Bolden, Connie E., 80:73 (biog.)
Bonk, John Wallace, 80:227 (obit., photo)
Boorstin, Daniel Joseph, 76:101 (biog., photo)
Boyd, Jessie Edna, 79:193 (biog.)

Brademas, John, 82:64 (biog., photo)
Brawley, Paul H., 89:176 (obit., photo)
Brecht, Albert, 88:70 (biog., photo)
Brink, Carol Ryrie, 82:198 (obit., photo)
Brooks, Hallie Beachem, 86:232 (obit.)
Brown, Marcia, 78:59 (biog., photo); 84:15 (biog.)
Buck, Paul H., 80:227 (obit., photo)
Bunge, Charles A., 81:73 (biog., photo)
Bunnell, William I., 79:48 (biog., photo)
Burkhardt, Frederick Henry, 76:102 (biog., photo)
Burns, Robert W., Jr., 79:48 (biog.)
Butler, Dorothy, 83:54 (biog., photo)
Byrnes, Hazel Webster, 82:198 (obit.)
Byrum, John Donald, Jr., 78:60 (biog., photo)
Capoor, Asha, 87:76 (biog.)
Carnovsky, Leon, 76:251 (obit., photo)
Carroll, Bonnie C., 85:7 (biog., photo)
Carroll, Martha S., 80:227 (obit., photo)
Carson, Johnny, 84:15 (biog., photo)
Carter, John Waynflete, 76:251 (obit.)
Carter, Julia Frances, 81:213 (obit., photo)
Cassell, Kay A., 87:76 (biog.)
Castagna, Edwin, 84:22 (obit., photo)
Chambers, Aidan, 87:76 (biog.)
Chambers, Bradford, 85:16 (obit., photo)
Chanin, Leah F., 83:55 (biog., photo)
Chelton, Mary K., 86:82 (biog., photo)
Cheney, Frances Neel, 77:54 (biog., photo); 79:49 (biog., photo)
Childs, James Bennett, 78:207 (obit., photo)
Chisholm, Margaret Elizabeth Bergman, 76:102 (biog., photo); 87:76 (biog., photo)
Clausman, Gilbert Joseph, 78:60 (biog., photo)
Cleary, Beverly Bunn, 76:102 (biog., photo); 81:74 (biog., photo); 85:7 (biog., photo)
Clifton, Joe Ann, 89:66 (biog., photo)
Coco, Alfred Joseph, 78:61 (biog., photo)
Colaianni, Lois Ann, 80:73 (biog., photo)
Cole, Fred Carrington, 77:54 (biog., photo); 79:49 (biog., photo); 87:227 (obit., photo)
Cole, John Y., 79:49 (biog., photo)
Comaromi, John P., 81:74 (biog., photo)
Converse, William, 88:71 (biog., photo)
Cooke, Eileen D., 79:49 (biog., photo)
Cooney, Barbara, 81:74 (biog., photo)
Cooney, Jane, 87:76 (biog.)
Cooper, Kenneth R., 85:7 (biog., photo)
Cooper, Sandra M., 79:49 (biog., photo)
Cooper, Susan, 77:55 (biog., photo)
Coral, Lenore, 88:71 (biog., photo)
Corrigan, John T., 88:71 (biog., photo)

Cory, John MacKenzie, 89:176 (obit., photo)
Cox, Carl Raymond, 77:221 (obit., photo)
Craig, Florence, 82:198 (obit.)
Critsos, James M., 80:74 (biog., photo)
Cronin, John William, 85:16 (obit., photo)
Culbertson, Don Steward, 81:213 (obit., photo)
Cunningham, George, 85:8 (biog.)
Curley, Arthur, 86:82 (biog., photo)
Currier, Lura Gibbons, 84:22 (obit., photo)
Custer, Arline Kern, 76:251 (obit., photo)
Daignese, Joseph M., 80:74 (biog., photo)
Dainton, Sir Frederick Sydney, 78:61 (biog., photo)
Dalgleish, Alice, 80:227 (obit.)
Dalton, Jack, 84:15 (biog., photo)
Danton, J. Periam, 84:15 (biog., photo)
David, Charles W., 85:17 (obit.)
Davidson, Mary Wallace, 83:55 (biog., photo)
Davis, Charles Hargis, 83:55 (biog., photo)
Day, Melvin S., 77:55 (biog., photo)
DeBerry, Joseph, 80:228 (obit., photo)
DeGennaro, Richard, 76:102 (biog., photo); 87:77 (biog., photo); 88:72 (biog., photo)
DePaola, Thomas Anthony, 84:16 (biog., photo)
DeProspo, Ernest R., 84:23 (obit.)
DeSolla Price, Derek John, 84:23 (obit., photo)
Dempsey, Frank J., 89:177 (obit., photo)
Dillon, Diane, 77:55 (biog., photo)
Dillon, Leo, 77:55 (biog., photo)
Dix, William Shepherd, 76:103 (biog., photo); 79:193 (obit., photo)
Dixon, Rebecca Danforth, 83:55 (biog., photo)
Dodd, James B., 81:74 (biog., photo)
Doms, Keith, 83:56 (biog., photo)
Dougherty, Richard M., 89:66 (biog., photo)
Douglas, William O., 76:103 (biog., photo)
Dowlin, Kenneth E., 88:72 (biog., photo)
Downs, Robert Bingham, 77:56 (biog., photo)
Doyle, Robert P., 85:8 (biog.)
Drennan, Henry Thomas, 79:50 (biog., photo)
Dubberly, Ronald A., 88:72 (biog., photo)
Duff, John B., 87:77 (biog., photo)
Dunlap, Connie, 80:74 (biog., photo)
DuMont, Rosemary Ruhig, 87:77 (biog., photo)
Dunkin, Paul Shaner, 76:252 (obit., photo)
Duran, Daniel Flores, 79:50 (biog., photo)
Echelman, Shirley, 78:62 (biog., photo); 82:65 (biog., photo)
Edge, Segrid, 82:198 (obit.)
Edwards, Margaret Alexander, 89:177 (obit., photo)

Index

Egielski, Richard, 88:72 (biog., photo)
Egoff, Sheila, 80:75 (biog., photo)
Eichenberg, Fritz, 85:8 (biog., photo)
Einhorn, Nathan R., 84:23 (obit.)
Ellenberger, Jack S., 77:56 (biog., photo)
Elliott, Carl Atwood, 83:56 (biog.)
Ellsworth, Ralph E., 89:66 (biog., photo)
Epstein, Dena Julia, 78:62 (biog., photo)
Eshelman, William R., 79:50 (biog., photo)
Estabrook, Leigh Stewart, 87:77 (biog.); 89:67 (biog., photo)
Evans, Luther, 82:198 (obit.)
Facente, Gary, 83:56 (biog., photo)
Fair, Ethel Marion, 81:213 (obit., photo)
Fast, Elizabeth, 78:207 (obit., photo)
Faust, Clarence Henry, 76:252 (obit.)
Fenner, Phyllis, 83:200 (obit.)
Fisher, Edith Maureen, 89:67 (biog., photo)
Fitzpatrick, Kelly, 82:65 (biog., photo)
Fleischman, Sid, 88:72 (biog.)
Fontaine, Everett O., 77:221 (obit., photo)
Ford, William D., 85:8 (biog.)
Foster, Eloise Cantzon, 89:67 (biog., photo)
Fox, Paula, 79:51 (biog., photo)
Franklin, John Hope, 76:104 (biog., photo)
Frantz, Ray W. Jr., 79:51 (biog.)
Frarey, Carlyle James, 77:221 (obit., photo)
Freedman, Russell, 89:67 (biog., photo)
Freehafer, Edward G., 87:227 (obit.)
Fritz, Jean, 77:56 (biog., photo); 86:82 (biog.); 87:78 (biog., photo)
Fussler, Herman Howe, 77:57 (biog., photo)
Futas, Elizabeth, 89:67 (biog., photo)
Gagliardo, Ruth Garver, 81:213 (obit., photo)
Gaines, Ervin J., 87:227 (obit., photo)
Galvin, Thomas J., 79:51 (biog., photo); 82:65 (biog.); 86:82 (biog., photo)
Garten, Edward D., 86:83 (biog., photo)
Gasaway, Laura N., 87:78 (biog., photo)
Gates, Francis L., 81:74 (biog.)
Gaver, Mary Virginia, 77:57 (biog., photo)
Geer, Helen, 85:17 (obit.)
Geh, Hans-Peter, 86:83 (biog.)
Geisel, Theodore Seuss, 81:75 (biog., photo); 83:59 (biog.)
Gell, Marilyn, 80:75 (biog., photo)
Giles, Louise, 77:222 (obit., photo)
Ginader, George Hall, 82:65 (biog., photo)
Goble, Paul, 80:75 (biog.)
Godfrey, Irma C., 88:72 (biog., photo)
Goff, Frederick, 83:200 (obit., photo)
Goldhor, Herbert, 89:68 (biog., photo)
Goldstein, Harold, 82:65 (biog., photo); 87:227 (obit., photo)
Goodrum, Charles A., 78:62 (biog., photo)
Gorman, Michael, 78:63 (biog., photo)
Graham, Mal L., 84:23 (obit.)
Grant, Mary A., 86:83 (biog., photo)
Greenaway, Emerson, 77:58 (biog., photo)
Gregorian, Vartan, 82:65 (biog.)
Grele, Ronald J., 89:68 (biog., photo)

Grosch, Audrey N., 79:51 (biog., photo)
Gross, Mason Welch, 78:208 (obit., photo)
Haas, Warren James, 79:52 (biog., photo); 85:9 (biog., photo)
Hamill, Harold, 87:227 (obit.)
Hamilton, Virginia, 76:104 (biog., photo)
Hammond, Jane Laura, 76:104 (biog., photo)
Hannigan, Jane Anne, 85:9 (biog.)
Harrar, Joanne, 84:16 (biog., photo)
Hashim, Elinor M., 84:16 (biog., photo)
Hatfield, Frances S., 88:237 (obit.)
Haviland, Virginia, 77:58 (biog., photo); 83:57 (biog.); 88:237 (obit., photo)
Haycock, Kenneth R., 78:63 (biog., photo)
Haycraft, Howard, 77:58 (biog., photo)
Hayes, Robert M., 86:83 (biog., photo)
Haygood, William C., 86:232 (obit.)
Hearne, Elizabeth G., 86:83 (biog., photo)
Heim, Kathleen M., 83:57 (biog., photo); 88:73 (biog., photo)
Henne, Frances Elizabeth, 77:59 (biog., photo); 79:52 (biog.); 86:232 (obit.)
Herring, Harold F., 85:9 (biog.)
Hewitt, Vivian D., 79:52 (biog., photo)
Hickey, Doralyn Joanne, 88:237 (obit.)
Higham, Norman, 84:17 (biog., photo)
Hill, Lister, 86:232 (obit.)
Hines, Theodore C., 84:24 (obit., photo)
Hinton, Frances, 81:75 (biog., photo)
Hirsch, Felix, 84:24 (obit.)
Hoagland, Sister Mary Arthur, 78:64 (biog., photo)
Hogan, Thomas H., 87:78 (biog., photo)
Holahan, Paulette H., 87:78 (biog., photo)
Holley, Edward Gailon, 76:105 (biog., photo); 84:17 (biog.); 88:73 (biog., photo); 89:68 (biog., photo)
Hookway, Sir Harry, 86:84 (biog., photo)
Horn, Andrew Harlis, 84:24 (obit.)
Horrocks, Norman, 86:84 (biog., photo)
Horton, Marion Louise, 85:17 (obit.)
Howard, Joseph H., 86:84 (biog., photo)
Humphry, John Ames, 78:64 (biog.)
Hunter, Molly, 76:105 (biog., photo)
Hurt, Charlie D., 87:78 (biog.)
Hyman, Trina Schart, 86:84 (biog.)
Immroth, John Phillip, 77:222 (obit., photo)
Intner, Sheila S., 88:73 (biog., photo)
Jackson, Sidney L., 80:228 (obit., photo)
Jackson, W. Carl, 82:199 (obit.)
Jacobs, Leland Blair, 84:17 (biog.)
Jacobs, Roger F., 82:66 (biog., photo)
Jacobstein, J. Myron, 79:52 (biog., photo)
Javits, Jacob Koppel, 82:66 (biog., photo)
Jensen, Kenneth, 87:79 (biog., photo)
Jensen, Mary Ann, 86:85 (biog.); 89:68 (biog.)
Jepson, William H., 83:57 (biog., photo)
Johnson, Barbara Coe, 76:105 (biog., photo)
Johnson, Herbert F., 87:79 (biog., photo)

Johnson, Mary Frances Kennon, 80:228 (obit., photo)
Johnson, Richard David, 76:105 (biog., photo)
Jonah, David Alonzo, 82:199 (obit., photo)
Jones, Clara Stanton, 76:106 (biog., photo); 79:53 (biog.); 84:17 (biog., photo)
Jones, Virginia Lacy, 77:59 (biog., photo); 81:75 (biog., photo); 85:17 (obit., photo)
Josephine, Helen B., 80:75 (biog., photo)
Josey, E. J., 81:75 (biog., photo); 84:17 (biog., photo)
Juergensmeyer, John E., 84:17 (biog., photo)
Jurkins, Jacquelyn J., 85:9 (biog.)
Kalp, Margaret Ellen, 79:194 (obit., photo)
Kaminstein, Abraham Louis, 78:208 (biog., photo)
Karpel, Bernard, 87:227 (obit.)
Kaye, Marilyn Janice, 83:57 (biog.)
Kegan, Elizabeth Hamer, 80:228 (obit., photo)
Kennedy, Anna Clark, 85:18 (obit.)
Kerker, Ann Elizabeth, 77:60 (biog., photo)
Kilburn, Peter, 87:228 (obit.)
Kilgour, Frederick Gridley, 76:106 (biog.); 83:58 (biog.)
Kimmel, Margaret Mary, 85:10 (biog.)
King, Donald W., 84:18 (biog., photo)
Kirkegaard, Preben, 76:106 (biog., photo)
Kirkus, Virginia, 81:214 (obit., photo)
Kitchen, Paul Howard, 76:106 (biog., photo)
Knox, William Tyndall, 79:194 (obit.)
Knutson, Linda J., 87:79 (biog., photo)
Kortendick, James J., 87:228 (obit.)
Kosse, Suzanne Jill, 88:73 (biog., photo)
Krug, Judith Fingeret, 77:50 (biog., photo)
Krug, Richard E., 84:24 (obit.)
Krummel, Donald W., 82:66 (biog., photo)
Kunze, Horst J., 81:76 (biog., obit.)
Kurth, William H., 78:209 (obit.)
Kushe, Lawrence David, 76:107 (biog., photo)
Lacy, Dan Mabry, 76:107 (biog., photo)
Ladenson, Alex, 88:237 (obit.)
Lamb, Gertrude, 81:76 (biog., photo)
Lancour, Harold, 82:199 (obit.)
Land, Brian, 76:107 (biog.)
Landau, Herbert B., 81:76 (biog., photo)
Lang, Sister Granz, 80:75 (biog., photo)
Lathem, Edward Connery, 78:64 (biog., photo)
Lathrop, Dorothy P., 81:214 (obit.)
Laughlin, Jeannine L., 87:79 (biog.)
Leary, Margaret A., 89:69 (biog., photo)
Lee, Chang C., 89:69 (biog., photo)
Lee, Joel M., 79:53 (biog., photo)
Lee, Mollie Huston, 83:200 (obit., photo)
Leeds, Byron, 84:18 (biog., photo)
L'Engle, Madeleine, 85:10 (biog.)
Lerner, Adele A., 85:10 (biog.)
Lerner, Louis Abraham, 78:65 (biog., photo); 85:18 (obit.)
Lester, June, 87:74 (biog., photo)
Levy, Evelyn, 78:209 (obit.)
Lewis, Peter Ronald, 78:65 (biog., photo)

Index

Li, Marjorie Hsu, 87:79 (biog., photo)
Liebars, Herman, 77:60 (biog., photo)
Lindberg, Donald Allan Bror, 85:11 (biog., photo)
Lindquist, Hennie D., 78:209 (obit.)
Lippincott, Joseph Wharton, 77:223 (obit., photo)
Livingston, Lawrence G., 79:194 (obit., photo)
Lobel, Arnold, 82:66 (biog., photo)
Longworth, Alan, 82:66 (biog.)
Lord, Milton E., 86:232 (obit., photo)
Lorenz, John George, 76:107 (biog., photo)
Lorenzi, Nancy M., 83:58 (biog., photo)
Love, Erika, 79:53 (biog., photo)
Low, Edmon, 76:108 (biog., photo); 84:25 (obit., photo)
Lowe, Mildred, 89:177 (obit., photo)
Lowrie, Jean, 79:53 (biog.)
Lucker, Jay K., 81:77 (biog., photo)
Luskay, Jack R., 80:76 (biog.)
Lyders, Josette Anne, 89:69 (biog., photo)
Lyman, Helen Huguenor, 80:76 (biog., photo)
Lynch, Beverly P., 85:11 (biog., photo)
Lynch, Mary Jo, 79:54 (biog., photo)
Lynch, Sister Mary Dennis, 84:18 (biog., photo)
McAnanama, Judith Eleanor, 85:11 (biog., photo)
McDermott, Gerald, 76:108 (biog., photo)
MacDonald, Alan, 81:77 (biog., photo)
McElderry, Margaret Knox, 76:108 (biog., photo)
McGregor, Della Louise, 79:194 (obit., photo)
McGregor, Jane Ann, 82:67 (biog., photo)
McGuire, Alice Brooks, 76:252 (obit., photo)
McKenna, Frank Eugene, 77:61 (biog., photo); 79:195 (obit.)
McKenzie, Dorothy C., 79:54 (biog., photo)
McKinley, Robin, 86:85 (biog.)
MacLachlin, Patricia, 87:80 (biog., photo)
McLarin, Edgar S., 88:74 (biog., photo)
Macleish, Archibald, 83:201 (obit., photo)
McNamara, Brooks, 78:65 (biog., photo)
McNamara, Margaret Craig, 76:109 (biog., photo); 82:200 (obit.)
Mahar, Mary Helen, 80:76 (biog.)
Malinowsky, H. Robert, 86:85 (biog., photo)
Markey, Karen, 89:70 (biog., photo)
Martell, Charles R., 85:11 (biog., photo)
Martin, Lowell A., 80:77 (biog., photo)
Martin, Susan Katherine, 89:70 (biog., photo)
Matheson, Nina W., 84:18 (biog., photo)
Mathews, Anne J., 87:80 (biog., photo)
Mearns, David C., 82:200 (obit., photo)
Mechanic, Sylvia, 87:80 (biog.)
Medina, Sue O'Neal, 84:19 (biog.)
Melcher, Daniel, 77:61 (biog., photo); 86:223 (obit.)
Melczewski, Marion A., 82:200 (obit., photo)
Meredith, Louise, 76:253 (obit.)
Messerle, Judith R., 87:80 (biog.)

Metcalf, Keyes DeWitt, 77:61 (biog., photo); 84:25 (obit., photo)
Metcalfe, John Wallace, 83:201 (obit., photo)
Metzdorf, Robert Frederic, 76:253 (obit.)
Meyer, Helen Honig, 77:61 (biog., photo)
Miller, Charles Edmond, 89:70 (biog., photo)
Miller, Frank Winston, 89:70 (biog.)
Miller, Jean K., 86:85 (biog.)
Mills, Shirley C., 79:54 (biog., photo)
Minudri, Regina, 86:85 (biog., photo)
Mirsky, Phyllis Simon, 85:12 (biog.)
Mish, John L., 84:25 (obit.)
Mitchell, Eleanor, 85:18 (obit.)
Mobley, Emily, R., 88:74 (biog., photo)
Molz, Kathleen R., 76:109 (biog., photo)
Monty, Vivienne, 89:71 (biog., photo)
Moon, Eric Edward, 77:62 (biog., photo); 82:67 (biog.); 88:74 (biog., photo)
Moon, Ilse, 89:71 (biog., photo)
Moore, Bessie Boehm, 81:77 (biog., photo); 85:12 (biog.)
Moore, Everett Thomson, 76:109 (biog.); 88:238 (obit.)
Morrison, Lillian, 88:74 (biog.)
Morrison, Samuel F., 88:75 (biog., photo)
Morton, Elizabeth Homer, 78:210 (obit.)
Moses, Sibyl Elizabeth, 88:75 (biog., photo)
Muller, Karen, 88:75 (biog., photo)
Mumford, Lawrence Quincy, 76:110 (biog., photo); 83:201 (obit., photo)
Munn, Ralph, 76:253 (obit., photo)
Naftalin, Frances Healy, 79:55 (biog., photo)
Nelson, Milo, 79:55 (biog.)
Nemeyer, Carol Anmuth, 76:110 (biog., photo); 82:67 (biog.)
Nesbitt, Elizabeth, 78:210 (obit., photo)
Neufeld, M. Lynne, 81:78 (biog., photo)
Newman, Jerald C., 84:19 (biog., photo); 88:75 (biog., photo)
Newman, Ralph G., 76:110 (biog., photo)
Norwood, Frank W., 84:25 (obit., photo)
Nyholm, Jens Peter, 84:26 (obit.)
Nyren, Karl, 89:178 (obit., photo)
O'Brien, Elmer John, 79:55 (biog., photo)
O'Dell, Scott, 79:55 (biog., photo)
Oboler, Eli M., 84:26 (obit.)
Ofek, Uriel, 79:55 (biog.)
Oman, Ralph, 86:85 (biog., photo)
Ott, Bill, 89:71 (biog., photo)
Owens, Major R., 88:75 (biog., photo)
Palmer, Raymond A., 83:58 (biog., photo)
Parent, Roger H., 80:77 (biog., photo); 85:12 (biog., photo)
Parks, Martha, 82:200 (obit., photo)
Patterson, Katherine Womeldorf, 79:56 (biog., photo); 82:67 (biog., photo)
Pell, Claiborne, 84:19 (biog.)
Pellowski, Anne, 80:77 (biog., photo); 81:78 (biog., photo)
Penney, Pearce J., 83:58 (biog.)
Penniman, W. David, 89:71 (biog., photo)
Perkins, Carl Dewey, 76:111 (biog., photo); 85:18 (obit., photo)

Person, Ruth Janssen, 87:81 (biog., photo)
Peterson, Carolyn Sue, 85:12 (obit., photo)
Phinazee, Annette L., 84:27 (obit., photo)
Phinney, Eleanor, 83:202 (obit., photo)
Pilpel, Harriet Fleischl, 77:62 (biog., photo)
Piternick, Anne B., 77:62 (biog., photo)
Pitts, Judy M., 89:72 (biog., photo)
Plaister, Jean M., 88:75 (biog.)
Poole, Jay Martin, 80:78 (biog.)
Posner, Ernst, 81:214 (obit.)
Posner, Marcia W., 89:72 (biog., photo)
Potter, William Gray, 84:20 (biog.)
Powell, Benjamin E., 82:20 (obit., photo)
Powell, Lawrence Clarke, 82:67 (biog., photo)
Powers, Sister Mary Luella, 84:27 (obit.)
Powers-Gibson, Marla, 88:76 (biog., photo)
Prentice, Ann E., 87:81 (biog.)
Price, Kathleen M., 84:20 (biog.)
Provenson, Alice and Martin, 85:12 (biog., photo)
Rachow, Louis August, 79:56 (biog., photo); 82:67 (biog., photo)
Randall, David Anton, 76:253 (obit.)
Ransom, Harry Huntt, 77:223 (obit.)
Raskin, Ellen, 80:78 (biog.)
Rayward, W. Boyd, 80:78 (biog.)
Reagan, Agnes L., 87:81 (biog.)
Reed, Sarah Rebecca, 79:195 (obit., photo)
Reese, Ernest J., 77:223 (obit., photo)
Resnik, Linda, 86:86 (biog.)
Rettig, James Robert, 89:72 (biog., photo)
Rhoads, Berton, 80:79 (biog.)
Ricardo, Ralph E., 89:72 (biog., photo)
Richards, John Steward, 80:229 (obit., photo)
Ricking, Myrl, 78:211 (obit., photo)
Riggs, Donald E., 87:81 (biog.)
Ringer, Barbara Alice, 76:111 (biog., photo)
Ritchie, Donald A., 87:81 (biog.)
Robbins-Carter, Jane, 85:13 (biog., photo)
Rodger, Eleanor Jo, 87:82 (biog.)
Rogers, A. Robert, 86:223 (obit.)
Rogers, Joseph W., 85:19 (obit.)
Rogers, Rutherford David, 78:65 (biog.)
Rollins, Charlemae Hill, 80:229 (obit., photo)
Roman, Susan, 87:82 (biog., photo)
Roos, Jean Carolyn, 83:202 (obit., photo)
Roper, Fred W., 87:82 (biog., photo)
Rossell, Beatrice Sawyer, 77:223 (obit., photo)
Roth, Harold Lee, 83:203 (obit., photo)
Rothrock, Mary U., 77:224 (obit., photo)
Rothstein, Samuel, 89:73 (biog., photo)
Ruffner, Frederick Gale, 88:76 (biog.); 85:13 (biog., photo)
Sabosik, Patricia, 86:86 (biog., photo)
Sargent, Charles W., 82:67 (biog., photo)
Saunders, Wilfred Leonard, 81:78 (biog.)
Scarry, Patricia, 81:78 (biog., photo)
Schindel, Morton, 80:79 (biog., photo)
Schmidt, C. James, 81:78 (biog., photo)

335

Index

Schoenherr, John, 89:73 (biog., photo)
Schon, Isabel, 87:82 (biog., photo)
Scott, Marianne Florence, 82:68 (biog.); 85:13 (biog., photo)
Sealock, Richard B., 85:19 (obit., photo)
Segal, Jo An S., 85:14 (biog.)
Sendak, Maurice Bernard, 84:20 (biog., photo)
Sessa, Frank Bowman, 88:258 (obit., photo)
Shactman, Bella Evelyn, 85:19 (obit.)
Shank, Russell, 78:66 (biog., photo)
Shaw, Spencer Gilbert, 83:59 (biog., photo); 89:73 (biog., photo)
Shaw, Thomas Shuler, 76:254 (obit., photo)
Sheehy, Eugene P., 78:66 (biog., photo)
Sheldon, Brooke E., 83:59 (biog., photo)
Shepard, Marietta Daniels, 85:19 (obit.)
Shera, Jesse Hauk, 77:62 (biog., photo); 83:203 (obit., photo)
Shipman, Joseph Collins, 78:211 (obit., photo)
Shores, Louis, 82:201 (obit., photo)
Sloan, Elaine F., 88:76 (biog., photo)
Smith, Lillian Helena, 84:27 (obit., photo)
Spalding, C. Sumner, 76:111 (biog., photo)
Spaulding, Frank H., 87:82 (biog., photo)
Spicer, Erik J., 80:79 (biog., photo)
Spier, Peter, 79:56 (biog., photo)
Spivacke, Harold, 78:211 (obit., photo)
Steinitz, Kate Trauman, 76:254 (obit.)
Steptoe, John Lewis, 89:74 (biog., photo)
Steuermann, Clara, 76:112 (biog., photo)
Stevens, Charles H., 80:230 (obit., photo)
Stevenson, Grace Thomas, 77:63 (biog., photo)
Stewart, Ruth Ann, 87:83 (biog., photo)
Stockham, Ken, 83:60 (biog.)
Stone, Elizabeth W., 77:63 (biog., photo); 81:79 (biog., photo); 87:83 (biog., photo)
Strip, A. C., 82:68 (biog., photo)
Stripling, Barbara K., 89:74 (biog., photo)
Stueart, Robert D., 84:20 (biog., photo)
Sullivan, Peggy, 80:80 (biog., photo)
Summers, F. William, 83:60 (biog., photo); 87:83 (biog., photo); 88:76 (biog., photo)
Surridge, Ronald George, 85:14 (biog., photo)
Sutherland, Zena B., 84:21 (biog., photo)
Swartz, Roderick G., 87:228 (obit., photo)
Swerdlove, Dorothy L., 85:15 (biog.)
Talbot, Richard J., 85:14 (biog., photo)
Tate, Elizabeth, 80:80 (biog., photo)
Tate, Horace E., 79:56 (biog., photo)
Tauber, Maurice F., 81:214 (obit.)
Taylor, Charles F., 81:214 (obit., photo)
Taylor, Mildred D., 78:67 (biog., photo); 89:75 (biog., photo)
Taylor, Nettie Bancroft, 85:15 (biog., photo)
Taylor, Rhonda Harris, 87:84 (biog.)
Tees, Miriam Hadley, 76:112 (biog., photo)
Thomas, Lucille Cole, 89:75 (biog., photo)
Thompson, William Godfrey, 79:56 (biog.)
Thorpe, Frederick A., 77:63 (biog., photo)
Tiffany, Burton Chatterton, 76:112 (biog., photo)
Tighe, Ruth Liepman, 82:68 (biog., photo)
Tocatlian, Jacques, 80:80 (biog.)
Tomlinson, Kenneth, 87:84 (biog.)
Torbert, Richard C., 87:84 (biog.)
Trezza, Alphonse Fiore, 76:113 (biog., photo); 84:21 (biog., photo)
Trotti, John Boone, 78:67 (biog., photo)
Tsai, Betty L., 88:76 (biog., photo)
Tscherny, Elena, 87:84 (biog., photo)
Tucker, Ben, 89:75 (biog.)
Ulveling, Ralph A., 81:215 (obit., photo)
Van Allsburg, Chris, 83:60 (biog.); 87:84 (biog.)
Van Jackson, Wallace, 77:64 (biog., photo)
Vann, Sarah Katherine, 83:60 (biog., photo); 88:77 (biog.)
Vedder, Marion H., 87:228 (obit.)
Veliotes, Nicholas A., 87:84 (biog.)
Virgo, Julie, A. C., 78:67 (biog., photo); 86:86 (biog., photo)
Vitz, Carl Peter Paul, 82:201 (obit., photo)
Voigt, Cynthia, 84:21 (biog., photo)
Vosper, Robert Gordon, 78:68 (biog., photo); 86:86 (biog., photo)
Waddell, John Neal, 76:254 (obit.)
Wallace, Linda K., 85:15 (biog., photo)
Waller, Theodore, 77:64 (biog., photo)
Waples, Douglas, 79:195 (obit.)
Warner, Robert M. 81:79 (biog., photo); 87:85 (biog., photo)
Watanabe, Ruth T., 79:57 (biog.)
Watanabe, Shigeo, 78:68 (biog., photo)
Webster, Duane E., 88:77 (biog., photo)
Wedgeworth, Robert, 87:85 (biog., photo)
Weeks, Ann Carlson, 83:61 (biog.); 87:85 (biog., photo)
Weibel, Kathleen, 89:75 (biog., photo)
Wezeman, Frederick, 82:202 (obit.)
White, Carl M., 84:28 (obit.)
White, Herbert S., 88:77 (biog., photo)
White, Lucien W., 76:254 (obit., photo)
Whiteley, Sandra M., 86:87 (biog., photo)
Whitenack, Carolyn I., 77:64 (biog., photo)
Whitney, Virginia P., 77:65 (biog., photo)
Wichers, Jean Elaine, 84:28 (obit.)
Wiese, Bernice (Marion), 78:212 (obit.)
Wijnstroom, Margreet, 77:65 (biog., photo)
Wilcox, Alice Erlander, 76:113 (biog.)
Willard, Nancy, 83:61 (biog., photo)
Williams, Mabel, 81:79 (biog., photo)
Williams, Martha E., 88:77 (biog., photo)
Wilmeth, Don Burton, 83:61 (biog.)
Wilson, Alexander, 87:85 (biog.)
Wilson, Don W., 88:78 (biog., photo)
Wilson, Jane Bliss, 76:113 (biog.)
Wilson, Louis Round, 80:230 (obit., photo)
Winchell, Constance M., 84:28 (obit., photo)
Winkler, Paul Walter, 76:113 (biog., photo)
Winnie-The-Pooh, 77:65 (biog., photo)
Winslow, Amy, 81:215 (obit.)
Wofford, Azile M., 78:212 (obit.)
Woodsworth, Anne, 86:87 (biog.)
Woodward, Rupert C., 82:202 (obit.)
Woodworth, Mary L., 87:228 (obit.)
Wright, Wyllis Eaton, 80:230 (obit., photo)
Wrightson, Patricia, 86:87 (biog.)
Wu, Julia Li, 84:22 (biog., photo)

ABBREVIATIONS AND ACRONYMS

Following are selected abbreviations and acronyms used in *The ALA Yearbook of Library and Information Services.*

AAHC—Association of Academic Health Centers
AAHSLD—Association of Academic Health Science Library Directors
AALL—American Association of Law Libraries
AAP—Association of American Publishers
AARP—American Association of Retired Persons
AASL—American Association of School Librarians
ABA—American Booksellers Association
ABC—American Broadcasting Company
ACLS—American Council of Learned Societies
ACRL—Association of College and Research Libraries
AECT—Association for Educational and Communications Technology
AFLS—Armed Forces Library Section
AIA—American Institute of Architects
AIIM—Association for Information and Image Management
AILA—American Indian Library Association
AJL—Association of Jewish Libraries
ALA—American Library Association
ALHRT—American Library History Round Table
ALISE—Association for Library and Information Science Education
ALMRS—Army Library Management Reporting System
ALSC—Association for Library Service to Children
ALTA—American Library Trustee Association
ANSI—American National Standards Institute
APALA—Asian/Pacific American Librarians Association
ARL—Association of Research Libraries
ARSC—Association for Recorded Sound Collections
ARLIS/NA—Art Libraries Society of North America
ASCLA—Association of Specialized and Cooperative Library Agencies
ASIS—American Society for Information Science
Aslib—Association for Information Management
ATLA—American Theological Library Association
BCEL—Business Council for Effective Literacy
BCR—Bibliographic Center for Research
BIS—Bibliographic Instruction Section
BLIS—Biblio-Techniques and Information Systems
CACUL—Canadian Association of College and University Libraries
CALA—Chinese-American Librarians Association
CAPL—Canadian Association of Public Libraries
CARL—Canadian Association of Research Libraries
CASLIS—Canadian Association of Special Libraries and Information Services
CBC—Children's Book Council
CCLM—Coordinating Council of Literary Magazines
CCRM—Center for Chinese Research Materials

CE—Continuing Education
CICI—Confederation of Information Communication Industries
CINE—Council on International Nontheatrical Events
CIS—Community Information Section
CLA—Canadian Library Association *also* Catholic Library Association
CLEI—U.S. Office of Education the Center for Libraries and Education Improvement
CLENERT—Continuing Library Education Network and Exchange Round Table
COA—Committee on Accreditation
COLT—Council on Library Media/Technical Assistants
CONSER—Committee on Notations for Serials Holdings Statements
COSLA—Chief Officers of State Library Agencies
COSWL—Committee on the Status of Women in Librarianship
CRL—Center for Research Libraries
CSLA—Canadian School Library Association
CUFT—Center for the Utilization of Federal Technology
DTRAD—Division of Technology, Resource Assessment and Development
EMIERT—Ethnic Materials and Information Exchange Round Table
ERIC—Educational Resource Information Center
ERT—Exhibits Round Table
FEDLINK—Federal Library Information Network
FLICC—Federal Library and Information Center Committee
FLRT—Federal Librarians Round Table
FOLUSA—Friends of Libraries USA
FRFDS—Fundraising and Financial Development Section
FTRT—Freedom to Read Foundation
GODORT—Government Documents Round Table
IBBY—International Board of Books for Young People
ICLIS—Intermountain Community Learning and Information Services
IFC—Intellectual Freedom Committee
IFLA—International Federation of Library Associations
IFRT—Intellectual Freedom Round Table
ILLINET—Illinois Library and Information Network
IRA—International Reading Association
IRC—International Relations Committee
IRRT—International Relations Round Table
JCP—Joint Committee on Printing
JMRT—Junior Members Round Table
LA—Library Association (British)
LAMA—Library Administration and Management Association
LC—Library of Congress
LHRT—Library History Round Table
LMPI—Library Materials Price Index Committee
LIRT—Library Instruction Round Table
LITA—Library and Information Technology Association
LOMS—Library Organization and Management Section
LRRT—Library Research Round Table
MAGERT—Map and Geography Round Table
MARC—Machine-Readable Cataloging
MLA—Medical Library Association *also* Music Library Association
MPLA—Mountain Plains Library Association
Multi-LINCS—Multitype Library Networks and Cooperatives Section
NABRIN—National Advisory Board on Rural Information Needs

NAC—Network Advisory Committee
NAL—National Agricultural Library
NARIC—National Rehabilitation Information Center
NASIG—North American Serials Interest Group
NCATE—National Council for Accreditation of Teacher Education
NCES—National Center for Education Statistics
NCLIS—National Commission on Libraries and Information Science
NEDCC—New England Document Conservation Center
NEH—National Endowment for the Humanities
NELA—New England Library Association
NFAIS—National Federation of Abstracting and Information Services
NIH—National Institutes of Health
NIOSH—National Institute of Safety and Health
NISO—National Information Standards Organization (formerly ANSI Z-39)
NLW—National Library Week
NTIS—National Technical Information Service
NYPL—New York Public Library
OCLC—Online Computer Library Center
OERI—Office of Educational Research Improvement
OFR—Office for Research
OHA—Oral History Association
OIF—Office for Intellectual Freedom
OLOS—Office for Library Outreach Services
OLPR—Office for Library Personnel Resources
OMB—Office of Management and Budget
OPM—Office of Personnel Management
PGI—General Information Program
PIO—Public Information Office
PLA—Public Library Association
PLMS—Preservation of Library Materials Section
PMRC—Parents' Music Resource Center
PNLA—Pacific Northwest Library Association
PRS—Public Relations Section
RASD—Reference and Adult Services Division
RBMS—Rare Book and Manuscript Section
RIAA—Recording Industry of America
RLAC—Research Libraries Advisory Committee
RLG—Research Libraries Group
RLIN—Research Libraries Information Network
RMLN—Regional Medical Library Network
RTSD—Resources and Technical Services Division
SAA—Society of American Archivists
SAC—Subject Analysis Committee
SASS—Systems and Services Section
SCOLE—Standing Committee on Library Education
SDC—Systems Development Corporation
SELA—Southeastern Library Association
SLA—Special Libraries Association
SOLINET—Southeastern Library Network
SORT—Staff Organization Round Table
SRRT—Social Responsibilities Round Table
SSLI—Society of School Librarians International
SWLA—Southwestern Library Association
TLA—Theatre Library Association
UBC—Universal Bibliographic Control
UBCIM—Universal Bibliographic Control and International MARC Program
ULC—Urban Libraries Council
UNESCO—United Nations Educational, Scientific, and Cultural Organization
USBE—Universal Serials and Book Exchange, Inc.
USDE—United State Department of Education
USIA—United States Information Agency
WHCLIST—White House Conference on Library and Information Services Task Force
WLN—Washington Library Network
WNBA—Women's National Book Association
WSS—Women Studies Section
YASD—Young Adults Services Division